# Contributions to Finance and Accounting

The book series 'Contributions to Finance and Accounting' features the latest research from research areas like financial management, investment, capital markets, financial institutions, FinTech and financial innovation, accounting methods and standards, reporting, and corporate governance, among others. Books published in this series are primarily monographs and edited volumes that present new research results, both theoretical and empirical, on a clearly defined topic. All books are published in print and digital formats and disseminated globally.

David Jamieson Bolder

# Modelling Economic Capital

## Practical Credit-Risk Methodologies, Applications, and Implementation Details

Springer

David Jamieson Bolder
Nordic Investment Bank
Helsinki, Finland

ISSN 2730-6038 ISSN 2730-6046 (electronic)
Contributions to Finance and Accounting
ISBN 978-3-030-95095-8 ISBN 978-3-030-95096-5 (eBook)
https://doi.org/10.1007/978-3-030-95096-5



This Springer imprint is published by the registered company Springer Nature Switzerland AG
The registered company address is: Gewerbestrasse 11, 6330 Cham, Switzerland

*Für Josefa und Susan Bolder, zwei außerordentlich starke Frauen, die mein Leben unendlich bereichert haben.*

*Nancy et Thomas, encore une fois, sans vous, je serais peu.*

# Foreword

Credit-risk management has always been a challenging task, but it remains as crucial as ever in modern banking. The requirements and expectations for solid, documented, and model-based credit-risk management have developed significantly since the 2008 financial crisis. Nowadays, the concept of credit-risk economic capital is deeply embedded in every bank's daily management and decision making. Chief risk officers are faced with the heavy responsibility of ensuring that their risk modelling provides an appropriate and sound foundation for their institution's decisions.

This book, written by David Bolder, on the topic of economic-capital risk modelling has been produced in parallel to, and in conjunction with, development of the Nordic Investment Bank's (NIB) own economic-capital model. This is where this book stands out and goes well beyond other literature written about the subject. David's book is based on the actual work carried out at NIB, and the real choices and situations we faced, during the process. While providing theoretical foundations and principles, the book also addresses the many questions and real-life decisions that needed to be made, all with the objective of "getting it right."

NIB is a AAA-rated international financial institution (IFI), owned by the eight Nordic and Baltic countries. In 2020, NIB concluded the modernization of its statutes, which now incorporate risk-based capital requirements into its legal foundation.[1] This decision would not have been possible without a solid foundation of risk-based capital-management practices, including a comprehensive set of relevant models at hand. As part of the process, NIB executive management wanted to ensure that our economic-capital model was mathematically sound, built on defensible risk parameters, and was overall deemed fit-for-purpose. Accordingly, we initiated the work to redesign as needed, to document, and to subsequently externally validate our new economic capital model for credit risk.

[1] NIB is, at the time of this book's publication, the only bank among its peers (the other IFIs) that has taken this route.

NIB has been fortunate to have David to lead this important work. While having both a strong academic background and solid financial-sector experience, David is also gifted in explaining the concepts, mathematical and statistical choices, and related impacts to decision makers and other stakeholders. This has been crucial for us during the new model's development and implementation phases.

The book provides an *end-to-end* view, diving into practical implementation details and extending beyond economic capital to cover other (related) critical banking applications such as risk-based loan pricing, expected credit loss (ECL) modelling, stress testing, and measurement of financial-derivative exposure. This makes David's work highly relevant not only for risk-management practitioners but also for a much broader group of readers. All those willing to put in the effort will be well rewarded with useful contextual knowledge, a structured approach to tackling complex issues, and applicable practical solutions.

Nordic Investment Bank
Helsinki, Finland
2021

Hilde Kjelsberg

# Preface

*[T]he best prize that life offers is the chance to work hard at work worth doing.*

*(Theodore Roosevelt)*

It is customary when writing a preface to provide some sort of explanation to why the book was written. Although this preface will not deviate from this pattern, we will *not* go about it in the usual, direct way. Instead, we will begin with a rather lengthy detour. It is more than just taking the scenic route; the truth is that it will simply take some time to get where we need to go. The trip is worth it.

The jumping-off point is the details of a quantitative analyst's job. This book is focused on financial risk management, so we will principally take this perspective.[2] Quantitative risk analysts frequently find themselves required to measure various dimensions of a firm's risk. This difficult, and often precarious, undertaking inevitably involves use of mathematical and statistical models.

The reason for use of models is easy to understand. Describing an intricate and multifaceted world is *not* feasible without some form of simplification and dimension reduction. Otherwise, one would be steamrolled by complexity. Creating logical parsimony is the central role of the model. In recent years, it has become well understood that models are a double-edged sword. They provide structure and insight, but embed their own risks.[3] As a consequence, every experienced quantitative risk analyst worries about one important issue: getting it wrong.

Claiming that an entire profession is profoundly concerned about making mistakes is a deeply depressing beginning. It would, however, be a bit surprising were this not the case. A quantitative analyst, whether in the risk-management area or not, performs technical analysis to support firm decision making. Poor analysis leads to correspondingly poor decisions. Enough bad decisions and the firm's future—not to mention the analyst's career—comes into question. Complicating matters, the task

[2] The following discussion relates equally well—with perhaps a few minor adjustments—to virtually any numerically minded industry: physics, engineering, statistics, genetics, computer science, or economics.

[3] Derman [1, 2] or Rebonato [3] are a great place to start for more background on these ideas.

is inherently difficult. Most financial analyses require fairly intimidating amounts of complex instruments, market data, and portfolio inputs. Modelling outputs are also typically highly involved non-linear functions of these inputs. To make matters worse, the principal modelling relationships in financial economics are not built upon physical laws, but human behaviour. It's often impossible to determine if one is using the *right* model.[4] There are thus a multitude of ways to get things wrong. A rational and conscientious quantitative analyst has literally no choice but to worry about this point.

## An Analyst's Objectives

Worrying is natural, but it won't solve any problems. How then does the quantitative analyst try to minimize their fears? It begins with a clear and practical description of one's objectives. It is admittedly presumptuous to describe an entire industry's ambitions, but we'll nonetheless try to hit the broad strokes. A working description of a quantitative analyst's objectives is given as:

> Perform defensible, replicable, robust, and conservative quantitative analysis to effectively inform management decision making.

This is a fairly short, but dense, sentence. It is easily read, confidently pronounced aloud in a meeting, or inserted into a team's mission statement. In practice, however, it is arduously achieved. This objective also merits some unpacking. Let's do this by considering the key underlined concepts in more detail:

- *Defensibility*: Our modelling choices and assumptions need to be based upon well-founded and plausible logical arguments. Equally importantly, there needs to be some understanding of the main choices and the principal alternatives. In short, one's analytic choices need to be reasonable and fit for purpose to the task at hand.
- *Replicability*: We generally do *not* know the truth, so it is difficult to speak of accuracy. Instead, we seek clear analysis that others can reproduce. The inability to recreate someone's analysis is an important red flag. Not incidentally, and for the same reasons, replicability is also a key principle in scientific discourse.
- *Robustness*: If we change the measurement technique or slightly change the inputs, a robust result does not vary dramatically. All else equal, this form of stability is a rather desirable characteristic in one's analysis.
- *Conservatism*: If we have to err, we prefer to systemically (but not excessively) overestimate our risks, rather than underestimate them. This can, of course, be taken too far. Taken in appropriate measure, it is a useful objective.

[4] One may even legitimately question if such a notion actually even exists.

A few ideas are conspicuous by their absence from our objectives. There is, for example, no explicit mention of accuracy or precision. We also avoid any language like "getting it right" or identification of the "correct model." This might be disappointing to some readers. In some ventures, such as the pricing of plain-vanilla financial instruments, there is more space for such ideas. These limited situations notwithstanding, we have explicitly steered clear of such words and concepts. The reason is an attempt to avoid overconfidence, arrogance, or hubris in our analysis. There is much that we do not know and perhaps more that is unknowable. Risk is basically about the *a priori* specification of future marginal and joint risk-factor and portfolio-value distributions. Founding one's objectives upon the assumption of precise knowledge of these distributions—with any significant degree of precision—seems like a singularly bad idea. These are hard words, but a failure to honestly describe what can be accomplished can lead to important misapprehensions about the value of risk-management analysis. Even within this relatively modest working definition, however, our objectives represent a pretty tall order.

## Analytic Axioms

We are still, the reader is certainly thinking, rather far from an explanation of why this book was written. That is true, but we are getting closer. The next step involves adding a more concrete dimension to this discussion. Objectives are great, but are of limited value absent some idea of how they can actually be attained. To help in this regard, we will now introduce *five* principles, or axioms, to guide our actions towards achievement of this objective. This is not something that one would typically find in a textbook. They are unwritten rules, or practices, that one will routinely discover underlying solid analysis and well-constructed systems. Some are gleaned from critical sources and practitioners such as Taleb [4], Knight [5], Box [6], or Derman [7]. Others are the result of my own hard-earned decades-long experience.[5]

Following these axioms is, unfortunately, no guarantee that a quantitative analyst will meet their objectives. If seriously followed, however, they will provide a road map towards our quantitative goals. The rest is hard work and sound judgement. Moreover, embedded in these principles—and intertwined with a strong desire to attain the preceding objectives—we will unearth the fundamental rationale for this book.

[5] This recalls Mark Twain's sage words on the value of experience: *"a man who carries a cat by the tail learns something he can learn no other way."*

## #1: Multiplicity of Perspective

Redundancy, in the world prior to the COVID-19 global pandemic, was something of a dirty word. Instead, the focus in past decades has been on concepts such as outsourcing, process optimization, and just-in-time resourcing. These ideas have left their mark on the overall business world and also influenced modelling practices. There is much merit to seeking to make optimal use of scarce resources, but these ideas do have an important weakness: they are typically not terribly robust. Small perturbations to highly optimized systems often lead to dramatic setbacks in performance. The COVID-19 pandemic—which was an admittedly large shock—has driven home this point in a variety of sectors.

Since robustness forms a key element of our quantitative analyst's objectives, the notion of redundancy matters to us. This leads us to our first axiom:

**If you can help it, never do anything just one way.**

Most production risk-management systems collect dizzying numbers of data records every day. Using these instrument, market-data, and portfolio inputs, they then proceed to perform millions of calculations yielding an array of key metrics. If we fear getting something wrong and value robustness, then a natural solution is the use of multiple models for the computation of pivotal quantities. One can, of course, have only one production model. There is dramatic value in also having a suite of challenger models; this involves the introduction of redundancy into one's risk-management system. Some alternative models can be very simple, while others might involve only a slight, but conceptually important, variation on the production model. There is particular value in models founded on fundamentally different assumptions from one's production choice. We can think of this as conceptually similar to including an outsider in a firm's board of directors. Multiple approaches built on conflicting assumptions can help to avoid *group-think* among our models.

To make this more concrete, imagine that you have a portfolio of complicated American-style options. Your production implementation likely needs to employ some kind of finite-difference algorithm to value the individual options in your portfolio. Use of analytic Black and Scholes's [8] formula or a simpler numerical Bermudan-option approach would represent interesting challenger models. They are both incorrect, and somehow insufficient, but they are easy to compute with fewer moving parts that can go wrong. More importantly, the final, complex result will deviate in expected ways from these calculations. Extra work and computation are involved, but the consequence is a powerful sanity (or robustness) check on one's results.

Our first axiom is essentially counselling analytic redundancy. This idea is *not* new. Critical systems—nuclear power plants, air-traffic control, and space-shuttle launches as a few examples—routinely build in redundancies to minimize the risk of failure.[6] It might seem excessive to apply such notions to financial risk management, but there are many conceptual parallels that suggest scope for similar solutions.

## *#2: Many Eyes*

Our second axiom is:

**Actively seek (and value) external review and criticism.**

Nobody likes criticism. It is hurtful to have someone pick apart—even with the best of intentions—something you've worked hard to build. It is nonetheless essential. Everyone makes mistakes. The idea that good analysts are impervious to important errors is a dangerous misconception. It has been long understood in psychological circles—see, for example, Reason [10]—that cognitive errors are an essential part of the creative process. These can be errors in one's mathematical development, conceptual argumentation, or simply bugs in one's implementation. They happen to every analyst and every team. Errors, whether we wish to admit it or not, are a natural (if unwelcome) by-product of quantitative analysis.

Accepting the (widespread) existence of cognitive error is the first step. The next course of action is to seek solutions. The principal tool to minimize such error is critical external oversight.[7] Critical review can, and should, occur in many layers. The starting point, of course, is a careful review of one's own work. Then, it naturally proceeds to one's colleagues. At this point, things get a bit more difficult. Much of what quantitative analysts do on a daily basis is simply too complicated and technical for non-expert audiences. For complex and critical models, sufficient in-house expertise often does not exist for examination beyond one's immediate colleagues. External review is thus necessary. This typically takes the form of model-validation via a specialized external firm.

To summarize, many eyes can really help to identify and mitigate cognitive error. That said, many eyes are not enough; it also has to be the right eyes. For this reason, when possible, it is preferable to also put key ideas into the public

[6] See Perrow [9] for a fascinating, and at times frightening, discussion of the ways that complex systems can go wrong.

[7] This notion goes by many names. Book editors call this manuscript proofing, computer software engineers refer to this activity as debugging, while academics use the term *peer review* to manage quality control for journal submissions.

domain.[8] Publication accomplishes both: it exposes one's work to many eyes while simultaneously getting it to the right ones. By making a contribution to the practitioner literature, there is a greater chance people with the proper experience and perspective will provide their invaluable input.[9]

## *#3: Pictures and Words*

One common theme, across all areas of quantitative endeavour, is the need to manage large amounts of input and output data. In the modern world of *big data*, this trend is only going one way: upwards. This brings us to our third axiom:

**Visualization is your (best) friend.**

Even a modest risk-management operation will write thousands of records to a variety of database tables on a daily basis. A small number of (lucky) individuals possess the ability to peruse large tables of data and identify issues; this is nonetheless a rare skill. The human eye, conversely, is pretty good at catching graphical patterns or anomalies. This argues for the liberal use of visualization tools to (regularly) examine the range of one's key inputs and outputs. It is also fruitfully applied to important intermediate calculations. Indeed, a fantastic application is visualization of one's production model differences with respect to the challenger models introduced in axiom #1.

Some aspects of visualization are intuitive. Even better, there are increasing numbers of helpful scientific computing and business intelligence tools to assist with this task. That said, there are numerous key principles and pitfalls associated with visualization. Tufte [11] is an excellent source of inspiration in this often underrated area. In Tufte's [11] words, "[a]t their best, graphics are instruments for reasoning about quantitative information." Is improved reasoning not essentially the end-game for the entire activity of quantitative analysis? Financial risk models are complex and decision making is difficult; any tool that can assist in this process is highly welcome. Visualization is, however, not just any tool. It is perhaps our most important ally.

---

[8] For a more thorough discussion on these ideas, please see Bolder [16].

[9] Propriety algorithms and models can complicate this process. Often, however, the issue relates principally to the sensitivity of the inputs and outputs. This challenge is readily managed by use of fabricated (but generally representative) data inputs.

## #4: The Three Little Pigs

In the late nineteenth century, inspired by the Grimm brothers, Jacobs [12] published the famous fairy tale: the three little pigs. Although this would appear to be almost as far away from quantitative analysis as one can possibly get, the story taught us that solid, well-built brick houses are best. The lesson applies, of course, more broadly. This indirectly leads us to our fourth axiom:

**When you construct something, build it to last**

It is simply astounding how often, in practical situations, temporary solutions become permanent. In today's business world, there are always ambitious work agendas and tight deadlines. Prototypes that are judged good enough can become production systems and remain so for years. This is not a jab against business processes or practices; it appears to be a combination of human nature and constrained resources. The consequence, however, is that quick and sloppy implementations can become weak links in one's analytic chain.

Understanding and accepting this fact is a stride in the right direction. What is the remedy? When building any system, it is advisable to proceed as if it will be permanent; it may very well be! In the best case, one will have a well-built, carefully constructed prototype to aid in the development of the final production system. In the worst case, the temporary but ultimately permanent model will have been built with care. This brings us back to Jacobs's [12] fundamental point about the shortcomings of straw and wooden homes: it is generally safer to have high construction standards.

## #5: The Best for Last

Our final axiom ties together many of the previous elements, and finally brings us to the point at hand: motivating the production of this book. It reads as a combination of a command and an imploration:

**Write it down!**

The preceding axioms simply cannot be accomplished without putting pen to paper. Multiplicity of perspective (axiom #1) requires understanding of key differences in alternative modelling approaches. External review and criticism (axiom #2) necessitate getting deeply into the details. Effective visualization and permanent, solid solutions (axioms #3 and #4) require planning and detailed descriptions of one's underlying methodologies. To repeat, none of the preceding axioms can be accomplished without detailed documentation.

In many organizations, models can be organized in generations. They are developed by one or more people, who eventually move on to other responsibilities within or outside the firm. They are then replaced by a second generation who, not having been involved in the construction, have less complete model understanding. Knowledge is lost with each successive generation. In many cases, by the time we arrive at the third or fourth heir, the model is effectively a *black box*. One manages the inputs and collects the outputs but lacks a clear idea of what is happening in between. The basic notion of a black box is illustrated schematically in Fig. 1.

Black boxes are dangerous. As a modeller, it is almost invariably a bad idea to use things you don't understand. Absent a comprehensive understanding, how can one properly interpret and communicate results? One might get away with it for short periods of time, but ultimately it will catch up with you. Fortunately, it's basically impossible to (correctly) document a black box. You can't sensibly write down what you don't comprehend. Documentation thus explicitly forces discipline and clarity regarding one's processes and assumptions. A detailed description of one's model—and associated visualizations with alternative challenger models—also goes a long way to resolving the generational decline in internal model knowledge. Documentation is, in many ways, the antidote to the black box.[10] To

**Fig. 1** *The root of much evil*: A black box takes a set of inputs and produces one or many outputs. The processing, or algorithmic, aspect is partly or completely unknown. This lack of clarity is highly problematic.

[10] This realization also lies at the heart of many detailed documentation initiatives surrounding model-risk management—see, for example, OCC [13]—and the increasingly extensive Pillar III requirements supported by the regulatory community.

bring our *fifth* crucial axiom to its logical extension, a model is not implemented until it is fully and conscientiously documented.[11]

## Why This Book?

This realization finally brings us to the origins of this book and the central point of this preface. Over the period from 2019 to 2021, the Nordic Investment Bank (NIB) embarked upon an important journey to modernize its statutes. This involved, among other things, the adoption of economic capital as a central tool in the management of its business. To support this initiative, detailed internal efforts were performed to simultaneously revise, refresh, and extend NIB's credit-risk economic-capital framework. This was a long and complicated journey that necessitated the use of many mathematical and statistical modelling techniques.

Why was this book written? It seeks to meet the aforementioned objectives by explicitly following the associated axioms. A commitment was made to do things the right way. This was not easy. Each axiom involves extra work above and beyond the already challenging day-to-day tasks faced by the quantitative analyst. Nevertheless, the choice was *not* difficult.[12] Within financial institutions, the days of implementing and using complex mathematical models without careful oversight have passed. One need not perhaps follow the letter of these five axioms, but there are increasing pressures—and, more importantly, good logical reasons—to follow their spirit. The preceding axioms thus form the guiding principles of our approach to quantitative analysis and, by extension, this book.

The forthcoming chapters chronicle the key elements of NIB's credit-risk economic-capital methodology. This incorporates important modelling details and assumptions as well as questions surrounding model parametrization and implementation, important applications, and a variety of related concepts. This book also explicitly covers multiple possible model implementations and challenger models and extensive visualization aids. It is not perfect, nor will any modelling framework ever be. Its publication is, however, strongly motivated by a desire to seek (and value) constructive external criticism and thereby help to gradually (and continuously) improve NIB's credit-risk economic-capital architecture. With luck, it will also contribute to the general conversation and assist other individuals and

[11] Proper model documentation includes many elements. A non-exhaustive list includes links to the academic and industry literature; the mathematical details of one's modelling choice(s); the rationale behind assumptions and implementation decisions; and visualization of actual calculation outcomes.

[12] This is reminiscent of Victor Hugo's thoughts on this subject: *"initiative is doing the right thing without being told."*

entities working in this important area. Perhaps the most important justification for writing this book, from NIB's institutional perspective, is the desire to build something that will last.

Helsinki, Finland David Jamieson Bolder

# Acknowledgements

Without Kai Arte, Matti Koivu, Björn Ordell, and Jari Lievonen, this book would not exist. These gentlemen took a rather big chance on hiring a (fairly random) Canadian outsider to come into the Nordic Investment Bank and help rethink, retool, and rebuild their (credit-risk) economic-capital framework. I deeply appreciate their vote of confidence and hope to have fulfilled their expectations. I have never lost sight of the fact that Kai, Matti, Jari, and Björn laid much of the groundwork for this book during the years prior to my arrival. Putting these ideas, in a structured and organized way, into the form of a book was actually Kai and Matti's idea. In many ways, therefore, it has been my task (and pleasure) to complete their vision.

A book like this, outlining the conceptual choices of an entire institution, cannot be written without strong encouragement from the top. Hilde Kjelsberg has been a constant source of support, confidence, and enthusiasm; she, as much as anyone, has helped make this project a reality. Henrik Normann's intellectual rigour, quick mind, and hard questions did not make defending model-development choices particularly easy, but it always improved the final product. André Küüsvek, Henrik's successor, and the current president of the NIB, has also been nothing other than fully supportive of this initiative.

To the extent that this book has value, it is as a practically minded guide to addressing important, but prickly, quantitative capital-related questions faced by real-life financial institutions. Such pragmatism can only come from the hard-earned experience of developing, building, testing, interpreting, communicating, maintaining, and basically sweating over associated production models. Practitioner work of this nature is never performed alone; it requires a team. In this respect, I have been very fortunate. My colleagues Jaakko Louekari, Svetlana Bryazgina, Janne Kunnas, Hanh Vo, Tlahui Bolaños, and Ming Yin have all contributed in very important ways to the success of this venture. I owe a particularly deep debt of gratitude to Aleksi Korpinen. Joining shortly after my arrival, Aleksi has been my partner in crime and has expertly handled much of the technical, systems-related heavy lifting thereby allowing me to focus more intently on the conceptual side of things.

This work has benefited immensely from many useful conversations and interactions with talented and generous colleagues across the entire NIB institution. There are thus many people who need to be recognized. Antti Miettunen's experience with stress-testing and rating agencies helped shape the final role of these topics in the following discussion. Mike Ryan and Christopher Mikander's patience in explaining the accounting side of (oft bewildering) loan-impairment computations was both invaluable and very much appreciated. Joe Wright and Shashvat Kapoor—along with a host of other lending professionals posing tricky, but very reasonable, questions regarding model results—have helped me to better appreciate the business side and thus construct more practically useful models. Michaela Kettner—with her diligence, professionalism, and support on the model-risk front—has been a godsend. Matti Koivu's technical expertise, guidance, and intuition was an enormous asset during the (far too short) time we worked together. Ville Väisänen's deep knowledge of the institution and his insights into capital structure and loan pricing (and many other things) helped me to build a more sensible overall framework. Last, but certainly not least, Pascal Gauthier's boundless energy, curiosity, eye for detail, and appetite to improve things assisted importantly in forging a stronger system and, ultimately, a much better book.

The opinions expressed in the following pages, it must be mentioned, are solely mine. While frequent reference is made to the NIB and I have aimed to sensibly (but not perfectly) depict its practices (at the time of writing) insofar as economic-capital modelling is concerned, no assurance is made with respect to institutional accuracy. The NIB should not be assigned any responsibility for any possible misrepresentation or deficiencies. All of my thanks and well-deserved acknowledgements are furthermore, I also hasten to stress, entirely free of implication. All errors, inconsistencies, typographical mistakes, shortcomings, design flaws, or faults in logic are to be placed squarely on my shoulders.

Finally, as always, I would like to thank my wife and son for their patience, assistance, and understanding with yet another book project. Without them behind me, the effort necessary to produce such a work would be simply unthinkable. After Bolder [14, 15], I swore that I was done with the book-writing business. I was wrong. I can now, with some definitiveness, state that this is the end of the road. To borrow a thought from distinguished statistician Patrick Billingsley that touched me many years ago, I would very much like these publications to be considered as my humble contribution to the "river of [practitioner] mathematics." While this is open to debate, we can all hopefully agree with Billingsley [17] that "although the contribution is small, the river is great."

## References

1. E. Derman. Model risk. Goldman Sachs Quantitative Strategies Research Notes, April 1996.
2. E. Derman. Models. *Financial Analysts Journal*, 65(1):28–33, 2009.
3. R. Rebonato. Theory and practice of model risk management. Quantitative Research Centre (QUARC) Technical Paper, 2003.

4. N. N. Taleb. *The Black Swan: The Impact of the Highly Improbable*. Random House, New York, NY, 2007.
5. F. H. Knight. *Risk, Uncertainty and Profit*. Houghton Mifflin Co, Boston, MA, 1921.
6. G. E. P. Box. Science and statistics. *Journal of American Statistical Association*, 71(356):791–799, 1976.
7. E. Derman. *Models Behaving Badly: Why Confusing Illusion with Reality Can Lead to Disaster, on Wall Street and in Life*. Free Press, New York, USA, 2012.
8. F. Black and M. S. Scholes. The pricing of options and corporate liabilities. *Journal of Political Economy*, 81:637–654, 1973.
9. C. Perrow. *Normal Accidents*. Princeton University Press, New York, NY, 1984.
10. J. Reason. *Human Error*. Cambridge University Press, New York, USA, 1990.
11. E. R. Tufte. *The Visual Display of Quantitative Information*. Graphics Press LLC, Chesire, Connecticut, second edition, 2001.
12. J. Jacobs. *English Fairy Tales*. David Nutt, London, England, 1898.
13. OCC. Supervisory Guidance on Model Risk Management. Technical report, Office of the Comptroller of the Currency, April 2011.
14. D. J. Bolder. *Fixed Income Portfolio Analytics: A Practical Guide to Implementing, Monitoring and Understanding Fixed-Income Portfolios*. Springer, Heidelberg, Germany, 2015.
15. D. J. Bolder. *Credit-Risk Modelling: Theoretical Foundations, Diagnostic Tools, Practical Examples, and Numerical Recipes in Python*. Springer-Nature, Heidelberg, Germany, 2018.
16. D. J. Bolder. Stealing Others' Strategies: Lessons on Model Risk. In *Evolving Practices in Public Investment Management: Proceedings of the Seventh Public Investors Conference*, 2020.
17. P. Billingsley. *Probability and Measure*. Wiley, Third Avenue, New York, New York, third edition, 1995.

# Testimonials

This is a very valuable book providing a comprehensive treatment of credit risk capital. The most fascinating and relatively unique aspect is the illustration of the practical development and implementation of a capital framework in an actual institution. It thus goes well beyond describing the concepts and derivations but also delves deeply into the actual choices that have to be made from beginning to end on all dimensions and how these decisions can be made. While rigorous and technical, the book is also layered with judgement, common sense, and honesty. This is a very welcome addition to the literature on this subject.

*- Lakshmi Shyam-Sunder, Chief Risk Officer, World Bank*

Dave Bolder's excellent new book describes how to model and compute a bank's economic capital. He starts with a broad overview of the issues, introduces the necessary technical tools, and provides practical advice garnered from his extensive experience. The models are first introduced at a high level and then they are carefully described and developed. The presentation is thorough and accessible to someone with an undergraduate degree in mathematics or statistics. Bolder's ongoing commentary is especially insightful in pointing out limitations and developing our intuition. The author's approach is well summarized by his five guiding principles outlined in the preface. With its solid theoretical foundation and its sensible practical suggestions, this volume is an important contribution to the risk management literature.

*- Phelim Boyle, Professor Emeritus, Pioneer in Quantitative Finance*

David J. Bolder's two previous books *Fixed-Income Portfolio Analytics and Credit-Risk Modelling* are valuable sources of information for academics and practitioners working in quantitative finance. This book, *Modelling Economic Capital*, will become an equally valuable resource as it is written with David's highly readable style that combines solid technical foundations, clear descriptions of real-world problems, modelling and risk-management approaches, and practical implementation, including key details often omitted in other sources. *Modelling*

*Economic Capital* is a comprehensive treatment that will be very useful in the research, education, and practice in modern quantitative finance.

- *Cody Hyndman, Chair, Department of Mathematics and Statistics, Concordia University*

Accessible, insightful, practical – a must-read for financial practitioners. The global financial and sovereign debt crisis has triggered the necessity of financial authorities and financial firms to develop and conceptualize risk exposures for safeguarding financial stability, reduce contingency risks, and for financial firms to master their economic capital models. Having worked in central banking for over 25 years, this book by David Bolder successfully provides a holistic view of the opportunities and challenges surrounding the modelling of economic capital in an increasing complex, heterogeneous, and global financial market. David, with his wealth of risk management knowledge, provides clear and pragmatic reflections of the credit risk economic capital framework, while transparently offering practical lessons from the Nordic Investment Bank. I highly recommend this book for risk management practitioners in private and public firms and as lecture material for graduate programmes as a forward guidance of managing economic capital.

- *Per Nymand-Andersen, Adviser to senior management at the ECB, Lecturer at Goethe University*

David J. Bolder, a leading risk-management expert, masterfully gives a complete guided tour of the Nordic Investment Bank's modelling and computation of economic capital. A unique look into the inner workings of a financial institution, Bolder covers important topics and intricate details not found in other texts. This book hits the modelling trifecta of what models are used, why those models are used, and how they are implemented, including simplifying assumptions and approximations, data requirements and availability, parameter specification and estimation, and computational methods and computing systems. Bolder skilfully guides us through the reasoning and justification for choices made at all stages in the process. Modellers from any discipline can benefit from the many discussions balancing rigour with practical considerations. Linking the models to business practice applications such as loan pricing, origination, and the connection to the lending firm's capital structure is a distinctive feature. This work is a notable contribution to the financial and regulatory community and should be on the shelf of every risk manager.

- *Professor R. Mark Reesor, Associate Professor and Chair, Department of Mathematics, Wilfrid Laurier University*

# Contents

# Chapter 1
# Introducing Economic Capital

*Just as a cautious businessman avoids investing all his capital in one concern, so wisdom would probably admonish us also not to anticipate all our happiness from one quarter alone.*

*(Sigmund Freud)*

This is a book with a central focus on the notion of economic capital and its applications. It thus makes good sense to begin with a clear description of this surprisingly complex concept. Our story begins with the banking business, although the following ideas will apply equally well—with some perhaps slight adjustments—to a broader range of financial institutions including insurance companies, investment dealers, or brokerages. Banks, as we all know, lend money. Such a mandate entails a number of ancillary financial activities. Loan origination and counterparty evaluation is a central preoccupation, cost-effective funds must be raised in local and international markets to finance these loans, short-term liquidity needs to be earmarked and invested to manage daily flows and unexpected outcomes, and key portfolio asset-and-liability mismatches need to be hedged.[1] In a few words, a modern bank needs to lend, fund, invest, and hedge. All of these efforts, even hedging, give rise to various financial (and non-financial) risks that need to be identified, measured, and managed. A bank's success, as a venture, depends importantly on its effectiveness in navigating these risks.

The first challenge facing a bank arises from the diverse nature of these risks. A movement in an interest or exchange rate, for example, is somehow different from the failure of a counterparty to meet their payment obligations. Measuring the former risk is quite likely to involve conceptual and practical differences from the latter one. This is only a simple example; the true range of risks is, in fact, much broader. Although they might arise and behave in different ways, it is useful and important to manage one's risks in a global sense. This idea is loosely referred to as enterprise risk management. A powerful tool for the joint management of these

[1] Many banks, of course, also raise funds via customer deposits.



D. Bolder, *Modelling Economic Capital*, Contributions to Finance and Accounting,
https://doi.org/10.1007/978-3-030-95096-5_1

risks is referred to as economic capital. Economic capital, to be criminally brief, is a firm-wide, model- and assumption-based measure of business risk.

Calculating economic capital requires not just one, but typically multiple financial models. The multiplicity of models arises precisely from the variety of risks that we seek to incorporate into the final measure. In a perfect world, a single, unified model would describe the totality of an institution's risks. The diversity of the underlying risks and, quite frankly, our shortcomings in measuring them makes such an approach practically unfeasible. The following chapters will focus principally on the credit-risk dimension, but we would be remiss if we did not touch upon—at least, conceptually—the other important sources of risk faced by financial institutions.

Although financial modelling is a crucial element in the computation of economic capital, jumping straight into technical considerations is probably not a great idea. Instead, to somewhat mangle a popular adage, we should *think before we model.*[2] With a clear view of what we wish to accomplish—and some of the potential stumbling blocks along the way—digestion of mathematical and statistical details can occur much more smoothly and naturally. This chapter, therefore, seeks to provide a gentle, but comprehensive, introduction to the key ideas, motivations, and concepts associated with the notion of economic capital.

## 1.1 Presenting the Nordic Investment Bank

Although our intention is to attack economic capital from a broad perspective, the ideas and methodologies presented in the following chapters are employed by a specific institution: the Nordic Investment Bank (NIB). NIB is an international financial institution focused—to put it very briefly—on environmental and productivity related lending activity in the Nordic and Baltic regions. Established in 1975 by the five Nordic countries, it makes loans to both private and public-sector entities, but not individuals.[3] It also finances its activities through market borrowing, not customer deposits. NIB's loans are offered on competitive market terms.

The NIB has been estimating, internally reporting, and using economic capital since 2004. Although not a regulated entity, it has nonetheless followed the Internal Capital Adequacy Assessment Process (ICAAP) since 2016.[4] ICAAP, as a concept and process, relates to the Basel Committee for Banking Supervision's Pillar 2 (i.e.,

---

[2] The typical advice is to *think before you speak*, but experience indicates that thinking is profitable before engaging in a rather wider set of activities from bungee jumping to financial modelling.

[3] The five Nordic countries include—moving from west to east—Iceland, Norway, Denmark, Sweden, and Finland. The three Baltic countries—from south to north, Lithuania, Latvia, and Estonia—joined the NIB in 2005.

[4] See ECB [15] for a useful guide to the occasionally byzantine world of ICAAP.

the supervisory review) aspect introduced in Basel II.[5] In 2020, through a desire to modernize its risk-governance framework, and precipitated by practical challenges associated with antiquated statutory gearing limits, the NIB introduced a number of changes to its statutes. A new set of economic-capital, leverage, and liquidity management principles—along with some associated changes in the responsibilities of its Control Committee—were introduced.

These statutory adjustments were, to put it mildly, a game changer. Prior to the revised statutes, the principal constraint on NIB's financial activity was a volume-based gearing ratio. While broadly effective, such an approach did not differentiate between the riskiness of each unit of lending or treasury activity to our overall activities. Volume certainly matters, but so does the underlying risk profile of what an institution adds to its balance sheet. Economic-capital offers an approach to capture both dimensions. It does so, however, at a cost. Volume-based ratios are typically easily defined and computed; economic-capital, by contrast, is a relatively complex and nuanced object. Its complexity, of course, is necessary to adequately reflect the intricacy of the risks facing a modern financial institution.

This book is, in many ways, a child of NIB's recent statutory change. While most of the elements described in the forthcoming chapters have been performed for years—if not decades—prior to the recent revision of its statutes, it was a natural moment to carefully rethink and revise the overall framework. Such an effort naturally involved careful documentation of the attendant choices; the result was this book. Putting these ideas into the public domain serves, at least, *two* purposes. First, and perhaps most centrally, it provides clarity about our modelling practices and permits qualified and interested external parties to provide useful constructive feedback on our choices. Placing these ideas into circulation is thus an important step towards mitigating the inherent model risk associated with construction and implementation of an economic-capital framework. Transparency is also a fundamental aspect in public discourse among NIB's member countries. Modelling practices, their mathematical complexity notwithstanding, are no exception.[6] Secondly, many practical lessons have been learned during this process that, in our view, will be of interest to a broader audience. Openness, sharing, and solicitation of external feedback are thus the key objectives in the production of this publication.

The following chapters, therefore, are not based upon theoretical examples of how one might possibly use economic capital. Instead, we will address these issues within the context of a real-life entity. Naturally, there are important limits to the amount of proprietary information that can be shared in such a publication. No customer information will be provided and most figures will be related to high-level values already found in other publications such as financial reports. In many cases,

---

[5] Basel II's introduction and discussion ranged from roughly 2004 to 2006.

[6] This relates to the idea—see, for example, Elmgren [16]—of open government. While open government is challenging, and not always uncontroversial, transparency has a long history in the Nordic region.

we will use fictitious (although illustrative) data to demonstrate our choices. Specific figures and details regarding credit obligors are, however, rather beside the point and *not* pertinent to a meaningful discussion of the topics. This is a book about choosing, parametrizing, implementing, and applying economic-capital methodologies. As in any large-scale financial modelling venture, both objective and subjective decisions must be taken. It will be useful for the reader to understand and experience how these methodological choices have been taken within the NIB context across the entirety of the credit-risk dimension. Great pains have nonetheless been taken to ensure that, despite the usefulness of a specific perspective, the notions considered in the coming chapters are of general interest and utility.

**Colour and Commentary 1** (SOME READING INSTRUCTIONS)*: This work has a lot of ground to cover. This makes it inevitably long and detailed. We can loosely think of reading this book as visiting a large touristic destination such as London, Paris, New York, or Beijing.*[a] *There is much to see, learn, and experience, but it can be difficult to get started and decide where to allocate one's time. Conceptualizing this book as a city visit, its consumption requires a plan. The preface and this first chapter set the stage: these are roughly equivalent to a short tourist guide. To complement the technical discussion, extensive mathematics, and examples found in each chapter, numerous distinct grey text boxes (such as this one) are provided.*[b] *Each box seeks to highlight various key points, takeaways, challenges, or observations. Their purpose is to help the reader to navigate, digest, and organize the material. To extend our tourist-attraction analogy, we can view these grey text boxes as the various destinations found on popular jump-on and jump-off bus tours offered to tourists in these major cities. Skipping through the boxes, in any given chapter, can assist the reader in deciding when (and where) to* jump *into the details.*

[a] No promise is made that exploring the coming pages will be anywhere near as exciting as your next vacation.

[b] There are, in fact, roughly 150 of these text boxes scattered over the forthcoming 12 chapters.

## 1.2 Defining Capital

Before there was economic capital, there was capital. As the introductory quote suggests—stemming from famed psychoanalyst, Sigmund Freud, whose contributions mostly occurred a century ago—the idea of capital is *not* new. A definition was provided by Adam Smith in his *Wealth of Nations* published in the late eighteenth

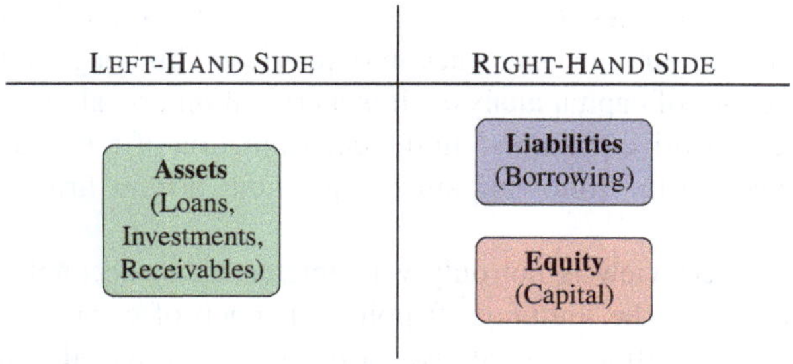


**Fig. 1.1** *A stylized balance sheet*: This schematic represents a (very) stylized firm balance sheet. It illustrates the conceptual interplay between assets, liabilities, and equity.

century.[7] The idea of capital, albeit with a strong political-economy dimension, is also treated extensively in the works of Karl Marx written during the 1880s.[8] There are many different definitions that one might consider, but they all basically boil down to an owner's investment or stake in an enterprise. Although it can be broken down more finely, this (slightly simplified) working definition amply serves our purposes.

It is, of course, useful to be slightly more concrete. Figure 1.1 provides a, certainly quite familiar, stylized view of a firm's balance sheet. The left-hand side illustrates firm assets such as loans, investments, and receivables. These are, more or less, the elements of the business that are used to generate revenues. The right-hand side basically deals with sources of financing associated with the revenue-generating left-hand side. It includes liabilities and the overall equity, or capital, position.

Capital (or equity) is, from double-entry book-keeping, a residual figure. It is the excess of a firm's assets over its liabilities. For an accounting scholar, using the terms capital and equity interchangeably is likely considered to be a grave act of negligence.[9] This not being an accounting treatise, a bit of simplification and cheating is permitted. Our objective is, in this regard, not precision, but rather illumination.

Accounting niceties aside, the important point from Fig. 1.1 is that the difference between a firm's assets and liabilities provides invaluable insight into a business' state of affairs. A large equity position indicates a comfortable distance between a firm's assets and its obligations. This is generally a good thing. If it is too large, however, then the efficiency and profitability of a firm can suffer. When this equity

[7] Although not the most famous event occurring in this year, this work—see Smith and Krueger [43]—was originally published in 1776. It defines capital as "that part of a man's stock, which expects to afford him revenue."

[8] The curious, and perhaps masochistic, reader is referred to the original source: Marx et al. [29].

[9] Specifically, the difference between assets and liabilities is referred to as shareholder's equity. Capital, in an accounting sense, is generally considered to be a technical subset of this equity position. Capital is thus viewed as the owner's ongoing investment in the firm, whereas equity is the owner's share of the business.

or capital position becomes too small, conversely, then a small bump in the road might put the firm's continued existence into question. This rough logic falls under the broader category of capital analysis; it is a critical pillar—along with solvency, liquidity, and competitive position—in the determination of a firm's overall credit quality. It reduces to the following simple question: does a firm have sufficient equity?

This balance-sheet view is not only very interesting to accountants and credit analysts, but it is also the jumping-off point for much of corporate finance. The appropriate mix of liabilities and equity, for example, is referred to as the capital-structure decision and is a rich area of research.[10] Dividend policy, the market for corporate control, corporate governance, and topics related to shareholder activism also all look at the firm through this lens.

Our viewpoint, with an eye on the notion of economic capital, is slightly different. We are looking for inherent limitations with this view of the firm. The missing ingredient, as one might expect, is *risk*. It turns out that—particularly for financial institutions—the risk dimension manifests itself primarily in a firm's assets. This makes eminent sense, since a corporation's revenues are typically generated from its assets. For most firms, assets include receivables, physical stock, cash, and inventory. Liabilities, conversely, include payables and bank and/or market debt. The riskiness of the assets of a generic firm—other than perhaps receivables—is typically not dramatic. These assets are, from an accounting perspective, usually held variously at historical or amortized cost.

The story is somewhat different for financial institutions. Some investments—including marketable securities—are held at fair value. This implies that, as market conditions change, valuation changes flow through profit-and-loss. This is useful, because it creates a link between asset riskiness and the firm's equity (or capital) position. Loan obligations, however, are not typically fair valued; the reasons are various, but the lack of liquid secondary markets for their resale is one important explanation. Changes in the (often difficult to assess) value of loan assets are thus not directly incorporated into the balance sheet. These changes do, however, make an indirect appearance. Loan impairments—often referred to as expected credit losses or ECL—attempt to capture average credit losses and impending credit deterioration. These impairment values also flow through the profit-and-loss statement and ultimately impact the firm's equity position.

### *1.2.1 The Risk Perspective*

Fair value and impairment calculations represent valiant efforts, on the behalf of the accounting community, to incorporate asset riskiness into a firm's financial statements. These are particularly helpful for financial institutions such as the

[10] The most sensible starting point in this area is Myers [33, 34].

NIB. There is, however, still something missing. Risk is, practically, a combination of outcomes and likelihood. Risk managers are typically worried about very negative outcomes with low likelihoods (or probability). To really assess the comfortableness—or, in more popular jargon, adequacy—of a firm's capital position, this extreme perspective needs to be incorporated.

What do we really mean by extreme? Let's consider some concrete examples of highly negative outcomes for a financial institution:

- one, or more, large, structurally important loan or bond obligors could simultaneously move into default and fail to pay the firm back;
- interest rates or exchange rates or credit spreads—or all of the above—could dramatically move against the firm;
- one or more large swap counterparties could go out of business forcing the firm to novate (i.e., liquidate and replace) an important part of their swap exposure; or
- key systems or controls could fail and/or large-scale fraudulent activity could occur.

These are all (rather disheartening) examples of credit, market, counterparty, and operational risk, respectively. Each depict adverse events that a firm might face, but which do not make any appearance in our schematic definition of capital from Fig. 1.1.

The balance-sheet equity or capital amount is thus, rather unfortunately, not particularly informative about such extreme down-side asset risks. Is such a pessimistic perspective simply a fiction of the minds of paranoid risk managers? Risk managers may indeed by overly suspicious by nature and training, but the last 25 years have offered no shortage of dramatic financial events: an incomplete (but still depressing) list includes the 1997 Asian crisis, the dot-com meltdown of 2000–2001, the global financial crisis of 2007–2009 and its decade long aftermath, at least two waves of European sovereign-debt crises, and the financial turmoil associated with the COVID-19 pandemic in 2020.[11] Really understanding and assessing the adequacy of firm's capital position thus requires us to systematically go beyond average, or expected, losses.

We have established the need, for the appropriate assessment of a firm's capital adequacy, to incorporate worst-case risks associated with the asset-side of the balance sheet. We have further established how this viewpoint is particularly important for financial institutions given the composition of their assets. There is, however, another important characteristic associated with financial institutions. Deposit-taking banks, investment banks, and insurance companies play a central role in any economy: credit intermediation. In other words, they facilitate the financing of firms and individuals either directly by extension of credit or insurance

[11] An excellent, if somewhat discouraging, broader view of the unnerving regularity of financial turbulence throughout history is Reinhart and Rogoff [38].

or indirectly through enabling financial transactions.[12] If such financial institutions fail or run into trouble, the effect on the economy is disproportionate. There is a knock-on effect to other firms through a reduced ability to efficiently, or cost-effectively, finance their continued operations. In really extreme situations, otherwise well-functioning firms can face dire solvency problems simply due to problems with financial institutions.

Financial firms thus have a high degree of systemic importance. This explains their preferential access to liquidity arrangements through central banks, deposit insurance, and, in extreme cases, direct government bailouts. While this is certainly a contentious area involving use of taxpayer money, these measures all arise from the unique centrality and importance of financial institutions in any given economy. As Peter Parker learned the hard way, however, *with great power, comes great responsibility.*[13] Systemically important financial institutions may have access to a broad range of (tax-payer funded) support functions, but there is a flip side to the coin. They also face disproportionately high levels of oversight and regulation. The regulatory community has thus been, virtually since its inception, at the forefront of the movement to incorporate this extreme-risk perspective into the assessment of a firm's asset riskiness and, by extension, its capital position. Our simple question, *"does a firm have enough capital?"*, takes on a new degree of importance in this setting.

### 1.2.2 Capital Supply and Demand

This detour through the origins of capital, as a financial concept and its potential shortcomings, has finally led us to the rationale for economic capital. Economic capital is basically an *economically* motivated alternative representation—working through the firm's assets—of the balance-sheet capital position. Abstracting (for the moment) from the details of its computation, imagine that we can actually calculate such an adjusted capital amount. What would be the point? We could directly compare this risk-adjusted capital figure to the actual balance-sheet capital (or equity) position. If our approximation was bigger than the balance-sheet value, it would be somewhat disappointing. It would mean that the firm would not have enough capital to weather really extreme worst-case risk outcomes. We would probably, by contrast, be encouraged if our asset-risk adjusted capital position exceeded the balance-sheet value. This is the heart of the economic-capital concept. It is a measure used by regulators—and indeed any interested internal or external

[12] For a much more complete review of the banking sector, and its economic centrality, see Siklos [42].

[13] This is a humorous, but still entirely pertinent, reference to Spider-Man. If you really desire some additional background on this, very tangential topic, it's easy to find. Bendis [2] is not a bad place to start.

stakeholder—to assess a firm's capital adequacy. Again, we return to our simple question: does the firm have enough capital?

Regulators have, in particular, a somewhat unique perspective on the idea of economic capital. Although they are certainly interested in understanding the sufficiency of a financial institution's capital position, they are also intimately concerned with the *minimum* amount of capital each firm should hold. This prescriptive way of looking at the problem makes sense; regulators are trying to create a level playing field among financial institutions within their jurisdiction. While minimum capital requirements and economic capital are intimately related, they are not precisely the same thing. The former is a lower bound, while the latter is a general concept.

To use economic capital to assess a firm's capital adequacy, it is helpful to introduce the notions of capital supply and demand. Capital supply is the actual amount of a firm's available capital; rather simply, it is the difference between balance-sheet assets and liabilities.[14] The capital demand is one's economic capital computation; it is an estimate of how much capital is potentially required, or demanded under adverse conditions, by the riskiness of the firm's assets. Capital adequacy analysis thus essentially reduces to the comparison of these two quantities. Capital supply less capital demand is often referred to as (capital or equity) headroom. In the unfortunate case of capital demand exceeding supply, we can speak of negative headroom or capital shortfall. As a general rule—which paves over much complexity and nuance—we would like a firm's headroom to be reasonably large and positive. Figure 1.2 provides a schematic illustration of the case when capital supply exceeds capital demand (and vice versa).

While hopefully helpful from a conceptual perspective, to this point we have only addressed why one might be interested in something like economic capital. The actual quantity, and how it is produced, probably remains frustratingly vague. Numerous questions arise. How do we, for example, actually adjust the specific assets? More structure is definitely needed in this area. What do we actually mean by worst-case extreme risk? This could clearly mean different things to different firms. We might also ask: how do we accommodate disparate types of risk? There is also the need to incorporate the interactions between individual assets in our portfolios. We are, after all, modern financial professionals concerned with the portfolio perspective. These are all important questions that we will seek to address in the following discussion.

[14] There are often slight technical adjustments to this figure, which are not to be ignored, but simple balance-sheet arithmetic gets us to the right order of magnitude.

**Colour and Commentary 2** (DEFINING CAPITAL): *Equity, in a balance-sheet sense, refers to an owner's share of the firm. Practically, it is the residual asset value after subtracting the firm's liabilities. Colloquially, this is referred to as the enterprise's capital position.*[a] *Accounting practices—such as fair valuation and loan-impairment calculations—take into account the average, or expected, riskiness in firm assets. They do not, however, address extreme worst-case risk outcomes. This perspective, given the depressingly regular incidence of financial crises, is important and cannot be ignored. Assessing a firm's capital adequacy—which is a fancy way of asking if it has enough capital—requires this extreme-risk perspective. Here enters the concept of economic capital. Economic capital is an* economically *motivated alternative representation—focused on the riskiness of the firm's assets—of the balance-sheet capital position. This reduces questions of capital adequacy to a comparison of actual balance-sheet equity values (i.e., capital supply) to one's economic-capital estimate (i.e., capital demand).*

[a] There are, from an accounting perspective, subtle and important differences between capital and equity. This fact notwithstanding, these two terms are treated as broadly synonymous in everyday financial parlance.

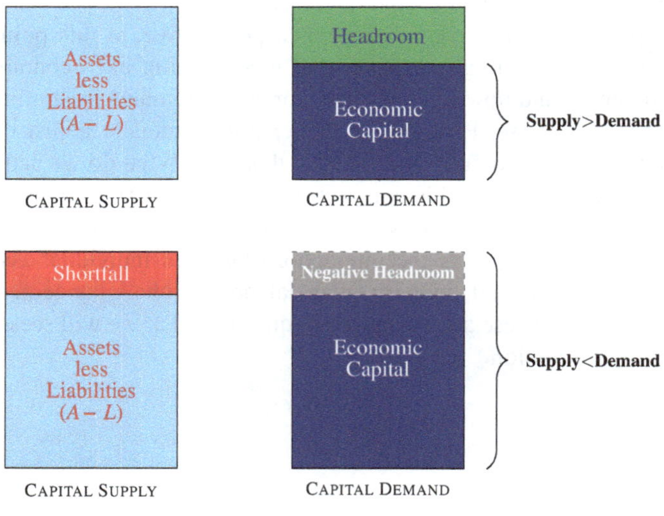


**Fig. 1.2** *Capital-adequacy mechanics*: The preceding schematic illustrates the interaction between the notions of capital supply, capital demand, and headroom. All else equal, we prefer that a firm's supply of capital exceeds the demands upon it.

## 1.3 An Enormous Simplification

Let us begin with a statement of full transparency: there does *not* exist a unique, correct way to compute economic capital. Any individual who claims otherwise is either being less than truthful, or trying to sell you something, or both. Economic capital is a model- and assumption-based metric. There is instead a range of possible choices with varying degrees of defensibility and potentially differing objectives. Depending on your perspective, this might be either refreshing or discouraging. The variability in economic-capital computations should nonetheless not be overstated. There do, of course, exist general principles and accepted practices for the measurement of economic capital. The Basel Committee on Banking Supervision, for example, has been a driving force, from the regulatory side, in finding a common language for economic capital and standardizing comparison across firms and jurisdictions.[15] This offers a useful backdrop for making decisions on one's economic-capital calculation, but it still represents a few options among many possible choices.

Despite its non-uniqueness and the potential complexity behind one's economic-capital risk model, computing economic capital is practically fairly easy to understand. To see this we introduce a simplification; this is not how economic capital is computed, but rather a conceptual tool. Imagine the following procedure. For each asset on a firm's balance sheet—be it a loan, a deposit, a corporate bond, or an interest-swap contract—we assign it a *number*. Not just any number, of course, but we follow some rather structured rules. In particular, each of our asset numbers takes a value between 0 and 1. More specifically,

1. a value of zero implies that the asset has no risk; and
2. a value of one implies that it has no value.

The obvious corollary of this property is that the greater the asset's risk, the larger our assigned number. The extremes, while informative, are likely not terribly interesting. A value of zero would probably only apply to local-currency cash position with a reputed central bank (and even this is debatable). Assigning a value of one, conversely, is basically equivalent to writing off the entire value of the asset. This would presumably only occur in the event of default with absolutely no prospect of any recovery through bankruptcy proceedings. In the vast majority of cases, our number will be comfortably in the unit interval with, in high-quality institutions, a fairly strong tendency to lie at the lower end of the scale.[16]

The reader is probably thinking that such a number assignment might be an interesting exercise, but how is it related to the idea of economic capital? The answer is surprisingly simple. If one multiplies this *number* by the asset value,

[15] Much has been written on the Basel accords; BIS [3, 4, 5] are excellent starting points for some of the practical elements of minimum regulatory capital requirement computations. Chapter 11 will delve much more deeply into the regulatory world.

[16] Different lending institutions, of course, specialize in different parts of the credit spectrum.

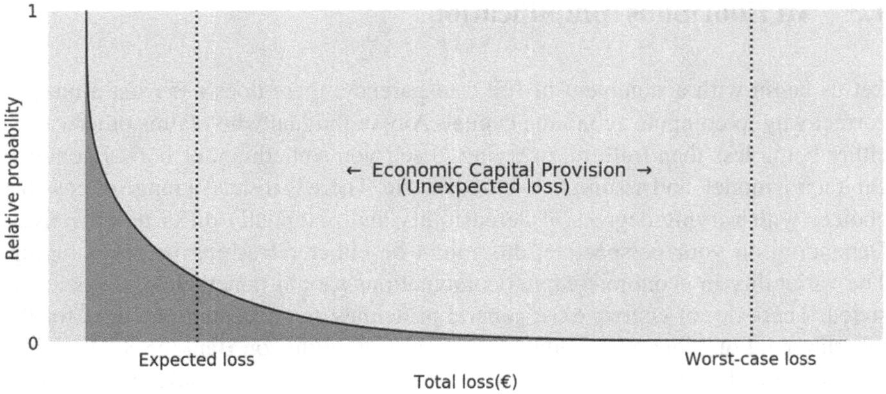


**Fig. 1.3** *Economic capital at a glance*: This figure illustrates a stylized portfolio loss distribution. Economic capital is defined, in a technical sense, as the difference between the worst-case outcome and the expected, or average, loss. This difference is often referred to as unexpected loss.

one arrives at its economic-capital figure. The total economic capital figure for a given firm is thus the sum of the product of these numbers—each between zero and one—and their asset values.[17] Consider a simple (aggregate) example: a firm's total assets are EUR 1 billion and each and every number is 8%. In this case, a firm's economic capital figure is EUR 80 million. If the firm's actual equity position is EUR 100 million, then it can be considered to have adequate (or even excess) capital. An equity position of EUR 60 million, however, would likely be considered problematic.

Our asset numbers are clearly related to the notion of risk. Bigger numbers, after all, are assigned to riskier assets. While useful to understand and interpret economic capital, these numbers are not used to compute it. Estimating economic capital requires wrestling with asset risk. Risk, when you get down to it, depends on the interplay between value outcomes and their associated probabilities and likelihoods. The collection of all possible outcomes (or events) and likelihood is referred to as a statistical distribution or probability law. We require such an object to assess the risk of our asset portfolio. Figure 1.3 illustrates a stylized, firm-wide, asset-portfolio loss distribution: for the moment, let's not worry about where it might come from.[18] This distribution will help us identify the actual practical definition of economic capital. It specifically outlines the various firm asset-loss outcomes along with an assessment of their relative probability. Low levels of loss occur with a high likelihood, while extreme (worst-case) losses are rare. The expected, or average, portfolio loss lies, as it should, at the centre of the overall probability mass.

[17] Those familiar with regulatory risk weights will recognize this idea.

[18] This is a job for future chapters.

As discussed previously, the main point of economic capital is to understand what happens to a firm's assets when things go really wrong. In the context of our asset-loss distribution in Fig. 1.3, it means considering events out in its far right-hand side. This is referred to as the tail of the distribution. It is in this unsavoury neighbourhood that we will meet extreme, worst-case losses. Inspection of Fig. 1.3 reveals that the further we move into the distribution's tail, the lower the probability of the loss outcome. This makes logical sense, but it strongly suggests that we cannot really talk about *worst-case* losses without also including some assessment of their probability. We could, for example, talk about a 0.1% worst-case loss. This basically suggests that portfolio losses of this magnitude would occur once out of every 1000 random draws from this firm-asset probability law. This worst-case probability is referred to as a confidence level and it is typically denoted by the first letter in the Greek alphabet, $\alpha$. Moreover, by convention, we talk about it as $1-\alpha$.[19] So, to return to our example, a 0.1% of a worst-case loss translates into a $1 - 0.1\% = 99.9\%$ confidence level.

It is tempting to characterize economic capital as this $1 - \alpha$ worst-case loss. This would not be quite correct. As we saw previously, the accounting community has already done a good job—through adjustments such as fair valuation and loan impairments—of incorporating expected loss. Economic capital, therefore, is defined as the $1 - \alpha$ worst-case outcome minus the expected loss. This difference—in an unfortunate choice of terminology—is often referred to as the unexpected loss. Conceptually, it is useful to think of economic capital as the additional reduction of asset value—over and above the expected loss already addressed by one's accountants—that might occur if things really get ugly.

Figure 1.3 and our recent definitions are practically quite helpful. The economic capital is thus formally defined as the $1 - \alpha$ confidence-level unexpected asset loss. To compute our number between zero and one, at the overall portfolio level, we simply evaluate the following ratio:

$$\text{Firm's Asset } \textit{Number} = \frac{\text{Asset Portfolio Unexpected Loss}}{\text{Asset Portfolio Value}}. \tag{1.1}$$

The larger this number, of course, the more capital a firm would require to insure, or cushion, itself against large losses associated with the inherent riskiness of its assets. This ratio also depends directly on the value of $\alpha$. As $\alpha$ gets smaller—and by extension, the larger our confidence level, $1 - \alpha$—the bigger the numerator in Eq. 1.1, and the more economic capital required.

The role of our confidence level, $1 - \alpha$, warrants further investigation. How, for example, does one choose $\alpha$? If left to anxious and distrustful risk managers, $\alpha$ might become infinitesimally small leading to astronomical levels of economic capital. Delegating this task to the marketing team, conversely, might very well

[19] Confidence level is admittedly not a great name, but the idea is to describe the degree of confidence that a firm's asset losses will not exceed $1 - \alpha$.

create the opposite result. Happily, in practice, $\alpha$ is *not* set by either party. The actual choice of $\alpha$ will typically depend on the current, or desired, credit quality of the firm. A firm with a AAA rating—or one that seeks to be considered among the ranks of AAA entities—will typically have a very low level of $\alpha$. Such firms, to warrant the strength of their rating, are expected to have a combination of asset quality and capital adequacy to weather a very severe financial storm. At a one-year horizon for AAA entities, for example, it is common to set $\alpha = 0.01\%$ leading to an intimidating 99.99% confidence interval. Indeed, the level of $\alpha$ can be considered to roughly correspond to the firm's probability of default over the time horizon under examination. This intuitive approach thus suggests very different levels of $\alpha$ for AAA or BBB or CCC firms.[20]

We have already discussed the importance of comparing economic capital to a firm's actual equity position, let's now make it a bit more precise. We define a firm's capital headroom as,

$$\text{Firm's Capital Headroom} = \underbrace{\text{Asset Portfolio Unexpected Loss}}_{\text{Economic Capital}} - \text{Firm's Equity Position}. \tag{1.2}$$

The economic capital is the unexpected loss associated with a $1-\alpha$ confidence level; it is an alternative, economically motivated representation of a firm's equity position informed by asset riskiness. The difference between a firm's actual equity position and its economic-capital estimate is highly informative. Headroom tells us a number of things. Its sign describes whether a firm is adequately capitalized for its asset risks or not. The magnitude of an institution's headroom speaks to its capacity to take new risks. Overly large or small levels of headroom will raise questions. In the former case, one might worry about the efficiency—and also potentially profitability—of the firm. In the latter, fears will arise about risk-taking capacity and a firm's ability to maintain their current credit rating.[21]

Our notion of economic capital as assigning a number, between zero and one, to each individual asset is represented in Eq. 1.1. That said, it isn't quite complete; Eq. 1.1 computes this number at the portfolio level. The portfolio level is useful and interesting for high-level oversight by regulators and credit analysts, but day-to-day management of economic capital requires more granularity. What we seek is

[20] Capital adequacy is a key—although certainly not the only—element in a credit agency's decision process. All else equal, for example, a downgrade is likely imminent (but not certain) for a AAA-rated firm that finds itself with AA levels of equity.

[21] If the headroom is large in either direction, one may be able adjust the confidence level, $1 - \alpha$, to generate a manageable, positive headroom level. When possible, and abstracting from other important determinants, one could impute the firm's implied credit rating associated with their equity position.

something more like:

$$\text{An Individual Asset's } \textit{Number} \approx \frac{\text{Individual Asset's Unexpected Loss}}{\text{Individual Asset's Value}}. \quad (1.3)$$

A closer look reveals, of course, that to get these numbers, we need some assessment of the individual asset's unexpected loss. Our economic-capital number and unexpected loss are thus two ways of describing the same underlying concept; the reader is invited to employ the perspective that feels most intuitive to them.

Equation 1.3 falls into the category of things that are relatively easy to write down, but rather harder to accomplish. There are, at least, *two* complicating factors:

1. identifying and measuring the unexpected losses associated with each individual asset; and
2. taking into account this asset-level risk within the context of the overall portfolio.

Both of these aspects are absolutely central. Different assets are naturally subject to varying types of risk. Our economic-capital measure would be incomplete if it did not incorporate these main risks. The second point is a bit more subtle, but equally important. Assets cannot generally be considered in isolation. A swap contract, for example, may be used to offset the interest- or exchange-rate risk associated with a bond. A loan in one sector or region may actually diversify a firm's overall lending portfolio.

The good news is that this chapter does not immediately attempt to provide specific technical answers to these thorny practical challenges. Instead, we will try to introduce a number of concepts that should help us motivate, evaluate, and understand the nature of these technical choices investigated in later chapters.

**Colour and Commentary 3** (ECONOMIC CAPITAL IS JUST A NUMBER)*: Classic, and technically correct, definitions of economic capital will focus on the unexpected element—defined at a specific level of confidence—of the firm's asset-loss distribution. This can be difficult to digest; an alternative conceptual notion might help. Extracting all of the complexity associated with models and assumptions from the discussion, it can be useful and illuminating to think about economic capital as a number between zero and one. Zero corresponds to an absence of risk, whereas one implies a complete lack of asset value. As a general rule, the larger the number, the riskier the assets. Whether this number is 0.1, 0.12, or 0.20, when it is multiplied by the firm's assets, the economic-capital value is revealed. Analytically, we can take this a step further and imagine that each individual asset is assigned its own economic-capital number. Practically, such a figure can be constructed by dividing the asset's worst-case (unexpected) loss—with a* $1 - \alpha$ *confidence*

(continued)

**Colour and Commentary 3** (continued)
*level—by the current asset value. This collection of numbers provides not only a recipe for computing overall economic capital, it also allows management to* slice-and-dice *the economic capital by different dimensions. Moreover, one can compare the relative riskiness of different assets within one's portfolio simply by using their assigned number. The individual asset-level description of economic capital is referred to as risk attribution (or allocation) and it is an invaluable tool in the management of economic capital.*

## 1.4 Categorizing Risk

Computation of economic capital is thus, in its essence, a risk-measurement problem. There are, sadly, many different types of risk. Indeed, classifying and constructing lists of different types of risk is a popular activity among risk managers. Borrowing the notion from the physical sciences—most particularly the study of biology—such lists are often referred to as risk taxonomies. Figure 1.4 provides a visualization of such a risk taxonomy for the individual risks embedded in a typical financial institution's assets.

The usual suspects make an appearance in our taxonomy: market, default and migration, counterparty, and operational risks.[22] We will have rather more to say about the similarities and differences between these risks in the coming pages. Capital buffers are, by contrast, rather specific to the calculation of economic capital. These are, as the name suggests, extra allocations towards the economic-capital calculation to account for uncertainty in its measurement. The core intention, which originated with financial regulators, is to ensure an abundance of caution into one's assessment of a firm's capital position.

There is, of course, more to the capital-buffer story than simply a regulatory recommendation to wear both a belt and suspenders. The rationale and reason for the presence of capital buffers is tightly linked to *two* extreme viewpoints to be considered in the parametrization of one's risk models. As highlighted in Fig. 1.3, risk requires working with asset-loss distributions. In other words, it is necessary to formulate forecasts of the range of possible asset values one's portfolio might take. The nature of our asset-loss distributions, or our range of estimates regarding the future, are based on parameters. These parameter choices depend importantly on the information available to us at the time of the calculation.[23]

[22] McNeil et al. [30] provide a nice description of financial risks for the reader seeking more colour and detail.

[23] We have much more to say on the question of parameter selection in Chap. 3.

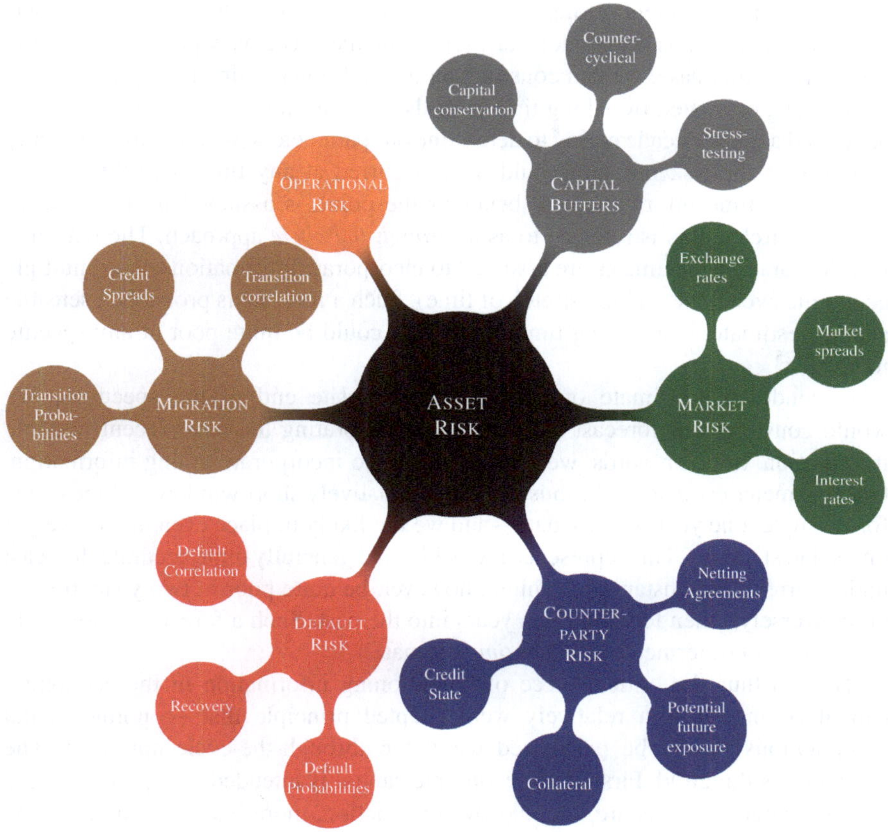


**Fig. 1.4** *A simple risk taxonomy*: The preceding figure describes, for a typical financial institution, a set of major risks that typically make an appearance in economic-capital calculations. Attached to each type of risk, where appropriate, are some key risk drivers.

Information and conditionality are two closely related topics. Imagine you were told that you needed to estimate the height of a 16-year-old girl. Absent any additional information, you would likely provide the average height for young women, of age 16, across the entire population. This is referred to as an unconditional estimate; you have limited information. Imagine further, however, that you were told this young woman played competitive basketball. You would likely *condition* upon (or take into account) this new information, and might revise your estimate upwards. This is called, unsurprisingly, a *conditional* estimate.[24] The quality of one's estimate is a separate question. The distinction, in this case, is information.

[24] If you also knew her position—an example of further conditioning information—you might further adjust your guess.

In a risk-management setting, we may use the same ideas to forecast our asset-portfolio losses. It is a bit more artificial, but the basic viewpoint remains the same. In the first case, we can construct an unconditional estimate by using model parameters, estimated over long time periods, to determine our risk metrics. If we have used a multi-decade period to determine our parameters, we are thus essentially acting as if the risk measure could have occurred at any time over this period. No specific time information, to belabour the point, is assumed in this case. In practical circles, this is referred to as a *through-the-cycle* approach. The reason is that the parameter estimates are assumed to incorporate information across multiple economic cycles (i.e., a long stretch of time). Such a forecast is probably a sensible average estimate, over a long time period, but could be quite poor at any specific moment.[25]

A conditional estimate operates at the opposite end of the spectrum. We would construct our forecast as of today, incorporating the most recent possible information. In other words, we actively decide to incorporate timing information. Our parameter estimates will thus use only a relatively short window of time—say, for example, one year of daily data—and we are likely to place even higher weight on the latest values. This represents a sensible, and generally quite accurate, forecast under current circumstances. It might, however, be quite poor in two years time—or, conversely, when looking three years into the past. Such a forecast is, for fairly obvious reasons, termed a *point-in-time* estimate.

Time is thus the critical piece of conditioning information in the economic-capital setting. It is a relatively well-accepted principle that economic-capital computations should be performed using the through-the-cycle approach. The reasoning is threefold. First of all, economic capital is intended to capture extreme events. Longer datasets are, literally by construction, more likely to capture some extreme observations. Second, point-in-time risk estimates tend to be procyclical. This means that in quiet economic conditions they tend to be low, while they increase rapidly under crisis conditions. The impact of risk-measure procyclicality is rapid increases in economic capital—and consequent model-driven deterioration of a firm's capital adequacy—in crisis conditions. This does not seem to be a particularly positive characteristic in an economic-capital estimator. Finally, there is a general desire to be able to compare economic-capital estimates across time. With the point-in-time approach, changes in economic capital might arise from either changes in the portfolio composition or market conditions. It is difficult to isolate these effects. Overall, therefore, a through-the-cycle estimator is better positioned to capture extremes, avoid procyclicality, and permit intertemporal comparison of a firm's economic-capital position.

Against this backdrop, we may now revisit the idea of a capital buffer. Although the through-the-cycle approach attempts to capture extreme outcomes, it does

[25] Just like using the average population height could fail rather seriously when forecasting the height of our 16-year old basketball player.

have an important long-term average element.[26] Capital buffers attempt to address this potential shortcoming by adding something extra to the economic-capital computation for the possibility of actual outcomes being somewhat worse than what the unconditional, through-the-cycle perspective might suggest. Indeed, in some regulatory environments, the level of these buffers is partially determined in a countercyclical manner. Such a mechanism, in the hands of regulators driving minimum regulatory capital requirements, is an example of a macroprudential tool.[27]

Capital buffers have the benefit of being based on easy-to-compute formulaic representations provided by the regulatory community. The other members of our risk taxonomy highlighted in Fig. 1.4 are not so lucky. They must be computed through the blood, sweat, and tears of mathematical and statistical assumption as well as often complex computational implementation. This might sound discouraging, but for some risk types, the situation is even worse. In the real world, risks can be usefully decomposed into *two* disparate groups:

- those that we can measure with some degree of confidence; and
- those that we cannot.

Our usual suspects—market, migration, default, and counterparty risks—are, even if it can be at times technical and difficult, bravely estimated with varying degrees of accuracy. Capital buffers, given their macroprudential perspective, are rather hard to handle. Since responsibility for this component has been co-opted by our friendly neighbourhood regulator, this is happily *not* our problem. This leaves us with operational risk; it is the canonical example of a risk that we cannot reliably estimate. Vast in scope, operational risk simultaneously encompasses loss-generating events such as innocent data-entry errors, holes in one's IT-security firewall, fraudulent activity, and so-called *acts of God* such as hurricanes, earthquakes, or pandemics. Each of these elements are difficult to understand and measure on a standalone basis; their joint examination quickly becomes a quantitative analyst's nightmare. The consequence is that operational-risk economic capital is typically computed in a highly simplified formulaic manner.[28]

The remainder of this chapter, and indeed the entire book, will focus on those risks that we can actually measure. Credit risks—migration, default, and counterparty—will take centre stage. Our discussion of the important market-risk dimension will remain at the conceptual level.[29] This is not to say that difficult-to-

[26] The ability to capture extremes is affected by parameter selection, but certainly goes beyond this choice. The mathematical and statistical structure of the model also impact this dimension in important ways.

[27] See ECB [14] for more background on this key aspect of financial-stability policy.

[28] The typical approach is to use some notion of the firm's size as a proxy for its exposure to operational risks.

[29] The reader is referred to Bolder [7] or Jorion [20] for much more discussion on the measurement of market risk.

measure risks—such of those of the operational flavour—are not important. On the contrary, they are central.[30] They nonetheless involve rather less internal modelling and computation, placing them somewhat outside of the scope of this discussion.

**Colour and Commentary 4** (RISK CONDITIONALITY)*: The nature of the data used to parametrize one's risk models has, rather unsurprisingly, an important influence on the result. This notion can be made more precise. Long-horizon, relatively low frequency datasets yield unconditional—or long-term average—estimates. Risk measures based on such data are referred to as* through-the-cycle *estimators. Short-horizon, higher frequency datasets lead to conditional (or local) estimates; the resulting risk measures are termed* point-in-time *metrics. The treatment of time is thus the critical difference between these alternative approaches. Both perspectives—and the many possible choices between these* two *extremes—are perfectly valid. Which approach one chooses will naturally depend on one's objectives. Economic capital tends to use the through-the-cycle lens, because it better captures extremes, avoids procyclicality, and permit intertemporal comparison of a firm's risk position. NIB, following this general practice, also adopts the through-the-cycle perspective. The through-the-cycle viewpoint—also widely employed by the regulatory community—is a key reason for the presence of the capital buffers arising in economic-capital calculations. These buffers thus attempt, to a certain extent, to carefully bring the point-of-time perspective into the analysis.*[a]

[a] The point-in-time angle will not be ignored. It plays a central role in loan-impairment and stress-testing analysis.

## 1.5 Risk Fundamentals

With the conceptual frame hopefully moderately clear in the reader's mind, it is time to turn our attention to the risk-measurement dimension. As should be abundantly clear, approximating the $1 - \alpha$ unexpected loss for each individual asset—and thereby the entire portfolio—will require some heavy machinery. Our immediate objective is not to describe the machine in detail, but rather outline some of its main design features.

Although certainly not exhaustive, *three* key risk questions will be addressed in this section:

[30] Chapelle [12] is an excellent starting point for the various strategies used by operational risk managers to overcome these challenges.

1. identifying a fundamental characterization of risk;
2. examining the inherent tension between portfolio diversification and concentration; and
3. reviewing *two* alternative approaches for the construction of financial models (or indeed, any type of mathematical model).

The disparate risks in our taxonomy behave in different ways. The first order of business is to gain an understanding of how precisely these risks might differ and what this implies for their measurement. Equally important, we will try to understand the commonalities—through a fundamental characterization of risk—between our disparate risks. The portfolio perspective is another area of correspondence between different risk types. The twin concepts of diversification and concentration provide important insights into the measurement of economic capital.

The final topic in this section relates to some foundational concepts in mathematical modelling. Financial modelling is *not*—to be brutally honest—everyone's favourite topic. Some view modelling with suspicion and distrust, others with open hostility, while many consider it to be a necessary evil.[31] The simple reality, however, is that mathematical models are tools. Their role is to illuminate and inform the decision-taking process, but certainly not to take the decisions themselves. Against this backdrop, discussion of possible modelling choices and their implications for economic-capital estimation should hopefully be welcome.

### *1.5.1 Two Silly Games*

The following exercise will require some patience from the reader. It has—at first blush, at least—no obvious link to finance or economics and is quite certainly not the classic approach towards introducing economic capital. There is, of course, some method to this madness. Hopefully the reader's patience will be rewarded and the process might even prove (moderately) entertaining.

We'd like to try playing *two* rather silly, and entirely fictitious, games of chance. Both games involve simultaneously rolling two (fair) dice as one might when playing a board game or visiting a casino.[32] The result of each roll of the dice has a financial consequence for the participant. The actual outcome depends on the sum of our dice values (or pips), which we will refer to as $\mathcal{S}$.

The rules—and specific results—of each game are summarized in Table 1.1. In the first game, one gains €0.05 if $\mathcal{S}$ is even and experiences a loss of equal and opposite sign when $\mathcal{S}$ is odd. In brief, even you win, odds you lose. The second game is only slightly more nuanced. If $\mathcal{S} = 2$, you lose a whopping €1.75, whereas

[31] A small minority, conversely, view mathematical models as the answer to all of our problems. For the quantitative analyst, this is more disturbing than scepticism and wariness, because it suggests a critical misunderstanding of the role of these tools.

[32] Each die is of the six-sided traditional variety, where the dots on each side are referred to as *pips*.

**Table 1.1** *The rules*: This table highlights the simple rules associated with our two silly games. The final outcome of each game is determined by the sum of the sides of two rolled dice, which is denoted as $\mathcal{S}$.

| Game #1 | Game #2 |
|---|---|
| If $\mathcal{S}$ is even, you win €0.05 | If $\mathcal{S} > 2$, you win €0.05 |
| If $\mathcal{S}$ is odd, you lose €0.05 | If $\mathcal{S} = 2$, you lose €1.75 |

**Table 1.2** *Game results*: The adjacent table provides a complete description of the full set of outcomes and likelihoods associated with a single realization of our two silly games. It also provides profit-and-loss results along with the expected financial receipt.

| | Dice outcomes | | Game P&L | | Expected P&L | |
|---|---|---|---|---|---|---|
| $\mathcal{S}$ | Count | Prob. | #1 | #2 | #1 | #2 |
| 2 | 1 | 0.03 | 0.05 | **−1.75** | 0.001 | **−0.049** |
| 3 | 2 | 0.06 | **−0.05** | 0.05 | **−0.003** | 0.003 |
| 4 | 3 | 0.08 | 0.05 | 0.05 | 0.004 | 0.004 |
| 5 | 4 | 0.11 | **−0.05** | 0.05 | **−0.006** | 0.006 |
| 6 | 5 | 0.14 | 0.05 | 0.05 | 0.007 | 0.007 |
| 7 | 6 | 0.17 | **−0.05** | 0.05 | **−0.008** | 0.008 |
| 8 | 5 | 0.14 | 0.05 | 0.05 | 0.007 | 0.007 |
| 9 | 4 | 0.11 | **−0.05** | 0.05 | **−0.006** | 0.006 |
| 10 | 3 | 0.08 | 0.05 | 0.05 | 0.004 | 0.004 |
| 11 | 2 | 0.06 | **−0.05** | 0.05 | **−0.003** | 0.003 |
| 12 | 1 | 0.03 | 0.05 | 0.05 | 0.001 | 0.001 |
| Total | 36 | 1.00 | – | – | 0.000 | 0.000 |

in all other dice outcomes, a small gain of €0.05 is achieved. In short, with *snake eyes* you lose big, in all other cases you win small.[33]

Playing each game a single time is probably fairly uninteresting, but imagine playing either game 25 times in a row. The final financial result will then simply be the sum of these 25 repetitions. Which game would you prefer to play? The profit-and-loss profiles of each game are quite different. One's choice will certainly depend on individual preferences and assessment of the relative odds of success.

There are, it turns out, no secrets about the throwing of two dice. Table 1.2 unpacks the full details of our two silly games. With two six-sided dice, there are 36 different possible combinations that might be obtained. There are only, however, 11 possible outcomes for the sum of both sides (i.e., $\mathcal{S}$). Some values of $\mathcal{S}$—such as two or 12—can only occur in a single way. Others—such as six, seven, and eight—arise through multiple variations of dice throws. Six possible values of $\mathcal{S}$ are even, while only five are odd. Adding up the probability of the odd and even outcomes, however, we find that they are equally likely.

Table 1.2 also helpfully displays the expected profit-and-loss associated with a single repetition of our silly games. This is simply, following from basic probability

[33] Rolling a pair of dice with a sum of two is colourfully referred to as snake eyes in the game of *craps*. This rather odd gambling activity incidentally seems to appear in a surprising number of Hollywood movies.

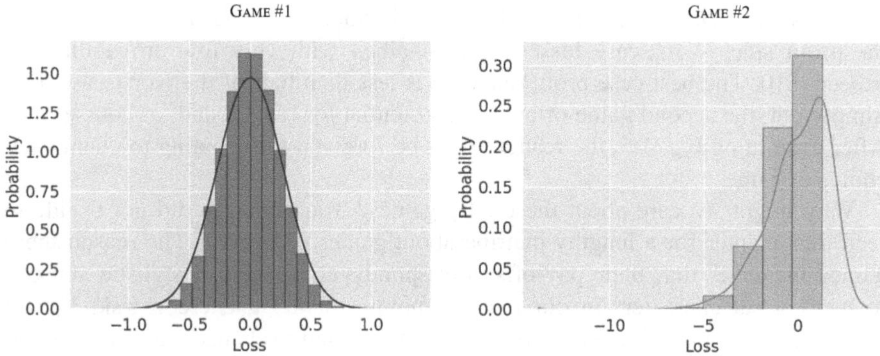


**Fig. 1.5** *Silly game pay-off profiles*: The two preceding graphics outline—across tens of thousands of simulated realizations—the distribution of the pay-off profiles associated with our two silly games.

and the discreteness of our sample space, the sum of the probability weighted outcomes.[34] To be honest, the game pay-offs were specifically selected so that expected profit-and-loss value of each game is equivalent; in short, these games were cooked. On average, there is *no* differences between these games.

Perhaps the reader, in light of this new information, has revised her choice of which game to play. After all, it seems that, on average, one should be indifferent between playing these two silly games. There is, nevertheless, ample scope *not* to be entirely detached. Even if the expected outcome agrees between these two games, they do not have the same *risk* characteristics. A single roll of the dice can create a loss of €1.75 in the second game. This admittedly occurs with a small (i.e., 3%) probability. To obtain such a loss in the first game, however, one would need 35 consecutive odd rolls of the dice! While not physically impossible, the probability of such an event is vanishingly small.[35] There is thus a dramatic difference between our two silly games.

Figure 1.5 helps us visualize the precise nature of these differences by displaying the pay-off distribution for our silly games. These graphics were produced by simulating, on a computer, hundreds of thousands of realizations of 25 consecutive repetitions of each game. Both are centred around zero; this is where the similarities end. The first game's profit-and-loss profile is symmetric—that is, there is an equally probability of gain and loss. Moreover, the most extreme gains or losses do not appear to exceed about €1. Our second game's loss distribution is, by contrast,

[34] It suffices to show the expected outcome for a single game, because each repetition of our silly games is independent. The pay-off for $n$ identical repetitions of our silly games is, therefore, merely the sum of their $n$ expected pay-outs. See Casella and Berger [11] for more background on the notion of statistical expectation.

[35] Specifically, it is $0.5^{35} = \frac{1}{34,359,738,368}$, which is effectively zero. Many popular lotteries, to provide some context, actually offer significantly higher probabilities of success. See Zabrocki [49] for a Canadian example.

highly asymmetric. The negative side of the distribution extends much further than the profit side. Worst-case losses appear—albeit with very low probability—to exceed €10. The best-case profit outcome is less than half of the worst-case loss. Simply put, the second game offers more potential for reward and, of course, risk. After examining Fig. 1.5, the reader might be forgiven for deciding to change her choice of game.

Why might we care about these silly games? You certainly did not decide to read this chapter for a lengthy diatribe about games of chance. The reason these games matter is that their pay-offs correspond—at least, in a stylistic sense—to *two* central characters in our risk taxonomy: market and credit risk. Market risk is, at least approximately, symmetric. Interest and exchanges rates or market-spread movements tend to have roughly equal probability of rising or falling. These market-risk factors can, and do, change in large, sudden swings. Most of the time, however, their movements are the sum of many, small cumulative up and down steps. Mechanically, this is the pay-off profile of the first game.

Credit risk is a different animal. The bond investor or lender earns a typically small credit spread or lending margin. Very occasionally, a credit obligor defaults and fails to meet part, or all, of its contractual obligation. In these rare cases, the loss outcome is very large. As a result, credit risk is occasionally described as picking up nickels in the dirt in front of a steamroller. One earns, with apparently low risk, a steady stream of small returns. In some rare cases, one slips and dismayingly meets the business end of the steamroller. This is, again approximately, a description of our second game's pay-off distribution. It also, fairly graphically, illustrates the inherent motivation for banks to have a firm handle on the credit risks embedded in their lending portfolios.

Figure 1.6 displays—to permit comparison with Fig. 1.5—illustrative market- and credit-loss distributions. Loss-centric risk managers have a tendency to write losses—unlike in the analysis of our two games—as a positive number. This

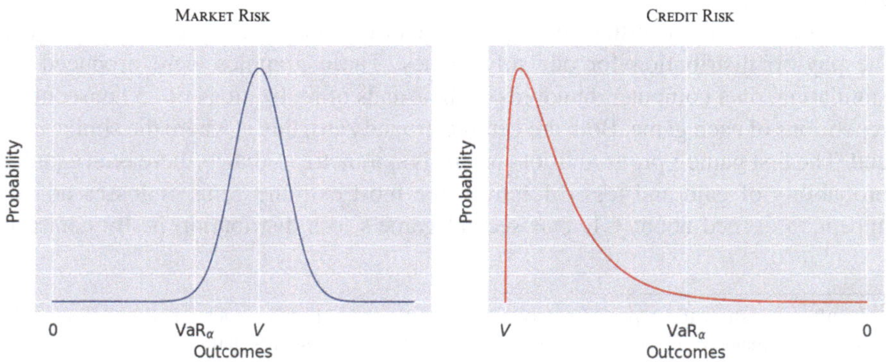


**Fig. 1.6** *Market- and credit-loss distributions*: These figures display illustrative market- and credit-loss distributions. Loss, following common practice, is displayed as a positive number. These distributions are, in a stylized way, roughly consistent with our silly game pay-off profiles from Fig. 1.5.

convention makes no practical difference; it simply leads to the classical right-skewed credit-loss distribution.

While our two dice-rolling games are certainly silly, the results are surprisingly consistent with the differences between credit and market risk. The relative outcomes and magnitudes are naturally somewhat exaggerated in the context of our silly games. The negative financial outcome in the second game has a probability of $\frac{1}{36} \approx 0.03$. In our current portfolio, on average, the default probability is about $\frac{60}{10{,}000} = 0.006$; for the highest quality credit countparties, it is only a fraction of this average amount. At the same time, the probability of market-risk gains and losses are *not*—at any given point in time—precisely equal. Furthermore, large jumps in market-risk factors can, and do, occur with some regularity. These practical differences notwithstanding, our two silly games can be considered as a useful analogy for these two risk archetypes. Credit and market-risk arise from *two* rather different investment strategies or, if you prefer, games.

As useful as the analogy posed by our simple games might be, the reality of financial-market risk is dramatically more complicated and nuanced. The set of possible financial outcomes, in our two silly games, is known and discrete.[36] We may count and assign a probability to every possible dice throw. Actual asset values, sadly, do not work this way. A virtual infinity of outcomes are possible, and in most cases, the assignment of probabilities is a subjective exercise. Even worse, we do *not* even know what it is that we do not know. In other words, in the real world there are possible, but perhaps very improbable, outcomes that we have not even thought to consider. This is Taleb [44]'s infamous black swan.[37] This unsettling situation is increasingly referred to as Knightian uncertainty after the influential publication, Knight [25]. This does not imply that our silly game analogies are without use, it merely counsels caution and humbleness in the face of the task ahead of us.

Understanding this distinction highlighted by our silly games, nonetheless has a number of benefits. The fundamental structure of market and credit risk is different. Market risk is comprised of large number of small positive, and negative, outcomes. Credit risk is dominated by a few large, but inherently rare, events. It thus makes complete sense that we, as risk managers, need to model and measure these divergent risks using distinct tools. With that important point in mind, characterization of both risks starts from the same place. It is necessary to identify the underlying economic factors that drive risk. This brings us to a fundamental decomposition of risk that impacts, you will not be surprised to hear, market and credit risk in alternative ways.

[36] Our ability to perfectly understand the associated sample space is a principal reason why games of chance are so beloved by statisticians and probabilists.

[37] Or, if you prefer another colour of swan, see Bolton et al. [10].

**Colour and Commentary 5** (RISK ARCHETYPES): *We introduced—to motivate how varying risks in our taxonomy might arise—two silly games involving the throwing of a pair of dice. The financial results of playing either game, in expectation at least, are equal. Their risk profiles differ dramatically. The first game—an allegory for market risk—involves a symmetric loss distribution constructed from the sum of many small positive and negative underlying drivers. Credit risk is encapsulated in the second game. It involves a modest positive return in most states of the world, but with the potential for a large, low-probability loss lurking in the background. This is intended to reflect the mechanics of default and the associated highly skewed credit-loss distribution. The morale of these silly games is that key asset-value risks arise in very different ways and, as a consequence, we require distinct strategies to estimate their contribution to our economic capital figures.*

### *1.5.2 A Fundamental Characterization*

The value of asset portfolios, for a variety of reasons, rise and fall over time. The underlying drivers of these changes in asset valuation are legion. One of the main objectives of a risk taxonomy is to classify and organize these so-called risk drivers. Our two silly games take this a step further by trying to stylistically describe the characteristics of different kinds of risk. These efforts are still lacking something concrete. They do *not* help us understand *why* certain asset values change differently from others. To address this point, we may decompose these asset-value movements into two (very) broad categories:

1. general, or *systemic*, market movements that impact the value of all (or most) assets; and
2. *idiosyncratic*, or specific, movements relating to a single (or only a few) assets.

This amounts to a categorization of changes in asset valuations into common and specific risk poles. This idea is far from new. It lies at the heart of the capital asset pricing model (CAPM) and arbitrage pricing theory (APT).[38]

Some concrete examples are useful. When the general level of interest rates rises in an economy, it affects many assets. Some might even argue that it impacts *all* assets. This is a case of a systemic risk. Similar situations occur with exchange rates,

[38] See, for more background on these classical although still very relevant financial theories, Treynor [45], Sharpe [40, 41], Lintner [26], and Ross [39].

commodity prices, or key macroeconomic variables such as inflation and output.[39] These quantities are correspondingly referred to as systemic risk factors.

On the other hand, some asset-value effects are associated with a specific entity. A given company—due to poor governance structures, failure of an important project, or simply bad luck—might run into financial difficulty. The impact of such financial distress, and associated asset-value movements, is typically restricted to the company in question. We refer to these firm-specific elements as idiosyncratic risk factors.

How might we make use this risk decomposition? It is very tempting to place market risk into the systemic category and assign credit risk to the idiosyncratic side. Market risk is, after all, largely about examining the effect of systemic factors on one's portfolio: interest rate, exchange rate, credit-spread, basis-swap, or market-volatility movements. Moreover, finance theory tells us that idiosyncratic market risk is, with a moderate amount of effort and organization, readily diversified away. As such, it is not compensated, or priced, in financial markets. Credit risk—often linked to a firm's liquidity, solvency, capital, and competitive positions—matches fairly closely to our firm-specific notion of idiosyncratic risk.

There is a significant amount of truth to this unequivocal, binary allocation of market and credit risk into these systemic and idiosyncratic buckets. Unfortunately, it is not quite true. Some element of what is typically classified as market risk can be considered to be quite idiosyncratic. Credit spreads do move in concert with other similar credits, but some (often variable and difficult-to-estimate) part of that spread remains firm specific. Moreover, bond yields are importantly influenced by security specific factors surrounding market-microstructure and liquidity.[40]

Credit risk is, of course, a bit more complicated. Much of what we think of as credit risk is clearly idiosyncratic. Firms have a strong tendency to run into trouble as a consequence of internal firm-specific choices. Nevertheless, firms do not operate in a vacuum. They have competitors who exert an important influence on their financial situation. They are also tied into a network of suppliers and clients. Competitive actions or the financial health of key members in their operating network can, and do, impact their fate. These important latter effects cannot be easily categorized as firm specific or idiosyncratic. Defaults are thus logically correlated through general economic conditions and industry interdependencies. Credit risk has—like its cousin, market risk—elements of both dimensions.

This latter point is the key message of Fig. 1.7. Neither systemic nor idiosyncratic are—despite their important conceptual differences—completely distinct. The corollary is that market and credit risk cannot be allocated, in a wholesale

---

[39] One can, and probably should, argue that it is actually the macroeconomic variables who are driving the financial outcomes.

[40] See Amihud et al. [1] for thoughts on liquidity and O'Hara [36] for an excellent entry point into the theory of market microstructure.

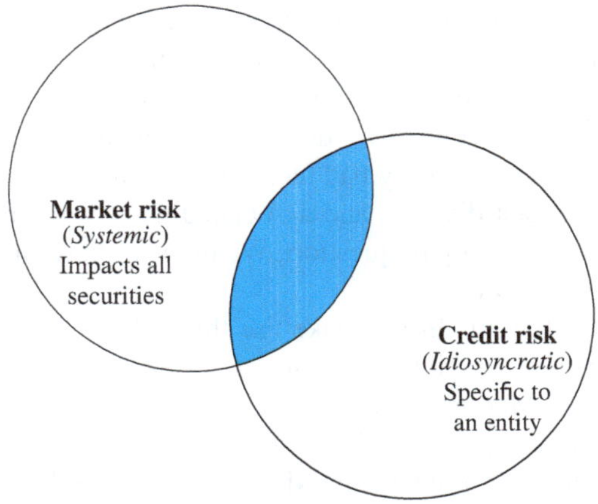


**Fig. 1.7** *Independent risks?*: This schematic is designed to help the reader appreciate the interplay between systemic and idiosyncratic risks. While a useful distinction, these two notions of risk are not truly independent. Market and credit risk accordingly inherit this overlap.

manner, to these broad categories. As we will see in the following section, this has important implications. The fundamental distinction relates back to a centrally important concept in both finance and economic-capital estimation: concentration and diversification.

**Colour and Commentary 6** (A BROAD RISK CATEGORIZATION)*: It is informative and useful to break the risk associated with asset-value movements into two broad categories: systemic and idiosyncratic. Systemic risk stems from underlying factors whose movements—naturally, in different ways—affect all assets. Idiosyncratic risk is specific and relates only to the individual firm. Conventional wisdom often seeks to categorize market risk as systemic and credit risk as idiosyncratic. There is some truth in this arrangement, but it is not quite correct. What is more, it is wrong in important ways. Idiosyncratic risk, in financial theory, is not rewarded. This is because, with sufficient effort, it can be diversified away. Following this logic, were credit risk to be entirely idiosyncratic, it could be safely ignored. This latter statement is patently false, implying the incorrectness of treating credit risk as an entirely idiosyncratic phenomena.*[a] *Indeed, investigation of the systemic nature of credit risk yields important insight into a key element of economic-capital calculations: portfolio concentration.*

[a] The implications of treating market risk as entirely systemic, however, are rather less severe.

### 1.5.3 Introducing Concentration

Almost everyone who has ever taken an introductory course in finance has performed a diversification exercise. It can take a variety of forms, but it essentially amounts to indicating how the variance of portfolio returns (i.e., risk) can be reduced by adding non perfectly correlated assets. This concept, first introduced by Markowitz [28], is the central idea behind diversification. There is, of course, a limit to the benefits of diversification. Systemic risk, which impacts all assets, simply cannot be fully diversified away.

Idiosyncratic risk is another matter. It can, and should, be eliminated through diversification. Credit and market risk, however, vary importantly along this perspective. The lion's share of diversification benefits in an equity portfolio appear to be achievable with a few dozen stocks. Replicating a sovereign-bond benchmark—that might include hundreds of individual instruments—can be achieved with only a handful of bond holdings. In short, the market-risk component of a fixed-income portfolio is readily diversified. Statements suggesting that idiosyncratic risk is not compensated are made, almost invariably, in a market-risk context.

Default- or credit-risk diversification turns out to be a bit more slippery. Why might this be the case? Our silly games can help provide us some insight. A market-risk loss represents, in most cases, only a small proportion of the instrument's value. Remember, market-risk movements are typically the sum of numerous, relatively small market movements. Multiple securities, being buffeted in different directions by the vagaries of market-risk factors, have many more opportunities to offset each others' gains and losses. Credit-risk losses, while rare, are also more sizable; in the worst case, you can lose the entire investment. Such rare events are not readily offset by other asset-price movements.

The consequence of this difference is that credit risk is significantly more sensitive—than its market-risk counterpart—to the composition of one's asset portfolio. In contrast to the market-risk setting, true diversification in credit-risk portfolios can require hundreds or even thousands of individual securities. Even then, it is necessary that no one single exposure dominates the portfolio.

This latter claim might be hard for some readers to accept. Even those who buy this idea might benefit from a demonstration. Let us, therefore, consider a concrete, motivational example. Imagine that we construct *two* portfolios where everything—with one important exception—is identical. The total values of the portfolios are equal and set to €1000.[41] Every instrument further shares the same probability of default at $\frac{50}{10{,}000} \approx 0.005$. Moreover, in the event of default, we assume that only 60% of the exposure's value will be recovered.

Despite these striking similarities, there is a key distinction. One portfolio has only 100 individual risk exposures of varying size; some are quite large, while others are relatively small. The other portfolio has 10,000 individual exposures.

[41] You may multiply this value by whatever value you wish to make it a bit more realistic.

**Table 1.3** *Competing portfolios*: What are the differences, in terms of credit risk, associated with diversified and concentrated portfolios? One way to find out is to construct two portfolios that differ solely along the concentration dimension. The underlying table summarizes two such example portfolios.

| Measure | Diversified | Concentrated |
|---|---|---|
| Total portfolio size | €1000 | |
| Number of positions | 10,000 | 100 |
| Mean position size | €0.10 | €10.00 |
| Minimum position size | €0.10 | €0.08 |
| Maximum position size | €0.10 | €47.80 |
| Default probability | 50 bps. | |
| Loss-given default | 40.00% | |
| Confidence level | 99.97% | |

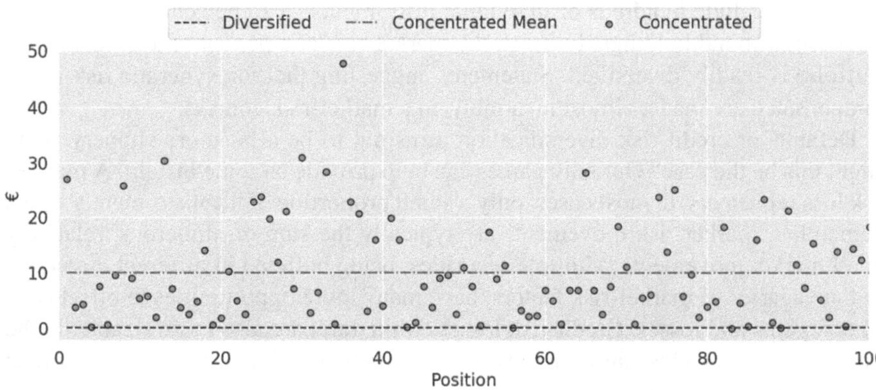


**Fig. 1.8** *Sample exposure profiles*: This graphic shows the distribution of exposure sizes associated with the diversified and concentrated portfolios introduced in Table 1.3. The distinction is visually striking.

Each exposure takes a value of $\frac{1}{10{,}000}$. To put it more directly, one set of exposures is diversified, while the other is rather concentrated. The key summary statistics associated with these two portfolios are summarized, for convenience, in Table 1.3.

Figure 1.8 helps out by illustrating the contrasting distributions of exposure sizes associated with our two sample portfolios. The diversified portfolio exposures are not terribly interesting; they all share the same value. The same is not true for our concentrated portfolio. One very large exposure accounts for almost 5% of the total portfolio. There is another handful of exposures in the 2 to 3% range. Others appear to be very close to zero.

One might legitimately ask if this is another cooked example. The simple answer is yes. At the same time, however, it is not so different from some real-world portfolios. The concentrated example might represent a corporate-bond book or

**Table 1.4** *Concentration results*: Here we observe the differences, in terms of idiosyncratic and systemic risk written in percentage terms of our portfolio value, for our competing portfolios. Systemic risks differ very little, whereas the idiosyncratic dimension diverges dramatically.

| | Diversified | Concentrated |
|---|---|---|
| Idiosyncratic | 0.1% | 3.1% |
| + Systemic | 7.6% | 9.0% |

a commercial lending portfolio.[42] Such portfolios typically include a relatively modest number of heterogeneous exposures; note, however, that these 100 positions are already substantially larger than what is typically required for a comfortable degree of diversification in the market-risk environment. The diversified case, conversely, might be a large credit-card or student-loan portfolio. It is comprised of many relatively homogeneous positions. It is extremely unlikely, of course, that either of these cases would involve identical default probabilities and loss-given-default assumptions. This aspect was definitely, and unapologetically, manipulated to focus our attention entirely on the concentration dimension.

The interesting question after having introduced these two portfolios, of course, is what is the impact on each portfolio's credit-risk economic capital calculation? To answer this query, we naturally need to compute their economic capital. Abstracting from the technical details, we use two alternative models. One, fairly unrealistic, model assumes that all credit risk is idiosyncratic in nature. The other includes both idiosyncratic and systemic elements in a sensible manner.[43] The utility of these two distinct models is to permit us to assess the impact of both systemic and idiosyncratic risks on our economic-capital estimates.

Table 1.4 summarizes the results of our experiment. The individual values are provided in percentage terms. As one would have expected, the idiosyncratic risk for the diversified portfolio approaches zero. The 10,000 position portfolio has thus succeeded in diversifying away idiosyncratic risk. The concentrated portfolio has not. Roughly one third of the total risk, for this 100 exposure portfolio, remains idiosyncratic. The full benefits of diversification thus remain at some distance. When we move to consider the full credit-risk model in the second line of Table 1.4, we see that the total risk of these two portfolios are surprisingly similar. The diversified portfolio is naturally less risky, but not dramatically so. Figure 1.9 strikingly visualizes this point.

There are, at least, three takeaways from this exercise. First, systemic risk simply cannot be diversified. This is hardly new—it is, in fact, a central lesson from the CAPM model—but it is reassuring to see it resurface in this context. It is

[42] In actuality, these would involve more positions, but stylistically they are similar.

[43] For the interested reader, the idiosyncratic choice is the binomial independent-default model, while the second (systemic and idiosyncratic) approach is a one-factor Gaussian threshold model. See Bolder [8, Chapters 2 and 4] for more background on these models. We will also revisit these general approaches, within the NIB setting, in Chap. 2.

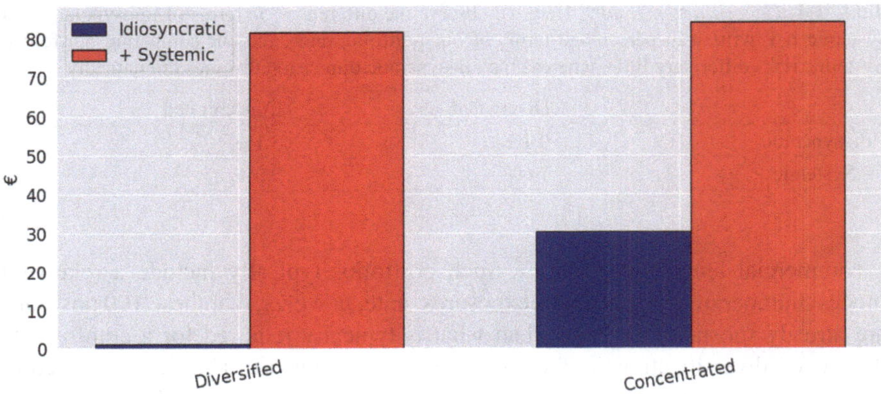


**Fig. 1.9** *Achieving diversification*: This figure provides, in currency terms, the idiosyncratic and systemic risk results for the two distinct portfolios introduced in Table 1.3. Total risk is not dramatically dissimilar, but the idiosyncratic elements differ. Concentration clearly matters.

furthermore hard work, as a second point, to diversify away idiosyncratic risk in the case of credit risk. 100 heterogeneous exposures does not even bring us close. Finally, the systemic aspect is definitely *not* restricted to the world of market risk. Indeed, our example and Table 1.4 clearly illustrate the fundamental importance of systemic factors in the estimation of credit-risk economic capital.

In this fabricated example, we have only examined the simplest type of concentration: that related to exposure size. Credit obligations also differ along a host of other dimensions such as their geographic region, industrial sector, credit category, default-recovery assumptions, or even firm size. The more similarities, within a portfolio, among these aspects, the greater the potential for concentration.[44] Diversification in a credit-risk setting is thus even more difficult than what is suggested in this example.

Concentration and diversification are opposite side of the same coin. Both are intimately related to the fundamental notions of idiosyncratic and systemic risks. Appreciating this fact is an important step towards understanding models of economic capital. A key responsibility of such models is to appropriately combine these two dimensions to describe our asset-loss distributions. For the measurement of market risk, this involves leaning strongly (or even completely) in the systemic direction. Credit risk, conversely, requires a careful hand to manage the interactions between idiosyncrasy and diversification on the one hand and systemic issues and concentration on the other.

[44] Concentration is consequently a core theme in the measurement of credit risk. See Lütkebohmert [27] for much more on strategies and techniques to manage it.

**Colour and Commentary 7** (ONE COIN, TWO SIDES)*: A cornerstone of finance theory holds that idiosyncratic risk, which is readily diversified, is not compensated. While true in a market risk sense, the narrative is somewhat more complicated in the credit-risk situation. A simple, stylized example of a concentrated and diversified portfolio illustrates that elimination of idiosyncratic risk is not trivial task for credit-risk portfolios. Hundreds, if not thousands, of positions are necessary. Moreover, an eye must be also be trained on other possible sources of concentration such as geographical location and industry. Asset riskiness, and thus estimation of economic capital, depends importantly on portfolio composition. This analysis indicates that the structure of one's portfolio also has different implications depending on the type of risk under examination.*

### *1.5.4 Modelling 101*

We now, in our quest to better understand economic-capital calculations, turn our attention to financial modelling. Let us begin with a wise statement from Holland [19]:

> Model building is the art of selecting those aspects of a process that are relevant to the question being asked.

To those less accustomed to working with mathematical models, it might be a bit startling to read about *selection* in this context. A bit of reflection, however, reveals that it is inevitable. Models are a simplified representation of a complex, indeed unknowable, reality. In the physical sciences, our understanding may be superior to that in the social realm, but it still remains far from perfect.[45] We simply cannot create models that encapsulate all of the complexity of the real world; choices must be made. Holland [19]'s basic point is that it's more important, in principle, to appreciate the problem and the conceptual logic behind one's modelling choice than the fine print of the mathematical details.[46]

This reasoning will help to explain why so much attention has been placed on the nature of the risks associated with a firm's assets. It also suggests that this (first) conversation about economic-capital models will focus, as intimated by Holland [19], on the selection of those relevant aspects. The technical details will be thoroughly covered in subsequent chapters.

---

[45] Compare this to our two silly games, where all possibilities and probabilities can be characterized to perfection.

[46] Naturally, the details are also important, but they quickly become irrelevant if high-level decisions are poorly taken.

There are many types and flavours of mathematical models, but one overriding classification can be helpful. The key distinction surrounds *why* certain events, which one is attempting to model, occur. One class of models—which we will refer to as *structural*—attempts to capture some aspects of the underlying mechanism driving key events. Imagine, for example, building a model of monetary policy. A structural approach would describe the logical linkages between central-bank rate decisions, the monetary transmission mechanism, and inflation outcomes. Structural models describe, in mathematical terms, how key variables *should* interact. This requires some theoretical foundations upon which the model can build. The alternative approach is data driven. Placing less weight on theoretical considerations, one uses statistical techniques to extract empirical relationships from the data. These are termed *reduced-form* models. Image and voice recognition software are excellent examples of reduced-form models; they use massive amounts of data to train algorithms to recognize certain combinations of events. The *why* aspect is not central.

Ultimately, all models have parameters. These parameters are, almost invariably, estimated from real-world data. One might justifiably enquire, in this context, as to the real difference between structural and reduced-form models. The key distinction is *causality*. A structural model attempts to describe causal relationships between variables within the real-world data-generating process. Reduced-form models are more agnostic about causality, they attempt to identify empirical relationships embedded in the data.

The difference may appear subtle and perhaps abstract, but it is a useful magnifying glass through which to examine and evaluate models. Neither approach, for example, is dominant. Both have their own strengths and weaknesses. Reduced-form models lean heavily on the data; they are, as a consequence, fairly sensitive to non-representative or erroneous inputs. They are also particularly vulnerable when predicting outcomes outside of one's data range. Structural models place a greater importance on theory. Should the theoretical relationships be flawed, these shortcomings will be inherited by the model. In most estimations of economic capital, however, both modelling techniques make an appearance.

Estimation of market-risk, to be more concrete, is typically performed with a reduced-form model. The value of financial instruments—be they loans, deposits, bonds, or swaps—practically depends on a host of underlying market-risk factors. Different financial instruments, however, have varying degrees of responsiveness to change in these factors. Some instruments might be very sensitive to exchange rates, whereas others are invariant to them. A common, and clever, approach to characterizing market risk thus involves writing

$$\text{Asset-value movements} = \sum_{k=1}^{K} \text{Factor Sensitivity}_k \cdot \text{Factor change}_k, \tag{1.4}$$

where we have $K$ distinct market-risk factors. In words, the contribution of various market-risk factors are assumed to be additive. Each individual market-risk factor

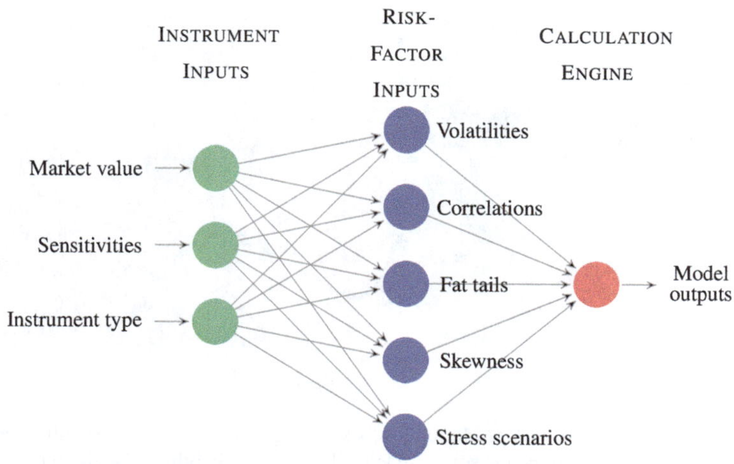


**Fig. 1.10** *A market-risk model*: The preceding schematic organizes the instrument- and risk-factor-level inputs into the typical market-risk calculation. The market-risk factor system is normally described using a data-driven reduced-form model.

contribution is simply the product of the instrument's factor sensitivity and the factor's movement.[47] A critical aspect of measuring market risk, therefore, involves the construction and management of these sensitivities.

Equation 1.4 has a convenient form, but it says nothing about the sign, magnitude, and interaction of these market-risk factor changes. Getting a handle on market risk will inevitably involve tackling this aspect. The reduced-form assumption enters at this point. Market-risk models rarely attempt to describe why interest rates, exchange rates, and key market spreads interact. Instead, they collect large amounts of market data including daily, weekly, or monthly observations of all important market-risk factors. Risk estimates are then based on estimation of the joint statistical properties of this data, or alternatively by extracting risk-factor movements from a period of extreme market turmoil.[48] In either case, the role of this complex system of market-risk factors is informed by observed, empirical data relationships.

Figure 1.10 provides a high-level schematic of the main ingredients involved in a typical market-risk calculation. Key inputs are profitably separated into *two* groups: those related to the financial instruments and those linked to the market-risk factors. Collecting and organizing the instrument sensitivities is hard work, but most of these

[47] See Bolder [7, Part I] for a more detailed discussion of these ideas.

[48] This is an almost criminally brief description. See Bolder [7, Part IV], and subsequent chapters, for more specifics.

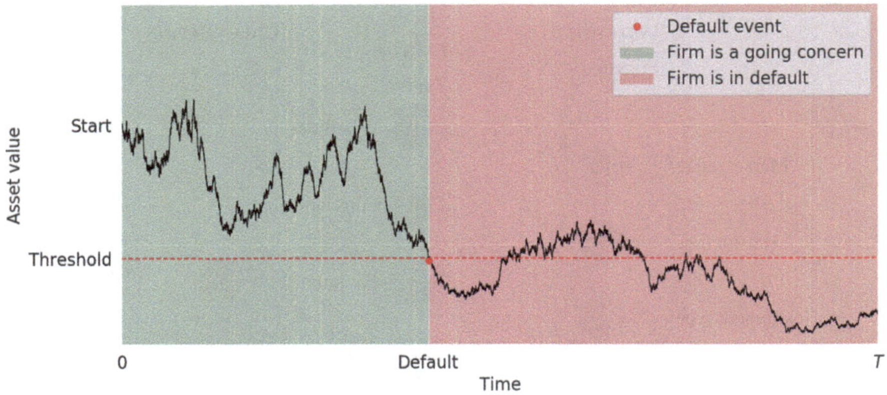


**Fig. 1.11** *A structural relationship*: Merton [31]'s key insight was to identify default as occurring when a firm's asset values fall below some predefined—typically liability related—threshold. This is a classical example of a theoretically motivated structural model.

values are readily available through internal systems. The art and science of market-risk modelling relate to the risk-factor system. By and large, this aspect is captured through a data-driven reduced-form model.

Market-risk measurement is thus predominately reduced-form and focused on systemic market risk factors.[49] What about credit risk? Measuring credit risk, the reader may not be surprised to learn, usually involves a different strategy relative to the market-risk case. NIB's credit-risk economic-capital model—similar to many other institutions—follows a structural approach.[50] The key theoretical insight dates back to Merton [31], who offered a clever, and intuitive, description of the underlying *cause* of firm default. It begins, as one would hope, with the firm's balance sheet. The insight is that default occurs when the firm's equity position hits zero; in other words, the asset value is equal to, or larger, than the firm's commitments. Using the language of the previous sections, the firm's supply of capital is exhausted. This observation yields a road map for modelling credit risk.

Figure 1.11 provides a useful visualization of Merton [31]'s theoretical conclusion. The firm's assets move over time in a random fashion. If, at any point, they fall below some predefined threshold, then default is assumed to have occurred. This threshold value needs to be determined, but it basically reduces to some function of the firm's liabilities and the firm's overall financial position. This idea, as is the case in all structural models, effectively endogenizes a key aspect of the phenomena one is trying to model. That is, default is determined inside the model through the interaction of other key variables.

---

[49] The canonical references in this area are Morgan/Reuters [32] and Jorion [21].

[50] There is, however, an entire class of reduced-form credit risk models. See, for example, Bolder [8, Chapter 3] for several concrete examples.

Merton [31]'s insight, while incredibly useful, still requires some polishing to make it a model. The classical structure continuous-time in Merton [31] is now rarely used, but has been supplanted with a number of practical points introduced by Vasicek [46, 47, 48] and Gupton et al. [17, 18]. Without getting to deeply into the details—covered amply in subsequent chapters—one asset-related quantity is particularly helpful in understanding the inner workings of this model. Each credit obligor is assigned a latent state variable closely related to its asset value. It is comprised of the following *two* familiar components:

$$\text{Asset-value index} = \text{Systemic element} + \text{Idiosyncratic element}. \tag{1.5}$$

This requires some unpacking. Each firm's asset-value index is the sum of a systemic and idiosyncratic component. The systemic factor impacts all firm assets; this is the mechanism driving default dependence in the model. The idiosyncratic piece is specific to the individual firm. The genius of Eq. 1.5 is that it explicitly incorporates our fundamental risk characterization.

The individual components of Eq. 1.5 are random and are assumed to be independent.[51] Equation 1.5 gives us what we need to build a proper model. Mechanically, we can think of the credit event as being determined by a number of random draws. We pick a common systemic value out of a hat; it is shared by all credit obligors. We then pull a separate idiosyncratic factor for each credit obligor out of a long line of hats and then proceed to construct our asset-value indices. There is a credit event for each credit counterpart with the following generic form:

$$\text{Credit Event} = \begin{cases} \text{Default} : \text{Asset-value index} \leq \text{Threshold} \\ \text{Survival} : \underbrace{\text{Asset-value index} > \text{Threshold}}_{\text{Otherwise}} \end{cases}. \tag{1.6}$$

Armed with a practical definition of each firm's credit event, the rest is (copious) mathematical and statistical detail. Unlike the market-risk setting, however, realistic implementations of Eqs. 1.5 and 1.6 involve some fairly heavy computations. Drawing random numbers from hats may be relatively easy on a computer, but extremely large numbers must be drawn from an almost breathtaking array of hats to obtain a reasonable degree of accuracy.[52] We will touch on the implementation challenges in Chap. 4.

Figure 1.12—constructed analogously to Fig. 1.11—organizes the instrument- and portfolio-level inputs into a visualization of the credit-risk calculation. The simulation engine, which is responsible for all of the random-number generation, requires many inputs. The first group relates to the individual instruments while the second involves instrument attributes central to systemic-risk considerations. As previously discussed, these instrument features help the model characterize the

[51] This basically means that the randomness of the systemic component is determined completely separately from the idiosyncratic element.

[52] There are probably enough hats involved to make even Britain's Queen Elizabeth II blush.

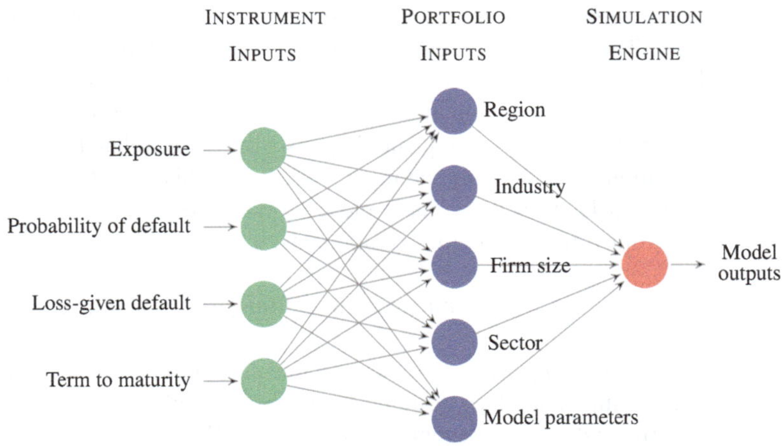


**Fig. 1.12** *A credit-risk model*: This schematic organizes the instrument- and portfolio-level inputs into a visualization of the credit-risk calculation. The instrument and portfolio data fields relate principally to the idiosyncratic and systemic dimensions, respectively. The simulation engine combines these inputs using a structural modelling approach.

degree of portfolio concentration. The simulation engine then collects and combines these inputs using a structural modelling approach to generate economic-capital estimates.

**Colour and Commentary 8** (HANDLING CAUSALITY)*: In this motivational introductory chapter, detailed technical model explanations and derivations are misplaced. A serious discussion of economic-capital estimation would be nonetheless incomplete without addressing the modelling dimension. At a high level, models are profitably characterized by how they handle causality. Structural models rely on theory to endogenize key aspects of the model; in this sense, they attempt to assign causality. Reduced-form models, conversely, rely on empirical data to exogenously describe these key relationships. No approach is, in a general sense, superior to the other and many practical implementations make comfortable use of both philosophies. Market-risk economic-capital model, in general, falls into the reduced-form camp; complex interactions of systemic market-risk factors are typically informed exogenously by empirical data. Credit-risk calculations, by contrast, are often structurally motivated. The structural, or endogenous, default element is theoretically determined through an (indirect) examination of each firm's balance sheet thereby linking back to the idea of capital supply and demand. This approach also easily incorporates both the systemic and idiosyncratic elements so important to credit risk.*

## 1.6 Managing Models

We have, in this discussion, only scratched the surface of the intricacies involved in computing credit-risk economic capital. We have followed Holland [19]'s advice and highlighted some of the relevant aspects. No responsible modelling discussion, however, would be complete without a few words on model governance. Computation of economic capital, in many organizations, is based on internal models. In the literature, these are typically referred to as decision-support models.[53] Decision-support models can be found in medical, agricultural, logistical, and business applications. Interesting and relevant examples might include a medical diagnosis tool, an early-warning tornado system, mergers-and-acquisition decision analysis, or selecting the optimal product mix in a pulp-and-paper mill.

Such models are typically developed internally when, as in the case of economic capital, their development and understanding has strategic importance. With the explicit introduction of economic capital into NIB's statutes, this hurdle would seem to have been comfortably cleared. Simply because a model is strategically important and merits internal development, however, does not imply a free pass. On the contrary, its criticality warrants sustained and careful oversight. The possibility that models are themselves a source of risk—as introduced by Derman [13] and Rebonato [37]—should not be taken lightly. Such model risk (perhaps) need not be directly incorporated into our economic-capital computations, but it definitely needs to be managed.

Managing model risk requires a governance structure. Any internal model—whether for decision support, regulatory oversight, or for policy making—is an ongoing work in progress. It consequently involves a continuous cycle of validation, analysis and improvement, verification, implementation, and usage. It never really ends; Fig. 1.13 reflects this fact with a circular schematic.

Managing model risk essentially amounts to an exercise in quality control.[54] As a consequence, much focus in model risk is assigned to the model-validation process. While the importance of independent, external validation cannot be denied, internal model developers and owners also have a number of additional responsibilities. These include the use of benchmark models, careful computer-code and system management, production of detailed diagnostics and sensitivity analysis, and ongoing stress testing. These are not part-time activities, but central aspects of a well-functioning internal modelling environment.[55] As a consequence, these ideas will show up repeatedly in the following chapters.

One additional model-owner responsibility towers over all others: documentation and transparency. Quality control is virtually impossible without clarity surrounding model choices and assumptions. Scientific discourse, which has proven rather effec-

[53] See Keen [22, 23] and Keen and Morton [24] for the origins of this interesting academic literature.

[54] See Bolder [9] for a more detailed argumentation of this point and its implications.

[55] This, in turn, ties back to the quantitative analysis axioms introduced in the preface.

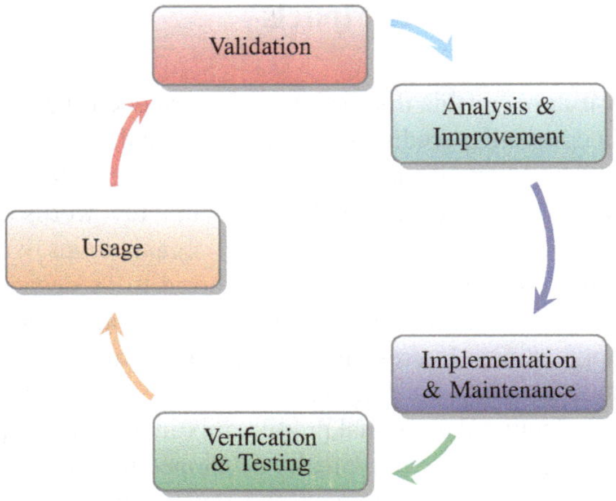


**Fig. 1.13** *Model-improvement cycle*: Any model, to be of practical usefulness, requires ongoing review, validation, and improvement. It also needs to be used. This cycle implies that no working model is a static entity, but rather a dynamic one.

tive in recent centuries, slavishly follows this principle. Scientific ideas are, literally by construction, forced to run the gauntlet of peer review and publication. Modelling ideas are also strengthened and improved through their explicit documentation and exposure to external consideration and critique. This reasoning is the driving force behind the production of this book and argues for its dissemination to the widest possible audience.[56]

**Colour and Commentary 9** (MODEL RISK): *Economic-capital computations depend critically on modelling assumptions and choices. Given their strategic importance, these models are typically internally developed in the form of decision-support systems. Perhaps somewhat ironically, these models are themselves a source of risk. Classified as model risk in our taxonomy, there are no current requirements to add it to economic capital. Common sense and sound business practice, however, argue strongly for extensive governance measures surrounding these models. This can take a range of forms. Model validation receives the most attention—and is certainly very important—but model owners also have numerous additional responsibilities. The most important, and perhaps least well appreciated, element relates to documentation and transparency. Carefully writing down one's methodologies is a valuable discipline. Model quality is moreover directly proportional to its degree of exposure to external critique. These reflections were the catalyst for the production of this book and the justification for its broad dissemination to an external audience.*

[56] Again, our axioms *"write it down"* and *"seek external criticism"* are clearly reflected in these actions.

**Table 1.5** *Economic-capital results*: This table illustrates NIB's economic-capital figures—from the 2020 annual report in NIB [35, pp. 21–23]—by their principal risk dimensions. All figures are denominated in EUR millions.

| Dimension | Subtotal | Total |
|---|---|---|
| *Default risk* | 1534 | |
| *Migration risk* | 487 | |
| **Credit risk** | | 2021 |
| **Market risk** | | 567 |
| **Operational risk** | | 101 |
| *Conservation buffer* | 306 | |
| *Countercyclical buffer* | – | |
| *Stress-test buffer* | 120 | |
| **Capital buffers** | | 426 |
| Economic capital (i.e., capital demand) | | 3115 |
| **Headroom** | | 697 |
| Adjusted common equity (i.e., capital supply) | | 3812 |

## 1.7 NIB's Portfolio

Remaining at the conceptual level can only take us so far, because economic capital is a concrete quantity. To complete this introductory chapter, therefore, it is interesting and useful to examine various perspectives on actual NIB economic-capital computations. Table 1.5 thus provides a bird's eye view illustrating the entire economic-capital computation of roughly EUR 3.1 billion as the end of 2020.[57] It also distinctly includes the various members of our risk taxonomy.[58]

The values from Table 1.5 are drawn from the 2020 NIB annual report. Other institutions provide similar disclosures both in their financial statements and Pillar 3 regulatory reports.[59] Although not a regulated entity, the spirit of the computations from Table 1.5 is consistent with fundamental regulatory principles and best practice.

A few useful conclusions can be drawn. Credit risk, through either default or migration, is the dominant risk in NIB's portfolio. This is the case for literally all lending institutions. It accounts, through NIB's lending and investment activities, for almost two thirds of the total. Moreover, the credit-risk component is multifaceted including both a default and a credit-migration dimension. As will be made much more precise in Chap. 2, default risk relates to an obligor not repaying their obligations whereas migration touches on the capital impact associated with a deterioration of borrower credit quality. Both elements are important, although the

[57] These values are found in NIB [35, pp. 21–23].

[58] Counterparty risk is embedded in the default and credit-migration figures.

[59] BIS [6] rather carefully outlines a publication template for the contents and format of key economic-capital metrics.

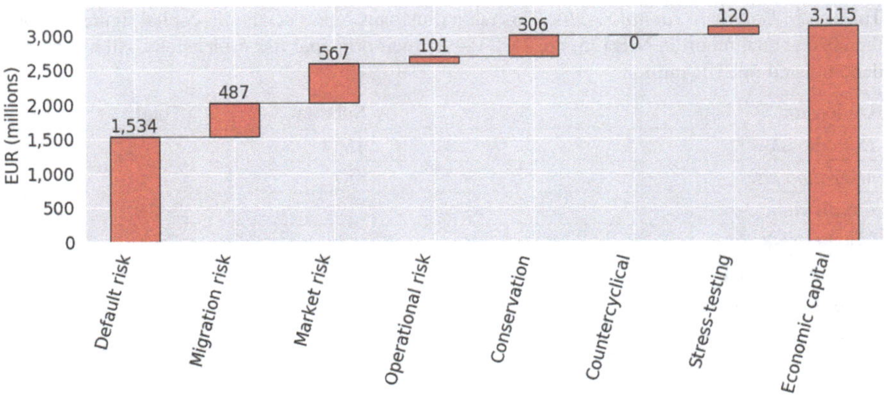


**Fig. 1.14** *The waterfall graphic*: The preceding figure illustrates the main results from Table 1.5 in graphic format; it is often referred to as a waterfall graphic. It underscores the central importance of the credit-risk dimension.

default aspect dominates NIB's portfolio. The size and complexity of the credit-risk aspect is the principal justification for the disproportionate amount of time and energy invested, in the following chapters, into the credit-risk dimension. There is simply much to discuss and analyze; this fact is further underscored visually by Fig. 1.14.

A second point is that Fig. 1.14 provides an opportunity to perform a rapid analysis of NIB's capital adequacy position. In short, it looks to be fairly healthy. The headroom is between 15 to 20% of the equity position providing scope to further grow lending and treasury activities. From NIB [35, pp. 25], we may also read the total NIB asset position as about EUR 35.4 billion. Using this fact and Table 1.5, we may also proceed to compute our economic-capital numbers. For the entire portfolio, it is about $\frac{3.1}{35.4} \approx 0.088$ or 8.8% if we represent it as a percentage. This suggests that, on average, about 9% of each asset's value needs to be set aside for their riskiness. A separate number can also usefully be computed, depending on how far one wishes to go, for taxonomy type, sub-portfolio, or risk factor. The credit and market-risk numbers, for example, amount to about 5.7% and 1.6%, respectively.

NIB's credit-risk economic-capital model is, as is common practice, based on a long-term, unconditional, through-the-cycle approach. To correct for this aspect, among other things, the regulatory community has introduced the notion of capital buffers. These represent an additional cushion to account for variations in current economic conditions. NIB, although not a regulated entity, also follows this regulatory practice. The buffers themselves come in three flavours: conservation, countercyclical, and stress-test. The conservation buffer is the closest thing to a pure through-the-cycle adjustment and is simply a linear multiple of the minimum regulatory capital requirements.[60] The countercyclical buffer, conversely, is an

[60] Again, we will turn our attention to the regulatory perspective in Chap. 11.

example of a macro-prudential tool. It is set by various jurisdictions—also as a percentage of regulatory capital—against the flow of current macroeconomic conditions. In other words, regulatory authorities build it up during good times, only to release it during period of economic downturn or crisis. This explains why it takes a value of zero in Table 1.5; the vast majority of authorities released the countercyclical buffer during March and April of 2020 at the inception of the global COVID-19 pandemic.

The final piece of the puzzle in Table 1.5 is the so-called stress-testing buffer. This is an additional contribution to overall economic capital, which is intended to capture the impact of severe adverse macro-financial conditions. It is basically another layer of prudence. It can feel somewhat excessive to add yet another safeguard to a collection of worst-case risk measures and regulator-specified buffers. While there is truth to this reflection, this buffer stems from a separate stress-testing exercise. There is value, and the potential for significant insight into the strengths and weaknesses of one's asset portfolio, in such an analysis. For regulated entities, the level of the stress-testing buffer is determined via assessment by one's supervisor. At the NIB, the level is specified by Board decision supported by quantitative analysis. A much more detailed discussion of this aspect is found in Chap. 12.[61]

**Colour and Commentary 10** (ASSESSING CAPITAL ADEQUACY)*: Financial institutions are constantly asked by key stakeholders—such as regulators, credit agencies, investors, borrowers, and indeed, themselves—a very simple question: do they have enough capital? The fancy term for attempts to answer this question is capital-adequacy analysis. It is not a simple question to answer, because it depends on the multidimensional risks faced by the firm's assets. Economic capital, as a concept, was developed to help by providing a lens through which one can holistically examine the riskiness of these assets. The preceding analysis of NIB's capital adequacy as of December 2020 is a good example of the various elements at play. Similar analyses are performed across literally thousands of financial institutions across the world. In the coming chapters, we will delve much more deeply into the mathematical structures and assumptions necessary to generate these high-level figures. Given that there is no shortage of details, a rather high amount of care needs to be given towards the organization of this discussion.*

[61] Treatment of stress testing in the final chapter of this work should not be seen as a commentary on its importance. It shows up last simply because, to adequately discuss it, one needs to have a firm global understanding of all the various elements.

## 1.8 Looking Forward

Having supplied some conceptual insight into the idea of economic capital and looked more concretely at the NIB situation, the final task in this chapter is to lay out the structure of the remaining discussion. Our stated objective is to provide a reasonably complete description of a framework for the measurement and practical application of credit-risk economic capital. A framework suggests multiple interdependencies between various components; this needs to be reflected in the organization of our exposition. Writing such a book is thus like building a conceptual house. Each chapter represents an important element of the overall construction; moreover, the chapters depend upon on another in a sequential fashion. It is difficult, for example, to discuss loan-pricing issues or parameter selection without a good understanding of the economic-capital model. Figure 1.15 correspondingly displays the forthcoming 11 chapters from the bottom upwards as building blocks.

Part I is the foundation of our conceptual house. It lays out the methodological details associated with our credit-risk economic-capital model. This covers *three* separate chapters: the model itself, the determination of model parameters, and details associated with the implementation. Following from the axioms introduced in the preface, although NIB has a single production model, two additional challenger models are computed on a daily basis.[62] This is to permit an ongoing point of comparison (or sanity check) for interpretation, trouble-shooting, and communication. The order of these three chapters is quite important. The base methodology is the natural starting point in Chap. 2. Since models are not particularly useful without parameters, Chap. 3 immediately addresses this question following the specification of the modelling details. Finally, model estimation involves stochastic simulation and, as a consequence, it is computationally intensive. Strategies for managing this complexity form a central part of Chap. 4.

Part II addresses the important economic-capital application of loan pricing. Loan pricing needs to be performed in a quick and flexible manner to permit loan originators to consider multiple financing alternatives with their clients. Any sensible assessment of loan pricing requires economic-capital inputs, which are the result of a reasonably slow and complex simulation procedure. This presents a fundamental problem. The classic solution—adopted in many institutions—involves use of an approximation for the economic-capital consumption associated with a specific loan. Chapter 5 is, therefore, dedicated to the construction of a (semi-)closed-form approximation of default and migration risk. This turns out to be both a worthwhile investment and a helpful tool, since we will also make liberal use of it in our loan-impairment and stress-testing calculations. Chapter 6 then turns our attention to the conceptual and practical details of loan pricing. This touches not

[62] This a direct application of our quantitative analysis axiom *"if you can help it, never do anything just one way."*

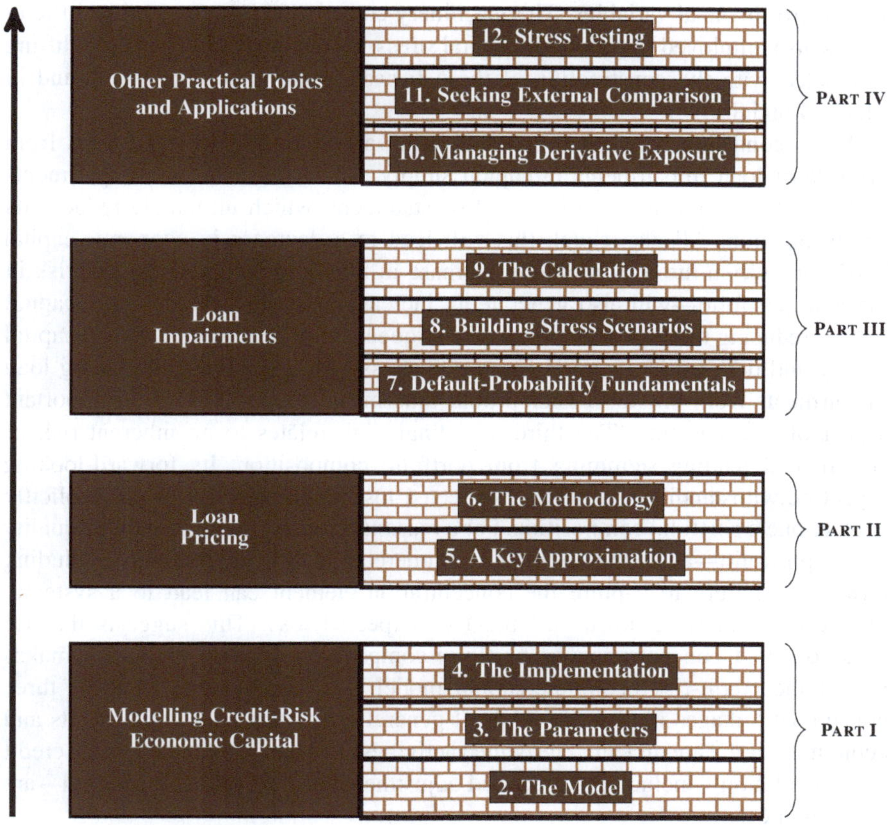


**Fig. 1.15** *Our chapter plan*: This schematic describes the organization of the forthcoming 11 chapters in this book. The overall credit-risk economic-capital framework—including models and applications—are organized into four logical sections. We have represented them from the bottom upwards as building blocks; each chapter thus represents a key step towards the subsequent discussion.

only on many key aspects of economic capital, but also extends into important ideas in corporate finance.

Part III of this book focuses on another application of economic capital: loan impairments. At first glance, the link to economic capital might seem tenuous. Loan impairments are an accounting measure that typically ignore the tail of the loss distribution, but instead focus on the expectation. Indeed, this is why loan impairments are also widely referred to as *expected* credit losses. There are, however, at least *three* conceptual linkages between economic capital and loan impairments. The first relates to the structure of the International Financial Reporting Standard #9 (IFRS 9). Launched in January 2018, IFRS 9 introduced an important forward-looking dimension into the computation of expected credit losses. Future default-probability outcomes need to be predicated on forecasts of key macro-financial variables. The machinery constructed to manage this difficult task is also employed in economic-capital stress-testing analysis. The heavy-lifting associated with the construction of these forward-looking scenarios is found in Chaps. 7 and 8.

The second link between economic capital and loan impairments stems from the role of loan impairments in capital supply. An increase in loan impairments will flow through a firm's profit-and-loss statement, which ultimately reduces its equity position. All else equal, this will lead to a decrease in economic-capital headroom. Often the reasons for an increase in loan impairments—greater risk in the loan portfolio—will also generate an increase in credit-risk economic capital further reducing the firm's headroom. This squeezing of headroom between capital supply and demand is a central feature of stress-testing analysis. Excluding loan impairments from this discussion would thus mean missing out on an important aspect of stress testing. The third, and final, link relates to an inherent risk of commercial lending stemming from portfolio composition. Its forward-looking aspect notwithstanding, the IFRS 9 expected-loss computation does not explicitly capture one's portfolio composition. For a reasonably concentrated and high-quality credit portfolio—as found in many commercial-lending institutions (including NIB)—the failure to capture the concentration element can lead to a systemic underestimation (i.e., downward bias) of expected loss. This suggests the use of a so-called concentration or portfolio-composition adjustment, which makes use of the credit-risk economic-capital model. The combination of these three conceptual linkages implies (in its most general form) that loan impairments and economic capital are, in fact, intertwined activities. The details of the expected credit loss calculation—including a proposed adjustment for portfolio composition—are covered in Chap. 9.

Part IV, the final section of this book, deals with a collection of (loosely related) practical topics and applications. Chapters 10 and 11, for example, both have their feet firmly anchored in the regulatory world. Chapter 10 addresses the fascinating and subtle realm of counterparty credit risk. Modern banks need to make use of derivative contracts—swaps, forwards, and in some cases, options—to manage their positions. Unlike loans, bonds, or deposits, the computation of credit exposures—a key input into the economic-capital calculation—is a challenge. The difficulty stems principally from the fact that, at any given point in time, a derivative contract may be either an asset or a liability to the firm. This status, of course, has rather important implications for credit risk. We thus dedicate the totality of Chap. 10 to a discussion of the (flexible and helpful) regulatory approach for the prudent, risk-based estimation of derivative exposures. Chapter 11 tackles a common challenge for an international institution. As a non-regulated entity, its actions are not prescribed by a supervisor. At the same time, regulatory guidance and rating agencies provide an essential external point of comparison for internal risk-management activities. Chapter 11 examines, therefore, multiple regulatory approaches and both Pillar I and II calculations as well as a well-known rating-agency methodology. It describes NIB's continuous effort to identify and evaluate external benchmarks. This is not, however, an NIB-specific undertaking; all institutions benefit from constructive external comparison. Chapter 12 concludes, building on much of the previous discussion, with a consideration of the stress-testing dimension. With the nominal goal of motivating the stress-testing buffer from Table 1.5, it also addresses the incorporation of severely adverse scenarios as well as the idea of reverse stress testing.

**Colour and Commentary 11** (A CONCEPTUAL HOUSE): *This work seeks to provide a reasonably complete description of a framework for the measurement and practical application of credit-risk economic capital. The very word, framework, suggests multiple pieces and interdependencies. The various elements of a framework cannot, unfortunately, be considered in just any order. Writing such a book is thus like building a conceptual house. This means that we need to deal with the basement before working on the roof. The organization of the remaining 11 chapters—organized in* four *distinct parts—attempt to reflect this fact. Part I is the foundation of our house; it deals with the credit-risk economic-capital model, its many parameters, and the implementation challenges stemming for the use of a simulation model. Parts II and III can be viewed as the walls and rooms of our conceptual structure. They focus on two important applications: loan pricing and impairments. In doing so, they also introduce some centrally important technical ideas—approximation of economic capital and macro-financial stress scenarios—for our practical toolbox. Part IV, let's call it the roof of our building, concludes with a collection of practical topics and applications. These are not least in importance—after all, they are keeping the rain off of our heads—but instead are best considered when equipped with a global understanding of the key concepts earned in the previous chapters.*

## 1.9 Wrapping Up

The principal objective of this chapter was to provide a comprehensive, although gentle, introduction to the computation of economic capital. A few key takeaways bear repeating. First of all, economic capital is basically a worst-case measure of asset riskiness used to complement the *average*, or expected, risk perspective provided in financial statements. The second key point is that economic capital is ultimately—for each individual asset, credit obligor, or sub-portfolio—simply a number between zero and one. An economic-capital number of zero implies a riskless position. Outside of this extreme case, the number increases proportionally with an asset's overall risk. Since asset risks are complex and multifaceted, we need to make use of fairly complex mathematical models to actually compute economic capital. The principal job of these models is to sensibly capture idiosyncratic and systemic effects, the actual portfolio composition, and notions of concentration and diversification. These models themselves, as a final point, also create their own risks. Model governance and oversight are key tools in managing this aspect. Two particularly important model-risk mitigants, documentation and model transparency, are key drivers behind the production of this book.

The forthcoming chapters consider *two* main perspectives: measurement and management of credit-risk economic capital. The economic-capital measurement chapters delve more deeply into methodological modelling questions as well practical parametrization and implementation issues. Other modelling chapters focus on the fast (semi-)closed-form approximation of economic capital and building stress scenarios consistent with macro-financial forecasts. This is the foundation of our credit-risk economic-capital framework. The management-focused chapters principally address key applications of economic capital: loan pricing, calculation of loan impairments, and stress testing. These aspects build on our modelling foundation and provide helpful tools to assist in guiding the lending organization.

## References


1. Y. Amihud, H. Mendelsohn, and L. P. Pedersen. Liquidity and asset prices. *Foundations and Trends in Finance*, 1(4):269–364, 2005.
2. B. M. Bendis. Ultimate Spider-Man. (1):1–52, 2000.
3. BIS. The internal ratings-based approach. Technical report, Bank for International Settlements, January 2001.
4. BIS. International convergence of capital measurement and capital standards: A revised framework. Technical report, Bank for International Settlements, January 2004.
5. BIS. An explanatory note on the Basel II IRB risk weight functions. Technical report, Bank for International Settlements, July 2005.
6. BIS. Pillar 3 disclosure requirements–updated framework. Technical report, Bank for International Settlements, December 2018.
7. D. J. Bolder. *Fixed Income Portfolio Analytics: A Practical Guide to Implementing, Monitoring and Understanding Fixed-Income Portfolios*. Springer, Heidelberg, Germany, 2015.
8. D. J. Bolder. *Credit-Risk Modelling: Theoretical Foundations, Diagnostic Tools, Practical Examples, and Numerical Recipes in Python*. Springer-Nature, Heidelberg, Germany, 2018.
9. D. J. Bolder. Stealing Others' Strategies: Lessons on Model Risk. In *Evolving Practices in Public Investment Management: Proceedings of the Seventh Public Investors Conference*, 2020.
10. P. Bolton, M. Despres, L. A. P. da Silva, F. Samama, and R. Svartzman. *The Green Swan: Central Banking and Financial Stability in the Age of Climate Change*. Bank for International Settlements, January 2020.
11. G. Casella and R. L. Berger. *Statistical Inference*. Duxbury Press, Belmont, California, 1990.
12. A. Chapelle. *Operational Risk Management*. John Wiley & Sons, Ltd, 2018.
13. E. Derman. Model risk. Goldman Sachs Quantitative Strategies Research Notes, April 1996.
14. ECB. Macro-Prudential Policies and Tools. Technical report, European Central Bank, June 2010. Financial Stability Review: Section IV.A.
15. ECB. ECB Guide to the Internal Capital Adequacy Assessment Process (ICAAP). Technical report, European Central Bank, November 2018.
16. A. Elmgren. *Open Government in the Nordics*. Aarhus University, Denmark, February 2019.

17. G. M. Gupton, G. Coughlan, and M. Wilson. *CreditMetrics — Technical Document*. Morgan Guaranty Trust Company, New York, 1997.
18. G. M. Gupton, C. C. Finger, and M. Bhatia. *CreditMetrics — Technical Document*. Morgan Guaranty Trust Company, New York, 2007.
19. J. H. Holland. *Hidden Order: How Adaptation Builds Complexity*. Addison-Wesley, New York, NY., 1995.
20. P. Jorion. Risk Management Lessons from Long-Term Capital Management. *European Financial Management*, 6:277–300, 2000.
21. P. Jorion. *Value at Risk: The New Benchmark for Managing Financial Risk*. McGraw-Hill Ryerson Limited, New York, NY, 2006.
22. P. G. W. Keen. *Decision Support Systems: A Research Perspective*. Center for Informations Systems Research. Afred P. Sloan School of Management, 1980.
23. P. G. W. Keen. Value Analysis: Justifying Decision Support Systems. *MIS Quarterly*, 5(1): 1–15, 1981.
24. P. G. W. Keen and M. S. S. Morton. *Decision support systems: an organizational perspective*. Addison-Wesley series on decision support. Addison-Wesley Pub. Co., 1978.
25. F. H. Knight. *Risk, Uncertainty and Profit*. Houghton Mifflin Co, Boston, MA, 1921.
26. J. Lintner. The valuation of risky asset and the selection of risky investments in stock portfolios and capital budgets. *The Review of Economics and Statistics*, 47(1):13–37, 1965.
27. E. Lütkebohmert. *Concentration Risk in Credit Portfolios*. Springer Verlag, Berlin, 2008.
28. H. Markowitz. Portfolio Selection. *The Journal of Finance*, 7(1):77–91, 1952.
29. K. Marx, R. Institut Marksizma-Leninizma (Moscow, I. für Marxismus-Leninismus beim ZK der SED., and I. Marx-Engels-Stiftung. *Karl Marx, Friedrich Engels Gesamtausgabe (MEGA): Abt. "Das Kapital" und Vorarbeiten*. Dietz, 2008. Original Publication Dates: 1867–1883.
30. A. J. McNeil, R. Frey, and P. Embrechts. *Quantitative Risk Management: Concepts, Tools and Techniques*. Princeton University Press, New Jersey, 2015.
31. R. Merton. On the pricing of corporate debt: The risk structure of interest rates. *Journal of Finance*, 29:449–470, 1974.
32. J. Morgan/Reuters. *RiskMetrics — Technical Document*. Morgan Guaranty Trust Company, New York, 1996.
33. S. C. Myers. Determinants of corporate borrowing. *Journal of Financial Economics*, (5): 147–175, 1977.
34. S. C. Myers. Still searching for optimal capital structure. *Journal of Applied Corporate Finance*, 1(6):4–14, 1993.
35. NIB. Nordic Investment Bank Financial Report 2020. URL: https://www.nib.int/filebank/a/1613377638/93a3a266fc787bb3e6dd86c3a2d563d3/10767-NIB_Financial_Report_2020.pdf, February 2020.
36. M. O'Hara. *Market Microstructure Theory*. Blackwell Publishers Cambridge, Massachusetts, 1995.
37. R. Rebonato. Theory and practice of model risk management. Quantitative Research Centre (QUARC) Technical Paper, 2003.
38. C. M. Reinhart and K. S. Rogoff. *This Time Is Different: Eight Centuries of Financial Folly*. Princeton University Press, Princeton, New Jersey, 2009.
39. S. A. Ross. The arbitrage theory of capital asset pricing. *Journal of Economic Theory*, 35(3): 341–360, 1976.
40. W. F. Sharpe. A simplified model for portfolio analysis. *Management Science*, 9(2):277–293, 1963.
41. W. F. Sharpe. Capital asset prices: A theory of market equilibrium under conditions of risk. *The Journal of Finance*, 19(3):425–442, 1964.
42. P. Siklos. *Money, Banking and Financial Institutions: Canada in the Global Environment*. McGraw-Hill Ryerson Limited, Toronto, Ontario, 1994.
43. A. Smith and A. B. Krueger. *The Wealth of Nations*. Bantam Classics, 2003. Original Publication Date: 1776.

44. N. N. Taleb. *The Black Swan: The Impact of the Highly Improbable*. Random House, New York, NY, 2007.
45. J. L. Treynor. Market value, time, and risk. Unpublished Manuscript, August 1961.
46. O. A. Vasicek. Probability of loss on loan distribution. KMV Corporation, February 1987.
47. O. A. Vasicek. Limiting loan loss probability distribution. KMV Corporation, August 1991.
48. O. A. Vasicek. The distribution of loan portfolio value. *Risk*, (12):160–162, December 2002.
49. M. Zabrocki. Calculating the Probabilities of Winning Lotto 6/49. York University: Mathematics and Statistics, March 2003.

# Part I
# Modelling Credit-Risk Economic Capital

# Chapter 2
# Constructing a Practical Model

*Don't always blindly follow guidance and step-by-step instructions; you might run into something interesting.*

*(Georg Cantor)*

As we saw in the introductory chapter, economic capital is a model-based approach to assess a firm's worst-case capital demand across a broad range of enterprise risks. The three largest elements are generally credit, market, and operational risk. While it is conceptually possible to try to describe some of these key risks in a *joint* manner, it is more typical to handle them separately. It is simply too difficult to construct a defensible simultaneous description of these three major risks. Moreover, estimating each piece separately and then simply adding them together takes a conservative stance on the interactions between these risks.[1]

For the vast majority of banking institutions, credit risk represents the single most important element of economic capital. The principal concern of a lending institution is (almost invariably) extending funds to another entity and ultimately not being paid back.[2] Depending on the size of the loan—and any amounts recovered during bankruptcy proceedings—the loss to the firm can be substantial. A second, related worry, is that the borrowing entity's financial situation worsens, making default (and attendant future losses) more likely. The deterioration in a borrower's creditworthiness also typically generates (unrealized) financial losses. This is because loan (and market) pricing—determined based on the borrower's situation at the time of the loan—is usually inadequate to cover the heightened risk of default. These two dimensions are referred to as default and credit-migration risk, respectively.

Lending and investing activities are nonetheless a banking institution's *daily bread*, so they cannot be simply avoided. Instead, they need to be managed. A critical aspect of lending, of course, is the initial assessment of a firm's financial

---

[1] In particular, it assumes no scope for diversification among these central risks.

[2] This can occur in a few ways: a direct loan, the purchase of a firm's bond, or even investment in a firm's equity. The mechanics of the extension of credit may differ, but the basic risks are the same.



D. Bolder, *Modelling Economic Capital*, Contributions to Finance and Accounting,
https://doi.org/10.1007/978-3-030-95096-5_2

position. This involves capturing all current information and also taking a forward-looking perspective. Such analysis allows the lender to determine if it makes sense to extend the loan in the first place. A second component is credit mitigation; these are features that safeguard the lender in the future. One important tool involves structuring the loan contract to provide recourse to the lending firm in specific situations. Broadly, such contractual features are referred to as loan covenants. These might take the form of limits on the lending firm's financial ratios or optionality in the loan contract permitting early termination and repayment.[3] An additional form of credit mitigation relates to assignment of collateral—in the form of other assets from the borrowing firm—to be collected in the event of default. A final aspect involves guarantees, where another entity steps in to fulfil the obligation in the event original borrower is not capable of meeting it.

Credit mitigation thus includes loan covenants, collateralization, and guarantees. These are standard credit-risk management tools for every lending institution, but some amount of risk always still remains. If the lending institution accepted no risk in a lending transaction, they could hardly expect to earn any return for their efforts.[4] At the same time, there is also competition among lenders in the economy. This mainly occurs along the pricing dimension, but it also naturally extends to the extent and severity of credit-mitigation measures.[5] In short, there are good reasons why credit risk can be mitigated, but not avoided. Managing credit risk must thus also extend beyond credit-risk mitigants. It also needs to be carefully measured; managing and balancing risk in a prudent fashion is dreadfully uncomfortable if you cannot measure it. Explaining how this might reasonably be performed is the principal task of this chapter.

## 2.1 A Naive, but Informative, Start

Every serious credit-risk economic capital model is complex and multifaceted. Jumping straight into the detail, without a bit of context, would be intimidating and counterproductive. Let's instead begin with a simpler, although admittedly somewhat naive, alternative modelling approach: the independent-default model.[6] As the name clearly indicates, it treats every default event as independent. The corollary of this central assumption is that it also entirely ignores systemic risk.

---

[3] These are only a few examples. Many other types of loan covenants are possible.

[4] As clichéd as it might sound, there is truth to the old saying "no risk, no reward." It also sounds far more serious and erudite in its original latin form, *periculum praemio*.

[5] Faced with two loans of the same price, a borrower will rationally accept the alternative offering the least number of constraints on its activities.

[6] In the spirit of full disclosure, this method represents one of our challenger models computed every day in our economic-capital framework as a comparator to the more complex production methodology.

**Table 2.1** *Important credit-risk variables*: This table introduces the three of the most important elements associated with the measurement of credit risk within any modelling venture: the exposure at default, (unconditional) default probability, and loss-given-default.

| Variable | Symbol | Acronym | Description |
|---|---|---|---|
| Exposure-at-default | $c_i$ | EAD | Magnitude of the loan at default |
| (Unconditional) default probability | $p_i$ | PD | Probability of default over a $(T-t)$-year horizon |
| Loss-given-default | $\gamma_i$ | LGD | Severity of the loss in the event of default |

This lack of realism makes it a poor choice of production model, but its associated simplicity makes it an excellent place to start.

To build this initial model, we require some ingredients. Imagine that one's portfolio consists of lending exposures to $I$ distinct credit obligors.[7] We require three pieces of information about each of these counterparties: the total amount of exposure at play, the likelihood (or probability) of default over a given time horizon, and the amount of recovery in the event of default. These are referred to as the exposure-at-default, (unconditional) probability of default, and loss-given-default; we will denote them—for the $i$th credit obligor—as $c_i$, $p_i$, and $\gamma_i$, respectively. Table 2.1 provides a detailed summary of these three central quantities. It is useful, for the less experienced reader, to gain a good familiarity with these objects from the start. They will be employed repeatedly, in a variety of different ways, during each of the following chapters.

In principle, all three elements outlined within Table 2.1 are random variables. This implies that their future values are unknown and their range of possible outcomes is described by some statistical distribution. Understanding this fact is critical, because it will colour important modelling efforts in later discussion. For this introductory discussion, however, we will unrealistically treat them as known, deterministic quantities.

The kernel of the independent-default model is dead simple. The default event associated with the $i$th credit obligor—which we will denote as $\mathcal{D}_i$—occurs with probability $p_i$. Survival, or non-incidence of default, naturally arrives with probability $1-p_i$. Default, in this context, is essentially a Bernoulli trial. Default either occurs or it does not; it is a binary state. We can succinctly (and conveniently) summarize this fact in the form of an indicator variable for each individual obligor,

$$\mathbb{I}_{\mathcal{D}_i} = \begin{cases} 1: & \text{default occurs during } (t, T] \text{ with probability } p_i \\ 0: & \text{survival until time } T \text{ with probability } 1-p_i \end{cases}. \tag{2.1}$$

[7] We might also refer to these as risk owners; the idea is that they should represent a collective entity for the determination of a default event. This can become rather involved in practice, but is conceptually easy to understand.

To be clear, we represent the current time as $t$ and the final time-point of our analysis as $T$. $T - t$ describes the length of risk horizon.[8]

This development directly leads to a description of the portfolio loss as,

$$L = \sum_{i=1}^{I} c_i \gamma_i \mathbb{I}_{\mathcal{D}_i}. \tag{2.2}$$

This short expression might not look like much, but it is actually the launch-site for all portfolio credit-risk models. It includes the exposures of all credit obligors, their loss-given-defaults, and a trigger describing when default occurs (or not). The objective is to characterize the distribution of the overall portfolio loss ($L$ as at time $T$) through a description of the statistical behaviour of each of the three elements on the right-hand side of Eq. 2.2. Given this loss distribution, we can compute a range of interesting metrics for use in the measurement (and ultimately) management of credit risk.

In the independent-default model, the only source of uncertainty arises from each $\mathbb{I}_{\mathcal{D}_i}$ term defined in Eq. 2.1. Since each $\mathbb{I}_{\mathcal{D}_i}$ is statistically independent, the problem is rather tractable. If we are willing to assume that all credit obligors have the same default probability—that is, $p_i = p$ for all $i = 1, \ldots, N$—we can even find a closed-form solution for the distribution of $L$.[9] Practically, characterization of the distribution of $L$ is readily determined via simulation methods. We can conceptualize this as a coin-tossing exercise. Imagine that we have an (unfair) coin where the probability of tails is $p_i$ and $1 - p_i$ is heads. Tails represents default and heads is survival. Now extend this to $I$ coins each with this property. If we independently flip all $I$ coins, we can evaluate one realization of the portfolio loss. If we flip this collection of coins thousands (or even millions) of times, we can trace out all the possible permutations and combinations of portfolio credit loss. Equipped with this information, we can proceed to estimate virtually any risk metric we might desire.

This brute-force solution clearly requires an intimidating amount of coin flipping.[10] The effort is completely justified. If our objective is to capture one of the most important risks to a lending institution, we need to answer the following question: how likely is the coincident default of multiple important credit obligors over the next $T - t$ periods of time? The independent-default model—which basically takes the simplest possible route—provides a first incomplete answer to this question. Blessed with simplicity, the independent-default model will nevertheless underestimate this risk. The reason is that we are ignoring any possible default

[8] It is often set to one-year, but it is regularly altered for different situations and applications.

[9] A collection of independent, identically distributed Bernoulli trials follows the binomial distribution. See Bolder [7, Chapter 2] for much more detail on this question. A semi-analytic solution is available in the more general case if one is willing to delve into more complicated mathematics. Bolder [7, Chapter 7] touches on this idea.

[10] Thankfully, we can comfortably delegate this daunting task to a computer.

dependence (or correlation) between our lending counterparties. The larger point is that even in the simplest setting, there is a surprising amount of complexity in tracing out the credit-loss distribution. This situation will only get worse as we add more realism to our modelling framework.

**Colour and Commentary 12** (THE INDEPENDENT-DEFAULT MODEL): *The simplest approach to the modelling of portfolio credit risk involves a very strong assumption: that the default events of each of one's credit obligors are independent. This is tantamount to assuming that all credit portfolio risk is idiosyncratic or, in other words, there is no systemic credit risk. The logical consequence of such a choice is somewhat ridiculous; it implies that with a sufficiently large and diversified portfolio one could completely eliminate credit risk. As discussed in the previous chapter, this is neither consistent with economic theory nor is it a particularly conservative stance. We can thus conclude that the independent-default model is* not *a serious option. This does not, however, imply that it is not useful. Its simplicity, its use of the bare minimum of inputs, and its (fairly radical) base assumptions make it easy to understand and compute. In other words, not much can go wrong in its calculation. This makes it an excellent choice of challenger model to assist in trouble-shooting, interpreting, and communicating one's production methodology.*

## 2.2 Mixture and Threshold Models

All production models—in an attempt to capture a higher degree of realism—involve a number of complicated twists and additions. Addressing and organizing this complexity is the main task of this chapter. It is nonetheless useful to quickly sketch out the details of a few competing approaches before we jump into a description of our actual choice. Serious candidates for the modelling of portfolio credit risk fall into *two* main categories: mixture and threshold models.[11] This section will touch on both of these modelling frameworks. To keep it brief and permit us to focus on the core concepts, we'll restrict our attention to the one-factor setting.

[11] An excellent overview of these two approaches is found in McNeil et al. [29, Chapter 11].

### 2.2.1 The Mixture Model

The principal shortcoming of the independent-default model is its failure to capture systemic risk. The question thus becomes: how might we capture this dimension in a portfolio credit-risk model? The mixture-model setting solves this problem through the randomization of the default probability. Instead of using the given value $p_i$ to describe the unconditional default probability, we cleverly replace it with something else that induces default correlation.

The general approach employed by all mixture models is to write each $p_i$ as $p_i(Z)$, where $Z$ is a random variable that is common to all credit obligors in one's portfolio. $Z$, which affects all variables—albeit in perhaps different ways—is the systemic risk factor. This trick leads to a revised definition of our default indicator from Eq. 2.2 as

$$\mathbb{I}_{\mathcal{D}_i} = \begin{cases} 1: & \text{default occurs during } (t, T] \text{ with probability } p_i(Z) \\ 0: & \text{survival until time } T \text{ with probability } 1 - p_i(Z) \end{cases}. \tag{2.3}$$

An entire family of models can be constructed involving various choices of $Z$ and alternative specifications of $p_i(Z)$. One simple, mathematically pleasant, and educational entry point is to set $p_i(Z) \equiv Z$ and $Z \sim \beta(\alpha, \beta)$. In plain English, the unconditional default probability is assumed to follow a beta distribution. The unit-interval support of the beta distribution makes it a natural candidate for a probability and, quite conveniently, also yields closed-form solutions for the loss distribution.[12]

The loss function remains unchanged from Eq. 2.2. Estimation of each mixture model loss distribution can always be performed numerically via stochastic simulation. It involves the same frenzy of coin-flipping as in the independent-default model with one important difference. At each iteration of the simulation model, one draws the common systemic random variable, $Z$, from a hat.[13] This value then resets the individual probabilities of various individual coin flips for that realization. It is useful to think of $Z$ as a global macroeconomic variable. Each draw of $Z$ thus tells us something about the state of the world. When $Z$ is large and positive, this pushes up the default probabilities for all credit obligors in the portfolio; this would be an adverse economic outcome. A small realization of $Z$ creates the reverse chains of events. In both cases, however, $Z$ is the object inducing default correlation within the model.

Given the value of $Z$, however, each coin flip is independent. This important property is referred to as conditional independence. It ensures that the model has both a systemic element—via the outcome of $Z$—and an idiosyncratic component that enters through the coin flip. A particularly interesting, and popular, choice of mixture model illustrates this fact very well. Consider the following default

---

[12] See Bolder [7, Chapter 3] for more details on this so-called beta-binomial mixture model.

[13] Or, if you prefer, it can be drawn from an urn or a bucket or from your favourite scientific computing software.

probability definition for the $i$th credit obligor:

$$p_i(Z) = p_i\left(\omega_{i0} + \omega_{i1} Z\right), \tag{2.4}$$

where $Z \sim \Gamma(a, b)$ and $\omega_{i0} + \omega_{i1} = 1$. This yields the gamma-Poisson mixture implementation, which is referred to as the CreditRisk+ model in practical applications.[14] Expanding Eq. 2.4, we arrive at a very useful decomposition,

$$p_i(Z) = \underbrace{p_i \omega_{i0}}_{\substack{\text{Idio-}\\ \text{syncratic}\\ \text{component}}} + \underbrace{p_i \omega_{i1} Z}_{\substack{\text{Systemic}\\ \text{component}}}, \tag{2.5}$$

The randomized default probability is broken into both idiosyncratic and systemic pieces. The unconditional default probability as well as the $\omega_{i0}$ and $\omega_{i1}$ parameters—termed factor loadings—determine the relative importance of these two key aspects of risk.[15] Determining the appropriate values of the $\omega$'s is a critical aspect of the practical model implementation.

Mixture or, as they are sometimes called, actuarial models approach the problem from a reduced-form perspective. That is, the default event as an exogenous occurrence. Although it certainly induces default dependence and thereby introduces a systemic-risk element, it is silent on how default actually happens. For some, this is a weakness, for others it is a strength. In reality, it is neither; it is simply a feature of mixture models. In the subsequent section, we introduce a competing approach that attacks this question from another (more structural) angle.

**Colour and Commentary 13** (MIXTURE MODELS)*: The family of mixture models represents a first possible step in extending the independent-default model into the realm of systemic risk. The origins of the term mixture model stem from the fact that the binomial structure of the model is* mixed *with another random variable driving the default probability.*[a] *There are thus two sources of uncertainty: the coin flips themselves and the probabilities of each coin. Both elements are, in the context of each simulation, in flux. Their combination yields a full-blown description of the permutations and combinations of default events incorporating ideas of both idiosyncratic and*

(continued)

[14] The model was first suggested and popularized by Wilde [43]. An excellent, and exhaustive, overview of this approach is found in Gundlach and Lehrbass [17].

[15] We can also see how this approach nests the independent-default model. It is readily recovered by setting $\omega_{i0} = 1$. The consequence of the condition $\omega_{i0} + \omega_{i1} = 1$ is that the systemic part falls out of the model.

**Colour and Commentary 13** (continued)
*systemic risk. CreditRisk+, a popular industrial model introduced by Wilde [43], falls into this class of portfolio credit-risk model.*

[a] The binomial structure of the independent-default model can also, by virtue of the law of small numbers, be written in terms of the Poisson distribution. See Bolder [7, Chapter 2] for more details on this important equivalency.

### *2.2.2 The Threshold Model*

Shortly after the introduction of the celebrated Black and Scholes [4] model, Merton [30] made a central contribution to the study of risk management. In an attempt to identify a general and consistent approach for the pricing of corporate debt, he provided the key notion underlying much of the credit-risk literature. The idea is that a firm practically enters into bankruptcy when its equity is exhausted. Or, in other words, when the value of its assets dip below its liabilities. In the language of the previous chapter, we can think of this as a situation when a firm's capital demand exceeds its supply.

The genius of this observation is that it provides a concrete path for the modelling of portfolio credit risk: one needs to describe the joint distribution of the individual credit-obligor assets in one's credit portfolio. Merton [30] offers a detailed approach—using continuous-time mathematics—to characterize, parametrize, and model this situation. Some years later, Vasicek [40, 41, 42] offered a simplification of the basic structure of Merton [30]'s proposal. Further contributions to the literature have lead to the current family of portfolio credit-risk threshold models.

The additional modelling element stems from a description of the firm's asset values.[16] We thus specify for the $i$th credit obligor in one's portfolio, the following variable:

$$y_i = \underbrace{a_i Z}_{\substack{\text{Systemic}\\ \text{component}}} + \underbrace{b_i \epsilon_i}_{\substack{\text{Idio-}\\ \text{syncratic}\\ \text{component}}}, \tag{2.6}$$

where $Z, \epsilon_i \sim \text{i.i.d.}\mathcal{N}(0, 1)$ and $a_i, b_i \in \mathbb{R}$ are selected such that $y_i \sim \mathcal{N}(0, 1)$. We are no longer flipping coins, but we are not completely in uncharted territory.

[16] Practically, these can also be viewed as asset returns. Sometimes this notion is generalized to the idea of creditworthiness index or latent state variable. The effect is the same and the details are important; for this introductory discussion, it is probably preferable to keep the logical, asset-related link to the original Merton [30] approach.

Inspection of Eq. 2.6 reveals that our variable, $y_i$, is the sum of two familiar components: systemic and idiosyncratic risk. A single realization of $Z$, which captures the systemic component, provides a common effect—experienced in potentially different ways—for all credit counterparties. Again, this can be viewed as a global macroeconomic variable. Each of the firm-specific $\epsilon_i$ terms describes the idiosyncratic effect. This explains why there are $I$ of them and they are all independent. Although the mechanics are very different, the $\epsilon$'s are conceptually not so far removed from our coin-flipping exercise. Finally, the parameters $a_i$ and $b_i$ (i.e., factor loadings) determine the relative importance of the systemic and idiosyncratic parts.[17]

It still requires a bit more discussion to get to our default event. We wish to describe default as the situation when a firm's assets are less than its liabilities. We view each $y_i$ as a (random) characterization of the firm's assets. Let's introduce the value $K_i$ to represent the liabilities. By extension, using the Merton [30] insight, we can (cheerfully) define the default event as,

$$\mathcal{D}_i \equiv \{y_i \leq K_i\}. \tag{2.7}$$

If, via the realizations of $Z$ and $\epsilon_i$, $y_i$ falls below the value $K_i$, then default will have occurred. The firm will have exhausted its equity and find itself in bankruptcy. This directly permits us to re-express our default indicator variable—from Eqs. 2.1 and 2.3—in the following form:

$$\mathbb{I}_{\mathcal{D}_i} \equiv \mathbb{I}_{\{y_i \leq K_i\}} = \begin{cases} 1: & \text{default occurs during } (t, T] \text{ when } y_i \leq K_i \\ 0: & \text{survival until time } T \text{ if } y_i > K_i \end{cases}. \tag{2.8}$$

Once again, the loss definition from Eq. 2.2 remains the same. We have simply provided an alternative characterization of the default event.

How might we now estimate the associated credit-loss distribution? Again, we use simulation. We begin by drawing the common $Z$ from the standard-normal distribution. This is the systemic piece, which determines the general state of the world. We then draw $I$ independent $\epsilon_i$ random variates; once again, from the standard normal distribution. These are the specific, firm idiosyncratic elements. Using Eq. 2.6, we combine these inputs to construct our collection of firm asset values, or $y_i$'s. Comparing these to their liability values permits us to evaluate our indicator variables from Eq. 2.8 and construct a single loss outcome.[18] This process is then repeated—more or less, *ad nauseum*—by a computer program until we have a sufficiently clear view of our loss distribution to estimate risk metrics.

---

[17] These coefficients should be linked back to the CreditRisk+ $\omega$ parameters introduced in Eq. 2.5. Do not forget that the $a_i$ and $b_i$ parameters are chosen to force $y_i \sim \mathcal{N}(0, 1)$; this, as we'll see in subsequent discussion, leads to some practical headaches.

[18] This also, of course, requires a sensible value for each threshold value, $K_i$.

The class of threshold models, in contrast to the mixture-model world, takes a structural approach to the characterization of credit risk. This means that it endogenizes the default event; or rather, default is determined within the model, not outside of it. Again, this does not make it necessarily superior to the mixture-model approach, just different. For multiplicity of perspective, different is good.

**Colour and Commentary 14** (THRESHOLD MODELS)*: The family of threshold models represents a second possible approach towards adding the systemic element into the independent-default model. The structure is, practically at least, rather different. It begins with the assignment of a latent state variable—conceptually related to the idea of a firm's assets—to each individual credit obligor. This state variable linearly combines two elements: a systemic and an idiosyncratic component. The term threshold model arises from the operation required to determine each individual default event. If a credit obligor's state variable falls below a pre-defined* threshold*—which is motivated by the firm's level of liabilities—then default is triggered. As in the mixture-model setting, there is a common element impacting all obligors; this induces default correlation and creates systemic risk. The independent, firm-specific elements represent idiosyncratic risk. CreditMetrics is a well-known industrial model, introduced by Gupton et al. [18], that uses the threshold-model methodology. A twist upon this approach will form the foundation of the our production credit-risk model.*

## 2.3 Asset-Return Dynamics

Equipped with this background, we can now proceed to examine—in rather greater detail and mathematical rigour—our specific choice. As previously indicated, the origin of capital modelling at the NIB dates back a few decades. As with most institutions, the framework has moved forward in a gradual—and sometimes uneven—manner. The bank's economic-capital model was initially implemented in, and around, 2004 using an external vendor tool. Some years later, an in-house approach was developed and brought into production. Over the course of time, improvements and adjustments to the basic methodology were introduced. We will refer to this as the *legacy* model. This situation continued until it received, during 2019 and 2020, a serious conceptual and practical overhaul. Following extensive statutory revision, a new implementation involving numerous methodological changes became a necessity. The remaining sections of this chapter seek to help the reader gain a better understanding of these choices, which together can be described as our *current* (or revised) production model.

While our legacy approach can be classified as a multivariate, multi-period Gaussian threshold model, it has a few features that differ from the general class of such models. As such, it is useful and important to review, motivate, and to the extent reasonable and feasible, derive the main elements of the legacy approach. This will provide some context and justification for the recently revised methodology.

NIB has, from the beginning, opted for a threshold model. Use of this approach requires one to introduce, as lightly introduced in the previous section, what is referred to as a latent creditworthiness index. In the parlance of the Merton [30] approach, this would be related to the value of an obligor's assets (or asset return).[19] The generalization to a creditworthiness index is thus sensible, but it naturally requires a mathematical structure. Specification of the mechanics of one's creditworthiness process is thus a *first* step into the construction of a threshold model. We are going to allocate quite a bit of effort into understanding this first step, because it has important implications for the overall development of the legacy (and revised) NIB credit-risk modelling framework.

The characterization of the asset or creditworthiness state variable has customarily been done in an industrial strength manner. The legacy approach does not deviate from this practice. A bit of formality is thus in order. On the probability space, $(\Omega, \mathcal{F}, \mathbb{P})$, a slight generalization of Merton [30]'s approach leads to the following stochastic differential equation (SDE) to describe the $i$th obligor's latent (i.e., unobserved) creditworthiness process,

$$d\tilde{X}_i(t) = \sum_{j=1}^{J} \tilde{\beta}_{ij} dZ_j(t) + \tilde{\sigma}_i dW_i(t). \tag{2.9}$$

These are the intertemporal dynamics of $\{\tilde{X}_i(t) : i = 1, \dots, I,\ t \geq 0\}$, which is a multivariate system of creditworthiness indices; there is one for each obligor. Equation 2.9 lies at the heart of the legacy modelling methodology; indeed, some variation on it is, in fact, the cornerstone of a sizable proportion of extant industrial and academic models.

Equation 2.9, despite being only a single expression, requires a fairly dramatic amount of explanation. The actual unpacking process will provide useful insight into the structure of the model. Let us, therefore, try to address each definitional and implicational point in turn:

1. **DRIFT**: The SDE in Eq. 2.9 does *not* have a drift term; as such, each increment of $X_i(t)$ should be centred around zero for all $i = 1, \dots, I$.[20] One could

[19] This latter interpretation makes logical sense in the context of a corporate entity, but can be a bit more complicated for a sovereign, municipality, or government agency.

[20] The actual individual values of the underlying process, $\{X_i(t) : i = 1, \dots, I,\ t \geq 0\}$, will however depend on the set of starting values for $X$. If they are all set to zero at inception, then the expected value of each $X_i$ will remain zero across time, although the actual outcomes will practically deviate from this point.

potentially imagine a generic drift term related to the business cycle, but not only would this be difficult to identify, its incorporation would create important challenges for the model's implementation.

2. **Systemic Factors**: The stochastic element in the first term in Eq. 2.9, $\{Z_j(t) : j = 1, \ldots, J, \ t \geq 0\}$, is a correlated system of Brownian motions with instantaneous correlation matrix, $\tilde{S}$. Each individual $Z_j$ is intended to represent a market-related systemic risk factor. In general, this could be related to macroeconomic outcomes, commodity prices, or even volatility. Practically, for the purposes of our model, these factors are considered to be regional- and industrial-related variables.
3. **Idiosyncratic Factors**: The second stochastic term in Eq. 2.9 is a standard scalar Wiener process, $\{W_i(t) : t \geq 0\}$ for $i = 1, \ldots, I$. Each $W_i$ is, by construction, independent of both one another and the correlated systemic risk factors. These elements, therefore, describe the idiosyncratic (i.e., specific) risks associated with each individual obligor.
4. **Factor Dimensionality**: As a practical matter, we have that $I \gg J$. The individual obligors in our portfolio are counted in hundreds, whereas the maximal number of correlated systemic factors is unlikely to exceed a few dozen. This is both conceptually important—that is, there are relatively few sources of systemic risk, but many types of idiosyncratic risk—and also of practical interest since it determines the dimensionality of one's parametrization.
5. **Properties of Brownian Motion**: The presence of the Brownian motions implies time-independent increments and Gaussianity. There is something for everyone. To be more specific—for the probabilist or statistician—the time-increment of a standard Wiener process associated with the $i$th credit obligor, $W_i(t) - W_i(s)$ with $t > s$, are independent and distributed as $\mathcal{N}(0, t - s)$. Moreover, given a set of time increments, $t > s > v$, then the increments $W_i(t) - W_i(s)$ and $W_i(s) - W_i(v)$ are independent. For an econometrician, this implies that the idiosyncratic factors are independent from both a cross-sectional and time-series perspective. The systemic factors, however, are *not* cross-sectionally independent; their linear dependence is captured by the instantaneous correlation matrix, $\tilde{S}$. Since the system $\{Z_j(t) : j = 1, \ldots, J, \ t \geq 0\}$ is a collection of Brownian motions, non-overlapping systemic increments remain independent over time. For the economist, this implies that—whether from an idiosyncratic or systemic perspective—shocks regarding the creditworthiness of our set of obligors in one period are independent of similar shocks received in other periods. In the real world, for the practitioner, this is quite unlikely to be true. There are probably temporal trends in the evolution of creditworthiness, but this model assumes them away. Even if you believed such trends exist, however, reliably identifying their magnitude and dynamics is likely to be empirically very difficult (or even impossible).
6. **Time Continuity**: In this general setting, Eq. 2.9 implies that our creditworthiness system has continuous sample paths. While this is an attractive theoretical property, practically we cannot observe the creditworthiness of any entity at each possible instant in time. Economic-capital is typically estimated

in annual increments; in some cases, one might wish to consider monthly credit migration, but this is probably the feasible lower limit of time granularity. The consequence is that it will be necessary to discretize Eq. 2.9 to create a workable implementation.

7. **Time Homogeneity**: The model parameters, $\tilde{\beta}_{ij}, \tilde{\sigma}_i \in \mathbb{R}$ for all $i = 1, \ldots, I$ and $j = 1, \ldots, J$, determine the instantaneous relative weight (or loading) of each systemic and idiosyncratic risk factor to an individual obligor's creditworthiness. They also, indirectly, determine the relative weights of the systemic and idiosyncratic risk factors for each individual obligor. Since these parameters are not indexed to time, we may safely surmise them to be time homogeneous. In other words, the importance of a given risk factor to a credit counterparty's creditworthiness is assumed to be constant over time. This, as a choice, is probably somewhat dubious; specification of meaningful time-varying parameters is, however, a daunting undertaking.
8. **Systemic Factor Loadings**: The systemic $\tilde{\beta}$ parameters and the correlated system of Brownian motions, $\{Z_j(t); j = 1, \ldots, J; t \geq 0\}$, are responsible for the portfolio effects. They do so, however, in different ways. The systemic risk factors describe the current state of regional and sectoral risk. The instantaneous correlation matrix, $\tilde{S}$, captures the dependence between these outcomes.[21] The $\tilde{\beta}$ parameters, as previously suggested, determine the loading of each risk factor onto a given obligor. The actual interdependence between the creditworthiness of each obligor thus depends on the $\tilde{\beta}$ values and the relevant entries in $\tilde{S}$. Were $\tilde{S}$ to be an identity matrix, then all of the cross-obligor correlations would be determined by the $\tilde{\beta}$ parameters. If, however, all of the $\tilde{\beta}$ parameters were set to zero, then systemic risk is removed from the model and creditworthiness can be considered to be entirely idiosyncratic. This would bring us back to the previously discussed independent-default model.[22]
9. **Parameter Dimensionality**: The theoretical number of model parameters is quite unsettling. There are, in principle, $J \times I$ systemic and $I$ idiosyncratic parameter values. For a representative portfolio of 500 obligors and 24 systemic risk factors—values roughly consistent with the current implementation—this amounts to in excess of 10,000 possible model parameters. This is a clearly unmanageable (even laughable) situation. Some form of defensible parametric restrictions will be required to manage the dimensionality needed to simultaneously inform the actual dependence structure between obligor creditworthiness and thus, indirectly, portfolio-level default and credit migration.

[21] One could—and many model implementations actually do—orthogonalize this collection of risk factors to create a set of independent systemic risk drivers. In this case, the factor loadings would solely determine the factor correlations.

[22] It is difficult to conceive of placing all of the responsibility upon the correlation matrix, $\tilde{S}$. Setting all $\tilde{\beta}$ parameters to unity (or some other fixed value) does not quite achieve this; instead such an action essentially reduces the model to a single factor structure, which is an equally weighted linear combination of all systemic factors.

10. **MAPPING $X_i$ TO CREDIT MIGRATION**: Each increment is a zero-mean, time-scaled Gaussian outcome. This implies that, over time, the $\tilde{X}$ values will cover the support of the Gaussian distribution. Each $\tilde{X}_i(t)$ can thus, in principle, take values over the interval, $(-\infty, \infty)$. In practice, assuming each $\tilde{X}_i(0)$ is normalized to zero and divided by the instantaneous volatility, actual simulated outcomes will cover the continuum from roughly $(-5, 5)$. There are, however, only $q$ discrete credit-state outcomes. An important element of the model will, therefore, involve creating a link between continuous creditworthiness and discrete credit-state outcomes. By necessity, given their differing scales, this will require a many-to-one mapping between the creditworthiness and credit-state values.

There are clearly many details and insights that can be drawn from this choice of creditworthiness process. Equation 2.9 is thus a critical foundational element of the legacy model, but by itself, it raises more questions than it actually answers. In the following sections, we will make numerous adjustments to Eq. 2.9 with a view towards addressing some of the previous points and, to the extent possible, simplifying and standardizing the development. This journey will bring us, rather better prepared and informed, to our production model.

**Colour and Commentary 15** (DISMANTLING THE CONTINUOUS-TIME MACHINERY): *The legacy approach attempted to make a clear link to the original Merton [30] framework replete with its continuous-time mathematical structure. The first step is the specification of a multivariate stochastic differential equation to describe the latent, creditworthiness state variable for each credit obligor. Indeed, this is a very standard beginning. While theoretically appealing, it is practically rather difficult to use. Most importantly, the incremental complexity does not provide significant, if any, additional value in terms of flexibility and descriptive improvement. As a consequence, it makes logical sense to move as quickly as possible to simplify a number of key aspects of the legacy structure. This constructive approach may, to some readers, seem a bit excessive and painful. There is certainly truth to that view, but this form of exposition was selected because it permits us, from a first-principles pedagogical perspective, to reveal, motivate, and resolve a range of important issues and choices.*

### *2.3.1 Time Discretization*

The continuous-time construction is a bit cumbersome. Using it will require potentially complex mathematics for little pay-off—a situation to be generally avoided—since the model will be implemented in discrete time.[23] Indeed, it is unlikely that more than one or two steps will be taken. As a consequence, before proceeding further, it makes logical and practical sense to discretize the creditworthiness SDE presented in Eq. 2.9. There are a few alternatives techniques for such an operation, but we opt for the simplest approach: the simple and intuitive Euler-Maruyama method.[24] The first step is to create a partition of our time horizon, $[0, T]$ into a collection of $\kappa$ sub-intervals:

$$0 = t_0 < t_1 < t_2 < \cdots < t_\kappa = T. \tag{2.10}$$

Generally, the length of each subinterval is equal. That is, $\Delta t = t_k - t_{k-1}$ is constant for all $k = 1, \ldots, \kappa$. Given this partition, we proceed to transform Eq. 2.9 over any arbitrary discrete time interval, $[t_{k-1}, t_k]$, into:

$$X_i(t_k) - X_i(t_{k-1}) = \sum_{j=1}^{J} \tilde{\beta}_{ij} \underbrace{\Big( Z_j(t_k) - Z_j(t_{k-1}) \Big)}_{\Delta Z_j(k)} + \tilde{\sigma}_i \underbrace{\Big( W_i(t_k) - W_i(t_{k-1}) \Big)}_{\Delta W_i(k)}, \tag{2.11}$$

$$\Delta X_i(k) = \sum_{j=1}^{J} \tilde{\beta}_{ij} \Delta Z_j(k) + \tilde{\sigma}_i \Delta W_i(k),$$

where the $\Delta$ operator is introduced to somewhat reduce the notational burden. Recall, that the variance of each Brownian increment remains $\Delta t$. We may, with the following adjustment, slightly simplify our life and take one step closer to more typical threshold models. In particular, we write

$$\Delta X_i(k) = \underbrace{\frac{\sqrt{\Delta t}}{\sqrt{\Delta t}}}_{=1} \underbrace{\left( \sum_{j=1}^{J} \tilde{\beta}_{ij} \Delta Z_j(k) + \tilde{\sigma}_i \Delta W_i(k) \right)}_{\text{Eq. 2.11}}, \tag{2.12}$$

$$= \sum_{j=1}^{J} \underbrace{\tilde{\beta}_{ij} \sqrt{\Delta t}}_{\beta_{ij}} \underbrace{\frac{\Delta Z_j(k)}{\sqrt{\Delta t}}}_{\Delta z_i(k)} + \underbrace{\tilde{\sigma}_i \sqrt{\Delta t}}_{\sigma_i} \underbrace{\frac{\Delta W_i(k)}{\sqrt{\Delta t}}}_{\Delta w_i(k)},$$

for $k = 1, \ldots, \kappa$ where $\Delta z_j(k) \sim \mathcal{N}(0, \Omega_{jj})$ and $\Delta w_i(k) \sim \mathcal{N}(0, 1)$ for all $i = 1, \ldots, I$ and $j = 1, \ldots, J$. The beauty of this trick is that the parameters have also been scaled by the square-root of the common time step so that we do not

[23] Continuous-time models are essential in pricing applications where arbitrage relationships need to hold constantly over time. In risk-management settings, such as this one, this property is rarely required permitting us to work freely in discrete time.

[24] See Oksendal [34] for more information on this technique.

need to carry this aspect around with us in our development.[25] For this reason, $\beta_{ij} = \tilde{\beta}_{ij}\sqrt{\Delta t}$ and $\sigma_i = \tilde{\sigma}_i\sqrt{\Delta t}$ thus represent the parametrization—which must be determined empirically—associated with our selected time step. We also replace the instantaneous correlation matrix (i.e., $\tilde{S}$) for the correlated Brownian system, $Z$, with a non-instantaneous correlation matrix, $\Omega$.

Since we will be taking annual time steps, let's simplify our life somewhat by setting $\Delta t = 1$; while this is not really in the spirit of discretization, this decision is easily relaxed and it rather dramatically eases the notational burden. Finally, since all time steps are assumed to be equal, we may drop the reference to the $k$th time step leading to the following streamlined, discrete-time representation of Eq. 2.9:

$$\Delta X_i = \sum_{j=1}^{J} \beta_{ij}\Delta z_j + \sigma_i \Delta w_i, \tag{2.13}$$

for $i = 1, \ldots, I$. Depending on the context, of course, it may be useful to reintroduce specific reference to the time step in the notation. One, for example, might wish to include some notion of time dependency in the economic-capital computations.[26]

To summarize, not only is Eq. 2.13 easier to work with—from a mathematical perspective—it finds itself in a more convenient, and realistic, form for the important task of model parametrization. We have basically taken—for better or for worse—a decisive step away from the world of continuous-time mathematics.

### *2.3.2 Normalization*

Equation 2.13 is qualitatively similar to the Vasicek [40, 41, 42] formulation—touched upon in the introductory section—but it is missing a few important elements. More specifically, there is a lack of clarity about the relative importance of the systemic and idiosyncratic elements and the creditworthiness increment, for a given obligor, is *not* standard normal. These two elements are, of course, determined by choices of the $\beta$ and $\sigma$ elements. Practically, it is extremely useful, for the interpretation of the model structure and its results, to directly handle these two aspects. It also indirectly solves issues surrounding the determination of the $\sigma$ parameters.[27]

[25] Indeed, from a statistical perspective, the parameters will be consistent with the time steps used in the underlying estimation data.

[26] Consider a financial instrument, with a maturity less than $T$, that needs to be reinvested. Deposits are one example, where the decision to reinvest would reasonably depend on the creditworthiness index—and associated credit state—in the previous period.

[27] As we'll see in later discussion, there are sensible proxies for the common, systemic sources of risk, but the idiosyncratic element is, by its very definition, much more difficult to manage.

The first stepping stone in this development involves computation of the variance of the systemic element in Eq. 2.13. Undeniably tedious—and frankly is much more naturally expressed in matrix notation—its derivation is both informative and essential. In particular, we have

$$\begin{aligned}
\operatorname{var}\left(\sum_{j=1}^{J}\beta_{ij}\Delta z_j\right) &= \mathbb{E}\left(\left(\sum_{j=1}^{J}\beta_{ij}\Delta z_j\right)^2 - \left(\mathbb{E}\left(\sum_{j=1}^{J}\beta_{ij}\Delta z_j\right)\right)^2\right), \qquad (2.14)\\
&= \mathbb{E}\left(\left(\sum_{j=1}^{J}\beta_{ij}\Delta z_j\right)^2 - \cancel{\left(\sum_{j=1}^{J}\beta_{ij}\underbrace{\mathbb{E}(\Delta z_j)}_{=0}\right)^2}\right),\\
&= \mathbb{E}\left(\left(\sum_{j=1}^{J}\beta_{ij}\Delta z_j\right)\left(\sum_{k=1}^{J}\beta_{ik}\Delta z_k\right)\right),\\
&= \mathbb{E}\left(\sum_{j=1}^{J}\sum_{k=1}^{J}\beta_{ij}\beta_{ik}\Delta z_j\Delta z_k\right),\\
&= \sum_{j=1}^{J}\sum_{k=1}^{J}\beta_{ij}\beta_{ik}\operatorname{cov}\left(\Delta z_j,\Delta z_k\right),\\
&= \sum_{j=1}^{J}\sum_{k=1}^{J}\beta_{ij}\beta_{ik}\Omega_{jk},
\end{aligned}$$

for $i = 1, \ldots, I$. The takeaway from Eq. 2.14 is that the variability in the systemic contribution to the creditworthiness of the $i$th obligor is a fairly complicated function of the $\beta$ choices and the covariance structure of the systemic risk factors.

The standard deviation of the systemic-risk contribution—which is essential for normalization—is now simply defined as

$$\sigma\left(\sum_{j=1}^{J}\beta_{ij}\Delta z_j\right) = \sqrt{\sum_{\ell=1}^{J}\sum_{k=1}^{J}\beta_{i\ell}\beta_{ik}\Omega_{\ell k}}. \qquad (2.15)$$

Putting this quantity in our back pocket for the moment, we now rewrite (rather boldly) Eq. 2.13 in the following form,

$$\Delta X_i = \alpha_i \sum_{j=1}^{J} \frac{\beta_{ij}}{\underbrace{\sqrt{\sum_{\ell=1}^{J}\sum_{k=1}^{J}\beta_{i\ell}\beta_{ik}\Omega_{\ell k}}}_{\text{Eq. 2.15}}}\Delta z_j + \sqrt{1-\alpha_i^2}\,\Delta w_i, \qquad (2.16)$$

where $\alpha_i \in (0, 1) \subset \mathbb{R}$ and $\sigma_i = \sqrt{1 - \alpha_i^2}$ for $i = 1, \ldots, I$. This is the *discretized* and *normalized* form of our creditworthiness indicator state variable. Although technically correct, the form of the factor loadings in Eq. 2.16 is in dire need of some simplification. Let's, therefore, define

$$\mathrm{B}_{ij} = \frac{\beta_{ij}}{\sqrt{\sum_{\ell=1}^{J}\sum_{k=1}^{J}\beta_{i\ell}\beta_{ik}\Omega_{\ell k}}} \equiv \frac{\beta_{ij}}{\sigma\left(\sum_{j=1}^{J}\beta_{ij}\Delta z_j\right)}, \tag{2.17}$$

for $i = 1, \ldots, I$ and $j = 1, \ldots, J$. This allows us to restate Eq. 2.16 more succinctly as

$$\Delta X_i = \alpha_i \sum_{j=1}^{J} \mathrm{B}_{ij}\Delta z_j + \sqrt{1-\alpha_i^2}\,\Delta w_i. \tag{2.18}$$

At first glance, this may not seem to be much in the way of progress. Indeed, it may appear to actually further complicate the creditworthiness process dynamics. Practically, we have introduced *two* important elements:

1. there is an $\alpha$ parameter, for each obligor, that determines the relative importance of the systemic and idiosyncratic contributions to the creditworthiness index—it is broadly referred to as the systemic weight; and
2. the normalized factor loadings (i.e., the B's) work along the specification of the systemic weights (i.e., the $\alpha$'s), ensure that each $\Delta X_i$ outcome has unit variance.[28]

Both of these points naturally require demonstration. Indeed, the systemic weights (i.e., the $\alpha_i$'s) have, more or less, fallen from the sky. The easiest place to start is to verify the zero expectation. In particular, for the set of $I$ credit counterparties,

$$\begin{aligned}
\mathbb{E}(\Delta X_i) &= \mathbb{E}\left(\underbrace{\alpha_i \sum_{j=1}^{J} \mathrm{B}_{ij}\Delta z_j + \sqrt{1-\alpha_i^2}\,\Delta w_i}_{\text{Eq. 2.18}}\right) \\
&= \alpha_i \sum_{j=1}^{J} \mathrm{B}_{ij}\underbrace{\mathbb{E}(\Delta z_j)}_{=0} + \sqrt{1-\alpha_i^2}\,\underbrace{\mathbb{E}(\Delta w_i)}_{=0}, \\
&= 0,
\end{aligned} \tag{2.19}$$

[28] As we'll see shortly, the cross correlation between any two increments—say $\Delta X_n$ and $\Delta X_m$, for example—will be more complicated.

as expected. This is a relatively obvious consequence of the previous structure, but is nonetheless usefully verified.

Let's now move on to the variance of the collection of creditworthiness increments. It has the following form,

$$
\begin{aligned}
\operatorname{var}(\Delta X_i) &= \operatorname{var}\left(\underbrace{\alpha_i \sum_{j=1}^{J} \mathrm{B}_{ij}\Delta z_j + \sqrt{1-\alpha_i^2}\Delta w_i}_{\text{Eq. 2.18}}\right) \qquad (2.20)\\
&= \underbrace{\operatorname{var}\left(\alpha_i \sum_{j=1}^{J} \mathrm{B}_{ij}\Delta z_j\right) + \operatorname{var}\left(\sqrt{1-\alpha_i^2}\Delta w_i\right)}_{\text{By independence}}\\
&= \alpha_i^2 \operatorname{var}\left(\sum_{j=1}^{J} \frac{\beta_{ij}}{\underbrace{\sqrt{\sum_{\ell=1}^{J}\sum_{k=1}^{J} \beta_{i\ell}\beta_{ik}\Omega_{\ell k}}}_{\text{Eq. 2.17}}}\Delta z_j\right) + (1-\alpha_i^2)\underbrace{\operatorname{var}(\Delta w_i)}_{=1}\\
&= \left(\frac{\alpha_i}{\sqrt{\sum_{\ell=1}^{J}\sum_{k=1}^{J} \beta_{i\ell}\beta_{ik}\Omega_{\ell k}}}\right)^2 \underbrace{\operatorname{var}\left(\sum_{j=1}^{J} \beta_{ij}\Delta z_j\right)}_{\text{Eq. 2.14}} + (1-\alpha_i^2)\underbrace{\operatorname{var}(\Delta w_i)}_{=1}\\
&= \frac{\cancel{\alpha_i^2}}{\cancel{\sum_{\ell=1}^{J}\sum_{k=1}^{J} \beta_{i\ell}\beta_{ik}\Omega_{\ell k}}} \underbrace{\left(\cancel{\sum_{\ell=1}^{J}\sum_{k=1}^{J} \beta_{i\ell}\beta_{ik}\Omega_{\ell k}}\right)}_{\text{Eq. 2.14}} + 1 - \cancel{\alpha_i^2}\\
&= 1,
\end{aligned}
$$

as desired. This is a rather more laborious computation, but it clearly illustrates the effectiveness of the normalization in the previous section. Each individual $\Delta X_i \sim \mathcal{N}(0, 1)$; this simple property, as will be demonstrated in a moment, dramatically streamlines the default and credit-migration computations.

Another rather unexciting computation involves identifying the specific form of the cross asset-correlation between the $n$th and $m$th arbitrary obligors in one's credit portfolio. Working from first principles, it is derived as[29]

$$
\begin{aligned}
\operatorname{cov}(\Delta X_n, \Delta X_m) &= \mathbb{E}\left(\left(\Delta X_n - \underbrace{\mathbb{E}(\Delta X_n)}_{=0}\right)\left(\Delta X_m - \underbrace{\mathbb{E}(\Delta X_m)}_{=0}\right)\right), \qquad (2.21)\\
&= \mathbb{E}\left(\Delta X_n \cdot \Delta X_m\right),\\
&= \mathbb{E}\left(\left(\alpha_n \sum_{j=1}^{J} \mathrm{B}_{nj}\Delta z_j + \sqrt{1-\alpha_n^2}\Delta w_n\right)\right.\\
&\quad \times \left.\left(\alpha_m \sum_{k=1}^{J} \mathrm{B}_{mk}\Delta z_k + \sqrt{1-\alpha_m^2}\Delta w_m\right)\right),\\
&= \underbrace{\mathbb{E}\left(\left(\alpha_n \sum_{j=1}^{J} \mathrm{B}_{nj}\Delta z_j\right)\left(\alpha_m \sum_{k=1}^{J} \mathrm{B}_{mk}\Delta z_k\right)\right)}_{\text{Cross terms vanish by independence}},\\
&= \alpha_n\alpha_m \mathbb{E}\left(\left(\sum_{j=1}^{J} \mathrm{B}_{nj}\Delta z_j\right)\left(\sum_{k=1}^{J} \mathrm{B}_{mk}\Delta z_k\right)\right),\\
&= \alpha_n\alpha_m \mathbb{E}\left(\left(\sum_{j=1}^{J} \frac{\beta_{nj}}{\underbrace{\sigma\left(\sum_{j=1}^{J} \beta_{nj}\Delta z_j\right)}_{\text{Eq. 2.17}}} \Delta z_j\right.\right.
\end{aligned}
$$

[29] In the underlying derivation, it is useful to recall that, due to previous independence assumptions, the terms $\mathbb{E}(\Delta Z_j \cdot \Delta W_i)$ and $\mathbb{E}(\Delta W_i \cdot \Delta W_j)$ vanish for all (distinct) choices of $i$ and $j$.

$$
\times \left( \sum_{k=1}^{J} \underbrace{\frac{\beta_{mk}}{\sigma\left(\sum_{j=1}^{J} \beta_{mj}\Delta z_j\right)}}_{\text{Eq. 2.17}} \Delta z_k \right) \Bigg) ,
$$

$$
\begin{aligned}
&= \left( \frac{\alpha_n}{\sigma\left(\sum_{j=1}^{J} \beta_{nj}\Delta z_j\right)} \right) \left( \frac{\alpha_m}{\sigma\left(\sum_{j=1}^{J} \beta_{mj}\Delta z_j\right)} \right) \\
&\quad \times \text{cov}\left( \sum_{j=1}^{J} \beta_{nj}\Delta z_j, \sum_{k=1}^{J} \beta_{mk}\Delta z_k \right), \\
&= \alpha_n \left( \frac{\text{cov}\left( \sum_{j=1}^{J} \beta_{nj}\Delta z_j, \sum_{k=1}^{J} \beta_{mk}\Delta z_k \right)}{\sigma\left(\sum_{j=1}^{J} \beta_{nj}\Delta z_j\right) \sigma\left(\sum_{j=1}^{J} \beta_{mj}\Delta z_j\right)} \right) \alpha_m, \\
&= \alpha_n \text{corr}\left( \sum_{j=1}^{J} \beta_{nj}\Delta z_j, \sum_{k=1}^{J} \beta_{mk}\Delta z_k \right) \alpha_m, \\
&= \alpha_n \cdot \rho_{nm} \cdot \alpha_m,
\end{aligned}
$$

where the final step follows from the definition of correlation. We use the succinct expression, $\rho_{nm}$, to describe the observed linear dependence between the factor-loaded systemic factors of the $n$th and $m$th credit obligors. This quantity can be referred to as factor correlation. Moreover, since $\text{var}(\Delta X_i) = 1$ for all choices of $i$, the covariance and correlation of the creditworthiness increments are equivalent. Practically, this means that

$$
\begin{aligned}
\text{cov}(\Delta X_n, \Delta X_m) &= \text{corr}(\Delta X_n, \Delta X_m), \\
&= \alpha_n \cdot \rho_{nm} \cdot \alpha_m.
\end{aligned}
\tag{2.22}
$$

As a quick sanity check, setting $n = m$, we have that $\rho_{nn} = 1$, by definition. The consequence is that $\alpha_n^2$ is the contribution to variance from the systemic factor.

When adding the idiosyncratic component of variance, $1 - \alpha_n^2$, we replicate the unit variance result from Eq. 2.20.[30]

The most important conclusion from Eq. 2.22 is the interpretation of the $\alpha$ parameters. The individual $\alpha_n$ terms, which we should get in the habit of referring to as systemic weights, can be viewed as driving the correlation between the $n$th creditworthiness increment and the systemic factor. An easy way to see this is to consider a classic one-factor model,

$$\Delta X_n = \alpha_n \Delta G + \sqrt{1 - \alpha_n^2} \Delta w_n, \tag{2.23}$$

where $\Delta G$ is a single global risk factor and we can assume that $\beta_n$ is equal to unity. If we compute the correlation of the creditworthiness increment with the single global factor, $G$, we have

$$\begin{aligned} \text{cov}(\Delta X_n, \Delta G) &= \text{cov}\left(\alpha_n \Delta G + \sqrt{1 - \alpha_n^2} \Delta w_n, \Delta G\right), \\ &= \mathbb{E}\left(\left(\alpha_n \Delta G + \sqrt{1 - \alpha_n^2} \Delta w_n\right) \Delta G\right), \\ &= \alpha_n \underbrace{\mathbb{E}\left(\Delta G^2\right)}_{=1}, \\ &= \alpha_n. \end{aligned} \tag{2.24}$$

A similar computation to that found in Eq. 2.21—in the univariate setting—reveals that $\text{cov}(\Delta X_m, \Delta X_n) = \alpha_n \alpha_m$. The idea is analogous in our multivariate case. To handle the additional complexity of the systemic factors, however, the $\alpha_n$ and $\alpha_m$ terms need to load onto the more involved cross-correlation term, $\rho_{nm}$. We thus have a parsimonious and intuitive interpretation of the pairwise correlation between obligors in our credit portfolio. Moreover, this addition brings our model much closer, from a practical perspective, to the standard threshold-model implementation.

The preceding pages have been a flurry of changing notation and derivations. It is not always easy to follow all of the various steps. Table 2.2 attempts to help by chronicling the evolution of our state variables and coefficients throughout the discretization and normalization processes. Although the final column is basically our end point, there is value in following the steps from our stochastic differential equation—analogous to the one found in the Merton [30] work and more common a few decades ago—and the Vasicek [40, 41, 42] style formulation.

[30] Recall that, by independence, the idiosyncratic element impacts the variance measure, but does *not* contribute to covariance.

**Table 2.2** *Keeping track of variables and coefficients*: This table helps us keep track of the various state variables, their sub-components, and coefficients as we work from the original stochastic differential equation to the final discretized and normalized form in Eq. 2.18.

| Variable | Continuous time | Discretized | Normalized |
|---|---|---|---|
| State-variable increment | $dX_i(t)$ | $\Delta X_i$ | $\Delta X_i$ |
| Systemic-factor increment | $dZ_j(t)$ | $\Delta z_j$ | $\Delta z_j$ |
| Idiosyncratic-factor increment | $dW_i(t)$ | $\Delta w_i$ | $\Delta w_i$ |
| Systemic-factor loading | $\tilde{\beta}_{ij}$ | $\beta_{ij}$ | $\mathrm{B}_{ij}$ |
| Idiosyncratic-factor loading | $\tilde{\sigma}_i$ | $\sigma_i$ | $\sqrt{1-\alpha_i^2}$ |
| Systemic weight | 1 | 1 | $\alpha_i^2$ |

**Colour and Commentary 16** (Gaussian-Threshold Model)*: Despite the heavy first step involving the introduction of Eq. 2.9, the situation has improved. Time discretization, factor-level normalization, and the introduction of a proper form for the systemic weights have had a useful effect. We can now clearly see that, at its heart, the legacy model essentially follows a multivariate Gaussian-threshold methodology.*[a] *Examination of the latent-variable correlation structure also reveals a rich interaction between systemic weights and systemic-factor correlations. Specifying these coefficients will actually bring the model to life. For the remainder of this chapter, we will keep the discussion fairly abstract. Chapter 3 will address the important question of model parametrization.*

[a] It is not, however, expressed in its canonical form. For readers interested in more background, Bolder [7, Chapter 4] examines the class of threshold models in significant detail.

### 2.3.3 A Matrix Formulation

Another awkward aspect of the base formulation is its scalar representation. Given the large potential numbers of correlated and independent risk drivers—along with their loadings—it makes much more sense to place our discretized creditworthiness system into matrix notation. This turns out, unfortunately, to be a bit complicated. Let us begin with the most natural representation

$$\underbrace{\begin{bmatrix}\Delta X_1\\ \vdots\\ \Delta X_I\end{bmatrix}}_{I\times 1}=\underbrace{\begin{bmatrix}\alpha_1 & \cdots & 0\\ \vdots & \ddots & \vdots\\ 0 & \cdots & \alpha_I\end{bmatrix}}_{I\times I}\underbrace{\begin{bmatrix}\mathrm{B}_{11} & \cdots & \mathrm{B}_{1J}\\ \vdots & \ddots & \vdots\\ \mathrm{B}_{I1} & \cdots & \mathrm{B}_{IJ}\end{bmatrix}}_{I\times J}\underbrace{\begin{bmatrix}\Delta z_1\\ \vdots\\ \Delta z_J\end{bmatrix}}_{J\times 1}$$

$$+\underbrace{\begin{bmatrix} \sqrt{1-\alpha_1^2} & \cdots & 0 \\ \vdots & \ddots & \vdots \\ 0 & \cdots & \sqrt{1-\alpha_I^2} \end{bmatrix}}_{I\times I} \underbrace{\begin{bmatrix} \Delta w_1 \\ \vdots \\ \Delta w_I \end{bmatrix}}_{I\times 1}. \tag{2.25}$$

If we define the base systemic weights as the following diagonal matrix,

$$A = \begin{bmatrix} \alpha_1 & \cdots & 0 \\ \vdots & \ddots & \vdots \\ 0 & \cdots & \alpha_I \end{bmatrix}, \tag{2.26}$$

then it naturally follows that $(I - A^2)^{\frac{1}{2}} \in \mathbb{R}^{I\times I}$ is readily calculated.[31] Assigning reasonable symbols to the remaining matrices and vectors in Eq. 2.25, we can concisely express Eq. 2.19 as

$$\Delta X = AB\Delta z + (I - A^2)^{\frac{1}{2}} \Delta w, \tag{2.27}$$

where $B \in \mathbb{R}^{I\times J}$ is a matrix of normalized factor loadings, $\Delta z \in \mathbb{R}^{J\times 1}$ is a column vector of systemic risk factors, and $\Delta w \in \mathbb{R}^{I\times 1}$ is a column vector of idiosyncratic risk variables. Equation 2.27 is basically a simplified recipe for describing the entire system, $\Delta X \in \mathbb{R}^{I\times 1}$, of latent creditworthiness state variables in a single step. This quantity falls into the *nice-to-have* category, but it is not used very frequently.

While we have Eq. 2.27, let's put it to good use. The asset-return (or creditworthiness index) correlation matrix is of central importance in simulating economic-capital outcomes, trouble-shooting simulation results, and interpreting and communicating the model values. The more we can learn about it, the better our overall understanding. Examination in matrix notation has an important advantage of allowing us to see the entire picture. Let's see where Eq. 2.27 takes us. By construction, we have that $\Delta z \sim \mathcal{N}(0, \Omega)$ and $\Delta w \sim \mathcal{N}(0, I)$. As a consequence, it follows that

$$\begin{aligned} \text{var}(\Delta X) &= \text{var}\left(AB\Delta z + \left(I - A^2\right)^{\frac{1}{2}} \Delta w\right), \\ &= AB \underbrace{\text{var}(\Delta z)}_{\Omega}(AB)^T + \left(I - A^2\right)^{\frac{1}{2}} \underbrace{\text{var}(\Delta w)}_{I} \left(\left(I - A^2\right)^{\frac{1}{2}}\right)^T \end{aligned} \tag{2.28}$$

[31] This follows from the fact that $A$ is diagonal, but also that each $\alpha_i$ falls in the unit interval. Any negative $\alpha_i$ would otherwise lead to complex values. It should also be clear, from context, that the identity matrix has dimensions $I \times I$, but we'll underscore that point here to be certain.

$$
\begin{aligned}
&= AB\Omega B^T A + \left( \left(I - A^2\right)^{\frac{1}{2}} \right) \left(I - A^2\right)^{\frac{1}{2}} \Big), \\
&= AB\Omega B^T A + I - \underbrace{AIA}_{A^2}, \\
&= I + A\left( B\Omega B^T - I \right) A,
\end{aligned}
$$

which is an interesting, and somewhat unexpected, form.[32] Although each $\Delta X_i$ has unit variance, the full asset-correlation matrix is rather more complicated. In particular, we have that $\Delta X \sim \mathcal{N}\left(0, I + A\left( B\Omega B^T - I \right) A\right)$. All the main characters—systemic weights, normalized factor loadings, and factor correlations—make an appearance. The basic pattern is, upon examination, rather similar to the results from Eq. 2.21.

Equation 2.28, while interesting and occasionally useful, is *not* the most typical mathematical representation of our creditworthiness index. In most calculations, we find ourselves working at the credit obligor level. We typical use the less elegant, but surprisingly helpful, mixed-matrix representation. To get to this point, we first define the following fairly trivial, but convenient, row-vector quantity:

$$
\beta_i = \left[ \beta_{i1} \cdots \beta_{iJ\cdot} \right]. \tag{2.29}
$$

This immediately allows us to restate the awkward double-sum in the factor-loading normalization from Eq. 2.17 as,

$$
\sqrt{\beta_i \Omega \beta_i^T} = \sqrt{\sum_{\ell=1}^{J} \sum_{k=1}^{J} \beta_{i\ell} \beta_{ik} \Omega_{\ell k}}. \tag{2.30}
$$

The normalized factor loadings thus become

$$
\begin{aligned}
\mathrm{B}_i &= \left[ \mathrm{B}_{i1} \cdots \mathrm{B}_{iJ} \right], \\
&= \frac{1}{\sqrt{\beta_i \Omega \beta_i^T}} \overbrace{\left[ \beta_{i1} \cdots \beta_{iJ} \right]}^{\beta_i}.
\end{aligned} \tag{2.31}
$$

[32] Indeed, it is hard to tell if it makes sense. The corner cases of $A \equiv 0$ and $A \equiv I$—representing the domination of idiosyncratic and systemic risk, respectively—collapse to values of $I$ and $B\Omega B^T$ for Eq. 2.28. This quick sanity check suggests that the formulation, at least for the extremes, is mathematically reasonable.

There is nothing new in this representation, but it is rather easier to read (and manipulate). Using these constructs, for each $i$, we may now write our discretized creditworthiness index as

$$\Delta X_i = \alpha_i \underbrace{\frac{\beta_i}{\sqrt{\beta_i \Omega \beta_i^T}}}_{\mathrm{B}_i} \Delta z + \sqrt{1-\alpha_i^2}\,\Delta w_i, \tag{2.32}$$

$$= \alpha_i \mathrm{B}_i \Delta z + \sqrt{1-\alpha_i^2}\,\Delta w_i.$$

In short, we have vectorized the interaction between the systemic variables and their factor loadings, but otherwise maintained a scalar structure.[33] Again, there is not much exciting going on here; Eq. 2.32 simply turns out to be both a convenient and parsimonious representation.

**Colour and Commentary 17** (MIXED MATRIX NOTATION)*: It is entirely possible—and indeed, even advisable—to write our collection of I discretized and normalized creditworthiness indices in matrix notation. The final result is a concise and interesting mathematical representation. There is, however, a problem. Most common mathematical operations, in this setting, tend to occur at the obligor level. This means that the full matrix form is seldom employed. Instead, it is more common to work with the mixed-matrix notation summarized in Eq. 2.32. The interaction between the systemic variables and their factor loadings is vectorized, but otherwise the scalar structure has been maintained. Slightly clumsy, it nevertheless turns out to be an efficient and pragmatic way to represent the individual latent creditworthiness indices. In particular, this layered approach to the problem turns out to be very helpful in managing the parametrization questions addressed in Chap. 3.*

## 2.3.4 Orthogonalization

Before jumping to the remainder of the proper model construction, we will take a short detour. In the base formulation, the systemic factors are correlated. Abstracting from the systemic weights, this implies that the actual factor structure depends on a complicated combination of the factor loadings and the factor correlation matrix. Many industrial applications are constructed such that the systemic factors are actually orthogonal. This clearly offers some conceptual advantages. The good news

[33] With $\mathrm{B}_i \in \mathbb{R}^{1\times J}$ and $\Delta z \in \mathbb{R}^{J\times 1}$, their dot product (i.e., $\mathrm{B}_i \Delta z$) happily reduces to a scalar.

is that, with a bit of work, Eq. 2.32 can be readily orthogonalized. In this brief aside, we will examine precisely how this might be done.

The discretrized systemic factor correlation matrix of $\Delta z$ is, by construction, symmetric, real-valued, and positive definite. The consequence is that we can decompose $\Omega$ as,

$$\Omega = CDC^T, \tag{2.33}$$

where $D \in \mathbb{R}^{I\times I}$ is a diagonal matrix of positive real-valued eigenvalues. $C \in \mathbb{R}^{I\times I}$ is the collection of orthonormal eigenvectors.[34] The properties of $D$ allow us to immediately rewrite Eq. 2.33 as

$$\begin{aligned} \Omega &= \overbrace{C \underbrace{D^{\frac{1}{2}} D^{\frac{1}{2}}}_{D} C^T}^{\text{Eq. 2.33}}, \\ &= CD^{\frac{1}{2}} I \left(CD^{\frac{1}{2}}\right)^T, \end{aligned} \tag{2.34}$$

where, once again, $I$ denotes the identity matrix.[35]

This might seem like a curiosity, but it is just what we need. Recall that $\Delta z \sim \mathcal{N}(0, \Omega)$. We can actually reconstruct this quantity starting from $\Delta v \sim \mathcal{N}(0, I)$; that is, a vector of $I$ i.i.d. standard normal variates. Indeed, we might simply define

$$\Delta z = CD^{\frac{1}{2}} \Delta v. \tag{2.35}$$

The expectation of $\Delta v$ is clearly zero, but what about its variance? This is easily verified:

$$\begin{aligned} \text{var}(\Delta z) &= \text{var}\left(CD^{\frac{1}{2}} \Delta v\right), \\ &= CD^{\frac{1}{2}} \underbrace{\text{var}(\Delta v)}_{I} \left(CD^{\frac{1}{2}}\right)^T, \\ &= CDC^T, \\ &= \Omega. \end{aligned} \tag{2.36}$$

[34] This is a special case of the eigenvalue problem, which is sometimes referred to as the spectral decomposition. Much more background can be found—in increasing levels of theoretical complexity—in Harris and Stocker [21, Section 9.9], Press et al. [35, Chapter 9], and Golub and Loan [15, Chapter 8].

[35] There are, it turns out, other ways to do this. We could define $U = CD^{\frac{1}{2}}$ implying that $\Omega = UU^T$, which is often referred to as the Cholesky decomposition of $\Omega$.

The consequence is that $\Delta z = CD^{\frac{1}{2}}\Delta v \sim \mathcal{N}(0, \Omega)$. The immediate corollary is that by introducing a slight variation on our normalized factor loadings as

$$\breve{\mathrm{B}}_i = \mathrm{B}_i C D^{\frac{1}{2}}, \tag{2.37}$$

we can restate Eq. 2.32 as,

$$\Delta X_i = \alpha_i \breve{\mathrm{B}}_i \Delta v + \sqrt{1-\alpha_i^2}\Delta w_i. \tag{2.38}$$

To avoid more repetitive calculations, we leave it as an exercise for the reader to verify that $\Delta X_i$ retains unit variance—that is, $\Delta X_i \sim \mathcal{N}(0, 1)$—under this transformation.[36]

Ultimately, it makes little practical difference if one defines the model using the $\mathrm{B}_i$ or $\breve{\mathrm{B}}_i$ formulation of the factor loadings. The orthogonalized implementation offers conceptual clarity in the interpretation of the coefficients, while parametrization is slightly easier to manage with the base approach. It is ultimately a question of taste. The current implementation employs the $\mathrm{B}_i$ definition, but we are keenly aware that both methods are entirely legitimate.[37]

## 2.4 The Legacy Model

Our legacy credit-risk economic capital model—used in production until late 2020—was a version of the multivariate Gaussian threshold model. Thus far, we have principally focused on the asset-return, or creditworthiness, state variables. In this section, we will incorporate the remaining elements required to flesh out the full-blown model.

### *2.4.1 Introducing Default*

Each individual default event is defined, in the spirit of the threshold model introduced in the first section, as

$$\mathbb{I}_{\{\Delta X_i \leq K_i\}}, \tag{2.39}$$

[36] As a hint, it suffices to show that $\breve{\mathrm{B}}_i \breve{\mathrm{B}}_i^T = 1$.

[37] In Chap. 11, we will actually exploit this orthogonalized form within some interesting Pillar II regulatory calculations.

where $K_i$ represents an as-yet-undefined default threshold. In words, this implies that if the realization of the creditworthiness index falls below $K_i$, then the obligor is deemed to have entered the default state. Following the Merton [30] logic, we can think of the $K_i$ value as being somehow related to the firm's liabilities.

The immediate challenge is to determine a sensible value for $K_i$. While there is a range of possible choices, one option dramatically simplifies the problem and provides an entirely logical answer. The basic idea is to calibrate the expected value of the default event to the probability of default associated with the $i$th credit obligor. Defining the one-period default probability of the $i$th credit counterpart as $p_i$, we have

$$\begin{aligned} \mathbb{E}\left(\mathbb{I}_{\{\Delta X_i \leq K_i\}}\right) &= p_i, \\ \underbrace{\mathbb{P}\left(\Delta X_i \leq K_i\right)}_{\Delta X_i \sim \mathcal{N}(0,1)} &= p_i, \\ \Phi\left(K_i\right) &= p_i, \\ \Phi^{-1}\left(\Phi\left(K_i\right)\right) &= \Phi^{-1}\left(p_i\right), \\ K_i &= \Phi^{-1}\left(p_i\right), \end{aligned} \tag{2.40}$$

where $\Phi(\cdot)$ and $\Phi^{-1}(\cdot)$ denote the cumulative and inverse cumulative standard normal distribution functions, respectively.[38] This allows us to directly restate the default event more concretely as,

$$\mathbb{I}_{\{\Delta X_i \leq \Phi^{-1}(p_i)\}}, \tag{2.41}$$

for $i = 1, \ldots, I$. In turn, this definition permits us to write down a straightforward expression for the total default loss in one's portfolio as,

$$L_{\mathcal{D}} = \sum_{i=1}^{I} c_i \underbrace{\left(1 - \mathcal{R}_i\right)}_{\gamma_i} \mathbb{I}_{\{\Delta X_i \leq \Phi^{-1}(p_i)\}}, \tag{2.42}$$

where—drawing from Table 2.1—$c_i$, $\mathcal{R}_i$, and $\gamma_i$ denote the $i$th counterparty's exposure, recovery rate, and loss-given-default, respectively. In a one-period, default-only setting, the distribution of $L_{\mathcal{D}}$ is precisely our modelling object of interest.

The default probability estimate, $p_i$, is an unconditional estimate of the failure of the $i$th obligor to meet its credit obligations—this value relates only to each counterpart on an individual basis. The entire justification for the addition of $\Delta X_i$, however, was to induce dependence between these default events. To understand

[38] In principle, the periodicity of the default probability should be consistent with the length of the discretized time step $\Delta X_i$.

better how this works, we can examine the probability of a default event conditional upon a given realization of the set of systemic risk factors. This is defined as,

$$\mathbb{P}\left(\Delta X_i \leq \Phi^{-1}(p_i) \middle| \Delta Z\right) = \mathbb{P}\left(\underbrace{\alpha_i \mathrm{B}_i \Delta z + \sqrt{1-\alpha_i^2}\Delta w_i}_{\text{Eq. 2.32}} \leq \Phi^{-1}(p_i) \middle| \Delta z\right), \tag{2.43}$$

$$\begin{aligned} p_i(\Delta z) &= \mathbb{P}\left(\Delta w_i \leq \frac{\Phi^{-1}(p_i) - \alpha_i \mathrm{B}_i \Delta z}{\sqrt{1-\alpha_i^2}} \middle| \Delta z\right), \\ &= \Phi\left(\frac{\Phi^{-1}(p_i) - \alpha_i \mathrm{B}_i \Delta z}{\sqrt{1-\alpha_i^2}}\right) \\ &\equiv \boxed{\Phi\left(\frac{\Phi^{-1}(p_i) - \alpha_i \breve{\mathrm{B}}_i \Delta v}{\sqrt{1-\alpha_i^2}}\right)}, \end{aligned}$$

which follows directly from the fact that the idiosyncratic shock, $\Delta w_i$, is a standard normal variate. Just for fun, Eq. 2.43 also includes the orthogonalized version of the model. In either case, the consequence is that large negative outcomes of the systemic risk factors will tend, for all obligors, to push the probability of default upwards. This is the source of default dependence. Since different obligors load onto the individual systemic risk factors in varying ways, the actual dependence structure is actually quite complex. Nevertheless, this quantity provides significant insight into the inner workings of our credit-risk model.

**Colour and Commentary 18** (DEFAULT CONDITIONALITY)*: The threshold model induces default correlation by conditioning each credit ogligor's latent creditworthiness state variable upon a common set of systemic risk factors. A positive systemic risk-factor realization will improve all credit counterparties' default probabilities, whereas a negative draw works in the opposite direction. Given the systemic risk-factor realization, however, all default events are independent. Moreover, each credit obligor—through the specification of the* $\alpha$ *and* B *parameters—are potentially impacted in a different way by the systemic values. The conditional default probability, as described in Eq. 2.43, is a rather useful object in understanding the impact of systemic risk-factor outcomes on a given credit obligor's risk profile. As a final point, the form changes only very slightly when using the dependent or orthogonalized formulations of systemic risk factors.*

### 2.4.2 Stochastic Recovery

The magnitude of the credit loss also depends, as suggested in Eq. 2.42, upon the amount of the total credit exposure *recovered* through the default process. The larger the amount recovered, of course, the lower the default loss. We can think of this recovery amount as taking a value from zero to unity. A recovery value of zero would imply that, in the event of default, one would be in the unfortunate situation of losing one's entire exposure. Conversely, a recovery value of one suggests that, happily, no loss is incurred.[39] The entire amount is recovered. Naturally, these are extremes. Typical values, therefore, fall in the open interval, $(0, 1)$.

For each exposure—similar to the default probability—one thus needs to estimate, determine, or otherwise assign a recovery rate in the event of default. Rather than recovery, which we might refer to as $\mathcal{R}$, it is more common to work with the loss-given-default. This latter quantity is simply $\gamma \equiv 1 - \mathcal{R}$; in essence, therefore, recovery and loss-given-default are opposite sides of the same coin.

The loss-given default associated with a credit obligation depends, again similar to the default probability, upon a complex interaction between a range of factors. The financial strength of the firm plays, of course, an important role. Perhaps equally important, however, are the seniority of the claim and the presence of any external guarantees or collateral attached to the loan or treasury asset. These latter points are intimately connected to the inevitable legal aspects associated with the default of any entity. Related to this point is the type of organization; a corporation, a financial institution, a public-sector entity, or a government. Each of these organizational types will, in principle, have different characteristics impacting the loss-given-default in varying ways. Most organizations, and NIB is no exception, have developed a fairly involved loss-given-default framework describing the underlying process of how these values are determined for each of their individual asset exposures.[40]

The simplest modelling treatment of this quantity would involve assignment of a constant loss-given default—let's assume, as is typically the case, that this value is determined by the firm's loss-given-default framework—to each of the individual exposures within one's portfolio. This is a sensible approach, but it ignores the potential uncertainty in the actual size of the final loss. As previously discussed, a multiplicity of factors exerts an influence on the final loss-given-default outcome.[41] Even the most detailed loss-given-default framework will struggle to determine

[39] Naturally, in reality, it is not quite so simple. There are often significant time lags, foregone cash-flows, and additional transaction costs. This is, however, a model and thus its representation is defensibly stylistic.

[40] How precisely this is performed at NIB is beyond the scope of this discussion, which focuses on the modelling dimension. This is not to say that no modelling is involved in LGD specifications, far from it, but this area often touches on rather proprietary dimensions.

[41] Altman et al. [2] provides a useful broad based analysis of the factors driving recovery with a particular focus on the link to default probabilities.

precisely the importance of each underlying driver to a specific credit obligor. Assignment of a single, deterministic loss-given-default value is thus probably overly simplistic. A more complicated, and perhaps more realistic, alternative would be to treat the actual loss-given default as a random variable. Such an approach would certainly complicate the model implementation, but it would directly address this important source of uncertainty. For this reason, the employment of stochastic loss-given-default values has become standard practice in credit-risk models.

How might this work? We can succinctly restate—from Eq. 2.42—the default-loss of our portfolio as,

$$L_{\mathcal{D}} = \sum_{i=1}^{I} c_i \gamma_i \mathbb{I}_{\mathcal{D}_i}, \tag{2.44}$$

where $\mathcal{D}_i \equiv \Delta X_i \leq \Phi^{-1}(p_i)$ and $\gamma_i \sim \mathcal{X}(\bar{\gamma}_i, \upsilon_{\gamma_i}, \cdots)$. In actuality, we have done relatively little with this restatement. The $i$th loss-given-default quantity has merely been specified as a yet-to-be-defined random variable given its first two moments: the mean, $\bar{\gamma}_i$ and the variance, $\upsilon_{\gamma_i}$. Clearly a choice is required regarding the distribution of each $\gamma_i$, but this is not the only choice required. One also needs to decide on the dependence between the default event, $\mathbb{I}_{\mathcal{D}_i}$, and the loss-given-default. Are they somehow related or are they independent? Moreover, it is necessary to decide upon any relationship between the loss-given-default of any two credit obligors, say $\gamma_i$ and $\gamma_j$.

Before exploring possible marginal distributions for each individual loss-given-default parameter, let us first consider questions of dependence. Common practice involves the assumption of independence between the loss-given-default outcome of any two arbitrary credit obligors, $i$ and $j$. Economic intuition aside, it is difficult to practically imagine how calibration of such dependence would work when examining relatively high credit-quality obligors. The loss-given default outcome comes into play only in the case of default. As default is rare, it only affects a small number of credit obligors—very often none—in any given simulation draw. Imposition of correlation at the individual credit obligor level is unlikely to have any appreciable impact on risk outcomes, quite simply because joint defaults are so rare. This is the same reasoning behind the use of global conditioning variables to induce default correlation; default correlation at the obligor level is relatively ineffective.

It is very common to assume that the loss-given-default is an entirely idiosyncratic affair. Although loss-given-default is a random variable, each outcome is independent of the set of global systemic variables, a firm's default probability, and the loss-given-default events associated with other credit obligors. We will also make this choice in our development. More complex and involved specifications are, indeed, possible.[42] The typical viewpoint leans on the fact that virtually any

[42] Frye [11], for example, offers an alternative in the one-factor setting that, like the conditional default probability, depends on the common global macroeconomic variable. Frye [12], conversely,

economic-capital model is already rather complex and parameter selection, in this setting, is extremely difficult. Moreover, it is important that the loss-given-default outcome employed in our economic-capital model is conceptually consistent with the assigned value from one's loss-given-default framework. This is not a deviation from general practice, it is principally a choice driven by a combination of analytic convenience and a lack of informative data.

One useful advantage of the assumption of independence is a relatively straightforward computation of the mean of the portfolio default loss. In particular, working from Eq. 2.44, the mean is given as,

$$\begin{aligned} \mathbb{E}(L_{\mathcal{D}}) &= \mathbb{E}\left(\sum_{i=1}^{I} c_i \gamma_i \mathbb{I}_{\mathcal{D}_i}\right), \\ &= \sum_{i=1}^{I} \mathbb{E}\left(c_i \delta_i \mathbb{I}_{\mathcal{D}_i}\right), \\ &= \sum_{i=1}^{I} c_i \underbrace{\mathbb{E}(\gamma_i)\,\mathbb{E}\left(\mathbb{I}_{\mathcal{D}_i}\right)}_{\text{By independence}}, \\ &= \sum_{i=1}^{I} c_i \bar{\gamma}_i \underbrace{\mathbb{P}(\mathcal{D}_i)}_{p_i}. \end{aligned} \tag{2.45}$$

The expected loss is thus simply the sum of the product of the exposures, the average loss-given-defaults, and the probabilities of default. This further underscores the central importance of these *three* fundamental quantities, which we introduced in Table 2.1.

The final decision involves a choice of distribution for each random loss-given-default variable. There are many possible choices. One important restriction, however, is that the support of this random variable is confined to the unit interval. A trivial possibility would involve the use of a standard uniform distribution. Such a choice implies that every point in the unit interval has an equal probability. This seems unreasonable and can be rejected out of hand, not least because it implies a common mean loss-given-default outcome of 0.5 for all credit obligors.

Ignoring the standard uniform distribution, there are two main approaches to the selection of a suitable distribution. One can find a distribution with support restricted to a fixed interval or transform a random variable with infinite support into the interval between zero and one. One could, for example, draw a random variable from the normal distribution and then map it to (0, 1) using a logistic or

offers another possibility where the loss-given-default is a stylized function of the conditional-default probability.

probit transformation.[43] There are rather fewer distributions with bounded support. The classic choice is the beta distribution.[44] There are numerous other choices that, upon closer inspection, are ultimately special cases of the beta distribution. Another, perhaps less common choice, is the so-called Kumaraswamy distribution; see Kumaraswamy [26] for more detail.

We have, once again, opted for simplicity. Each individual loss-given-default random variable is assumed to follow an independent beta distribution. The parameters of each beta distribution are informed, at least in part, from one's internal loss-given-default framework. The specific parametric choices are discussed, in much more detail, in Chap. 3.[45] The important takeaway, at this point, is that our approach incorporates random recovery in a relatively straightforward—and to the extent possible—conservative fashion.

**Colour and Commentary 19** (PARAMETRIZING RECOVERY)*: The management of the recovery dimension in the measurement of credit risk is a complicated task. The amount recovered subsequent to a default event—or, closely related, the notion of loss-given-default—is* not *known in advance: it is a stochastic quantity. Although ultimately random, it nevertheless depends upon a range of factors: an obligor's organizational structure, its financial strength, its legal domicile, and any credit-mitigation measures to name a few important elements. Taking this into account, our methodology assigns a separate marginal distribution—describing the interaction between recovery outcomes and likelihoods—to each credit obligor. These marginal distributions, while important, do not tell the entire story. It is also necessary to specify any dependence between the various recovery processes and the default outcomes. Our production model, consistent with general practice, assumes independence between recovery and default. This enhances model tractability and avoids some rather thorny parametric questions. It is an expedient choice, forced upon us by practical data constraints, but it is important to be aware that it is probably not quite correct.*

[43] These, of course, are only two popular transformations of a continuous-valued variable into (0, 1); there are many others.

[44] See Johnson et al. [22, Chapter 25] for significantly more background on this distribution.

[45] This discussion incorporates a unique angle that attempts to capture an important stylized fact about loss-given-default.

### 2.4.3 Risk Metrics

As highlighted in the previous chapter, the economic capital calculation is the distance between a worst-case measure of risk and the accounting- or valuation-based expected loss. Equation 2.45 provides clear direction for the computation of expected loss. To determine the credit-risk economic capital estimate—and complete the basic structure of our model—we still need a worst-case loss quantity. Since there are multiple possible candidates to measure worst-case losses, a few decisions need to be taken. In this brief section, we'll consider *two* main alternatives to motivate our choice.

Using the Gaussian threshold model outlined in the previous sections, we use simulation to trace out the entire credit loss distribution. This provides all of the ingredients required to actually compute virtually any desired measure of portfolio riskiness. We do not, however, typically consider the entire loss distribution. As rather pessimistic risk-management professionals, we invariably focus our attention on the tail of the loss distribution. This is, after all, where all the bad things happen. The classic measure is referred to as Value-at-Risk or VaR. Originally suggested by Morgan/Reuters [32], within the market-risk setting, it is described mathematically as

$$\text{VaR}_\alpha(L) = \inf\left(x : \mathbb{P}\left(L \leq x\right) \geq 1-\alpha\right), \tag{2.46}$$

where $\inf(\cdot)$ denotes the infimum operator.[46] Equation 2.46 depends on *two* parameters: $\alpha$ a threshold for the probability on the right-hand side and the default loss, $L$. The first is a parameter, whereas the second is a random variable: portfolio default-loss. $\alpha$ is also referred to as the confidence level. Imagine it is 0.99. With this parameter choice, $\text{VaR}_\alpha(L)$ describes the largest default-loss outcome exceeding 99% of all possible losses, but is itself exceeded in 1% of all cases. When computed for default or migration risk, it is often referred to as credit VaR.[47]

With a bit of additional effort, we may simplify our abstract specification of VaR. From Eq. 2.46, the VaR measure, by definition, satisfies the following relation,

$$\int_{\text{VaR}_\alpha(L)}^{\infty} f_L(\ell)d\ell = \alpha, \tag{2.47}$$

$$1-\mathbb{P}\left(L \geq \text{VaR}_\alpha(L)\right) = 1-\alpha,$$

[46] The infimum is basically—avoiding lots of mathematical formalism—a set-theoretical generalization of the minimum operator. See Royden [37] for the important details.

[47] An excellent reference for all things related to VaR is Jorion [23].

$$\mathbb{P}\Big(L \leq \text{VaR}_\alpha(L)\Big) = 1 - \alpha,$$
$$F_L\Big(\text{VaR}_\alpha(L)\Big) = 1 - \alpha,$$

where $F_L(\cdot)$ denotes the cumulative default-loss distribution function. The natural solution is thus,

$$\text{VaR}_\alpha(L) = F_L^{-1}(1-\alpha). \tag{2.48}$$

In words, Eq. 2.48 verifies that $\text{VaR}_\alpha(L)$ is nothing other than the $(1-\alpha)$-quantile of our portfolio credit-loss distribution. Since we are already in the business of running millions of simulations of our model, quantiles are readily estimated by simply ordering the simulation results. Readily computed, easy-to-use, understand, and communicate, it is no wonder that VaR has become such a popular risk measure.

A few decades prior to the writing of this book, Artzner et al. [3] produced a very useful paper providing, in an axiomatic manner, the main desirable properties of a risk metric. Risk measures that fulfil all properties are referred to as *coherent*. VaR was, unfortunately, found wanting along one important dimension.[48] This has led to a search for alternatives. An increasingly common (and coherent) measure, is defined as the following conditional expectation

$$\begin{aligned}\mathcal{E}_\alpha(L) &= \mathbb{E}\left(L \,\middle|\, L \geq \text{VaR}_\alpha(L)\right), \qquad (2.49)\\ &= \frac{1}{1-\alpha}\int_{\text{VaR}_\alpha(L)}^{\infty} \ell f_L(\ell)d\ell,\end{aligned}$$

where $f_L(\ell)$, as before, represents the default-loss density function. Equation 2.49 describes the expected default-loss given that one finds oneself at, or beyond, the $(1-\alpha)$-quantile (i.e., $\text{VaR}_\alpha(L)$) level. This quantity is, as a consequence, termed the conditional VaR, the tail VaR, or the expected shortfall. We predominately use the term expected shortfall and refer to it symbolically as $\mathcal{E}_\alpha(L)$ to explicitly include the desired quantile defining the tail of the return distribution.[49] Figure 2.1 provides a visualization of the difference between these two central measures of risk.

There are, of course, other possible choices of risk metric that one might consider. Boyle et al. [8] chronicle the disadvantages of VaR—in terms of coherence—and offer a twist on the idea of expected shortfall. Gilli and Këllezi [13] propose

[48] In particular, VaR is not sub-additive. See McNeil et al. [29, Chapter 2.3] for a nice exposition of this point.

[49] Given a closed-form expression for the default-loss density, Eqs. 2.48 and 2.49 can often be manipulated to derive analytic formulae for the VaR and expected-shortfall measures. In practical industrial applications, unfortunately, we rarely find ourselves in this happy situation.

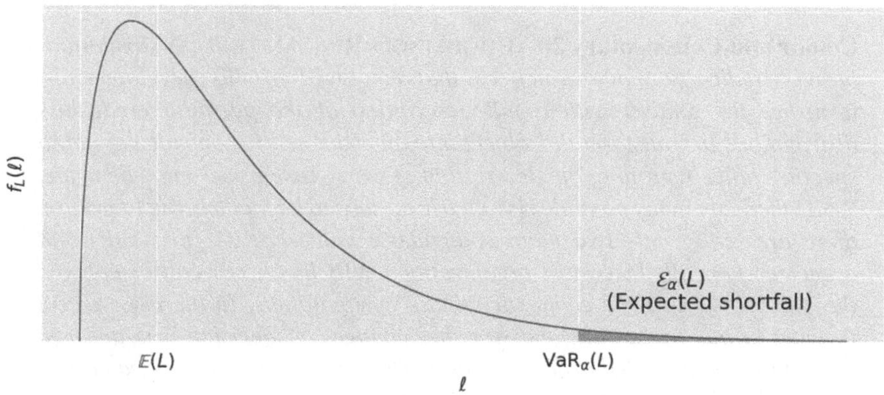


**Fig. 2.1** *Visualizing risk metrics*: This graphic, via the illustration of a generic credit-loss density $f_L(\ell)$, illustrates the VaR and expected shortfall measures. VaR is a quantile of the loss distribution, while expected shortfall is the *average* at or beyond a specific quantile.

some ideas from extreme-value theory. Although quite interesting, and potentially powerful, these notions have not yet found popularity in industrial applications. For the moment, therefore, the principal alternatives used in practical circles are the presented VaR and expected-shortfall measures.

Traditionally, like most organizations, NIB has used the VaR measure with varying confidence levels for alternative applications. The production measure in the revised credit-risk economic capital model has nonetheless broken with tradition and moved to expected-shortfall measure. VaR's non-coherence does give some reason for pause, and was certainly a contributing factor in the final decision, but it is not the key factor. A more convincing motive is the inherent conservatism associated with expected shortfall. Instead of looking at losses associated with a fixed quantile, it considers the average losses beyond this point. To put it bluntly, *all* of the really bad outcomes are structurally incorporated into the calculation of expected shortfall. This is, for a risk manager, an attractive perspective.

The final deciding factor in favour of expected shortfall, however, relates to a practical point. A useful, well-functioning, credit-risk economic capital model requires attribution of overall capital to individual loans and treasury instruments. This process is referred to risk attribution; the actual approach will be addressed in the final section of this chapter. VaR-measure risk attribution in the simulation setting turns out to be a messy and noisy affair. Conversely, the same computation applied to expected shortfall is significantly more robust and stable. The central importance of risk attribution, along with the theoretical advantages of expected shortfall, ultimately tipped the scales in favour of this coherent risk measure.

**Colour and Commentary 20** (CHOOSING A RISK METRIC)*: A simulation-based, credit-risk model—such as that employed in this development—furnishes the analyst with a full description of the portfolio credit-loss distribution. To transform this object into an estimate of economic capital, a specific choice regarding the description of worst-case losses must be made. While there are many possible risk-metric options to be found in the literature, there are really only* two *main contenders: Value-at-Risk (i.e., VaR) and expected shortfall. Like most organizations, NIB has historically employed the VaR metric in their economic-capital computations. In the most recent revision of our framework, the situation changed. A decision was taken to move to the expected-shortfall measure. Three main reasons motivated this choice. The first is theoretical; in the jargon of Artzner et al. [3] expected shortfall is—unlike VaR—a* coherent *risk measure. The second reason is conceptual. By incorporating all extreme tail observations into its calculation, expected shortfall is both a more complete and conservative description of downside risks. The final reason is practical; simulation-based methods for attribution of risks to individual loans and investments are dramatically more robust for expected shortfall.*[a] *This combination of sensible reasons feels like sufficient justification for the move.*

[a] The precise details of this calculation follow in the final section of this chapter.

## 2.5 Extending the Legacy Model

Starting from a generic description of creditworthiness dynamics, we have established that the legacy model is a (non-canonical) multivariate, Gaussian threshold model with stochastic recovery. We have introduced a detailed notation, identified the key aspects of the model and even motivated our choice of risk metric. With the important question of parameter selection relegated to Chap. 3, this might conclude our discussion. As indicated on numerous occasions in previous sections and chapters, however, our 2020 statutory change (quite naturally) prompted reflection on the structure of the credit-risk economic capital model. The reflection lead to action. The *two* central consequences were associated with the choice of threshold-model copula function and the incorporation of credit migration. This section walks through the details, and implications, of these two central elements.

### 2.5.1 Changing the Copula

The legacy credit-risk economic-capital model was founded on the assumption that both the idiosyncratic and systemic risk factors are normally distributed. This choice is, in a general sense, referred to as the Gaussian copula. The Gaussian copula, following the recent financial crisis starting in 2008, has nonetheless come under strong criticism. The source of this disapproval relates to some very strong assumptions about default correlation. A well-cited article—see MacKenzie and Spears [28]—has even made the Gaussian-copula specification rather infamous. The main problem is that it ignores the idea of *tail dependence*. The basic idea is that as we move far enough into the tail of the credit-loss distribution, default becomes independent in the Gaussian copula. This is hardly confidence inspiring. One practical solution, offered in the literature, is to use the so-called $t$-copula; this means that idiosyncratic and systemic risk factors follow a $t$ distribution.[50]

The notion of tail dependence is neither particularly well known nor is it extremely straightforward to explain without resort to rather technical arguments.[51] It is nonetheless worth deeper reflection. Tail dependence is conceptually analogous to more commonly used notions of correlation such as linear or rank correlation coefficients. Typically, one begins with two random variables. In our case, let's give these random variables specific names, $\mathbb{I}_{\mathcal{D}_i}$ and $\mathbb{I}_{\mathcal{D}_j}$, naturally representing the default events of two arbitrarily selected credit obligors. Default correlation considers the simple linear dependence between these two random quantities. Tail dependence, conversely, considers the relationship between these two events as we move arbitrarily far into the tail of their joint credit-loss distribution.

Default is, for almost any credit obligor, a rare event. A joint default is worse: it is the coincidence of two rare (i.e., tail) events. The incidence of joint default tells us something about the notion of tail dependence. The Gaussian copula implies, unfortunately, by its very mathematical structure, that as the two events become sufficiently rare, they tend towards independence. In most portfolios, however, it is precisely the multiplicity of default that generates sizable risk scenarios. Since the probability of two independent events is their product, and default is by definition a low-probability outcome, joint defaults are structurally underestimated in the Gaussian setting. Although the notion is quite technical, the impact is easy to understand.

An example provides a useful demonstration of the difference associated with one's choice of copula function. Figure 2.2 provides the results associated with a simple experiment. We examine our credit portfolio for a given date in the spring of 2020. Two credit counterparties were arbitrarily selected. We then investigate the joint default outcomes associated with one million simulations. Using the same

[50] Kuhn [25] and Kostadinov [24] both make compelling cases for the benefits of the $t$-distributed threshold implementation.

[51] For the reader interested in a more formal description, please see Bolder [7, Chapter 4] and the multiple references it contains.

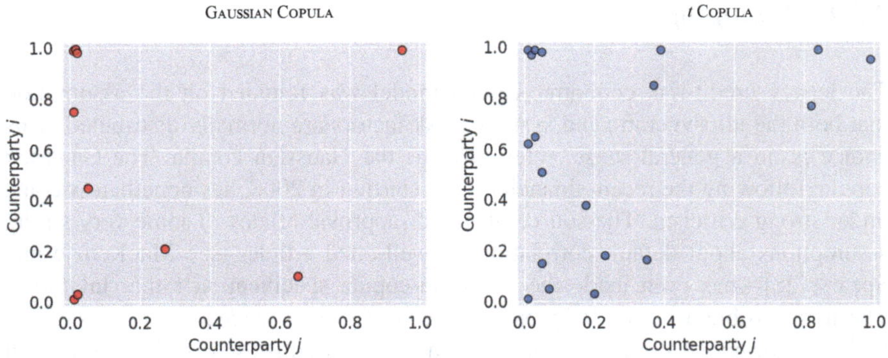


**Fig. 2.2** *Joint default*: Joint defaults lie at the heart of default correlation and the conservative description of the worst-case credit-loss outcomes. This figure provides a visual perspective on the differences between the distribution of joint defaults under the Gaussian- and $t$-copula specifications of the threshold model. In each case, the proportional joint-default losses of two arbitrarily selected obligors are displayed under our competing copula functions.

randomly simulated outcomes *two* copula functions are employed: the presented Gaussian and the $t$ copulas. To be clear, therefore, the only difference relates to the choice of copula function.[52] There are, of course, cases where one credit counterparty defaults, whereas the other does not. Only those situations, to be clear, where both of the obligors experience a default outcome are presented. Generally, of course, there are far fewer incidences of two counterparties defaulting concurrently. In the Gaussian case, there are precisely 10 joint defaults. The $t$-copula case, conversely, exhibits a twofold increase in the incidence of joint default. This is precisely the impact of (non-zero) tail dependence; a more realistic, and conservative, description of joint default is created.

The results presented in Fig. 2.2 might not seem like a dramatic difference, but expanding this notion across all pairs of credit counterparts across an entire portfolio can, and does, have an important impact on the final risk figures. There is, at the portfolio level given the parameter settings, only about a 20% increase in joint default. At the individual obligor level, however, when joint default does occur, on average it leads to a sizable increase in the number of joint defaults. This, of course, varies from a small reduction in some cases to increases on the order of many multiples of the base number of Gaussian-copula joint defaults. The bottom line, therefore, is that tail dependence matters quite importantly in terms of joint default and, ultimately, practical portfolio-level default correlation. The final consequence is a more realistic and conservative estimate of economic capital.

[52] There is also some noise associated with the random draws associated with the recovery outcomes, but this only impacts the magnitude of the loss, not their incidence.

## 2.5.2 Constructing the t Copula

To construct the $t$-copula model, the vast majority of the model infrastructure remains unchanged. The creditworthiness process is slightly adjusted as follows,

$$\Delta X_i = \sqrt{\frac{\nu}{W}} \underbrace{\left(\alpha_i \mathrm{B}_i \Delta z + \sqrt{1-\alpha_i^2}\Delta w_i\right)}_{\text{Eq. 2.32}}. \tag{2.50}$$

where $W \sim \chi^2(\nu)$ is referred to as the mixing variable. In other words, $W$ is a common variable shared across all risk obligors within a given simulation that follows a $\chi^2$ distribution with $\nu$ degrees of freedom. Equation 2.50 is a special case of what is generally referred to as a normal-variance mixture model.[53]

While it is not obvious from Eq. 2.50, the $\sqrt{\frac{\nu}{W}}$ terms transforms each $y_n$ into a univariate standard $t$-distributed random variable.[54] This implies that $\mathbb{E}(y_n) = 0$ and $\text{var}(y_n) = \frac{\nu}{\nu-2}$ for all $n = 1, \ldots, N$. In other words, the marginal distribution of each $\Delta X_i$ follows a standard $t$ distribution, while simultaneously moving the joint distribution of the collection of $\{\Delta X_i \ : \ i = 1, \ldots, I\}$ to a multivariate $t$ distribution. The final result is the so-called $t$-threshold model.

The new moments of $\Delta X_i$ merit demonstration. The expected value of Eq. 2.50 is,

$$\begin{aligned}
\mathbb{E}\left(\Delta X_i\right) &= \mathbb{E}\left(\sqrt{\frac{\nu}{W}}\left(\alpha_i \mathrm{B}_i \Delta z + \sqrt{1-\alpha_i^2}\Delta w_i\right)\right), \qquad (2.51)\\
&= \alpha_i \cdot \overbrace{\mathbb{E}\left(\sqrt{\frac{\nu}{W}}\right)\mathrm{B}_i \underbrace{\mathbb{E}\left(\Delta z\right)}_{=0}}^{\text{By independence}} + \sqrt{1-\alpha_i^2}\cdot \overbrace{\mathbb{E}\left(\sqrt{\frac{\nu}{W}}\right)\underbrace{\mathbb{E}(\Delta w_i)}_{=0}}^{\text{By independence}},\\
&= 0,
\end{aligned}$$

as expected.

Finding the variance of $\Delta X_i$ is a bit more work,

$$\text{var}\left(\Delta X_i\right) = \mathbb{E}\left(\Delta X_i^2 - \underbrace{\mathbb{E}(\Delta X_i)^2}_{=0}\right), \tag{2.52}$$

[53] Quite simply, different choices of $W$ and $\nu$ induce alternative copula functions. See Bolder [7, Chapter 4] for much more information on this notion (and many other helpful references).

[54] See Bolder [7, Appendix A] for a detailed description of the construction of the $t$-distribution.

$$
\begin{aligned}
&= \mathbb{E}\left(\left(\sqrt{\frac{\nu}{W}}\left(\alpha_i \mathrm{B}_i \Delta z + \sqrt{1-\alpha_i^2}\Delta w_i\right)\right)^2\right),\\
&= \underbrace{\mathbb{E}\left(\frac{\nu}{W}\cdot\alpha_i^2\cdot \mathrm{B}_i \Delta z \Delta z^T \mathrm{B}_i^T\right) + \mathbb{E}\left(\frac{\nu}{W}\cdot(1-\alpha_i^2)\cdot\Delta w_i^2\right)}_{\text{Cross terms vanish by independence and zero expectations}},\\
&= \alpha_i^2\cdot\nu\cdot\mathbb{E}\left(\frac{1}{W}\right)\mathrm{B}_i \underbrace{\mathbb{E}\left(\Delta z\Delta z^T\right)}_{\Omega}\mathrm{B}_i^T\\
&\quad +(1-\alpha_i^2)\cdot\nu\cdot\mathbb{E}\left(\frac{1}{W}\right)\underbrace{\mathbb{E}\left(\Delta w_i^2\right)}_{=1},\\
&= \alpha_i^2\cdot\nu\cdot\mathbb{E}\left(\frac{1}{W}\right)\underbrace{\mathrm{B}_i\Omega\mathrm{B}_i^T}_{=1} + (1-\alpha_i^2)\cdot\nu\cdot\mathbb{E}\left(\frac{1}{W}\right),\\
&= \cancel{\alpha_i^2\cdot\nu\cdot\mathbb{E}\left(\frac{1}{W}\right)} + \nu\cdot\mathbb{E}\left(\frac{1}{W}\right) - \cancel{\alpha_i^2\cdot\nu\cdot\mathbb{E}\left(\frac{1}{W}\right)},\\
&= \nu\cdot\mathbb{E}\left(\frac{1}{W}\right),
\end{aligned}
$$

where we need to observe that $\mathrm{B}_i\Omega\mathrm{B}_i^T = 1$; this is the normalized, factor-loaded variance.[55] Resolving this expression now reduces to evaluating the reciprocal of a chi-squared distribution with $\nu$ degrees of freedom. Although tedious, it is readily determined from first principles by solving the following integral,

$$
\begin{aligned}
\mathbb{E}\left(\frac{1}{W}\right) &= \int_{\mathbb{R}_+} \frac{1}{w} f_W(w)dw, \qquad (2.53)\\
&= \int_{\mathbb{R}_+} \frac{1}{w} \underbrace{\frac{1}{2^{\frac{\nu}{2}}\Gamma\left(\frac{\nu}{2}\right)} w^{\frac{\nu}{2}-1} e^{-\frac{w}{2}}}_{W\sim\chi^2(\nu)} dw,\\
&= \frac{1}{2^{\frac{\nu}{2}}\Gamma\left(\frac{\nu}{2}\right)} \int_{\mathbb{R}_+} w^{\frac{\nu-2}{2}-1} e^{-\frac{w}{2}} dw,
\end{aligned}
$$

[55] It was, in fact, constructed in such a way to be equal to one.

$$
\begin{aligned}
&= \frac{2^{\frac{\nu-2}{2}}\Gamma\left(\frac{\nu-2}{2}\right)}{2^{\frac{\nu}{2}}\Gamma\left(\frac{\nu}{2}\right)} \underbrace{\int_{\mathbb{R}_+} \overbrace{\frac{1}{2^{\frac{\nu-2}{2}}\Gamma\left(\frac{\nu-2}{2}\right)} w^{\frac{\nu-2}{2}-1} e^{-\frac{w}{2}}}^{\chi^2(\nu-2)} dw}_{=1}, \\
&= \frac{1}{2}\frac{\Gamma\left(\frac{\nu-2}{2}\right)}{\Gamma\left(\frac{\nu}{2}\right)}, \\
&= \frac{1}{2}\frac{\left(\frac{\nu-2}{2}-1\right)!}{\left(\frac{\nu}{2}-1\right)!}, \\
&= \frac{1}{2}\frac{1}{\left(\frac{\nu}{2}-1\right)}, \\
&= \frac{1}{\nu-2},
\end{aligned}
$$

which directly implies from Eq. 2.52 that, indeed as we claimed, $\text{var}(\Delta X_i) = \frac{\nu}{\nu-2}$. The final line of Eq. 2.53 follows from two useful facts: $\nu \in \mathbb{N}_+$ and $\Gamma(n) = (n-1)!$.

The marginal systematic and idiosyncratic variable distributions of the $t$-distributed model remain Gaussian. The joint and marginal distributions of the latent default-state variables (i.e., $\{\Delta X_i \ : \ i = 1, \ldots, I\}$) follow a $t$-distribution. At the joint distribution level, of course, the covariance—and correlation—between any two arbitrary latent creditworthiness state variables, $\Delta X_n$ and $\Delta X_m$, are also slightly transformed.

Recycling our analysis from Eq. 2.21 on page 72 with our new definition in Eq. 2.50, we have

$$
\begin{aligned}
\text{cov}(\Delta X_n, \Delta X_m) &= \mathbb{E}(\Delta X_n \Delta X_m), \qquad (2.54) \\
&= \mathbb{E}\left( \underbrace{\sqrt{\frac{\nu}{W}}\left(\alpha_n \text{B}_n \Delta z + \sqrt{1-\alpha_n^2}\Delta w_n\right)}_{\Delta X_n} \underbrace{\sqrt{\frac{\nu}{W}}\left(\alpha_m \text{B}_m \Delta z + \sqrt{1-\alpha_m^2}\Delta w_m\right)}_{\Delta X_m} \right), \\
&= \mathbb{E}\left(\frac{\nu}{W}\left(\alpha_n\alpha_m \text{B}_n \Delta z \Delta z^T \text{B}_m^T\right)\right), \\
&= \nu \mathbb{E}\left(\frac{1}{W}\right) \alpha_n \text{B}_n \underbrace{\mathbb{E}(\Delta z \Delta z^T)}_{\Omega} \text{B}_m^T \alpha_m, \\
&= \nu \mathbb{E}\left(\frac{1}{W}\right) \alpha_n \underbrace{\text{B}_n \Omega \text{B}_m^T}_{\rho_{nm}} \alpha_m, \\
&= \left(\frac{\nu}{\nu-2}\right) \alpha_n \rho_{nm} \alpha_m,
\end{aligned}
$$

where $\rho_{nm} = B_n \Omega B_m^T$ is the normalized, factor-loaded correlation between the $n$th and $m$th creditworthiness latent state variables.[56] With the exception of the coefficient involving $\nu$, this looks very similar to the structure found in Eq. 2.21. To get to the correlation coefficient, we need only normalize by the volatility of $\Delta X_n$ and $\Delta X_m$ as follows:

$$
\begin{aligned}
\rho(\Delta X_n, \Delta X_m) &= \frac{\mathrm{cov}(\Delta X_n, \Delta X_m)}{\sqrt{\mathrm{var}(\Delta X_n)}\sqrt{\mathrm{var}(\Delta X_m)}}, \qquad (2.55)\\
&= \frac{\left(\frac{\nu}{\nu-2}\right)\alpha_n \rho_{nm} \alpha_m}{\sqrt{\frac{\nu}{\nu-2}}\sqrt{\frac{\nu}{\nu-2}}},\\
&= \frac{\cancel{\left(\frac{\nu}{\nu-2}\right)}\alpha_n \rho_{nm} \alpha_m}{\cancel{\frac{\nu}{\nu-2}}},\\
&= \alpha_n \rho_{nm} \alpha_m,
\end{aligned}
$$

which happily corresponds exactly with the Gaussian model analogue derived in Eq. 2.22. We may continue to interpret the correlation between two arbitrary latent creditworthiness variables—often referred to as asset correlation—as the product of their respective systemic weight parameters and systemic correlation coefficient. This latter quantity is also sometimes called the factor correlation.

There are a few other small practical differences in the implementation. The default indicator of the $i$th obligor, $\mathcal{D}_i$, has the same conceptual definition as in the Gaussian case, but the default threshold is somewhat different. Specifically, following the logic from Eq. 2.40, we have

$$
\begin{aligned}
p_i &= \mathbb{E}(\mathbb{I}_{\mathcal{D}_i}), \qquad (2.56)\\
&= \mathbb{P}(\mathcal{D}_i),\\
&= \mathbb{P}(\Delta X_n \leq K_i),\\
&= F_{\mathcal{T}_\nu}(K_i),
\end{aligned}
$$

implying directly that $K_i = F_{\mathcal{T}_\nu}^{-1}(p_n)$. We will use, for lack of better notation, $F_{\mathcal{T}_\nu}$ and $F_{\mathcal{T}_\nu}^{-1}$ to denote the cumulative and *inverse* cumulative distribution functions of the standard $t$-distribution with $\nu$ degrees of freedom, respectively. This threshold adjustment is necessary and makes logical sense given that we've actually changed the underlying marginal and joint distributions.

[56] Because of the normalization, $\rho_{nm}$ is conveniently both the correlation coefficient and covariance.

### 2.5.3 Default Correlation

Default correlation is a critically important quantity; inducing some degree of correlation between the default of individual credit obligors has been the motivating factor in the construction of the threshold model. To this point, we have seen both systemic factor and asset correlation, but have not examined the precise form of default correlation. We can no longer postpone consideration of this point. Proper treatment begins with the covariance between the $n$th and $m$th default events. From first principles, we have

$$\begin{aligned} \text{cov}\left(\mathbb{I}_{\mathcal{D}_n}, \mathbb{I}_{\mathcal{D}_m}\right) &= \mathbb{E}\left(\mathbb{I}_{\mathcal{D}_n}\mathbb{I}_{\mathcal{D}_m}\right) - \mathbb{E}\left(\mathbb{I}_{\mathcal{D}_n}\right)\mathbb{E}\left(\mathbb{I}_{\mathcal{D}_m}\right), \\ &= \mathbb{P}\left(\mathcal{D}_n \cap \mathcal{D}_m\right) - \mathbb{P}\left(\mathcal{D}_n\right)\mathbb{P}\left(\mathcal{D}_m\right). \end{aligned} \tag{2.57}$$

Normalizing the covariance to arrive at the default correlation,

$$\begin{aligned} \rho\left(\mathbb{I}_{\mathcal{D}_n}, \mathbb{I}_{\mathcal{D}_m}\right) &= \frac{\text{cov}\left(\mathbb{I}_{\mathcal{D}_n}, \mathbb{I}_{\mathcal{D}_m}\right)}{\sqrt{\text{var}(\mathbb{I}_{\mathcal{D}_n})}\sqrt{\text{var}(\mathbb{I}_{\mathcal{D}_m})}}, \\ &= \frac{\mathbb{P}\left(\mathcal{D}_n \cap \mathcal{D}_m\right) - \mathbb{P}\left(\mathcal{D}_n\right)\mathbb{P}\left(\mathcal{D}_m\right)}{\sqrt{\mathbb{P}(\mathcal{D}_n)(1-\mathbb{P}(\mathcal{D}_n))}\sqrt{\mathbb{P}(\mathcal{D}_m)(1-\mathbb{P}(\mathcal{D}_m))}}. \end{aligned} \tag{2.58}$$

Recalling that the variance of an indicator variable coincides with a Bernoulli trial permits a return to our simpler notation. We thus have

$$\rho\left(\mathbb{I}_{\mathcal{D}_n}, \mathbb{I}_{\mathcal{D}_m}\right) = \frac{\mathbb{P}\left(\mathcal{D}_n \cap \mathcal{D}_m\right) - p_n p_m}{\sqrt{p_n p_m (1-p_n)(1-p_m)}}. \tag{2.59}$$

Default correlation thus depends on the unconditional default probabilities as well as the joint probability of default between counterparties $n$ and $m$. This definition is model independent. The choice of model, however, will determine the form of the joint default probability, $\mathbb{P}\left(\mathcal{D}_n \cap \mathcal{D}_m\right)$.

In the Gaussian threshold model, it should be no surprise that the joint distribution of $\Delta X_n$ and $\Delta X_m$ is also Gaussian. In this case, $\mathbb{P}\left(\mathcal{D}_n \cap \mathcal{D}_m\right)$ is described by the bivariate normal distribution. It has the following mathematical form,

$$\begin{aligned} \mathbb{P}\left(\mathcal{D}_n \cap \mathcal{D}_m\right) &= \mathbb{P}\bigg(\Delta X_n \leq \Phi^{-1}(p_n), \Delta X_m \leq \Phi^{-1}(p_m)\bigg), \\ &= \frac{1}{2\pi\sqrt{1-(\alpha_n \rho_{nm} \alpha_m)^2}} \int_{-\infty}^{\Phi^{-1}(p_n)} \\ &\quad \times \int_{-\infty}^{\Phi^{-1}(p_m)} e^{-\frac{\left(u^2 - 2\alpha_n \rho_{nm} \alpha_m uv + v^2\right)}{2(1-(\alpha_n \rho_{nm} \alpha_m)^2)}} du dv, \\ &= \Phi\left(\Phi^{-1}(p_n), \Phi^{-1}(p_m); \alpha_n \rho_{nm} \alpha_m\right). \end{aligned} \tag{2.60}$$

This expression easily permits us—with the help of a good numerical integration library—to directly compute the default correlation between counterparties $n$ and $m$ using Eq. 2.59.

It is helpful to put Eq. 2.60 into matrix form. Define the correlation matrix as,

$$\Omega_{nm} = \begin{bmatrix} 1 & \mathbf{r}_{nm} \\ \mathbf{r}_{nm} & 1 \end{bmatrix}, \tag{2.61}$$

where the asset-correlation coefficient is denoted as $\mathbf{r}_{nm} = \alpha_n \rho_{nm} \alpha_m$ to slightly ease the notational burden. The determinant of $\Omega_{nm}$ is given as,

$$\det(\Omega_{nm}) = |\Omega_{nm}| = 1 - \mathbf{r}_{nm}^2, \tag{2.62}$$

and the inverse is simply,

$$\begin{aligned} \Omega_{nm}^{-1} &= \frac{1}{|\Omega_{nm}|} \begin{bmatrix} 1 & -\mathbf{r}_{nm} \\ -\mathbf{r}_{nm} & 1 \end{bmatrix}, \\ &= \begin{bmatrix} \frac{1}{1-\mathbf{r}_{nm}^2} & \frac{-\mathbf{r}_{nm}}{1-\mathbf{r}_{nm}^2} \\ \frac{-\mathbf{r}_{nm}}{1-\mathbf{r}_{nm}^2} & \frac{1}{1-\mathbf{r}_{nm}^2} \end{bmatrix}. \end{aligned} \tag{2.63}$$

Defining $x = \begin{bmatrix} u & v \end{bmatrix}^T$, then

$$\begin{aligned} x^T \Omega_{nm}^{-1} x &= \begin{bmatrix} u & v \end{bmatrix} \begin{bmatrix} \frac{1}{1-\mathbf{r}_{nm}^2} & \frac{-\mathbf{r}_{nm}}{1-\mathbf{r}_{nm}^2} \\ \frac{-\mathbf{r}_{nm}}{1-\mathbf{r}_{nm}^2} & \frac{1}{1-\mathbf{r}_{nm}^2} \end{bmatrix} \begin{bmatrix} u \\ v \end{bmatrix}, \\ &= \frac{u^2 - 2\mathbf{r}_{nm} uv + v^2}{1 - \mathbf{r}_{nm}^2}. \end{aligned} \tag{2.64}$$

Our bivariate Gaussian joint-default probability, from Eq. 2.60, can be more succinctly rewritten as,

$$\begin{aligned} \Phi\left(\Phi^{-1}(p_n), \Phi^{-1}(p_m); \mathbf{r}_{nm}\right) &= \frac{1}{2\pi\sqrt{1-\mathbf{r}_{nm}^2}} \int_{-\infty}^{\Phi^{-1}(p_n)} \\ &\quad \times \int_{-\infty}^{\Phi^{-1}(p_m)} e^{-\frac{\left(u^2 - 2\mathbf{r}_{nm} uv + v^2\right)}{2(1-\mathbf{r}_{nm}^2)}} du dv, \\ &= \frac{1}{2\pi\sqrt{|\Omega_{nm}|}} \int_{-\infty}^{\Phi^{-1}(p_n)} \int_{-\infty}^{\Phi^{-1}(p_m)} e^{-\frac{x^T \Omega_{nm}^{-1} x}{2}} dx. \end{aligned} \tag{2.65}$$

This is referred to as the Gaussian copula. Copula functions essentially describe dependence between random variables. The job of a copula function is to map a collection of marginals into a joint distribution. This notion—which was originally introduced by Sklar [38]—is the definitive way to describe dependence between random variables.

It is naturally possible to generalize the joint dependence across all of our credit counterparties. Equation 2.65, with $I$ counterparties, where $R$ is the asset correlation matrix between the $I$ counterparties, is then

$$\begin{aligned}\Phi\left(\Phi^{-1}(p_1),\cdots,\Phi^{-1}(p_I);R\right) = & \frac{1}{(2\pi)^{\frac{I}{2}}\sqrt{|R|}}\int_{-\infty}^{\Phi^{-1}(p_1)}\cdots \\ & \times\int_{-\infty}^{\Phi^{-1}(p_I)} e^{-\frac{x^TR^{-1}x}{2}}dx, \end{aligned} \tag{2.66}$$

where,

$$R = \begin{bmatrix} 1 & \mathbf{r}_{12} & \cdots & \mathbf{r}_{1(I-1)} & \mathbf{r}_{1I} \\ \mathbf{r}_{21} & 1 & \cdots & \mathbf{r}_{2(I-1)} & \mathbf{r}_{2I} \\ \vdots & \vdots & \ddots & \vdots & \vdots \\ \mathbf{r}_{I1} & \mathbf{r}_{I2} & \cdots & \mathbf{r}_{I(I-1)} & 1 \end{bmatrix} \tag{2.67}$$

summarizes the asset-correlation coefficients for every pair of credit obligors in one's portfolio. Equation 2.66 is a function, defined on the unit cube $[0,1]^I$, transforming a set of marginal distributions into a single joint distribution.

Equation 2.59, as previously mentioned, applies to any choice of threshold model. In the $t$-threshold setting, however, the joint distribution of $\Delta X_n$ and $\Delta X_m$ is now assumed to follow a bivariate $t$-distribution with $\nu$ degrees of freedom. Mathematically, such an object is written as

$$\begin{aligned}\mathbb{P}\left(\mathcal{D}_n\cap\mathcal{D}_m\right) &= \mathbb{P}(y_n\leq F_{\mathcal{T}_\nu}^{-1}(p_n), y_m\leq F_{\mathcal{T}_\nu}^{-1}(p_m)), \\ &= \frac{\Gamma\left(\frac{\nu+d}{2}\right)}{\Gamma\left(\frac{\nu}{2}\right)(\nu\pi)^{\frac{d}{2}}|\Omega_{nm}|^{\frac{1}{2}}}\int_{-\infty}^{F_{\mathcal{T}_\nu}^{-1}(p_n)} \\ &\quad\times\int_{-\infty}^{F_{\mathcal{T}_\nu}^{-1}(p_m)}\left(1+\frac{x^T\Omega_{nm}^{-1}x}{\nu}\right)^{-\left(\frac{\nu+d}{2}\right)}dx, \end{aligned} \tag{2.68}$$

where $\Gamma(\cdot)$ represents the gamma function,

$$\Gamma(u) = \int_0^\infty x^{u-1}e^{-x}du. \tag{2.69}$$

and $\Omega_{nm}$ is unchanged from the definition in Eq. 2.61, $x \in \mathbb{R}^2$ and $d = 2$. This is the classic, direct form.[57]

An alternative description of the joint default probability, which we provide for completeness and future usage, makes use of the conditional default probability in the $t$-threshold setting. That is,

$$\begin{aligned}
p_i(\Delta z, W) &= \mathbb{E}\left(\mathbb{I}_{\mathcal{D}_i} \,\middle|\, \Delta z, W\right), \qquad (2.70)\\
&= \mathbb{P}\left(\mathcal{D}_i \,|\, \Delta z, W\right),\\
&= \mathbb{P}\left(\Delta X_i \leq F_{\mathcal{T}_\nu}^{-1}(p_i) \,\middle|\, \Delta z, W\right),\\
&= \mathbb{P}\left(\underbrace{\sqrt{\frac{\nu}{W}}\left(\alpha_i \mathrm{B}_i \Delta z + \sqrt{1-\alpha_i^2}\Delta w_i\right)}_{\text{Eq. 2.50}} \leq F_{\mathcal{T}_\nu}^{-1}(p_n) \,\middle|\, \Delta z, W\right),\\
&= \mathbb{P}\left(\Delta w_i \leq \frac{\sqrt{\frac{W}{\nu}} F_{\mathcal{T}_\nu}^{-1}(p_i) - \alpha_i \mathrm{B}_i \Delta z}{\sqrt{1-\alpha_i^2}} \,\middle|\, \Delta z, W\right),\\
&= \Phi\left(\frac{\sqrt{\frac{W}{\nu}} F_{\mathcal{T}_\nu}^{-1}(p_i) - \alpha_i \mathrm{B}_i \Delta z}{\sqrt{1-\alpha_i^2}}\right).
\end{aligned}$$

To determine the conditional probability of $y_n$, both the global systematic factor, $\Delta z$, and the mixing random variate, $W$, must be revealed. Our desired joint-default probability, for arbitrarily selected counterparties $n$ and $m$, is thus determined as,

$$\begin{aligned}
\mathbb{P}\left(\mathcal{D}_n \cap \mathcal{D}_m\right) &= \mathbb{E}\left(\mathbb{I}_{\mathcal{D}_n} \cap \mathbb{I}_{\mathcal{D}_m}\right), \qquad (2.71)\\
&= \underbrace{\mathbb{E}\left(\mathbb{E}\left(\mathbb{I}_{\mathcal{D}_n} \cap \mathbb{I}_{\mathcal{D}_m}\right) \,\middle|\, \Delta z, W\right)}_{\text{By iterated expectations}},\\
&= \mathbb{E}\left(\underbrace{\mathbb{E}\left(\mathbb{I}_{\mathcal{D}_n} \,\middle|\, \Delta z, W\right) \cdot \mathbb{E}\left(\mathbb{I}_{\mathcal{D}_m} \,\middle|\, \Delta z, W\right)}_{\text{By conditional independence}}\right),\\
&= \mathbb{E}\left(p_n(\Delta z, W) \cdot p_m(\Delta z, W)\right),
\end{aligned}$$

[57] One can loosely think of the gamma function as a continuous-valued extension of the integer-valued factorial function. See Abramovitz and Stegun [1, Chapter 6] for more information on this mathematical object.

$$= \int_{-\infty}^{\infty} \cdots \int_{-\infty}^{\infty} \int_{0}^{\infty} p_n(z, w) \cdot p_m(z, w) \cdot f_W(w)$$
$$\cdot \phi_{\Delta z}(z_1, \cdots, z_J) dw dz_1 \cdots dz_J.$$

This approach exploits the conditional independence of the latent state variables to find an alternative, but equivalent, representation of the joint default probability. Since resolution of this expression requires numerical integration, the catching point is the dimensionality of $\Delta z \in \mathbb{R}^J$. If $J = 1$, then Eq. 2.71 reduces to a very manageable two-dimensional integral. If not, then it may very well be computationally impractical to use this trick; in this case, Eq. 2.68 is the appropriate choice for evaluating the joint default probability and, by extension, the pairwise default correlation.

As a final point, the joint-default density under the $t$-threshold model has the following form

$$F_{\mathcal{T}_\nu}\left(F_{\mathcal{T}_\nu}^{-1}(p_1), \cdots, F_{\mathcal{T}_\nu}^{-1}(p_I); R\right) = \frac{\Gamma\left(\frac{\nu+d}{2}\right)}{\Gamma\left(\frac{\nu}{2}\right)(\nu\pi)^{\frac{d}{2}}|R|^{\frac{1}{2}}} \int_{-\infty}^{F_{\mathcal{T}_\nu}^{-1}(p_1)} \cdots \int_{-\infty}^{F_{\mathcal{T}_\nu}^{-1}(p_I)} \times \left(1 + \frac{x^T R^{-1} x}{\nu}\right)^{-\left(\frac{\nu+d}{2}\right)} dx, \tag{2.72}$$

where $R$ remains as in the definition in Eq. 2.67. This copula function, defined on the unit cube $[0, 1]^I$, is the $t$-distributed analogue of the Gaussian equivalent in Eq. 2.66. The mathematical structure does not provide an enormous amount of insight, but the key difference is that the $t$-copula has non-zero tail dependence, whereas the Gaussian copula does not. Ultimately, this makes a rather important distinction in the specification of credit-default risk.

**Colour and Commentary 21** *($t$-THRESHOLD MODEL): The great financial crisis, beginning in 2007–2008, exposed some important statistical flaws in the Gaussian threshold model. Most importantly, it has a structural lack of* tail dependence. *In a modelling framework where attention is consistently focused on the extremes of the credit-loss distribution, zero tail dependence moves from a theoretical peculiarity to a serious problem. A practical solution is required to address this serious shortcoming. It turns out that relatively few members of the elliptical family of distributions—those distributions typically best suited for the threshold framework—actually have non-zero tail dependence. The $t$ distribution—induced in this case through a $\chi^2$ mixing variable in the normal-variance mixture setting—fortunately represents one*

(continued)

**Colour and Commentary 21** (continued)
*tractable candidate exhibiting non-zero tail dependence. For this reason, along with the fact that the necessary model adjustments are relatively modest, we have opted to employ this version of the threshold model. The driving rationale behind this choice is a desire to simultaneously enhance the realism and conservatism of our credit-risk economic-capital estimates.*

### 2.5.4 Modelling Credit Migration

If one assumes that credit losses are experienced only in the event of default, then the previous framework would be sufficient to describe our methodological approach. There is nevertheless, as hinted at previously, another dimension to credit risk. Financial losses are also logically possible in the event that a credit counterparty is downgraded. Credit deterioration implies that one needs to reassess the relative likelihood of repayment and, in general, correspondingly write down the value of one's assets. This occurs even when the attendant obligor continues to properly service its credit obligation. Improvement in a credit obligor's credit status will, of course, have a positive valuation impact. The possibility of one's obligors to move up or down the credit spectrum is referred to, in general, as credit migration. Default is, in fact, simply a special case of this general behaviour—it considers only the transition from the current credit state to the default state.

Dealing with this generalization does not dramatically change the model structure, but it does require some additional overhead. Given $q$ discrete credit-quality states, or rating categories, we assume that each obligor's credit status follows a discrete-time Markov chain. This basically means that the only information required to determine an obligor's credit status in the next period is its current credit status. This so-called Markov property practically implies that, for a given obligor $i$, currently in state $m$ at time $t$, the probability it finds itself in state $n$ at time $t+1$ is written as,

$$\begin{aligned} p_{mn} &= \mathbb{P}\left(\text{Going } \textbf{to } n \middle| \text{ Coming } \textbf{from } m\right), \\ &= \mathbb{P}\left(S_{i,t+1} = n \middle| S_{i,t} = m\right), \end{aligned} \tag{2.73}$$

for $n, m = 1, \ldots, q$. $S_{i,t}$ denotes the credit state of the $i$th obligor at time $t$. This generic form describes all obligors, time points, and constellations of starting and ending points. The driving idea is that a Markov chain characterizes the *transitions* between various states over time. These are also referred to as transition probabilities, of which default probabilities are a special case (i.e., transition directly into the default state).

The collection of so-called *transition* probabilities, associated with a given Markov chain, are collected into the transition matrix, $P$. For our $q$-state process, it is summarized as

$$P = \begin{bmatrix} p_{11} & p_{21} & \cdots & p_{q1} \\ p_{12} & p_{22} & \cdots & p_{q2} \\ \vdots & \vdots & \ddots & \vdots \\ p_{1q} & p_{2q} & \cdots & p_{qq} \end{bmatrix}. \tag{2.74}$$

This notation can, given it is essentially the opposite of what is used in matrix algebra to refer to specific elements, be somewhat confusing. It does, however, have its own useful internal logic. Each row relates to the state of an obligor as of time $t$. If counterparty $i$ is classified in the second credit state at time $t$, then only the *second* row is relevant to determining the relative probabilities of transition into the set of $q$ credit states at time $t + 1$. When examining only the default perspective, we ignore all the other elements in this second row and consider only the $p_{q2} = \mathbb{P}\left(S_{i,t+1} = q \,\middle|\, S_{i,t} = 2\right)$. This is, to be very explicit, the probability that a credit-counterpart currently in state 2 will transition into default (i.e., state $q$) in the next period. Naturally, if we sum across all the transition probabilities for the next period, the row must sum to unity. That is,

$$\sum_{n=1}^{q} p_{nm} = 1, \tag{2.75}$$

for $m = 1, \ldots, q$.[58] The point is that the rows of the transition matrix, $P$, must sum to one.[59] Figure 2.3 illustrates—in a schematic manner, again starting from $S_{i,t} = 2$—how the transition probabilities describe the movement from the current credit state to the range of possible state values in the next period. If we wish to capture the full range of possible movements to other credit states, then it will be necessary to make intelligent use of the entire transition matrix.

The transition matrix will inform—as did the default probabilities in the default-only setting—the specific thresholds. Before we examine precisely how, it is preferable to first build the general framework. Clearly, by construction, we have $S_{i,t} \in \{1, \ldots, q\}$ for each $i = 1, \ldots, I$. This portfolio-level credit-obligor knowledge, along with $P$, is all that is required to simulate the portfolio counterparties' credit states in the next period.[60] The actual computation, however, is somewhat more complicated.

[58] In our simple example, $m = 2$.

[59] There are many excellent references on the theory and practice of Markov chains; a few recommended choices include Brémaud [9], Hamilton [20], and Meyn and Tweedie [31].

[60] More information, as we'll see in upcoming discussion, is required to determine the credit losses (or gains) associated with these transitions.

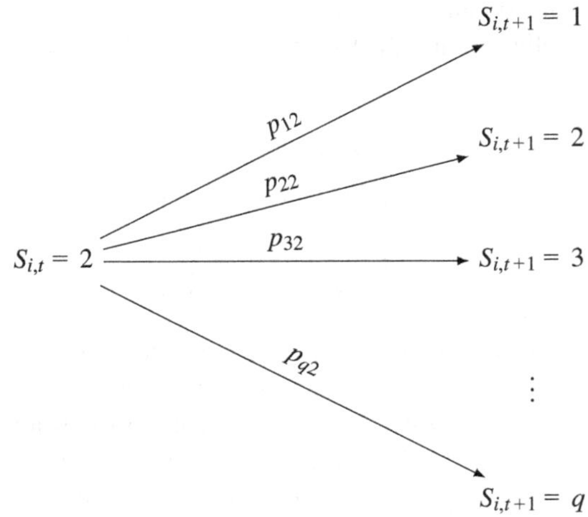


**Fig. 2.3** *Transition probabilities*: This schematic illustrates, given the current state of the $i$th obligor is 2, the range of transition probabilities into the other $q$ states. This is, quite simply, the second row of the transition matrix, $P$.

In Eq. 2.40, we calibrated the $i$th default threshold as using an indicator variable. We can generalize this approach somewhat. We need a more flexible definition of the default threshold. Let us, therefore, define $K_{S_{i,t}}(j)$ as the threshold of an obligor in state $i$ as of time $t$, for moving to state $j$ as of time $t+1$. In the default setting, we only consider the situation of $j = q$; that is, movement from state $i$ to default. The introduction of the transition matrix, however, shows us that transition is possible to any of the individual credit states $j = 1, \ldots, q$. Using this idea, we may redefine the notion of the *default* threshold as follows,

$$\begin{aligned} \mathbb{E}\left(\mathbb{I}_{\left\{\Delta X_i \in \left[-\infty, K_{S_{i,t}}(q)\right]\right\}}\right) &= p_{q,S_{i,t}}, \\ \mathbb{P}\left(\Delta X_i \in \left[-\infty, K_{S_{i,t}}(q)\right]\right) &= p_{q,S_{i,t}}, \\ \mathbb{P}\bigg(-\infty \leq \Delta X_i \leq K_{S_{i,t}}(q)\bigg) &= p_{q,S_{i,t}}, \end{aligned} \tag{2.76}$$

recalling that $p_{q,S_{i,t}}$ is the probability of default, but also the $(S_{i,t}, q)$ element of the transition represented in Eq. 2.74.[61] This might not seem like much progress, but if we recall that $\Delta X_i$ is a continuous, one-dimensional random variable and, rather

[61] Don't forget that the transition probability notation is the exact opposite of matrix notation; this often leads to confusion (and occasionally mistakes).

vacuously, $-\infty < K_{S_{i,t}}(q)$, then

$$
\begin{aligned}
\mathbb{P}\left(\Delta X_i \leq K_{S_{i,t}}(q)\right) - \mathbb{P}\left(\Delta X_i \leq -\infty\right) &= p_{q,S_{i,t}}, \\
F_{\Delta X_i}\left(K_{S_{i,t}}(q)\right) - \underbrace{F_{\Delta X_i}(-\infty)}_{=0} &= p_{q,S_{i,t}}, \\
\Phi\left(K_{S_{i,t}}(q)\right) &= p_{q,S_{i,t}}, \\
K_{S_{i,t}}(q) &= \Phi^{-1}(p_{q,S_{i,t}}).
\end{aligned}
\tag{2.77}
$$

While we have not learned anything new relative to the development in Eq. 2.40, we have transformed a threshold into an interval. We also generalized the notation. In particular, we write the default probability using its true identity: a transition probability. That is, $p_i$ is replaced with $p_{q,S_{i,t}}$. The threshold is also not simply linked to the $i$th obligor, but also includes information on their current credit state, $S_{i,t}$, and the targeted credit-state threshold.

The development summarized in Eq. 2.77, as the reader has certainly noticed, applies to the Gaussian threshold model. The same basic logic applies in the $t$-threshold setting, but the distributions differ. In this case, the generalized default threshold simply becomes,

$$
K_{S_{i,t}}(q) = F_{\mathcal{T}_\nu}^{-1}(p_{q,S_{i,t}}). \tag{2.78}
$$

These generalizations permit us to consider credit-migration for non-default states. Returning to the Gaussian case, a specific example will be helpful. Again, conditioning on the $i$th credit counterpart currently finding itself in state $S_{i,t}$, we would like to link the (possible) migration to state 3 with the probability of transitioning from state $S_{i,t}$ to 3. This transition probability is simply denoted as $p_{3,S_{i,t}}$. The starting point is inspired by Eq. 2.76,

$$
\begin{aligned}
\mathbb{E}\left(\mathbb{I}_{\left\{\Delta X_i \in \left[K_{S_{i,t}}(4), K_{S_{i,t}}(3)\right]\right\}}\right) &= p_{3,S_{i,t}}, \\
\mathbb{P}\left(K_{S_{i,t}}(4) \leq \Delta X_i \leq K_{S_{i,t}}(3)\right) &= p_{3,S_{i,t}}, \\
\mathbb{P}\left(\Delta X_i \leq K_{S_{i,t}}(3)\right) - \mathbb{P}\left(\Delta X_i \leq K_{S_{i,t}}(4)\right) &= p_{3,S_{i,t}}, \\
\Phi\left(K_{S_{i,t}}(3)\right) - \Phi\left(K_{S_{i,t}}(4)\right) &= p_{3,S_{i,t}},
\end{aligned}
\tag{2.79}
$$

since, by construction, $K_{S_{i,t}}(4) < K_{S_{i,t}}(3)$. There does not, however, appear to be any obvious approach to isolate the $K$ terms; this is a situation of a single equation in two unknowns. The solution involves rewriting the right-hand side transition probability, $p_{3,S_{i,t}}$, in an alternative, perhaps initially non-intuitive form.

In particular, we redefine it as,

$$p_{3,S_{i,t}} = \sum_{w=3}^{q} p_{w,S_{i,t}} - \sum_{w=4}^{q} p_{w,S_{i,t}}. \tag{2.80}$$

These are simply the differences in the sum of elements across a given row of the transition matrix, $P$, with different index starting points. If we plug our definition from Eq. 2.80 into Eq. 2.79, we have that

$$\Phi\left(K_{S_{i,t}}(3)\right) - \Phi\left(K_{S_{i,t}}(4)\right) = \underbrace{\sum_{w=3}^{q} p_{w,S_{i,t}} - \sum_{w=4}^{q} p_{w,S_{i,t}}}_{\text{Eq. 2.80}}. \tag{2.81}$$

If we equate the two corresponding terms on the right- and left-hand sides of Eq. 2.81, then we can identify our thresholds as,

$$K_{S_{i,t}}(3) = \Phi^{-1}\left(\sum_{w=3}^{q} p_{w,S_{i,t}}\right), \tag{2.82}$$

and

$$K_{S_{i,t}}(4) = \Phi^{-1}\left(\sum_{w=4}^{q} p_{w,S_{i,t}}\right). \tag{2.83}$$

More generally, of course, we can conclude that the $j$th boundary for the $i$th credit obligor is,

$$K_{S_{i,t}}(j) = \Phi^{-1}\left(\sum_{w=j}^{q} p_{w,S_{i,t}}\right). \tag{2.84}$$

In this manner, the set of finite, real-valued thresholds

$$-\infty < K_{S_{i,t}}(q) < K_{S_{i,t}}(q-1) < \cdots < K_{S_{i,t}}(2) < K_{S_{i,t}}(1) \equiv \infty. \tag{2.85}$$

A bit of reflection reveals that we have created $I$ partitions of the support of a standard normally distributed state variable—each conditioned on the current credit state of the $i$th counterparty, $S_{i,t}$—informed by the appropriate transition probabilities. Although we have $I$ individual partitions, there are only $q$ unique cases, each linked to a separate row in the transition matrix, $P$. This represents a large, and messy, number of partitions of the real-number line, $\mathbb{R}$. We can simplify our life somewhat by cumulating, or summing, the transition-matrix entries across each row from right to left. This operation significantly eases working with quantities like those found on the right-hand side of Eq. 2.80 and leads to the so-called cumulative transition matrix, G, which we define as

$$G = \begin{bmatrix} (p_{11} + p_{21} + \cdots + p_{q1}) & (p_{21} + \cdots + p_{q1}) & \cdots & p_{q1} \\ (p_{12} + p_{22} + \cdots + p_{q2}) & (p_{22} + \cdots + p_{q2}) & \cdots & p_{q2} \\ \vdots & \vdots & \ddots & \vdots \\ (p_{1q} + p_{2q} + \cdots + p_{qq}) & (p_{2q} + \cdots + p_{qq}) & \cdots & p_{qq} \end{bmatrix}, \tag{2.86}$$

$$= \begin{bmatrix} \sum_{w=1}^{q} p_{w1} & \sum_{w=2}^{q} p_{w1} & \cdots & \sum_{w=q}^{q} p_{w1} \\ \sum_{w=1}^{q} p_{w2} & \sum_{w=2}^{q} p_{w2} & \cdots & \sum_{w=q}^{q} p_{w2} \\ \vdots & \vdots & \ddots & \vdots \\ \sum_{w=1}^{q} p_{wq} & \sum_{w=2}^{q} p_{wq} & \cdots & \sum_{w=q}^{q} p_{wq} \end{bmatrix},$$

Each one of the values in this cumulative transition matrix, $G$, lies in the interval, $[0, 1]$—they are, in the end, probabilities. As we saw from the previous development, the cumulative transition matrix is an intermediate step. The next step in determining the appropriate partition requires transforming these probability quantities into the domain of $\Delta X_i$. The entries in $G$ are thus mapped back into the values of the standard normal distribution using the inverse standard normal cumulative distribution function following the basic logic found in Eqs. 2.76 to 2.80. This leads to,

$$G_{\Phi^{-1}} = \begin{bmatrix} \Phi^{-1}\left(\sum_{w=1}^{q} p_{w1}\right) & \Phi^{-1}\left(\sum_{w=2}^{q} p_{w1}\right) & \cdots & \Phi^{-1}\left(\sum_{w=q}^{q} p_{w1}\right) \\ \Phi^{-1}\left(\sum_{w=1}^{q} p_{w2}\right) & \Phi^{-1}\left(\sum_{w=2}^{q} p_{w2}\right) & \cdots & \Phi^{-1}\left(\sum_{w=q}^{q} p_{w2}\right) \\ \vdots & \vdots & \ddots & \vdots \\ \Phi^{-1}\left(\sum_{w=1}^{q} p_{wq}\right) & \Phi^{-1}\left(\sum_{w=2}^{q} p_{wq}\right) & \cdots & \Phi^{-1}\left(\sum_{w=q}^{q} p_{wq}\right) \end{bmatrix}, \tag{2.87}$$

$$= \begin{bmatrix} \Phi^{-1}(g_{11}) & \Phi^{-1}(g_{21}) & \cdots & \Phi^{-1}(g_{q1}) \\ \Phi^{-1}(g_{12}) & \Phi^{-1}(g_{22}) & \cdots & \Phi^{-1}(g_{q2}) \\ \vdots & \vdots & \ddots & \vdots \\ \Phi^{-1}(g_{1q}) & \Phi^{-1}(q_{2q}) & \cdots & \Phi^{-1}(g_{qq}) \end{bmatrix},$$

$$
= \begin{bmatrix} K_1(1) & K_1(2) & \cdots & K_1(q) \\ K_2(1) & K_2(2) & \cdots & K_2(q) \\ \vdots & \vdots & \ddots & \vdots \\ K_q(1) & K_q(2) & \cdots & K_q(q) \end{bmatrix}.
$$

The individual entries of the matrix, $G_{\Phi^{-1}}$, thus represent the collection of boundaries, or thresholds, for the determination of credit migration as described in Eq. 2.85. Each row, which captures the current state of the $i$th counterpart, describes the partition of the $\Delta X_i$ space.

The previous development applies to the Gaussian threshold implementation. Virtually identical logic, in the $t$-threshold approach, brings us to,

$$
G_{\mathcal{T}_\nu^{-1}} = \begin{bmatrix} F_{\mathcal{T}_\nu}^{-1}(g_{11}) & F_{\mathcal{T}_\nu}^{-1}(g_{21}) & \cdots & F_{\mathcal{T}_\nu}^{-1}(g_{q1}) \\ F_{\mathcal{T}_\nu}^{-1}(g_{12}) & F_{\mathcal{T}_\nu}^{-1}(g_{22}) & \cdots & F_{\mathcal{T}_\nu}^{-1}(g_{q2}) \\ \vdots & \vdots & \ddots & \vdots \\ F_{\mathcal{T}_\nu}^{-1}(g_{1q}) & F_{\mathcal{T}_\nu}^{-1}(q_{2q}) & \cdots & F_{\mathcal{T}_\nu}^{-1}(g_{qq}) \end{bmatrix}. \tag{2.88}
$$

The only difference associated with a change in copula function is the choice of inverse cumulative distribution function to employ. It needs to be consistent with the underlying latent creditworthiness variable definition.

Irrespective of one's choice of copula function, a modicum of computational caution is required. Since the sum of each row of the transition matrix is unity, each element in the first column of $G$ takes the value of one. That the support of the normal distribution is $(-\infty, \infty)$ implies, however, that one would assign a value of $\infty$ to the elements in the first column of $G$. This will, of course, inevitably lead to numerical problems. Instead, we assign a value of 10, because the probability of observing an outcome from a standard normal or $t$ distribution behind these values is vanishingly small.[62]

Figure 2.4 provides a visualization of how, for a counterparty currently in credit state $S_{i,t}$, the partition of the $\Delta X_i$ space is constructed. We observe the relation to the cumulative transition probabilities and how, stylistically at least, the individual thresholds are placed. The random draw of $\Delta X_i$ determines, for the $i$th counterparty, the location in the interval, $(-\infty, \infty)$. The specific sub-interval that this random draw enters thus determines the $i$th credit obligor's $t + 1$ credit state. This is a very clever idea. It allows us to map a real-valued variable that might take an uncountable range of values—the creditworthiness index—into a small, finite set of $q$ credit categories.

Figure 2.4 also illustrates how the default outcome, $\Delta X_i \leq K_{S_{i,t}}(q)$, is simply a special case of this more general framework. The size of each individual interval—which is hard to illustrate in a schematic diagram like Fig. 2.4—is directly

[62] Any sufficiently large positive number will, of course, work.

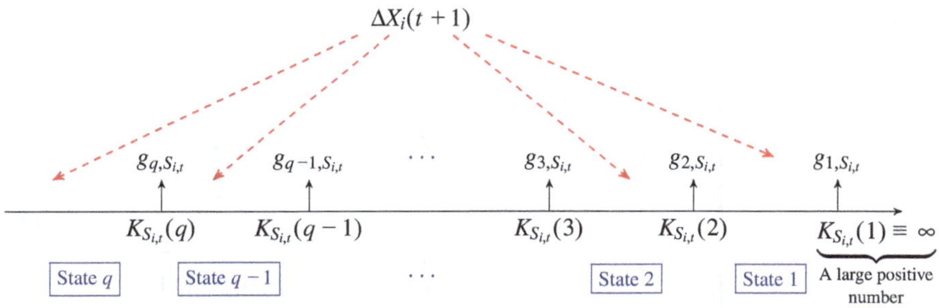


**Fig. 2.4** *Partitioning the $\Delta X_i$ space*: This figure visually illustrates, for a counterparty currently in credit state $S_{i,t}$, the partition of the $\Delta X_i(t+1)$ space, its relation to the cumulative transition probabilities, and how the individual thresholds are placed. All the necessary information stems directly, or indirectly, from the transition matrix, $P$.

proportional to the associated probability of transition. Improbable outcomes are assigned sliver thin intervals, while very likely outcomes have significant distance between the two end-points. The idea is to ensure that the final transition outcomes are numerically consistent with a random draw from the distribution of each $\Delta X_i$ and that simulated credit-state mappings are driven by the values in our transition matrix, $P$.

**Colour and Commentary 22** (DEFAULT AS SPECIAL CASE)*: A credit-risk model is, quite naturally, centrally concerned with the idea of default. This is, of course, the principal avenue through which loss is experienced by the firm. It is nonetheless, from an analytic perspective, rather useful to think of default as a special case of credit-migration. The default threshold is particularly important, because it involves negotiating repayment and, in some cases, losing one's entire investment. At the same time, movement from one credit state to another (including default) can be viewed a sequence of economically meaningful intervals. Each sub-interval maps the creditworthiness index into a credit state. Default is easy to understand, since it conceptually involves the firm's assets falling below its liabilities. Credit deterioration (or improvement), however, can be seen to follow a similar pattern. The required level of assets associated with these internals are, by contrast, a bit more difficult to define. Ultimately, they are inferred, as the default case, from transition-probability estimates. This generalization forms the central logic of credit-migration modelling.*

Naturally, we need to construct a mathematical formulation of Fig. 2.4. Given the simulated outcome $\Delta X_i(t+1)$ associated with the $i$th counterparty currently in credit state $S_{i,t}$, we may determine the credit state in the next period, $S_{i,t+1}$ as follows,

$$
S_{i,t+1} = \begin{cases} 1 : \Delta X_i(t+1) \in \left[ K_{S_{i,t}}(2), K_{S_{i,t}}(1) \equiv \infty \right] \\ 2 : \Delta X_i(t+1) \in \left( K_{S_{i,t}}(3), K_{S_{i,t}}(2) \right] \\ \vdots \\ q-1 : \Delta X_i(t+1) \in \left( K_{S_{i,t}}(q), K_{S_{i,t}}(q-1) \right] \\ q : \Delta X_i(t+1) \in \left( -\infty, K_{S_{i,t}}(q) \right] \end{cases}, \tag{2.89}
$$

for $i = 1, \ldots, I$. This intuitive expression can be further simplified—with a significant computational advantage for practical implementation—by exploiting the monotonicity of the threshold definitions introduced in Eq. 2.85 and assured from the structure in Eqs. 2.87 and 2.88. A bit of reflection reveals that the credit state in the next period is determined by the smallest threshold which exceeds, or is equal to, $\Delta X_i(t+1)$. This is defined as,

$$
S_{i,t+1} = \sum_{\ell=1}^{q} \mathbb{I}_{\left\{ \Delta X_i(t+1) \leq K_{S_{i,t}}(\ell) \right\}}. \tag{2.90}
$$

While somewhat less intuitive, Eq. 2.90 permits a more parsimonious representation of the credit-state transition process.[63] Not great from a pedagogical perspective, this form saves a significant amount of computational complexity and expense.

## 2.5.5 *The Nuts and Bolts of Credit Migration*

The previous section provides a detailed, and workable, description of the link between firm creditworthiness and the underlying credit state associated with each individual obligor in one's portfolio. An important question remains: what happens in the event that a credit counterpart changes credit state? We have already seen the implications—in Eqs. 2.41 and 2.42—of a credit default. One loses some portion of the total exposure; the exact amount depends upon one's assumptions regarding recovery. Considering (non-default) migration, of course, an alternative strategy is required. Practically, we would expect that:

[63] Other (probably more clever) computational tricks are possible; one alternative, for example, has a specific structure involving the supremum operator. The important point is to define this condition in an efficient manner consistent with one's definitions.

1. a credit loss (gain) to be recognized in the event of credit deterioration (improvement);
2. the magnitude of the credit loss (or gain) should be consistent with market-valuation effects associated with similarly rated entities;
3. the specific size and interest-rate sensitivity of the obligor's exposures to be incorporated into any credit loss (or gain); and
4. neither gain nor loss is to occur in the event an obligor remains in the same credit state.

A critical aspect of this development is the creation of a link between the value of an obligor's exposures and changes in the market value of these exposures. Given that loan exposures are not (typically) traded in liquid markets, this is something of a challenge. For traded instruments, however, it is rather more straightforward. Any credit-risky security trades at a premium over the lowest-risk borrower—almost always the government—in that currency. The difference between actual bond yields and the government, or Treasury, yield for a similar maturity is referred to as the credit spread.[64] Conceptually, the credit spread is decomposed into two separate components: a general and an idiosyncratic element. The general aspect describes the global risk associated with the entity's credit state or rating. The idiosyncratic element, conversely, is unique to the issue and may incorporate specific risks—and also, more practically, liquidity—associated with its debt claims. For the purposes of credit-migration modelling, a few assumptions are typical. First, only the global or general credit-spread risk is considered.[65] Second, we will assume that spread movements can also be used to model valuation gains and losses for both marketable bonds and non-marketable loans. We further assume—although this is principally for the purposes of simplicity—that the credit spread is constant across the entire maturity spectrum.[66]

A further, perhaps more difficult-to-defend, assumption is the time homogeneity of these credit spreads. Credit spreads clearly vary across time due to investment flows, changes in relative liquidity and variation in aggregate risk preferences. There is also evidence that credit spreads are correlated with the general business cycle. One could clearly attempt to model these dynamics, but the entire credit-risk economic-capital approach seeks to generate long-term, through-the-cycle estimates of the credit-loss distribution. In other words, transition probabilities, correlation parameters, loss-given-default estimates, and assumed credit-spread values are,

[64] It is also possible, of course, to define the spread relative to another reference curve. A popular choice, given its liquidity, is the LIBOR-based swap curve. Given ongoing and forthcoming LIBOR-market reform, the plumbing of the swap market is likely to change, but its central role and usefulness for spread computations likely will not.

[65] There is, as an empirical reality, a significant amount of heterogeneity with a given credit rating. Modelling this aspect is complex, noisy, and unlikely to dramatically influence the results. As such, it makes logical sense to exclude it.

[66] Empirically, we do observe a term structure of credit spreads for each credit rating, which varies across the credit spectrum.

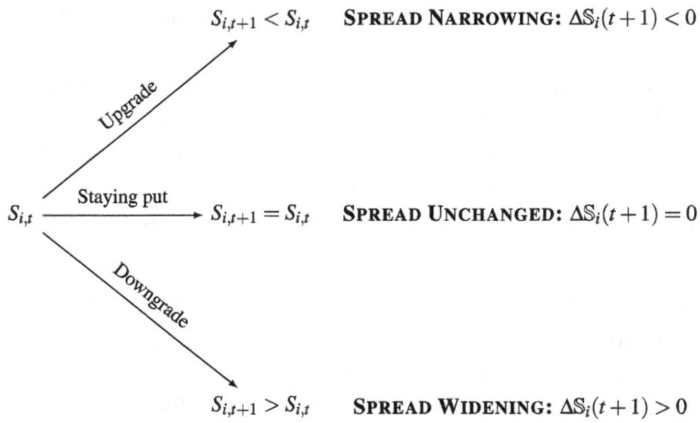


**Fig. 2.5** *Credit-spread cases*: In the credit migration setting, there are three disjoint outcomes: upgrade, downgrade, or staying put. These naturally translate into three associated credit-spread cases: spread narrowing, spread widening, and no change at all. This figure visualizes, in a schematic manner, this situation.

by construction, unconditional.[67] Time homogeneity thus implies that the credit spreads are estimated using long-term, low-frequency data, and are relatively infrequently updated. Much more on this exercise is found in Chap. 3.

To make this more concrete, let us define the credit spread associated with the $i$th credit counterpart in credit state, $S_{i,t}$ as $\mathbb{S}_{S_{i,t}}$ for $i = 1, \ldots, I$. In fact, there are only $q - 1$ actual credit values; we ignore the default state, $q$, because it does logically require a spread and the loss implications are fundamentally different. For any time step, therefore, the spread change for a given counterparty can be written as,

$$\Delta\mathbb{S}_i(t+1) = \mathbb{S}_{S_{i,t+1}} - \mathbb{S}_{S_{i,t}}. \tag{2.91}$$

Recall that $S_{i,t} = 1$ describes the highest level of credit quality, $S_{i,t} = 20$ is the lowest, and $S_{i,t} = 21$ denotes default.[68] If $\mathbb{S}_{S_{i,t+1}} < \mathbb{S}_{S_{i,t}}$ (i.e., $\Delta\mathbb{S}_i(t+1) > 0$) then we have a spread widening associated with credit deterioration (i.e., downgrade); this further implies that $S_{i,t+1} > S_{i,t}$. Conversely, $\mathbb{S}_{S_{i,t+1}} > \mathbb{S}_{S_{i,t}}$ ((i.e., $\Delta\mathbb{S}_i(t+1) < 0$) represents a spread tightening with credit improvement (i.e., upgrade), $S_{i,t+1} < S_{i,t}$. Naturally, $\mathbb{S}_{S_{i,t+1}} = \mathbb{S}_{S_{i,t}}$ (i.e., $\Delta\mathbb{S}_i(t+1) = 0$) can only occur when there is no change in underlying credit state. There are thus three disjoint cases for each credit obligor migration in every possible state of the world: downgrade, upgrade, and staying put. Figure 2.5 provides a visualization of these three credit-migration outcomes and the associated credit-spread implications.

---

[67] A number of regulatory mandated buffers attempt to incorporate the, potentially important, consequences of the business cycle for one's economic-capital estimates. These were discussed, in greater length and detail, in Chap. 1.

[68] Other firms will naturally follow differing scales, but the idea is the same.

The definition in Eq. 2.91 permits a straightforward expression for the migration loss associated with the $i$th credit obligor's migration,

$$-D_{m,i} \cdot \underbrace{\left(\mathbb{S}_{S_{i,t+1}} - \mathbb{S}_{S_{i,t}}\right)}_{\Delta \mathbb{S}_i(t+1)} \cdot c_i, \tag{2.92}$$

where $D_{m,i}$ and $c_i$ denote the modified spread duration and exposure of the $i$th credit obligor, respectively. The modified spread duration measure is generally defined as,

$$D_{m,i} = \frac{1}{V_{i,t}} \frac{\partial V_{i,t}}{\partial S_{i,t}}, \tag{2.93}$$

where $V_{i,t}$ represents the value of the $i$th credit obligation. While relatively easy to find or compute for market-traded instruments, this value is slightly more difficult to source for non-marketable loan contracts. Our approach to this computation will be discussed in the following chapter.[69]

Given the credit state associated with the $i$th counterpart in the start and end of each period—which is provided using the ideas from the previous section—determining the credit-spread movement involves looking up one of $q-1$ values. A simple example may be useful. Imagine that the $i$th counterparty has a € 15 million exposure with an average modified duration of 4.75 years. At time $t$, it was in credit state 2 with a (fictitious) credit spread of 100 basis points. In period $t+1$, obligor $i$th moved to credit state 3, which has a (equally invented) 120 basis-point spread. From Eq. 2.92, the credit loss amounts to

$$\begin{aligned} -D_{m,i} \cdot \left(\mathbb{S}_{S_{i,t+1}} - \mathbb{S}_{S_{i,t}}\right) \cdot c_i &= -4.75 \cdot (1.20\% - 1.00\%) \cdot (€\ 15,000,000), \quad (2.94) \\ &= -0.95\% \cdot (€\ 15,000,000), \\ &= -€\ 142,500. \end{aligned}$$

We thus estimate the credit loss to be approximately € 142,500. Use of the modified duration implies a good first-order approximation of the credit loss and permits a parsimonious, computationally efficient implementation.

The total credit-migration loss is thus,

$$L_{\mathcal{M}} = \sum_{i=1}^{I} D_{m,i} \cdot \Delta \mathbb{S}_i(t+1) \cdot c_i, \tag{2.95}$$

[69] See Bolder [6, Chapter 3] for much more detail on fixed-income instrument sensitivities in general and spread duration in particular.

or, rather, the sum across all credit migrations. We have dispensed with the negative sign in Eq. 2.95 because, as in the default setting, we treat loss as a positive quantity. This is simply convention, but we need to be cautious to treat default and migration losses in a consistent manner. As with the default case, many of the contributions to the sum in Eq. 2.95 will be zero. Transition, however, is typically significantly more probable than default, so relatively speaking, a higher proportion will be non-zero. The overall migration effect—depending, of course, on the overall size of the credit spreads—should involve a smaller magnitude; moreover, there is always the possibility of credit gains to offset loss outcomes. Thus, while the exact size of the migration effect will depend on the portfolio composition, it is generally expected to be somewhat smaller than default losses.[70]

Combining the default and migration losses into a single expression, total credit losses can be defined as,

$$\begin{aligned} L &= L_{\mathcal{D}} + L_{\mathcal{M}}, \qquad (2.96)\\ &= \sum_{i=1}^{I} c_i \left( \underbrace{\gamma_i \mathbb{I}_{\left\{\Delta X_i(t+1) \leq K_{S_{i,t}}(q)\right\}}}_{\text{Default}} - \underbrace{D_{m,i} \Delta \mathbb{S}_i(t+1) \mathbb{I}_{\left\{\Delta X_i(t+1) > K_{S_{i,t}}(q)\right\}}}_{\text{Migration}} \right). \end{aligned}$$

This representation describes default and credit migration as disjoint, or mutually exclusive, events.[71] This is useful, because although default is a special case of migration, the loss implications are substantially different and need to be modelled separately. The incorporation of migration losses to one's credit-risk modelling framework adds a significant amount of richness to the results.

Both default and migration losses—as highlighted in Eq. 2.96—depend on the systemic and idiosyncratic elements embedded in $\Delta X_i$. This computation continues to be performed with stochastic simulation. We conceptualized the default simulation as pulling systemic variables from hats and then flipping very large numbers of unfair coins. The incorporation of credit migration slightly changes the game. Default is a binary event, whereas migration is multifaceted. While the general anatomy of the simulation approach remains the same, it might help to imagine moving from coins to a dice. With both default and migration, we still draw our (common) systemic factors from a hat. We then proceed to use this outcome

[70] The level of confidence also plays a role. A very high-level of confidence will tend to bring out the relatively rare incidence of multiple defaults. Lower levels of confidence may, by this logic, lead to dominance of migration risk in the final economic-capital values.

[71] More specifically, by construction, we have that

$$\left\{\Delta X_i(t+1) \leq K_{S_{i,t}}(q)\right\} \cap \left\{\Delta X_i(t+1) > K_{S_{i,t}}(q)\right\} = \emptyset. \qquad (2.97)$$

**DEFAULT**: COIN TOSS **MIGRATION**: MULTI-SIDED DIE

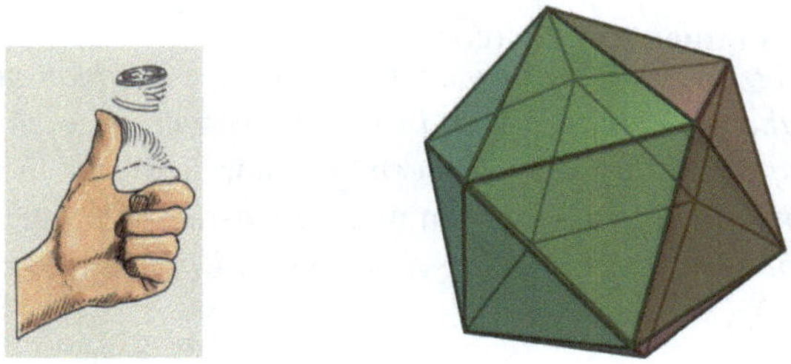

**Fig. 2.6** *Adding migration*: Default, as a binary event, is well conceptualized as an (unfair) coin toss. Migration does not quite work in this setting. It is easier to think about migration as the roll of a large die with many uneven sides where the outcome determines the next period's credit state.

to construct a die with $q + 1$ sides. If the die falls on side 1, the obligor moves to the first credit state; landing on side 2 implies a transition to credit state 2 and so on.[72] Such multi-sided dice actually do exist, but we would need $q$ of them; one corresponding to each row of our transition matrix. Moreover, some of the sides would be incredibly small.[73] Figure 2.6 provides a brief visualization of this important practical twist on the model implementation.

> **Colour and Commentary 23** (THE IMPORTANCE OF MIGRATION): *Each firm, when wrestling with the computation of credit-risk economic capital, needs to reflect on the inclusion of migration risk. Historically, our economic-capital computations did not consider the profit-and-loss consequences of credit downgrade or upgrade; only default was considered. During the run-up to statutory change, a decision was taken to incorporate this dimension and capitalize for migration risk. The reasoning was twofold. First of all, our portfolio is, by both construction and mandate, of relatively high credit quality. The risk of default is, for most loan exposures, correspondingly low. Risk of credit deterioration is not.*[a] *There is a consequent danger of missing a (potentially) important risk dimension. A second rationale arises indirectly through credit impairments or loan-loss provisioning. The loan-loss provision will, in the event of a material deterioration of an obligor's credit quality, lead to an increase in associated impairments. Since this increase will flow through to the profit-and-loss statement, credit-migration has an indirect financial-statement impact.*[b] *Credit migration has thus been incorporated into our economic capital model with a view towards ensuring greater consistency*

(continued)

[72] Default occurs by rolling $q + 1$ on our die.

[73] So small, in fact, that physically our die idea would never actually work.

**Colour and Commentary 23** (continued)
*of loan-pricing, creating better incentives for loan-origination, and helping to recognize the potential profit-and-loss implications associated with loan-obligor downgrades. In short, the general view was that incorporation of credit migration provides a more* complete *credit-risk characterization. Other firms, depending on their specific situation and objectives, may very well arrive at a different decision.*

[a] Although, it should be stressed, the financial consequences of downgrade are typically rather smaller for downgrade than default.

[b] We return to the interesting question of computing loan impairments in Chap. 9.

## 2.6 Risk Attribution

This final discussion point in this chapter relates to the notion of risk attribution. Management of economic capital requires us to understand how various sub-components of our portfolio contribute to overall capital demand. This is necessary for loan pricing and capital budgeting. To a certain extent, it also proves helpful in loan-impairment calculations.[74] More simply, it facilitates a better understanding of how risks are distributed throughout one's portfolio. The ability to perform such central analysis requires an allocation, or attribution, of economic capital to individual loans and financial investments. Easy to motivate and understand, it turns out to be a surprisingly mathematically complicated venture. The complexity is, in this case, unavoidable. The simple reason is that, in a practical setting, an economic-capital framework will not get very far without the ability to attribute risks to various aspects of one's portfolio.

In most cases, although not always, risk attribution reduces to an application of Euler's theorem for homogeneous functions. The popularity of this method stems from the fact that it is not only mathematically plausible, but it also ensures both existence and uniqueness. In other words, there are many possible ways one might decompose an aggregate risk metric down to the instrument level, but the standard approach is the most natural and defensible.

To employ the Euler method, we need our risk measure to be a homogeneous function of the portfolio weights or exposures. Homogeneity is a natural feature of a coherent risk measure—this is one of Artzner et al. [3]'s desirable axiomatic properties—and essentially amounts to the idea that if one doubles one's portfolio exposure, all else equal, one doubles the risk.[75] It is hard to argue against such logic.

[74] To see precisely how, please take a look at Chap. 9.

[75] Mathematically, $f(x)$ is termed a homogeneous function of the first order if,

$$f(\lambda x) = \lambda f(x), \tag{2.98}$$

Assuming that one's risk measure, call it $\Xi(c)$, is a first-order homogeneous function of the obligor exposures, $c \in \mathbb{R}^I$, the Euler's result implies that

$$\begin{aligned}\Xi(c) &= \sum_{i=1}^{I} \Xi(c_i), \\ &= \sum_{i=1}^{I} c_i \frac{\partial \Xi(c)}{\partial c_i}.\end{aligned} \tag{2.99}$$

The partial derivative, $\frac{\partial \Xi(c)}{\partial c_i}$, is termed the marginal risk associated with $\Xi$. Conceptually, it is the change in risk associated with an infinitesimally small movement in the underlying exposure of the $i$th credit counterpart. Both Value-at-Risk (VaR) and expected shortfall, like volatility, are first-order homogeneous risk measures ensuring that Euler decomposition can be employed.[76] Equation 2.99 is an equality; given homogeneity, it must hold. Consequently, one need only identify the marginal risk—that is, partial derivatives—and one has a sensible risk decomposition. In some cases, finding the partial derivatives is straightforward, while in others it can be quite challenging. There are *two* broad approaches to obtaining these partial derivatives in the credit-risk setting: numerical approximation or use of analytical tricks. We'd prefer to use the latter, but sadly we are stuck managing the former.

Despite the usefulness of this general approach to the question of risk attribution, it is not a panacea. Caution is required. The presence of partial derivatives should be, if not a red flag, then a reason for increased attention. By its very construction, a partial derivative is a marginal quantity. In other words, it represents the reasonable approximation of a change in the overall risk for a *small* movement in the exposure of a given contract, or region, or industry. When one considers large changes, however, all bets are off. Zhang and Rachev [44, Page 8] offer a nice overview of the key questions and some of the existing associated research. The proposed risk attribution makes logical and mathematical sense for our purposes, but it important to keep in mind that it is a subtle quantity.

### 2.6.1 The Simplest Case

The most straightforward setting arises where the partial derivatives can be written in closed form. A good example, which sadly is unavailable to us, is the parametric

---

for any choice of $\lambda \in \mathbb{R}$. See Loomis and Sternberg [27] for more discussion on homogeneous functions.

[76] Bolder [6, Chapter 11] provides, from a market-risk perspective, rather more background on the origins and defensibility of this approach.

market-risk measure. Let's briefly examine the logic. Imagine a portfolio with a vector of $K$ risk-factor weights $\zeta \in \mathbb{R}^K$ along with variance-covariance matrix, $\Omega$. Assuming zero return and abstracting from the (thorny) question of length of time horizon, the parametric VaR, at confidence level $\alpha$ for our imaginary portfolio is typically written as,

$$\text{VaR}_\alpha(L) = \Phi^{-1}(1-\alpha)\sqrt{\zeta^T\Omega\zeta}. \tag{2.100}$$

The VaR, as we saw previously, is simply the appropriate quantile of the return distribution; given the assumption of Gaussianity, it reduces to a multiple of the portfolio-return variance, $\sqrt{\zeta^T\Omega\zeta}$. Similar expressions are available for expected shortfall. We can, without loss of generality, assume this to be the economic-capital, since subtracting the expected loss (a constant) changes nothing.

The hard work in the risk-factor decomposition of $\text{VaR}_\alpha(L)$ is to compute the marginal value-at-risk. As seen in Eq. 2.99, this is merely the gradient vector of partial derivatives of the VaR measure to the risk-factor exposures summarized in $\zeta$. Mathematically, it has the following form,

$$\frac{\partial \text{VaR}_\alpha(L)}{\partial \zeta} = \Phi^{-1}(1-\alpha)\frac{\partial\sqrt{\zeta^T\Omega\zeta}}{\partial \zeta}. \tag{2.101}$$

Let's see if we can quickly derive the result in Eq. 2.101 and demonstrate its reasonableness as a risk-attribution method. Directly computing $\frac{\partial\sqrt{\zeta^T\Omega\zeta}}{\partial\zeta}$ is not so straightforward. Instead, define the portfolio volatility as,

$$\sigma_p(\zeta) = \sqrt{\zeta^T\Omega\zeta}. \tag{2.102}$$

Working with the square-root sign is annoying, so let's work with the square of the portfolio volatility (or, rather, variance),

$$\begin{aligned}
\frac{\partial\left(\sigma_p(\zeta)^2\right)}{\partial\zeta} &= 2\sigma_p(\zeta)\frac{\partial\sigma_p(\zeta)}{\partial\zeta}, \\
\frac{\partial\sigma_p(\zeta)}{\partial\zeta} &= \frac{1}{2\sigma_p(\zeta)}\frac{\partial\left(\sigma_p(\zeta)^2\right)}{\partial\zeta}, \\
\frac{\partial\sqrt{\zeta^T\Omega\zeta}}{\partial\zeta} &= \frac{1}{2\sigma_p(\zeta)}\frac{\partial\left(\sqrt{\zeta^T\Omega\zeta}^2\right)}{\partial\zeta}, \\
&= \frac{1}{2\sigma_p(\zeta)}\frac{\partial\left(\zeta^T\Omega\zeta\right)}{\partial\zeta}, \\
&= \frac{\Omega\zeta}{\sqrt{\zeta^T\Omega\zeta}},
\end{aligned} \tag{2.103}$$

which is a vector in $\mathbb{R}^K$. Plugging this result into Eq. 2.101, we have our desired result,

$$\frac{\partial \text{VaR}_\alpha(L)}{\partial \zeta} = \Phi^{-1}(1-\alpha) \underbrace{\frac{\Omega\zeta}{\sqrt{\zeta^T\Omega\zeta}}}_{\text{Eq. 2.103}}. \tag{2.104}$$

An element-by-element multiplication of these marginal value-at-risk values and the vector, $\zeta$, provides the contribution of each risk-factor to the overall risk. That is,

$$\text{Contribution of } i\text{th risk factor to } \text{VaR}_\alpha(L) = \zeta_i \cdot \frac{\partial \text{VaR}_\alpha(L)}{\partial \zeta_i}, \tag{2.105}$$

where $\zeta_i$ refers to the $i$th element of the risk-weight vector, $\zeta$. Does the sum of these individual risk-factor contributions actually lead us to the overall risk-measure value? Consider the dot product of the sensitivity vector, $\zeta$, and the marginal value-at-risk gradient,

$$\begin{aligned}
\zeta^T \frac{\partial \text{VaR}_\alpha(L)}{\partial \zeta} &= \zeta^T \underbrace{\left(\Phi^{-1}(1-\alpha)\frac{\Omega\zeta}{\sqrt{\zeta^T\Omega\zeta}}\right)}_{\text{Eq. 2.104}}, \\
&= \Phi^{-1}(1-\alpha)\frac{\zeta^T\Omega\zeta}{\sqrt{\zeta^T\Omega\zeta}}, \\
&= \underbrace{\Phi^{-1}(1-\alpha)\sqrt{\zeta^T\Omega\zeta}}_{\text{Eq. 2.100}}, \\
&= \text{VaR}_\alpha(L).
\end{aligned} \tag{2.106}$$

In a few short lines, we have found a sensible and practical approach for the allocation of VaR to individual market-risk factors. Regrettably, while promising and intuitive, this expedient path is not available to us in the credit-risk setting. The threshold and mixture models used for credit-risk measurement do not generally lend themselves to parametric forms, which in turn forces us to rely upon simulation methods for risk-measure estimation.

### 2.6.2 An Important Relationship

If the partial derivatives cannot be computed analytically, then their numerical computation would appear to be a reasonable solution. Estimating numerical derivatives in a simulation setting, however, is a bit daunting. There is, happily, a surprising relationship which facilitates the computation of the marginal-risk figures.[77] Its statement requires a bit of background. Let us, as before, define the total default credit loss as the following sum over the $I$ counterparties in the credit portfolio,

$$L = \sum_{i=1}^{I} \underbrace{c_i \gamma_i \mathbb{I}_{\mathcal{D}_i}}_{X_i}, \tag{2.107}$$

where $\mathbb{I}_{\mathcal{D}_i}$, $\gamma_i$, and $c_i$ represent our now familiar default-event, loss-given-default, and exposure quantities, respectively. We can use our Gaussian or $t$-threshold definition of the default event if you like, or imagine something else entirely. Consider Eq. 2.107 to be a general statement.

We now introduce the key relationship. Under positive homogeneity conditions, the VaR measure for the portfolio loss, $L$, can be written as the sum of the marginal value-at-risk values. That is,

$$\begin{aligned} \text{Contribution of } i\text{th counterparty to } \text{VaR}_\alpha(L) &= \left.\frac{\partial \text{VaR}_\alpha(L + hX_i)}{\partial h}\right|_{h=0} \\ &= \mathbb{E}\left( X_i \,\middle|\, L = \text{VaR}_\alpha(L) \right), \end{aligned} \tag{2.108}$$

where $h$ is a small positive constant. It is also possible to show that,

$$\text{VaR}_\alpha(L) = \sum_{i=1}^{I} \mathbb{E}\left( X_i \,\middle|\, L = \text{VaR}_\alpha(L) \right). \tag{2.109}$$

That is a lot to swallow and does not appear to be particularly believable at first glance. In words, Eq. 2.109 implies that the loss contribution associated with each of the $I$ counterparties—where the total loss exactly coincides with the VaR measure—is equivalent to their overall contribution. Computationally, therefore, one need only use a Monte-Carlo engine to simulate the loss distribution and examine the set of losses at the VaR outcome to determine their individual contributions.

An analogous result is also available for the expected shortfall. In particular,

$$\begin{aligned} \text{Contribution of } i\text{th counterparty to } \mathcal{E}_\alpha(L) &= \left.\frac{\partial \mathcal{E}_\alpha(L + hX_i)}{\partial h}\right|_{h=0}, \\ &= \mathbb{E}\left( X_i \,\middle|\, L \geq \text{VaR}_\alpha(L) \right). \end{aligned} \tag{2.110}$$

[77] See Tasche [39], Gourieroux et al. [16], and Rau-Bredow [36] for much more detail.

It can also be analogously shown that

$$\mathcal{E}_\alpha(L) = \sum_{i=1}^{I} \mathbb{E}\left(X_i \middle| L \geq \text{VaR}_\alpha(L)\right). \tag{2.111}$$

The difference in the expected-shortfall case—which is not unimportant—is that one needs to compute the average losses greater than or equal to the VaR for the decomposition of this measure. It thus also readily lends itself to extraction from one's Monte-Carlo engine. Derivation of this result is far from trivial, but it is outlined in detail in Bolder [7, Chapter 7]. The reader unfamiliar with these results—and not entirely convinced by their statement without proof—is recommended to invest a bit of time in reviewing their mathematical logic and justification.

### 2.6.3 The Computational Path

Despite the powerful relationship between conditional expectation and partial derivatives introduced in the previous section, evaluation of the conditional expectation in the case of VaR, from Eq. 2.109, is not terribly straightforward. Algorithms do exist. In the most direct manner, one proceeds in two steps. First, given $M$ simulations, one orders the loss vectors for each iteration in ascending order. Second, using the choice of $\alpha$, one identifies $\text{VaR}_\alpha(L)$ and then selects the *single* loss vector, $L_m$, consistent with this VaR estimate. This is, by definition, a singleton set. The losses associated with each instrument—or dimension of interest—are extracted from the loss vector. That is, according to Eq. 2.109, each contribution is equal to $\mathbb{E}\left(L_i \,|\, L = \text{VaR}_\alpha(L)\right)$. It basically comes for free from one's simulation engine. Naturally, there is a catch. This is an incredibly *noisy* estimator of the true risk attributions. As bluntly, but very accurately, stated by Glasserman [14],

> each contribution depends on the probability of a rare event conditional on an even rarer event.

An alternative is to repeat our $M$-iteration simulation a large number of times and average the resulting portfolio-loss vectors. While this basically works, a depressingly large number of repetitions is required to achieve convergence. In short, the computational expense is exorbitant.

Hallerbach [19] offers an alternative.[78] It is an approximation that begins from the $M$ simulations. Given a small positive number $\epsilon$, the following set is defined

$$\mathcal{L}_{\text{VaR}_\alpha}(\epsilon) = \left[\text{VaR}_\alpha(L) - \epsilon, \text{VaR}_\alpha(L) + \epsilon\right]. \tag{2.112}$$

[78] This approach, described recently in Mossessian and Vieli [33], appears to still be in broad use in industrial applications.

Each element of $\mathcal{L}_{\text{VaR}_\alpha}(\epsilon)$ is thus a portfolio-loss vector in the neighbourhood of one's VaR estimate. The average across all elements in the portfolio-loss vectors of $\mathcal{L}_{\text{VaR}_\alpha}(\epsilon)$ is a *biased* estimator for the overall VaR and the conditional expectations found in Eq. 2.109. Defining $M^*$ as the number of elements in $\mathcal{L}_{\text{VaR}_\alpha}(\epsilon)$, our estimate of our desired conditional expectations—or equivalently marginal VaR values—is

$$\mathbb{E}\left(L_i \middle| L = \text{VaR}_\alpha(L)\right) \approx \frac{1}{M^*} \sum_{\ell \in \mathcal{L}_{\text{VaR}_\alpha}(\epsilon)} \ell_i. \tag{2.113}$$

for $i = 1, \ldots, I$. The trick is to find the value of $\epsilon$ that increases the number of loss vectors to sufficiently reduce the noise, but not introduce an unreasonable amount of bias. These effects move, of course, in opposite directions. Reducing bias comes at the cost of increased estimation variance and vice versa.[79]

A challenge of this approach is that the sum of approximated conditional expectations will, in principle, no longer sum to the observed VaR. Hallerbach [19] thus, quite practically, suggests rescaling the individual contributions in a proportionate manner to force them back to the desired VaR estimate. If this sounds slightly *ad hoc*, it is because it is. There are, to be honest, not many alternatives.[80]

One legitimate option is to change the risk measure to the expected shortfall. Approximation of its conditional expectation is much more natural. Again, starting from $M$ simulations, the following set is defined

$$\mathcal{L}_{\text{E}_\alpha} = \left\{ L \geq \text{VaR}_\alpha(L) \right\}. \tag{2.114}$$

In this case, we collect all of the portfolio-loss vectors exceeding the designated VaR level. This set, virtually by definition, contains multiple elements. With $M = 10{,}000$ and $\alpha = 0.99$, it will include by construction, $(1 - 0.99) \cdot 10{,}000 = 100$ portfolio-loss vectors. If we reduce $\alpha$ to the 99.97th quantile, of course, this falls to just 3.[81] The point nonetheless remains valid. With a judicious choice of $M$, we can ensure a sufficient number of elements in $\mathcal{L}_{\text{ES}_\alpha}$. The necessity of introducing $\epsilon$ and its attendant bias is thus precluded.

---

[79] While practically feasible, the author's personal experience reveals finding the appropriate balance to be a frustratingly slow exercise.

[80] Fan et al. [10] offer an approach exploiting the multivariate copula functions of one's model dependence structure. In a complex, multiple-step simulation, this is unlikely to be extremely helpful.

[81] Naturally, at the 99.99th quantile with $M = 10{,}000$ we have that $\mathcal{L}_{\text{ES}_\alpha}$ is a singleton set. The interplay between the number of iterations and one's confidence level is, thus, critically important. More on this point in Chap. 4.

Defining $\tilde{M}$ as the number of elements in $\mathcal{L}_{\text{ES}_\alpha}$, our estimate of our desired conditional expectations—or equivalently marginal expected-shortfall values—is

$$\mathbb{E}\left(L_i \middle| L \geq \text{VaR}_\alpha(L)\right) \approx \frac{1}{\tilde{M}} \sum_{\ell \in \mathcal{L}_{\text{ES}_\alpha}} \ell_i. \tag{2.115}$$

for $i = 1, \ldots, I$. This is thus both a sharper and unbiased estimate of the risk contribution associated with our expected-shortfall measure. It is also consistent with findings in the literature of greater robustness of expected-shortfall risk measure and attribution estimates.

### *2.6.4 A Clever Trick*

To summarize the previous discussion, the risk-attribution computation for expected shortfall is significantly more stable than its VaR equivalent. The reason, of course, is that our expected-shortfall estimates are an *average* over the values beyond a certain quantile. The VaR figures, conversely, depend on the values *at* a specific quantile. This latter quantile is harder to pinpoint and subject to substantial simulation noise.

Bluhm et al. [5, Chapter 5], keenly aware of the inherent instability of Monte-Carlo-based VaR risk attribution, offer a possible solution. The idea is to find the quantile that equates one's VaR-based economic-capital estimate to the shortfall. They refer to this as *VaR-matched* expected shortfall. Conceptually, it is straightforward. One computes, using the predetermined level of confidence $\alpha$, the usual VaR-based economic capital.[82] We seek, however, a new quantile, let's call it $\alpha^*$, that equates expected shortfall with $\text{VaR}_\alpha(L)$. Mathematically, we seek the $\alpha^*$ root of the following equation,

$$\text{VaR}_\alpha(L) - \mathcal{E}_{\alpha^*}(L) = 0. \tag{2.116}$$

In some specialized situations, Eq. 2.116 may have an analytic solution. More pragmatically, however, it is readily solved numerically. $\alpha^*$ can be identified, in fact, as the solution to the following one-dimensional non-linear optimization problem

$$\min_{\alpha^*} \left\| \text{VaR}_\alpha(L) - \mathcal{E}_{\alpha^*}(L) \right\|_p, \tag{2.117}$$

[82] Ignoring again, without loss of generality, the constant expected-loss term.

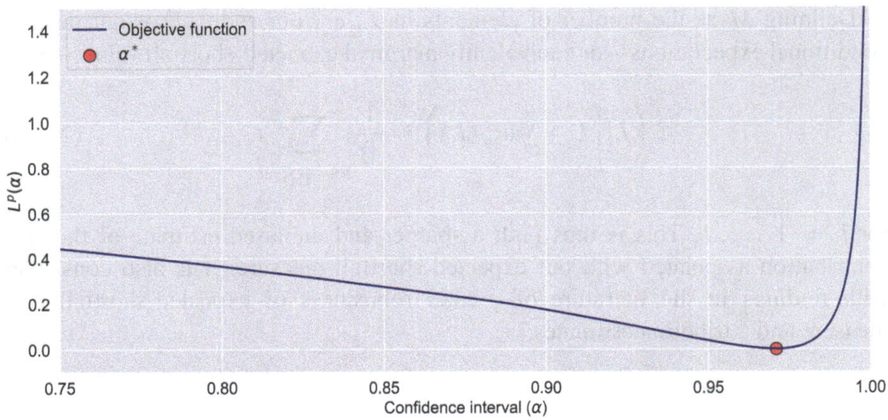


**Fig. 2.7** *Equating VaR and expected shortfall*: This graphic highlights the least-squares motivated objective function used to identify the expected-shortfall quantile, $\alpha^*$ that equates the expected shortfall with the 99th quantile VaR estimate.

where $\alpha^* \in (0, 1)$ and $\|\cdot\|_p$ describes the p-norm used to characterize distance. One could, given its low dimensionality, use a brute-force, grid-search algorithm to resolve Eq. 2.117; the ultimate result is conceptually identical.

Figure 2.7 displays the objective function—using the $L^2$ norm to describe the distance between our two risk measures—for a sample threshold model implementation. The choice of $L^2$ reduces $\alpha^*$ to a least-squares estimator.[83] $L^p(\alpha)$, as evidenced in Fig. 2.6, demonstrates both a smooth shape and clear minimum highlighted with a red star.

To summarize, an efficient alternative is to identify the $\alpha^*$ equating one's VaR-based economic-capital estimate and the associated expected shortfall. Then one employs this quantity to approximate the VaR-matched expected shortfall contributions. One does not, therefore, directly compute a true VaR risk attribution, but rather accepts Bluhm et al. [5, Chapter 5]'s advice. While numerically defensible, this choice is not without empirical repercussions. Most importantly, a small sleight of hand has been performed. We have quietly switched our risk metric—for risk attribution purposes—from VaR to expected shortfall. While not a criminal act, it is still hard to precisely understand the ultimate consequences.

Despite the cleverness of this trick, there is already a clean logical solution: simply use expected shortfall as one's economic-capital measure. This avoids the need to use mathematical tricks and ensures a structural consistency between one's economic-capital metrics and the associated risk-attribution calculations.[84] Since

[83] Other choices of $p$ are, of course, possible, but this option is numerically robust and easily understood.

[84] The remaining issue to keep in mind is the choice of $M$ to ensure adequate numbers for the robust estimation of the risk attributions. This important question is addressed in Chap. 4.

this represents an important change to the economic-capital framework—which is always daunting to revise—it is understandable that one might be reluctant to make a change of this magnitude. Since NIB was already in the midst of a large-scale review of their credit-risk economic capital methodology, it was less difficult. Indeed, this practical risk-attribution advantage—combined with the coherence of expected shortfall and its inherent conservatism—made moving to a new risk metric a relatively easy choice.

**Colour and Commentary 24** (RISK ATTRIBUTION)*: The analytic advantages of one's economic-capital framework are severely limited without an ability to attribute overall risk to individual financial instruments. Absent this capability, there is simply no way to understand how capital demand is distributed across one's portfolio. Although essential, in the credit-risk setting this is* not *a trivial task. Useful and tractable semi-analytic methods exist, but are not available in the multivariate setting.*[a] *We need, therefore, to take recourse to numerical methods. In practice, these methods are much more stable for expected shortfall relative to the VaR metric. Numerous clever tricks exist to improve the situation, but the simplest solution is to use expected shortfall as one's principal economic-capital metric. Accepting this fact—while taking into consideration the other conceptual advantages of the expected-shortfall measure—is precisely what we have done.*

[a] Saddlepoint methods, for example, work exceptionally well in low-dimensional cases; see Bolder [7, Chapter 7] for an introduction.

## 2.7 Wrapping Up

This mathematics-heavy chapter focuses principally on the methodological structure and choices associated with our credit-risk economic-capital model. The entry point is a general, intimidating, and frankly fairly impractical stochastic differential equation describing the creditworthiness (i.e., asset-return) dynamics for the $I$ credit obligors in one's portfolio. Appropriate time discretization, normalization, and notational adjustment reveal the skeleton of a Gaussian threshold model. Some additional machinery—including stochastic recovery—brought us to our legacy implementation. The current economic-capital framework involves two revisions to this basic structure: a new copula function that permits tail dependence and credit migration. This long, and at times winding, road leads us to the final production model.

There are, unfortunately, a multiplicity of moving parts. It is easy to lose the forest for the trees. Table 2.3 thus attempts to help us summarize the key decisions by chronicling the key methodological facts about our model. In one phrase, the

**Table 2.3** *Methodology fact sheet*: The underlying table provides, at a glance, a summary of the key methodological choices associated with our credit-risk economic-capital model.

| Dimension | Description |
|---|---|
| Model type | Multivariate threshold model |
| Time perspective | Discrete time |
| Horizon | One-year, single step |
| Copula | $t$ |
| Credit migration | Yes |
| Risk metric | Expected shortfall |
| Confidence level | 99.97th quantile |
| Parameter perspective | Long-term, through-the-cycle approach |
| Loss-given-default | Random following independent beta distributions. |
| Transition matrix | 20-state NIB master scale |

current credit-risk production model is a one-period, multivariate $t$-threshold model with stochastic recovery and credit migration.

This chapter's objective was to introduce the credit-risk economic capital model. Although these details are absolutely necessary for an understanding of our proposed model, they are *not* sufficient. As every mathematician knows, we need both necessity and sufficiency to be really satisfied.[85] Two additional pieces of the puzzle are required. As a first point, the model does not really come alive until the specific parameters are identified. We would be, in other words, hard-pressed to use the model without clear and concrete coefficients. Model parametrization, which brings many practical challenges and involves numerous decisions, is the focus of the next chapter. The second requirement touches upon model implementation questions. Even if you have all of the mathematics and parameters sorted out, the computations still need to be performed. This task can be categorized as conceptually easy, but practically hard. It is a bit like climbing a mountain. We know that we need only put one foot, and hand, in front of the other. That knowledge, while perhaps comforting in some sense, doesn't necessary ease the difficulty of actually getting up the mountain. Chapter 4 thus acts as our mountain-climbing guide.

## References

1. M. Abramovitz and I. A. Stegun. *Handbook of Mathematical Functions.* Dover Publications, New York, 1965.
2. E. I. Altman, B. Brady, A. Resti, and A. Sironi. The link between default and recovery rates: Theory, empirical evidence, and implications. *The Journal of Business*, 78(6):2203–2228, 2005.

[85] Even then, one can usually find something to complain about.

3. P. Artzner, F. Delbaen, J.-M. Eber, and D. Heath. Coherent measures of risk. *Mathematical Finance*, 9(3):203–228, July 2001.
4. F. Black and M. S. Scholes. The pricing of options and corporate liabilities. *Journal of Political Economy*, 81:637–654, 1973.
5. C. Bluhm, L. Overbeck, and C. Wagner. *An Introduction to Credit Risk Modelling*. Chapman & Hall, CRC Press, Boca Raton, first edition, 2003.
6. D. J. Bolder. *Fixed Income Portfolio Analytics: A Practical Guide to Implementing, Monitoring and Understanding Fixed-Income Portfolios*. Springer, Heidelberg, Germany, 2015.
7. D. J. Bolder. *Credit-Risk Modelling: Theoretical Foundations, Diagnostic Tools, Practical Examples, and Numerical Recipes in Python*. Springer-Nature, Heidelberg, Germany, 2018.
8. P. P. Boyle, M. Hardy, and T. C. Vorst. Life after var. *The Journal of Derivatives*, 13(1):48–55, 2005.
9. P. Brémaud. *Markov Chains: Gibbs Fields, Monte Carlo Simulation and Queues*. Springer Verlag, 175 Fifth Avenue, New York, NY, 1999. Texts in Applied Mathematics.
10. G. Fan, Y. Zeng, and W. K. Wong. Decomposition of portfolio VaR and expected shortfall based on multivariate copula simulation. *International Journal of Management Science*, 7(2): 153–160, 2012.
11. J. Frye. Depressing recoveries. Federal Reserve Bank of Chicago, October 2000.
12. J. Frye. Loss given default as a function of the default rate. Federal Reserve Bank of Chicago, September 2013.
13. M. Gilli and E. Këllezi. An application of extreme value theory for measuring financial risk. *Computational Economics*, 27(1):207–228, 2006.
14. P. Glasserman. Measuring marginal risk contributions in credit portfolios. Risk Measurement Research Program of the FDIC Center for Financial Research, January 2006.
15. G. H. Golub and C. F. V. Loan. *Matrix Computations*. The John Hopkins University Press, Baltimore, Maryland, 2012.
16. C. Gourieroux, J. Laurent, and O. Scaillet. Sensitivity analysis of values at risk. *Journal of Empirical Finance*, 7(3-4):225–245, November 2000.
17. M. Gundlach and F. Lehrbass. *CreditRisk+ in the Banking Industry*. Springer Verlag, Berlin, first edition, 2004.
18. G. M. Gupton, G. Coughlan, and M. Wilson. *CreditMetrics — Technical Document*. Morgan Guaranty Trust Company, New York, 1997.
19. W. G. Hallerbach. Decomposing portfolio value-at-risk: A general analysis. Erasmus University Rotterdam, October 2002.
20. J. D. Hamilton. *Time Series Analysis*. Princeton University Press, Princeton, New Jersey, 1994.
21. J. W. Harris and H. Stocker. *Handbook of Mathematics and Computational Science*. Springer Verlag, New York, New York, 1998.
22. N. L. Johnson, S. Kotz, and N. Balakrishnan. *Continuous Univariate Distributions: Volume 2*. John Wiley and Sons, New York, NY, 1997. Wiley Series in Probability and Statistics.
23. P. Jorion. Risk Management Lessons from Long-Term Capital Management. *European Financial Management*, 6:277–300, 2000.
24. K. Kostadinov. Tail approximation for credit-risk portfolios with heavy-tailed risk factors. Zentrum Mathematik, Technische Universität München, December 2005.
25. G. Kuhn. Tails of credit default portfolios. Zentrum Mathematik, Technische Universität München, December 2005.
26. P. Kumaraswamy. A generalized probability density function for double-bounded random processes. *Journal of Hydrology*, 46(1):79–88, 1980.
27. L. H. Loomis and S. Sternberg. *Advanced Calculus*. World Scientific Publishing, Inc., Hackensack, New Jersey, 2014.
28. D. MacKenzie and T. Spears. "The Formula That Killed Wall Street?" The Gaussian Copula and the Material Cultures of Modelling. University of Edinburgh, June 2012.
29. A. J. McNeil, R. Frey, and P. Embrechts. *Quantitative Risk Management: Concepts, Tools and Techniques*. Princeton University Press, New Jersey, 2015.

30. R. Merton. On the pricing of corporate debt: The risk structure of interest rates. *Journal of Finance*, 29:449–470, 1974.
31. S. P. Meyn and R. L. Tweedie. *Markov Chains and Stochastic Stability*. Springer-Verlag, 175 Fifth Avenue, New York, NY, 1993.
32. J. Morgan/Reuters. *RiskMetrics — Technical Document*. Morgan Guaranty Trust Company, New York, 1996.
33. D. Mossessian and V. Vieli. Decomposing portfolio risk using Monte Carlo estimators. FactSet Research Systems Inc., 2017.
34. B. K. Oksendal. *Stochastic Differential Equations*. Springer Verlag, Berlin, fourth edition, 1995.
35. W. H. Press, S. A. Teukolsky, W. T. Vetterling, and B. P. Flannery. *Numerical Recipes in C: The Art of Scientific Computing*. Cambridge University Press, Trumpington Street, Cambridge, second edition, 1992.
36. H. Rau-Bredow. Value-at-risk, expected shortfall, and marginal risk contribution. In G. Szegö, editor, *Risk Measures for the 21st Century*. John Wiley & Sons, 2004.
37. H. L. Royden. *Real Analysis*. Prentice-Hall Inc., Englewood Cliffs, New Jersey, 1988.
38. A. Sklar. Fonctions de répartition à *n* dimensions et leurs marges. *Publications de l'Institut de Statistique de L'Université de Paris*, 8:229–231, 1959.
39. D. Tasche. Risk contributions and performance measurement. Zentrum Mathematik, Technische Universität München, February 2000.
40. O. A. Vasicek. Probability of loss on loan distribution. KMV Corporation, February 1987.
41. O. A. Vasicek. Limiting loan loss probability distribution. KMV Corporation, August 1991.
42. O. A. Vasicek. The distribution of loan portfolio value. *Risk*, (12):160–162, December 2002.
43. T. Wilde. CreditRisk+: A credit risk management framework. Credit Suisse First Boston, January 1997.
44. Y. Zhang and S. Rachev. Risk Attribution and Portfolio Performance Measurement: An Overview. University of California, Santa Barbara, September 2004.

# Chapter 3
# Finding Model Parameters

*If you have a procedure with ten parameters, you probably missed some.*

*(Alan Perlis)*

We can loosely think of a firm-wide credit-risk economic-capital model as a complicated industrial system, such as a power plant, an air-traffic control system, or an interconnected assembly line. The operators of such systems typically find themselves—at least, conceptually—sitting in front of a large control panel with multiple switches, levers, and buttons.[1] Getting the system to run properly, for their current objective, requires setting everything to its proper place and level. Failure to align the controls correctly can lead to inefficiencies, defective results, or even disaster. In a modelling setting, unfortunately, there is no exciting control room. There are, however, invariably a number of important parameters to be determined. It is useful to imagine the parameter selection process as being roughly equivalent to adjusting the switches, levers, and buttons in an industrial process. There are many possible combinations and their specific constellation depends on the task at hand. Good choices require experience, reflection, and judgement. Transparency and constructive challenge also contribute importantly to this process.

The previous chapter identified a rich array of parameters associated with our large-scale industrial model. The principal objective of this chapter is to motivate our actual parameter choices. It is neither particular easy nor terribly relaxing to walk through a detailed explanation of such a complex system. The labyrinth of questions that need to be answered can easily lead us astray or obscure the thread of the discussion. Figure 3.1 attempts to mitigate this problem somewhat through the introduction of a parameter tree. It highlights *five* main categories of parameters: credit states, systemic factors, portfolio-level quantities, recovery rates, and credit

[1] This old-fashioned control panel is fun to envision, but sadly, in today's world, most of these things are probably run via computer.



D. Bolder, *Modelling Economic Capital*, Contributions to Finance and Accounting,
https://doi.org/10.1007/978-3-030-95096-5_3

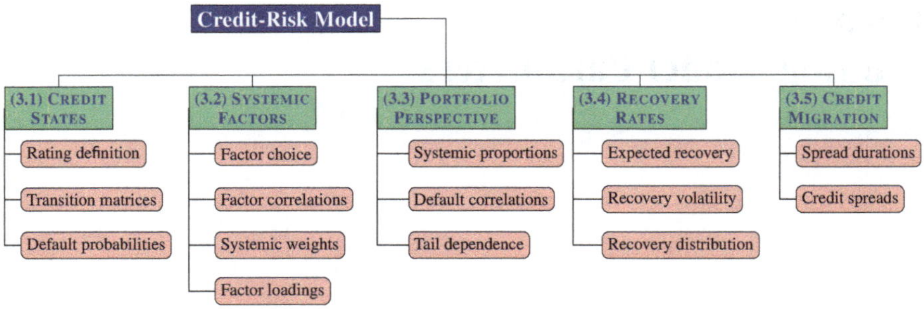


**Fig. 3.1** *A parameter tree*: This schematic highlights *five* main classes of parameters and further illustrates the key questions associated with each grouping. This parameter tree forms a rough outline of this chapter—providing the main sections—and acts as a logical guide through the complexity of our credit-risk economic capital *control panel*.

migration. Each of the five divisions of Fig. 3.1 corresponds to one of the main sections of this chapter. These categories are further broken down into a number of sub-categories identifying the specific parameter questions to be answered. Overall, there more than a dozen avenues of parameter investigation to be covered. Figure 3.1 thus forms not only a rough outline of this chapter, but also a logical guide for navigating the complexity of our credit-risk economic capital *control panel*.

Before jumping in and answering the various parameter questions raised in Fig. 3.1, it is useful to establish a few ground rules. The first rule, already highlighted in previous chapters, is that economic capital is intended to be a long-term, unconditional, or through-the-cycle estimate of asset riskiness. This indicates that we need to ensure a long-term perspective in our parameter selection. A second essential rule is that, wherever possible, we wish to select our parameters in an objective, defensible fashion. In other words, we need to rely on data. Data, however, brings its own set of challenges. We will not always be able to find the perfect dataset to precisely measure what we wish; as a small institution with limited history, NIB often finds itself faced with such challenges. This suggests the need to employ some form of logical proxy. Moreover, consistency of data for different parameters types, the choice of time horizons, and the relative weight on extreme observations are all tricky questions to be managed. We will *not* pretend to have resolved all of these questions perfectly, but will endeavour to be transparent about our choices.

A final rule, or perhaps guideline, is that a model owner or operator needs to be keenly aware of the sensitivity of model outputs to various parameter choices. This is exactly analogous to our industrial process. The proper setting for a lever is hard to determine absent knowledge of how its setting impacts one's production process. Such analysis is a constant component of our internal computations and regular review of parameter choices. It will not, however, figure much in this chapter.[2]

[2] Section 3.3, highlighting the portfolio perspective, does take a few steps in this important direction.

The reason is twofold. First of all, such an analysis inevitably brings one into the specific details of the portfolio: regional and industrial breakdowns and the impact on specific clients. Such information is naturally sensitive and, as such, cannot be shared in such a forum. The second, more practical, reason relates to the volume of material. This chapter is already extremely long and detailed—perhaps too much so—and adding analysis surrounding parameter sensitivity will only make matters worse. Let the reader be nonetheless assured that parameter sensitivity is an important internal theme and forms a central component of the parameter-selection process.

The mathematical structure of any model is deeply important, but it is the specific values of the individual parameters that really bring it to life. The remaining sections of this chapter will lean upon the structure introduced in Fig. 3.1 to describe and motivate our parametric choices. Necessarily very NIB-centric, the general themes and key questions apply very widely to a broad range of financial institutions.

## 3.1 Credit States

As is abundantly clear in the previous chapter, the default and migration risk estimates arising from the $t$-threshold model depend importantly on the obligor's credit state. One can make a legitimate argument that this is the most important aspect of the credit-risk economic capital model. The corollary of this argument is the treatment of credit states—and their related properties—is the natural starting point for any discussion on parameterization.

### 3.1.1 *Defining Credit Ratings*

NIB has, for decades, made use of a 21-notch credit-rating scale.[3] This is a fairly common situation among lending institutions; control over one's internal rating scale is a very helpful tool in loan origination and management. For large institutions, it is also the source of rich internal firm-specific data on default, transition, and recovery outcomes. NIB—as are many other lending organizations—is unfortunately too small to enjoy such a situation. The consequence is a lack of sufficient internal credit-rating data and history to estimate firm-specific quantities. It is thus necessary to identify and use longer and broader external credit-state datasets for this purpose. A natural source for this data is the large credit-rating agencies: S&P, Moodys, or Fitch. We have taken the decision to generally rely upon

[3] This is often referred to as a 20-notch system, with the exclusion of default from the scale. As default is a naturally legitimate credit-state outcome in the credit-risk economic-capital model, we will use 21 distinct notches.

**Table 3.1** *An internal credit scale*: This table introduces the 21-notch NIB rating scale and maps it to the 18-notch S&P and Moody's credit categories. Both Moody's and S&P and have many additional speculative-grade groupings below the B3 and B- levels, respectively. These are, however, outside of NIB's investment range and thus not explicitly considered. PD20 is thus a catch-all category for everything below the B3 and B-cut-offs.

| | NIB Code | S&P | Moody's | |
|---|---|---|---|---|
| | PD01 | AAA | Aaa | |
| | PD02 | AA+ | Aa1 | |
| | PD03 | AA | Aa2 | |
| | PD04 | AA- | Aa3 | |
| | PD05 | A+ | A1 | |
| | PD06 | A | A2 | |
| | PD07 | A- | A3 | |
| | PD08 | BBB+ | Baa1 | |
| | PD09 | BBB | Baa2 | |
| | PD10 | BBB- | Baa3 | |
| PD11–PD13 | PD11 | BB+ | Ba1 | |
| PD11–PD13 | **PD12** | **BB+/BB** | **Ba1/Ba2** | |
| PD11–PD13 | PD13 | BB | Ba2 | |
| | PD14 | BB- | Ba3 | PD14–PD16 |
| | **PD15** | **BB-/B+** | **Ba3/B1** | PD14–PD16 |
| | PD16 | B+ | B1 | PD14–PD16 |
| PD17–PD19 | PD17 | B | B2 | |
| PD17–PD19 | **PD18** | **B/B-** | **B2/B3** | |
| PD17–PD19 | PD19 | B- | B3 | |
| | PD20 | CCC | Caa | |
| | | Default | | |

S&P transition probabilities, but we also examine Moodys' data for comparison purposes. One can certainly question the representativeness of this data for our specific application, but there are unfortunately not many legitimate alternatives. We will attempt to make adjustments for data representation as appropriate.

Both Moody's and S&P also allocate 19 and 20 non-default credit ratings, respectively; each is described with a different alphanumeric identifier as shown in Table 3.1. Typically, we refer to the top-ten ratings—in either scale—as *investment grade*. The remaining lower groups are usually called *speculative grade*. The most obvious solution—for small- to medium-sized firms—would be to create a one-to-one mapping between one's internal scale and the S&P and Moody's categories; this would ultimately preclude managing different numbers of groupings. This is, however, a problem for NIB (and many other lending institutions), since the very lower end of the S&P and Moody's scales are simply too far outside of our typical lending risk appetite.[4] These categories are referred to as either *"extremely speculative"* or in *"imminent risk of default."* This is simply not representative of

[4] Other lenders' internal scales, of course, may deviate from the external-rating universes for rather different reasons.

our business mandate and practice. For this reason, everything below S&P's B- and Moody's B3 categories are lumped together into the final PD20 NIB credit rating. This makes the mapping rather more difficult. We need to link 20 (non-default) NIB categories into 17 (non-default) S&P and Moody's credit notches.

Finding a sensible mapping between these two mismatched scales requires some thought. As an over-specified problem, a unique mapping solution naturally does not exist. Some external logic or justification is required to move forward.[5] The first ten (investment-grade) categories are easy. They are simply matched on a one-to-one basis among the S&P, Moody's and NIB scales. The hard part relates to the speculative grade. Our practical solution to this mapping problem involves sharing of a pair of S&P and Moody's rating categories between three triplets of NIB groupings. This links six credit-rating agency groups into nine NIB categories; the three-notch mismatch is thus managed. The overlap occurs for rating triplets PD11-13, PD14-16, and PD17-19. The specific values are summarized in Table 3.1. As a final step, PD20 maps directly to the CCC and Caa S&P and Moody's categories, respectively.

**Colour and Commentary 25** (CREDIT RATING SCALE AND MAPPINGS): *NIB's internal 21-notch credit scale is* not *a modelling choice. It was designed, and has evolved over the years, to meet its institutional needs. This includes the creation of a common language around credit quality, the need to support the loan-origination process, and also to aid in risk-management activities.*[a] *Our modelling activities need to reflect this internal reality. Our position as a small lending institution nonetheless requires looking outwards for data. To do this, explicit decisions about the relationships between the internal scale and external ratings need to be established. This is a modelling question. The solution is a rather practical mapping between NIB's 20 non-default notches and the first 17 non-default credit ratings for S&P and Moody's. Its ultimate form, summarized in Table 3.1, was designed to manage the notch mismatch and the nature of our internal rating scale. We will return to this decision frequently in the following parameter discussion as well as in subsequent chapters.*

[a] Internal rating scales are a common tool among lending institutions all over the world.

[5] Mathematically, one could potentially seek to simplify the problem or provide additional constraints to lead to a unique solution. This process is generally referred to as regularization. While such formalization might be helpful, we have opted for a rather simpler approach.

### 3.1.2 Transition Matrices

The previous credit-rating categorization has some direct implications. In particular, it implicitly assumes that the credit quality of its obligors can be roughly described by a small, discrete and finite set of $q$-states. From a mathematical modelling perspective, this strongly suggests the idea of a discrete-time, discrete-state Markov-chain process.[6] While there are limits to how far we can push this idea—Chap. 7 will explore this question in much more detail—treating the collection of credit states as a Markov chain is a useful starting point. It immediately provides a number of helpful mathematical results. In particular, the central parametric object used to describe a Markov chain is the transition matrix. Denoted as $P \in \mathbb{R}^{q \times q}$, it provides a full, parsimonious characterization of the one-period movements from any given state to all other states (including default). Chapter 2 has already demonstrated the central role that the transition matrix plays in determining default and migration thresholds. The question we face now is how to defensibly determine the individual entries of $P$.

One might, very reasonably, argue for the use of multiple transition matrices differentiated by the type of credit obligor. There are legitimate reasons to expect that transition dynamics are *not* constant across substantially different business lines. A very large lending institution, for example, may employ a broad range of transition matrices for different purposes. In our current implementation, however, only *two* transition matrices are employed for all individual obligors; one for corporate borrowers and another for sovereign obligors. This allows for a slight differentiation in transition dynamics between these two classes of credit counterparty.[7] With $q \times q$ individual entries, a transition matrix is already a fairly high-dimensional object. This discussion will focus principally on the corporate transition matrix; the same ideas, it should be stressed, apply equally in the sovereign setting.

Prior to the data analysis, we seek some clarity on what we expect to observe in a generic credit-migration transition matrix. Kreinin and Sidelnikova [31], a helpful source in this area, identify *four* properties of a *regular* credit-migration model.[8] These include:

1. There exists a single absorbing, default state. In other words, once default occurs, it is permanent. While in real life there may be the possibility of workouts or negotiations, this is an extremely useful abstraction in a modelling setting.
2. There exists some $\tilde{t}$ such that $p_{qi}(\tilde{t}) > 0$ for all $i = 1, \ldots, q-1$. In words, this means that all states will, at some time horizon, possess a positive probability of

[6] For a comprehensive discussion of the theory of Markov chains, please see Hamilton [19], Brémaud [8], and Meyn and Tweedie [36].

[7] In both cases, the calibration is structured so that they share the same set of common default probabilities.

[8] They actually identify only three. At the risk of diluting their definition, we have added a fourth, potentially redundant, but still descriptive, property.

default. Empirically, $\tilde{t}$ is somewhere between one to three or four years, even for AAA rated credit counterparts.

3. The $\det(P) > 0$ and all of the eigenvalues of $P$ are distinct. These are necessary conditions for the computation of the matrix logarithm of $P$, which is important if one wishes to compute a generator matrix to lengthen (or shorten) the time perspective.[9]
4. The matrix, $P$, is diagonally dominant. Since each entry, $p_{ij} \in (0, 1)$, for all $i, j = 1, .., q$ and each row sums to unity, this implies that the majority of the probability mass is assigned to a given entity remaining in their current credit state. Simply put, credit ratings are characterized by a relatively high degree of inertia.

These specific properties, for credit-risk analysis, are useful to keep in mind. An important consequence of the second point, and the existence of an absorbing default state is that,

$$\lim_{t\to\infty} P^t \equiv \begin{bmatrix} 0 & 0 & \cdots & 1 \\ 0 & 0 & \cdots & 1 \\ \vdots & \vdots & \ddots & \vdots \\ 0 & 0 & \cdots & 1 \end{bmatrix}. \tag{3.1}$$

That is, eventually everyone defaults.[10] In practice, of course, this can take a very long time and, as a consequence, this property does not undermine the usefulness of the Markov chain for modelling credit-state transitions.

Discussing and analyzing actual transition matrices is a bit tricky given their significant dimension. Our generic transition matrix, $P \in \mathbb{R}^{21\times 21}$, has 441 individual elements. This does not translate into 441 model parameters, but it is close. The absorbing default state makes the final row redundant reducing the total parameter count to 420. The final column, which includes the default probabilities, is specified separately. This is discussed in the next section. This still leaves a dizzying 400 transition probability parameters to be determined.

How do we go about informing these 400 parameters? Despite seeming like an insurmountable task, the answer is simple. These values are borrowed, and appropriately transformed, from rating agency estimates.[11] The principal twist is that some logic is required, as previously discussed, to map the low-dimensional rating agency data into NIB's 21-notch scale. This important question, along with a

---

[9] We'll expand much more on these ideas in Chap. 7.

[10] Recall that for $t \in \mathbb{N}$, the $t$-period transition matrix is simply computed by raising the one-period transition matrix to the power of $t$; that is, $P^5$, is an example of the five-period transition matrix. This is, of course, predicated on the assumption that the credit-state process does indeed follow Markov-chain dynamics. Chapter 7 addresses this question in detail.

[11] Given adequate data, transition matrices can be readily estimated via the method of maximum likelihood; see Bolder [7, Chapter 9] for more details.

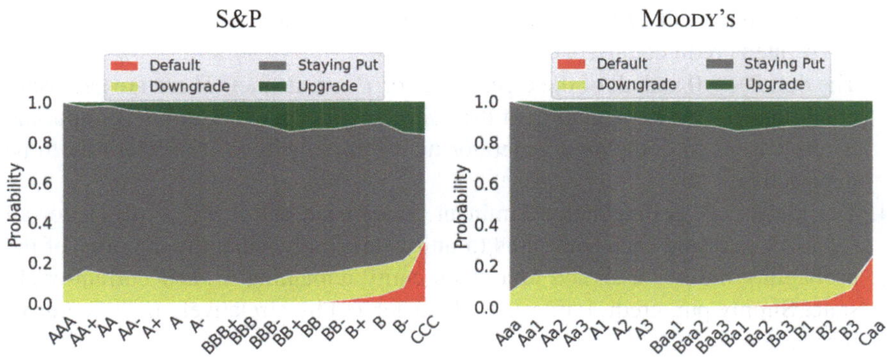


**Fig. 3.2** *A low-dimensional view*: This figure breaks out the long-term S&P and Moody's transition matrices into four categories: the probabilities of upgrade, downgrade, default, and staying put. This dramatically simplifies the matrices and permits a meaningful visual comparison.

number of other key points relating to default and transition properties, is relegated to Chap. 7.[12] In this parametric discussion, we will examine the basic statistical properties of these external transition matrices. In doing so, an effort will be made to verify, where appropriate, Kreinin and Sidelnikova [31]'s properties. We will also decide if there is any practical difference in employing S&P or Moody's transition probabilities.

Such a large collection of numbers does not really lend itself to conventional analysis. In such situations, it consequently makes sense to make an attempt at dimension reduction. For each rating category, over a given period of time, there are only four *logical* things that can happen: an entity can downgrade, upgrade, move into default, or stay the same. While there is only way to default or stay the same, there are typically many ways to upgrade or downgrade. If we sum over all of these potential outcomes, and stick with the four categories, the result is a simpler viewpoint. Figure 3.2 illustrates these *four* possibilities for each of the pertinent 18 S&P and Moody's credit ratings.

Figure 3.2 illustrates a number of interesting facts. First, far and away the most probable outcome is staying put. This underscores our fourth property; each transition matrix is diagonally dominant. As an additional point, the probability of downgrade increases steadily as we move down the credit spectrum. Downgrade remains nonetheless substantially more probable than default until all but the lowest credit-quality categories. Indeed, the probability of default is not even visible until we reach the lower five rungs on the credit scale. Interestingly, the probability of upgrade tends down as credit quality decreases, but it appears to be generally more flat than for downgrades. The final, and perhaps most important, conclusion is that there does not appear to be any important qualitative differences between the S&P

[12] This is such a big topic that it merits a separate discussion.

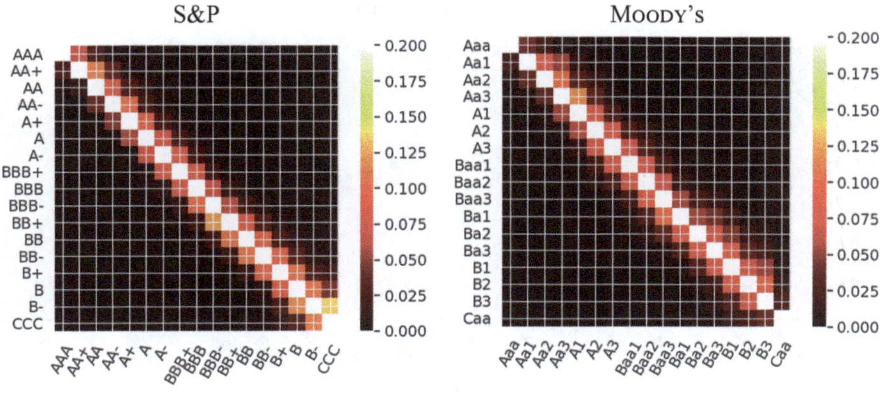


**Fig. 3.3** *The heat map*: This figure illustrates a colour-based visualization of our high-dimensional transition matrices. It includes the long-term S&P and Moody's estimates along our abbreviated 18-notch scale(s).

and Moody's transition-probability estimates. This does not immediately imply that there are no differences, but suggests broad similarity at this level of analysis.

Figure 3.3 employs the notion of a heat map to further illustrate the long-term one-year, corporate S&P and Moody's transition matrices. A heat map uses colours to represent the magnitude of the 400+ individual elements in both matrices; lighter colours indicate a high level of transition probability, whereas darker colours represent lower probabilities. The predominance of light colors across the diagonal of both heat maps underscores the strong degree of diagonal dominance in both estimates already highlighted in Fig. 3.2; indeed, most of the action is in the neighbourhood of the diagonal. Comparison of the right- and left-hand side graphics in Fig. 3.3 reveals that, visually at least, the two matrices seem to be quite similar. This is additional evidence suggesting that we need not be terribly concerned which of these two data sources is employed.

One final technical property needs to be considered. Figure 3.4 illustrates the $q$ eigenvalues associated with our S&P and Moody's transition matrices. All eigenvalues are comfortably positive, distinct, and less than or equal to unity. The eigenvalue structure of our two alternative transition-matrix estimates are quite similar. Moreover, the determinant of both matrices is a small positive number with condition numbers of less than 3.[13] All of these attributes—consistent with Kreinin and Sidelnikova [31]'s third property—can be interpreted in many ways when combined with the theory of Markov chains. For our purposes, however, we may conclude that $P$ is non-singular and can be used with both the matrix exponential and natural logarithm. These technical properties are not of immediate

[13] See Golub and Loan [17] for much more background on these matrix concepts.

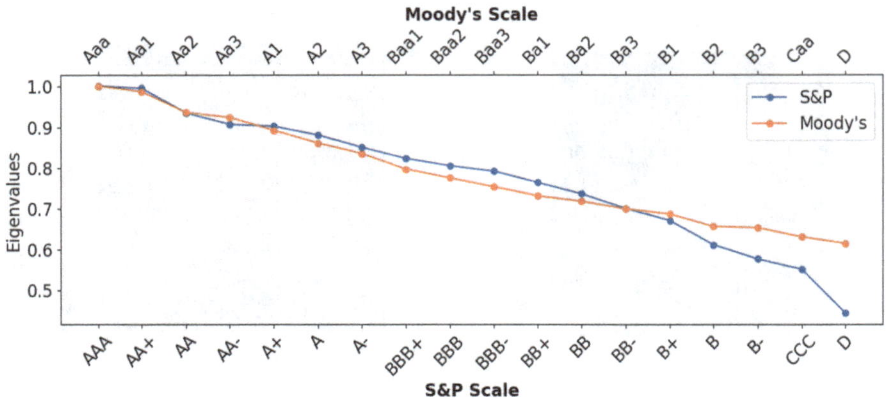


**Fig. 3.4** *Transition-probability eigenvalues*: This figure illustrates the $q$ eigenvalues associated with each of our S&P and Moody's transition matrices. All eigenvalues are positive, distinct, and less than one. Moreover, the eigenvalue structure of our two estimates is quite similar.

usefulness, but will prove very helpful in Chap. 7 when building forward-looking stress scenarios.

**Colour and Commentary 26** (THE TRANSITION MATRIX)*: Our t-threshold credit-risk economic capital model, as the name clearly indicates, requires the specification of a large number of default and migration* thresholds. *These are inferred from estimated transition probabilities, which are traditionally stored and organized in a transition matrix. A transition matrix is a wonderfully useful object, which has a number of important properties. The most central is the existence of a permanent absorbing default state that is accessible from all states. Despite all of its benefits, the transition matrix has one drawback: it includes a depressingly large number of parameters. With 20 (non-default) credit states, about 400 transition probabilities need to be determined. We, like (almost) all small lending institutions, simply do not have sufficient internal data to defensibly estimate these values. The solution is to look externally. Examination of comparable S&P and Moody's transition matrices happily reveals that both sources provide results that are qualitatively very similar. This supports our decision to adopt—subject to an appropriate transformation to our internal scale—the long-term, through-the-cycle transition probabilities published by S&P.*

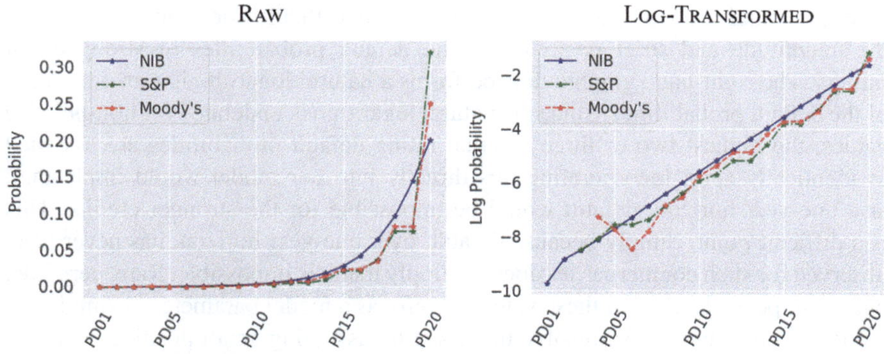


**Fig. 3.5** *Default probabilities*: The raw values in the left-hand graphic illustrate the exponentially increasing trend in default probabilities as we move down the credit spectrum. The right-hand graphic performs a natural logarithmic transformation of these values; its linear form verifies the exponential observation. Internal NIB values are compared to the implied S&P and Moody's estimates.

### 3.1.3 Default Probabilities

Default probabilities are quietly embedded in the final column of our transition matrix. For credit-risk economic-capital they play a starring role; their determination of the default threshold is tantamount to describing each obligor's distance to default. As a consequence, they merit special examination and attention. We have thus constructed a separate logical approach to their determination. This is an important distinction from the remaining transition probabilities, which are adopted (fairly) directly from external rating agency estimates.

Default is—at least, for investment-grade loans—a rather rare event. To this point, given their relatively small values, it is difficult for us to assess the default-probability assumptions embedded in our transition matrix. Indeed, they were hardly visible in Fig. 3.2. Figure 3.5 rectifies this situation with a close up of the S&P and Moody's default probabilities. Unlike our previous analysis, these 18 credit notches have been projected onto the 20-step NIB scale using the mapping logic from Table 3.1.[14] The right-hand graphic illustrates the raw values, which exhibit an exponentially increasing trend in default probabilities as we move down the credit spectrum. This is the classical form of default probabilities; each step out the credit-rating scale leads to a multiplicative increase in the likelihood of default.[15]

[14] The basic consequence is some overlapping of the speculative-grade default probabilities. We'll address this point in much more detail in Chap. 7.

[15] The credit-rating scale is thus highly non-linear in default probabilities. If it helps, you can think of it as being analogous to the famous Richter—or local magnitude—scale (classically) used by seismologists to measure the strength of earthquakes.

Exponential growth is tough to visualize. It is difficult, for example, to verify the magnitude and strict positivity of the default probabilities of strong credit ratings. The right-hand graphic thus performs a natural logarithmic transformation of the default probabilities. Since the natural logarithm is undefined for non-positive values, the highest two or three external rating default probabilities are assigned to identically zero. Incorporating this directly into our model would imply that, at a one-year horizon, default would be impossible for the stronger credits. This is a difficult point. Simply because default, over one-year horizon, has never been observed for such counterparties does *not* imply that it is impossible. Rare, certainly, but not impossible. Setting these values to zero, as a model parameter, is simply not a conservative choice. We resolve this issue by assigning small positive values to the first three default-probability classes.

How does this assignment occur? The data provides a helpful clue. If we divide each successive (non-zero) default probability by its adjacent value, we arrive at a constant ratio of roughly 1.5; in other words, the exponential growth factor is about 1.5. Extrapolating forwards and backwards using this trend yields the blue line in Fig. 3.5. This might seem a bit naive, but it actually yields values that are highly consistent with—and even slightly more conservative than–those produced by S&P and Moody's. The only exception is the final category, which is termed PD20. This corresponds to S&P's CCC and Moody's Caa, which is basically an amalgamation of lowest rungs in their credit scale. It is simply *not* representative of our lending business. For this reason, the PD20 default-probability value has been capped at 0.2. This is an example of using modelling judgement and business knowledge to tailor the results to one's specific circumstances.

**Colour and Commentary 27** (DEFAULT PROBABILITIES)*: Not all transition probabilities—from an economic-capital perspective, at least—are created equally. Default probabilities, used to determine the distance to default, play a disproportionately important role in our risk computations. Their central importance motivates a deviation from broad-based adoption of external credit-rating agency estimates. The set of default probabilities is determined by exploiting the empirical exponential form. Each subsequent rating is simply assumed to be a fixed multiplicative proportion of the previous value. Some additional complexity occurs at the end points. External rating agencies' estimates—due to lack of actual observations—imply* zero *(one-year) default probabilities for the highest credit-quality obligors. In the spirit of conservatism, we allocate small positive values—consistent with the multiplicative definition—to these rating classes. At the other end of the spectrum, the lowest rating category is simply* not *representative of the credit quality in our portfolio. Consequently, the 20th NIB default-probability estimate is capped at 0.2. The end product is a logically consistent, conservative, and firm-specific set of default-probability estimates.*

## 3.2 Systemic Factors

Although the assumption of default independence would dramatically simplify our computations, it is inconsistent with economic reality. A modelling alternative is an absolute necessity. The introduction of systemic factors is the mechanism used to induce default (and migration) correlation among the credit obligors in our portfolio. While conceptually clear and rather elegant, it immediately raises a number of practical questions. What should be the number and composition of these factors? How do we inform their dependence structure? What is the relative importance of the individual factors for a given credit obligor. All of these important queries need to be answered before the model can be implemented. This section addresses each in turn.

### *3.2.1 Factor Choice*

The systemic factors driving default correlation are—unlike many popular model implementations—assumed to be correlated. With orthogonal factors, it is possible to maintain a latent (or unobservable) form. This choice is unavailable in this setting. Since we ultimately need to estimate the cross correlations between these factors, it will be necessary to give them concrete identities. Our credit-risk economic-capital model thus includes a total of $J = 24$ systemic factors; these fall into industrial and regional (or geographic) categories. There are 11 industrial sectors and 13 geographic regions. The dependence structure between these individual factors is, as is often the case in practice, informed by analysis of equity index returns. This means that we require historical equity indices for each of our systemic factors; this constrains somewhat the choice.

Even within these constraints, there is a broad range of choice. Were you to place *five* people into a room and ask them to give their opinion on the correct set of systemic factors, you would likely get *five*, or more, opinions. The reason is simple; there is no one correct answer. On one hand, completeness argues for the largest possible factor set. Too many factors, however, will be difficult to manage. Judiciously managing the age-old trade-off between granularity and parsimony is *not* easy. It ultimately comes down to a consideration of the costs and benefits of including each systemic factor.

These specific sector systemic-factor choices are summarized in Table 3.2. Such an approach requires some kind of internal or external industrial taxonomy, which may, or may not, be specialized for one's purposes.[16] With one exception, our industrial classification is mapped to a rather high level. Paper and forest products, which can probably be best viewed as a sub-category of the material or industrial

[16] Many alternative industrial classifications are available.

**Table 3.2** *Industrial systemic factors*: This table summarizes the industrial systemic factors employed in our credit-risk economic-capital model implementation.

| # | Industry |
|---|---|
| 1 | Energy (oil and gas) |
| 2 | Materials |
| 3 | Paper and forest products |
| 4 | Industrials |
| 5 | Consumer discretionary |
| 6 | Consumer staples |
| 7 | Health care |
| 8 | Financials |
| 9 | Information technology |
| 10 | Telecommunication services |
| 11 | Utilities |

**Table 3.3** *Geographic systemic factors*: This table summarizes the various systemic factors associated with geographic regions employed in our credit-risk model implementation. Shaded regions represent NIB member countries.

| # | Region |
|---|---|
| 1 | Africa and Middle East |
| 2 | Baltics |
| 3 | Denmark |
| 4 | Developed Asia |
| 5 | Emerging Asia |
| 6 | Europe |
| 7 | Finland |
| 8 | Iceland |
| 9 | Latin America |
| 10 | New Europe |
| 11 | North America |
| 12 | Norway |
| 13 | Sweden |

groupings, is further broken out due to its importance to the Nordic region. This is another clear example of tuning the level of model granularity required for the analysis of one's specific problem.

Table 3.3 provides an visual overview of the set of 13 *geographic* systemic factors. A very broad or detailed partition along this dimension is possible, but the granularity is tailored to meet specific business needs. Roughly half of the regional systemic factors, as one would expect with our mandate-driven focus, fall into the Baltic and Nordic sectors. Europe is broken down into two main categories: Europe and new Europe. The latter category relates primarily to Eurozone ascension countries in central and eastern Europe. The remaining geographic factors split the globe into a handful of large, but typical, zones.

**Colour and Commentary 28** (NUMBER OF SYSTEMIC FACTORS)*: Selecting the proper set of systemic risk factors is not unlike putting together a list of invitees for a wedding. The longer the list, the greater the cost. Some people simply have to be there, some would be nice to have but are unnecessary, while others might actually cause problems. Finally, different people are likely to have diverging opinions. We have opted for 24 industrial and regional factors. This is a fairly large wedding, but it is hard to argue for a much smaller one. With one exception, the lowest level of granularity is used for the industrial classification. On the regional side, roughly one half of the factors relate to NIB member countries. The remaining geographic factors are important for liquidity investments on the treasury side of the business. While there is always scope for discussion and disagreement, from a business perspective, the majority of the selected systemic factors are necessary guests.*

### 3.2.2 Systemic-Factor Correlations

Having determined the identity of our systemic factors, we move to the central question of systemic-factor dependence. These so-called asset correlations are sadly *not* observable quantities. Default data can be informative in this regard.[17] We have elected to follow the well-accepted approach of informing asset correlation through a readily available proxy: equity prices. This is not a crazy idea. Equity prices, and more particularly returns, communicate information about the value of a firm. Cross correlations between movements in a given firm's value and other firm-value movements provide some insight into the question at hand. Moreover, a broad range of firm level, geographic, and industry equity return data is available.

The logical reasonableness of the link between asset and equity data, as well as its ready availability, should not lure us into believing that equity data does not have its faults. Equities are bought and sold in markets; these markets may react to general macroeconomic trends, supply and demand, and investor sentiment in ways *not* entirely consistent with asset-value dynamics. The inherent market-based interlinkages between individual equities will tend to overstate the true dependence at the firm level. By precisely how much, of course, is rather difficult to state with any degree of accuracy.[18] The granularity and dimensionality of the model construction, however, leaves us with no other obvious alternatives. It is nonetheless important to be frank and transparent about the quality of equity data as a proxy. In short, it is useful, available, and logically sensible, but far from perfect.

---

[17] See, for example, Bolder [7, Chapter 10] for an introduction to this area.

[18] This question has, however, been addressed in the academic literature. Frye [16], for example, finds evidence of overstatement of correlation associated with the use of equity correlations.

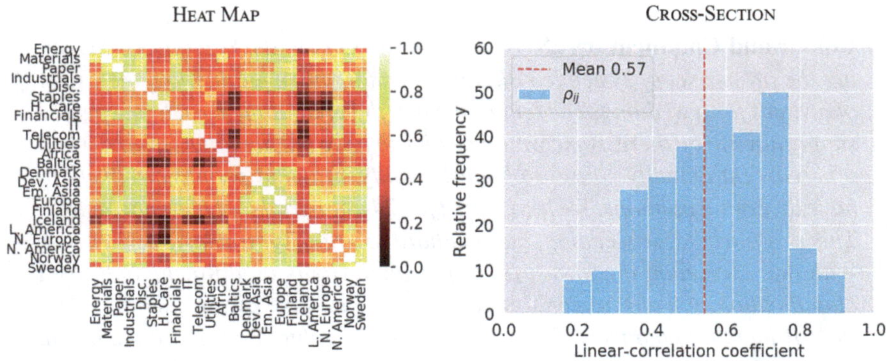


**Fig. 3.6** *(Linear) Systemic correlations*: This figure attempts to graphically illustrate the roughly 300 distinct pairwise estimated product-moment (or Pearson) correlation-coefficient outcomes associated with our system of $J = 24$ industrial and geographic systemic factors. The left-hand side provides a heat map of the correlation matrix, while the right-hand side focuses on the cross section.

Risk-factor correlations are thus proxied by equity returns; these returns are, practically, computed as logarithmic differences of equity indices. Armed with a matrix of equity returns, $X \in \mathbb{R}^{\tau \times J}$, where $\tau$ represents the number of collected equity return time periods, we may immediately write $S = \text{cov}(X) \in \mathbb{R}^{J \times J}$. Technically, it is straightforward to decompose our covariance matrix, $S$, as follows:

$$S = V \Omega V^T, \tag{3.2}$$

where $V \in \mathbb{R}^{J \times J}$ is a diagonal matrix collecting the individual volatility terms associated with each systemic factor and $\Omega \in \mathbb{R}^{J \times J}$ is a positive-definite, symmetric correlation matrix. $\tau$, for this analysis, is set to 240 months or 20 years of index data.

Analogous to the transition-matrix setting, it is not particularly informative to examine large-scale tables with literally hundreds of pairwise correlation estimates. Figure 3.6 attempts to gain visual insight into this question through another application—in the left-hand graphic—of a heat map. The lighter the shading of the colour in Fig. 3.6, the closer the correlation is to unity. This explains the light yellow—or almost white—stripe across the diagonal. The right-hand graphic examines the distribution of all (roughly 300) distinct off-diagonal elements.[19] Overall, the smallest pairwise correlation between two systemic factors is roughly 0.15, with the largest exceeding 0.90. The average lies between 0.5 and 0.6. This supports the general conclusion that there is a strong degree of positive correlation between the selected systemic factors.

[19] The precise number is $\frac{J \cdot (J-1)}{2} = \frac{24 \cdot 23}{2} = 276$.

This is hardly a surprising observation. All variables are equity indices, which have structural similarities due to typical co-movements of equity markets. The high concentration in the Nordic sector, with strong regional interdependencies, further complicates matters. Many institutions would gather together all Nordic and Baltic factors under the umbrella of a single European risk factor. NIB does not have this luxury. The granularity in this region can hardly be avoided if we desire to distinguish between member country contributions to economic capital—its centrality to our mission makes it a modelling necessity. Nevertheless, this is a highly positively correlated collection of random financial-market variables. It will be important to recall this fact when we turn to the question of systemic-factor loadings.

The next step involves examining the factor volatilities. Figure 3.7 illustrates the elements of our diagonal volatility matrix; each can be allocated to an individual equity return series. The average annualized return volatility is approximately 19%, which appears reasonable for equities. Consumer staples, health care and utilities—as one might expect—appear to have the most stable returns with volatility in the 10–15% range. On the upper end of the volatility scale, exceeding 20%, are paper-and-forest products and IT. Generally, deviations of the regional indices from the overall average level are relatively modest. The exception is Iceland with annualized equity return volatility of approximately 45%, which is approaching three times the average. This is certainly influenced by the relative small size of the Icelandic economy, its large financial sector, and Iceland's macroeconomic challenges in the period following the 2008 financial crisis.

A legitimate question, which will be addressed in the following sections, is whether or not we have any interest in the volatility of these systemic risk factors.

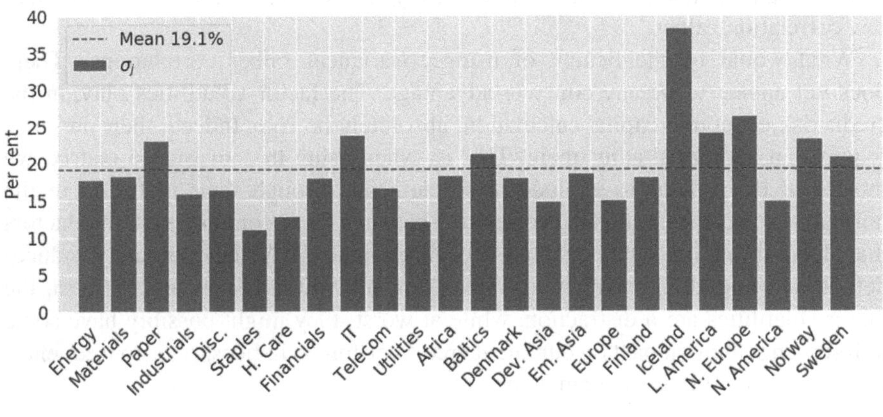


**Fig. 3.7** *Factor volatilities*: This figure illustrates the annualized-percentage factor (i.e., equity index return) volatility of each of the $J = 24$ industrial and geographic systemic factors. This information is only pertinent if we employ the covariance matrix rather than the correlation matrix for describing the systemic-risk factor dependence.

Equity return data is a convenient and sensible proxy for our systemic risk factors. In principle, however, this proxy seeks to inform the dependence between these factors, not their overall level of uncertainty. Volatility is centrally important in market-risk computations, but the threshold-model approach actually involves normalizing away these volatilities.

Outfitted with 20 years of monthly equity index data for 24 logically sensible geographical and industrial systemic-risk factors, a number of practical decisions still need to be taken. Indeed, one could summarize these decisions in the form of *three*, important, and interrelated questions:

1. Should we employ the covariance or correlation matrices to model the dependence structure of our systemic risk-factor system?
2. If we opt to use correlation, should we use the classical, product-moment Pearson correlation coefficient or the rank-based, Spearman measure?
3. Should we employ our full 20-year dataset or some sub-period?

While these are all pertinent questions that need answering, let us begin with the first question. This is more of a mathematical choice and, once answered, we may turn our attention of the latter *two* more empirical decisions.

### Which Matrix?

Should we employ a covariance or a correlation matrix? This might, to the reader, appear to be a rather odd question.[20] In principle, if managed properly, it should not really matter. Equation 3.2 illustrates, rather clearly, that the same information is found in both matrices. The only difference is scaling; covariances are adjusted, in a quadratic manner, for the factor volatility. The correlation matrix summarizes raw correlation values.

What would be the benefit of using covariances rather correlations? There does not appear to be any concrete advantage. The factor volatilities play, in the credit-risk economic-capital calculation, absolutely no role. Indeed, their presence requires an additional adjustment. That is, when using the covariance matrix, we must take extra pains to exclude these elements through their inclusion in the normalization constant. It is the correlation between these common systemic factors that bleeds through to our latent creditworthiness index, $\Delta X$, and ultimately, induces default and migration correlations among our individual risk owners. At best, the factor volatilities are a distraction, while at worst, they might possibly have some unforeseen scaling impact on our latent creditworthiness indices. As a consequence, we may as well eliminate them at the outset.

[20] In the spirit of full disclosure, the legacy implementation of the credit-risk economic capital model used covariance information. This question thus became a source of (friendly) internal debate.

Use of the covariance matrix may also confuse the interpretation of the factor-loading parameters. One would conceptually prefer that, in the final implementation, the factor loadings are *not* quietly being modified by the factor volatilities. Overall, the difference is not dramatic, but anything that simplifies our understanding of the model and the interpretation of model parameters—without undermining the basic requirements of the model—is difficult to argue against. For this reason, we have definitively elected to use the correlation matrix as the fundamental measure of systemic risk-factor dependence.

### Which Correlation Measure?

The classical notion of correlation, often referred to as the product-moment definition, is typically called Pearson correlation.[21] It basically compares, for a set of observations associated with two random variables, how each pair of joint outcomes deviates from their respective means. The classic construction, for two arbitrary random variables $X$ and $Y$, is described by the following familiar (and already employed) expression

$$\rho = \frac{\mathbb{E}\left(\left(X - \mathbb{E}(X)\right)\left(Y - \mathbb{E}(Y)\right)\right)}{\sqrt{\text{var}(X)\text{var}(Y)}}. \tag{3.3}$$

An alternative approach, termed rank correlation, approaches the computation in an alternative manner. The so-called Spearman's rank correlation is defined as

$$r = \frac{\mathbb{E}\left(\left(r(X) - \mathbb{E}(r(X))\right)\left(r(Y) - \mathbb{E}(r(Y))\right)\right)}{\sqrt{\text{var}(r(X))\text{var}(r(Y))}}, \tag{3.4}$$

where $r(\cdot)$ denotes the rank outcome of random variable.[22] Instead of comparing the distance of each observation from its mean, it compares the rank of each observation

[21] Named after Karl Pearson who—see, for example, Magnello [33]—has had a significant influence upon modern statistics.

[22] An unbiased estimator, for this rank-correlation quantity, is often written for a sample of size $N$ as,

$$r = 1 - \frac{6\sum_{k=1}^{N} d_k^2}{N(N^2 - 1)}, \tag{3.5}$$

where $d_k$ is the difference in rank between the $k$th pair of observations. Chambers [10] provides a proof of this result.

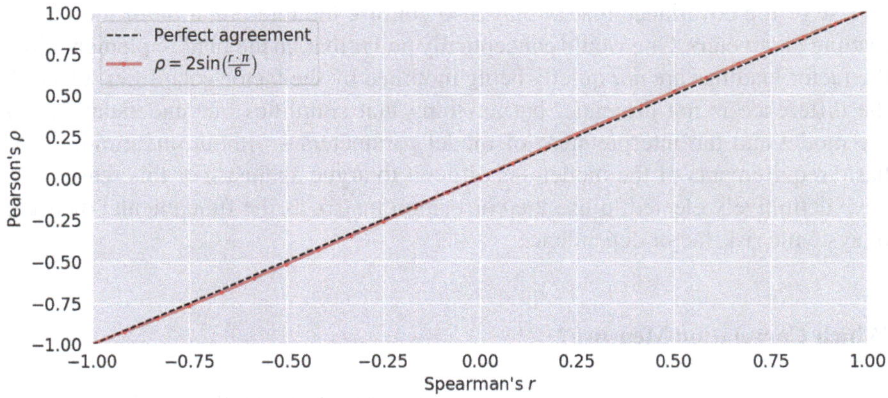


**Fig. 3.8** *Comparing Pearson's* $\rho$ *to Spearman's* $r$: The preceding figure examines, across the range of $-1$ to 1, the link between two notions of correlation for bivariate Gaussian data: Pearson's $\rho$ and Spearman's $r$. While they do not match perfectly, the differences are minute; consequently, imposition of Spearman's rank correlation—in a Gaussian setting—will imply a rather similar level of correlation relative to the typical Pearson definition. In non-Gaussian settings, the differences can be more important.

to the mean rank. It is thus basically an order-statistic version of the correlation coefficient.[23] Otherwise, Eqs. 3.3 and 3.4 are structurally identical.

Spearman's coefficient is popular due to its lower degree of sensitivity to outliers; broadly speaking, it has many parallels, in this regard, to the median. For relatively well-behaved random variables, there is only a modest amount of difference between the two measures. Indeed, for bivariate Gaussian random variates, the relationship between Spearman's $r$ and Pearson's $\rho$ is given as,[24]

$$r = \frac{6}{\pi}\arcsin\left(\frac{\rho}{2}\right), \tag{3.6}$$

which directly implies that

$$\rho = 2\sin\left(\frac{r\pi}{6}\right). \tag{3.7}$$

This may appear to be a complicated relationship, but practically, over the domain of the coefficients, $[-1, 1]$, there is not much difference. Figure 3.8 provides a graphical perspective on Eq. 3.7. While they do not match perfectly, the differences are minute; consequently, imposition of Spearman's rank correlation—in a Gaussian

---

[23] Analogous to the difference between the mean and the median or the volatility and the inter-quartile range.

[24] See McNeil et al. [34, Theorem 7.42] for a proof of this result; these ideas are also explored in Kendall and Stuart [29, Chapter 31].

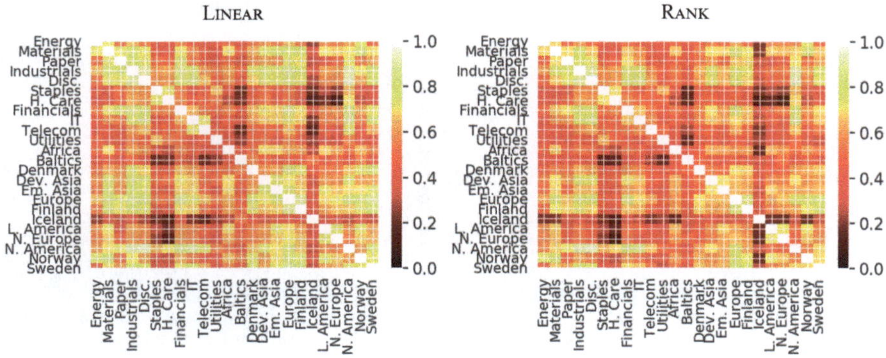


**Fig. 3.9** *Competing heat maps*: The preceding heat maps compare the roughly 300 pairwise linear and rank correlation coefficients across our 24 separate systemic risk variables. There is little in the way of qualitative difference between the two measures, but due to their lower sensitivity to outliers, the rank correlation coefficients are slightly lower than their linear compatriots.

setting—will imply an extremely similar level of correlation along the typical Pearson definition. The point of this discussion is to indicate that the decision to use rank or product-moment correlation, in a Gaussian setting, is more a logical than an empirical choice. In a non-Gaussian setting, however, differences can be more important. It becomes particularly pertinent—as is common in financial-market data—in the presence of large, and potentially, distorting outlier observations.

Figure 3.9 provides two heat maps comparing the roughly 300 pairwise linear and rank correlation coefficients across our 24 separate systemic risk variables. While there is little in the way of qualitative difference between the two measures, due to their lower sensitivity to outliers, the rank correlation coefficients are slightly lower than their linear compatriots. The rank correlation coefficients have distinctly, albeit not dramatically, more darker colour in their heat map. Both figures are computed using 20 years of monthly equity return data; this leads to a total of 240 observations for each pairwise correlation estimate. The first twenty years of the twenty-first century have not been, from a financial perspective at least, particularly calm. Equity markets have experienced a number of rather extreme events during this period. The rank correlation will capture these extremes, but in a less dramatic way, given the relative stability of the rank of return relative to its level. This stability property is rather appealing.

We wish these crisis periods to have an impact on the final results, but not to potentially dominate them. To judge this question, however, we need a bit more information than is found in Fig. 3.9. Figure 3.10 accordingly attempts to help by examining the cross section of off-diagonal elements of $\Omega$. The centres of these two cross-section correlation-coefficient distribution are rather close: in the linear case it is 0.57 and 0.52 in the rank setting. The range of correlation values are qualitatively quite similar, spanning the values of about 0.1 to 0.9. There is, however, a slight difference. The cross section of rank correlation coefficients appears to be somewhat more symmetric than with the linear estimates. Both sets of values lean

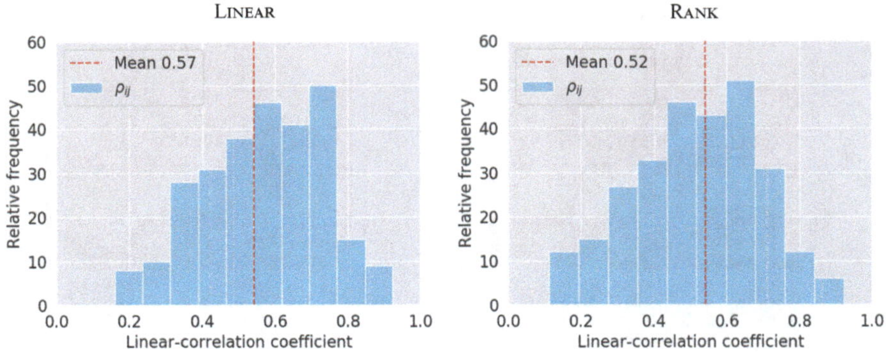


**Fig. 3.10** *Competing cross sections*: This figure illustrates, again for linear and rank dependence measures, the cross section of pairwise correlation coefficients. On average, the rank correlation is about 0.05 less than the linear metric. Visually, however, relatively little separates these two estimators.

somewhat towards the upside of the unit interval, but the rank correlation graphic is less extreme.[25] This is, in fact, exactly how the rank correlation is advertised.

There does not appear to be an unequivocally correct choice. The product-moment definition of correlation allows the extremes to exert more influence on the final results; as a risk manager, this has some value, because crisis episodes receive a larger weight. The rank correlation approach—like its sister measure, the median—attempts to generate a more balanced view of dependence. The lower impact of data outliers—typically, in this case, stemming from crisis outcomes—implies slightly lower and more symmetric correlation estimates. We seek, in our economic-capital estimates, to construct a long-term, unconditional estimate of risk consumption.[26] With this in mind, given the preceding conclusions, we have a preference for the rank correlation.

There are also more technical arguments. Both correlation matrices, as previously indicated, exhibit a significant number of individual correlation coefficient entries exceeding 0.75. Such a highly correlated system is often referred to as multi-collinear.[27] If we were using this system to estimate a set of statistical parameters, this could potentially pose serious problems. Although this is not our specific application of $\Omega$, even a slight dampening of the high level of correlations implies a greater numerical distinction between our $J = 24$ individual systemic risk factors. Many models, after all, impose orthogonality on their systemic state variables to avoid such issues. On this dimension, therefore, we also have a slight preference for the rank-correlation measure.

[25] To be more precise, about one quarter of the linear correlation figures exceed 0.70, while this percentage is closer to 13% in the rank case.

[26] This is, as previously mentioned, often referred to as the through-the-cycle approach.

[27] See Judge et al. [27, Chapter 22] for much more on this topic.

**Colour and Commentary 29** (FLAVOUR OF CORRELATION): *Correlation refers to the interdependence between a pair of random variables. There are a variety of ways that it might be practically measured. Two well-known alternatives are the product-moment and rank correlation coefficients. Although they attempt to address the same question, they approach the problem from different angles. Since we find ourselves in the business of computing a large number of pairwise systemic-factor correlations, this distinction is quite relevant for us. On the basis of lower sensitivity to extreme events, greater cross-sectional symmetry, and a modest dampening of the highly collinear nature of our systemic risk-factor system, we have opted to employ the rank-correlation measure to estimate systemic-factor correlations. In the current analysis, the difference is relatively small. Moreover, nothing suggests that these two measures will deviate dramatically in the future. Our choice is thus based upon the perceived conceptual superiority of the rank-correlation measure.*

### What Time Period?

There are two time-related extremes to be considered in the measurement of risk: long-term unconditional and short-term conditional. A virtual infinity of possible alternatives exists for a spectrum between these two endpoints. Following basic regulatory principles, an economic-capital model is a long-term, unconditional, through-the-cycle risk estimator. This implies that a relatively lengthy time period should be employed for the estimation of our systemic risk-factor correlations. While helpful to understand this choice, it does not entirely answer our question. We have managed to source 20 years of monthly equity time-series data for each of our $J = 24$ systemic risk factors. Should we use it all, or should we employ some subset of this data? A 10-, 15-, or 20-year period would still be consistent, at least in principle, with through-the-cycle estimation.

Figure 3.11 illustrates, one final time, two rank correlation heat maps for our $J = 24$ systemic risk factors. The only distinction between the two heat maps is that they are estimated using varying time periods. The 10-year values are based on the months from January 2010 to December 2019, while the 20-year period utilizes the 240 monthly observations from January 2000 to December 2019. On a superficial level, the colour patterns in the two heat maps look highly similar. The 20-year estimates, however, look to be, on average, a bit lighter. This implies higher levels of correlation, which is not terribly surprising, given that the longer period incorporates the most severe parts of the great financial crisis. There is general agreement that

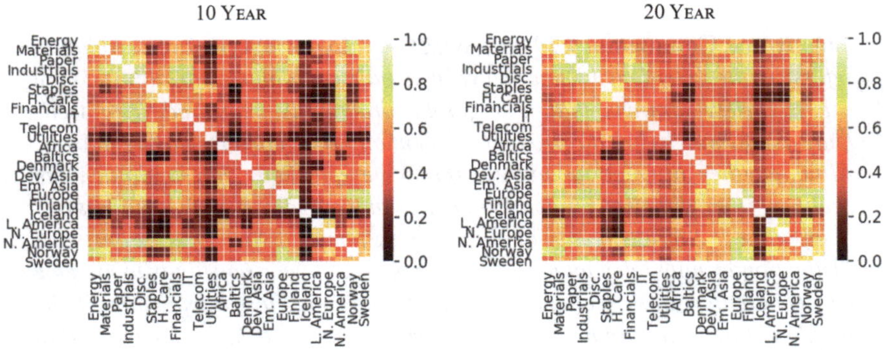


**Fig. 3.11** *Time-indexed heat maps*: These heat maps compare the roughly 300 pairwise *rank* correlation coefficients—over the last 10 and 20 years working backwards from December 2019—across our 24 separate systemic risk variables. The most recent 10-year period appears structurally similar, but exhibits significantly lower levels of correlation than the associated 20-year time horizon.

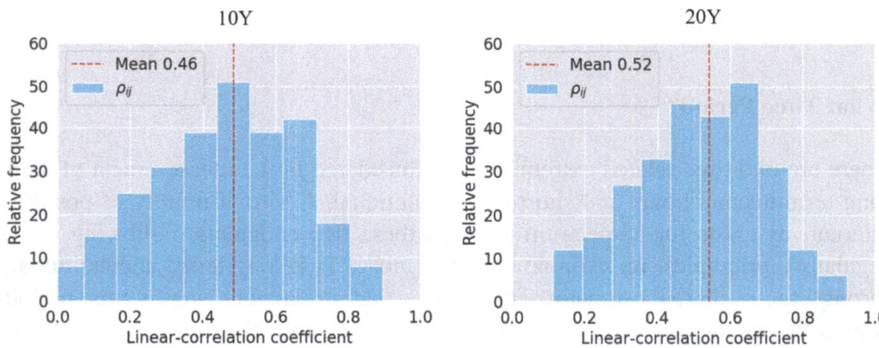


**Fig. 3.12** *Time-indexed cross sections*: This figure illustrates, again using the rank dependence measure, the cross section of pairwise correlation coefficients over the 10- and 20-year periods working backwards from December 2019, respectively. Both the location and dispersion the two cross sections appear to differ; the last 10-year period exhibits generally lower levels of systemic-risk factor dependence.

financial-variable correlations tend to trend higher—thereby reducing the value of diversification—during periods of turmoil.[28]

Figure 3.12 illustrates, again using only the rank dependence measure, the cross section of pairwise (rank) correlation coefficients over our 10- and 20-year periods, respectively. Average correlation, as we've seen before, is roughly 0.52 over the full 20-year period. It falls to 0.46 when examining only the last 10 years. We further observe that both the location and dispersion of the two cross sections appear to

[28] See Chesnay and Jondeau [12] and Sandoval and Franca [37] for a detailed analysis of this phenomenon.

differ; the most recent 10-year period exhibits generally lower levels of systemic-risk factor dependence.

Few logical arguments speak for the preference of the 20-year period, relative to the shorter 10-year time span, other than conservatism. Either time interval fulfils the basic requirements of a through-the-cycle risk estimator. A 20-year period could, of course, be considered more appropriate for a long-term unconditional correlation estimate. More importantly, the full 20-year period includes a broader range of equity return outcomes—including the great financial crisis—and consequently generates slightly more conservative estimates. For this reason, the decision is to use the full 20-year period and, over time, simply continue to add to the existing dataset. Each year, this decision on the overall span of data is revisited to ensure both representativeness and consistency with our economic-capital objectives.

**Colour and Commentary 30** (LENGTH OF PARAMETER-ESTIMATION HORIZON)*: When estimating parameters for a long-term through-the-cycle perspective, we would theoretically prefer the longest possible collection of historical time series. Such a dataset is likely to permit an average of the greatest possible number of observed business cycles. There are two catches. First, pulling together such a dataset can be both difficult and expensive. Second, even if you succeed, there are dangers in going far back in time. Too far into the past and—due to structural changes in economic relationships—the data may not be representative of current conditions. This forces the analyst into an awkward dance: the through-the-cycle requires lengthy data history, but not too long. Our approach is, where available, to start with a roughly 20-year time horizon. We then work with this data and carefully examine various sub-periods to understand the implications of different choices. Endeavouring to find conservative and defensible parameters, an appropriate horizon is ultimately selected.*

### *3.2.3 Distinguishing Systemic Weights and Factor Loadings*

Systemic-factor weights and loading parameters, while related, are asking *two* slightly different questions. The systemic weight attempts to answer the following query:

> How important is the overall systemic component, in the determination of the creditworthiness index, relative to the idiosyncratic dimension?

The systemic weight is, following from this point, simply a number between zero and one. These are the parameter values, $\{\alpha_1, \ldots, \alpha_I\}$, introduced in Chap. 2. A value of zero, for a given credit obligor, suggests that only idiosyncratic risk matters for determination of its migration and default risk outcomes. Were this to apply to all credit counterparties, we would, in essence, have an independent-default model. On the other hand, a systemic weight of unity places all of the importance on the systemic factor. Gordy [18]'s asymptotic single-risk factor model is an example of an approach that implies the presence of only systemic risk.[29] A defensible position, of course, lies somewhere in between these two extremes.

Factor loadings focus on a different, but again related, dimension. They seek to answer the following question:

> How important is each of the $J$ individual systemic risk factors—again, for the calculation of the creditworthiness index—to a given credit obligor?

Factor loadings, for a given counterparty, are thus not, as in the systemic-weight case, a single value, but rather a vector in $\mathbb{R}^J$. Let's continue to refer to each of these vectors as $\beta_i \in \mathbb{R}^{1\times J}$ for the $i$th credit counterpart; this allows us to consistently write the entire matrix of factor loadings as,

$$\beta = \begin{bmatrix} \beta_1 \\ \beta_2 \\ \vdots \\ \beta_I \end{bmatrix} \in \mathbb{R}^{I\times J}. \tag{3.8}$$

Such a constellation of parameters, for each $i = 1, \ldots, I$, implies a potentially very rich mathematical structure. With $J = 24$ and $I \approx 600$, our $\beta$ factor loading matrix contains almost 15,000 individual entries. Such flexibility can offer benefits, but it may also dramatically complicate matters.

The structure of each $\beta_i$ essentially creates a linear combination of our $J$ risk factors to act as the systemic contribution for that obligor. Let's consider a few extreme cases, since they might provide a bit of insight. Imagine that each $\beta_i$ was constant—however, one might desire to define it—across all counterparties. The consequence would be, in fact, a single-factor model. We could easily, in this case, simply replace our $J$ factors with a single linear combination of these variables. Each pair of obligors in the model would thus have a common level of factor-, asset-, and default correlation. Such an approach would, of course, undermine the whole idea of introducing a collection of $J$ systemic variables.

At the opposite end of the spectrum, one could assign distinctly different non-zero values to each of the roughly 15,000 elements in $\beta$. The implication—setting aside the practical difficulties of such an undertaking for the moment—is that each obligor's systemic contribution would be a unique linear combination of our $J$ systemic variables. Given two obligors, $i$ and $j$, the vectors $\beta_i$ and $\beta_j$ would play a central role in determining their level of default correlation. Indeed, this latter point holds in a general sense.

---

[29] This limiting case can only be attained with some mathematical caution. Naively setting all systemic weights to one in the multivariate $t$-threshold model yields, as one might expect, fairly nonsensical results.

Once again, an appropriate response to this challenge certainly lies somewhere between these two extreme ends of the spectrum. The actual estimation of the factor loadings and systemic weights should also be informed, in principle, by empirical data. A significant distinction between the factor loadings and systemic weights is that the former possesses dramatically greater dimensionality. The specific data that one employs and, perhaps equally importantly, how the structure of these parameters are organized are important questions. The following sections outline our choices, and the related thought processes, in both of these related areas.

### 3.2.4 Systemic-Factor Loadings

Let us begin with the factor loadings; these values are—algebraically speaking—closer to the actual systemic factor. Determination of our factor loadings will, as a consequence, turn out to be rather important in the specification of the systemic weights. As indicated, each $\beta_i$ vector determines the relative weight of the individual systemic factors in the creditworthiness of the $i$th distinct credit obligor. Some procedure is required to determine the magnitude of each $\beta_{ij}$ parameter for $i = 1, \ldots, I$ and $j = 1, \ldots, J$.

#### Some Key Principles

When beginning any modelling effort, it is almost invariably useful to give some thought to one's desired conceptual structure. In this case, there is a potentially enormous number of parameters involved, which will create problems of dimensionality and, more practically, statistical identification. Some direction would be helpful. A bit of reflection reveals a few logical principles that we might wish to impose upon this problem:

1. *Obligors with the same sectoral and geographical profiles should share the same loadings onto the systemic factors.* If this did not hold, it would be very difficult, or even impossible, to interpret and communicate the results.[30]
2. *A given obligor should load* only *onto those sectoral and geographical factors to which it is directly exposed.* The correlation matrix, $\Omega$, describes the dependence structure of the underlying equity return factors. As a consequence, the interaction between the factors is already captured. If an obligor then proceeds to load onto all factors, untangling the dependence relationships would become rather messy. This principle can thus inform sensible parameter restrictions.

[30] These obligors, of course, will naturally differ along the idiosyncratic dimension.

3. *Factor loadings should be both positive and restricted to the unit interval.* There is no mathematical or statistical justification for this principle; it stems solely from a desire to enhance our ability to interpret and communicate these choices.
4. *A minimal number of systemic factors should be targeted; this is the principal of model parsimony.* Not only does this facilitate implementation—in terms of dimensionality and computational complexity—but it also minimizes problems associated with collinearity.
5. *To the extent possible, the factor loadings should be informed by empirical data.* Since asset returns are not, strictly speaking, observable, it is necessary to identify a sensible proxy. Moreover, the previous principles may restrict the *goodness of fit* to this proxy data. Nonetheless, this would form an important anchor for the estimates.

While each of these principles make logical sense, nothing suggests that all can be simultaneously achieved. It may be the case, for example, that some of these principles are mutually exclusive.

### A Loading Estimation Approach

The structure of the threshold model provides clear insights into a possible estimation procedure for the factor loadings. In particular, for a given obligor $i$, we have that

$$\beta_i \Delta z = \sum_{j=1}^{J} \beta_{ij} \Delta z_j, \tag{3.9}$$

where $\Delta z \in \mathbb{R}^{J\times 1}$. The right-hand side of Eq. 3.9 clearly illustrates the fact that each column of the $\beta_i$ row vector is a linear weight upon the systemic factors. Imagine that we could identify $K$ individual equities with similar properties. That is, stemming from the same geographic region, operating in the same region, and possessing similar overall size. Given $T$ return observations of the $k$th equity—corresponding to the equivalent time periods for our systemic factors—we could construct the following equation:

$$r_{kt} = \sum_{j=1}^{J} \beta_{ijk} \Delta z_{jt} + \epsilon_{kt}, \tag{3.10}$$

for $t = 1, \ldots, \tau$ and $k = 1, \ldots, K$ and where $r_{kt}$ is the $t$-period return of the $k$th equity in our collection. This is, of course, an ordinary least squares (OLS) problem.[31] In this setting, the $\beta$'s simply reduce to regression coefficients. Further

[31] Note, however, that the typical intercept value has been excluded.

inspection of Eq. 3.10 reveals a certain logic; the return of the $k$th equity is written as a linear combination of the set of systemic factors plus an idiosyncratic component. This is rather close to what we seek. Again, this amounts to using equity behaviour to estimate asset returns.

Equation 3.10, while logically promising, is not without problems. First of all, there are $K$ equities in each category. The natural consequence is thus $K \times J$ individual factor-loading estimates. One could presumably solve this problem by taking an average—basically integrating out the $K$ dimension—of the individual $\hat{\beta}_{ijk}$ parameters over each $j$ in $J$.

The second problem, however, is dimensionality. Use of Eq. 3.10 implies a separate weight on each of the $J$ systemic risk factors. Such a complex structure is not easy to interpret. The larger number of parameters also raises issues of parameter robustness. Estimating $J = 24$ separate parameters with perhaps 10 or 20 years of monthly data is certainly possible, but the sheer number of regression coefficients, the high degree of collinearity between the systemic-risk explanatory variables, and the necessity of averaging estimates collectively represent significant estimation challenges. Computing standard errors is not easy is such a setting and, more importantly, they are unlikely to be entirely trustworthy.

A third problem, making matters even worse, is the fact that nothing in the OLS framework hinders individual $\beta_{ij}$ values from taking negative values further complicating clarification. Some additional normalization is possible to force positivity, of course, but this only adds to the overall complexity and adds an *ad hoc*, and difficult-to-justify, element to the estimation procedure.

There are, therefore, at least *three* separate problems: averaging, dimensionality, and non-positivity. Some of these problems can be mitigated with clever tricks, but the point is that estimating factor-loading coefficients—even with strong simplifying assumptions—is fraught with practical headaches. The results are neither particularly robust nor satisfying. We will, in a few short sections, find ourselves in a similar situation with regard to the systemic weights. In this case the complexity and dimensionality is unavoidable, which argues for maximal simplicity.

### A Simplifying Assumption

These sensible reasons to strongly restrict systemic-factor loadings lead to the fairly reasonable question: should we even formally estimate these parameters? One might simply load—for these non public-sector cases—equally onto each obligor's geographic and industrial systemic factors. The consequence of this legitimate reflection is the following extremely straightforward set of factor-loading coefficients:

- only a credit entity's geographic and industrial factor loadings are non-zero;
- each non-zero factor loading is set to 0.5; and
- the only exception is a weight of unity on a public-sector counterpart's geographic loading.

The consequence is a sparse $\beta$-matrix entirely populated with non-estimated parameters.[32] This approach allows us to fulfil four of our five previously highlighted principles. It controls the number of parameters, creates consistency, ensures positivity, and dramatically aids interpretability. The only shortcoming is that the parameter values are not informed by empirical data. This would appear to be the price to be paid for the attainment of the other points.

There is another constructive way to think about this important simplifying assumption. The systemic risk-factor correlation matrix, $\Omega$, possesses a certain dependence structure. The choice of factor loadings further combines our systemic factors to establish some additional variation of obligor-level correlations. There are, however, many possible combinations of factor-loading parameters that achieve basically the same set of results. In a statistical setting, such a situation is referred to as overidentification.[33] To simplify this fancy term, we can imagine a situation of trying to solve two equations in three unknowns. The problem is not it cannot be solved, but rather the existence of an infinity of possible solutions. Resolving such a situation typically requires restricting it somewhat through the imposition of some kind of constraint.[34] The current set of non-estimated factor loadings can thus be thought of as a collection of constraints, or over-identifying restrictions, used to permit a sensible model specification.

> **Colour and Commentary 31** (FACTOR-LOADING CHOICES): *Having established a set of five key principles for the specification of factor-loading parameters, a number of potential estimation options are found wanting. They require averaging, lead to relatively high degrees of dimensionality, and pose difficulties for statistical inference. Dimension reduction and normalization solve some of these problems, but this leads to relatively small degrees of (economic) variation between individual obligors. Ultimately, therefore, we have decided to employ a simple set of rules for the specification of the factor-loading parameters. This choice fulfils all of our principles, save one: the desire to empirically estimating our factor-loading values. This choice was not taken lightly and can, conceptually, be viewed as a set of overidentifying restrictions upon the usage of our collection of systemic risk factors.*

### Normalization

Introduction of correlated systemic factors, without some adjustment, will distort the variance structure of our collection of latent creditworthiness state variables. Unit variance of these threshold state variables is necessary for the straightforward

---

[32] With $J = 24$, only about $\frac{1}{12}$th of $\beta$'s elements is non-zero.

[33] See Judge et al. [27, Chapter 7] for more information on the notion of identification.

[34] Such a process can also be termed regularization.

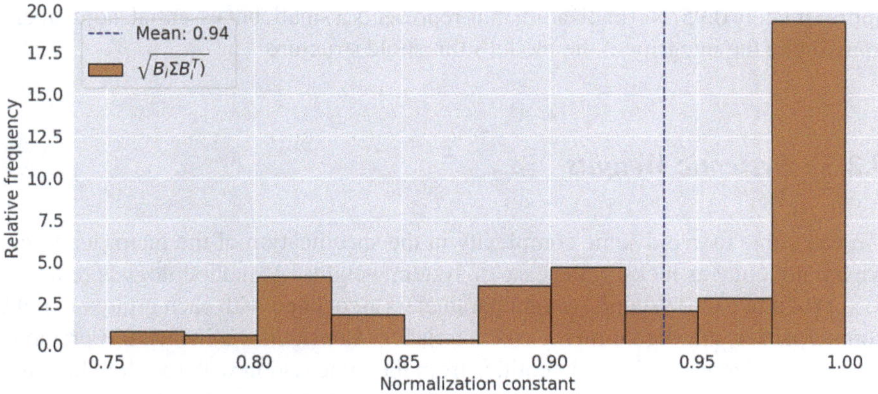


**Fig. 3.13** *Normalization constants*: Since the introduction of factor loadings distorts the variance of the systemic risk factors, it is necessary to perform a normalization to preserve unit variance. This graphic provides an illustration of the resulting normalization constants.

determination of default and migration events. A small correction is consequently necessary to preserve this important property of each systemic random observation. Mathematically, the task is relatively simple. For the $i$th risk obligor, the contribution of the systemic component—abstracting, for now, from the systemic-weight parameter—is given as,

$$\mathrm{B}_i = \frac{\beta_i}{\sqrt{\beta_i \Omega \beta_i^T}}, \tag{3.11}$$

where $\beta_i \in \mathbb{R}^{1\times J}$ is the $i$th row of the $\beta \in \mathbb{R}^{I\times J}$ matrix.[35]

The definition in Eq. 3.11 was already introduced in Chap. 2. Equipped with our factor correlations and loading choices, it is interesting to examine the magnitude of these normalization constants (i.e., the denominator of Eq. 3.11). Figure 3.13 displays the range of these values—for an arbitrary date in 2020—used to ensure that the systemic component has unit variance. The impact is rather a gentle. The span of adjustment factors ranges from roughly 0.75 to one; the average value is

[35] The effectiveness of this normalization is readily verified:

$$\mathrm{var}\left(\mathrm{B}_i \Delta z\right) = \mathrm{var}\left(\frac{\beta_i}{\sqrt{\beta_i \Omega \beta_i^T}} \Delta z\right) = \left(\frac{1}{\sqrt{\beta_i \Omega \beta_i^T}}\right)^2 \beta_i \, \mathrm{var}\left(\Delta z\right) \beta_i^T = \frac{\beta_i \overbrace{\cancel{\mathrm{var}\left(\Delta z\right)}}^{\Omega} \beta_i^T}{\cancel{\beta_i \Omega \beta_i^T}} = 1. \tag{3.12}$$

approximately 0.95. Normalization thus represents a small, but essential, adjustment to maintain the integrity of the model's threshold structure.

### 3.2.5 Systemic Weights

We were able to avoid some complexity in the specification of the factor loadings; we are not quite as lucky in the case of system weights. A methodology is required to approximate the systemic-weight parameters associated with each group of credit counterparties sharing common characteristics. Consider, similar to the previous setting, a collection of $N$ credit entities from the same region with roughly the same total amount of assets (i.e., firm size) and the same industry classification. Let us begin with a proposition. Imagine that the following identity holds:

$$\alpha_N^2 \equiv \frac{1}{\frac{1}{2}N(N-1)} \underbrace{\sum_{n=1}^{N}\sum_{m=1}^{N}}_{n\neq m, m<n} \text{corr}\left(\Delta X_n, \Delta X_m\right). \tag{3.13}$$

What does this mean? First, we are assuming that each the $N$ individual obligors in this sub-category have a common systemic weight, $\alpha_N$. The proposition holds that a reasonable estimator for $\alpha_N$ is the average correlation between these $N$ assets. There are, of course, $N^2$ possible pairwise combinations of these $N$ entities. If we subtract the $N$ diagonal elements, this yields $N(N-1)$ combinations. Only half of these elements, of course, are unique. We need only examine the lower off-diagonal elements, which explains the conditions on the double sum and the $\frac{1}{2}$ in the denominator of the constant.

Under what conditions is Eq. 3.13 true? This requires a bit of tedious algebra and a few observations. First, the expected value of each $\Delta X_n$ and $\Delta X_m$ is, by construction, equal to zero for all $n, m = 1, \ldots, N$. Second, the idiosyncratic factors, $\{\Delta w_n; n = 1, \ldots, N\}$ are independent of all of the systemic factors; the expectation of the product of any idiosyncratic and systemic factor will thus vanish. Finally, we recall that only two factor loadings, as highlighted in previous discussion, are non-zero. These final happy facts eliminate many terms from our development.

Let's begin with the correlation term in the double sum of our identity from Eq. 3.13 and see how it might be simplified. Working from first principles, we have

$$\begin{aligned}\text{corr}\left(\Delta X_n, \Delta X_m\right) \\ &= \frac{\mathbb{E}\left(\left(\Delta X_n - \overbrace{\mathbb{E}(\Delta X_n)}^{=0}\right)\left(\Delta X_m - \overbrace{\mathbb{E}(\Delta X_m)}^{=0}\right)\right)}{\underbrace{\sqrt{\text{var}(\Delta X_n)}}_{=1}\underbrace{\sqrt{\text{var}(\Delta X_m)}}_{=1}}, \end{aligned} \tag{3.14}$$

$$
\begin{aligned}
&= \mathbb{E}\left(\Delta X_n \cdot \Delta X_m\right), \\
&= \underbrace{\mathbb{E}\left(\left(\alpha_N \sum_{j=1}^{J} \mathrm{B}_{nj}\Delta z_j + \sqrt{1-\alpha_N^2}\Delta w_n\right)\left(\alpha_N \sum_{j=1}^{J} \mathrm{B}_{mj}\Delta z_j + \sqrt{1-\alpha_N^2}\Delta w_m\right)\right)}_{\text{Because of common characteristics, they share a common } \alpha_N}, \\
&= \mathbb{E}\left(\left(\alpha_N \sum_{j=1}^{J} \mathrm{B}_{nj}\Delta z_j\right)\left(\alpha_N \sum_{j=1}^{J} \mathrm{B}_{mj}\Delta z_j\right)\right), \\
&= \alpha_N^2 \underbrace{\mathbb{E}\left(\left(\mathrm{B}_{I_n}\Delta z_{I_n} + \mathrm{B}_{G_n}\Delta z_{G_n}\right)\left(\mathrm{B}_{I_m}\Delta z_{I_m} + \mathrm{B}_{G_m}\Delta z_{G_m}\right)\right)}_{=1?},
\end{aligned}
$$

where $I_k$ and $G_k$ denote the industrial and geographic loading from the $k$th equity series, respectively. We now have a clearer idea of the condition required to establish our identity in Eq. 3.13. If the expectation equates to unity, then the identity holds. In this case, the double sum yields the same value as the denominator in the constant preceding the sum. These terms cancel one another out establishing equality between the left- and right-hand sides indicating that our proposition holds.

Under what conditions does the expectation in Eq. 3.14 reduce to one? It turns out that the collection of $N$ equity series needs to share the same industrial *and* geographic factors (and factor loadings). In other words, the factor correlations among the $N$ members of our dataset must be identical. Practically, this means that $\mathrm{B}_{I_m} = \mathrm{B}_{I_n}$ and $\mathrm{B}_{G_m} = \mathrm{B}_{G_n}$.[36] In this case, we have that

$$
\begin{aligned}
\operatorname{corr}(\Delta X_n, \Delta X_m) &= \mathbb{E}\left(\left(\mathrm{B}_{I_n}\Delta z_{I_n} + \mathrm{B}_{G_n}\Delta z_{G_n}\right)^2\right), \qquad (3.15)\\
&= \operatorname{var}\left(\mathrm{B}_{I_n}\Delta z_{I_n} + \mathrm{B}_{G_n}\Delta z_{G_n}\right), \\
&= \operatorname{var}\left(\mathrm{B}_n \Delta z\right), \\
&= 1,
\end{aligned}
$$

by construction from Eq. 3.12. Naturally, this choice of estimation is applied under the assumption that the model actually holds.

The consequence of this development is that if we organize our estimation categories into a grid with each square sharing a common industrial and geographic systemic factor, then Eq. 3.13 will provide a reasonable estimate of the equity-

[36] We also naturally require that $\Delta z_{I_m} = \Delta z_{I_n}$, and $\Delta z_{G_m} = \Delta z_{G_n}$, but this happens naturally if the region and industrial classifications coincide.

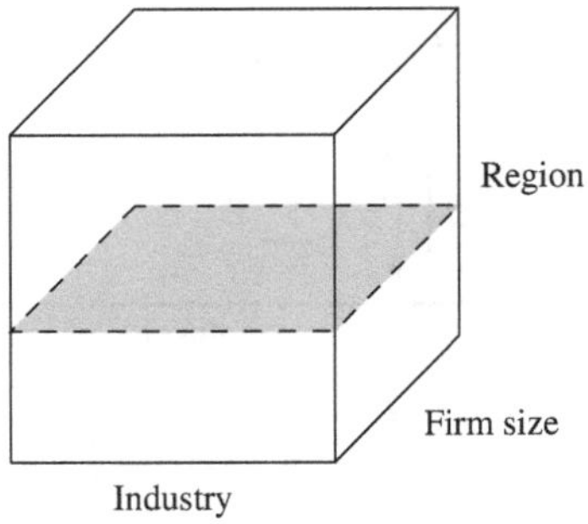


**Fig. 3.14** *A cube of systemic weights*: To include the notion of firm size and respect the estimation method introduced in Eq. 3.13, we have elected to create a cube of systemic-weight parameters.

based systemic weight. In a more general sense, it would appear that as long as the granularity of the systemic-weight estimation matches that of the systemic factor structure, this estimator will work. The analysis thus strongly suggests the use of a regional-sectoral grid to inform the various systemic-weight parameters.

Geographical and industrial identities are sensible and desirable categorizations for systemic weights. They are not, however, the only dimensions that we would like to consider. There is, for example, a reasonable amount of empirical evidence suggesting that systemic importance is also a function of firm size.[37] Adding a size dimension to the determination of systemic weights is possible, but it transforms a region-industry grid into a cube including region, industry and firm size.

Figure 3.14 provides a schematic view of this systemic-weight cube. It clearly nests the industrial sector and geographical region grid introduced in the derivation of the systemic-weight estimator. With 11 sectors and 13 regions, this yields 143 individual systemic weights. For each firm-size dimension, therefore, it is necessary to add an additional 143 parameters. Each additional firm-size category must thus be selected judiciously. Not only would too many firm-size groups violate the principle of model parsimony, but would also create a significant data burden. As a consequence, we have opted to employ only *three* firm size groups:

**Small:** total assets size in the interval of EUR $(0, 1]$ billion;
**Medium:** total firm assets from EUR $(1, 10]$ billion; and
**Large:** total firm assets is excess of EUR 10 billion.

One can clearly dispute the size of the thresholds separating these *three* categories, but it is hard to disagree that this represents a minimal characterization of the firm-size dimension. Any smaller than three size categories and this dimension would best be ignored; a larger set of groups, on the other hand, would only magnify existing issues surrounding data parsimony and sufficiency.

Although this cube format provides a sensible decomposition of the main factors required to inform systemic weights and offers a convenient representation—along

[37] BIS [3, Section 4.5] addresses this very issue and, attempts, in an admittedly limited manner, to incorporate this idea into regulatory computations.

these three dimensions—it is not without a few challenges. The following sections detail the measures taken to address them.

### A Systemic-Weight Dataset

There is no way around it: estimation of systemic weights requires a significant amount of data. With 11 industries, 13 regions, and 3 firm-size categories, a set of $K = 11 \times 13 \times 3 = 429$ cube sub-categories sharing common characteristics is required. If we hope to have 15–30 equity time series in each sub-category—to ensure a reasonably robust estimate of its average equity return cross correlations—this would necessitate roughly 6000 to 12,000 individual equity time series.

While the actual parameters are determined annually based on an extensive internal analysis, we will use a sample dataset to illustrate the key elements of the estimation procedure.[38] Our starting point is a collection of 20,000 individual, 120-month, equity index time series across various industries, regions, and firm sizes.[39] At first glance, this would appear to fall approximately within our (overall) desired dataset size. This is only true, of course, if the underlying equity time series are uniformly distributed across our 429 cube entries. The first order of business, therefore, is to closely examine our dataset to understand how it covers our three cube dimensions.

Table 3.4 takes the first step in exploring our dataset.[40] It examines, from a marginal perspective, the total number of equity series within each region, industry, and firm-size classification. Our hope of a uniform distribution along our key dimensions does not appear to be fulfilled. Along the regional front, Developed Asia and North America dominate the equity series; they account for roughly 40% of the total. Some important regions for NIB—such as the Baltics and Iceland—are only very lightly represented. With only two equity series, for example, we have virtually no information for Iceland. Indeed, both the Nordic and Baltic regions—as one might expect by virtue of their size—exhibit only a modest amount of data. Given the central importance of these member countries to our mandate, and the need to have granularity for these regions within the economic capital model, it will be necessary to adapt to these data deficiencies.

The industrial and size dimensions look to have, in general, a rather broader range of equity series. Financials and industrials are, by a sizable margin, the largest

---

[38] The presented figures are thus *not* quite our internal systemic-weight parameters, but the actual computations follow an almost identical logic.

[39] The attentive reader might ask why we employ 20 years of data for the systemic correlations, but only 10 years for systemic weights. In practice, we currently use a longer horizon. As we move back in time, however, it becomes rather challenging to maintain a continuous price history for such a large number of equities. Although interesting, such issues would detract from a clear description of the methodology.

[40] With a cross sectional size of 20,000 and a time-series dimension of 120 months, this yields a total panel dataset of about 2.4 million individual return observations.

**Table 3.4** *Equity series by dimension*: The underlying tables illustrate—along the region, industry, and size dimensions—the marginal distributions of equity series. Some geographic regions, such as Iceland and the Baltics, are quite thin. The coverage of industrial sectors, with the possible exception of paper, is rather better.

| Region | Count |
|---|---|
| Africa and Middle East | 642 |
| Baltics | 21 |
| Denmark | 86 |
| Developed Asia | 4295 |
| Emerging Asia | 6452 |
| Europe | 2677 |
| Finland | 86 |
| Iceland | 2 |
| Latin America | 336 |
| New Europe | 635 |
| North America | 3925 |
| Norway | 101 |
| Sweden | 227 |
| Total | 19,485 |

| Industry | Count |
|---|---|
| Energy | 707 |
| Materials | 1954 |
| Paper | 113 |
| Industrials | 4103 |
| Discretionary | 1648 |
| Staples | 2825 |
| Health care | 1244 |
| Financials | 3818 |
| IT | 1986 |
| Telecom | 614 |
| Utilities | 473 |
| Total | 19, 485 |

| Size | Count |
|---|---|
| Small | 11,421 |
| Medium | 5515 |
| Large | 2549 |
| Total | 19,485 |

categories accounting for almost one half of all series. The paper industry looks somewhat thin, but appears to be in better shape than the worst regional categories. Finally, the size decomposition is not exactly split into equally sized groups, but there are substantial numbers of series observations in each group.

While the marginal perspective is a useful starting point, it does not tell the full story. Table 3.5 illustrates the first of *three* pairwise joint perspectives. It shows the number of equities found within a two-dimensional grid of geographic and industry categories. Again, we see our roughly 20,000 time series in a manner that helps us understand how uniformly distributed they are along our dimensions of interest. 15 grid entries, or about 10% of the total, are empty. More than half of these, of course, stem from the Icelandic region. Numerous individual grid points have hundreds of observations. About one third of the grid entries, conversely, has five or less equity series. It is possible to construct an estimate in this cases, but it will not necessarily be the strongest signal of equity return correlations in this sub-sector.

Since we are considering a cube, there are two other possible two-dimensional viewpoints to be examined: region versus size and sector versus size. Table 3.6 outlines the equity counts for these perspectives. Once again, the regional aspect is the most problematic. Slicing each region into three size categories does not, of course, help out the situation in Iceland and the Baltics. Denmark, Finland, and Norway also exhibit a rather small number of individual series within the largest size category. The sector-size breakdown is somewhat less problematic; again, the paper industry has relatively few equity series. From each of our three two-dimensional perspectives, the number of equity series is far from equally spread among our three

**Table 3.5** *Sector-region grid*: The underlying table illustrates the number of equities found within a grid based on geographic and industry categories.

| Sector | Africa and Middle East | Baltics | Denmark | Developed Asia | Emerging Asia | Europe | Finland | Iceland | Latin America | New Europe | North America | Norway | Sweden | Total |
|---|---|---|---|---|---|---|---|---|---|---|---|---|---|---|
| Energy | 26 | – | 2 | 87 | 118 | 126 | 2 | – | 10 | 28 | 275 | 28 | 5 | 707 |
| Materials | 47 | – | 1 | 433 | 799 | 190 | 4 | – | 38 | 61 | 361 | 7 | 13 | 1954 |
| Paper | 4 | 1 | – | 18 | 52 | 12 | 2 | – | 4 | 4 | 13 | – | 3 | 113 |
| Industrials | 116 | 5 | 25 | 1067 | 1531 | 496 | 26 | 1 | 53 | 140 | 562 | 24 | 57 | 4103 |
| Discretionary | 43 | 3 | 7 | 563 | 382 | 248 | 6 | 1 | 30 | 37 | 309 | 2 | 17 | 1648 |
| Staples | 82 | 6 | 8 | 687 | 1230 | 267 | 14 | – | 63 | 116 | 321 | 10 | 21 | 2825 |
| Health care | 29 | 2 | 14 | 210 | 363 | 179 | 4 | – | 6 | 16 | 387 | 4 | 30 | 1244 |
| Financials | 234 | 1 | 23 | 626 | 748 | 730 | 8 | – | 79 | 141 | 1169 | 19 | 40 | 3818 |
| IT | 27 | – | 4 | 447 | 852 | 260 | 14 | – | 3 | 29 | 315 | 6 | 29 | 1986 |
| Telecom | 29 | 1 | 1 | 92 | 234 | 89 | 5 | – | 12 | 21 | 118 | 1 | 11 | 614 |
| Utilities | 5 | 2 | 1 | 65 | 143 | 80 | 1 | – | 38 | 42 | 95 | – | 1 | 473 |
| Total | 642 | 21 | 86 | 4295 | 6452 | 2677 | 86 | 2 | 336 | 635 | 3925 | 101 | 227 | 19,485 |

**Table 3.6** *Region and sector-size grid*: The underlying tables illustrate the number of equities found within a two-dimensional grid based on firm size versus geographic and industry categories. The Baltics, Iceland, and the paper industry remain problematic in terms of numbers of equity series.

| Region | Small | Medium | Large | Total |
|---|---|---|---|---|
| Africa and Middle East | 411 | 178 | 53 | 642 |
| Baltics | 19 | 2 | – | 21 |
| Denmark | 41 | 24 | 21 | 86 |
| Developed Asia | 2736 | 1146 | 413 | 4295 |
| Emerging Asia | 4470 | 1606 | 376 | 6452 |
| Europe | 1267 | 872 | 538 | 2677 |
| Finland | 46 | 26 | 14 | 86 |
| Iceland | 1 | 1 | – | 2 |
| Latin America | 127 | 150 | 59 | 336 |
| New Europe | 474 | 123 | 38 | 635 |
| North America | 1649 | 1290 | 986 | 3925 |
| Norway | 63 | 28 | 10 | 101 |
| Sweden | 117 | 69 | 41 | 227 |
| Total | 11,421 | 5515 | 2549 | 19,485 |

| Region | Small | Medium | Large | Total |
|---|---|---|---|---|
| Energy | 419 | 164 | 124 | 707 |
| Materials | 1276 | 499 | 179 | 1954 |
| Paper | 66 | 37 | 10 | 113 |
| Industrials | 2600 | 1121 | 382 | 4103 |
| Discretionary | 1004 | 463 | 181 | 1648 |
| Staples | 1791 | 680 | 354 | 2825 |
| Health care | 638 | 376 | 230 | 1244 |
| Financials | 1851 | 1344 | 623 | 3818 |
| IT | 1286 | 473 | 227 | 1986 |
| Telecom | 344 | 155 | 115 | 614 |
| Utilities | 146 | 203 | 124 | 473 |
| Total | 11,421 | 5515 | 2549 | 19,485 |

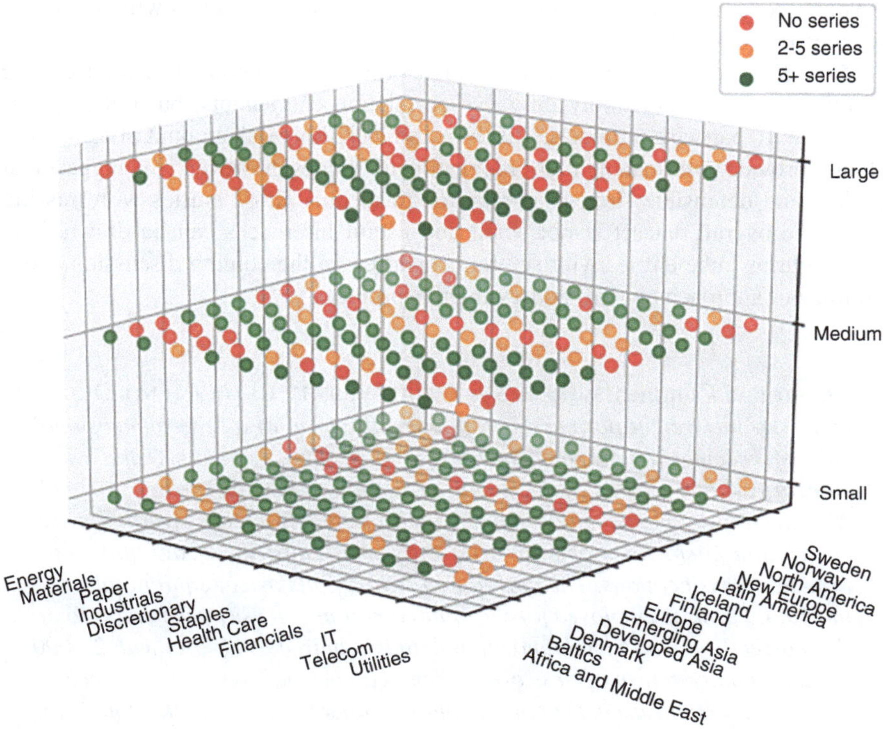


**Fig. 3.15** *A cube perspective*: The preceding figure attempts to provide a useful visualization of the number of equity series associated with each of the 429 individual cube elements. Colours are used to organize entries into *three* categories: red for no series, yellow for 2 to 5 series, and green for more than 5 equity series. The number of red dots clearly increases as we move from small to large firm size.

dimensions. This is less a data quality issue and more a feature of the regional, sectoral, and size distributions of listed equities.

With 20,000 total series and 429 entries, a uniform distribution would place about 45 equity series in each individual cube entry. Our preliminary analysis has made it clear that this will *not* occur. Figure 3.15 thus attempts to examine how far we are from this ideal. It provides a visualization of the number of equity series associated with each of the 429 individual cube elements. Colours—using a familiar traffic-light scheme—are used to organize entries into *three* categories. Red, the most problematic, represents zero equity series associated with a given entry. Yellow, which suggests that an estimate is possible although perhaps not terribly robust, is applied for cases of 2 to 5 equity series. Finally, the colour green indicates the presence of more than 5 equity series; this is a desired outcome. The results are as expected. While we observe substantial amounts of green and yellow, the number of problematic red dots clearly increases as we move from small to large firm size.

It is consequently difficult to imagine that each of our cube points will be equally well informed by our dataset.

This does not mean that our estimation procedure is doomed to failure. Five equity series does not imply only *five* correlation coefficients, but rather yields $\frac{5\cdot(5-1)}{2} = 10$ pairwise estimates. This is *not* an incredibly rich amount of data, but it should provide a reasonable first-order estimate. It does, however, still suggest that a clear and defensible strategy is required to identify those entries with missing data. The overall dataset is not small and useful inferences can be drawn from neighbouring cube entries with similar properties. In the coming discussion, we'll outline our approach towards addressing this problem.

> **Colour and Commentary 32** (SYSTEMIC-WEIGHT CHOICE AND DATA)*: Our systemic weight parametrization takes the form of a three-dimensional cube of systemic-weight coefficients. With 11 sectors, 13 regions, and 3 size categories, however, this choice implies a daunting 429 values to be estimated. A systemic-weight estimator can be constructed from the average cross correlation coefficients of firms with the same industrial, geographic, and firm-size classifications. The correlation between historical equity returns of individual firms is employed for the approximation of these parameters. To do this correctly, a non-trivial amount of data is required. A dataset with 20,000 monthly equity return series, over a ten-year period, has been sourced to outline the various aspects of the estimation process. Although the data is far from uniformly distributed across our three dimensions, it provides significant cross-correlation information. A clear strategy is nonetheless required to manage those cube entries with little or no data.*

## Estimating Correlations

Logistically, the job before us is rather simple. We need only compute a correlation coefficient for each of the pairs of equity series allocated to each entry in our cube definition. These collections of estimates for each grid point then need to be aggregated somehow to a single estimate representing our associated systemic weight. As is often the case in practice, there are a few complications. *Four* methodological questions arise:

1. What measure of correlation is to be employed?
2. How should we aggregate the pairwise correlation estimates for each cube entry?
3. How are we to manage cube entries without any data?
4. Should any constraints or logical relationships be imposed on the cube structure?

As always, when taking these decisions, we endeavour to be consistent with previous solutions. In the area of missing data, it makes sense to impose the smallest possible non-empirical footprint on the parameters. This implies leveraging the existing dataset, to the extent possible, to inform our cube entries absent equity series data. This is a fine line to successfully walk. The general approach is to reflect carefully, take a judicious choice, and then provide full transparency about the process.[41]

The first question—which correlation coefficient to use—can be conceptually difficult. Having wrestled with this point in the determination of the systemic correlation matrix, we have elected to use the rank (i.e., Spearman) correlation across the $K$ equity series in each cube point. The underlying argument of less sensitivity to outliers applies equally well in this context. It is further strengthened by a general desire to take consistent choices across the various elements of the economic-capital model.

The second question would appear to be directly answered by Eq. 3.13. It clearly suggests that we average our individual pairwise correlation estimates. Use of rank correlation, which belongs to the family of order statistics, is justified on the basis of the reduced impact of outliers. Use of the median, rather than the mean, would further insulate our estimates of pairwise correlation coefficients for each cube entry against outliers. This would appear to be particularly important given the relatively sparse amount of data associated with many of our cube points. For this reason, we use the median for cube-entry aggregation.

How do we handle missing data entries? The cube is essentially three slices of a sector-region grid, each indexed to one of the size categories. A missing data point is essentially an empty grid entry. The other median correlation entries occurring within the missing data-point's grid are the most natural source of information to approximate the missing entry. Often in such problems, from a mathematical perspective, one would approximate the missing point with a two dimensional plane estimated using surrounding non-empty points. In this setting, this is *not* a particularly sensible strategy. The adjacent cells could be from quite different regions and industries. Only the parallel adjacent cells, relating to the same industry or region, are logically informative. The likelihood of similarities, in terms of cross correlation, would appear to be highest along the industrial rather than the geographic dimension.[42] We've also seen that our industrial equity series are more equally distributed along the sector aspect. Missing data entries are, therefore, replaced using the (non-empty) industry median systemic-weight grid estimates for the same size category.

The fourth, and final, practical question is the most difficult, the most heuristic, and has the greatest potential for criticism. Relying entirely on the previous computational logic may still provide unreasonable results. Such unreasonableness may manifest itself in different ways. Regulatory guidance, for example, suggests that systemic weights should fall into the range of $[0.12, 0.24]$. It is entirely possible,

[41] This permits others to decide for themselves as to whether we have succeeded in this regard.

[42] This implicitly assumes that firms in the same industry, but different regions, have more commonalities than those in the same region, but different industries. This is, of course, debatable.

however, for a given estimate to fall below the lower bound of this interval. Another example relates to the size dimension. Nothing in the current estimate approach ensures, as one would expect, that the medium-size systemic weight—for a given region and sector—exceeds the small-size estimate. Economically, we expect systemic weights to be a monotonically increasing function of firm size. Some, hopefully sensible, manipulation is required should we desire to ensure this idea is incorporated into our final cube estimate.

To this end, we impose the following additional constraints onto our individual systemic-cube entries:

- a minimum systemic weight of 0.12, which is the bottom of the regulatory requirement;
- a maximum value of 0.40, which also represents the systemic weight applied to all public-sector entities; and
- a monotonic relationship between systemic weight and firm size.

The final point suggests that the systemic weight cannot decrease—for a given industrial sector and geographic region—as the firm size increases. The first two elements are relatively easy to implement, while the final aspect will require a bit of justification.

Before getting to these key points, let us first examine the first-order systemic-weight approximations. These do not yet include an application of the minimum and maximum values, but they do handle the missing data with industry medians. They also impose a very simple, and logical, monotonicity constraint. As we move along the size dimension—for fixed sector and region—the systemic weight estimate must be greater than, or equal, to the value from the previous size grouping.

Table 3.7 illustrates, along our first two-dimensional sector-region grid, the raw median rank correlation estimates. Despite the wall of numbers, it does provide a useful perspective. The overall median value is 0.17 with a minimum value of 0.01 and a maximum of 0.76. The median values, across each region and sector slice, are not terribly far from the regulatory interval of [0.12, 0.24]. The highest systemic weights appear to occur in Finland, Sweden, Norway, and the Baltics. Africa and Middle East and Emerging Asia are at the lower end of the regional spectrum. Along the sector aspect, financials, paper, and energy exhibit higher systemic weights, while telecommunications, health care, and utilities receive lower estimates.

Table 3.8 provides similar median rank correlation coefficients for the remaining two-dimensional grids: region- and sector-size combinations. The first interesting point is the relationship—be it by region or sector—between systemic weight and firm size. There is a fairly convincing increasing trend in systemic weights as we increase firm size. It holds in aggregate and, with one exception, at each regional and sectoral level. One might argue that this is an artifact of our monotonicity constraint. This was only imposed in a limited set of cases. Our analysis, while hardly a solid academic finding, does provide some comfort that inclusion of the firm-size dimension is a sensible choice.

**Table 3.7** *Sector-region correlations*: The underlying table outlines the median pairwise (rank) cross correlations for each of the equity series along the sector and region dimensions. Missing data points are replaced with industry medians and a weak monotonicity constraint is imposed. Red, yellow, and green shading indicate below, within, and above regulatory guidance, respectively.

| Sector | Africa and Middle East | Baltics | Denmark | Developed Asia | Emerging Asia | Europe | Finland | Iceland | Latin America | New Europe | North America | Norway | Sweden | Median |
|---|---|---|---|---|---|---|---|---|---|---|---|---|---|---|
| Energy | 0.09 | 0.22 | 0.29 | 0.18 | 0.14 | 0.16 | 0.24 | 0.22 | 0.22 | 0.17 | 0.27 | 0.25 | 0.23 | 0.22 |
| Materials | 0.13 | 0.16 | 0.16 | 0.17 | 0.13 | 0.17 | 0.23 | 0.16 | 0.19 | 0.15 | 0.20 | 0.14 | 0.15 | 0.16 |
| Paper | 0.18 | 0.19 | 0.19 | 0.19 | 0.11 | 0.27 | 0.76 | 0.19 | 0.01 | 0.17 | 0.26 | 0.19 | 0.39 | 0.19 |
| Industrials | 0.08 | 0.32 | 0.19 | 0.22 | 0.12 | 0.20 | 0.27 | 0.20 | 0.16 | 0.15 | 0.23 | 0.11 | 0.27 | 0.20 |
| Discretionary | 0.08 | 0.32 | 0.20 | 0.17 | 0.09 | 0.14 | 0.26 | 0.17 | 0.17 | 0.17 | 0.18 | 0.26 | 0.14 | 0.17 |
| Staples | 0.07 | 0.17 | 0.17 | 0.17 | 0.10 | 0.16 | 0.21 | 0.16 | 0.14 | 0.15 | 0.16 | 0.21 | 0.20 | 0.16 |
| Health Care | 0.09 | 0.45 | 0.21 | 0.12 | 0.11 | 0.11 | 0.11 | 0.12 | 0.20 | 0.12 | 0.14 | 0.09 | 0.13 | 0.12 |
| Financials | 0.10 | 0.20 | 0.20 | 0.18 | 0.12 | 0.21 | 0.26 | 0.20 | 0.20 | 0.16 | 0.23 | 0.34 | 0.32 | 0.20 |
| IT | 0.08 | 0.16 | 0.15 | 0.21 | 0.16 | 0.14 | 0.22 | 0.16 | 0.19 | 0.12 | 0.19 | 0.13 | 0.19 | 0.16 |
| Telecom | 0.13 | 0.12 | 0.12 | 0.12 | 0.11 | 0.12 | 0.21 | 0.12 | 0.09 | 0.12 | 0.14 | 0.12 | 0.12 | 0.12 |
| Utilities | 0.08 | 0.04 | 0.14 | 0.11 | 0.11 | 0.18 | 0.14 | 0.14 | 0.17 | 0.20 | 0.21 | 0.14 | 0.14 | 0.14 |
| Median | 0.09 | 0.19 | 0.19 | 0.17 | 0.11 | 0.16 | 0.23 | 0.16 | 0.17 | 0.15 | 0.20 | 0.14 | 0.19 | 0.17 |

**Table 3.8** *Region and sector-size correlations*: The underlying tables provides raw median rank-correlation estimates—similar to Table 3.7—along the region-size and sector-size dimensions; the colour scheme is also the same.

| Region | Small | Medium | Large | Median |
|---|---|---|---|---|
| Africa and Middle East | 0.07 | 0.10 | 0.12 | 0.10 |
| Baltics | 0.21 | 0.32 | 0.27 | 0.27 |
| Denmark | 0.14 | 0.20 | 0.22 | 0.20 |
| Developed Asia | 0.17 | 0.17 | 0.18 | 0.17 |
| Emerging Asia | 0.11 | 0.13 | 0.13 | 0.13 |
| Europe | 0.13 | 0.19 | 0.22 | 0.19 |
| Finland | 0.22 | 0.29 | 0.27 | 0.27 |
| Iceland | 0.00 | 0.00 | 0.00 | 0.00 |
| Latin America | 0.15 | 0.16 | 0.17 | 0.16 |
| New Europe | 0.14 | 0.16 | 0.18 | 0.16 |
| North America | 0.11 | 0.22 | 0.25 | 0.22 |
| Norway | 0.13 | 0.17 | 0.15 | 0.15 |
| Sweden | 0.15 | 0.24 | 0.29 | 0.24 |
| Median | 0.14 | 0.17 | 0.18 | 0.17 |

| Sector | Small | Medium | Large | Median |
|---|---|---|---|---|
| Energy | 0.14 | 0.20 | 0.31 | 0.20 |
| Materials | 0.11 | 0.16 | 0.27 | 0.16 |
| Paper | 0.11 | 0.15 | 0.29 | 0.15 |
| Industrials | 0.11 | 0.15 | 0.23 | 0.15 |
| Discretionary | 0.09 | 0.12 | 0.19 | 0.12 |
| Staples | 0.09 | 0.10 | 0.13 | 0.10 |
| Health Care | 0.07 | 0.10 | 0.15 | 0.10 |
| Financials | 0.11 | 0.16 | 0.24 | 0.16 |
| IT | 0.12 | 0.14 | 0.22 | 0.14 |
| Telecom | 0.10 | 0.10 | 0.12 | 0.10 |
| Utilities | 0.08 | 0.10 | 0.17 | 0.10 |
| Median | 0.11 | 0.14 | 0.22 | 0.13 |

The range of values in Table 3.8 are qualitatively similar to those found in Table 3.7. The vast majority of the systemic-weight estimates are also entirely consistent with regulatory guidance. Finland, Sweden, and the Baltics also exhibit higher levels of systemic weights, when we examine the size dimension. On the industry side, the paper, energy and IT sectors continue to exhibit higher levels of

**Table 3.9** *Raw-cube summary statistics*: The adjacent table houses a broad range of summary statistics related to our raw systemic-weight cube estimates in aggregate and along the size dimension.

| | Firm size | | | |
|---|---|---|---|---|
| Measure | Small | Medium | Large | Total |
| Mean | 0.15 | 0.20 | 0.27 | 0.21 |
| Median | 0.15 | 0.20 | 0.24 | 0.19 |
| 75th Percentile | 0.17 | 0.23 | 0.30 | 0.24 |
| Minimum | 0.01 | −0.06 | −0.00 | −0.06 |
| Maximum | 0.45 | 0.59 | 0.76 | 0.76 |
| Volatility | 0.06 | 0.09 | 0.12 | 0.10 |
| IQR | 0.06 | 0.08 | 0.11 | 0.10 |
| Percentage <0.12 | 27% | 12% | 6% | 15% |
| Percentage >0.40 | 1% | 2% | 13% | 5% |

systemic weight. Not everything completely matches up, since it is entirely possible to view different dependence structures as we organize our data along varying dimensions.[43]

Having examined all of the possible two-dimensional views of our systemic-weight estimates, we may now turn our attention to the cube values. Using the same basic approach outlined previously—without yet imposing upper or lower bounds on the results—Table 3.9 provides a number of summary statistics. These are computed across the region-sector grids, each holding the size dimension constant, and also at the overall level. The mean and median figures appear to be generally consistent with the two-dimensional analysis. In particular, the minimum and maximum values remain quite extreme. Moreover, the percentage of values outside of our predefined limits is significantly higher than in the two-dimensional settings.

What is driving this small number of extreme results? Only a small fraction of the 215 two-dimensional estimates fall outside of our limits, whereas about one fifth does in the cube setting. The situation appears to be magnified when moving from the grid to cube perspectives. This stems from the decrease in entry sample sizes associated with moving to a cube. As we have fewer equity series to inform a given cube entry, there is an increased possibility of a small number of fairly extreme pairwise correlation estimates dominating the outcome.

Setting bounds, in this context, would thus appear to be a reasonable solution. Presumably, the lower bound, by virtue of its increased conservatism, would not expose us to undue amounts of criticism. The upper bound, however, is another matter. It could, at worst, be seen as a non-conservative action. There are at least *three* compelling reasons to envisage placing a cap on our systemic weight estimates. The first is a structural question. Systemic weights ultimately play a critical role in the correlation of the underlying model default events; indeed, this is the entire point of the introduction of systemic risk factors. Many systemic-weight

[43] Some of this effect certainly stems from a lack of uniformity in the underlying grid categories. Large categories can dominate along some slices, but have a restricted influence among others.

estimation procedures, therefore, use default incidence data among various rating classes, to inform these parameters.[44] The results associated with such default-based estimation approaches, relative to the use of equity data, typically generate significantly lower systemic-weight values. The reason is a global, persistent level of cross correlation between general equity prices and returns.[45] When using equity data as a proxy, the consequence is an upward bias in our systemic-weight estimates. Although the magnitude of this bias is difficult to determine, it does argue for eliminating some of the more extreme upside estimates.

The second point relates to a category of credit counterparty that has not yet been discussed: public-sector entities. Such credit obligors do not, unfortunately, possess a public-listed stock and, as such, we may not use equity price returns as a proxy. There are relatively few good alternatives. One could try to infer public-sector correlations from bond or credit-default-swap (CDS) spreads. Both ideas, while containing some information on inter-entity correlations, raise many technical challenges. Moreover, many public-sector exposures have neither liquid bond issues nor listed CDS contracts.[46] This would then suggest using sovereign proxies; thereby creating an awkward situation of layering multiple data sources. The solution is a logical, and conservative, simplification. All public-sector entities—irrespective of region, sector, or size—are allocated a systemic-weight equal to the upper bound on our systemic cube.

Is this a good decision? There are sensible reasons to expect a high level of systemic weight for public-sector entities. Their revenues are highly related to tax receipts, whereas their expenditures are significantly linked to various social programs. Both items are macroeconomically procyclical, presumably creating important common systemic linkages. To avoid a potential error-prone and uninformative estimation approach, placing all public-sector obligors into the highest systemic-weight group is a clean solution. It does, of course, strongly argue for the establishment of a reasonable upper limit.

The third and final point has already been addressed. As we chop up our 20,000 equity series into 429 distinct sub-buckets, the average behaviour appears to be fairly reasonable. There are, however, a minority of fairly extreme outcomes that appear to be driven by issues associated with small sample sizes. Regulatory guidance caps systemic weights at 0.24. The data, and economic logic, would appear to suggest that a practical estimate could exceed this level. We have, not completely arbitrarily but also not completely defensibly, placed our upper bound at slightly above $1\frac{1}{2}$ times the regulatory upper bound.

---

[44] Bolder [7, Chapter 10] provides a fairly detailed overview of popular techniques in this area and numerous references for further reading.

[45] Our analysis underscores the empirical literature. With roughly 200 million possible pairwise correlation coefficients from our collection of 20,000 equity series, only a very small proportion is negative.

[46] There are also important questions about the strength of the overall (pure) credit-risk signal in CDS spreads. See, for example, Arakelyan and Serrano [2] for a detailed analysis of CDS-market liquidity.

**Colour and Commentary 33** (AN UPPER BOUND ON SYSTEMIC WEIGHTS): *Arbitrarily setting a key model parameter can be a controversial undertaking. Done correctly, it can help one's model implementation. Done poorly, it can almost be considered a criminal act. In all cases, however, it needs to be done in a transparent and defensible manner. The application of an upper bound on systemic weights exhibits this element of arbitrariness.* Three *main reasons argue for this choice. First, there is a general tendency of equity based systemic-weight estimates—relative to default correlation-based techniques—to be structurally higher. Conservatism is a fine objective, but anything in excess can be a problem. Second, due to difficulties in finding good proxy data and their strong systemic linkages, all public-sector entities are assigned systemic weights at the upper bound. This practice argues for a reasonable maximum level of systemic weight. Finally, we need to be symmetrical in our logic. If we are comfortable with a lower bound for reasons of conservatism, then a (reasonable) upper bound should not be overly difficult to digest.*

### Imposing Strict Monotonicity

The final step in the specification of the systemic-weight cube relates to monotonicity constraints. Thus far, only a weakly monotonic relationship has been imposed along the size dimension. That is, as we move from small- to large-sized firms, the systemic weight must be greater than or equal to the previous entry. This implies that, practically, for some region-sectors pairs, the systemic weight may be flat along the size dimension. In principle, we would prefer a strictly monotonous relationship. This means that a large firm's systemic weight, for each combination of region and sector, would always be greater than for a smaller one.

For about one quarter of the 143 distinct region-sector pairs, upward steps along the size dimension are not strictly monotonous. Our desired strict monotonicity is imposed using a simple heuristic method. We first compute the slope among those region-sector pairs with increasing systemic weights along the size dimension. This mean slope is subsequently imposed along each of the flat aspects; caution, of course, is taken to ensure that the upper bound remains respected.[47] Although definitely *ad hoc*, the rationale behind this adjustment is related to logical consistency and conservatism. Systemic weights do generally increase in a strictly monotonic manner, *ceteris paribus*, as we increase firm size. When this does not occur naturally, it appears defensible to (gently) force this condition.

[47] Imposition of the upper bound does imply that, in a small number of cases, strict monotonicity is not achieved.

**Table 3.10** *Size-slope adjustment summary*: The underlying table describes, for each fixed sector-region pair, the average systemic weight parameter. Values are provided before and after the adjustment along with the scaling factor employed. On average, the adjustment is small, but it adds logical consistency and conservatism to the model.

| Perspective | Small | Medium | Large |
|---|---|---|---|
| Starting point | 0.16 | 0.22 | 0.27 |
| Scaling factor | 1.00 | 1.43 | 1.82 |
| Final result | 0.16 | 0.22 | 0.28 |

Table 3.10 describes the results of this process. It begins by illustrating, for each fixed sector-region pair, the mean systemic weight parameter. These outcomes are utilized to construct a scaling factor. The systemic-weight of a medium-sized firm, for a given pair of regions and sectors, should be 43% greater than the small-sized equivalent; this rises to more than 80% from small to large firms. The final average results are presented. On average, the adjustment is small, because it only impacts a small subset of the entries. Although the change is modest in aggregate, this adjustment nonetheless ensures an important logical consistency to the model. Its limited size, upon consideration, is actually a feature. It implies that only modest adjustment is required to the empirical estimates.

Figure 3.16 provides a visualization of this heuristic operation. The left-hand graphic illustrates the initial, unadjusted, situation. A small number of flat size-dimension slopes can be identified. The right-hand graphic repeats the analysis after the adjustment; with a few exceptions around the upper limit, all firm-size slopes along fixed sector-region pairs have a strict increasing monotonic form. At the same time, we observe that the overall impact is relatively modest and the majority of cube entries remains untouched.

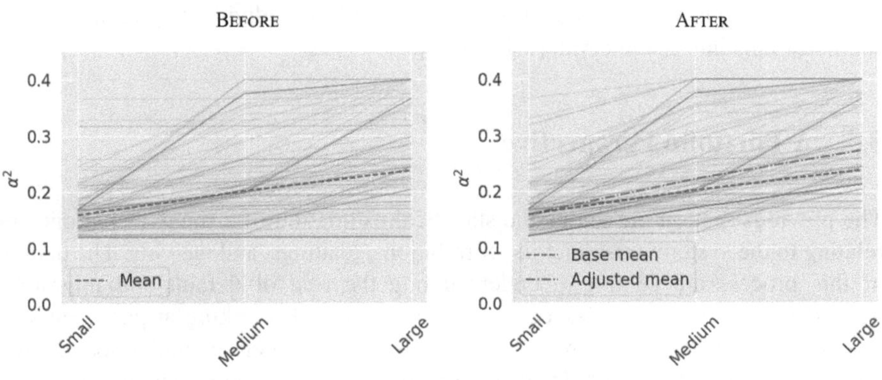


**Fig. 3.16** *Size-slope adjustment*: These graphics illustrate, for each fixed sector-region pair, the systemic-weight slope along the size aspect. A before-and-after perspective is provided to help understand the impact of the heuristic adjustment used to impose strict monotonicity over this dimension.

### A Final Look

Specification of systemic weights is a critical aspect of a credit-risk economic-capital model. The relative importance of the common systemic component is a key driver of default correlations and, ultimately, the form of the credit-loss distribution. With 11 regional and 13 sectoral systemic state variables, the process is a particular challenge. Following regulatory guidance to further introduce the notion of firm size does not make the task any easier. A desire for modelling accuracy nevertheless makes us reluctant to forego this (size) aspect of the model.

A principal objective in the systemic-weight estimation process is to allow the data to inform, to the extent possible, the final results. Any heuristic adjustments should, in principle, minimally impact the outcomes. Although our degree of success in this venture is an open question, *four* main interventions were imposed. The first is that missing data points—identified for a fixed firm size along the sector-region grid—are replaced with the median industry outcome. The second and third are systemic-weight constraints. A minimum systemic weight of 0.12—the lower bound of the regulatory interval—is imposed in conjunction with an upper bound of 0.4. The former, by virtue of its conservatism, is uncontroversial. The latter, which is defended by a range of arguments, provides fuel for debate. The final adjustment is the imposition of strict monotonicity—for each sector-region pair—along the size dimension. This final choice also introduces additional prudence into the systemic-weight parametrization.

Figure 3.17 provides a last view on the final set of cube systemic-weight estimates. Similar to Fig. 3.15, it permits a full visualization of our 429 cube elements. Once again, colours are used to organize the entries. Light blue indicates values falling into the regulatory range, regular blue describes estimates from 0.24 to 0.34, while dark blue describes estimates exceeding 0.34. The general trend involves dots getting darker as we move up the size dimension. Nevertheless, consistent with our previous analysis, a significant number of the individual systemic-weight estimates falls into the interval, $[0.12, 0.34]$.

## 3.3 A Portfolio Perspective

The previous section highlights the statistical estimation of a range of parameters relating to the systemic risk factors: correlations, loadings, and weights. The details of this process are central to understanding the role of default and migration dependence in any credit-risk economic capital model. Looking at parameters in isolation, however, rarely provides deep insight into their overall impact. Two notions, in particular, can help in this regard: systemic proportions and a deeper examination of default correlation. Both require a portfolio perspective and, in the following sections, will be investigated.

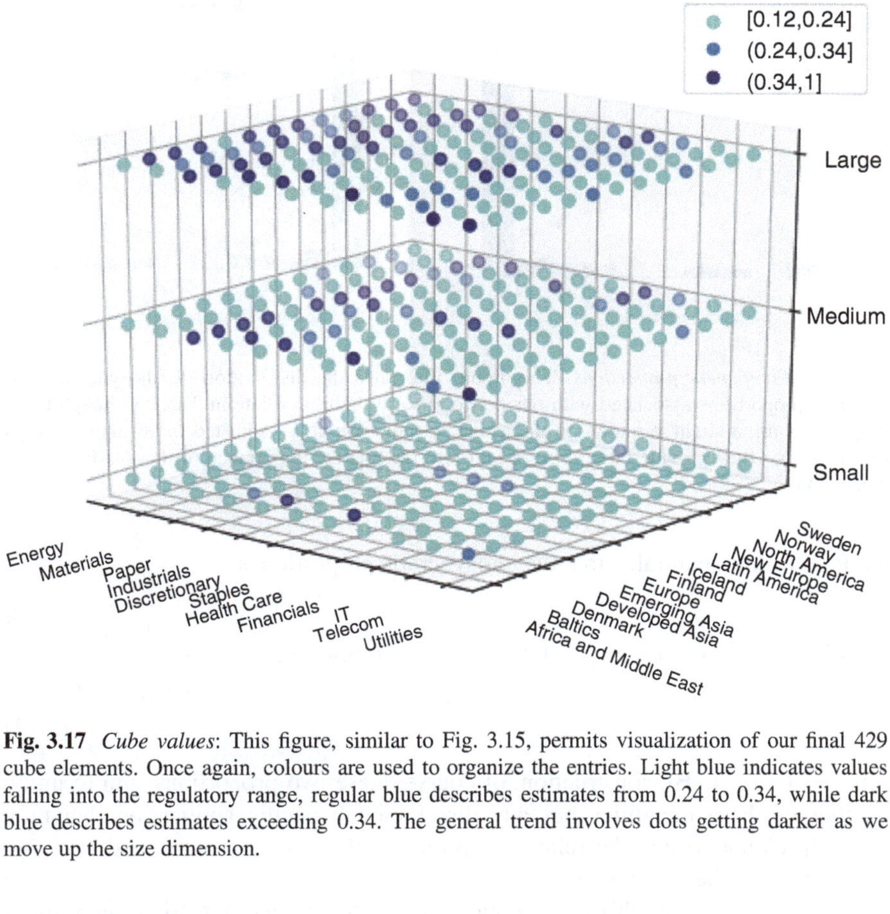


**Fig. 3.17** *Cube values*: This figure, similar to Fig. 3.15, permits visualization of our final 429 cube elements. Once again, colours are used to organize the entries. Light blue indicates values falling into the regulatory range, regular blue describes estimates from 0.24 to 0.34, while dark blue describes estimates exceeding 0.34. The general trend involves dots getting darker as we move up the size dimension.

### *3.3.1 Systemic Proportions*

The $\alpha$ coefficients, as already highlighted in detail, specify the relative weight on the systemic and idiosyncratic weights. The systemic-weight coefficients themselves are not true weights. $\alpha_i$ and $\sqrt{1-\alpha_i^2}$, while fairly close, cannot be interpreted as the weight on the systemic and idiosyncratic components, respectively. They have, instead, been constructed to ensure the unit variance of the creditworthiness index. To provide a clean description of the *true* weights on our two principal risk dimensions, we introduce the idea of systemic proportions. It involves a simple, even trivial, adjustment. The systemic proportion is simply,

$$\text{Systemic proportion}_i = \frac{\alpha_i}{\alpha_i + \sqrt{1-\alpha_i^2}}, \tag{3.16}$$

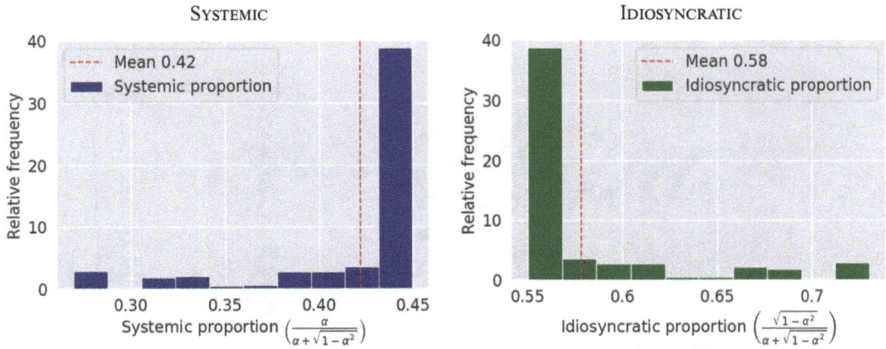


**Fig. 3.18** *Component proportions*: This figure illustrates the distribution of idiosyncratic and systemic proportions associated with our portfolio for an arbitrary date in 2020. Although these proportions are a slight variation on the actual systemic weights—adjusted to be interpreted as true weights—they provide interesting insight into the relative importance of these two key risk dimensions.

while, it follows naturally, that the idiosyncratic proportion is

$$\text{Idiosyncratic proportion}_i = \left(1 - \text{Systemic proportion}_i\right) = \frac{\sqrt{1-\alpha_i^2}}{\alpha_i + \sqrt{1-\alpha_i^2}}, \tag{3.17}$$

for $i = 1, \ldots, I$. By construction, of course, these two proportions sum to unity. Neither of these quantities has any direct model-specific application, but they can help us understand the relative importance of the idiosyncratic and systemic components in the threshold model.

Figure 3.18 provides histograms summarizing the observed distribution of these systemic and idiosyncratic proportions for an arbitrary date in 2020; these values naturally depend on the confluence of firm size, region, and industry within the underlying portfolio. The average systemic proportion is roughly 0.4 with values ranging from as low as 0.3 and up to 0.45. There is a significant amount of probability at the upper end of this range. This clustering is related to the imposition of an upper bound on the systemic weight and the assignment of all public-sector entities—an important part of our portfolio, as is the case with most international financial institutions—to this maximum value.

The idiosyncratic proportions are, by their very definition, the mirror image of the systemic proportions. The average value is roughly 0.60, with a significant amount of probability mass in the neighbourhood of 0.55, which naturally corresponds to the clump of systemic proportions in the region of 0.45. Values range from around 0.55 to slightly more than 0.7. We can approximately conclude that common systemic factors drive roughly 40% of the risk, with the remainder described by specific, idiosyncratic elements. This is, as a point of comparison, significantly more

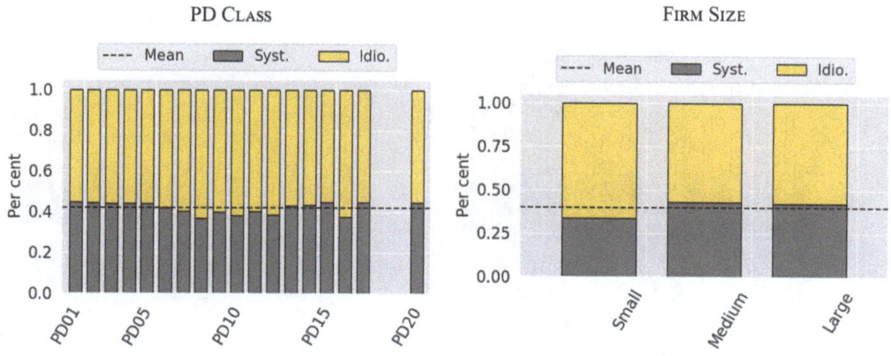


**Fig. 3.19** *Weighting perspectives*: This figure breaks out the average idiosyncratic and systemic weights by rating category and firm size; the weights were adjusted to sum to one to ease the interpretation. Again, we see that on average about 40% the weight is allocated to the idiosyncratic factor. This ratio is not, however, constant across the PD-class and firm-size dimensions.

conservative than the regulatory guidance. Use of the lower bound, $\alpha_i^2 = 0.12$, leads to a split of roughly 0.3 to 0.7 for the systemic and idiosyncratic components, respectively. This rises to about 0.35 to 0.65 if we use the regulatory upper bound, $\alpha_i^2 = 0.24$.[48]

Figure 3.19 takes the analysis a step further by illustrating the systemic and idiosyncratic proportions by default-probability class and firm size. To anchor our perspective, the roughly 40% mean systemic proportion is provided. PD classes one through five appear to be slightly above this average, while the classes 7 to 12 are somewhat below.[49] A gradual increase in systemic proportion is evident when moving from small to large firms; medium and large firms, however, do not manifest any (material) visual difference.

Figure 3.20 extends the view from Fig. 3.19 to include the systemic and idiosyncratic proportions by region and sector. The majority of regions does not visually deviate from the overall average. New Europe and Africa and Middle East are somewhat higher than the mean, whereas Iceland and Developed Asia are somewhat below this level. IT, public-sector entities, and financials exhibit higher than average systemic proportions; this is sensible, since these firms exhibit strong macroeconomic linkages. Health care, utilities, and telecommunication firms, conversely, exhibit a higher weight on the idiosyncratic dimension. Again, this appears reasonable, since such firms often operate in controlled, regulated environments reducing the role of systemic factors.

[48] Interestingly, to flip the ratio to a 60%-to-40% mix for systemic and idiosyncratic risk, an eye-watering $\alpha_i^2$ parameter of roughly 0.67 is required.

[49] This is consistent with the regulatory formula, where systemic weight is directly proportional to rating quality. This is discussed in more detail in Chap. 11.

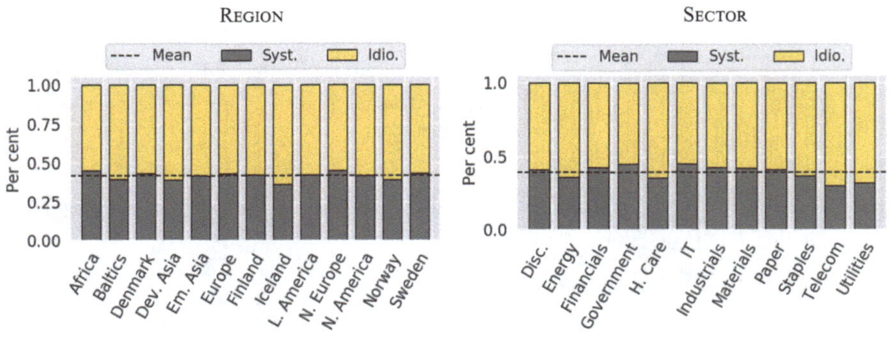


**Fig. 3.20** *More weighting perspectives*: This figure, building on Fig. 3.19, breaks out the average idiosyncratic and systemic proportions by region and industrial sectors. Differences in systemic proportions are visible, but individual values do not appear to vary dramatically from the mean values.

**Colour and Commentary 34** (SYSTEMIC-WEIGHT REASONABLENESS): *With even a modest number of systemic-risk factors, it is hard to definitively opine on the magnitude of the systemic weights in one's credit-risk model. Regulatory guidance places the* $\alpha_i^2$ *values in the interval,* $[0.12, 0.24]$ *with higher credit-quality firms tending towards the upper end. This argues for systemic proportions in the range of 0.3 to 0.35. On average, in this case, about two thirds of default and migration events are driven by systemic factors. The remainder thus stems from idiosyncratic elements. Our systemic-weight parametrization moves this average value up to approximately 0.4. On the surface, therefore, one may conclude that a conservative approach to internal modelling has been taken.*[a] *On the systemic-weight dimension, at least, a compelling argument can be made for the prudence of the systemic parameters.*

[a] While this was the intention, the reasonableness of this choice also needs to be considered with other modelling alternatives—such as inclusion or exclusion of migration effects and the form of copula function. Conservatism is best assessed through joint examination of the entire set of modelling decisions.

In the following section, we will turn our attention towards understanding how these systemic-weight choices impact the central driver of credit-risk interdependence; the notion of default correlation. The mathematical chain from systemic correlations to systemic weights to default correlations is not particularly direct, but it merits careful examination. It is, after all, the nucleus of the threshold model.

### 3.3.2 Factor-, Asset-, and Default-Correlation

Correlations, as we've seen in the context of a threshold model, come in a variety of flavours. Factor correlation refers to the pairwise dependence between the loaded systemic-risk factors associated with two credit obligors. Asset correlation addresses—also for an arbitrarily selected pair of credit counterparts—the interdependence between latent creditworthiness index variables. The final, and perhaps most interesting quantity, is the pairwise correlation between underlying default events; we call this default correlation. Each of these *three* elements provides an alternative perspective into our model's interactions between any two obligors.

Our objective in this section is to examine, to the best of our ability, the various definitions of correlation at the portfolio level. This will require re-organizing some of our previous definitions. Let us begin by repeating the generic definition of the $i$th obligor's creditworthiness index,

$$\Delta X_i = \sqrt{\frac{\nu}{W}}\left(\alpha_i \mathrm{B}_i \Delta z + \sqrt{1-\alpha_i^2}\epsilon_i\right). \tag{3.18}$$

This expression illustrates all of the characters within our threshold-model implementation: systemic and idiosyncratic elements, factors loadings, systemic weights, systemic-factor correlations, and the mixing variable employed to induce a multivariate $t$ distribution. In Chap. 2, we demonstrated that $\Delta X_i \sim \mathcal{T}_\nu\left(0, \frac{\nu}{\nu-2}\right)$.

The systemic-risk factor correlation between any two obligors, $n$ and $m$, is a function of its systemic factor loadings and the common systemic-risk factor outcomes. The covariance between these two quantities is,

$$\begin{aligned}
\mathrm{cov}(\mathrm{B}_n\Delta z, \mathrm{B}_m\Delta z) &= \left(\left(\mathrm{B}_n\Delta z - \mathbb{E}(\mathrm{B}_n\Delta z)\right)\left(\mathrm{B}_m\Delta z - \mathbb{E}(\mathrm{B}_m\Delta z)\right)^T\right), \qquad (3.19)\\
&= \left(\left(\mathrm{B}_n\Delta z - \mathrm{B}_n\underbrace{\cancel{\mathbb{E}(\Delta z)}}_{=0}\right)\left(\mathrm{B}_m\Delta z - \mathrm{B}_m\underbrace{\cancel{\mathbb{E}(\Delta z)}}_{=0}\right)^T\right),\\
&= \mathbb{E}\left(\mathrm{B}_n\Delta z\Delta z^T\mathrm{B}_m^T\right),\\
&= \mathrm{B}_n\Omega\mathrm{B}_m^T,\\
&= \underbrace{\rho(\mathrm{B}_n\Delta z, \mathrm{B}_m\Delta z)}_{\rho_{nm}}
\end{aligned}$$

where the last step follows from the previously established fact that $\text{var}(\text{B}_i \Delta z) = 1$ for all $i = 1, \ldots, I$. The factor correlation is thus a rather complicated cocktail of systemic-factor loadings and correlations.[50]

The asset correlation, as derived in the previous chapter, has a fairly elegant form. It is written as $\alpha_n \rho_{nm} \alpha_m$. Given the dimensionality of our systemic factors, most of the complexity is embedded in the factor correlation term, $\rho_{nm}$. The pair of systemic weights works together to complete the picture. If there is a high degree of factor correlation and both systemic weights are large, then the asset correlation will be correspondingly high. A few simple examples can help build some intuition. Imagine that the factor correlation is 0.75 and both credit obligors share systemic weights at the upper bound of $\alpha_i^2 = 0.4$. The asset correlation would then become,

$$\begin{aligned} \text{Case 1}_{\text{Asset correlation}} &= \alpha_n \rho_{nm} \alpha_m, \\ &= \sqrt{0.4} \cdot 0.75 \cdot \sqrt{0.4} = 0.30. \end{aligned} \tag{3.21}$$

If only one of the obligors is at the lower bound of 0.12, then we observe,

$$\text{Case 2}_{\text{Asset correlation}} = \sqrt{0.4} \cdot 0.75 \cdot \sqrt{0.12} \approx 0.16, \tag{3.22}$$

which amounts to a twofold decrease in overall asset correlation between these two credit counterparts. Following this to the lower limit, when both parties have systemic weights at the lower bound, then

$$\text{Case 3}_{\text{Asset correlation}} = \sqrt{0.12} \cdot 0.75 \cdot \sqrt{0.12} \approx 0.09. \tag{3.23}$$

Naturally, this is scaled upwards and downwards by the factor correlation, but these simple examples illustrate the critical role of the systemic weights in the determination of asset correlations.[51]

The final object of interest is the default correlation. This quantity, also derived in the previous chapter, has the following model-independent form,

$$\rho\left(\mathbb{I}_{\mathcal{D}_n}, \mathbb{I}_{\mathcal{D}_m}\right) = \frac{\mathbb{P}\left(\mathcal{D}_n \cap \mathcal{D}_m\right) - p_n p_m}{\sqrt{p_n p_m (1 - p_n)(1 - p_m)}}. \tag{3.24}$$

---

[50] With the parametric factor loading restrictions introduced in the previous sections, this can be considerably simplified. If we let $I_k$ and $G_k$ represent the industry and geographic location associated with the $k$th credit obligor, then we may rewrite Eq. 3.19 as,

$$\rho_{nm} = \text{cov}\left(\text{B}_{I_n} \Delta z_{I_n} + \text{B}_{G_n} \Delta z_{G_n}, \text{B}_{I_m} S_{I_m} + \text{B}_{G_m} \Delta z_{G_m}\right). \tag{3.20}$$

Although this reduces the sheer number of individual terms, it has not proven more useful, in our experience at least, for analyzing the overall portfolio.

[51] Incidentally, following this simple calculation with $\max(\alpha_n^2) = \max(\alpha_m^2) = 0.4$ and $\max(\rho_{nm}) = 1$, the maximal asset correlation coefficient is 0.4.

**Table 3.11**
*Cross-correlation cases*: We can identify 14 logical distinct cross-correlation cases—along the public-sector, industry, regional, and size dimensions—to analyze the degree of factor, asset, and default correlation embedded in the current model parameters.

| Case | Public-sector | Industry | Region | Size |
|---|---|---|---|---|
| 1 | Both | n/a | Different | n/a |
| 2 | Both | n/a | Same | n/a |
| 3 | One | Different | Different | Different |
| 4 | One | Different | Same | Different |
| 5 | One | Different | Different | Same |
| 6 | One | Different | Same | Same |
| 7 | Neither | Different | Different | Different |
| 8 | Neither | Same | Different | Different |
| 9 | Neither | Different | Same | Different |
| 10 | Neither | Same | Same | Different |
| 11 | Neither | Different | Different | Same |
| 12 | Neither | Same | Different | Same |
| 13 | Neither | Different | Same | Same |
| 14 | Neither | Same | Same | Same |

Given the $t$-copula implementation, the joint distribution of $\Delta X_n$ and $\Delta X_m$ follows a bivariate-$t$ form. This helps us evaluate the tricky quantity $\mathbb{P}(\mathcal{D}_n \cap \mathcal{D}_m)$.[52] Specifically, from the previous chapter, it has the following generic form,

$$\begin{aligned} \mathbb{P}(\mathcal{D}_n \cap \mathcal{D}_m) &= \mathbb{P}\bigg(\Delta X_n \leq \Phi^{-1}(p_n), \Delta X_m \leq \Phi^{-1}(p_m)\bigg), \\ &= F_{\mathcal{T}_\nu}\left(F_{\mathcal{T}_\nu}^{-1}(p_n), F_{\mathcal{T}_\nu}^{-1}(p_m); \alpha_n \rho_{nm} \alpha_m\right). \end{aligned} \tag{3.25}$$

The final expression for default correlation, within the credit-risk model is thus

$$\rho\left(\mathbb{I}_{\mathcal{D}_n}, \mathbb{I}_{\mathcal{D}_m}\right) = \frac{F_{\mathcal{T}_\nu}\left(F_{\mathcal{T}_\nu}^{-1}(p_n), F_{\mathcal{T}_\nu}^{-1}(p_m); \alpha_n \rho_{nm} \alpha_m\right) - p_n p_m}{\sqrt{p_n(1-p_n)}\sqrt{p_m(1-p_m)}}. \tag{3.26}$$

This expression is readily computed with the use of numerical integration.[53]

The preceding ingredients are everything that is needed to compute factor, asset, and default correlations for each pair of credit obligors. There is, however, a problem. With 500+ obligors, this amounts to approximately 140,000 distinct pairs of counterparties to examine. Even for the hardest-working and most committed quantitative analyst, this is a tad too much to visually wade through and digest. What is required is some conceptual organization. Table 3.11 lessens the burden somewhat

[52] The specific mathematical form of this bivariate distributional function is outlined in the previous chapter. The reader interested in dramatically more detail on the multivariate $t$ distribution, in all its forms, is referred to Kotz and Nadarajah [30].

[53] See Bolder [7, Chapter 4] for practical details.

by introducing a logical partition of our collection of credit counterparties using the model structure; this amounts to public-sector status, industrial sector, geographical region, and firm size. These divisions were, of course, not selected by random. They relate to the differences in the key drivers of our correlation quantities: systemic weights and loadings.[54]

Let's work through the basic logic of our partition:

- In the first two cases, both entities are in the public sector. In this case, the industry designation and firm size do not matter. There are *two* cases: the counterparts share the same geographic region or they do not.
- In the second setting, only one of the obligors falls in the public sector. Since only one member of the pair has an industry identity, they can only differ along the regional and firm size dimensions. This amounts to *four* possible cases.
- The final part is perhaps the most interesting. Both counterparties are in the corporate sector implying potential differentiation along the industrial, regional, and firm-size categories. The consequence is *eight* distinct cases.

The result is a reduction of 140,000 correlation pairs into 14 logical cases.[55] While losing a significant amount of information, hopefully we gain a bit of perspective.

Each group is mutually exclusive and covers all possible outcomes; that is, no obligor pair can fall into more than one group. Equally importantly, each sub-group exhibits a link to the lending business. It is interesting and sensible, for example, to consider the set of public-sector obligor pairs falling into the same geographic region. Similarly, we care about the nature of default correlation between two non-public-sector entities in the same industry, but stemming from different geographic regions. Practically, we would expect to observe a greater degree of factor correlation associated with obligors sharing a greater number of characteristics. Two obligors in the same industry and region should, in principle, be more correlated than two entities dissimilar along these dimensions. This analysis can, hopefully, shed some light onto the economic reasonableness of these empirically driven parameter estimates. We can thus think of this as a kind of parameter sanity check.

Despite our logical breakdown, there remains a substantial amount of heterogeneity within each of our sub-groups. Even if they fall into the same industry, region, and asset-size category, they can potentially have very different default probabilities, exposure, and loss-given default settings. This means that they may exhibit significant correlation, but impact the overall portfolio risk in quite distinct ways. This does not negate this analysis, but it is useful in understanding and interpreting the results.

[54] Individual systemic correlations and default probabilities also matter importantly, but are rather more difficult to logically organize.

[55] The overidentifying restrictions on the factor loadings also play a role in making this a meaningful logical partition.

**Table 3.12** *Correlation analysis*: The underlying table describes the number and percent of obligor pairs falling into each logical class along with their respective average factor-, asset-, and default-correlation values.

| | | Obligor pairs | | Type of correlation | | |
|---|---|---|---|---|---|---|
| Extreme | Case | Count | % | Factor | Asset | Default |
| Low agreement | 1 | 24,954 | 17.8% | 0.71 | 0.28 | 0.015 |
| High agreement | 2 | 7686 | 5.5% | 1.00 | 0.40 | 0.029 |
| Low agreement | 3 | 27,562 | 19.7% | 0.68 | 0.23 | 0.014 |
| | 4 | 4694 | 3.3% | 0.88 | 0.29 | 0.019 |
| | 5 | 31,261 | 22.3% | 0.72 | 0.26 | 0.016 |
| High agreement | 6 | 6627 | 4.7% | 0.90 | 0.33 | 0.024 |
| Low agreement | 7 | 14,903 | 10.6% | 0.72 | 0.21 | 0.017 |
| | 8 | 4852 | 3.5% | 0.89 | 0.29 | 0.024 |
| | 9 | 2069 | 1.5% | 0.86 | 0.24 | 0.023 |
| | 10 | 784 | 0.6% | 1.00 | 0.32 | 0.029 |
| | 11 | 8443 | 6.0% | 0.74 | 0.22 | 0.020 |
| | 12 | 3711 | 2.6% | 0.89 | 0.29 | 0.025 |
| | 13 | 1822 | 1.3% | 0.87 | 0.27 | 0.026 |
| High agreement | 14 | 817 | 0.6% | 1.00 | 0.32 | 0.032 |
| Total/Average | | 140,185 | 100.0% | 0.76 | 0.26 | 0.018 |

Table 3.12 provides a daunting number of correlated-related figures organized by our previously defined cases using our portfolio on an arbitrary date during 2020. With so many numbers, it is useful to examine the extremes. In particular,

- Cases 1, 3, and 7 represent situations of correspondence along the public-sector dimension, but literally no overlap among the other three categories. These cases, logically at least, have the lowest amount of agreement in terms of correlation outcomes. We will refer to these as *low-agreement* cases.
- Cases 2, 6, and 14, in contrast, after public-sector correspondence, involve the greatest degree of overlap among our three categories. Conceptually, we would expect them to exhibit the highest amount of agreement in terms of cross-correlation coefficients. Let's call these *high-agreement* cases.

With only 14 cases, were the portfolio to be uniformly distributed along our key dimensions, we would expect about 7% of the pairs in each case. Interestingly, our three low-agreement cases represent about half of the total number of obligor pairs. This is significantly above what one would expect under uniformity. If we add in case 5—where the only level of dimensional agreement is firm size—this rises to about 70%. The high-agreement cases appear to be relatively less frequently occurring; all together they amount to about 10% of the individual counterparty pairs. This does suggest, at least along these dimensions, a reassuringly low level of concentration.

Factor correlation is, across all 14 cases, quite high. The lowest average value is about 0.7. Indeed, our low-agreement cases—as we had suspected—exhibit the lowest levels of factor correlation. On the other hand, Cases 2, 6, and 14 show the highest levels of factor correlation with levels approaching unity. Cases 2 and 14, by construction, load onto the same factors in the same way and, as such, have perfect factor correlation. At the factor correlation level, therefore, the trend in factor correlations is as expected. The overall factor-correlation levels remain quite high due to significant positive correlation among our systemic risk factors stemming from the use of equity returns in their parametrization.

The asset-correlation coefficients, which work from the factor correlation and add the systemic weights, tell a similar story. Cases 1, 3, and 7—we could also add case 5 to this group—possess lower asset-correlation values relative to the others. The average asset-correlation coefficient for these cases appears to be between 0.2 and 0.25. The high agreement group displays values in excess of 0.32. Again, we observe consistent, and expected, behaviour among our logical cases. Asset correlation levels are also, if somewhat differentiated among cases, generally quite high.

Moving to default correlation, the same trend persists, albeit at significantly lower levels. Default correlation coefficients in a threshold setting, even in the most aggressively parametrized situations, rarely exceed about 0.05. The average level, across all obligor pairs, is roughly 0.02. The low-agreement cases all display average default-correlation coefficients south of this figure. The high-agreement cases, however, each exhibit values almost twice the overall average.

**Colour and Commentary 35** (A PARAMETRIC SANITY CHECK)*: Parameter selection is a tricky business and any tools that can help us assess the consistency of our choices are very welcome. Sorting out factor, asset, and default correlation, for example, is* not *trivial. Each quantity is a complicated combination of factor correlation, factor-loading, and systemic-weight model parameters. Moreover, with even a modest number of credit obligors, there are many possible pairwise interactions. One can, in our specific case, organize the (intimidatingly large) number of obligor pairs into 14 logical cases along the type-of-entity, industry, geographic-region, and firm-size dimensions. This helps to organize our thinking and formulate expectations regarding the level of correlation within the model. Counterparties with stronger agreement along these dimensions should reveal higher degrees of default dependence. To test this proposition, we compute the average levels of factor, asset, and default correlation across each of these logical cases. At all levels, the various correlation coefficients appear to be consistent with our presuppositions; greater agreement among our predefined key dimensions appears to lead to a higher degree of model dependence. This analysis, which basically amounts to something of a sanity check on the model calibration, helps us to conceptualize and judge the reasonableness of the current parameters.*

### 3.3.3 *Tail Dependence*

Equation 3.18 describes the latent creditworthiness state variable associated with each of the individual obligors in our portfolio. Quietly, in the background, sits a difficult to manage parameter, $\nu$. This is the degrees-of-freedom parameter of the chi-squared (mixing) random variable used to generate marginal and joint $t$ distributions for our state-variable system. The strategic business rationale for this specific implementation of threshold model is the inclusion of non-zero tail dependence. In this respect, the $t$-copula model is a significant conceptual improvement over the Gaussian version.

To actually use the model, of course, one needs to select a value for $\nu$. This is easier said than done. Bluhm et al. [6], in their excellent text on credit risk, state that:

> We do not know about an established standard calibration methodology for fitting $t$-copulas to a credit portfolio.

Neither do we. This is, therefore, a challenge faced by any user of the $t$-threshold model. Central to the problem is the fundamental notion of tail dependence. Since it relates to the joint incidence of extreme outcomes, data is understandably very scarce. As a consequence, this parameter is determined by a combination of expert judgement and trial and error.

What we do know is that $\nu$ should not be a very large value—say 100 to 300—because this practically amounts to a Gaussian copula model with its attendant shortcomings. On the other hand, a very low value of $\nu$—below, for example, about 30 or 40—is really quite aggressive. The current parameter value has been set to 70. It is certainly easy to throw rocks at this choice.[56] Why not 65 or 75? Or 50 or 90? There is no good objective rationale that can be used to defend this decision. It amounts to walking a fine line between being sufficiently *or* overly conservative. Ultimately, it is about model judgement and risk-management needs. It is, in our view, logically preferable to incorporate positive tail dependence into our model—and live with a hard-to-calibrate parameter—than not to have it at all.

## 3.4 Recovery Rates

Recovery, as discussed in Chap. 2, is assumed to be a stochastic quantity. For each default outcome, a simultaneous random variable is drawn from a distribution to determine the amount recovered. Naturally, this raises two important questions: how is the recovery aspect distributed and is it somehow related to the default element? Both questions are, from an empirical perspective, a bit difficult to answer. Default

[56] Internally, of course, a detailed analysis of the impact of different choices of $\nu$ upon credit-risk economic capital is performed on a periodic basis.

is a generally rare event making estimation of default probabilities a challenging problem; recovery is an outcome conditional on default. Thus, we are trying to estimate the distribution of an outcome conditional on another rather rare event. Availability and richness of data is thus the principal problem in this area.

To handle these problems, *three* main assumptions are typically made:

1. the recovery rate, which varies among obligors, is assumed to be function of numerous elements of counterparty's current general creditworthiness;
2. the recovery process is assumed to be independent of the default mechanics; and
3. the stochastic element of recovery is described by the beta distribution.

All three of these assumptions can be relaxed and other choices are, of course, possible. These common assumptions, however, represent reasonable choices in the face of limited data.

A key follow-up question is how does one specify the stochastic dynamics of the recovery elements. Moreover, once a specific choice is made, how is the parametrization performed? This can, in principle, be as complex as one desires. These objects, for example, could be treated as multivariate stochastic processes; that is, they could possess randomness across both the cross-sectional and time dimensions. This would, not to mention the challenges of parameter estimation, likely be overkill. Instead, recovery values are typically drawn from a convenient time-invariant distribution.

**The Beta Distribution**

To operationalize this general notion, it is necessary to specify the distribution of each individual recovery variable, $\mathcal{R}_i$; in our case, the beta distribution. Let us first consider this decision generically; afterwards, we can specialize it to our needs and desires. Consider the following random variable,

$$X \sim \text{Beta}(a, b), \tag{3.27}$$

where $a$ and $b$ are parameters in $\mathbb{R}_+$.[57] In words, $X$ is beta distributed. The density of $X$ is summarized as,

$$f_X(x) = \frac{1}{\beta(a, b)} x^{a-1}(1-x)^{b-1}, \tag{3.28}$$

for $x \in (0, 1)$. That is, the support of $X$ is the unit interval.[58] $\beta(a, b)$ denotes the so-called beta function, which is described as,

$$\beta(a, b) = \int_0^1 t^{a-1}(1-t)^{b-1} dt, \tag{3.29}$$

[57] $a$ and $b$ are referred to as shape parameters; they are not, as is the case with many common distributions, directly mapped to a distributional moment.

[58] This is the standard density function, although it is readily generalized to any finite interval, $[v, u]$, where $u > v$.

which bears a strong resemblance to the form of the beta density. The beta function is also closely related to the gamma function. In particular,

$$\beta(a, b) = \frac{\Gamma(a)\Gamma(b)}{\Gamma(a+b)}. \tag{3.30}$$

The gamma function, which can be seen as a continuous analogue of the discrete factorial function, is written as[59]

$$\Gamma(t) = \int_{\infty}^{\infty} x^{t-1} e^{-x} dx. \tag{3.31}$$

The beta distribution, given its finite support, is often used in statistics and engineering to model proportions. Interestingly, if one sets $a = b = 1$, then the beta distribution collapses to a continuous uniform distribution.[60] Moreover, it can easily be constructed from the generation of gamma random variates.[61] Finally, the mean of a beta-distributed random variable, $X$, with parameters $a$ and $b$ is,

$$\mathbb{E}(X) = \frac{a}{a+b}, \tag{3.32}$$

while its variance is,

$$\text{var}(X) = \frac{ab}{(a+b)^2 (a+b+1)}. \tag{3.33}$$

So much for the mathematical background on the beta distribution. The key question is: how precisely is this choice utilized in a default credit-risk model? It basically comes down to parameter choice. In principle, one could expect to have slightly different parameters for each region, industry, or business line. As one would expect, however, a number of simplifying assumptions are imposed. Each individual credit obligor is assigned to a loss-given-default value following from an internal framework. We then transform this loss-given-default value into an recovery amount.

To simulate recoveries, which is our ultimate goal, we need to establish a link between the moments furnished by internal assignment and the model parameters. This is basically a calibration exercise. We denote $M_i$ and $V_i$ as the mean and

[59] The role of the gamma and beta functions in density functions is basically to appropriately assign probability mass to events. See Abramovitz and Stegun [1, Chapter 6] for a detailed description of the gamma function.

[60] It is easy to see, from Eqs. 3.28 and 3.29, that when $a = b = 1$, then $f_X(x) \equiv 1$ consistent with the standard uniform density.

[61] See Casella and Berger [9, Chapter 3], Johnson et al. [26, Chapter 25], and Fishman [15, Chapter 3] for much more technical information and background on the beta distribution.

variance conditions associated with the $i$th credit obligor.[62] $M_i$ is directly informed by the policy; the choice of $V_i$, however, is less obvious. A common value might be assigned to all individual credit obligors. We could also use this parameter to target specific characteristics of the recovery distribution. In the forthcoming analysis, we will explore the implications of both choices. For the time being, let's just think of it as a generic value.

We thus view $M_i$ and $V_i$ as economically motivated moment conditions for the recovery variable. The idea is to determine how we might transform these values into beta-distribution shape parameters, $a_i$ and $b_i$, for employment in our model. Using the definitions provided in Eqs. 3.32 and 3.33, we construct a system of (non-linear) equations. The first expression equates the first moments

$$\begin{aligned} M_i &= \frac{a_i}{a_i + b_i}, \\ M_i(a_i + b_i) &= a_i, \\ a_i &= \frac{b_i M_i}{1 - M_i}. \end{aligned} \tag{3.34}$$

The second piece, equating the variance terms, is a bit more complex

$$V_i = \frac{a_i b_i}{(a_i + b_i)^2 (a_i + b_i + 1)}. \tag{3.35}$$

If we substitute Eq. 3.34 into 3.35, a tiresome calculation reveals

$$\begin{aligned} V_i &= \frac{b_i \overbrace{\frac{b_i M_i}{1 - M_i}}^{a_i}}{\left( \underbrace{\frac{b_i M_i}{1 - M_i}}_{a_i} + b_i \right)^2 \left( \underbrace{\frac{b_i M_i}{1 - M_i}}_{a_i} + b_i + 1 \right)}, \\ &= \frac{\frac{b_i^2 M_i}{1 - M_i}}{\left( \frac{\cancel{b_i M_i} + b_i - \cancel{b_i M_i}}{1 - M_i} \right)^2 \left( \frac{\cancel{b_i M_i} + b_i - \cancel{b_i M_i} + (1 - M_i)}{1 - M_i} \right)}, \\ &= \frac{\cancel{b_i^2} M_i}{\cancel{1 - M_i}} \cdot \frac{(1 - M_i)^{\cancel{3}}}{\cancel{b_i^2} (b_i + (1 - M_i))}, \end{aligned} \tag{3.36}$$

[62] Although it is more common to talk about volatility, we need only square it to arrive at the desired variance condition.

$$
\begin{aligned}
&= \frac{M_i(1-M_i)^2}{b_i + (1-M_i)}, \\
b_i &= \frac{(1-M_i)(M_i(1-M_i) - V_i)}{V_i}.
\end{aligned}
$$

Now plugging this quantity back into Eq. 3.34, we recover the required value of $a_i$ as,

$$
\begin{aligned}
a_i &= \frac{\left(\overbrace{\frac{(1-M_i)(M_i(1-M_i)-V_i)}{V_i}}^{b_i}\right) M_i}{1-M_i}, \qquad (3.37)\\
&= \frac{M_i\cancel{(1-M_i)}(M_i(1-M_i)-V_i)}{V_i} \cdot \frac{1}{\cancel{1-M_i}}, \\
&= \frac{M_i(M_i(1-M_i)-V_i)}{V_i}.
\end{aligned}
$$

We thus have a concrete link between the beta-distribution parameters and the provided moment conditions. This is, in fact, a closed-form application of the method-of-moments estimation technique.[63]

While technically correct, this result is not terribly intuitive. If, however, we introduce the term,

$$
\xi_i = \frac{M_i(1-M_i) - V_i}{V_i}, \qquad (3.38)
$$

then we can rewrite our recovery model parameter choices as,

$$
\begin{aligned}
a_i &= M_i \xi_i, \qquad (3.39)\\
b_i &= (1-M_i)\xi_i.
\end{aligned}
$$

We can interpret $\xi_i$ in Eq. 3.38 as the normalized distance between the provided value and the variance of a Bernoulli trial with parameter, $M_i$. This is not a coincidence since the beta distribution approaches the Bernoulli distribution as the shape parameters, $a_i$ and $b_i$, approach zero. This would be precisely the case, as is clear from Eq. 3.38, should we set $M_i(1-M_i) = V_i$. That is, this is the variance of a Bernoulli trial, with parameter, $M_i$. In this situation, which is the point, both $a_i$ and $b_i$ reduce to zero.

[63] See Casella and Berger [9] for more background on this parameter-estimation technique.

One way to see that these are equivalent conditions is to re-examine the definition of the beta distribution's variance from Eq. 3.35,

$$\begin{aligned} V_i &= \frac{a_i b_i}{(a_i + b_i)^2 (a_i + b_i + 1)}, \\ &= \frac{M_i \xi_i (1 - M_i)\xi_i}{(M_i \xi_i + (1 - M_i)\xi_i)^2 (a_i + b_i + 1)}, \\ &= \frac{M_i \xi_i^2 (1 - M_i)}{(\cancel{M_i \xi_i} + \xi_i - \cancel{M_i \xi_i})^2 (a_i + b_i + 1)}, \\ &= \frac{M_i (1 - M_i)}{(a_i + b_i + 1)}. \end{aligned} \tag{3.40}$$

As long as the sum of the two parameters $a_i$ and $b_i$ remains greater than zero, then the denominator of Eq. 3.40 exceeds unity. This, by extension, ensures that $V_i < M_i(1 - M_i)$.

The Bernoulli trial limiting case is, however, practically rather unsatisfactory. It is conceptually equivalent to flipping a coin. The outcome is binary; heads with probability $M_i$ and tails with $1 - M_i$. Instead of heads and tails, however, we have values 0 and 1. That is, the probability of the full recovery of a claim is $M_i$; the corollary is that our recovery takes the value of zero (i.e., we lose the entire exposure) with probability $1 - M_i$. This is probably not a reasonable recovery model, but it is interesting that it is embedded in the structure of the beta-distribution approach.[64] If we avoid this unrealistic extreme case, then the beta distribution will permit the recovery of any claim to, in principle, take any value in the unit interval.

**Fixed Recovery Volatility**

The uncertainty surrounding the mean recovery rate—referred to previously as $\sqrt{V_i}$—is not obviously determined. We have, in the past, experimented with the assignment of a value of $\sqrt{V_i} \equiv 0.25$ to all counterparties. Why might one do this? The simple, and perhaps not very satisfying, answer is that one lacks sufficient information to empirically differentiate between individual obligors. Small to medium institutions will generally have a correspondingly modest—and typically uninformative, default and loss-given-default—data history.

Using the method-of-moments estimator derived in Eqs. 3.38 and 3.39, Fig. 3.21 summarizes the associated beta-distribution parameters utilized to generate beta-distributed random variates arising from the blanket assumption of $\sqrt{V_i} \equiv 0.25$. Since each $a_i$ and $b_i$ parameter is a function of both moment conditions, we cannot

64 The beta-distribution approach to recovery thus nests *two* additional, and fairly extreme, models: a Bernoulli trial and a uniform distribution. The former occurs when the shape parameters take the values of zero, whereas the latter arises when both are set to one.

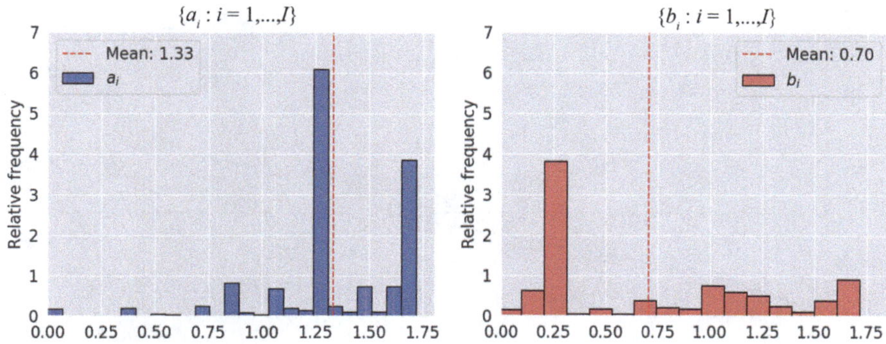


**Fig. 3.21** *Fixed $V_i$ Beta-distribution parameters*: Using a method-of-moments approach, this figure illustrates the mapping of $M_i$ choices and fixed $V_i \equiv 0.25$ into a collection of the beta distribution's two shape parameters, $a_i$ and $b_i$.

speak of a mapping between the beta parameters and assumed moments.[65] The $a_i$ values take an average value of roughly 1.3; observed values range from close to zero to about 1.75. The $b_i$ values, conversely, exhibit a mean value of about 0.7; again, observations range from 0 to almost 2. The $a_i$ outcomes are clustered around the mean, while the $b_i$'s appear to have a multimodal form with probability mass around 0.25, 1, and 1.75.

How does the beta distribution take these two shape parameters and determine the relative probabilities of an outcome? Since the standard beta distribution is restricted to the unit interval, we seek to understand how probability mass is spread over this region. Figure 3.22 helps us answer this question by plotting a broad range of beta densities. The first uses the mean shape parameters—in particular, $a = 1.3$ and $b = 0.7$—to describe the average density associated with a fixed choice recovery volatility. This outcome, summarized by the red line, places a significant amount of probability mass around unity and gradually falls down towards zero; in this case, the mean appears to lie between 0.65 and 0.7. The blue line repeats this analysis, but uses financial exposures to find a weighted set of beta parameters.[66] There is very little difference, although the weight on higher recoveries falls slightly with a modest impact on the mean outcome. The final high-level point of comparison is the uniform density, where all values in [0, 1] are equally likely.

In addition to these three high-level comparative densities, every single observed pair of $a$ and $b$ shape parameters are used to display the entire range of employed densities. A broad range of shapes are evident. Some look flat, others have the standard upward-sloping shape found in the average density, a few bell-shaped densities can be identified, others exhibit a $u$-shaped form, while another group

[65] Each $a_i$ and $b_i$ value is, to repeat, a shape parameter and cannot, as in some distributions, be easily equated with a distributional moment.

[66] The difference is not dramatic: $\bar{a} \approx 1.37$ and $\bar{b} \approx 0.80$.

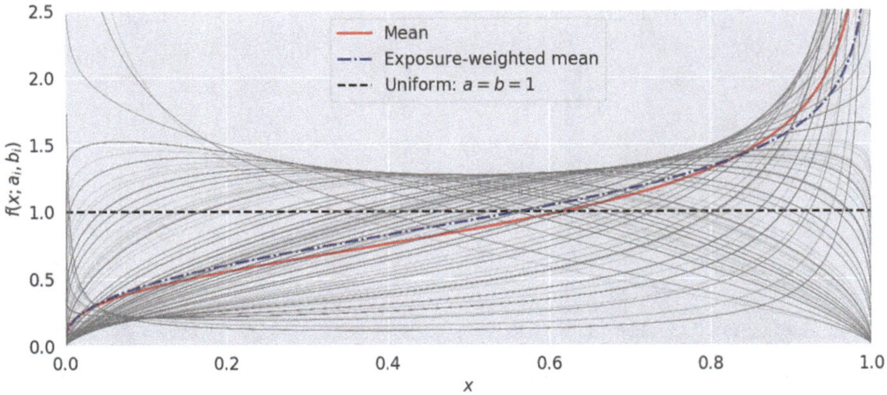


**Fig. 3.22** *Fixed $V_i$ beta densities*: The preceding figure plots the entire range of beta densities associated with the (indirectly) assumed shape parameters. For reference, the beta densities associated with the simple-mean and exposure-weighted mean shape parameters are also provided. On average, a higher probability of large recovery is assumed.

looks to be downward sloping.[67] There is a fairly rich range of assumed beta densities. Empirically, there is some evidence that actual recovery rates are actually bimodal; this implies that there is a disproportionately high probability of quite large or quite small recoveries.[68] This is a rather stark deviation between this empirical finding and the constant recovery-variance assumptions illustrated in Fig. 3.22.

**Colour and Commentary 36** (FIXED RECOVERY VOLATILITY)*: Determination of recovery volatility is hard. One might quite reasonably opt to make a common assessment of recovery uncertainty for all one's credit obligors. Although not terribly defensible, it has the benefit of simplicity. The resulting beta densities are helpful in assessing this choice. While a range of beta densities is observed with varying forms, the average result places a relatively high degree of probability mass on high-recovery outcomes. Empirical evidence suggests that actual recovery rates are actually bimodal; the consequence is a disproportionately high probability of quite large or quite small recoveries. This would appear to be something of a shortcoming of the constant recovery volatility assumption. To resolve this, we need to identify an approach permitting the introduction of recovery bimodality. The*

(continued)

[67] As a general rule, if $a = b$, then the density will be symmetric, whereas if $a \neq b$, then it will be skewed in one direction or another.

[68] See Schuermann [38] for a nice overview of the stylized empirical facts about loss-given-default (and recovery).

**Colour and Commentary 36** (continued)
*consequence, of course, will be more extreme recovery and loss-given-default outcomes with a commensurate increase in one's associated economic-capital estimates.*

**Bimodal Recovery**
The method-of-moments technique provides a useful link between the desired recovery moments and these shape parameters. The mean of this distribution (i.e., $M_i$) should be clearly provided by one's loss-given-default framework, but its variance (i.e., $V_i$) may not be known. While this feels problematic, it represents something of an opportunity. We might treat the $V_i$ value as a free parameter. It could be selected to obtain desired distributional characteristics; such as, quite pertinent in our situation, bimodality.

A bimodal beta distribution is consistent with a so-called $U$-shaped density function. That is, there is a preponderance of probability mass at the lower and upper—or extreme—ends of the distribution's support. Practically, this means that, irrespective of the mean, large or small recoveries are relatively more probable. It turns out that there is a convenient condition ensuring that a beta density has a $U$-shaped form: both the $a$ and $b$ parameters must be less than 1. The imposition of a bi-model recovery distribution thus reduces to something like the following optimization problem:

$$\begin{aligned} \min_{a_i(M_i,V_i),b_i(M_i,V_i)} \quad & V_i, \\ \text{subject to:} \quad & \\ a_i(M_i, V_i), b_i(M_i, V_i) &\in (0, 1), \\ \frac{a_i(M_i, V_i)}{a_i(M_i, V_i) + b_i(M_i, V_i)} &= M_i, \\ V_i &> 0. \end{aligned} \tag{3.41}$$

In words, therefore, we seek the smallest variance value that would lead to a $U$-shaped beta density. Inspection of Eq. 3.41 suggests that it is not much of an optimization problem. Indeed, there exists a (hopefully, non-empty) set of possible $V_i$ values that respect our three constraints. This set is defined—in what basically amounts to a simple manipulation of Eq. 3.41—as follows:

$$\mathcal{V}_i = \left\{ V_i : \underbrace{a_i(M_i, V_i), b_i(M_i, V_i) \in (0, 1)}_{U\text{-shaped condition}}, \underbrace{\frac{a_i(M_i, V_i)}{a_i(M_i, V_i) + b_i(M_i, V_i)} = M_i}_{\text{Preserve mean}}, \underbrace{V_i > 0}_{\substack{\text{Positive}\\ \text{variance}}} \right\}. \tag{3.42}$$

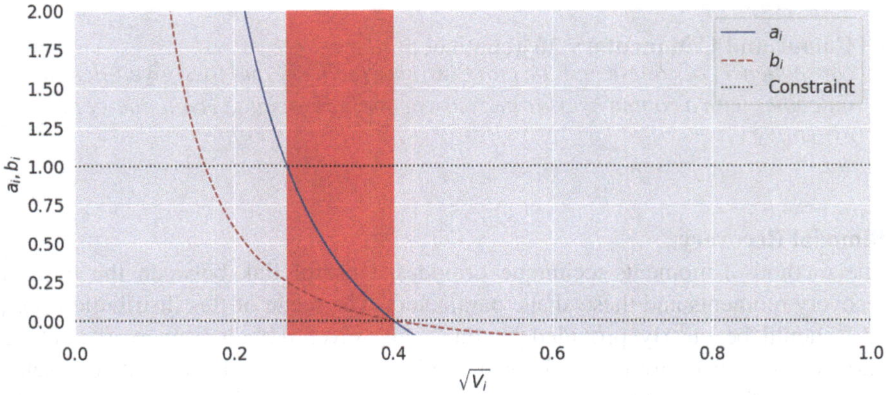


**Fig. 3.23** *Visualizing* $\mathcal{V}_i$: For the $i$th arbitrarily selected credit obligor, this figure provides a visualization of the set $\mathcal{V}_i$ defined in Eq. 3.42. The red-shaded area represents the confluence of $a_i$, $b_i$, and $\sqrt{V_i}$ values that preserve the mean, provide positive variance, and permit a $U$-shaped beta density function.

Any member of this set—that is, $V_i \in \mathcal{V}_i$—will respect one's internal loss-given-default framework, provide a $U$-shaped or bimodal beta distribution, and involve a mathematically legitimate choice for the second moment of the recovery distribution.

Figure 3.23 provides a graphical visualization of this set for an arbitrarily selected credit obligor; it is, however, quite representative of the general problem faced by obligors. The red-shaded area in Fig. 3.23 represents the confluence of $a_i$, $b_i$, and $\sqrt{V_i}$ values that preserve the mean, provide positive variance, and permit a $U$-shaped beta density function. Permissible values of $\sqrt{V_i}$, in this case, appear to range from about 0.25 to roughly 0.4.

A bit of effort can help us identify the boundaries of the set defined in Eq. 3.42. This means working with the $U$-shaped condition constraints to understand what they imply for the possible values of $V_i$. Let's start with the $a_i$ parameter. It has to be strictly less than unity, which implies, from our previous definitions, that

$$\begin{aligned} a(M_i, V_i) &< 1, \\ M_i \xi_i &< 1, \\ M_i \left( \frac{M_i(1-M_i) - V_i}{V_i} \right) &< 1, \\ \frac{M_i(1-M_i)}{V_i} &< \frac{1}{M_i} + 1, \\ V_i &> \frac{M_i^2(1-M_i)}{1+M_i}. \end{aligned} \tag{3.43}$$

This suggests a lower bound on $V_i$, based on the specification of $a$, which depends entirely on the mean recovery value. A corresponding upper bound can be derived from the second constraint condition as follows,

$$\begin{aligned} a(M_i, V_i) &> 0, \\ M_i\left(\frac{M_i(1-M_i)-V_i}{V_i}\right) &> 0, \\ \frac{M_i(1-M_i)}{V_i} &> 1, \\ V_i &< M_i(1-M_i). \end{aligned} \tag{3.44}$$

Combining these two values together, and applying the square-root operator to return to volatility space, the $a_i$-parameter bounds on the $V_i$ parameter are defined by the following open interval

$$\sqrt{V_i} \in \left(\sqrt{\frac{M_i^2(1-M_i)}{1+M_i}}, \sqrt{M_i(1-M_i)}\right). \tag{3.45}$$

Interestingly, the (unattainable) upper bound is the volatility of a Bernoulli trial with parameter, $M_i$.

We also may similarly compute a similar set of $b$-parameter induced bounds. The lower bound is given as,

$$\begin{aligned} b(M_i, V_i) &< 1, \\ (1-M_i)\xi_i &< 1, \\ (1-M_i)\left(\frac{M_i(1-M_i)-V_i}{V_i}\right) &< 1, \\ \frac{M_i(1-M_i)}{V_i} &< \frac{1}{1-M_i}+1, \\ V_i &> \frac{M_i(1-M_i)^2}{2-M_i}, \end{aligned} \tag{3.46}$$

while the upper bound is,

$$\begin{aligned} b(M_i, V_i) &> 0, \\ (1-M_i)\left(\frac{M_i(1-M_i)-V_i}{V_i}\right) &> 0, \\ \frac{M_i(1-M_i)}{V_i} &> 1, \\ V_i &< M_i(1-M_i). \end{aligned} \tag{3.47}$$

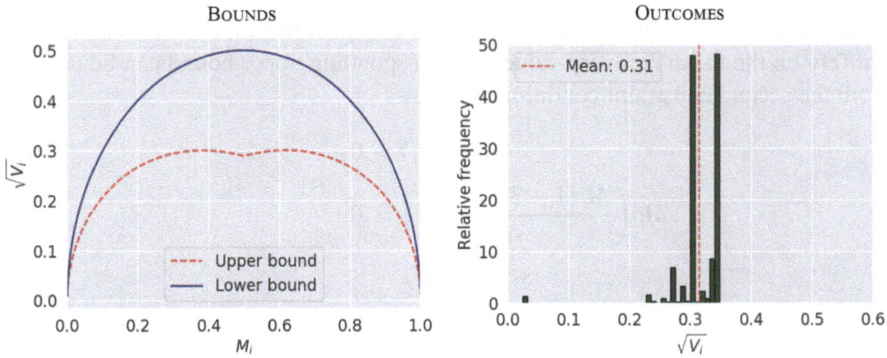


**Fig. 3.24** *Identifying* $V_i$: Respecting our constraints, explicit upper and lower bounds, for a given level of $M_i$, can be traced out. We seek to avoid being too close to the upper bound, which approaches the Bernoulli-trial case, so we select one quarter of the distance between the lower and upper bounds. The final results are presented in the right-hand graphic.

Combining, these two values together yields a second interval

$$\sqrt{V_i} \in \left(\sqrt{\frac{M_i(1-M_i)^2}{2-M_i}}, \sqrt{M_i(1-M_i)}\right). \tag{3.48}$$

The Bernoulli-trial variance upper bound is common between both the $a_i$ and $b_i$ calculations. Overall, since both $a_i$ and $b_i$ constraints need to be jointly respected, the final set of parameter-induced bounds, in terms of $M_i$, are

$$\sqrt{V_i} \in \left(\max\left(\sqrt{\frac{M_i(1-M_i)^2}{2-M_i}}, \sqrt{\frac{M_i^2(1-M_i)}{1+M_i}}\right), \sqrt{M_i(1-M_i)}\right) \equiv \left(\underline{V_i}, \overline{V_i}\right). \tag{3.49}$$

The left-hand graphic in Fig. 3.24 examines the practical upper and lower bounds on $\sqrt{V_i}$ for the full range of mean recovery values, $M_i$, over the unit interval. The broadest range of possible $V_i$ values occurs when $M_i = 0.5$. As $M_i$ moves to its lower and upper extremes, the set of permissible values shrinks asymptotically to zero.[69]

The previous bound derivations are tedious, but provide some useful insight into the problem. As we move towards the upper bound, our beta-distribution structure tends towards a Bernoulli trial with parameter, $M_i$. This coin-flip approach pushes

[69] As a practical matter, this suggests that mean recovery values of one or zero are not really workable. In the unlikely case such values might arise, they can be replaced with 0.01 and 0.99, respectively. This makes no material economic change in the parameter values and happily avoids mathematical headaches.

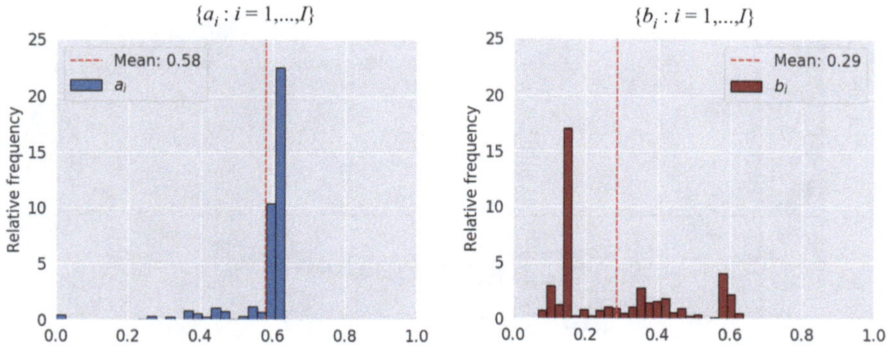


**Fig. 3.25** *Revised beta-distribution parameters*: Using the modified method-of-moments approach from Eq. 3.50, this figure illustrates the mapping of $M_i$ and $V_i$ choices into a collection of the beta distribution's two shape parameters, $a_i$ and $b_i$.

the $a_i$ and $b_i$ shape parameters, as previously seen, towards zero. This is the ultimate bimodal distribution; full or zero recovery.[70] While it makes logical sense that our investigation would take us towards this approach, we prefer to avoid its extreme nature. Instead, we opt for neither extreme, but exhibit a bias for the lower end. Our selected recovery volatility for the $i$th credit obligor is thus defined as,

$$\sqrt{V_i} = \sqrt{\underline{V_i} + 0.25 \cdot \left(\overline{V_i} - \underline{V_i}\right)}. \tag{3.50}$$

There is nothing particularly special about the choice of 0.25. It was intended to represent a compromise between the extremes with a preference for slightly more distance from the Bernoulli-trial case. One could, of course, argue for a value of 0.5. Ultimately, the impact on the final parameter values and, by extension, the economic-capital results is rather modest.

The right-hand graphic in Fig. 3.24 illustrates the range of $\sqrt{V_i}$ associated with Eq. 3.50. There is not a dramatic difference in the average outcome—of about 0.3—and the common legacy setting of 0.25. With the exception of an outlier or two, the computed values lie comfortably from about 0.2 to 0.35 with peaks in probability mass around 0.3 and 0.35, respectively.

The shape parameters associated with the approach highlighted in Eq. 3.50 are presented in Fig. 3.25. No individual $a_i$ or $b_i$ value exceeds one or falls below zero. The mean $a_i$ parameter is roughly 0.6, which compares to the fixed-$V_i$ average outcome of 1.3. The $b_i$ parameters exhibit an average of about 0.3, which is less than half of what was observed in the constant-recovery-volatility approach. The bottom line is that the imposition of $U$-shaped density constraints on our

[70] This would be consistent with the (naive) minimization approach suggested in Eq. 3.41.

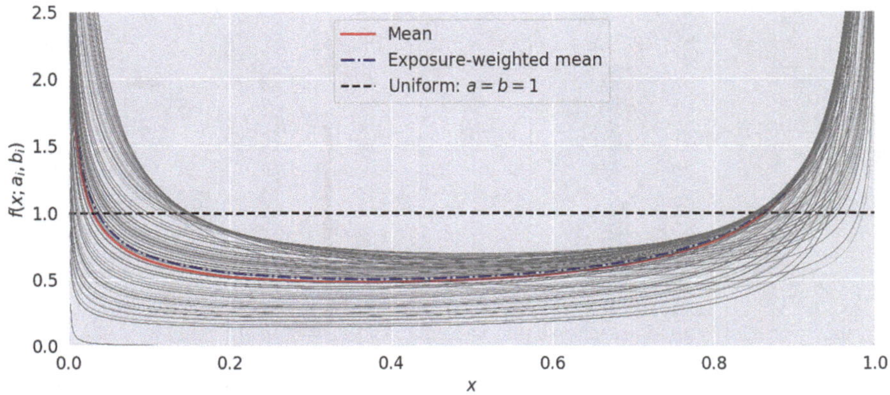


**Fig. 3.26** *Revised beta densities*: This figure plots the entire range of beta densities associated with the (indirectly) assumed shape parameters. For reference, the beta densities associated with the simple-mean and exposure-weighted mean shape parameters are also provided. On average, this approach implies a relatively higher probability of extreme—large loss or recovery—outcomes, which is consistent with empirical evidence surrounding recoveries.

method-of-moments estimator leads to fairly important changes in the associated beta-distribution shape-parameter estimates.

Figure 3.26 completes the picture. It provides—analogous to Fig. 3.22 for the constant-recovery-volatility case—an illustration of the entire population of beta densities associated with our $U$-shaped constrained method-of-moments estimator. The results are visually quite striking. Not only do the mean and exposure-weighted mean densities demonstrate a $U$-shaped form, every single beta density exhibits the desired bimodal structure. This was accomplished while preserving the mean recovery rate and generating recovery volatility estimates that are generally consistent with the constant $\sqrt{V_i}$ approach. This clearly exemplifies the ability of our constraint set to achieve our targeted beta-density outcomes.

**Colour and Commentary 37** (BIMODAL RECOVERY)*: Empirical evidence—see, for example, Chen and Wang [11]—suggests that the recovery rate distribution is bimodal. In plain English, this means there is a disproportionately high probability of extreme (i.e., high or low) outcomes. Practically, the bimodal property enhances model conservatism by increasing the global probability of extremely low levels of default recovery. Bimodal beta densities are mathematically attainable through restriction of the shape ($a_i$ and $b_i$) parameters to the unit interval. Incorporating these constraints into the method-of-moments estimator, and using the recovery volatility as a free parameter, permit imposition of a bimodal form. Under this approach, the mean recovery rate is preserved, all beta densities are bimodal, and*

(continued)

**Colour and Commentary 37** (continued)
*reasonable recovery volatility estimates are generated. Beyond a desire to meet an empirical stylized fact, however, this is not an economically motivated parametrization; it is a mathematical trick to induce bimodality. The main alternative, a constant and common recovery volatility parameter, provides no logical competition. Absent another clear justification for the choice of recovery volatility, this parameter-estimation technique would thus appear to be a judicious choice.*

## 3.5 Credit Migration

Incorporation of credit migration into the credit-risk economic capital model necessitates a number of parametric ingredients. The central quantity, the transition matrix, has already been identified and examined in detail. Two additional variables are necessary. The first is a description of the spread implications of moving from one credit state to another. The second requirement is some notion of the sensitivity of individual loan prices to changes in their discount rate. This section will explore how one might estimate both of these important modelling inputs.

### 3.5.1 *Spread Duration*

Let us begin with the easier quantity: the current sensitivity or modified spread-duration assumption. Spread duration is readily available for instruments traded in active secondary markets, but it rather less obviously computed for untraded loans. We thus employ the cash-flow weighted average maturity as a spread-duration proxy for each of our loan obligors. This involves an embedded assumption, which requires some explanation. To help understand our choice, let's return to first principles. The value of a fixed-income security at time $t$ with yield $y$ and $N$ remaining cash-flows is simply,

$$V(y) = \sum_{i=1}^{N} \frac{c_{t_i}}{(1+y)^{t_i - t}}, \tag{3.51}$$

where each $c_{t_i}$ represents an individual cash-flow. In other words, the value is merely the sum of the discounted individual cash-flows. The yield, $y$, is the common discount rate for all individual cash-flows that provides the observed valuation.

Equation 3.51 is silent on the credit spread, which complicates computation of spread duration. It is thankfully possible to decompose—for a given underlying tenor—any fixed-income security's yield into two logical parts: the risk-free yield and its associated credit spread. More concretely, we write:

$$y = \hat{y} + s, \tag{3.52}$$

where $\hat{y}$ and $s$ denote the risk-free yield and credit spread, respectively.[71] This permits us to rewrite the pricing, or valuation, function of an arbitrary loan as,

$$V \equiv V(\hat{y}, s) = \sum_{i=1}^{N} \frac{c_{t_i}}{\underbrace{\left(1 + \hat{y} + s\right)^{t_i - t}}_{\text{Eq. 3.52}}}, \tag{3.53}$$

The advantage of this formulation is that it directly includes the credit (or lending) spread.[72]

The modified spread-duration is defined as the normalized first derivative of our loan-price relation with respect to the credit spread, $s$. It is written as,

$$\begin{aligned} D_m &= \left| \frac{1}{V(\hat{y}, s)} \frac{\partial V(\hat{y}, s)}{\partial s} \right|, \qquad (3.54)\\ &= \left| \frac{1}{V(\hat{y}, s)} \frac{\partial}{\partial s} \left( \underbrace{\sum_{i=1}^{N} \frac{c_{t_i}}{(1 + \hat{y} + s)^{t_i - t}}}_{\text{Eq. 3.53}} \right) \right|, \\ &= \frac{1}{V(\hat{y}, s) \cdot (1 + \hat{y} + s)} \sum_{i=1}^{N} \frac{(t_i - t) c_{t_i}}{(1 + \hat{y} + s)^{t_i - t}}, \\ &= \frac{1}{V(y) \cdot (1 + y)} \sum_{i=1}^{N} \frac{(t_i - t) c_{t_i}}{(1 + y)^{t_i - t}}, \end{aligned}$$

where the absolute-value operator is introduced because, in practice, we typically treat this as a positive quantity and introduce the negative sign as required by the context. The product of Eq. 3.54 and a given spread perturbation provides an approximation of the percentage return change in one's loan value. This explains its usefulness for the credit-migration computation.[73]

---

[71] This need not be an actual risk-free rate, but could also be some form of lower risk reference rate. It may be more useful to characterize $\hat{y}$ as the corresponding LIBOR-based swap rate.

[72] See Bolder [7, Part I] for more information on fixed-income security sensitivities in general and spread duration in particular.

[73] As some of the spread movements can be quite large, this linear approximation may overestimate some of the valuation losses. There is thus an argument to compute a convexity term to capture the

While Eq. 3.54 provides a direct, practical description for the first-order, linear, credit-spread sensitivity of a loan, it is not easy for us to employ. For a given loan, it may be difficult to clearly identify the specific credit spread and risk-free rates, which makes the determination of $y$ a rather noisy and uncertain affair. A set of cash-flow forecasts are, however, available for every individual loan based on forward interest rates and actual loan margins. This permits a simple proxy representation of Eq. 3.54. It is conceptually similar and has the following form:

$$\begin{aligned} D_m &= \frac{1}{V(y)(1+y)} \sum_{i=1}^{N} \frac{(t_i - t)c_{t_i}}{(1+y)^{t_i - t}}, \\ &\approx \frac{1}{V(0)(1+\not{y})} \sum_{i=1}^{N} \frac{(t_i - t)c_{t_i}}{(1+\not{y})^{t_i - t}}, \\ &\approx \frac{1}{V(0)} \sum_{i=1}^{N} (t_i - t)c_{t_i}, \\ &\approx \left( \sum_{i=1}^{N} c_{t_i} \right)^{-1} \sum_{i=1}^{N} (t_i - t)c_{t_i}. \end{aligned} \tag{3.55}$$

This proxy is simply the cash-flow weighted average tenor. We can see, of course, that our proxy stems from setting $y = 0$; in this case, Eqs. 3.54 and 3.55 coincide exactly. For any non-negative yield, however, the modified spread duration will be inferior to this weighted average cash-flow proxy. The magnitude of this difference is, in the ongoing low-yield environment, likely to be rather small. One useful characteristic of this proxy choice is that it forms a conservative spread-duration estimator for any (non-negative) loan yield.

Some NIB loan contracts have an interesting, and important, feature that has practical implications for the spread-duration calculations. In particular, various individual loans possess what is contractually referred to as a negotiation date. This future date, typically occurring a few years after disbursement, but a number of years before final maturity, offers both parties an opportunity to revisit the details of the loan. The consequence may involve re-pricing, repayment, or ultimately no change. It basically offers a potential loan reset; as such, it makes sense to consider this negotiation date as the effective maturity date of the loan for spread-duration purposes.

Practically, the presence of a pre-maturity negotiation feature makes very little difference to our sensitivity formula. If, for our generic loan, we define the number

---

non-linear relationship between yield and price movements to somewhat offset this overestimation effect. We avoid this correction, which lends a conservative aspect to this calculation.

of cash-flows associated with the negotiation date as $\tilde{N} \leq N$, then

$$D_m = \frac{1}{V(y)(1+y)} \sum_{i=1}^{\tilde{N}} \frac{(t_i - t)c_{t_i}}{(1+y)^{t_i - t}}, \tag{3.56}$$

$$\approx \left( \sum_{i=1}^{\tilde{N}} c_{t_i} \right)^{-1} \sum_{i=1}^{\tilde{N}} (t_i - t)c_{t_i}.$$

The structure of the spread-duration approximation is unchanged, it is merely truncated when the negotiation date is inferior to the true maturity date. For those loans without such a feature in their contract—where $N = \tilde{N}$—then no difference in the spread-duration measure is observed.

**Colour and Commentary 38** (SPREAD DURATION): *The estimation of credit migration requires, for each individual loan obligation, an estimate of its sensitivity to credit-spread movements. In other words, we require spread-duration estimates. A proxy for modified spread duration is employed that assumes a zero overall yield level. The linear nature of this assumption and the consequent overestimate of sensitivity for any non-negative yield imply that this is a relatively conservative estimator. One additional, firm-specific, adjustment is involved. Many loans involve a negotiation date—typically occurring several years prior to final maturity—that provides both parties the opportunity, in the event of material changes to their position, to revise the contractual details. When such a feature is present, a revised cash-flow stream to this intermediate date is employed.*[a] *Ultimately, the computation of spread duration is a simple, but data-intensive affair.*

[a] More generally, any lending entity engaged in such calculations will need to take into account any important firm-specific contractual details.

### 3.5.2 *Credit Spreads*

Logically, one could imagine the specification of a separate loan-spread value for each credit class *and* loan. This would quickly become practically unmanageable. Instead, the typical approach is to specify a generic credit-spread level for each of one's credit categories. Were a loan to migrate from one credit class to another, it would experience an associated change in its category specific credit-spread level with a corresponding valuation effect.

There is a broad range of sources one might use to inform credit spreads: internal lending spreads, observed corporate bond prices, the credit-default swap (CDS) market, and even model-based implied values. Each offers advantages and disadvantages and, unfortunately, there is no one dominant data source. Bond-market information is a useful benchmark for comparative purposes, but these values are computed in an overly broad-based manner. That is, the range of entities within a credit-rating class used to estimate generic bond spreads are surprisingly heterogeneous and *not* necessarily representative of firm-specific business exposure. For this reason, we argue that internal lending spreads are the most sensible source for determination of credit spreads.

Data alone will not resolve the problem. We also require a theoretical, and economically motivated, approach towards the description of credit spreads. This turns out to a surprisingly deep question. To make progress, one must touch upon a variety of areas: bond pricing, corporate finance, credit-risk models, probability theory, and statistics. The following sections, accepting this challenge, offer a simplified, workable implementation for use in our economic-capital framework.

## The Theory

The hazard rate is a central character in the modelling of credit spreads. Loosely speaking, it can be thought of as the default probability over a (very) short time period. Bolstered with this concept, the credit spread of the $i$th entity—following from Hull and White [23]—can be profitably described by the following identity,

$$h_i \approx \frac{\mathbb{S}_i(t, T)}{1 - \gamma_i}, \tag{3.57}$$

where $h_i$ denotes the hazard rate, $\mathbb{S}_i(t, T)$ is the credit spread for the time interval $(t, T)$ and $\gamma_i$ is the loss-given-default. This expression also plays a central role in fitting hazard-rate functions for the valuation of loan and other credit-risky portfolios.[74] It also highlights an important, but intuitive, notion: the credit spread depends on one's assessment of the firm's creditworthiness and, in the event of default, recovery assumptions.

Equation 3.57 is the key character for an empirical estimation of credit spreads—and indeed it will prove useful in latter discussion for verification purposes—but we seek a theoretical approach. Merton [35] remains, to this day, the seminal theoretical work in the area of credit-risk modelling. It forms the foundation of the entire branch of structural credit-risk models. The key idea is that a default occurs when

[74] The level of $h_i$, more specifically, is often determined from credit-default swap contracts. See Bolder [7, Chapter 9] for more details.

the value of the firm's asset dip below their liabilities. Framed in a continuous-time mathematical setting, this logical idea permits derivation of a host of useful relationships for computation of credit-risk-related prices and risk measures. We will lean on it heavily in the following development.

The Merton [35] approach begins by defining the intertemporal dynamics of an arbitrary firm's assets on the probability space $(\Omega, \mathcal{F}, \mathbb{P})$ as

$$\frac{dA_t}{A_t} = \mu dt + \sigma dW_t, \tag{3.58}$$

where $A_t$ denotes the asset value, while $\mu$ and $\sigma$ represent the expected asset return and volatility, respectively. $\{W_t, \mathcal{F}_t\}$ is a standard, scalar Wiener process on $(\Omega, \mathcal{F}, \mathbb{P})$.[75] Operationalizing this key idea leads to the second ingredient in our recipe: the default condition. Practically, the default event over $(t, T]$ is written as,

$$\{A_T \leq K\}, \tag{3.59}$$

where $K$ represents the firm's liabilities. Practically, and this is Merton [35]'s central insight, it occurs when the value of a firm's assets fall below its liabilities. Succinctly put, default is triggered when equity is exhausted.[76]

With a gratuitous amount of mathematics and some patience, one can describe the probability of default in this structure, over the time interval $(t, T]$, as

$$\mathbb{P}(A_T \leq K) \equiv p(t, T) = \Phi\left(\underbrace{\frac{-\ln\left(\frac{A_t}{K}\right) - \left(\mu - \frac{\sigma^2}{2}\right)(T-t)}{\sigma\sqrt{T-t}}}_{\delta_t(\mu)}\right), \tag{3.60}$$

where $\Phi$ denotes the cumulative distribution function of the standard univariate Gaussian probability law.[77] The fairly unwieldy ratio in Eq. 3.60—which we have called $\delta_t(\mu)$—is a quite famous output from the Merton [35] framework. $\delta_t$ is the so-called distance to default. This quantity plays an important role in industrial credit-analytic methodologies.[78] As the name suggests, distance-to-default is a standardized measure of how far away a firm is from default. It seems quite natural that it would show up in a default-probability definition. Mechanically, the larger

[75] See Karatzas and Shreve [28] for much more information on stochastic processes in general and Brownian motions in particular.

[76] We have, in fact, already a (multivariate) version of these ideas in our development of the threshold model in Chap. 2. That is not an accident.

[77] See Bolder [7, Chapter 5] for the details of this derivation.

[78] See, for example, Crosbie and Bohn [13].

the distance to default, the lower the probability of default. It depends, again quite intuitively, on the current value of firm assets (i.e., $A_t$), the length of the time horizon under consideration (i.e., $T-t$), the size of the liabilities ($K$), and the risk and return characteristics of the firm's assets (i.e., $\mu$ and $\sigma$).

One of the challenges of using Eq. 3.60 is that determination of asset returns and volatilities can be practically quite challenging. This is because firm assets are not—outside infrequent balance-sheet disclosures—observed with any regularity. Resolving this problem involves turning to firm equity values, which, in contrast to their asset equivalents, are readily and frequently observable. This brings us into the realm of asset pricing and necessitates moving to a new probability measure. More specifically, we need to use the equivalent martingale measure, $\mathbb{Q}$, induced with the choice of money market account as the numeraire asset; this is often termed the risk-neutral measure. This takes us off onto another mathematical foray, but with some persistence we may actually write the risk-neutral default probability as,

$$\mathbb{Q}\left(A_T \leq K\right) \equiv q(t,T) = \Phi\left(\underbrace{\frac{-\ln\left(\frac{A_t}{K}\right) - \left(r - \frac{\sigma^2}{2}\right)(T-t)}{\sigma\sqrt{T-t}}}_{\delta_t(r)}\right), \tag{3.61}$$

where $r$ represents the risk-free interest rate.[79] Under the $\mathbb{Q}$ measure, by construction, all assets return the risk-free rate. This is a core idea behind risk-neutrality.

What has all this provided? In Eqs. 3.60 and 3.61, we have two alternative default-probability definitions that apply under two different probability measures. Their forms are essentially identical, up to the expected asset returns. Beyond their obvious utility as default-probability estimates, Eqs. 3.60 and 3.61 provide the first step towards a more general credit-spread definition. This begins with understanding that the risk-neutral default probability is also closely related to the credit spread. Both are involved in pricing activities and both depend on the firm's basic creditworthiness. With a bit of basic algebraic manipulation, we can simplify the risk-neutral default probability in Eq. 3.61 to help us with our objective of creating a sensible credit-spread estimator.

Reorganizing Eq. 3.60, we can identify the following relationship

$$-\ln\left(\frac{A_t}{K}\right) = \Phi^{-1}\Big(p(t,T)\Big)\sigma\sqrt{T-t} + \left(\mu - \frac{\sigma^2}{2}\right)(T-t). \tag{3.62}$$

[79] This turns out to be tightly linked to the Black and Scholes [5] option-pricing model. Once again, the reader is referred to Bolder [7, Appendix B] for the graphic details and multiple additional references.

If we insert this expression into Eq. 3.61, we may write the *risk-neutral* default probability as a function of the *physical* probability of default. The result is,

$$q(t,T) = \Phi\left(\frac{\overbrace{\Phi^{-1}\Big(p(t,T)\Big)\sigma\sqrt{T-t} + \left(\mu - \frac{\sigma^2}{2}\right)(T-t)}^{\text{Eq. 3.62}} - \left(r - \frac{\sigma^2}{2}\right)(T-t)}{\sigma\sqrt{T-t}}\right), \tag{3.63}$$

$$= \Phi\left(\Phi^{-1}\Big(p(t,T)\Big) + \left(\frac{\mu - r}{\sigma}\right)\sqrt{T-t}\right).$$

This is quite elegant. If $\mu = r$, then the two default probability definitions coincide. Since in the face of risk aversion, $\mu > r$, we find ourselves in a situation where risk-neutral default probabilities are systemically greater than physical default likelihoods. A crucial factor in Eq. 3.63 is the $\frac{\mu-r}{\sigma}$ term, which is broadly known as the Sharpe ratio.[80] The difference between these two default quantities thus basically boils down to a risk-adjusted return ratio.[81]

Although this result depends upon the underlying assumption of asset returns, it does have a fairly general applicability. Bluhm et al. [6], who explore this idea in detail, also offer a variety of options to expand and motivate Eq. 3.63. Most of them are related, in one way or another, to the well-known Capital Asset Pricing Model (or CAPM) introduced decades ago by Treynor [43], Sharpe [39, 40] and Lintner [32]. For our purposes, we will examine this in a rather more blunt fashion. In particular, we rewrite Eq. 3.63 as,

$$q(t,T) = \Phi\left(\Phi^{-1}\Big(p(t,T)\Big) + \lambda\sqrt{T-t}\right), \tag{3.64}$$

where $\lambda \in \mathbb{R}_+$. This step involves basically rolling the $\mu$, $r$, and $\sigma$ values into a single parameter. Capturing each individual quantity in an accurate manner is not a trivial undertaking; a single-parameter approach, as we'll see soon, turns out to be practical for calibrating credit spreads.

The consequence of the previous development is an economically motivated description of the relationship between physical and risk-neutral default probabilities. Arriving at Eq. 3.64 has touched upon a variety of foundational contributions to the finance literature: Merton [35]'s structural-default model, Black and Scholes

[80] Refer to Sharpe [41, 42] for the history of this important quantity.

[81] This formulation also arises in the interest-rate literature and, with a similar form, is referred to as the market price of risk; this is, in fact, the motivation for use of the (forthcoming) $\lambda$ notation. See, for example, Björk [4, Chapter 16].

[5]'s option-pricing formula, Sharpe [41]'s famous ratio, the market price of risk formulation found the short-rate model literature launched by Vasicek [44], and the omnipresent CAPM model. The next step is to link this definition more closely to the credit spread.

### Pricing Credit Risky Instruments

Asset-pricing, in its most formal sense, entails the evaluation of the discounted expected cash-flows associated with a given financial instrument. In a no-arbitrage pricing—see, for example, Harrison and Kreps [20] and Harrison and Pliska [21]—this expectation must be evaluated with respect to the equivalent martingale measure, $\mathbb{Q}$. This may seem to be an excessive amount of financial-economic machinery, but it is important to ensure that the foundations of our proposed method are solid.

Our credit-spread proposal is best understood, in this specific context, using a zero-coupon bond. In the absence of credit risk, one need only discount the one unit of currency pay-off back to the present time. In the presence of a possible firm default, an adjustment is necessary. Let's denote the cash-flow profile of this instrument as $C(t, T)$. Following from Duffie and Singleton [14, Chapter 5], this can be succinctly described as,

$$C(t,T) = \underbrace{e^{-\int_t^T r_u du}}_{\substack{\text{Risk-free} \\ \text{part}}} - \underbrace{\gamma \cdot \mathbb{I}_{A_T \leq K} \cdot e^{-\int_t^T r_u du}}_{\substack{\text{Adjust for} \\ \text{default risk}}}, \tag{3.65}$$

where

$$\mathbb{I}_{A_T \leq K} = \begin{cases} 1 : \text{Default (i.e., } A_T \leq K) \\ 0 : \text{Survival (i.e., } A_T > K) \end{cases}, \tag{3.66}$$

and $r$ is the instantaneous short-term interest rate. To simplify things somewhat, we will assume that $r$ is deterministic. As previously discussed, the price of the cash-flows in Eq. 3.65 is simply the expectation under $\mathbb{Q}$. The result is,

$$\begin{aligned} \mathbb{E}_t^{\mathbb{Q}}\Big(C(t,T)\Big) = \hat{P}(t,T) &= \mathbb{E}_t^{\mathbb{Q}}\left(e^{-\int_t^T rdu} - \gamma \cdot \mathbb{I}_{A_T \leq K} \cdot e^{-\int_t^T rdu}\right), \\ &= e^{-r(T-t)} - \gamma \cdot \mathbb{Q}(A_T \leq K) \cdot e^{-r(T-t)}, \\ &= e^{-r(T-t)}\Big(1 - \gamma \cdot q(t,T)\Big). \end{aligned} \tag{3.67}$$

If we are willing to assume the reasonableness of the structural Merton [35] model, then we could introduce the definition of $q(t, T)$ from Eqs. 3.61 or 3.64. Using the latter version, we can write the price of a zero-coupon bond as,

$$\hat{P}(t,T) = e^{-r(T-t)}\left(1-\gamma\cdot\overbrace{\underbrace{\Phi\left(\Phi^{-1}\Big(p(t,T)\Big)+\lambda\sqrt{T-t}\right)}_{\text{Eq. 3.64}}}^{q(t,T)}\right). \tag{3.68}$$

This is progress. We have represented the price of an, admittedly simple, credit-risky fixed-income security as a function of its tenor, physical default probability, and loss-given-default values. This is not the typical pricing relationship, but it is both consistent with first principles and well suited to our specific purposes. All that is missing is an explicit connection to the credit spread.

The price of a zero-coupon bond can always be represented as,

$$\hat{P}(t,T) = e^{-y(T-t)}, \tag{3.69}$$

where $y$ is essentially an unknown that is used to solve for the price. $y$, of course, is generally termed the bond yield. A common, and powerful, decomposition of the bond yield is,

$$y \approx r + \mathbb{S}, \tag{3.70}$$

where $r$ and $\mathbb{S}$ denote the risk-free rate and credit spread, respectively.[82] Quite simply, the yield of any fixed-income security can be allocated into two portions: the risk-free, time-value-of-money component and an adjustment for potential default.[83]

With this decomposition, we are only a few steps from our destination. Combining Eqs. 3.68 to 3.70 and simplifying, we have

$$\begin{aligned}
\underbrace{e^{-(\cancel{r}+\mathbb{S})(T-t)}}_{\hat{P}(t,T)} &= \underbrace{\cancel{e^{-r(T-t)}}\left(1-\gamma\cdot\Phi\left(\Phi^{-1}\Big(p(t,T)\Big)+\lambda\sqrt{T-t}\right)\right)}_{\text{Eq. 3.68}}, \qquad (3.71)\\
e^{-\mathbb{S}(T-t)} &= \left(1-\gamma\cdot\Phi\left(\Phi^{-1}\Big(p(t,T)\Big)+\lambda\sqrt{T-t}\right)\right),\\
\mathbb{S}(t,T,\gamma,p,\lambda) &= -\frac{1}{T-t}\ln\left(1-\gamma\cdot\Phi\left(\Phi^{-1}\Big(p(t,T)\Big)+\lambda\sqrt{T-t}\right)\right).
\end{aligned}$$

---

[82] We just used this fact in the previous section to derive an expression for spread duration.

[83] This is a bit of a simplification, since actual bond prices also incorporate risk adjustments for maturity, liquidity, and other market-microstructure effects. For this reason, in the interest of full transparency, Eq. 3.70 should be thought of a high-level approximation.

The consequence is a defensible expression for the credit spread as a direct function of bond tenor, loss-given-default, physical default probability, and a risk-related tuning parameter, $\lambda$. The first three quantities—for a given instrument—can be directly estimated. The tuning parameter, however, needs to be calibrated to current—or average—market conditions.

Equation 3.71 may look somewhat messy; one might worry that it is not completely intuitive. A quick sanity check can help. Let's set $\gamma = 1$ and return to the first line of Eq. 3.71. A bit of manipulation reveals,

$$
\begin{aligned}
e^{-(r+\mathbb{S})(T-t)} &= e^{-r(T-t)}\left(1 - \underbrace{1}_{=\gamma} \cdot \underbrace{\Phi\left(\Phi^{-1}\Big(p(t,T)\Big) + \lambda\sqrt{T-t}\right)}_{q(t,T)}\right), \quad (3.72)\\
e^{-(r+\mathbb{S})(T-t)} &= e^{-r(T-t)}\Big(1 - q(t,T)\Big),\\
\hat{\delta}(t,T) &= \delta(t,T)S(t,T),
\end{aligned}
$$

where $S(t, T)$ and $\hat{\delta}(t, T)$ are the survival and risky discount functions over $(t, T]$, respectively. Here we see the classical construction of the credit-risky discount curve. We can take comfort that this relationship—only a step or two from our formulation—lies at the heart of modern loan and corporate-bond valuation methodologies.

## The Credit-Spread Model

Equation 3.71 offers a succinct, economically plausible analytic link between the credit spread and our key economic-capital model variables: physical default probabilities and loss-given-default values. This functional form offers a path to enhancing the generality and robustness of a firm's credit-spread estimates. It is not, however, without a few drawbacks. As always, the principal drawbacks of any mathematical model are found in the assumptions. Establishment of Eq. 3.71 involved the following key choices:

1. a log-normal distributional assumption (i.e., geometric Brownian-motion dynamics) for the firm's asset prices;
2. use of a simplified zero-coupon bond structure for its construction;
3. collapsing the entire market-price of risk, or Sharpe ratio, structure into a single parameter; and
4. assumption of a constant risk-free interest rate.

All of these assumptions, with patience and hard work, could potentially be relaxed. The cost, however, would be incremental complexity. We actually desire to move in the opposite direction; that is, introduce more simplicity.

The credit-spread estimates within our credit-risk economic capital model are, by construction, independent of tenor. The principal reason is to manage conceptual and computational complexity. It also helps to keep the results reasonable intuitive and easier to communicate with various stakeholders. For this reason, we propose effectively eliminating the time dimension by setting $T - t = 1$. We furthermore select a common loss-given-default parameter for all issuers. Let's call this $\hat{\gamma}$. This permits us to immediately simplify Eq. 3.71 to

$$\mathbb{S}_i(\hat{\gamma}, p_i, \lambda) = -\ln\left(1 - \hat{\gamma} \cdot \Phi\left(\Phi^{-1}(p_i) + \lambda\right)\right), \tag{3.73}$$

for the $i$th credit-spread observations. As a practical matter, we set $\hat{\gamma} = 0.45$. This value is close to the historical portfolio average, reasonably conservative, and consistent with regulatory guidance.[84]

The next point is that a single market price of risk parameter, $\lambda$, is not sufficiently flexible to fit either the observed internal margin or bond-market data. It can fit either the investment grade or speculative grade credit spreads, but not both. As a consequence, we have elected to make $\lambda$ a function of the rating class to permit sufficient flexibility to accurately fit the observed data. This can, of course, be accomplished in a number of ways. The simplest would be to assign a separate parameter to each of our 20 distinct notches. Such an approach raises *two* issues. First, it gives rise to a large number of parameters. Second, it does not constrain the interaction between the credit-rating-related $\lambda$ values in any way. Economically, for example, we would anticipate reasonably smooth risk-preference movements across the credit scale.

Our solution is to construct the following non-linear market price of risk function:

$$\lambda(p_i) = \varsigma_0 + \varsigma_1 p_i + \varsigma_2 p_i^2. \tag{3.74}$$

Other choices are certainly possible, but this form is parsimonious and provides a reasonable degree of smoothness. The non-linearity does not play a central role, but appears to add a bit of additional flexibility to the overall fit.

Equation 3.74 permits us to restate our credit-spread representation in its final form as

$$\mathbb{S}_i(\hat{\gamma}, p_i, \varsigma_0, \varsigma_1, \varsigma_2) = -\ln\left(1 - \hat{\gamma} \cdot \Phi\left(\Phi^{-1}(p_i) + \underbrace{\left(\varsigma_0 + \varsigma_1 p_i + \varsigma_2 p_i^2\right)}_{\text{Eq. 3.74}}\right)\right), \tag{3.75}$$

[84] As discussed in Chap. 11, this is the setting for the foundational Basel IRB method.

for $i = 1, \ldots, K$ internal credit-margin observations in our dataset. If we use $\mathbb{S}_i$ to denote the $i$th observed credit-margin value, then our three $\varsigma$ parameters can be estimated by solving the following optimization problem:

$$\min_{\varsigma_0,\varsigma_1,\varsigma_2} \sum_{i=1}^{K} \left( \mathbb{S}_i - \mathbb{S}_i\left( \hat{\gamma}, p_i, \varsigma_0, \varsigma_1, \varsigma_2 \right) \right)^2. \tag{3.76}$$

The least-squares or $\mathcal{L}_2$ objective function was selected for its mathematical advantages.

As a final practical (and technical) matter, the problem can be solved in the raw form presented in Eq. 3.76 or the squared differences can be weighted by the position sizes. The discrepancy between the two approaches is not particularly large, but we adopt the weighted estimator to lend a bit more importance to the larger disbursements. This necessitates a small change to the optimization problem in Eq. 3.76. To accommodate this, we denote $\vec{\mathbb{S}} \in \mathbb{R}^{K\times 1}$ as the column vector of observed and estimated spread deviations as

$$\vec{\mathbb{S}} = \begin{bmatrix} \mathbb{S}_1 - \mathbb{S}_1\left( \hat{\gamma}, p_1, \varsigma_0, \varsigma_1, \varsigma_2 \right) \\ \mathbb{S}_2 - \mathbb{S}_2\left( \hat{\gamma}, p_2, \varsigma_0, \varsigma_1, \varsigma_2 \right) \\ \vdots \\ \mathbb{S}_K - \mathbb{S}_K\left( \hat{\gamma}, p_K, \varsigma_0, \varsigma_1, \varsigma_2 \right) \end{bmatrix} \tag{3.77}$$

and introduce $W \in \mathbb{R}^{K\times K}$ as a diagonal matrix of loan exposures with the following form:

$$W = \begin{bmatrix} c_1 & 0 & \cdots & 0 \\ 0 & c_2 & \cdots & 0 \\ \vdots & \vdots & \ddots & \vdots \\ 0 & 0 & \cdots & c_K \end{bmatrix}, \tag{3.78}$$

where $c_i$ represents the exposure of the $i$th lending position. Using these two components, our revised optimization problem becomes:

$$\min_{\varsigma_0,\varsigma_1,\varsigma_2} \vec{\mathbb{S}}^T W \vec{\mathbb{S}}. \tag{3.79}$$

The only difference with this latter representation—beyond the introduction of matrix notation—is that smaller loans play a slightly less important role in the final estimates than their larger equivalents.

### Credit-Spread Estimation

The credit spread incorporates *four* key elements: the nature of the default event, an assessment of the entity's default probability, the magnitude of loss given default, and an approximation of general risk preferences. Our methodology incorporates all four pieces. First, it leans on the structural default definition that colours much of modern financial literature and practical applications. Non-coincidentally, it also sits at the heart of our economic-capital framework. Second, it employs the same default probabilities found in the final column of our transition matrix. Third, it makes a generic assumption for the loss-given-default of all counterparties.[85] Finally, the actual credit-spread calibration occurs through the risk-preference parameters.

It is rather difficult, given the high sensitivity of internal credit spread data, to provide any significant degree of transparency regarding the actual parameter-selection process. As a consequence, we will focus principally on the final results. A few global comments are, however, entirely possible. First of all, consistent with the long-term through-the-cycle approach, the internal margin dataset spans the last two decades. A second point is that, in accordance with lending mandate and policies, it is rather skewed towards the investment and high-quality speculative grades. Since credit-risk estimates are necessary for the entire range of credit-rating classes, this precludes a simply curve-fitting approach to the problem.[86] This underscores the value of an economically motivated approach.

Figure 3.27 provides the resulting credit spreads associated our approach. The credit spread increases in a monotonic fashion from roughly 40 basis points at the highest level of credit quality to approximately 10% at the lower end of the scale. Reassuringly, broad-based bond-spread averages—collected over the same period as the internal spread data—are qualitatively similar to the final results.

Circling back to Eq. 3.57, an additional sanity check on our spread estimates is also possible. Following our characterization of the hazard rate in Eq. 3.57—also offered by Hull et al. [24]—a quick, but meaningful, approximation of the risk-neutral probability is given as

$$
\begin{aligned}
Q_i &= \mathbb{Q}(\tau \leq T), \\
&\approx 1 - \mathbb{Q}(\tau > T), \\
&\approx 1 - e^{-h_i},
\end{aligned}
\tag{3.80}
$$

where, in this example, $T - t = 1$ and $\tau$ denotes the default event. Taking this a step further, actual and risk-neutral default probabilities are linked—see, for example,

[85] Relaxing this assumption does not significantly change the overall fit and merely leads to additional complexity in the model implementation.

[86] In particular, the high-quality credit ratings can be fit quite readily, but extrapolation would be required to fill the entire scale. Extrapolation so far outside of one's data range is typically a fairly sketchy practice, which we would prefer to avoid.

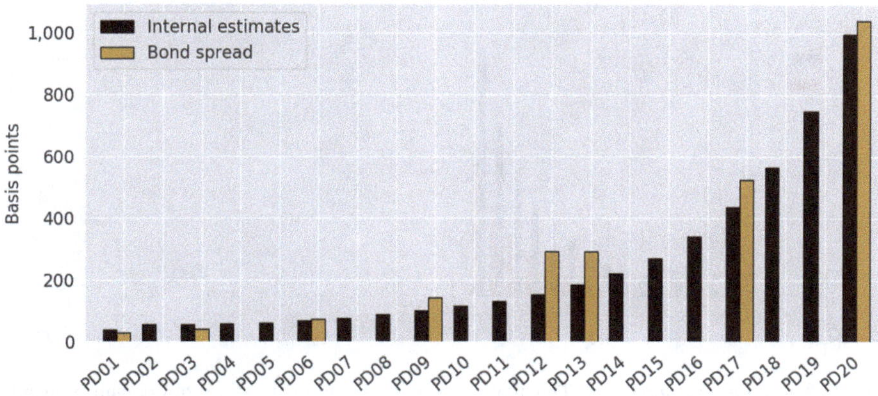


**Fig. 3.27** *Credit-spread estimates*: This graphic illustrates the estimated credit spreads, organized by credit-risk rating, stemming from the previously described methodology. Corporate bond spreads, where available, are included for comparison purposes.

Jarrow [25] for more detail—by the following identity:

$$\mathcal{Q}_i = \vartheta_i \mathcal{P}_i, \tag{3.81}$$

where $\vartheta_i > 0$ is yet another representation of the risk premium. Less accurate (and formal) than the Sharpe ratio structure found in Eq. 3.63, it nonetheless captures the distance between the physical and risk-neutral default probabilities. This (model-independent) form is often used in empirical academic studies. Equation 3.81 further suggests that if we compute the physical and risk-neutral probabilities, their ratio will provide some insight into the level of the risk premium (i.e., $\vartheta_i = \frac{\mathcal{Q}_i}{\mathcal{P}_i}$).

All we need are the risk-neutral default probabilities. Incorporating our estimated spreads into Eq. 3.80 provides the solution. Embedded, quite naturally, in our economically motivated credit-spread methodology are both flavours of default probability. From Eq. 3.57, we have that

$$\mathcal{Q}_i \approx 1 - \exp\underbrace{\left(-\frac{\mathbb{S}_i}{\mathcal{R}}\right)}_{\substack{\text{Eq.}\\ 3.57}}, \tag{3.82}$$

for $i = 1, \ldots, q$. This provides all of the necessary ingredients to calculate the inferred risk premium.

Figure 3.28 summarizes the results. The left-hand graphic explicitly compares the physical—extracted from the final column of our transition matrix—and the implied risk-neutral default probabilities. In all cases, the risk-neutral values dominate the physical default probabilities; the magnitude of the dominance, however, decreases as we move out the credit spectrum. The right-hand figure displays the

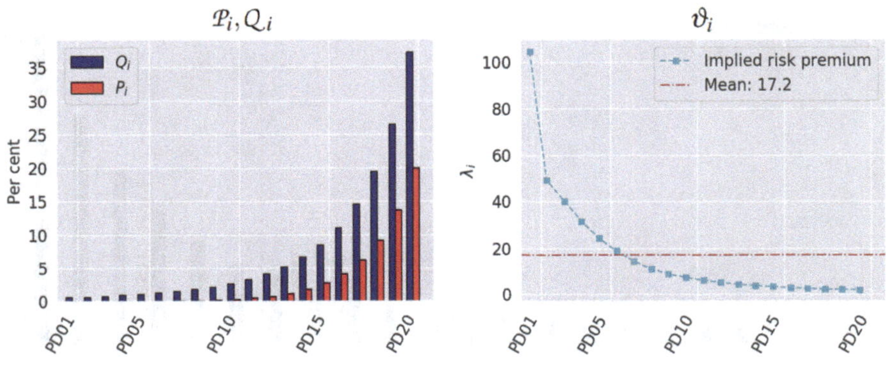


**Fig. 3.28** *A point of comparison*: This figure examines the implied risk-neutral default probabilities and inferred risk premia associated with the estimated internal-margin-based credit-spreads. The results are broadly consistent with empirical evidence in this area.

ratio of these two default probabilities—in this manner, we may infer the risk premium. The average value—across all credit classes—is approximately 17 units. At the short end, however, it approaches 100 and it falls to less than 2 for credit category 20.

A number of empirical studies examine this relationship. Heynerickx et al. [22] is a good example. This work performs a rather involved study using a broad range of credit classes and tenors over the period from 2004–2014. Referring to the risk premium as the coverage ratio, they present a similar pattern to that found in Fig. 3.28. Over the entire period, for example, risk premia range from more than 200 for AAA issuers to roughly 2 for CCC entities.[87] In the post-crisis period, however, the general levels are somewhat lower, although the basic shape remains consistent. In this framework, the general form of our results appears to be consistent with this (and other) empirical work.

**Colour and Commentary 39** (CREDIT-SPREAD ESTIMATION)*: Estimation of long-term, through-the-cycle, unconditional credit spread levels is, under any circumstances, a serious undertaking. Closely linked to macroeconomic conditions and the vagaries of financial markets, credit spreads are observably volatile over time. Broad-based credit indices, observed bonds spreads, and credit-default swap contracts can provide insight into credit spread levels. The specificity of one's lending activities and pricing policies nonetheless renders it difficult to make direct use of these values. We present an economically*

(continued)

[87] Aiming for a through-the-cycle estimate of credit spreads suggests that we focus on the longer, approximately unconditional, perspective.

**Colour and Commentary 39** (continued)
*motivated approach that uses one's history of internal lending margins. While the actual implementation is relatively straightforward, the underpinnings of the model take us on a whirlwind tour of central theoretical finance results over the last four or five decades. An interesting, and useful, sanity check on the final results involves direct comparison of the physical default probabilities from our transition matrix with the risk-neutral equivalents implied by our credit-spread estimates. In this regard, the final results appear to be broadly consistent with extant empirical evidence.*

## 3.6 Wrapping Up

This long and detailed chapter focuses on the specific choices one needs to take in determining the parametric structure of a large-scale credit-risk economic capital model. There is no shortage of moving parts. Table 3.13 tries to help manage all of this complexity by summarizing the key decisions; these are the main settings of our control panel.

**Table 3.13** *Parametric fact sheet*: The underlying table provides, at a glance, a summary of the key methodological choices associated with our credit-risk economic-capital model.

| Dimension | Description |
|---|---|
| Transition matrix | • Internal 21-state credit-state scale<br>• Corporate and sovereign matrices<br>• Common probabilities based on long-term S&P estimates |
| Systemic factors | • Geographic region and industrial sector<br>• 13 regional, 11 industrial, 1 public-sector |
| Systemic correlations | • Based on 20-year monthly equity-series data<br>• Use Spearman's rank correlation |
| Factor loadings | • Overidentified: 50% weight on region and sector<br>• Unit weight to region if public sector<br>• All other factor loadings set to zero |
| Systemic weights | • Cube based on region, sector, and firm size<br>• Values must fall in [0.12, 0.4] |
| Tail dependence | • Use of expert judgement to set $\nu = 70$ |
| Recovery | • Mean value from internal loss-given-default framework<br>• Recovery uncertainty calibrated to ensure bimodal recovery density |
| Instrument tenor | • Spread duration proxied with weighted average cash-flows<br>• Use (when appropriate) negotiation date instead of final maturity |
| Credit spreads | • Based upon internal lending margin data<br>• Calibrated via an economically motivated (theoretical) approach |

When combined with Chap. 2, a fairly complete and practical credit-risk model view should be emerging. The remaining missing point—before we can turn our attention to a collection of interesting and helpful applications—relates to the actual implementation. With some models, such questions are not terribly interesting; many possible approaches are possible and can be considered broadly equivalent. In this case, the combination of simulation methods with even a moderately sized portfolio imply the need to think hard about questions of model implementation. Industrial economic capital, along with many related applications, is required on a daily basis to properly manage our portfolios; as a consequence, computational speed matters. One also needs a plan to organize and build the factory performing these ongoing calculations.

## References


1. M. Abramovitz and I. A. Stegun. *Handbook of Mathematical Functions*. Dover Publications, New York, 1965.
2. A. Arakelyan and P. Serrano. Liquidity in Credit Default Swap Markets. *Journal of Multinational Financial Management*, 37-38:139–157, 2016.
3. BIS. An explanatory note on the Basel II IRB risk weight functions. Technical report, Bank for International Settlements, July 2005.
4. T. Björk. *Arbitrage Theory in Continuous Time*. Oxford University Press, Great Clarendon Street, Oxford, first edition, 1998.
5. F. Black and M. S. Scholes. The pricing of options and corporate liabilities. *Journal of Political Economy*, 81:637–654, 1973.
6. C. Bluhm, L. Overbeck, and C. Wagner. *An Introduction to Credit Risk Modelling*. Chapman & Hall, CRC Press, Boca Raton, first edition, 2003.
7. D. J. Bolder. *Credit-Risk Modelling: Theoretical Foundations, Diagnostic Tools, Practical Examples, and Numerical Recipes in Python*. Springer-Nature, Heidelberg, Germany, 2018.
8. P. Brémaud. *Markov Chains: Gibbs Fields, Monte Carlo Simulation and Queues*. Springer Verlag, 175 Fifth Avenue, New York, NY, 1999. Texts in Applied Mathematics.
9. G. Casella and R. L. Berger. *Statistical Inference*. Duxbury Press, Belmont, California, 1990.
10. L. G. Chambers. Spearman's rank correlation coefficient. *The Mathematical Gazette*, 73: 331–332, December 1989.
11. R. Chen and Z. Wang. Curve Fitting of the Corporate Recovery Rates: The Comparison of Beta Distribution Estimation and Kernel Density Estimation. *PLOS One*, 7(8):1–9, 2013.
12. F. Chesnay and E. Jondeau. Does correlation between stock returns really increase during turbulent periods? *Economic Notes*, 30:53–80, February 2001.
13. P. J. Crosbie and J. R. Bohn. Modeling default risk. KMV, January 2002.
14. D. Duffie and K. Singleton. *Credit Risk*. Princeton University Press, Princeton, first edition, 2003.
15. G. S. Fishman. *Monte Carlo: Concepts, Algorithms, and Applications*. Springer-Verlag, 175 Fifth Avenue, New York, NY, 1995. Springer Series in Operations Research.
16. J. Frye. Correlation and asset correlation in the structural portfolio model. Federal Reserve Bank of Chicago, April 2008.
17. G. H. Golub and C. F. V. Loan. *Matrix Computations*. The John Hopkins University Press, Baltimore, Maryland, 2012.
18. M. B. Gordy. A risk-factor model foundation for ratings-based bank capital rules. *Journal of Financial Intermediation*, 12:199–232, 2003.
19. J. D. Hamilton. *Time Series Analysis*. Princeton University Press, Princeton, New Jersey, 1994.

20. J. Harrison and D. Kreps. Martingales and arbitrage in multiperiod security markets. *Journal of Economic Theory*, 20:381–408, 1979.
21. J. Harrison and S. Pliska. Martingales and stochastic integrals in the theory of continuous trading. *Stochastic Processes and Their Applications*, 11:215–260, 1981.
22. W. Heynerickx, J. Carboni, W. Schoutens, and B. Smits. The relationship between risk-neutral and actual default probabilities: the credit risk premium. *Applied Economics*, 48(42):4066–4081, 2016.
23. J. Hull and A. White. Cva and wrong-way risk. *Financial Analysts Journal*, 68(5):58–69, 2012.
24. J. Hull, M. Predescu, and A. White. Bond prices, default probabilities, and risk premiums. Technical report, University of Toronto, January 2005.
25. R. A. Jarrow. Problems with using CDS to infer default probabilities. Technical report, Johnson Graduate School of Management, Cornell University, January 2012.
26. N. L. Johnson, S. Kotz, and N. Balakrishnan. *Continuous Univariate Distributions: Volume 2*. John Wiley and Sons, New York, NY, 1997. Wiley Series in Probability and Statistics.
27. G. G. Judge, W. Griffiths, R. C. Hill, H. Lütkepohl, and T.-C. Lee. *The Theory and Practice of Econometrics*. John Wiley and Sons, New York, New York, second edition, 1985.
28. I. Karatzas and S. E. Shreve. *Brownian Motion and Stochastic Calculus*. Springer-Verlag, Berlin, second edition, 1991.
29. S. M. Kendall and A. Stuart. *The Advanced Theory of Statistics*, volume 2. Charles Griffin & Company Limited, London, UK, 4 edition, 1979.
30. S. Kotz and S. Nadarajah. *Multivariate t Distributions and Their Applications*. Cambridge University Press, New York, 2004.
31. A. Kreinin and M. Sidelnikova. Regularization algorithms for transition matrices. *Algo Research Quarterly*, 4(1/2):23–40, 2001.
32. J. Lintner. The valuation of risky asset and the selection of risky investments in stock portfolios and capital budgets. *The Review of Economics and Statistics*, 47(1):13–37, 1965.
33. M. E. Magnello. Karl Pearson and the establishment of mathematical statistics. *International Statistical Review*, 77(1):3–29, 2009.
34. A. J. McNeil, R. Frey, and P. Embrechts. *Quantitative Risk Management: Concepts, Tools and Techniques*. Princeton University Press, New Jersey, 2015.
35. R. Merton. On the pricing of corporate debt: The risk structure of interest rates. *Journal of Finance*, 29:449–470, 1974.
36. S. P. Meyn and R. L. Tweedie. *Markov Chains and Stochastic Stability*. Springer-Verlag, 175 Fifth Avenue, New York, NY, 1993.
37. L. Sandoval and I. D. P. Franca. Correlation of financial markets in times of crisis. *Physica A: Statistical Mechanics and its Applications*, 391, February 2011.
38. T. Schuermann. What do we know about loss-given default? In D. Shimko, editor, *Credit Risk Models and Management*. Risk Books, 2004.
39. W. F. Sharpe. A simplified model for portfolio analysis. *Management Science*, 9(2):277–293, 1963.
40. W. F. Sharpe. Capital asset prices: A theory of market equilibrium under conditions of risk. *The Journal of Finance*, 19(3):425–442, 1964.
41. W. F. Sharpe. Mutual fund performance. *The Journal of Business*, 39(1):119–138, 1966.
42. W. F. Sharpe. The Sharpe Ratio. *The Journal of Portfolio Management*, 21(1):49–58, 1994.
43. J. L. Treynor. Market value, time, and risk. Unpublished Manuscript, August 1961.
44. O. Vasicek. An equilibrium characterization of the term structure. *Journal of Financial Economics*, 5:177–188, November 1977.

# Chapter 4
# Implementing the Model

*Ideas are useless unless used. The proof of their value is in their implementation. Until then, they are in limbo.*

*(Theodore Levitt)*

It is entirely natural, when asked to describe a modelling venture, to spend the vast majority of time on the *what* and the *why*. What specific models were selected? Why was one model preferred over another? What parameters were selected and why? This has been the principal focus of the preceding three chapters. Rather less time is spent on the *how*? There are good reasons for this. How precisely one implements a given model is viewed, to be blunt, as the analyst's own business. Books on home auto repair, to make a perhaps strange analogy, rarely tell their readers how to organize their garage. There is, in actual fact, probably no such thing as an optimal workshop layout. There is simply too much variability in physical layouts and individual preferences for such a thing. The same principle applies to the organization of a financial modelling framework.

There are limits to this do-it-yourself auto-repair analogy: we are *not* changing spark plugs or cleaning a carburetor. Instead, we are computing daily risk-management figures to support large-scale lending and investment operations. This undertaking is more aligned with an automobile assembly line than leisurely tuning one's vehicle. Regular computation of credit-risk economic capital is thus conceptually similar to running a factory.[1] With such an industrial process, there is a premium on efficiency and robustness. In other words, our factory (or computation) needs to do what it was designed to do (every single day) while consuming a minimum of resources. The capacity to achieve these objectives depends importantly on *how* the system is designed. Efficiency, as will soon become clear in our credit-risk setting, is a central issue with resource-hungry simulation-based methods.

There is another important driving reason for explicit consideration of the *how* dimension. A decade or two ago, such questions were rarely raised. Since the great financial crisis, however, questions surrounding model risk have attracted

[1] Or running a large, and very busy, commercial auto shop.



D. Bolder, *Modelling Economic Capital*, Contributions to Finance and Accounting,
https://doi.org/10.1007/978-3-030-95096-5_4

increasing attention by regulators and financial-institution managers. In brief, there has been increasing scrutiny on *how* the risk-management factory is being run. Much attention is, quite defensibly, focused on questions of model design and parametrization. Implementation has *not* escaped attention. OCC [32], a very influential document on the topic of model risk, reads:

> Model risk management should include disciplined and knowledgeable development and implementation processes that are consistent with the situation and goals of the model user and with bank policy.

The regulatory community thus has a close eye not just on the what and why, but also on the *how*.

As a final argument, this book is *not* an academic treatise: it is intended to be practical. Practicality starts with what we are modelling and why we have made these choices. It also extends, of course, to encompass *how* these quantities are computed. We would be remiss, and this book would be missing something important, if we glossed over the main implementation issues. This chapter thus seeks—with the why and what elements addressed in the previous chapters firmly in mind—to provide an overview of the high-level system architecture, information on the base algorithms, and a detailed analysis of model convergence. It thus represents a broad-based description of some central implementation choices associated with our central portfolio credit-risk computations.

## 4.1 Managing Expectations

A few prefatory comments are nevertheless warranted. Most specifically, we need to temper expectations of what can be reasonably accomplished in this chapter. Implementation can be messy. There is often a rather sizable distance between the what and how of any given undertaking. It is neither possible, nor desirable, to walk through all of the gory details. We will need to choose our spots carefully.

Risk-management computations invariably sit atop of a much larger collection of systems managing key activities such as trade capture, valuation, payment processing, and the general ledger.[2] This arises from the necessity of capturing an enterprise-wide perspective on risk. There is inevitably a firm-specific element to any implementation. Firms naturally do things in different ways.[3] This nonetheless complicates comparison. The NIB approach, described in the following sections, may thus legitimately vary in critical ways from other firms. While this discussion will seek to maintain a generic perspective, there will inevitably be some degree

[2] Most financial institutions have, in fact, a veritable jungle of important in-house and vendor-based front-, middle-, and back-office systems to handle these tasks.

[3] Some firms are centralized, for example, whereas others have operations in multiple hubs. This has significant implications for the design of a risk-management system.

of specificity that may not widely generalize. This is natural, but needs to be understood.

Another element relates to resources. Large and small firms face rather different challenges. The large firm, of course, has more resources. They have teams of people working on tasks that might be a part-time responsibility for a staff member in a smaller firm. This advantage is offset by vastly larger volumes and organizational complexity.[4] The small firm faces smaller volumes, but is challenged to perform the same basic tasks with fewer resources. NIB, as a small to medium sized institution, fits more into one end of this size-resource spectrum. Again, this merely needs to be appreciated when reading the forthcoming discussion.

Our high-level description of modelling algorithms will include, where deemed necessary, stylized extracts of computer-code. This last aspect is reserved for only the most important and central computations. The motivation is to help the reader gain an in-depth understanding of key implementation choices. However helpful, it does raise a few issues. First, it explicitly suggests a particularly programming language. Our selected programming language offers numerous practical benefits, but it is far from the only sensible alternative.[5] Every analyst, and institution, should make their own programming language choice based on their preference set. The second point refers to arm-chair programming experts.[6] There are certainly other (very clever) ways to organize the presented stylized code; our approach places a strong premium on clarity and readability, but makes no claim regarding superiority.

**Colour and Commentary 40** (DISCUSSING MODEL IMPLEMENTATION): *Broadly speaking, prior to the great financial crisis, model implementation was viewed as an institution-specific affair. In recent years—as a greater appreciation of model risk has developed—interest in these questions has broadened. Regulators, in particular, have taken a keen interest in model implementation. The factory analogy is quite powerful in this regard. Inputs enter through the front door and exit as manufactured outputs. Attempts to ensure the quality, efficiency, and robustness of the outputs necessitate careful examination of inputs and the associated industrial processes. The same applies to modelling practice. This chapter correspondingly turns our attention to this dimension, but a few words of caution are required. Financial institutions vary dramatically in their system architectures, organizational structures, and resource availability. It is impossible to construct a one-size-*

(continued)

[4] Indeed, for very large institutions, some of the elements in this chapter might actually fall *outside* of the risk-management area.

[5] We'll soon return to this interesting question.

[6] This is basically like the back-seat driver or the arm-chair football manager (or, for Americans and Canadians, arm-chair quarterback).

**Colour and Commentary 40** (continued)
*fits-all implementation solution. This needs to be understood before getting started. Nonetheless, a description of our implementation choices, with a focus on the general issues, will hopefully prove broadly useful.*

## 4.2 A System Architecture

Even a modestly sized credit-risk economic capital model will have multiple modules and thousands of lines of code. Adding in a collection of associated applications—such as pricing, loan impairments, or stress testing—and the situation only gets worse. Starting work on the various components and hoping for the best is generally a bad idea. You need a plan. This makes sense; building and running a factory are complicated tasks. A well-designed system needs to be based on a logical architecture. NIB has found that it is conceptually, and practically, useful to consider *three* functional layers:

1. a first layer concerned with input data collection, transformation, and integrity;
2. a second layer focused on the calculation, or modelling, methodologies; and
3. a final layer dealing with the delivery of results (i.e., model outputs) to internal and external stakeholders.

This structure—originally introduced by Ramirez [34]—is broadly referred to as a three-tier approach or architecture. This is, of course, not the only avenue one can take to system design. There are many other viable competing alternatives. The key point is that, irrespective of your choice, one needs an explicit blueprint to follow.

The three-tier approach—displayed schematically in Fig. 4.1—offers a number of conceptual and practical advantages. The first is rather obvious. The *three* layers map directly into the key aspects of any model: inputs, processing, and outputs. This commonsensical model decomposition dates back, at least, to OCC [31]. Each element requires rather different treatment and, more often than not, are the responsibility of various teams within the financial institution. A system architecture that maps one-to-one onto the modelling structure is both appealing and convenient.

The main idea (and advantage) of the three-tier architecture is that the functionality from each of the layers is kept separate from one another. Although naturally interdependent, the data layer is constructed and run separately from the application and reporting layers. All the necessary data inputs for the core applications are collected once daily.[7] Each application could, of course, also collect its own data from the source systems. While possible, this approach is inefficient.

[7] In some risk-management applications, the frequency of data collection may be more frequent, although rarely less so.

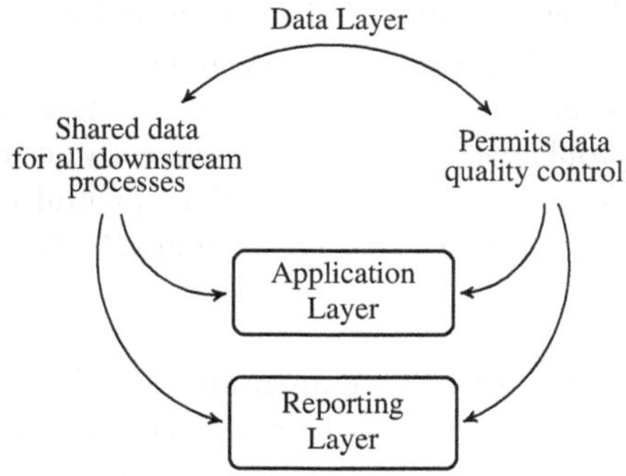


**Fig. 4.1** *Three-tier architecture*: Originally introduced by Ramirez [34], this graphic provides a schematic of the three-tier architecture. This conceptual structure represents a compelling plan for the design of our credit-risk economic capital calculations along with its various applications.

Should something change in the data representation, for example, then each of the other code elements would need to be rewritten. System maintenance is difficult enough. Moreover, a single global data layer permits better economies of scale for data oversight and quality assurance.[8]

The reporting layer is also practically independent of the model applications. A report should not, in principle, need to worry about how the key inputs are computed.[9] More often than not, in fact, the data structure required for one's reporting is actually at odds with efficient storage of the outputs. It is preferable to store model outputs in an efficient logical format.[10] The reporting layer can then exploit this structure and collect what it needs for a given report. The reporting element often also uses rather different technologies: such as a business-intelligence tool for interactive reporting or a rendering software for permanent, periodic reports. Keeping the reporting element separate generally reduces both complexity and practical headaches.

There are also scheduling benefits. Should problems arise with the input data, for example, one can easily halt the entire production run. The data issues can be resolved without having to cancel any applications or reporting flows. Once the problem is resolved, the entire system can be triggered from the start. While this might not sound particularly exciting, the separation of these conceptual layers simply makes the production system easier to manage when things inevitably go wrong.

This architecture is not, however, without some inconveniences. During application development, for example, it is often tempting to directly source a missing field without passing through the data layer. Instead, one needs to contact a colleague—or perhaps even a separate team—and negotiate inclusion of the desired input into the data layer; this can be time-consuming and is admittedly somewhat bureaucratic.

[8] Many financial institutions have data-quality teams, but a risk manager is always well counselled to perform some sanity checks on her input data.

[9] Or indeed, how the models inputs are sourced and prepared.

[10] This touches on the important topic of data normalization. Carpenter [7] is a good source for more background on this question.

Another example relates to a desire to perform certain computations within the reporting layer. Simple manipulation of key outputs cannot be considered a criminal breach of the three-layer architecture, but more complex calculations might be problematic. There are consequently occasional incentives to deviate from the three-tier approach. While sometimes painful, carefully following its discipline ultimately bears fruit in a cleaner, maintainable, and more readily manageable implementation.

**Colour and Commentary 41** (THREE-TIER ARCHITECTURE): *Nobody builds a house, or a factory, without first developing a plan.*[a] *This applies equally to the construction of a credit-risk economic-capital management framework. NIB makes use of a stylized version of Ramirez [34]'s three-tier architecture, which was originally offered as an approach for software development.*[b] *The guiding principle is that the three tiers—data, application, and reporting—are treated as conceptually separate layers. Each tier, rather conveniently, maps directly into OCC [31]'s three central parts of any model: inputs, processing, and outputs. Although interdependent, each piece is designed, organized, and executed separately. This discipline has some costs, but ultimately leads to greater ease and clarity in system development, maintenance, and execution.*

[a] Or, at the very least, they never do it *twice*.

[b] It may be surprising to see a software-development technique in a modelling discussion, but in the sage words of Derman [9], "financial models are software."

## 4.3 The Data Layer

Before any credit-risk economic capital computations can be performed, the input data needs to be collected and prepared. This involves detailed information regarding the features of individual firm assets, the characteristics of credit obligors, and cash-flow data.[11] The consequence is a broad range of descriptive data fields and records.[12] Since NIB is a relatively small organization, the daily amount of data required and consumed is fairly modest compared to a large financial institution. Even small portfolio-level computations still involve material complexity along the

[11] The latter quantities turn out to be rather important for associated applications such as loan pricing and impairments.

[12] Data can be conceptually organized as a table or matrix. A data field is a characteristic (i.e., a column), while a data record is a specific instance of a data field (i.e., a row). During 2021 at NIB, the credit-risk economic capital computation necessitated the capture of roughly 50,000 (non-cash-flow) data elements (columns times rows) each day.

data dimension. Regulators are also very aware of this fact as is echoed by OCC [32]:

> The data and other information used to develop a model are of critical importance; there should be rigorous assessment of data quality and relevance, and appropriate documentation.

Big-, medium- and small-sized firms thus need to take data seriously.

As with many other institutions, various required quantities are managed in different source systems.[13] This creates inevitable inconsistencies in data storage and challenges in aggregating inherently diverse data into a common form. In other words, getting our required data (at the right time) into the proper format is *not* an easy task. This is an age-old problem for practical modellers. Generically referred to as extract-transform-load or ETL, it is a common burden involved in the construction of enterprise-wide risk systems. If the you are thinking that this is rather an IT topic than a modelling question, then you are entirely correct.[14] In a perfect world, ensuring data quality and robustness would not be the concern of the risk manager or quantitative analyst. The world, of course, is imperfect and it is consequently dangerous to ignore this dimension. Even those organizations with large teams of highly qualified data-quality experts are well advised to allocate some time to this dimension.

Figure 4.2 describes, in a schematic way, a reasonably generic daily ETL process. Each day, typically late in the evening or the early morning, an automated data-capture module is launched to collect the full set of required data. This is linked to the completion of the necessary computations found in one's (presumably vendor-based) source systems and generally involves pulling data from various database locations. It is natural, and understandable, that different system vendors use varying conceptual data representations, identifiers, and formats. Appreciating this fact does *not* make it easier to manage. Aggregation of data and enforcement of consistency is thus a central task. How specifically this is done, of course, is extremely system and situation specific. The final step of the ETL is to populates one's input database tables—stored in an modelling-area sandbox or in a formal data warehouse—for use by *all* downstream applications.

Figure 4.2 with its boxes and arrows makes the ETL process seem straightforward, even easy. It is not. It is unglamourous, painstaking work. Working with real-world systems means that errors will arise. A good ETL process thus includes a battery of (logged) technical, consistency and business-logic-related data-quality checks. Outliers and inconsistencies are flagged and sent to team members for follow up and correction. This adds value to the organization, despite not always being terribly exciting, because the risk manager's global perspective can highlight

[13] The specific constellation of source systems is naturally slightly different in each institution, but similar things are being done in different ways. Everyone, for example, needs to value marketable securities, produce financial statements, and make payments.

[14] See Kimball and Caserta [24] for a deep dive into this world.

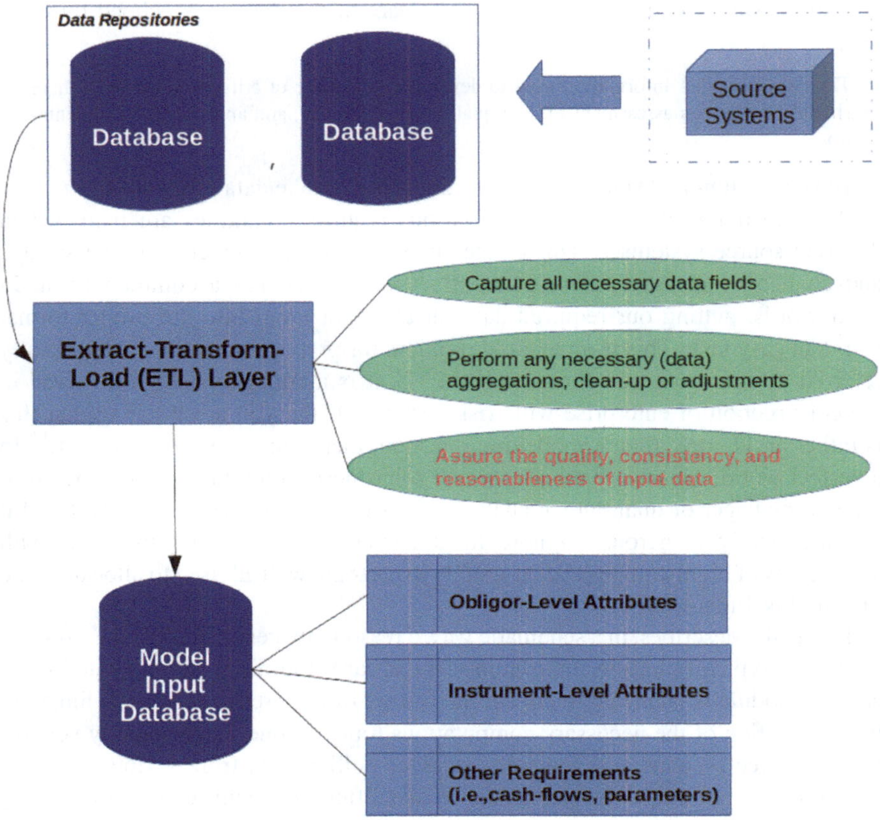


**Fig. 4.2** *Data-capture process*: There are many ways to collect and organize one's data; it very much depends on the structure of one's internal systems. The preceding schematic nonetheless outlines—in a stylized manner—the basic steps involved in a daily data-capture, or ETL, process.

issues that are simply not visible at lower levels. A clear understanding of one's data, and its potential issues, also pays dividends for model design and reporting.

NIB, as have many other institutions, has invested a significant amount of time and effort into its economic-capital ETL process. A central tool in this effort is a collection of dashboards permitting the visual examination of tabular and graphical input data along both cross-sectional and time-series dimensions. The construction of such dashboards is rather resource-intensive, but it dramatically simplifies the trouble-shooting process. In the author's experience, the more you look for data issues, the more you find them. And, happily, the more you find, the more you can fix. The consequence is steady progress towards the (unattainable) ideal of perfect data.

**Colour and Commentary 42** (THE DATA LAYER): *An old adage in computer science, familiar to most, is* "garbage in, garbage out." *It colourfully expresses the well-grounded idea that meaningful computations are impossible without high-quality inputs.*[a] *This principle holds equally well for risk-management computations. Indeed, this situation is often rather acute for risk managers due to their need to take an enterprise-wide viewpoint. Practically, enterprise risk-management means managing multiple source systems—at times in different physical locations—with inconsistent data formats, identifiers, and conventions. The first job in computation of economic capital thus involves the collection and processing of one's input data. Referred to as extract-transform-load or ETL, this task is the bane of analysts responsible for large-scale computations across the world. Although every firm's situation is slightly different, a single, and separate daily data ETL process for economic-capital and related calculations provides numerous benefits. It streamlines complex interaction with internal databases, allows the heavy lifting to be undertaken by query languages, reduces the potential for inter-model inconsistencies, permits imposition of extensive (one-time) data-robustness checks, and allows application code to proceed independently.*

[a] Charles Babbage, arguably the father of modern computing, when asked "if you put into the machine wrong figures, will the right answers come out?" famously responded "I am not able rightly to apprehend the kind of confusion of ideas that could provoke such a question."

### 4.3.1 Key Data Inputs

Within the first few pages of the second chapter, we had already established the critical importance of three data quantities: default probability, loss-given-default, and exposure. Figure 4.3 provides a schematic description of these key data inputs.

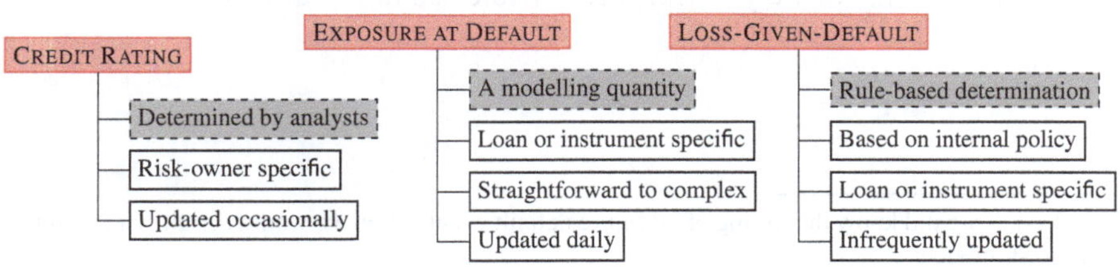


**Fig. 4.3** *Key Data Inputs*: This schematic highlights the situation for the *three* most important credit-risk modelling inputs. Getting all of these quantities—for each individual instrument—is hard work, but they are sourced in varying ways.

The first element determines the likelihood of a default event—and the associated threshold—while the latter two describe the magnitude of the loss. When internal analysts assign a credit rating to a given risk owner, or defaultable entity, it immediately inherits a default probability according to the logic in Chap. 3. Loss-given-default works in a similar manner; a loan or financial instrument is given an average loss-given-default value depending on its specific characteristics. The associated uncertainty around this central estimate was also motivated and derived in Chap. 3. Although extensive internal structures and policies (as well as some modelling assumptions) sit behind these two important inputs, there is not a huge amount of work involved for the quantitative risk analyst. The data need only be collected, verified for accuracy, and properly organized.

The situation with exposure is sadly not as straightforward. Choices need to be made and some challenges need to be addressed. The first point relates to the formal name of this object: exposure at default. It refers to the size of the exposure at the specific time of default. Since we do not know if and when default might occur, this is a fundamentally unknown quantity.[15] From this first-principles perspective, therefore, exposure at default should always be treated as a random variable. This viewpoint may be a bit excessive. Some instruments have relatively stable exposures. A coupon-bearing bond, a loan, or a deposit are all quite well approximated—for the purposes of credit-risk measurement—by their notional value.[16] The uncertainty around the loss-given-default value will, in any event, quite likely dominate any possible market-value deviations. Finally, since we do not have any good idea about when default might occur, the current notional (or market) value is a fairly defensible simplifying assumption.[17] This is a rather important deviation from the market-risk setting.

For other instruments, such as derivative contracts, use of current notional (or market) value can be woefully inadequate. Consider a simple interest-rate swap. Its market value is, almost certainly, only a small proportion of its notional value. Use of the notional value would thus dramatically overestimate potential default losses. Even worse, from one day to the next, it is entirely possible for a swap exposure to move from an asset to a liability. Thus, not only is the notional value uninformative about the size of the exposure, it cannot even help to determine its sign. Derivative contracts, therefore, must be modelled as a random variable. Determining reasonable derivative exposure turns out, in fact, to be such a heavy undertaking that the entirety of Chap. 10 is dedicated to this question.

[15] Indeed, if we did know the timing of all future default events, then we would certainly not require credit-risk models.

[16] The market value is also a quite sensible quantity—and perhaps superior in some ways—but is difficult to reliably obtain for non-traded loan assets.

[17] This basically amounts to assuming that one's instrument exposure follows the martingale property.

### Peculiarities of Loan Exposures

Loan exposures are, for the most part, easily handled. One merely assigns the current notional value—or a market-equivalent, if desired and available—as the exposure at default. There are nonetheless a few exceptions. The first relates to a popular, and effective, credit mitigation method: guarantees. The second relates to how one might handle loans sitting in the twilight between contractual agreement and the actual disbursement of funds. Both cases are interesting and require different solutions.

Guarantees, while definitely valued by bankers, do present a few issues for the computation of loan exposures. Imagine a EUR 100 potential loan to a rather poor credit counterparty. The lending institution, given this situation, may be understandably reluctant to extend any credit. This might change if another third party offers to guarantee, say, 40% of the loan.[18] While this may very well facilitate the loan contract, it poses a problem for the quantitative analyst. How should the exposure be split, if at all, between these two entities? Ultimately, it depends on the nature of the guarantee. If the guarantor is only liable for a fixed part of the loan contract, it makes sense to split the exposure into two parts: one EUR 40 loan to the guarantor with the remaining EUR 60 to the original obligor.[19] Theoretical *pro rata* exposures are thus constructed. This is motivated by the so-called substitution approach outlined in regulatory capital calculations.[20]

Conversely, if both parties to this loan contract are considered *joint and severally* liable, then another strategy is required.[21] In this case, splitting up the exposures will not be very helpful. The only way one does not receive any payment is if both obligors simultaneously default. This joint event will always be less (or equally) likely than either marginal event.[22] The general practice is to assign the entire exposure to the more creditworthy counterparty, which should invariably be the guarantor.[23]

---

[18] This is, of course, the same idea behind having a generous parent co-sign for a student loan or a first mortgage.

[19] They will also certainly have different credit ratings—or there is little economic justification—and potentially different loss-given-default values.

[20] See, for example, BIS [3, Section C].

[21] With the important caveat that a really good definition requires speaking with a lawyer or consulting a legal text, the basic idea is that both parties are on the hook for the whole thing.

[22] To see this, we only require a bit of simple probability. Consider two (default) events $A$ and $B$. By Bayes famous rule, the joint probability is

$$\mathbb{P}(A \cap B) = \mathbb{P}(A|B) \cdot \mathbb{P}(B) = \mathbb{P}(B|A) \cdot \mathbb{P}(A). \tag{4.1}$$

If the events perfectly coincide, then $\mathbb{P}(A|B) = \mathbb{P}(B|A) = 1$ and the joint probability, $\mathbb{P}(A \cap B) = \mathbb{P}(A) = \mathbb{P}(B)$. In all other (more normal) cases, $\mathbb{P}(A|B), \mathbb{P}(B|A) < 1$. From Eq. 4.1, and simple arithmetic, it thus follows that $\mathbb{P}(A \cap B)$ is less than either of the marginal probabilities, $\mathbb{P}(A)$ or $\mathbb{P}(B)$.

[23] Again, were this not the case, there would not be much point to the guarantee.

Another credit-mitigation technique, the posting of collateral, can play a role. For loans, this typically does *not* directly effect the credit rating or exposure at default, but rather influences the loss-given-default estimate.[24] For derivative contracts, however, collateral becomes an intimate part of the exposure computation. While this discussion is relegated to Chap. 10, the collateral issue also arises with a rather special type of money market instrument: a repurchase agreement. A repurchase agreement or repo contract is a simultaneous sale and repurchase of high-quality, usually sovereign, securities.[25] Since the time horizon is typically very short—often only one day—the value of the cash and the securities generally only differ by a small amount. Using the notional amount to describe the exposure at default thus seems rather excessive. In the worst case, one is left holding the cash (or the securities) if one's counterparty fails to meet their obligations. If what you hold is worth less than what you expected to receive, then you have experienced a credit loss. We could—and large players in these markets certainly do—try to model this difference as a random variable and use worst-case outcomes to inform one's exposure at default. NIB, as do many other institutions with modest exposure to these instruments, takes a simpler approach. The exposure at default is fixed as a relatively modest percentage of the notional amount. What this approach lacks in elegance, it makes up for in practical expedience.

The final issue associated with credit exposures relates to timing. Loans have a life cycle as they move from idea to active instrument to maturity. There are, to begin, a variety of steps in the origination process: initial client discussions, negotiation, and deliberation at one's internal credit committee. From an economic-capital perspective, however, a loan really comes alive when there is a formal agreement between the client and the bank. At this point, we can begin to think of an economic commitment. Some loans are disbursed shortly after agreement, while others take more time; some, in fact, may never actually disburse. Loans, where the funds have not yet been paid out to the client, but have also not been officially cancelled, are referred to as agreed-not-disbursed instruments.

Agreed-not-disbursed loans are further broken down into two sub-categories: committed and uncommitted. Committed instruments represent an economic obligation to the lending institution. Failure to honour the agreement to disburse could have financial and reputational implications. Uncommitted loans are typically linked to a broader arrangement with an obligor whereby additional discussion and agreement are required before disbursement. Such instruments do *not* represent a financial commitment. As a result, uncommitted agreed-not-disbursed loans do not

[24] The presence of collateral should not, in principle, impact the likelihood of default, but rather the magnitude of the loss.

[25] Depending upon whether you are the seller or buyer of the securities, this is referred to as a repo or reverse-repo, respectively. In the first case, you are borrowing money, whereas in the latter you are lending it. Readers seeking more background on repurchase are referred to Fabozzi [13, Chapter 9].

(typically) figure into economic-capital computations. Their committed equivalents are a different story. Committed agreed-not-disbursed contracts are, from a life-cycle perspective, nevertheless not yet actual loans. In other words, these are *off-balance* sheet items. This raises an important question: how should they be treated for the purposes of economic-capital?

Any healthy lending institution will have a stock of agreed-not-disbursed loans. Such instruments can be viewed as an off-balance-sheet inventory of loans awaiting disbursement to offset ongoing loan amortizations and prepayments. Since the latter are definitively exiting the balance sheet, they need to be replaced with the former. To the extent that these agreed-not-disbursed quantities represent a financial commitment, however, they need to be considered as a firm asset. As a firm asset, they contribute to overall risk and must be incorporated into one's economic-capital computations.[26]

The regulatory community firmly agrees with this point. The Basel Committee on Banking Supervision (BCBS) has, in its regulatory guidance, a long-standing approach to the treatment of off-balance-sheet exposures. It is well described by the following quotation from BIS [4]:

> In the risk-based capital framework, [off-balance-sheet] items are converted under the standardised approach into credit exposure equivalents through the use of credit conversion factors.

The *credit-conversion factor* is thus, to be very clear, simply a number between zero and one that, when multiplied by the notional amount of the off-balance-sheet item, yields the associated credit exposure.

The more difficult question is the appropriate choice of credit-conversion factor. A clear upper bound is the value of one; this essentially amounts to treating undisbursed and disbursed loans in an identical fashion. The lower bound, from the regulator's perspective, varies with the computation and the nature of the off-balance-sheet item. Current guidance suggests a lower bound, for agreed-not-disbursed loans with a maturity exceeding one year, of 0.5. This does not imply that a financial institution may freely select the lower bound; the specific choice must be justified by historical experience. As a practical matter, the credit conversion factor for computation of economic-capital exposures of agreed, but not-yet-disbursed, loan commitments lies in the interval, [0.5, 1]. Our current choice, revised periodically based on analysis of actual disbursement patterns, lies at the higher end of this interval.[27]

---

[26] Here we use the term asset in the broader sense; it may not precisely agree with the accounting perspective.

[27] It is also entirely possible, and in many cases quite reasonable, to have an alternative credit-conversion factor for different types of lending activity.

**Colour and Commentary 43** (MODELLING EXPOSURES): *Although exposure at default is, strictly speaking, a random variable, it is typically treated as deterministic. The reason is simple. For normal bonds, loans, and deposits there are few advantages, but clear costs, associated with this more general treatment. Instead, the nominal (or market) value at the data-capture time is employed. There are, of course, some important exceptions. Agreed, but not yet disbursed, loans as well as loans with explicit third-party guarantees require special treatment; both cases are fortunately addressed by the regulatory community. Only a moderate proportion of notional value is used to approximate the exposure at default for repurchase agreements, whose risk is dramatically curtailed via collateral. These exceptions involve some effort, but the basic logic is reasonably straightforward. Derivative contracts represent an entirely different level of exception. The capacity of such instruments to (quickly) move from asset to liability necessitates a rather different approach. Chapter 10 deals with this question, which is often referred to using the moniker of* countparty credit risk.

## 4.4 The Application Layer

Having sorted, to the best of our ability, the data inputs, we turn our attention to the second layer in Ramirez [34]'s architecture: the applications. At this point, it is useful to reflect on the fundamental nature of our credit-risk economic capital models. *Is it a custom, firm-specific solution or is it a generic problem?* This is not a random, theoretical question and its answer has a number of implications for one's choices within the application layer. It is also an occasionally controversial discussion; individuals and organizations can have quite distinct views.

The deviation of outlook makes sense; the stakes are quite high. Allocation of scarce firm resources are involved. The nature of this question manifests itself in *two* important, related issues:

1. Should one purchase or build one's credit-risk economic capital system?
2. If a decision is taken to build a system, what programming environment makes the most sense?

These are highly practical challenges without obvious, correct solutions.[28] Before proceeding to address our choices, it is useful to put some structure on these important questions. This type of discussion might be something of a surprise in a modelling treatise, but it is an important implementation issue. Failure to effectively and seriously address these issues can create fairly big headaches.

[28] These points also apply much more widely beyond credit-risk economic capital models.

### 4.4.1 Purchase or Build Application Software?

Our first question is a classic corporate dilemma. Does the firm build a key input internally or contract an external company to do it on their behalf? This make-or-buy decision is, by no means, unique to our situation. Engineers, building complex manufacturing goods, worry about this question all the time. An auto manufacturer, for example, faces this question again and again. Sometimes, such as in the case of car tires, the decision to outsource is easy. More central components—such as the vehicle's powertrain—probably need to be insourced. Numerous other parts can potentially go either way. Given that this is a common problem, we need not necessarily solve it ourselves. There is, in fact, a fairly extensive literature relating to this question. Fine and Whitney [14] claim that a firm's ability to effectively make this decision is actually a *core competence*. While ultimately a financial decision, outsourcing also creates some potential for external dependency. They introduce *two* categories of dependency on external suppliers:

1. dependency for capacity; and
2. dependency for knowledge.

In the first case, a firm could do it itself, but judges outsourcing as a better use of resources. In the second case, the firm cannot perform the task and relies on an external expert. This is a useful distinction. Dependencies associated with using an external product are not, therefore, uniformly bad.

To help assess the acceptability of an external dependence, Fine and Whitney [14] raise another important dimension: centrality of the component to your business. The logic is quite compelling. If something is complex, but well understood and easily extracted from your business process, then it is not central. Such elements are often referred to as *commodities*. Our auto manufacturer does not typically make their own tires, because this product is not central to their business and there are many excellent external vendors. These are good candidates for outsourcing. In contrast, if something is integral to your business, you may want to avoid *dependency for knowledge*. It is unlikely, to consider a slightly silly example, that a fast-food firm would assign the production of their *secret hamburger sauce* to an external vendor.

Figure 4.4 introduces Fine and Whitney [14]'s centrality and dependency trade-off. If a product has low centrality and creates few dependencies, then its external purchase makes logical sense. On the other hand, a central task whose outsourcing creates important dependencies is advisedly built in-house. Low-dependency and high-centrality—or high-dependency and low-centrality—cases are less obviously determined.

While Fine and Whitney [14]'s structure is helpful, physical and software engineering are *not* the same thing. There are, fortunately, no shortage of references on building or buying software tools. Some examples include Hung [20], Perception Software [33], Cohn [8], and Sefferman [37]. There is sadly relatively little from the academic side; instead, much of the discussion is generated from the software

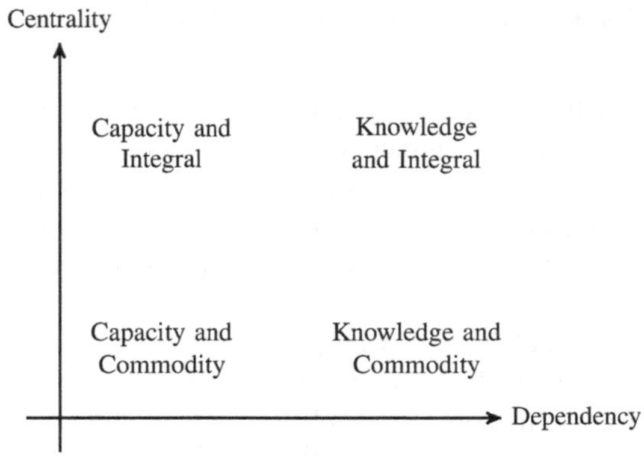


**Fig. 4.4** *Dependency vs. centrality*: This schematic, borrowed from Fine and Whitney [14], introduces two key dimensions for the make-buy decision: centrality and dependency. This logical distinction can support one's thinking about in-house or vendor-based development.

industry. Most of what you read on this question correspondingly has implicit, or explicit, bias.[29] This does not mean such sources are useless. It just implies a bit of caution.

Every situation is a bit different, but some general arguments merit consideration. Many elements speak for the purchase of software. In particular, external solutions are typically somewhat lower cost and generally faster to implement. They allow one to cheerfully assign the tedious responsibility of upgrades and maintenance to someone else. The strongest argument is that it allows you to focus on your main business and not on software development. Most of these arguments are related, in one way or another, to the benefits of specialization and economies of scale.

We also need to consider the other side of the question. Arguing for building your own software are that it lends the firm complete control of development and ensures that system knowledge stays in-house. It also avoids dependency on external resources and allows one to transform a system into a core competency. Finally, although this is a bit controversial, it may actually be less expensive.[30] Arguments to build your own system thus turn around control and independence. Both sides are compelling. Ultimately, the choice depends upon the value of these points to your situation and organization.

Resources are scarce, so cost-benefit analysis is essential. Keen [23] raises the important distinction between value and cost. He argues that traditional cost-benefit analysis is not terribly applicable for systems related to decision support. These tools are used to assist in taking decisions under uncertainty in often semi-structured settings. The difference between *good* and *bad* decisions can have enormous financial consequences. It is hard, or even impossible, to incorporate this element

[29] Software vendors naturally have inherent incentives to lean towards the buy decision. Tool vendors, of course, naturally tilt in the other direction.

[30] Predictably, both make and buy camps argue that their approach is less expensive. In reality, the actual cost probably depends significantly on how the development project is structured. There is an infamous project-development adage that provides some insight on this point: *"Fast, good or cheap. Pick two."*

into one's cost function. It cannot, however, be ignored. Keen [23]'s basic (and compelling) thesis provides some useful practical advice: *"value first, cost second."*

Equipped now with some background thinking for this decision, we can now turn to our situation. Internal credit-risk economic capital computations are rather unique to the institution. A deep understanding of modelling assumptions and techniques is necessary. As we've seen in the previous chapters, there are countless small decision points in both model construction and parametrization. Outsourcing this task would potentially create dangerous knowledge dependencies (or gaps). Economic-capital applications also do not generally lend themselves to economies of scale. One-size-fits-all solutions are to be considered with some caution.[31] NIB thus views this application as falling firmly in the upper right-hand quadrant of Fig. 4.4: centrally important and with strong potential for key external dependencies. This supports the decision to internally develop these tools.

**Colour and Commentary 44** (MAKE OR BUY?)*: To make or buy an internal component or system is an age-old corporate decision. Unsurprisingly, there is an extensive academic literature addressing this question. Fine and Whitney [14], for example, provide a helpful logical structure around the trade-off of centrality of the element to one's business and any dependencies created by outsourcing. The information-system literature, while helpful, also tends to be vendor-driven and, as a result, is often rather biased. It nonetheless helps tease out the key advantages and disadvantages of this decision. NIB has consciously opted for internal development of its credit-risk economic capital framework. Economic-capital is centrally important for internal steering, decision-making, and risk-management within our operations. At the same time, model construction and parametrization are highly nuanced. Effective use of the model would be hampered without full understanding and control of these technical elements. The confluence of these two elements ultimately drove our insourcing decision.*

## 4.4.2 Which Programming Environment?

Having decided to build an internal system, we are immediately faced with a second question: what programming language or environment should we use? This is an admittedly highly technical and painfully practical business. One might argue that it does not matter. Such a line of reasoning is disingenuous: how things are

[31] The Pillar I regulatory solution, addressed in Chap. 11, is an example of a *one-size-fits-all* solution. It does this for good reason, but it also needs to be complemented with (firm-specific) Pillar II analysis to tell the whole story.

implemented clearly makes a difference. One might further argue that this is the development team's choice. This is a fair point, because they are doing the job after all. They should be able to select their tools. Unfortunately, it is not so simple. The consequences of this decision are significant. In particular, there are *three* main elements to consider:

1. development, testing, and implementation;
2. maintenance and extension; and
3. model-owner succession.

It is possible that the development team may actually only be involved in (or around for) the first step. The decision, however, needs to be made with a firm eye on all *three* of these dimensions. If not, there is a risk of an optimal decision for the model developer, but a sub-optimal situation for the overall firm.

There are dozens of potential programming environments. Each has its own strengths and weaknesses. These advantages and disadvantages will, depending on the problem and application, come to play in different ways. Beyond the technical, there are important staffing and resourcing implications. Maintenance and extension is, quite likely, the lion's share of one's system effort. Building one's credit-risk economic capital model is not, after all, a one-off exercise. It requires consistent review, validation, adjustment, and improvement. Its lifetime will necessarily span multiple generations of analysts over many years. A really unhappy outcome would involve a very specialized, or difficult-to-follow, modelling implementation. Subsequent analysts would be consequently challenged to effectively use and maintain it. This question is thus best considered, and addressed, before one actually develops the system.

What is the conventional academic wisdom in this area? Regrettably, there is *not* very much available direction. Meador and Mezger [30] and Elfring [12] date back to the 1980s. Both works are, as one might expect, very focused on the specific tasks involved in the software project. More recent publications—such as Imamgoglu and Cetinkaya [21] and Gupta [17]—are more specialized. The former proposes a software to select a language. Elfring [12] makes a valid point. They argue that "if you were a carpenter building a new house, the first thing you would do is collect your tools." We'll try to follow this advice and consider the range of possible choices available to us.

Although there are many different possible candidates, programming solutions can be usefully organized into *three* possible lanes.[32] The first, and simplest, alternative involves *interactive GUI-based applications*. The classic example is spreadsheet applications and their associated scripting languages. Easy to use and broadly available, these are often treated as a default choice. The second alternative includes *scientific computing languages*. These come in a variety of forms and include both third-party and open-source tools. These all have proper programming

[32] This is not an official organization of the universe of programming languages, but rather a helpful categorization for this particular task.

syntax and are (almost) always interpreted languages. The final category are the most serious: *professional programming languages*. The usual suspects in this area would include the C, C++, C#, and Java languages, although there are many more examples. As the name suggests, these compiled languages are employed for large-scale software development.

It is relatively easy to exclude the first approach. Spreadsheets and their scripting languages are certainly a useful computing tool, but they are not well suited for large-scale numerical applications. This leaves us with a (broad) choice between interpreted and compiled languages. What is the difference? All programming languages need to provide direction to the computer in a way that it can understand. Compiled languages transform the computer code—via an extra step called compilation—into machine-readable object code. Interpreted languages follow an alternative strategy: they use an interpreter to translate their commands to the computer. This is a very fast, loose, and not-entirely true definition.[33] This separation of interpreted and compiled languages—despite being slightly artificial—is nonetheless useful.

Compiled professional programming languages, by almost any criterion, are the *right* choice. They are faster, more efficient, and offer much greater flexibility. This is why they are the virtually universal solution for large-scale software development. There is, however, one important catch: a careful and experienced hand is required.[34] Interpreted scientific programming languages offer an alternative. They provide complex programming constructs, interpreted code, built-in numerical and statistical functionality, and generally excellent visualization tools. There is disappointingly a tragic flaw with interpreted languages: they are relatively slow. We can loosely think of the programming-language choice as falling along a spectrum with performance and ease-of-use located at opposite ends of the scale.[35]

This reduces the programming language question to a determination of where one would like to be along this spectrum. This essentially makes it a staffing question. What is the typical profile of a quantitative risk analyst? Figure 4.5 highlights three broad required skillsets: finance and economics, mathematics and statistics, and computer science. It is hard to be a quantitative analyst without knowledge in all *three* of these areas. Unfortunately, accumulation of knowledge and skills in these domains often pulls people in different directions.[36] Since the technical burden associated with scientific programming languages is not as high, it broadens the universe of possible quantitative analysts. Use of a more accessible scientific

---

[33] Some languages, for example, can actually do both. See Kwame et al. [25] for a useful, and much more accurate, description of this distinction.

[34] The reason is that compiled code typically runs more efficiently, but the compilation process is technical and involved. Extra, hard-to-acquire skills are required to master the use of compiled languages.

[35] There are certainly other ways to frame this question, but these two dimensions are the most centrally important for quantitative analysts.

[36] This is why individuals with skills at the intersection of the three sets in Fig. 4.5 are both hard to find and well compensated.

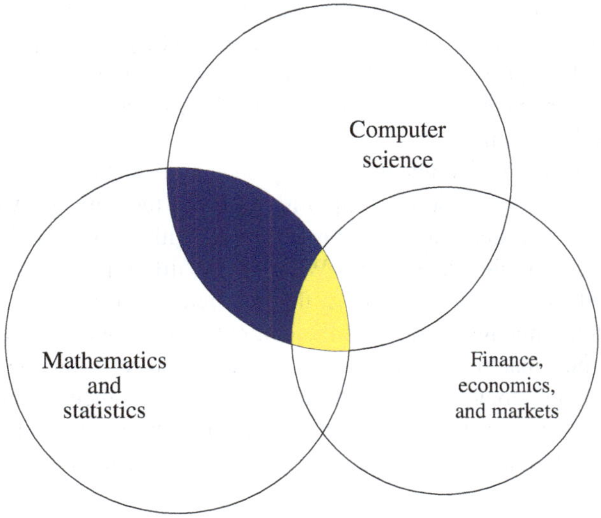


**Fig. 4.5** *Quantitative analyst skills*: This picture displays the three diverse skillsets required by a quantitative risk analyst. Finding someone strong in all areas—in the yellow-shaded intersection of all three sets—is extremely challenging (and often expensive).

computing language thus makes it easier to hire staff capable of maintaining and extending existing systems. We wish to avoid developing a fantastic, high-performance economic capital system that only a handful of people within (or without) the organization can readily understand and use.

We have, when considering this question, elected to trade-off ease-of-use for performance. The credit-risk economic-capital framework, described in this work, is implemented with a scientific computing language. This does not imply that this decision represents the right choice for every financial institution. Larger firms can achieve economies of scale allowing them to achieve greater staff specialization. This permits them to hire individuals outside of the intersection of the three skillsets in Fig. 4.5. Practically, this might involve a development team—using high-performance professional languages—that has relatively limited knowledge of financial mathematics and theory. Development would be guided through prototypes and specifications provided by the modelling team. Such solutions, however, require a certain firm size and critical mass.

There is still one remaining question. Should one use a third-party or open-source scientific computing language? Ultimately, this is more than just a resource question.[37] The open-source software movement has provided a broad range of very useful tools—from the Linux operating system to the Apache web server to

[37] This simple query can easily bring us into controversial territory. The uninitiated reader might be surprised by the strength of the emotional response to this question. Stallman [38] is an excellent entry point into this ongoing debate.

GCC compilers—used by many professional programmers. Open-source scientific computing software do offer some direct cost benefits, but they provide neither customer service nor support. Third-party solutions involve direct licensing costs, but they offer assistance, training, useful manuals, and an implicit promise of continuity. It is not an easy decision and will depend on the firm's specific situation. We have, on the basis of reflection and experience, adopted the open-source Python programming language. Its popularity, relatively straightforward syntax, large-user community, and many useful libraries were the driving reasons behind this choice.[38]

**Colour and Commentary 45** (THE PYTHON PROGRAMMING LANGUAGE)*: When selecting a programming language for the development of a large-scale economic capital system, there are many dimensions to be considered: performance, richness of existing function libraries, the size of the user community, the critical role of staffing, and the open-source vs. vendor-based debate. Every choice will invariably do well on some dimensions and worse on others. Professional-programming languages—such as C++, C#, or Java—typically offer superior performance and syntactical flexibility, but at the cost of complexity. Finding staff with a combination of professional programming and business skills is correspondingly challenging. Python—as an open-source, interpreted, scientific-computing language—is relatively easy to use, has a large and active user community, numerous helpful libraries, and is inexpensive compared to other vendor-based solutions. NIB has, with this selection, explicitly accepted the trade-off between these advantages and the performance disadvantages relative to compiled professional programming frameworks.*

### *4.4.3 The Application Environment*

Our credit-risk economic capital framework is, by conscious decision, implemented as an internally developed system using the open-source (interpreted) Python programming language. While important decisions, they nonetheless only represent the jumping-off point for the construction of one's application environment. It is analogous to, when building a house, having made a decision on the neighbourhood and style of one's construction. There still remain a depressing number of large and small choices.

Delving into the minute detail of our internal credit-risk economic-capital system would not add tremendous value to our discussion. There are, however, some key

[38] See McKinney [28], VanderPlas [39], and Hilpisch [18, 19] for some useful background on this scientific computing language.

elements that are worth discussing. Since our focus lies firmly with quantitative modelling, we'll touch on those system design aspects that have the most important implications for model governance. Owners, designers, and implementers of internal analytics (i.e., models) have numerous responsibilities. One of the first elements touches upon coding practice and maintenance. Returning again to OCC [32], it turns out that regulators have quite a bit to say on this topic:

> Computer code implementing the model should be subject to rigorous quality and change control procedures to ensure that the code is correct, that it cannot be altered except by approved parties, and that all changes are logged and can be audited.

In short, this basically means that computer code needs to be accessible and readable. It also strongly suggests that it must be stored in repositories for security, back-up, and auditability.

A model repository is a powerful tool. It is basically a carefully organized, time-indexed library for one's software development. One can check in and check out various aspects of a project, make changes, branch out in different directions, and merge these branches together. Various levels of permissioning and access can be added to this structure. Model repositories are precisely what OCC [32], and other regulators, have in mind when they speak about change management and auditability. NIB makes use of the very popular open-source solution, *Git*, for this purpose.[39] Figure 4.6 schematically describes our application environment and specifically highlights the role of the code repositories.

Writing software is a tricky business. Going into this endeavour, one thing is clear: there will be errors (or bugs) in your programs. While this may sound defeatist, it is a simple fact. Reason [35], coming at this question from a psychological perspective, indicates that errors are unavoidable. Indeed, he takes this a step further with the following statement:

> Correct performance and systematic error are two sides of the same coin.

Beizer [1], the author of an excellent treatise on software testing, suggests that roughly 2-4% of lines of raw computer programs have errors. In other words, it is not *if* one has a bug in one's code implementation, but rather *when*.

Forewarned, as they say, is forearmed. What, therefore, can we do about the inevitability of coding errors? There are *three* main tools: validation (i.e., debugging), testing and diagnostics, and documentation. These elements work together. Validation is the first step. After development of a code module, it is best passed to another team member for review. The simple act of justifying one's implementation to a colleague can significantly reduce error. This can, as resources permit, be formalized by a periodic code review by an external party.[40]

---

[39] This tool was proposed almost 20 years ago by Linus Torvalds for use in development of the Linux operating system. See Loeliger and McCullough [26] for much more detail on its use and functionality.

[40] These typically occur through regular model-validation exercises.

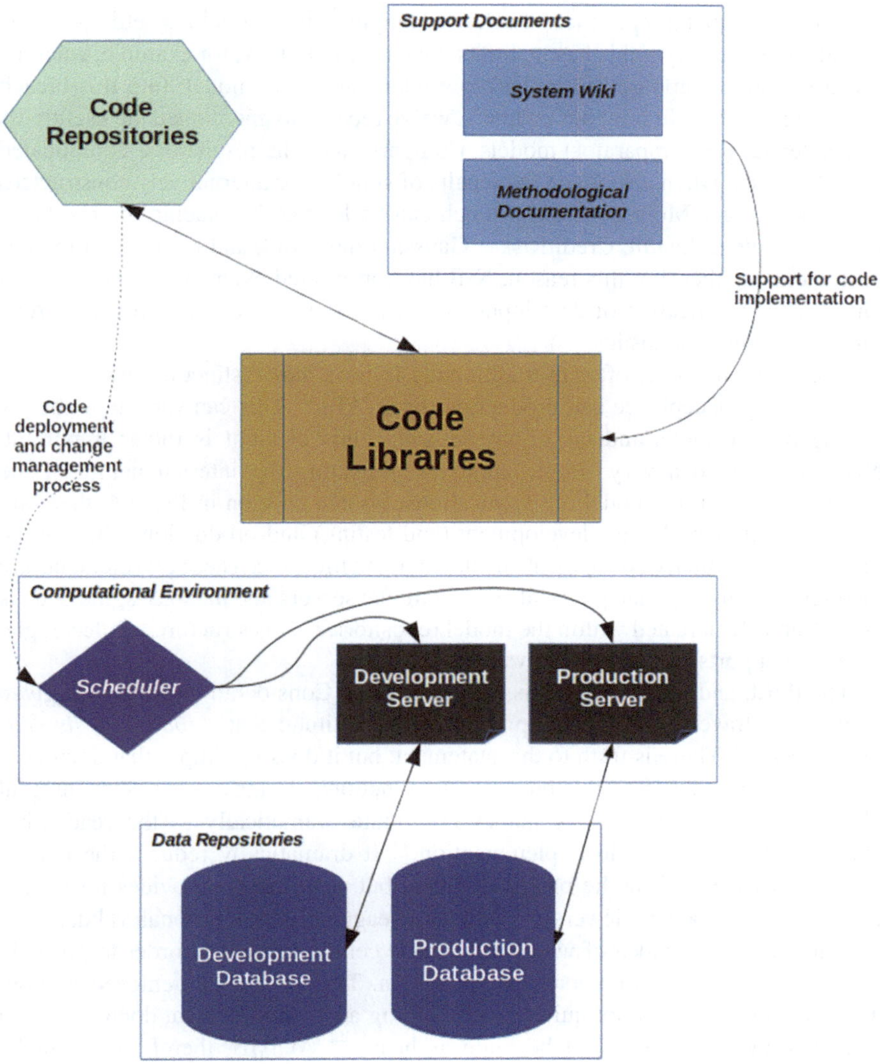


**Fig. 4.6** *Application environment*: The schematic above outlines the basic sub-components associated with our credit-risk economic-capital application environment. These include the role of code repositories, the software development lifecycle, and supporting documentation.

The second step is testing and diagnostics. Testing—see again, Beizer [1] for much more on this dimension—is a field unto itself. The basic idea is that one predefines a set of tasks that one's code is intended to perform. This is constructed so that one already knows what the proper outputs should look like. One then *tests* the code to ensure that it reproduces the desired output.[41] In a modelling setting—while useful and necessary—this has its limits. One may not know, for example, what the precise result is supposed to be before implementing the model. Into this breach comes diagnostics. In previous chapters, we've repeatedly mentioned the usefulness of challenger (or comparator) models. Comparison of the results of a complicated model is eased when also given the results of simpler (or alternatively constructed) implementations. More concretely, much can be learned by placing the results of the independent-default, CreditRisk+, Gaussian threshold, and $t$ threshold models beside one another. For this reason, NIB has constructed extensive dashboards not only for the verification of data inputs, but also to review and investigate a broad range of output diagnostics.

The deployment of software traditionally follows *four* distinct phases: development, testing, acceptance and production (or DTAP).[42] This can vary dramatically among organizations and tasks, but designing this element is rather important. NIB has adopted a very simple approach, reflecting the internal nature of the development and the modelling applications. As can be seen in Fig. 4.6, there are only *two* separate phases: development (and testing) and production. This can be viewed as a minimal development and deployment lifecycle. These two elements are distinguished by separate physical computational servers and databases; the code is also clearly demarcated within the model repositories. This structure, while simple, strongly supports our testing and validation efforts.

The third, and final, mitigant is documentation. Considerable attention is given to the well-travelled, computer programming platitude that *"good code is self-documenting."* There is truth to this statement, but it does *not* imply that documentation is unnecessary. Sensible program and functional design as well as meaningful object, function, and variable names contribute dramatically to the readability and usability of any code implementation.[43] It dramatically reduces the burden towards describing *how* the program works, but nevertheless provides no insight into the *why*. Code reviewers—whether colleagues or professional validators—need to have a clear idea of *why* you've made certain choices in order to properly judge the correctness of your implementation. This cannot be achieved without documentation. This is not quite the same thing as methodological documentation and, in principle, should not be quite as heavy.[44] At NIB, therefore, we make extensive use of an internal web-browser-based Wiki to document our coding structure. This ensures broad accessibility, while keeping the documentation burden

[41] While this is the essence of the idea, there are many related variations and nuances to be considered.

[42] For professional software developers, this leads to important ideas such as the software development lifecycle. It probably also brings one to the notion of agile development. This is quickly moving beyond the author's area of expertise. For more reliable information on this important field, the reader is handed over to Ruparelia [36] and Lwakatare [27] and their associated references.

[43] For this reason, it is useful to establish (within reason) internal coding standards.

[44] You can think of this book as, broadly speaking, representing the methodological documentation.

within bounds. Figure 4.6, our schematic of the application architecture, thus also has an explicit reference to documentation.

**Colour and Commentary 46** (MODEL GOVERNANCE VIA APPLICATION ENVIRONMENT)*: Regulators have dramatically increased their focus on the correctness and robustness of modelling-code implementation. Numerous strategies exist for mitigating potential issues in this area. As a first step, we employ an industrial-strength model-repository tool to facilitate code development and auditability. A second step relates to testing and diagnostics. The use of challenger models, diagnostic dashboards as well as separate testing and production computational servers and databases naturally support this dimension. The final component relates to documentation. Model documentation facilitates validation, training of new staff, understanding of the model owner's thought process, and ongoing model maintenance. Only when key decisions are clearly and carefully documented, can an organization truly open themselves up to constructive criticism and OCC [32]'s notion of effective challenge.*[a] *It also creates a corporate memory in the event of the departure of key modelling staff. NIB makes a distinction between methodological and implementation documentation; the burden associated with the latter dimension is reduced through use of an internal web-browser-based Wiki.*

[a] The preface of this book and Bolder [6] also discuss these issues in significant detail.

### *4.4.4 A High-Level Code Overview*

Having danced around it now for quite some time, we are finally ready to descend into the actual code structure. We'll try hard not to dive too deeply, since the value of line-by-line description of computer code is limited.[45] Some understanding of the fundamental code structure is, however, useful insofar as it has implications for questions of model governance and, ultimately, the convergence of our simulation methods. It also helps, to a certain extent, to create concrete links to the mathematical and parametric discussions found in Chaps. 2 and 3.

The workhorse of the credit-risk economic capital model is the Python function, `ecMain.py`. Figure 4.7 provides an algorithmic description of this function. It can logically be broken down into *five* separate steps of which, the first four, can be considered to be the central part of the computation. The first two steps involve

[45] The presented algorithms represent only a fraction of the total implementation and have been stripped of important, but distracting, error-handling elements.

```
begin algorithm (ecMain.py)
    (1) Read configuration file
    (2) Source necessary input data
    (3) Execute numerous book-keeping operations
        (3.1) Define key constants
        (3.2) Determine systemic risk-factor identifiers
        (3.3) Assign model parameters
    (4) Perform the simulation
    (5) Write final results to a set of database tables
end algorithm
```

**Fig. 4.7** *The main function*: The daily economic-capital model implementation involves *five* distinct steps each involving, of course, numerous sub-steps. This schematic highlights these key steps; each aspect will be further explored in turn.

**Table 4.1** *Configuration settings*: This table summarizes the most important configuration settings found in a `.json` input file. These are semi-static variables of global importance that should not be hard-coded into the model implementation. As such, they can be changed—after, of course, proper reflection and analysis—without altering the base code structure.

| Setting | Value | Description |
|---|---|---|
| `V` | 1000 | Number of repetitions |
| `M` | 500,000 | Simulations per repetition |
| `systMaxVal` | 0.40 | Maximum systemic-weight parameter |
| `nu` | 70 | $t$-distribution degrees-of-freedom parameter |
| `modelList` | `["i", "g", "t"]` | Number of models to estimate |
| `numProcesses` | 60 | Processes to employ in multiprocessing implementation |
| `lowMemory` | 1 | Default- migration-loss calculation to employ |
| `esQuantile` | 0.9997 | Expected-shortfall quantile |

*getting* the configuration settings and model inputs data. The third step involves *setting* a variety of risk-owner parametric values. Step four handles the stochastic simulation; this is the heart of `ecMain` and, indeed, the credit-risk economic-capital model. The fifth, and final, step involves *writing* the risk-owner, exposure, and parametric results to the necessary output database tables for use by the reporting layer.

Each of these steps merits a bit of additional description and colour. We will thus walk through each in turn, albeit with varying degrees of detail. The configuration file is the most sensible starting point. It contains a collection of base variables that may, for various reasons, change over time. Generally, however, we think of them as being static model-level inputs. The most pertinent configuration settings, for this discussion, are summarized in Table 4.1.

The *two* perhaps most critical configuration settings relate to the variables, `V` and `M`. This provides a first peek into the inner workings of the simulation engine. If

```
begin sub--algorithm (ecMain.py)
    (2.1) getPartyData: assigns risk-owner data to pf data object
    (2.2) getRegionMap: puts link between country codes and regions into regionMap
    (2.3) getExposureData: populates tf dataframe with exposure-level data
    (2.4) getCreditSpreadData: places credit-spread levels into sprd
    (2.5) getSystemicCube: populates cube with the systemic-weight parameters
    (2.6) getCorrMatrix: builds correlation matrix, cMat, and Cholesky decomposition, cholMat
    (2.7) getRegionSectorMappings: Puts regional and sectoral information into rsMap
    (2.8) getTransitionMatrices: allocates the NIB and S&P transition matrices to P
end sub--algorithm
```

**Fig. 4.8** *Source key data inputs*: Each of the `get` functions source different inputs data elements. Various degrees of processing are involved across the functions.

one needs to run one hundred million simulations—to achieve a desired degree of convergence—there are a few ways this can be achieved. One might simply run the whole thing in one go. This would probably, depending on how you do it, require a fairly shocking amount of memory and processing power. Alternatively, one could perform 10 repetitions of 10 million iterations; since each individual simulation is independent, they are easily recombined. This second strategy might, again if organized correctly, lead to more efficient use of one's computing source. In the NIB setting, `V` describes the number of repetitions, whereas `M` is the number of iterations. The total number of independent simulations, therefore, is their product: `V` · `M`. Determining the appropriate choices of `V` and `M` to achieve the best possible use of our computing environment will be discussed in (significant) detail later in this chapter. The configuration settings, `numProcesses` and `lowMemory` also feed into this question.

The remaining settings in Table 4.1 should be changed only sparingly. They all relate to fairly self-explanatory model parameters or constraints that will only change infrequently after appropriate discussion and management approval.[46] The `modelList` setting illustrates list of challenger (and production) models to be run. This list will also only change infrequently.

Figure 4.8 provides more colour on the second logical step: *sourcing* the necessary input data. Each function is prefixed with the verb, `get`.[47] This is because they each involve the extraction of data from a corresponding database table and assigning it to an appropriate data structure. These data structures, in turn, represent critical inputs into downstream computations. All of these `get` functions take

[46] They can also, be adjusted upon occasion for the purposes of sensitivity analysis.

[47] This simple naming convention is, incidentally, a double example of self-documenting code and imposition of coding standards.

a database-connection and a date argument, and source their inputs exclusively, following the three-tier architecture, from the data layer.[48]

The results of these queries are used to populate two fundamental data structures—`pandas` dataframes—representing the risk-owner (i.e., counterparty or obligor) and exposure (i.e., instrument or trade or transaction) level data.[49] These dataframes play a central role in the code implementation. To the extent possible, all risk-owner and exposure information—both original inputs and computed fields—are placed in these data objects. One can think of them, very loosely of course, as an ice-hockey puck being passed from one function to another throughout the entire programmatic implementation.[50] This approach allows for brief function input arguments and a clear idea of the final output variables. It also dramatically simplifies the input and output management surrounding risk-owner and exposure records.

In addition to these core inputs, there is a wide range of model-specific data tables. Some of these, such as `getRegionMap`, are essential to organizing region and sectoral identities. Others relate to economic-capital model parameters—discussed in Chap. 3—including systemic weights, transition probabilities, systemic risk-factor correlations, and credit spreads. These slow-moving parameters are nonetheless expected to be adjusted, at least, on an annual basis. These parameter records are, as a consequence, stored in the database environment with a start and end date. In this manner, the necessary model parameters can be selected to be consistent with the portfolio-computation date.[51]

### 4.4.5 Book-Keeping and Parameter Assignment

Having sourced the necessary data, a number of set-up operations must be performed. We refer to this collection of functions as *book-keeping*. The intention behind this term is to refer to putting various essential quantities and numerical ingredients, such as parameter values and identifiers, in the correct places. All of

[48] In other words, the responsibility for sourcing, cleaning and organizing this data is the responsibility of the ETL process illustrated in Fig. 4.2.

[49] Every programming language provides various objects to store one's data. The `pandas` dataframe is one of the most flexible and convenient of such data structures within the Python programming language. VanderPlas [39] provides an excellent introduction for interested readers.

[50] This example will probably mostly speak to Canadian or Nordic readers. Feel free to insert the appropriate object—football, baseball, rugby ball, or whatever—from your favourite sport into this analogy.

[51] This also represents a clean repository for historical parameter choices serving as an important modelling audit trail.

```
begin sub--algorithm (ecMain.py)
    (3.1) Define key constants
        N, t: number of risk-owners and exposures, respectively
        q: number of credit states or PD classes
        J: the number of systemic risk factors
    (3.2) Determine systemic risk-factor identities
        setSectorCode: assigns industrial category to each risk owner
        setRegionCode: gives each risk owner a regional category
        setSizeCode: puts each risk owner into three categories: small, medium, and large
    (3.3) Assign model parameters
        buildBetaMatrix: constructs the N×J factor-loading matrix, B
        setSystemicWeights: extracts risk-owner systemic-weight parameter from cube
        setLGDParameters: performs method-of-moments estimation of LGD beta distribution
        setCreditState: transforms string-valued PD class to integer value
        buildTenor: allocates modified spread-duration estimates by lending and Treasury books
        constructCumulativeTransitionMatrices: both Gaussian and t versions
end sub--algorithm
```

**Fig. 4.9** *Book-keeping operations*: Each of the `set` functions allocate key identifier and parameter values to the individual risk owners sent to the simulation engine. Ultimately, these values take the form of additional fields in the party (or risk-owner) `pandas` dataframe. This is a central data object in the credit-risk computation.

the functions in this step, therefore, are prefixed with verbs such as `set`, `build`, or `construct`.[52]

Figure 4.9 provides a high-level overview of these book-keeping operations. After setting a few useful constants, each risk owner needs to be assigned a sector, a region, and a size code.[53] As we saw in Chap. 3, the systemic weights and correlations are determined based upon these identities. These fields also serve as important fields for downstream analysis and reporting applications. Assigning the wrong parameter to a given counterparty is a typical (and very avoidable) source of model error. It is, therefore, critically important that a clear and consistent approach is implemented to manage these parameters.

Step 3.3, as represented in Fig. 4.9, gets to the business of parameter assignment. The non-normalized factor-loading matrix, $\mathtt{B} \in \mathbb{R}^{\mathtt{N}\times\mathtt{J}}$, is manufactured in `buildBetaMatrix`. Each row of `B` represents the relative weight imposed on the $J$ systemic factors. Recall from Chap. 3 that, for each risk-owner, only a maximum of two elements of each row of `B` is non-zero: one relating to the sector and another

---

[52] Again, the choice of verb in one's function name might feel unimportant, but it represents a (low-cost) opportunity for self-documentation and, thus, additional clarity.

[53] In the (relatively rare) event of a missing total-asset record, a firm is conservatively assigned to the medium-size category. This is an example of a fall-back value.

to the region.[54] The results from the `setSectorCode` and `setRegionCode` functions are essential in the determination of the precise locations of these non-zero factor-loading values.

The systemic weights are also assigned using the `cube` object employing the same sector, region and firm-size classifications. Unlike the factor loadings, however, each risk owner only receives a single systemic-weight value. This information is stored in the `alpha_squared` field of the `pf` dataframe.

This brings us, for the first time in this chapter, back to the mathematical and statistical part of the model. Let's quickly recall that the asset-return, or creditworthiness index, for each individual risk owner depends—in the full $t$-threshold model—on three random variables: $W \sim \chi^2(\nu) \in \mathbb{R}$, $\Delta z \sim \mathcal{N}(0, \Omega) \in \mathbb{R}^{\mathrm{J}\times 1}$, and $\Delta w_i \sim \mathcal{N}(0, 1) \in \mathbb{R}$ for $i = 1, \ldots, \mathrm{N}$. These are the $\chi^2$ mixing variable for the $t$ distribution, the multivariate normal set of systemic risk factors, and the independent idiosyncratic risk drivers, respectively. $W$ and $\Delta z$ are common to all credit obligors, whereas the $\Delta w_i$'s are risk-owner specific. The actual construction of $\Delta X_i$, an arbitrary risk-owner's creditworthiness index, is simply

$$\Delta X_i = \sqrt{\frac{\nu}{W}} \left( \alpha_i \underbrace{\frac{\beta_i}{\sqrt{\mathrm{diag}(\beta\Omega\beta^T)_{ii}}}}_{\mathrm{B}_i} \Delta z + \sqrt{1-\alpha_i^2}\Delta w_i \right), \tag{4.2}$$

where $\beta_i \in \mathbb{R}^{1\times \mathrm{J}}$ denotes the $i$th row of $\beta$ for $i = 1, \ldots, \mathrm{N}$. Each $\Delta X_i$ requires unit variance. Having each $\alpha_i \in [0, 1]$ maintains this property, but the factor-loadings embedded in $\beta$ unfortunately do not. As a consequence, to restore unit variance of $\Delta X$, each $i$th systemic-risk contribution needs to be normalized by $\sqrt{\mathrm{diag}(\beta\Omega\beta^T)_{ii}}$. This quantity is computed for each credit counterparty, or risk owner, and assigned to the `norm_constant` field.

Translating into our computer implementation, the main parametric components in Eq. 4.2 thus take the following practical form

$$\begin{aligned} \mathtt{dX[i]} = \sqrt{\frac{\mathtt{nu}}{\mathtt{W}}} \Bigg( & \frac{\sqrt{\mathtt{alpha\_squared[i]}}\ \overbrace{\mathtt{B[i,:]}}^{i\text{th row of } \mathtt{B}}}{\mathtt{norm\_constant[i]}} \mathtt{dZ} \\ & + \sqrt{1-\mathtt{alpha\_squared[i]}}\mathtt{dW[i]} \Bigg), \end{aligned} \tag{4.3}$$

for `i`=1,...`N`. There is literally a one-to-one correspondence between the terms in Eqs. 4.2 and 4.3.

[54] Public-sector entities, who do not have a clear industrial classification, load entirely onto the regional systemic factor.

The next step involves setting the recovery-related parameters. The average risk-owner recovery field is derived from the ETL process. Recovery is treated as a random variable following a beta distribution with two shape parameters for each risk owner. As we saw in Chap. 3, we treat the recovery volatility as a free parameter and exploit (a variation upon) the method-of-moments estimation technique to determine these shape parameters. The consequence of this computation is some new fields for our `pandas` dataframe. Average recovery and volatility are assigned the field name `recovery_mu` and `recovery_vol`, respectively. The two shape parameters are described as `recovery_alpha` and `recovery_beta`.[55]

The `buildTenor` function essentially does a bit of organization for the spread-duration fields constructed within the ETL process. A key secondary objective of `buildTenor` is to assign a modified spread-duration proxy to loans absent cash-flows. These off-balance-sheet items, due to their contribution to risk, are formally included in our calculations. The complication is that because they have not disbursed, they naturally do not have any cash-flows within our source systems. Rather than ignore the migration element for these transactions, we simply assign them the average spread duration for disbursed loans within the portfolio. Other assumptions are, of course, possible, but this is both expedient and conservative.[56]

The final parametric effort relates to the `constructCumulativeTransitionMatrices` function. These values represent, for the current rating of each owner, the default and migration thresholds used to compare against the `dX` outcomes. A separate set of thresholds are, of course, required for the Gaussian and $t$-threshold models. As a consequence, this function returns two arguments each relating to the model implementations: `GInv` and `GInv_t`. The only tricky element in this computation is setting the boundary values of unity, to which the inverse cumulative distribution function values assign a value of $\infty$. We sidestep this problem by arbitrarily setting these value to 10 and 15 for the Gaussian and $t$-threshold implementations, respectively.[57]

### *4.4.6 The Simulation Engine*

The fourth step from Fig. 4.7 represents the heart and soul of the economic-capital model: it deals with the simulation engine. Everything up to this point is basically preamble and, to be frank, everything succeeding it is basically processing or expanding, in some way or another, upon the credit-risk economic-capital results.

---

[55] These names where selected because the two shape parameters, in the one dimensional beta distribution, are typically (but unimaginatively) referred to as $\alpha$ and $\beta$.

[56] Once these loans disperse the full cash-flow information is available and the calculation proceeds in the normal way.

[57] Any sufficiently large positive number, of course, will do the job.

```
begin runSimEngine                                                    1st loop: for each
    Initialize key variables including key output, ecObj               credit-risk model
    for j in range(0, numModels):
        for v in range(0, V):                                         2nd loop:
            simulateDX(j): generates random scenarios, dX∈ℝ^{N×M}      for each
            getK(j): identifies the default thresholds                repetition
            computeCreditEvents: uses dX to determine new credit states
                and store in mI and dI for migration and default, respectively
            computeMigrationLoss: contains logic to compute migration losses
            computeDefaultLoss: computes random LGD and default losses
            Various tasks: collect and order migration and default losses, compute and store
                expected-shortfall, expected losses, and allocations at v level
        Populate ecObj: the function output is a Python dictionary of simulation results
            averaged over the V repetitions for each model
end runSimEngine
```

**Fig. 4.10** *The simulation engine*: This schematic outlines the main steps involved in the heart of the credit-risk economic-capital computation: `runSimEngine`. It involves two main loops—one for each model and another for the repetitions—and assigns the main results to the `ecObj` data object.

The actual simulation calculation is governed by the function `runSimEngine` conceptually summarized in Fig. 4.10.

**Colour and Commentary 47** (CENTRALITY OF SIMULATION ENGINE)*: NIB's internal modelling framework includes a broad range of competing and related calculations, but the undisputed championship belt belongs to the credit-risk simulation engine. Risk-owner (i.e., credit-obligor) default and migration-risk allocations stemming from this model permeate all downstream applications. Economic-capital approximations, expected credit-loss calculations, risk-adjusted returns, and stress-testing results are all either derivatives or extensions of this central computation. Even regulatory capital computations, while important in their own right, are principally computed for comparative benchmarking purposes. While reviewing the following pages, therefore, the reader should endeavour to understand this point and, whenever it becomes unclear, actively seek to identify the practical or conceptual link back to the credit-risk simulation engine.*

The simulation engine was constructed with the flexibility to manage *three* individual models: the independent-default, Gaussian-threshold, and $t$-threshold models.[58] In principle, the computation of default and migration losses do not

[58] It is also entirely possible that we might decide to add another challenger model in the future.

differ among models. The random-variate generation and threshold computations, however, are model specific. This implies that `runSimEngine` needs awareness of which particular model is being run. Under normal circumstances, of course, each model is computed in a sequential manner.

Why, might one legitimately ask, is the model constructed to compute *three* distinct credit-risk models when a decision was already taken to employ the $t$-threshold implementation as the production choice? The answer is simple: to bake explicit trouble-shooting and model diagnostics into our framework.[59] There is always a risk of error and misunderstanding of results when performing large-scale complex calculations. The inclusion of the independent-default model, with its simple structure, provides a lower bound for both default and migration-risk estimates. Moreover, the complete lack of systemic risk in this approach yields rather different and predictable, albeit less realistic, risk estimates. The Gaussian threshold model is computed as a more direct comparator; it also permits direct assessment of the impact of non-zero tail dependence.

**Colour and Commentary 48** (MODEL MULTIPLICITY): *Model risk is mitigated by understanding of our quantitative limitations and careful oversight.*[a] *Given their relative closeness to the proceedings, model owners are well advised to take this responsibility seriously and incorporate a multiplicity of perspective directly into their modelling frameworks. A relatively low cost, but high impact, approach used by NIB involves the simultaneous computation and analysis of comparator models. In addition to the minimum regulatory capital requirements and rating agency perspectives—discussed in Chap. 11—two additional benchmark models are computed and stored on a daily basis: the independent-default and Gaussian threshold models.*[b] *Although extra effort and computational expense is required, these supporting calculations are central in assessing, trouble-shooting, and communicating the magnitude of dependence, diversification, and distributional effects within the official t-threshold setting.*

[a] This relates to Derman [10]'s caution about the idolatry of models. What better way to avoid this issue than to explicitly recognize their functional multiplicity?

[b] We can thus speak of a suite of credit-risk economic capital models of which the production model is *"first among equals."*

The first aspect of the actual calculation is generating the random variates: `W`, `dZ`, and `dW`. A stylized Python code implementation is provided in Algorithm 4.1. Taking a range of key inputs—relating to systemic weights, factor loadings, and

[59] This links directly back to our first quantitative analysis axiom introduced in the preface: *"if you can help it, never do anything just one way."*

correlations—it performs the dirty work of random-variable generation. This code, as well as the remaining algorithms displayed in this chapter, are *not* intended to be a full-blown, recommended implementation. The idea is rather to provide a bit of practical insight into the key parts of the simulation engine.

There are different strategies, as touched upon earlier, for approaching the problem of generating large numbers of random-variable outcomes. One might compute them, for all risk owners and `M` iterations, in a single step. Conversely, one might elect to loop over the `M` scenarios and compute random variates *on-the-fly* over each iteration. The former is typically rather more computationally efficient, but has dramatically higher memory requirements. Our implementation employs, given access to rather significant amounts of memory in our server environment, the former strategy. The function `simulateX` returns the `numpy` array, `dX`$\in \mathbb{R}^{\mathtt{N}\times\mathtt{M}}$. With `M` = 1,000,000 and assuming roughly 600 individual risk-owners, the result is an array with in excess of 500 million elements. This is clearly memory intensive and its proper use requires caution.[60]

The exceptional amount of memory required by this approach explains the necessity of repeating the `V` repetitions of the `M` iterations. Since each simulation is, by construction independent, these `V` repetitions can be collected together by averaging the individual results. This is essentially a computational trick to permit the requisite amount of total simulations—to obtain convergence—within system constraints. The results of each repetition are stored in the Python `ecObj` dictionary object at each step in the loop; the `ecObj` is then used to perform the averaging. `V` repetitions of `M` iterations also provides the possibility of computing the variability of one's estimator. This notion of uncertainty is a key input into the, practically essential, custom of computing error bounds on one's simulation estimates. This aspect will be discussed in the next section when we address model convergence.

**Algorithm 4.1** (*Building our state variables*) `N`, `J`, and `M` are the number of credit obligors, systemic variables, and simulations, respectively. `myA` and `myB` are the systemic weights, `BMat` are the factor loadings, `cholMat` is the Cholesky decomposition of the correlation matrix (i.e., $\Omega$), and `myNu` is the $t$-distribution degrees-of-freedom parameter. Finally, `myModel` is a flag to determine the underlying model.

```
def simulateDX(N, M, J, myA, myB, BMat, cholMat, myModel, myNu):
    if myModel == 'i': # Independent default
        dX = np.random.normal(0,1,[N,M])
    elif myModel == 'g':   # Gaussian-threshold
        dZ = np.dot(np.random.normal(0, 1, [M, J]), cholMat.T)
        dW = np.random.normal(0, 1, [N, M])
        dX = np.tile(myA, [M, 1]).T*np.dot(BMat, dZ.T) + \
             np.tile(myB, [M, 1]).T*dW
    elif myModel == 't':   # t-threshold
        dZ = np.dot(np.random.normal(0, 1, [M, J]), cholMat.T)
        dW = np.random.normal(0, 1, [N, M])
```

[60] Depending on the computer implementation, this can requires 20 to 40 gigabytes of cache memory. A memory flood is the typical punishment for a poor choice of `N`.

```
        W = np.sqrt(myNu/np.tile(np.random.chisquare(myNu, M), (N
            , 1)))
        dX = np.multiply(W, np.tile(myA, [M, 1]).T*np.dot(BMat,
            dZ.T) \
                              + np.tile(myB, [M, 1]).T*dW)
    return dX
```

No fixed simulation seed is employed in the generation of the random numbers.[61] The intention of production implementation is *not* to generate reproducible results, but rather to run a sufficient number of simulations to attain a reasonable degree of convergence. Such an approach requires true randomness.[62] Additionally, at this point, no attempts have been made to introduce variance-reduction techniques. This is not due to the inefficiency of such approaches, but it is instead motivated by a desire to avoid complicating an already complex implementation. Variance-reduction techniques are, at their essence, mathematical tricks. The cost of such tricks is often complexity and difficult-to-follow code solutions. Optimally, one would employ both approaches, but clarity of implementation takes precedence.[63]

Figure 4.10 indicates that the `runSimEngine` involves *two* separate embedded loops: one for the specific model and the other for the repetition. The first two function calls, `simulateDX` and `getK`, take the model iteration, `j`, as an input argument. This is because, as mentioned, these aspects of the simulation algorithm depend on the model. The remaining function calls are basically agnostic about the underlying model. They operate, in the same manner, irrespective of the model choice.

**Algorithm 4.2** (*Default and migration indicators*) `N`, `q`, and `M` are the number of credit obligors, credit-rating states, and simulations, respectively. `dX` is the matrix of threshold state variables while `K` denotes the thresholds.

```
def computeCreditEvents(N, M, q, dX, K):
    dI = np.less(dX.T, K[:, -1]).T # Default indicators
    mI = np.empty([N, M], dtype=np.float64) # Migration
        indicators
    for m in range(0, M):
        mI[:, m] = np.sum(np.tile(dX[:, m], (q, 1)).T<K, 1)
    return dI, mI
```

Algorithm 4.2 is called `computeCreditEvents`; it returns *two* $N \times M$ `numpy` arrays of default and migration indicators. These are referred to `dI` and `mI`, respec-

[61] See Fishman [15, Chapter 7] for more background on the notion of a simulation seed.

[62] Or, at least, as close to pure randomness as can be achieved using computer-based simulation.

[63] Importance sampling techniques such as those introduced by Glasserman and Li [16] work rather naturally in the default-risk setting—see also Bolder [5, Chapter 8]—but it is rather difficult to (easily) extend these ideas to joint consideration of random recovery and migration risk.

tively. dI—readily computed in a single line—is essentially a matrix of zeroes and ones. A one indicates a default event, whereas a zero denotes survival. Given the relatively low incidence of default—as evidenced by the generally low one-year probabilities of default—dI is mostly comprised of zeroes. Under the current portfolio composition and parametrization—and assuming M = 1,000,000—only slightly more than three million of 500 million (or so) elements in dI are assigned a non-zero value. By any measure, this is a sparse matrix.

The migration indicator adds up, across the rows, the creditworthiness index outcomes less than each obligor's fixed threshold. This sum leads to an identification of the new credit state. This computational trick avoids having to perform a more tedious, and time-consuming, case-by-case identification of each new credit state. Instead of zeros and ones, mI consists of the new credit-state outcomes after migration. By their construction, the mI outcomes will also include the default events. Default is, after all, simply a special case of migration.[64] For this reason, we need to use both dI and mI when computing migration losses to exclude the default losses, which require separate handling.

Algorithm 4.2 indicates that the migration indicator is computed with a loop over each of the M iterations. This would appear to be a rather slow and inefficient approach to this problem. It is, indeed, possible to compute the migration indicator in a single step as follows:

$$\texttt{mI} = \texttt{np.sum(dX.reshape((n, M, 1))} < \texttt{K.reshape((n, 1, q)), axis} = 2) \tag{4.4}$$

While convenient and succinct, this approach can, for large values of M, lead to run-time errors. The reason is its fairly extreme memory consumption. For relatively small numbers of iterations—that is, for M < 200,000—it provides a significant increase in computational speed. At M ≈ 1,000,000, given our hardware, it can unfortunately generate memory errors. Understanding this fact, the base implementation employs the less elegant loop over M employed in Algorithm 4.2.

Algorithm 4.3 provides the Python code associated with the computeMigrationLoss function. The implementation is fairly transparent. An N × M array, termed mLoss, is populated with the migration losses for each risk owner across each individual stochastic scenario. c represents the risk-owner exposure, while dSpread is the modified spread-duration proxy. deltaS is the spread movement determined with the use of mI. The overall migration loss (or gain) is thus simply the product of the spread duration, spread movement, and credit exposure; a small condition ensures that this computation vanishes in the event of default.

---

64 Instead of taking the value of one as in dI, however, default amounts to migration into the 21st (i.e., default) credit state.

**Algorithm 4.3** (*Computing migration losses*) `dI` and `mI` are the matrices of default and migration indicators. `sprd` includes the credit-spread levels for each rating class, `S0` are the credit ratings, `dSpread` are spread durations, and `c` are the credit exposures.

```
def computeMigrationLoss(dI, mI, sprd, S0, c, dSpread):
    N, M = mI.shape
    mLoss = np.zeros([N, M]) # Migration losses
    for m in range(0,M):
        deltaS = sprd[mI[:,m].astype(int)-1,1]-sprd[S0-1,1] #
            Spread movement
        mLoss[:,m] = (1-dI[:,m])*dSpread*deltaS*c
    return mLoss
```

The final key function in the simulation engine is `computeDefaultLoss`. The Python code is found in Algorithm 4.4. If we had opted to generate an `N × M` array of recovery outcomes, then this entire computation could be performed in a single line. This is *not* the most reasonably approach since it requires sampling, irrespective of the default outcome, a stochastic recovery value for all outcomes. Generating a huge number of beta-distributed random variates—and making use of only about a very small fraction of them—is conceptually wasteful and computationally expensive. Instead, therefore, the random recovery outcomes are computed only when the default indicator takes the value of unity.

**Algorithm 4.4** (*Computing default losses*) `N` and `M` are the number of credit obligors and simulations, respectively. `dI` are the default indicators. `myAlpha` and `myBeta` represent the recovery beta-distribution shape parameters and `c` are the credit exposures.

```
def computeDefaultLoss(N, M, dI, myAlpha, myBeta, c):
    dLoss = np.empty([N, M], dtype=np.float64) # Default losses
    for m in range(0, M):
        I = np.where(dI[:, m] > 0) # Subset of default events
        if not is_empty(I):
            lossGivenDefault = 1-np.random.beta(myAlpha[I],
                myBeta[I])
            dLoss[I, m] = c[I]*lossGivenDefault
    return dLoss
```

The two loops for computing migration and default losses, summarized in Algorithm 4.2 to 4.4, are responsible for the vast majority of the computational effort. Looping over millions of iterations is bound to be time-consuming.[65] It is, of course, possible within Python to avoid the necessity of looping. Algorithm 4.5 presents an alternative implementation—combining all of the previous algorithms—via vectorization.[66] This provides a significant speed (and readability) improvement

[65] With a non-compiled, interpreted programming language such as Python, this is an extremely sub-optimal implementation decision.

[66] Vectorization is a generic term—which may mean slightly different things depending on the context—that basically refers to the performance of a looped operation in a single step.

for lower numbers of iterations, but it has a tendency to create memory problems as we increase `M` into the neighbourhood of one million or more.[67]

**Algorithm 4.5** (*Computing migration and default losses*) `N`, `q`, and `M` are the number of credit obligors, credit-rating states, and simulations, respectively. `dX` and `K` are the state variables and thresholds. `sprd` include the credit-spread levels for each rating class, `S0` are the credit ratings, `dSpread` are spread durations, and `c` are the credit exposures. `myAlpha` and `myBeta` represent the recovery beta-distribution shape parameters.

```
def calculateLosses(N, M, q, dX, K, sprd, S0, dSpread, c, myAlpha
    , myBeta):
    mLoss = np.zeros((N, M)) # Migration losses
    dLoss = np.zeros((N, M)) # Default losses
    # Construct indicators
    mI = np.sum(dX.reshape((N, M, 1)) < K.reshape((n, 1, q)),
        axis=2)
    dI = np.equal(mI, q)
    # Migration losses
    deltaS = sprd[mI-1, 1]-sprd[S0-1, 1][:, None]
    mLoss = (1-dI)*dSpread[:, None]*deltaS*c[:, None]
    # Default losses
    I = np.where(dI > 0)
    if not is_empty(I):
        I_n, I_M = I
        lossGivenDefault = 1-np.random.beta(myAlpha[I_n], myBeta[
            I_n])
        dLoss[I_n, I_M] = c[I_n]*lossGivenDefault
    return mLoss, dLoss
```

The decision on the specific algorithm used in the computation of default and migration losses—either by loop or in one step—is governed by the `lowMemory` configuration flag identified in Table 4.1. Depending on the memory constraints of the specific hardware set-up, it has proven rather useful to be able to toggle back and forth between these two extremes. When using parallel-processing techniques, for example, memory is a scarce resource and, consequently, the `lowMemory` flag is typically set to one.

Once the migration and default losses are computed, the remainder of the computation involves simply collection of results, ordering, and computation of the risk metrics. The `ecObj` dictionary has *three* main fields: expected losses, risk-owner-level economic-capital allocations, and risk-owner-level standard errors. The first two elements are computed and assigned to every iteration over `V`. The standard errors, centrally important to the computation of confidence intervals for our risk-owner economic-capital allocations, can only be determined once all `V` looping iterations are complete. It is simply the risk-owner-wise standard deviation of the

[67] The actual location of the upper bound on `M` depends, of course, on the amount of cache memory available on one's computation server. It will vary by the server's configuration—these observations are predicated on a test server with 48 gigabytes of random-access memory.

allocations.[68] With a fully populated `ecObj`, the fourth step in Fig. 4.7 is readily performed, thus completing the simulation algorithm.

**Colour and Commentary 49** (MEMORY VS. PROCESSORS)*: In any computational setting, random access (or cache) memory and processing power are scarce resources. In an ideal world, of course, one would have an extremely generous amount of both. In the real world, this utopic ideal is unattainable.*[a] *Practically, however, these two quantities may act in competing, or perhaps less obvious, ways. This manifests itself, in our implementation, through the choice of* `M` *and* `V`*. A large setting of* `M` *needs to be offset with a lower choice of* `V`*. Such a strategy will generally involve significant consumption of memory, but underuse of processors. A lower* `M` *permits a larger* `V`*, but inverts the importance of memory and processor resources. Related to this point is also the code implementation: should one, for example, vectorize the code or use an iterative looping strategy or a bit of both? Finding the appropriate trade-off along these dimensions requires trial-and-error investigation and varies by one's hardware choices. These questions are intimately related to the critical question of model convergence addressed in the following section.*

[a] At least, it is not attainable for a reasonable price.

## 4.5 Convergence

Stochastic simulation is a legitimate technique for the estimation of any industrial credit-risk economic-capital model, but an open question remains. How many individual simulations are required to ensure a *satisfactory* level of convergence? Irrespective of the number of simulations, the credit-risk economic-capital estimations will differ with each computation. The key is the magnitude of the deviation. Adequate convergence, from a pragmatic perspective, basically means that the difference between consecutive estimates is relatively small.[69] The level of acceptability of these differences is thus less a mathematical question and more of an economic one.

[68] Naturally, for the result to be meaningful—and this is probably somewhat debatable—-we require that `V` be larger than about 20 or so.

[69] McLeish [29] is an excellent source for the use of simulation methods in a financial setting. Bolder [5, Chapter], and its associated references, provides some additional colour on the credit-risk problem.

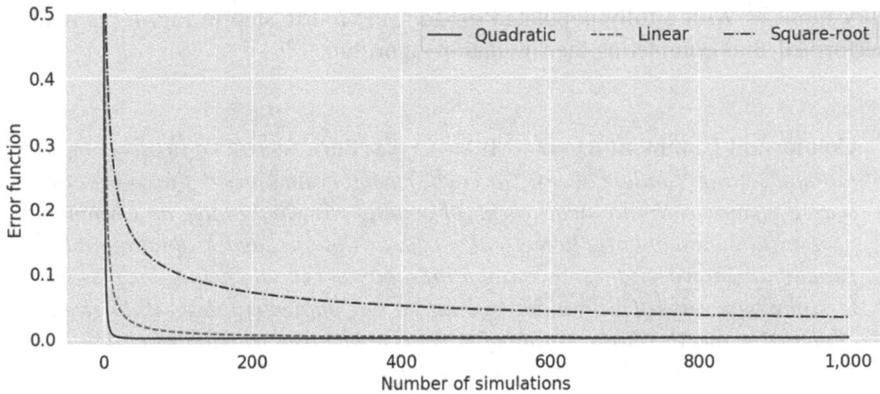


**Fig. 4.11** *Theoretical simulation error function*: This figure illustrates the theoretical relationship between total simulations and convergence error. Although in specific problems, the rate of convergence may slightly deviate, simulation error tends to zero at the speed of $\frac{1}{\sqrt{M}}$. We refer to this as $\mathcal{O}\left(\frac{1}{\sqrt{M}}\right)$ convergence; it is a bit depressing to compare it to linear or quadratic convergence.

Optimization of a stochastic-simulation code implementation, in general, involves one of *two* alternative approaches:

1. (SOFTWARE) the use of mathematical techniques to reduce the variance of the simulation estimate; or
2. (HARDWARE) the clever application of more computational power—that is, additional processing power and random-access memory—to the problem.

Naturally, it is entirely possible to appeal to both solutions. It is, nevertheless, sensible to keep these two aspects, from a conceptual perspective, separate. The following discussion directly tackles the second issue using raw stochastic simulation.

Let us begin with the theoretical relationship between the total number of $M$ independent simulations and convergence. Simulation error tends to zero at the speed of $\frac{1}{\sqrt{M}}$; we refer to this as $\mathcal{O}\left(\frac{1}{\sqrt{M}}\right)$ convergence. Figure 4.11 provides a visualization of the rate of error convergence to zero. In a word, it is slow. To reduce the error in half, for example, it is necessary to increase the total number of simulations by a factor of four.[70] A natural question is: why would one use a technique with such a painfully slow level of convergence? The answer is that the convergence rate of stochastic simulation, unlike other much faster techniques, is independent of the problem dimension. Our multivariate $t$-threshold model simply cannot be solved using faster grid-based numerical-integration techniques. Despite

[70] Contrasting this with (appreciably faster) linear and quadratic convergence in Fig. 4.11 is not terribly fun.

faster convergence rates, such methods regrettably fail miserably for dimensionality greater than about three or four.[71]

Despite our theoretical understanding of the convergence rate, each problem is slightly different. Accordingly, an assessment of the relative uncertainty for one's simulation problem is required. Such an assessment can typically—for problems such as ours without a readily manipulated analytic form—only be acquired by actually running the simulation multiple times in different ways. If one runs a simulation, say V times, then the standard deviation of these V simulation outcomes is a useful uncertainty measure. Experimentation is thus the central point around which one may measure the uncertainty of our simulation estimates—it will also form the backbone of the remaining sections of this chapter.

### 4.5.1 Constructing Confidence Bands

To evaluate our experiments, we require a bit of statistical machinery. How, for example, might one employ the standard error of our (portfolio and obligor-level) simulation estimates to produce a sensible and reliable confidence interval? The answer to this question is based on the theory of sums of independent random variables; that is, the central limit theorem.[72] This can be described in full generality, but we will specialize it for our purposes.

Our first object of interest is the credit-risk economic capital at a given point in time, which we will denote as $P$. This is a random variable whose value is never truly known, but only observed with measurement (i.e., simulation) error. We construct V independent (noisy) observations of $P$, which we'll refer to as $\hat{P}_v$ for $v = 1, \ldots, \text{V}$.[73] Using these, we may construct the following estimator

$$\bar{P} = \frac{1}{\text{V}} \sum_{v=1}^{\text{V}} \hat{P}_v. \tag{4.6}$$

[71] This depressing fact—an example of Bellman [2]'s *curse of dimensionality*—remains despite enormous increases in computational efficiency in recent decades.

[72] See Durrett [11] for a variety of flavours of this important probabilistic result.

[73] Each $\hat{P}_v$ is, for completeness, constructed as

$$\hat{P}_v = \frac{1}{M} \sum_{m=1}^{M} \hat{P}_{m,v}, \tag{4.5}$$

for $v = 1, \ldots, \text{V}$. This is a key benefit of simulation techniques: we may construct our own experiments through the choice of V and M.

$\bar{P}$ is our estimator for the unknown $P$. That is, for a given value of $\mathtt{M}$, we compute a simulation-based portfolio credit-risk economic capital estimate, $\hat{P}_v$. We then repeat this $\mathtt{V}$ times and construct Eq. 4.6. The key question is: how good is $\bar{P}$?

$\bar{P}$ is, most importantly for this exercise, the (normalized) sum of a sequence of independent random variables; which is, of course, itself also a random variable. The central-limit theorem, very loosely, holds that the probability law of such sums tends towards the normal distribution. To exploit this fact and to be able to say something about our confidence of this estimate, however, we first need to compute the standard error of the measurement. We define it as,

$$s_P = \sqrt{\sum_{v=1}^{\mathtt{V}} \frac{(P_v - \bar{P})^2}{\mathtt{V}-1}}. \tag{4.7}$$

This quantity is thus the simple standard deviation of our estimator in Eq. 4.6. Clearly the larger the value of $\mathtt{V}$, the sharper the estimate in Eq. 4.7.

The associated $\gamma$ confidence interval for $P$ is now simply

$$\bar{P} \pm \mathcal{T}_{\mathtt{V}-1}^{-1}(1-\gamma)\frac{s_P}{\sqrt{\mathtt{V}}}, \tag{4.8}$$

where $\mathcal{T}_{\mathtt{V}-1}^{-1}(1-\gamma)$ is the inverse Student-t distribution with $\mathtt{V}-1$ degrees of freedom evaluated at the given level of confidence, $\gamma$.[74] If we set $\gamma = 0.90$, then we have built a 90% confidence interval for $\bar{P}$.[75]

We are also interested in obligor-level economic capital allocations. Define the (unknown) random vector of the $\mathtt{N}$ risk-owner-level credit-risk economic capital values as,

$$C = \begin{bmatrix} C_1 \\ \vdots \\ C_{\mathtt{N}} \end{bmatrix}. \tag{4.9}$$

It follows immediately that

$$P = \sum_{n=1}^{\mathtt{N}} C_n. \tag{4.10}$$

[74] The $t$ distribution arises due to the need to offset the bias arising from our potentially small-sample estimate of the volatility of $\bar{P}$. As $\mathtt{V}$ gets reasonably large, this converges to the Gaussian distribution permitting replacement of $\mathcal{T}_{\mathtt{V}-1}^{-1}(\cdot)$ with $\Phi^{-1}(\cdot)$.

[75] In other words, the idea is that with a 90% level of confidence the true $P$ will lie within the interval described in Eq. 4.8.

This necessary link between the risk-owner and portfolio levels is ensured by the risk-attribution methodology introduced in Chap. 2.

Since vector $C$ is unknown, we play the same game as before. For a given $\mathtt{M}$, we construct $\mathtt{V}$ estimates of $C$, which we will refer to as $\hat{C}_v$ for $v = 1, \ldots, \mathtt{V}$. Our estimator for $C$ is thus

$$\begin{aligned}\bar{C} &= \frac{1}{\mathrm{V}} \sum_{v=1}^{\mathrm{V}} \hat{C}_v, \quad (4.11)\\ &= \frac{1}{\mathrm{V}} \sum_{v=1}^{\mathrm{V}} \begin{bmatrix} \hat{C}_{1,v} \\ \vdots \\ \hat{C}_{\mathrm{N},v} \end{bmatrix}, \\ &= \begin{bmatrix} \bar{C}_{1,v} \\ \vdots \\ \bar{C}_{\mathrm{N},v} \end{bmatrix}.\end{aligned}$$

Allowing us to define the following standard-error economic-capital allocation vector as,

$$\begin{aligned}s_C &= \begin{bmatrix} s_{C_1} \\ \vdots \\ s_{C_{\mathrm{N}}} \end{bmatrix}, \quad (4.12)\\ &= \begin{bmatrix} \sqrt{\frac{1}{\mathrm{V}-1} \sum_{v=1}^{\mathrm{V}} \left( \hat{C}_{1,v} - \bar{C}_1 \right)^2} \\ \vdots \\ \sqrt{\frac{1}{\mathrm{V}-1} \sum_{v=1}^{\mathrm{V}} \left( \hat{C}_{\mathrm{N},v} - \bar{C}_{\mathrm{N}} \right)^2} \end{bmatrix}.\end{aligned}$$

where clearly $s_C \in \mathbb{R}^{\mathrm{N} \times 1}$. There is nothing particularly interesting, or new, in the risk-owner allocation computations. It is simply the multivariate version of the portfolio result. Accordingly, the allocation-level $\gamma$ confidence interval is now simply

$$\bar{C}_n \pm \mathcal{T}_{\mathrm{V}-1}^{-1}(1-\gamma) \frac{s_{C_n}}{\sqrt{\mathrm{V}}}, \quad (4.13)$$

for $n = 1, \ldots, \mathtt{N}$.

It is interesting, and rather useful, to understand the link between the uncertainty associated with each simulated economic-capital (risk-owner) allocation and the overall portfolio value. To accomplish this, we need to gather these quantities together in some fashion to get to a portfolio perspective. Since we are not weighting, but rather summing, across the economic-capital allocations, we collect the individual volatility contributions with the following vector of ones:

$$\omega = \begin{bmatrix} 1 \\ \vdots \\ 1 \end{bmatrix}, \tag{4.14}$$

where $\omega \in \mathbb{R}^{\mathrm{N}\times 1}$. The standard-error of the portfolio economic-capital estimate, extracted from the individual allocations standard errors, might be postulated as,

$$s_P \stackrel{?}{=} \underbrace{\omega^T \operatorname{diag}(s_C)\omega}_{\sum_{n=1}^{\mathrm{N}} s_{C_n}}, \tag{4.15}$$

The claim is that the standard error of the portfolio is simply the sum of the standard error of the individual risk-owner allocations. This would require a fairly strong assumption; Eq. 4.15 is tantamount to assuming that the simulation error of the $i$th and $j$th arbitrary risk-allocations are statistically independent. The correlation structure, to the extent one exists, relates to simulation error. Since simulation error should be independent of the model structure, independence is not a terrible *a priori* assumption. To be on the safe side, however, one should probably rewrite Eq. 4.15 as,

$$s_P = \sqrt{\omega^T \operatorname{cov}(\hat{C}_{\mathrm{V}})\omega}, \tag{4.16}$$

where

$$\hat{C}_{\mathrm{V}} = \begin{bmatrix} \hat{C}_{1,1} & \cdots & \hat{C}_{1,\mathrm{V}} \\ \vdots & \ddots & \vdots \\ \hat{C}_{\mathrm{N},1} & \cdots & \hat{C}_{\mathrm{N},\mathrm{V}} \end{bmatrix}, \tag{4.17}$$

is the full $\mathrm{N} \times \mathrm{V}$ set of risk-owner economic-capital allocation simulation estimates. The practical difference between Eqs. 4.15 and 4.16 is an empirical question.

**Colour and Commentary 50** (CONFIDENCE BOUNDS)*: Computation of confidence bounds—due to the inherent independence of distinct simulation runs—is a relatively straightforward calculation. Their deceptively simple form should not, however, lead us to underestimate their importance to the*

(continued)

**Colour and Commentary 50** (continued)
*simulation exercise. Unadorned simulation estimates, absent an associated assessment of their uncertainty, are of questionable usefulness to the quantitative analyst. Confidence bounds, built up from simulation-estimator standard errors, are an extremely valuable model-implementation diagnostic. It is certainly possible to verify convergence periodically via a separate exercise, but it is more convenient—not to mention, reassuring—to organize one's approach to provide daily confidence bounds. Our basic simulation approach involving* V *repetitions of* M *iterations—for a total of* V·M *simulations—readily enables the inclusion of both portfolio and risk-owner level confidence into our collection of daily model diagnostics. The computation of standard errors is thus not a part-time occupation, but rather an integral part of the base daily computation. This permits ongoing assessment and oversight of model convergence.*

### *4.5.2 Portfolio-Level Convergence*

Our first experiment involves repeated computation and comparison of simulation results across a range of V values. We fix M = 250,000, but slowly and steadily increase the number of repetitions, V. We begin with V = 4, for a total number of one million simulations. We then increase V, in discrete steps, all the way up to 4000 for a total of one billion simulations. Although this is a laborious process, it provides priceless information about our problem.

The total economic-capital estimate is the average of the individual V repetitions. Since the actual amount of economic capital is irrelevant in this exposition, the *true* economic capital value is normalized to unity.[76] All of our estimates, irrespective of the value of V, turn around this central value. As we can see in Fig. 4.12, when V = 4, the standard deviation of this estimate—which is also referred to as standard error—is roughly 1.5% of the true value. For V = 2000, by contrast, the standard error falls to about 6–7 basis points.

The principal conclusion from Fig. 4.12, computed using these ideas, is that when V·M > 100 million or so, then we have a rather tight estimate of the *total* economic-capital consumption. The 90% confidence interval has a breadth of only a few basis points. Thus, were we interested solely in the accuracy of the overall economic-capital estimate, a total number of simulations in and around the neighbourhood of 100 million would look to be roughly sufficient. Again, if this was our only objective, then we would essentially be done with our convergence analysis. In reality, however, the model's key output is a separate economic-capital allocation

[76] This value is estimated using an irresponsibly large number of simulations.

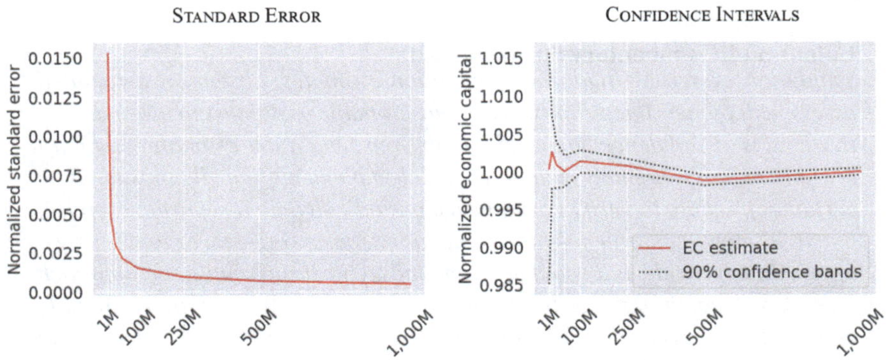


**Fig. 4.12** *Convergence analysis*: The graphics highlights, for an arbitrary date in 2020, the convergence of a normalized economic-capital estimate as a function of the number of simulation runs, V·M. The left-hand graphic is the standard deviation of our (normalized) estimates, while the right-hand graphic summarizes a 90% confidence interval of the total estimates.

for each individual risk owner. A useful implementation, therefore, requires a satisfactorily high degree of convergence for each of these N obligor-level estimates.

## 4.5.3 Obligor-Level Convergence

Given that N exceeds about 500, attaining overall convergence is a bit more complex than in the total economic-capital case. At the aggregate level, lots of small differences, in different directions, will act to offset one another. At the obligor level, this effect is less present. Working in EUR space is difficult, because of the broad range of differences in individual risk-owner allocations. Some obligors have economic-capital consumption in the ten of millions of EUR, whereas others have values in the thousands; this complicates comparison. A bit of structure—and normalization—is thus required. Using our previous methodology, we may easily compute $\gamma$ confidence interval as,

$$\left(\underbrace{\bar{C}_n - \mathcal{T}_{\mathrm{V}-1}^{-1}(1-\gamma)\frac{s_{C_n}}{\sqrt{\mathrm{V}}}}_{\text{Lower bound}},\ \underbrace{\bar{C}_n + \mathcal{T}_{\mathrm{V}-1}^{-1}(1-\gamma)\frac{s_{C_n}}{\sqrt{\mathrm{V}}}}_{\text{Upper bound}}\right), \tag{4.18}$$

for $n = 1, \ldots, \mathrm{N}$. Examination of Eq. 4.18 reveals rather clearly that the breadth of the confidence interval is easily calculated. Dividing this breadth by the original point estimate provides a reasonable assessment of the range of worst-case percentage error associated with a given simulation. Specifically, we propose the following

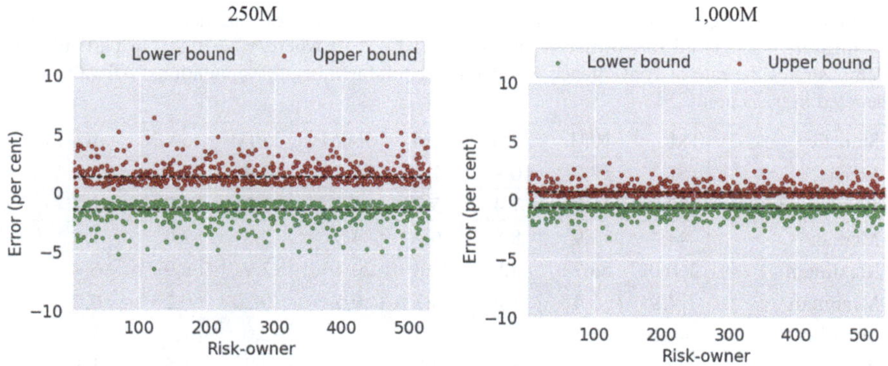


**Fig. 4.13** *Percentage risk-owner allocation errors*: The preceding graphics display—for 250 and 1 billion simulations, respectively—the percentage risk-owner allocations for each of the N estimates. In all cases, the confidence level is $\gamma = 0.90$.

measure of individual obligor-level convergence

$$\begin{aligned}\epsilon_n &= \frac{1}{\bar{C}_n}\overbrace{\left(\underbrace{\left(\bar{C}_n + \mathcal{T}_{\mathrm{V}-1}^{-1}(1-\gamma)\frac{s_{C_n}}{\sqrt{\mathrm{V}}}\right)}_{\text{Upper bound}} - \underbrace{\left(\bar{C}_n - \mathcal{T}_{\mathrm{V}-1}^{-1}(1-\gamma)\frac{s_{C_n}}{\sqrt{\mathrm{V}}}\right)}_{\text{Lower bound}}\right)}^{\text{Width of confidence interval}}, \quad (4.19)\\ &= \frac{2\cdot\mathcal{T}_{\mathrm{V}-1}^{-1}(1-\gamma)\frac{s_{C_n}}{\sqrt{\mathrm{V}}}}{\bar{C}_n}.\end{aligned}$$

The normalization of each confidence-interval breadth by the overall estimated allocation permits us to compare small and large estimates on equal footing. Let's call it the percentage economic-capital allocation error.

Figure 4.13 employs our newly minted percentage economic-capital allocation error measure, defined in Eq. 4.19, to illustrate the range of outcomes for 250 million and one billion total simulations. In both cases, the confidence level is 90%. The fourfold increase from the left- to right-hand graphics cuts, by $\mathcal{O}\left(\frac{1}{\sqrt{\mathrm{M}}}\right)$ convergence, the breadth of the confidence interval in half. Even in the 250 million simulation case, the error bound rarely deviates from the mid-point by more than a few percentage points. This implies a relatively tight estimate for the majority of the risk-owner allocations.

Table 4.2 provides a broad range of summary statistics for our error terms. The average percentage confidence-interval width is greater than 50% with one million

**Table 4.2** *Convergence statistics*: This provides a broad range of summary statistics for the $\epsilon_n$ measure—across all risk owners—introduced in Eq. 4.19 where $\gamma = 0.90$. In particular, it demonstrates the rate of convergence for increasing total numbers of simulations. All values are denoted in basis points.

| Statistic | 1M | 10M | 25M | 50M | 100M | 250M | 500M | 1000M |
|---|---|---|---|---|---|---|---|---|
| Mean | 55.4 | 17.3 | 10.9 | 7.7 | 5.5 | 3.4 | 2.4 | 1.7 |
| Weighted-mean | 37.0 | 11.7 | 7.4 | 5.2 | 3.7 | 2.3 | 1.7 | 1.2 |
| Median | 44.4 | 13.9 | 8.8 | 6.4 | 4.5 | 2.8 | 2.0 | 1.4 |
| Maximum | 260.0 | 58.7 | 42.8 | 28.8 | 20.4 | 12.9 | 8.9 | 6.4 |
| Minimum | 4.9 | 1.4 | 1.0 | 0.7 | 0.5 | 0.3 | 0.2 | 0.2 |
| Volatility | 40.2 | 10.1 | 6.4 | 4.5 | 3.1 | 2.0 | 1.4 | 1.0 |
| IQR | 37.2 | 10.7 | 7.3 | 4.8 | 3.5 | 2.2 | 1.5 | 1.1 |

simulations.[77] This is dramatically far from convergence. Increasing the simulations by a factor of 100 leads, as expected by theory, to a roughly tenfold decrease in the error estimate.

The mean error estimate is useful, but it is rather sensitive to outliers and, perhaps more importantly, it treats all economic-capital allocations equally. In real-life portfolios, it is typical for a relatively modest proportion of exposures to drive a significant part of the overall risk in one's portfolio.[78] Getting the large allocations correct is thus, all else equal, more important than getting them all right.[79] Percentage error can be economically misleading when applied to small allocations. A large percentage confidence interval to a vanishingly small allocation does not create, from an economic perspective, the same level of concern as even moderate uncertainty in a large individual contribution estimate. It is thus encouraging to observe that the weighted-average percentage confidence-interval width is systemically smaller than the simple average. This strongly suggests the convergence uncertainty is lower in large allocations.

Examination of Table 4.2 in more detail also reveals that extreme errors—as measured by the minimum and maximum—as well as error volatility are also a predictably decreasing function of the number of simulations. This provides comfort that the overall implementation and convergence behaviour are consistent with our theoretical expectations.

Figure 4.14 provides a second perspective on Fig. 4.13 by ordering the errors estimates by the magnitude—measured in terms of standard deviations from the average allocation—of the underlying economic-capital estimate and the internal PD class, respectively. Clear patterns are evident. The confidence bound appears to

[77] On a median or weighted-average basis, it is somewhat lower, but still generally unacceptably high.

[78] This appears to be a practical example of the so-called Pareto principle, or 80-20 rule, which holds that about 80% of the results come from 20% of the causes. This is perhaps a bit too precise, but the general principle often holds, at least approximately.

[79] If you really had to choose, you would presumably like to get them all about right.

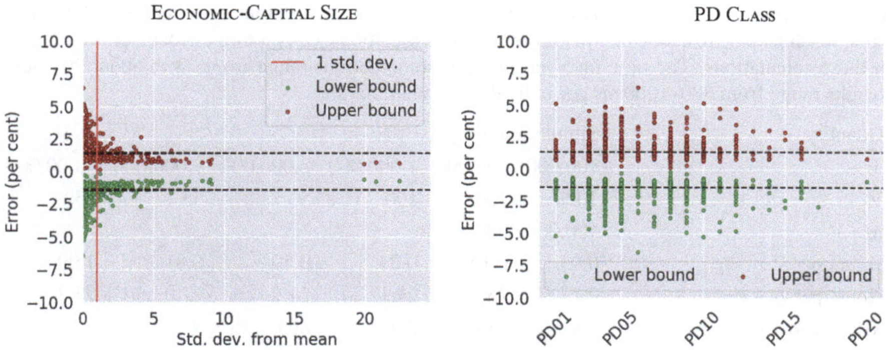


**Fig. 4.14** *Organizing risk-owner allocation errors*: The preceding graphics provide a second perspective on Fig. 4.13 by ordering the percentage confidence-interval breadths by the magnitude of the economic-capital estimate and PD class, respectively. In general, the larger the allocation, the lower the overall error. Conversely, high-quality credit-allocation estimates are noisier than their lower-quality compatriots. These values were computed with 250 million simulations and $\gamma = 0.9$.

be a decreasing function of the size of the economic-capital allocation. Logically, this is presumably due to the fact that these larger exposures are more consistently represented in the tails of the loss distribution. The corollary is that the least precise estimates occur predominately among the smallest allocations. We may thus, fairly confidently, conclude that at around 250 million simulations, the largest (and thus most important) allocations receive a satisfactorily tight estimate.

In the right-hand-side of Fig. 4.14, there appears to be a trend towards improvement in simulation accuracy as we move down the credit spectrum. A bit puzzling at first, this is a feature of the credit-risk problem. Default probabilities increase roughly exponentially as we move from PD classes one to 20. The incidence of default in our simulation model is thus markedly higher for a PD13 than for a PD04 credit obligor. Not only is the incidence of default higher, but this permits more frequent draws from the random recovery distribution. The combination of these elements should help to yield less noisy estimates at the lower end of the credit scale. High-quality credit obligors get hit along both dimensions; there is a low prevalence of default and correspondingly fewer draws from the recovery distribution. Although it is structurally more difficult to generate tight economic-capital estimates of high credit-quality risk owners, Fig. 4.14 suggests that this effect is relatively constrained in our case.

### *4.5.4 Computational Expense*

This brings us back to our original *two* solutions to this problem: brawn or brains. To this point, we have relied on brawn, but have said relatively little about

**Table 4.3** *Single-processor speed*: This table summarizes *six* different combinations of `M` and `V` values each leading to a total of 100 million overall simulations. Only a *single* processor is employed in these calculations. The time involved in these computations range from 23 to about 30 hours. Results range from 800–1000 ms per individual simulation run.

| Quantity | Simulation perspective | | | | | |
|---|---|---|---|---|---|---|
| $M$ | 100,000 | 500,000 | 1,000,000 | 2,000,000 | 3,000,000 | 4,000,000 |
| $V$ | 1000 | 200 | 100 | 50 | 33 | 25 |
| $M \cdot V$ | 100,000,000 | | | | | |
| Hours per $V$ | 0.03 | 0.12 | 0.24 | 0.50 | 0.81 | 1.09 |
| Hours per $M \cdot V$ | 29.7 | 23.2 | 24.1 | 24.9 | 27.0 | 27.3 |
| Microseconds per $m \in M \cdot V$ | 1068 | 836 | 866 | 895 | 971 | 981 |

computational cost. It is useful to understand precisely how much brawn we are taking about. The reader, when examining Fig. 4.12, may have been a bit shocked to observe a *billion* total simulations. This is, by almost any standard, a ridiculous amount of computational effort. The natural question follows: is it reasonable, or even feasible, to regularly incur such a dramatic amount of computational expense? This query cannot, of course, be answered without some review of the computation times.

It is difficult to discuss calculation speeds without reference to hardware choices and one's computational strategy. A server environment with 48 virtual processors and 256 gigabytes of cache memory was configured for testing purposes.[80] In brief, this is a fairly powerful set-up that permits a performance of a significant number of simulations in, hopefully, reasonably short time periods.

We follow *two* alternative computational strategies: single and multiprocessing. Let us begin with the single-processor approach. *Six* different combinations of `M` and `V` settings were selected, each leading to a total of `M` $\cdot$ `V` $=$ 100 million overall simulations. On one end of the spectrum, we consider 1000 `V` repetitions of `M` $=$ 100,000 iterations. On the other end, instead of many repetitions of a small number of iterations, we consider `V` $=$ 25 repetitions of four million iterations. Naturally, as we increase `M`, there is an increased memory burden. It was not possible to reliably use an `M` greater than about 4,000,000 without program failure due to memory errors.[81]

The results are rather disappointing. Table 4.3 summarizes a variety of statistics related to this single-processor experiment. The time required for each of these computations ranges from 23 to about 30 hours. This translates into 800–1000 ms

[80] Each individual CPU is relatively small with a clockspeed of roughly 2.1 gigahertz (GHz). Although it is difficult to compare processors strictly by their clock speed, it is a rough measurement of processor capacity. Most modern i7 chips, as a point of comparison, have clock rates in excess of 3 GHz.

[81] `numpy` arrays do not appear to have any explicit size limits, but, by trial and error, we found that array operations are somewhat fragile when operating on the boundaries of memory consumption.

**Table 4.4** *Multi-processor speed*: This table fixes `M` at 250,000 and considers increasing levels of `V` covering a range from one million to one billion total simulations. 35 separate processors are employed in these calculations. The time involved spans six minutes to about 13 hours; this amounts to 50–300 ms per individual simulation run.

| Quantity | Simulation perspective | | | | | | | |
|---|---|---|---|---|---|---|---|---|
| $M$ | 250,000 | | | | | | | |
| $V$ | 4 | 40 | 100 | 200 | 400 | 1000 | 2000 | 4000 |
| $M \cdot V$ (millions) | 1 | 10 | 25 | 50 | 100 | 250 | 500 | 1000 |
| Hours per $V$ | 0.0003 | 0.0001 | 0.0001 | 0.0001 | 0.0001 | 0.0001 | 0.0001 | 0.0001 |
| Hours per $M \cdot V$ | 0.1 | 0.2 | 0.4 | 0.7 | 1.4 | 3.3 | 6.5 | 12.8 |
| Microseconds per $m \in M \cdot V$ | 288 | 68 | 53 | 51 | 49 | 48 | 47 | 46 |

per individual simulation run.[82] In all cases, therefore, each simulation experiment requires literally one full day. Given that 100 million simulations, from our previous analysis, is at lower end of what is necessary to achieve a minimally acceptable level of uncertainty, the single-processor strategy does *not* appear to be viable.

The multiprocessor approach, as the name suggests, involves making practical use of the 48 cores available on our testing server. Employing the `Pool` functionality from Python's `multiprocessing` library, 35 of 48 processors were employed for this experiment.[83] There is certainly much more to the implementation of parallel processing—and many alternative platforms and strategies—but a detailed discussion would take us quite far afield.[84] The practical consequence is a slight reorganization of the code implementation, but it remains largely similar and eminently readable.

The second multiprocessor, or parallel processing, experiment holds the value of `M` fixed at 250,000. Larger, or smaller, values are possible, but this appears—within current memory constraints—to a rather sensible setting.[85] With fixed `M`, we then gradually increase the value of `V` to raise the total number of simulations. `V` $= 4$, for example, yields only one million simulations, whereas setting `V` to 4000 brings us back to our one billion total simulations.

Table 4.4 summarizes the, much more encouraging, results of this second exercise. The amount of simulation time has been considerably reduced. One hundred million total simulations requires less than 90 minutes, whereas the fastest

[82] A microsecond is one millionth of a second.

[83] More processors can, of course, be employed, but practical testing revealed that, to avoid memory errors, it is sensible to *not* use all available processors.

[84] A good introduction—within the context of the Python programming language—into this field of endeavour is Zaccone [40].

[85] Setting `M` to a larger value, for example, requires more memory and, to respect the overall constraint, can only be accommodated by using fewer cores. This, in turn, essentially defeats the purpose of using multiple processors. On the other hand, if `M` is too small, we need more processors to accommodate all of the resulting effort. We'll return to the (pseudo-optimal) selection of `M` in the next section.

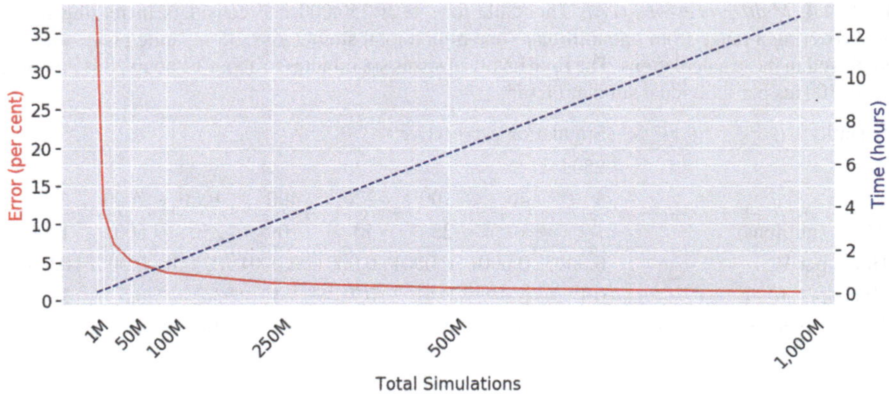


**Fig. 4.15** *Convergence-time trade-off*: This graphic provides visual insight into the trade-off between simulation accuracy, or degree of convergence, and the amount of required computational time. As previously discussed, simulation errors go to zero at roughly the same speed of $\frac{1}{\sqrt{M}}$, while the computational costs increase linearly.

single-processor implementation from Table 4.3 required close to 24 hours. This represents a roughly 17-fold increase in computational speed. Why, we might legitimately ask, if we use 35 processors instead of just one, do we not see speed increases on the magnitude of 35? The reasons relates to the overhead associated with multiprocessing. Upfront costs are involved in partitioning the work to various processors, while back-end costs are required to redistribute the results to our `ecObj` object. We can think of these as fixed costs associated with parallel processing. This explains the steady decrease in microseconds for each individual simulation in $\mathtt{M} \cdot \mathtt{V}$; as we increase `V`, we are spreading the fixed costs among a larger number of repetitions. The inherent overhead, therefore, explains implementation improvements on the order of 20 times rather than 30.

Although parallel processing permits pronounced reductions in computational expense, it does not come entirely for free. Total simulations in the neighbourhood of 250 to 500 million—which appear, based on the previous analysis, to be roughly necessary for manageable levels of convergence—require between about 4–7 hours of computational time.[86]

Figure 4.15 attempts to visually describe this practical trade-off between level of convergence, or accuracy, and computational time. There is something of a mismatch between computational time and noise reduction: as previously discussed, simulation errors go to zero at roughly the same speed of $\frac{1}{\sqrt{\mathtt{M}}}$, while the computational costs increase linearly. To cut the simulation noise in half, to view this from a depressing standpoint, four times more computational expense is incurred.

[86] This, of course, only applies on this relatively small test server. In our production setting, using a reasonably high performance hardware set-up, the computational time associated with 500 million simulations is roughly 90 minutes.

**Colour and Commentary 51** (CONVERGENCE REQUIREMENTS): *Simulation techniques admirably manage high dimensionality, but do so relatively slowly. Simulation can definitely be cast in the role of the tortoise in Aesop's legendary fable.*[a] *Cutting simulation errors in half requires a quadrupling of one's computational efforts. At a reasonable tolerance for error, our credit-risk economic-capital model requires somewhere between about 250 and 500 million simulations to obtain acceptable levels of convergence. While we admire the tortoise's perseverance, we are nonetheless interested in ways to speed him up. Our strategy to manage this challenge is threefold. First, the code implementation makes use of parallel-processing techniques to actively employ available computing resources. Second, investment in memory and processors has been made through a powerful computational server. Third, and finally, standard error estimates are produced daily for all models and individual allocations. The combination of these elements permits timely and affordable computations along with continuous oversight of convergence performance.*

[a] For a serious discussion of the tortoise, the hare, and their much celebrated race, please see Jacobs and Heighway [22].

### 4.5.5 *Choosing* M

So far, we have typically set $\mathtt{M} = 250{,}000$ and used V to achieve the desired number of total simulations. It turns out that the results are not invariant to the choice of M. To understand why, we need to return to our underlying credit-risk economic capital metric: expected shortfall. Discussed in detail in Chap. 2, it is the average loss at and beyond a given quantile, $\alpha$. Setting $M = 100{,}000$ and $\alpha = 0.99$ means that we will have

$$\begin{aligned}(1-\alpha)\cdot\mathtt{M} &= (1-0.99)\cdot 100,000, \\ &= 1000,\end{aligned} \tag{4.20}$$

available *tail* observations to inform our expected shortfall estimate. This is more than sufficient to construct a robust estimator of one's expected-shortfall measure.

At a confidence level of $\alpha = 0.9997$, we are operating quite far out in the tail of the loss distribution. Table 4.5, replicating the simple arithmetic in Eq. 4.20 for various choices of M and $\alpha$, displays the sample size available for the computation of the expected-shortfall metric. For any combination of M and $\alpha$, this will be repeated over each iteration of $v = 1, \ldots, \mathtt{V}$. Using the standard setting to this point—$\mathtt{M} = 250,000$ and $\alpha = 0.9997$—reveals a working sample size of 75 loss observations

**Table 4.5** *Expected-shortfall estimator sample size*: This table, for various choices of M and $\alpha$, displays the sample size available for the computation of the expected-shortfall metric over each iteration of $v = 1, \ldots, \mathrm{V}$. Too big and it can create resource issues. Too small and it may bias the final credit-risk economic-capital estimates.

| M | $\alpha$: Level of confidence | | | |
|---|---|---|---|---|
| | 0.9900 | 0.9990 | 0.9997 | 0.9999 |
| 1000 | 10 | 1 | 0 | 0 |
| 10,000 | 100 | 10 | 3 | 1 |
| 100,000 | 1000 | 100 | 30 | 10 |
| 250,000 | 2500 | 250 | 75 | 25 |
| 500,000 | 5000 | 500 | 150 | 50 |
| 750,000 | 7500 | 750 | 225 | 75 |
| 1,000,000 | 10,000 | 1000 | 300 | 100 |

for each iteration of our simulation algorithm. While not tremendously small, it cannot be considered enormous.

The interesting, and pertinent, question is: how do our economic-capital estimate change as we increase M. This brings us to a final, rather industrial strength, experiment. The idea is to fix V at 250 and consider *three* alternative choices of M: 250,000; 500,000; and one million. This yields a modest total of 62.5, 125, and 250 million simulations, respectively. The catch is that each of these experiments is then repeated $\mathrm{K} = 50$ times.[87] While extremely computationally intensive, this extra work permits us to examine the distribution of our combinations of V and M.

Figure 4.16 visually summarizes the high-level results. For each choice of M, we can construct the empirical distribution of both default and migration-risk economic-capital estimators.[88] The left-hand side graphics in Fig. 4.16 chronicle the evolution of default risk as one moves sequentially from $\mathrm{M} = 250{,}000$ to one million. At $\mathrm{M} = 250{,}000$, the values vary from the central estimate by up to about 50 basis points. As we move to $\mathrm{M} = 500{,}000$, the dispersion visibly tightens; indeed, it looks to be cut almost in half. At $\mathrm{M} = 1{,}000{,}000$, there appears to be less volatility relative to $\mathrm{M} = 500{,}000$. The improvement, however, is much smaller in magnitude. A analogous pattern is visible in the migration-risk estimates, albeit with lower overall dispersion from the outset.[89]

Figure 4.16 indicates that the choice of M makes a difference in the general uncertainty around the central estimate. Does it have an impact on the level? The answer is yes, albeit slightly. We will take the truth of the credit-risk economic-

[87] This leads to a staggering total number of $3\frac{1}{8}$, $6\frac{1}{4}$, and $12\frac{1}{2}$ billion simulations for each experiment.

[88] One might argue that $\mathrm{K} = 50$ is a fairly modest sample to specify a distribution. While we always wish for more, these estimates are not easily acquired. It took several days of computation for each choice of M.

[89] This supports the notion that migration risk, by virtue of its basic characteristics, converges more quickly than the default side.

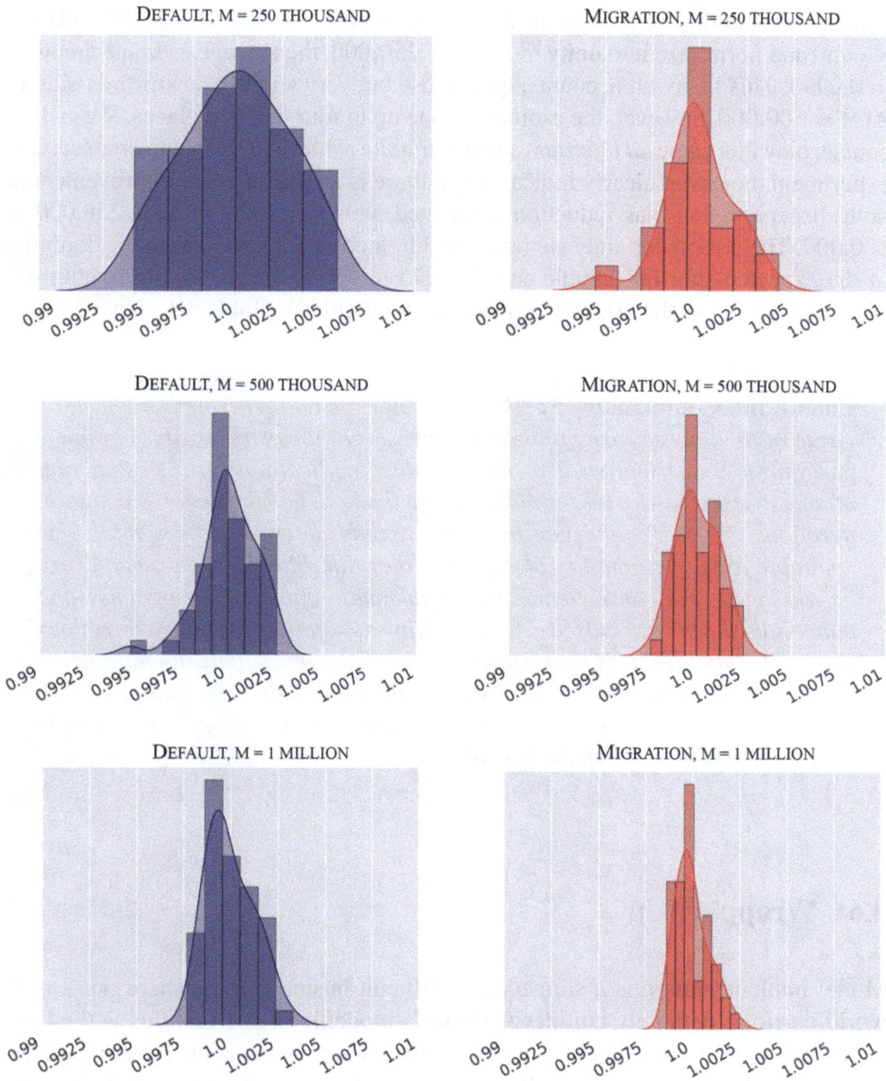


**Fig. 4.16** *The impact of* `M`: The graphics above examine, for a fixed `V` $=$ 250, the impact of different choices of `M` on the distribution of our default and migration estimators. The combination of `V` and `M` are repeated `K` $=$ 50 times and the economic-capital results are normalized to unity.

capital value, in this exercise, to be the average across V $= 250$, M $= 1{,}000{,}000$ and K $= 50$ and normalize it to unity.[90] For M $= 250{,}000$, the average estimate amounts to 0.9990. This is, by all accounts, quite close but very slightly downwards biased. At M $= 500{,}000$, however, the estimate is one up to four decimal places. We can, of course, play this game *ad infinitum* and never quite achieve perfect convergence. Our experiment, however, clearly indicates that there is an unequivocal improvement in both dispersion and bias reduction associated with increasing M from 250,000 to 500,000. The reason certainly stems, as highlighted in Table 4.5, from the doubling of the expected-shortfall sample size from 75 to 150 extreme-loss observations.[91] This analysis forms the original choice of M highlighted in Table 4.1 on page 246.

**Colour and Commentary 52** (CHOICE OF M): *Credit-risk measurement, by virtue of the intense rarity of default, operates at the extreme edges of one's portfolio-loss distribution. This has practical implications for the estimation of one's risk metrics via simulation methods. The choice of simulation iterations, M, and confidence level, $\alpha$, directly determine the sample size available for the estimation of expected shortfall. Should one's sample size be too small, the consequence is a problematic combination of noisy and potentially downward biased estimates. Unfortunately, prescriptive directions cannot be provided. It is necessary to periodically investigate the interaction between various reasonable values of M and one's estimates. Equipped with this information, one may find the appropriate trade-off between estimate uncertainty, bias, and computational expense.*

## 4.6 Wrapping Up

Model implementation is a slippery and difficult business. It is where one's real-world portfolio definitely collides with one's modelling structure; this is the busy workshop floor of our economic-capital factory. Thorny questions regarding implementation infrastructure, data collection and quality control, software choice, and staffing policy become surprisingly important. The pressure to get this right has only intensified in recent years with an increased emphasis on model governance and oversight. This naturally spills over into coding and documentation practice. Credit-risk measurement has an additional level of implementation complexity. Since one invariably employs simulation methods, model convergence is a central concern.

---

[90] This is still not the absolute truth of our unknown random variable $P$, but with 12.5 billion total simulations, it's a pretty tight estimate.

[91] The marginal impact of increasing the expected-shortfall sample size from 150 to 300, by contrast, appears to be limited.

This leads to an awkward, but important, tension between the need for a high level of certainty in one's estimates and the efficient use of (expensive) computing resources. There are many possible solutions depending on one's portfolio, resources, and personal taste. Our solution, presented in the previous discussion, centres around a parallel-processing structure that explicitly permits daily computation of standard errors and confidence bounds at both the portfolio and obligor levels. This direct incorporation of the model-convergence dimension into our model implementation is entirely consistent with emerging best practice in model oversight and has served us well.

## References


1. B. Beizer. *Software Testing Techniques*. Wiley India, New Delhi, India, 2008.
2. R. Bellman. *Adaptive Control Processes: A Guided Tour*. Princeton University Press, 1961.
3. BIS. Supervisory framework for measuring and controlling large exposures. Technical report, Bank for International Settlements, March 2013.
4. BIS. Basel III leverage ratio framework and disclosure requirements. Technical report, Bank for International Settlements, January 2014.
5. D. J. Bolder. *Credit-Risk Modelling: Theoretical Foundations, Diagnostic Tools, Practical Examples, and Numerical Recipes in Python*. Springer-Nature, Heidelberg, Germany, 2018.
6. D. J. Bolder. Stealing Others' Strategies: Lessons on Model Risk. In *Evolving Practices in Public Investment Management: Proceedings of the Seventh Public Investors Conference*, 2020.
7. D. A. Carpenter. Clarifying Normalization. *Journal of Information Systems Education*, 19(4): 379–382, 2008.
8. C. Cohn. Build vs. buy: How to know when you should build custom software over canned solutions, 2014.
9. E. Derman. Model risk. Goldman Sachs Quantitative Strategies Research Notes, April 1996.
10. E. Derman. *Models Behaving Badly: Why Confusing Illusion with Reality Can Lead to Disaster, on Wall Street and in Life*. Free Press, New York, USA, 2012.
11. R. Durrett. *Probability: Theory and Examples*. Duxbury Press, Belmont, California, second edition, 1996.
12. G. Elfring. Choosing a Programming Language. *Byte*, 10(6):235–236, 1985.
13. F. J. Fabozzi. *The Handbook of Fixed Income Securities*. Irwin, Chicago, Illinois, fifth edition, 1997.
14. C. H. Fine and D. E. Whitney. Is the Make-Buy Decision Process a Core Competence? MIT Center for Technology, February 1996.
15. G. S. Fishman. *Monte Carlo: Concepts, Algorithms, and Applications*. Springer-Verlag, 175 Fifth Avenue, New York, NY, 1995. Springer Series in Operations Research.
16. P. Glasserman and J. Li. Importance sampling for portfolio credit risk. *Management Science*, 51(11):1643–1656, 2005.
17. A. Gupta. How to Select a Simulation Software. *International Journal of Engineering Research and Development*, 10(3):35–41, 2014.
18. Y. Hilpisch. *Derivative Analytics with Python: Data Analysis, Models, Simulation and Hedging*. Wiley, West Sussex, United Kingdom, 2015.
19. Y. Hilpisch. Computational Finance: Why Python is Taking Over. *Wilmott Magazine*, 2016: 43–44, 2016.
20. C. Hung. Software Buyer's Guide: Build vs. Buy. RL Solutions, January 2017.

21. M. Y. Imamgoglu and D. Cetinkaya. A Rule Based Decision Support System for Programming Language Selection. *Proceedings of the Second International Conference on Knowledge Engineering and Applications*, 1:71–75, 2017.
22. J. Jacobs and R. Heighway. *The Fables of Æsop, Selected, Told Anew and their History Traced.* Macmillan & Company, London, UK, 1950.
23. P. G. W. Keen. Value Analysis: Justifying Decision Support Systems. *MIS Quarterly*, 5(1): 1–15, 1981.
24. R. Kimball and J. Caserta. *The Data Warehouse ETL Toolkit: Practical Techniques for Extracting, Cleaning, Conforming, and Delivering Data.* Wiley Publishing, Inc., Indianapolis, USA, 2004.
25. A. E. Kwame, E. M. Martey, and A. G. Chris. Qualitative Assessment of Compiled, Interpreted and Hybrid Programming Languages. *Communications on Applied Electronics*, 7(7), October 2017.
26. J. Loeliger and M. McCullough. *Version Control with Git : Powerful Tools and Techniques for Collaborative Software Development.* O'Reilly Media, Inc., Sebastopol, California, 2012.
27. L. E. Lwakatare. *DevOps Adoption and Implementation in Software Development Practice: Concept, Practices, Benefits and Challenges.* PhD thesis, University of Oulu, 2017. Unpublished Thesis.
28. W. McKinney. *Python for Data Analysis.* O'Reilly Media, Inc., Sebastopol, California, 2013.
29. D. McLeish. *Monte Carlo Simulation and Finance.* Wiley, first edition, 2005.
30. C. L. Meador and R. A. Mezger. Selecting an End User Programming Language for DSS Development. *MIS Quarterly*, 8(4):267–281, 1984.
31. OCC. OCC Bulletin 2000–16 on Risk Modeling: Model Validation. Technical report, Office of the Comptroller of the Currency, May 2000.
32. OCC. Supervisory Guidance on Model Risk Management. Technical report, Office of the Comptroller of the Currency, April 2011.
33. Perception Software. Decision Support: Building vs. Buying. Encompass White Paper, January 2014.
34. A. O. Ramirez. Three-tier architecture. *Linux Journal*, 2000(75), 2000.
35. J. Reason. *Human Error.* Cambridge University Press, New York, USA, 1990.
36. N. B. Ruparelia. Software Development Lifecycle Models. *ACM SIGSOFT Software Engineering Notes*, 35(3):8–13, 2010.
37. A. Sefferman. Build vs. buy: When to buy software or build it yourself, 2017.
38. R. Stallman. The free universal encyclopedia and learning resource, 2000. URL https://www.gnu.org/encyclopedia/anencyc.txt.
39. J. VanderPlas. *Python Data Science Handbook.* O'Reilly Media, Inc., Sebastopol, California, 2017.
40. G. Zaccone. *Python Parallel Programming Cookbook.* Packt Publishing, Birmingham, UK, 2015.

# Part II
# Loan Pricing

# Chapter 5
# Approximating Economic Capital

*It has long been an axiom of mine that the little things are infinitely the most important.*

*(Arthur Conan Doyle)*

As the previous chapter makes abundantly clear, the computation of credit-risk economic capital is, irrespective of the approach taken, computationally intensive and slow. This is simply a fact of life. Clever use of parallel-processing and variance-reduction techniques can improve this situation, but they cannot entirely alleviate it. In some settings, however, speed matters. It would be extremely useful—and, at times, even essential—for certain applications, to perform large numbers of *quick* credit-risk economic-capital estimates. *Two* classic applications include:

- LOAN PRICING: computing the marginal economic-capital impact of adding a new loan, or treasury position, to the current portfolio; and
- STRESS TESTING: assessing the impact of a (typically adverse) global shock to the entire portfolio—or some important subset thereof—upon one's overall economic-capital assessment.

The needs of these applications are slightly different. Loan pricing examines a single, potential addition to the lending book; not much change is involved, but the portfolio perspective is essential.[1] Time is also very much of the essence. One simply cannot wait for 90 minutes (or so) every time one wishes to consider an alternative pricing scenario.[2] Stress-testing involves many, separate portfolio and instrument-level calculations; significant portfolio change and dislocation generally occurs.[3] One might be ready to wait a few days for one's stress-testing results, but if one desires frequent, sufficiently nuanced, and regular stress analysis, such

[1] Chapter 6 considers this application in much more detail.

[2] Even waiting 10 minutes would (eventually) make loan originators crazy and stifle their ability to consider a broad range of potential loan structures for their clients.

[3] Chapter 12 is dedicated to the discussion of stress testing.

 
D. Bolder, *Modelling Economic Capital*, Contributions to Finance and Accounting,
https://doi.org/10.1007/978-3-030-95096-5_5

slowness is untenable. To be performed effectively—albeit for different reasons—both applications thus require swiftness.

Sadly, speed of execution is one element woefully lacking from our large-scale industrial credit-risk economic capital model. What is to be done? Since it is simply unworkable to use the simulation engine to inform these estimates, an alternative is required. The proposed solution involves the construction of a *fast*, first-order, instrument-level *approximation* of one's economic-capital allocation. Approximation suggests the presence of some error, but in both applications an immediate, but slightly noisy, estimate is vastly superior to a more accurate, but glacially slow value.

This might seem a bit confusing. The economic-capital model is, itself, a simulation-based approximation. We would, in essence, be performing an approximation of an approximation. While there is some truth to this criticism, there is no other reasonable alternative. Failure to find a fast, semi-analytic, approximation would undermine our ability to sensibly employ our credit-risk economic capital model in a few important, and highly informative, applications.

Such an approach to this underling problem is *not* without precedent. Bolder and Rubin [7], for example, investigate a range of flexible high-dimensional approximating functions—in a rather different analytic context—with substantial success. Ribarits et al. [25] present—based on Pykhtin [23]—precisely such an economic-capital approximation for loan pricing. This work is a generalization of the so-called granularity adjustment—initially proposed by Gordy [13]—for Pillar II concentration-risk calculations.[4] This regulatory capital motivated methodology, while powerful, is *not* directly employed in our approach for one simple reason: we wish to tailor our approximation to our specific modelling choice and parametrization. A second reason is that we will require separate, although certainly related, approximations for both default and credit-migration risk. The consequence is that, although motivated by the general literature, much of this chapter is specific to the NIB setting. It will hopefully, however, stimulate ideas and provide a conceptual framework for others facing similar challenges.

## 5.1 Framing the Problem

Before jumping into specific approximation techniques, let's try to frame the problem. To summarize, we require a *fast* assessment of the marginal economic-capital consumption—at a given point in time—operating at the individual loan and obligor level. We may ultimately apply it at the portfolio level, but it needs to operate at the individual exposure level.[5] The plan is to construct a closed-form—or, at

[4] This area, an important part of the regulatory world, is covered extensively in Chap. 11.

[5] A portfolio analysis would, consequently, involve summing the implications across a range of individual positions.

least, semi-analytical—mathematical approximation of the economic-capital model allocations. There are, fortunately, many possible techniques in the mathematical and statistical literature that might be useful in this regard. Broadly speaking, there are *two* main approaches to such an approximation:

1. a structural description; or
2. a reduced-form—or, empirically motivated—approach.

The proposed economic-capital approximation methodology in this chapter is based, more or less, on the former method. That said, this need not be so. The sole selection criterion—ignoring, for the moment, speed—is predication accuracy. This suggests that we might legitimately consider reduced-form techniques as well.

This brings us to the general approximation problem. Let us begin by defining $y \in \mathbb{R}^{I \times 1}$ as the vector-quantity that we are trying to approximate; this is basically our collection of $I$ economic-capital estimates at a given point in time. We further denote $X \in \mathbb{R}^{I \times \kappa}$ as a set of explanatory, or instrument, variables that can act to describe the current economic-capital outcomes.[6] Good examples of instruments would include the size of the position, its default probability, assumed recovery rate, industrial sector, and geographic region. Our available inputs thus involve $I$ economic-capital allocations along with $\kappa$ explanatory variables for each observation.

The (slow) simulated-based economic-capital model, $f(X)$, is a complicated function of these explanatory variables. Conceptually, it is a mapping of the following form:

$$y \leftarrow \boxed{\text{Economic-Capital Model: } f(X) + \epsilon} \leftarrow X \tag{5.1}$$

where $\epsilon$ is observation or measurement error.[7] In words, therefore, $f(X)$ is basically the economic-capital model. Regrettably, we do not have a simple description of $f$; if we did, of course, we would not find ourselves in this situation! Practically, our approximation is attempting to bypass the unknown function, $f$, and replace it with an approximator. Conceptually, this replaces Eq. 5.1 with

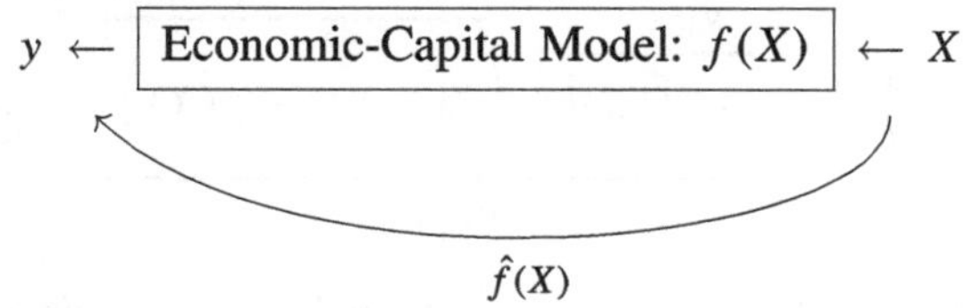


[6] In a machine-learning context, these are typically referred to as features.

[7] In our case, of course, this is more readily conceptualized as simulation error.

where we denote our approximation as $\hat{f}(X)$. The trick, and our principal task in this chapter, is to find a sensible, rapidly computed, and satisfactorily accurate choice of $\hat{f}$. There are no shortage of potential candidates. Function approximation is a heavily studied area of mathematics. Much of the statistics literature relating to parameter estimation touches on this notion and the burgeoning discipline of machine learning is centrally concerned with prediction of (unknown and complicated) functions.[8]

If $y$ is the true model output, then our approximation can be characterized as:

$$\hat{y} = \hat{f}(X). \tag{5.2}$$

We write this value without error, which is a bit misleading. There is, quite naturally, error associated with our new approximation. We prefer, however, to describe this directly in comparison to the observed $y$. Indeed, a useful choice $\hat{f}$ involves a small distance between $y$ and $\hat{y}$; this includes the approximation error. There are a variety of ways to measure this distance, but one common, and useful, metric is defined as:

$$\mathbb{E}\left[\left(y - \hat{y}\right)^2\right] = \mathbb{E}\left[\left(f(X) + \epsilon - \hat{f}(X)\right)^2\right]. \tag{5.3}$$

This is referred to as the mean-squared error. It is basically the average distance between the sum of the squared approximation errors. Squaring the errors has the desirable property of transforming both over- and underestimates into positive figures; it also helpfully generates a continuous and differentiable error function. The measurement error is also clearly inherited from the original (unknown) function $f$. The bottom line is that we seek an approximator, $\hat{y}$, that keeps the error definition in Eq. 5.3 at a relatively acceptable level.

With some patience, the mean-squared error can also tell us something useful about our problem. Employing a few algebraic tricks, we may re-write the previous expression as:

$$\mathbb{E}\left[\left(y - \hat{y}\right)^2\right] = \underbrace{\overbrace{\text{var}[\hat{f}(X)]}^{\text{Variance}} + \overbrace{\left(\mathbb{E}[\hat{f}(X)] - f(X)\right)^2}^{\text{Bias}^2}}_{\text{Reducible}} + \underbrace{\text{var}(\epsilon)}_{\text{Irreducible}}. \tag{5.4}$$

Our measure of distance between the observed and approximated economic-capital values can be generally categorized into *two* broad categories: reducible and

[8] There are many good references for the area of machine, or statistical, learning. A natural starting point, however, is Hastie et al. [16]. A more introductory version of this material is found in James et al. [17].

irreducible error.[9] Reducible error, which itself can be broken down into variance and bias—can be managed with intelligent model selection. Irreducible error stems from observation error; in our case, this relates to simulation noise.[10] This is something we need to either live with or, when feasible, actively seek to reduce. Bias describes fundamental differences between our approximation and true model. We might, for example, use a linear model to approximate something that is inherently non-linear. Such a choice would introduce bias. Variance comes from the robustness of our estimates across datasets. It seeks to understand how well, if we reshuffle the cards and generate a new sample, our approximator might perform. A low-variance estimator would be rather robust to changes in one's observed data-set.

Statisticians and data scientists speak frequently of a variance-bias trade-off. This implies that simultaneous reduction of both aspects is difficult (or even impossible). Statisticians, with their focus on inference, tend to accept relatively high bias for low variance. Machine-learning algorithms, due to their flexibility, tend to have lower bias, but the potential for higher bias.[11] The proposed approximation model—leaning towards the classical statistical school of thought—employs a multivariate linear regression with structurally motivated response variables. In principle, therefore, this choice involves a reasonable amount of bias. Our credit-risk economic-capital model is not, as we've seen, particularly linear in its construction. The implicit logic behind this choice, of course, is that it provides a stable, low-variance estimator.

**Colour and Commentary 53** (Approximating Economic Capital): *There is a certain irony in expending—in the previous chapters—such a dramatic amount of mental and computational resources for the calculation of economic capital, only to find it immediately necessary to approximate it. This is the dark side associated with the centrality of credit-risk economic capital. Determining the marginal economic-capital consumption associated with adding (or changing) one, or many, loans has a broad range of useful appli-*

(continued)

[9] To arrive at the decomposition in Eq. 5.4, one needs to rewrite the right-hand-side of Eq. 5.3 as,

$$\mathbb{E}\left[\left(f(X)+\epsilon-\hat{f}(X)\underbrace{+\mathbb{E}[\hat{f}(X)]-\mathbb{E}[\hat{f}(X)]}_{=0}\right)^2\right], \tag{5.5}$$

and recall that, through independence and zero expectation, the product of $\epsilon$ with any term—save itself—vanishes. The rest is expansion, simplification, and tedium. See again Hastie et al. [16] or James et al. [17] for more detail, and useful colour, on this computation.

[10] In our case, this can be controlled—albeit not without cost—by increasing the total number of simulations. This is an important practical application of the convergence discussion in Chap. 4.

[11] See Breiman [8] and Bolder [6] for more detailed background on the relative differences between statistical and machine-learning approaches to this general problem.

**Colour and Commentary 53** (continued)
*cations. Examples include risk-adjusted return computations, loan pricing, stress testing, sensitivity analysis, and even loan impairments. The slowness of the base simulation-based computation makes—using the simulation engine—such rapid and flexible marginal computations practically infeasible. Their impossibility does not, of course, negate their usefulness. As such, the most logical, and pragmatic, course of action is to construct a fast, accurate, semi-analytic approximation to permit such analysis. Moreover, such effort is not wasted. Not only does it facilitate a number of productive computations, but it also provides welcome, incremental insight into our modelling framework.*

## 5.2 Approximating Default Economic Capital

We've established that we need an approximation technique that, given the existing portfolio, can operate at the instrument level. As established in previous chapters, there are *two* distinct flavours of credit-risk economic capital: default and migration. While we need both, different strategies are possible. We could group the two together and construct a model to approximate the *combined* default and migration economic capital. Alternatively, we could build separate approximators for each element. Neither approach is right or wrong; it depends on the circumstances. Our choice is for distinct treatment of default and migration risk.[12] As a consequence, we'll develop our approximators separately beginning with the dominant source of risk: default.

### 5.2.1 *Exploiting Existing Knowledge*

As a general tenet, if you seek to perform an approximation of some object, it is wise to exploit whatever knowledge you have about it. Specific qualities and attributes about the economic-capital model can thus help inform our approximation decisions. We know that our production credit-risk model is a multivariate $t$-threshold model. We also know that threshold models essentially randomize the conditional probability of default—and thereby induce default correlation—through the introduction of common systemic variables.[13] Extreme realizations of these systemic variables push up the (conditional) likelihood of default and dispropor-

[12] We'll defend this choice later in the discussion, once we've built a bit more understanding of the general approximation approach.

[13] See Bolder [5, Chapter 4] for more colour on the global properties of threshold models.

tionately populate the tail of any portfolio's loss distribution. This link between systemic factors and tail outcomes seems like a sensible starting point.

This brings us directly to the latent creditworthiness state variable introduced in Chap. 2. To repeat it once again for convenience, it has the following form:

$$\Delta X_i = \sqrt{\frac{\nu}{W}}\left(\alpha_i \mathrm{B}_i \Delta z + \sqrt{1-\alpha_i^2}\Delta w_i\right), \tag{5.6}$$

for $i = 1, \ldots, I$. For our purposes, it will be useful to simplify somewhat the notation and structure of the model. These simplifications will enable the construction of a stylized approximator. In particular, the product of systemic factors and their loadings is, by construction, standard normally distributed; that is, $\mathrm{B}_i \Delta z \sim \mathcal{N}(0, 1)$. To reduce the dimensionality, we simply replace this quantity with a single standard normal random variable, $z$. Moreover, to underscore the distance to the true model and make it clear we are operating in the realm of approximation, let us set $\Delta w_i = \upsilon_i$ and $\Delta X_i = y_i$. This yields

$$y_i = \sqrt{\frac{\nu}{W}}\left(\alpha_i z + \sqrt{1-\alpha^2}\upsilon_i\right), \tag{5.7}$$

which amounts to a univariate approximation of our multivariate $t$-threshold model. Some information is clearly lost with these actions, most particularly relating to regional and sectoral aspects of each credit obligor. This will need to be addressed in the full approximation.

A few additional components bear repeating from Chap. 2. The default event (i.e., $\mathcal{D}_i$) occurs if $y_i$ falls below a pre-defined threshold, $K_i = F_{\mathcal{T}_\nu}^{-1}(p_i)$ or,

$$\mathbb{I}_{\mathcal{D}_i} = \mathbb{I}_{\left\{y_i \leq F_{\mathcal{T}_\nu}^{-1}(p_i)\right\}}. \tag{5.8}$$

which allows to get a step closer to our object of interest. The default loss for the $i$th obligor, $L_i^{(d)}$, can be written as

$$\begin{aligned} L_i^{(d)} &= \mathbb{I}_{\mathcal{D}_i} \overbrace{(1-\mathcal{R}_i)}^{\gamma_i} c_i, \\ &= \underbrace{\mathbb{I}_{\left\{y_i \leq F_{\mathcal{T}_\nu}^{-1}(p_i)\right\}}}_{\text{Equation 5.8}} \gamma_i c_i, \end{aligned} \tag{5.9}$$

where $\mathcal{R}_i$, $\gamma_i$, and $c_i$ denote (as usual) the recovery rate, loss-given-default, and exposure-at-default of the $i$th obligor, respectively. The $d$ superscript in Eq. 5.9 explicitly denotes default to keep this estimator distinct from the forthcoming migration case; despite the additional notational clutter, it will prove useful throughout the following development. The magnitude of the default loss thus ultimately depends upon the severity of the common systemic-state variable (i.e., $z$ and $W$) outcomes. Equations 5.6 to 5.9 thus comprise a brief, somewhat stylized representation of our current production model.

The kernel of previous knowledge that we wish to exploit relates to the interaction between systemic variable outcomes and the conditional probability of default. This relationship is captured via the so-called conditional default loss. Conditionality, in this context, involves assuming that our common random variates, $z$ and $W$, are provided in advance; we will refer to these given outcomes as $z^*$ and $w^*$. Under this approach to the problem, we can derive a fairly manageable expression for this quantity as

$$\begin{aligned}
\underbrace{\mathbb{E}\left(L_i^{(d)}\bigg| z = z^*, W = w^*\right)}_{\text{Conditional default loss}} &= \mathbb{E}\left(\underbrace{\mathbb{I}_{\left\{y_i \leq F_{\mathcal{T}_\nu}^{-1}(p_i)\right\}}\gamma_i c_i}_{\text{Equation 5.9}}\Bigg| z = z^*, W = w^*\right), \quad (5.10)\\
&= \mathbb{P}\left(\underbrace{\sqrt{\frac{\nu}{W}}\left(\alpha_i z + \sqrt{1-\alpha_i^2}\upsilon_i\right)}_{y_i} \leq F_{\mathcal{T}_\nu}^{-1}(p_i)\Bigg| \right.\\
&\qquad \left. z = z^*, W = w^*\right)\mathbb{E}(\gamma_i)c_i,\\
&= \mathbb{P}\left(\upsilon_i \leq \frac{\sqrt{\frac{W}{\nu}}F_{\mathcal{T}_\nu}^{-1}(p_i) - \alpha_i z}{\sqrt{1-\alpha_i^2}}\Bigg| z = z^*, W = w^*\right)\\
&\qquad \mathbb{E}(\gamma_i)c_i,\\
&= \underbrace{\Phi\left(\frac{\sqrt{\frac{w^*}{\nu}}F_{\mathcal{T}_\nu}^{-1}(p_i) - \alpha_i z^*}{\sqrt{1-\alpha_i^2}}\right)}_{p_i(z^*,w^*)}\mathbb{E}(\gamma_i)c_i,
\end{aligned}$$

given that $\upsilon_i$ follows, by construction, a standard normal distribution. This expression—or, at least, a variation of it—forms the structural basis for much of current regulatory guidance.[14] Equation 5.10 also plays a central role in our *default* economic-capital approximation.

To move further, we first need to be a bit more precise on the actual values associated with our conditioning variables. Equation 5.10 applies to any loss associated with arbitrary systemic-variable realizations. If we may select any choice of $z^*$ and $w^*$—and we're interested in worst-case default losses—why not pick

[14] See BIS [2, 3, 4] for rather more detail. We will turn to regulatory questions in Chap. 11.

really bad ones? Indeed, why not use the same level of confidence (i.e., 0.9997) embedded in our economic-capital metrics, which we will generically denote as $\alpha^*$. If we seek an extreme downside observation for the common systemic risk factor, a sensible choice is

$$z^* = \Phi^{-1}(1 - \alpha_z^*), \tag{5.11}$$

where $\alpha_z^*$ denotes the confidence level associated with $z$. For the common mixing variable, a natural choice would be

$$w^* = \text{Inv} - \chi^2(1 - \alpha_w^*, \nu), \tag{5.12}$$

where again $\alpha_w^*$ is separately defined. In principle, we would prefer that $\alpha_z^* = \alpha_w^*$. As is often the case, the situation is a bit more nuanced. While the choice of systemic-state variable outcome is quite reasonable, unfortunately, the value in Eq. 5.12 does not perform particularly well for estimating worst-case default loss. In some cases, it works satisfactorily, whereas in other settings it is far too extreme and leads to dramatic overestimates of the conditional default loss.

This brings us to an interesting insight into the $t$-threshold model. The larger the confidence interval used to evaluate Eq. 5.12, the smaller the value of the common mixing variable, $w^*$. The smaller the $w^*$ outcome, the smaller the ratio $\sqrt{\frac{w^*}{\nu}}$, which in turn modifies the default threshold. Reducing the size of the threshold, essentially amounts to a reduction in the creditworthiness of the obligor; making default more probable.[15] The conditional default probability associated with extreme outcomes of $z^*$ and $w^*$ is thus hit from both ends: on one side there is a nasty systemic state variable outcome, while on the other the threshold goal-line has been moved closer. Setting them both to extreme values can, in many cases, lead to really dramatic default losses.

The best way, perhaps, to understand the nature of this calculation is to consider a practical example. Table 5.1 summarizes all of the key inputs for an illustrative, but arbitrary, credit obligor. Three levels of $\alpha_w^*$ confidence interval are provided for the $w^*$ outcomes, but the $z^*$ outcomes are held constant. Key components of the computation are displayed illustrating the impact of $w^*$ and the sensitivity of overall results to this choice. Innocently moving $\alpha_w^*$ from 0.6667 to 0.9997—all else equal—leads to fairly dramatic increases in the default loss estimate.

Figure 5.1 explores this question in more detail by widening our gaze. It displays, for three different choices of $\alpha_w^*$, the *normalized* estimated and observed default loss values across the entire portfolio.[16] The clear conclusion is that the estimated value increases steadily—and ultimately rather significantly exceeds the observed

[15] Low levels of confidence have the opposite effect; they increase the ratio $\sqrt{\frac{w^*}{\nu}}$, pushing out the threshold, and effectively increasing the credit quality for all obligors.

[16] Normalized, in this context, means that the the average *observed* values are subtracted and the result is divided by the volatility of the *observed* default losses; this essentially means that the axes

**Table 5.1** *A simple example*: The underlying table summarizes, for an arbitrary and illustrative exposure, the various quantities and calculations involved in the construction of a conditional probability of default with the preceding conditioning variables, $z^*$ and $w^*$.

| | | Severity of $w^*$ | | |
|---|---|---|---|---|
| Quantity | Definition | $\alpha_w^* = 0.6667$ | $\alpha_w^* = 0.9000$ | $\alpha_w^* = 0.9997$ |
| Degrees of freedom | $\nu$ | 70 | | |
| Confidence level | $\alpha^* \equiv \alpha_z^*$ | 0.9997 | | |
| Exposure | $c_i$ | 65,000,000 | | |
| Credit state | $S_i$ | 11 | | |
| Loss-given-default | $\mathbb{E}(\gamma_i)$ | 0.52 | | |
| Default probability | $p_i$ | 0.55% | | |
| Systemic weight | $\alpha_i$ | 0.19 | | |
| Systemic shock | $z^* = \Phi^{-1}(1 - \alpha_z^*)$ | −3.43 | | |
| Mixing-variable shock | $w^* = \text{Inv} - \chi^2(1 - \alpha_w^*, \nu)$ | 64.39 | 55.33 | 36.39 |
| Threshold value | $F_{\mathcal{T}_\nu}^{-1}(p_i)$ | −2.61 | | |
| Mixing ratio | $\sqrt{\frac{w^*}{\nu}}$ | 0.96 | 0.89 | 0.72 |
| Key ratio | $\frac{\sqrt{\frac{w^*}{\nu}} F_{\mathcal{T}_\nu}^{-1}(p_i) - \alpha_i z^*}{\sqrt{1 - \alpha_i^2}}$ | −1.11 | −0.42 | 0.00 |
| Conditional default probability | $p_i(z^*, w^*)$ | 13.37% | 33.85% | 50.00% |
| Conditional default loss | $\mathbb{E}\left(L_i^{(d)} \middle\| z = z^*, W = w^*\right)$ | 4,519,809 | 11,442,358 | 16,900,000 |

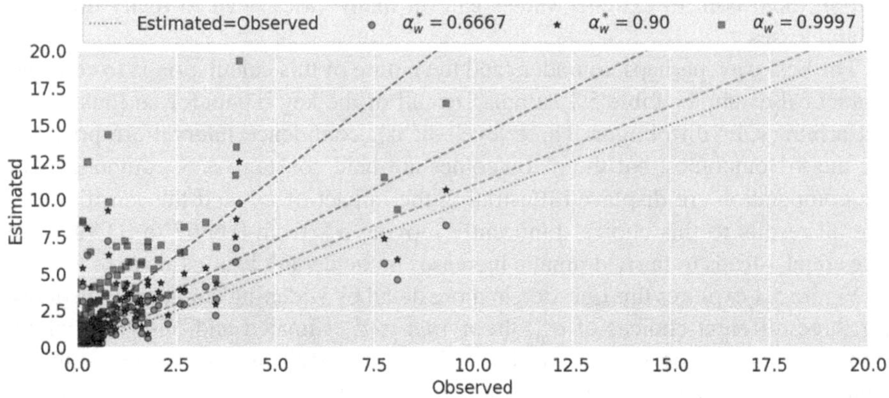


**Fig. 5.1** *Choosing* $\alpha_w^*$: The preceding graphic displays, for three different choices of $\alpha_w^*$ used to identity $w^*$, the *normalized* estimated and observed default loss values. The larger the choice of $\alpha_w^*$, the more extreme the default-loss estimates.

outcomes—for larger values of $\alpha_w^*$. The degree of sensitivity of the conditional default probability to the choice of confidence level for the mixing variable is rather surprising. It seems that this variable's principle role is not to generate extreme loss outcomes, but rather simply to induce a joint $t$ distribution; and, as a result, tail dependence.[17] For the remainder of this analysis, therefore, we will use the more neutral, but slightly conservative, value of $\alpha_w^* = 0.6667$. Different values are naturally possible, and this is by no means an optimized choice, but it performs quite reasonably.

**Colour and Commentary 54** (THE $t$-THRESHOLD MIXING VARIABLE)*: In the Gaussian threshold model, the conditional probability of default depends solely on the provided realization of the systemic risk factor (or factors). Intuition about the randomization of the (conditional) default probability—and the inducement of default correlation—is straightforward: extreme systemic factor realizations lead to correspondingly high probabilities (and magnitudes) of default loss. Moving to the t-threshold setting complicates things. A second conditioning variable—the $\chi^2$-distributed quantity—must also be revealed. One's first reaction is to simultaneously draw an extreme mixing-variable outcome. Our analysis demonstrates that this yields unrealistically large default loss probabilities.*[a] *This appears to suggest that the mixing variable's role is* not *to generate extreme outcomes, but rather to alter the joint distribution and induce tail dependence. For this reason, when using the conditional default probability of the t-threshold model for our approximation analysis, we assume a relatively neutral draw from the $\chi^2$-distributed mixing variable.*

[a] Effectively, extreme mixing variable outcomes pull in the default threshold for all obligors. Combined with a simultaneously bad draw from the systemic state variable, obligors are hit from both sides and the impact is excessive.

## 5.2.2 *Borrowing from Regulatory Guidance*

Equation 5.10 actually turns out to be a critical ingredient of our initial closed-form—although, admittedly simple—approximation of the marginal economic-capital consumption associated with a given exposure. A few additional steps are

in Fig. 5.1 denote standard deviations from the observed mean. We'll use this idea throughout the chapter.

[17] Moreover, given their independence, the joint extreme coincidence of systemic and mixing variable outcomes should be exceedingly rare. Forcing them both to the extremes clearly scales up the default-loss outcomes in an unrealistic manner.

nonetheless required. Let us define $\mathcal{A}_i^{(d)}(\alpha^*)$ as the observed *default* economic-capital allocation associated with the $i$th obligor computed at confidence level, $\alpha^*$. Recall that economic-capital is, conceptually, written as

$$\mathcal{A}_i^{(d)}(\alpha^*) = \underbrace{\text{Worst-Case Loss}_i(\alpha^*) - \text{Expected Loss}_i}_{\text{Unexpected Loss}_i(\alpha^*)}. \tag{5.13}$$

For the (Pillar I) computation of minimum regulatory capital requirements—see Chap. 11 for much more on these ideas—the internal ratings-based approach offers the following exposure-level formula for the direct computation of this quantity:

$$\mathcal{A}_i^{(d)}(\alpha^*) \approx \underbrace{\overbrace{\mathbb{E}\left(L_i^{(d)} \middle| z = z^*, W = w^*\right)}^{\text{Equation 5.10}} - \mathbb{E}\left(L_i^{(d)}\right)}_{\text{Unexpected Loss}_i(\alpha_z^*)}, \tag{5.14}$$

which basically amounts to the difference between conditional and unconditional default loss. This quantity is, in the classical sense, a VaR-related measure of risk.[18]

Exploitation of Eq. 5.14 leads us to the kernel of the approximation method. The mathematical structure of the approximation is

$$\begin{aligned}
\underbrace{\mathcal{A}_i^{(d)}(\alpha_z^*)}_{\equiv \mathcal{A}_i^{(d)}(\alpha^*)} &\approx \mathbb{E}\left(L_i^{(d)} \middle| z = z^*, W = w^*\right) - \mathbb{E}\left(L_i^{(d)}\right), \\
&\approx \underbrace{\mathbb{E}\left(L_i^{(d)} \middle| \alpha_z^*\right)}_{\text{Equation 5.10}} - p_i \cdot \mathbb{E}(\gamma_i) \cdot c_i, \\
&\approx \underbrace{\Phi\left(\frac{\sqrt{\frac{w^*}{\nu}} F_{\mathcal{T}_\nu}^{-1}(p_i) - \alpha_i z^*}{\sqrt{1-\alpha_i^2}}\right)}_{p_i(\alpha_z^*)} \mathbb{E}(\gamma_i) c_i - p_i \cdot \mathbb{E}(\gamma_i) \cdot c_i, \\
&\approx \left(p_i(\alpha_z^*) - p_i\right) \cdot \mathbb{E}(\gamma_i) \cdot c_i,
\end{aligned} \tag{5.15}$$

for $i = 1, \ldots, I$ risk-owner risk contributions. To be fair, the previously described unexpected loss expression does not precisely coincide with the regulatory definition in Eq. 5.14. The $t$-threshold model leads to a few conceptual changes. The most

[18] Our interest is in an expected-shortfall metric, but we will address this issue in a moment.

important is the presence of our common mixing variable, $w^*$. For this computation, as already indicated, we will set $w^*$ at a fixed, reasonably neutral quantity—to induce tail dependence—and treat the $\alpha_z^*$ and $z^*$ as the true variables of interest.[19] Collecting our thoughts, Eq. 5.15 is an analytical representation of a regulatory capital, VaR-based economic-capital allocation. The intuition is that a worst-case outcome for the default loss is inferred from a catastrophically bad outcome of the systemic variable, $z^*$. Subtracted from this is the expected loss computed by averaging over all possible outcomes of the systemic state variable.[20]

There is a definitional issue associated with the approximation in Eq. 5.15: it is based on the idea of a VaR unexpected-loss estimator. We use, as highlighted in previous chapters, the expected-shortfall metric. Using the definition of expected-shortfall, and applying it to Eq. 5.15, this can be rectified as

$$\underbrace{\frac{1}{1-\alpha_z^*}\int_{\alpha_z^*}^1 \mathcal{A}_i^{(d)}(x)dx}_{\mathcal{E}_i^{(d)}(\alpha_z^*)} \approx \frac{1}{1-\alpha_z^*}\int_{\alpha_z^*}^1 \underbrace{\left(p_i(x)-p_i\right)\cdot\mathbb{E}(\gamma_i)\cdot c_i\,dx}_{\text{Equation 5.15}}, \tag{5.16}$$

$$\begin{aligned}
\mathcal{E}_i^{(d)}(\alpha_z^*) &\approx \mathbb{E}(\gamma_i)\cdot c_i\cdot\underbrace{\frac{1}{1-\alpha_z^*}\int_{\alpha_z^*}^1 p_i(x)dx}_{\tilde{p}_i(\alpha_z^*)} - \frac{p_i\mathbb{E}(\gamma_i)\cdot c_i}{1-\alpha_z^*}\int_{\alpha_z^*}^1 dx,\\
&\approx \mathbb{E}(\gamma_i)\cdot c_i\cdot\tilde{p}_i(\alpha_z^*) - \frac{p_i\mathbb{E}(\gamma_i)\cdot c_i}{1-\alpha_z^*}\Big[x\Big]_{\alpha_z^*}^1,\\
&\approx \mathbb{E}(\gamma_i)\cdot c_i\cdot\tilde{p}_i(\alpha_z^*) - \frac{p_i\mathbb{E}(\gamma_i)\cdot c_i}{\cancel{1-\alpha_z^*}}\cancel{(1-\alpha_z^*)},\\
&\approx \left(\tilde{p}_i(\alpha_z^*)-p_i\right)\cdot\mathbb{E}(\gamma_i)\cdot c_i.
\end{aligned}$$

There is both good and bad news. The good news is that, when moving to the expected-shortfall setting, the basic form of our approximation is preserved. The bad news is that the integral $\tilde{p}_i(\alpha_z^*)$ is not, to the best of our knowledge, available in closed form. Computation of this quantity requires solving a one-dimensional numerical-integration problem. To solve 500+ individual problems, this takes a bit less than 2 seconds. For large-scale approximations—such as stress-testing calculations—this has the potential to slow things down somewhat, but no real damage is involved. For an individual loan, thankfully, this numerical element

[19] There is, therefore, a small mathematical sleight of hand with the confidence levels.

[20] For this reason, each $\mathbb{E}\left(L_i^{(d)}\right)$ is independent of $z$.

**Table 5.2** *Simple economic-capital estimates*: This table illustrates some key results of using Eq. 5.10 and 5.16 to estimate the default-related economic-capital consumption associated with the simple example introduced in Table 5.1.

| Quantity | Definition | Value |
|---|---|---|
| Model default economic capital | $\mathcal{E}_i^{(d)}(\alpha^*)$ | 4,314,601 |
| Model default economic-capital ratio | $\frac{1}{c_i}\mathcal{E}_i^{(d)}(\alpha^*)$ | 6.6% |
| VaR regulatory-capital approximation | $\mathcal{A}_i^{(d)}(\alpha_z^*) = \left(p_i(\alpha_z^*) - p_i\right) \cdot \mathbb{E}(\gamma_i) \cdot c_i$ | 4,333,909 |
| VaR regulatory-capital ratio | $\frac{1}{c_i}\mathcal{A}_i^{(d)}(\alpha_z^*)$ | 6.7% |
| Expected-shortfall regulatory-capital approximation | $\mathcal{E}_i^{(d)}(\alpha_z^*) = \left(\tilde{p}_i(\alpha_z^*) - p_i\right) \cdot \mathbb{E}(\gamma_i) \cdot c_i$ | 5,358,698 |
| Expected-shortfall regulatory-capital ratio | $\frac{1}{c_i}\mathcal{E}_i^{(d)}(\alpha_z^*)$ | 8.2% |

requires only a fraction of a second.[21] As a consequence, this semi-analytic twist to our approximation does not delay the associated applications in any appreciable way.

Table 5.2 takes the simple example introduced in Table 5.1 and—with the help of Eqs. 5.10 and 5.16—provides some insight into how well the approximations actually work. The true model-based default economic-capital value is about EUR 4 million amounting to roughly $6\frac{1}{2}\%$ of the position's overall exposure. This figure seems sensible for a position falling, albeit slightly, below investment grade. The VaR-based approximation, from Eq. 5.15, also generates an estimate a bit north of EUR 4 million or around 6.7%. The VaR estimator, in this case, thus generates a marginal over-estimate. Incorporation of the expected-shortfall element—using, in this case, the numerical-integration estimator introduced in Eq. 5.16—yields a rather higher estimate of about EUR 5.4 million or in excess of 8%. This represents a rather significant overstatement of the model-based economic capital.

Our simple example illustrates that, as a generic approximation, the presented results appear to be in the vicinity. That said, the VaR estimator seems to outperform the expected-shortfall calculation. To make a more general statement, of course, it is necessary to look beyond a single instance. We need to systemically examine the relationship between actual economic-capital estimates and our approximating expressions. Figure 5.2 consequently compares our regulatory motivated economic-capital approximations—computed with Eq. 5.16—to the true simulation-model outcomes. Since the actual levels of economic capital are unimportant, the results

[21] The implementation makes use of `scipy`'s `quadrature` function. See Ralston and Rabinowitz [24] for more on Gaussian quadrature and numerical integration.

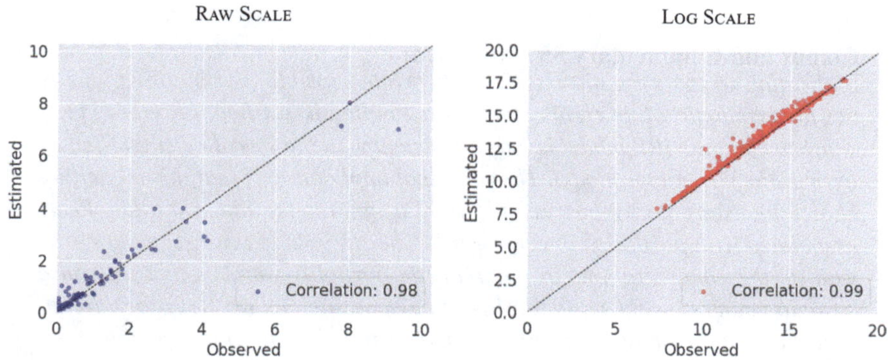


**Fig. 5.2** *Degree of agreement*: The preceding graphics, in raw and logarithmic terms, illustrate the degree of agreement between our (normalized) approximation in Eq. 5.16 and the (normalized) observed simulation-based economic-capital contributions. The overall level of linear correlation is fairly respectable.

have again been normalized. The left-hand graphic outlines the comparative results on a normalized basis similar to Fig. 5.1. Visually, the agreement appears sensible, although there are numerous instances where individual estimates deviate from the observed values by a sizable margin. Interestingly, at the overall portfolio level, despite the approximation noise, there is a really quite respectable cross-correlation coefficient of 0.98. This suggests that, although Eq. 5.16 may not always capture the level of default risk, it does catch the basic pattern.

A related issue is the broad range of economic-capital values. For some obligors, the allocation approaches zero, whereas for others it can be one (or more) orders of magnitude larger. This stems from the exponential form of default probabilities as well as concentration in the underlying portfolio. This fact, combined with the the patchy performance of the approximation in Eq. 5.16, can lead to scaling problems. As a consequence, the right-hand graphic illustrates the approximation fit when applying natural logarithms to both (normalized) observed and approximated default-risk values. This simple transformation smooths out the size dimension and increases the correlation coefficient to 0.99. Although far from perfect, we may nonetheless cautiously conclude that there is some merit to this basic approach.

**Colour and Commentary 55** (THE APPROXIMATION KERNEL)*: The central component of the default economic capital approximator is pinched directly from the logic employed in the Basel Internal-Rating Based (or IRB) approach. More specifically, worst-case default losses are approximated via the conditional probability of default associated with a rather highly adverse*

(continued)

**Colour and Commentary 55** (continued)
*realization of the systemic risk factor.*[a] *While sensible and intuitive, this is* not *an assumption-free choice. As covered in detail in Chap. 11, Gordy [13] shows us that the IRB model is only consistent with the so-called single-factor asymptotic risk-factor model. The principal implication is that this modelling choice focuses* entirely *on systemic risk; it ignores the idiosyncratic effects associated with portfolio concentrations. The strength of this assumption—as well as the concentrations in our real-life portfolio—implies that this base structure can only take us so far. It will be necessary, as we move forward, to adjust our approximation to capture the ignored idiosyncratic elements.*

[a] We also draw a more neutral-valued $\chi^2$ mixing variable to accommodate the $t$-threshold structure of our production model.

### 5.2.3 A First Default Approximation Model

Raw use of Eq. 5.16 is likely to be sub-optimal. Its high correlation with observed values, however, suggests that it makes for a useful starting point. What we need is the ability to allow for somewhat more approximation flexibility in capturing individual differences. In other words, we seek an approximation model. This is the underlying motivation behind transforming Eq. 5.16 into an ordinary least-squares (OLS), or regression, estimator. The presence of regression coefficients allows us to exploit the promising correlation structure and also increases the overall fit to the observed data.

The basic linear structure follows from Eq. 5.16 and we use the logarithmic operator to induce an additive form as

$$\mathcal{E}_i^{(d)}(\alpha_z^*) \approx \underbrace{\bigg(\tilde{p}_i(\alpha_z^*) - p_i\bigg)\mathbb{E}(\gamma_i)c_i}_{\text{Equation 5.16}}, \tag{5.17}$$

$$\mathcal{E}_i^{(d)}(\alpha_z^*) \approx \tilde{p}_i(\alpha^*)\mathbb{E}(\gamma_i)c_i - \underbrace{p_i\mathbb{E}(\gamma_i)c_i}_{\mathbb{E}\left(L_i^{(d)}\right)},$$

$$\mathcal{E}_i^{(d)}(\alpha_z^*) + \mathbb{E}\left(L_i^{(d)}\right) \approx \tilde{p}_i(\alpha_z^*)\mathbb{E}(\gamma_i)c_i,$$

$$\ln\left(\mathcal{E}_i^{(d)}(\alpha_z^*) + \mathbb{E}\left(L_i^{(d)}\right)\right) \approx \ln\left(\tilde{p}_i(\alpha_z^*)\mathbb{E}(\gamma_i)c_i\right),$$

$$\ln\left(\mathcal{E}_i^{(d)}(\alpha_z^*) + \mathbb{E}\left(L_i^{(d)}\right)\right) \approx \ln\left(\tilde{p}_i(\alpha_z^*)\right) + \ln\left(\mathbb{E}(\gamma_i)\right) + \ln(c_i).$$

Equation 5.17 is an approximation. If we re-imagine this linear relationship with an intercept and error, we have

$$\underbrace{\ln\left(\mathcal{E}_i^{(d)}(\alpha_z^*) + \mathbb{E}\left(L_i^{(d)}\right)\right)}_{y_i^{(d)}} = \xi_0 + \xi_1 \underbrace{\ln\left(\tilde{p}_i(\alpha_z^*)\right)}_{X_{i,1}^{(d)}} + \xi_2 \underbrace{\ln\left(\mathbb{E}(\gamma_i)\right)}_{X_{i,2}^{(d)}} + \xi_3 \underbrace{\ln(c_i)}_{X_{i,3}^{(d)}} + \epsilon_i^{(d)}, \tag{5.18}$$

for $i = 1, \ldots, I$ risk-owner risk contributions.[22] The left-hand side of Eq. 5.18 is a transformation of the observed default economic-capital estimates, while the elements of our approximation from Eq. 5.16 have become additive explanatory variables.

Equation 5.18 directly translates, of course, into the classical ordinary least squares setting and reduces to the familiar model,

$$y^{(d)} = X^{(d)}\Xi + \epsilon^{(d)}, \tag{5.19}$$

where

$$y^{(d)} = \begin{bmatrix} \ln\left(\mathcal{E}_1^{(d)}(\alpha_z^*) + \mathbb{E}\left(L_1^{(d)}\right)\right) \\ \vdots \\ \ln\left(\mathcal{E}_I^{(d)}(\alpha_z^*) + \mathbb{E}\left(L_I^{(d)}\right)\right) \end{bmatrix}, \tag{5.20}$$

and

$$X^{(d)} = \begin{bmatrix} 1 & \ln\left(\tilde{p}_1(\alpha_z^*)\right) & \ln\left(\mathbb{E}(\gamma_1)\right) & \ln(c_1) \\ \vdots & \vdots & \vdots & \vdots \\ 1 & \ln\left(\tilde{p}_I(\alpha_z^*)\right) & \ln\left(\mathbb{E}(\gamma_I)\right) & \ln(c_I) \end{bmatrix}, \tag{5.21}$$

and $\epsilon^{(d)} \sim \mathcal{N}(0, \sigma^2 I)$ for $\sigma \in \mathbb{R}_+$. The OLS estimator for $\Xi = \begin{bmatrix} \xi_0 & \xi_1 & \xi_2 & \xi_3 \end{bmatrix}^T$ determined, as usual, through the minimization of $(y^{(d)} - X^{(d)}\Xi)^T(y^{(d)} - X^{(d)}\Xi)$

[22] It is customary to use the symbol $\beta$ for regression coefficients. Since we already employ this character to denote factor loadings, we will use an alternative esoteric Greek letter to avoid confusion.

**Table 5.3** *A first default-approximation model*: This table summarizes the results of the base default economic-capital approximation model. It has an intercept and *three* regulatory capital requirement motivated explanatory variables. The amount of variance explained is fairly encouraging, but the proportional errors are depressingly (even frighteningly) large.

| Quantity | Description | Estimate | Standard error | $t$-statistic | $p$-value |
|---|---|---|---|---|---|
| $\xi_0$ | Intercept | −0.91 | 0.13 | −7.06 | 0.00 |
| $\xi_1$ | (Extreme) conditional default probability | 0.92 | 0.02 | 53.18 | 0.00 |
| $\xi_2$ | Loss-given-default | 1.08 | 0.03 | 35.10 | 0.00 |
| $\xi_3$ | Exposure | 1.04 | 0.01 | 158.95 | 0.00 |
| Root mean *squared* error | | 45% | | | |
| *Mean* absolute error | | 18% | | | |
| *Median* absolute error | | 10% | | | |
| $R^2$ | | 0.923 | | | |

is thus simply the well-known least-squares solution:

$$\hat{\Xi} = \left( X^{(d)^T} X^{(d)} \right)^{-1} X^{(d)^T} y^{(d)}. \tag{5.22}$$

Standard errors and test-statistic formulae also follow from similarly well-known results.[23] As discussed previously, this does not imply that our model is inherently linear, but rather that we are knowingly accepting a certain degree of model bias for low variance and the ability to use statistical-inference techniques.

Table 5.3 summarizes the results of fitting the previously described approximation model to observed economic-capital allocation data associated with an arbitrary date in 2020. All *four* of the parameter estimates are strongly statistically significant. The actual parameter values are also positive for the conditional default probability, loss-given-default, and exposures, which seems plausible. The $R^2$ statistic of roughly 0.9 suggests that the amount of total variance explained by a simple linear model is encouraging.

The actual calculation of approximated (i.e., predicted) default-risk values actually involves a small bit of algebraic gymnastics. In particular,

$$\begin{aligned} \hat{y}^{(d)} &= X^{(d)}\hat{\Xi}, \\ e^{\hat{y}^{(d)}} &= e^{X^{(d)}\hat{\Xi}}, \\ e^{\ln\left(\widehat{\mathcal{E}^{(d)}(\alpha_z^*)} + \mathbb{E}(L^{(d)})\right)} &= e^{X^{(d)}\hat{\Xi}}, \\ \widehat{\mathcal{E}^{(d)}(\alpha_z^*)} &= e^{X^{(d)}\hat{\Xi}} - \mathbb{E}\left(L^{(d)}\right), \end{aligned} \tag{5.23}$$

[23] For much more detailed background on the rudiments of OLS, please see Judge et al. [19].

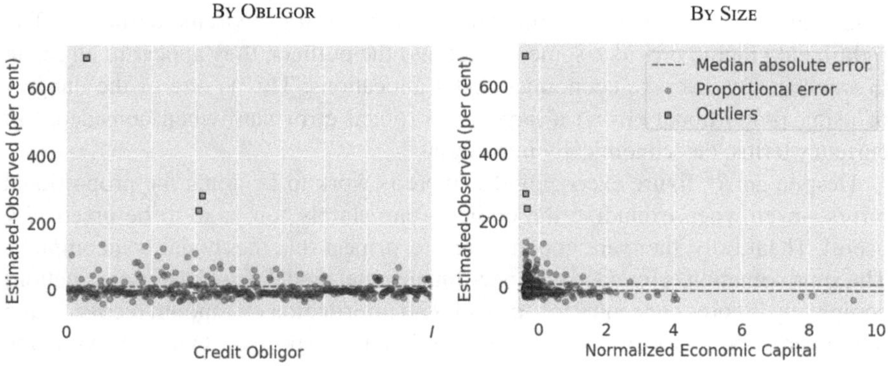


**Fig. 5.3** *Initial error analysis*: The preceding graphics display the model errors—estimated less observed values—organized by both individual credit obligor and normalized default economic capital. The handful of extreme outliers are presented separately.

where $\widehat{\mathcal{E}^{(d)}(\alpha_z^*)}$ and $\mathbb{E}\left(L^{(d)}\right)$ denote the $I$-dimensional vectors of approximated default economic-capital values and expected losses, respectively. Equation 5.23 permits computation of root-mean-squared, mean-absolute and median-absolute error measures. The results are provided, in Table 5.3, in (proportional) percentage terms rather than logarithmic or currency space.[24] These goodness-of-fit measures—assessing the (in-sample) correspondence between observed and predicated values—unfortunately paint a less rosy picture. The mean-absolute error is roughly 20%; implying that, on average, the approximation misses its mark by about one fifth. If we turn to the median-absolute error, it improves to one tenth; this strongly suggests the presence of a few large outliers. Our suspicion is confirmed with the—notoriously sensitive to outliers—root-mean-squared error taking a dreadful value of 45%.[25]

Figure 5.3 looks into the outlier question more carefully by illustrating the collection of proportional approximation errors.[26] The left hand graphic indicates

---

[24] The logarithmic-transformation is helpful to manage scale discrepancies between economic-capital allocations, but it is essentially a statistical trick to improve the overall fit. Since we ultimately require currency estimates, model diagnostics in logarithmic space are *not* terribly helpful and thus excluded.

[25] Outlier sensitivity is easily seen from the definition. Given $\epsilon^{(d)} \in \mathbb{R}^{I\times 1}$, then

$$\text{RMSE} = \sqrt{\frac{\epsilon^{(d)T}\epsilon^{(d)}}{I}}. \tag{5.24}$$

The squared term in the numerator places rather heavy weight on any individual and extreme error (i.e., outlier).

[26] The errors are defined as estimated less observed default economic values divided by their true observed outcome.

a general trend towards over-estimation and a handful of extreme outliers.[27] The right-hand graphic provides some insight into the outliers; they appear to all relate to small, below average economic-capital allocations. This is one of the dangers of using proportional errors; a large proportional error can, when considered in currency terms, be economically immaterial.

Despite an $R^2$ figure exceeding 0.9, there is work to be done; the proportional errors—even when excluding the outliers—are simply too large to be practically useful. Thankfully, there are good reasons to suspect that the model is incomplete. The approximation is founded on a one-dimensional model, which (by construction) completely ignores concentration, provides no information on random recovery, and fails to incorporate a broader default-correlation perspective. Our approximation model can thus be further improved.

**Colour and Commentary 56** (A FIRST DEFAULT APPROXIMATION MODEL): *Our regulatory capital motivated first-order approximation of default economic capital is readily generalized into a linear regression model. This permits calibration to daily data and provides diagnostics on the strength of specific parts of the approximation. The initial results are mixed. On the positive side, the percentage of variance explained exceeds 90% and the individual regression variables are highly statistical significant. More negatively, proportional goodness-of-fit measures suggest an unacceptable level of inconsistency. Part of the problem is explained by a handful of outliers, but the model also has difficulty with a sizable subset of individual obligors. In many ways, this is not a surprise. The explanatory variables in this initial model capture, literally by their definition, only the systemic aspect of economic capital. This suggests identification and incorporation of idiosyncratic and concentration related explanatory variables as a sensible avenue towards improvement of our initial model.*

### 5.2.4 Incorporating Concentration

Our first naive default approximation model is unfortunately, in its current form, not quite up to the task. This is not just due to a deficiency of the underlying regulatory capital computation, but it is rather a structural issue. Gordy [13]—in his excellent first-principle analysis of the Basel-IRB methodology—demonstrates that this regulatory formula is equivalent to using Vasicek [28]'s single-factor asymptotic risk-factor model (ASRF). This has two immediate consequences. First, it requires

[27] Outliers, in this context, were (somewhat arbitrarily) identified as a proportional error exceeding 200%.

that one's portfolio is—in practical terms—extremely well diversified across many credit obligors. Second, as the name suggests, there is only a single source of risk. As such, there is simply no mechanism to capture regional, sectoral, or firm-size effects. To be blunt, this implies that our initial model in Eq. 5.18 is simply not equipped to capture concentration effects.

Most real-world financial institutions—and NIB is no exception in this regard—have regional and sectoral concentrations. Ignoring this dimension leads, as became clear in the previous section, to structural bias in our economic-capital approximations. The most natural route, remaining in the regulatory area, would involve the so-called granularity adjustment. This quantity, introduced by Gordy [13], is an add-on to the base regulatory capital computation to account for concentration.[28] After significant experimentation, we rejected this path. The principal issue is that it does not (easily, at least) have the requisite flexibility to handle either multiple risk factors or readily incorporate regional and sectoral information.[29]

We opt to follow an alternative, and perhaps more intuitive, strategy. The idea is to assign a concentration score to each individual set of lending exposures sharing similar regional and structural characteristics. We can then include this score as an explanatory variable in our regression model in Eq. 5.18. If done correctly, this would help to incorporate important idiosyncratic features of one's exposures into our approximation.

There is a rich literature on concentration. Concentration and Lorenz curves, Herfindahl-Hirschman indices and Gini coefficients are popular tools in this area.[30] The challenges with these methods, for our purposes, are twofold. First, they require full knowledge of the economic-capital weights, which will not always be (logically) available to us. Second, and perhaps more importantly, we seek a concentration measure that incorporates aspects of our current model with a particular focus on sectoral and regional dimensions.

The proposed score, or index, is a function of *three* pieces of information about the obligor. These include:

1. geographic region;
2. industrial sector; and
3. public-sector or corporate status.

The measure is specialized to the current credit-risk economic-capital model's factor structure. It does not stem from any current literature, but should rather be viewed as something of a heuristic concentration metric.

---

[28] This interesting and important area is addressed in Chap. 11. If you cannot wait to dig into this fascinating area, you are immediately referred to Lütkebohmert [20, Chapter 11], Gordy and Lütkebohmert [14, 15], Martin and Wilde [21], Emmer and Tasche [9], and Torell [27].

[29] Pykhtin [23] does offer a multivariate approach, which is explored in Chap. 11.

[30] For more background on this fascinating field of study, please see Yitzhaki and Olkin [29], Figini and Uberti [10], Bellalah et al. [1], Milanovic [22], and particularly the extremely useful Lütkebohmert [20].

We take a slow, methodical, and constructive approach to development of our concentration metric. The first step in the fabrication of our index begins by assigning, at a given point in time, total portfolio exposure (i.e., exposure-at-default) to our $J$ systemic state variables. Since our $I$ credit obligors may simultaneously be members of both a region and an industrial sector, managing this seems a bit challenging. How, for example, do we allocate our exposure to these risk factors? The solution is to use the factor loadings—these quantities determine the relative importance of the region and industry systemic factors. Recall, from Chap. 3, that one half of an obligor's weight is allocated to its geographic region, while the remaining half is assigned to its industrial sector. At most, therefore, an individual obligor's exposure can be assigned to two distinct factors. A public-sector entity, which has no obvious industrial classification, receives a full weight to its region. An advantage of this approach is the incorporation of the obligor's factor loadings (indirectly) into our index.

Mathematically, this $j$th risk factor's exposure assignment—which we will denote as $\bar{\mathcal{V}}_j$—is thus simply,

$$\bar{\mathcal{V}}_j = \sum_{i=1}^{I} \mathrm{B}_{ij} c_i, \tag{5.25}$$

for $j = 1, \ldots, J$ and where, as usual, $c_i$ denotes the $i$th obligor's exposure at default. In other words, we basically weight the individual exposure estimates by their factor loadings. In practice, this is a very straightforward matrix multiplication,

$$\bar{\mathcal{V}} = \mathrm{B}^T c, \tag{5.26}$$

where $\bar{\mathcal{V}} \in \mathbb{R}^{J \times 1}$, $c \in \mathbb{R}^{I \times 1}$ are $\mathrm{B} \in \mathbb{R}^{I \times J}$.[31] One might be tempted to replace exposure with economic capital (i.e., $\mathcal{E}_i(\alpha^*)$) in Eq. 5.26; it is, in fact, economic-capital concentration that we seek to describe. This turns out to be a bad idea. Were we to use economic-capital in the construction—even indirectly—in the establishment of our concentration metric, we would find ourselves awkwardly having economic-capital embedded in both sides of our regression relationship. Lesser indiscretions have been classified as a criminal act in statistical circles.

Figure 5.4 summarizes, for an arbitrary portfolio during 2020, the percentage allocation of exposure—following from Eq. 5.26—to our $J = 24$ regional and sectoral categorizations. Since the actual amounts and systemic-risk factor identities are relatively unimportant—but we wish to be able to compare to further transformations—the values are illustrated in numbered percentage terms. The top four categories consume almost half of the total exposure. While concentration is typical in most real-life commercial lending and investment portfolios, we should

[31] Many, or even most, of the B factor-loading values are zero. This is a consequence of the overidentifying factor-loading constraints introduced in Chap. 3. Incidentally, it makes no practical difference if one uses the raw factor loadings, $\beta$, or their normalized equivalents, B.

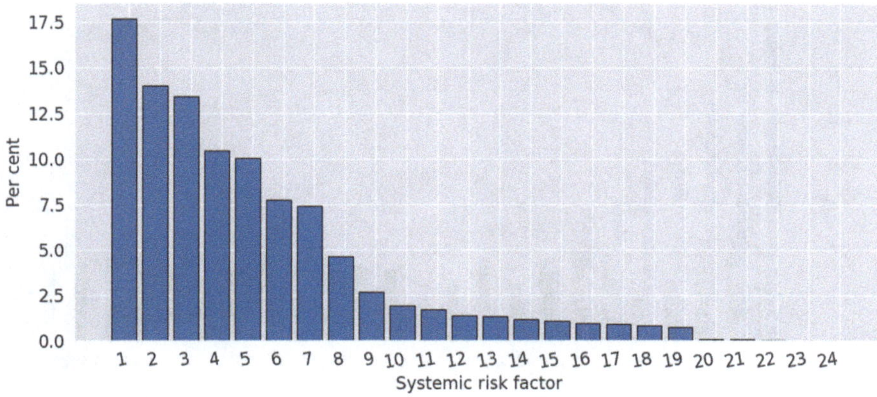


**Fig. 5.4** *Exposure by risk factor*: The preceding graphic displays, for an arbitrarily selected portfolio from 2020, the percentage factor-loaded exposure allocations by systemic risk factor computed using Eq. 5.26.

be cautious to read too much into Fig. 5.4. In this intermediate step, we use only the relatively uninformative factor loadings.

Having used factor loadings to aggregate portfolio exposure, the next step involves the incorporation of the systemic-factor dependence structure. Technically, this takes the form of a projection. In particular, the next step is

$$\begin{aligned}\tilde{\mathcal{V}} &= \underbrace{\begin{bmatrix} 1 & \rho_{12} & \cdots & \rho_{1J} \\ \rho_{21} & 1 & \cdots & \rho_{2J} \\ \vdots & \vdots & \ddots & \vdots \\ \rho_{J1} & \rho_{J2} & \cdots & 1 \end{bmatrix}}_{\Omega} \begin{bmatrix} \mathcal{V}_1 \\ \vdots \\ \mathcal{V}_J \end{bmatrix}, \\ &= \Omega\bar{\mathcal{V}}. \end{aligned} \tag{5.27}$$

where $\Omega \in \mathbb{R}^{J \times J}$ is the factor-correlation matrix estimated in Chap. 3 and $\tilde{\mathcal{V}} \in \mathbb{R}^{J \times 1}$ is a projected vector of exposure amounts. Technically, $\tilde{\mathcal{V}}$ is a linear projection of $\bar{\mathcal{V}}$ using the projection matrix, $\Omega$—it is essentially a linear (dimension-preserving) mapping from $\mathbb{R}^{J \times 1}$ to $\mathbb{R}^{J \times 1}$. If all of the systemic factors were to be orthonormal, then $\Omega$ would be an identity matrix, and the original exposure figures would be preserved. If there is strong positive correlation between the systemic risk factors, conversely, we would expect to see a relative increase in the relative allocation to each risk-factor category.

To see the implications of projecting correlation information onto our factor-arranged exposure outcomes, let's directly compare the allocations $\bar{\mathcal{V}}$ and $\tilde{\mathcal{V}}$ in percentage terms. These results are summarized in Fig. 5.5. Projecting the correlation matrix onto the exposure amounts clearly, and dramatically, changes

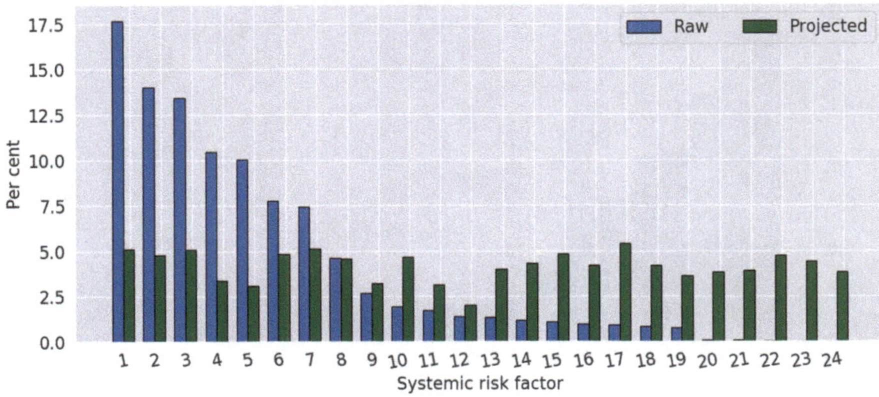


**Fig. 5.5** *Incorporating systemic dependence*: The preceding graphic reproduces the percentage factor-loaded exposure allocations from Fig. 5.4, but also adds in the percentage correlation-matrix projected outcomes from Eq. 5.27. The positively correlated risk-factor system flattens out the concentration profile.

the concentration profile. Specifically, projecting $\bar{V}$ flattens out the profile implying, when taking into account factor correlations, that the deviations in concentration are rather different than those suggested by the factor-loading-driven result in Fig. 5.4.

What exactly is going on? The answer, of course, begins with the structure of the systemic risk-factor correlation matrix itself. The risk factors are, as indicated and discussed in previous chapters, a positively correlated system. We can make this a bit more precise. Using an eigenvalue decomposition, it is possible to orthogonalize a correlation matrix into a set of so-called principal components.[32] A useful byproduct of this computation is that one can estimate the amount of variance, in the overall system, explained by each individual orthogonal factor. This provides useful insight into the degree of linear correlation between the raw variables in one's system. Table 5.4 reviews the results of this analysis—applied to our factor correlation matrix, $\Omega$—for the five most important orthogonal factors. The single, most important, orthogonal factor explains in excess of 50% of the overall variance, while the top five (of 24) principal components cover about three quarters of total system variance.

The results in Table 5.4 strongly underscore the rather dependent nature of our risk-factor system and help explain Fig. 5.5. A few systemic risk factors appear to demonstrate a high degree of correlation when we simply sum over the exposures. Controlling for the (generally high) level of linear dependence between these individual systemic risk factors, however, is essential to capturing the model's picture of portfolio concentration.

The final step involves the transformation of the individual values in Eq. 5.27 into a readable and interpretable index. This basically amounts to normalization; it

---

[32] A fantastic reference for this practical statistical technique is Jollliffe [18]. See Golub and Loan [12] for more on the eigenvalue decomposition.

**Table 5.4** *Systemic correlation*: The underlying table illustrates, using the principal-components technique, the amount of variance explained by the five most important orthogonalized factors derived from our systemic correlation matrix, $\Omega$. These results strongly underscore the rather dependent nature of our risk-factor system.

| Principal component | % variance explained |
|---|---|
| 1 | 55.6% |
| 2 | 8.8% |
| 3 | 4.6% |
| 4 | 4.3% |
| 5 | 3.3% |
| Total | 76.7% |

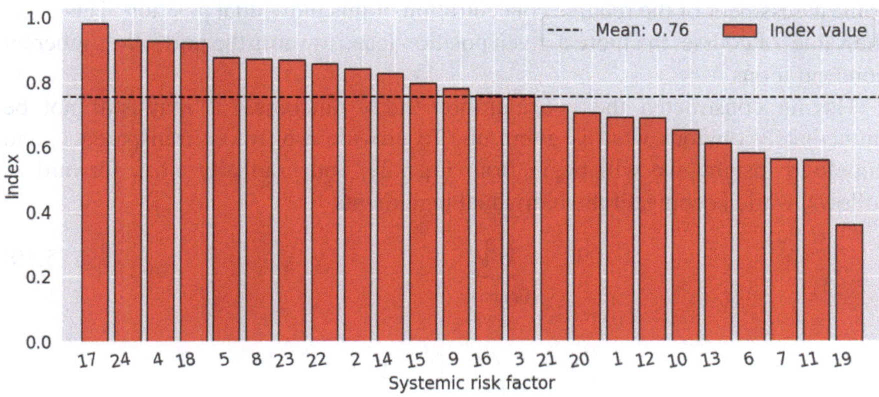


**Fig. 5.6** *The concentration index*: The preceding graphic displays—conditional on our arbitrarily selected portfolio from 2020—the set of $J$ distinct concentration index values arranged in descending order.

is consequently transformed into a value in the unit interval as,

$$\hat{\mathcal{V}} = \frac{\tilde{\mathcal{V}}}{\max(\tilde{\mathcal{V}})}. \tag{5.28}$$

Other normalizations are certainly possible. The largest concentration index value takes, of course, a value of unity. $\hat{\mathcal{V}}_j$ thus represents the final concentration-index value for the $j$th risk factor.

Figure 5.6 illustrates, using Eq. 5.28, the set of $J$ distinct concentration index values displayed in descending order. These values are, once again, conditional on our arbitrary 2020 portfolio, although the results do not appear to vary considerably across time. This is certainly due to high levels of persistence in the portfolio and infrequently updated through-the-cycle parameters.[33] Actual concentration values

[33] It takes time to change the composition of any buy-and-hold portfolio.

for a given risk-owner, or exposure, fall in the range [0.36,1] with a mean of about 0.75. The ordering is broadly similar to that observed in Fig. 5.4, but there are a few surprises.

A separate concentration index is required for each individual credit obligor, but there are only $J$ concentration-index values. The factor-loading matrix comes, once again, to the rescue by offering a logical approach to allocation of the sectoral and regional concentration values to the obligor level. Practically, this amounts to (yet) another matrix multiplication,

$$\mathcal{V} = \mathrm{B}\hat{\mathcal{V}}, \tag{5.29}$$

where $\mathcal{V} \in \mathbb{R}^{I\times 1}$ is the final concentration index. Each element of $\mathcal{V}$ thus provides some assessment of the relative concentration of this individual position. The larger the value, of course, the more a given position leans towards the portfolio's inherent concentrations.

Having constructed the concentration index outcomes, it may still not be immediately obvious what is going on. To provide a bit more transparency, and hopefully insight, we will begin from Eq. 5.29, and gradually work forward as follows, while keeping all the individual ingredients

$$\begin{aligned} \mathcal{V} &= \underbrace{\mathrm{B}\hat{\mathcal{V}}}_{\substack{\text{Equation}\\ 5.29}}, \\ &= \underbrace{\mathrm{B}\left(\frac{\tilde{\mathcal{V}}}{\max(\tilde{\mathcal{V}})}\right)}_{\substack{\text{Equation}\\ 5.28}}, \\ &= \frac{\mathrm{B}}{\max(\Omega\bar{\mathcal{V}})}\underbrace{\Omega\bar{\mathcal{V}}}_{\substack{\text{Equation}\\ 5.27}}, \\ &= \frac{\mathrm{B}\Omega}{\max\left(\Omega\mathrm{B}^T c\right)}\underbrace{\mathrm{B}^T c}_{\substack{\text{Equation}\\ 5.26}}, \\ &= \left(\frac{\overbrace{\mathrm{B}\Omega\mathrm{B}^T}^{I\times I}}{\underbrace{\max\left(\Omega\mathrm{B}^T c\right)}_{\text{Scalar: }1\times 1}}\right)c. \end{aligned} \tag{5.30}$$

An element in the preceding decomposition of the $\mathcal{V}$ computation should look familiar. $B\Omega B^T \in \mathbb{R}^{I\times I}$ is the normalized, factor-loaded, systemic risk-factor correlation matrix. A standardized factor-loaded correlation matrix is thus projected onto the vector of exposure contributions, $c$, to yield our proposed concentration index. While not perfect, it does appealingly capture a number of key elements of concentration: current portfolio weights, systemic factor loadings, and the correlation structure of these common factors.

**Colour and Commentary 57** (INDEXING CONCENTRATION)*: A central task of the credit-risk economic-capital simulation engine is to capture the interplay between diversification and concentration in one's portfolio. This aspect needs to be properly reflected in any approximation method. It takes on particular importance given our previous decision to lean heavily upon a regulatory motivated approximation that entirely assumes away idiosyncratic risk. A possible solution to this question involves the construction of a* concentration *index, which can act as an additional explanatory variable in our regression model. Our proposed choice involves a linear projection of the individual credit obligor exposures at default. The projection matrix is a function of the (normalized) factor loadings and the factor correlation. In this way, the resulting index directly incorporates three important drivers of concentration risk: the factor loadings, systemic correlations, and the current portfolio composition.*

### *5.2.5 The Full Default Model*

We've clearly established the need to incorporate additional idiosyncratic explanatory variables into our base regression model. The previously defined concentration index is a natural candidate; there are many others. Indeed, there is no shortage of possibilities. This means that model selection is actually hard work. The consequence is a very large set of possible extensions and variations to consider.[34] This situation can only be resolved with a significant amount reflection, examination of error graphics and model-selection criteria as well as trial-and-error. Ultimately, we have opted for six *new* explanatory variables to add to our original Eq. 5.18. Despite our best efforts, the revised and extended model should not be considered as an optimal choice. It is better to view it as a sensible element of the set of possible

[34] Even with a few dozen possible explanatory variables, the power set (i.e., set of all possible subsets) is depressingly large.

approximation models. With this in mind, it is described as

$$\overbrace{\ln\left(\mathcal{E}_i^{(d)}(\alpha^*) + \mathbb{E}\left(L_i^{(d)}\right)\right)}^{y_i^{(d)}} = \overbrace{\underbrace{\xi_0 + \xi_1 \ln\left(\tilde{p}_i(\alpha_z^*)\right) + \xi_2 \ln\left(\mathbb{E}(\gamma_i)\right) + \xi_3 \ln(c_i)}_{\text{Base default model}} + \underbrace{\sum_{k=4}^{\kappa} \xi_k X_k^{(d)}}_{\substack{\text{Additional}\\ \text{explanatory}\\ \text{variables}}}}^{\sum_{k=0}^{\kappa} \xi_k X_i^{(d)}} + \epsilon_i^{(d)}, \tag{5.31}$$

for $i = 1, \ldots, I$ risk-owner risk contributions.

Table 5.5 summarizes the parameter and goodness-of-fit statistics associated with the revised model. Comparing the results to the base approximation summary found in Table 5.3 on page 298, we observe a number of differences. First of all, there is significant improvement in the (in-sample) goodness-of-fit measures. The proportional root-mean squared error is reduced by a factor of five, while our two proportional *absolute* errors are cut by more than half. The median absolute error

**Table 5.5** *Full default-approximation model*: This table summarizes the results of the full-blown default economic-capital approximation model including a number of additional regressors as described in Eq. 5.31. The overall fit is substantially improved relative to the base model displayed in Table 5.3.

| Quantity | Description | Estimate | Standard error | $t$-statistic | $p$-value |
|---|---|---|---|---|---|
| $\xi_0$ | Intercept | −4.02 | 0.09 | −45.20 | 0.00 |
| $\xi_1$ | (Extreme) conditional default probability | 0.80 | 0.01 | 81.18 | 0.00 |
| $\xi_2$ | Loss-given-default | 1.04 | 0.01 | 87.51 | 0.00 |
| $\xi_3$ | Exposure | 1.02 | 0.00 | 312.38 | 0.00 |
| $\xi_4$ | Obligor credit rating | 0.03 | 0.00 | 13.53 | 0.00 |
| $\xi_5$ | Concentration index | 3.03 | 0.06 | 52.87 | 0.00 |
| $\xi_6$ | Public-sector indicator variable | 0.15 | 0.04 | 4.31 | 0.00 |
| $\xi_7$ | Large exposure indicator variable | 0.16 | 0.02 | 9.25 | 0.00 |
| $\xi_8$ | Small exposure indicator variable | 0.05 | 0.02 | 2.69 | 0.01 |
| Root mean *squared* error | | 9% | | | |
| *Mean* absolute error | | 6% | | | |
| *Median* absolute error | | 4% | | | |
| $R^2$ | | 0.988 | | | |

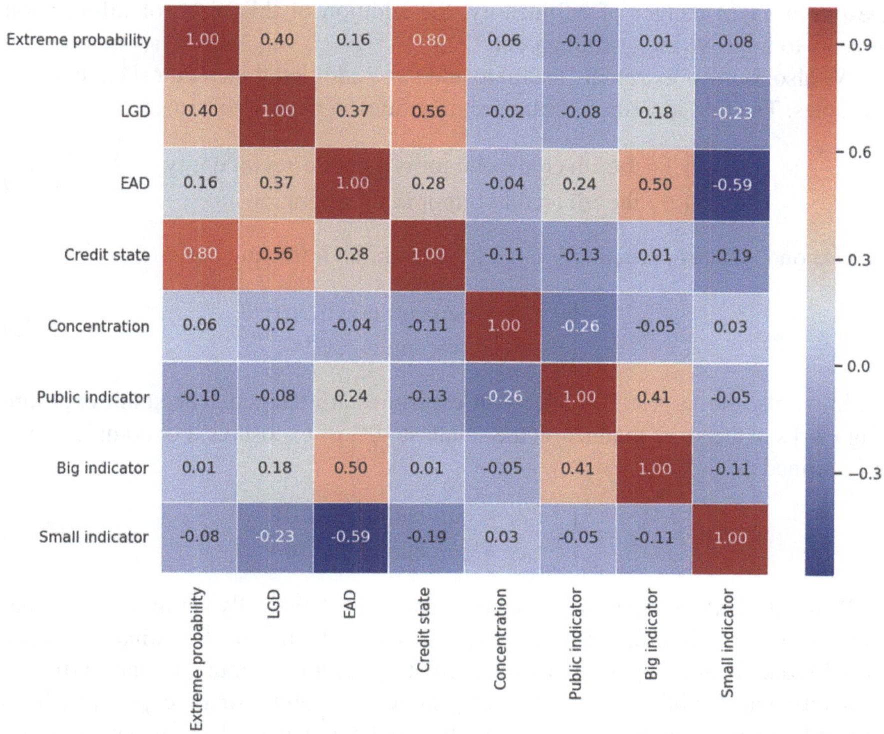


**Fig. 5.7** *Default instrument correlation*: This heat-map illustrates the cross-correlation between the key explanatory variables included in the extended regression model summarized in Table 5.5.

is now only about 4% of the base estimate. The amount of variance explained also increases sharply to 0.99. Finally, all of the new parameters are statistically significant and there is no dramatic (economic) change in the $\xi_1$ to $\xi_3$ parameters.[35] By almost any metric, the extended model represents a serious upgrade.

The new explanatory variables warrant some additional explanation beyond the brief descriptions provided in Table 5.5. The concentration index was already defined in the previous section and, as we had hoped, turns out to be extremely statistically significant. It clearly provides additional information to the model not encapsulated in the systemic-risk-focused extreme conditional default probability. The obligor credit rating, entered as an integer from 1 to 20, somewhat surprisingly improves the overall fit. We would expect—and, in fact, find in Fig. 5.7—positive correlation between the credit rating and the extreme conditional default probability.

[35] The intercept variable does, however, change significantly.

Despite a slight danger of collinearity, the addition of this piece of information appears to improve the overall model.[36]

We also found it extremely useful to add *three* additional indicator (i.e., dummy) variables. The first identifies public-sector entities in the portfolio as

$$\mathbb{I}_{P_i} = \begin{cases} 1 : \text{the } i\text{th credit obligor is a public-sector entity} \\ 0 : \text{the } i\text{th credit obligor is a corporation} \end{cases} . \tag{5.32}$$

The second isolates particularly large firms with the following logic:

$$\mathbb{I}_{B_i} = \begin{cases} 1 : c_i \geq \text{percentile}(c, 0.90) \\ 0 : c_i < \text{percentile}(c, 0.90) \end{cases} , \tag{5.33}$$

or, in words, the largest 10% of credit exposures are flagged. The small exposure flag works in the same manner on the smallest 10% of exposures. For completeness, it is defined as

$$\mathbb{I}_{S_i} = \begin{cases} 1 : c_i \leq \text{percentile}(c, 0.10) \\ 0 : c_i > \text{percentile}(c, 0.10) \end{cases} . \tag{5.34}$$

While these three choices are clearly important, statistically significant explanatory variables, it is difficult to directly understand their role. Examination of the initial model results suggests that the regulatory capital computation has particular difficulty with public-sector, unusually large, and quite small exposures. This probably relates to underlying concentration and parameter-selection questions. We can conceptualize these final three explanatory variables as allowing the model to better handle exceptions. These indicator variables also do not, as seen in Fig. 5.7, exhibit much correlation with the other explanatory variables. The only exception is, unsurprisingly, the large-exposure indicator and the exposure-at-default variable.

One area of investigation is conspicuous by its absence: random recovery. Nothing in our instrument-variable selection provides any insight into this important dimension. A number of avenues was nonetheless investigated. Key parameters—such as the shape parameters of the underlying beta distribution or the recovery volatility—were added to the model without success. Modified, more severe, loss-given-default values were also explored—again using the characteristics of the underlying beta distributions—without any improvement in model results. On the contrary, these efforts generally led to a deterioration of the overall fit.

Figure 5.8 revisits the error analysis performed in Fig. 5.3 using our extended regression model summarized in Eq. 5.31. To aid in our interpretation, the original outliers—from the base default model—are also displayed. Although the general pattern is qualitatively similar, the range of estimation error is reduced by an order of magnitude. While much of the impact relates to improved handling of the outliers,

[36] This high level of cross correlation should nonetheless be flagged as a potential weak link in the extended regression model.

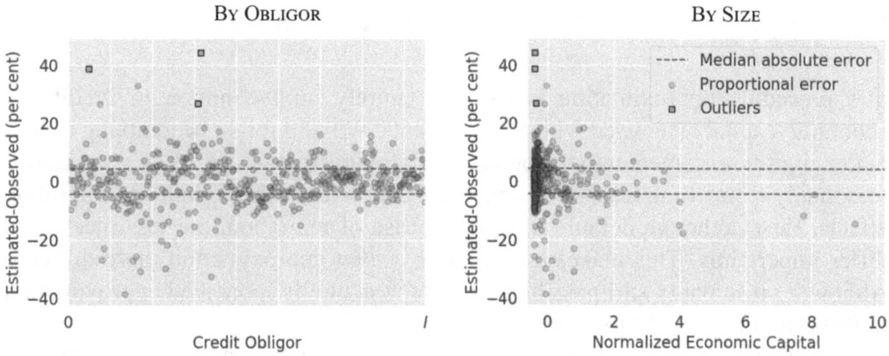


**Fig. 5.8** *Revised default-error analysis*: The preceding graphics replicate the analysis displayed in Figure 5.3 using the extended regression model summarized in Eq. 5.31. The original outliers—from the initial model—are displayed to illustrate the overall improvement.

there is also a more general effect. The difficulty of approximating small, below-average economic-capital allocations is not entirely resolved; part of the issue relates to the proportional nature of the error measure, but it remains a weakness.

While imperfect, we conclude that this is a satisfactory approximation model. It exploits some basic relationships involved in the computation of economic capital, is relatively parsimonious, and generates a reasonable degree of fit and statistical robustness. Some weaknesses remain; most particularly relatively high cross correlation between a few explanatory variables as well as a tendency to significantly overestimate a subset of below-average exposures.

**Colour and Commentary 58** (A Workable Default Approximation Model): *Given the complexity of the credit-risk economic-capital model, we should not expect to be able to construct a perfect approximator.*[a] *Exploiting our knowledge of the problem nonetheless allows us to build a regression model with fairly informative systemic and idiosyncratic explanatory variables. The final result is a satisfactory description of the underlying model. Satisfactory, in this context, implies a median proportional approximation error in the neighbourhood of 4%. While a lower figure would naturally be preferable, we can live with this result. Construction of such models, it should be stressed, is* not *a one-off exercise. The approximation model is re-estimated daily and the error structure is examined within our internal diagnostic dashboards. On an annual basis, a more formal model-selection (or rather verification) procedure is performed. Ultimately, we are always on the lookout for ways to improve this approximation.*

[a] If we could, then we might wish to dramatically rethink our model-estimation approach.

## 5.3 Approximating Migration Economic Capital

The preceding approximation is focused entirely on the notion of credit-risk economic-capital associated with default events. While it might be tempting to fold in the migration element into the previous approximation model, there, at least, *two* reasonably compelling reasons to separately approximate the default and migration effects. First, although default is a special case of migration, the loss mechanics differ importantly. This makes constructing a joint approximation more difficult. Although presumably still possible, separate structurally motivated approximation models are more natural to construct and easier to follow.

The second reason is more practical. Distinct default and migration models permit autonomous prediction of these two effects. This may be interesting for analytic purposes; understanding the breakdown between these two sources of risk can provide, for example, incremental insight into the model outcomes. It may also be necessary from a portfolio perspective. In certain stress testing or loan-impairment calculations, for example, we may not be directly interested in the migration allocation. In other cases, we may be interested *only* in migration effects. A joint model would make it difficult to manage such situations.

### 5.3.1 Conditional Migration Loss

Having justified this choice, let us turn our attention to a possible migration-approximation model. We begin, as in the default setting, by trying to exploit our knowledge of the basic calculation and adding some structure to the migration problem. Denoting $L_i^{(m)}$ as the credit-migration loss associated with the $i$th credit obligor at time $t+1$, we recall that it has the following form,

$$L_i^{(m)} = \underbrace{\left(\mathbb{S}\left(S_{i,t+1}\right) - \mathbb{S}\left(S_{i,t}\right)\right)}_{\Delta\mathbb{S}_i} \tau_i c_i, \tag{5.35}$$

where $\mathbb{S}_i$ is the credit spread, $S_{i,t}$ is the credit state at time $t$, $\tau_i$ is the modified spread duration, and $c_i$ is the exposure of the $i$th position. The time-homogeneous credit spread, of course, is determined directly by the credit state.[37] The spread change (i.e., $\Delta\mathbb{S}_i$) is thus determined by any movement in an obligor's credit state from one time step to the next. The spread movement is then multiplied by the modified spread duration and position exposure to yield an approximation of the migration loss.

Can we construct, using similar logic to the default case, a conditional migration loss estimate? The short answer is yes, there is clearly some conditionality in the

[37] The actual parametrization of these spreads is described in Chap. 3.

migration loss. We will denote, to ease the notation, the current credit state, at time $t$, as $S_{i0}$. This is known. The actual loss outcome depends upon the credit-state value at time $t+1$; we'll call this $S_{i+}$. To formalize this idea, let us rewrite Eq. 5.35 in a similar form and applying the expectation operator to both sides,

$$
\begin{aligned}
L_i^{(m)} &= \underbrace{\Big(\mathbb{S}(S_{i+}) - \mathbb{S}(S_{i0})\Big)\tau_i c_i}_{\text{Equation 5.35}}, && (5.36)\\
\mathbb{E}\left(L_i^{(m)}\middle| S_{i+}=s\right) &= \mathbb{E}\left(\Big(\mathbb{S}(S_{i+}) - \mathbb{S}(S_{i0})\Big)\tau_i c_i\middle| S_{i+}=s\right),\\
&= \left(\underbrace{\mathbb{E}\left(\mathbb{S}(S_{i+})\middle| S_{i+}=s\right)}_{\text{This is a random variable}} - \underbrace{\mathbb{S}\left(S_{i0}\middle| S_{i+}=s\right)}_{\text{This is a constant}}\right)\tau_i c_i,\\
&\approx \Big(\mathbb{S}(s) - \mathbb{S}(S_{i0})\Big)\tau_i c_i.
\end{aligned}
$$

While perhaps not earth-shattering, this expression underscores the fact that the only really uncertain element in the credit-migration calculation is the future credit-state value, $S_{i+}$.[38] The million dollar question relates to our choice of conditioning variable, $s$. One option would be to set $s=\mathbb{E}(S_{i+})$.

For most credit counterparties—save those already at the extremes of the credit scale—credit migration can involve either an improvement or deterioration of their credit quality. This, in turn, implies either profit or loss associated with the associated credit-migration effects described in Eq. 5.36. Naturally, when looking to the extreme tail of the loss distribution, we would expect the vast majority of credit-migration outcomes to involve downgrade, credit-spread widening, and ultimately loss. We will thus, for our purposes, focus our attention predominately on extreme downside outcomes.

Let's begin with the basics. $S_{i+}$ is a random variable and its expectation will depend upon an entity's appropriate transition probabilities. Its unconditional expectation is

$$
\begin{aligned}
\mathbb{E}(S_{i+}) &= \sum_{k=1}^{q} \underbrace{\mathbb{P}\left(S_{i,t+1}=k\middle| S_{i,t}=S_{i0}\right)}_{\text{Transition probability}}\cdot k, && (5.37)\\
&= \sum_{k=1}^{q} p_{kS_{i,t}}\cdot k,
\end{aligned}
$$

[38] The final step is something of an approximation. Although we developed an expression for the credit spreads in Chap. 3, it does not turn out to be helpful in this case.

recalling that $q = 21$ is the number of distinct credit states (including default) and where the individual transition probabilities (i.e., the $p$'s) are simply elements from the $S_{i,t}$th row of the transition matrix, $P$. The expected one-step forward credit state is simply the transition-probability-weighted sum of the possible future credit states. Transition matrices nonetheless exhibit a significant amount of inertia.[39] The actual expected credit state, in one period's time, is unlikely to stray very far away from the current credit state. Consequently, Eq. 5.37—in its current form—will generally *not* be terribly informative about credit-migration economic-capital outcomes.

How might we resolve this issue? The worst-case migration loss should logically occur when the (unknown) future credit state, $S_{i+}$, takes its worst possible level. Under our $t$-threshold credit risk model, the actual credit-state outcome depends on draws from the systemic-risk and mixing-variable distributions. We might, therefore, employ the same trick as we used in the default setting; select an extreme systemic risk-factor variable outcome, $z^*$. The conditional expectation of $S_{i+}$ for the $i$th credit obligor, given $z^*$ is a better candidate for the as-yet-undetermined $s$ in Eq. 5.36. It can be correspondingly written as

$$
\begin{aligned}
\mathbb{E}(S_{i+}|z^*) &= \sum_{k=1}^{q} \mathbb{P}\left( S_{i,t+1} = k \middle| S_{i,t} = S_{i0}, z^* \right) \cdot k, \qquad (5.38)\\
&= \underbrace{\sum_{k=1}^{q-1} \mathbb{P}\left( K_{S_{i,t}}(k) \leq \Delta X_i \leq K_{S_{i,t}}(k+1) \middle| z^* \right) \cdot k}_{\text{Migration}} \\
&\quad \underbrace{+\mathbb{P}\left( \Delta X_i \leq K_{S_{i,t}}(q) \middle| z^* \right) \cdot q}_{\text{Default}}, \\
&= \sum_{k=1}^{q-1} \left( \mathbb{P}\left( \Delta X_i \leq K_{S_{i,t}}(k+1) \middle| z^* \right) - \mathbb{P}\left( \Delta X_i \leq K_{S_{i,t}}(k) \middle| z^* \right) \right) \\
&\quad \cdot k + \mathbb{P}\left( \Delta X_i \leq K_{S_{i,t}}(q) \middle| z^* \right) \cdot q, \\
&= \sum_{k=1}^{q-1} \underbrace{\left( \Phi\left( \frac{\sqrt{\frac{w^*}{\nu}} K_{S_{i,t}}(k+1) - \alpha_i z^*}{\sqrt{1-\alpha_i^2}} \right) - \Phi\left( \frac{\sqrt{\frac{w^*}{\nu}} K_{S_{i,t}}(k) - \alpha_i z^*}{\sqrt{1-\alpha_i^2}} \right) \right)}_{p_i(z^*,k)}
\end{aligned}
$$

[39] We saw this behaviour in Chap. 3 and will discuss it again in Chap. 7.

$$
\cdot k + \underbrace{\Phi\left(\frac{\sqrt{\frac{w^*}{\nu}}F_{\mathcal{T}_\nu}^{-1}(p_i) - \alpha_i z^*}{\sqrt{1-\alpha_i^2}}\right)}_{p_i(z^*,q)\equiv p_i(\alpha^*)} \cdot q,
$$

$$
= \underbrace{\sum_{k=1}^{q-1} p_i(z^*,k)\cdot k}_{\text{Migration}} + \underbrace{p_i(z^*,q)\cdot q}_{\text{Default}},
$$

where

$$
K_{S_{i,t}}(j) = F_{\mathcal{T}_\nu}^{-1}\left(\sum_{w=j}^{q} p_{w,S_{i,t}}\right), \tag{5.39}
$$

is the $i$th obligor credit-migration threshold for movement into state $j$.[40] As in the default setting, we use a fixed, relatively neutral realization of the mixing variable, $w^*$. Equation 5.38 is a rather unwieldy expression, but we already have experience with these conditional-default probability expressions and, perhaps most importantly, they are readily and quickly computed.

We are not quite ready for prime-time usage. The approximation in Eq. 5.38 is a bit too conservative; the simple reason is that it includes the default probability. This component, by construction, will be carved out of the credit-migration economic-capital and allocated to the default category. If we exclude the final default term, however, our expectation will lose a significant amount of probability mass. To solve this, we simply rescale our conditional probabilities excluding the default element. This amounts to an expected downside non-default transition. Practically, this is easily accomplished by defining,

$$
\tilde{p}_i(z^*,k) = \frac{p_i(z^*,k)}{\sum_{j=1}^{q-1} p_i(z^*,j)}, \tag{5.40}
$$

for $k = 1,\ldots,q-1$ and then writing our (revised) conditional non-default credit state expectation as,

$$
\mathbb{E}\left(S_{i+}^{(m)}\middle| z^*\right) = \sum_{k=1}^{q-1} \tilde{p}_i(z^*,k)\cdot k. \tag{5.41}
$$

[40] These credit migration notions and thresholds are extensively discussed in Chap. 2.

We have thus made a slight, but important change, from the base definition in Eq. 5.38. Equation 5.41 describes the expected (non-default) credit state for the $i$th obligor in the next period, conditional on an unpleasant realization of the systemic risk factor.[41] This shift in focus is captured by the use of $S_{i+}^{(m)}$ rather than the original $S_{i+}$ notation.

Equipped with this, model consistent, estimator for the worst-case (non-default) credit deterioration, we may return to the business of approximating credit-risk economic-capital allocation. Again, we motivate our approach through the Basel IRB method. If we denote the capital allocation associated with migration risk as $\mathcal{A}_i^{(m)}(\alpha_z^*)$, we might approximate it as,

$$
\begin{aligned}
\mathcal{A}_i^{(m)}(\alpha_z^*) &\approx \overbrace{\underbrace{\mathbb{E}\left(L_i^{(m)}\middle|\mathbb{E}\left(S_{i+}^{(m)}\middle|z^*\right)\right)}_{\text{Worst-case loss}} - \underbrace{\cancel{\mathbb{E}\left(L_i^{(m)}\middle|\mathbb{E}(S_{i+})\right)}}_{\mathbb{E}\left(L_i^{(m)}\right)\approx 0}}^{\text{Unexpected loss}}, \qquad (5.42)\\
&\approx \underbrace{\left(\mathbb{S}\left(\mathbb{E}\left(S_{i+}^{(m)}\middle|z^*\right)\right) - \mathbb{S}\left(S_{i0}\right)\right)}_{\Delta\mathbb{S}_i(z^*)\text{: Worst-case spread movement}}\tau_i c_i,\\
&\approx \Delta\mathbb{S}_i(z^*)\tau_i c_i.
\end{aligned}
$$

Unlike the default case, we ignore the unconditional expected loss. Since it is generally quite close to zero, we exclude it from our basic structure.[42]

While Eq. 5.42 appears to be a sensible construct—built in the image of the default-risk approximation—it has an important potential structural disadvantage. There are only 20 (non-default) credit states that can be forecast with a correspondingly small number of spread outcomes. Equation 5.40 will, without some form of intervention, thus produce only a small number of discrete credit-spread outcomes for a given obligor's modified spread duration and exposure. The credit-migration economic-capital engine, however, operates under no such constraint. It can provide a (quasi-)continuum of possible migration–risk allocations. This would suggest that our approximation—even if it differs by one notch on the credit-state forecast—can exhibit rather important approximation errors. Our solution is to simply permit non-integer (i.e., fractional) credit-state forecasts and determine the appropriate spread outcome through the use of linear interpolation. This is essentially a trick—a fractional credit rating does not really exist—permitting us to transform our estimator from discrete to continuous space. This small adjustment provides our estimator with significantly more flexibility.

---

[41] As in the default section, $z^*$ is the $\alpha_z^*$ quantile of the underlying systemic risk factor distribution.

[42] This stems from the high degree of inertia in credit-rating transition and, for most obligors, the relatively symmetric probability of upgrade and downgrade.

We have also ignored the expected-shortfall dimension. Practically, Eq. 5.42 is a quantile-based estimator. If we wish to consider the expected shortfall metric, then we will need to solve the following integral:

$$\begin{aligned}\mathcal{E}_i^{(m)}(\alpha_z^*) &= \frac{1}{1-\alpha_z^*}\int_{\alpha_z^*}^1 \mathcal{A}_i^{(m)}(x)dx, \qquad (5.43)\\ &= \tau_i c_i \cdot \underbrace{\frac{1}{1-\alpha_z^*}\int_{\alpha_z^*}^1 \Delta\mathbb{S}_i\Big(\Phi^{-1}(1-x)\Big)dx}_{\Delta\tilde{\mathbb{S}}_i(z^*)}.\end{aligned}$$

Practically, only a small amount of incremental effort is required to numerically integrate Eq. 5.43. We thus employ the integrated worst-case spread change, $\Delta\tilde{\mathbb{S}}_i(z^*)$, as the base migration loss estimator found in Eq. 5.43.

To better understand the kernel of our approximation, we return to our simple example introduced in Table 5.1 on page 290. Naturally, we will now consider the case of credit-migration economic capital. Some of the credit obligor's details are reproduced for convenience and its modified spread duration has also been added. Unsurprisingly, the unconditional expected rating remains extremely close to the original level. Conditional on extreme outcomes of our systemic and mixing variables, however, the expected (or shocked) credit state belongs to PD class 13. If we use the integrated, expected-shortfall form, from Eq. 5.43, this increases to a 13.2 rating. Of course, such a PD categorization does not actually exist. Through appropriate interpolation along the spread curve, however, this leads to a 56 and 63 basis-point credit widening for the VaR-motivated and integrated worst-case spread movements, respectively. These values translate into forecast credit losses of about EUR 0.94 and 1.05 billion. Since the actual economic-capital value is roughly EUR 0.87 million, both of these forecasts appear to overshoot the target.[43]

Figure 5.9 provides a potentially helpful visualization of the difference between unconditional and conditional (non-default) transition probabilities. Using our sample obligor from Table 5.6, the three flavours of transition probability are plotted side-by-side across the entire (non-default) credit spectrum. The unconditional transition probabilities, as one would expect, are roughly symmetric and centred around the current credit state: PD11.[44] The $\alpha^*$ confidence-level (non-default) migration probabilities—both VaR-motivated and integrated from Eqs. 5.42 and 5.43—behave in a decidedly different fashion. The likelihood of remaining in the current credit state is dramatically reduced and the remaining probability

[43] Interestingly, the model-based worst-case credit-spread widening, imputed from the true credit-migration estimate, is readily calculated from Table 5.6 as $\frac{\mathcal{E}_i^{(m)}(\alpha^*)}{c_i\tau_i} = \frac{868{,}247}{65{,}000{,}000\times 2.6} \approx 51$ basis points.

[44] For this credit rating, upgrade and downgrade probabilities, on an unconditional basis, appear to be roughly equivalent. This is usually true, but it starts to break down as one moves to the boundaries of the credit spectrum.

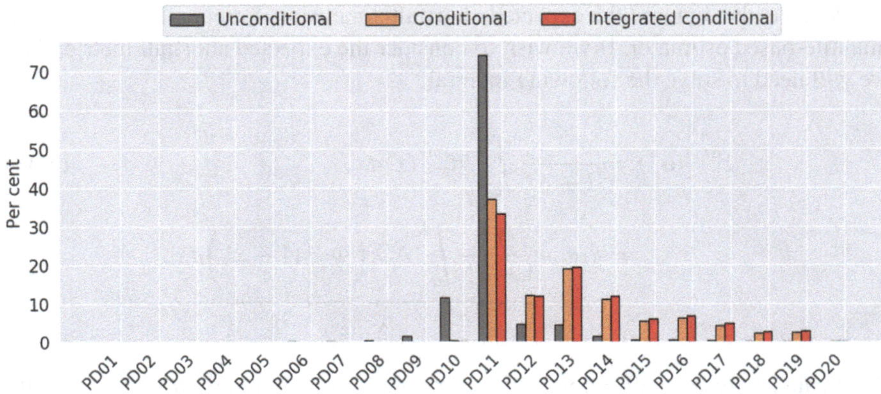


**Fig. 5.9** *Credit-migration conditionality*: The preceding figure compares the unconditional transition probabilities to the $\alpha_z^* = 0.9997$ confidence-level (non-default) conditional transition probabilities for the sample obligor highlighted in Table 5.6. The unconditional, VaR-motivated, and integrated versions of these migration probabilities are displayed. The conditional quantities are, in stark contrast to their rather symmetric unconditional equivalents, skewed towards credit deterioration.

**Table 5.6** *Extending our simple example*: The underlying table summarizes, for the same specific exposure illustrated in Tables 5.1 and 5.2, the various quantities and calculations involved in the construction of a conditional forecast of the migration loss.

| Quantity | Definition | Value |
|---|---|---|
| Degrees of freedom | $\nu$ | 70 |
| Confidence level | $\alpha_z^*$ | 0.9997 |
| Exposure | $c_i$ | 65,000,000 |
| Modified spread duration | $\tau_i$ | 2.6 yrs. |
| Original credit state | $S_{i0}$ | 11.0 |
| (Unconditional) expected (non-default) rating | $\mathbb{E}\left(S_{i+}^{(m)}\right)$ | 11.0 |
| (Conditional) expected (non-default) rating | $\mathbb{E}\left(S_{i+}^{(m)} \middle\vert z^*\right)$ | 13.0 |
| (Conditional) integrated expected (non-default) rating | $\frac{1}{1-\alpha_z^*}\int_{\alpha_z^*}^{1} \mathbb{E}\left(S_{i+}^{(m)} \middle\vert \Phi^{-1}(1-x)\right) dx$ | 13.2 |
| Worst-case spread | $\Delta\mathbb{S}_i(z^*)$ | 56 bps. |
| Integrated worst-case spread | $\Delta\tilde{\mathbb{S}}_i(z^*)$ | 63 bps. |
| VaR-based forecast | $\widehat{\mathcal{A}_i^{(m)}(\alpha_z^*)}$ | 940,704 |
| Expected-shortfall-based forecast | $\widehat{\mathcal{E}_i^{(m)}(\alpha_z^*)}$ | 1,059,842 |
| Credit-migration economic-capital | $\mathcal{E}_i^{(m)}(\alpha^*)$ | 868,247 |

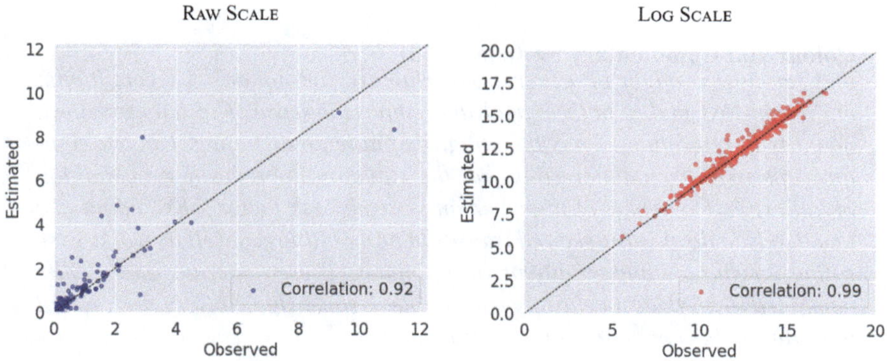


**Fig. 5.10** *Degree of migration agreement*: The preceding graphics, in raw and logarithmic normalized units, illustrate the degree of agreement between our approximation in Eq. 5.43 and the observed simulation-based economic-capital contributions. The overall level of linear correlation is fairly respectable, although there is a decided tendency to overstate the level of risk.

mass is skewed strongly toward downgrade. The skew is slightly more pronounced for the integrated conditional transition likelihoods. It is precisely this information that we are attempting to harness for the approximation of credit migration. These worst-case transition probabilities thus—in a manner similar to conditional default probabilities in our earlier discussion—form the kernel of the migration-loss approximation.

Figure 5.10 generalizes the single obligor example in Table 5.6 to the entire portfolio. As before, the results are provided in raw and logarithmic normalized units. The idea is to help understand the general degree of agreement between our approximation in Eq. 5.43 and the observed simulation-based migration economic-capital contributions. The overall level of linear correlation is fairly respectable at 0.92 and 0.99 on the raw and logarithmic scales, respectively.

Our base migration-risk approximator has, similar to the result from Table 5.6, a decided tendency to somewhat misstate the precise level of risk. This is likely a structural feature of the approach culminating in Eq. 5.43. As in the default setting, conditioning solely on the systemic risk factor ignores idiosyncratic effects. Given the more symmetric nature of migration risk—relative to the skewed nature of default—restricting our approximation to downside systemic risk appears to manifest itself as overly conservative initial estimates. Figure 5.10 nonetheless suggests that, these shortcomings aside, it is a useful starting point.

**Colour and Commentary 59** (THE MIGRATION KERNEL)*: The decision to separately approximate migration and default, while sensible, presents a dilemma. We need to identify a reasonable first-order migration-loss approximator. A natural starting point is to lean on the default-approximation kernel*

(continued)

**Colour and Commentary 59** (continued)
*and see how it might be generalized. Happily, the notion of a conditional migration loss makes both logical and empirical sense. The only unknown quantity in migration loss is the obligor's future credit rating. Unconditionally, this is rather uninteresting, but the situation improves if we condition on an extreme outcome of the common systemic risk factor.*[a] *Extending this idea leads to downward-skewed transition probabilities as well as worst-case rating downgrade and credit-spread estimates. These quantities are readily combined to produce an entirely reasonable, if somewhat conservative, initial migration-risk economic-capital approximator.*

[a] As in the default setting, the $\chi^2$-distributed mixing variable is fixed at a fairly neutral value.

### 5.3.2 A First Migration Model

It will come as no surprise that we use the same linear regression structure—given its reasonable degree of success—as employed in the default setting. Indeed, we now have all of the necessary constituents to construct a base credit-migration approximation model. Consider the following form:

$$\begin{aligned}
\mathcal{E}_i^{(m)}(\alpha^*) &\approx \tau_i c_i \cdot \underbrace{\frac{1}{1-\alpha_z^*}\int_{\alpha_z^*}^{1} \Delta\mathbb{S}_i\left(\Phi^{-1}(1-x)\right)dx}_{\text{Equation 5.43}}, \qquad (5.44)\\
&\approx \Delta\tilde{\mathbb{S}}_i(z^*)\tau_i c_i,\\
\underbrace{\ln\left(\mathcal{E}_i^{(m)}(\alpha^*)\right)}_{y_i^{(m)}} &\approx \ln\underbrace{\left(\Delta\tilde{\mathbb{S}}_i(z^*)\tau_i c_i\right)}_{\text{Equation 5.43}},\\
y_i^{(m)} &= \theta_0 + \theta_1\underbrace{\ln\left(\Delta\tilde{\mathbb{S}}_i(z^*)\right)}_{X_{i,1}^{(m)}} + \theta_2\underbrace{\ln(\tau_i)}_{X_{i,2}^{(m)}} + \theta_3\underbrace{\ln(c_i)}_{X_{i,3}^{(m)}} + \epsilon_i^{(m)},
\end{aligned}$$

for $i = 1, \ldots, I$. Again applying natural logarithms, we have a similar form to the earlier default approximation in Eq. 5.18. This directly translates, of course, into the familiar OLS setting and reduces to the usual linear model,

$$y^{(m)} = X^{(m)}\Theta + \epsilon^{(m)}, \qquad (5.45)$$

where

$$y^{(m)} = \begin{bmatrix} \ln\left(\mathcal{E}_1^{(m)}(\alpha^*)\right) \\ \vdots \\ \ln\left(\mathcal{E}_I^{(m)}(\alpha^*)\right) \end{bmatrix} \tag{5.46}$$

and

$$X^{(m)} = \begin{bmatrix} 1 \ln\left(\Delta\tilde{\mathbb{S}}_1(z^*)\right) \ln(\tau_1) \ln(c_1) \\ \vdots \quad \vdots \quad \vdots \quad \vdots \\ 1 \ln\left(\Delta\tilde{\mathbb{S}}_I(z^*)\right) \ln(\tau_I) \ln(c_I) \end{bmatrix}. \tag{5.47}$$

As before, we need only employ the standard OLS estimator for $\Theta = \left[\theta_0\ \theta_1\ \theta_2\ \theta_3\right]^T$. Although the inputs are rather different, the base migration model is conceptually equivalent to the default case.

Table 5.7 provides the usual summary for our base, structurally motivated, credit-migration model shown in Eq. 5.45. All *four* regression coefficients are strongly statistically significant. The percentage of variance explained (i.e., $R^2$) attains a decent level. The other goodness-of-fit measures, however, show room for improvement. The proportional root-mean-squared value of almost 40% is somewhat better than in the base default model, but it suggests the presence of important outliers. Having already been in this situation, let's skip directly to the extension of Eq. 5.45 to include a wider range of idiosyncratic explanatory variables.

**Table 5.7** *A first migration-approximation model*: This table summarizes the results of the base migration economic-capital approximation model. It has an intercept and three logically motivated explanatory variables. The results, while not overwhelming, are reasonably encouraging.

| Quantity | Description | Estimate | Standard error | $t$-statistic | $p$-value |
|---|---|---|---|---|---|
| $\theta_0$ | Intercept | −2.04 | 0.17 | −11.90 | 0.00 |
| $\theta_1$ | Worst-case spread | 0.69 | 0.02 | 29.37 | 0.00 |
| $\theta_2$ | Spread duration | 1.01 | 0.02 | 64.62 | 0.00 |
| $\theta_3$ | Exposure | 1.01 | 0.01 | 143.70 | 0.00 |
| Root mean *squared* error | | 40% | | | |
| *Mean* absolute error | | 23% | | | |
| *Median* absolute error | | 17% | | | |
| $R^2$ | | 0.886 | | | |

### 5.3.3 *The Full Migration Model*

As in the default case, an extension of the base model is necessary. The full migration-risk regression model—which is once again the result of a significant amount of analysis—is described as:

$$\overbrace{\ln\left(\mathcal{E}_i^{(m)}(\alpha^*)\right)}^{y_i^{(m)}} = \overbrace{\underbrace{\theta_0 + \theta_1 \ln\left(\Delta\tilde{\mathbb{S}}_i(z^*)\right) + \theta_2 \ln(\tau_i) + \theta_3 \ln(c_i)}_{\text{Base migration model}} + \underbrace{\sum_{k=4}^{\kappa} \theta_k X_k^{(m)}}_{\substack{\text{Additional}\\ \text{explanatory}\\ \text{variables}}}}^{\sum_{k=0}^{\kappa} \theta_k X_i^{(m)}} + \epsilon_i^{(m)}, \tag{5.48}$$

for $i = 1, \ldots, I$ risk-owner risk contributions. The interesting part of Eq. 5.48 relates to the identity of the additional explanatory variables.

Table 5.8 displays the results of the final credit-migration economic-capital approximation model. All model parameters are statistically significant. Coincidentally, *five* additional explanatory variables were also selected. As in the default setting, the integer-valued credit rating and the concentration index turn out to be surprisingly useful in explaining credit-migration risk outcomes. Two additional indicator (i.e., dummy) variables also prove helpful. The first identifies public-sector

**Table 5.8** *Full migration-approximation model*: This table provides the key summary statistics for the full credit-migration economic-capital approximation model. It does not fit quite as well as the default approach, but it appears to do reasonably well.

| Quantity | Description | Estimate | Standard error | $t$-statistic | $p$-value |
|---|---|---|---|---|---|
| $\theta_0$ | Intercept | −0.62 | 0.17 | −3.70 | 0.00 |
| $\theta_1$ | Worst-case spread | 0.93 | 0.02 | 51.40 | 0.00 |
| $\theta_2$ | Spread duration | 0.98 | 0.01 | 123.43 | 0.00 |
| $\theta_3$ | Exposure | 1.01 | 0.00 | 239.04 | 0.00 |
| $\theta_4$ | Obligor credit rating | −0.08 | 0.00 | −17.66 | 0.00 |
| $\theta_5$ | Concentration index | 1.42 | 0.07 | 19.74 | 0.00 |
| $\theta_6$ | Public-sector indicator variable | −0.33 | 0.03 | −12.32 | 0.00 |
| $\theta_7$ | High-risk indicator variable | −0.27 | 0.05 | −4.98 | 0.00 |
| $\theta_8$ | Systemic weight | −1.73 | 0.13 | −13.03 | 0.00 |
| Root mean *squared* error | | 15% | | | |
| *Mean* absolute error | | 11% | | | |
| *Median* absolute error | | 9% | | | |
| $R^2$ | | 0.978 | | | |

entities in the portfolio exactly as in Eq. 5.32 in the default setting.[45] The second high-risk indicator is defined as

$$\mathbb{I}_{H_i} = \begin{cases} 1 : S_i \geq \text{PD14} \\ 0 : S_i < \text{PD14} \end{cases}. \tag{5.49}$$

Obligors at the very low end of the credit spectrum are, as one might expect, dominated by default risk. As a consequence, identifying them for different treatment improves the overall approximation. As before, these indicator variables are based on a certain logic, but their success likely depends on rather complicated non-linear aspects of the production $t$-threshold model.

The systematic weight parameter, the final addition to our approximating regression, also provides value in describing migration risk. Its role in determining the relative importance of systemic and idiosyncratic factors makes it important in both the migration and default settings. It is excluded in the full default model, because it is ultimately captured by other explanatory variables.

Figure 5.11 provides a heat-map of the cross correlation associated with our migration explanatory variables. The only potential danger point—in terms of multicollinearity—arises between the credit rating and public-sector variables. With this borderline exception, the remaining descriptive variables all appear to capture different systemic and idiosyncratic elements of migration-risk economic capital. This is underscored by the goodness-of-fit measures in Table 5.8. In addition to a fairly healthy increase in the $R^2$ measure, the proportional root-mean-square errors are reduced by a factor of three; the mean and median absolute errors, perhaps the most important dimensions, are cut in half. The results are broadly comparable—although marginally worse—than the full-default model outcomes presented in Table 5.5.

Figure 5.12 concludes our examination of the migration-approximation model through a detailed examination of the error profiles. In particular, it highlights the error plots (estimated less observed) for the base and full migration-risk approximation models. Each perspective considers the individual obligor and (normalized) size dimensions. A small number of model outliers are identified in the base model and inherited in the extended model graphics; in all cases, the additional explanatory variables improve the situation. Overall, a threefold reduction in the scale of error is provided with the extended model. Although it struggles in certain situations, and there is stubborn tendency to overestimate risk, the general performance of the approximation can be considered to be satisfactory.

[45] There are, it should be stressed, the only four of eight (non-intercept) variables arising in both default and migration models. This observation underscores the benefits of separate treatment of migration and default risk.

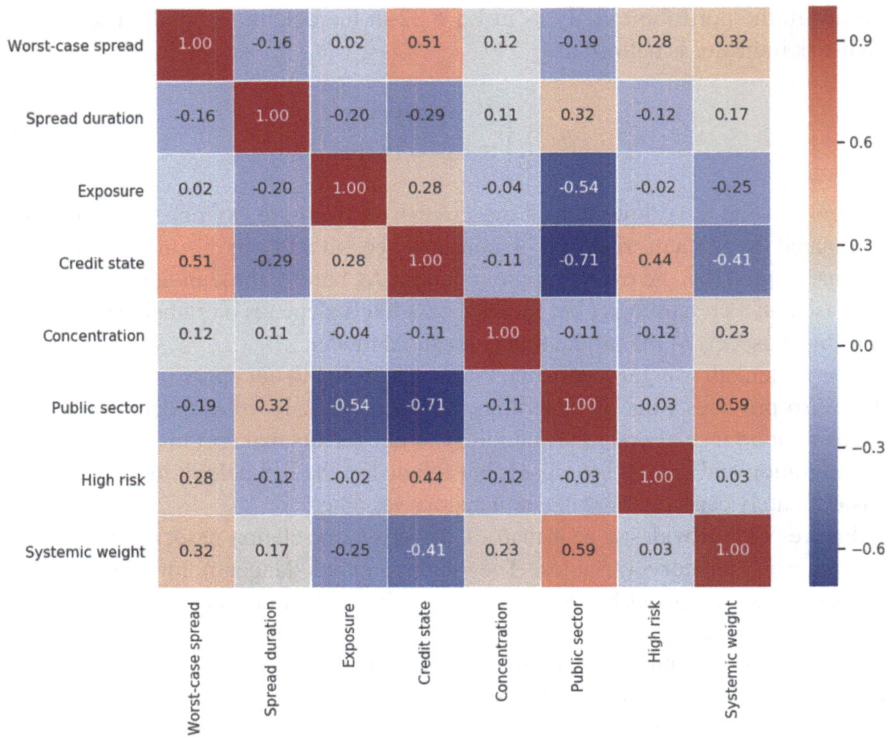


**Fig. 5.11** *Migration instrument correlation*: This heat-map illustrates the cross-correlation between the key migration risk explanatory variables included in the extended regression model summarized in Table 5.8.

**Colour and Commentary 60** (A WORKABLE MIGRATION APPROXIMATION MODEL)*: Migration-risk economic capital is not easier to predict than its default equivalent.*[a] *Analogous to the default case, one can nonetheless construct a fairly defensible regression model involving meaningful systemic and idiosyncratic explanatory variables. The results are satisfactory; in particular, the* $R^2$ *approaches 0.98 and the median proportional approximation error comes out—not quite on par with the full default model—at around 9%. Migration risk approximation nevertheless remains a constant struggle. The model is re-estimated daily, parameters are stored in our database, and the results are carefully monitored via our internal diagnostic dashboards. A more formal model-selection procedure is performed on an annual basis.*

[a] To repeat, if it was, then we could perhaps dispense with our complicated simulation algorithms.

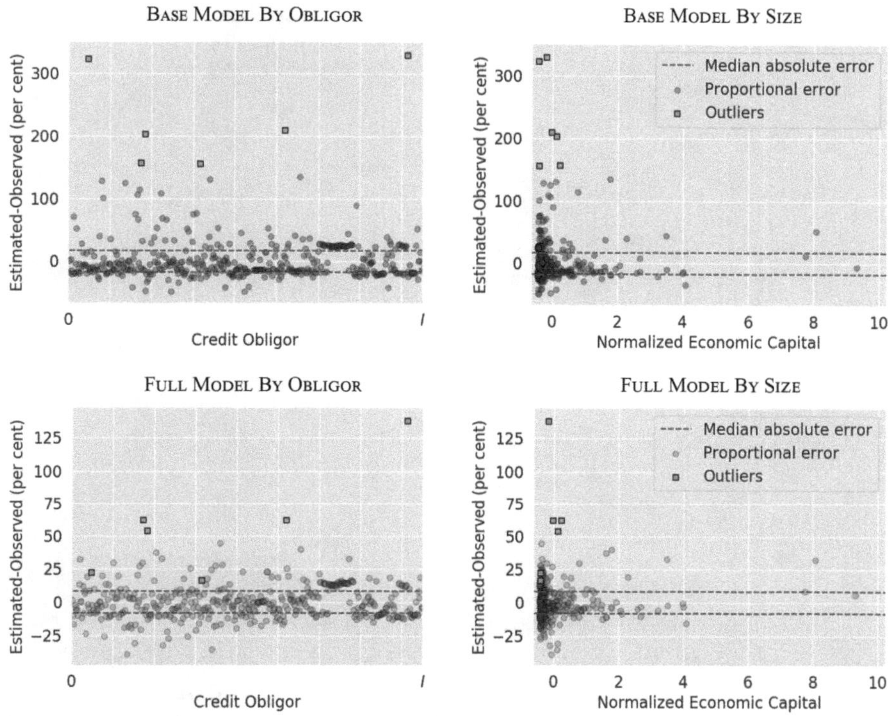


**Fig. 5.12** *Migration-error analysis*: The preceding graphics highlight the error plots (estimated less observed) for the base and full migration-risk approximation models. Each perspective consider the individual obligor and (normalized) size dimensions. A threefold reduction in the scale of error is provided with the extended model.

## 5.4 Approximation Model Due Diligence

Lawyers talk about the idea of a standard of care and due diligence in a very technical and specific way. These ideas can, if we're careful with them, be meaningfully applied to the modelling world. We have, as model developers, a certain responsibility to exercise a reasonable amount of *prudence and caution* in model selection and implementation. Despite having invested a significant amount of time motivating and deriving our approximation models, we cannot yet be considered to have entirely performed our due diligence. The reasons are fairly simple: to this point, we have only examined their performance on an in-sample basis for a single point in time. To appropriately discharge our responsibility for due diligence, this section will address the *two* following questions:

1. How do our default and model approximations perform over a lengthier time interval?

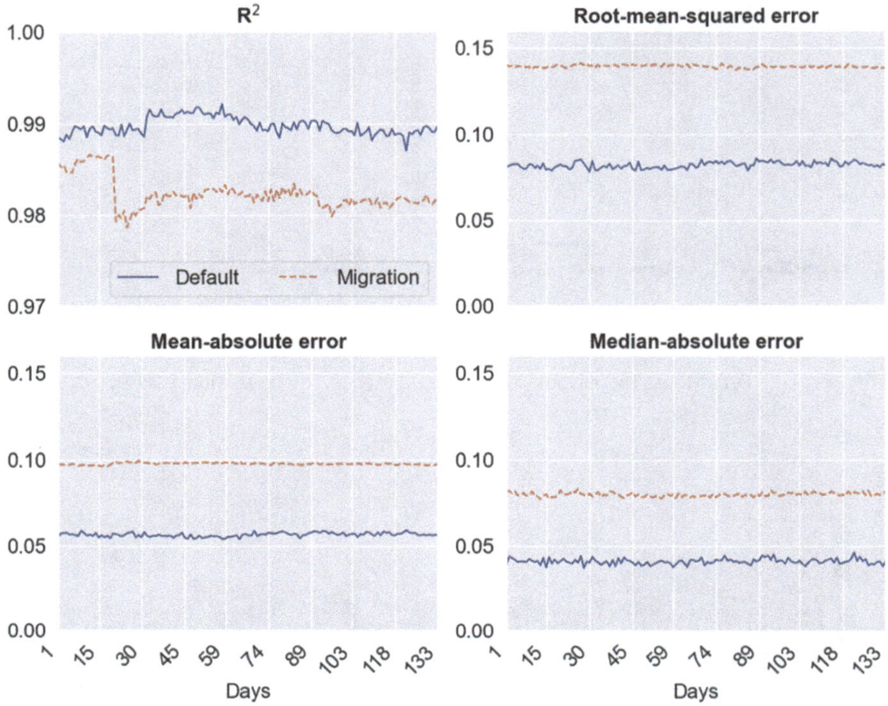


**Fig. 5.13** *A historical perspective*: Using the portfolio data over each date in a six-month period straddling 2020 and 2021, the full default and migration models are estimated and the evolution of our four main goodness-of-fit measures are displayed. The results indicate a relatively high degree of stability over time.

2. What is the relative performance of our approximations—again over a reasonable length of time—along *both* the in- and out-of-sample dimensions?

Let's begin with the first, more easily addressed, issue. The default and migration approximation models were fit—using the ideas from the previous sections—to a sequence of portfolios. Figure 5.13 illustrates the results by focusing on the daily evolution of the four resulting goodness-of-fit criteria over a roughly 130 business-day (i.e., six-month) period. The results are fairly boring; the root-mean, mean-absolute, and median-absolute error estimates remain resolutely stable over the entire period. The default $R^2$ never deviates, in any meaningful way, from 0.99. The only slightly interesting result is a downward jump in the migration $R^2$ stemming from a hard-to-approximate addition to the portfolio earlier during our horizon of analysis.

Boring, in the context of Fig. 5.13, is a good thing. The results strongly suggest that our two approximations are satisfactorily robust. Caution is, of course, required. A few new observations could undermine these positive results and lead us to question our conclusion. This is important to keep in mind and argues for constant oversight. This point notwithstanding, we may cautiously infer, from the analysis in Fig. 5.13, that our approximations have value beyond the single datapoint presented in the previous sections.

The second question is harder to answer and takes us further afield. The natural starting point is to provide a bit more precision on the difference between in- and out-of-sample estimates. As the name suggests, in-sample fit describes errors stemming from observations used to fit (or train) one's approximation algorithm. Out-of-sample fit, by extension, applies to errors for observations falling outside, or excluded from, the estimation dataset. Any information embedded in out-of-sample observations is not, literally by construction, captured in one's model parameters. It is precisely this characteristic that makes out-of-sample prediction both difficult and interesting.

Out-of-sample prediction is a powerful technique to guard against the over-fitting of an estimation model. This is a concern shared by both statisticians and data scientists. Over-fitting basically describes an excessive specialization of the model parameters to one's specific data sample; the consequence is the identification of trends that do not generalize more broadly to other samples or the overall data population.[46] It is easy to see how out-of-sample error analysis is precisely the right tool to assess the degree of model over-fitting in one's approach.

Over-fitting is a particularly depressing and dangerous model shortcoming. One's in-sample goodness-of-fit measures look great, but the model actually fails dreadfully out of sample. Given the high levels of $R^2$ and low proportional errors in the preceding approximation models, it is entirely natural to worry about this problem. Have we, for example, over-specialized our model structure to the provided sample data? Addressing this entirely rationale fear is an important part of our due-diligence process. Moreover, given that the loan-pricing problem is, by definition, an out-of-sample prediction problem, we cannot ignore this dimension.

How should we proceed? Stone [26] and Geisser [11], almost 50 years ago, proposed a general technique to systemically manage in- and out-of-sample datasets and thereby control the over-fitting problem. The idea is quite simple: one first partitions the given dataset into $k$ (roughly) equally sized subsets. Each of these subsets is referred to as a *fold*. One then excludes one of these folds—let's start with $k = 1$—and uses the remaining data to estimate the model. In statistical or machine learning, these are generally referred to as the training and testing datasets, respectively. One proceeds to compute two sets of goodness-of-fit measures: one for the estimation dataset and another for the set of excluded data. These are the in- and out-of-sample measures, respectively. One then puts the excluded data back into the sample, and excludes another fold (say, $k = 2$) and repeats the exercise. This is performed $k$ times until each of the partitions has been excluded once. The result is

46 A less charitable way to describe over-fitting is the characterization of trends that do *not* actually exist.

**Table 5.9** *Goodness-of-fit statistics*: This table summarizes a range of goodness-of-fit summary statistics for both in- and out-of-sample estimates. The values are based on a five-fold cross-validation exercise performed for every business day over a six-month period.

| | | Default | | | | Migration | | | |
|---|---|---|---|---|---|---|---|---|---|
| Measure | Perspective | Mean | $\sigma$ | Min | Max | Mean | $\sigma$ | Min | Max |
| $R^2$ | In-sample | 0.990 | 0.002 | 0.982 | 0.996 | 0.982 | 0.004 | 0.969 | 0.994 |
| | Out-of-sample | **0.990** | **0.007** | **0.965** | **0.999** | **0.979** | **0.013** | **0.927** | **0.999** |
| Root-mean-squared error | In-sample | 0.081 | 0.004 | 0.066 | 0.091 | 0.137 | 0.008 | 0.114 | 0.150 |
| | Out-of-sample | **0.086** | **0.015** | **0.050** | **0.158** | **0.149** | **0.039** | **0.092** | **0.309** |
| Mean absolute error | In-sample | 0.056 | 0.002 | 0.047 | 0.062 | 0.097 | 0.003 | 0.085 | 0.106 |
| | Out-of-sample | **0.059** | **0.006** | **0.041** | **0.090** | **0.102** | **0.011** | **0.073** | **0.145** |
| Median absolute error | In-sample | 0.041 | 0.002 | 0.035 | 0.047 | 0.080 | 0.003 | 0.069 | 0.092 |
| | Out-of-sample | **0.042** | **0.005** | **0.028** | **0.059** | **0.081** | **0.008** | **0.056** | **0.105** |

a broad range of both in- and out-of-sample estimates.[47] This is referred to—again following from Stone [26] and Geisser [11]—as $k$-fold cross validation.[48]

Table 5.9 illustrates the results of a $k$-fold cross validation exercise performed for every day during the same six-month time interval employed for the construction of Fig. 5.13. On each distinct date, the original dataset was randomly reshuffled to ensure different fold compositions over time. With roughly 130 days and $k = 5$ folds per dataset, the consequence is about $5 \times 130 = 650$ separate sets of in- and out-of-sample goodness-of-fit statistics. In Table 5.9 we find the mean, volatility (i.e., $\sigma$), minimum and maximum in- and out-of-sample good-of-fit measures for both migration and default approximation models.

Although there are admittedly many numbers to peruse, a few conclusions are possible. First of all, there is a universal degradation of fit when moving from the in- to the out-of-sample perspective. Second, and more interestingly, the magnitude of the deterioration of fit is (for the most part) relatively modest. Finally, the default model appears to be more robust, along this dimension, than their migration equivalents.

Figure 5.14 seeks to help us better digest all of the figures in Table 5.9 by illustrating the competing distributions of in- and out-of-sample good-of-fit measures for the default approximation model. Visually, the in-sample fit measures are clearly tighter than the out-of-sample values. The centre of the two distributions do not appear to be dramatically different, although there is a decided right skew.[49] In the default setting, the overall worsening of out-of-sample prediction accuracy appears to be reasonably limited.

[47] It is also possible to repeat this again by randomly reshuffling one's original dataset and repartitioning.

[48] See Hastie et al. [16, Section 7.2] for a helpful introduction to cross validation.

[49] Or, in the case of the $R^2$, a left skew.

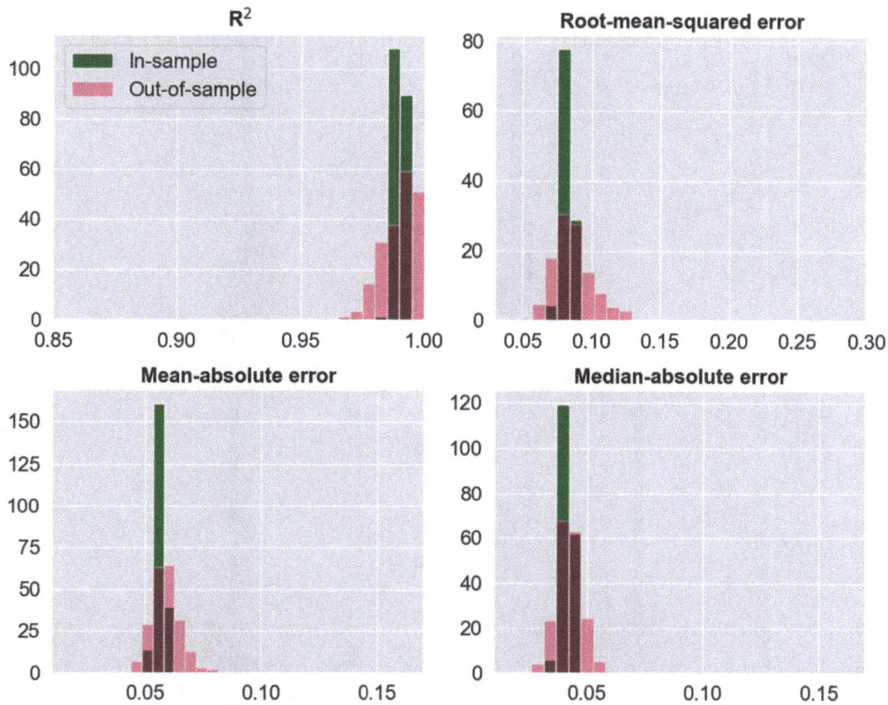


**Fig. 5.14** *Default out-of-sample fit*: Computed using a five-fold cross validation of the full default approximation model for each day over a six-month period, the graphics display the distribution of in- and out-of-sample goodness-of-fit measures. Each day, the order of the observations using the cross validation were randomly shuffled.

Figure 5.15 repeats the analysis found in Fig. 5.14, but instead examines the *migration* approximation model. Once again, the in-sample fit measures are fairly closely clustered around a central point. The dispersion of the out-of-sample metrics is qualitatively similar, but substantially broader than in the default case. The root-mean-squared error, in particular, exhibits a bimodal distribution. This stems from the inclusion or exclusion of certain outlier observations from the training and testing samples. While the out-of-sample performance of the migration approximation is significantly worse than the default model, the analysis does not reveal any terrible surprises. We may, therefore, cautiously provide fairly positive responses to the two due-diligence questions posed at the beginning of this section.

**Colour and Commentary 61** (DUE-DILIGENCE RESULTS): *The notion of due-diligence basically sets a standard for the requisite degree of caution and prudence for a reasonable person finding themselves in a position of*

(continued)

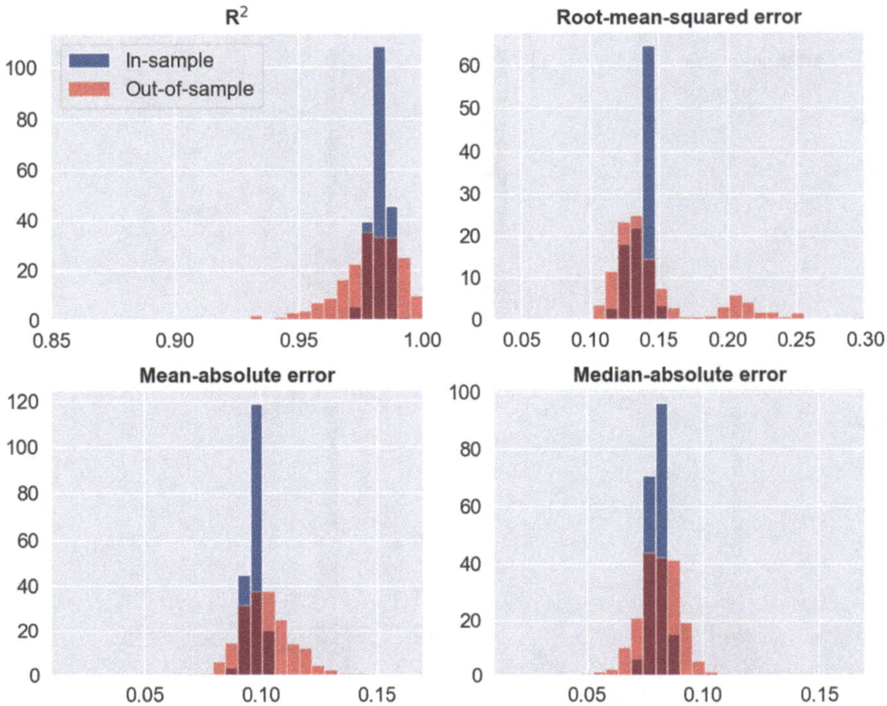


**Fig. 5.15** *Migration out-of-sample fit*: Analogous to Fig. 5.14, the graphics apply to the migration case. Computed using a five-fold cross validation of the full migration approximation model for each day over a six-month period, the graphics display the empirical distribution of in- and out-of-sample goodness-of-fit measures. Each day, the order of the observations using the cross validation were randomly shuffled.

**Colour and Commentary 61** (continued)
*responsibility. Given its central importance for a range of important credit-risk economic capital applications—including, most centrally, loan pricing and stress testing—we identify a strong need for model due-diligence. This is operationalized in* two *questions: model-prediction observations over a broader time period* and *out-of-sample performance. Examining daily portfolios over a six-month period reveals an admirable degree of robustness in our in-sample goodness-of-fit measures. Analyzing the same six-month data window within the context of a (daily) five-fold cross validation exercise further demonstrates only moderate degradation associated with out-of-sample goodness-of-fit in our approximation models.*[a] *This extensive due-diligence analysis provides a degree of comfort in our approximation models.*

[a] The default model nonetheless significantly outperforms the migration approximator.

## 5.5 The Full Picture

The previous discussion hopefully underscores that, despite rather strenuous analytical efforts and a small amount of creativity, it is *not* particularly easy to construct a fast, accurate, and defensible semi-analytic approximation of the default and migration economic-capital estimates. If it was, of course, then we might ultimately be able to avoid lengthy and computationally expensive simulation algorithms. The challenges certainly stem from the many complex non-linear relationships between the individual obligors and their characteristics. Despite these complications, we are able to offer *two* fairly defensible approximation approaches.

It should be fairly obvious, by this point, how total credit-risk economic capital is approximated. Nevertheless, for completeness, the full approximator is written as

$$\begin{aligned}\mathcal{E}_i(\alpha^*) \approx \widehat{\mathcal{E}_i(\alpha_z^*)} &= \underbrace{\sum_{k=0}^{\kappa} \hat{\xi}_k X_{i,k}^{(d)}}_{\substack{\text{Default}\\ \text{risk}}} + \underbrace{\sum_{k=0}^{\kappa} \hat{\theta}_k X_{i,k}^{(m)}}_{\substack{\text{Migration}\\ \text{risk}}}, \\ &= \widehat{\mathcal{E}_i^{(d)}(\alpha_z^*)} + \widehat{\mathcal{E}_i^{(m)}(\alpha_z^*)},\end{aligned} \tag{5.50}$$

for $i = 1, \ldots, I$. This requires two main inputs: the regression coefficients and the explanatory variables. For various downstream applications the parameters—estimated and stored daily—are readily available. Separate functions, involving a modicum of numerical integration, are available to collect the descriptive variable matrices (i.e., $X^{(d)}$ and $X^{(m)}$) as required.

Both approximations rely upon structurally motivated linear-regression estimators. This offers an important advantage: it allows us to exploit our knowledge of the underlying problem. Other choices are nonetheless possible. The presence of complex non-linear relationships strongly suggests consideration of other, perhaps more empirically motivated, techniques. The area of machine-learning, for example, offers a number of potential methods to address these features of our model. Internal assessment of popular machine-learning approaches has, in the current implementation, nevertheless been somewhat disheartening. While generally reasonable, they fail to outperform the previously presented techniques. One reason appears to relate to relatively small datasets; this is, to a certain extent, a constraint associated with the need to condition on the current portfolio structure. Another explanation is that our proposed approximators are actually rather sensible and correspondingly difficult to beat.

**Colour and Commentary 62** (ECONOMIC-CAPITAL APPROXIMATION CHOICES)*: Building a defensible and workable mathematical approximation of a complicated object is part art and part science. Numerous choices are required. The current economic-capital approximation model is no exception. At least* three *explicit strategies have been followed. First of all, separate approximation models are constructed for both default and migration effects. This enhances analytical flexibility, but roughly doubles the total amount of effort. Structurally motivated linear models, as a second point, have been employed. These high-bias (hopefully low-variance) estimators permit exploitation of model knowledge, but may ignore important non-linear elements.*[a] *Finally, and perhaps most importantly, model selection was verified over an extended time period with the consideration of both in- and out-of-sample perspectives. The combination of these three elements does not guarantee optimal approximation models—far from it—but it does represent a comprehensive framework for their defence and ultimate improvement.*

[a] There is, for example, no reason one might not be able to exploit model knowledge in the context of more flexible estimators.

### *5.5.1 A Word on Implementation*

The actual implementation of the migration and default approximation models is, after all the detailed discussion of their construction and defensibility, rather anticlimactic. Figure 5.16 summarizes the various algorithmic steps. Conceptually, the code follows the same *three* steps for each model: compute and collect the instrument (or explanatory) variables, calculate the dependent variables, and then estimate the regression coefficients. All these activities are assigned to separate functions since each requires a reasonable amount of effort. `getXDefault` and `getXMigration`, which manage the computation of response variables, perform a moderate number of numerical integrations. Moreover, the logarithmic transformations require a bit of caution.

The primary output of the approximation algorithm takes the form of two Python dictionaries: `vd` and `vm`. These two objects are populated with the default and migration economic-capital estimates, respectively. Although they usefully contain model forecasts, residuals, standard errors, test statistics and $p$ values, the most important data members are the parameters.[50] These are used extensively in

[50] In addition, all of these diagnostics are computed in both logarithmic and currency space. Although our principal focus is the currency estimates, there is useful information in both perspectives.

```
begin approximateEc
```

| | |
|---|---|
| `getXDefault`: this function collects the default instrument variables and places the result into `Xd`$\in \mathbb{R}^{n\times\kappa}$<br>`getY`: assigns the dependent variable to `Yd`$\in \mathbb{R}^{n\times 2}$; we need two dimensions to represent logarithmic and transformed currency space<br>`estimateModel`: solves multivariate regression `Yd` $= \beta_d$`Xd`$+ \varepsilon_d$ and places parameters and goodness-of-fit results into `vd` data object | DEFAULT LOGIC |
| `getXMigration`: this function collects the migration response variables and places the result into `Xm`$\in \mathbb{R}^{n\times\kappa}$<br>`getY`: assigns the dependent variable to `Ym`$\in \mathbb{R}^{n\times 2}$; the same function is employed with a different input flag<br>`estimateModel`: solves multivariate regression `Ym` $= \beta_m$`Xm`$+ \varepsilon_m$ and places parameters and goodness-of-fit results into `vm` data object; the same estimation logic (and function) used for both default and migration approximation | MIGRATION LOGIC |

**Clean-up**: Write the regression coefficients to the appropriate database

```
end approximateEc
```

**Fig. 5.16** *The EC approximation*: Using instrument variables derived from the structural elements of the default and migration computations, economic-capital is approximated using a standard OLS framework. Since a logarithmic transformation is employed and it is useful to separately predict their outcomes, the default and migration approximations are individually performed.

subsequent applications and, upon the completion of `approximateEc`, are saved into their own database table.

Having computed the approximation models, we can immediately put them to work. More complex approximation-related applications are considered in future chapters, but a small question needs to be addressed. The first application of our approximation methodologies, touches on the relationship between credit obligors and individual loans (or treasury) positions.

### 5.5.2 An Immediate Application

Credit-risk economic-capital computations operate, as previously discussed, at the risk owner level. A risk owner, to be clear, is an entity whose credit deterioration, or failure to pay, would lead to financial loss. It may be a single corporation or public institution or, in some cases, it can cover a parent company and its individual subsidiaries. While these details are important, for the purposes of this discussion, one simply needs to understand the relationship between risk-owner and individual exposures. Finding the correct terminology for this latter quantity is a challenge; we might refer to it as a trade, a transaction, an instrument, or a position. None of these is entirely satisfactory. However you wish to refer to it, it is the most atomistic element of one's portfolio. In the lending book, these are essentially loans. On the treasury side, however, this can involve a broad range of positions in various

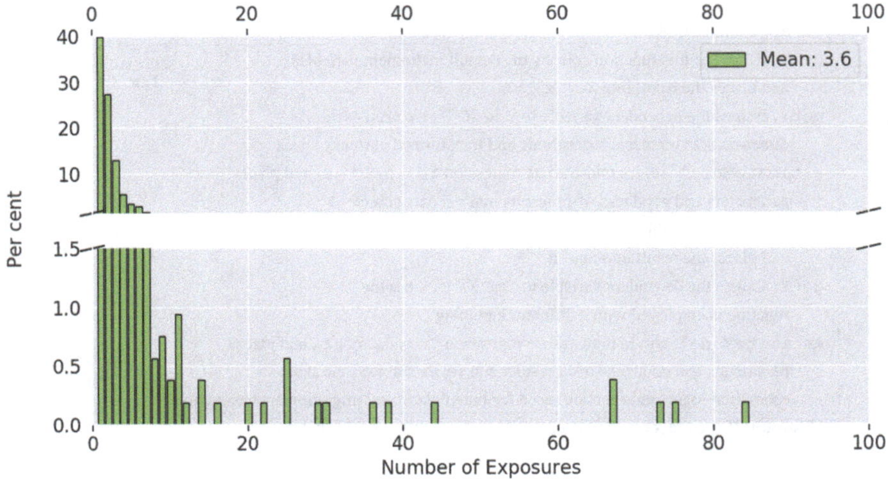


**Fig. 5.17** *Exposure counts*: Each individual risk owner has, on average, four separate individual exposures. The preceding graphic illustrates the significant dispersion around this central value. Two thirds of the portfolio's risk owners have only one or two exposures, whereas others have dramatically more.

instruments such as swaps, bonds, forward contracts, repos, or deposits. At the NIB, for lack of a better term, we use *individual exposure* (or just exposure) to refer to these elements of our portfolio.[51]

To actually compute economic capital, these individual exposures are aggregated to the risk-owner level. In recent years, our portfolio has had in the neighbourhood of 600 individual risk owners, but more than 2000 exposures implying roughly four exposures per risk owner.[52] In its base implementation, however, economic-capital is only assigned at the risk-owner level; it is, after all, at this level where default (or credit transition) occurs. This creates a small challenge. For analytic purposes, reporting, and loan-pricing activities, it is necessary to allocate the risk-owner economic capital to each of its underlying exposures.

How are these exposures distributed by risk owner? Figure 5.17 answers this question by displaying, for the usual arbitrary date in 2020, the range of exposure numbers across individual risk owners. These results are presented as a percentage of the total number of exposures. Although the mean outcome is roughly four, it varies dramatically. About two thirds of the portfolio's risk owner have only one or two exposures, whereas some have dozens. The largest number of exposures per risk owner approaches 100. These are certainly associated with treasury counterparties

[51] The reader should, of course, feel free to use (or invent) a better descriptor.

[52] Other financial institutions may have different distributions, but face the same conceptual issue.

and include a range of instruments such as swaps, deposits, and repo exposures.[53] Given the presence of netting and collateral arrangements, the sheer number of exposures, in isolation, does not tell a very useful story.[54]

Since the model does not provide any explicit guidance as to how we should allocate the overall risk-owner economic-capital to individual exposures, we need to address this ourselves. After some deliberation, a few general allocation principles were identified to guide us. More specifically, there are *three* key elements, in our view, that are required:

1. **Conservation of Mass**: Economic-capital can be neither created, nor destroyed, by the allocation procedure.
2. **Risk Proportionality**: Riskier exposures, all else equal, should receive a larger proportion of the risk allocation than their safer equivalents.
3. **Weak Positivity**: A lower bound on the exposure-level risk allocation is zero; we do *not* allocate negative economic capital to an exposure. This might appear somewhat controversial. Negative economic capital, after all, is frequently assigned in a market-risk setting. Such positions, or risk-factor exposures, can broadly be interpreted as a form of hedge. Outside of default insurance, which we have not traditionally employed, such dynamics do not appear to be sensible in the credit-risk setting.

We will employ these basic axioms to direct our choice of allocation methodology.

Some notation is now required. Let us represent risk-owner economic capital, once again, as $\mathcal{E}_i$ for $i = 1, \ldots, I$. Here we refer to the total risk-owner economic-capital allocation including both default and credit-migration effects. Our task is to attribute $\mathcal{E}_i$ to each of its $\mathrm{N}_i \geq 1$ exposures. Clearly, if $\mathrm{N}_i = 1$, this is a trivial task. If $\mathrm{N}_i = 10$, however, it will be rather less obvious how to apportion the total economic capital.

Whatever approach one selects, it is basically a weighting problem. Practically, therefore, any allocation algorithm can be described as

$$\mathcal{E}_{ij} = \omega_{ij}\mathcal{E}_i, \tag{5.51}$$

where $\mathcal{E}_{ij}$ is the $j$th exposure's allocation of the $i$th risk-owner's economic capital. $\omega_{ij}$ is the weight of the $j$th exposure to the $i$th risk owner. These weights need to be identified. In other words, the entire exercise is about finding sensible $\omega$'s.

The good news is that we may now employ our previously described principles to identify reasonable $\omega$ choices. The conversation-of-mass axiom, for example, can be translated into a requirement that the full risk-owner level economic capital (i.e.,

[53] In some large institutions, there may be thousands of exposures with a single risk-owner.

[54] This question is addressed in detail in Chap. 10.

$\mathcal{E}_i$) is assigned to the exposures. Mathematically, this amounts to

$$\begin{aligned} \mathcal{E}_i &= \sum_{j=1}^{\mathrm{N}_i} \mathcal{E}_{ij}, \\ &= \sum_{j=1}^{\mathrm{N}_i} \underbrace{\omega_{ij}\mathcal{E}_i}_{\substack{\text{Equation}\\ 5.51}}, \\ &= \mathcal{E}_i \underbrace{\sum_{j=1}^{\mathrm{N}_i} \omega_{ij}}_{\substack{\text{Our}\\ \text{choice}}}, \end{aligned} \tag{5.52}$$

which implies that we merely require that

$$\sum_{j=1}^{\mathrm{N}_i} \omega_{ij} = 1, \tag{5.53}$$

for $i = 1, \ldots, I$. Quite simply, the condition in Eq. 5.53 ensures that the total economic-capital amount is assigned.

If we define $\mathcal{R}_{ij}$ as the riskiness of the $j$th exposure associated with the $i$th risk-owner, then we also require that:

$$\mathcal{R}_{ij} \geq \mathcal{R}_{ik} \Rightarrow \omega_{ij} \geq \omega_{ik}. \tag{5.54}$$

for all $j, k = 1, .., \mathrm{N}_i$. A riskier exposure receives a greater economic-capital allocation; this addresses the risk-proportionality principle. Our final axiom, which deals with weak positivity, implies that the individual weights must respect:

$$\omega_{ij} \in [0, 1], \tag{5.55}$$

for all $j = 1, \ldots, \mathrm{N}_i$ and $i = 1, \ldots, I$.

The three conditions in Eqs. 5.53 to 5.55 provide us with all that we require to write a concrete expression for our individual weights. The weights must be positive, sum to unity, and respect our risk ordering. The following expression is consistent with all of these constraints:

$$\omega_{ij} = \frac{\max\left(\mathcal{R}_{ij}, 0\right)}{\sum_{k=1}^{N_i} \max\left(\mathcal{R}_{ik}, 0\right)} \tag{5.56}$$

The only element that is missing is a choice of risk assessment. There exist a number of possibilities—such as the total exposure or market value—but there is already an obvious candidate. In the previous sections, a detailed description of the default and migration economic-capital approximations was provided. These would appear to be a highly sensible choice for each individual $\mathcal{R}_{ij}$ assessment. More specifically, using Eq. 5.50, we require that

$$\begin{aligned} \mathcal{R}_{ij} &= \overbrace{\underbrace{\sum_{k=0}^{\kappa} \hat{\xi}_k X_{ij,k}^{(d)}}_{\substack{\text{Default}\\ \text{risk}}} + \underbrace{\sum_{k=0}^{\kappa} \hat{\theta}_k X_{ij,k}^{(m)}}_{\substack{\text{Migration}\\ \text{risk}}}}^{\widehat{\mathcal{E}_{ij}(\alpha_z^*)}}, \\ &= \widehat{\mathcal{E}_{ij}^{(d)}}(\alpha_z^*) + \widehat{\mathcal{E}_{ij}^{(m)}}(\alpha_z^*). \end{aligned} \tag{5.57}$$

In short, we first compute the necessary instrument variables for each $i$th risk owner and $j = 1, \ldots, N_i$ exposures. We then use our regression coefficients to produce associated migration and default economic-capital estimates; this serves admirably as a consistent measure of position risk for our allocation algorithm.[55]

**Colour and Commentary 63** (EXPOSURE-LEVEL ALLOCATION)*: Since default and migration occur at the risk-owner level, they must be computed and allocated from a risk-owner perspective. Economic-capital allocations—for a variety of practical applications—are nonetheless required at the*

(continued)

[55] Our estimation algorithms are indifferent as to whether they are performed at the risk-obligor or instrument level. One need only be able to compute the necessary explanatory variables. We can also, should we so desire, separately allocate default and migration economic capital.

**Colour and Commentary 63** (continued)
*individual exposure level.*[a] *A downgrade or a default will impact all of a risk-owner's underlying exposures, albeit in potentially different ways.*[b] *In other words, not all exposures possess the same risk profile and, as a consequence, assignment of risk-owner economic-capital is not an uninteresting and routine task. Identifying three commonsensical principles governing this operation and, leaning heavily on our approximation models, an internally consistent methodology is presented. We can see that our extensive effort to construct a reasonable economic-capital estimator is already bearing fruit.*

[a] Individual exposure is a potentially confusing term. As a trade, transaction, position, or instrument, it refers to the most atomistic elements of our portfolio.

[b] Different loans, for example, may exhibit differences in guarantees or collateral thus influencing loss-given-default values.

## 5.6 Wrapping Up

After having gone to such lengths to construct a functioning simulation-based engine for our credit-risk economic-capital model in Chap. 4, it is somewhat peculiar to immediately allocate an entire chapter towards finding semi-closed-form analytic approximations of the same object. The driving reason is speed. Even with clever use of parallel-processing and variance-reduction techniques, we cannot produce credit-risk economic capital estimates in seconds.[56] Certain applications, however, demand rapidity. On one hand, it is necessary to perform timely and flexible loan-pricing computations. Loan origination, as a fundamental activity, simply cannot operate without the ability to quickly consider a multitude of lending options. On the other hand, some endeavours (such as stress-testing) involve a huge scale of calculation that cannot be handled at simulation-model speeds. Whatever the reason, there is a clear demand for a reasonably accurate, instrument-level, fast, semi-analytical approximation of both default and migration economic capital. Their construction is tedious, time-consuming, and we are ultimately never entirely satisfied with their performance. The effort is nonetheless worthwhile. Our investment in this chapter—which has already found one small application—will pay generous dividends as we turn to various economic-capital applications in the forthcoming discussion and analysis.

[56] Even doing so in a small number of minutes is, for a reasonable price, almost impossible.

## References


1. M. Bellalah, M. Zouari, A. Sahli, and H. Miniaoui. Concentration measures in risk management. *International Journal of Business*, 20(2):110–127, 2015.
2. BIS. The internal ratings-based approach. Technical report, Bank for International Settlements, January 2001.
3. BIS. International convergence of capital measurement and capital standards: A revised framework. Technical report, Bank for International Settlements, January 2004.
4. BIS. An explanatory note on the Basel II IRB risk weight functions. Technical report, Bank for International Settlements, July 2005.
5. D. J. Bolder. *Credit-Risk Modelling: Theoretical Foundations, Diagnostic Tools, Practical Examples, and Numerical Recipes in Python*. Springer-Nature, Heidelberg, Germany, 2018.
6. D. J. Bolder. Statistics and Machine-Learning: Variations on a Theme. In P. Nymand-Andersen, editor, *Data Science in Economics and Finance for Decision Makers*. Risk Books, 2021.
7. D. J. Bolder and T. Rubin. Optimization in a Simulation Setting: Use of Function Approximation in Debt-Strategy Analysis. Bank of Canada: Working Paper 2007-13, February 2007.
8. L. Breiman. Statistical Modeling: The Two Cultures. *Statistical Science*, 16(3):199–231, 2001.
9. S. Emmer and D. Tasche. Calculating credit risk capital charges with the one-factor model. Technical report, Deutsche Bundesbank, January 2005.
10. S. Figini and P. Uberti. Concentration measures in risk management. *The Journal of the Operational Research Society*, 64(5):718–723, May 2013.
11. S. Geisser. The predictive sample reuse method with applications. *Journal of the American Statistical Association*, 70(350):320–328, 1975.
12. G. H. Golub and C. F. V. Loan. *Matrix Computations*. The John Hopkins University Press, Baltimore, Maryland, 2012.
13. M. B. Gordy. A risk-factor model foundation for ratings-based bank capital rules. *Journal of Financial Intermediation*, 12:199–232, 2003.
14. M. B. Gordy and E. Lütkebohmert. Granularity Adjustment for Basel II. Deutsche Bundesbank, Banking and Financial Studies, No 01-2007, January 2007.
15. M. B. Gordy and E. Lütkebohmert. Granularity adjustment for regulatory capital assessment. University of Freiburg, January 2013.
16. T. Hastie, R. Tibshirani, and J. Friedman. *The Elements of Statistical Learning: Data Mining, Inference and Prediction*. Springer-Verlag, New York, first edition, 2001.
17. G. James, D. Witten, T. Hastie, and R. Tibshirani. *An Introduction to Statistical Learning*. Springer-Verlag, New York, first edition, 2013.
18. I. T. Jollliffe. *Principal Component Analysis*. Springer, New York, New York, 2002.
19. G. G. Judge, W. Griffiths, R. C. Hill, H. Lütkepohl, and T.-C. Lee. *The Theory and Practice of Econometrics*. John Wiley and Sons, New York, New York, second edition, 1985.
20. E. Lütkebohmert. *Concentration Risk in Credit Portfolios*. Springer Verlag, Berlin, 2008.
21. R. J. Martin and T. Wilde. Unsystematic credit risk. *Risk*, pages 123–128, November 2002.
22. B. Milanovic. The Gini-type functions: An alternative derivation. *Bulletin of Economic Research*, 46(1):81–89, 1994.
23. M. Pykhtin. Multi-factor adjustment. *Risk*, (3):85–90, March 2004.
24. A. Ralston and P. Rabinowitz. *A First Course in Numerical Analysis*. Dover Publications, Mineola, New York, second edition, 1978.
25. T. Ribarits, A. Clement, H. Seppälä, H. Bai, and S.-H. Poon. Economic Capital Modeling: Closed form approximation for real-time applications. European Investment Bank and Manchester University, June 2014.
26. M. Stone. Cross-validatory choice and assessment of statistical predictions. *Journal of the Royal Statistical Society. Series B (Methodological)*, 36(2):111–147, 1974.

27. B. Torell. Name concentration risk and pillar 2 compliance: The granularity adjustment. Technical report, Royal Institute of Technology, Stockholm, Sweden, January 2013.
28. O. A. Vasicek. Limiting loan loss probability distribution. KMV Corporation, August 1991.
29. S. Yitzhaki and I. Olkin. Concentration indices and concentration cures. *Stochastic Orders and Decision under Risk*, IMS Lecture Notes – Monograph Series 1991.

# Chapter 6
# Loan Pricing

*Look beneath the surface; let not the several quality of a thing nor its worth escape thee.*

*(Marcus Aurelius)*

Loan origination is the lifeblood of any lending institution. This activity involves an enormous range of complicated and difficult qualitative elements that go far beyond any financial modelling discussion.[1] It should be evident, by this point in the proceedings, that the ideas discussed in this book are ill-equipped to tackle the non-technical aspects of loan origination. Skipping over these important—and not-to-be-ignored details—we will focus on the aspect where quantitative tools can add value: the lending decision point. When faced with a potential loan proposal, a lending institution ultimately has to determine to extend credit or not. From a quantitative perspective, it is immensely useful to conceptualize the possible addition of each individual loan to one's portfolio as a distinct investment decision or project. This allows us to frame this choice within a wider framework of very useful ideas in corporate finance and risk management.

Informing investment decisions is a fundamental branch of the corporate-finance literature.[2] Sometimes more broadly referred to as capital budgeting, it addresses the central question of how a firm should prioritize the allocation of its assets to risky, but potentially profit-generating activities. Brealey et al. [11] describe it as the answer to the following question:

> [H]ow much should the firm invest, and what specific assets should the firm invest in?

This is necessarily very broad. Taking a medium to long-term perspective, typical examples include whether or not to build a new manufacturing facility, trial a new drug, or develop a new product brand. This idea applies equally well to potential

[1] The reader is directed to EBA [16] for an interesting (and timely) dip into these conceptual waters.

[2] There are literally too many references to effectively cite. There is a deep and extensive discussion ranging from a 50-year chestnut in Mao [26] to the standard textbook treatment found in Peterson and Fabozzi [31].

 
D. Bolder, *Modelling Economic Capital*, Contributions to Finance and Accounting,
https://doi.org/10.1007/978-3-030-95096-5_6

mergers and acquisitions. While the possible variations are endless, it is not terribly difficult to see how the loan decision fits into this broad mould. Each loan spans a reasonable amount of time, consumes a firm's scarce resources and any decision can, quite possibly, crowd out other lending prospects. A clear and consistent approach is thus required to rank various lending options and ultimately ensure that good lending decisions are taken.

The lending institution, as is often the case in capital budgeting, has limited power over the circumstances surrounding lending decisions.[3] When granting a loan, the Bank has no appreciable control over the firm's current creditworthiness, its competitors, its operating environment nor over the future development of economic conditions. It does, however, control some aspects. A lending institution can, within reason, exert some influence on the term, the pricing, and the convenants of the loan. These are the basic parameters of a lending institution's capital-budgeting activity.

We will, in this chapter, operationalize the lender's control, or choice, variable as the magnitude of its lending margins.[4] In short, every financial institution requires a holistic approach towards setting sensible lending margins (i.e., prices)—for all of its stakeholders—for each loan that it extends to a credit obligor. This is a particularly challenging task for, at least, *three* reasons. A loan price:

1. has to cover the institution's costs including a required return on capital;
2. must be broadly consistent with market prices; and
3. has to be consistent with the institution's mandate or strategy.

Every financial institution thus needs to walk a fine line between cost recovery, market consistency, and strategic direction. Figure 6.1 provides a schematic description of this challenge. Costs, to be clear, need to be defined in a larger sense. They naturally need to include funding costs, administration expenses, and expected credit losses. Loans also need to be priced to recover the cost of capital allocated to them. If this is not the case, then eventually loan activity will need to be curtailed. This links the pricing of a given loan closely to its consumption of capital as well as the balance-sheet composition of the institution. Indeed, as will soon become evident, the simple question of accepting or rejecting a loan proposal encompasses almost every aspect of the lending institution's structure.

The principal objective of this chapter is to describe the conceptual framework underlying NIB's loan-pricing methodology in significant detail; this development will, nonetheless, apply more generally to a broad range of financial institutions. We will begin with some fundamental notions associated with asset pricing; this will provide us with the necessary machinery for the construction of loan-pricing

[3] This may be hard to believe for a reader having struggled to get a mortgage loan, but this point is quite true in commercial lending.

[4] It is, as we'll see, broader than just the lending margin. Tenor, for example, is also quite important. Lending margin, however, is a useful one-dimensional description of the principal lever in the lending decision.

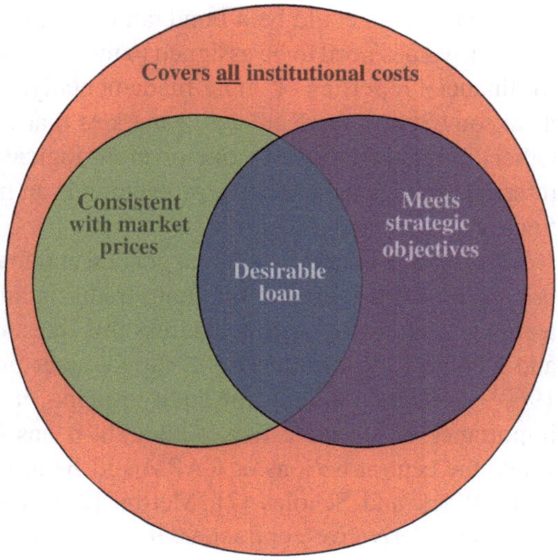


**Fig. 6.1** *Key lending criteria*: This picture displays, in a simplified and schematic manner, the three key criteria involved in identifying a desirable loan: cost recovery, market consistency, and strategic relevance. Finding the intersection of all three elements is often challenging.

expressions. The next step involves a close look at the lender's balance-sheet. This provides insight into the interlinkages between assets, liabilities, and equity. Ultimately, the lessons learned in this section will permit us to confidently estimate the financing costs associated with an arbitrary loan transaction. The final sections handle the fine print of marrying notions of risk and return within the context of the firm's capital structure.

The end product is a risk-adjusted return measure that seeks to (fairly) inform the appropriate choice of lending margin (i.e., price). One can think of this as a common yardstick, or benchmark, permitting impartial comparison between disparate loan proposals, thereby supporting the capital-budgeting process. To do this sensibly requires both the incorporation of various specialized pricing features and explicit links back to the institution's strategic objectives and economic-capital framework. While helpful and centrally important, it bears repeating that this analysis captures only the quantitative dimension of the lending decision. Numerous other qualitative factors enter into these decisions that, although not addressed in this chapter, play a central role in this process. Returning to Fig. 6.1, this chapter will have much to say about the outer circle, but rather little to add regarding the important inner circles touching on market conditions and strategic objectives.

## 6.1 Some Fundamentals

People have been valuing assets as long as assets have existed. Barter and trade would hardly be possible absent such practice; our focus, however, is on financial assets. Consider some arbitrary contingent claim; an asset whose value depends (i.e., is contingent) upon the realization of some future (unknown) financial-market event (or events). This could be a bond, an equity, a deposit or some form of derivative product. Values need to be assigned to these assets. Said valuation might be required for financial reporting or, more fundamentally, because we wish to sell or purchase it. In some cases, there are active markets that can be used to determine this value. Other times, we must take one or more logical steps to infer a valuation. This is referred to as the asset-pricing problem; it is an important sub-field of mathematical finance.

Our focus is financial assets in general and loan contracts in particular. The loan-pricing problem falls into this long tradition and the finance literature is literally teeming with useful tools to address this question.[5] Treynor [39], Sharpe [33, 34] and Lintner [25] introduced the capital-asset pricing model (CAPM) in the early 1960's. Designed mainly for equity pricing, it clearly illustrates the fundamental importance of systemic risk. Although, it has been twisted and revised over the years, the central notions of CAPM still lie at the heart of many modern financial tools. Black and Scholes [7], Merton [28], and Vasicek [40] ushered in the era of modern derivative-contract asset-pricing in the early to mid 1970's. Exploiting the notions of arbitrage and market completeness, and using continuous time mathematics, this work set the stage for most current valuation models. In the economics literature, conversely, general equilibrium approaches are used (mostly in theoretical settings) for price determination.[6]

Although our application is less complex than many pricing problems, it still fits into the general asset-valuation framework. As a consequence, this framework sets the stage for the subsequent discussion. Let us introduce these ideas in the context of pricing a risk-free bond. Ultimately, once you peel away all the details, pricing involves the discounting of cash-flows. This case is no exception. Managing the book-keeping of these cash-flows, however, requires organization and clarity. Pinching some common, but useful, notation from Brigo and Mercurio [12], we can establish some important basic quantities.

Many commercial loans have amortized notional repayment schedules, which implies a need to be quite cautious about the outstanding amounts on payment dates. To sort this out, let $\beta$ denote the total number of payment dates and define the notional payment schedule as

$$\left\{-N_0, N_1, N_2, \cdots, N_\beta\right\}, \tag{6.1}$$

for payment dates $\left\{t \equiv T_0, T_1, T_2, \cdots, T_\beta \equiv T\right\}$ where $-N_0$ is the initial disbursement. We define

$$X_i = \sum_{j=i}^{\beta} N_j, \tag{6.2}$$

[5] It's hard to be entirely definitive, but modern asset pricing probably started with Williams [41].

[6] See Mas-Colell et al. [27, Part IV] for more on this important, but complex question.

as the notional between the $(i-1)$th and $i$th payment dates.[7] $X_i$ thus denotes the outstanding loan amount associated with the $i$th payment.

Let us further write $c_i$ as the coupon rate for the $i$th payment date.[8] The (ex-disbursement) loan cash-flow stream would look something like:

$$\left\{\underbrace{c_1X_1 + N_1}_{\substack{\text{Coupon and}\\ \text{Principal}}}, c_2X_2 + N_2, \cdots, c_\beta X_\beta + N_\beta\right\}, \tag{6.3}$$

where

$$c_i = \underbrace{\Delta(T_{i-1}, T_i)}_{\Delta_i} K_i. \tag{6.4}$$

$K_i$ is the $i$th coupon rate and $\Delta_i \equiv \Delta(T_{i-1}, T_i)$ is the day-count convention.[9] Understanding the cash-flow stream, three challenges immediately arise. First, the coupon element must be represented in a less vague manner to provide insight into the lending margins. Second, we need to determine how to actually discount these future values back to the current time. Finally, it will be necessary to incorporate the potential for credit default. Let's examine each in turn.

The first challenge is easy to handle. Our loans—as is the case with many international financial institutions—typically pay a floating-rate coupon based on a reference index.[10] When $K_i \neq K$—that is, the coupon is not a fixed rate—then we have that

$$K_i = \underbrace{L(T_{i-1}, T_i)}_{L_i} + m, \tag{6.5}$$

where $L_i$ is a—typically six-month—LIBOR tenor and $m$ is a lending spread or margin. With the advent of reference-rate reform—see, for example, Hou and Skeie [20], Duffie and Stein [15], or Bailey [5]—the structure of the LIBOR is changing.[11] Conceptually, however, the notion of some common underlying reference rate will not. We can, therefore, think of $L_i$ as a generic floating reference rate; currently, it is

[7] During the grace period, where the loan outstanding does not change, the associated $N$ values can naturally be zero.

[8] Strictly speaking, the term *coupon* should be used exclusively with bonds, not loans. Old habits, and expressions, nevertheless die hard. The reader should feel free to replace the term "coupon" with *interest-rate payment* as desired.

[9] This is the concrete representation of the number of days between payment dates used to determine the magnitude of the cash-flow.

[10] There is the possibility of providing fixed-rate loans to lending clients, but these would be swapped back to floating anyway.

[11] Moreover, by the publication of this book, it will certainly have been replaced.

traditional LIBOR, in the future it will take an alternative (but conceptually similar) form.

The second challenge involves, in principle, a huge amount of finance theory. Pricing a loan-commitment might look like the simple discounted sum of cash-flows, but a startling amount of complexity is lurking just under the surface. We will not grapple with all of it, but some of it will be necessary for our purposes. Formally, the price of any contingent claim can, on the probability space, $(\Omega, \mathcal{F}, \mathbb{P})$, be written as its expectation taken with respect to the equivalent martingale measure, $\mathbb{Q}$.[12] This is quite a mouthful, but it is the result of a significant amount of practical and theoretical research.[13]. The consequence is that the price of our loan may be written as,

$$
\begin{aligned}
\mathbb{E}^{\mathbb{Q}}\left(P \middle| \mathcal{F}_t\right) &= \mathbb{E}^{\mathbb{Q}}\left(\sum_{i=1}^{\beta}\left(\underbrace{\Delta_i(L_i+m)X_i}_{\text{Coupon}} + N_i\right)e^{-\int_t^{T_i} r_u du}\middle| \mathcal{F}_t\right), \qquad (6.6)\\
&= \sum_{i=1}^{\beta}\mathbb{E}^{\mathbb{Q}}\left(\left(\Delta_i(L_i+m)X_i + N_i\right)e^{-\int_t^{T_i} r_u du}\middle| \mathcal{F}_t\right),\\
&= \sum_{i=1}^{\beta}\underbrace{\mathbb{E}^{\mathbb{Q}^{T_i}}\left(\left(\Delta_i(L_i+m)X_i + N_i\right)\middle| \mathcal{F}_t\right)P(t,T_i)}_{\text{Björk [6, Proposition 19.12]}},\\
&= \sum_{i=1}^{\beta}\left(\Delta_i\left(F(t,T_{i-1},T_i)+m\right)X_i + N_i\right)\underbrace{P(t,T_i)}_{\delta_i},\\
P_t &= \underbrace{\sum_{i=1}^{\beta}\Delta_i\left(F(t,T_{i-1},T_i)+m\right)X_i\delta_i}_{\text{Coupons}} + \underbrace{\sum_{i=1}^{\beta}N_i\delta_i}_{\text{Principal}},
\end{aligned}
$$

where $r_t$ denotes the instantaneous, risk-free, short-term interest rate at time $t$. This requires some unpacking.[14] Much of Eq. 6.6—such as notional amounts, spreads,

[12] We further assume that this (transformed) measure is induced with the money-market account as the choice of numeraire asset. This is typically generically referred to as the risk-neutral measure.

[13] See Harrison and Kreps [18], Harrison and Pliska [19], and Duffie [13] for foundational discussion on asset-pricing theory.

[14] The measure $\mathbb{Q}^{T_i}$ is induced with the zero-coupon bond with maturity $T_i$ as the choice of numeraire asset. This is typically referred to as the forward measure; see, for example, Brigo and Mercurio [12, Section 2.5] or Björk [6, Chapter 19]. Implicitly, there is a change-of-measure from $\mathbb{Q}$ to $\mathbb{Q}^{T_i}$; this is accomplished with none other than the Radon-Nikodym derivative, $\frac{d\mathbb{Q}^{T_i}}{d\mathbb{Q}}$. This clever choice of numeraire allows us to simplify dramatically our integrands by separating out the dependent instantaneous short rate, $r$, and the LIBOR rate, $L_i$.

and day-count fractions—is deterministic. These values are constant under the expectation operator. The only random variables are the future LIBOR rates and the path of the instantaneous risk-free, short rate. The (forward-measure) expectation of future LIBOR is written as,

$$\mathbb{E}^{\mathbb{Q}^{T_i}}\left(L_i \middle| \mathcal{F}_t\right) \equiv \mathbb{E}^{\mathbb{Q}^{T_i}}\left(L(T_{i-1}, T_i) \middle| \mathcal{F}_t\right) = F(t, T_{i-1}, T_i), \tag{6.7}$$

where $F(t, \tau, T)$ denotes the forward interest rate prevailing at time $t$ for a contract starting at time $\tau \geq t$ with a tenor $T - \tau$.[15] In plain English, therefore, this confirms the common practice of using implied forward rates to represent (unknown) future LIBOR rates when generating loan cash-flows. The following quantity is another well-known character in asset-pricing circles,

$$\delta_i \equiv P(t, T_i) \equiv \delta(t, T_i) = \mathbb{E}_t^{\mathbb{Q}}\left(e^{-\int_t^{T_i} r_u du}\right). \tag{6.8}$$

Depending on your perspective and preferences, this might be referred to as the pure-discount bond price, an Arrow-Debreu security, or the pricing kernel. For the purposes of loan pricing, we will unceremoniously refer to it as the discount factor.[16]

The important takeaway from this unprovoked application of financial theory is a pricing relationship that is on firm ground. We may replace unknown future LIBOR outcomes with the implied forward rates extracted from the swap curve and discount future cash-flows using the risk-free overnight-index-swap (OIS) interest rate.[17]

**Colour and Commentary 64** (RISK-FREE PRICING)*: Every student who has taken a base course in finance is aware that the price of a risk-free, fixed-income security is simply the discounted sum of its cash-flows. The theoretical foundations of this general approach are often less well understood. There is a random element to both the magnitude and form of future cash-flows and their associated discount factors. More formally, the price of a fixed-income security is characterized as its* expected *discounted cash-flows under the appropriate pricing measure discounted at the risk-free interest rate. Both quantities must be inferred from the financial market. In the loan-pricing setting, this reduces to a replacement of (unknown) future LIBOR rates with*

(continued)

[15] Brigo and Mercurio [12] provide much more background and detail on this point.

[16] An Arrow-Debreu security is, of course, rather more general; this would be a special case. See Arrow and Debreu [3] for the gory details.

[17] OIS discounting remains a relatively recent practice and is (probably) poised to change somewhat with the advent of reference-rate reform. See Hull and White [21] for a discussion of its origins.

**Colour and Commentary 64** (continued)
*implied forward rates and discounting with risk-free rates.*[a] *This may feel like financial semantics, but appreciating this aspect is central to placing our upcoming risk-adjusted return calculation on a sound theoretical footing.*

[a] Overnight-interest-rate swaps rates, while not entirely risk-free, are generally employed as an acceptable proxy.

If there was no possibility of default from the loan obligor, we would be done. Default is possible, of course, so it cannot be ignored. Following Jeanblanc [23], we can explicitly introduce the default time $\tau$ as a positive-valued random-variable defined on the probability space, $(\Omega, \mathcal{F}, \mathbb{Q})$. You can think of it as a random future time. Defining $t$ as the current time and $T$ as the loan's terminal date, then default occurs if $\tau \in (t, T]$. Practically, therefore, this random default time shows up in pricing formulae as the following indicator variable,

$$\mathbb{I}_{\tau>T} = \begin{cases} 1 : \tau > T \text{ (or survival to } T) \\ 0 : \tau \leq T \text{ (or default prior to } T) \end{cases}. \tag{6.9}$$

This a useful object taking the value of one if default occurs over $(t, T]$ and zero otherwise. It is the main tool for the incorporation of default into pricing logic.

Making generous use of Eq. 6.6—and leaning on the theoretical background from Duffie and Singleton [14] and Bluhm et al. [8]—we can re-write our pricing expression—without expectation—as,

$$P = \underbrace{\sum_{i=1}^{\beta} \mathbb{I}_{\tau>T_i} \left( \Delta_i \left( L_i + m \right) X_i + N_i \right) e^{-\int_t^{T_i} r(u)du}}_{\text{Conditional interest and principal payments}} + \underbrace{R(\tau)X(\tau)e^{-\int_t^{\tau} r(u)du}}_{\text{Conditional default recovery}}, \tag{6.10}$$

where $R \equiv R(\tau)$ is the amount of the defaulted loan one expects to recover. Default conditionality has now been introduced.

The remaining effort involves computation, as done in Eq. 6.6, of the $\mathbb{Q}$-expectation of Eq. 6.10. This requires a few assumptions. The first, common choice is to assume that $\tau$ and $r(t)$ are independent. That is, that the default event does not depend upon risk-free interest rates.[18] This means that we can readily evaluate

[18] The link between short-term interest rates, the business cycle, and default probabilities probably argues against this decision. For simplicity of pricing, however, it is probably best to avoid this potential rabbit hole of complex economic relationships.

Eq. 6.10 as

$$
\begin{aligned}
\mathbb{E}_t^{\mathbb{Q}}(P) &= \mathbb{E}_t^{\mathbb{Q}}\left(\sum_{i=1}^{\beta} \mathbb{I}_{\tau>T_i}\left(\Delta_i\left(L_i+m\right)X_i+N_i\right)e^{-\int_t^{T_i} r(u)du}\right. \\
&\quad \left. + R(\tau)X(\tau)e^{-\int_t^{\tau} r(u)du}\right), \qquad (6.11) \\
&= \sum_{i=1}^{\beta} \mathbb{E}_t^{\mathbb{Q}}\left(\mathbb{I}_{\tau>T_i}\left(\Delta_i\left(L_i+m\right)X_i+N_i\right)e^{-\int_t^{T_i} r(u)du}\right) \\
&\quad + \mathbb{E}_t^{\mathbb{Q}}\left(R(\tau)X(\tau)e^{-\int_t^{\tau} r(u)du}\right), \\
&= \sum_{i=1}^{\beta} \underbrace{\mathbb{E}_t^{\mathbb{Q}}\left(\mathbb{I}_{\tau>T_i}\right)\cdot \mathbb{E}_t^{\mathbb{Q}}\left(\left(\Delta_i\left(L_i+m\right)X_i+N_i\right)e^{-\int_t^{T_i} r(u)du}\right)}_{\text{By independence}} \\
&\quad + \mathbb{E}_t^{\mathbb{Q}}\left(R(\tau)X(\tau)e^{-\int_t^{\tau} r(u)du}\right), \\
&= \sum_{i=1}^{\beta} \mathbb{Q}(\tau>T_i)\underbrace{\left(\Delta_i\left(F(t,T_{i-1},T_i)+m\right)X_i+N_i\right)\underbrace{P(t,T_i)}_{\delta_i}}_{\text{Equation 6.6}} \\
&\quad + \mathbb{E}_t^{\mathbb{Q}}\left(R(\tau)X(\tau)e^{-\int_t^{\tau} r(u)du}\right), \\
&= \underbrace{\sum_{i=1}^{\beta} \left(\Delta_i\left(F(t,T_{i-1},T_i)+m\right)X_i+N_i\right)\overbrace{\delta_i\mathbb{Q}(\tau>T_i)}^{\tilde{\delta}_i}}_{\text{Regular cash-flows}} \\
&\quad + \underbrace{\mathbb{E}_t^{\mathbb{Q}}\left(R(\tau)X(\tau)e^{-\int_t^{\tau} r(u)du}\right)}_{\text{Recovery}},
\end{aligned}
$$

where we use $\mathbb{E}_t^{\mathbb{Q}}(\cdot) \equiv \mathbb{E}^{\mathbb{Q}}(\cdot|\mathcal{F}_t)$ to (slightly) ease the notation. Equation 6.11 looks qualitatively quite similar to the risk-free setting summarized in Eq. 6.6. There are *two* main differences: the discount factors have an alternative form and there is an ugly recovery expression hanging around at the end.

The discount factors are the easiest to explain. From first principles, we have that

$$\begin{aligned}\mathbb{Q}(\mathbb{I}_{\tau>T_i}) &= \underbrace{\mathbb{Q}(\tau > T_i)}_{S(T_i)},\\ &= 1 - \underbrace{\mathbb{Q}(\tau \leq T_i)}_{F_\tau(T_i)},\end{aligned} \tag{6.12}$$

where risk-neutral $S(T_i)$ and $\mathbb{Q}(\tau \leq T_i)$ represent the survival and default probabilities, respectively.[19] The survival probability is, of course, a number between zero and 1. If $S(T) = 0.9$, then we would conclude that there is a 90% probability of survival between $t$ and $T$. It works much like a discount factor. If we take the product of a survival probability and risk-free discount factors yield, we get the following, very useful, object

$$\tilde{\delta}_i \equiv \tilde{\delta}(t, T_i) = \underbrace{\delta(t, T_i)}_{\delta_i} S(T_i). \tag{6.13}$$

This is referred to as the credit-risk-adjusted discount factor. It is quite intuitive. If the survival probabilities are always and everywhere equal to one, then we recover the risk-free discount rates. If they all take the value of zero, conversely, the security has no value. Under normal circumstances, their values are not so extreme. Instead, in the context of Eq. 6.13, they act as a modifier to the risk-free discount rate. They push down the discount function in a manner directly proportionate to the credit risk of the obligor.[20]

The final, less obvious term, in Eq. 6.11 requires a bit of algebraic wrestling. Making a few assumptions and recalling the basic principles of statistical distributions, it is accurately approximated as

$$\begin{aligned}\mathbb{E}_t^{\mathbb{Q}}\left(R(\tau)X(\tau)e^{-\int_t^\tau r(u)du}\right) &= \int_t^T R(u)X(u)\overbrace{e^{-\int_t^u r(v)dv}}^{\delta(t,u)} f_\tau(u)du,\\ &= \underbrace{\sum_{i=1}^{\beta}\int_{T_{i-1}}^{T_i} R(u)X(u)\delta(t,u)f_\tau(u)du,}_{\text{Partition the integral range}}\end{aligned} \tag{6.14}$$

[19] $F_\tau(\cdot)$ denotes the cumulative distribution function of $\tau$. The default probability is, by its very form, equivalent to this (as-yet-unspecified) function of $\tau$.

[20] Indeed, one can think of the difference between the risk-free and survival rates as a kind of representation of the individual firm's credit spread.

$$\approx \underbrace{\sum_{i=1}^{\beta} R \int_{T_{i-1}}^{T_i} X(u)\delta(t,u) f_\tau(u) du}_{\text{Assume constant recovery}},$$

$$\approx \underbrace{\sum_{i=1}^{\beta} R X_i \delta_i \int_{T_{i-1}}^{T_i} F'_\tau(u) du}_{\substack{\text{Constant exposure and discount}\\ \text{factor on each sub-interval}}},$$

$$\approx \sum_{i=1}^{\beta} R X_i \delta_i \bigg( F_\tau(T_i) - F_\tau(T_{i-1}) \bigg),$$

$$\approx \sum_{i=1}^{\beta} R X_i \delta_i \underbrace{\bigg( \mathbb{Q}(\tau \leq T_i) - \mathbb{Q}(\tau \leq T_{i-1}) \bigg)}_{\text{Equation 6.12}},$$

$$\approx \sum_{i=1}^{\beta} R X_i \delta_i \mathbb{Q}\bigg( \tau \in [T_{i-1}, T_i] \bigg).$$

This approximation has a very practical form; it permits us to write the recovery aspect as a simple product of recovery rates, exposures, risk-free discount factors, and risk-neutral default probabilities.[21]

Gathering all of the details together, we arrive at the final product. The (risk-neutral) expectation of a floating-rate loan obligation can be approximated as,

$$\mathbb{E}_t^{\mathbb{Q}}(P) \equiv P_t \approx \sum_{i=1}^{\beta} \underbrace{\left( \Delta_i \bigg( F(t, T_{i-1}, T_i) + m \bigg) X_i + N_i \right) \tilde{\delta}_i}_{\text{Discounted (risky) expected cash-flows}} + \underbrace{R X_i \mathbb{Q}\bigg( \tau \in [T_{i-1}, T_i] \bigg) \delta_i}_{\text{Expected recovery}}. \tag{6.15}$$

The logic is that the individual cash-flows are discounted at a rate that reflects the creditworthiness of the underlying obligor. It also includes a conditional amount for the recovery of any funds in the event of default.

---

[21] It is common, at this point in most default-risk pricing discussions, to place some additional structure onto the survival probabilities. This involves the (very useful) notion of the hazard function. For our purposes, however, this quantity will not be required. The interested reader is referred to Taylor and Karlin [38, Chapter 1] or Stuart and Ord [37, Section 5.34] for more background on hazard functions.

This is not quite the end of the story. Equation 6.15 can also be (usefully) written in an alternative, but equivalent form. We could discount the cash-flows, without any notion of default, as in Eq. 6.6. If we did that, however, we would have to subtract off the expected credit loss and then, as before, add back the expected recovery. Let's try this with Eq. 6.15,

$$\begin{aligned} P_t &\approx \sum_{i=1}^{\beta} \underbrace{\left(\Delta_i\left(F(t,T_{i-1},T_i)+m\right)X_i+N_i\right)\delta_i}_{\text{Equation 6.6}} - \underbrace{X_i\mathbb{Q}\left(\tau\in[T_{i-1},T_i]\right)\delta_i}_{\text{Expected loss}} \\ &\quad + \underbrace{RX_i\mathbb{Q}\left(\tau\in[T_{i-1},T_i]\right)\delta_i}_{\text{Expected recovery}}, \qquad (6.16) \\ &\approx \sum_{i=1}^{\beta} \underbrace{\left(\Delta_i\left(F(t,T_{i-1},T_i)+m\right)X_i+N_i\right)\delta_i}_{\text{Discounted (riskless) expected cash-flows}} \\ &\quad - \underbrace{\overbrace{(1-R)}^{\text{LGD}}X_i\mathbb{Q}\left(\tau\in[T_{i-1},T_i]\right)\delta_i}_{\text{Net expected loss}}, \end{aligned}$$

where the well-known quantity, loss-given-default or LGD, makes a surprise appearance. While Eqs. 6.15 and 6.16 are equivalent, the latter expression offers the (not-to-be-underestimated) benefit of being able to adjust all cash-flows directly using risk-free discount factors.

**Colour and Commentary 65** (DEFAULT-RISK PRICING)*: A second financial pricing adage is that cash-flows should be discounted with a rate that is commensurate to their riskiness. How such discount rates are constructed requires theoretical structure. It turns out that these rates are based on the interaction between risk-free rates and survival probabilities. The risk-free dimension captures the time value of money, while the survival aspect explicitly addresses the payment-default dimension. This clever decomposition has useful consequences. It permits us—when making the appropriate adjustments for default and recovery—to continue to discount expected future cash-flows at risk-free rates. In other words, as long as the key actors are present in the correct form, there are a number of possible configurations for their representation. We will make generous use of this flexibility in the construction of risk-adjusted loan returns.*

Actually evaluating Eq. 6.16 requires some effort. One needs to identify cash-flows dates, outstanding amounts, margins, and day-count fractions. These will need to be sourced from internal systems. Risk-free discount, implied LIBOR forward-rate, and (risk-neutral) default probability curves will also be required. This likely involves additional systems and input data. Discount and projection curves need to be extracted from market instruments such as overnight-index and interest-rate swap securities.[22] Risk-neutral default probabilities are, most typically, extracted from credit-default-swap markets. This requires some additional theoretical machinery and statistical assumptions.[23]

The bigger question relates the conceptual notion of so-called risk-neutral default probabilities. The risk-neutral, or pricing, or equivalent martingale measure—which we have denoted as $\mathbb{Q}$—is a central object in asset pricing. It is a subtle object arising from assumptions about arbitrage and market completeness. Risk-neutral probabilities are the correct quantity for pricing, but they unfortunately do not correspond to one's typical idea of a default probability. We generally like to think of a probability in relative frequency terms. That is, if a random event was repeated 100 times, then a specific outcome might be sensibly assigned a probability of 0.1 if it occurs on ten occasions. In a financial setting, this more natural definition of probability is—in a loose sense—referred to as the natural or physical probability measure. We write it as $\mathbb{P}$ to differentiate it from the equivalent martingale measure, $\mathbb{Q}$.

These probability measures, quite simply, serve different purposes. The risk-neutral measure arises naturally in pricing applications, whereas the physical probability measure stars in strategic and risk-management settings.[24] Often both make an appearance in a given analysis, but when this occurs, they stick to their area of relevance. While this is a well-understood area of finance theory, it bears repeating and underscoring in this analysis. The computation of risk-adjusted rates of return—the objective of this chapter—involves both pricing and risk-management dimensions. Particular care will need to be taken to use the correct quantity in the correct place.

**Colour and Commentary 66** *($\mathbb{P}$'S AND $\mathbb{Q}$'S): To* mind your p's and q's *is an old-fashioned English expression counselling caution and attentiveness in one's behaviour. It presumably comes from the fact that these two letters*

(continued)

[22] This can get quite involved. See, for example, Ametrano and Bianchetti [2] for a discussion of some of the finer points involved in this exercise.

[23] More details can be found in Bolder [10, Chapter 9].

[24] Meucci [29] provides an insightful description of these two different *tracks* in quantitative financial analysis.

**Colour and Commentary 66** (continued)
*look strikingly similar, but mean rather different things.*[a] *A similar degree of vigilance is recommended when working with risk-neutral and physical probabilities—denoted as* $\mathbb{P}$ *and* $\mathbb{Q}$*, respectively—in financial problems. Analogous to our English proverb, these measures serve rather different purposes despite some structural parallels. The risk-neutral measure applies when pricing securities; quantities computed under this measure cannot be interpreted in the typical way. The physical measure applies to real-world empirical problems such as risk measurement or strategic analysis. Using the wrong measure in the wrong context can lead to potentially disastrous results. Since computation of risk-adjusted returns touch on both these areas, we are well advised to tread carefully.*

[a] The actual origins of this saying, as one might expect, are a matter of some debate. See Knight [24] for some (rather old) thoughts on the matter.

## 6.2 A Holistic Perspective

The determination of appropriate lending margins needs to capture both risk and return dimensions. As a result, we do *not* face a pure loan-pricing problem. Equation 6.16 is certainly useful and (if) applied correctly, were we so inclined, would represent an excellent starting point for the fair-value liquidation of a lending asset. Most financial institutions are not in the business, however, of liquidating their lending assets.[25] Loan-price valuations have many applications, but they are not directly informative to lending decisions. Why, therefore, have we invested several pages of effort in rather dense asset-pricing theory? The answer is that the forthcoming analysis will incorporate an important pricing dimension. We will need this knowledge. There is, nevertheless, an important dimension *not* directly present in our pricing formulae: worst-case risk.

Asset pricing incorporates average, or expected, risk. It does not include any explicit notion of extreme, downside (or worst-case) risks. This is the job of economic capital. Risk-adjusted pricing might incorporate this aspect, conceptually at least, as follows:

$$\text{Risk-adjusted price} = \underbrace{\text{Risk-free price} - \text{Expected loss}}_{\text{Equation 6.16}} - \text{Worst-case loss}. \tag{6.17}$$

[25] Nor are these loans typically fair-valued, beyond informational purposes, in financial reporting. The clear exception is loan securitization, of course, but that is not the current topic of discussion.

This might be a useful quantity, but it is denominated in currency terms making comparison between individual loans somewhat difficult. A risk-adjusted return might solve this issue with the following (very generic form):

$$\text{Risk-adjusted return} = \frac{\overbrace{\text{Risk-free price} - \text{Expected loss}}^{\text{Equation 6.16}} - \text{Other relevant costs}}{\text{Worst-case loss}}. \tag{6.18}$$

Risk-adjusted returns have a long history in finance. The Sharpe ratio, which is a rather famous case of the more general information ratio, is still used extensively in asset-management circles and dates back to the late 1960s.[26] The usefulness of these ratios is that they normalize some notion of return by some measure of risk. The return is thus deflated, or discounted, by the amount of risk it generates. High-return, but high risk investments are thus made comparable to their low-return, low-risk equivalents in a consistent manner. Such a quantity is thus of significant usefulness in informing investment, or lending, decisions. We thus find ourselves back to the firm's capital budgeting problem, thus explaining our interest.

The big question, of course, is what precisely to put into the numerator and denominator of Eq. 6.18 to make the precise structure of risk-adjusted return the most meaningful and representative of one's business. The key to answering these questions is found in the financial statements. We need to understand how lending activities are financed. How much is financed, for example, by liabilities and how much by equity? This is a capital structure question. We also need to investigate how an individual loan contributes to the firm's overall equity position. What, therefore, are the relevant revenues and expenses associated with an individual loan? This is a profit-and-loss question. Finally, we must identify the specific risks that need to be compensated. This goes somewhat beyond the firm's financial statements and enters into the realm of economic capital.

### *6.2.1 The Balance-Sheet Perspective*

The most natural starting place is the firm's balance sheet. Among other things, a balance sheet illustrates asset composition and capital structure. These two dimensions provide useful insight into investment and financing decisions, which will help us organize the actors appearing in the numerator of Eq. 6.18.

Figure 6.2 begins this process with the graphical representation of two stylized balance sheets. The left-hand graphic includes the useful high-level view of assets, liabilities, and shareholder's equity. The right-hand side specializes to the type of

[26] See Sharpe [35, 36] for the origins of the Sharpe ratio and Bacon [4] for a good discussion on the information ratio. Bolder [9, Chapter 14] also touches on these ratios and some of their cousins.

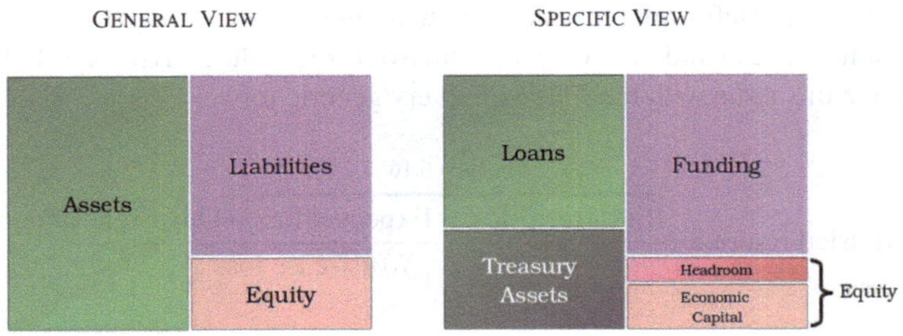


**Fig. 6.2** *Asset composition and capital structure*: The preceding graphics illustrate—from a few complementary perspectives—the typical (albeit somewhat stylized) balance sheet of a lending institution.

balance sheet one would expect to see from a garden-variety lending institution.[27] The asset side is broken into two main categories: lending and treasury assets. Loans, appearing in amortized-cost form, are probably best treated as a monolithic category. It is useful, conversely, to consider the various fair-valued elements of treasury assets. Many of these instruments will serve short-term liquidity needs—such as facilitating loan disbursements and financing repayments—but some portion will also relate to medium-term investments. A fraction of the treasury assets will also include derivative securities—such as interest-rate or cross-currency swaps—employed to hedge various aspects of the lending operations. The market values of such instruments are generally only a small proportion of their notional values and, depending on market conditions, they may appear as either assets or liabilities.[28]

As we move to the specific balance-sheet view in Fig. 6.2, it is also helpful to broadly characterize firm liabilities as funding. While some other liabilities naturally occur, the vast majority relates to financial-market funding. NIB, like most international financial institutions, funds itself in global capital markets at various tenors across a range of currencies.[29] The equity allocation is also further subdivided into two categories: economic-capital and headroom. The magnitude of the economic-capital value is, of course, directly proportional to the riskiness of the assets on the left-hand side of the balance sheet. Recall further that the headroom is defined as the residual between a firm's actual equity position and its economic-capital consumption. A positive headroom indicates capacity for further risk taking, while a small or negative figure often spells trouble.

[27] This viewpoint would, with a few small label changes and brushing over some firm-specific elements, equally apply to virtually any financial institution.

[28] Typically, derivative valuations on both sides of the balance sheet roughly cancel one another out. While centrally important for the operations of almost any financial institution, they do not figure importantly in this discussion. Chapter 10 touches on how derivative contracts enter into the economic-capital picture.

[29] For many financial institutions, funding is typically augmented by (or even predominately comprised of) client deposits.

While it is obvious that the right-hand side of the balance sheet finances the left-hand assets, it is less evident what specifically finances what. It is not uncommon for financial institutions to, conceptually at least, imagine that lending activity is financed by funding, whereas treasury investments are funded with equity. A firm may, through their asset-and-liability management function, build explicit (albeit partial) links between the two sides of the balance sheet. Conceptually, however, this is something of a fiction. A firm should be viewed, and is typically managed, from a holistic or macro perspective. Each asset held by a firm is being financed by both funding and equity. This is, in many ways, the central message of any balance sheet and the reason for the primacy of capital-structure questions in the corporate-finance literature.

This seemingly innocuous conclusion—that assets are financed by the entire right-hand side of the balance sheet—nonetheless has some important ramifications. Most particularly, the revenues generated by the firm's assets need to cover one's costs. Funding costs, while potentially multifaceted and complex, are readily tabulated and determined. The cost of equity, however, is rather less clear cut. In the simplest sense, assets need to generate sufficient revenues to pay an annual dividend. This, however, is only part of the equation. If the firm wishes to grow its balance sheet—as most do—the assets also need to permit corresponding growth in the equity position.[30] Increasing levels of assets will—even at unchanged levels of riskiness—consume more economic capital. Absent a commensurate increase in equity, the headroom will shrink and, ultimately, business activity will likely need to be curtailed.

The actual required level of equity growth is something of an open question. Some firms, and industries, have a broad range of growth prospects. Others do not. These prospects are generally somehow linked to their products' life cycles, the competitive structure of the industry, and the state of technology. It is probably a reasonable assumption that, over the medium to long-term, all firms should seek to grow, at least, at the same pace as their general macroeconomy.[31] Over shorter time periods, of course, firms might target higher (or lower) levels of growth. Again, if assets do not generate sufficient revenues to fund the necessary degree of equity growth then—without an external injection of capital—challenges may arise. For a financial institution, the shrinkage in headroom might ultimately lead to foregoing future lending opportunities, issues with regulators, or even downgrade by credit agencies.

What precisely is the mechanism for equity growth? It follows a rather well-known channel through the firm's profit-and-loss statement. The generation of

[30] An old paper—which still nicely frames the key issues—about the interplay between growth, dividends, and stocks prices is found in Gordon [17].

[31] A randomly selected Swedish firm's long to medium-term growth target, for example, should probably not be determined independently of the expected evolution of Swedish output.

asset revenues involves incurrence of costs. For a financial institution, the revenue element will take the form of loan margins, associated lending fees, and financial security coupon payments.[32] The expense side will include financing costs, administrative expenses, fair-value adjustments, and loan impairments.[33] On a periodic basis, the asset revenues and expenses are summed and netted, the dividend payment is subtracted and the remainder is added to the equity position. The consequence is an adjustment—made on a quarterly or annual basis—to the equity position; this is often referred to as retained earnings. More simply, these retained earnings are an internal asset-driven source of financing. In principle, a firm can only grow in two ways: via this internal, organically driven, route or from additional external injections of capital.

**Colour and Commentary 67** (GROWING A FIRM)*: There are, when you sift through all of the details, only* two *possible ways to grow a firm. The first involves organically increasing one's equity position through retained earnings. The second requires an external injection of capital. Both, as is usual, offer advantages and disadvantages. External injections can lead to issues surrounding information asymmetries between management and shareholders.*[a] *For international financial institutions, with government shareholders, capital replenishment can also become a political question. These issues notwithstanding, new external capital can be extremely effective in helping an entity expand its activities. Internal growth has fewer implications for the institution's status quo, but it can limit growth opportunities and, in certain situations, prove rather slow. In day-to-day loan pricing discussions—given the infrequent and unpredictable nature of external equity inflows—it is nonetheless customary to abstract from possible future capital injections and focus on internal growth. Organic capital expansion places a burden on firm assets to contribute sufficient return to make one's desired growth possible; one's loan-pricing framework must reflect this central fact.*

[a] This relates to Akerlof [1]'s famous lemons problem.

[32] If a firm owns equity assets, this would also include dividend income. Marketable securities' revenue is also a bit more complex than simply coupons, but here we seek to keep it conceptually simple.

[33] Because loans are typically held at amortized cost, changes in their fair value do not flow through profit-and-loss. To account for expected lending losses, a separate loan-impairment computation is performed. While structurally slightly different, it is conceptually analogous to the final *net expected loss* term in Eq. 6.16. This element, in all its glory, will be considered more formally in Chap. 9.

### 6.2.2 Building the Foundation

The discussion in the preceding section will, almost certainly for most readers, contain few (if any) new ideas. These details nevertheless bear explicit repetition, because they provide part of the foundation for the computation of risk-adjusted returns. The fundamental assumption, at this point, is that a firm's assets need to internally create sufficient return to finance current and future growth prospects. Let us try to work out, from first principles, what precisely these assets need to return. We begin with the definition of a firm's return on equity:

$$\text{Return on equity (ex dividend)} = \frac{\overbrace{\text{Revenues} - \text{Expenses}}^{\text{Firm P\&L}} - \text{Dividends}}{\text{Equity}},$$

$$\underbrace{\text{Return on equity (ex dividend)} + \frac{\text{Dividends}}{\text{Equity}}}_{\text{Return on equity}} = \frac{\overbrace{\text{Revenues} - \text{Expenses}}^{\text{Firm Net income}}}{\text{Equity}}. \tag{6.19}$$

This is a familiar ratio; it is simply the quotient of net income and equity. Equation 6.19 attempts to include dividend policy and raises the point that it may be—according to one's tastes and objectives—placed on either side of the identity. Moreover, Eq. 6.19 also explicitly incorporates the central role of assets in the generation of net income. This is important, because asset composition is our main focus of attention and principal decision variable.

The return on equity identity, from Eq. 6.19, is a good jumping off point. One can establish a sensible growth target for this quantity. That said, it has a few critical shortcomings; these are the same issues that precipitated the construction of the economic-capital measure. In particular, it is silent on worst-case risk. One (perhaps slightly dodgy) strategy to meet a return-on-equity target would be to add very risky assets to one's balance sheet. In the short term, at least, this would—despite increased loan impairments and fair-value volatility—typically enlarge net income. It would, however, expose the firm to greater risk and potentially disastrous future net-income outcomes. This argues against the use of the return-on-equity measure for decisions on asset allocation.[34]

Wholesale addition of riskier assets to one's balance sheet is *not* necessarily a sub-optimal strategy. The important element, of course, is that the asset return is commensurate to the risk taken; moreover, the portfolio-level implications of these risks need to be understood.[35] This argues, therefore, for an adjustment—or perhaps restatement—of Eq. 6.19 introducing the risk dimension. Abstracting from dividend

[34] It is naturally part of the analysis, but it should not be the sole decision criterion.

[35] It also must be consistent with the firm's overall risk appetite and capital position.

policy, let us consider:

$$\text{Return on economic capital} = \frac{\overbrace{\text{Asset revenues} - \text{Asset (and other) expenses}}^{\text{Net asset income}}}{\text{Economic capital}}, \tag{6.20}$$

with a slight specialization relative to Eq. 6.19 towards the asset dimension. The differences between Eqs. 6.19 and 6.20 are not dramatic, but they are nonetheless definitive. The revised denominator captures the riskiness of the assets. The high asset-risk strategy, mentioned above, can only work if those assets also generate a correspondingly high degree of return. Conversely, low-risk assets—that in the previous analysis might look uninteresting—can also usefully contribute to this ratio. Equation 6.20 thus appears to be a sensible candidate for a risk-adjusted return ratio.

While a portfolio level risk-adjusted return ratio is fantastic, actually decisions occur by individual asset. Somehow, therefore, we need to break Eq. 6.20 out by asset. With $N$ individual assets, the following decomposition is always possible,

$$\underbrace{\text{Return on economic capital}}_{\text{RAROC}} = \sum_{n=1}^{N} \frac{\overbrace{\text{Asset revenues}_n - \text{Asset (and other) expenses}_n}^{\text{Net asset income}_n}}{\text{Economic capital}}. \tag{6.21}$$

The numerator in Eq. 6.21 represents the marginal contribution to net income (and eventually equity) from each asset, whereas the denominator is unchanged. This is progress. Equation 6.21 tells us how each asset contributes, on a risk-adjusted basis, to the total return. This is referred to as the risk-adjusted return on capital or RAROC. It has a long and storied history in the banking community; it was initially developed roughly 50 years ago by Banker's Trust.[36] Depending on the exact construction of the numerator and denominator of Eq. 6.21, this measure can provide rather different guidance. Thus, while we will use the generic term RAROC throughout the following discussion, be aware that there is no unique definition.[37]

Equation 6.21, while respecting the rules of algebra, does *not* quite go far enough. Our ultimate interest would involve the marginal contribution to *both* return and risk

[36] James [22] is an interesting look into the genesis and rationale behind this measure.

[37] As usual, it is always a good idea to understand the specific recipe used to cook the dish.

at the asset level. We thus propose something like the following:

$$\underbrace{\text{Return on economic capital}_n}_{\text{RAROC}_n} = \frac{\overbrace{\text{Asset revenues}_n - \text{Asset (and other) expenses}_n}^{\text{Net asset income}_n}}{\text{Economic capital}_n},$$

$$= \frac{\text{Marginal asset-income contribution}_n}{\text{Marginal asset-risk consumption}_n}, \tag{6.22}$$

for $n = 1, \ldots, N$ individual assets. This is precisely what we seek. The numerator of Eq. 6.22 captures an asset's marginal contribution to income, while the denominator normalizes by its risk consumption.

Sadly, although Eq. 6.22 is conceptually ideal, it an arithmetic mess. It is clear that

$$\underbrace{\text{Return on economic capital}}_{\text{Portfolio RAROC}} \neq \sum_{n=1}^{N} \frac{\text{Marginal asset-income contribution}_n}{\text{Marginal asset-risk consumption}_n}. \tag{6.23}$$

In plain English, our preferred asset-level, risk-adjusted return measure cannot be summed, in an intuitive way, to yield the overall portfolio metric. Instead, a bit more flexibility is required. Equation 6.22 is aggregated to the portfolio level by summing over both the numerator and denominator simultaneously. More specifically, this looks like

$$\underbrace{\text{Return on Economic Capital}}_{\text{Portfolio RAROC}} = \frac{\sum_{n=1}^{N} \text{Marginal asset-income contribution}_n}{\sum_{n=1}^{N} \text{Marginal asset-risk consumption}_n},$$

$$= \frac{\sum_{n=1}^{N} \text{Asset revenues}_n - \text{Asset expenses}_n}{\sum_{n=1}^{N} \text{Economic capital}_n},$$

$$= \underbrace{\frac{\text{Net income}}{\text{Economic capital}}}_{\text{Equation 6.20}}. \tag{6.24}$$

This minor inconvenience would seem to be the price to pay for a meaningful working definition of risk-adjusted return (or RAROC).[38]

[38] In practice, Eq. 6.24 allows us to compute the RAROC of any possible sub-portfolio. It is only necessary to keep track of the marginal contribution and consumption to economic capital for each individual asset.

**Colour and Commentary 68** (A MARGINAL PERSPECTIVE): *In our search for a sensible risk-adjusted return ratio, a natural point of departure is the return on equity. Sole examination of return on equity is nonetheless sub-optimal, because it ignores important (worst-case) aspects of the underlying asset risks. This argues for updating the return-on-equity ratio's denominator with economic capital. This small change permits explicit consideration of asset riskiness. A further adjustment reduces this to the individual asset level. Our proposed risk-adjusted return—or risk-adjusted return on capital (RAROC)—measure is thus the ratio of an asset's marginal contribution to asset income divided by its marginal consumption of economic capital. This RAROC measure provides a sensible, risk-adjusted metric for asset-selection decisions. A bit of caution and extra arithmetical gymnastics are nonetheless required when aggregating this measure over individual assets or subsets of one's portfolio.*

## 6.3 Estimating Marginal Asset Income

Equipped with a workable and concrete risk-adjusted ratio, we may proceed beyond word equations and build a specific prescription for its calculation. This process will bring us back to the previously introduced fundamentals of loan pricing. A few new bells and whistles will, however, be added. The typical loan-valuation problem, for example, does not concern itself with how the loan is actually financed. Equation 6.22 involves the explicit inclusion of relevant asset expenses. This will be our starting point.

Figure 6.3 provides a high-level schematic of the typical inflows and outflows of a lending transaction. As highlighted in the initial section of this chapter, loan obligors pay (usually six-month) LIBOR plus a lending margin denoted $m$. These

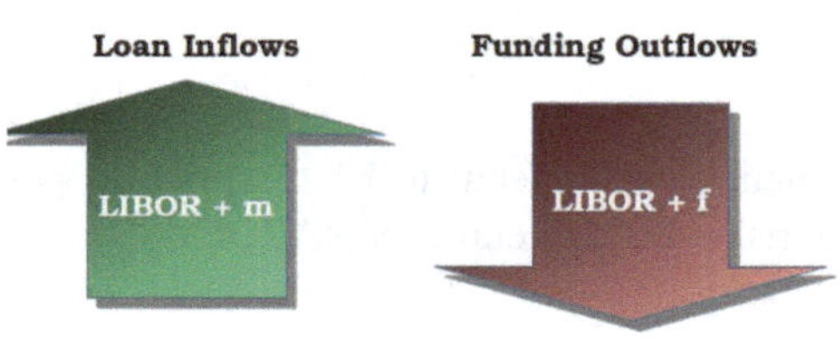


**Fig. 6.3** *Loan mechanics*: This graphic provides a simplified schematic of the principal elements of loan profit-and-loss in a LIBOR-based—or, if you prefer, reference-rate-based—financial institution.

loans are funded with a (typically three-month) LIBOR-based funding transaction plus a funding spread, which we'll call $f$. A few points arise. First of all, there may be some form of basis risk between the six-month LIBOR lending rate and the three-month LIBOR funding values. While important, let us collect this aspect and push it into the funding spread, $f$. The second point relates to an institution's attitude towards interest-rate risk. Many financial institutions immunize themselves from interest rate movements by hedging all lending and funding activity back into some fixed (typically LIBOR) reference rate. This also helps manage tenor mismatches between assets and liabilities.[39] Occasionally, however, some aspect is not completely hedged. This amounts to a perfectly legitimate view on interest rates, but it does complicate our analysis.

Let's take the perspective, for the moment at least, of a fully LIBOR-based bank.[40] Any fixed-rate loans, funding, and (most) investment operations are dully swapped—individually or on a macro basis—back into either three- or six-month LIBOR.[41] For the purposes of determining the numerator of our risk-adjusted ratio in Eq. 6.22, even when this hedging does not occur, we may always conceptually determine the equivalent $m$ and $f$ values associated with any position. This relatively straightforward computation involves the instrument's cash-flows flows and the appropriate swap curve. On this basis, we may (cautiously) conclude that Fig. 6.3 provides a reasonable characterization of lending inflows and outflows.[42]

To arrive at a sensible expression for the numerator of our risk-adjusted return ratio, we will begin slowly. We attend first to the loan revenues less funding expenses. This has the following form,

$$\begin{aligned}\begin{array}{c}\text{Loan}\\ \text{Revenues}\end{array} - \begin{array}{c}\text{Funding}\\ \text{Expenses}\end{array} = \sum_{i=1}^{\beta} & \underbrace{\left(\Delta_i\left(L_i + m\right)X_i\right)e^{\int_t^{T_i} r(u)du}}_{\text{Discounted (riskless) inflows}} \\ & - \underbrace{\left(\Delta_i\left(L_i + f\right)X_i\right)e^{\int_t^{T_i} r(u)du}}_{\text{Discounted (riskless) outflows}},\end{aligned} \tag{6.25}$$

[39] Most retail commercial banks, for example, fund themselves with short-term deposits, but make long-term mortgages loans. Swapping both sides back into a common reference rate enormously helps manage net margins.

[40] This is defensible, because the hedging decision can be thought of separately and independently from the lending choice.

[41] Exchange-rate risks are also hedged, but even if they were not, this element would show up in the economic-capital calculation.

[42] Following this reasoning, an $m$ value is also readily calculable for fixed-rate treasury asset investments. This would permit extension of these ideas across all firm assets.

$$\mathbb{E}_t^{\mathbb{Q}}\left(\begin{array}{c}\text{Loan}\\ \text{Revenues}\end{array} - \begin{array}{c}\text{Funding}\\ \text{Expenses}\end{array}\right) = \mathbb{E}_t^{\mathbb{Q}}\left(\sum_{i=1}^{\beta}\left(\Delta_i\left(L_i + m\right)X_i\right)e^{\int_t^{T_i} r(u)du}\right.$$
$$\left. - \left(\Delta_i\left(L_i + f\right)X_i\right)e^{\int_t^{T_i} r(u)du}\right),$$
$$\begin{array}{c}\text{Expected}\\ \text{Marginal}\\ \text{Loan Income}\end{array} = \sum_{i=1}^{\beta}\Delta_i\underbrace{\left(m - f\right)}_{\substack{\text{Internal}\\ \text{margin}}}X_i\delta_i.$$

This is a lovely result. Abstracting from other expenses and impairments, the economic lending contribution to net income is simply the exposure-weighted, discounted sum of net margins over the loan's lifetime. This expression does, however, require some additional explanation. The notional repayments—from both loan and funding perspectives—are not considered because they do not have a profit-and-loss impact. We apply the (risk-neutral) expectation operator, because we are trying to compute market-consistent economic values for these cash-flows. The structural relationships are, of course, motivated by financial-statement accounting principles, but this remains (at least, partially) a pricing problem. The pleasant aspect of Eq. 6.25 is the cancellation of the LIBOR component.[43] This is a practical and conceptual benefit of running a LIBOR-based financial institution.[44] The other important dimension is that, unlike the accounting problem, we are not focusing on a single reporting period. We seek to consider the financial impact of the loan instrument over its entire tenor; this further supports the application of (risk-neutral) expectations.

Unfortunately, it is necessary to complicate the marvellously parsimonious expression from Eq. 6.25. Embedded in its construction is an important, and debatable, assumption. It assumes that the loan is entirely funded with market-based liabilities. As explicitly highlighted in Fig. 6.3, however, loan financing stems from both funding and equity. This would imply that both these elements need to be incorporated. We can take another crack at the form of the expected marginal loan income through a slight restatement of Eq. 6.25. This simply requires the

[43] We need not even make use of the change-of-measure trick to evaluate our expectation taken with respect to the equivalent martingale measure (induced by a collection of forward measures).

[44] Recall that the (expected) basis risk associated with the different LIBOR tenors is embedded in $f$. The worst-case aspect of this risk should also find its way into the market-risk component of economic capital.

re-weighting of a loan's financing sources as,

$$\begin{aligned}\text{Marginal Loan Income} &= \sum_{i=1}^{\beta}\left[\underbrace{\Delta_i\left(L_i+m\right)X_i}_{\text{Inflows}}-\underbrace{\Delta_i\left(\overbrace{(1-\xi_i)\left(L_i+f\right)}^{\text{Funding}}+\overbrace{\xi_i\mathcal{H}}^{\text{Equity}}\right)X_i}_{\text{Financing outflows}}\right]e^{\int_t^{T_i}r(u)du},\end{aligned} \tag{6.26}$$

$$\begin{aligned}\mathbb{E}_t^{\mathbb{Q}}\left(\text{Marginal Loan Income}\right) &= \mathbb{E}_t^{\mathbb{Q}}\left(\sum_{i=1}^{\beta}\left[\Delta_i\left(L_i+m\right)X_i-\Delta_i\left((1-\xi_i)\left(L_i+f\right)+\xi_i\mathcal{H}\right)X_i\right]e^{\int_t^{T_i}r(u)du}\right),\\ &= \sum_{i=1}^{\beta}\mathbb{E}_t^{\mathbb{Q}}\left(\left[\Delta_i\left(L_i+m\right)X_i-\Delta_i\left((1-\xi_i)\left(L_i+f\right)+\xi_i\mathcal{H}\right)X_i\right]e^{\int_t^{T_i}r(u)du}\right),\\ &= \underbrace{\sum_{i=1}^{\beta}\mathbb{E}_t^{\mathbb{Q}^{T_i}}\left(\left[\Delta_i\left(L_i+m\right)X_i-\Delta_i\left((1-\xi_i)\left(L_i+f\right)+\xi_i\mathcal{H}\right)X_i\right]\right)\underbrace{P(t,T_i)}_{\delta_i},}_{\text{Using the logic in Eq. 6.6}}\end{aligned}$$

$$\text{Expected Marginal Loan Income} = \sum_{i=1}^{\beta}\Delta_i\left(m-\underbrace{(1-\xi_i)f}_{\substack{\text{Funding}\\\text{financed}}}-\underbrace{\xi_i\left(\mathcal{H}-F(t,T_{i-1},T_i)\right)}_{\substack{\text{Equity}\\\text{financed}}}\right)X_i\delta_i,$$

where $\xi_i$ denotes the proportion of equity financing associated with the $i$th loan payment and $\mathcal{H}$ represents the target rate of return on equity. This restatement is not as immediately intuitive as Eq. 6.25. As we can see, the LIBOR based element does not completely cancel out.[45] We are also left to interpret the new equity financing term.

[45] This consequently forces us to make use of the forward-measure numeraires introduced in our initial loan-pricing development.

If we set $\xi_i = 0$ then Eq. 6.26 collapses to Eq. 6.25. This is reassuring. Conversely, setting $\xi_i$ to unity (i.e., fully financing the loan with equity) yields,

$$\begin{aligned}\begin{array}{c}\text{Expected}\\ \text{(Equity-Financed)}\\ \text{Marginal}\\ \text{Loan Income}\end{array} &= \sum_{i=1}^{\beta} \Delta_i \left( m - \left( \mathcal{H} - F(t, T_{i-1}, T_i) \right) \right) X_i \delta_i, \\ &= \sum_{i=1}^{\beta} \Delta_i \left( m + \underbrace{F(t, T_{i-1}, T_i)}_{\text{Expected LIBOR}} - \mathcal{H} \right) X_i \delta_i. \end{aligned} \tag{6.27}$$

How should we interpret this result? If the loan was entirely financed with equity, it would (as usual) earn the margin *plus* expected LIBOR. These inflows would need to be compared to the expected return on equity, $\mathcal{H}$. In the more general case, however, the funding costs—with a weight of $(1 - \xi)$—need to be offset. The difference between expected LIBOR and the required equity return also arises. The larger point is that, in a LIBOR bank, the equity financed proportion of a loan—or an investment for that matter—earns LIBOR.[46]

**Colour and Commentary 69** (LIABILITY VS. EQUITY FINANCING)*: If we assume that a loan obligation is solely financed with market funding, we may derive a streamlined representation of expected marginal loan income. It is essentially the sum of the discounted differences between lending and funding margins over the instrument's lifetime. In reality, however, a proportion of every loan is also financed through equity. Inclusion of this dimension creates two practical problems: determination of the required return for equity and assignment of appropriate weights to the funding and equity components. Leaving these practical details for future sections, a revised loan-income expression may be derived. While less parsimonious, the result is nonetheless quite interesting. While the reference rate (i.e., LIBOR) component cancels out from the funding-only perspective, it remains for the equity. This implies that, in addition to the margin, the equity financed aspect of any loan earns the full amount of LIBOR. This naturally leads to a comparison of this LIBOR amount to the expected return associated with equity. Both the funding and equity sources of financing, of course, earn the lending margin.*

[46] Funding financed lending activity also, of course, earns LIBOR. Since it simultaneously costs LIBOR, this effect cancels out.

### 6.3.1 Weighting Financing Sources

Equation 6.26, despite its useful structure, cannot be implemented without a clearer view on the value of each $\xi_i$. This quantity tells us the proportion of loan financing stemming from equity. In any introductory corporate finance textbook—Brealey et al. [11] is an excellent choice—one can find a treatment of the so-called *weighted-average cost of capital*. As the name strongly suggests, this involves weighting the relative costs of market funding and equity. If we denote $D_t$ and $E_t$ as the time $t$ balance-sheet values of the firm's debt and equity, respectively, then a possible candidate for the equity weight is

$$\xi_t = \frac{E_t}{D_t + E_t}. \tag{6.28}$$

This particular choice offers a number of benefits. It is easy to compute and intuitive. Moreover, it directly reflects the balance-sheet structure of the financial institution. This makes it an excellent choice for computation of a firm's cost of capital.

For our purposes, however, there are also a few shortcomings. Logistically, we need to consider future cash-flows over potentially long-term horizons. The precise capital structure, at these future points, will be difficult or impossible to know. A possible solution would be to fix our weight, $\xi$, to the current time. Perhaps more worrying, however, is the relatively homogeneous treatment of all loans implied by Eq. 6.28. Irrespective of the loan's riskiness, it will be financed in the same proportions with funding and equity. This does not follow the spirit of the calculation. Some loan transactions will consume—through their inherent riskiness—more of the firm's equity. As a consequence, they need not cover only their funding costs, but also contribute more to equity than less risky substitute loans.

An alternative weighting scheme that explicitly incorporates the (worst-case) risk dimension might look like

$$\xi_t = \frac{\mathcal{E}_t}{X_t}, \tag{6.29}$$

where $\mathcal{E}_t$ and $X_t$ represent the loan's economic capital and outstanding notional values at time $t$, respectively. The intuition, and logic, behind this choice is that a loan's amount of equity financing is directly proportional to its consumption of equity.[47] Equity consumption is proxied with its economic-capital allocation. A low-risk loan might only have an equity financing weight of a few percentage points, whereas this could rise to 20 or even 30% for highly risky lending ventures. The corollary—which will be addressed in later sections—is that the required return on

[47] These asset-specific values are also, from a logistical perspective, more readily available over time for inclusion in the calculation.

equity for such loans may be higher than that necessitated by market-based funding. It also means that riskier assets face a higher burden.

Using Eq. 6.29, we may return to our expression for expected marginal loan income and make it a bit more concrete. In particular,

$$\begin{aligned}
\begin{array}{c}\text{Expected}\\ \text{Marginal}\\ \text{Loan Income}\end{array} &= \underbrace{\sum_{i=1}^{\beta} \Delta_i \left( m - \left( 1 - \underbrace{\frac{\mathcal{E}_i}{X_i}}_{\xi_i} \right) f - \underbrace{\frac{\mathcal{E}_i}{X_i}}_{\xi_i} \Big( \mathcal{H} - F(t, T_{i-1}, T_i) \Big) \right) X_i \delta_i}_{\text{Equation 6.26}}, \qquad (6.30)\\
&= \sum_{i=1}^{\beta} \Delta_i \left( \underbrace{\left( m - \left( 1 - \frac{\mathcal{E}_i}{X_i} \right) f \right) X_i}_{\text{Funding component}} - \underbrace{\Big( \mathcal{H} - F(t, T_{i-1}, T_i) \Big) \mathcal{E}_i}_{\text{Equity component}} \right) \delta_i .
\end{aligned}$$

The result is quite sensible. The funding component involves the lending and (weighted) funding margins relative to the outstanding loan amount. The equity piece, as before, describes the difference between the required equity return and expected forward LIBOR rates. The magnitude of this component, however, depends on the loan's economic-capital consumption. If we set $\mathcal{E}_i$ to zero—the loan is considered to be riskless—this is equivalent to a zero weight on equity financing. In this case, the equity piece vanishes and Eq. 6.30 collapses to Eq. 6.25.

**Colour and Commentary 70** (FINANCING WEIGHTS): *The firm's current capital structure is a natural touchstone for the determination of the relative weights on the cost of funding and equity. While simple and intuitive, this approach fails to capture the specific risks associated with a given credit obligor. In other words, the static, homogeneous nature of the capital structure doesn't allow us to differentiate loan riskiness. We resolve this issue by specifying the weight on equity financing as the ratio of the loan's economic capital to its outstanding amount. The consequence of this choice is that the cost of equity financing is directly proportional to a loan's economic-capital allocation. Alternative choices are naturally possible, but this appears to provide an intuitive link to worst-case risk and questions of capital adequacy. In other words, it establishes a logical correspondence between determination of one's lending margin and the riskiness of the firm's balance sheet.*

### 6.3.2 Other Income and Expenses

Before moving to actually construct our risk-adjusted return ratio, some additional elements must be incorporated into loan income. These have been ignored, up to this point, to avoid notational clutter. At this point, however, it is necessary to ensure that all possible cost and revenue criteria are included.

Let us begin with an important source of expense: administration. There are various ways to describe this, but our approach is to denote administrative expenses in percentage terms. We will denote it as $a$. This is multiplied—as with lending and funding margins—by the current loan outstanding amount. The actual magnitude of a specific loan's administrative expenses can, and does, depend upon a number of things: creditworthiness, tenor, or geographical location to name a few. These would, of course, have some link to, or influence on, the composition of administrative expenses. Since we are focused on recurring (discounted) administrative expenses over the loan's lifetime, we can embed it into the existing machinery as,

$$\begin{matrix}\text{Administrative}\\ \text{Expenses}\end{matrix} = \sum_{i=1}^{\beta} \Delta_i a X_i \delta_i. \tag{6.31}$$

The next element relates to a feature of certain loans, which certainly also applies in other lending settings. This is referred to as an up-front fee; we will denote it as $u$. Again, it is a percentage quantity that is conceptually similar to lending or funding margins or administrative expenses. The twist in this case, as the name implies, is that it is a one-time event.[48] An upfront-free occurs only at inception. We can readily handle this with an appropriately structured indicator function. $\mathbb{I}_{i=1}$ dutifully takes a value of unity at the first cash-flow date and zero everywhere else. This permits us to write the lifetime loan income associated with up-front fees as,

$$\begin{matrix}\text{Up-front}\\ \text{Fee Income}\end{matrix} = \sum_{i=1}^{\beta} \Delta_i \left( \mathbb{I}_{i=1} u \right) X_i \delta_i. \tag{6.32}$$

This might seem like overkill, but the intention is to inject this aspect organically into our risk-adjusted return ratio formula.

The notion of (expected) default risk—introduced in the first section—has not yet been included into our net loan-income construction.[49] If we let $\gamma$ represent our estimated loss-given-default value, then we could simply borrow the formally derived expected credit loss expression from Eq. 6.16 on page 352. For convenience,

[48] Indeed, in many cases, we may have $u \equiv 0$.

[49] This idea is intimately related to loan impairments, covered in great detail in Chaps. 7 to 9. In loan pricing, we use a stylized statistical measure of expected default loss and assume away the complex accounting details.

we restate its approximate form

$$\begin{array}{c}\text{Risk-Neutral}\\\text{Expected}\\\text{Loss}\end{array} \approx \sum_{i=1}^{\beta} \Delta_i \gamma \mathbb{Q}\Big(\tau \in [T_{i-1}, T_i]\Big) X_i \delta_i. \tag{6.33}$$

This structure, while technically correct for pricing, is not ideal for our purposes. We will need to make some concessions for the financial-statement perspective adopted in the construction of our ratio. In brief, we seek to maintain the spirit of Eq. 6.33, but simultaneously bring it closer to the loan-impairment computation flowing through the profit-and-loss statement.

Practically, this transformation is accomplished by simply replacing the risk-neutral default probabilities with their real-world equivalents. The result is,

$$\begin{array}{c}\text{Loan}\\\text{Impairment}\end{array} \approx \sum_{i=1}^{\beta} \Delta_i \gamma \underbrace{\mathbb{P}\Big(\tau \in [T_{i-1}, T_i]\Big)}_{p_i} X_i \delta_i. \tag{6.34}$$

The loan-impairment calculation is not a price; it is a risk measure. As a consequence, we need to change our underlying probability measure. Instead of extracting our probabilities from financial markets, they now need to be estimated from historical data. This implies a slightly lower degree of flexibility in their form. These physical-measure default probabilities are typically estimated at an annual frequency. To ease the notational burden somewhat, we will denote $p_i$ as the appropriate annual default rate associated with the $i$th cash-flow date.[50]

Pulling all of these disparate pieces together, we finally arrive at a comprehensive—if somewhat stylized—description of the marginal income associated with a specific loan. It takes the following, admittedly noisy, form

$$\begin{aligned}\begin{array}{c}\text{Expected}\\\text{Marginal}\\\text{Loan}\\\text{Income}\end{array} &= \begin{array}{c}\text{Upfront}\\\text{Fees}\end{array} + \begin{array}{c}\text{Lending}\\\text{Margin}\end{array} - \begin{array}{c}\text{(Weighted)}\\\text{Funding}\\\text{Margin}\end{array} - \begin{array}{c}\text{Admin}\\\text{Expenses}\end{array}\\ &\quad - \begin{array}{c}\text{Loan}\\\text{Impairments}\end{array} - \begin{array}{c}\text{(Weighted)}\\\text{Equity}\\\text{Cost}\end{array}, \qquad (6.35)\\ &= \sum_{i=1}^{\beta} \Delta_i \Bigg[\Bigg(\mathbb{I}_{i=1} u + m - \left(1 - \frac{\mathcal{E}_i}{X_i}\right) f - a - \gamma p_i\Bigg) X_i\\ &\quad -\Big(\mathcal{H} - F(t, T_{i-1}, T_i)\Big)\mathcal{E}_i\Bigg] \delta_i.\end{aligned}$$

[50] This necessitates the scaling by the appropriate day count.

Equation 6.35 represents the numerator of our risk-adjusted return ratio. All that remains is to identify the appropriate denominator.

## 6.4 Risk-Adjusted Returns

Equation 6.22 indicates that the RAROC computation requires the marginal asset-risk contribution in the denominator; in short, it is the economic capital. That much is obvious. The practical challenge, however, is to find the most reasonable possible form for our purposes. The key questions surround timing and discounting.

Economic capital is computed at a given point in time, with a fixed portfolio composition, and with a predefined set of model parameters. Equation 6.35, which is the comparable term for the numerator of our risk adjusted ratio, involves the discounted sums of cash-flows over a single loan's lifetime. This puts us in something of an apples-and-pears situation.

The most natural solution to this mismatch is to organize the denominator in a similar manner. We seek the total marginal economic-capital consumption of a given loan over its lifetime. A direct way to construct such a quantity would look like:

$$\begin{matrix}\text{Discounted} \\ \text{Marginal} \\ \text{Economic-Capital} \\ \text{Consumption}\end{matrix} = \sum_{i=1}^{\beta} \mathcal{E}_i \delta_i. \tag{6.36}$$

This is basically the sum of discounted future economic-capital consumptions associated with each individual payment date. This would create a logical correspondence between the numerator and denominator.

There is just one problem: we do not know the future economic-capital consumptions associated with a given loan at each of its future cash-flow dates. There are, at least, *two* annoying reasons. First, we simply do not know the portfolio composition at these future times. This implies that we cannot really accurately determine future concentration effects. Second, even if we did have this information, we do not have the computational capacity to perform so many complex stochastic simulations. Economic capital, after all, is *not* a fast computation.

The first annoyance can be solved by assuming that future portfolio will have a similar composition to the current portfolio. This is something of a heroic assumption and is subject to criticism, but there are really no other practical alternatives. The second issue requires some mathematical machinery. It is solved with the use of a complex, non-linear approximation of the economic-capital consumption.[51] This approximation depends on a set of regression parameters and explanatory variables

[51] The mathematical structure of this approximation—treated here in a very abstract manner—is discussed in detail in Chap. 5.

as well as the specific details of the loan.[52] These parameters are updated every day to reflect the current structure of the portfolio; forecasts of *future* economic capital, to repeat, necessarily assume a similar portfolio composition. Denoting all of this approximation-level information as $\theta$, we may write the economic-capital approximation at the $i$th payment date as $\hat{\mathcal{E}}_i(\theta)$.

Using our approximation, we can rewrite Eq. 6.36 as,

$$\begin{array}{c}\text{Estimated}\\ \text{Discounted}\\ \text{Marginal}\\ \text{Economic-Capital}\\ \text{Consumption}\end{array} = \sum_{i=1}^{\beta} \hat{\mathcal{E}}_i(\theta)\delta_i. \tag{6.37}$$

This is an object that can be sensibly computed.[53] Equation 6.37 will play the role of denominator for our risk-adjusted return ratio. We will also use this approximation, where appropriate, to replace the funding-and-equity cost weights introduced in Eqs. 6.29 and 6.30.

We now have all the necessary components to actually explicitly write out a possible RAROC computation for an arbitrary loan obligation. Combining our previous development, we have

$$\text{RAROC} = \frac{\overbrace{\text{Asset revenues} - \text{Asset expenses}}^{\text{Marginal net asset income: Eq. 6.35}}}{\underbrace{\text{Economic capital}}_{\text{Equation 6.37}}}, \tag{6.38}$$

$$\approx \frac{\sum_{i=1}^{\beta} \Delta_i \left( \left( \mathbb{I}_{i=1} u + m - \left(1 - \frac{\hat{\mathcal{E}}_i(\theta)}{X_i}\right) f - a - \gamma p_i \right) X_i - \Big(\mathcal{H} - F(t, T_{i-1}, T_i)\Big) \hat{\mathcal{E}}_i(\theta) \right) \delta_i}{\sum_{i=1}^{\beta} \hat{\mathcal{E}}_i(\theta)\delta_i},$$

$$\approx \frac{\sum_{i=1}^{\beta} \Delta_i \overbrace{\left( \mathbb{I}_{i=1} u + m - \left(1 - \frac{\hat{\mathcal{E}}_i(\theta)}{X_i}\right) f - a - \gamma p_i \right)}^{\eta_i} X_i \delta_i}{\sum_{i=1}^{\beta} \hat{\mathcal{E}}_i(\theta)\delta_i}$$

$$- \frac{\sum_{i=1}^{\beta} \Delta_i \Big(\mathcal{H} - F(t, T_{i-1}, T_i)\Big) \hat{\mathcal{E}}_i(\theta)\delta_i}{\sum_{i=1}^{\beta} \hat{\mathcal{E}}_i(\theta)\delta_i},$$

[52] A non-exhaustive list would include the regional and sector identity of the obligor, the amount outstanding, the credit class, the loss-given-default, the and size of firm.

[53] Albeit subject to the reasonableness of the variety of assumptions made in Chap. 5.

$$
\approx \underbrace{\frac{\sum_{i=1}^{\beta} \Delta_i \eta_i X_i \delta_i}{\sum_{i=1}^{\beta} \hat{\mathcal{E}}_i(\theta)\delta_i}}_{\text{Lending RAROC}}
- \underbrace{\left( \frac{\sum_{i=1}^{\beta} \Delta_i \mathcal{H} \hat{\mathcal{E}}_i(\theta)\delta_i}{\sum_{i=1}^{\beta} \hat{\mathcal{E}}_i(\theta)\delta_i} - \frac{\sum_{i=1}^{\beta} \Delta_i F(t, T_{i-1}, T_i) \hat{\mathcal{E}}_i(\theta)\delta_i}{\sum_{i=1}^{\beta} \hat{\mathcal{E}}_i(\theta)\delta_i} \right)}_{\text{Equity-return target}},
$$

where we have tried to reduce the notational clutter with the following definition,

$$
\begin{aligned}
\eta_i &\triangleq \underbrace{\eta_i\left(u, m, f, a, \gamma, p_i, X_i, \theta\right)}_{i\text{th payment loan profit-and-loss}}, \\
&= \mathbb{I}_{i=1} u + m - \left(1 - \frac{\hat{\mathcal{E}}_i(\theta)}{X_i}\right) f - a - \gamma p_i .
\end{aligned}
\tag{6.39}
$$

The result is a prescriptive—if not necessarily parsimonious—formula for the construction of a risk-adjusted return on (economic) capital.

The lending RAROC piece of Eq. 6.38 is relatively intuitive. It is a risk-deflated (marginal) net loan income. The equity return aspects on the right-hand-side, however, are independent of the size of the position. They are also, approximately at least, independent of the loan's riskiness. This requires a bit of effort to see. Inspection reveals that both elements of the equity-return target are essentially weighted averages. Let's begin with the required equity return piece, where

$$
\mathcal{H}\bar{\Delta} \approx \mathcal{H} \underbrace{\left( \frac{\sum_{i=1}^{\beta} \Delta_i \hat{\mathcal{E}}_i(\theta)\delta_i}{\sum_{i=1}^{\beta} \hat{\mathcal{E}}_i(\theta)\delta_i} \right)}_{\approx \bar{\Delta}},
\tag{6.40}
$$

which is a kind average payment-period return; $\bar{\Delta}$ is a kind of scaling for the payment frequency.[54]

The second term is a bit more unpleasant since it relates to the economic-capital weighted implied forward rate component. This relationship between the spot rate and the future path of forward rates—and the assumption of their equality—is referred to as the expectations hypothesis. A huge literature—starting with Modigliani and Shiller [30]—deals with this issue. In a nutshell, it does not really hold, but the difference is typically small and relates to term premia. For our conceptual purposes, we can probably safely abstract from this element. LIBOR-based forward rates could thus usefully be replaced with averaged expected interest rates over the loan's lifetime (i.e., $T - t$). We might denote this rate as $\overline{L(t,T)}$ to reflect its origins in the LIBOR market.[55] We thus opt to approximate this LIBOR-related element as,

$$\overline{L(t,T)}\bar{\Delta} \approx \frac{\sum_{i=1}^{\beta} \Delta_i F(t, T_{i-1}, T_i)\hat{\mathcal{E}}_i(\theta)\delta_i}{\sum_{i=1}^{\beta} \hat{\mathcal{E}}_i(\theta)\delta_i}. \tag{6.41}$$

Using these simplifications, the implication for our RAROC computation is a significantly simplified more compact form,

$$\text{RAROC} \approx \frac{\sum_{i=1}^{\beta} \Delta_i \eta_i X_i \delta_i}{\sum_{i=1}^{\beta} \hat{\mathcal{E}}_i(\theta)\delta_i} - \left(\mathcal{H} - \overline{L(t,T)}\right)\bar{\Delta}. \tag{6.42}$$

Once again, the main contribution stems from the funding-financed net-income contribution; this is unchanged. Subtracted from this component is the difference between the required rate of return on equity and the loan's LIBOR-related earnings. The second aspect represents, in a simplified and approximate way, the required return on equity (approximately) decoupled from both the size and riskiness of the loan. As we will see in the following section, it may be useful to think of these two aspects as being conceptually distinct.

[54] Equation 6.40 would hold with equality if $\Delta_i \equiv 1$ for all $i = 1, \ldots, \beta$ or the payments are made annually. When the payment frequency is *not* annual, we will almost invariably annualize the RAROC estimate anyway.

[55] It is admittedly a kind of risk-weighted average, but this effect is relatively small and we'll ignore it for our purposes.

**Colour and Commentary 71** (THE ROLE OF LIBOR)*: Working from a combination of asset-pricing and corporate-finance first principles, a risk-adjusted return ratio for loan obligations can be constructed. Interestingly—when explicitly allocating the financing costs into funding and equity proportions—the ratio can be split into* two *distinct parts. The first piece describes risk-adjusted net-income return; this is basically the ratio of marginal loan contribution to the marginal consumption of capital. The second aspect, however, is approximately equal to the difference between the expected cost of equity and the reference rate (i.e., LIBOR).*[a] *This has a pair of important implications. The expected rate of return on equity can be examined either together or separately from the main RAROC computation. Indeed, it can be considered as a kind of RAROC target. The second point has already been touched upon. Each loan contributes, for its equity component, an amount roughly equal to the full LIBOR rate. This quantity correspondingly represents the relevant point of comparison for the determination of an expected equity return.*

[a] Subject to simplifying assumptions surrounding payment frequencies and intertemporal risk weighting.

## 6.5 The Hurdle Rate

When firms are examining investment projects, a natural outcome is the associated expected rate of return. Indeed, this is precisely what we have been doing in the context of a specific loan project. Having computed such a return leads to the next inevitable question: is it sufficient? There is certainly some floor on the return below which the firm would simply not accept the project. Such a floor is often colloquially referred to as a *hurdle rate*.[56] Hence the use of the suggestive symbol, $\mathcal{H}$, to represent this quantity.

The most obvious choice for a hurdle rate is the firm's cost of capital. In practice, however, it is generally set to a level somewhat north of the cost-of-capital figure. The reasons relate to a focus on profit generation and a desire to incorporate the risk dimension. In our setting, these aspects have a different relevance. The risk component, to begin with, is already explicitly incorporated into our RAROC calculation; it need not be considered twice. The pure profit motive, as previously

[56] Presumably, although it is not easily verified, the origin of the term stems from the need for a project's expected return to *jump* over this rate to be accepted.

alluded to, does not entirely fit at the NIB. As an international financial institution, the mandate is not—unlike most commercial organizations—to maximize profit. Instead, it seeks to provide additionality in its area of operations—with a focus on productivity and the environment—in a (financially) sustainable manner.[57] Financial sustainability might also be interpreted as not needing to return to one's shareholders—outside of exceptional circumstances—for injections of capital. With this in mind, each firm needs (on a risk-adjusted basis) to generate a sufficient equity return to permit its targeted level of growth and relevance. Nevertheless, some lower-return loans with very high degrees of additionality might be considered. These, to meet the overall objectives and constraints, would need to be offset by other activities generating higher levels of return. This balance is central for attaining sustained organic growth.

There is a number of possible ways to derive such a hurdle rate. We will avoid the weighed average cost of capital approach, because we seek an ex-funding perspective.[58] Instead, our focus is rather on a required equity return. A default approach, as previously discussed, would be to focus on the (predicted or historical average) rate of economic growth, above the risk-free time value of money, in the firm's area of operation. If we denote this as $\pi$, then we might write our hurdle rate as

$$\mathcal{H}(t, T) = r(t, T) + \pi(t, T), \tag{6.43}$$

where $T - t$ is the horizon under consideration and $r$ represents a risk-free interest rate.[59] Practically, therefore, if one expected the Nordic and Baltic regions to have medium to long-term economic growth in the neighbourhood of 3% with 2% risk-free interest rates, then the hurdle rate would take a value of about 5%.

The role of the risk-free rate is interesting. Equation 6.42 indicates that equity financed lending or treasury activity contributes, at least, LIBOR. For analytic purposes, we can consider this to be roughly equivalent to a risk-free rate. If we assume that our hurdle rate is equal to this risk-free rate, then the lending-financed RAROC calculation could be used on a standalone basis since—from Eq. 6.42—we have that $\mathcal{H} - L(t, T) \approx \mathcal{H} - r(t, T) = 0$. Since an entity's shareholders can earn the risk-free rate on their own, of course, this is a relatively poor choice of hurdle rate. The consequence, therefore, is that it makes logical sense to judge a hurdle rate relative to the risk-free rate.

---

[57] Other entities can, and certainly do, have analogous strategic objectives to be attained.

[58] This piece is, in fact, already incorporated into our net lending income.

[59] Whatever the time horizon, we have an annualized rate in mind.

To hammer down this point, let's revisit our RAROC calculation using the concrete definition of the hurdle rate from Eq. 6.43. Restating Eq. 6.42, we have

$$
\begin{aligned}
\text{RAROC} &\approx \frac{\sum_{i=1}^{\beta} \Delta_i \eta_i X_i \delta_i}{\sum_{i=1}^{\beta} \hat{\mathcal{E}}_i(\theta)\delta_i} - \Bigg( \underbrace{r(t,T) + \pi(t,T)}_{\text{Equation 6.43}} - \overbrace{L(t,T)}^{\approx r(t,T)} \Bigg) \bar{\Delta}, \qquad (6.44) \\
&\approx \frac{\sum_{i=1}^{\beta} \Delta_i \eta_i X_i \delta_i}{\sum_{i=1}^{\beta} \hat{\mathcal{E}}_i(\theta)\delta_i} - \Big( \cancel{r(t,T)} + \pi(t,T) - \cancel{r(t,T)} \Big) \bar{\Delta}, \\
&\approx \frac{\sum_{i=1}^{\beta} \Delta_i \eta_i X_i \delta_i}{\sum_{i=1}^{\beta} \hat{\mathcal{E}}_i(\theta)\delta_i} - \pi(t,T)\bar{\Delta}.
\end{aligned}
$$

Using this form, in this case, the decision point is a RAROC of zero. That is, if the funding financed component covers $\pi(t, T)$, then the proposed lending project should—at least, on purely financial-return grounds—be accepted. This is because, once having covered all loan-related costs, its overall contribution meets the corporate equity return target. This result naturally leans on a few mathematical choices. One may naturally question the assumption that the risk-free and LIBOR rates roughly coincide.[60] Mechanically, however, this would lead to a slightly more conservative form for Eq. 6.44. So, while the assumption is clearly incorrect, it should not bias our decision-making in the wrong direction.

A challenge with the hurdle-rate definition in Eq. 6.43 relates to the level of risk-free rates. We have established that equity funded assets, in a LIBOR-based lending institution, are (at least) earning something roughly equivalent to the risk-free rate. For this reason, the risk-free rate falls out of our direct comparison. The issue is that this property makes LIBOR-based firms' overall income levels rather sensitive to the level of interest rates. If interest rates are zero—or, in some cases, negative as is the case in the current environment—focusing on long-term economic growth for one's hurdle rate definition may be insufficient. A firm will also require a general level of income to meet dividend obligations and basic absolute levels of balance-sheet growth.

[60] In reality, due to term premia and credit risk, the LIBOR rate should exceed the risk-free rate.

Another alternative, that might slightly assuage this aspect, would relate the hurdle rate to the firm's medium-term growth targets. Imagine, for example, that the institution wishes to attain an annual growth rate of $g(t, T)$ over the risk-free rate over the next $T - t$ years. This figure could come from internal analysis, mandate-driven objectives, or shareholder guidance. The logical process for selecting $g(t, T)$ could, and should, also incorporate assumptions and expectations regarding the path of risk-free interest rates. In this case, we could write our hurdle rate in a manner similar to Eq. 6.43 as,

$$\mathcal{H}(t, T) = r(t, T) + g(t, T). \tag{6.45}$$

Over the short-term, it is certainly possible for $g(t, T)$ to differ from $\pi(t, T)$. Over the medium to long-term, however, it will be difficult for any firm to attain growth levels that deviate importantly from broad-based economic growth.

**Colour and Commentary 72** (SPECIFYING A HURDLE RATE): *The choice of hurdle rate, defined as $\mathcal{H}$ in the previous discussion, is not specific to the individual loan under investigation. It is more broadly related to the general level of return required on a firm's equity. It must, therefore, be determined by reflection of firm-wide objectives. Two key elements enter into this choice. First, the equity financed component of asset returns—in a LIBOR-matched lending institution—will earn approximately the risk-free rate.*[a] *This argues for the specification of the hurdle rate relative to the general level of (risk-free) interest rates. The second point is that while it is difficult to target overall returns in excess of economic growth in the long term, any functional hurdle rate certainly needs to be calibrated to a firm's current and targeted growth objectives. Selection of one's hurdle rate is thus a central part of a lending institution's annual planning process; the corollary is that, depending on circumstances and future plans, it may vary over time.*

[a] There is a credit premium embedded in the LIBOR setting. During the reference-rate reform process as predominately overnight-funding, transaction-based replacements assume the role of reference rates, we should expect this risk-free assumption to move closer to the truth.

## 6.6 Allocating Economic Capital

Having covered the majority of the structural elements in the risk-adjusted capital return calculation, a bit more practical specificity regarding the economic-capital is required. Economic capital is, after all, a key component in the calculation. The question is: how precisely do we determine which elements of economic capital to include? Do we include everything—including regulatory or internal management buffers—for every type of asset investment? This would imply allocating all market, credit, and operational risk as well as the full set of buffers to every individual loan and treasury investment.

Some guidance would be welcome. If this was an accounting exercise, then full allocation might be a sensible objective. There is, however, also a behavioural aspect to a firm's RAROC calculation. It is, in fact, trying to help support sensible decision making. Aspects outside the decision-maker's control might not be useful inclusions into the calculation.[61] To reflect this fact, the basic premise is thus proposed:

> Economic capital should be allocated to those areas responsible for its management.

How this principle manifests itself depends, of course, on a firm's organizational structure. Asset-investment decisions are, after all, made in differing ways across institutions. At most lending institutions, for example, a lending origination department (or function) makes (most) loan proposals. They are not, however, responsible for determining how the associated financing is sourced and hedged. Loans also give rise to liquidity needs; again, the lending originator does not decide on the specific investment profile of these liquidity securities. The counterparty, default-credit, and market risk associated with borrowing, hedging, and liquidity investments are correspondingly not sensibly allocated to lending decisions.

A similar argument, operating in the opposite direction, applies to treasury operations. Treasury staff have no influence on the idiosyncratic credit-risk characteristics of a given loan investment. As a consequence, they should not be allocated lending related credit-risk economic capital. This makes sense despite the fact that treasury activity is largely driven, indeed caused, by lending business.

Operational risk and the capital buffers, conversely, are shared by both business lines.[62] It thus makes sense to allocate them accordingly. Moreover, both are readily determined through either an estimate of net interest income or risk-weighted assets. The (management) stress-testing buffer, however, is unallocated.[63] Figure 6.4 summarizes how the various elements of economic capital might sensibly be allocated to the lending and treasury business lines. This is merely one example that fits relatively well into our setting; compelling arguments can be made for alternative forms of risk allocation.

---

[61] Such questions, often referred to as risk budgeting, can become quite involved. See Scherer [32] for a useful entry point into this world.

[62] Countercyclical buffers are (typically) excluded to avoid introduction of economic cyclicality into the pricing decision. This point, depending on one's perspective and objectives, is open to debate.

[63] Refer to Chap. 1 for a review of these economic-capital buffers.

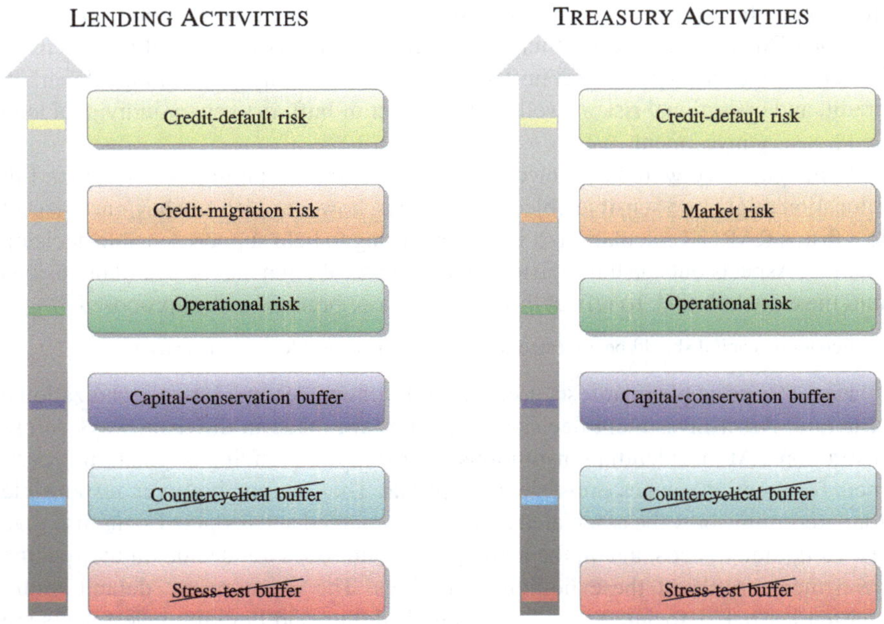


**Fig. 6.4** *Business-line allocation*: The preceding schematic summarizes the allocation of economic capital by the abovementioned business lines. The amounts allocated, by risk and buffer type, are only those specific to assets within that business area.

## 6.7 Getting More Practical

To this point, our discussion has been heavy on the theoretical dimension, but rather light on practicalities. To really get a feel for the RAROC computation, it is thus useful to examine a detailed, practical example. Not only does an example make things more concrete, it also allows us to examine a few twists and turns in the computation presented by real-life situations. Due to privacy concerns, however, it is impossible to examine a real loan. To that end, Fig. 6.5 outlines the details of an entirely fictitious loan.

Our fabricated case takes the form of a Norwegian industrial corporate considering a five-year maturity loan with a total exposure of EUR 60 million. It furthermore resides in internal credit-rating class PD06, and has a loss-given-default value of 0.45. The range of fees and costs are also summarized in Fig. 6.5. This collection of data represents the information available to the loan originator. The key question is: how can we think about the return associated with this constellation of loan details on a risk-adjusted basis?

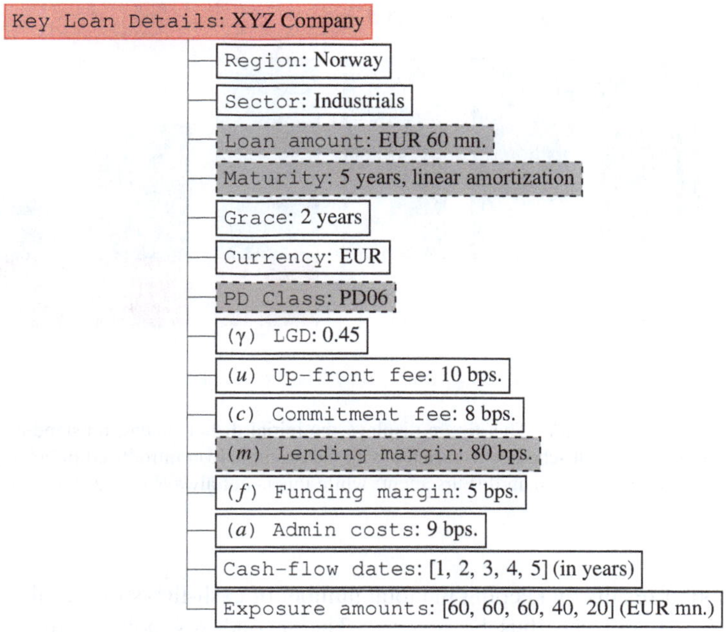


**Fig. 6.5** *A concrete example*: This schematic outlines the qualitative and quantitative details associated with a fictitious, but illustrative and concrete, loan example.

## 6.7.1 *Immediate Disbursement*

The first step in addressing this question involves understanding the intertemporal structure of implied loan cash-flows. Figure 6.6 illustrates the expected cash-flows associated with our five-year loan, its two-year grace period, and a linear amortization structure. A key underlying assumption is that the full amount of the loan is immediately disbursed. Practically, this is a not only unlikely, but probably even impossible. For loans that are expected to disburse in the iminent future, however, this is a sensible simplification.[64]

Figure 6.6 clearly displays the equal capital repayment of EUR 20 million during the final three years of the loan's life. This creates a step-down effect on the loan outstanding, which needs to be reflected in the cash-flow and economic-capital values.

Table 6.1 jumps right to the details of the RAROC computation. In particular, it focuses attention on the various elements of the ratio's numerator. These aspects of expected marginal loan income were introduced in Eq. 6.35. The first point is that we assume each cash-flow occurs on an annual basis; this simplifies the

[64] We will relax this assumption in a moment and explore the implications for the RAROC calculation.

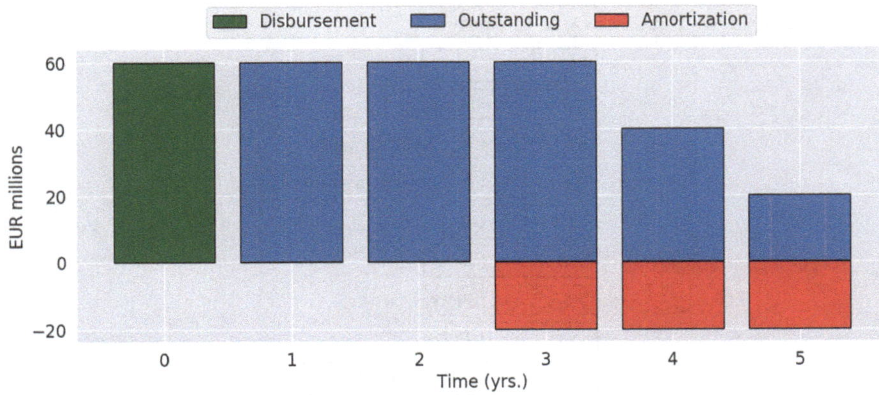


**Fig. 6.6** *Outstanding profile*: This figure displays the initial disbursement, outstanding amount, and amortization payment schedule associated with the example loan introduced in Fig. 6.5. In this case, we observe immediate loan disbursement; while this is not always the case, it simplifies the computation.

illustration of results by keeping the total number of cash-flows low. It also implies that $\Delta_i = 1$ and can thus be ignored. The second key point is that the loan outstanding amounts—from Fig. 6.6—are summarized in the second column. These $\{X_i; i = 1, \ldots, 5\}$ quantities play a central role in determining each subsequent column.

The remaining values in Table 6.1 should be relatively self-explanatory. A 10 basis-point up-front fee, on a EUR 60 million loan, amounts to a single payment of EUR 60,000 on the first cash-flow date. The funding margin is slightly more complex since it involves weighting its values by the associated economic-capital consumption at period $i$.[65] Overall, on a discounted basis, the total (lifetime) marginal contribution to capital is roughly EUR 1.8 million. This forms the numerator of our RAROC ratio.

Table 6.2 turns our attention to the various components comprising the denominator of our RAROC calculation. The actual economic capital estimate at time $i$ is written as,

$$\begin{aligned}\underbrace{\text{Economic Capital}}_{\mathcal{E}_i(\theta)} &= \bigg(\text{Default Risk}\bigg) + \bigg(\text{Migration Risk}\bigg)\\ &\quad + \bigg(\text{Buffers \& Operational Risk}\bigg), \qquad (6.46)\\ \mathcal{E}_i(\theta) \approx \hat{\mathcal{E}}_i(\theta) &= \hat{\mathcal{D}}_i(\theta) + \hat{\mathcal{M}}_i(\theta) + \hat{\mathcal{B}}_i,\end{aligned}$$

[65] These values will be addressed in the subsequent table.

**Table 6.1** *The RAROC numerator*: The underlying table illustrates, in the context of our practical example outlined in Fig. 6.5, the various elements of the RAROC numerator organized by individual cash-flow date.

| $i$ | $X_i$ | $\mathbb{I}_{i=1} \cdot u \cdot X_i$ | $m \cdot X_i$ | $\left(1 - \frac{\hat{\mathcal{E}}_i(\theta)}{X_i}\right) \cdot f \cdot X_i$ | $-a \cdot X_i$ | $-\gamma \cdot p_i \cdot X_i$ | $\eta_i \cdot X_i$ | $\eta_i \cdot X_i \cdot \delta_i$ |
|---|---|---|---|---|---|---|---|---|
| 1 | 60,000,000 | 60,000 | 480,000 | 26,375 | −54,000 | −18,225 | 494,150 | 495,036 |
| 2 | 60,000,000 | 0 | 480,000 | 26,199 | −54,000 | −21,776 | 430,422 | 431,622 |
| 3 | 60,000,000 | 0 | 480,000 | 26,130 | −54,000 | −23,500 | 428,630 | 428,334 |
| 4 | 40,000,000 | 0 | 320,000 | 17,419 | −36,000 | −16,893 | 284,526 | 282,359 |
| 5 | 20,000,000 | 0 | 160,000 | 8727 | −18,000 | −9099 | 141,628 | 139,174 |
| Total | 240,000,000 | 60,000 | 1,920,000 | 104,849 | −216,000 | −89,493 | 1,779,356 | **1,776,525** |

**Table 6.2** *The RAROC denominator*: This table outlines, following from the example in Fig. 6.5, the different aspects of the RAROC denominator organized by individual cash-flow date.

| $i$ | $X_i$ | $\hat{\mathcal{D}}_i(\theta)$ | $\hat{\mathcal{M}}_i(\theta)$ | $\hat{\mathcal{B}}_i$ | $\hat{\mathcal{E}}_i(\theta)$ | $\hat{\mathcal{D}}_i(\theta) \cdot \delta_i$ |
|---|---|---|---|---|---|---|
| 1 | 60,000,000 | 7,136,138 | 113,521 | 1,296,378 | 8,546,037 | 8,561,362 |
| 2 | 60,000,000 | 7,515,214 | 87,218 | 1,296,378 | 8,898,810 | 8,923,618 |
| 3 | 60,000,000 | 7,680,664 | 60,154 | 1,296,378 | 9,037,197 | 9,030,964 |
| 4 | 40,000,000 | 5,132,042 | 30,390 | 864,252 | 6,026,684 | 5,980,788 |
| 5 | 20,000,000 | 2,536,025 | 10,236 | 432,126 | 2,978,388 | 2,926,779 |
| Total | 240,000,000 | 30,000,083 | 301,519 | 5,185,513 | 35,487,115 | **35,423,511** |

for $i = 1, \ldots, \beta$. In words, there are three main components to the approximated *lending* economic-capital consumption for each time period.[66] The first two relate to the default and migration credit-risk allocations; these are both based on separate approximation algorithms and depend on a parameter vector.[67] The final component combines the non-stress-test capital buffers and operational risk. It does not depend on the parameter vector, $\theta$, since it does not involve any complicated mathematical approximations. The capital buffers, based on risk-weighted assets, are known with precision.[68] The overall quantity is still designated as a percentage, because determination of the operational risk is not exactly computed. It depends on a firm's historical accounting-based net-interest income, which can be readily determined in aggregate, but is less exact at the loan level.

Examination of Table 6.2 (unsurprisingly) reveals that the majority of economic capital, for this loan, stems from credit-default risk. Credit-migration risk is relatively modest for this loan; capital buffers and operational risk are also fairly small. The total (discounted) lifetime economic-capital consumption amounts to about EUR 35 million.

The RAROC estimate, quite mechanically, is simply the ratio of the total discounted capital contribution and consumption. This amounts to about $\frac{1.78}{35.4} \approx 5.0\%$. This result is displayed, more precisely, in Table 6.3, which further illustrates a separate RAROC figure for each individual cash-flow period. These annual figures do not have a direct application, but they are nonetheless interesting. They provide some insight into the evolution of annual capital contribution and consumption over the loan's lifetime. The various components of the numerators and denominators are also displayed. The elements of the numerator will change along with key inputs such as lending margin, administrative expenses, funding margin, and other fees. The denominator, which scales the income contribution by risk, varies by

[66] If we wish to compute a RAROC for a treasury investment, the denominator would include slightly different ingredients. See Fig. 6.4 for more detail.

[67] To be really precise, we should write the set of approximation parameters as $\theta_0 \equiv \theta$ to reflect their link to the starting time point—that is, $i = 0$—associated with the calculation.

[68] This depends on the level of the loan's associated risk-weighted assets; this quantity is extensively discussed in Chap. 11.

**Table 6.3** *The RAROC calculation*: The underlying table combines the results from Tables 6.1 and 6.2 to illustrate the overall RAROC estimate along with associated values for each individual year.

| $i$ | $X_i$ | $\eta_i \cdot X_i \cdot \delta_i$ | $\hat{\mathcal{E}}_i(\theta) \cdot \delta_i$ | $\text{RAROC}_i = \frac{\eta_i \cdot X_i \cdot \delta_i}{\hat{\mathcal{E}}_i(\theta) \cdot \delta_i}$ |
|---|---|---|---|---|
| 1 | 60,000,000 | 495,036 | 8,561,362 | 5.78% |
| 2 | 60,000,000 | 431,622 | 8,923,618 | 4.84% |
| 3 | 60,000,000 | 428,334 | 9,030,964 | 4.74% |
| 4 | 40,000,000 | 282,359 | 5,980,788 | 4.72% |
| 5 | 20,000,000 | 139,174 | 2,926,779 | 4.76% |
| Total | 240,000,000 | 1,776,525 | 35,423,511 | **5.02%** |

what specific risks are allocated, the riskiness of the loan, and the current portfolio composition. The actual economic-capital computation also importantly takes into account any existing exposure to the same credit obligor. Adding EUR 60 million of new loan exposure is rather different—in terms of incremental economic capital—from combining this exposure to existing loans of, let's say, EUR 300 million. In the former case, this is a relatively average new exposure. In the latter, it appends to an already fairly important concentration. The consequence is a higher level of risk and thus a larger economic-capital allocation.

### 6.7.2 *Payment Frequency*

Questions naturally arise regarding the frequency of payments. The preceding illustrative calculations operate on the assumption that cash-flows occur only on an annual basis. Most real-life loans, however, actually pay on a semi-annual basis. In some institutions, payments might even occur at a quarterly, or even monthly, frequency. How would this impact the actual RAROC computation? We would hope that the impact would be minimal. The situation is analogous to the role of payment frequency on bond-yield calculations; there is an effect, but the result is modest. In the RAROC setting, the magnitude of this effect needs to be determined.

Figure 6.7 addresses this potential concern by illustrating the path of RAROC from the displayed annual frequency incrementing towards a daily payment. While daily payments are obviously somewhat extreme, we see a clear limiting behaviour in the RAROC evolution. The biggest jump occurs from annual to semi-annual payment frequency, although the total change is only a matter of a handful of basis points. Beyond monthly, the change is almost imperceptible as it tends towards continuous compounding. We can conclude, therefore, that there is no material difference between the use of annual or semi-annual cash-flows in the RAROC computation.

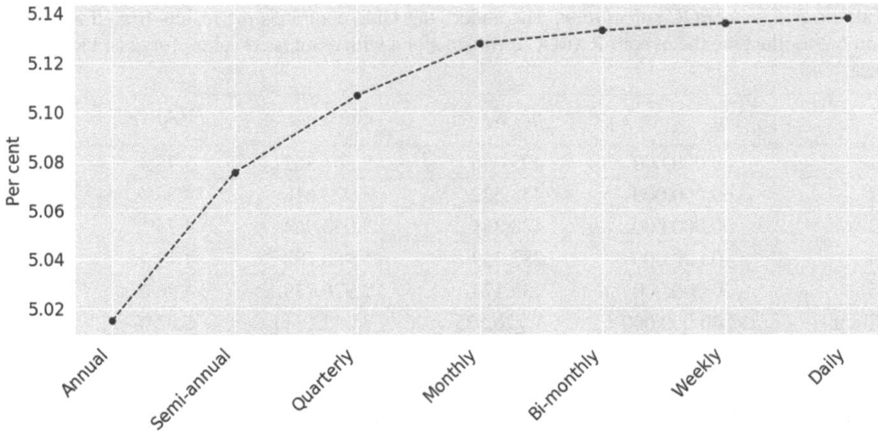


**Fig. 6.7** *The role of payment frequency*: This graphic repeats the computation from Table 6.3 for an array of possible payment frequencies ranging from annual to daily. The impact on the final RAROC outcome is modest amounting to only a handful of basis points.

### *6.7.3 The Lending Margin*

The risk-adjusted return on capital calculation is, at its core, a tool to determine an appropriate level of lending margin. Administrative expenses, discount factors, funding margins, and loan impairments are beyond the loan originator's control. Economic capital, determined principally by the obligor-level attributes, is also a given. The size and tenor of the loan are, of course, subject to some degree of negotiation. These are, however, largely determined by the obligor's preferences and the requirements of the underlying project. The only remaining degree of freedom for the loan originator relates to the income component: upfront and commitment fees as well as lending-related margins. Among these quantities, the lending margin has the greatest impact and, as a consequence, plays the most important role. Indeed, loan pricing is principally about finding an appropriate lending margin. As indicated in the introduction to this chapter, the lending margin is basically our *choice* variable.

Mechanically, loan pricing could be quite easy. One need only find the lending margin that equates the RAROC calculation with the firm's internal hurdle rate. Any level of lending margin above that point would meet the institution's internal growth target. The seemingly simple procedure masks an underlying problem: the lending institution does not operate in a vacuum. For many loan transactions, more specifically, there is an external market price. In some cases, this price relates to a deep and liquid set of external sources of financing. In others, it might represent a few indicative quotes from other potential lenders. Thus, although the depth of

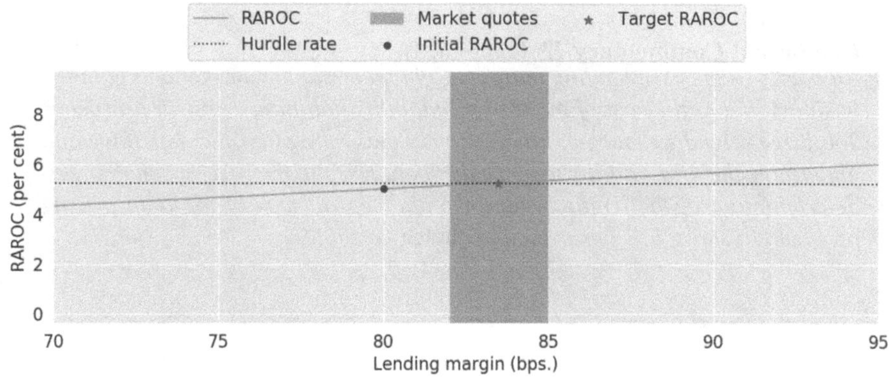


**Fig. 6.8** *Finding the lending margin*: Finding the lending margin is a tricky affair. The lending originator must negotiate between meeting the firm hurdle rate and setting a margin consistent with market pricing. The lack, in many cases, of a single clear signal from the market confuses the task. The example above attempts, in an illustrative manner, to describe this process.

the market is variable, there is almost invariably an external comparator for loan pricing.[69] Lending margins need to be determined within this context.

Figure 6.8 highlights—within our simple loan example—the relationship between the lending margin and the RAROC value. Assuming an invented hurdle rate of $5\frac{1}{4}\%$, the lending margin would need to be increased from 80 to about 84 basis points. This is the simple intersection of the RAROC curve—as a function of lending margin—and the hurdle rate. For illustrative purposes, a range of possible market quotes are presented in Fig. 6.8 in the neighbourhood of 82 to 85 basis points. In a real-life situation, these could possibly deviate importantly from this hurdle-rate break-even point. The loan originator needs to find a balance between the internal-growth requirements of the lending institution and the competitive forces summarized by external market prices.

**Colour and Commentary 73** (THE KEY CHOICE VARIABLE): *Many elements in the loan origination process are beyond the lender's control. Administrative costs and funding margins are, in principle, controllable, but they involve larger processes outside the lending area. Loan impairments and economic-capital consumption relate principally to the riskiness of the credit obligor. The principal area of choice relates to the lending margin. Even in this case, however, flexibility is limited. Selection of the lending margin involves walking a fine line between the firm's hurdle rate and market prices.*

(continued)

[69] For small to medium firms, the process of price discovery is complicated by a relatively small number of potential lenders. Moreover, the flow of information regarding these lender's pricing intentions is not entirely transparent.

**Colour and Commentary 73** (continued)
*An overly aggressive lending margin might undercut the market and gain the business, but at the cost of internal profitability and future growth prospects. Too large a lending margin, however, may make the offer uncompetitive and undermine the firm's ability to make the loan. Despite the inherent challenges, determination of the lending margin is the central task of the loan-pricing problem. In short, it is our principal* choice *variable.*

### *6.7.4 Existing Loan Exposure*

In our straightforward example, the EUR 60 million deal was assumed to represent *new* lending for the institution. In other words, the loan portfolio does not include any other exposure to the same credit obligor. This is not always the case. Indeed, it is not uncommon for a firm to engage in multiple loans of various sizes and tenors with a single counterpart. Leveraging existing client relationships is, after all, simply good business. From a risk perspective, this is not immediately problematic, but it does require some adjustments. In particular, a large concentration with a single client involves more risk than numerous smaller exposures with a range of obligors. The RAROC calculation, and more particularly the economic-capital computation, needs to take this dimension into account.

Figure 6.9 illustrates the impact of varying levels of existing exposure—holding all other variables constant—associated with our sample loan.[70] The first point, which involves no existing client exposure, corresponds to the roughly 5% RAROC estimate from Table 6.3. As we increase existing obligor loans gradually to EUR 500 million, the RAROC falls non-linearly to approximately 4.3%. While this general trend will apply for other loans, the specific shape of the curve will depend on the obligor's risk attributes and the general composition of the portfolio.

The initial economic-capital consumption—as a percentage of the loan exposure—is also presented for the various existing loan values. We see that it starts around 14% (i.e., EUR 8.5 million) and increases (also non-linearly) by about 2.5% points to 16.5% (i.e., almost EUR 10 million). The concentration effect is thus sufficiently large that it cannot be ignored in the RAROC computation.[71]

[70] In this example, the existing loans are assumed to have an average maturity of four years.

[71] Practically, the calculation of this effect is conceptually straightforward. If $N$ and $O$ denote the *new* and *existing* (i.e., old) loan exposures, respectively, then

$$\hat{\mathcal{E}}_\theta(N) = \hat{\mathcal{E}}_\theta(O + N) - \hat{\mathcal{E}}_\theta(O), \tag{6.47}$$

where, $\hat{\mathcal{E}}_\theta(\cdot)$ denotes the economic-capital approximation. This computation thus requires *three* separate evaluations of the approximation approach from Chap. 5.

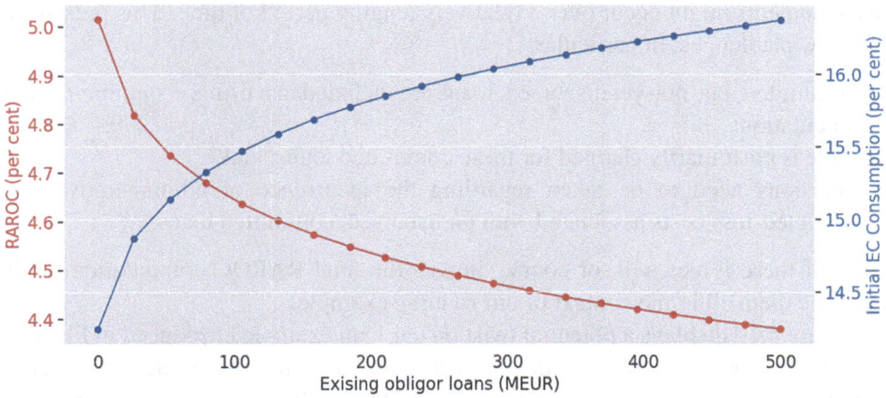


**Fig. 6.9** *Concentration effects*: Economic-capital consumption is a (complicated) non-linear function of the overall exposure to an obligor. New loans, therefore, must be handled differently from loans adding to existing exposures. The preceding graphic outlines the RAROC impact, for our example loan, associated with varying levels of existing exposure (all else equal).

**Colour and Commentary 74** (CONCENTRATION EFFECTS)*: The preceding chapters describe, in great detail, the technical aspects of the computation of economic capital. Much of this discussion surrounded the role of single-name and portfolio concentrations. The loan-pricing problem—and more particularly, the impact of existing obligor exposure for new loans—is a concrete, practical application of this modelling dimension. Incorporation of existing and outstanding loans into the economic-capital estimates within the RAROC computation is* not *optional. A simple example illustrates clearly that the economic-capital consumption increases significantly (and non-linearly), with a corresponding decrease in the associated RAROC value. This information is critical in the determination of efficient lending margins reflecting existing portfolio concentrations.*[a]

[a] This simple fact also explains why multiple lenders, when asked to provide quotes on a given deal, often provide such a surprisingly wide range of values. A given loan can, and will, impact their own portfolios in different ways.

### 6.7.5 *Forward-Starting Disbursements*

Not all loans disburse quickly after performance of one's RAROC analysis. Indeed, not all loans disburse in their entirety at one point in time. In some cases, multiple disbursements might occur over a relatively lengthy period of time. This presents a few new challenges. In particular,

1. committed, but-not-yet disbursed, loans are included in a firm's economic-capital calculation;
2. a fee is customarily charged for these committed loans; and
3. decisions need to be taken regarding the incurrence of administrative and expected-loss costs associated with undisbursed, committed loans.

Each of these issues will, of course, impact the final RAROC computation. Let's examine them all in the context of our running example.

Figure 6.10 displays a potential twist on our loan example introduced in Fig. 6.5. One half of the loan disburses in one year, with the remainder going out the door in two years' time. At the time of final disbursement, the five-year loan tenor clock begins. The final maturity occurs after seven years, but the basic amortization profile remains unchanged; it is simply shifted forward two years.

To accommodate this dimension, it is necessary to introduce two new concepts: the disbursement and the commitment. These have, of course, always been lurking around in the background. We now simply need to make them more visible. On the same time grid—$i = 0, 1, \ldots, \beta$—we can denote the loan disbursement at time $i$ as $D_i$. If we let $X$ represent the total loan notional amount, then the commitment amount at time $i$—referred to as $C_i$—can be inferred as,

$$\text{Commitment}_i = \text{Notional amount} - \text{Cumulative disbursements up until time } i,$$

$$C_i = X - \sum_{k=0}^{i-1} D_i, \tag{6.48}$$

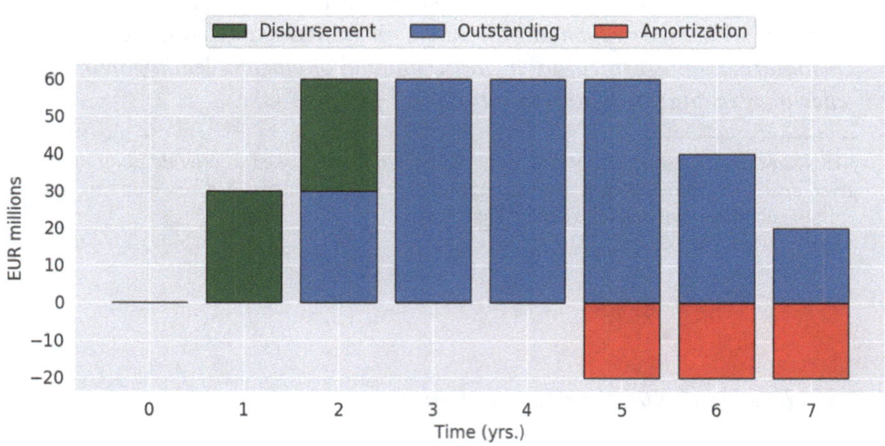


**Fig. 6.10** *A forward starting loan*: This graph illustrates the same basic loan example, introduced in Figure 6.5, but changes the starting conditions. The disbursement occurs in two steps: one- and two-years in the future, respectively.

for $i = 1, \ldots, \beta$. The loan commitments, as we would expect, decrease as the amount of loan disbursements approach the agreed total loan level.[72] In our previous five-year, immediate-disbursement loan example, $D_0 = X$. The consequence was the rather uninteresting case of $C_i$ being identically zero for all $i$. Naturally, in such cases, there is little incremental value associated with including them in the RAROC calculation. When disbursements are spread out over future periods, conversely, the commitments play a rather more important role.

To properly accommodate the fee income associated with these commitments, it is necessary to update Eq. 6.35 to include the associated fees. The expected marginal loan income thus becomes

$$\begin{aligned}\begin{array}{c}\text{Expected}\\\text{Marginal}\\\text{Loan}\\\text{Income}\end{array} &= \begin{array}{c}\text{Commit-}\\\text{ment}\\\text{Fees}\end{array} + \begin{array}{c}\text{Upfront}\\\text{Fees}\end{array} + \begin{array}{c}\text{Lending}\\\text{Margin}\end{array} - \begin{array}{c}\text{(Weighted)}\\\text{Funding}\\\text{Margin}\end{array} - \begin{array}{c}\text{Admin}\\\text{Expenses}\end{array}\\ &\quad - \begin{array}{c}\text{Loan}\\\text{Impair-}\\\text{ments}\end{array} - \begin{array}{c}\text{(Weighted)}\\\text{Equity}\\\text{Cost}\end{array}, \qquad (6.49)\\ &= \sum_{i=1}^{\beta} \Delta_i \left( cC_i + \left( \mathbb{I}_{i=1} u + m - \left(1 - \frac{\mathcal{E}_i}{X_i}\right) f - a - \gamma p_i \right) X_i \right.\\ &\quad \left. - \left( \mathcal{H} - F(t, T_{i-1}, T_i) \right) \mathcal{E}_i \right) \delta_i,\end{aligned}$$

where the RAROC computation itself has the following revised form:

$$\text{RAROC} \approx \frac{\sum_{i=1}^{\beta} \Delta_i \left( cC_i + \eta_i X_i \right) \delta_i}{\sum_{i=1}^{\beta} \hat{\mathcal{E}}_i(\theta) \delta_i} - \left( \mathcal{H} - L(t, T) \right), \qquad (6.50)$$

where, to be clear, $c$ represents the percentage commitment fee.

Table 6.4 provides a revised version of Table 6.1 for this two-year, gradual forward-start version of our loan. Beyond two additional years of cash-flows, there are new columns for commitments and commitment fees. After one year, the loan commitment remains at EUR 60 million. Half of the loan was disbursed on this date, but the commitment fee is earned on the undisbursed balance over the entire first year. In the second year, by contrast, the commitment fees are only earned

[72] A lag is necessary, since these values are used for cash-flows and economic-capital calculations. At time $i$, we need to know the commitment as of time $i - 1$ to properly compute these quantities.

**Table 6.4** *The forward RAROC numerator*: The underlying table illustrates, in the context of our practical example outlined in Fig. 6.5, the various elements of the RAROC numerator organized by individual cash-flow date. It compares to Table 6.1, but has been modified to incorporate a gradual two-year forward start.

| $i$ | $C_i$ | $X_i$ | $\mathbb{I}_{i=1} u \cdot X_i$ | $c \cdot C_i$ | $m \cdot X_i$ | $\left(1 - \frac{\hat{\mathcal{E}}_i(\theta)}{X_i}\right) \cdot f \cdot X_i$ | $-a \cdot X_i$ | $-\gamma \cdot p_i \cdot X_i$ | $c \cdot C_i + \eta_i \cdot X_i$ | $\eta_i \cdot X_i \cdot \delta_i$ |
|---|---|---|---|---|---|---|---|---|---|---|
| 1 | 60,000,000 | 0 | 60,000 | 48,000 | 0 | 0 | -0 | -0 | 108,000 | 108,194 |
| 2 | 30,000,000 | 30,000,000 | 0 | 24,000 | 240,000 | 11,644 | -27,000 | -10,888 | 237,755 | 238,418 |
| 3 | 0 | 60,000,000 | 0 | 0 | 480,000 | 26,116 | -54,000 | -23,500 | 428,616 | 428,320 |
| 4 | 0 | 60,000,000 | 0 | 0 | 480,000 | 26,047 | -54,000 | -25,340 | 426,707 | 423,458 |
| 5 | 0 | 60,000,000 | 0 | 0 | 480,000 | 25,978 | -54,000 | -27,297 | 424,681 | 417,323 |
| 6 | 0 | 40,000,000 | 0 | 0 | 320,000 | 17,310 | -36,000 | -19,586 | 281,725 | 273,500 |
| 7 | 0 | 20,000,000 | 0 | 0 | 160,000 | 8675 | -18,000 | -10,528 | 140,146 | 134,136 |
| Total | 90,000,000 | 270,000,000 | 60,000 | 72,000 | 2,160,000 | 115,770 | -243,000 | -117,139 | 2,047,631 | **2,023,349** |

**Table 6.5** *The forward RAROC denominator*: This table outlines, following from the example in Fig. 6.5, the different aspects of the RAROC denominator organized by individual cash-flow date.

| $i$ | $\mu \cdot C_i + X_i$ | $\hat{\mathcal{D}}_i(\theta)$ | $\hat{\mathcal{M}}_i(\theta)$ | $\hat{\mathcal{B}}_i$ | $\hat{\mathcal{E}}_i(\theta)$ | $\hat{\mathcal{D}}_i(\theta) \cdot \delta_i$ |
|---|---|---|---|---|---|---|
| 1 | 46,200,000 | 5,427,769 | 106,294 | 998,211 | 6,532,274 | 6,543,987 |
| 2 | 53,100,000 | 6,612,889 | 100,051 | 1,147,295 | 7,860,234 | 7,882,147 |
| 3 | 60,000,000 | 7,680,664 | 87,218 | 1,296,378 | 9,064,260 | 9,058,009 |
| 4 | 60,000,000 | 7,846,209 | 60,154 | 1,296,378 | 9,202,742 | 9,132,658 |
| 5 | 60,000,000 | 8,011,438 | 31,875 | 1,296,378 | 9,339,692 | 9,177,858 |
| 6 | 40,000,000 | 5,348,804 | 30,390 | 864,252 | 6,243,446 | 6,061,186 |
| 7 | 20,000,000 | 2,640,509 | 10,236 | 432,126 | 3,082,871 | 2,950,648 |
| Total | 339,300,000 | 43,568,281 | 426,217 | 7,331,019 | 51,325,518 | **50,806,493** |

on the EUR 30 million committed balance. The total marginal economic-capital contribution associated with the revised example increases to about EUR 2 million.

The remaining non-commitment column calculations in Table 6.4 operate in the same manner as before, but with one important exception. The assumption is that the administrative expenses and expected loss are only allocated to the disbursed loan amounts. This choice can be disputed. One might legitimately argue that administrative costs are also incurred for undisbursed loans. Moreover, there is typically an allowance for committed loans in the loan-impairment calculation. Arguments can be made in either direction and ultimately it comes down to a trade-off between accuracy and desired organizational incentives. Overloading forward-start loans with excessive costs might discourage such activity; this might create structural disadvantages for certain types of loans and obligors. Excluding these costs could, however, encourage them and lead to lower profitability and reduced capacity for capital growth.

Table 6.5—which is directly comparable to Table 6.2—turns to the denominator of our forward-start example. The same characters are present, albeit with two additional years of calculations. The second column has a slightly different form. A central input to the economic-capital calculation—often referred to as the exposure-at-default—is redefined as,

$$\text{Economic Capital Exposure}_i = \mu C_i + X_i, \tag{6.51}$$

where $\mu \in [0, 1]$. The remaining approximation inputs are unchanged. Loan commitments are an economic obligation on the part of the lending institution. To the extent that they earn commitment fees and represent potential future earnings, they are also a firm asset. As an (off-) balance sheet asset, it is logically important to also capture their risks. Ignoring them completely would be incorrect. The question is: to what extent should we incorporate these inherently uncertain commitments into our risk calculations? The constant, $\mu$, is a multiplier that attempts to address this question. It modifies the commitments by a value in the unit interval. A value of zero ignores them, while a value of unity implies certain disbursement. In regulatory

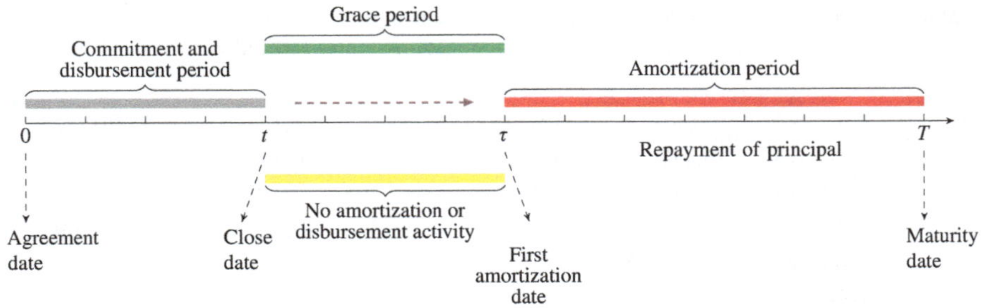


**Fig. 6.11** *Loan life-cycle schematic*: This schematic illustrates, in a stylized manner, the life cycle of a loan. It helps us to visualize the commitment, grace, and amortization periods.

circles, this constant is referred to as a credit-conversion factor or CCF.[73] This example sets this value to 0.75. The consequence of this setting, and Eq. 6.51, is that despite the forward start, economic-capital is consumed from the agreement date of this loan. The total, discounted, marginal lifetime economic-capital consumption from the forward-start version of the loan is about EUR 50 million.

Figure 6.11 helps to visualize all of these moving parts by providing a schematic of the loan life cycle. It begins with the agreement date, followed by the commitment period. As we saw earlier, the loan is disbursed in one or more instalments during this time interval. Once the loan closes—or, alternatively, is fully disbursed—the grace period follows. During this time span, interest payments proceed as normal, but no principal is repaid.[74] After the expiry of the grace period, each payment is a combination of principal and interest until final maturity. Often the agreement and close dates are very close together—as in our original version of the loan example—so the commitment period is not particularly exciting. When this is not the case, however, this loan schematic needs to be kept in mind to correctly manage the RAROC calculation.

Table 6.6 closes out our loan example—in a manner similar to Table 6.3—by summarizing all of the numerator and denominator elements and combining them to illustrate the annual, and overall, RAROC figures. The total RAROC is mechanically computed as $\frac{2.0}{50.8} \approx 4.0\%$. This is significantly lower than in the immediate disbursement case. Examining the annual RAROC values explains the difference: the first few years—when we earn only the commitment fees—have a significantly lower level of return. This should be no surprise. The commitment fee is a relatively small value compared to the $\mu = 75\%$ consumption of economic capital. If

[73] As one would expect, regulators also put limits and provide guidance on the appropriate choice of $\mu$. Chapter 4 discusses this point in more detail.

[74] For a bullet-style loan, the grace period extends to the final maturity, when the full notional amount is repaid.

**Table 6.6** *The forward RAROC calculation*: The underlying table combines the results from Tables 6.4 and 6.5 to illustrate the overall RAROC estimate along with associated values for each individual year.

| $i$ | $C_i$ | $X_i$ | $\mu \cdot C_i + X_i$ | $c \cdot C_i + \eta_i \cdot X_i \cdot \delta_i$ | $\hat{\mathcal{E}}_i(\theta) \cdot \delta_i$ | $\text{RAROC}_i = \frac{(c \cdot C_i + \eta_i \cdot X_i) \cdot \delta_i}{\hat{\mathcal{E}}_i(\theta) \cdot \delta_i}$ |
|---|---|---|---|---|---|---|
| 1 | 60,000,000 | 0 | 46,200,000 | 108,194 | 6,543,987 | 1.65% |
| 2 | 30,000,000 | 30,000,000 | 53,100,000 | 238,418 | 7,882,147 | 3.02% |
| 3 | 0 | 60,000,000 | 60,000,000 | 428,320 | 9,058,009 | 4.73% |
| 4 | 0 | 60,000,000 | 60,000,000 | 423,458 | 9,132,658 | 4.64% |
| 5 | 0 | 60,000,000 | 60,000,000 | 417,323 | 9,177,858 | 4.55% |
| 6 | 0 | 40,000,000 | 40,000,000 | 273,500 | 6,061,186 | 4.51% |
| 7 | 0 | 20,000,000 | 20,000,000 | 134,136 | 2,950,648 | 4.55% |
| Total | 90,000,000 | 270,000,000 | 339,300,000 | 2,023,349 | 50,806,493 | **3.98%** |

administrative and impairment costs were included, this would act to further reduce the risk-adjusted return associated with this forward-start loan example.

### *6.7.6 Selecting Commitment Fees*

In their basic form, the RAROC estimates of the immediate-disbursement and forward-start versions of our loan example differ by about 100 basis points. The reason stems from the inability of the 8 basis-point fee to compensate for the loan-commitment economic capital and the reduced lending-margin receipts during the commitment period. This raises an interesting question: what level of commitment fees would make the firm indifferent between the immediate and forward-start versions of our sample loan?

Figure 6.12 attempts to answer this question by illustrating the RAROC—under *ceteris paribus* conditions—of our forward-start loan for commitment fees ranging from zero to 80 basis points. The initial RAROC of 4% relates to a commitment fee, as seen previously, of eight basis points. The break-even commitment fee amounts to roughly 65 basis points. This makes logical sense; it is roughly equal to the product of the credit-conversion factor ($\mu = 0.75$) and the original lending margin of 75 basis points.

This analysis suggests that a likely unreasonably high level of commitment fee would be necessary to compensate for the forward-start nature of the loan. In practice, however, the commitment fee is not the only tool available to the loan originator. A combination of a small increase in lending margin and upfront fee—in addition to an augmentation of the commitment fee—might also accomplish the

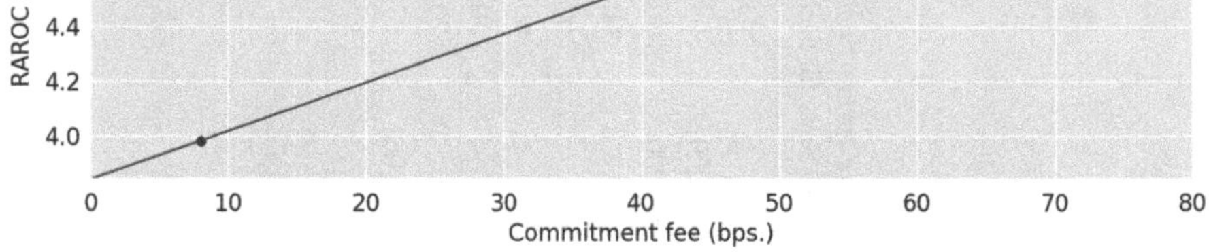


**Fig. 6.12** *The commitment fee*: The difference between the commitment fee and the lending margin tends to lead, for forward-start loans, to a drop-off in risk-adjusted returns on capital. The preceding graphic illustrates the relationship between the RAROC and the commitment fee. All else equal, a value of approximately 65 basis points is required to break-even with the immediate disbursement loan.

same result. Naturally, the institution (and the client) may not view these various fee elements as equivalent, but the option still remains. The larger picture is that, without some adjustment, a forward-start loan appears to structurally lead to lower RAROC outcomes.

**Colour and Commentary 75** (NON-IMMEDIATE LOAN DISBURSEMENT): *Not all loans are immediately, or rather quickly, disbursed. Some involve a rolling forward start with multiple disbursement instalments ranging over a relatively lengthy time period. These loans, once agreed, find themselves in a kind of limbo. They are not fully loans, but they do represent an economic obligation to the lending institution. We refer to the associated undisbursed loan balances as* commitments. *Computation of risk-adjusted return on capital for such forward-starting loans requires making practical (and defensible assumptions) regarding these loan commitments. In particular, one needs to decide upon the amount of capital they consume, how much fee income they earn, and the treatment of administrative and loan-impairment expenses during the commitment period. These choices have an important influence on the RAROC computations and, ultimately, the desirability of such forward-starting loan activity.*

## 6.8 Wrapping Up

This chapter addresses the thorny, but central, question of loan pricing. Determining an appropriate pricing structure for a given loan includes both qualitative and quantitative elements. Although extremely important, the preceding discussion does not spend much time on the qualitative dimension. Exclusion of these strategic elements from our focus—principally due to difficulties in their quantitative model-based assessment—should *not* be interpreted as a statement on their importance. On the contrary, we must not lose sight of their central role in the loan-origination process.

This chapter is essentially about building a supporting quantitative infrastructure for the complicated business of originating loans. Some heavy lifting was required. The core idea is to treat each loan decision as an investment project or, as it is referred in the literature, as a capital-budgeting decision. Asset-pricing theory and key corporate-finance concepts were combined to construct a structural description of the risk-adjusted return on capital. Further embedded in this calculation is the full machinery of the economic-capital simulation engine and associated approximations developed in Chaps. 2 to 5. Such technical detail is inevitable for building a coherent approach to loan pricing; the consequence of this effort is the useful and flexible RAROC calculation.

The embedded theoretical elements of the RAROC calculation provide insight into a range of practical questions. Where should one set the lending margin to meet internal growth targets? What is the impact associated with delayed disbursement, or forward-start, loans? How might the magnitude of the commitment fee influence the forward-start decision? Does the payment frequency make an important difference? How should existing loans with a given obligor influence our decision to extend additional credit? These, and many more, legitimate queries need to be addressed in the loan-origination process. While they need to be married with a range of important qualitative factors, these critical practical questions build the foundation for supporting decisions on lending proposals.

## References

1. G. A. Akerlof. The Market for "Lemons": Quality Uncertainty and the Market Mechanism. *The Quarterly Journal of Economics*, 84(3):488–500, August 1970.
2. F. Ametrano and M. Bianchetti. Everything You Always Wanted to Know About Multiple Interest Rate Curve Bootstrapping but Were Afraid to Ask. April 2013.
3. K. J. Arrow and G. Debreu. Existence of an equilibrium for a competitive economy. *Econometrica*, 22(3):265–290, 1954.
4. C. R. Bacon. *Practical Portfolio Performance Measurement and Attribution*. John Wiley & Sons, Ltd, New York, NY, 2008.
5. A. Bailey. The Future of LIBOR. Financial Conduct Authorty, Chief Executive Speech, 27 July 2017.
6. T. Björk. *Arbitrage Theory in Continuous Time*. Oxford University Press, Great Clarendon Street, Oxford, first edition, 1998.
7. F. Black and M. S. Scholes. The pricing of options and corporate liabilities. *Journal of Political Economy*, 81:637–654, 1973.
8. C. Bluhm, L. Overbeck, and C. Wagner. *An Introduction to Credit Risk Modelling*. Chapman & Hall, CRC Press, Boca Raton, first edition, 2003.
9. D. J. Bolder. *Fixed Income Portfolio Analytics: A Practical Guide to Implementing, Monitoring and Understanding Fixed-Income Portfolios*. Springer, Heidelberg, Germany, 2015.
10. D. J. Bolder. *Credit-Risk Modelling: Theoretical Foundations, Diagnostic Tools, Practical Examples, and Numerical Recipes in Python*. Springer-Nature, Heidelberg, Germany, 2018.
11. R. A. Brealey, S. C. Myers, and F. Allen. *Principles of Corporate Finance*. McGraw-Hill, New York, New York, 2011.
12. D. Brigo and F. Mercurio. *Interest-Rate Models: Theory and Practice*. Springer Verlag, Berlin, Germany, first edition, 2001.
13. D. Duffie. *Dynamic Asset Pricing Theory*. Princeton University Press, Princeton, New Jersey, second edition, 1996.
14. D. Duffie and K. Singleton. *Credit Risk*. Princeton University Press, Princeton, first edition, 2003.
15. D. Duffie and J. C. Stein. Reforming LIBOR and Other Financial Market Benchmarks. *The Journal of Economic Perspectives*, 29(2):191–212, 2015.
16. EBA. Guidelines on loan origination and monitoring. European Banking Authority, May 2020.
17. M. J. Gordon. Dividends, Earnings, and Stock Prices. *The Review of Economics and Statistics*, 41(2):99–105, 1959.
18. J. Harrison and D. Kreps. Martingales and arbitrage in multiperiod security markets. *Journal of Economic Theory*, 20:381–408, 1979.

19. J. Harrison and S. Pliska. Martingales and stochastic integrals in the theory of continuous trading. *Stochastic Processes and Their Applications*, 11:215–260, 1981.
20. D. Hou and D. Skeie. LIBOR: Origins, Economics, Crisis, Scandal, and Reform. Federal Reserve Bank of New York Staff Report, March 2014.
21. J. Hull and A. White. LIBOR vs. OIS: The Derivatives Discounting Dilemma. *Journal of Investment Management*, 11(3):14–27, 2012.
22. C. James. RAROC Based Capital Budgeting and Performance Evaluation: A Case Study of Bank Capital Allocation. Wharton Financial Institions Center Working Paper: 96-40, September 1996.
23. M. Jeanblanc. Credit risk. Université d'Evry, April 2002.
24. C. Knight. Mind your Ps and Qs. *Notes and Queries*, 4(88):11, 1851.
25. J. Lintner. The valuation of risky asset and the selection of risky investments in stock portfolios and capital budgets. *The Review of Economics and Statistics*, 47(1):13–37, 1965.
26. J. C. T. Mao. Survey of capital budgeting: Theory and practice. *The Journal of Finance*, 25(2): 349–360, 1970.
27. A. Mas-Colell, M. D. Whinston, and J. R. Green. *Microeconomic Theory*. Oxford University Press, New York, NY, 1995.
28. R. Merton. On the pricing of corporate debt: The risk structure of interest rates. *Journal of Finance*, 29:449–470, 1974.
29. A. Meucci. 'P' Versus 'Q': Differences and Commonalities between the Two Areas of Quantitative Finance. GARP Risk Professional, January 2011.
30. F. Modigliani and R. J. Shiller. Inflation, Rational Expectations and the Term Structure of Interest Rates. *Economica*, 157(40):12–43, 1973.
31. P. P. Peterson and F. J. Fabozzi. *Capital Budgeting: Theory and Practice*. John Wiley and Sons, New York, NY, 2002.
32. B. Scherer. *Portfolio Construction & Risk Budgeting*. Risk Books, London, UK, 2007.
33. W. F. Sharpe. A simplified model for portfolio analysis. *Management Science*, 9(2):277–293, 1963.
34. W. F. Sharpe. Capital asset prices: A theory of market equilibrium under conditions of risk. *The Journal of Finance*, 19(3):425–442, 1964.
35. W. F. Sharpe. Mutual fund performance. *The Journal of Business*, 39(1):119–138, 1966.
36. W. F. Sharpe. The Sharpe Ratio. *The Journal of Portfolio Management*, 21(1):49–58, 1994.
37. A. Stuart and J. K. Ord. *Kendall's Advanced Theory of Statistics*, volume 1. Oxford University Press, New York, 5 edition, 1987.
38. H. M. Taylor and S. Karlin. *An Introduction to Stochastic Modeling*. Academic Press, San Diego, California, 1994.
39. J. L. Treynor. Market value, time, and risk. Unpublished Manuscript, August 1961.
40. O. Vasicek. An equilibrium characterization of the term structure. *Journal of Financial Economics*, 5:177–188, November 1977.
41. J. B. Williams. *The Theory of Investment Value*. Harvard University Press, Boston, MA, 1938.

# Part III
# Modelling Expected Credit Loss

# Chapter 7
# Default-Probability Fundamentals

> *Get the fundamentals down and the level of everything you do will rise.*
>
> *(Michael Jordan)*

Two critical credit-risk economic capital applications remain to be addressed: loan-impairments and stress testing. Both involve a significant conceptual deviation from the base economic-capital framework: conditionality. By a combination of logical agreement and regulatory guidance—stemming from a global desire to avoid procylicality in capital requirements—economic-capital is computed from a long-term, unconditional or through-the-cycle perspective. Loan-impairment and stress-testing computations, by stark contrast, depend importantly on (typically adverse) macro-financial economic outcomes. By their very structure, to be interesting and useful, they must deviate from the through-the-cycle perspective. These applications must grapple with the point-in-time, or conditional, viewpoint. Their appropriate consideration—in conjunction with our economic-capital framework—will require some mathematical machinery permitting us to toggle back and forth between the through-the-cycle and point-in-time frames of reference.

Before we can sensibly consider strategies for the construction of point-in-time scenarios, we'll need to take a step or two backward and solidify our understanding of through-the-cycle default and transition probabilities. In particular, the forward-looking aspect must be properly developed. This will lead to an extended trip into the world of default probability term structures and surfaces. This under-appreciated area will be examined in the context of a modelling horse-race. Finally, we will touch upon a tedious, but essential, issue: managing the inherent mismatch between the number of external-agency ratings and the notches on the internal NIB scale. This problem—in two distinct forms—is rather NIB-specific, but will also apply more generally to many small-to-medium firms unable to use their own internal data to inform these default and transition probability quantities.

Default probabilities, from both an object and concept perspective, are the cornerstone of this chapter. The idea is simple enough; a default probability denotes the likelihood of a credit obligor's failure to make good on their obligations



D. Bolder, *Modelling Economic Capital*, Contributions to Finance and Accounting,
https://doi.org/10.1007/978-3-030-95096-5_7

over a specific time period. Unfortunately, despite their intuitive nature, such default probabilities are *not* directly observable; they must be inferred from either market prices or firm default history. Statistical estimation of individual default and transition probabilities, while interesting, is not our focus.[1] We will rely on external-rating agencies to provide these important inputs. What then is our interest? It relates to extensively-studied, but often misunderstood, fundamental quantities and empirical stylized facts regarding the time-related properties of default probabilities. Mastery of these concepts—and their practical extensions—will provide a solid foundation for later development of stress-testing and loan-impairment tools.

**Colour and Commentary 76** (LOOSE ENDS): *Before departing on any serious voyage on a sailing vessel, an experienced crew has much work to do. Many pieces of rope need to be tied or fastened to their correct place; failure to do so can result in disaster. These elements of string, cord, or rope are often referred to as* loose ends. *The expression* tying up loose ends, *therefore, describes the necessity of managing many small, but important, details prior to a big event.*[a] *This chapter can, in a global sense, be viewed in the same manner. The basics of default probabilities, the identification and management of original default-probability data sources, the derivation and estimation of various surface-fitting techniques, and the construction of firm-specific default surfaces and transition matrices are oft-overlooked details. They nonetheless need to be as carefully and correctly tied off as the sailor's ropes. While not terribly exciting, failure to properly manage them can, and will, lead to serious issues in our stress-testing and loan-impairment model implementation.*

[a] In the same spirit, it can relate to unfinished business. See Merriam-Webster [34, Page 705].

## 7.1 The Basics

It is always advisable to begin from the beginning.[2] Common practice—see, for example, Jeanblanc and Rutkowski [26], Jeanblanc [25], or Duffie and Singleton

[1] Those interested in the statistical estimation dimension are referred to Bolder [6, Chapter 9] and the many useful sources that it references.

[2] Or, as the King of Hearts in Alice's Adventures in Wonderland (Carroll [12]), so clearly states:

> 'Begin at the beginning,' the King said gravely, 'and go on till you come to the end: then stop.'

[18]—involves the treatment of default as a random variable, $\tau$, conceptualized as a specific point in time; we already saw this idea in Chap. 6 within the asset-pricing context. This formulation turns out to be both analytically tractable and conceptually powerful. In particular, it allows us to compare the incidence of default relative to the current point in time, which is typically denoted as $t$. If $\tau > t$, for example, default has not yet occurred. Conversely, when $\tau < t$, then the firm has already defaulted on their obligations.[3]

As a random variable, our default time $\tau$, has all of the necessary statistical machinery for its application in a wide range of situations. We may define its cumulative distribution function as,

$$F_\tau(t) = \mathbb{P}(\tau \leq t), \tag{7.1}$$

which immediately—under the assumption of absolute continuity and some other important technical details—yields the probability density function,

$$f_\tau(t) = \frac{d}{dt}F_\tau(t). \tag{7.2}$$

These two statistical objects provide a detailed description of the combination of outcomes and likelihoods associated with our default event, $\tau$.

**Colour and Commentary 77** (The Default Event)*: Treatment of the default event, denoted $\tau$, as a random variable opens up a number of mathematical modelling opportunities. In a perfect world, we would work with a set of correlated default events, $\{\tau_i : i = 1, ..., I\}$, where $I$ denotes the number of obligors in one's portfolio or analysis set. In practice, this can be rather unwieldy. The rareness of default makes it challenging, from a statistical point of view, to assign default and transition probabilities to individual obligors.*[a] *Instead, it is common to assign each of one's obligors to a set of predefined common credit classes. Conceptually, this reduces the computation of default probabilities to the set of $\{\tau_r : r = 1, ..., \mathcal{R}\}$, where $\mathcal{R}$ denotes the number of (non-default) rating categories in one's portfolio or analysis set.*[b] *Each of our $I$ obligors, it should be stressed, still has its own default event. The probabilities that one attaches to it are simply common among all entities within a shared credit class.*

[a] It can, to be fair, be done using market and financial-statement data, but it is a fairly messy (and noisy) business.

[b] Note that $r = 1$ relates to the high-quality credit and $r = \mathcal{R}$ denotes the worst-quality category. This ordinality of our rating set, while arbitrary, is practically useful.

[3] To extend this idea, a risk-free entity—although such a thing does not truly exist other than as a theoretical ideal—is achieved by setting $\tau = +\infty$.

A popular, and quite central, default-event-related quantity is defined as,

$$
\begin{aligned}
S(t,T) &= \mathbb{P}(\tau > T), \\
&= 1 - \underbrace{\mathbb{P}(\tau \le T)}_{\text{Eq. 7.1}}, \\
&= 1 - F_\tau(T),
\end{aligned} \tag{7.3}
$$

where $t$, as before, is the current point in time and $t \le T$. This quantity is referred to, for obvious reasons, as the survival probability or function.[4] Although it is simply a variation upon existing definitions, it is highly useful.[5] It basically turns the default probability on its head and asks: what is the probability that the credit obligor does *not* default? One can think of the second time argument (i.e., $T$) in Eq. 7.3 as a dial that can be turned gradually forward in time. Indeed, the first time argument $t$ is not typically included in the definition of the survival probability. We explicitly include it for two reasons. First of all, it is always useful to keep track of the current point in time.[6] Secondly, it will later help us establish a conceptual link to another important financial object.

The next definition brings us to a fundamental notion of default probability. Specifically,

$$
p(t,T) = \mathbb{P}\bigg(\tau \in (t,T]\bigg), \tag{7.5}
$$

for any $t \le T$. $p(t,T)$ essentially describes the likelihood of a default at any point during the interval $(t,T]$. Again, we are careful to explicitly include the starting point, $t$. This object has a variety of possible names. When $t$ is the current point in time, it is often referred to as the *cumulative* default probability.[7] Given its lack of conditionality, it is sometimes also called the unconditional default probability.

There are a number of important links between default and survival probabilities. A nice way to see one aspect of this relationship is to somewhat generalize Eq. 7.5. In particular, if we select two future points—$u$ and $v$—such that $t \le u \le v$, then we

---

[4] The cumulative distribution function of $\tau$ can thus also (rather obviously) be written in terms of the survival probability as,

$$
F_\tau(T) = 1 - S(t,T). \tag{7.4}
$$

[5] Equation 7.3 is, in fact, the jumping-off point for an entire sub-field of statistics: survival analysis. See Kleinbaum and Klein [29] for a good introduction.

[6] It should be clear, to provide a practical instance, that $S(t,t) = 1$ for any non-defaulted firm.

[7] In this case, where $t$ is the current point in time, we have that $p(t,t) = 0$ for the non-defaulted credit obligor. Conversely, we would expect that $\lim_{T\to\infty} p(t,T) = 1$. Such attention to the boundary conditions might appear pedantic, but their proper definition is essential.

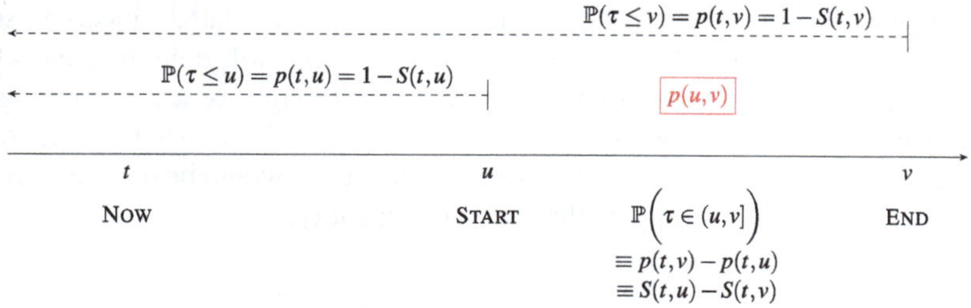


**Fig. 7.1** *Some helpful default-probability relationships*: This schematic outlines—for a default probability, $p(u, v)$—the linkages between cumulative-default and survival probabilities. The current point in time, $t$, is explicitly provided. For this example to work, we require that $t \leq u \leq v$.

may be interested in the probability of default during the interval $(u, v]$. This might be written as,

$$p(u, v) = \mathbb{P}\Big(\tau \in (u, v]\Big). \tag{7.6}$$

This is a kind of unconditional—since there is no conditioning information—marginal, or forward, default probability. It turns out that there a few ways that this value can be determined from our existing definitions.

Figure 7.1 provides a schematic for the determination of $p(u, v)$. Working from our previous quantities, however, it is determined simply as,

$$\begin{aligned} p(u, v) &= \mathbb{P}(u < \tau \leq v), \qquad (7.7)\\ &= \underbrace{\mathbb{P}(\tau \leq v)}_{F_\tau(v)} - \underbrace{\mathbb{P}(\tau \leq u)}_{F_\tau(u)},\\ &= p(t, v) - p(t, u),\\ &= \Big(\not{1} - S(t, v)\Big) - \Big(\not{1} - S(t, u)\Big),\\ &= S(t, u) - S(t, v). \end{aligned}$$

These unconditional marginal, or forward, default probabilities can be represented as the difference between cumulative default or survival probabilities anchored to the current point in time, $t$.

Knowledge of cumulative default (or survival) probabilities for a broad range of future values thus provides useful information regarding forward default likelihoods. Thus we see for the first time in this chapter—but certainly not the last—a link between default-probability calculations and the term structure of interest rates. In fact, the result of fixing $t$ to the current point of time, and computing the cumulative default probabilities for various choices of $T \geq t$, is generally referred to as the term structure of default probabilities.

All that is lacking in the previous default-probability related objects is some notion of conditionality. Our previous marginal, or forward, default rate—which we had called $p(u, v)$—is unconditional. That is, although we are computing the probability of default during interval $(u, v]$, we have not introduced any notion of its defaulting prior to time $u$. Such information, however, would be quite useful. We might, therefore, seek to compute the following quantity,

$$p(t, u, v) = \mathbb{P}\left(\tau \in (u, v] \middle| \tau > u\right), \tag{7.8}$$

for any $t \leq u \leq v$. This is not, of course, quite the same notion of probability as introduced in Eqs. 7.5 to 7.7. It is a conditional marginal, or forward, default probability. It specifies the probability of default over $(u, v]$ assuming survival to time $u$. Equation 7.8 is also, thankfully, readily computed through the use of Bayes' theorem.[8] The result, using a few of our previous definitions, is thus simply

$$\begin{aligned} p(t, u, v) &= \mathbb{P}\left(\tau \in (u, v] \middle| \tau > u\right), \\ &= \frac{\mathbb{P}\Big(\{\tau \in (u, v]\} \cap \{\tau > u\}\Big)}{\mathbb{P}(\tau > u)}, \\ &= \frac{\overbrace{\mathbb{P}\Big(\{\tau \leq v\} \cap \{\tau > u\}\Big)}^{\text{Eq. 7.7}}}{S(t, u)}, \\ &= \frac{S(t, u) - S(t, v)}{S(t, u)}, \\ &= 1 - \frac{S(t, v)}{S(t, u)}. \end{aligned} \tag{7.10}$$

Our conditional forward default probability is thus simply a function of the appropriate survival rates. Given the established link between survival rates

[8] Recall that for random events, $A$ and $B$, the conditional default probability is written as,

$$\mathbb{P}(A|B) = \frac{\mathbb{P}(A \cap B)}{\mathbb{P}(B)}. \tag{7.9}$$

This is referred to as Bayes' rule or theorem in honour of Sir Thomas Bayes, although there is apparently some uncertainty about his exact role in Eq. 7.9's discovery. See, for example, Stigler [46].

and cumulative default probabilities, one may naturally also write Eq. 7.10 as,

$$\begin{aligned} p(t,u,v) &= \mathbb{P}\left(\tau \in (u,v] \,\Big|\, \tau > u\right), \\ &= \frac{p(t,v) - p(t,u)}{1 - p(t,u)}. \end{aligned} \tag{7.11}$$

The basic format is not as condensed as in Eq. 7.10, but the two definitions are equivalent.[9]

**Colour and Commentary 78** (DEFAULT-PROBABILITY VERNACULAR)*: A word on terminology is in order. Different terms are used, in a baffling array of ways, to describe the various default-probability related quantities. The words cumulative and marginal, for example, appear to be applied with little discrimination. Furthermore, the role of conditionality is also not always entirely clear. The consequence is the potential for confusion and misapplication of a particular variation of default probability. In our treatment, therefore, we propose a simple solution. The notation will do the talking. We are unlikely to resolve the broad range of terms employed in this field, but the mathematical definitions can speak for themselves.* $p(t,u)$ *will refer to cumulative default probabilities anchored to the current point in time,* $t$*, over the full time interval* $t-u$*.* $p(u,v)$ *is essentially the same object, but with the potential for a forward start to the extent that* $t \leq u \leq v$*. Finally, the conditional forward or marginal default probability will be denoted as* $p(t,u,v)$*; the three arguments underscore the nature of the conditionality (i.e., survival to, at least, time* $u$*).*

## 7.1.1 *The Limiting Case*

The forward default probability, $p(t,u,v)$, is a useful object. It tells us, as previously described, the likelihood of a default within the interval $(u,v]$ conditional upon survival (i.e., non-default) up until time $u$. This computation depends, of course, on the size of the interval. $v-u$ could be a year, a month, or a day. It might be interesting to generalize this idea. That is, we could write our conditional

[9] In practical applications, it is not uncommon to see a combination of both cumulative default and survival probabilities for the computation of conditional marginal default probabilities.

forward default probability as,

$$\begin{aligned} p(t,u,u+\Delta t) &= \mathbb{P}\left(\tau \in (u,u+\Delta t] \middle| \tau > u\right), \quad (7.12) \\ &= \underbrace{\frac{S(t,u)-S(t,u+\Delta t)}{S(t,u)}}_{\text{Eq. 7.10}}, \\ &= \frac{\overbrace{F_\tau(u+\Delta t)-F_\tau(u)}^{\text{Eq. 7.4}}}{S(t,u)}, \end{aligned}$$

assuming that $F_\tau$ is a continuous, strictly positive, and differentiable function.[10] Although this is essentially just a manipulation of previously introduced objects, a rather new idea can be introduced through the following limit:

$$\begin{aligned} h(t,u) &= \lim_{\Delta t\to 0}\frac{p(t,u,u+\Delta t)}{\Delta t}, \quad (7.13) \\ &= \frac{1}{S(t,u)}\lim_{\Delta t\to 0}\underbrace{\frac{F_\tau(u+\Delta t)-F_\tau(u)}{\Delta t}}_{\substack{\text{Formal definition}\\ \text{of a derivative}}}, \\ &= \frac{F_\tau'(u)}{S(t,u)}. \end{aligned}$$

$h(\cdot)$ is referred to as the hazard rate (or function). In financial settings, it is occasionally termed the forward default rate. It should be viewed as an instantaneous default rate, which is essentially a mathematical trick to allow for the modelling of default probabilities in continuous time.

With a bit of manipulation, we can exploit the continuous time aspect of Eq. 7.13. It leads to a particularly elegant definition of the survival probabilities. More specifically,

$$\begin{aligned} h(t,u) &= \frac{1}{S(t,u)}\frac{d}{du}F_\tau(u), \quad (7.14) \\ &= \frac{1}{S(t,u)}\frac{\partial}{\partial u}\left(1-S(t,u)\right), \\ &= -\frac{1}{S(t,u)}\frac{\partial S(t,u)}{\partial u}, \end{aligned}$$

[10] These conditions certainly do not apply to all cumulative distribution functions, but they should not restrict our choice too dramatically.

$$\int_t^u h(t,x)dx = -\int_t^u \frac{1}{S(t,x)}\frac{\partial S(t,x)}{\partial x}dx,$$

$$S(t,u) = e^{-\int_t^u h(t,x)dx},$$

where the (straightforward) steps in the solution to the ensuing (first-order, homogeneous) differential equation are found in Bolder [6, Chapter 9]. As before, we can think of the current time, $t$, as a fixed parameter and not a variable. Its explicit inclusion does clutter the notation, but the reason will soon become evident.

A few practical elements can be gathered from Eq. 7.14. First of all, as we would expect, we have that $S(t,t) = 1$. Second, if the hazard rate is a constant—or rather, $h(t,u) \equiv h$—then $S(t,u) = e^{-h(t-u)}$. If $h = 0.01$ and $t - u = 3$ years, for example, then $S(t,u) \approx 0.97$. Our previous quantities can also be reexamined in this continuous-time setting. The cumulative default probability can now be written as,

$$\begin{aligned} p(t,u) &= \underbrace{1 - S(t,u)}_{\text{Eq. 7.7}}, \\ &= 1 - e^{-\int_t^u h(t,x)dx}, \end{aligned} \tag{7.15}$$

while the forward default probability is simply,

$$\begin{aligned} p(t,u,v) &= \underbrace{1 - \frac{S(t,v)}{S(t,u)}}_{\text{Eq. 7.10}}, \\ &= 1 - \frac{e^{-\int_t^v h(t,x)dx}}{e^{-\int_t^u h(t,x)dx}}, \\ &= 1 - e^{-\int_u^v h(t,x)dx}. \end{aligned} \tag{7.16}$$

This discussion suggests that, silently in the background of one's default and survival probability definitions, there is always some hazard function lurking about. Whether one chooses to circumvent it or handle it directly is, naturally, the choice of the individual quantitative analyst.

### 7.1.2 An Extended Aside

There is, as previously hinted at, a strong conceptual link between default and survival probabilities and key ideas in the term structure of interest rates literature.[11] It is helpful to walk through—albeit as an aside—the basics of interest-rate term-structure modelling to clarify the connection between these two areas of study.

The two most fundamental interest-rate objects are the so-called risk-free zero-coupon rates and bond prices. A zero-coupon (or pure-discount) bond has a single, certain cash-flow at maturity; it is often normalized, for convenience, to be a single unit of currency. If, as before, we denote the current point in time as $t$, then the yield on this coupon-less bond with maturity $u$ is written as $z(t,u)$; we consequently require that $t \leq u$. This is the annualized rate of interest earned over the time interval $u - t$. Its (continuously compounded) price is written as,

$$P(t,u) = e^{-z(t,u)(u-t)}, \tag{7.17}$$

implying immediately that

$$z(t,u) = -\frac{\ln P(t,u)}{u-t}. \tag{7.18}$$

Outside of short-term treasury bills, these zero-coupon bond rates (or prices) are not directly observable. They can, however, be inferred from the prices of sovereign coupon bonds.[12]

In a world of non-negative interest rates, it is necessary for $P(t,t) = 1$. Interest-rate negativity has, of course, become a 21st century commonality. In these cases, then $P(t,u)$ can exceed unity for a range of values of $u$. We also typically see that the pure-discount bond function is (weakly) decreasingly monotonous in $u$. The path of $z(t,u)$ can nonetheless take various forms as we vary $u$; it might be flat, upward-sloping, humped, or even downward shaped.

The next key notion is the forward interest rate. It represents the current interest rate, which one might transact at, for a contract starting (and maturing) in the future. Like the forward default probability, it takes three arguments: the current time, the forward start date, and the final maturity. Let us denote these as $t$, $u$, and $v$, respectively. The only condition on these time points is, as in the forward default probability setting, $t \leq u \leq v$. The forward rate is thus written as $f(t,u,v)$.[13] In a continuously compounded setting, the forward rate is determined by solving the

[11] Duffie and Singleton [18] have exploited this link to build an entire practical structure for jointly modelling interest-rate and credit-risk dynamics.

[12] Sovereigns are naturally not risk-free, but they are close as we can get in real-life. If you doubt the ability of sovereigns to default, please read Reinhart and Rogoff [41, 42].

[13] To underscore the parallel to the default case, we also use similar notation.

following break-even equation:

$$\begin{aligned} e^{z(t,v)(v-t)} &= e^{z(t,u)(u-t)} e^{f(t,u,v)(v-u)}, \\ e^{f(t,u,v)(v-u)} &= \frac{e^{z(t,v)(v-t)}}{e^{z(t,u)(u-t)}}, \\ f(t,u,v) &= \frac{z(t,v)(v-t) - z(t,u)(u-t)}{v-u}. \end{aligned} \tag{7.19}$$

Analogous to the forward default probability, forward interest rates are derived as a function of more fundamental building blocks. Zero-coupon rates are used to infer forward interest rates. Interestingly, if we use the definition of Eq. 7.18, we may directly redefine Eq. 7.19 directly as,

$$\begin{aligned} f(t,u,v) &= \frac{\overbrace{\left(-\frac{\ln P(u,v)}{\cancel{v-t}}\right)}^{\text{Eq. 7.18}}\cancel{(v-t)} - \overbrace{\left(-\frac{\ln P(t,u)}{\cancel{u-t}}\right)}^{\text{Eq. 7.18}}\cancel{(u-t)}}{v-u}, \\ &= -\frac{\left(\ln P(t,v) - \ln P(t,u)\right)}{v-u}. \end{aligned} \tag{7.20}$$

This demonstrates that the forward rate can also be represented as a function of pure-discount bond prices.

The distance between $u$ and $v$—the length of the forward interest-rate contract—can take various values; $v-u$ might be a year, a month, or a day. As with forward default probabilities, there is value in examination of the limiting case. Following from Eq. 7.12 (and naturally our definition in Eq. 7.20), one might write the forward interest rate as

$$f(t,u,u+\Delta t) = -\frac{\left(\ln P(t,u+\Delta t) - \ln P(t,u)\right)}{\Delta t}. \tag{7.21}$$

If we proceed, as previously in Eq. 7.13, to take the limit as $\Delta t$ tends to zero, then

$$\begin{aligned} f(t,u) &= \lim_{\Delta t \to 0} -\frac{\left(\ln P(t,u+\Delta t) - \ln P(t,u)\right)}{\Delta t}, \\ &= -\left(\underbrace{\lim_{\Delta t \to 0} \frac{\ln P(t,u+\Delta t) - \ln P(t,u)}{\Delta t}}_{\substack{\text{Formal definition} \\ \text{of a derivative}}}\right), \\ &= -\frac{\partial \ln P(t,u)}{\partial u}. \end{aligned} \tag{7.22}$$

This quantity is referred to as the instantaneous forward interest rate.[14] As in the hazard-rate situation examined in the previous sections, this is a differential equation. We may solve for the pure-discount bond price with a bit of calculus. In particular,

$$\begin{aligned}
\int_t^u f(t,x)dx &= -\int_u^t \frac{\partial \ln(t,x)}{\partial x}dx, \quad (7.24)\\
\Big[\ln P(t,x)\Big]_t^u &= -\int_t^u f(t,x)dx,\\
\ln P(t,u) - \underbrace{\ln P(t,t)}_{=0} &= -\int_t^u f(t,x)dx,\\
P(t,u) &= e^{-\int_t^u f(t,x)dx}.
\end{aligned}$$

This development underscores the correspondence between the default and interest-rate fields. Although an instantaneous forward rate does not actually exist—and, as such, Eq. 7.24 is basically a trick to permit use of continuous-time mathematics—it is practically very useful.[15]

**Colour and Commentary 79** (AN UNEXPECTED, BUT WELCOME, LINK): *As hinted at, and ultimately demonstrated in the preceding pages, there is a concrete conceptual connection between default and interest rates. There are, in fact, at least three points of commonality. First, the forward default and interest rates exhibit many similarities. Both take three distinct time arguments, refer to future occurrences as of the current point in time, and can be made time continuous with essentially equivalent limiting arguments. Second, the survival and pure-discount bond functions are conceptual analogues. Both are—barring negative interest rates—restricted to the unit interval, decrease monotonically over time, and can be written as an integrated negative exponential function of their respective forward quantity. Finally, the*

(continued)

[14] Interestingly, if we set $u = t$, we arrive at

$$r(t) \equiv f(t,t) = -\frac{\partial \ln P(t,t)}{\partial t}, \quad (7.23)$$

which is typically called the instantaneous short-term interest rate. This object is basically the point of departure for the entire field of dynamic interest-rate modelling.

[15] See Bolder [4, 5], Bolder and Gusba [7], or Bolder and Liu [8] for much more information on interest-rate modelling.

**Colour and Commentary 79** (continued)
*instantaneous forward interest and hazard rates play a comparably central role. Survival analysis begins with specification of a statistical form for the hazard function. Interest-rate modelling, unsurprisingly, leans heavily on assumptions regarding the mathematical form of the instantaneous forward rate.*[a] *Understanding these linkages is not only intellectually interesting, it also widens the set of possible tools for use in default-probability modelling. We can, and will, borrow methods from the field of interest rates in the forthcoming analysis.*

[a] Or, as introduced in Eq. 7.23, its related entity: the instantaneous short-term interest rate.

## 7.2 A Thorny Problem

It is common practice to use the theory of Markov chains to organize and describe the credit categories of obligors in one's portfolio. NIB is no exception. As highlighted in previous chapters, the transition matrix plays a central role in the computation of migration risk and embeds the one-year default probabilities. This structure works quite well in the context of the one-period, through-the-cycle economic-capital model. As we move to stress-testing and loan-impairment computations—multiple periods into the future and along the point-in-time dimension—some challenges arise. Pushing the point-in-time discussion to Chap. 8, let's restrict our focus to the forward-looking aspect. The base Markov-chain assumptions are sadly inconsistent with empirical multiperiod default probabilities across the rating-category spectrum. This depressing shortcoming—which we will demonstrate shortly—makes the construction of a term-structure of default probabilities rather more complex than one might have initially suspected. Understanding where and how things go wrong with the time-homogeneous Markov-chain approach is the first step in resolving this issue. It does, however, require some background development and explanation.

### *7.2.1 Set-Up*

Imagine that you have a large collection of individual credit obligors in your portfolio. This is a potentially difficult, or intimidating, situation if you seek to mathematically characterize the individual creditworthiness of each entity. Thankfully this is neither a new problem, nor is it necessary for you to find a solution. Large credit-rating agencies solved, at least approximately, this problem in and around WWI. They brilliantly opted to place individual credit obligors into a relatively small number of pre-defined groups or categories. This effectively reduces the dimensionality of the problem from potentially 1000s to about 20. Not a bad trade.

White [52] provides some interesting background on the rating agencies and highlights their dubious role in the 2008–2009 financial crisis. While these criticisms are certainly well-founded, it does not detract from the general cleverness and usefulness of the credit rating as a concept. Its consequences in terms of dimension reduction, for quantitative practitioners, are literally a godsend. The notion of credit rating is, of course, imperfect. It ignores the natural heterogeneity of creditworthiness *within* credit categories. It is also subject to timing problems and misclassification. While it is important to be aware of these caveats, it remains a powerful and important tool.

It is thus common to assume that each of one's obligors (i.e., counterparties) can be allocated to a finite set of $\kappa$ credit categories.[16] Each category represents a distinct level of credit risk ranging from the highest credit quality to actual default. Although each obligor has its own idiosyncratic credit characteristics—and this is clearly a simplification—such an organization is convenient. It represents a gateway to a number of formidable mathematical tools to describe the dynamic behaviour of one's set of obligors. In particular, a typical assumption is that the collection of credit states follows a $\kappa$-dimensional, discrete-time Markov-chain process. An enormous benefit of this choice is that the probability of default and migration between credit states can be described with a $\kappa \times \kappa$ transition matrix, which is denoted as $P$.

There are many useful references on the theory and practice of Markov chains: Brémaud [10], Taylor and Karlin [48] or Meyn and Tweedie [35] are very helpful in terms of the theoretical basics, whereas Jarrow et al. [24] and Gupton et al. [21] provide an introduction to their use in a financial setting. Bolder [6, Chapter 9] works through the maximum-likelihood approach commonly employed for the determination of the elements of the empirical transition matrix. More details can also be found in Jafry and Schuermann [23], Schuermann [43], and Lando and Skødeberg [32].

### 7.2.2 Some Theory

We make full use of the $\kappa$-state, discrete-time Markov-chain assumption for describing the credit-quality dynamics of our obligors. We also source, like many other market participants, the required transition matrices from the credit-risk agencies. Whether Moody's, Standard and Poor's or Fitch, the transition matrices produced by these entities are available on an *annual basis*. In

[16] This is not the only way to solve this problem. ECB [19] is a useful reference on the credit-risk modelling practices of public institutions.

other words, the transition probabilities—be they associated with migration, default, or remaining in the current state—are all defined over a one-year period.

This creates a challenge: transition matrix elements are available at an annual (or perhaps quarterly) frequency, but we wish to employ a time step in our credit-risk model that is longer.[17] To get started, let us first introduce some basic concepts and notation. The set of $\kappa$ Markov-chain credit states is defined as,

$$S = \{1, 2, ..., \kappa\}. \tag{7.25}$$

It is common to identify credit-quality states with alphanumeric characters—such as AAA, Aa, or A1—but these may always be mapped into an appropriate set of integers.[18] We denote the initial probabilities of falling in a particular state as,

$$p_0 = \left\{\mathbb{P}\left(S_0 = 1\right), \mathbb{P}\left(S_0 = 2\right), \cdots, \mathbb{P}\left(S_0 = \kappa\right)\right\}, \tag{7.26}$$

where

$$\sum_{i=1}^{\kappa} \mathbb{P}\left(S_0 = i\right) = 1. \tag{7.27}$$

Each individual transition probability is described as,

$$\mathbb{P}\left(S_t = j \mid S_{t-1} = i\right) = p_{ij}, \tag{7.28}$$

for $i, j = 1, ..., \kappa$. Using this idea, we may define the transition matrix for this $\kappa$-dimensional Markov chain as,

$$\underbrace{\{p_{ij}\}_{i,j=1,2,...,\kappa}}_{\text{Transition probabilities}} \equiv \underbrace{\begin{bmatrix} p_{11} & p_{12} & \cdots & p_{1\kappa} \\ p_{21} & p_{22} & \cdots & p_{2\kappa} \\ \vdots & \vdots & \ddots & \vdots \\ p_{\kappa 1} & p_{\kappa 2} & \cdots & p_{\kappa\kappa} \end{bmatrix}}_{P} \tag{7.29}$$

[17] It turns out to be even more difficult to manage a shorter time period. Resolving this situation involves scaling down the annual transition matrix to a shorter time horizon. Stated in this way, it sounds easy, but it turns out to be a surprisingly thorny problem.

[18] In our case, as seen in previous chapters, we simply employ the first 20 integers.

where,

$$p_{i1} + p_{i2} + \cdots + p_{i\kappa} = \sum_{j=1}^{\kappa} p_{ij} = 1 \tag{7.30}$$

for all $i = 1, ..., \kappa$. Or, more simply, each row of the transition matrix must sum to unity—this is a kind of conservation of mass constraint. Starting in state $i$, the probability of moving to any other state in the subsequent period must be equal to one.

The transition matrix involves, by convention, one-year transition probabilities—we will take this quantity as given, although typically some effort is required to obtain it. Let us further use $P_t$ to more generally denote the $t$-period transition matrix.[19] Given $t \in \mathbb{N}$ and $t \geq 1$, determination of $P_t$ is, with an additional common assumption, relatively straightforward. Specifically, if we assume that the Markov chain is also *time-homogeneous*, then

$$P_t = P^t, \tag{7.31}$$

and, by extension,

$$p_t = p_0 P^t, \tag{7.32}$$

where, as in Eq. 7.26,

$$p_t = \left\{ \mathbb{P}\left( S_t = 1 \right), \mathbb{P}\left( S_t = 2 \right), \cdots, \mathbb{P}\left( S_t = \kappa \right) \right\}. \tag{7.33}$$

Time homogeneity essentially implies that the transition probabilities are independent of $t$. Iterating over powers of $P$, therefore, provides us with all of the information necessary to describe the time evolution of any individual entry in our transition matrix. Our interest, for the moment, is in the final column, which contains the default probabilities. The key point, however, is that this result is conditional on default-probability dynamics being consistent with a time-homogeneous Markov-chain process.

Treating of each time step, $t \in \mathbb{N}$, as a natural number amounts to a discrete-time Markov-chain process. It is also quite possible to define a Markov chain in continuous time; technical details aside, this essentially implies that time can take any positive real value (i.e., $t \in \mathbb{R}_+$). Scaling up one-period transition matrices works a bit different in this setting. This brings us to a final quantity, which will

[19] Using this notation, it follows easily that $P \equiv P_1$.

prove helpful in resolving our problem: the so-called generator matrix. A generator matrix, denoted $G \in \mathbb{R}^{\kappa \times \kappa}$, has two key properties. First, the rows sum to zero. That is,

$$g_{i1} + g_{i2} + \cdots + g_{i\kappa} = \sum_{j=1}^{\kappa} g_{ij} = 0, \tag{7.34}$$

for $i = 1, ..., \kappa$. The second point is that *all* non-diagonal elements must be greater than or equal to zero; or, more specifically,

$$g_{ij} \geq 0, \tag{7.35}$$

for $i, j = 1, ..., \kappa$ where $i \neq j$. This implies, of course, that the diagonal elements must be less than or equal to zero.

If $P$ is a transition matrix, then $P - I_\kappa$ is a generator matrix, where $I_\kappa$ denotes the $\kappa \times \kappa$ identity matrix. It should be noted, however, that $P - I_\kappa$ is not an excellent choice. Nonetheless, if $G$ is a generator matrix, then

$$P = e^G, \tag{7.36}$$

is a transition matrix, where $e$ denotes the matrix exponential.[20] If we raise both sides to some $t \in \mathbb{N}$, then

$$\begin{aligned} P^t &= (e^G)^t, \\ P_t &= e^{tG}, \end{aligned} \tag{7.38}$$

which offers an alternative (continuous-time) representation of Eq. 7.31. In fact, the generator matrix is a key object in the definition of a continuous-time Markov chain. Without getting too deeply into the theory of Markov chains, if $G$ is a true generator

[20] The matrix exponential, the multivariate analogue of the exponential function, is formally defined as

$$e^{At} = \sum_{k=0}^{\infty} \frac{(At)^k}{k!}. \tag{7.37}$$

See Golub and Loan [20, Chapter 9] or Moler and Loan [36] for a discussion of various algorithms for its computation. Incidentally, Moler and Loan [36] almost certainly win the prize for the mathematics paper with the most honest (and amusing) title of all time.

matrix, then Eq. 7.38 holds for all $t \geq 0$.[21] That is, one can freely scale up (or down) one's transition matrix over the full time spectrum.

The deal-breaker, however, is that given a transition matrix, $P$, it does not necessarily follow that $\ln(P)$—as strongly suggested by Eq. 7.36—is a generator matrix.[22] It is very possible, for example, to have negative off-diagonal elements. This leads, rather annoyingly, to obstacles in the determination of the generator matrix.

### 7.2.3 Regularization

As succinctly stated in Kreinin and Sidelnikova [30]

> Computing the generator of an existing transition matrix by taking the logarithm still raises the issues of existence and uniqueness.

To repeat, a generator matrix need not be unique nor is it necessary that $\ln(P)$ actually be a generator matrix. Proving these results is not trivial; the reader is referred to Kingman [28] for a taste of the complexity involved.

Kreinin and Sidelnikova [30] offer an alternative strategy, which they refer to as their regularization approach. Regularization is a general term in mathematics referring to making adjustments—in terms of structure or information—to help solve ill-posed problems. It is particularly, although certainly not exclusively, found in optimization problems. Regularization is particularly relevant in this case, given the failure of the straightforward and conceptually reasonable method to yield results; in other words, the basic problem is ill-posed.

---

[21] If $P_t$ is the transition matrix of the Markov-chain process, $S_t$, then $G$ is the generator of $S_t$ if

$$\frac{dP_t}{dt} = P_t G. \tag{7.39}$$

It is immediately clear that the solution to this differential equation is, as in Eq. 7.38,

$$\begin{aligned} P_t &= e^{tG}, \\ P_t' &= \underbrace{e^{tG}}_{P_t} G, \\ &= P_t G. \end{aligned} \tag{7.40}$$

[22] In this case, as in Eq. 7.36, $\ln(\cdot)$ refers to the matrix logarithm. This is not a particularly straightforward object to compute and there are a number of possible approximations for its value. See Golub and Loan [20, Section 9.4.4] for more information.

The trick is to re-state or adjust the basic problem. Kreinin and Sidelnikova [30] offer a quasi-optimization of the generator. It involves the following, slightly heuristic, modification the original problem as,

$$G^* = \arg \min_{G \in \mathcal{G}(\kappa)} \|G - \ln(P)\|, \tag{7.41}$$

where $\|\cdot\|$ is some notion of distance for the class of $\kappa \times \kappa$ matrices.[23] $\mathcal{G}(\kappa)$ denotes the set of $\kappa$-dimensional generators. The idea is quite intuitive. Since $\ln(P)$ does not necessarily offer a sensible result, we find a true generator matrix that is as close as possible—in terms of distance—from $\ln(P)$.

It turns out, Eq. 7.41 can be solved on a row-by-row basis. Kreinin and Sidelnikova [30] and Torrent-Gironella [49] offer an iterative pseudo closed-form solution to the problem in Eq. 7.41. We solve the problem numerically by the constrained minimization of the Euclidean distance between each row of $G^*$ and the matrix logarithm of our one-year transition matrix. This appears to be both efficient and robust. Even better, the computation is extremely fast; it requires only a second or two of computational expense.

**Colour and Commentary 80** (A CENTRAL OBJECT)*: The study of Markov chains is both deep and subtle, but fortunately its full complexity is not necessary for our purposes. Some aspects, however, cannot be avoided. Although it might appear to be a mathematical curiosity, for instance, the generator matrix of a transition matrix is a critical part of any continuous-time Markov chain. It serves as a lever to scale up and down the individual transition (and default) probabilities over various time intervals. The term structure of default probabilities—across all rating categories—is intimately related to this notion of scaling. As will soon become clear, the time-homogeneous version of the Markov chain is not up to the task. Relaxation of time homogeneity, however, offers a potential solution to redeem the Markov-chain model. The generator matrix will play a central role in this rescue operation.*

### 7.2.4 Going to the Data

The major rating agencies collect, and have been in the business of collecting, rating and default data for large numbers of firms for many decades. They provide

[23] An obvious choice to describe the distance between the two matrices is the Frobenius norm; see Golub and Loan [20, Chapter 2] for more details.

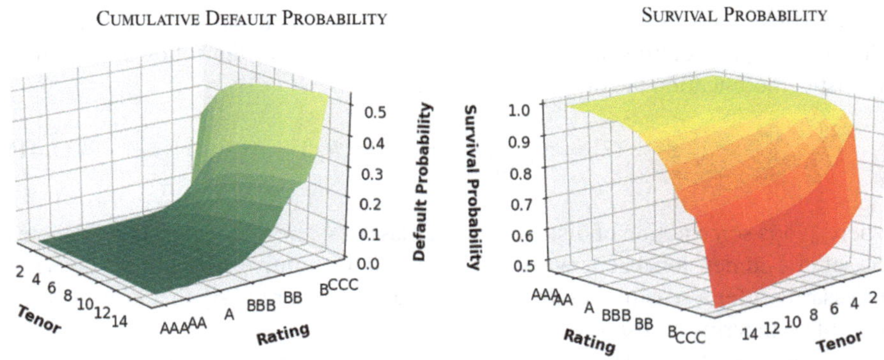


**Fig. 7.2** *Empirical default-probability term structures*: The preceding graphics illustrate the empirical multiperiod default and survival probability estimates stemming from S&P [45, Table 26]. It is precisely these observed data patterns that our internal models strive to capture.

information—in a variety of raw and processed forms—to their clients and the general public. Each rating agency, on an annual basis, publishes a high-level overview of their analysis. These sources are of primordial importance for small institutions, such as the NIB, with insufficient internal data to inform robust default-probability estimates. The following analysis is based on S&P [45], although the results do not differ dramatically if one were to rely upon Moody's or Fitch data.

S&P [45, Table 26] describes for each of S&P's 17 pertinent, non-default rating categories, the empirical probability of default for one to 15 years.[24] Using the terminology from the previous sections, these are long-term, (i.e., through-the-cycle) cumulative default probabilities. Mathematically, we can denote them as,

$$\{p_r(t,u)\ :\ u = 1, ..., T\}, \tag{7.42}$$

where $T = 15$ and $r = 1, ..., \mathcal{R}$. We can think of these results as the truth; or, at least, some first-order approximation of it. Our internal models need to correspondingly strive to capture the basic features of these empirical estimates.

Figure 7.2 illustrates, for each time step and credit-rating category, the cumulative default and survival probabilities from S&P [45, Table 26]. A number of

[24] As indicated in Chap. 3, we do not employ the entire S&P scale. Since the very low end of the scale is outside of our area of operation, the five categories below B- (i.e., CCC+, CCC, CCC-, CC and C in descending order) are aggregated into a single catch-all, CCC category. This explains the use of only 17 non-default S&P rating categories; we might refer to this as a truncated S&P scale.

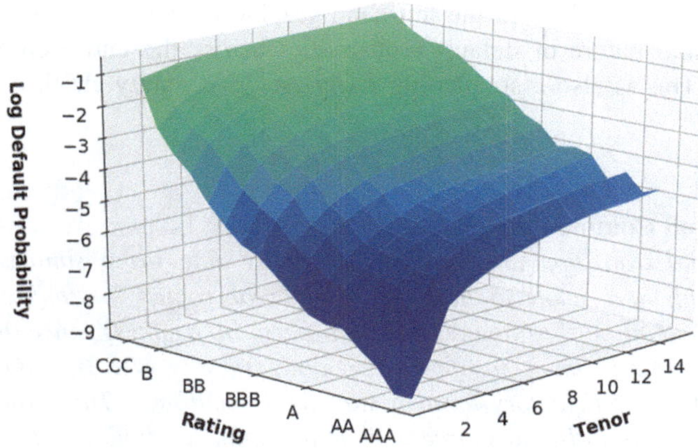


**Fig. 7.3** *Default-probability exponentiality*: This cumulative default probability surface is computed by applying natural logarithms to the left-hand graphic in Fig. 7.2. It clearly indicates the exponential nature of default probabilities over the entire empirical term structure.

points are worth addressing. These estimates are updated annually, but are very slow-moving since they represent a long-term, or through-the-cycle, estimate of these default-probability term structures. This may seem to be of limited interest, but these values actually form the foundation for movement—in Chap. 8—to the point-in-time perspective required for stress-testing and loan-impairment analytics.

As a second point, it is probably preferable to think of Fig. 7.2 as representing a default-probability *surface* rather than term structures. For a given credit rating, say AA+, we can speak of a term structure. When we consider all possible rating categories and tenors, it becomes a surface. This is particularly important given that we expect to have interactions—or rather restrictions—between these credit states and tenors. The five-year cumulative BB default probability should not exceed, for example, the A equivalent. In other words, we expect that for a given tenor, the default probabilities increase monotonically as we move out the credit spectrum.[25] At the same time, for a given credit state, the cumulative-default probability needs to increase (at least, weakly) monotonically as we increase the tenor.[26] This is, in fact, precisely what we observe in Fig. 7.2. The final point is that default probabilities increase exponentially as we move out the credit scale. This admittedly makes it somewhat difficult to visualize the entire surface. Figure 7.3

---

[25] Of course, when speaking of survival probabilities, we require a monotonically decreasing relationship.

[26] Again, the direction of the monotonicity is opposite for survival probabilities.

applies natural logarithms to the left-hand graphic in Fig. 7.2 clearly indicating the exponential nature of default probabilities across the entire empirical term structure.[27] This is also a simple, but fairly effective, sanity check on S&P [45, Table 26].

**Colour and Commentary 81** (A NOTE ON S&P DATA): *We rely heavily on external transition and default probability data for a simple reason: it is simply too small to produce sensible or robust internal estimates of these quantities. Although NIB has been in business since the mid-1970s, there are simply too few credit obligors, observed transitions, and defaults for a satisfactory level of statistical accuracy.*[a] *This explains the recourse to external-data sources. While a helpful solution, it is not without its drawbacks. The first, conceptual issue, is that one worries about the representativeness of large global datasets for our specific regional and industrial activities. Little can be done to assuage this concern. The second point is practical; at some point soon, the 18-notch S&P categorization will need to be mapped into the 21-step internal master scale. This needs to be resolved with some mathematical gymnastics and common sense. Neither drawback is an insurmountable obstacle, but both need to be kept firmly in mind.*

[a] With 20 non-default categories, there are 420 (non-default) transition probabilities to estimate; literally thousands of obligors across the entire credit spectrum over decades are necessary to adequately inform these parameters.

The next step involves extracting a sensible long-term, (one-year) corporate transition matrix from the data provided in S&P [45, Table 23]. Examination of the specific figures isn't terribly helpful, so we've used colour-coding to provide better insight. Equation 7.43 provides this information, in its full glory, for those with reading spectacles at the ready. The black values describe transition probabilities exceeding 0.5, orange denotes values from $[0.05, 0.5)$, the gray figures fall into the interval $[0.01, 0.05)$, while the remaining entries are roughly equal to zero (to

[27] If the default surface was indeed exponential across each credit rating, we would expect the log-transformation to generate a plane in $\mathbb{R}^3$ (i.e., a sheet of paper in three-dimensional space). While this is not quite true, as we can see in Fig. 7.3, it is qualitatively close.

decimal places, at least).

$$
\hat{P} = \begin{array}{cccccccccccccccccc}
>0.5 & & & & \approx 0 & \approx 0 & \approx 0 & \approx 0 & \approx 0 & \approx 0 & \approx 0 & \approx 0 & \approx 0 & \approx 0 & \approx 0 & \approx 0 & \approx 0 & \approx 0 \\
 & >0.5 & & & & \approx 0 & \approx 0 & \approx 0 & \approx 0 & \approx 0 & \approx 0 & \approx 0 & \approx 0 & \approx 0 & \approx 0 & \approx 0 & \approx 0 & \approx 0 \\
\approx 0 & & >0.5 & & & & \approx 0 & \approx 0 & \approx 0 & \approx 0 & \approx 0 & \approx 0 & \approx 0 & \approx 0 & \approx 0 & \approx 0 & \approx 0 & \approx 0 \\
\approx 0 & \approx 0 & & >0.5 & & & & \approx 0 & \approx 0 & \approx 0 & \approx 0 & \approx 0 & \approx 0 & \approx 0 & \approx 0 & \approx 0 & \approx 0 & \approx 0 \\
\approx 0 & \approx 0 & \approx 0 & & >0.5 & & & & \approx 0 & \approx 0 & \approx 0 & \approx 0 & \approx 0 & \approx 0 & \approx 0 & \approx 0 & \approx 0 & \approx 0 \\
\approx 0 & \approx 0 & \approx 0 & \approx 0 & & >0.5 & & & & \approx 0 & \approx 0 & \approx 0 & \approx 0 & \approx 0 & \approx 0 & \approx 0 & \approx 0 & \approx 0 \\
\approx 0 & \approx 0 & \approx 0 & \approx 0 & \approx 0 & & >0.5 & & & & \approx 0 & \approx 0 & \approx 0 & \approx 0 & \approx 0 & \approx 0 & \approx 0 & \approx 0 \\
\approx 0 & \approx 0 & \approx 0 & \approx 0 & \approx 0 & & & >0.5 & & & \approx 0 & \approx 0 & \approx 0 & \approx 0 & \approx 0 & \approx 0 & \approx 0 & \approx 0 \\
\approx 0 & \approx 0 & \approx 0 & \approx 0 & \approx 0 & \approx 0 & & & >0.5 & & & & \approx 0 & \approx 0 & \approx 0 & \approx 0 & \approx 0 & \approx 0 \\
\approx 0 & \approx 0 & \approx 0 & \approx 0 & \approx 0 & \approx 0 & \approx 0 & & & >0.5 & & & & \approx 0 & \approx 0 & \approx 0 & \approx 0 & \approx 0 \\
\approx 0 & \approx 0 & \approx 0 & \approx 0 & \approx 0 & \approx 0 & \approx 0 & \approx 0 & & & >0.5 & & & & & \approx 0 & \approx 0 & \approx 0 \\
\approx 0 & \approx 0 & \approx 0 & \approx 0 & \approx 0 & \approx 0 & \approx 0 & \approx 0 & & & & >0.5 & & & & \approx 0 & & \\
\approx 0 & \approx 0 & \approx 0 & \approx 0 & \approx 0 & \approx 0 & \approx 0 & \approx 0 & \approx 0 & \approx 0 & & & >0.5 & & & & & \\
\approx 0 & \approx 0 & \approx 0 & \approx 0 & \approx 0 & \approx 0 & \approx 0 & \approx 0 & \approx 0 & \approx 0 & \approx 0 & & & >0.5 & & & & \\
\approx 0 & \approx 0 & \approx 0 & \approx 0 & \approx 0 & \approx 0 & \approx 0 & \approx 0 & \approx 0 & \approx 0 & \approx 0 & \approx 0 & & & >0.5 & & & \\
\approx 0 & \approx 0 & \approx 0 & \approx 0 & \approx 0 & \approx 0 & \approx 0 & \approx 0 & \approx 0 & \approx 0 & \approx 0 & \approx 0 & & & & >0.5 & & \\
\approx 0 & \approx 0 & \approx 0 & \approx 0 & \approx 0 & \approx 0 & \approx 0 & \approx 0 & \approx 0 & \approx 0 & \approx 0 & \approx 0 & \approx 0 & & & & >0.5 & \\
0 & 0 & 0 & 0 & 0 & 0 & 0 & 0 & 0 & 0 & 0 & 0 & 0 & 0 & 0 & 0 & 0 & \mathbf{1}
\end{array} \tag{7.43}
$$

In this form, the full one-year S&P transition matrix, offers little insight into the problem. There are $18 \times 18 = 324$ individual elements and many of the entries do not have sufficient digits to practically distinguish them from zero; there are also, however, a significant number of entries assigned an identically zero value.[28] Indeed, in the spirit of full transparency, the actual data is not actually found in quite the (conceptual) form presented in Eq. 7.43. An additional category of *not-rated* entities is provided by S&P. This extra column encapsulates firms that started in the sample, but, for various reasons, did not receive a rating. While it is useful to receive this data, it presents us with something of a conundrum. While there are numerous possibilities to use this information, it is common practice to proportionally spread this probability mass—on a row-by-row basis—across the remaining credit states. As a final step, some additional normalization is performed to ensure that the result is a true transition matrix.

Equation 7.43 does nonetheless permit some useful observations. The diagonals are clearly dominant, implying that the probability of *not* transitioning—that is, staying put in one's current credit state—is quite high at a one-year horizon. To the extent transition occurs, it appears to be principally restricted to one or two-notch

[28] At a one-year frequency, for example, there are few or no cases of a AAA rating moving to CCC or D. At the same time, movement from CCC to AAA, over a single year, is vanishingly rare. These facts are reflected in S&P statistical estimates.

upgrades and downgrades. It is thus interesting to compare—for a given row—the immediate entries to the left and right of the diagonal. These describe the main downgrade and upgrade probabilities, respectively.

The last element of interest in Eq. 7.43 relates to the final column; these are the default probabilities. Up until the 11th row—corresponding to the rating category, BB+—the one-year value is zero to two decimal points. This underscores the rareness of default and the fundamental challenges of using internal firm data for their estimation.

As previously discussed, it is generally not possible to compute the generator matrix associated with $\hat{P}$ through a simple application of the matrix logarithm. Using the transition matrix from Eq. 7.43 and the regularized optimization approach introduced in Eq. 7.41, however, we may construct a reasonable approximation of the associated generator matrix. It has the following form:

$$\hat{G} = \begin{bmatrix}
\mathbf{-0.1} & 0.1 & 0.0 & 0.0 & 0.0 & 0.0 & 0.0 & 0.0 & 0.0 & 0.0 & 0.0 & 0.0 & 0.0 & 0.0 & 0.0 & 0.0 & 0.0 & 0.0 \\
0.0 & \mathbf{-0.2} & 0.1 & 0.0 & 0.0 & 0.0 & 0.0 & 0.0 & 0.0 & 0.0 & 0.0 & 0.0 & 0.0 & 0.0 & 0.0 & 0.0 & 0.0 & 0.0 \\
0.0 & 0.0 & \mathbf{-0.2} & 0.1 & 0.0 & 0.0 & 0.0 & 0.0 & 0.0 & 0.0 & 0.0 & 0.0 & 0.0 & 0.0 & 0.0 & 0.0 & 0.0 & 0.0 \\
0.0 & 0.0 & 0.0 & \mathbf{-0.2} & 0.1 & 0.0 & 0.0 & 0.0 & 0.0 & 0.0 & 0.0 & 0.0 & 0.0 & 0.0 & 0.0 & 0.0 & 0.0 & 0.0 \\
0.0 & 0.0 & 0.0 & 0.1 & \mathbf{-0.2} & 0.1 & 0.0 & 0.0 & 0.0 & 0.0 & 0.0 & 0.0 & 0.0 & 0.0 & 0.0 & 0.0 & 0.0 & 0.0 \\
0.0 & 0.0 & 0.0 & 0.0 & 0.1 & \mathbf{-0.2} & 0.1 & 0.0 & 0.0 & 0.0 & 0.0 & 0.0 & 0.0 & 0.0 & 0.0 & 0.0 & 0.0 & 0.0 \\
0.0 & 0.0 & 0.0 & 0.0 & 0.0 & 0.1 & \mathbf{-0.2} & 0.1 & 0.0 & 0.0 & 0.0 & 0.0 & 0.0 & 0.0 & 0.0 & 0.0 & 0.0 & 0.0 \\
0.0 & 0.0 & 0.0 & 0.0 & 0.0 & 0.0 & 0.1 & \mathbf{-0.2} & 0.1 & 0.0 & 0.0 & 0.0 & 0.0 & 0.0 & 0.0 & 0.0 & 0.0 & 0.0 \\
0.0 & 0.0 & 0.0 & 0.0 & 0.0 & 0.0 & 0.0 & 0.1 & \mathbf{-0.2} & 0.1 & 0.0 & 0.0 & 0.0 & 0.0 & 0.0 & 0.0 & 0.0 & 0.0 \\
0.0 & 0.0 & 0.0 & 0.0 & 0.0 & 0.0 & 0.0 & 0.0 & 0.1 & \mathbf{-0.3} & 0.1 & 0.0 & 0.0 & 0.0 & 0.0 & 0.0 & 0.0 & 0.0 \\
0.0 & 0.0 & 0.0 & 0.0 & 0.0 & 0.0 & 0.0 & 0.0 & 0.0 & 0.2 & \mathbf{-0.4} & 0.1 & 0.0 & 0.0 & 0.0 & 0.0 & 0.0 & 0.0 \\
0.0 & 0.0 & 0.0 & 0.0 & 0.0 & 0.0 & 0.0 & 0.0 & 0.0 & 0.0 & 0.1 & \mathbf{-0.3} & 0.1 & 0.0 & 0.0 & 0.0 & 0.0 & 0.0 \\
0.0 & 0.0 & 0.0 & 0.0 & 0.0 & 0.0 & 0.0 & 0.0 & 0.0 & 0.0 & 0.0 & 0.1 & \mathbf{-0.4} & 0.1 & 0.0 & 0.0 & 0.0 & 0.0 \\
0.0 & 0.0 & 0.0 & 0.0 & 0.0 & 0.0 & 0.0 & 0.0 & 0.0 & 0.0 & 0.0 & 0.0 & 0.1 & \mathbf{-0.4} & 0.1 & 0.0 & 0.0 & 0.0 \\
0.0 & 0.0 & 0.0 & 0.0 & 0.0 & 0.0 & 0.0 & 0.0 & 0.0 & 0.0 & 0.0 & 0.0 & 0.0 & 0.1 & \mathbf{-0.4} & 0.2 & 0.1 & 0.0 \\
0.0 & 0.0 & 0.0 & 0.0 & 0.0 & 0.0 & 0.0 & 0.0 & 0.0 & 0.0 & 0.0 & 0.0 & 0.0 & 0.0 & 0.2 & \mathbf{-0.5} & 0.2 & 0.0 \\
0.0 & 0.0 & 0.0 & 0.0 & 0.0 & 0.0 & 0.0 & 0.0 & 0.0 & 0.0 & 0.0 & 0.0 & 0.0 & 0.0 & 0.0 & 0.2 & \mathbf{-0.7} & 0.4 \\
0.0 & 0.0 & 0.0 & 0.0 & 0.0 & 0.0 & 0.0 & 0.0 & 0.0 & 0.0 & 0.0 & 0.0 & 0.0 & 0.0 & 0.0 & 0.0 & 0.0 & \mathbf{0.0}
\end{bmatrix}. \tag{7.44}$$

Equation 7.44 is certainly less visually useful—beyond serving as an eye test—than Eq. 7.43. It does underscore the negativity of the diagonal elements and the necessity of having a sensible algorithm for their construction.

Armed with $\hat{P}$ and $\hat{G}$, we can proceed to compare our time-homogeneous Markov-chain assumption to the empirical default-probability surface values provided by S&P [45, Table 26]. We construct two potential estimators: discrete- and continuous versions. The discrete-time case simply raises Eq. 7.43 to consecutive powers $t = 1, ..., T$ and extracts the final column at each step.[29] The continuous-time estimates use the generator matrix, displayed in Eq. 7.44, and the relationship from Eq. 7.38 (i.e., $e^{t\hat{G}}$) to build an estimated default surface.[30]

Figure 7.4 displays a selection of the results. Seven distinct credit-rating cumulative default probability term structures—across the entire spectrum—are presented along with the average across all 17 non-default credit classes. At the upper end of the scale, the fit between discrete- and continuous-time Markov-chain outputs does not appear to deviate dramatically from the empirical estimates. With the exception of the AAA category, there is virtually perfect agreement between the discrete- and continuous-time Markov-chain estimates. This suggests that time continuity is a not a terribly controversial assumption in this setting and that the generator matrix, $G$, has been reasonably identified; these conclusions will be helpful in later analysis.

That is the end of the good news. As we move to the lower end of the investment-grade credits and into speculative grade, the situation degrades. The Markov-chain assumption implies a smooth upward growth—concave at the higher end of the scale, but convex for weaker credits—in default probabilities that is simply inconsistent with the empirical evidence. The basic curve shapes are not particularly similar, but most damagingly, the implied Markov-chain term structures are simply far too high. In other words, the Markov-chain results are overly conservative relative to the estimates provided by S&P [45, Table 26]. To be more blunt, the time-homogeneous Markov-chain model must be viewed as an abject failure when applied to actual, real-world default probability term structures. The consequence is that, when moving multiple periods forward in time, we unfortunately cannot lean on the standard time-homogeneous Markov chain model.

**Colour and Commentary 82** (AN ANALYTIC DISAPPOINTMENT)*: The time-homogeneous Markov-chain model—as embodied by a fixed transition matrix—has a major flaw. It does not permit the generation of a default-probability surface—across multiple periods and rating classes—that is even weakly consistent with empirical estimates. It thus cannot be used directly in the determination of through-the-cycle default-probability surfaces, which form the foundation for stress-testing and loan-impairment analysis. This is a disappointing revelation given the centrality of the transition matrix in our economic-capital framework. It is consequently necessary to investigate alternative approaches for the construction of the requisite default-probability surfaces. This basically means that we need to go back to the modelling drawing board.*

[29] We can, however, ignore the final absorbing default state.

[30] Naturally, the latter approach further assumes time-continuity of our Markov chain.

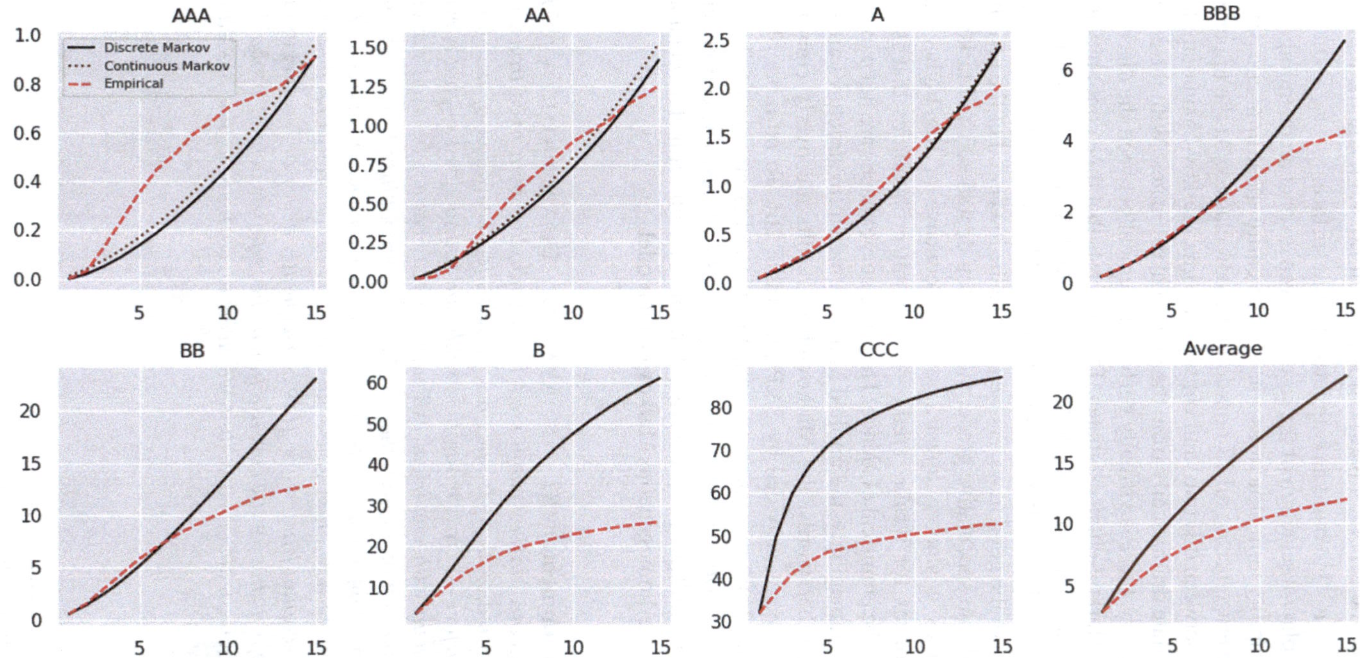


**Fig. 7.4** *The Markovian assumption*: The graphic above illustrates—for a number of selected credit-rating categories—the relationship between empirical default-probability term structures and two possible Markov-chain estimates. The link at higher levels of investment grade is not terrible, but as we move out the spectrum, the abject failure of the time-homogeneous Markov-chain assumption appears to be beyond dispute.

## 7.3 Building Default-Probability Surfaces

The (rather spectacular) failure of the time-homogeneous Markov-chain assumption leads us to a quandary: a sensible approach is required to fit the empirical default-probability surfaces found in S&P [45, Table 26] and summarized in Fig. 7.2. Without a mathematical specification of through-the-cycle default surfaces, we cannot even begin to consider the construction of point-in-time scenarios for our loan-impairment and stress-testing applications.

There is, thankfully, a bright side. At its heart, this is basically a curve-fitting problem. Curve or surface-fitting is, perhaps surprisingly, an area of mathematical endeavour offering many flexible and accurate techniques.[31] We could, therefore, certainly find a method to fit Fig. 7.2 to a very high degree of accuracy. The important question, however, is: what precisely are we looking for in an estimator? In other words, before jumping into possible techniques, it is always a good idea to identify what a sensible approach might look like. This is particularly important given that curve-fitting is a mathematical exercise that, in general, contains relatively little economic intuition.

After some reflection, our shopping list for a default-surface estimator has *three* items on it. In particular, we seek:

1. a relatively parsimonious, or low-dimensional, approach that permits us to readily extend our default surfaces to other applications;
2. a reasonable—although not necessarily, perfect—degree of fit to the empirical data found in S&P [45, Table 26]; and
3. if possible, an approach that nests the time-homogeneous Markov-chain transition matrix sitting at the foundation of our economic-capital framework.

To summarize, we are seeking a workable trade-off between goodness of fit, parsimony, and theoretical consistency. The ability to fit a default-probability surface under these three conditions would position us quite well for future stress-testing and loan-impairment computations.

In the preface, we counselled that, "if you can help it, never do anything just one way." Here we find ourselves in precisely such a situation. In the following sections, in an attempt to follow our starting axiom, we will consider three alternative approaches to fitting our through-the-cycle default-probability surface. Each has its own advantages and disadvantages; along the way, we will examine both their mathematical structure and how they address our three selection principles. Informally, we can think of this as a race with *three* different horses.

[31] Lancaster and Salkauskas [31] is an excellent starting point for this literature.

### 7.3.1 A Low-Dimensional Markov Chain

The first approach has previously been used at NIB. This legacy implementation attempts to simplify the problem, while at the same time maintaining some semblance of a Markov-chain structure. It proposes, for each credit category, three distinct credit states: an initial (or starting), an asymptotic, and a default state. We will denote each as $I_r$, $A_r$ and $D_r$, respectively, for $r = 1, ..., \mathcal{R}$. As the name suggests, all credit categories begin in the initial state. From here, there are three possible destinations. It is possible to stay put, move to the asymptotic state, or default. Default is, as usual, an absorbing state. Once a rating class enters default, there is no exit. The asymptotic state offers only two possible outcomes: remaining in the asymptotic state or default.

This simple model basically peels back all of the complexity of the various rating classes and reduces it to three outcomes. The initial and default states remain basically unchanged; it is the so-called asymptotic position that is new. Conceptually, it appears to be a transition state on the way from the initial setting to default. This is underscored by the inability to move backwards from the asymptotic state to the initial point. Its name, however, would seem to suggest that it is some kind of long-term average outcome for a given rating class. Although its precise interpretation is somewhat unclear, its principal role is undoubtedly to reduce dimensionality. From this perspective, this approach meets our parsimony criterion. While it does not fully nest the our time-homogenous Markov-chain implementation, it does have a link, however tenuous, to this world.

Figure 7.5 provides a classical schematic for this low-dimensional Markov-chain process. Given the fairly significant restrictions, there are only three parameters associated with each individual credit state. These include:

- $p_d(r)$: the probability of the $r$th rating class moving from the initial to the default state;

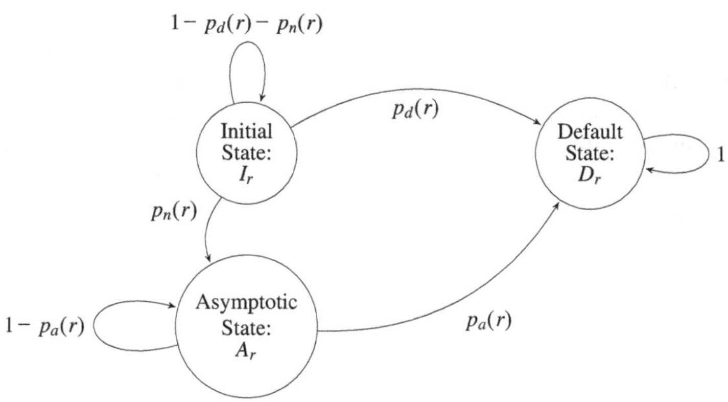


**Fig. 7.5** *A simple Markov chain*: The preceding schematic illustrates the basic properties of a low-dimensional Markov-chain process used—in our traditional implementation—to fit the default-probability surface introduced in Fig. 7.2. There are three states: initial, asymptotic, and default.

- $p_n(r)$: the probability of the $r$th rating class transitioning from the initial to the asymptotic state; and
- $p_a(r)$: the probability of the $r$th rating class advancing from the asymptotic to the default state,

for $r = 1, ..., \mathcal{R}$.

To actually estimate these parameters, in manner consistent with the observed default-probability surface, we need to infer the transition matrix associated with this low-dimensional Markov-chain process. The actual state structure, in a more mathematical format, is written as

$$S_t^{(r)} = \begin{cases} I_r : \text{Initial state} \\ A_r : \text{Asymptotic state} \\ D_r : \text{Default state} \end{cases}, \tag{7.45}$$

for $r = 1, ..., \mathcal{R}$ and $t \geq 0$. Using Fig. 7.5, we may infer the transition matrix as,

$$P^{(r)} = \begin{bmatrix} \mathbb{P}\left(S_t^{(r)} = I_r \middle| S_{t-1}^{(r)} = I_r\right) & \mathbb{P}\left(S_t^{(r)} = A_r \middle| S_{t-1}^{(r)} = I_r\right) & \mathbb{P}\left(S_t^{(r)} = D_r \middle| S_{t-1}^{(r)} = I_r\right) \\ \mathbb{P}\left(S_t^{(r)} = I_r \middle| S_{t-1}^{(r)} = A_r\right) & \mathbb{P}\left(S_t^{(r)} = A_r \middle| S_{t-1}^{(r)} = A_r\right) & \mathbb{P}\left(S_t^{(r)} = D_r \middle| S_{t-1}^{(r)} = A_r\right) \\ \mathbb{P}\left(S_t^{(r)} = I_r \middle| S_{t-1}^{(r)} = D_r\right) & \mathbb{P}\left(S_t^{(r)} = A_r \middle| S_{t-1}^{(r)} = D_r\right) & \mathbb{P}\left(S_t^{(r)} = D_r \middle| S_{t-1}^{(r)} = D_r\right) \end{bmatrix}, \tag{7.46}$$

$$= \begin{bmatrix} 1 - p_n(r) - p_d(r) & p_n(r) & p_d(r) \\ 0 & 1 - p_a(r) & p_a(r) \\ 0 & 0 & 1 \end{bmatrix},$$

for $r = 1, ..., \mathcal{R}$. While the notation is not particularly welcoming, the ultimate structure of our transition matrix is actually quite simple. Due to the restrictions between state movements, it has an upper-triangular form and, as promised, only three parameters per credit category.

The actual parameter identification process uses a recursive technique. All recursion relations depend on the specification of a clear set of starting conditions. We begin by setting $S_0^{(r)} = I_r$, which is a fairly defensible beginning point. Indeed, it is hard to argue that all credit categories should *not* start in their initial state. This directly implies that $\mathbb{P}(S_0^{(r)} = I_r) = 1$ and, of course, that $\mathbb{P}(S_0^{(r)} = A_r) = \mathbb{P}(S_0^{(r)} = D_r) = 0$. We have thus essentially also provided a clear picture of the initial unconditional low-dimensional Markov-chain state probabilities.

To further improve our situation, we fix one of the three parameters by setting $p_d(r) = \mathbb{P}(\tau_r \in (0, 1])$. That is, the probability of default, from the initial state, is linked to that state's one-year default probability from our full-blown transition matrix, $\hat{P}$, summarized in Eq. 7.43. Not only does this create a link to our base implementation, but it also further reduces the dimensionality of our estimation problem. Now, we have to identify only *two* parameters per rating class.

The next element associated with a recursive method is a set of dynamic equations—or recursion relations—with a clear link to the starting conditions. This involves the description of our unconditional state probabilities incorporating the necessary elements from our simplified transition matrix in Eq. 7.46. Specifically, we have that

$$\mathbb{P}\left(S_t^{(r)} = I_r\right) = \underbrace{\left(1 - p_n(r) - p_d(r)\right)\mathbb{P}\left(S_{t-1}^{(r)} = I_r\right)}_{\text{Staying in } I_r}, \tag{7.47}$$

$$\mathbb{P}\left(S_t^{(r)} = A_r\right) = \underbrace{p_n(r)\mathbb{P}\left(S_{t-1}^{(r)} = I_r\right)}_{\text{Coming from } I_r} + \underbrace{\left(1 - p_a(r)\right)\mathbb{P}\left(S_{t-1}^{(r)} = A_r\right)}_{\text{Staying in } A_r},$$

$$\mathbb{P}\left(S_t^{(r)} = D_r\right) = \underbrace{p_d(r)\mathbb{P}\left(S_{t-1}^{(r)} = I_r\right)}_{\text{Coming from } I_r} + \underbrace{p_a(r)\mathbb{P}\left(S_{t-1}^{(r)} = A_r\right)}_{\text{Coming from } A_r} + \underbrace{\mathbb{P}\left(S_{t-1}^{(r)} = D_r\right)}_{\text{Staying in } D_r},$$

$r = 1, ..., \mathcal{R}$ and $t = 1, ..., T$. All of these values follow logically from Fig. 7.5 and Eq. 7.46. The desired result for a given rating class, $r$, and for fixed choices of $p_n(r)$ and $p_a(r)$ is,

$$\hat{p}_r(0, t) = \mathbb{P}\left(S_t^{(r)} = D_r\right), \tag{7.48}$$

for $t = 1, ..., T$. More simply, recursing over Eq. 7.47 provides us with an estimate—for each individual rating category—of the set of cumulative default probabilities anchored to the current point in time. This is our default-probability surface.

The most obvious approach to solving this problem involves solving the following set of minimization problems,

$$\min_{p_n(r), p_a(r)} \sum_{t=1}^{T} \left(\hat{p}_r(0, t) - p_r(0, t)\right)^2, \tag{7.49}$$

subject to:

$$p_n(r), p_a(r) \in [0, 1],$$

for $r = 1, ....\mathcal{R}$.[32] The approach presented in Eq. 7.49, while fairly sensible, treats each individual credit class on a standalone basis. Economic logic—not to mention the results in Figs. 7.2 and 7.3—suggests that the collection of default probability term structures should be handled as a system; that is, as a default-probability surface.

This argues for the construction of a single joint optimization problem. We can thus think of identifying vectors of $p_n$ and $p_a$ parameters. To keep our variable book-keeping clean and transparent, let us define,

$$\vec{p}_x = \left[p_x(1)\ p_x(2)\cdots p_x(\mathcal{R})\right]^T, \tag{7.50}$$

for $x \in \{n, a\}$. This allows us to restate Eq. 7.49 as,

$$\min_{\vec{p}_n,\vec{p}_a} \sum_{r=1}^{\mathcal{R}} \sum_{t=1}^{T} \left(\hat{p}_r(0,t) - p_r(0,t)\right)^2, \tag{7.51}$$

subject to:

$$p_n(r), p_a(r) \in [0, 1] \text{ for } r = 1, ...\mathcal{R},$$
$$p_x(r+1) \geq p_x(r) \text{ for } r = 1, ...\mathcal{R} - 1 \text{ and } x \in \{n, a\}.$$

The final constraints represent monotonicity conditions for the resulting default-probability surface. These ensure the economic reasonableness of the final result.

Figure 7.6 graphically illustrates the results associated with this approach. For selected credit-rating categories, it investigates the goodness of fit between our empirical default-probability term structures and the low-dimensional legacy Markov-chain model. To better understand the role of the monotonicity constraints, it further displays the results of the separate and joint optimization problems introduced in Eqs. 7.49 and 7.51. The first observation is that this model provides a dramatically improved fit relative to the time-homogeneous model examined in Fig. 7.4. The low-dimensional model nonetheless continues to generate concave term structures among investment-grade ratings and convex estimates as we move into speculative-grade territory. This contrasts with the empirical values, which appear to be essentially convex across all rating classes.

As a second point, the low-dimensional Markov-chain approach appears to systematically overestimate longer-term cumulative default probabilities. This occurs across virtually all individual credit-rating classes in Fig. 7.6. It is clearly evident when considering the average across all categories. Thus, although there is a significant improvement in overall performance, the low-dimensional fit still faces a few challenges matching both the overall shape and level of the empirical default-surface estimates.

---

[32] Any notion of distance will do, but the sum of squared errors (or the $\mathcal{L}^2$ norm) has a number of mathematical advantages.

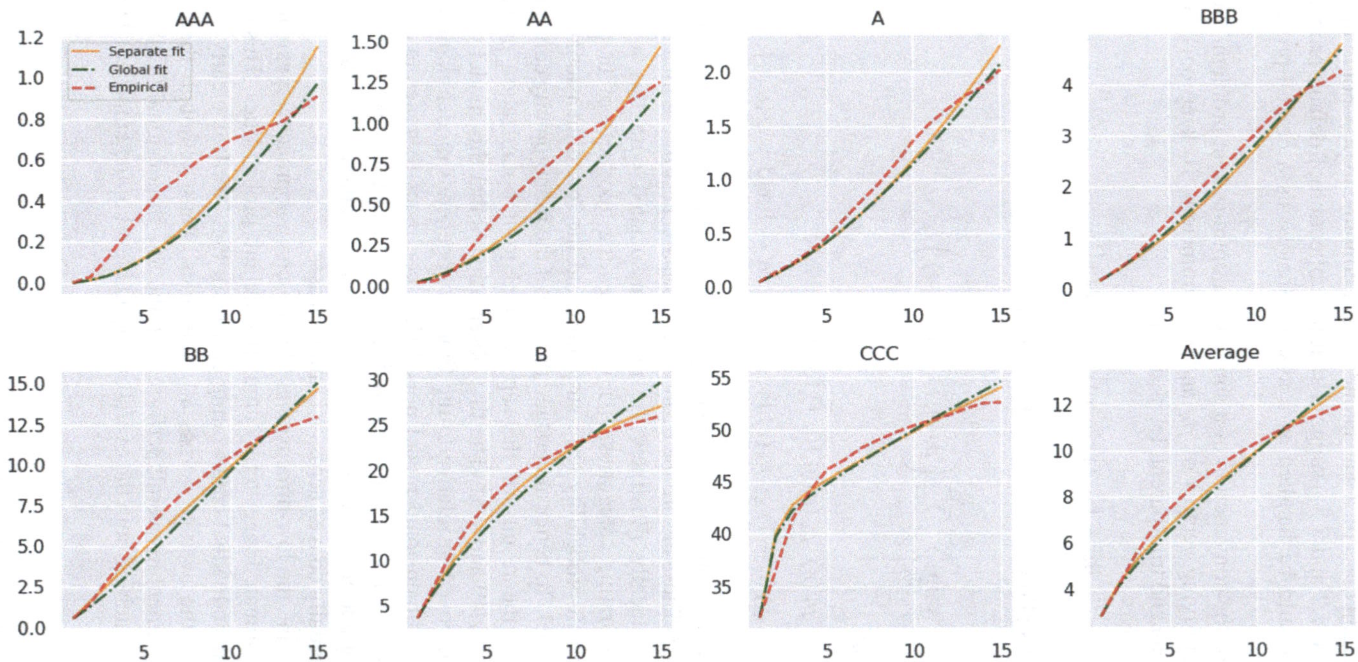


**Fig. 7.6** *The low-dimensional fit*: The graphic above illustrates—for selected credit-rating categories—the goodness of fit between empirical default-probability term structures and the low-dimensional legacy Markov-chain model. The role of the monotonicity constraints are investigated by displaying the results of the separate and joint optimization problems from Eqs. 7.49 and 7.51.

**Table 7.1** *Selected low-dimensional parameters*: This table outlines the individual parameters, organized by the separate and joint optimization approaches, used to fit the default-probability term structures in Fig. 7.6.

| $r$ | Rating | Separate | | Joint | |
|---|---|---|---|---|---|
| | | $p_n(r)$ | $p_a(r)$ | $p_n(r)$ | $p_a(r)$ |
| 0 | AAA | 0.011 | 0.011 | 0.002 | 0.056 |
| 2 | AA | 0.011 | 0.011 | 0.002 | 0.056 |
| 5 | A | 0.013 | 0.013 | 0.003 | 0.078 |
| 8 | BBB | 0.019 | 0.014 | 0.004 | 0.128 |
| 11 | BB | 1.000 | 0.005 | 0.012 | 0.279 |
| 14 | B | 0.000 | 0.076 | 0.019 | 0.279 |
| 16 | CCC | 0.017 | 0.451 | 0.019 | 0.468 |

A final observation relates to the differences between the separate and joint optimization results described in Eqs. 7.49 and 7.51, respectively. Not surprisingly, the separate and distinct optimization of each default-probability term structure has, in general, a better fit. With fewer constraints, it has the flexibility to better specialize the individual credit-category observations. Overall, however, the two approaches do not differ in any important respect. On average, across all individual credit classes, the results agree almost exactly. The fact that the monotonicity constraints do not have a significant impact suggests that they are fairly natural in this setting. That is, there appears to be a high degree of monotonicity already present in the data.

Table 7.1 provides the actual parameter values—again for a selected number of rating classes to avoid overwhelming the reader with numbers—for both the separate and joint optimization problems. The monotonicity constraints are clearly satisfied in the joint problem. Interestingly, the parameter values differ significantly in the two settings despite their generally consistent overall default-probability surface estimates. This leads us to conclude that many constellations of parameters might be consistent with the fitted model. This is further justification for the imposition of constraints; it provides some order and structure to the individual parameter values.

To link back to the original structure of this low-dimensional Markov-chain model, we may construct an (implied) separate transition matrix for each individual rating class. Showing them all would be rather tedious, but a single example can provide some useful insight. Setting $r = 8$, we have S&P's BBB credit class. The associated one-period (jointly optimized) transition matrix—introduced in Eq. 7.46—is given as

$$\begin{aligned} P^{(BBB)} &= \begin{bmatrix} 1 - p_n(BBB) - p_d(BBB) & p_n(BBB) & p_d(BBB) \\ 0 & 1 - p_a(BBB) & p_a(BBB) \\ 0 & 0 & 1 \end{bmatrix} \\ &= \begin{bmatrix} \mathbf{0.994} & 0.004 & 0.002 \\ 0.000 & \mathbf{0.872} & 0.128 \\ 0.000 & 0.000 & \mathbf{1.000} \end{bmatrix}. \end{aligned} \tag{7.52}$$

The $(1, 2)$th and $(2, 3)$th elements can be recovered directly from Table 7.1. Raising $p^{(BBB)}$ to consecutive powers $t = 1, ..., T$ and extracting the $(1, 3)$th element (i.e., $p_d(BBB)$) will provide a reasonable approximation of the default-probability term-structure estimate found in Fig. 7.6. This approximation, however, deteriorates as we move out the credit spectrum. The reason relates to the same time-homogeneous concerns that arose in the context of the full transition matrix considered in Eq. 7.43.

**Colour and Commentary 83** (A LOW-DIMENSIONAL MARKOV CHAIN): *Our legacy, through-the-cycle, default-surface estimates have been computed with a simple three-dimensional Markov-chain model. The three states—initial, asymptotic, and default—are highly restricted to provide a parsimonious description of each rating class. Through some sensible starting conditions and a recursion relationship, it is possible to fit this approach to the empirical default-probability surfaces provided in S&P [45, Table 26]. Even better, the entire system can be jointly estimated with a set of (non-onerous) monotonicity constraints to maintain sensible intra-rating and tenor relationships. The overall goodness of fit, while dramatically better than the full time-homogeneous Markov model, does exhibit some difficulty matching the shape and level of observed default-probability term structures. It thus meets two our three selection criteria: it is parsimonious and provides a (fairly) reasonable fit to the empirical data. This leads to the final criterion. On the surface, its Markov-chain structure appears to provide a low-dimensional link to our initial transition matrix. Ultimately, however, the connection is only tenuous. There does not appear to exist—for each rating class—a transition matrix that can replicate the default-probability surface. We ultimately conclude that this method, despite its promise, is merely an elaborate curve-fitting technique.*

### 7.3.2 A Borrowed Model

Concluding that the previously discussed low-dimensional Markov-chain model is essentially a disguised curve-fitting technique, we may very well wish to consider a method that leans unapologetically in this direction. Given the strong conceptual links between default and interest rates, it is sensible to look to the interest-rate literature for inspiration. Building zero-coupon interest-rate term structures is a classic curve-fitting exercise offering a broad range of flexible techniques. Nelson and Siegel [37] springs immediately to mind given its history. It was designed expressly to introduce a degree of parsimony into the common task of interest-rate term structure fitting.[33] It begins with a four-parameter functional form for the instantaneous forward interest-rate curve.[34] Using a variation of Eq. 7.24, this structure is integrated to build an associated zero-coupon function. This model was such a success that it was extended in a number of ways. Svensson [47] offered a more complex implementation with additional parameters, while Diebold and Li [15] cleverly extended it for us into the dynamic term-structure setting.

Its flexibility, popularity, and parametric frugality thus makes the Nelson and Siegel [37] an excellent candidate for fitting our individual empirical default-probability term structures. If we adapt their model to the problem at hand, we might write the cumulative default-probability term structures as,

$$\begin{aligned} p_r\,(t, u|\,\theta, \lambda_r) &= \theta_0^{(r)} + \theta_1^{(r)} \left( \frac{1 - e^{-\lambda_r(u-t)}}{\lambda_r(u-t)} \right) + \theta_2^{(r)} \left( \frac{1 - e^{-\lambda_r(u-t)}}{\lambda_r(u-t)} - e^{-\lambda_r(u-t)} \right), \\ &= \begin{bmatrix} 1 & \frac{1-e^{-\lambda_r(u-t)}}{\lambda_r(u-t)} & \frac{1-e^{-\lambda_r(u-t)}}{\lambda_r(u-t)} - e^{-\lambda_r(u-t)} \end{bmatrix} \begin{bmatrix} \theta_0^{(r)} \\ \theta_1^{(r)} \\ \theta_2^{(r)} \end{bmatrix}, \end{aligned} \tag{7.53}$$

for $u = 1, ..., T$ and $r = 1, ..., \mathcal{R}$ where $\theta_r = \begin{bmatrix} \theta_0^{(r)} & \theta_1^{(r)} & \theta_2^{(r)} \end{bmatrix}^T$. There is some economic insight to be gleaned from interpretation of the exponentially motivated expression in Eq. 7.53. In the term-structure literature, these terms are considered to represent the level, slope, and curvature of the yield curve. This resonates in the interest-rate world, but might be less applicable in this setting. It may thus be easier to think of this approximation as a linear combination—in $\theta_r$—of some complicated set of basis functions.[35]

A troublesome aspect of this model stems from the fourth parameter: $\lambda_r$. This is the only non-linear choice variable in the model and has been known—see, for example, Cairns and Pritchard [11] and Bolder and Stréliski [9]—to cause annoying optimization stability problems. A typical pragmatic solution—which we will employ here—is to simply fix it to a constant value.[36] For this curve-fitting exercise, therefore, we simply set

$$\lambda_r \equiv \lambda = 0.12, \tag{7.54}$$

[33] The gold standard, at and around the time of this model's introduction, was the so-called cubic-spline model. See, for example, McCulloch [33] or Bliss [2]. While very useful, cubic-spline models are not known for their parametric simplicity.

[34] The approximation is, in fact, based on the use of the first three Laguerre polynomials. See Hurn et al. [22] or Bolder and Liu [8, Appendix C] for the bloody details.

[35] We will further investigate this interesting aspect in more detail in Chap. 8.

[36] Diebold and Rudebusch [16, Section 2.4.1] offer some justification for precisely this advice.

for all $r = 1, ..., \mathcal{R}$. Relaxing this assumption might permit a slightly better fit, but will involve significant computational headaches. From a cost-benefit perspective, this seems a defensible choice.[37]

Fitting the default-probability surface thus simply reduces to solving the following optimization problem

$$\min_{\theta_1,\cdots,\theta_{\mathcal{R}}} \sum_{r=1}^{\mathcal{R}} \sum_{t=1}^{T} \left( p_r\,(0,t\,|\,\theta,\lambda) - p_r(0,t) \right)^2, \tag{7.55}$$

subject to:

$$\theta_0^{(r+1)} \geq \theta_0^{(r)} \text{ for } r = 1, ...\mathcal{R} - 1.$$

Again, we are simply tuning our choice of the individual $\theta_r$ vectors by minimizing the Euclidean distance between our estimated model and the observed multi-period default-probability term structure outcomes. The entire problem is, as before, solved as a single system. The constraints ensure that the first Nelson and Siegel [37] parameter—relating to the level of the overall cumulative default-probability curve—rises (weakly) monotonically over the credit spectrum. These monotonicity conditions are introduced in the same spirit as the previously examined low-dimensional Markov-chain method.

Figure 7.7 illustrates the now-familiar visualization of the Nelson and Siegel [37] fit to our selection of empirical default-probability term structures. The fit is remarkably good. To get to this point required a bit of brute-force intervention. Solving the raw optimization problem in Eq. 7.55 provided an excellent overall match to the empirical data, but resulted in a systemic underestimate to the one-year default probabilities at the higher end of the credit scale. This shortcoming was resolved by placing an arbitrarily large weight to the first-period squared errors—as described in Eq. 7.55 where $t = 1$—to encourage the optimizer to properly capture the initial default probabilities.[38] The consequence, however, is a slight deterioration in the fit of other default-probability tenors.

Despite this initial challenge, the Nelson-Siegel model offers a substantial improvement—along the goodness-of-fit dimension—relative to the low-dimensional Markov-chain method. It captures the convexity across all credit classes and appears to almost flawlessly describe the overall level of default probabilities. On average, the Nelson and Siegel [37] and empirical values are almost indistinguishable. One potential issue arises at S&P's CCC rating. The estimated cumulative default-probability curve clearly falls as we move from the 12- to 15-year tenors. Such behaviour is perfectly acceptable in the interest-rate

[37] Fixing of $\lambda$ can also, in a loose manner, be thought of as taking a choice of (perhaps imperfect) basis for the infinite dimensional function space represented by the set of default-probability curves. For a much better (and rigorous) treatment of these ideas, please see Björk [1].

[38] Although this amounts to a heuristic intervention, this is a fairly common practical approach towards solving such issues.

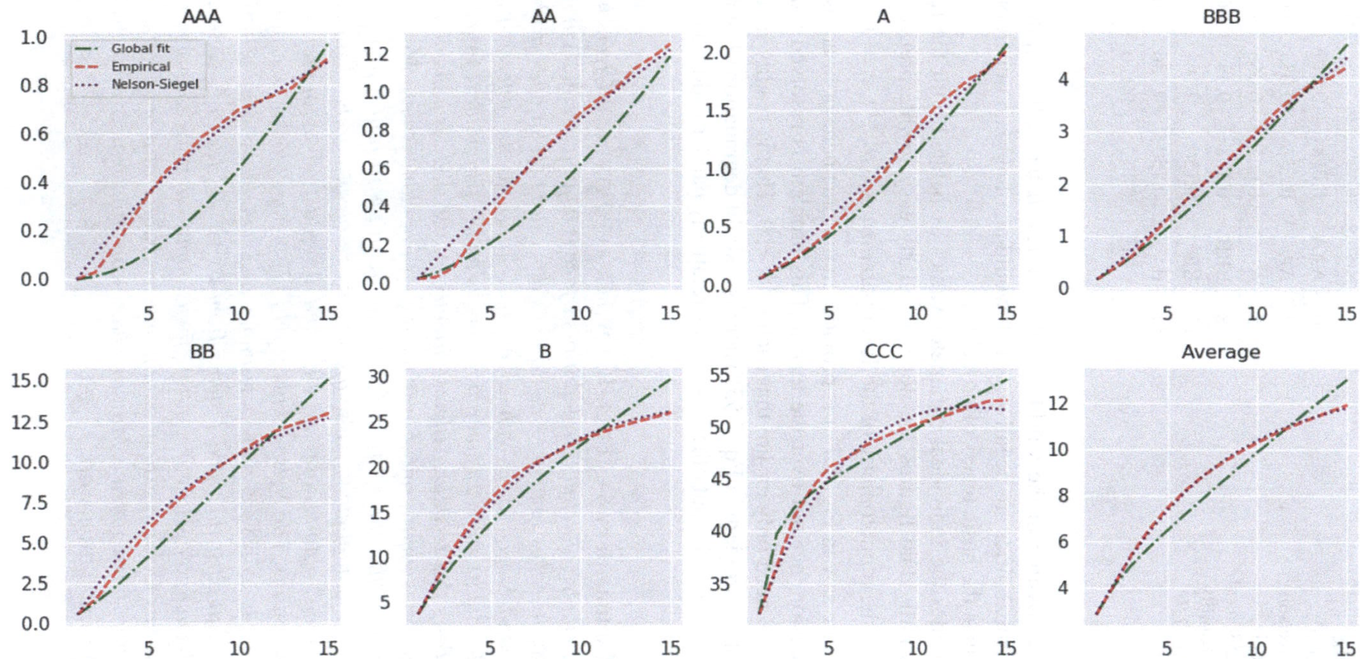


**Fig. 7.7** *Pure curve-fitting results*: The graphic above illustrates—for selected credit-rating categories—the goodness of fit between empirical default-probability term structures and the Nelson and Siegel [37] approach used principally in interest-rate modelling. The globally fit low-dimensional Markov-chain model is also included to permit easy comparison.

**Table 7.2** *Selected Nelson-Siegel parameters*: This table outlines the individual parameters, stemming from the Nelson and Siegel [37] model introduced in Eq. 7.53, used to fit the default-probability term structures in Fig. 7.7.

| $r$ | Rating | Parameters $\theta_0^{(r)}$ | $\theta_1^{(r)}$ | $\theta_2^{(r)}$ |
|---|---|---|---|---|
| 0 | AAA | 0.018 | −0.019 | −0.000 |
| 2 | AA | 0.032 | −0.033 | −0.016 |
| 5 | A | 0.065 | −0.066 | −0.049 |
| 8 | BBB | 0.138 | −0.139 | −0.099 |
| 11 | BB | 0.150 | −0.164 | 0.177 |
| 14 | B | 0.150 | −0.156 | 0.616 |
| 16 | CCC | 0.150 | 0.120 | 1.042 |

setting, but is not possible in the world of default rates. It basically implies that forward default probabilities are negative, which would amount to an unpardonable transgression against the basic tenets of probability.

Table 7.2 provides the individual parameter values associated with the results in Fig. 7.7. The individual figures are not particularly easy to interpret, but we do clearly observe the monotonicity of the level parameters, $\left\{\theta_0^{(r)} : r = 1, \ldots \mathcal{R}\right\}$. Unfortunately, as we saw in Fig. 7.7, this provides monotonic behaviour across the credit-class dimension, but not over the tenors. This problem is resolved with an extra constraint; we need only ensure that each $\theta_1^{(r)} < 0$. This is readily included into our optimization problem in Eq. 7.55. There is a slight degradation of fit at the lower end of the credit scale, but otherwise it is a relatively painless addition.

**Colour and Commentary 84** (FULL-BLOWN CURVE FITTING)*: Given that describing the empirical default-probability surface is a quintessential curve-fitting exercise, it makes logical sense to consider extant techniques in this area. Nelson and Siegel [37], with its extensive links to the interest-rate modelling field and its emphasis on parsimony, is an ideal candidate for consideration. Taking this technique almost directly off the shelf, it immediately offers a conspicuous improvement over the legacy low-dimensional Markov-chain approach. While there are a few issues relating to fitting first-year default rates and monotonicity, these are readily resolved through heuristic adjustments to the optimization weights and introduction of appropriate parameter constraints. The Nelson and Siegel [37] methodology correspondingly scores high marks on our parsimony and goodness-of-fit criteria. The only knock against this model stems from its virtual lack of economic justification. Its unapologetic curve-fitting focus implies that we cannot hope, through use of this technique, to maintain any semblance of a connection to the standard time-homogeneous Markov-chain transition matrix underlying our economic-capital framework.*

### 7.3.3 Time Homogeneity

As a final alternative towards fitting our default-probability surface, we consider going straight to the source of the problem with our original Markov-chain process: time homogeneity. Bluhm and Overbeck [3] offer an interesting alternative to the standard time-homogeneous Markov-chain model used in the literature. The idea is to use a continuous-time version of the Markov chain and, with some clever mathematical gymnastics, permit the entries of our transition matrix to adjust over time in a non-homogenous manner. In short, the transition parameters—and thus default probabilities—are no longer assumed to be fixed in time.

The basic implementation is deceptively simple. The necessary theory—relating to the link between transition and generator matrices for continuous-time Markov chains—has already been covered in previous sections. Ultimately, the main contribution relates to the construction of a time varying generator matrix. This requires restatement of Eq. 7.38 as

$$P_t = e^{tG_t}, \tag{7.56}$$

where

$$G_t = \Phi(t)G. \tag{7.57}$$

The good news is that our original generator matrix, $G$, is preserved. All of the time-varying behaviour is collapsed into the matrix function, $\Phi(t) \in \mathbb{R}^{(\mathcal{R}+1)\times(\mathcal{R}+1)}$.[39] The heavy lifting is embedded in the choice of $\Phi(t)$. Bluhm and Overbeck [3] suggest the following diagonal specification

$$\Phi_{ij}(t, \alpha_i, \beta_i) = \begin{cases} \dfrac{(1-e^{-\alpha_i t})t^{\beta_i - 1}}{1-e^{-\alpha_i}} : i = j \\ 0 : i \neq j \end{cases}, \tag{7.58}$$

for $i, j = 1, ..., \mathcal{R}$. This implies that, with $2 \cdot \mathcal{R}$ parameters, we may transform $P$ into a time-inhomogeneous Markov chain. Let us place, for convenience, all of these coefficients into two vectors $\vec{\alpha}$ and $\vec{\beta}$.

What exactly is Eq. 7.58 doing? It is easy to see that when $t = 1$, $\Phi(t)$ reduces to an identity matrix. This demonstrates that when $t = 1$, the original (unadjusted) transition matrix is recovered. In other words, this approach *nests* the time-homogeneous approach. Moreover, when $t = 0$, then $\Phi$ is a matrix of zeros. In general, for all positive choices of $\alpha_i$ and $\beta_i$, $\Phi$ is an increasing function of $t$. It is not mapped to the unit interval nor, despite Bluhm and Overbeck [3]'s arguments to the

[39] It is not immediately obvious that $G_t$ remains a generator matrix. Bluhm and Overbeck [3, Appendix] sketch a proof of this result.

contrary, is Eq. 7.58 motivated by probability theory.[40] It is probably best to think of the structure in Eq. 7.58 as being selected by Bluhm and Overbeck [3]—through some combination of trial-and-error and hard-won mathematical experience—for its flexibility. Here we see that this approach is, at its heart, also a curve-fitting method.

As usual, the model parameters need to be selected. This is accomplished by solving the following optimization problem,

$$\min_{\vec{\alpha},\vec{\beta}} \sum_{r=1}^{\mathcal{R}} \sum_{t=1}^{T} \left( \exp\left( \underbrace{t\,\Phi\Big(t, \vec{\alpha}(r), \vec{\beta}(r)\Big) G}_{G_t} \right) - p_r(0,t) \right)^2, \tag{7.59}$$

subject to:

$$\vec{\alpha}(r+1) \geq \vec{\alpha}(r) \text{ for } r = 1, \ldots \mathcal{R} - 1,$$

which is profitably compared to Eqs. 7.51 and 7.55. The constraint on the $\alpha$ values is not provided in Bluhm and Overbeck [3] and, in actual fact, is probably not even necessary. It nonetheless adds some additional structure to the parameter values without any obvious deterioration of overall fit.

Figure 7.8 provides the usual comparison of the non-homogeneous Markov-chain model relative to the usual selection of observed default-probability term structures. The other competitors—the low-dimensional Markov chain and Nelson and Siegel [37]—are also provided for context. The results are quite encouraging. The functional form in Eq. 7.58 is sufficiently pliable to capture the variety of empirical shapes and levels. The overall goodness of fit is superior to the low-dimensional Markov-chain approach, but not quite as tight as the Nelson and Siegel [37] approach. Problems with the non-homogeneous Markov model's fit, however, seem to be restricted to the top few highest-quality credit categories. On average, across all credit classes, there seems to be little to distinguish between the empirical observations, the Nelson and Siegel [37] model, and Bluhm and Overbeck [3]'s suggestion. As a final point, the non-homogeneous Markov-chain method displays no challenges with monotonicity either at the credit category or tenor level. This aspect appears to be handled directly by the model structure—which happily manoeuvres the entire default-probability surface as a single system—and the calibration to observed data.

Table 7.3 illustrates a set of selected parameters associated with Bluhm and Overbeck [3]'s specification in Eq. 7.58. As usual, it is hard to directly interpret these values. We do observe, however, the impact of the constraints on $\alpha$. The $\beta$ parameters remain free to allow flexibility to fit the empirical term structures.

[40] That said, as indicated by Bluhm and Overbeck [3], Eq. 7.58 does have terms reminiscent of the exponential and gamma distributions; they are nevertheless not playing a probabilistic role. See Johnson et al. [27, Chapters 17 and 19] for much more on these distributions.

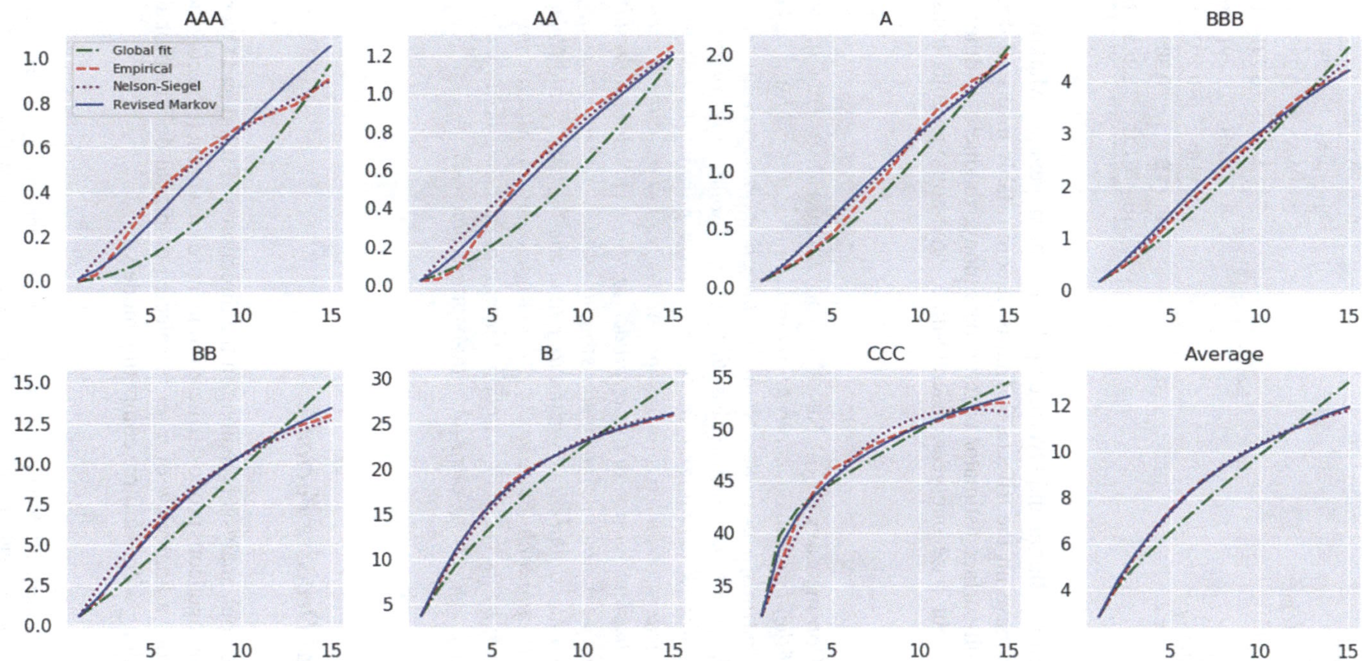


**Fig. 7.8** *Non-homogeneity*: The graphic above illustrates—for selected credit-rating categories—the goodness of fit between empirical default-probability term structures and the Bluhm and Overbeck [3] suggested non-homogeneous Markov-chain parametrization. The globally fit low-dimensional Markov-chain model and Nelson and Siegel [37] methods are also included to permit easy comparison.

**Table 7.3** *Selected non-homogeneous Markov parameters*: This table outlines the individual parameters, stemming from Bluhm and Overbeck [3]'s non-homogeneous Markov-chain model, used to fit the default-probability term structures in Fig. 7.8.

| $r$ | Rating | Parameters | |
|---|---|---|---|
| | | $\alpha_r$ | $\beta_r$ |
| 0 | AAA | 0.283 | 0.956 |
| 2 | AA | 0.283 | 0.736 |
| 5 | A | 0.291 | 0.676 |
| 8 | BBB | 0.291 | 0.457 |
| 11 | BB | 0.292 | 0.532 |
| 14 | B | 0.309 | 0.198 |
| 16 | CCC | 2.288 | 0.226 |

Overall, therefore, Bluhm and Overbeck [3]'s non-homogeneous Markov-chain model appears to have hit the trifecta.[41] That is, it comfortably meets all three of our desired default-surface estimator criteria: parsimony, goodness-of-fitness, and consistency with our base one-year, discrete-time, time-homogeneous transition matrix.

**Colour and Commentary 85** (A NON-HOMOGENEOUS MARKOV CHAIN): *The failure of the time-homogeneous Markov-chain model provides a rather obvious hint towards a possible solution: a time non-homogeneous implementation. The traditional drawback of this potential solution is complexity. Bluhm and Overbeck [3] suggest, however, a clever parametrization for a time-varying generator matrix in a discrete-state, continuous-time Markov-chain setting. Implementation of this approach provides encouraging results. In addition to a parsimonious parameter structure, the overall goodness-of-fit appears to be only slightly less satisfactory than the highly flexible Nelson and Siegel [37] approach. Even better, the non-homogeneous Markov implementation nests, by its very construction, the one-period time-homogeneous transition matrix underlying our economic-capital framework.*

### *7.3.4 A Final Decisive Factor*

Although the previous analysis is leaning in the direction of Bluhm and Overbeck [3]'s time non-homogeneous proposal, there is one more viewpoint to be considered. Figure 7.9 provides a final view of a set of selected empirical default-probability term structures along with our three competing models.

[41] For non-gambling readers, a trifecta is a winning (typically horse-racing) bet that successful identifies the correct first, second, and third place finishers. It is, as one would expect, rather hard to do and pays quite well.

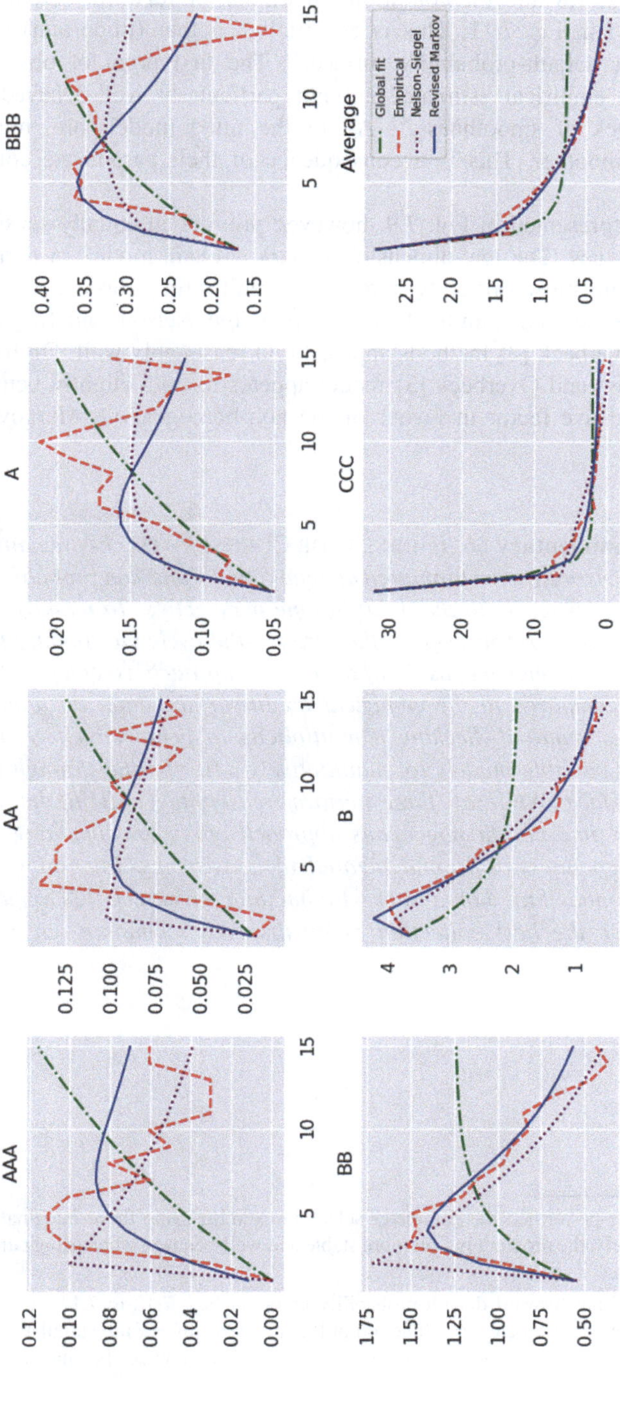


**Fig. 7.9** *An alternative perspective:* The graphic above transforms the cumulative default-probability term structures in Fig. 7.8 into the conditional marginal, or forward, default probabilities introduced in Eq. 7.11.

Figure 7.9, in particular, transforms the cumulative default-probability term structures from Fig. 7.8 into the conditional marginal, or forward, default probabilities introduced in Eq. 7.11. This is essentially another (important) way of visualizing on our default-probability surface.[42] The first point of observation is that the actual empirical estimates are not particularly well-behaved. This is due to their lack of smoothness.[43] All of the fitted models are, relatively speaking, much smoother. This is a consequence of their parametric construction.

Not all models presented in Fig. 7.9, however, provide an equally sensible fit to the observed values. The low-dimensional Markov-chain model, in particular, appears to have the most difficulty across all credit-rating classes. While the empirical estimates are an admittedly hard target, the Nelson and Siegel [37] and Bluhm and Overbeck [3] methods appear to do reasonably well. On balance, however, the Bluhm and Overbeck [3] model appears to do a slightly better job. This is a final decisive factor in favour of the non-homogeneous Markov-chain model.

**Colour and Commentary 86** (HORSES FOR COURSES): *Our key remaining applications necessitate transformation of default and transition probabilities from the through-the-cycle to the point-in-time perspective. To manage this successfully, we need a firm grip on the through-the-cycle viewpoint. Since the standard time-homogeneous Markov chain approach is categorically rejected when compared to the empirical credit-surface data, an alternative approach is required. Seeking a multiplicity of perspective, we have identified* three *possible models to quantitatively describe the through-the-cycle credit surface. While all three perform reasonably well, Bluhm and Overbeck [3]'s time non-homogeneous approach offers an appealing mix of parsimony, goodness-of-fit, and theoretical consistency. Imagining this exercise as a modelling horse race, Bluhm and Overbeck [3]'s model appears to have the best collection of attributes to dominate our race-course.*

[42] We could also have performed the parameter selection exercise using these marginal default probabilities. Ultimately, the problem is a bit more stable and well-behaved when using cumulative values.

[43] As seen in the limiting forward default-probability case—in Eqs. 7.12 to 7.14—the forward default probability can be interpreted as a function of the first derivative of the cumulative default probabilities. Non-smoothness in an underlying function will, of course, be magnified in its derivative.

## 7.4 Mapping to One's Master Scale

If we used, in a precise manner, the S&P (truncated) 18-notch scale for its internal rating structure, this would be the end of the story associated with through-the-cycle default-probability surfaces. In actuality, however, there are two important differences with the NIB case. As previously discussed, we use

- a firm-specific 21-step master rating scale; and
- an internal set of one-year default-probability values.

Both of these issues imply that it is not possible to adopt, in a wholesale manner, the through-the-cycle default surface model estimates developed in the previous section. Adjustments will be required to be able to sensibly proceed towards the construction of an NIB-based default-probability surface. This final section of the chapter is thus dedicated to resolving these issues.

Two points are worth raising. First, the following discussion is unfortunately rather NIB-centric. As many institutions operate under schemes that differ from the large credit-rating firms, however, generalization of these ideas may be of wider usefulness and applicability. The second point is that there is no general literature on moving from a $n$- to an $m$-notch rating scale—for any arbitrary $n \neq m$—either on the basis of default or transition probabilities. Indeed, this is not a terribly natural process. The following development, therefore, is a collection of *ad hoc* and heuristic adjustments. While motivated by general logic and a desire to maintain the basic features of the S&P transition matrix and default-probability surface, there is nothing unique or theoretically guided about this approach. In the spirit of full transparency, there are certainly other competing approaches that might reasonably be employed (and, if we are honest, may even be superior to what is presented).

Our starting point is a need to create a link between 17 S&P and 20 non-default internal rating categories. Given the mismatch between the number of classes, it is clear that there does not exist a one-to-one mapping between these two sets. Chapter 3 presents—including the S&P, Moody's and internal scales—a conceptual link. It is sadly imperfect, because it can be interpreted in a number of alternative ways. Figure 7.10 illustrates two possible ways this proposed link might be interpreted. The left-hand graphic highlights a one-to-many mapping from the domain (i.e., S&P) to the codomain or target set (i.e., NIB). As the name suggests, a single S&P rating can yield multiple internal ratings, but two different S&P ratings cannot lead to the same internal classification.[44] While certainly not perfect for our purposes, the one-to-many mapping does offer a moderate degree of clarity.

An alternative linkage, in the right-hand graphic of Fig. 7.10, involves a more literal translation of the original table in Chap. 3. It is a many-to-many mapping. In this case, not only can a single S&P rating map to multiple internal values, but other

[44] The S&P BB category, for example, is mapped to both PD12 and PD13. No other S&P rating links to these internal classes. In Fig. 7.10, this is evident from the lack of horizontal lines.

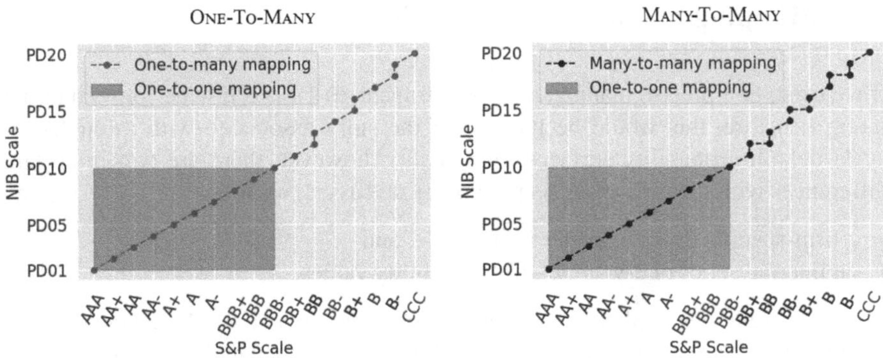


**Fig. 7.10** *Linking the external and internal scales*: With 17 (non-default) S&P ratings and 20 (non-default) internal notches, there is no unique way to link these two scales. The preceding graphics illustrate, using the language of function mappings, two distinct possibilities. Such questions inevitably arise when combining internal and external rating scales.

S&P ratings can also map to those classes.[45] It is, to put it colourfully, the functional equivalent of a free-for-all.

While we will make use of both of these mappings in the sequel, we do have a strong conceptual preference for the one-to-many form. We can think of it as a one-to-one mapping with *three* notable exceptions. To be very specific, from Fig. 7.10, these cases are: BB maps to PD12 and PD13, B+ is linked to PD15 and PD16, and B- connects to PD18 and PD19. In the following discussion, when we make use of the one-to-many mapping, we are referring to this object.

## *7.4.1 Building an Internal Default Probability Surface*

As introduced in Chap. 3, internal one-year, default probability estimates—for each point along the internal 21-notch master scale—follow a decades-old approach. To keep this chapter reasonable self-contained, we'll quickly trace out the basic idea. The individual values are not determined through an estimation technique, but rather follow from a combination of S&P rating data and economic logic. The two highest quality credit categories—PD01 and PD02—are assigned value of 0.6 and 1.45 basis points, respectively. This is necessary since usage of S&P statistics would involve assigning a zero value to these—AAA and AA+ equivalent—categories.[46] Internal

[45] Once again, the S&P BB category is mapped to both PD12 and PD13, but BB+ also maps to PD12. No other S&P rating links to these internal classes. Returning to Fig. 7.10, this is evidenced by the presence of both horizontal and vertical lines.

[46] For analytic purposes, a one-year, zero default probability, for any credit classification, is practically and economically problematic.

rating classes PD03 to PD07 are approximately assigned—on a one-to-one basis following from Fig. 7.10—the corresponding S&P AA to BBB+ through-the-cycle, default probability estimates. PD08 to PD20 are then simply computed as a multiple of the previous value. Practically, this amounts to $\text{PD}(k) = (1 + \xi)\text{PD}(k - 1)$ for $k = 8, ..., 20$. The traditional (and current) value of $\xi$ is $\frac{1}{2}$; this means that one-year default probabilities double with each step along the internal master scale. A upper bound of 20% is imposed, which has a modest impact on the PD20 credit category. This approach has served us quite well over the years, is broadly consistent with empirical data, and is straightforward to understand and communicate.

While our one-to-many mapping logical link between the S&P and internal rating scales will prove central to the construction of an NIB-scale transition matrix, it is not particularly helpful at the default-surface level. The reason stems from our one-year default probabilities. Up until about PD10, there is a very high level of agreement between the S&P and internal values. These are easily managed. Beyond about PD10, the situation becomes less obvious. From PD11 to PD19, the internal default probability estimates are slightly more conservative than the (mapped) S&P equivalents. At PD20, which is directly linked to S&P's CCC category, the internal value is substantially smaller than the S&P value. In particular, the PD20 default probability is about 15 percentage points lower than the 0.35 S&P value.[47] Neither a one-to-one nor a one-to-many link between the internal and S&P scales will be able to reproduce these differences.

The proposed solution is relatively simple and entirely heuristic. The internal default probability—for each tenor—is written as the linear combination of two adjacent S&P categories; we can think of this as an application of (a slight variation on) our many-to-many mapping from Fig. 7.10. This pair of weights—again for each internal rating class—are required to be positive and sum to unity. These conditions are not strictly mathematically necessary, but they certainly aid in interpreting and communicating the results. The weights are determined by creating a direct match between the internal default probability and the linear combination of the two associated S&P categories.

Instead of introducing complicated—and non-standard—notation for the description of this small optimization problem, it is easier to simply examine the results. Table 7.4 illustrates the final (optimized) one-to-many mappings between the internal and S&P scales. It should be fairly easy to read. The PD11 default probability is, for example, comprised of about 6% and 94% of S&P's BB+ and BB classes, respectively. The PD20 category, conversely, is roughly equal parts of B- and CCC. While the figures are fairly transparent and easy to interpret, we should not lose sight of the fact that this is an *ad hoc* exercise. No theoretical arguments lie underneath this approach to linking the two default scales.

---

[47] To repeat, the CCC is something of a catch-all category including all of the five C-level ratings. It is, therefore, not unreasonable to have differences of views as to what precisely this category entails.

**Table 7.4** *A possible default-probability mapping matrix*: This matrix in $\mathbb{R}^{21\times 18}$ provides a set of possible weights to map between the S&P and master internal-rating scales. There is no theoretical basis for this choice, nor is this a unique specification.

| NIB \S&P | AAA | AA+ | AA | AA− | A+ | A | A− | BBB+ | BBB | BBB− | BB+ | BB | BB− | B+ | B | B− | CCC | D |
|---|---|---|---|---|---|---|---|---|---|---|---|---|---|---|---|---|---|---|
| PD01 | 1.00 | – | – | – | – | – | – | – | – | – | – | – | – | – | – | – | – | 0.00 |
| PD02 | – | 1.00 | – | – | – | – | – | – | – | – | – | – | – | – | – | – | – | 0.00 |
| PD03 | – | – | 1.00 | – | – | – | – | – | – | – | – | – | – | – | – | – | – | 0.00 |
| PD04 | – | – | – | 1.00 | – | – | – | – | – | – | – | – | – | – | – | – | – | 0.00 |
| PD05 | – | – | – | – | 1.00 | – | – | – | – | – | – | – | – | – | – | – | – | 0.00 |
| PD06 | – | – | – | – | – | 1.00 | – | – | – | – | – | – | – | – | – | – | – | 0.00 |
| PD07 | – | – | – | – | – | – | 1.00 | – | – | – | – | – | – | – | – | – | – | 0.00 |
| PD08 | – | – | – | – | – | – | – | 1.00 | – | – | – | – | – | – | – | – | – | 0.00 |
| PD09 | – | – | – | – | – | – | – | – | 1.00 | – | – | – | – | – | – | – | – | 0.00 |
| PD10 | – | – | – | – | – | – | – | – | – | 1.00 | – | – | – | – | – | – | – | 0.00 |
| PD11 | – | – | – | – | – | – | – | – | – | – | 0.06 | 0.94 | – | – | – | – | – | 0.00 |
| PD12 | – | – | – | – | – | – | – | – | – | – | – | 0.42 | 0.58 | – | – | – | – | 0.00 |
| PD13 | – | – | – | – | – | – | – | – | – | – | – | – | 0.81 | 0.19 | – | – | – | 0.00 |
| PD14 | – | – | – | – | – | – | – | – | – | – | – | – | 0.32 | 0.68 | – | – | – | 0.00 |
| PD15 | – | – | – | – | – | – | – | – | – | – | – | – | – | 0.64 | 0.36 | – | – | 0.00 |
| PD16 | – | – | – | – | – | – | – | – | – | – | – | – | – | – | 0.87 | 0.13 | – | 0.00 |
| PD17 | – | – | – | – | – | – | – | – | – | – | – | – | – | – | 0.33 | 0.67 | – | 0.00 |
| PD18 | – | – | – | – | – | – | – | – | – | – | – | – | – | – | – | 0.93 | 0.07 | 0.00 |
| PD19 | – | – | – | – | – | – | – | – | – | – | – | – | – | – | – | 0.75 | 0.25 | 0.00 |
| PD20 | – | – | – | – | – | – | – | – | – | – | – | – | – | – | – | 0.49 | 0.51 | 0.00 |
| D | – | – | – | – | – | – | – | – | – | – | – | – | – | – | – | – | – | 1.00 |

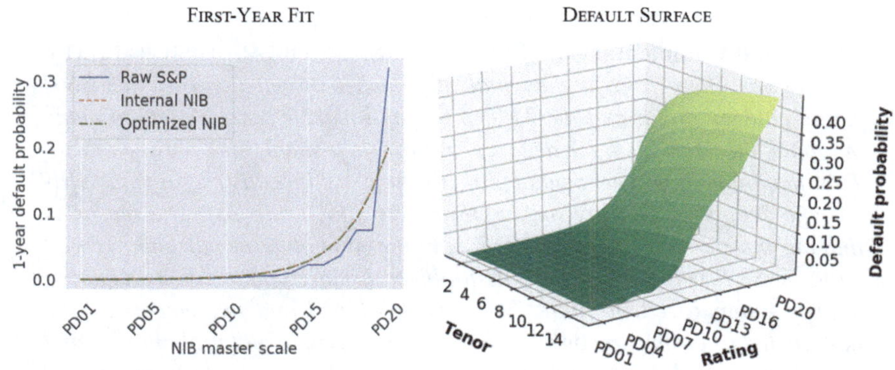


**Fig. 7.11** *Default-surface matching*: The preceding graphics illustrate the consequences of matching the internal and S&P default scales. The left-hand graphic illustrates the connection between the one-year default probabilities based on the weights described in Table 7.4. The right-hand graphic displays the default probability surface arising from the application of these weights to the S&P surface drawn from S&P [45, Table 26] and introduced in Fig. 7.2.

The logic is simple. From S&P [45, Table 26], we have a dataset of 15 years of cumulative default probabilities over 18 S&P credit states; let's call this $D \in \mathbb{R}^{15\times 18}$. If we define the mapping matrix in Table 7.4 as $M \in \mathbb{R}^{21\times 18}$, then $DM^T \in \mathbb{R}^{15\times 21}$ represents the heuristic transformation (or projection) of the raw S&P default surface data to the internal scale. $M$ basically serves a dual purpose; it links the two scales and preserves the basic structure of the one-year internal default probabilities across the entire time horizon.

Figure 7.11 provides a visualization of the usage of Table 7.4's results for matching the internal and S&P default scales. The left-hand graphic illustrates the connection between the one-year default probabilities. Here we see clearly the differences between the internal one-year default probabilities and the equivalent S&P [45, Table 26] results.[48] The internal and optimized (using Table 7.4) values agree almost perfectly.

The right-hand graphic of Fig. 7.11 displays the default probability surface arising from the application of these weights to the S&P surface. This derived internal default-probability surface compares favourably to the empirical results drawn from S&P [45, Table 26] and introduced in Fig. 7.2. The starting point is slightly different—as required by the internal transition-probability estimates—and this has a modest impact on the overall level. It is precisely this default-probability surface that will be used—with the help of the previously described models—to construct NIB-specific through-the-cycle default-probability term structure estimates.

[48] Our one-to-many mapping from Fig. 7.10 is used to project the 18-notch S&P categorization onto the 21-step internal scale. Close examination reveals that the PD12-13, PD15-16, and PD18-19 default-probability pairs are equal.

**Colour and Commentary 87** (AN INTERNAL DEFAULT-PROBABILITY SURFACE): *There is a fundamental mismatch between the 18-notch S&P rating categorization and the 21-step internal master scale. A one-to-many mapping has been used, for decades, to provide a simple link between them. This mapping, however, cannot directly help us in constructing an NIB-specific default probability surface from S&P [45, Table 26]. The reason is that our internal one-year default probabilities do not agree particularly well with the S&P values. To solve this problem, a more complicated weighting matrix—summarized in Table 7.4—was developed and implemented. This approach thus permits recovery of one-year internal default probabilities and a straightforward construction of an S&P-equivalent (or consistent) internal default surface. Across all tenors, we observe* three *distinct trends driven by this matching approach and the one-year internal default probabilities. The PD01 to PD10 categories agree with the S&P estimates. PD11 to PD19 are slightly more conservative than their S&P equivalents, while PD20 is rather smaller than the CCC S&P credit class.*[a] *Although convenient, it should be stressed that this is a heuristic computation absent any theoretical arguments for linking the two default scales.*

[a] This is ultimately due to the fact that we do not view S&P's catch-all CCC category as being entirely representative of the credit quality in our PD20 rating class.

### *7.4.2 Building an Internal Transition Matrix*

The low-dimensional Markov-chain and Nelson and Siegel [37] models can now be directly fit to the internal default-probability surface in Fig. 7.11 (i.e., $DM^T$). Unfortunately, the same is not true for Bluhm and Overbeck [3]'s non-homogeneous Markov-chain approach; it requires a transition matrix with the same 21 credit classes as found in our internal default-probability surface. While somewhat annoying, this direct relationship to the fundamental transition matrix used in our economic-capital model is actually a strength of this technique. Moreover, our economic-capital model also requires an empirically consistent, NIB-specific transition matrix.

The consequence is that, before we can complete this chapter, we will present a methodology for connecting the S&P transition matrix displayed in Eq. 7.43 and the internal default-probability estimates. In short, we need to transform $\hat{P} \in \mathbb{R}^{18\times 18}$ onto the 21-notch internal scale. Naively, we might seek a mapping $f$ such as

$$f : [0, 1]^{18\times 18} \rightarrow [0, 1]^{21\times 21}. \tag{7.60}$$

This will not quite do the job. That our matrix entries must fall into the unit interval to represent probabilities is a necessary, but not sufficient, condition. We also need to ensure that we are dealing with transition matrices. If we let $\mathcal{P}^{m\times n}$ denote the collection of transition matrices with $m$ rows and $n$ columns. We can thus revise our desired mapping to:

$$f : \mathcal{P}^{18\times 18} \rightarrow \mathcal{P}^{21\times 21}. \tag{7.61}$$

This is not a particularly natural thing to do. Nor is there, to the best of our knowledge, any literature suggesting how such a task should be accomplished. We should thus not expect an elegant analytic specification of $f$. Instead, we propose a second heuristic approach that attempts to meet the following criteria:

- preservation of the internal default probabilities;
- each row of the target matrix sums to unity;
- a (weakly) monotonically decreasing (non-default) diagonal;
- upgrade probabilities for each credit class increase in a monotonic manner towards the diagonal, while default likelihood falls monotonically as we move away from the diagonal;
- assignment of some minimal amount[49] (possibly very small) of transition probability mass to every (non-absorbing) element; and
- consistency, to the extent possible, with the S&P transition matrix.

These criteria are certainly not written in stone and, as such, could be subject to (possibly heated) discussion. They do seem reasonable, however, and consequently act as the foundation for the overall approach.

The details of the proposed mapping $f$ are highly technical and, consequently, not particularly exciting. Indeed, it looks rather more like an algorithm than a mapping. Moreover, it is difficult to follow precisely what is going on without jumping into the details. These points notwithstanding, the transition matrix is a critical element of our economic-capital framework and its construction merits a clear description. The actual mapping algorithm thus involves the following *eight* steps:

1. **Initialization:** Create an empty $P_N \in \mathcal{P}^{21\times 21} \subset [0, 1]^{21\times 21}$ matrix of zeros; let's call this the internal transition matrix.
2. **Default Probabilities:** We may then directly place all of the internal default-probability estimates—from PD01 to PD20—into the 21st column. Since default is an absorbing state, we can simply set element $(21, 21)$ to unity.
3. **Diagonals:** The next step is to directly place the diagonal elements from the S&P matrix $\hat{P} \in \mathcal{P}^{18\times 18}$, using the previously introduced one-to-many mapping from Fig. 7.10, into the first 20 rows of $P_N$.

[49] There are, with the exception of default, no logical economic restriction on moving from any given rating class to another. Moreover, there is no defensible, economic argument—again excluding defaulted entities—for a zero probability of any transition matrix event.

4. **Diagonal Smoothing:** We then, to impose some structure onto the transition matrix, use a smoothing $B$-spline model to ensure monotonically decreasing diagonals. Another fitting technique could certainly be used, but spline models are very good at this sort of task.[50] The diagonals are then replaced—across the first 20 rows and columns—with these smoothed values.
5. **Residual Probability Mass:** We now have default probabilities and a diagonal. Since each row needs to sum to unity, we may now comfortably compute the remaining probability mass that needs to be assigned to each individual row for it to be a true transition matrix. These values are calculated and stored for use in subsequent calculations.
6. **Upgrade and Downgrade Proportions:** The next step, for each (non-default) credit state, is to compute the probability of upgrade and downgrade from our original S&P transition matrix.[51] To preserve this feature of the S&P matrix, we estimate the proportional probability—in percentage terms summing to one—of upgrade and downgrade for each S&P rating class. Again using our simple one-to-many mapping, these percentages are used to determine the relative proportion of remaining probability mass—computed in the previous step—to assign for each row in $P_N$.
7. **Upgrade and Downgrade Distributions:** We now know how much probability mass to assign to each side of the (non-default) off-diagonals. The remaining question is: how should it be distributed across the various columns of $P_N$? We use a monotone $I$-spline model to fit the transition-probability profile of each row in the S&P transition matrix.[52] These estimates—and, for a final time, our simple one-to-many mapping—are used to spread out the upgrade and downgrade probability mass across the (non-default) off-diagonal elements of $P_N$. The monotone characteristic of this fitting approach further ensures defensible economic behaviour of the downgrade and upgrade probabilities across each row of $P_N$.
8. **Zero-Valued Transition Probabilities:** As a final step, we wish to avoid any zero transition probabilities.[53] The minimum transition probability is set to the default probability of PD01, which is currently about 0.6 basis points. For the sovereign transition matrix, which has some almost sparse segments, this value is set to 0.1 basis points. All other zero entries in $P_N$ are set to this value; the required probability mass for this adjustment is drawn from the row's diagonal element.

[50] For much more information on splines in general—and the $M$- and $B$-spline bases, in particular—see de Boor [13], Nürnberger [38], Lancaster and Salkauskas [31], Dierckx [17], Schumaker [44], and Wegman and Wright [51].

[51] AAA has, of course, a zero probability of upgrade, while CCC has a zero probability of (non-default) downgrade.

[52] Also called monotone splines, the reader is referred to Ramsay [40], Wright and Wegman [53], Tutz and Leitenstorfer [50], Ramsay [39], and de Leeuw [14] for more background on this helpful tool.

[53] The only exception relates to the absorbing default state.

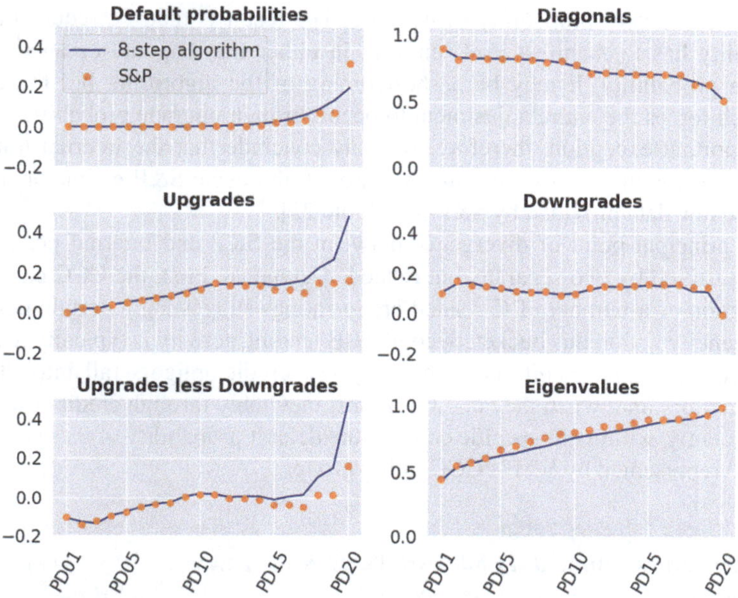


**Fig. 7.12** *Key transition-matrix matching criteria*: The preceding graphics provide a visual comparison of six alternative comparison criteria between the S&P and proposed internal transition matrices. Overall agreement is quite good; the biggest difference stems from the discrepancy between CCC and PD20 default probability values.

Figure 7.12 displays the results of *six* key criteria in our transition-matrix matching algorithm. Each criterion relates to a key, and familiar, aspect of a transition matrix.[54] The solid blue line is associated with the (derived) internal transition matrix, while the orange dots represent the one-to-many mapped S&P values from the matrix shown in Eq. 7.43.

We could present, in their full glory, each of the elements of $P_N$ to numerous decimal places. While useful perhaps for posterity, such a table would be neither useful nor terribly pleasant to examine. Figure 7.12, in contrast, provides an instructive visual comparison by permitting inspection of the individual internal default probabilities, the diagonal values, and (with the assistance of a calculator) permits computation of implicit upgrade and downgrade probabilities for each rating category.

There is a fairly high degree of overall agreement—along the selected six key dimensions in Fig. 7.12—between S&P's $\hat{P}$ and our internal $P_N$ transition matrices. The largest source of deviation stems from the discrepancy between the CCC and PD20 default-probability values. The CCC category—standing directly before

[54] The only exception might relate to the eigenvalues. These quantities, however, are a central aspect of the description of any square matrix; see Golub and Loan [20] for much more background on this important concept in linear algebra.

default—has a zero probability of upgrade. The result is that the reduced default probability has to manifest itself entirely in either the diagonal or an increased upgrade probability. It may be a shortcoming of the algorithm, but the current approach forces the entire adjustment to occur through upgrade probabilities. With this important exception, therefore, we may conclude that the internal transition matrix is generally consistent with the through-the-cycle S&P estimator inferred from the raw data provided by S&P [45, Table 23].

The principal point of divergence between the S&P and internal perspectives can be justified by two separate, but related, arguments. First, the CCC category is a collection of a number of C-related credit ratings suggesting a certain degree of heterogeneity within this bucket. Second, NIB lending activity is typically restricted to upper end of the credit spectrum; very few credit obligors fall into PD18 to PD20 territory and, when they do, it is almost inevitably through credit downgrade. Consequently, within our specific context, the default probability of these entities is not well represented by S&P's CCC rating group.

**Colour and Commentary 88** (AN INTERNAL TRANSITION MATRIX)*: A second fundamental mismatch occurs between the* $\mathcal{P}^{18\times 18}$ *S&P and* $\mathcal{P}^{21\times 21}$ *internal transition matrices. Linking these two matrices is neither natural nor particularly easy. One has to manage default probabilities, the magnitude of diagonals, and the relative upgrade and downgrade likelihoods. The decades-old one-to-many mapping can help with this problem, but some additional structure is required. In particular, any algorithm should preserve the internal default probabilities, but otherwise match* $\hat{P}$ *characteristics derived from the raw output from S&P [45, Table 23] as closely as possible. An eight-step heuristic algorithm was constructed for this purpose. Overall—when considering a set of six comparison criteria—the agreement between the original S&P and derived-internal-scale transition matrices is quite high. The largest point of disagreement stems from the previously discussed difference between S&P's CCC one-year default probability and our internal PD20 value. As in the previous section, the heuristic (or* ad hoc*) nature of this computation needs to be highlighted. The existence of other, perhaps superior, approaches is entirely possible.*

Outfitted with the necessary default-probability surface and transition matrices mapped to the internal scale, we may finally close out this chapter by proceeding to compute a set of internal, through-the-cycle, default-probability term structure estimates. The actual implementation is conceptually identical to the S&P setting.[55] The results are summarized—again for a selected set of internal credit classes—in Fig. 7.13. This result is directly comparable to the values displayed in Fig. 7.8.

[55] We do need, before getting started, to compute the generator matrix for $P_N$ using our previously discussed regularization algorithm.

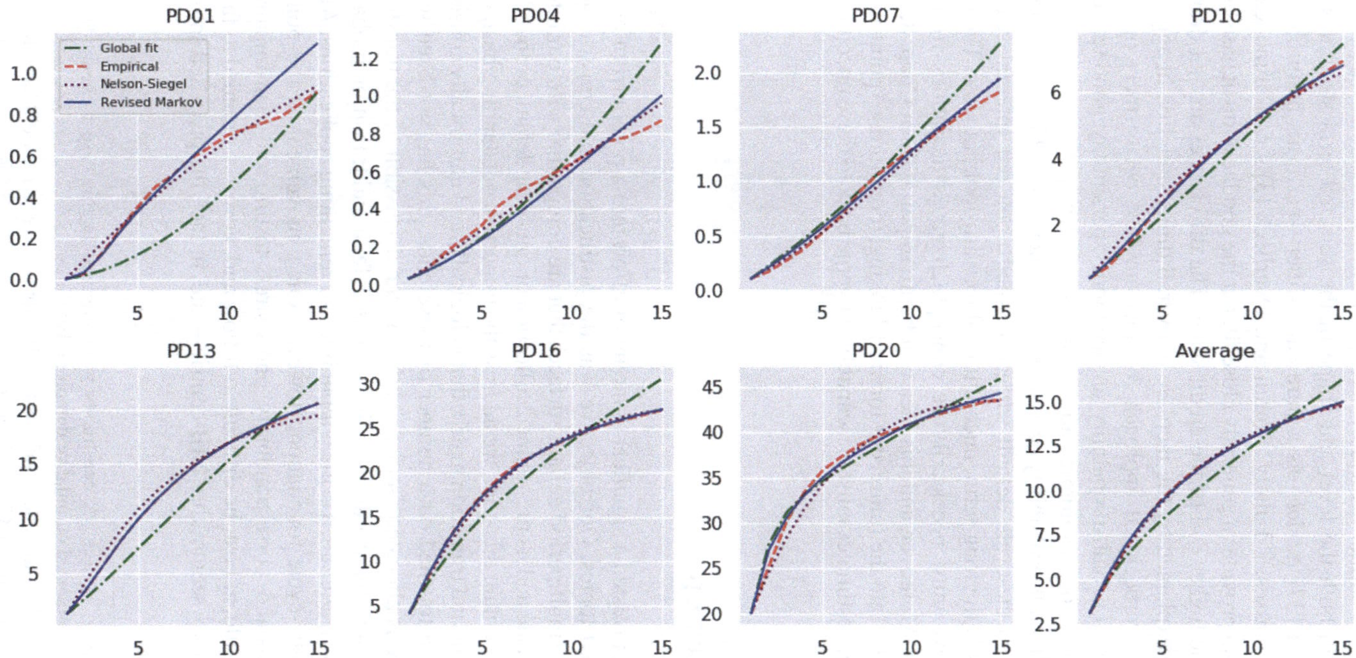


**Fig. 7.13** *The last word*: The figure above illustrates—for selected credit-rating categories on our internal scale—the goodness of fit between model results and empirical default-probability term structures. The actual implementation is conceptually identical as in the S&P setting. The globally fit low-dimensional Markov-chain, Nelson and Siegel [37], and Bluhm and Overbeck [3]'s non-homogeneous Markov-chain parametrizations are all included.

Qualitatively, the results of applying our surface-fitting models to internal-scale mapped data are very similar to the S&P setting. The low-dimensional Markov chain has difficulty with both the level and shape of the selected term structures. The Nelson and Siegel [37] model—as a pure curve-fitter—performs admirably well across all credit classes.[56] Finally, Bluhm and Overbeck [3]'s non-homogeneous Markov-chain also provides a generally close fit, but the goodness-of-fit has slightly deteriorated at the higher end of the credit scale. The differences are not dramatic and appear to be explained by the increase in overall dimensionality. In aggregate, the Bluhm and Overbeck [3] approach remains our best bet to meet our *three* distinct criteria for a default-probability surface model: parsimony, goodness-of-fit, and consistency with our economic-capital transition matrix.

The separate default-probability curves, or term structures, in Fig. 7.13 represent together a through-the-cycle default surface defined upon our internal scale. In other words, this is the long-term, unconditional forward-looking view. The point-in-time perspective must necessarily be conceptualized as deviations from this long-term anchor. Moreover, and this idea will figure importantly in Chap. 8, as we move arbitrarily far into the future, our forward-looking, (conditional) point-in-time default-probability estimates must inescapably converge back to these unconditional values.[57]

## 7.5 Wrapping Up

This chapter has invested a significant amount of effort into a potpourri of default-probability related topics. Our objective was the justification and construction of through-the-cycle multiperiod default surfaces that are compatible with our internal 21-notch rating scale and its pre-defined collection of one-year default probabilities. Along the way, to obtain this goal, we address the important outstanding business of determining an internal transition matrix that is logically and empirically consistent. Although we have touched on a number of loose ends, this has not been wasted effort. Much time is allocated—quite rightly—to the discussion of the transformation between through-the-cycle and point-in-time default and transition probability estimates.[58] This is, after all, a critical input into our remaining applications. Absent a solid through-the-cycle foundation, however, one's movement to the point-in-time perspective—and, correspondingly, one's stress-testing and loan-impairment frameworks—would, at best, be difficult to follow and, at worst, doomed to failure. These problems may seem rather NIB-centric—and, in fact, the proposed solutions

[56] The $\theta_1^{(r)} < 0$ for $r = 1, \ldots, \mathcal{R}$ constraints were imposed in this case to guarantee tenor monotonicity among associated cumulative default probabilities.

[57] The simple reason is that the value of information deteriorates over time; we'll have much more to say on this fundamental idea in Chaps. 8 and 9.

[58] This important topic is, in fact, the central focus of Chap. 8.

necessarily are—but these are general problems faced by most small to medium-sized financial institutions.

## References

1. T. Björk. *On the Geometry of Interest Rate Models*, pages 133–215. Springer Berlin Heidelberg, Berlin, Heidelberg, 2004.
2. R. R. Bliss. Testing term structure estimation methods. Federal Reserve Bank of Atlanta: Working Paper 96-12, 1996.
3. C. Bluhm and L. Overbeck. Calibration of PD Term Structures: to be Markov or not to be. *Risk*, 20(11):98–103, November 2007.
4. D. J. Bolder. Affine Term-Structure Models: Theory and Implementation. Bank of Canada: Working Paper 2001-15, October 2001.
5. D. J. Bolder. Modelling Term-Structure Dynamics for Portfolio Analysis: A Practitioner's Perspective. Bank of Canada: Working Paper 2006-48, December 2006.
6. D. J. Bolder. *Credit-Risk Modelling: Theoretical Foundations, Diagnostic Tools, Practical Examples, and Numerical Recipes in Python*. Springer-Nature, Heidelberg, Germany, 2018.
7. D. J. Bolder and S. Gusba. Exponentials, Polynomials, and Fourier Series: More Yield Curve Modelling at the Bank of Canada. Bank of Canada: Working Paper 2002-29, October 2002.
8. D. J. Bolder and S. Liu. Examining Simple Joint Macroeconomic and Term-Structure Models: A Practitioner's Perspective. Bank of Canada: Working Paper 2007-49, October 2007.
9. D. J. Bolder and D. Stréliski. *Yield Curve Modelling at the Bank of Canada*. Technical Report No. 84. Ottawa: Bank of Canada, 1999.
10. P. Brémaud. *Markov Chains: Gibbs Fields, Monte Carlo Simulation and Queues*. Springer Verlag, 175 Fifth Avenue, New York, NY, 1999. Texts in Applied Mathematics.
11. A. J. G. Cairns and D. J. Pritchard. Stability of descriptive model for the term structure of interest rates with application to german market data. Department of Actuarial Mathematics and Statistics, Heriot-Watt University, 2000.
12. L. Carroll. *Alice's Adventures in Wonderland*. Wisehouse Classics, Sweden, 1865.
13. P. de Boor. *A Practical Guide to Splines*. Springer Verlag, Berlin, Germany, 1978.
14. J. de Leeuw. Computing and fitting monotone splines. University of California, Los Angeles, 2017.
15. F. X. Diebold and C. Li. Forecasting the term structure of government bond yields. University of Pennsylvania Working Paper, 2003.
16. F. X. Diebold and G. D. Rudebusch. *Yield Curve Modeling and Forecasting: The Dynamic Nelson-Siegel Approach*. Princeton University Press, Princeton, New Jersey, 2013.
17. P. Dierckx. *Curve and Surface Fitting with Splines*. Clarendon Press, Walton Street, Oxford, 1993.
18. D. Duffie and K. Singleton. *Credit Risk*. Princeton University Press, Princeton, first edition, 2003.
19. ECB. The Use of Credit Risk Models in Central Banks. Occasional Paper Series, No, 64, July 2007.
20. G. H. Golub and C. F. V. Loan. *Matrix Computations*. The John Hopkins University Press, Baltimore, Maryland, 2012.
21. G. M. Gupton, G. Coughlan, and M. Wilson. *CreditMetrics — Technical Document*. Morgan Guaranty Trust Company, New York, 1997.
22. A. S. Hurn, K. A. Lindsay, and V. Pavlov. Smooth estimation of yield curves by laguerre functions. Queensland University of Technology Working Paper, 2005.

23. Y. Jafry and T. Schuermann. Measurement, estimation, and comparison of credit migration matrices. *Journal of Banking & Finance*, 28(11):2603–2639, 2004.
24. R. A. Jarrow, D. Lando, and S. M. Turnbull. A markov model for the term structure of credit risk spreads. *Review of Financial Studies*, 10(2):481–523, Summer 1997.
25. M. Jeanblanc. Credit risk. Université d'Evry, April 2002.
26. M. Jeanblanc and M. Rutkowski. Modelling of default risk: An overview. Université d'Evry and Warsaw University of Technology, September 1999.
27. N. L. Johnson, S. Kotz, and N. Balakrishnan. *Continuous Univariate Distributions: Volume I*. John Wiley & Sons, New York, NY, second edition, 1994.
28. J. Kingman. The imbedding problem for finite Markov chains. *Zeitschrift für Wahrscheinlichkeitstheorie und verwandte Gebiete*, 1(1):14–24, 1962.
29. D. G. Kleinbaum and M. Klein. *Survival Analysis: A Self-Learning Text*. Springer, Heidelberg, Germany, 2012.
30. A. Kreinin and M. Sidelnikova. Regularization algorithms for transition matrices. *Algo Research Quarterly*, 4(1/2):23–40, 2001.
31. P. Lancaster and K. Salkauskas. *Curve Fitting and Surface Fitting: An Introduction*. Academic Press, Orlando, Florida, 1986.
32. D. Lando and T. M. Skødeberg. Analyzing rating transitions and rating drift with continuous observations. *Journal of Banking & Finance*, 26(2-3):423–444, 2002.
33. J. H. McCulloch. Measuring the term structure of interest rates. *Journal of Business*, 44:19–31, 1971.
34. Merriam-Webster. *Webster's Ninth New Collegiate Dictionary*. Merriam-Webster, 9th edition, 1991.
35. S. P. Meyn and R. L. Tweedie. *Markov Chains and Stochastic Stability*. Springer-Verlag, 175 Fifth Avenue, New York, NY, 1993.
36. C. Moler and C. V. Loan. Nineteen dubious ways to compute the exponential of a matrix. *SIAM Review*, 20(4):801–836, 1978.
37. C. R. Nelson and A. F. Siegel. Parsimonious modeling of yield curves. *Journal of Business*, 60:473–489, 1987.
38. G. Nürnberger. *Approximation by Spline Functions*. Springer Verlag, Berlin, Germany, 1980.
39. J. Ramsay. Monotone regression splines in action. *Statistical Science*, 3(4):425–441, 1988.
40. J. Ramsay. Estimating smooth monotone functions. *Journal of the Royal Statistical Society*, 60(2):365–375, 1998.
41. C. M. Reinhart and K. S. Rogoff. The forgotten history of domestic debt. Working Paper 13946, National Bureau of Economic Research, April 2008.
42. C. M. Reinhart and K. S. Rogoff. *This Time Is Different: Eight Centuries of Financial Folly*. Princeton University Press, Princeton, New Jersey, 2009.
43. T. Schuermann. Credit migration matrices. In E. Melnick and B. Everitt, editors, *Encyclopedia of Quantitative Risk Assessment*. John Wiley & Sons, 2008.
44. L. L. Schumaker. *Spline Functions: Basic Theory*. John Wiley and Sons, West Sussex, England, 1978.
45. S&P. 2019 Annual Global Corporate Default And RatingTransition Study. Technical report, S&P Global Ratings, April 2020.
46. S. M. Stigler. Who Discovered Bayes's Theorem? *The American Statistician*, 37(4a):290–296, 1983.
47. L. E. O. Svensson. Estimating and interpreting forward interest rates: Sweden 1992-1993. Institute for International Economic Studies, Stockholm University, January 1994.
48. H. M. Taylor and S. Karlin. *An Introduction to Stochastic Modeling*. Academic Press, San Diego, California, 1994.
49. G. Torrent-Gironella. Quantifying Portfolio Credit Risk. CCruncher Technical Document, Version 2.5.1 2018.
50. G. Tutz and F. Leitenstorfer. Smooth monotonic regression in additive modelling. *Journal of Computational and Graphical Statistics*, 16(1):165–188, 2007.

51. E. J. Wegman and I. W. Wright. Splines in statistics. *Journal of American Statistical Association*, 78:351–365, 1983.
52. L. J. White. Markets: The Credit Rating Agencies. *The Journal of Economic Perspectives*, 24 (2):211–226, Spring 2010.
53. I. W. Wright and E. J. Wegman. Isotonic, convex and related splines. *The Anals of Statistics*, 8 (5):1023–1035, 1980.

# Chapter 8
# Building Stress Scenarios

*Probable impossibilities are to be preferred to improbable possibilities.*

*(Aristotle)*

A symbiotic relationship refers—according to Merriam-Webster [32]—to an intimate, long-term, mutually beneficial interaction between two distinct organisms. A classic example is the association between the shark and the remora. A remora is a small fish typically living on the back of a shark and feeding opportunistically off surplus food from a shark's prey and, more usefully, parasites on its skin. Both organisms benefit from this interaction. It is perhaps not a common analogy, but the relationship between financial markets and the real economy can also be viewed as symbiotic.[1] The real economy depends importantly upon financial markets to provide funding sources for ongoing business and projects. Financial markets, conversely, rely upon real businesses to generate activity and profitability. Unlike the shark and the remora, however, their relationship is somewhat more complicated. It is, at times, difficult to determine where one entity ends and the other begins.

Understanding this complex interaction between financial markets and the real economy is, believe it or not, a critical element in the construction of stress scenarios. Lending institutions, such as the NIB, are in the business of providing loans and credit to firms (and other entities) operating in the real economy. The success of this venture depends importantly on these firms' ability to service and repay their debt commitments. This is hardly breaking news. Indeed, we have already invested significant time and effort—within our economic-capital framework—in the computation of the expected and unexpected losses that might occur in the event of firm credit deterioration or default. This task, however, has been performed using long-term, unconditional estimates of general credit conditions and firm creditworthiness; this latter aspect can, in fact, be viewed as a dimension of the real economy. Our risk computations have thus, to this point, been performed using

[1] The reader will be left to decide which party, in this example, is most closely aligned with the shark.



D. Bolder, *Modelling Economic Capital*, Contributions to Finance and Accounting,
https://doi.org/10.1007/978-3-030-95096-5_8

the previously defined *through-the-cycle* perspective. There is nothing wrong with this approach. Regulators actually prefer, and suggest, the use of a through-the-cycle approach for the computation of economic capital.[2] The problem arises when we wish to consider stress scenarios. A long-term, unconditional viewpoint—by its very construction—averages across the ups and downs associated with business-cycle movements, financial-market turmoil, and full-blown economic crises. Our heretofore employed through-the-cycle approach is actually antithetical to stress-testing analysis.

This leads us to a simple conclusion. If we wish to construct and employ stress scenarios, then we need to understand and investigate the so-called *point-in-time* perspective. Point-in-time is, as defined in previous chapters, a short-term, current, conditional estimate. No long-term averaging is going on. It incorporates the most recent information about financial-market, general-credit, and macroeconomic conditions. Point-in-time analysis is thus, from an informational point of view, the polar opposite of the through-the-cycle approach. The current level of economic output, inflation, and interest rates will matter. Contemporaneous financial-market volatility, monetary policy, and employment levels are important. Recent default rates, for firms across the entire credit spectrum, also play a central role. There are, in fact, myriad financial-market and real-economy variables that contribute to the fabric of a point-in-time description.

The objective of this chapter is thus to construct a workable, empirically consistent description of point-in-time credit conditions. As has become our habit, drawn from our initial axioms, we will actually consider a few alternative approaches to this task. Each characterization must be built upon information from the real economy and financial markets. Only this way can we understand how a shock, or stress, arising from these variables would impact credit conditions and, ultimately, the risk of our lending portfolio.[3] Stress-related analysis thus follows a clear chain of logic: a scenario (often negative, but not always) outcome for one, or more, important financial-economic variables triggers a change in credit conditions leading to a commensurate change in one's risk estimates. One predicts an economic stress, infers credit conditions via a mapping model, and computes the implied risk. A visualization of this idea is found in Fig. 8.1.

Stress-testing is thus a concrete manifestation of so-called *what-if* questions. What if, for example, financial-market volatility increases dramatically? What if interest rates double or global output falls by half? What if the consensus forecast is realized? What would happen to our portfolio? Answering these valid, and important, questions is the core of stress testing. It requires a solid understanding of the relationships between these variables. In other words, it requires a model. This brings us back to the shark and the remora: the relationship between financial mar-

[2] While this appears to be the general consensus, the actual picture is admittedly a bit muddled. See Aguais et al. [1] for a useful discussion of the point-in-time and through-the-cycle debate.

[3] Stress, in this context, tends to refer to a generic deterioration or worsening of macro-financial conditions. It can, of course, move in the opposite direction.

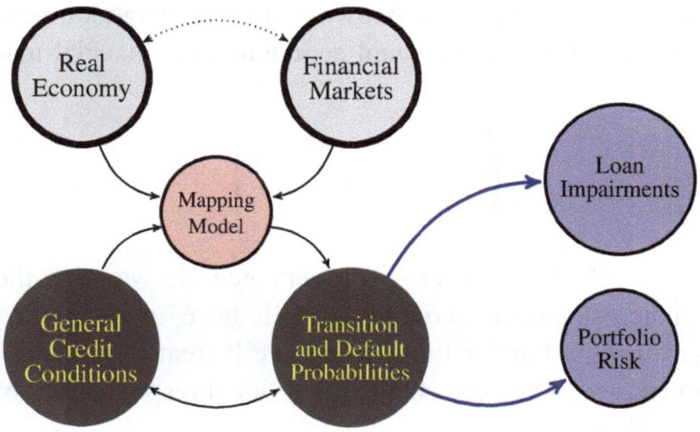


**Fig. 8.1** *A stress-scenario schematic*: This schematic provides a visualization of the logical interactions between the key elements in stress-testing analysis. It begins with an economic stress from the real economy or financial markets, infers (via a model) general credit conditions, and computes the implied portfolio risk. The glue holding it all together is the mapping (or linking) model.

kets and the real economy. There is invaluable point-in-time information regarding general credit conditions embedded in both entities. Successfully modelling these point-in-time dynamics—to support stress-testing analysis—requires capturing this information in a statistically and economically convincing manner. This assignment is the central focus of this chapter.

## 8.1 Our Response Variables

The first order of business in the development of any empirical model generally relates to identification of what we wish to describe. In most problems, this is sufficiently obvious that little, or no, time is allocated to it. This case, however, is less evident. We know that we seek to describe general credit conditions, but this is vaguely defined. It could refer to the general willingness of credit institutions to lend or the ability of firms to meet their lending obligations. Our focus is on the later, but, of course, these aspects are two sides of the same coin.

The ability of firms to meet and service their debt is clearly tied up with the probability of default. The central object in this area, discussed in detail in preceding chapters, is the transition matrix. It collects, in one single convenient location, not only the default probabilities for each credit class, but also all of the relevant probabilities associated with a firm's credit categorization being upgraded, downgraded, and staying put. These are referred to as transition probabilities. We can thus probably agree that, for our purposes, general credit conditions would be well described by a time-varying transition matrix. That is, the individual entries of this dynamic transition matrix would depend on the state of the real economy and financial markets.

Let us introduce a bit of notation that we will use throughout the entire chapter. We will write the set of informative real-economic and financial market variables as,

$$\left\{X_t \ : \ t = 1, \ldots, T\right\}, \tag{8.1}$$

where each $X_t \in \mathbb{R}^{\kappa \times 1}$. We refer—in a very generic way—to these $\kappa$ entities as the set of macro-financial variables.[4] We'll have much more to say about these characters shortly, but for the moment we'll treat them as given. For risk-management purposes, to be very concrete, our ideal response variable would be a sequence of transition matrices,

$$\left\{P_t(X_t) \ : \ t = 1, \ldots, T\right\}, \tag{8.2}$$

where each $P_t(X_t) \in \mathbb{R}^{(\mathcal{R}+1)\times(\mathcal{R}+1)}$ and $\mathcal{R}$, as before, represents the number of distinct (non-default) credit states. We can see, from Eq. 8.2, that each transition matrix is a function of our macro-financial variable vector, $X_t$. This is practically very useful. If we shock our macro-financial variables, say as $\hat{X}_{t+1}$, we could immediately compute the associated predicted transition matrix, $\hat{P}_{t+1}(\hat{X}_{t+1})$. This latter quantity could flow directly into our stress-testing and loan-impairment analysis.

Equation 8.2 is the end game; this is what we seek to construct. It is, in fact, the foundation of our stress-testing framework. It is not, sadly, particularly workable in this form. A transition matrix is a complicated object. NIB's internal scale has 20 non-default categories, while we use 17 from S&P and Moody's.[5] Including default probabilities, this leads to 420 and 306 meaningful NIB and agency transition matrix entries, respectively, for each point in time. This daunting amount of complexity makes direct use of Eq. 8.2 virtually impossible.[6] There are few, if any, sensible statistical techniques that one can use to describe an $(\mathcal{R}+1) \times (\mathcal{R}+1)$ matrix as a function of a $\kappa$-dimensional vector when $\mathcal{R}$ and $\kappa$ have a reasonable size. Even given such a technique, the amount of data required to inform the associated parameters would dramatically surpass what is currently available.

A simplified version of this problem involves consideration of a sub-component of our transition matrix: the default probabilities. Some applications, most particularly loan-impairment computations, only require this dimension. This definitely

[4] This construction joins the real-economic and financial-market variables together, but we need to keep in mind that they are quite different, albeit interrelated, animals.

[5] S&P and Moody's have, in fact, rather more rating categories. As introduced in Chap. 7, we collect the lower credit ratings into a single catch-all category to better describe NIB's lending universe.

[6] This is a practical example of Bellman [2]'s curse of dimensionality.

simplifies the problem somewhat: as the final column of $P_t(X_t)$, we have only to manage $\mathcal{R}$ elements.[7] Much of the following discussion, in fact, will focus on this important sub-problem. This is not only due to its importance for our applications, but also because it helps us better understand and grapple with the base concepts. Jumping straight into the transition matrix description is probably, in any event, a bad idea.

**Colour and Commentary 89** (A DYNAMIC MACRO-FINANCIAL TRANSITION MATRIX)*: To permit sensible stress-testing analysis, from a credit-risk perspective, our objective is to construct a dynamic corporate transition matrix conditional on the state of the real economy and financial markets (i.e., a point-in-time quantity). This would allow us to consider—for various constellations of the driving macro-financial variables—the impact on firm default and credit-migration. These values, in turn, could be transferred to our economic-capital and loan-impairment calculation engines. If we could reasonably characterize such dynamic, conditional transition matrices, stress analysis would hold no secrets for us. After such a statement, there is naturally a catch. The transition matrix is simply too complex an object—as a consequence of its literally hundreds of entries—to be directly modelled as a function of macro-financial outcomes. This does not mean that we need to change our objective, but it does suggest that we need to be rather more clever in our approach to it. Certain applications—such as loan-impairments—depend, in fact, only on a subset of the transition matrix: the default probabilities. This tends to be the typical (and perhaps somewhat more gentle) entry point into the general problem.*

### 8.1.1 Simplifying Matters

Only one alternative offers a reasonable possibility of preserving our desired relationship in Eq. 8.2: dimension reduction. We need to simplify the problem into fewer, and more manageable, moving parts. In other words, this approach essentially requires breaking down a transition matrix into its minimally useful representation. One might argue that this is the quintessential aspect of model construction.

A simple starting point begins with the reflection that a generic firm's credit quality—as summarized by its current categorization—can only do one of *four* things: it can improve, deteriorate (but not default), stay the same, or move into default. Since the probability of all four of these (disjoint) actions must sum to unity, it is sufficient to know three out of four. The fourth can be inferred by subtracting

[7] The probability of default in the absorbing state can be ignored, since it is always unity.

the sum of the other three from one. We can profitably exploit this basic idea. Instead of considering a single firm, however, we might examine the aggregate set of all firms over a given time interval. We can count, for example, the total number of firms that are upgraded, downgraded, and defaulted in a given quarter or year. Dividing this by the number of firms—and simultaneously inferring the number of unchanged credit classifications—yields an interesting low-dimensional description of our transition matrix. We will use the symbols $u_t$, $d_t$, and $c_t$ to denote the time $t$ aggregate upgrade, downgrade, and default rates, respectively. The unchanged, or stay-put, rate is corresponding defined as

$$s_t = 1 - u_t - d_t - c_t. \tag{8.3}$$

Repeating this for many time intervals should thus provide a degree of insight into transition-matrix dynamics.

Huge amounts of data are nonetheless necessary to perform this computation. Fortunately, the regular heavy lifting, necessary to derive these statistics, is already periodically performed by the major rating agencies. We use quarterly data sourced via Moody's for the aggregate upgrade, downgrade, and default percentages from 1992 to present.[8] The right-hand graphic in Fig. 8.2 displays the quarterly evolution of these four aggregate transition metrics over the last 30 years. The period-to-period changes are not enormous, but changes are certainly evident. There is a particular spike in downgrades—and, to a lesser extent, default—over 2008 to 2010 during the great financial crisis. Defaults and downgrades also appear to increase during the aftermath of the Asian crisis and the most recent COVID pandemic. While very preliminary, this simple graphic appears to suggest an empirical relationship between general credit conditions and the business cycle.[9]

The left-hand-graphic of Fig. 8.2 takes an alternative perspective. It displays the Moody's quarterly, through-the-cycle transition matrix and computes the average (annualized) upgrade, downgrade, and default probability; the average staying-put, or diagonal, element is computed using the logic from Eq. 8.3.[10] These are the unconditional, or averaged, values for these quantities over the almost 30-year period; this is the reason that they are constant over time. The left- and right-hand graphics of Fig. 8.2, therefore, provide a stark visualization of the differences between the through-the-cycle and point-in-time perspectives. The through-the-cycle viewpoint is the focus of Chap. 7.

[8] It also includes unchanged and withdrawn ratings. As in the construction of the through-the-cycle transition matrix, the probability mass associated with withdrawn ratings is (following general convention) proportionally allocated to the four main transition categories.

[9] Although this question does not appear to have been answered definitively in the literature, there is certainly a relationship between these quantities. See Koopman and Lucas [28] for a useful analysis.

[10] The displayed values can also be approximated by averaging over the 30 years of quarterly transition quantities in the right-hand of Fig. 8.2.

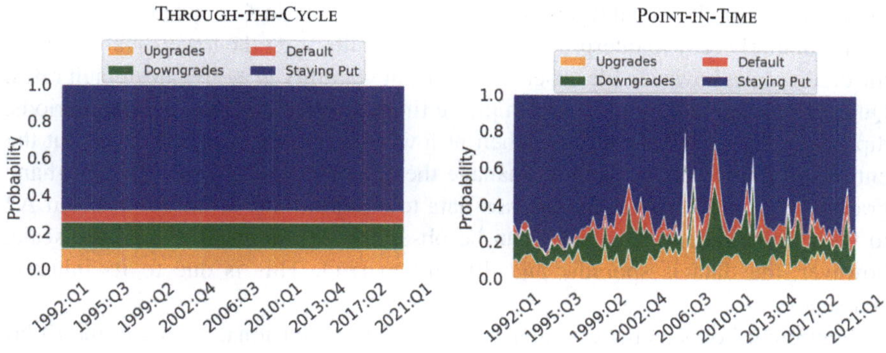


**Fig. 8.2** *A low-dimensional picture*: The preceding graphics illustrate a low-dimensional (quarterly, but annualized) time-varying view—under the through-the-cycle and point-in-time perspectives—of a global, aggregate, corporate transition matrix. Only four dimensions are included: upgrades, downgrades, default, and staying put.

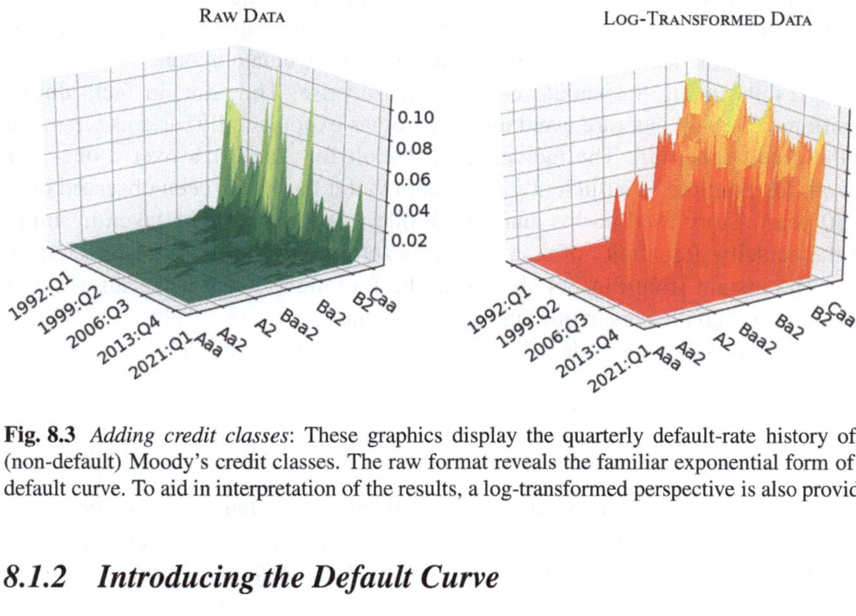


**Fig. 8.3** *Adding credit classes*: These graphics display the quarterly default-rate history of 17 (non-default) Moody's credit classes. The raw format reveals the familiar exponential form of the default curve. To aid in interpretation of the results, a log-transformed perspective is also provided.

### 8.1.2 Introducing the Default Curve

Figure 8.2, while a useful start, is probably too minimalistic. It provides a useful time-varying view into aggregate credit conditions, but it tells us very little about the individual credit classes. We simply do not have sufficient information to determine—without making heroic assumptions—how changing credit conditions impact various elements across the full credit spectrum. Let's, therefore, specialize to default probabilities. Again, our credit-rating agency colleagues have done the hard work by publishing quarterly, global corporate default rates for each of Moody's 17 distinct (non-default) credit classes.

Historical rating-level default results, again from 1992, are summarized in Fig. 8.3. The left-hand graphic displays the raw results. Given the exponential increase in default probabilities as we move from Aaa to Caa-rated entities, it is not particularly easy to interpret the individual results.[11] At the lower-quality end of the credit scale, however, we observe significant volatility in aggregate default rates. Quarterly Caa default rates, for example, at times approach $\frac{1}{10}$ and, in other periods, dip below 2%. Similar patterns, albeit at lower levels, are evident throughout the entire speculative grade. To help manage the exponential structure, the right-hand graphic of Fig. 8.3 transforms the raw data to a logarithmic scale. From about A2 to Caa, a familiar linear pattern can be observed. At the upper end of the scale, however, the data is sporadic and difficult to read. This is due to its inherent sparseness.

Figure 8.4 helps us better understand the high-dimensional results in the right-hand graphic of Fig. 8.3. It chronicles the individual non-zero, default rates from our Moody's dataset since 1992. What is striking is the sheer number of zero entries in this dataset; of almost 2000 possible observations, slightly less than one in five takes a non-zero value.[12] The entire Aaa, Aa1, and Aa2 categories are identically zero. Up until about Baa2, a zero value is vastly more likely than an observed default outcome. Beyond about Baa3, moving into the speculative grade, the incidence of default rises dramatically along with the richness of the data outcomes.

The results in Fig. 8.4 should come as no surprise. They are, in fact, almost definitional. Default is a rare event and it becomes exponentially rarer as we move out the credit spectrum. The incidence of default for Aaa firms over a one-year horizon, for example, is sufficiently infrequent that it has *never* been observed over the 30-year history used in this analysis. While this should not be taken to imply that the actually probability of Aaa default is zero, it does strongly underscore its rarity. The insight from Fig. 8.4 should not be forgotten, however, because it will pose numerous challenges in our later development.

Let us refer to the time-indexed collection of rating-level default rates as

$$\left\{c_{r,t} \,:\, t = 1, \ldots, T\right\}, \tag{8.4}$$

$r = 1, \ldots, \mathcal{R}$. Let us refer to each time $t$ collection of default rates as the point-in-time *default curve*. They are logically linked to the aggregate default rates, $c_t$, introduced in the previous section.[13] In statistical settings, $c_t$ is termed a simple

---

[11] Caa is not a real Moody's rating grade; it is NIB's amalgamation of the Caa1, Caa2, Caa3, Ca, and C classes. We used the same trick in Chap. 7 with the S&P scale to reflect the needs of our internal risk profile.

[12] The poor behaviour of the log transformation at zero explains the choppy behaviour in Fig. 8.3.

[13] While not precise, we can think the aggregate default rate as being a kind of average across the individual rating-level values. That is,

$$c_t \approx \sum_{r=1}^{\mathcal{R}} \omega_r \frac{c_{r,t}}{\mathcal{R}}, \tag{8.5}$$

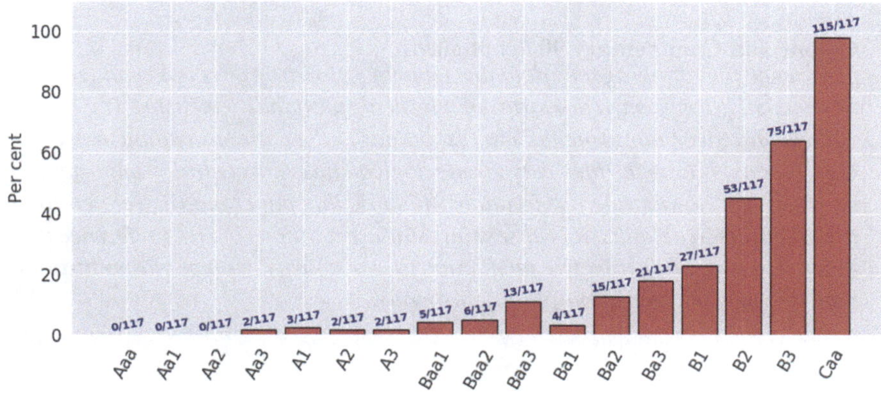


**Fig. 8.4** *Sparse rating-level data*: This graphic provides a visualization of the non-zero, quarterly, Moody's credit-rating level default rates displayed in Fig. 8.3. The point of this display is to help the reader under the sheer number of zero observations.

time series, whereas the full dataset—described in Eq. 8.4—is referred to as panel data. For each point in time, $t$, we have a cross section of default rates across the credit spectrum.

The cross-sectional, or panel, data in Figs. 8.3 and 8.4 provide a critical step towards establishing a time-varying transition matrix. In its raw form, this data is rather difficult to work with and interpret. The reasons are, at least, twofold. First, as highlighted in Fig. 8.4, there are many zero values. Second, we return to our common theme of dimensionality. There is simply too much data—17 credit ratings over 30 years—to easily manage. The raw data can, and will, be used. There are, however, some analytical techniques that might be profitably employed to improve this situation and simultaneously manage our dimensionality problem.

**Colour and Commentary 90** (RATING-LEVEL DEFAULT RATES): *Our Moody's dataset provides, quarterly over a 30-year period, a cross-sectional view of rating-level default rates. We will refer to the slice of default rates, for a given point in time, as a* default curve. *These values represent our principal source of data for inference of time-varying (i.e., point-in-time) default probabilities (and ultimately transition probabilities) across the credit spectrum. There are alternatives. Using corporate-bond or credit-default-swap spreads, it is also possible to gain insight—albeit under the pricing measure, $\mathbb{Q}$—into default-probability dynamics. We have, however, a strong*

(continued)

for some set of weights, $\{\omega_r : r = 1, \ldots, \mathcal{R}\}$, which might not be immediately obviously determined.

**Colour and Commentary 90** (continued)
*preference for rating-agency data for a number of reasons. As risk managers, our focus is firmly on real-world, or physical, probability measure (i.e., $\mathbb{P}$) values. Moreover, our principal interest relates to the entire transition matrix. Our Moody's data set also has strong logical links to centrally important upgrade and downgrade observations. Finally, this panel data is related to actual observed defaults. It is absent investor expectations or risk preferences; as such, it is a solid, objective foundation for the construction of our point-in-time default- and transition-probability model.*

### *8.1.3 Fitting Default Curves*

The interest-rate literature, as already seen in Chap. 7, offers numerous analogues to the analysis of default rates. Conditional forward-default and survival rates are closely linked to forward-interest rates and pure-discount bonds prices, respectively. Cross-sectional default rates appear to offer another point of agreement. The term structure of interest rates is, in fact, a cross section; it is often described as the credit curve.[14] When we index these cross sections to time, it becomes panel data. The key difference is that the cross-sectional variable for interest rates is the term to maturity, while it is credit quality in the default setting.

Why does this matter? It is often the case, with dynamic systems, that there are cross-sectional relationships that can be captured. In the yield-curve setting, this relates to the interaction between short-term and long-term interest rates. With default rates, this is likely to manifest itself in terms of monotonicity constraints.[15] The Aa1 default rate, for example, should be less than the Aaa value, which in turn should be inferior to the Ba1 observation and so on. The existence of such relationships implies that neither interest nor default rates may—from an economic perspective—jump around independently from adjacent values within the cross section. In short, such restricted interaction creates order from a potential chaos. Understanding this order, and describing it mathematically, is typically very helpful in the reduction of dimensionality.

In the early 1990s, Litterman and Scheinkman [31] published an influential analysis of the American sovereign yield curve. Using a (then rather obscure) statistical technique—termed principal components analysis—they demonstrated

[14] This should be a hint that our recently introduced nomenclature, default curve, was not selected at random.

[15] Jollliffe [25, Section 4.1] provides, moving away from finance and economics, an interesting example of cross-sectional patterns in human anatomical measurements (i.e., hand, wrist, forearm, head sizes, and so on).

**Table 8.1** *Explained default-curve variance*: This table illustrates the percentage of overall system variance that is explained by the first four orthogonal factors in a principal-components analysis of the default-curve data. This analysis was performed using the raw (although demeaned) Moody's default-curve data.

| Quantity | Eigenvalue | var($C$) explained | Cumulative var($C$) explained |
|---|---|---|---|
| Factor 1 | 0.000695 | 76% | 76% |
| Factor 2 | 0.000169 | 18% | 95% |
| Factor 3 | 0.000028 | 3% | 98% |
| Factor 4 | 0.000010 | 1% | 99% |
| Total | 0.000913 | 100% | 100% |

that the majority of variance in observed yield-curve movements could be described by three linear latent factors.[16] The consequences of this study were significant. The high-dimensional yield-curve object could be summarily reduced to a linear combination of three variables with little reduction in overall accuracy. Although these are purely statistical factors, they came to be referred to as level, slope, and curvature for the manner in which they influenced the shape of the yield curve.

An interesting question thus arises: can something similar be performed with the observed Moody's default-curve data? Table 8.1 provides a quick answer. Most of the overall default-curve variance can be explained by the first *four* orthogonal factors drawn from principal components analysis.[17] This is, on the surface, as convincing as the results from Litterman and Scheinkman [31]—where the first *three* factors typically explain in excess of 95% of total variance—suggesting the potential for dimension reduction.

Almost as important as the amount of variance explained is the nature of the loading vectors associated with each principal component. To understand this requires quickly delving into the algorithm. We define, from Eq. 8.4, the default-curve vector at time $t$ as,

$$\vec{c}_t = \begin{bmatrix} c_{1,t} \\ c_{2,t} \\ \vdots \\ c_{\mathcal{R},t} \end{bmatrix}, \tag{8.6}$$

[16] The idea behind principal components analysis is to find a subset of orthogonal factors that explain the maximum amount of variance in a system. See Jollliffe [25] for an excellent introduction and many practical examples.

[17] The analysis was performed on the demeaned default-curve data. We can, if we wish, set the zero-valued entries to a small positive number or attempt to work in logarithmic space; these slightly change the results, but get us to a similar terminal point.

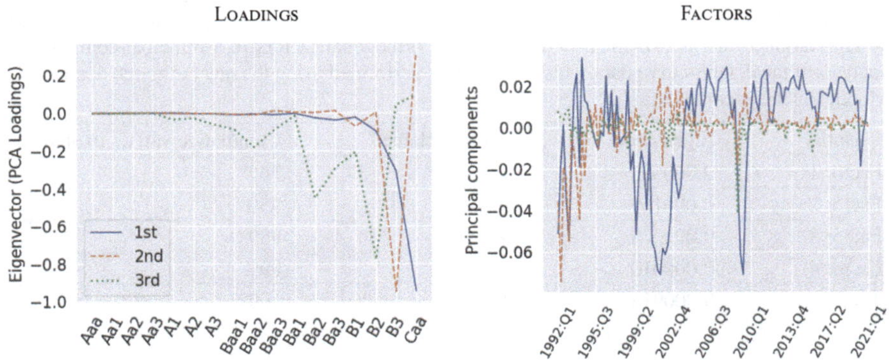


**Fig. 8.5** *Default-curve principal components*: This figure illustrates the values and loadings associated with the three most important orthogonal factors extracted from an application of principal-components analysis to our default-curve data set.

for $t = 1, \ldots, T$. In simple English, $\vec{c}_t$, is the cross section as at time $t$. Collecting the cross sections, we have

$$C = \begin{bmatrix} \vec{c}_1 \ \vec{c}_2 \cdots \vec{c}_T \end{bmatrix}. \tag{8.7}$$

The matrix, $C \in \mathbb{R}^{\mathcal{R}\times T}$, is thus our panel data. Principal components analysis seeks to find a projection vector, call it $a \in \mathbb{R}^{\mathbb{R}\times 1}$, that maximizes

$$\text{var}(a^T C) = a^T \text{var}(C) a, \tag{8.8}$$

subject to $a^T a = 1$ to normalize the projection vector to unit length. The first-order conditions of this problem are,

$$(C - \lambda I)a = 0, \tag{8.9}$$

which turns out to be the eigenvalue problem.[18] The factor loadings of the $n$ most important orthogonal factors, in the principal components analysis, are merely the $n$ eigenvectors associated with the $n$ largest eigenvalues of var$(C)$.

Figure 8.5 displays the loadings associated with the three most important orthogonal factors extracted from our application of principal-components analysis. The results are rather different from those presented in Litterman and Scheinkman [31]. The narrative, however, is rather similar. The first factor—representing about 75% of total variance—only affects all credit categories south of about B2. This looks to be a kind of high-risk credit effect. Incidentally, this factor correlates about 0.7 with the aggregate default rate (i.e., $c_t$), which is also dominated by the lower

[18] $\lambda$ is the constant in the method of Lagrange multipliers. See Golub and Loan [15] for more on the eigenvalue problem.

end of the credit spectrum. The second factor has an odd $V$-shaped impact over the B2 to Caa categories. Finally, the third factor impacts the speculative-grade credit—from about Baa2. None of these elements bear any resemblance to the level, slope, and curvature factors seen in interest-rate settings. Importantly, the factor loadings are essentially silent on the higher quality end of the credit curve; this is certainly an artifact of extremely sparse default observations in this sector.

The right-hand graphic in Fig. 8.5 illustrates the evolution, over our 30-year horizon, of the first three principal components. On their own, these are difficult to interpret. The first factor, at least, tends to dip down sharply during periods of economic distress and high levels of aggregate default.[19]

We should be cautious not to push this analogy too far nor to celebrate too soon. There are also important differences between yield and default curves that impact this analysis. Yield-curve values are based on bond prices; if fundamental relationships get too far out of line, they tend to be rectified by market participants buying and selling these securities. In other words, key yield-curve relationships are shaped by market actors. Default curves are based on observed default outcomes across the credit curve. The rarity of default makes these observations lumpy and noisy. From this perspective, default and interest rate curves are apples and pears. Interactions between points along the yield curve should thus, from a first-principles perspective, be significantly stronger than in the default-curve setting.

A second issue stems from the sparseness of our credit-curve data. Equation 8.8 demonstrates that principal components analysis seeks to find projection vectors that maximize the amount of variance explained. Many of our default curves, due to the lack of data, exhibit very little or no variance. This means that the natural dimensionality of our system is already quite low. We cannot really raise our glasses to toast our ability to explain the majority of the variance in a system with three factors, when in actuality, there are only six or seven elements exhibiting any meaningful dispersion. This is a very real consequence of data sparseness and a challenge that will need to be managed in constructing default-related stress scenarios.

**Colour and Commentary 91** (DEFAULT-CURVE DIMENSIONALITY)*: A default curve is defined as the observed incidence of default—for each credit category across the credit spectrum—over a specific period of time. Economic logic strongly suggests that default outcomes should be monotonically increasing as credit quality deteriorates. Inspired by the interest-rate literature—most particularly, Litterman and Scheinkman [31]—we use the principal-components technique to investigate how much structure*

(continued)

[19] This is supported by its, previously mentioned, strong positive correlation with $c_t$ as introduced in Eq. 8.3.

**Colour and Commentary 91** (continued)
*these logical restrictions impose on the observed data. With 17 possible credit states, the four largest principal components explain almost all of the total system variance. Moreover, the factor loadings of the three largest components appear to operate almost solely in the realm of speculative-grade credits. The results, while promising, are not as compelling as those found in Litterman and Scheinkman [31]'s yield-curve setting. The reason is evident: the empirical data does not always play along with economic logic. Sparseness, lumpiness and noisiness in real-world default-curve implies that, while monotonicity generally holds, it is occasionally violated. Moreover, it is difficult to construct a signal for a given credit category absent any meaningful default observations. This is a fundamental feature of default data that cannot be avoided. The results are sufficiently interesting, however, to cautiously move forward to consider functional forms for fitting individual default curves.*

Extending the analogy to the interest-rate environment, it is common to fit the cross-section of the spot yield curve with easier-to-manage mathematical forms. Examples include the previously discussed Nelson and Siegel [35], the exponential-spline, and smoothing-spline models.[20] Such fitting techniques serve a variety of purposes. They provide a simplified view of the term structure, they assist in interpolating (and, at times, extrapolating) interest-rate levels, they permit ready computation of associated interest-rate quantities (such as discount factors for forward rates), and they provide useful inputs into dynamic term-structure models. All of these advantages would be equally welcome within the default-curve setting.

A spot yield curve may take a variety of shapes: upward or downward sloping, steep or flat, normal or inverted, $U$-shaped, and may even exhibit humps. Interest rates, however, are typically fairly strictly bounded. Outside economies with rampant inflation, observed spot rates rarely exceed 20%. Furthermore, while nominal interest rates can take negative values, there also appear to be limits to the magnitude of their negativity. Finally, and rather importantly, the difference between short- and long-term spot interest rates rarely exceed more than a few hundred basis points. Extant yield-curve fitting models—and there are many of them—are specialized to these characteristics.[21]

Default curves, despite their conceptual similarities, have a rather different form. The most striking feature is the exponential growth in default incidence as one moves down the credit scale. As discussed, quarterly and annual Aaa to Aa2

[20] See Li et al. [30] and Shea [39] for more on exponential splines. Fisher et al. [14] is a helpful source on smoothing splines. See also Bolder and Gusba [7] and Bolder [5, Chapter 5] for many practical details on these approaches.

[21] A useful compendium of a wide range of models is found in Hagan and West [16].

default rates have been uniformly zero over the past 40 years. Theoretically they are not zero, but practically should not exceed a handful of basis points. Quarterly Caa default outcomes, by contrast, range from as low as about $\frac{1}{50}$ to almost $\frac{1}{10}$. The deviation between the two ends of the credit scale, therefore, is measured in orders of magnitude. The credit scale—like seismological scales used to measure earthquakes—is exponentially constructed. It is correspondingly unlikely that direct application of yield-curve fitting models will prove effective with default curves.

Some practical efforts confirm this suspicion. The Nelson and Siegel [35] and Li et al. [30] approaches are simply incapable of capturing the exponential form without generating negative default-rate estimates. Slightly more success can be achieved with smoothing-spline techniques, but the missing data points create problems and the overall number of parameters is simply too large. Fitting default curves will thus require a slightly different approach.

The basic fitting structure proposed in this chapter—which, with additional reflection and experience, can presumably be improved upon—is based on the idea of what is sometimes referred to as an exponential regression. More specifically, we might approximate each time $t$ default curve in Eq. 8.4 as

$$c_{r,t} = e^{\zeta_{t,0}+\zeta_{t,1}r}, \tag{8.10}$$

for $r = 1, \ldots, \mathcal{R}$. The associated parameter vector,

$$\zeta_t = \begin{bmatrix} \zeta_{t,0} \\ \zeta_{t,1} \end{bmatrix}, \tag{8.11}$$

needs to be estimated by fitting our data set for each $t = 1, \ldots, T$. If we apply natural logarithms to both sides, we can write this as the following generalized linear model,

$$\begin{aligned} \ln\left(\begin{bmatrix} c_{1,t} \\ c_{2,t} \\ \vdots \\ c_{\mathcal{R},t} \end{bmatrix}\right) &= \begin{bmatrix} 1 & 1 \\ 1 & 2 \\ \vdots & \\ 1 & \mathcal{R} \end{bmatrix} \begin{bmatrix} \zeta_{t,0} \\ \zeta_{t,1} \end{bmatrix} + \begin{bmatrix} \epsilon_{1,t} \\ \epsilon_{2,t} \\ \vdots \\ \epsilon_{\mathcal{R},t} \end{bmatrix}, \\ \ln(\vec{c}_t) &= X_{\mathcal{R}}\zeta_t + \epsilon_t, \end{aligned} \tag{8.12}$$

where $\epsilon_t \in \mathbb{R}^{\mathcal{R}\times 1}$ is our quantity to minimize through the selection of $\zeta_t$. The classic estimator for Eq. 8.10 is thus,

$$\hat{\zeta}_t = \left(X_{\mathcal{R}}^T X_{\mathcal{R}}\right)^{-1} X_{\mathcal{R}}^T \ln(\vec{c}_t), \tag{8.13}$$

where $\hat{\vec{c}}_t = e^{X_{\mathcal{R}}\hat{\zeta}_t}$.

This seems rather straightforward, but there are a few practical issues. While Eq. 8.13 illustrates the log-linearity of our model, the multiple zero values render its direct usage impossible. This can be solved by setting the zero values to a sufficiently small positive value.[22] A more important issue is that, without some sort of constraints, the least-squares approach has difficulty with lumpy or noisy data. Squaring errors places large portions of weight, in the selection process, on outliers. Some sort of anchoring is thus required. As a final issue, the log-linear format summarized in Eq. 8.12 lacks somewhat in flexibility. It is a completely linear form. Some limited amount of curvature, as suggested by our principal-component factor loadings in Fig. 8.5, would be helpful.

Taking these elements into account, the formal proposed default-curve fitting model is extended to include an additional curvature term,

$$c_{r,t} = e^{\zeta_{t,0}+\zeta_{t,1}r+\zeta_{t,2}\sin\left(\frac{r}{\omega}\right)}, \tag{8.14}$$

where $\omega$ is a wave-length parameter.[23] The term $\sin\left(\frac{r}{\omega}\right)$ is admittedly somewhat *ad hoc* in nature, but it is motivated by the idea of a Fourier-series expansion.[24] Other choices are certainly possible, but this selection appears to be fairly successful in inducing additional flexibility into our estimates.

Practically, Eq. 8.14 implies the following matrix structure,

$$\ln\left(\begin{bmatrix} c_{1,t} \\ c_{2,t} \\ \vdots \\ c_{\mathcal{R},t} \end{bmatrix}\right) = \begin{bmatrix} 1 & 1 & \sin\left(\frac{1}{\omega}\right) \\ 1 & 2 & \sin\left(\frac{2}{\omega}\right) \\ \vdots & & \\ 1 & \mathcal{R} & \sin\left(\frac{\mathcal{R}}{\omega}\right) \end{bmatrix} \begin{bmatrix} \zeta_{t,0} \\ \zeta_{t,1} \\ \zeta_{t,2} \end{bmatrix} + \begin{bmatrix} \epsilon_{1,t} \\ \epsilon_{2,t} \\ \vdots \\ \epsilon_{\mathcal{R},t} \end{bmatrix}, \tag{8.15}$$

for $t = 1, .., T$. The log-transformed default curve can accordingly be considered as a linear combination of the three pseudo-basis functions summarized in $X_{\mathcal{R}}$.

[22] We use one half of a basis point or 0.00005. This seems, for practical purposes, to be close enough to zero but also economically plausible.

[23] With $\mathcal{R} = 17$, a choice of $\omega \approx 12$ or 13 appears to be sensible given the form of the first factor loadings in Fig. 8.5. This corresponds to a curvature point centred around Ba2 or Ba3.

[24] See, for example, Davis [10] for more background on Fourier series.

Selection of our three-dimensional parameter vector arises, at time $t$, from the solution to the following minimization problem:

$$\min_{\zeta_t} \underbrace{\left(\ln(\vec{c}_t) - e^{X_{\mathcal{R}}\zeta_t}\right)^T \left(\ln(\vec{c}_t) - e^{X_{\mathcal{R}}\zeta_t}\right)}_{\epsilon_t^T \epsilon_t}, \tag{8.16}$$

subject to:

$$\underbrace{\exp\left(\zeta_{0,t} + \zeta_{1,t} + \zeta_{2,t}\sin\left(\frac{1}{\omega}\right)\right)}_{\hat{c}_{1,t}} \in \left[\frac{1}{10}, 2\right] \text{ basis points,}$$

$$\underbrace{\exp\left(\zeta_{0,t} + \zeta_{1,t}\mathcal{R} + \zeta_{2,t}\sin\left(\frac{\mathcal{R}}{\omega}\right)\right)}_{\hat{c}_{\mathcal{R},t}} \geq c_{\mathcal{R},t},$$

$$\zeta_{1,t} + \zeta_{2,t}\left(\sin\left(\frac{r+1}{\omega}\right) - \sin\left(\frac{r}{\omega}\right)\right) \geq 0 \text{ for } r = 1, \ldots, \mathcal{R}.$$

The first two constraints act as anchors. The highest-rated (i.e., AAA) default rate must fall in the interval of 0.1 to 2 basis points. The lowest-rate (i.e., Caa) default value, by contrast, needs to be at least as large as the observed default incidence during that period. The final set of constraints ensure monotonicity.[25]

Figure 8.6 illustrates—for a selected number of years over the almost 30-year time span—the visual fit of the solution to Eq. 8.16. The bottom, right-hand graphic provides the average fit across all time periods; this can be roughly considered as the through-the-cycle default curve. A few observations can be made. First of all, despite the lumpiness of the underlying data, the overall fit seems quite reasonable; to be fair, however, no monotonic form can provide a perfect fit to the data. The second observation—also evident in Fig. 8.3—is the significant variation in observed default curves. Empirically, therefore, deviations between the through-the-cycle default curve and periodically observed point-in-time equivalents are significant.

Figure 8.6 is rather difficult to read as the credit category falls below about Ba2 or so. To provide a bit more insight into the entire range of the default curve, Fig. 8.7 also displays the results in logarithmic space. Actual observed zero-valued

[25] To see where these inequalities come from, we begin with the idea that

$$\hat{c}_{r+1,t} \geq \hat{c}_{r,t}, \tag{8.17}$$

for each $r = 1, \ldots, \mathcal{R}$. One then replaces the estimated values in Eq. 8.17 with our functional form from Eq. 8.14 and simplifies.

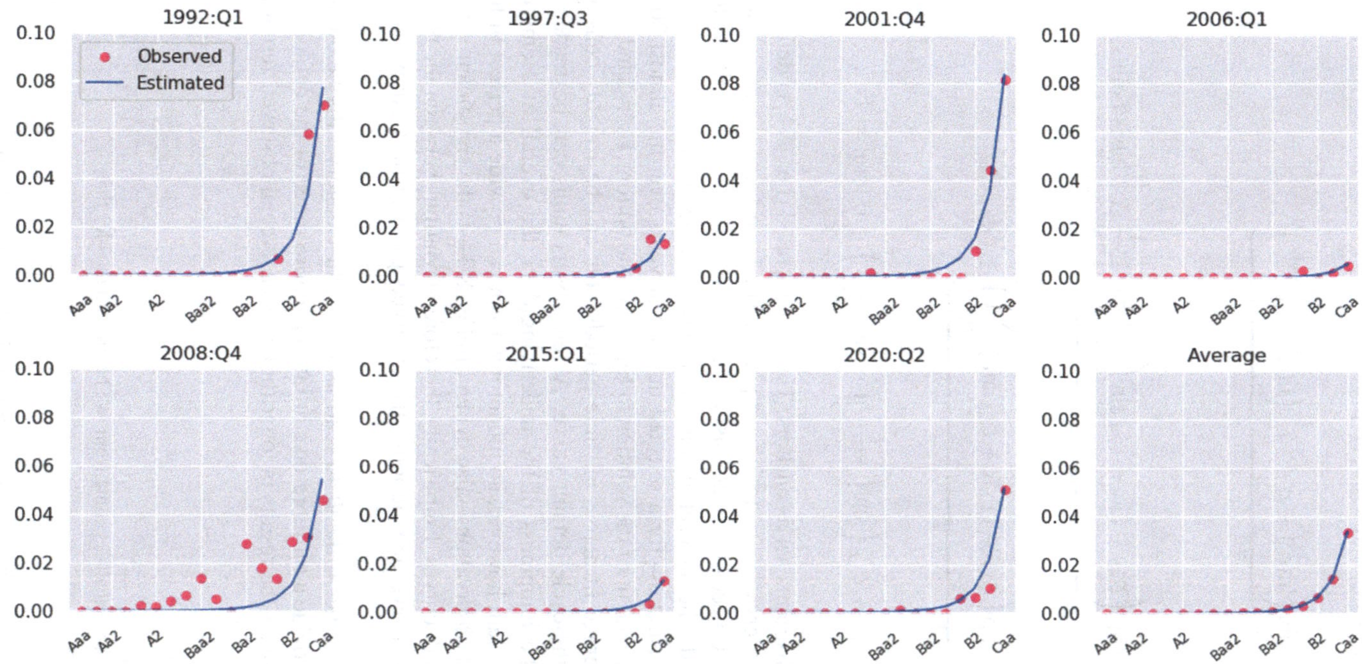


**Fig. 8.6** *Selected default-curve fits*: The collection of graphics above displays the observed and fitted default-curve values—for a selection of interesting periods—using our simple constrained exponential regression model. Although the fitting approach has difficulty capturing the lumpiness of observed default incidence, it does appear to describe the general trend.

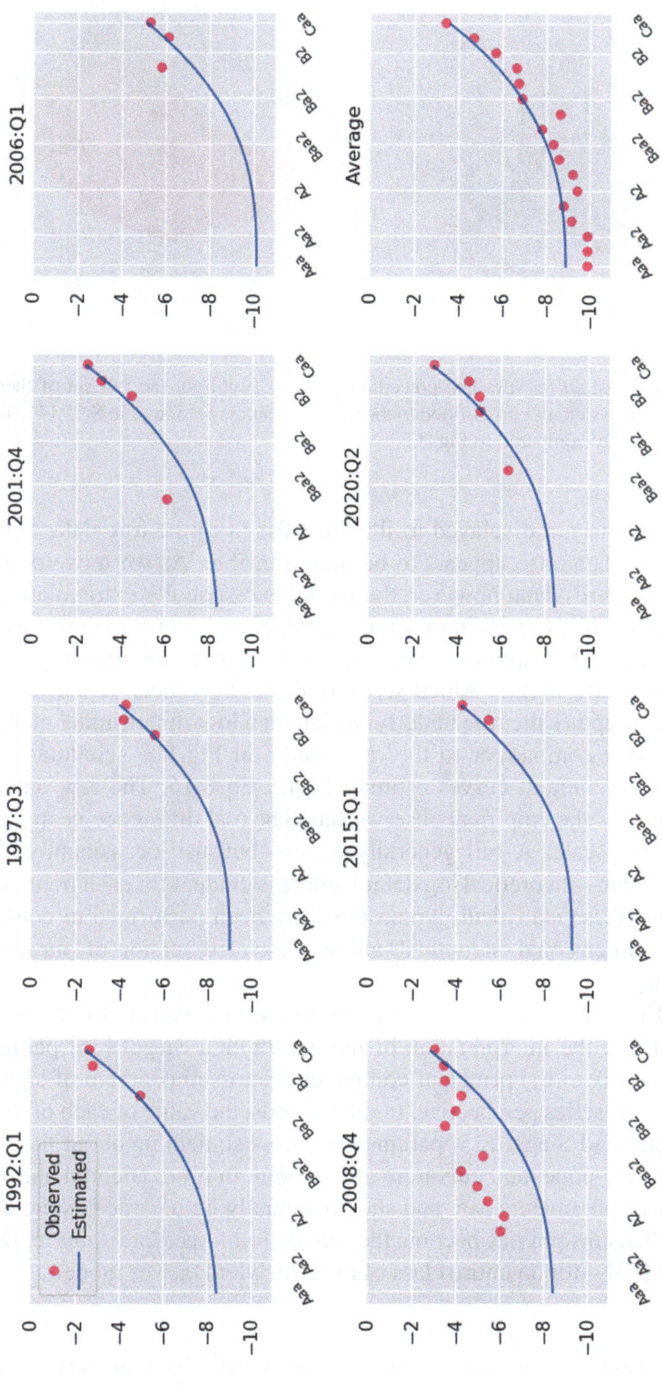


**Fig. 8.7** *Selected log default-curve fits*: The collection of graphics above replicates the results from Fig. 8.6 in logarithmic space. Zero-valued default incidences are not displayed to illustrate the fit to the true data.

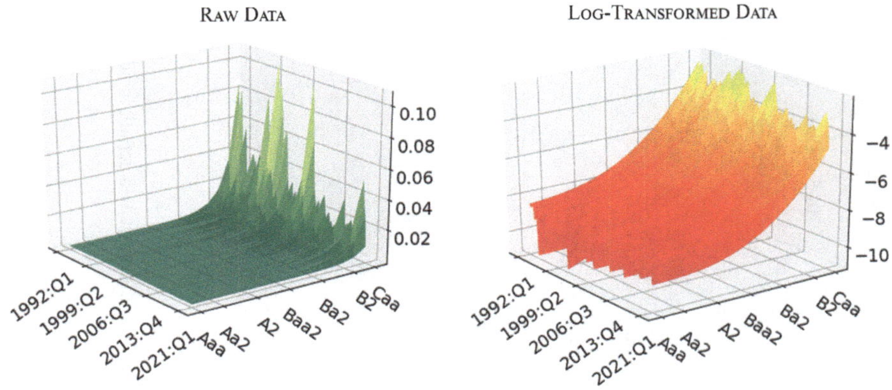


**Fig. 8.8** *Theoretical default curves*: The preceding graphics highlight the full set of theoretical raw and log-transformed default curves fitted to the observed outcomes found in S&P [41, Table 9]. These results are usefully compared to Fig. 8.3.

default incidences are not displayed to illustrate the fit to the true data.[26] The fit, in the presence of data, also appears to be quite sensible. As we move outside of the available (non-zero) data, however, the model is essentially extrapolating from the observed data. This, depending on one's perspective, can be viewed as either a feature or a bug of the estimation approach. On balance, the advantages appear to outweigh the disadvantages. Albeit stylized, these theoretical default curves do appear to broadly capture the true underlying data in a low-dimensional manner.

Figure 8.8—as a comparator to the raw results in Fig. 8.3—contains the full fitted time series of default curves estimated with Eq. 8.16. The raw data looks basically the same as the empirical observations. The real difference is only visible on the logarithmic scale. A full generally linear—but also occasionally slightly (concave) non-linear—theoretical log default curve is evident for each point in time. In essence, all of these statistical gymnastics have been performed to construct a reasonably low-dimensional, smoothed, and extrapolated version of our quarterly credit-curve data.

Diebold and Li [12]—to return once again to the interest-rate literature—offer a clever insight into the interpretation of the Nelson and Siegel [35] parameters. Their conceptual link to the principal-component factors make them of significant interest from a time-series perspective. In other words, the value of each of the three non-linear Nelson and Siegel [35] parameters tell us something about the relative importance of level, slope, and curvature at that point in time. Diebold and Li [12] show us that these parameters can, and should, actually be regarded as yield-curve state variables. This insight has become the foundation—see, for example, Diebold and Rudebusch [13]—for an entire class of dynamic yield curves models.

---

[26] Recall that, to aid estimation and avoid numerical problems, these zero values were (arbitrarily) set to 0.00005.

We might, pushing the default- and interest-curve analogy to its very limit, attempt to consider our $\zeta_t$ parameters in a similar manner. Our rather limited success with principal-components analysis should nonetheless temper our expectations; that said, it is worth a try. Each element of $\zeta_t$ tells us something via Eq. 8.14 about the relative form—in log terms, at least—of the default curve at that point in time. As a consequence, they do have the potential to act as state variables for the default-curve system.

Figure 8.9 plots, over our roughly 30-year history, the individual fitting parameter (i.e, $\zeta_t$) values. The results are quite interesting. The $\zeta_{0,t}$ parameter, a constant, appears to provide some insight the level of the highest quality default outcomes.[27] Its general stability is punctuated by occasional sharp increases for single quarter or two. The $\zeta_{1,t}$ coefficients, conversely, appear to be more strongly correlated with the lower end of the credit spectrum.[28] $\zeta_{0,t}$ and $\zeta_{1,t}$, interestingly, exhibit virtually no correlation over time. The final parameter, $\zeta_{2,t}$, describes the impact of the curvature function. Although this factor is rather strongly negatively correlated with the first and second factors, it does not vary importantly over time. Its role essentially relates to imposing some curvature (i.e., concavity) in the log-linear credit curves. Most of the work appears to be performed by $\zeta_{1,t}$, which is also strongly related to the first principal component from Fig. 8.5.

The main objective in fitting stylized credit curves, which seems to have been attained with a moderate degree of success, has been to build a low-dimensional and manageable response, or independent variable, for the construction of a point-in-time default and transition probabilities. These default-curve outcomes—both in their raw and theoretical form—will, along with observed upgrades and downgrades, form the foundation of our point-in-time model. These fitted values will also help us propose an alternative mapping, if only as a sanity check, between general (point-in-time) credit conditions and our description of the macro-financial situation.

**Colour and Commentary 92** (THEORETICAL DEFAULT CURVES)*: Inspired by the interest-rate literature—and with an eye towards increasing manageability and reducing dimensionality—a functional form was constructed and fit to our empirical default-curve data. A three-parameter model, in particular, was expressly designed to describe the exponential form of default-curve values over the credit scale. The overall fit of this approach appears to be fairly reasonable. Most importantly, it addresses a number of key shortcomings with the raw data. It provides—by moving from 17 credit categories to three model coefficients—a parsimonious description of our*

(continued)

[27] There is a very high positive correlation between the fitted Aaa rate and the $\zeta_{0,t}$ parameter.

[28] The $\zeta_{1,t}$ state variable correlates strongly and positively with the fitted Caa values.

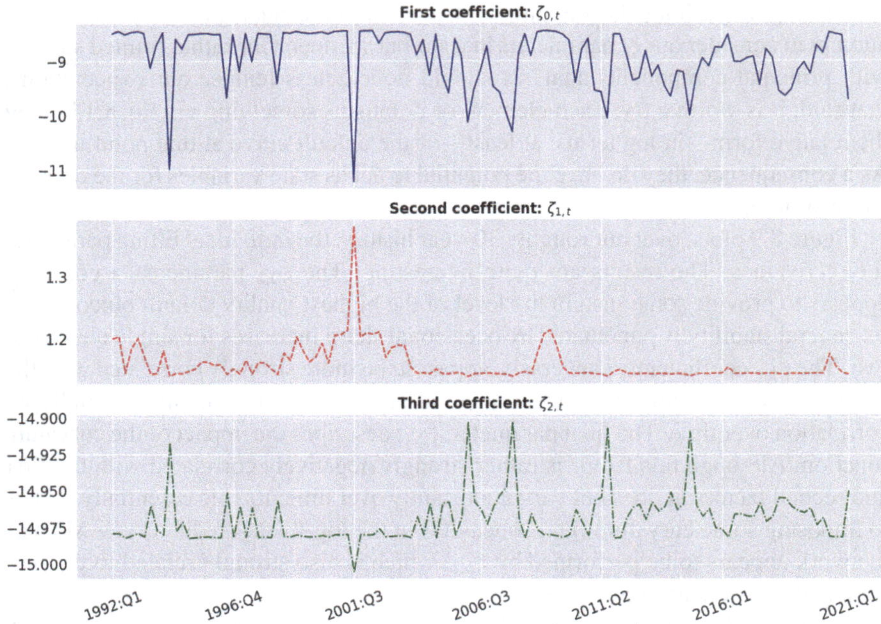


**Fig. 8.9** *Examining* $\zeta_t$: These plots describe the time evolution of our three $\zeta_t$ parameters—introduced in Eq. 8.14—used to fit observed default curve data. In principle, these parameter values could be used as state variables for the default-curve system.

**Colour and Commentary 92** (continued)
*data. Through imposition of constraints, it further allows us to anchor the overall default curve and eliminate observed incidences of zero default. This helps to attenuate the natural lumpiness or noisiness of the data in a manner that is (broadly) consistent with the empirical data. In other words, it acts as a consistent extrapolation method for missing data. Finally, the time-series evolution of these parameters has the potential to—reminiscent of Diebold and Li [12]—play the role of state variable in our point-in-time transition matrix model. The sparsity of our credit-curve data nonetheless makes this exercise somewhat difficult. It is, at this point, unclear if raw or theoretical default curves are preferable for our final application. Having the luxury of choice, however, is rather useful.*

## 8.2 Our Explanatory Variables

Having established that we will employ (either raw or theoretical) default curves as well as observed upgrades and downgrades to describe our point-in-time transition matrices, we now need to determine the underlying driving macro-financial variables. Choosing these variables is nonetheless *not* immediately straightforward. There is an enormous range of possible real-economic and financial-market data that might prove helpful for describing general credit conditions. There are also various approaches that one might follow. One could, as has become fairly commonplace in macroeconomic analysis, extract common factors from literally hundreds of economic indicators.[29] Alternatively, one might simply select (and, of course, test) a subset of potential meaningful explanatory variables.

The big-data, common-factor approach, while quite powerful, is unlikely to be particularly useful for this application. Ultimately, we wish to characterize key state variables—across various potential future states of the world—and examine the impact on our point-in-time estimates and portfolio risk. Common factors—generally built using principal-components analysis—are complex combinations of many other variables. As such, they are not readily predicted. This sadly precludes the use of this technique. As a consequence, we will find ourselves in the position of hand-selecting individual macro-financial variables for this analysis.

Let's begin with the real economy. A minimal small macroeconomic model typically includes, at least, three main variables: output, inflation, and monetary policy. Monetary policy, in turn, is generally well captured by the level of short- and long-term interest rates. Some measure of gross-domestic product is helpful for describing output, while base or core consumer-price indices do a sensible job for inflation. Productivity growth and employment figures are also useful additions to a general description of economic conditions.

On the financial side, there is literally a ridiculous amount of choice. A useful way to proceed is to think about the main sub-markets: fixed-income, equity, commodity, and foreign exchange. Interest rates and credit spreads, index levels, key commodities prices, and composite exchange rates, respectively, are sensible candidates to describe the state of each sub-market.

Table 8.2 provides an illustrative summary of ten key macro-financial variables used, broadly consistent with those used in the current NIB methodology, to describe general credit conditions. It also includes the necessary adjustments, if any, required to ensure their stationarity.[30] These choices are admittedly rather America-centric and might not include the reader's favourite element. The list does, however, a reasonable job of including those variables one would expect to make an appearance; it captures overall economic growth, inflation, financial-market

[29] These are referred to as dynamic factor models. See Stock and Watson [42] for a gentle introduction by the researchers who have played such a central role in this literature.

[30] We used the so-called augmented Dickey-Fuller (ADF) test—see, for example, Dickey and Fuller [11]—to test for a unit root in each of these macro-financial time series.

**Table 8.2** *Explanatory variable notation*: This table provides a description—and the notation employed—for the main macro-financial explanatory variables used in this analysis. The data is admittedly rather America-centric, but it is expected to be a reasonable global proxy.

| Description | Symbol | Stationarity adjustment |
|---|---|---|
| 10-year industrial BBB bond spread over US treasuries | $\varphi_t$ | None |
| US gross domestic product (GDP) implicit price deflator | $\pi_t$ | $\pi_t - \pi_{t-1}$ |
| Effective federal funds rate | $r_t$ | $r_t - r_{t-1}$ |
| US real gross domestic product (GDP) | $\theta_t$ | None |
| US civilian unemployment rate | $k_t$ | $\ln\left(\frac{k_t}{k_{t-1}}\right)$ |
| Global (non-fuel) commodities price index | $w_t$ | None |
| S&P 500 composite | $m_t$ | $\ln\left(\frac{m_t}{m_{t-1}}\right)$ |
| World oil-price index | $h_t$ | $h_t - h_{t-1}$ |
| US 10-year constant maturity, three-month LIBOR yield curve slope | $s_t$ | $s_t - s_{t-1}$ |
| VIX index | $\sigma_t$ | $\sigma_t - \sigma_{t-1}$ |

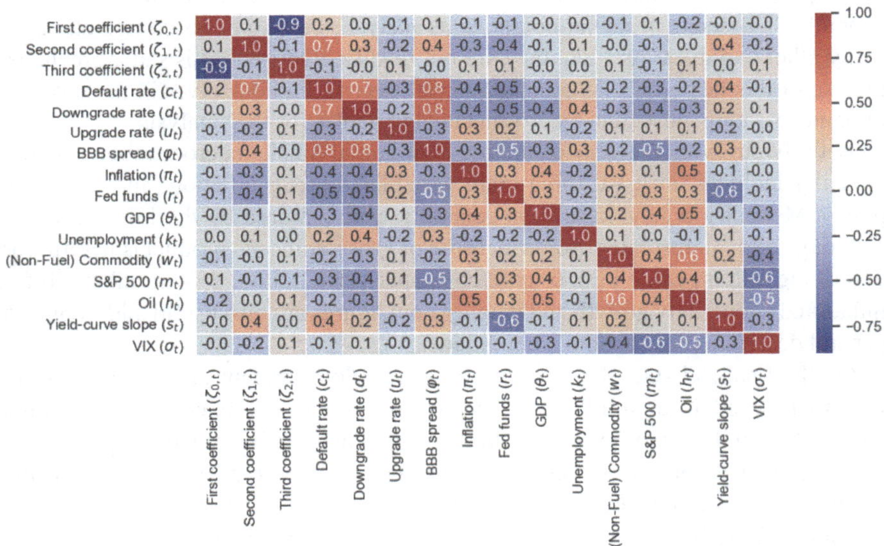


**Fig. 8.10** *Level cross correlation*: This figure provides—in a haze of numbers and colours—the (level) cross correlation between our key response and explanatory variables. The warmer the colour, the higher the positive correlation.

volatility, commodity prices, equity valuations, interest-rate levels, monetary policy, and credit spreads. The critical element is the existence of some concrete statistical relationship between these potential explanatory quantities and our previously discussed general-credit response variables.

Figure 8.10 attempts to address this question by highlighting the level-based cross correlation between our key response and explanatory variables. The default-curve model parameters, the observed aggregate default rate, and actual upgrade and downgrade percentages form our set of response variables. The ten variables in Table 8.2 represent our explanatory factors. The density of numbers makes Fig. 8.10 non-trivial to interpret. A few interesting conclusions can nonetheless, with a bit of patience, be drawn. In particular,

- no dramatic collinearity appears to be present in this collection of variables;
- the second $\zeta_t$ parameter appears to correlate quite highly (positively and negatively) with a number of macro-financial variables as well as the aggregate default rate;
- the aggregate default and downgrade rates—and to a lesser extent upgrades—appear to depend upon most of our macro-financial variables;
- commodity and equity prices are positively correlated, but both correlate negatively with market volatility; and
- credit spreads, inflation, and the Fed funds rates are related—with a few modest exceptions—to virtually all response and explanatory variables.

There are certainly more insights in Fig. 8.12, but this should provide a reasonable overview. One could also perform an identical correlation analysis with the first-differences of these variables. The story does not change dramatically.

**Colour and Commentary 93** (CREDIT-CONDITION EXPLANATORY VARIABLES): *Our principal task involves building a model of point-time credit conditions. Practically, this amounts to the construction of a time-varying transition matrix, $P(X_t)$, or the simpler problem of time-varying default probabilities, $c_t(r, X_t)$, for $r = 1, \ldots, \mathcal{R}$. In both cases, however, the vector $X_t$ denotes a set of explanatory macro-financial variables. What makes a sensible collection of explanatory variables? The most obvious criterion is a statistical relationship—and perceived economic causality—with our credit-condition response variables.*[a] *In addition to a statistical link, we also seek high-profile variables that can inform* what-if *stress-testing analysis. Finally, and not completely unrelated to the previous point, we are hunting for a relatively small system of explanatory variables. Too many individual drivers will not only complicate the analysis, it will confuse the stress-scenario process. We have, using basic economic logic, constructed a set of 10 macro-financial variables covering various elements of the real economy and financial markets. Admittedly America-centric, these quantities should nonetheless offer a reasonable global proxy. Moreover, no important collinearities appear to be present in the proposed system of explanatory variables.*[b]

[a] While causality would be fantastic, it is almost impossible to demonstrate. We will thus be satisfied with statistical dependence.

[b] Neither entirely exhaustive nor yet subjected to a proper selection process, this list of macro-financial variables will nonetheless perform admirably in our illustration of the key concepts.

### 8.2.1 Data Issues

Working with real-world data always presents challenges. Financial-market data is available at high frequency; it is up to the minute and noisy. Real economic data comes out, at best, on a monthly basis, but is typically only available on a quarterly frequency. It is also often subject to revision, making it somewhat less reliable. There is, therefore, a fundamental data-frequency mismatch between these two worlds. Working with macro-financial models invariably leads to compromises in both directions.

Causality is a second difficult area. Do financial markets drive the real economy or vice versa? This may feel like an unanswerable academic question, but it has practical implications for modelling stress scenarios. Good arguments can be made in either direction, but the reality is that it likely goes both ways and varies over time. Ultimately, uncertainty with regard to this question argues for the use of informative variables along both dimensions in our analysis. As a general principle, therefore, it is a bad idea—in the selection of our final set of explanatory variables—to specialize entirely to either real-economic or financial-market variables. The previously mentioned differences in the nature of underlying data sources for financial markets and the real economy nevertheless complicate this task.

Representativeness and stability are two final key challenges facing any empirical analysis. Quantitative analysts should always be worried about how well their selected data describes, or represents, the phenomena they are trying to model. This problem is no exception. We are trying to construct a meaningful bridge (or map) between general credit conditions on the one hand and financial and real-economy variables on the other. Our response variables reach back to the early 1990s. One could easily argue that key macro-financial relationships differ in important ways for portions of this 30-year time interval. The post-crisis period from 2010—to be a bit more precise—looks to be different than in preceding times. There is, therefore, always the danger of structural breaks in our underlying data. These potential pitfalls cannot be entirely avoided, but they can be managed. Cautious examination of our data and construction of relatively simple, and robust, statistical models can help.

## 8.3 An Empirically Motivated Approach

Our task is to describe and predict our variables of interest with another set of instruments or explanatory variables.[31] We've already engaged in a similar process within Chap. 5. Denote $y_t$ as what we're trying to explain, understand, or predict and

[31] See Breiman [8] for a powerful abstract description of this process in the context of statistical models and machine-learning algorithms.

$X_t$ as the explanatory variables, or simply things that could potentially influence the $y$'s. The (unknown) real-world time-series data-generating process looks something like this:

$$y_t \leftarrow \boxed{\text{The Real World}} \leftarrow X_t \tag{8.18}$$

for all choices of $t$. We can make educated guesses about Eq. 8.18, but we truly don't really know what is going on. Rewriting Eq. 8.18, we may schematically describe the statistician's approach to this problem as

$$y_t \leftarrow \boxed{\text{Data assumptions and a model}} \leftarrow X_t \tag{8.19}$$

Faced with uncertainty about our black box, we replace it with a useful approximation of a complex reality (i.e., a model). This is essentially our mapping model. Not a bad strategy, actually.[32]

There are, of course, different possible sets of data assumptions and models that one might select to fill the box in Eq. 8.19. As this is a difficult question with not terribly cooperative data, it is a good idea to somewhat hedge our bets. For this reason—and also naturally to be consistent with the axioms introduced in the preface—we will examine two broad modelling strategies for the construction of time-varying (i.e., point-in-time) transition and default probabilities. The first, considered in this section, is rather heuristic in nature and proceeds essentially via dimension reduction and empirical methods. While there are numerous possible variations, this first heuristic and empirically driven approach has traditionally been the model of choice at NIB. The second modelling strategy, addressed in the subsequent section, makes clever use of some theoretical ideas to build a link (or map) between our response and explanatory variables. Given a range of advantages, that will become evident in the following discussion, a version of this approach has become our production model. It is nonetheless rather useful, and informative, to understand and appreciate both modelling strategies.

[32] Machine-learning algorithms, incidentally, use a different strategy. They circumvent the black box with an algorithm and tune it (in a loose sense) through prediction accuracy. For more on these ideas, see Bolder [6].

### 8.3.1 A Linear Model

Within the context of the empirically motivated approach to building point-in-time transition and default probabilities, our specific choice of $y_t$ is,

$$y_t = \begin{bmatrix} c_{1,t} \\ \vdots \\ c_{\mathcal{R},t} \\ u_t \\ d_t \end{bmatrix} \equiv \begin{bmatrix} y_{1,t} \\ \vdots \\ y_{\mathcal{R},t} \\ y_{\mathcal{R}+1,t} \\ y_{\mathcal{R}+2,t} \end{bmatrix}, \tag{8.20}$$

for $t = 1, \ldots, T$. $y_t$ includes all of the default-curve values along with the upgrade and downgrade percentages for a particular point in time. Here we have written the raw default curve values, but we could also replace each $c_{r,t}$ with our fitted $\hat{c}_{r,t}$ values. Either way, these are the fundamental components of our time-varying transition matrix.[33] Importantly, to ensure that our dimensions are consistent in subsequent calculations, we note that $y_t \in \mathbb{R}^{(\mathcal{R}+2)\times 1}$.

Our specific choice of $X_t$, in its maximal sense, is written as,

$$X_t = \begin{bmatrix} 1 \\ x_{1,t} \\ \vdots \\ x_{\kappa,t} \end{bmatrix}. \tag{8.21}$$

This indicates that $X_t \in \mathbb{R}^{(\kappa+1)\times 1}$ where $X_t$ has been augmented to include a constant term. In full generality, the set of explanatory variables could be expanded or reduced to include a larger or smaller number of choices. For this reason, we denote the number of actual employed explanatory variables as $\kappa$. In practice, the actual elements of Eq. 8.21 will be populated by some constellation—or function—of the variables found in Table 8.2. Depending on one's variable-selection process, one might even opt to include a new explanatory variable or two.

[33] We will explore in a later section precisely how the transition matrix is approximated from these quantities.

The most obvious possible model between $y_t$ and $X_t$ would probably look something like

$$\underbrace{\begin{bmatrix} c_{1,t} \\ \vdots \\ c_{\mathcal{R},t} \\ u_t \\ d_t \end{bmatrix} \equiv \begin{bmatrix} y_{1,t} \\ \vdots \\ y_{\mathcal{R},t} \\ y_{\mathcal{R}+1,t} \\ y_{\mathcal{R}+2,t} \end{bmatrix}}_{y_t} = \begin{bmatrix} \gamma_{0,1} & \gamma_{1,1} & \cdots & \gamma_{\kappa,1} \\ \gamma_{0,2} & \gamma_{1,2} & \cdots & \gamma_{\kappa,2} \\ \vdots & \vdots & \ddots & \vdots \\ \gamma_{0,\mathcal{R}} & \gamma_{1,\mathcal{R}} & \cdots & \gamma_{\kappa,\mathcal{R}} \\ \gamma_{0,\mathcal{R}+1} & \gamma_{1,\mathcal{R}+1} & \cdots & \gamma_{\kappa,\mathcal{R}+1} \\ \gamma_{0,\mathcal{R}+2} & \gamma_{1,\mathcal{R}+2} & \cdots & \gamma_{\kappa,\mathcal{R}+2} \end{bmatrix} \begin{bmatrix} 1 \\ x_{1,t} \\ \vdots \\ x_{\kappa,t} \end{bmatrix} + \begin{bmatrix} \nu_{1,t} \\ \vdots \\ \nu_{\mathcal{R}+2,t} \end{bmatrix}, \tag{8.22}$$

$$y_t = \Gamma X_t + \nu_t,$$

for $t = 1, \ldots, T$, where $\Gamma \in \mathbb{R}^{(\mathcal{R}+2)\times(\kappa+1)}$ is a matrix of model parameters linking general credit conditions with our explanatory variables, and $\nu_t \in \mathbb{R}^{(\mathcal{R}+2)\times 1}$ is an error vector. Equation 8.22 basically postulates a linear relationship; it is a multivariate linear regression model.[34] Moreover, Eq. 8.22 is also simply a convenient way of writing $\mathcal{R} + 2$ separate regressions in a single format. Beyond simple convenience, this structure also permits imposition of constraints on parameters to ensure monotonicity between our default-curve entries. To make this very clear, Eq. 8.22 is also legitimately written as,

$$\begin{aligned} y_{k,t} &= \gamma_{0,k} + \gamma_{1,k}x_{1,t} + \cdots + \gamma_{\kappa,k}x_{\kappa,t} + \nu_{k,t}, \\ &= \gamma_k X_t + \nu_{k,t}, \end{aligned} \tag{8.23}$$

for $t = 1, \ldots, T$, $k = 1, \ldots, \mathcal{R} + 2$, and where $\gamma_k \in \mathbb{R}^{1\times(\kappa+1)}$ is a vector representation of the $k$th row of $\Gamma$.

Before we proceed to the estimation of the individual entries in $\Gamma$, there is an annoying problem with the specification of Eq. 8.22. It has nothing to do with the mathematics, but rather stems from the properties of our response variables. Each default-curve observation as well as the upgrade and downgrade rates must take values between zero and one. It is, of course, possible to impose additional parameter constraints to preserve this property. When combined with our monotonicity constraints, however, determining the parameters can subsequently become quite difficult.

It turns out to be significantly more effective to embed these (0, 1) constraints into the model, in an indirect fashion, through a transformation of the explanatory variables. Any mapping of $\gamma_k X_t$ into the unit interval will suffice. A common

[34] It is also, as we will see in latter sections, the first step towards the development of a state-space model.

approach makes use of the so-called logistic function. Specifically, we rewrite Eq. 8.23 as,

$$
\begin{aligned}
y_{k,t} &= \frac{e^{\gamma_k X_t}}{1+e^{\gamma_k X_t}}, \\
&= \frac{1}{1+e^{-\gamma_k X_t}}, \\
&= f(\gamma_k X_t),
\end{aligned} \tag{8.24}
$$

for $t = 1, \ldots, T$ and $k = 1, \ldots, \mathcal{R}+2$. Both forms of the logistic function, $f$, are equivalent. The second form is more common, and somewhat more parsimonious. The first form, however, is arguably somewhat more stable numerically and makes for a better choice when numerical optimization is involved.

The specification in Eq. 8.24 should not be confused with the related logistic distribution.[35] Nor can Eq. 8.24 be considered, however tempting, as a logistic regression.[36] In this case, the logistic function handily transforms any real-valued argument into the unit interval. More technically, any function $f$ where $f : \mathbb{R} \rightarrow (0, 1)$ would serve our purposes.[37]

The use of the logistic function does have some additional interesting characteristics—not unrelated to the logistic distribution and regression—that are worth briefly investigating. If we slightly re-arrange Eq. 8.24, we arrive at

$$
\frac{y_{k,t}}{1-y_{k,t}} = e^{\gamma_k X_t}. \tag{8.25}
$$

The left-hand side of Eq. 8.25 is referred to as the odds. Very popular in gambling circles, we can see that it is essentially the probability of event occurring divided by the probability that it doesn't occur. The higher the probability of an event, the smaller the denominator, and thus the greater the odds. Taking natural logarithms of both sides of Eq. 8.25 leads to

$$
f^{-1}(y_{k,t}) = \ln\left(\frac{y_{k,t}}{1-y_{k,t}}\right) = \gamma_k X_t, \tag{8.26}
$$

where, unsurprisingly, the left-hand side quantity is termed the log odds.[38] Use of a logistic transformation in Eq. 8.24 thus amounts—in addition to constraining our response variables to the unit interval—to writing the log odds as a linear function of our macro-financial factors.

---

[35] See Johnson et al. [24, Chapter 23] for much more detail on this continuous distribution.

[36] In a true logistic regression, the response variable can take only discrete—the most common case is binary, zero or one—values. See Judge et al. [26, Chapter 18] or Hastie et al. [19, Section 4.4] for a detailed description of this popular and powerful statistical technique.

[37] As a consequence, virtually any continuous cumulative distribution function with $\mathbb{R}$-valued support would do the trick.

[38] See James et al. [22, Chapter 4] for a nice description of these ideas.

Returning to our original model in Eq. 8.22, we may use these ideas to redefine it slightly as,

$$f^{-1}(y_t) = \Gamma X_t + \nu_t, \tag{8.27}$$

for $t = 1, \ldots, T$ with $f^{-1}$ defined in Eq. 8.26 as the log odds.[39] This formulation—despite the consideration of a number of variations—is the foundation of our first point-in-time description of our general credit conditions.[40]

Before proceeding to the actual estimation algorithm, it is first important to determine our monotonicity constraints. Logically, we require—for each time period—that the credit-rating level default rates increase in a (weakly) monotonic manner as we move down the credit spectrum. Practically, this amounts to,

$$c_{r,t} \leq c_{r+1,t}, \tag{8.29}$$

for $r = 1, \ldots, \mathcal{R} - 1$ and $t = 1, \ldots, T$. These constraints are unnecessary for the upgrade and downgrade variables. While technically correct, Eq. 8.29 is not immediately helpful. It does not refer to the model parameters and it applies to each individual time step. Using our model specification, we can simplify matters as

$$\begin{aligned} c_{r,t} &\leq c_{r+1,t}, \\ \gamma_r X_t &\leq \gamma_{r+1} X_t, \\ (\gamma_r - \gamma_{r+1}) X_t &\leq 0, \end{aligned} \tag{8.30}$$

for $r = 1, \ldots, \mathcal{R} - 1$ and $t = 1, \ldots, T$. This is modest progress, since we have introduced the model parameters. We still have to manage these constraints for each time step. Examination of Eq. 8.30 reveals, however, that if the values in $X_t$ are positive, we can exclude them. While it is not true that our macro-financial variables are uniformly positive, they do generally take non-negative values. This suggests the following proposed set of monotonicity constraints,

$$\gamma_{k,r} - \gamma_{k,r+1} \leq 0, \tag{8.31}$$

[39] Another popular choice of $f$ is the cumulative distribution function for the normal distribution, $\Phi$. This would lead to the following model,

$$\Phi^{-1}(y_t) = \Gamma X_t + \nu_t, \tag{8.28}$$

which is called the probit transformation. Again, this specification is conceptually linked to probit regression, but is not quite the same thing. A variant of this form will arise in the theoretically motivated approach covered in the next section.

[40] A bit of abuse of notation, in full transparency, has occurred since the structure of $\nu_t$ is not quite the same in Eqs. 8.22 and 8.27; its basic interpretation as an error vector nonetheless does not change.

for $k = 0, \ldots, \kappa$ and $r = 1, \ldots, \mathcal{R} - 1$. This leads to $(\kappa + 1) \times (\mathcal{R} - 1)$ linear parameter constraints. It is not a completely foolproof guarantee of monotonicity—given the possibility of negative $X_t$ outcomes—but it should typically provide sensible results.

Pulling all of these elements together, the collection of model parameters linking together our general credit conditions and explanatory macro-financial variables is determined through the solution of the following optimization problem:

$$\min_{\Gamma} \sum_{t=1}^{T} \underbrace{\left(f^{-1}(y_t) - \Gamma X_t\right)^T \left(f^{-1}(y_t) - \Gamma X_t\right)}_{\nu_t^T \nu_t}, \tag{8.32}$$

subject to:

$$\gamma_{k,r} - \gamma_{k,r+1} \leq 0 \text{ for } k = 0, \ldots, \kappa \text{ and } r = 1, \ldots, \mathcal{R} - 1.$$

One is, of course, free to either apply $f^{-1}$ to $y_t$ or $f$ to each $\gamma_k X_t$ dot product. Both are mathematically equivalent. The latter approach is practically preferable, however, when using raw default-curve data. This is because applying logarithms to zero-valued default incidences creates predictable numerical headaches.

**Colour and Commentary 94** (A CENTRAL RELATIONSHIP)*: We have established the set of key general credit condition variables and the macro-financial factors intended to explain them. To institute a proper point-in-time model, it is necessary to create a statistical link (or map) between these two quantities. The obvious starting point is a linear model. More complex mappings are certainly possible. Linear models—despite their shortcomings—offer a number of advantages: they are simple, robust (i.e., low variance), and permit extensive statistical inference.*[a] *Given the interpretation of our general credit condition variables as a probability—and their associated restriction to the unit interval—direct application of the linear model eludes us. This issue is, thankfully, resolved with a judicious transformation of our explanatory variables. This final transformed linear expression also readily permits the imposition of global monotonicity constraints to maintain presumed economic relationships between our rating-level default values. This general formulation will form the foundation of our first point-in-time transition matrix model. Variations in possible implementation relate to the choice of macro-financial factors and precisely how they enter into the model.*

[a] Linear models do, however, exhibit higher levels of bias on the variance-bias trade-off. See Hastie et al. [19] for more on this important concept.

### 8.3.2 An Indirect Approach

In our legacy implementation, the macro-financial variables do not appear directly in Eq. 8.27. Instead, they enter indirectly through a back-door route. They pass, in fact, through the aggregate default rate, $c_t$. It begins with the following transformed linear model,

$$f^{-1}(c_t) = \begin{bmatrix}\lambda_0 \; \lambda_1 \cdots \lambda_\kappa,\end{bmatrix}\begin{bmatrix}1\\ x_{1,t}\\ \vdots\\ x_{\kappa,t}\end{bmatrix} + \varepsilon_t, \tag{8.33}$$

$$f^{-1}(c_t) = \lambda X_t + \varepsilon_t,$$

for $t = 1, \ldots, T$ where $f^{-1}$ refers to the inverse of the logistic function.[41] The idea is that estimation algorithm works in two steps. First, the macro-financial variables are linked to the aggregate default rate through Eq. 8.33 and $\lambda$. Then, for a given realization of $X_t$, $\lambda X_t$ is used to revise our original model from Eq. 8.27. Re-arranging the dimensionality somewhat to make things fit together properly, we can write this approach in a single expression as,

$$f^{-1}\left(\begin{bmatrix}y_{1,t}\\ \vdots\\ y_{\mathcal{R},t}\\ y_{\mathcal{R}+1,t}\\ y_{\mathcal{R}+2,t}\end{bmatrix}\right) = \begin{bmatrix}\gamma_{0,1} & \gamma_{1,1} & \cdots & \gamma_{\kappa,1}\\ \gamma_{0,2} & \gamma_{1,2} & \cdots & \gamma_{\kappa,2}\\ \vdots & \vdots & \ddots & \vdots\\ \gamma_{0,\mathcal{R}} & \gamma_{1,\mathcal{R}} & \cdots & \gamma_{\kappa,\mathcal{R}}\\ \gamma_{0,\mathcal{R}+1} & \gamma_{1,\mathcal{R}+1} & \cdots & \gamma_{\kappa,\mathcal{R}+1}\\ \gamma_{0,\mathcal{R}+2} & \gamma_{1,\mathcal{R}+2} & \cdots & \gamma_{\kappa,\mathcal{R}+2}\end{bmatrix}\overbrace{\underbrace{\begin{bmatrix}\lambda_0 & 0 & \cdots & 0\\ 0 & \lambda_1 & \cdots & 0\\ \vdots & \vdots & \ddots & \vdots\\ 0 & 0 & \cdots & \lambda_\kappa\end{bmatrix}}_{\Lambda\equiv\text{diag}(\lambda)}\begin{bmatrix}1\\ x_{1,t}\\ \vdots\\ x_{\kappa,t}\end{bmatrix}}^{\widehat{f^{-1}(c_t)}}$$

$$+\begin{bmatrix}\nu_{1,t}\\ \vdots\\ \nu_{\mathcal{R}+2,t}\end{bmatrix}, \tag{8.34}$$

$$f^{-1}(y_t) = \Gamma\Lambda X_t + \nu_t.$$

In short, this is an alternative strategy to characterize the link between general credit conditions and macro-financial outcomes. Instead of $\Gamma \in \mathbb{R}^{(R+2)\times(\kappa+1)}$ as our linear-projection matrix, we have instead $\Gamma\Lambda \in \mathbb{R}^{(R+2)\times(\kappa+1)}$. It is nonetheless important to note that $\Lambda$ is estimated first—using Eq. 8.33—and then fixed when we estimate $\Gamma$.

[41] Although, as seen previously, other choices of $f$ are entirely possible.

While this might seem like an unnecessary complication, it does have some advantages. It permits the direct introduction of aggregate credit conditions—which is a useful response variable—into the process. It further introduces the idea of a composite state variable. The quantity, $\lambda X_t$, is a linear combination—under the logit transformation—of our macro-financial explanatory variables. Using the aggregate credit rate, $c_t$, is not so far (conceptually speaking) from the construction of principal components or dynamic factors found in Stock and Watson [42]. Indeed, the predicted result from Eq. 8.33 is referred to as a *credit-cycle index*.[42]

The credit-cycle approach also offers some potential reduction in the number of actual model parameters to be estimated. Not true in the general implementation, summarized in Eq. 8.34, it is possible in the specialized case of our legacy model. In particular, Eq. 8.34 is represented in a slightly different fashion as,

$$f^{-1}\left(\begin{bmatrix} y_{1,t} \\ \vdots \\ y_{\mathcal{R},t} \\ y_{\mathcal{R}+1,t} \\ y_{\mathcal{R}+2,t} \end{bmatrix}\right) = \begin{bmatrix} \gamma_{0,1} & \gamma_{1,1} \\ \gamma_{0,2} & \gamma_{1,2} \\ \vdots & \vdots \\ \gamma_{0,\mathcal{R}} & \gamma_{1,\mathcal{R}} \\ \gamma_{0,\mathcal{R}+1} & \gamma_{1,\mathcal{R}+1} \\ \gamma_{0,\mathcal{R}+2} & \gamma_{1,\mathcal{R}+2} \end{bmatrix} \underbrace{\begin{bmatrix} 1 \\ \hat{\lambda} X_t \end{bmatrix}}_{X_t(\hat{\lambda})} + \begin{bmatrix} \nu_{1,t} \\ \vdots \\ \nu_{\mathcal{R}+2,t} \end{bmatrix}, \tag{8.35}$$

$$f^{-1}(y_t) = \Gamma X_t(\hat{\lambda}) + \nu_t.$$

In the general case, there are $(\kappa + 1)$ non-zero $\Lambda$ parameters and $(\mathcal{R} + 2) \cdot (\kappa + 1)$ parameters in $\Gamma$. In the restricted version from Eq. 8.35, the $(\kappa + 1)$ parameters are unchanged, but one only needs to estimate $2 \cdot (\mathcal{R} + 2)$ individual $\Gamma$ coefficients. The number of general model parameters increases multiplicatively in $\kappa$, whereas in this specific model, it increases only linearly.[43] The principal justification for the restricted model version presented in Eq. 8.35—and, more broadly, the use of a credit-cycle index—is to keep the numbers of model parameters under control.

Figure 8.11 displays the so-called credit-cycle index from Eq. 8.33. One—of many—possible options are considered. We present the maximal model, which involves setting $\kappa = 10$ and including all elements from our set of macro-financial variables from Table 8.2. Figure 8.11 illustrates the in-sample fit associated with the quarterly data from 1992 to 2021. The overall model seems to provide a generally reasonable fit to the peaks and valleys observed in the aggregate default rates, but

[42] The fact that the left-hand side default-curve variables—$c_{r,t}$ for $r = 1, \ldots \mathcal{R}$—are essentially a kind of average of the aggregate default rate, $c_t$, is something of a problem. It amounts, indirectly at least, to including our independent variable into our set of explanatory factors. In statistical circles, this might be considered—-if not a criminal act—a venial sin.

[43] For $\mathcal{R} + 2 = 19$ and $\kappa = 10$, which correspond to a fairly reasonable model size, the general model requires $19 \cdot 11 + 11 = 220$ parameters. The restricted version, conversely, involves only $2 \cdot 19 + 11 = 49$ estimated coefficients.

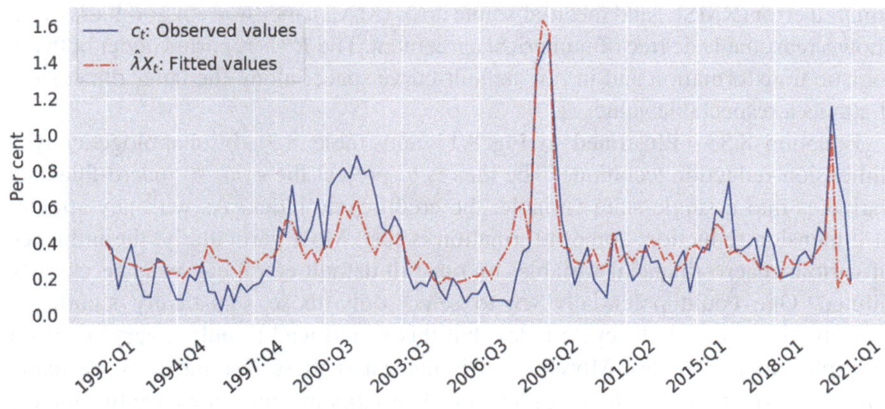


**Fig. 8.11** *Aggregate-level fit*: This figure examines the visual consistency of the linear model of aggregate default rates (i.e., $c_t$) introduced in Eq. 8.33. The maximal number of $\kappa = 10$ macro-financial variables are included in the analysis.

**Table 8.3** *Aggregate model results*: This table provides a range of detailed parametric- and model-level summary statistics for the maximal implementation of Eq. 8.33. Although we incorporate all variables from Table 8.2, not all of the variables are statistically significant in this intermediate step. We are reluctant to exclude individual variables, at this stage, because they may prove useful in the next step. This is nonetheless an important part of one's variable-selection process.

| Measure | Maximal Model | | | | | | | | | | |
|---|---|---|---|---|---|---|---|---|---|---|---|
| | $\lambda_0$ | $\lambda_1$ $(\varphi_t)$ | $\lambda_2$ $(\pi_t)$ | $\lambda_3$ $(r_t)$ | $\lambda_4$ $(\theta_t)$ | $\lambda_5$ $(k_t)$ | $\lambda_6$ $(w_t)$ | $\lambda_7$ $(m_t)$ | $\lambda_8$ $(h_t)$ | $\lambda_9$ $(s_t)$ | $\lambda_{10}$ $(\sigma_t)$ |
| Estimate | −5.80 | 0.29 | −0.79 | −0.07 | −0.01 | −0.02 | −0.02 | 0.01 | 0.68 | 0.26 | 0.01 |
| Standard Error | 0.34 | 0.11 | 0.35 | 0.23 | 0.02 | 0.04 | 0.01 | 0.02 | 0.60 | 0.21 | 0.02 |
| $t$-Statistic | −16.84 | 2.61 | −2.23 | −0.32 | −0.89 | −0.58 | −1.11 | 0.43 | 1.14 | 1.25 | 0.48 |
| $p$-Value | 0.00 | 0.01 | 0.01 | 0.38 | 0.19 | 0.28 | 0.13 | 0.33 | 0.13 | 0.11 | 0.32 |
| RMSE | 0.17% | | | | | | | | | | |
| MAE | 0.13% | | | | | | | | | | |
| $R^2$ (Log-transformed space) | 0.33 | | | | | | | | | | |
| $R^2$ (Non-transformed space) | 0.65 | | | | | | | | | | |

it is far from perfect. In particular, it seems to understate some spikes and overstate some of the lower default periods.

Table 8.3 provides a range of detailed parametric- and model-level summary statistics for our implementation of Eq. 8.33. The parameter values themselves are not terribly engaging, but the standard errors, $t$-statistics, and associated $p$-values tell an interesting story. Only the constant, corporate-bond spread, and inflation-rate parameters can be considered to be statistically significant at a 5% level. The importance of the bond-spread could have been predicted from Fig. 8.10, where we observe a linear correlation coefficient in excess of 0.8 between $c_t$ and $\varphi_t$.

It is thus disappointingly difficult to construct a robust statistical relationship between the aggregate default rate and our full set of macro-financial variables. The final four rows of Table 8.3 consider the overall model performance. Root-mean squared error (RMSE) and mean-absolute error (MAE), measures of goodness of fit, show a reasonable degree of numerical agreement. The $R^2$ is reported under both the logistic transformation and in raw default-curve space; along the latter dimension, it attains a respectable value.

Equation 8.33—illustrated in Fig. 8.11 and Table 8.3—is unapologetically a dimension-reduction technique. The idea is to project the $\kappa = 10$ macro-financial variables into a single state variable: the credit-cycle index. As with any attempt at dimension reduction, some information is lost. Most particularly, the influence of various macro-financial variables on our full default credit curves is necessarily diluted. One could potentially try to select only those statistically significant contributors to the credit-cycle index, but this would lead to only a very small set of explanatory variables. Moreover, it is unclear if these test statistics are really entirely pertinent for our final application. This explains our reluctance to trim any macro-financial explanatory variables at this step in the process.[44]

Understanding the limitations of our choice of dimension-reduction technique, the next step involves the use of the credit-cycle index to estimate—under fixed choices of λ—the individual Γ parameters. They are found as the solution to the constrained optimization problem following from Eq. 8.35

$$\min_{\Gamma} \sum_{t=1}^{T} \underbrace{\left(f^{-1}(y_t) - \Gamma X_t(\hat{\lambda})\right)^T \left(f^{-1}(y_t) - \Gamma X_t(\hat{\lambda})\right)}_{\nu_t^T \nu_t}, \tag{8.36}$$

subject to:

$$\gamma_{0,r} - \gamma_{0,r+1} \leq 0 \text{ for } r = 1, \ldots, \mathcal{R} - 1,$$
$$\gamma_{1,r} - \gamma_{1,r+1} \leq 0 \text{ for } r = 1, \ldots, \mathcal{R} - 1.$$

There are $2 \cdot (\mathcal{R} + 2)$ (non-fixed) coefficients embedded in this problem, making investigation of each individual parameter—and determination of significance—a fairly tedious task. There are, however, some basic trends worth describing. The results differ rather importantly depending on whether, or not, one uses raw or fitted default-curve data. Using the raw default-curve data, the first three credit classes have difficulty given the lack of data. The constant parameter is uniformly significant, but the slope parameter on the credit-cycle index is only significant for the two weakest credits. Moreover, the $R^2$ values start from essentially zero and increase inversely proportional to credit quality. The highest level is only about 0.2. If we use the fitted data, the results are moderately better. The overall fit is vaguely superior and the four weakest credit-class slope coefficients are significant. Moreover, it is possible to reasonably fit all credit categories within the default curve.

[44] Still, despite our failure to do so in this pedagogical discussion, some (at least, semi-formal) process is required to identify the most useful subset of macro-financial variables.

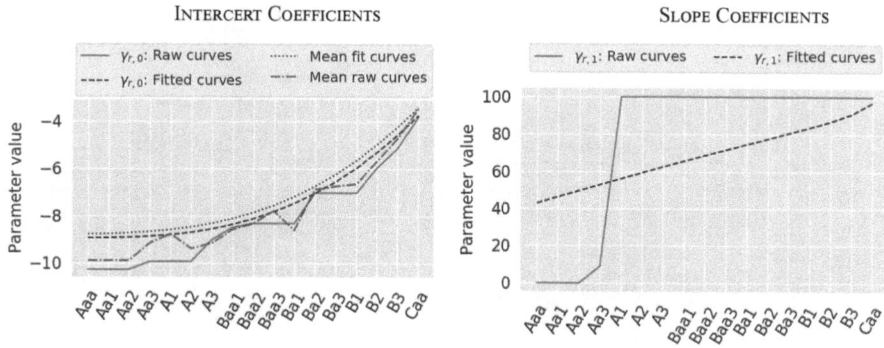


**Fig. 8.12** *Restricted* Γ *Parameters*: These graphics illustrate the individual default-curve Γ parameters from the solution of the restricted (and constrained) model presented in Eq. 8.36. Values from use of raw and fitted default-curve data are provided.

Figure 8.12 illustrates the individual default-curve estimated Γ parameters from Eq. 8.36. The left-hand graphic displays the intercept parameter (i.e., the $\gamma_{0,r}$'s) results using both the raw and fitted default-curve data, whereas the right-hand graphic illustrates the slope coefficients (i.e., the $\gamma_{1,r}$'s). Along with the intercepts, to provide some perspective, are the average fitted and raw (logarithmic) default curves. The similarities between these two quantities are striking; we can correspondingly conclude that the intercept essentially plays the role of the through-the-cycle default probability term structure. The slope coefficients, modified by the credit-cycle index from Eq. 8.33, thus manage the point-in-time adjustments. Using the fitted curves, the slope coefficients increase smoothly over the credit spectrum suggesting that the credit-cycle index becomes more important with decreasing credit quality. A similar pattern is evident for the estimates derived using the raw credit-curve data, but it essentially follows a kind of step function.[45]

Although it is not a direct consequence of the model structure, the empirical results shown in Fig. 8.12 suggest the following (rather appealing) logical decomposition of our statistical model:

$$f^{-1}(y_t) \approx \overbrace{\underbrace{\Gamma_0}_{\substack{\text{Through-}\\\text{the-}\\\text{cycle}}} + \underbrace{\Gamma_1 X_t(\hat{\lambda})}_{\substack{\text{Point-}\\\text{in-}\\\text{time}}}}^{\text{Equation 8.35}}, \tag{8.37}$$

where $\Gamma_0$ and $\Gamma_1$ represent the first and second columns of our Γ parameter matrix, respectively. Quite sensibly, the through-the-cycle aspect is fixed across all time

[45] This is almost certainly a consequence of the monotonicity constraints in Eq. 8.36 and the dominance of speculative-grade defaults highlighted in Figs. 8.4 and 8.5.

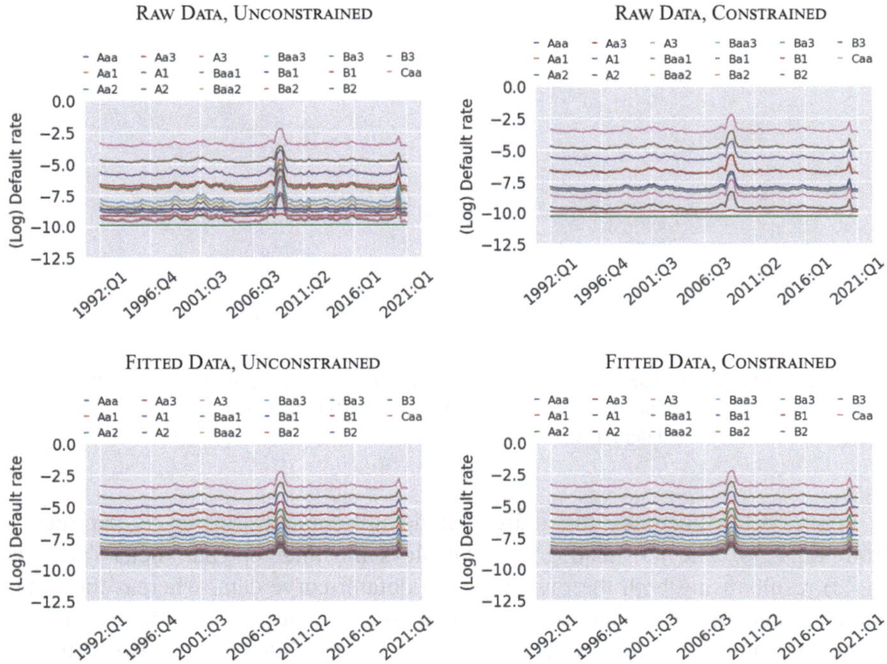


**Fig. 8.13** *Class-level fit*: The adjacent graphics provide—in logarithmic space, to permit interpretation—the estimated quarterly default curves from 1992 to early 2021. Both constrained and unconstrained values using the raw and fitted default curves are included.

periods, whereas the point-in-time contribution varies with our credit-cycle index. A similar form, albeit through intentional construction, will arise in our second theoretical-motivated approach addressed in the following section.

It is also useful to investigate the importance of the parameter monotonicity constraints. Figure 8.12 clearly illustrates that all $\gamma_0$ and $\gamma_1$ are—as required by Eq. 8.36—weakly increasing functions of $r$. What precisely does this mean, however, for default-curve estimates? Figure 8.13 attempts to answer this question in four separate graphics. The left-hand quadrants display the default-curve estimates associated with an unconstrained implementation of Eq. 8.36 using raw and fitted data, respectively. To permit visual examination, the usual logarithmic scale is employed. For the most part, predicted category level default rates are distinct, non-overlapping and monotone. At the upper end of the credit scale there are a few cases—when employing the raw data—where monotonicity is violated. The two right-hand quadrants of Fig. 8.13 are a copy of the left-hand side with one important difference: the constraints are imposed. We clearly observe how the imposition of constraints ensures distinct and non-overlapping time evolution of individual credit-rating default rates. The constraints thus not only appear to be doing their job, they can be deemed useful.

Equally interesting in Fig. 8.13 is the difference between the two upper and lower quadrants. This reflects the impact of using raw or fitted default-curve data.

**Table 8.4** *Upgrade and downgrade results*: This table provides a list of parametric- and model-level summary statistics for upgrade and downgrade proportion estimates embedded in Eq. 8.35. Neither appear to be particularly well explained by our credit-cycle index.

| Measure | Upgrade | | Downgrade | |
|---|---|---|---|---|
| | $\gamma_0$ | $\gamma_1$ | $\gamma_0$ | $\gamma_1$ |
| Estimate | −1.44 | −192.19 | −2.35 | 139.82 |
| Standard error | 0.09 | 20.84 | 0.08 | 18.18 |
| $t$-statistic | −16.09 | −9.22 | −30.02 | 7.69 |
| $p$-value | 0.00 | 0.00 | 0.00 | 0.00 |
| RMSE | 5.97% | | 5.67% | |
| MAE | 3.19% | | 4.03% | |
| $R^2$ | 0.11 | | 0.49 | |

In the two northernmost quadrants, the highest quality credit classes—Aaa to Aa2—exhibit no variability. The default curves associated with the fitted values, conversely, produce time-varying estimates for all credit classes. Most strikingly, during the great financial crisis, the two datasets produce contradictory results. The raw data suggests that all credit classes move (mostly) in tandem. The fitted data, in contrast, appears to predict a deviation between investment and speculative grade credits. Speculative-grade default incidence increases, but the highest credit categories rise only slightly; this would appear to be a consequence of the step-function form of the slope coefficients displayed in Fig. 8.12. This point is worth remarking and reflecting upon, since it has important implications for one's ultimate point-in-time probability model.

We may now turn our attention to the final two aspects of our categorization of general credit conditions: upgrade and downgrade incidences. Table 8.4 chronicles a number of parametric- and model-level summary statistics for the upgrade and downgrade proportion estimates embedded in Eq. 8.35 and 8.36. Neither appear to be particularly well explained by our credit-cycle index; in both cases, however, all estimated parameters are statistically significant. The $R^2$ value is not unreasonable for downgrades, but is quite low on the upgrade side. The prediction errors are—in both settings—also somewhat underwhelming.

To summarize, our first point-in-time model is a restricted version of the general linear model in Eq. 8.22. Equation 8.33 is used to construct a composite macro-financial variable entitled the credit-cycle index. Conditioning on this value, Eq. 8.35 proceeds to link this composite index (in a dimension-reduced manner) to our desired response variables. Two practical questions arise in this setting and remain outstanding. First, what set of explanatory variables should be employed? Second, is it preferable to use raw or fitted default-curve data in our response variable set? Neither are particularly easy to address and are left somewhat open. While important—due to their complexity, trial-and-error nature, and the role of one's specific objectives—they are not well-suited for discussion in a textbook setting.

**Colour and Commentary 95** (A RESTRICTED MODEL): *The general linear model—linking our general credit-condition response variables and our macro-financial explanatory factors—is rather high-dimensional. Even with three decades of quarterly data, the sheer number of associated model parameters makes robust practical implementation a serious challenge. The legacy NIB model thus employs a statistical twist to make the situation more manageable. It operates in* two *steps. First, it uses the aggregate default rate to construct a composite measure of general macro-financial conditions. This linear combination of our explanatory variables—under a logit transformation—is referred to as the credit-cycle index. This is basically a dimension-reduction trick, which inevitably involves some loss of information. In the second step, each response variable from our general credit condition vector is then linked to this single composite macro-financial variable. Practically, the intercept in this model (roughly) captures the through-the-cycle component, while the slope coefficient (and the credit-cycle index) incorporate the point-in-time aspect. The key advantage of this—admittedly circuitous approach—is a dramatic reduction in the number of model parameters. On the down side, however, the statistical power of the credit-cycle index for explaining our response variables appears to be somewhat limited.*

### *8.3.3 An Alternative Formulation*

The general model from Eq. 8.22 is unavailable for practical use by virtue of its (excessive) parameter dimensionality. The restricted approach, discussed in the previous section, makes a valiant effort towards resolving this challenge. There are, however, alternative techniques that one might employ to address this problem. One promising avenue, which we will explore and consider, follows from the interest-rate literature. A combination of the work of Litterman and Scheinkman [31], Nelson and Siegel [35], and Diebold and Li [12] has led to a rich array of low-dimensional yield-curve models cleverly circumventing a very similar issue.[46] Although there are good reasons to expect an analogous approach to be less effective in the default curve environment, it nonetheless merits consideration.

The core idea is to construct a lower dimensional set of response variables. In particular, we might replace our $\mathcal{R}$ default-curve variables with their three time-indexed $\zeta_t$ fitting variables from Fig. 8.9. This was, in fact, the principal objective

[46] One should also mention the important influence of Vasicek [43] towards the general development of dynamic yield-curve models.

of our efforts towards building a default-curve model. We denote this new response vector as $z_t \in \mathbb{R}^{J\times 1}$. This permits us to rewrite Eq. 8.22 as follows,

$$\underbrace{\begin{bmatrix}\zeta_{0,t}\\ \zeta_{1,t}\\ \zeta_{2,t}\\ u_t\\ d_t\end{bmatrix} \equiv \begin{bmatrix} z_{1,t}\\ \vdots \\ z_{J,t}\end{bmatrix}}_{z_t} = \begin{bmatrix}\gamma_{0,1} & \gamma_{1,1} & \cdots & \gamma_{\kappa,1}\\ \gamma_{0,2} & \gamma_{1,2} & \cdots & \gamma_{\kappa,2}\\ \vdots & \vdots & \ddots & \vdots\\ \gamma_{0,J} & \gamma_{1,J} & \cdots & \gamma_{\kappa,J}\end{bmatrix}\begin{bmatrix}1\\ x_{1,t}\\ \vdots\\ x_{\kappa,t}\end{bmatrix} + \begin{bmatrix}\nu_{1,t}\\ \vdots\\ \nu_{J,t}\end{bmatrix}, \tag{8.38}$$

$$z_t = \Gamma_z X_t + \nu_t,$$

for $t = 1, \ldots, T$, where $\Gamma_z \in \mathbb{R}^{J\times(\kappa+1)}$ is a matrix of model parameters linking general credit conditions with our explanatory variables, and $\nu_t \in \mathbb{R}^{J\times 1}$ is an error vector. The fundamental difference is between $z_t$ and $y_t$. Given that $J \ll \mathcal{R}$, the number of parameters in $\Gamma_z$ become significantly more manageable. In our case, for example, $\kappa = 10$—and given $J = 5$—Eq. 8.38 gives rise to 55 parameters for estimation.[47] The implementation of the restricted model in the previous section actually, if we recall, requires 49 parameters. The parametric burden is thus roughly equivalent in these two approaches.[48]

$z_t$ needs, however, to transformed into $y_t$ so that it can actually be employed in our framework. This effort has already been resolved in our previous analysis. In particular,

$$y_t = g(z_t), \tag{8.39}$$

where the specific form of $g$ is simply,

$$y_{i,t} = \begin{cases} e^{z_{1,t}+z_{2,t}i+z_{3,t}\sin\left(\frac{i}{\omega}\right)} : i = 1, \ldots, \mathcal{R}\\ z_{4,t} : i = \mathcal{R}+1\\ z_{5,t} : i = \mathcal{R}+2\end{cases}, \tag{8.40}$$

which follows directly from Eq. 8.14. In other words, our default-curve mapping permits us to almost effortlessly move between the first three values of $z_t$ and the predicted default curves.

While this is a pleasant idea, it remains to be seen if—at least, in principle—it actually works. To permit a reasonable comparison to the restricted model

[47] Since $\Gamma$ has $J \cdot (\kappa + 1)$ individual entries, $J = 5$, and $\kappa = 10$, then the total parameters are simply $5 \cdot (10 + 1) = 55$.

[48] We have also dispensed with the logistic transformation in Eq. 8.38. Practically, it is no longer possible (or necessary) since the $\zeta$ parameters—as illustrated in Fig. 8.9—may take both positive and negative values.

**Table 8.5** *Alternative-model results*: This table provides the $p$-values and overall $R^2$ statistics for the $J$ regression estimates stemming from our alternative, low-dimensional, model formulation presented in Eq. 8.38. The entire set of macro-financial variables was employed. Parameter estimates significant at more than the 5% level are highlighted in blue.

| Quantity | $\zeta_{0,t}(z_{1,t})$ | $\zeta_{1,t}(z_{2,t})$ | $\zeta_{2,t}(z_{3,t})$ | $u_t(z_{4,t})$ | $d_t(z_{5,t})$ |
|---|---|---|---|---|---|
| $\gamma_0$ | 0.00 | 0.00 | 0.00 | 0.00 | 0.48 |
| $\gamma_1(\varphi_t)$ | 0.03 | 0.33 | 0.20 | 0.17 | 0.00 |
| $\gamma_2(\pi_t)$ | 0.08 | 0.00 | 0.10 | 0.00 | 0.17 |
| $\gamma_3(r_t)$ | 0.08 | 0.09 | 0.10 | 0.29 | 0.13 |
| $\gamma_4(\theta_t)$ | 0.12 | 0.14 | 0.24 | 0.03 | 0.10 |
| $\gamma_5(k_t)$ | 0.34 | 0.13 | 0.26 | 0.21 | 0.04 |
| $\gamma_6(w_t)$ | 0.37 | 0.42 | 0.32 | 0.50 | 0.20 |
| $\gamma_7(m_t)$ | 0.06 | 0.01 | 0.34 | 0.36 | 0.26 |
| $\gamma_8(k_t)$ | 0.45 | 0.10 | 0.49 | 0.43 | 0.36 |
| $\gamma_9(s_t)$ | 0.23 | 0.08 | 0.48 | 0.27 | 0.24 |
| $\gamma_{10}(\sigma_t)$ | 0.22 | 0.07 | 0.06 | 0.29 | 0.46 |
| $R^2$ | 0.16 | 0.31 | 0.14 | 0.19 | **0.64** |

introduced in the previous section, we keep $\kappa = 10$ and include the entire set of macro-financial variables in our implementation of Eq. 8.38. The coefficients are readily estimated by minimizing $\sum_{t=1}^{t} v_t^T v_t$ with no monotonicity constraints.[49]

Table 8.5 provides a selection of key results helping us assess parameter significance and overall model fit. In all cases, save the downgrade proportion, the constant term is strongly significant. Otherwise, just a handful of parameters exhibit statistical significance across the range of macro-financial variables; this situation does appear somewhat, although not dramatically, better than in Table 8.3. While there is some value in linking our response vector directly to the macro-financial explanatory variables, we should not overstate the benefits of this structure. The overall model fit is also not terribly encouraging. The $R^2$ of the first and second default-curve state variables is quite weak, but the important second variable falls in the neighbourhood of 0.4. The upgrade $R^2$ result is not much better; only the downgrade series exhibits a strong overall model fit.

When examining Table 8.5, we might conversely argue against overstating the importance of any individual parameter. Various constellations of our macro-financial variables are being combined to describe our low-dimension representation of each individual default curve. Similar to typically rather parameter-heavy vector-autoregressive models, statistical inference on model parameters might not prove terribly helpful; we should alternatively allow it to operate as a general system.

[49] This means that each row of Eq. 8.38 may be independently estimated with the classic analytic least-squares estimator.

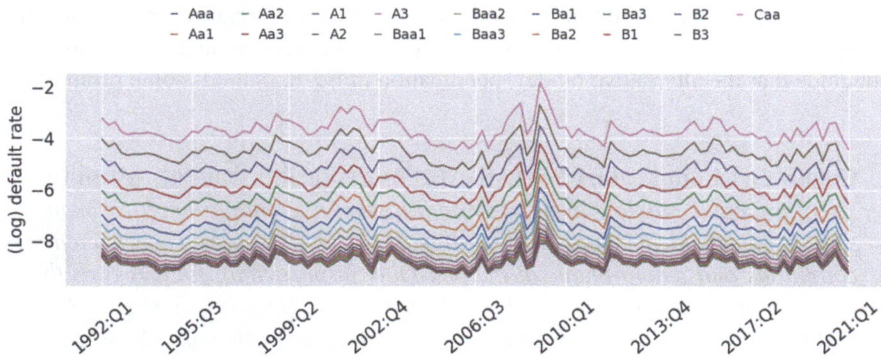


**Fig. 8.14** *Revised class-level fit*: This figure provides the predicted default curve outcomes, presented on a logarithmic scale, associated with our alternative legacy model representation from Table 8.5.

Analogous to our previous construction in Eq. 8.37, a similar logical decomposition is possible:

$$z_t \approx \overbrace{\underbrace{\Gamma_{z,0}}_{\substack{\text{Through-}\\\text{the-}\\\text{cycle}}} + \underbrace{\Gamma_{z,X}\begin{bmatrix} x_{1,t} \\ \vdots \\ x_{\kappa,t} \end{bmatrix}}_{\substack{\text{Point-}\\\text{in-}\\\text{time}}}}^{\text{Equation 8.38}}, \tag{8.41}$$

where, as before, $\Gamma_{z,0}$ and $\Gamma_{z,X}$ represent the first and remaining columns of our $\Gamma_z$ parameter matrix, respectively. The key question is: does our system of macro-financial parameters provide a meaningful categorization of general credit conditions?

To allow some insight into this question, Fig. 8.14 provides the usual predicted default curve outcomes presented on a logarithmic scale. Each curve is distinct, non-overlapping, and monotone along the credit spectrum. Interestingly, this was achieved without the imposition of any parametric constraints. Figure 8.14 naturally invites comparison to Fig. 8.13. Overall, the alternative model outcomes are noisier and more cyclical than the restricted-model equivalents. In Fig. 8.13, to be more concrete, the only significant event appears to occur during 2008 to 2010. Figure 8.14 indicates the presence of more complex dynamics; from this viewpoint, our parametric system from Table 8.5 seems more realistic. Most particularly, as suggested by Fig. 8.8, high-quality credit default rates are much more volatile.[50]

[50] This presumably comes from the implicit extrapolation of these values in the default-curve fitting algorithm.

Which is the most appropriate specification, of course, requires reflection and comparison with one's stress-testing objectives. We may nonetheless cautiously conclude that the alternative model specification in Eq. 8.38 holds some promise.

**Colour and Commentary 96** (AN ALTERNATIVE RESTRICTED MODEL): *There are other possible avenues to address the inherent parametric dimensionality embedded in our general linear model mapping between credit conditions and macro-financial factors. One, in particular, follows directly from the work of Litterman and Scheinkman [31], Nelson and Siegel [35], and Diebold and Li [12] in the interest-rate literature. Applying these ideas to our setting involves using our $\zeta_t$ fitting parameters as a low-dimensional representation of the default curve. This allows us—within the context of the minimal implementation of the restricted model—to cut the total number of parameters by a factor of three. Moreover, it allows direct use of macro-financial variables and permits elimination of the monotonicity constraints. In principle, this involves less loss of information relative to the restricted linear model presented in the previous section. Implementation of this model reveals (at times) encouraging levels of parameter significance and interesting default-curve dynamics. On the down side, the overall model fit is not particularly impressive. It also depends rather importantly—by construction—on the defensibility of the default-curve fitting algorithm.*

### *8.3.4 A Short Aside*

Our various implementations of the general linear model—in Eq. 8.22—have been skirting around a fundamental statistical structure: the state-space model.[51] This idea, which originated in physics and engineering, specifies a structural relationship—within a dynamic system—between a set of observed outcomes and set of (often unobserved or latent) state variables. Typically, these two levels are motivated by some set of underlying physical linkages.[52] The key point, however, is that a state-space formulation is a convenient, and powerful, description of a set of response values—such as general credit conditions—as a function of some

[51] There are many useful sources regarding state-space models. Two excellent starting points are Kim and Nelson [27] and Hamilton [17, Chapter 13].

[52] These often take the form of a set of differential (or difference) equations driven by theory or observation.

collection of underlying state (i.e., macro-financial) variables. In short, it closely matches with our modelling objectives.[53]

The state-space representation begins with the so-called measurement equation. This describes the observable quantities as a function of the underlying state variables. Specializing it to our situation, we have

$$\begin{aligned}\begin{bmatrix} z_{1,t} \\ \vdots \\ z_{J,t} \end{bmatrix} &= \begin{bmatrix} a_1 \\ \vdots \\ a_J \end{bmatrix} + \begin{bmatrix} H_{1,1} & \cdots & H_{1,\kappa} \\ \vdots & \ddots & \vdots \\ H_{J,1} & \cdots & H_{J,\kappa} \end{bmatrix} \begin{bmatrix} x_{1,t} \\ \vdots \\ x_{\kappa,t} \end{bmatrix} + \begin{bmatrix} \nu_{1,t} \\ \vdots \\ \nu_{J,t} \end{bmatrix}, \\ z_t &= A + HX_t + \nu_t, \end{aligned} \tag{8.42}$$

where $z_t$ is defined as in Eq. 8.38, $A \in \mathbb{R}^{J\times 1}$, $H \in \mathbb{R}^{J\times\kappa}$, and $X_t \in \mathbb{R}^{\kappa\times 1}$. This looks suspiciously like Eq. 8.38; indeed, the only real difference relates to pulling out the constant term from the $\Gamma_z$ matrix.

The key difference in the state-space model, with our development so far, relates to the second state, or transition, equation. In our case, it might be written as,

$$\begin{aligned}\begin{bmatrix} x_{1,t} \\ \vdots \\ x_{\kappa,t} \end{bmatrix} &= \begin{bmatrix} c_1 \\ \vdots \\ c_\kappa \end{bmatrix} + \begin{bmatrix} F_{1,1} & \cdots & F_{1,\kappa} \\ \vdots & \ddots & \vdots \\ F_{\kappa,1} & \cdots & F_{\kappa,\kappa} \end{bmatrix} \begin{bmatrix} x_{1,t-1} \\ \vdots \\ x_{\kappa,t-1} \end{bmatrix} + \begin{bmatrix} \eta_{1,t} \\ \vdots \\ \eta_{\kappa,t} \end{bmatrix}, \\ X_t &= C + FX_{t-1} + \eta_t, \end{aligned} \tag{8.43}$$

where $C \in \mathbb{R}^{\kappa\times 1}$, $F \in \mathbb{R}^{\kappa\times\kappa}$, and $\eta_t \in \mathbb{R}^{\kappa\times 1}$. Practically, Eq. 8.43 amounts to a vector auto-regression specification of our system of macro-financial explanatory variables.[54] The benefits of this choice are, at least, threefold. First, one can extend the definition of $X_t$ to include both observable macro-financial variables and latent unobservable factors. This lends greater flexibility to the model. The specification of the structure of the $H$ and $F$ matrices also allows for imposition of key constraints and interactions. The second benefit is the parameters embedded in Eqs. 8.42 and 8.43 can be estimated via a recursive technique referred to as the Kalman filter.[55] Finally, and perhaps most importantly, the dynamic interactions of the macro-financial state variables can help inform the measurement equation parameters.

The state-space representation may, or may not, prove helpful in this setting. It has, however, been prowling beneath the surface of our general linear model and

[53] This structure has also been profitably used in the interest-rate literature. See James and Webber [23, Chapter 18] and Bolder [4]—as well as the many sources found in these works—for more detail.

[54] For more detail on this popular time-series model, see Hamilton [17, Chapter 11] or Judge et al. [26, Section 12.3]. We will also work extensively with auto-regressive models—within the context of stress-testing analysis—in Chap. 12.

[55] Harvey [18] is the inevitable starting point for all matters related to this statistical technique.

the two associated specialized cases analyzed in previous sections. In any event, a serious investigation of the proposed alternative version of our legacy point-in-time model probably merits further consideration of the state-space form.

**Colour and Commentary 97** (THE STATE-SPACE REPRESENTATION): *Our general linear model linking credit conditions and macro-financial factors is not as broadly defined as we have believed. With a modest effort, it can be written in more general state-space formulation. This powerful description of a dynamic system—founded in the physical sciences—offers conceptual and practical analytic advantages in terms of model communication, estimation, and implementation. The state-space form consists of two dynamic equations. The first, measurement equation, basically corresponds to our general linear model. The second, so-called state equation, introduces a dynamic description of our set of macro-financial explanatory variables. It also opens the door to extension of our explanatory variables to include latent, or unobserved, factors. Irrespective of whether or not this state-space form is exploited, it is nonetheless important to understand that—like it or not—it underlies our general linear formulation.*

### 8.3.5 Building a Point-in-Time Transition Matrix

The information in $y_t$ or $z_t$—or simple transformations thereof—represents the general credit conditions central to the construction our time-varying transition matrices. As desired from the outset, these values are a function of some set of underlying macro-financial variables. This linkage can be built in a number of different ways: the composite credit-cycle index, a direct linear function of the macro-financial state variables, or through a reduced-form state space model.[56] These model choices matter since they have an impact as to how predicted macro-financial-variable shocks manifest themselves into general credit conditions and, subsequently, into our default and transition probabilities. The default probabilities essentially fall directly from our previous development. Getting to a full-blown transition matrix requires a bit more dirty work. The good news is that—given perturbed general credit conditions—our proposed mechanics for building future transition matrices are the same across all of our previously described restricted linear models falling into the empirically motivated approach.

Our vector of credit-condition response variables has $\mathcal{R} + 2$ entries: $\mathcal{R}$ default-curve values in addition to the upgrade and downgrade percentages. A transition

[56] There are simply the three possibilities identified in previous sections; many other choices are possible.

matrix, by contrast, has $(\mathcal{R}+1) \times (\mathcal{R}+1)$ individual elements. The final row—relating to the absorbing default state—is completely determined. The consequence is that, practically, only $\mathcal{R} \times (\mathcal{R}+1)$ transition-matrix entries need to be actively determined.[57] To be very concrete about our task, therefore, we seek a mapping of the form,

$$h : \mathbb{R}^{\mathcal{R}+2} \rightarrow \mathbb{R}^{(\mathcal{R}+1)\times(\mathcal{R}+1)}, \qquad (8.44)$$
$$h : y_t \rightarrow P_t,$$

where we will use the abbreviated notation $P_t \equiv P_t(y_t) \equiv P_t(f(X_t))$ to describe our target value. The important point is that—as desired from the beginning of this chapter—$P_t$ is time varying and a function of our macro-financial state variables.

Not any choice of $h$ will do. There are a number of restrictions that we would like (or need) to impose. Some are logical, but most are required to ensure that $P_t$ is a proper transition matrix. These include:

1. each individual element of $P_t$ must fall in the unit interval;
2. each row of $P_t$ must sum to unity;
3. the majority of probability mass should fall into the diagonal elements;
4. none of the entries in $P_t$ may take a zero value, although individual values can be vanishingly small;
5. the default probabilities in $P_t$ must be consistent with the default-curve estimates in $y_t$; and
6. the proportion of upgrade and downgrade probability mass in each row of $P_t$ is compelled to be compatible with the $u_t$ and $d_t$ values found in $y_t$.

The challenge is thus to identify a reasonable mapping function, $h$, that respects these *six* conceptual restrictions.

### The Role of $P$

Central to this endeavour is the through-the-cycle transition matrix, $P$, introduced and estimated in the previous chapter. Both objects are, after all, transition matrices. The crucial difference between $P$ and $P_t$ relates to information. $P$ has no specific knowledge of current macro-financial activities—beyond their long-term average values—whereas $P_t$ does. Most importantly, the two matrices are related as follows:

$$\lim_{s\rightarrow\infty} P_{t+s} \rightarrow P. \qquad (8.45)$$

Despite the formalism of Eq. 8.45, this is not a mathematical result, but rather an economic statement. Anchored at time $t$, moving forward our time horizon—as

[57] This, admittedly, does not materially help our situation, but every little bit of structure helps.

described by $s$—naturally involves a decay in the value of information. A one-year macro-financial prediction is already somewhat challenging; at a five- or seven-year horizon, the views of even the most seasoned economic forecaster become highly speculative. After a sufficient passage of time, our scenarios must thus logically converge to the unconditional, through-the-cycle estimator. This insight has important implications for our construction of long-term loan-impairment estimates. It also suggests—given the intertwined nature of $P$ and $P_t$—that the through-the-cycle estimator can prove helpful in the specification of our mapping function, $h$. With this in mind, it would be more appropriate to write Eq. 8.44 as,

$$P_t = h\left(y_t, P\right) \equiv h\left(f(X_t), P\right), \tag{8.46}$$

to explicitly reflect the role of the through-the-cycle transition matrix in this process. It is precisely for this reason that one speaks of a through-the-cycle to point-in-time transformation.

### Upgrades and Downgrades

Another critical part of this mapping relates to the management of upgrade and downgrade probabilities. The actual probability of upgrade or downgrade is directly difficult to use. Instead, it is useful to compare the time $t$ upgrade or downgrade proportion relative to the long-term average. We thus define the following two quantities

$$\mathcal{U}_t = \frac{u_t}{\frac{1}{T}\sum_{i=1}^{T} u_i} \equiv \frac{u_t}{\bar{u}}, \tag{8.47}$$

and

$$\mathcal{D}_t = \frac{d_t}{\frac{1}{T}\sum_{i=1}^{T} d_i} \equiv \frac{d_t}{\bar{d}}, \tag{8.48}$$

for $t = 1, \ldots, T$. The are referred to as the upgrade and downgrade multipliers, respectively. On average, by construction, both Eqs. 8.47 and 8.48 are both equal to one. Their actual level, therefore, describes—for a given point in time—the multiplicative deviation from average conditions. A value of $\mathcal{D}_t = 1.5$, for example, indicates that downgrades are 50% more likely than one would expect over the long term. These two simple transformations of elements of our response-variable vector, $y_t$, turn out to be quite useful. Figure 8.15 illustrates the evolution of these multipliers over our analysis horizon. Literally by definition, these two variables move in opposite directions.

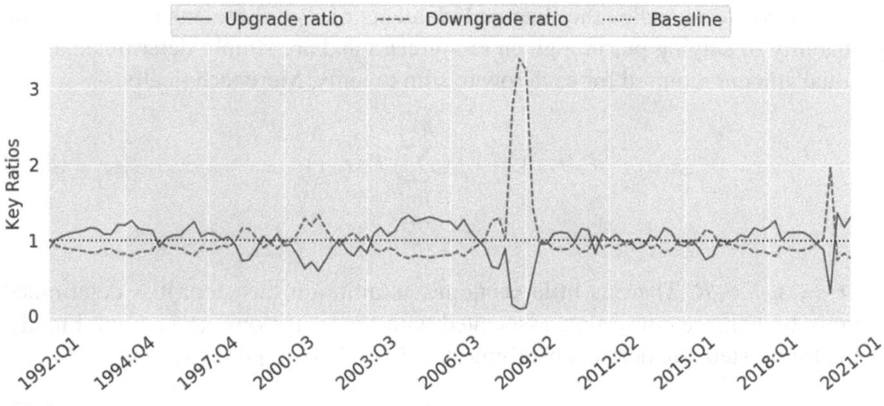


**Fig. 8.15** *Upgrade and downgrade ratios*: The upgrade and downgrade multipliers—illustrated over our data sample from 1992—were estimated using Eqs. 8.47 and 8.48. Given their contradictory nature, it is not surprising to observe that they are strongly negatively correlated.

## Building *h*

We now have all the necessary ingredients and background for the construction of $h$. It, unfortunately, does not possess a convenient functional form, but instead manifests itself as a *four*-step algorithm. In the first step, we initialize an empty matrix of dimensions $(\mathcal{R}+1) \times (\mathcal{R}+1)$ with zeros. That is,

$$P_t(r, j) = 0, \tag{8.49}$$

for $r, j = 1, \ldots, \mathcal{R}+1$. This is the object that we seek to populate. The second step concerns itself with the off-diagonal elements of the first $\mathcal{R}$ rows. These are defined as,

$$P_t(r, j) = \begin{cases} y_{r,t} : j = \mathcal{R}+1 \text{ (Default case)} \\ \mathcal{U}_t \cdot P(r, j) : j > r \text{ (Upgrade case)} \\ \mathcal{D}_t \cdot P(r, j) : j < r \text{ (Downgrade case)} \end{cases}, \tag{8.50}$$

for $r = 1, \ldots, \mathcal{R}$ and $j = 1, \ldots, \mathcal{R}+1$. This requires a bit of unpacking. Three things are happening. The default probabilities of $P_t$ are, first of all, inherited directly from the default-curve entries in $y_t$; this underscores how these quantities fall directly out of the base model. Second, the amount of through-the-cycle upgrade and downgrade probability mass is scaled by our multipliers defined in Eqs. 8.47 and 8.48. This treatment impacts all credit classes in the same manner.[58] How specifically this scaled probability mass is distributed, as a final point, is determined by the through-the-cycle transition probabilities.

[58] A higher dimensional model—at the cost of more parameters and more complexity—might attempt to model the upgrade and downgrade probabilities at the credit-rating level.

The third step handles the diagonal elements of $P_t$. These entries capture the probability of staying put in a given rating class and are simply determined as the residual amount required for each row to sum to unity. More technically,

$$P_t(r,r) = 1 - \underbrace{\sum_{j=1}^{\mathcal{R}+1}}_{j \neq r} P_t(r,j) \tag{8.51}$$

for $r = 1, \ldots, \mathcal{R}$. There is little economic intuition in this step; it is determined entirely by balance constraints associated with the transition-matrix from. Finally, in the fourth step, the default absorbing state is trivially imposed as,

$$P_t(\mathcal{R}+1, \mathcal{R}+1) = 1. \tag{8.52}$$

The final result is a legitimate point-in-time transition matrix whose structure is determined by macro-financial conditions and the through-the-cycle estimator.

Figure 8.16 provides a schematic illustrating our four-step algorithm. In particular, it graphically demonstrates the through-the-cycle to point-in-time transformation for a stylized version of the Baa2 rating category during 2009. This specific period, falling in the middle of the great financial crisis, was selected to demonstrate an extreme point-in-time transformation. Upgrade probabilities are cut almost in half, while there is a corresponding doubling of downgrade likelihood. Coupled with a precipitous increase in default probabilities, the diagonal element falls by about 5% points.

**Colour and Commentary 98** (CONSTRUCTING POINT-IN-TIME TRANSITION MATRICES): *While the various empirically motivated approaches essentially provide us with macro-financial-variable-informed (i.e., point-in-time) default-probability estimates essentially for free, more work is required to tease out a reasonably consistent associated point-in-time transition matrix. There does not exist, regrettably, any unique approach towards populating the entries of an* $(\mathcal{R}+1) \times (\mathcal{R} \times 1)$ *transition matrix with a (low-dimensional) vector of response variables. Instead, the link must rely upon economic common sense and lean upon the through-the-cycle estimator. Our proposed approach, for this collection of empirically motivated models, is a four-step algorithm with an equal number of corresponding fundamental assumptions. Default probabilities are inherited from the default-curve estimates embedded in* $y_t$*, upgrade and downgrade probability scaling factors are shared across all rating categories, the distribution of upgrade and downgrade probability mass are informed by the through-the-cycle matrix, and the diagonal elements are computed as a residual ensuring each row sums to one. Each of these basic assumptions can rightly be questioned, but*

(continued)

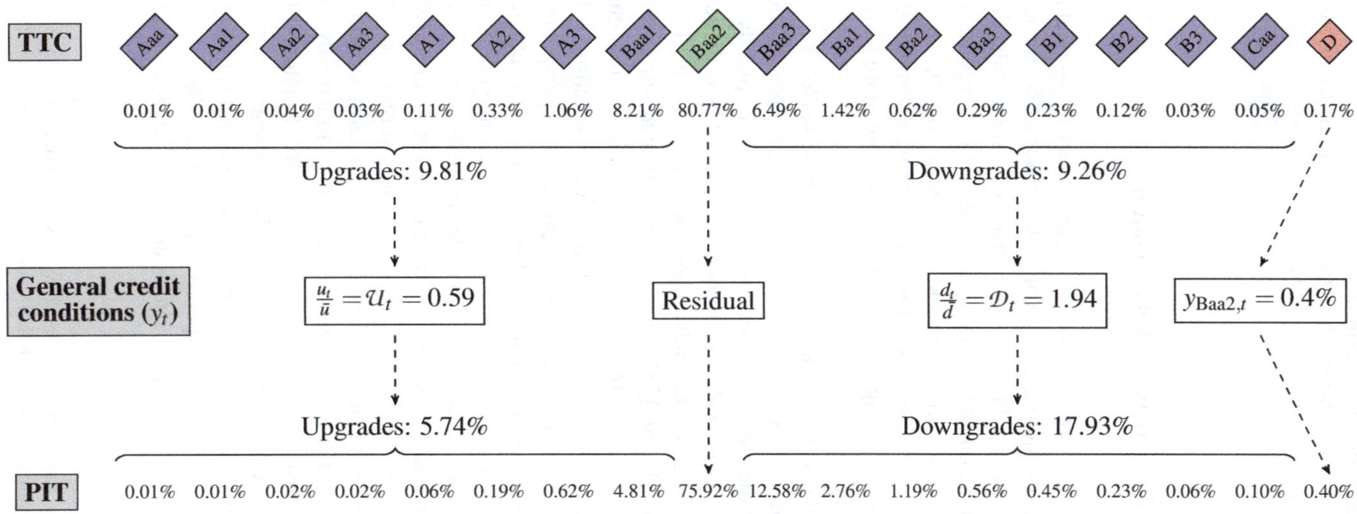


**Fig. 8.16** *Schematic h Mapping for Baa2 category*: This schematic provides a stylized description of how our $h$ mapping uses the $y_t$ general credit condition vector to transform the Baa2 row, or category, of the through-the-cycle transition matrix into a 2009 point-in-time estimator. This extreme example—occurring in the heat of the great financial crisis—illustrates how much individual transition-matrix entries can be transformed.

**Colour and Commentary 98** (continued)
*potential improvement necessitates increasing the complexity of our (already somewhat unwieldy) general credit-condition factors.*

## 8.4 A Theoretically Motivated Approach

The empirically motivated approach offers a concrete, workable—if, at times, rather heuristic—recipe for constructing a logical link between the through-the-cycle and point-in-time perspectives. The principal characters are a collection of macro-financial parameters on the one hand and a panel data set of corporate credit curves on the other. In this section, employing the same basic inputs, we will examine a more theoretically motivated approach towards building a through-the-cycle and point-in-time connection. In doing so, we will also borrow more heavily from the extant literature in this area.

Yang [49], in particular, offers a pathway to another, quite clever and interesting, approach to the problem of linking default (and migration) probabilities to macro-financial variables.[59] In the end, it turns out to be closely conceptually related to the previously considered models; both approaches, after all, address the same question with the same basic inputs. Its key advantage, however, is that it builds on the fundamental ideas from Merton [33], which have motivated our economic-capital framework (as well as many others) extensively discussed in previous chapters. Such consistency is valuable. A second key strength is a clear distinction, within a united framework, between the point-in-time and through-the-cycle perspectives.

Yang [49]'s approach is predicated on the idea of the forward default probability; by this, he is referring to what we describe in Chap. 7 as the conditional marginal (or forward) probability of default. In principle, there is nothing stopping him from working with cumulative or unconditional marginal (or forward) default probabilities; these are essentially different ways to express the same thing.[60] More generally, the model intends to describe the full term structure of default probabilities. While a laudable and sensible idea, it is practically very difficult to directly estimate. It essentially requires a time-indexed history of these term structures; such an object either does not exist or is so sparse as to be of little use. We will, however, borrow the kernel of Yang [49]'s approach for our purposes. At first we will put aside the forward perspective and consider the contemporaneous relationship between default incidence and our macro-financial variables. Once

---

[59] Related work by the same author also includes Yang [48] and Wu et al. [47]; Miu and Ozdemir [34] also looks to be a motivating influence in their work. We will borrow a number of ideas from each of these helpful publications.

[60] In other words, once you specify one of these quantities, it is straightforward to derive the others. These relationships are detailed in Chap. 7.

we've built this structure, we will then reintroduce the term structure of default probabilities from the (clearly distinguished) through-the-cycle and point-in-time perspectives. This will then allow us to confidently look forward and describe future (macro-financial-based) stress scenarios.

### 8.4.1 Familiar Terrain

Yang [49]'s model builds on the familiar Gaussian threshold model introduced by Merton [33]. Let us begin with a re-definition of the classic Gaussian latent state variable as

$$z_i(t) = \underbrace{\sqrt{\rho_i} s(t)}_{\text{Systemic}} + \underbrace{\sqrt{1-\rho_i}\epsilon_i(t)}_{\text{Idiosyncratic}} \sim \mathcal{N}(0,1), \tag{8.53}$$

for $t > 0$, $i = 1, \ldots, \mathcal{R}$ credit-rating categories, and $\rho_i \in (0,1)$.[61] We interpret the $s(t)$ as the global or systemic state variable, whereas $\{\epsilon_i(t)\}_{i=1,\ldots,\mathcal{R}}$ represents the set of idiosyncratic components. We explicitly include the current point of time, $t$, to underscore the importance of the evolution of $s(t)$.

Also consistent with the practical implementation of the Gaussian threshold model—see, for example, Vasicek [44, 45, 46]—there exists a collection of threshold values

$$\left\{ b_i(t) : i = 1, \ldots, \mathcal{R} \right\}, \tag{8.54}$$

where default occurs if

$$z_i(t) \leq b_i(t), \tag{8.55}$$

for $i = 1, \ldots, \mathcal{R}$ credit-rating classes. Over a one-period time horizon, the value of $b_i(t)$ is typically calibrated to the one-period *unconditional* default probability or $p_i(t)$. In this case, we might set

$$\begin{aligned} \mathbb{P}\left( \underbrace{z_i(t) \leq b_i(t)}_{\text{Equation 8.55}} \right) &= p_i(t), \\ \Phi(b_i(t)) &= p_i(t), \\ b_i(t) &= \Phi^{-1}(p_i(t)). \end{aligned} \tag{8.56}$$

[61] More generally, the $i$ index should apply at the risk-owner or firm level. This analysis needs, however, to operate for individual credit ratings. We can thus think of the $i$th latent variable as a representative firm from the $i$th rating class.

In the economic-capital setting, $p_i(t) \equiv p_i$ is time-homogeneous. In later discussion, we will explore a more general notion of $b_i(t)$ that nests this definition, but also captures time non-homogeneity. For the moment, for reasons that will become clear later in our investigation, we will simply use the general definition of $b_i(t)$.

This permits us to define the familiar conditional default probability as,

$$\begin{aligned} p_{i,s}(t) &= \mathbb{P}\left(z_i(t) \leq b_i(t) \middle| s(t)\right), \qquad (8.57)\\ &= \mathbb{P}\left(\underbrace{\sqrt{\rho_i}s(t) + \sqrt{1-\rho_i}\epsilon_i(t)}_{\text{Equation 8.53}} \leq b_i(t) \middle| s(t)\right), \\ &= \mathbb{P}\left(\epsilon_i(t) \leq \frac{b_i(t) - \sqrt{\rho_i}s(t)}{\sqrt{1-\rho_i}} \middle| s(t)\right), \\ &= \Phi\left(\frac{b_i(t) - \sqrt{\rho_i}s(t)}{\sqrt{1-\rho_i}}\right). \end{aligned}$$

This is another classical quantity in the threshold-model setting. It is, in fact, the mechanism for the creation of default correlation.

To reduce the clutter, Yang [49]'s defines

$$r_i = \frac{\sqrt{\rho_i}}{\sqrt{1-\rho_i}}. \qquad (8.58)$$

With a bit of algebra, we can show that $\rho_i = \frac{r_i^2}{1+r_i^2}$ and $\sqrt{1+r_i^2} = \frac{1}{\sqrt{1-\rho_i}}$. Using these results, we arrive at a new presentation of the conditional default probability from Eq. 8.57 as

$$p_{i,s}(t) = \Phi\left(\sqrt{1+r_i^2}b_i(t) - r_i s(t)\right). \qquad (8.59)$$

So far, other than slightly different notation, there is nothing particularly new. At this point, furnished with this necessary background, the unique development begins.

### *8.4.2 Yang [49]'s Contribution*

The essence of Yang [49]'s model is the role of conditionality.[62] The idea is that $p_{i,s}(t)$ denotes the point-in-time perspective. This makes sense, since it depends

[62] This point is perhaps best expressed in an early work, Yang [48].

upon the outcome of the systemic factor, $s$. To recover the through-the-cycle perspective, one needs to average over all possible outcomes of the systemic variable. That is, the through-the-cycle default probability is

$$p_i(t) = \mathbb{E}\bigg(p_{i,s}(t)\bigg) = \int p_{i,s}(t) f_s(x) dx, \tag{8.60}$$

where $f_s(\cdot)$ denotes the density function of the systemic variable, $s$. This is the unconditional default probability; we have *no* knowledge of the systemic variable's outcome. The idea is that one can use the expectation operator to toggle back and forth between the point-in-time and through-the-cycle default probabilities.[63] In an economic-capital setting, Eq. 8.59 is mostly a modelling mechanism that focuses on the interaction between systemic and idiosyncratic sources of risk. For stress-testing and loan-impairment computations, however, the accent is principally on managing the interaction between the through-the-cycle and point-in-time perspectives. Equation 8.60, while conceptually helpful, is not yet in a form that we can sensibly use for our purposes. Yang [49]'s main contribution involves building a structure to help in this regard.

This takes a few steps. First of all, the systemic variable is somewhat coarsely defined for our needs. To solve this shortcoming, a credit-condition index is introduced as

$$C(X_t) = \sum_{k=1}^{\kappa} a_k X_{k,t}, \tag{8.61}$$

where $X_{1,t}, \cdots, X_{\kappa,t}$ is our collection of $\kappa$ macro-financial scenarios.[64] Yang [49]'s credit-condition index is thus simply a (familiar) linear combination of a set of explanatory variables. This is certainly not dissimilar to Eq. 8.33 used in the previous approach.

Equation 8.61 is then used to provide a more nuanced definition of the systemic variable,

$$s(t) = -\left(\lambda \underbrace{\sum_{k=1}^{\kappa} a_k X_{k,t}}_{C(X_t)} + \sqrt{1-\lambda^2}\xi\right), \tag{8.62}$$

[63] Although to practically do this, one needs quite a bit of information: a clear description of the point-in-time default probability and the distributional characteristics of the systemic risk factor.

[64] Yang [49]'s development incorporates the normalization of the macro-financial state variables. While certainly practically important, and used in our implementation, such details add little to our conceptual understanding of the model.

where $\lambda \in (0, 1)$ and $\xi \sim \mathcal{N}(0, 1)$ is independent of the $X_t$ variables. The systemic factor is thus, itself, a combination of the macro-financial variables and an idiosyncratic component (i.e., $\xi$). The $\lambda$ coefficient essentially determines the relative importance of these two pieces. This is basically a trick to move from a one-dimensional source of systemic risk to a multi-factor setting.

Plugging this definition back into our conditional default probability from Eq. 8.59—and slightly adjusting the notion to reflect the dependence on our vector of macro-financial variables rather than the scalar, $s$—we have

$$\begin{aligned} p_{i,X}(t) &= \overbrace{\Phi\left(\sqrt{1+r_i^2}\,b_i(t) - r_i\left(\underbrace{-\left(\lambda C(X_t) + \sqrt{1-\lambda^2}\,\xi\right)}_{\text{Equation 8.62}}\right)\right)}^{\text{Equation 8.59}}, \qquad (8.63) \\ &= \Phi\left(\sqrt{1+r_i^2}\,b_i(t) + r_i\lambda C(X_t) + r_i\sqrt{1-\lambda^2}\,\xi\right). \end{aligned}$$

The result is a fairly ugly link to a broad set of components: the default threshold, the macro-financial variables, and a source of idiosyncratic systemic risk, $\xi$.

If we are to avoid Eq. 8.63 from becoming a dead-end, we need find a defensible way to eliminate $\xi$, the idiosyncratic component of the systemic variable. This can, fortunately, be achieved by exploiting an interesting property of the Gaussian distribution. Yang [49] pinched this trick from Rosen and Saunders [38], who in turn borrowed it from Kreinin and Nagi [29]. Let's first examine it in a generic setting. Define $Z \sim \mathcal{N}(0, 1)$ and $a, b \in \mathbb{R}$. The idea is to take the expectation of the cumulative distribution function of $a + bZ$. With a bit of work—which is mostly definitional—we can reveal a surprisingly elegant form. In particular,

$$\begin{aligned} \mathbb{E}\left(\Phi(a+bZ)\middle|\, Z\right) &= \mathbb{E}\left(\mathbb{P}(X \leq a+bZ)\middle|\, Z\right), \qquad (8.64) \\ &= \mathbb{E}\left(\mathbb{E}\left(\mathbb{I}_{\{X \leq a+bZ\}}\right)\middle|\, Z\right), \\ &= \underbrace{\mathbb{E}\left(\mathbb{E}\left(\mathbb{I}_{\{X-bZ \leq a\}}\middle|\, Z\right)\right)}_{\substack{\text{By the law of} \\ \text{iterated expectations}}}, \\ &= \mathbb{E}\left(\mathbb{I}_{\{X-bZ \leq a\}}\right). \end{aligned}$$

At this point, observing that $X$ and $Z$ are independent, we take note that $X - bZ \sim \mathcal{N}(0, 1 + b^2)$. Exploiting this fact, we can further simplify our previous expression as,

$$\begin{aligned}\mathbb{E}\Big(\Phi(a+bZ)\Big) &= \mathbb{E}\left(\mathbb{I}_{\left\{\frac{X-bZ}{\sqrt{1+b^2}} \leq \frac{a}{\sqrt{1+b^2}}\right\}}\right), \\ &= \mathbb{P}\left(\frac{X-bZ}{\sqrt{1+b^2}} \leq \frac{a}{\sqrt{1+b^2}}\right), \\ &= \Phi\left(\frac{a}{\sqrt{1+b^2}}\right).\end{aligned} \tag{8.65}$$

This result turns out to be quite handy.

This property of the Gaussian distribution is particularly useful in evaluating the conditional expectation of $p_{i,X}(t)$ given the idiosyncratic component of the systemic risk defined in Eq. 8.62, $\xi$. More specifically, $\xi$ plays the role of $Z$, $a = \sqrt{1 - r_i^2} b_i(t) + r_i \lambda C(X_t)$, and $b = r_i \sqrt{1 - \lambda^2}$. The consequence for Eq. 8.63 is

$$\begin{aligned}p_i(X_t) &= \mathbb{E}\left(\overbrace{\Phi\left(\underbrace{\sqrt{1+r_i^2}b_i(t) + r_i\lambda C(X_t)}_{a} + \underbrace{r_i\sqrt{1-\lambda^2}}_{b}\underbrace{\xi}_{Z}\right)}^{\text{Equation 8.63}}\right), \\ &= \Phi\left(\frac{\overbrace{\sqrt{1+r_i^2}b_i(t) + r_i\lambda C(X_t)}^{a}}{\underbrace{\sqrt{1+r_i^2(1-\lambda^2)}}_{\sqrt{1+b^2}}}\right), \\ &= \Phi\left(\frac{\sqrt{1+r_i^2}}{\sqrt{1+r_i^2(1-\lambda^2)}}b_i(t) + \frac{r_i\lambda}{\sqrt{1+r_i^2(1-\lambda^2)}}C(X_t)\right).\end{aligned} \tag{8.66}$$

Once again, there is a slight shift in notation. $p_i(X_t)$ denotes the (one-period) default probability of the $i$th credit class at time $t$ *given* the $X_t$ macro-financial vector outcome—this is the only remaining source of uncertainty. $p_{i,X}(t)$ is the same conceptual quantity, but it includes the awkward $\xi$ variable. This distinction is a subtle, but very important element of Yang [49]'s approach.

Our conditional default probability outcome is still a bit unwieldy. It can be streamlined by defining $\tilde{r}_i = \frac{r_i\lambda}{\sqrt{1+r_i^2(1-\lambda^2)}}$ and recognizing—after a bit of algebra—that $\sqrt{1+\tilde{r}_i^2} = \frac{\sqrt{1+r_i^2}}{\sqrt{1+r_i^2(1-\lambda^2)}}$. The consequence is

$$p_i(X_t) = \Phi\left(\sqrt{1+\tilde{r}_i^2}b_i(t) + \tilde{r}_i C(X_t)\right). \tag{8.67}$$

After a fair bit of development, we have arrived at a flavour of default probability that is a combination of our default threshold, $b_i(t)$, and the credit-quality index, $C(X_t)$. This is the central result.

Particularly interesting about Eq. 8.67 is that this default-probability definition is neither entirely based on the through-the-cycle nor the point-in-time perspective. It is, in fact, a bit of both. Precisely how much, it turns out, depends on the choice of $\tilde{r}_i$. This is best understood by considering extreme values of this mixing parameter, $\tilde{r}_i$. Let's begin with $\tilde{r}_i = 0$. This yields,

$$\begin{aligned} p_i(X_t) &= \Phi\left(\sqrt{1+\cancel{0^2}}b_i(t) + \cancel{0\cdot C(X_t)}\right), \quad (8.68)\\ &= \Phi\left(b_i(t)\right),\\ &= \Phi\left(\underbrace{\Phi^{-1}(p_i(t))}_{\text{Equation 8.56}}\right),\\ &= p_i(t). \end{aligned}$$

In this case, we recover the one-period through-the-cycle default probability. A value of $\tilde{r}_i = 0$ thus nests the intuitive notion of the through-the-cycle perspective as the average over all of the systemic outcomes; the point-in-time perspective disappears.

What happens, however, if we move to the other extreme and set $\tilde{r}_i = 1$? The consequence is,

$$\begin{aligned} p_i(X_t) &= \Phi\left(\sqrt{1+1^2}b_i(t) + 1\cdot C(X_t)\right), \quad (8.69)\\ &= \Phi\left(\underbrace{\sqrt{2}\cdot b_i(t)}_{a_{i,0}} + C(X_t)\right),\\ &= \Phi\left(a_{i,0} + \sum_{k=1}^{\kappa} a_k X_k\right),\\ \Phi^{-1}\left(p_i(X_t)\right) &= a_{i,0} + \sum_{k=1}^{\kappa} a_k X_k. \end{aligned}$$

In this case, the Yang [49] model can be viewed as a *probit* model of the default rate for each credit class $r = 1, \ldots, \mathcal{R}$. It is, in fact, a probit variation of the logit implementation of the first step in the empirically motivated approach in Eq. 8.33. What is slightly different is that the coefficients on the macro-financial variables are common across *all* credit categories; it is only the intercept term that varies over this dimension. Embedded in the Yang [49] model is thus an econometric specification of the point-in-time default probability. The through-the-cycle perspective does not (fully) disappear—it is embedded in our $a_{i,0}$—but it definitely slips firmly into the background.

Yang [49]'s proposed approach is thus essentially a pragmatic structure that, by the choice of $\tilde{r}_i$, allows the user to dial (or specify) the relative importance of both the through-the-cycle and point-in-time perspectives. This logic allows us to re-write the conditional probability of default—from Eq. 8.67—for the $i$th credit class given $X_t$ as

$$p_i(X_t) = \Phi\left(\underbrace{\sqrt{1+\tilde{r}_i^2}b_i(t)}_{\text{Through-the-cycle component}} + \underbrace{\tilde{r}_i C(X_t)}_{\text{Point-in-time component}}\right). \tag{8.70}$$

This idea already made an appearance in our previous discussion. In contrast to its implicit form identified in the empirically motivated setting, here it arises explicitly.

Equation 8.70 is, it bears repeating, Yang [49]'s principal contribution. It is a parsimonious, conceptually elegant, theoretically motivated, and pragmatic description of the default probability as a combination of both through-the-cycle and point-in-time perspectives. We will exploit this idea to build a practical link between macro-financial shocks and the future term structure of default probabilities.

**Colour and Commentary 99** (A THEORETICAL STRUCTURE): *Exploiting the basic structure of Merton [33]'s threshold model along with a few clever twists, Yang [49] offers a description of the contemporaneous (conditional) default probability as an explicit combination of the through-the-cycle and point-in-time perspectives. Unlike the use of the threshold-approach in our economic capital model, which was principally interested in capturing the distinction between systemic and idiosyncratic risk, Yang [49]'s proposal thus decomposes the default probability by time conditionality. This distinct separation is not only conceptually attractive, it also significantly aids in model interpretation and implementation. The through-the-cycle component is linked back to long-term unconditional default probabilities already addressed in Chap. 7, whereas the point-in-time contribution depends upon*

(continued)

**Colour and Commentary 99** (continued)
*a set of macro-financial variables. Both pieces can be derived from different, albeit related, sources.*

### 8.4.3 Adding Time

This structure also allows one, as will become clear in a moment, to naturally incorporate the time horizon into our analysis. So far, we have implicitly considered a one-period (i.e., one month or quarter or year) time horizon. We need—to build a usable stress-scenario model—to look one, two, 10, or even 40 years into the future. Our proposed approach, which is a slight variation (indeed, simplification) of Yang [49]'s proposal, has the following restatement of Eq. 8.67:

$$p_i(X_{t+\tau}) = \Phi\left(\sqrt{1+\tilde{r}_{i,\tau}^2}\, b_i(t+\tau) + \tilde{r}_{i,\tau} C(X_{t+\tau})\right), \tag{8.71}$$

for $\tau = 1, \ldots, T$ periods into the future and $i = 1, \ldots, \mathcal{R}$. This is a characterization, at time $t$, of the full term structure of default probabilities over the coming $T$ time periods. We have added a time subscript to the $\tilde{r}_i \equiv \tilde{r}_{i,\tau}$ parameters; this will turn out to be rather important.

Before proceeding to the practical details of making this expression actually work, we need to again reflect a bit on the value of macro-financial information.[65] The simple fact is that it degrades over time. At time $t$, given $X_t$, we are fully in the point-of-time perspective. Setting $\tau = 1$, we still lean strongly toward a point-in-time probability, but our estimate will rely on a forecast of $X_{t+\tau}$. Every step into the future leads to a degradation in the accuracy of our macro-financial forecasts. At some point, after some unknown number of periods, we need to admit that any macro-financial forecast has no value. The best we can do, in this case, is to use the long-term unconditional average macro-financial outcomes; such a forecast, however, is no forecast at all. This, in turn, should conceptually bring us back to the through-the-cycle perspective.

This natural deterioration in the value of information has important practical implications. Making this more precise, it implies a mathematical restriction something like:

$$\lim_{\tau \to \bar{\tau}} p_i(X_{t+\tau}) = p_i(t+\bar{\tau}), \tag{8.72}$$

[65] Or, indeed, information more generally.

where $p_i(t+\tau)$ denotes the $\tau$th period's through-the-cycle default probability for the $i$th credit class and $\bar{\tau}$ is some (unknown) number of steps into the future. In other words, as $\tau$ gets large, and our ability to forecast future outcomes worsens, we converge back to the through-the-cycle perspective. We can think of $\bar{\tau}$ as the finite threshold beyond which current information has lost its value.

The simplest way to accomplish this involves the use of the $\tilde{r}_{i,\tau}$ parameter. This value, after all, determines the relative importance of the point-in-time and through the cycle perspectives. Mechanically, we propose operationalizing the previous limit as,

$$\lim_{\tau \to \bar{\tau}} \tilde{r}_{i,\tau} = 0. \tag{8.73}$$

This is simply a more formal way to state that, as we move forward in time, we converge to the through-the-cycle perspective. Taking a step further, if we generalize Eq. 8.56 such that

$$b_i(t+\tau) = \Phi^{-1}(p_i(t+\tau)), \tag{8.74}$$

then Eq. 8.73 directly implies Eq. 8.72. This structure has the conceptual benefit of nesting our through-the-cycle term structure of default probability model. Recall, from Chap. 7, that we employ the time-nonhomogeneous Markov chain model suggested by Bluhm and Overbeck [3] for this task. The set of through-the-cycle values

$$\left\{ b_i(t+\tau) : \tau = 1, \ldots, T \right\}, \tag{8.75}$$

for $i = 1, \ldots, \mathcal{R}$ are thus readily available.

To actually implement this model, therefore, one basically needs a short list of ingredients:

- an initial set of $\tilde{r}_i(t+1)$ parameters determining the starting weights on the point-in-time and through-the-cycle perspectives;
- an estimate of the common $a_1, \ldots, a_\kappa$ macro-financial loadings;
- some (presumably expert-judgement-determined) estimate of $\bar{\tau}$; and
- a (again, probably heuristic) description for the nature of convergence of the $\tilde{r}_i$ coefficients towards zero at time $\bar{\tau}$.

The first two elements can be determined through statistical estimation, whereas the latter two choices are based on a combination of assumption, expert judgement, and common sense.

### 8.4.4 Parameter Estimation

To employ our variation of Yang [49]'s method, we will need to use our macro-financial and default data sets to determine the necessary parameters. Unlike the empirically motivated approach, however, we will not make use of constrained least-squares estimates. Instead, borrowing heavily from Yang [49], we employ the method of maximum likelihood in *two* separate stages. While this estimation strategy is a bit more involved, it also permits a slightly more fundamental treatment of our data.

There are *three* main elements that require estimation: the through-the-cycle and the point-in-time descriptions as well as the relative weight of the two viewpoints. A description of each is essential for every rating class. The through-the-cycle element is captured by the $b_i$ parameters; these are readily estimated and, indeed, even ultimately replaced with our own through-the-cycle model in the final implementation. The point-in-time dimension relates to the $a_k$ parameters, or macro-financial loadings. Finally, the $\tilde{r}_i$'s—which we will also refer to as the point-in-time weights—determine the relative importance of these two central perspectives.[66] It turns out, however, that simultaneous estimation of the factor loadings and point-in-time weights is not particularly effective. To resolve this, a two-step procedure is employed. In the first step, we use a rough approximation of the point-in-time weights and focus principally on the factor loadings (i.e., the $a_k$'s). At the second step, with already determined and fixed factor loadings, we then proceed to estimate the point-in-time weights (i.e., $\tilde{r}_i$'s). A few intermediate parameters show up along the way to facilitate this process.

To understand precisely how this works, we need to introduce some notation and establish a few basic facts. We will, as in the previous derivation of the Yang [49] model, let $i \in \{1, \ldots, \mathcal{R}\}$ denote the credit state and $t \in \{1, \ldots, T\}$ represent the various time steps over our data horizon. For each $i$ and $t$, we observe—within our Moody's data—$N_{i,t}$ firms and $d_{i,t}$ defaults. This is a slightly new twist on our data. To link back to our previous discussion—in Eqs. 8.6 and 8.7, for example—the combination of these quantities leads us to the individual default-curve entries. In particular,

$$c_{i,t} = \frac{d_{i,t}}{N_{i,t}}, \tag{8.76}$$

for $i = 1, \ldots, \mathcal{R}$ and $t = 1, \ldots, T$. The number of firms and default incidences in each period are thus essentially the building blocks underlying our default curves.

[66] We could also refer to these as the through-the-cycle weights, of course, since they describe both aspects. Loosely speaking, we can think of these as being roughly equivalent to the systemic-weight parameters in a threshold credit-risk economic-capital model.

The core idea of maximum likelihood is to find the set of parameters that *maximize* the probability of having observed one's data.[67] To get a handle on this probability, however, one needs a clear idea of how one's data is distributed. In our case, this is fortunately rather well understood. The probability of observing $d_{i,t}$ defaults among $N_{i,t}$ firms follows a binomial distribution with density function,

$$f_t^{(k)}\left(d_{i,t}, N_{i,t} \middle| \theta^{(k)}, X_t\right) = \binom{N_{i,t}}{d_{i,t}} \underbrace{p_i^{(k)}(\theta^{(k)}, X_t)}_{p}{}^{d_{i,t}} \left(1 - \underbrace{p_i^{(k)}(\theta^{(k)}, X_t)}_{p}\right)^{N_{i,t}-d_{i,t}}, \tag{8.77}$$

where $p_i^{(k)}(\theta^{(k)}, X_t)$ and $\theta^{(k)}$ denote the default probability (i.e., binomial parameter, $p$) and parameter vector associated with the $k$th step of the estimation algorithm, respectively. Under the assumption of conditional independence[68] between each rating class and time period, the complete joint density function—again, at the $k$th step—is written as

$$\prod_{t=1}^{T}\prod_{i=1}^{\mathcal{R}} f_t^{(k)}\left(d_{i,t}, N_{i,t} \middle| \theta^{(k)}, X_t\right). \tag{8.78}$$

The trick is simply to find the parameter set, $\theta^{(k)}$, that maximizes this joint density function.

## Preparation

In the initial set-up, before we actually get to the first step, we fix values for the through-the-cycle (i.e., the $b_i$'s) and intermediate point-in-time weight (i.e., $r_i$) parameters. The intuitive through-the-cycle coefficients are quite sensibly defined as,

$$\hat{b}_i = \Phi^{-1}\left(\frac{1}{T}\sum_{t=1}^{T}\frac{d_{i,t}}{N_{i,t}}\right), \tag{8.79}$$

for $i = 1, \ldots, \mathcal{R}$. This is nothing other than the long-term, unconditional average default rate for each credit-rating class. The first-step point-in-time weight locks in the initial importance of the systemic factors. It is defined in Eq. 8.58 as a function

[67] For much more on this concept, the reader is referred to Pawitan [37].

[68] Within the threshold model, default is *not* independent; this would ignore the critically important notion of default dependence. Given, or conditional on, the realization of the systemic-risk factor, however, they are independent. This is what we mean by conditional independence.

of the threshold model asset-correlation parameters. We fix it as,

$$\hat{r}_i = \frac{\sqrt{\hat{\rho}\left(\Phi(\hat{b}_i)\right)}}{\sqrt{1-\hat{\rho}\left(\Phi(\hat{b}_i)\right)}}, \tag{8.80}$$

using the Basel IRB guidance where $\hat{p}_i = \Phi(\hat{b}_i)$, from Eq. 8.79, is a long-term default probability estimate.[69] Again, these are mostly a placeholder—or rather rough first-order approximation—permitting us to focus our initial attention on the factor loadings. In the second step, we will have the opportunity to sharpen these values.

### The First Step

In the first step, as already discussed, we seek to estimate the $\lambda$ and $a_1, \ldots, a_\kappa$ macro-financial factor loading parameters. This leads us to define the binomial default probability with the following functional form:

$$p_i^{(1)}\left(\theta^{(1)}, X_t\right) = \Phi\left(\sqrt{1+\hat{r}_i^2}\hat{b}_i + \lambda\hat{r}_i\sum_{j=1}^{\kappa} a_j X_{j,t}\right), \tag{8.83}$$

implying that

$$\theta^{(1)} = \left[\lambda \; a_1 \; \cdots \; a_\kappa\right]. \tag{8.84}$$

The first-step default probability is essentially a restriction of the full-blown definition derived in Eq. 8.70. All the pieces are basically in place, but not all are yet permitted to vary. Moreover, the intermediate $\lambda$—which will not appear in the final result—is present to scale the point-in-time importance.

---

[69] This is discussed in rather more detail in Chap. 11. For completeness, each $\rho(p_i)$ is approximated as,

$$\hat{\rho}(\hat{p}_i) \approx \rho^- q(\hat{p}_i) + \rho^+\left(1 - q(\hat{p}_i)\right), \tag{8.81}$$

where

$$q(\hat{p}_i) = \frac{1 - e^{h\hat{p}_i}}{1 - e^h}, \tag{8.82}$$

and $h$ is a weighting parameter. The value $q(p_i)$ is confined to the unit interval, which ensures the asset-correlation coefficient lies in the interval, $\rho(p_i) \in [\rho^-, \rho^+] = [0.12, 0.24]$.

Using Eq. 8.78 to build the log-likelihood function associated with the $k$th step, we have

$$\mathcal{L}^{(k)}\left(\theta^{(k)}\right) = \ln\left(\underbrace{\prod_{t=1}^{T}\prod_{i=1}^{\mathcal{R}} f_t^{(k)}\left(d_{i,t}, N_{i,t} \middle| \theta^{(k)}, X_t\right)}_{\text{Equation 8.78}}\right), \tag{8.85}$$

$$= \sum_{t=1}^{T}\sum_{i=1}^{\mathcal{R}} \ln\left(\underbrace{\binom{N_{i,t}}{k_{i,t}} p_i^{(k)}(\theta^{(k)}, X_t)^{d_{i,t}} \left(1 - p_i^{(k)}(\theta^{(k)}, X_t)\right)^{N_{i,t}-d_{i,t}}}_{\text{Equation 8.77}}\right),$$

$$= \sum_{t=1}^{T}\sum_{i=1}^{\mathcal{R}} \Bigg[\cancel{\ln\binom{N_{i,t}}{k_{i,t}}} + d_{i,t}\cdot\ln\left(p_i^{(k)}(\theta^{(k)}, X_t)\right)$$

$$+ \left(N_{i,t} - d_{i,t}\right)\ln\left(1 - p_i^{(k)}(\theta^{(k)}, X_t)\right)\Bigg],$$

$$= \sum_{t=1}^{T}\sum_{i=1}^{\mathcal{R}} d_{i,t}\cdot\ln\left(p_i^{(k)}(\theta^{(k)}, X_t)\right)$$

$$+ \left(N_{i,t} - d_{i,t}\right)\ln\left(1 - p_i^{(k)}(\theta^{(k)}, X_t)\right),$$

where, by convention, we eliminate any constant terms since they do not impact the final optimization results.

The desired parameters for the first step in our procedure are estimated by solving a numerical optimization problem of this form:

$$\hat{\theta}^{(1)} = \arg\max_{\theta^{(1)}} \mathcal{L}^{(1)}\left(\theta^{(1)}\right), \tag{8.86}$$

subject to:

$$\lambda \in [0, 1].$$

To recap, therefore, given the through-the-cycle and point-in-time weights, the macro-financial factors are identified in this first step. Since we can also think of the $\lambda$ parameter as simultaneously determining the relative importance of the point-in-time component, we can see that the initial (fixed) choices of $\hat{r}_i$ are not terribly important. The $\lambda$ coefficient does this, however, in a fairly crude manner by treating all of the credit classes in an identical fashion. Indeed, all of the parameters in the first stage operate only at the global level; they do not make any distinctions between the individual rating classes. The second stage takes the opposite tack; the global parameters are fixed and it focuses on the distinctions between rating categories.

When working with maximum-likelihood estimators, a useful diagnostic is the so-called partial-likelihood function. Given a particular starting value, one first solves the non-linear optimization problem in Eq. 8.86.[70] Working from this optimal solution, we then select the first parameter (i.e., $a_1$). Holding all other parameters fixed, we then proceed to consider how the log-likelihood changes as we systematically change the value of $a_1$. Since we are already at the optimum, it should naturally get worse. An encouraging result would involve a tent-like (i.e., quadratic) function centred around our final $\hat{a}_1$ estimate. The steeper the tent, the happier we will be. We then reset $a_1$ back to its original (optimized) value and move to $a_2$. This is repeated sequentially for all of our $a_k$ parameter values. Disarmingly simple, this is essentially a trick for visualizing—something that would otherwise be impossible—the properties of our high-dimension log-likelihood surface.

The results of this exercise are summarized in Fig. 8.17. Output, unemployment, non-fuel commodities, equity and oil prices, and the VIX index all exhibit encouraging behaviour. These parameter estimates are rather sharp; indeed, the greater the curvature around the maximum of our (partial) likelihood function, the higher the implied level of parameter certainty.[71] The desired parabolic form is also evident for credit spreads and the US yield-curve slope, but the form is much flatter implying rather less conviction about our parameter values. The Fed funds rate parameter is convincingly negative, but rather flat from roughly -50 onwards. Finally, inflation does not appear, in this setting at least, to exert a strong impact on general credit conditions. To conclude, the overall first-step, factor-loading $a_k$ parameters look fairly sensible, but before putting this model into actual production, an explanatory variable selection process is required.

### 8.4.5 The Second Step

Having determined the factor loading parameters (i.e., the $a_k$'s), the final step turns its attention to the point-in-time weights. We already have the basic form of the log-likelihood function, we need only describe the form of the default probability. It is

---

[70] Our starting point is selected from the best objective function associated with several thousand randomly generated $\theta^{(1)}$ parameter vectors. Virtually all non-linear optimization algorithms perform better when launched with a good first guess.

[71] When the log-likelihood function is well-behaved with a quadratic form (i.e., regular), the square-root of the (negative) inverse of the diagonal of the Hessian (i.e., second-derivative) matrix of the likelihood function evaluated at its maximum, $\hat{\theta}$, is a sensible estimate of the asymptotic, estimation-error. The so-called Cramér-Rao bound holds that this quantity is actually a lower bound for the (unknown) variance of our maximum-likelihood estimator. There is, of course, rather more to the story and the interested reader is referred to DasGupta [9, Chapter 16], Held and Bové [20] or Pawitan [37, Chapter 8] for additional generality, much more rigour, and technical details.

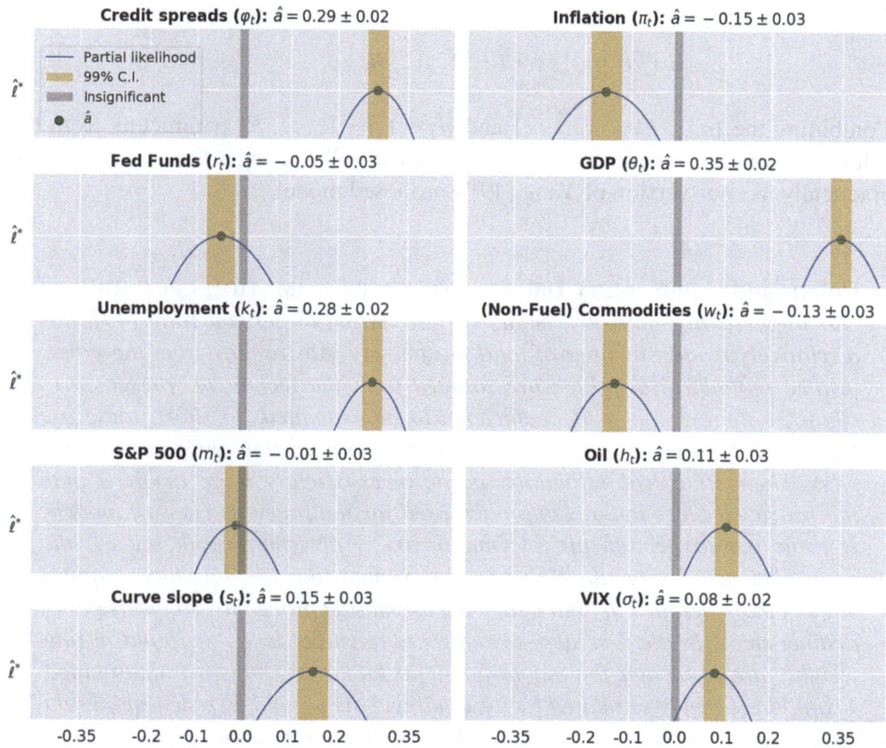


**Fig. 8.17** *Factor-weight partial likelihoods*: These graphics illustrate the partial likelihoods associated with our $\kappa$ distinct factor-weight parameters (i.e., $a_k$ for $k = 1, \ldots \kappa$) in the Yang [49] model. Most parameters appear to be well-identified (and regular), whereas question marks arise for a few others.

given as,

$$p_i^{(2)}\left(\theta^{(2)}, X_t\right) = \Phi\left(\sqrt{1+\tilde{r}_i^2}\hat{b}_i + \tilde{r}_i \sum_{j=1}^{\kappa} a_j X_{j,t}\right), \tag{8.87}$$

where

$$\theta^{(2)} = \left[\tilde{r}_1 \cdots \tilde{r}_{\mathcal{R}}\right]. \tag{8.88}$$

The $\lambda$ parameter, having done its job, is eliminated. The factor loadings are also fixed at their estimated values from the previous step. The only remaining moving part stems from the credit-rating specific point-in-time weights. This leads to the second-step optimization problem,

$$\hat{\theta}^{(2)} = \arg\max_{\theta^{(2)}} \mathcal{L}^{(2)}\left(\theta^{(2)}\right), \tag{8.89}$$

subject to:

$$\tilde{r}_i \in [0, 1] \text{ for } i = 1, \ldots, \mathcal{R}.$$

Combining the $\{a_k : k = 1, \ldots \kappa\}$ and $\{\tilde{r}_i : i = 1, \ldots, \mathcal{R}\}$ parameters from the solutions to Eqs. 8.86 and 8.89 provides us with all the ingredients necessary to practically use our version of Yang [49]'s proposed model.

**Colour and Commentary 100** (A TWO-STEP ESTIMATION PROCEDURE): *Our theoretically motivated model variant, based largely on Yang [49], has a relatively modest number of total parameters. Abstracting from the point-in-time probabilities—which are sourced from the techniques presented in Chap. 7—there are $\kappa + \mathcal{R}$ coefficients to be estimated. In short, these are the factor loadings (i.e., the $a_k$'s) and the point-in-time weights (i.e., the $\tilde{r}_i$'s). Their statistical estimation is, however, slightly more involved than the restricted least-squares approach used for the previous class of models. It turns out to be difficult to simultaneously determine both the $a_k$ and $\tilde{r}_i$ coefficients. Using the method of maximum likelihood—which requires slightly more detailed default data—the estimation procedure proceeds in two distinct steps. In the first step, working at the global level, the point-in-time weights are fixed and the macro-financial factor loadings are determined. Fixing these newly estimated factor loadings, the second step determines the credit-rating level point-in-time weights. A few intermediate parameters, that do not survive to the end of the estimation method, facilitate this process.*

### 8.4.6 To a Point-in-Time Transition Matrix

Unlike the empirically motivated set of models, the construction of a point-in-time transition matrix is readily performed within Yang [49]'s framework. Under the assumption that the macro-financial factor loading and point-in-time weight parameters from the previous method can be used more broadly across the entire transition matrix, the extension is rather straightforward. We could also, if we so desire, update our two-step maximum-likelihood estimator by moving from the binomial to the multinomial distribution. This would incorporate both the default and transition outcomes into the overall estimation procedure. The actual logic, involved in the construction of point-in-time transition matrices, would nonetheless remain the same. It would only lead to a change in the parameter estimates.

The actual model-related transition probability construction begins with a twist on Eq. 8.70, by defining the $ij$th transition probability as

$$p_{ij}(X_t) = \Phi\left(\underbrace{\sqrt{1+\tilde{r}_i^2}P_{ij}}_{\substack{\text{Through-the-}\\\text{cycle component}}} + \underbrace{\tilde{r}_i C(X_t)}_{\substack{\text{Point-}\\\text{in-time}\\\text{component}}}\right). \tag{8.90}$$

where $P_{ij}$ represents the $ij$th through-the-cycle transition probability. The consequence is a very intuitive explicit link between our vector of macro-financial variables and the transition matrix.

Since we will inevitably be looking several steps into the future, we also need to incorporate the time dimension into our construction. Generalizing Eq. 8.71 and combining it with Eq. 8.90, we arrive at

$$p_{ij}(X_{t+\tau}) = \Phi\left(\sqrt{1+\tilde{r}_{i,\tau}^2}P_{ij} + \tilde{r}_{i,\tau} C(X_{t+\tau})\right), \tag{8.91}$$

for $\tau = 1, \ldots, T$ where, as before, $\tilde{r}_{i,\tau} \rightarrow 0$ and $\tau \rightarrow \bar{\tau}$. This slight adjustment ensures a certain degree of time consistency in our construction.

Given the commonality of the factor-loading parameters across all transition probabilities and the inherent monotonicity in the through-the-cycle estimates, the monotonic nature of the transition matrix is preserved. To ensure that the final result remains a true transition matrix, however, some (slight) rescaling is typically necessary. We use the following rather obvious approach:

$$\hat{p}_{ij}(X_{t+\tau}) = \frac{p_{ij}(X_{t+\tau})}{\sum_{i=1}^{\mathcal{R}+1} p_{ij}(X_{t+\tau})}, \tag{8.92}$$

for $\tau = 1, \ldots, T$. In short, therefore, establishment of a point-in-time transition matrix follows almost directly from the default case.

## 8.5 Constructing Default-Stress Scenarios

In this final section, we will attempt to pull the previous discussion together and illustrate the practical construction of some default-probability stress scenarios.[72]

[72] We'll return to the transition matrix perspective in Chap. 12, when we consider stress testing.

The main objective is to set the stage for the loan-impairment discussion in Chap. 9. No new tools or objects require introduction. All of the necessary elements are already in place. The principal aspect of discussion centres, once again, around the role of time and information. As with the various mappings between macro-financial variables and credit conditions, there are no hard and fast rules. Our approach is consequently logic- and assumption-based with an important element of pragmatism.

**Colour and Commentary 101** (FORECAST OR SCENARIO?): *A word on terminology might be helpful. To this point, we've been fairly loose on the distinction between a forecast and a scenario. While there is some logical overlap, they are not entirely synonymous.*[a] *A bit of structure is required. Imagine you are working with some random process—it could be an exchange rate or the temperature in your hometown or something else entirely—and have some (hopefully reasonable) description of how it moves through time.*[b] *Given its inherent uncertainty, there is a broad (possibly infinite) range of future sample paths that it might take over the coming days, weeks, or months. Each possible sample path can be viewed as a scenario. A scenario is thus a single possible sequence of time-indexed outcomes, which may (or may not) be viewed as probable. Conversely, a forecast is typically considered to be one's best guess regarding the future values of this process. It could be determined as the most likely outcome—in an expected value sense—or it might be a guess.*[c] *Forecasting, in normal English language speech, also implies looking into the future. From this perspective, both a scenario and a forecast can easily get confounded. To minimize confusion, we'll try to use the (more formal) term* scenario *for a specific (typically extreme) sample path and employ* forecast *to describe the act of looking into the future.*

[a] There is not, in the spirit of full disclosure, complete agreement on their precise difference. Huss [21], for the curious reader, appears to be one of the first academic works addressing the idea of scenario analysis.

[b] This could be in the form of a stochastic differential equation, a transition density, or reduced-form statistical model.

[c] A (potentially quite poor) forecast can be constructed with little or no information; although, when done well, forecasting can be very complex. Identifying a scenario (typically) requires a more extensive understanding of the full range of possible outcomes and their probabilities. Scenario construction is thus (almost) always a more formal activity.

Stress-testing analysis is typically performed at the current point of time, which also coincides with the end of our data set. We will denote this as $T$. The decay of information value over time is hard to assess, but this question also depends on the nature of analysis we are performing. For a classical stress-testing exercise, the time horizon is probably only two or three years. In this case, our forecasting and analysis horizons probably coincide; *forecasting*, in this sense, refers to the time period over which forward-looking scenarios are produced. That is, we likely produce (more or less) sensible macro-financial scenarios for this period and use them—through our previously discussed channels—to construct associated point-in-time (default and transition) probabilities.

In loan-impairment analysis, however, the story is a bit different. In this setting, we typically require forward-looking estimates (i.e., scenario-conditional forecasts) of cumulative and conditional forward-default probabilities for 20+ years into the future. No self-respecting macroeconomist or financial-market practitioner would construct forecasts for such a horizon.[73] As we've seen, common sense argues that, after a certain amount of time, our best-guess future scenarios would converge to our long-term, unconditional, through-the-cycle estimates.[74]

We thus have a difference between the forecasting horizon for our macro-financial scenarios and the analysis period required for our loan-impairment application. Conceptually, to manage this situation, we will break out analysis period into *three* sections: a forecasting, a convergence, and a final through-the-cycle period. The first forecasting period directly maps our macro-financial scenarios into our desired default probabilities. In the convergence period, as the name suggests, our required values slowly converge back to the through-the-cycle estimates. In the final period, our future default probability estimates correspond to our through-the-cycle values.

Let's begin with the forecasting period, which we will denote as $\tau_p$ units of time.[75] In this analysis, given our data, the unit of time is one quarter (i.e., 3 months). Moreover, the specific setting using in our loan-impairment analysis is $\tau_p = 12$ quarters or three years. Again to link up better with the loan-impairment calculation, three different scenario viewpoints are employed: baseline, upside, and downside.[76] The idea with such an approach is to cover a broad range of outcomes and avoid over-weighting a particular (either positive or negative) perspective. Figure 8.18 displays the time-series history and a set of (home-made) mid-2021 scenarios for the main macro-financial variables used in our implementation.[77] We can think of

---

[73] For an enlightening discussion of techniques from a real-world, forecasting practitioner, see Silver [40].

[74] This should not be taken to mean that we should expect this to actually occur. It simply implies that, sufficiently far into the future, there is no grounds for an alternative supposition due to lack of information.

[75] The $p$ is intended to represent *prediction*. It could be denominated in years, quarters, or months depending on the specific situation.

[76] Using the previously introduced ideas, the baseline is conceptually close to a *forecast*. The upside and downside sample paths should be viewed as *scenarios*.

[77] The upside and downside scenarios are simply $\pm$ one standard deviation movements around a fairly benign (vector-autoregressive model constructed) baseline. The actual sign of the shocks is determined from the individual $\hat{\lambda}$ parameters. These invented (and non-professional) scenarios are generally sensible, but should not be taken very seriously. For actual applications, these scenarios are produced by serious financial forecasters.

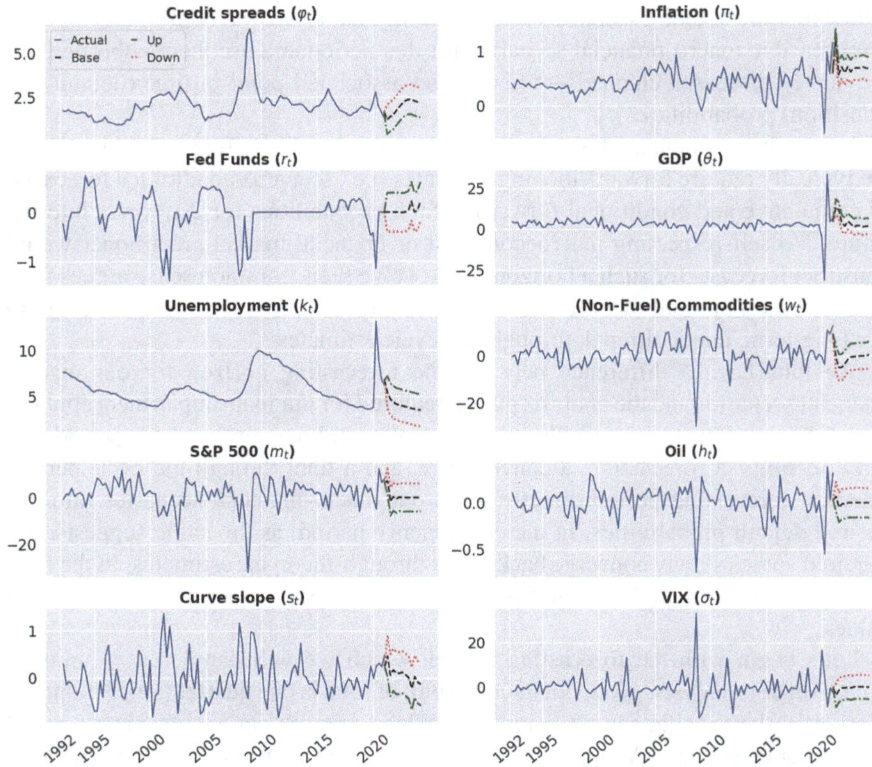


**Fig. 8.18** *Macro-financial scenarios*: These graphics provide the history of our macro-financial variables along with 12 quarters (i.e., three years) of (essentially fabricated) predicted values. A baseline, upside, and downside scenario is provided for each explanatory variable.

the results in Fig. 8.18, in a general sense, as being

$$\left\{ \hat{X}_t \; : \; t = T + 1, \ldots, T + \tau_p \right\}. \tag{8.93}$$

These scenarios could be purchased, produced in-house, drawn from thin air, or downloaded from some disreputable internet site.[78] However procured, these form the backbone of one's stress scenarios.

The macro-financial scenarios then—through one of the various empirically and theoretically motivated mappings illustrated in previous sections—directly permit the determination of our general credit-condition response variables. Figure 8.19 displays a selection of associated credit-condition scenarios derived from the values presented in Fig. 8.18. Here we see the credit-cycle index and the $\zeta_1$

[78] One might even draw them from the state-space transition equation presented in Eq. 8.43.

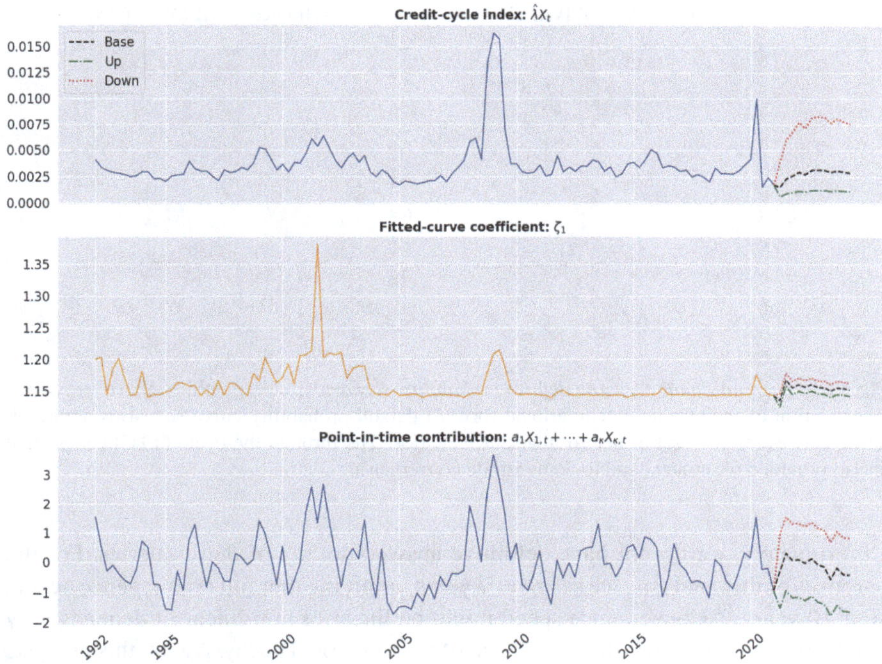


**Fig. 8.19** *Response-variable scenarios*: Conditioning on the macro-financial scenarios presented in Fig. 8.18, the preceding graphics illustrate a selection of the corresponding general credit-condition scenarios. These quantities, as discussed in the previous sections, directly contribute to the construction of time-varying default probabilities.

dimension-reducing variable from the empirically motivated setting. The point-in-time contribution from our variation of Yang [49]'s model is also presented.

Interestingly, the various driving state variables from Fig. 8.19 digest the macro-financial scenarios in different ways. Although we need to be somewhat cautious, given different scales, the credit-cycle index appears to treat the downside and upside in an asymmetric manner, while the other approaches are rather more symmetric. The overall dispersion in outcomes also varies. This is not necessarily bad—multiplicity of perspective is valuable—but it needs to be clearly understood.

If the term of one's analysis exceeds $\tau_p$, then additional complications arise. Let us define the convergence period as $\tau_c$ units of time. After $\tau_p + \tau_c$ periods, therefore, we expect a full convergence of scenarios back to the through-the-cycle case. The idea of convergence—as conceptually defensible as it might seem—raises *three* difficult, if not almost unanswerable, questions:

1. How long is the convergence period?
2. At what speed does convergence occur?
3. What specific quantity should be used to impose the convergence?

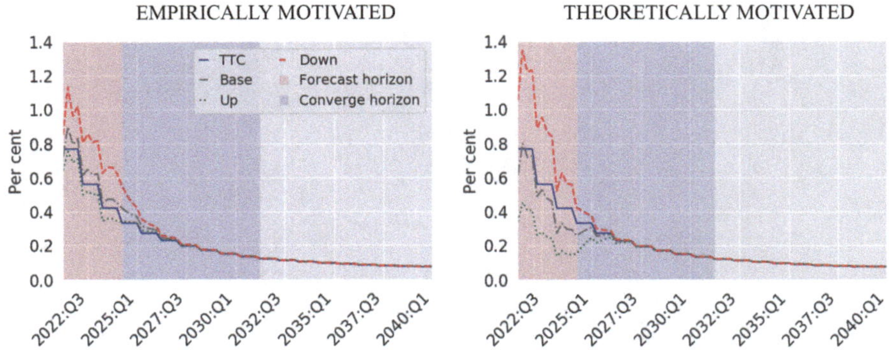


**Fig. 8.20** *Unconditional forward default-probability scenarios*: The graphics above provide a visualization of the average unconditional forward default-probability curve scenarios across all rating classes for each set of macro-financial scenarios. The through-the-cycle (TTC) perspective is also provided for context and to demonstrate convergence.

Unfortunately, we do not have definitive answers to any of these queries. For the purposes of this analysis, we set $\tau_c = 7$ years, implying that full convergence occurs after 10 years.[79] Convergence speed might be linear or non-linear; it depends very much on one's view regarding the speed of informational decay. Again, this analysis assumes a relatively fast non-linear speed of convergence.

Depending on the specific choice of model, we have slightly different answers to the third question. In the empirically motivated setting, convergence is imposed directly upon the marginal default probabilities estimated within the model. Our theoretically motivated approach encapsulates the time convergence element, as already discussed, through changes in the point-in-time weight coefficients (i.e., the $\tilde{r}_i$'s). In both cases, however, convergence is based on the idea that the value of information decays exponentially.[80] While we have no concrete justification for this choice in our setting, Olariu et al. [36] and Yu and Placide [50] are interesting (and generally supportive) examples of assessing the time value of information in rather different settings.

Figure 8.20—which illustrates the average default outcomes across all rating categories for each of our three scenarios—is computed in two steps. First, the point-in-time default probabilities are used to construct the unconditional forward

[79] Other than it being a nice round figure, this choice is difficult to defend.

[80] A simple exponential decay model is used. In particular, the convergence weight is defined as

$$\omega(t) = 1 - a \cdot (1 - b)^t, \tag{8.94}$$

for $t \geq 0$ where $a = 1$ is the starting point, and $b = 0.25$ is the rate of decay. The choice of $b$ parameter is not estimated, but simply chosen as a reasonably pragmatic value.

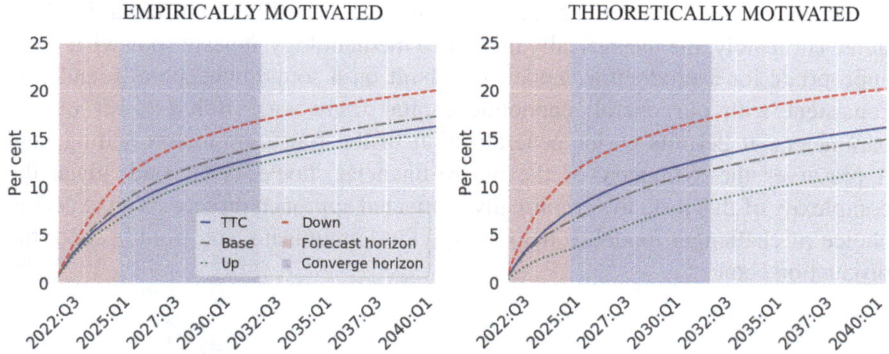


**Fig. 8.21** *Cumulative default-probability scenarios*: The graphics above display the average cumulative default-probability curve scenarios across all rating classes for each set of macro-financial scenarios—these outcomes are directly derived from the results in Fig. 8.20. Once again, the through-the-cycle (TTC) perspective is included to ease interpretation.

default probabilities for each credit class out to period $\tau_p$.[81] In the second step, a gradual convergence is imposed assuming the exponential decay of information value of time. After $\tau_p + \tau_c$ periods, the through-the-cycle term structures dominate the remainder of the time horizon.

The selected empirically motivated approach is based upon the reduced-form Diebold and Li [12] motivated model introduced in Eq. 8.38. While the three models introduced in this class provide broadly similar results, the fitted-curve dimension reduction technique generates the most reasonable results. It is nevertheless rather striking to examine the differences in average default probability implications across the empirically and theoretically motivated approaches. Yang [49]'s proposal, in particular, implies a rather wider dispersion of outcomes relative to the alternative specification.

Figure 8.21 provides, for comparison purposes, associated cumulative default probabilities. In many ways, the cumulative perspective is easier to visually interpret. Again, the differences in the two approaches are quite apparent. The empirical downside probabilities are somewhat less conservative than the theoretical equivalents. Moreover, in the empirical setting, the baseline scenario is slightly higher than the through-the-cycle case; the opposite occurs in Yang [49]'s model. Finally, asymmetry in treatment of the upside and downside scenarios is quite apparent in the empirically motivated estimates.

It is not terribly helpful to attempt to determine which of these two perspectives is closest to the absolute truth. Using the same basic inputs, but rather different fundamental assumptions, these two lanes of analysis provide qualitatively similar

[81] We could also easily compute, and display, the conditional forward default probabilities. As we'll see in Chap. 9, however, the unconditional version is the quantity of interest for loan-impairment computations.

results. When one scratches a bit, however, they do have slightly different implications. Ultimately, the theoretically motivated methodology appears somewhat more appropriate for a production model. It is built on a sound conceptual foundation consistent with our overall economic capital framework, it has fewer overall parameters, it permits easier generalization to the transition-matrix setting, and it preserves the symmetry of the macro-financial shocks. That said, given the complexity of this task, the empirically motivated approach represents an excellent choice of challenger model to help interpret, communicate, and trouble-shoot the production choice.

**Colour and Commentary 102** (STRESS-SCENARIO CONSTRUCTION)*: The mechanics of forecasting—after the complexity of building the framework—are blissfully straightforward. One buys, builds, invents, begs, or steals a set of macro-financial scenarios. Conditional on these scenarios—and one's choice of mapping to the model's response variables—an associated prediction of general credit conditions is produced. These general credit conditions—with aid of one's mapping—lead to a sequence of point-in-time default probabilities. If one's horizon of analysis exceeds the forecasting horizon for the macro-financial variables, then some additional—and generally indefensible—convergence assumptions are required. Sooner or later, of course, informational value decays and convergence between the point-in-time and through-the-cycle perspectives is inevitable.*[a] *Having examined multiple models in the preceding development, it is also time to make some decisions. Given its theoretical footing, parsimony, and more sensible outputs, the nod goes to our variation on Yang [49]'s model as a production choice. The empirically motivated approach, borrowing from the fundamental ideas introduced by Diebold and Li [12], offers a rather sensible challenger model. Significant practical legwork nevertheless remains—in the form of explanatory variable selection, detailed sensitivity analysis, and out-of-sample back-testing—before one can actually put either proposed model into daily production.*

[a] The timing and speed of this convergence is, however, entirely debatable.

## 8.6 Wrapping Up

The mission of this chapter was to provide a framework for incorporating macro-financial information into our description of general credit conditions and, by extension, default and transition probabilities. The utility of such a link arises from a consequent ability to investigate the impact of shocks or perturbations to our macro-financial variables upon various dimensions of portfolio risk. Such a capability is the very nucleus of stress testing. It is not, unfortunately, a trivial undertaking. Construction of this framework is plagued with issues of data sparsity, representativeness, and dimensionality. The proposed solution is a collection of transformations, approximations, and possible statistical descriptions to permit a manageable degree of model robustness and pragmatism. The resulting structure is both reasonable and defensible, but, to be continuously useful, requires ongoing oversight and challenge from key stakeholders. The next chapter immediately employs these ideas within the context of the loan-impairment calculation. Stress scenarios will also make another appearance in Chap. 12 as we turn to consider a range of stress-testing techniques.

## References


1. S. Aguais, L. R. F. Jr, M. King, M. C. Lennnon, and B. Lordkipanidze. Designing and Implementing a Basel II Compliant PIT-TTC Ratings Framework. MPRA Paper No. 6902, January 2008.
2. R. Bellman. *Adaptive Control Processes: A Guided Tour*. Princeton University Press, 1961.
3. C. Bluhm and L. Overbeck. Calibration of PD Term Structures: to be Markov or not to be. *Risk*, 20(11):98–103, November 2007.
4. D. J. Bolder. Affine Term-Structure Models: Theory and Implementation. Bank of Canada: Working Paper 2001-15, October 2001.
5. D. J. Bolder. *Fixed Income Portfolio Analytics: A Practical Guide to Implementing, Monitoring and Understanding Fixed-Income Portfolios*. Springer, Heidelberg, Germany, 2015.
6. D. J. Bolder. Statistics and Machine-Learning: Variations on a Theme. In P. Nymand-Andersen, editor, *Data Science in Economics and Finance for Decision Makers*. Risk Books, 2021.
7. D. J. Bolder and S. Gusba. Exponentials, Polynomials, and Fourier Series: More Yield Curve Modelling at the Bank of Canada. Bank of Canada: Working Paper 2002-29, October 2002.
8. L. Breiman. Statistical Modeling: The Two Cultures. *Statistical Science*, 16(3):199–231, 2001.
9. A. DasGupta. *Asymptotic Theory of Statistics and Probability*. Springer-Verlag, New York, 2008.
10. H. F. Davis. *Fourier Series and Orthogonal Functions*. Dover Publications, 1989.
11. D. A. Dickey and W. A. Fuller. Distribution of the estimators for autoregressive time series with a unit root. *Journal of the American Statistical Association*, 74(366):427–431, 1979.
12. F. X. Diebold and C. Li. Forecasting the term structure of government bond yields. University of Pennsylvania Working Paper, 2003.
13. F. X. Diebold and G. D. Rudebusch. *Yield Curve Modeling and Forecasting: The Dynamic Nelson-Siegel Approach*. Princeton University Press, Princeton, New Jersey, 2013.
14. M. Fisher, D. Nychka, and D. Zervos. Fitting the term structure of interest rates with smoothing splines. U.S. Federal Reserve Board Working Paper, 1994.
15. G. H. Golub and C. F. V. Loan. *Matrix Computations*. The John Hopkins University Press, Baltimore, Maryland, 2012.
16. P. S. Hagan and G. West. Interpolation methods for curve construction. *Applied Mathematical Finance*, 13(2):89–129, 2006.
17. J. D. Hamilton. *Time Series Analysis*. Princeton University Press, Princeton, New Jersey, 1994.
18. A. C. Harvey. *Forecasting, Structural Time Series Models and the Kalman Filter*. Cambridge University Press, Cambridge, first edition, 1990.
19. T. Hastie, R. Tibshirani, and J. Friedman. *The Elements of Statistical Learning: Data Mining, Inference and Prediction*. Springer-Verlag, New York, first edition, 2001.

20. L. Held and D. S. Bové. *Applied Statistical Inference*. Springer-Verlag, Berlin, Germany, 2014.
21. W. R. Huss. A move toward scenario analysis. *International Journal of Forecasting*, 4(3): 377–388, 1988.
22. G. James, D. Witten, T. Hastie, and R. Tibshirani. *An Introduction to Statistical Learning*. Springer-Verlag, New York, first edition, 2013.
23. J. James and N. Webber. *Interest-Rate Modelling*. John Wiley & Sons, Ltd, West Sussex, England, 2000.
24. N. L. Johnson, S. Kotz, and N. Balakrishnan. *Continuous Univariate Distributions: Volume 2*. John Wiley and Sons, New York, NY, 1997. Wiley Series in Probability and Statistics.
25. I. T. Jollliffe. *Principal Component Analysis*. Springer, New York, New York, 2002.
26. G. G. Judge, W. Griffiths, R. C. Hill, H. Lütkepohl, and T.-C. Lee. *The Theory and Practice of Econometrics*. John Wiley and Sons, New York, New York, second edition, 1985.
27. C.-J. Kim and C. R. Nelson. *State-Space Models with Regime Switching*. The MIT Press, Cambridge, Massachusetts, 1999.
28. S. J. Koopman and A. Lucas. Business and Default Cycles for Credit Risk. Tinbergen Institute Discussion Paper, 2003.
29. A. Kreinin and A. Nagi. Calibration of the default probability model. *European Journal of Operational Research*, 185(3):1462–1476, 2004.
30. B. Li, E. DeWetering, G. Lucas, R. Brenner, and A. Shapiro. Merrill lynch exponential spline model. Merrill Lynch Working Paper, 2001.
31. R. Litterman and J. Scheinkman. Common factors affecting bond returns. *The Journal of Fixed Income*, 1:54–61, 1991.
32. Merriam-Webster. *Webster's Ninth New Collegiate Dictionary*. Merriam-Webster, 9th edition, 1991.
33. R. Merton. On the pricing of corporate debt: The risk structure of interest rates. *Journal of Finance*, 29:449–470, 1974.
34. P. Miu and B. Ozdemir. Stress-Testing Probability of Default and Migration Rate with respect to Basel II Requirements. Technical report, DeGroote School of Business, McMaster University, October 2008.
35. C. R. Nelson and A. F. Siegel. Parsimonious modeling of yield curves. *Journal of Business*, 60:473–489, 1987.
36. S. Olariu, S. Mohrehkesh, X. Wang, and M. Weigle. On aggregating information in actor networks. *ACM SIGMOBILE Mobile Computing and Communications Review*, 18:85–96, February 2014.
37. Y. Pawitan. *In All Likelihood: Statistical Modelling and Inference Using Likelihood*. Clarendon Press, Oxford, 2001.
38. D. Rosen and D. Saunders. Analytical Methods for Hedging Systemic Credit Risk with Linear Factor Portfolios. Technical report, Fields Institute for Research in Mathematical Sciences, November 2006.
39. G. S. Shea. Interest rate term structure estimation with exponential splines: A note. *The Journal of Finance*, 40:319–325, 1985.
40. N. Silver. *The Signal and the Noise: Why So Many Predictions Fail, But Some Don't*. Penguin Publishing Group, 2012.
41. S&P. 2019 Annual Global Corporate Default And RatingTransition Study. Technical report, S&P Global Ratings, April 2020.
42. J. H. Stock and M. W. Watson. Twenty years of time series econometrics in ten pictures. *Journal of Economic Perspectives*, 31(2):59–86, May 2017.
43. O. Vasicek. An equilibrium characterization of the term structure. *Journal of Financial Economics*, 5:177–188, November 1977.
44. O. A. Vasicek. Probability of loss on loan distribution. KMV Corporation, February 1987.
45. O. A. Vasicek. Limiting loan loss probability distribution. KMV Corporation, August 1991.
46. O. A. Vasicek. The distribution of loan portfolio value. *Risk*, (12):160–162, December 2002.

47. B. Wu, B. H. Yang, K. Cui, Z. Du, and G. Fei. IFRS9 Expected Credit Loss Estimation: Advanced Models for Estimating Portfolio Loss and Weighting Scenario Losses. MPRA Paper 93634, University Library of Munich, Germany, April 2019.
48. B. H. Yang. Modeling Systemic Risk and Point-in-Time Probability of Default under the Vasicek Asymptotic Single Risk Factor Model Framework. MPRA Paper 59025, University Library of Munich, Germany, March 2014.
49. B. H. Yang. Point-in-time PD term structure models for multi-period scenario loss projection: Methodologies and implementations for IFRS 9 ECL and CCAR stress testing. MPRA Paper 76271, University Library of Munich, Germany, January 2017.
50. L. Yu and M. Placide. Information decay in building predictive models using temporal data. *Journal of Software*, 7(2):479–484, 2012.

# Chapter 9
# Computing Loan Impairments

*The general who wins a battle makes many calculations in his temple before the battle is fought. The general who loses a battle makes but few calculations beforehand.*

*(Tzu [26], The Art of War)*

When a financial institution issues a loan or purchases a fixed-income security, they are accepting a certain degree of credit and market risk. This uncertainty is necessarily incorporated into the pricing associated with these instruments. The general rule is the greater the risk, the lower the price and, thus, the higher the associated yield (or margin). In financial theory, as discussed in previous chapters, this pricing notion has been extensively formalized.[1] The price, or value, of any security is its expected value taken with respect to the equivalent martingale, or pricing, measure. Evaluating such an expectation—which can, at times, be quite analytically or computationally heavy—involves consideration of the interaction between individual cash-flows and the joint distribution of underlying (credit and market) risk factors. In short, although it can be a complicated business, we know quite a bit about pricing financial assets.

The larger point is that compensated, or priced, risk—associated with loans, bonds, swaps, or deposits—is intimately related to expected future outcomes. These expectations, in tandem with market prices, naturally move over time in response to general economic and firm-specific conditions. This explains the mechanics associated with daily changes in asset-portfolio valuations. There is nothing new in these ideas; these are very high-level financial concepts. Such general principles do motivate, however, much of the accounting treatment associated with financial instruments. Exactly how, and to what precise end, is useful to understand.

The accounting practice faces a few unique challenges in the treatment of financial instruments. Most importantly, it needs to ensure that the financial-instrument asset values found in financial statements provide a fair representation

[1] See, for example, Harrison and Kreps [19], Harrison and Pliska [20], or Duffie [9] for the key entry points into this theory.

 
D. Bolder, *Modelling Economic Capital*, Contributions to Finance and Accounting,
https://doi.org/10.1007/978-3-030-95096-5_9

of their true worth. Moreover, changes in these asset values need to be appropriately reflected in profit-and-loss outcomes. For instruments traded regularly in liquid financial markets, this is a reasonably straightforward task. The strong, third-party arm's length market signal of associated asset values can be used to inform the appropriate balance-sheet values.[2] Even this case can be confused by complexities in pricing or the specific role of the security. Some financial instruments, to be more specific, are naturally linked. A swap, for example, might be used to hedge a bond or loan exposure. The area of hedge accounting attempts to capture these interactions.

Another serious complication—and the main focus of this chapter—relates to instruments not traded in financial secondary markets. Absent the ability to directly apply market prices or risk-factor changes, informing financial valuations becomes a *much* less obvious undertaking. A loan asset—which is a critical object for any lending institution—is a posterchild for such instruments. Loans are typically represented on the balance sheet at amortized cost. In other words, the balance-sheet value is a deterministic function of time and initial conditions. It does not react to stochastic market outcomes. Since one expects to hold these loans to maturity, changes in market risk factors—such as interest rates—can generally be safely ignored. The same is *not* true for credit quality. Some accounting mechanism is required to capture both the initial and time-varying aspect of financial instruments held at amortized cost. It is simply unfair to ignore this dimension when reporting asset values in one's balance sheet.

Into this breach enters the loan-impairment calculation. A loan impairment, in its simplest form, is an estimate of the instrument's expected credit loss or, to use the popular acronym, ECL. Deducting the impairment amount from a loan's amortized cost provides an approximation of its credit-risk-adjusted value or net carrying value; the sum across all positions provides a view of the overall loan book. The loan-impairment computation is performed periodically and any changes flow through the income statement. Loan impairments, in a nutshell, represent the accountant's solution to the unresponsiveness of amortized-cost balance-sheet values to changes in creditworthiness. The net-asset-value perspective is also a very useful metric for managing one's lending portfolio.

While the conceptual and practical utility of loan impairments are clear, the specifics of how this quantity should be computed are rather less so. The impairment of financial instruments is handled in various ways by different standard setters. The International Accounting Standards Board (IASB) employs International Financial Reporting Standard (IFRS) 9 for this purpose.[3] The American Financial Accounting Standards Board (FASB) guidance regarding loan impairments, conversely, is found in the Current Expected Credit Loss (CECL) standard. Both standards are relatively new and incorporate significant changes to the traditional approach to loan impair-

[2] Market prices happily incorporate both market- and credit-risk effects. An interest-rate movement, a credit-spread change, or a rating transition—each stemming from rather diverse sources of risk—will immediately (in their own way) impact the instrument's market price.

[3] See, for example, EY [14, 15].

ments; the implications for the banking community have been significant. Many of the adjustments stem from shortcomings in previous practice that became evident—like so many aspects in current financial markets—during and after the great financial crisis of 2008 to 2010. Shocking amounts of ink have correspondingly been dedicated to the discussion of both standards and their respective development paths.[4] NIB, as a European-based international financial institution, follows IASB's IFRS 9 standard.

This chapter focuses on the specifics associated with the loan-impairment computation. While accounting practice colours much of the discussion, this is not an accounting document. It is, instead, written from the perspective of a quantitative risk manager. It is reasonable to ask: why risk management? Despite their differences, IFRS 9 and CECL both require the incorporation of forward-looking information into the loan-impairment computation. This is new. This seemingly innocuous change in perspective (generally) necessitates the use of advanced statistical techniques and dramatically increases the complexity of this area.[5] Risk-management staff in many institutions, already traditionally accustomed to use of such tools, have naturally found themselves recruited to assist with this task.[6]

**Colour and Commentary 103** (ANALYTIC PERSPECTIVE)*: It is a very good idea, when discussing loan-impairment calculations, to clearly and loudly announce one's analytic perspective. In recent years—due to (generally welcome and sensible) revisions in loan-impairment accounting standards—there has been a significant increase in complexity. It has thus become common for both accountants* and *risk-management professionals to be involved in this area. Very often, however, neither one has the full picture. Quantitative risk professionals are typically well positioned to opine on the underlying statistical and mathematical techniques, but often experience difficulties with the underlying accounting principles. Accountants face the opposite challenge. By declaring one's perspective, it helpfully forewarns one's interlocutor of one's potential strengths and weaknesses. Following this advice, therefore, we formally proclaim our (quantitative) risk-management perspective in this chapter. The reader is now free to appropriately adjust her expectations regarding the ensuing development and discussion.*

---

[4] Gornjak [17] provides a concise overview of the standard and a useful description of the existing literature.

[5] Chapters 7 and 8 have already illustrated the depth and complexity associated with one of the key inputs to this computation: forward-looking, point-in-time, scenario-based default probabilities.

[6] ECL is also part of the supervisory remit given its importance for the management of credit risk, which further explains the inclusion of both accounting and risk-management perspectives. The difference with IFRS 9, in the author's view at least, is the complexity of the base computation.

## 9.1 The Calculation

It is educational to take a constructive approach to the expected-loss calculation. We could simply write out the final formula, but it would not provide much insight. Without a bit of context, it is actually a somewhat confusing computation. A sensible starting point involves deriving a reasonably general definition of expected credit loss. This is, after all, the quantity that any self-respecting loan-impairment calculation is attempting to approximate. The actual application required by a specific accounting standard will invariably be a special case or variation of this general structure. A first-principle definition will nevertheless help us understand where we are coming from and—in most cases—can assist in judging the reasonableness of specific guidance.

Equipped with a general definition, we can proceed to pose a range of practical questions. These include:

1. PROBABILITY MEASURE: What probability measure should we employ for the evaluations of future expected outcomes?
2. MANAGING EXPOSURE: Do we work with cash-flows or exposures and does it make any difference?
3. TIME INCREMENTS: If we manage financial instruments by their exposures, how do we consistently manage the time dimension?
4. DEFAULT-PROBABILITY CHOICE: Which flavour of default probability is required in our computations?
5. DISCOUNTING: How do we determine the discount rate used to manage the time value of money?
6. INCORPORATING SCENARIOS: How does the forward-looking element—constructed in Chap. 8—enter into the overall calculation?

The reader may be left scratching her head at some of the preceding queries, but answering them in an organized (if not necessarily sequential) fashion will lead us to the final expected-credit loss definition. To the best of the author's knowledge, such a formalistic approach to the derivation of the expected-credit loss methodology has never been performed. While its technical nature may dismay some stakeholders, hopefully it will also appeal to (and stimulate discussion among) quantitative practitioners working in this area. To make things as concrete as possible, we will also introduce a fictitious, but realistic, practical example.

### *9.1.1 Defining Credit Loss*

The good news is that vast majority of mathematical machinery needed to attack the idea of expected credit loss has already been introduced in previous chapters. The most obvious starting point is to extend the ideas from our credit-risk economic capital model. Let's restate the default event as $\mathcal{D}_i$ and represent it in the following generic manner:

$$\mathbb{I}_{\mathcal{D}_i} = \begin{cases} 1 : \text{Default} \\ 0 : \text{Survival} \end{cases}, \tag{9.1}$$

for the $i$th exposure in one's asset portfolio. Default is a binary outcome; you either find yourself in default or you don't. This makes it ideally represented in indicator-variable form as in Eq. 9.1. The actual default loss has the familiar form,

$$L_i = \mathbb{I}_{\mathcal{D}_i} c_i \gamma_i, \tag{9.2}$$

where, as before, $c_i$ and $\gamma_i$ denote the $i$th exposure-at-default and loss-given default of the $i$th asset, respectively.

Equation 9.2 permits, in principle, the direct evaluation of expected credit losses. While convenient, it is missing an important element: it is absent any direct description of time. All three quantities in Eq. 9.2 can, at least in principle, be expected to vary over time. This dimension is consequently also quite interesting for practical computations.

In the economic-capital setting—and, more particularly, in our threshold-based model—the time dimension enters into the default indicator introduced in Eq. 9.1 as

$$\mathbb{I}_{\mathcal{D}_i(t,T)} \equiv \mathbb{I}_{\{y_i(t,T) \leq \mathcal{X}^{-1}(p_i(t,T))\}} = \begin{cases} 1 : y_i(t,T) \leq \mathcal{X}^{-1}\Big(p_i(t,T)\Big) \\ 0 : y_i(t,T) > \mathcal{X}^{-1}\Big(p_i(t,T)\Big) \end{cases}, \tag{9.3}$$

where $y_i(t,T)$ is an $\mathcal{X}$-distributed random variable describing $i$th firm's creditworthiness and $p_i(t,T)$ is the associated probability of default.[7] Both quantities are defined over the time interval $(t,T]$. In other words, if the realization of a creditworthiness state variable falls below a certain pre-defined threshold—which is a function of the firm's probability of default—over the interval $(t,T]$, then default occurs.

The economic-capital-motivated development, while useful and consistent with our overall framework, is likely to confuse things. The accounting guidance is rather more general in nature and makes no reference to specific model implementations. An alternative, more empirically motivated, approach is warranted. In the context of loan pricing, we defined the default event as a random time, $\tau$. This seems a bit

[7] In our production model, as described in Chap. 2, the generally defined $\mathcal{X}$ is a univariate $t$ distribution with $\nu$ degrees of freedom.

more appropriate for this setting. Using this idea, we may redefine Eq. 9.3 as

$$\mathbb{I}_{\mathcal{D}_i(t,T)} \equiv \mathbb{I}_{\{t<\tau_i\leq T\}} = \begin{cases} 1 : \tau_i \in (t,T] \\ 0 : \tau_i > T \end{cases}. \tag{9.4}$$

In this case, the $i$th default time (i.e., $\tau_i$) depends directly on the characteristics of the $i$th obligor; unlike Eq. 9.3, it does not pass through a structurally defined creditworthiness factor. This latter definition, given its broader generality, is probably more useful for the loan-impairment problem.[8]

Using Eq. 9.4, we may rewrite the credit loss associated with the $i$th credit obligor as,

$$L_i(t,T) = \mathbb{I}_{\{t<\tau_i\leq T\}} c_i(t,T)\gamma_i(t,T). \tag{9.5}$$

To permit full generality, we have also written the exposure and loss-given-default values as functions of time. It remains to be seen if these quantities will be stochastic or deterministic. For the moment, in the interests of a general treatment, let us imagine that they are random. To permit a more convenient evaluation of the expectation of Eq. 9.5, we will nonetheless assume that the default event, exposure-at-default, and loss-given-default are all statistically independent quantities.[9]

Before we can proceed to actually evaluate the expectation of Eq. 9.5, there is one final element to consider. Do we wish to examine the credit loss in present or future value terms? This question is actually quite important. Since $t$ denotes the current point in time, then virtually by construction, any default event will occur after $t$. If we wish to measure the magnitude of these future events, it will be necessary to discount them back to time $t$. Adding a stochastic discount rate into Eq. 9.5 leads to

$$L_{t,i}(t,T) = \underbrace{\mathbb{I}_{\{t<\tau_i\leq T\}} c_i(t,T)\gamma_i(t,T)}_{\text{Eq. 9.5}} e^{-\int_t^T r_u du}, \tag{9.6}$$

where $r_t$ denotes the stochastic instantaneous interest rate. A few points are worth addressing. We've added a $t$ subscript to the credit-loss quantity to underscore its anchoring to the current point in time. A second issue relates to how this quantity is connected to the discount rate. Will it yield a risk-free rate or will risk preferences be embedded into the outcome? This will ultimately depend on our choice of probability measure. The interaction between these two quantities—the default

[8] This is not to say, however, that Eqs. 9.3 and 9.4 are somehow inconsistent with one another. It is better to think of them as structural and reduced-form representations of the same phenomena.

[9] This is unfortunately not, strictly speaking, true. Altman et al. [1] address the relationship between default and recovery. In counterparty risk, there are a variety of potential interactions between default and exposure; see Gregory [18] for an excellent introduction to these questions. We'll come back to this question in Chap. 10.

event and the discount factor—also, as we will soon see, reveals some interesting relationships.

### 9.1.2 Selecting a Probability Measure

We have all the necessary ingredients for the evaluation of the expectation of Eq. 9.6. The expectation, however, needs to be taken with respect to a particular choice of probability measure. This brings us to our first question: what is the correct choice? Should we use the pricing measure, $\mathbb{Q}$, or the physical probability measure, $\mathbb{P}$? An argument could be made in either direction. The use of $\mathbb{Q}$ would generate a valuation, or pricing, loss. This result would be comparable to the impact associated with a fair-value adjustment inferred from financial-market prices. Employment of $\mathbb{P}$, however, would be more consistent with a risk-management perspective. To the best of our knowledge, the accounting standards do not provide any direct guidance on this question.

When in doubt, it makes sense to try both. Let us begin with taking conditional expectations of Eq. 9.6 with respect to the equivalent martingale measure induced with the money-market account as choice of numeraire,

$$\begin{aligned} \mathbb{E}_t^{\mathbb{Q}}\bigg(L_{t,i}(t,T)\bigg) &= \mathbb{E}_t^{\mathbb{Q}}\bigg(\mathbb{I}_{\{t<\tau_i\leq T\}}c_i(t,T)\gamma_i(t,T)e^{-\int_t^T r_u du}\bigg), \\ &= \mathbb{Q}\left(t<\tau_i\leq T\right)\cdot\bar{c}_i(t,T)\cdot\bar{\gamma}_i(t,T)\cdot\delta(t,T), \end{aligned} \tag{9.7}$$

where $\bar{c}$ and $\bar{\gamma}$ are the average exposure and loss-given-default values on the interval, $(t, T]$.[10] $\delta(t, T)$ is the risk-free pure-discount bond price, or discount function, for maturity $T$. Implicit in this development, it should be stressed, is the independence of the default event and the evolution of the instantaneous short rate.[11]

Equation 9.7 is very intuitive. The product $\bar{c}\cdot\bar{\gamma}$ describes the magnitude of the loss in the event of default. $\mathbb{Q}(t < \tau_i \leq T)$ modifies this value by the probability of default occurrence and $\delta(t, T)$ brings the entire amount back into present-value terms.

It is helpful to recall that the default probability is simply one less the survival probability or more technically,

$$\begin{aligned} \mathbb{Q}\left(t<\tau_i\leq T\right) &= 1-\mathbb{Q}(\tau_i>T), \\ &= 1-S_i(t,T). \end{aligned} \tag{9.8}$$

[10] Note that $\mathbb{E}_t^{\mathbb{Q}}(\cdot)$ is shorthand for $\mathbb{E}^{\mathbb{Q}}(\cdot|\mathcal{F}_t)$; for notational convenience and readability, we suppress the $\sigma$-algebra. It is still, however, present in the background.

[11] Duffie and Singleton [10] would, very rightly, contest this assumption.

This simple fact provides some welcome insight into our final result. Plugging this value back into Eq. 9.7 and simplifying, generates

$$\begin{aligned}\mathbb{E}_t^{\mathbb{Q}}\Big(L_{t,i}(t,T)\Big) &= \underbrace{\Big(1 - S_i(t,T)\Big)}_{\mathbb{Q}(t<\tau_i\leq T)} \cdot \bar{c}_i(t,T)\cdot\bar{\gamma}_i(t,T)\cdot\delta(t,T), \qquad (9.9)\\ &= \bar{c}_i(t,T)\cdot\bar{\gamma}_i(t,T)\cdot\left(\delta(t,T) - \underbrace{S_i(t,T)\delta(t,T)}_{\tilde{\delta}_i(t,T)}\right),\\ &= \bar{c}_i(t,T)\cdot\bar{\gamma}_i(t,T)\cdot\underbrace{\Big(\delta(t,T) - \tilde{\delta}_i(t,T)\Big)}_{\substack{\text{Difference between}\\ \text{risk-free and risky}\\ \text{discount factors}}}.\end{aligned}$$

This is not a typical representation of default losses, but it is nonetheless informative. If the instrument is risk-free, then $\delta(t,T) \equiv \tilde{\delta}_i(t,T)$ and the expected credit loss vanishes. In all other cases, $\delta(t,T) > \tilde{\delta}_i(t,T)$ implying a positive expected credit loss. Moreover, the greater the probability of default, the lower the survival probability and consequently, the larger the expected credit loss. Practically, the distance between the risk-free and risky discount functions (i.e., $\delta(t,T) - \tilde{\delta}_i(t,T)$) could be inferred from bond or credit default-swap spreads. This quantity is, after all, a present-valued adjusted risk-neutral default probability.

Changing tactics, we may also readily compute the expectation of Eq. 9.6 with respect to the real-world, or physical, probability measure. The result is

$$\begin{aligned}\mathbb{E}_t^{\mathbb{P}}\Big(L_{t,i}(t,T)\Big) &= \mathbb{E}_t^{\mathbb{P}}\Big(\mathbb{I}_{\{t<\tau_i\leq T\}}c_i(t,T)\gamma_i(t,T)e^{-\int_t^T r_u du}\Big), \qquad (9.10)\\ &= \mathbb{P}(t<\tau_i\leq T)\cdot\bar{c}_i(t,T)\cdot\bar{\gamma}_i(t,T)\cdot\mathbb{E}_t^{\mathbb{P}}\Big(e^{-\int_t^T r_u du}\Big),\\ &= p_i(t,T)\cdot\bar{c}_i(t,T)\cdot\bar{\gamma}_i(t,T)\cdot\hat{\delta}_i(t,T),\end{aligned}$$

where, as in previous chapters, $p_i(t,T)$ denotes the cumulative default probability of the $i$th credit obligor over the interval $(t,T]$. The principal difficulty of this formulation relates to the interest-rate element. In particular, the $\mathbb{P}$-expectation of the path associated with the instantaneous interest rate does not reduce to the risk-free discount factor.[12] $\hat{\delta}_i(t,T)$ is, consequently, not readily determined. The appropriate discount rate would need, in principle at least, to be estimated through

[12] The difference relates to risk preferences. The $\mathbb{P}$-dynamics of $r_t$ cannot be uniquely specified; see Björk [5, Chapter 16] or Bolder [7] for more detail. In interest-rate theory, this issue is closely linked to the so-called market price of risk.

an econometric, time-series model. This is consistent with the cumulative default probability values, which must also be determined in a similar fashion.

**Colour and Commentary 104** (CHOOSING A PROBABILITY MEASURE): *The discounted credit loss is a fairly intuitive function of* four *components: the default event, asset exposure, loss-given-default, and the path of future interest rates. Transforming this quantity into an expected value, however, requires a choice. One must decide under what probability measure to take the expectation. This is not merely a theoretical choice. It has important implications for how one computes key calculation inputs and the overall magnitude of one's estimates. Use of the pricing measure, $\mathbb{Q}$, allows one to infer risk-neutral default probabilities from market data and discount directly with risk-free interest rates. Application of the physical measure, $\mathbb{P}$, requires use of an econometric technique to determine real-world default probabilities and discount factors. The former case involves calibration, while the latter requires statistical estimation. A final point, which should not be ignored, is the size of the corresponding credit-loss expectation. Risk-neutral default probabilities are typically significantly higher than their real-world equivalents; use of the $\mathbb{Q}$ measure will thus result in a systemically higher estimate of expected default losses. Whatever the choice, one point is clear: one cannot cherrypick elements from both perspectives in one's expected-loss calculation. Put succinctly, one has to pick a lane.*

The final choice of probability measure must ultimately come from the accounting guidance. The $\mathbb{Q}$-measure values are, conceptually at least, much closer to the market-price adjustments associated with fair-valued balance-sheet assets. This would seem to argue for evaluation of Eq. 9.6 with the pricing measure. The IFRS 9 standard is nonetheless extremely clear about the need for loan-impairment computations to incorporate a forward-looking viewpoint. This manifests itself through the incorporation of—internal or external—macro-financial scenarios into one's default probability inputs.[13] Indeed, the entire related distinction—discussed at length in previous chapters—between *through-the-cycle* and *point-in-time* perspectives has no obvious meaning in the risk-neutral setting. This brings us firmly into the domain of statistical estimation and, by logical extension, the physical probability measure. Although the accounting standard—and associated literature—does not speak to the probability measure question explicitly, the choice is implicitly driven by the underlying requirements. Some effort will nonetheless be required to identify a sensible discount rate under the physical probability measure.

[13] We have, in fact, already dedicated the entirety of Chap. 8 to the details of how one might construct such a statistical relationship.

### 9.1.3 Managing the Time Horizon

Each loan has its own cash-flow profile. Some are bullet loans with a single repayment at maturity, while others have an amortizing schedule. Some pay annual coupons, whereas other have a semi-annual (or higher) payment frequency. Coupon payments can be fixed or based on some floating reference rate. In principle, each individual ECL computation could, or should, be performed at the instrument level using its individual cash-flows. This should be the end of the story, but unfortunately it is a bit more complicated. As will be discussed later, the IFRS 9 guidance incorporates some logic as to just how far into the future one needs to consider credit losses; the consequence is that our various quantities—exposures, probabilities, loss-given-defaults, and discount factors—are required at much higher (and common) levels of granularity. Given this twist, the time aspect matters. This dimension thus needs to be explicitly managed, from the beginning, within the context of our expected-loss calculation. It is not a particularly fascinating area of discussion, but robust loan-impairment estimates depend importantly on getting it right.

Let's begin with some notation. In general, our analysis occurs over the time interval, $(t, T]$. $T - t$ might be a week, a month, a year, or a decade; it will depend on the individual loan instrument. The first order of business is to partition $(t, T]$ into $n \in \mathbb{N}$ sub-intervals as follows:

$$\left\{ t = t_0, t_1, \ldots, t_{n-1}, t_n = T \right\} \tag{9.11}$$

This can be done in many ways, but we will employ an evenly spaced grid where $t_k - t_{k-1}$ is a fixed constant for all $k = 1, \ldots, n$. Again, our choice of $n$ need not be immediately specified. The key point, however, is that the time partition (or grid) in Eq. 9.11 is absolutely central to the loan-impairment calculation. Looking to Eq. 9.10, we need to be able to defensibly assign a value—for each of our four main quantities—to each individual associated point in time. This will involve a bit of effort and reflection.

The default-probability element in Eq. 9.10 is written in cumulative form. That is, it begins at time $t$ and ends at time $T$. It is quite natural, in light of our time partition, to extend this idea to

$$p(t, t_k) \equiv p(t_0, t_k), \tag{9.12}$$

for $k = 1, \ldots, n$. In our practical example, we will make use of a sequence of cumulative default probabilities—each anchored to the current point in time, $t_0$—(mostly) defined on an *annual* grid.[14] The most sensible solution is to interpolate

[14] The final, official computations, start from—as discussed in Chaps. 7 and 8—a quarterly grid. We use the annual grid in this example, because it is easier, within visualizations, to see what is

any necessary intermediate values on our arbitrary partition in Eq. 9.11. Linear interpolation springs to mind, but this leads to discontinuities in the cumulative default curve. This is probably acceptable, in a general sense, but it does create issues for the computation of other default quantities. A smoother form of interpolation, as we will examine in a moment, turns out to be practically preferable.

### Time-Frequency, Interpolation and Bootstrapping

Cumulative default probabilities will not be entirely sufficient for our computations. We also require the probability of default associated with each slice of our partition; that is, $(t_{k-1}, t_k]$ for $k = 1, ..., n$. This variation of default likelihood—introduced in previous chapters—is referred to as the forward default probability. It is, however, an open question—raised in the introduction to this section—as to whether we require conditional or unconditional forward probabilities. It will be useful to consider both to arrive at the correct choice. If we start with the conditional forward probabilities, we require the values

$$p(t, t_{k-1}, t_k) \equiv p(t_0, t_{k-1}, t_k), \tag{9.13}$$

for $k = 1, ..., n$. This is the probability of default over the interval $(t_{k-1}, t_k]$, assuming survival to time $t_{k-1}$.

The obvious way to procure these conditional forward default probabilities would be to compute them from our annual (or quarterly) cumulative default probabilities and then interpolate these values to our grid. This almost works, but it unfortunately fails to preserve the arithmetic relationship between cumulative and conditional forward default probabilities. In particular, we require that

$$p(t_0, t_k) = 1 - \left( \prod_{i=1}^{k} \left( 1 - p(t_0, t_{i-1}, t_i) \right) \right), \tag{9.14}$$

for all $k = 1, ..., n$. If this does not hold, then our grid interpolation approach will have introduced an inconsistency between cumulative and forward default probabilities. This might not appear important, but getting this even slightly wrong can bring us rather far afield. Since we will need to examine the implications of this choice, we require the highest degree of equivalence possible.

Imagine that we have a smooth—cubic-spline or otherwise—interpolated set of cumulative default probabilities in the form of Eq. 9.12. We may then proceed to compute, in a recursive manner, a consistent set of conditional forward default

going on. For production computations, a finer grid is employed although, in principle, the final choice is a matter of taste.

probabilities from Eq. 9.14. To start, we set $k = 1$ then we immediately find that,

$$p(t_0, t_1) = 1 - \left(\prod_{i=1}^{1}\left(1 - p(t_0, t_{i-1}, t_i)\right)\right), \tag{9.15}$$

$$p(t_0, t_0, t_1) = p(t_0, t_1).$$

In other words, the first term on the grid is equal for both flavours of probability. Let iterate forward to $k = 2$, which yields

$$\begin{aligned} p(t_0, t_2) &= 1 - \left(\prod_{i=1}^{2}\left(1 - p(t_0, t_{i-1}, t_i)\right)\right), \\ &= 1 - \underbrace{\left(1 - p(t_0, t_1, t_2)\right)}_{\text{Unknown}} \cdot \underbrace{\prod_{i=1}^{1}\left(1 - p(t_0, t_{i-1}, t_i)\right)}_{\text{Known}}, \\ p(t_0, t_1, t_2) &= 1 - \frac{1 - p(t_0, t_2)}{\prod_{i=1}^{1}\left(1 - p(t_0, t_{i-1}, t_i)\right)}. \end{aligned} \tag{9.16}$$

This illustrates that, having already determined the value for $t_1$, the general expression from Eq. 9.14 reduces to one equation with a single unknown. This allows us to easily determine the $t_2$ value. If we increment to $k = 3$, logic tells us that given the $t_1$ and $t_2$ probabilities, we can figure out the $t_3$ figure. The general expression follows. The $k$th conditional forward default probability depends on the $k$th cumulative default quantity and the other, already computed, $k - 1$ forward likelihoods as

$$p(t_0, t_{k-1}, t_k) = 1 - \frac{1 - p(t_0, t_k)}{\prod_{i=1}^{k-1}\left(1 - p(t_0, t_{i-1}, t_i)\right)}, \tag{9.17}$$

for $k = 2, ..., n$. This, admittedly tedious, computation is strongly reminiscent of the so-called bootstrapping calculation used to infer zero-coupon interest rates from bond or swap yields.[15]

[15] See Bolder and Stréliski [8] for a description of this practice. A bit of caution is, however, required to avoid confusing this practice with statistical bootstrapping as introduced by Efron [11].

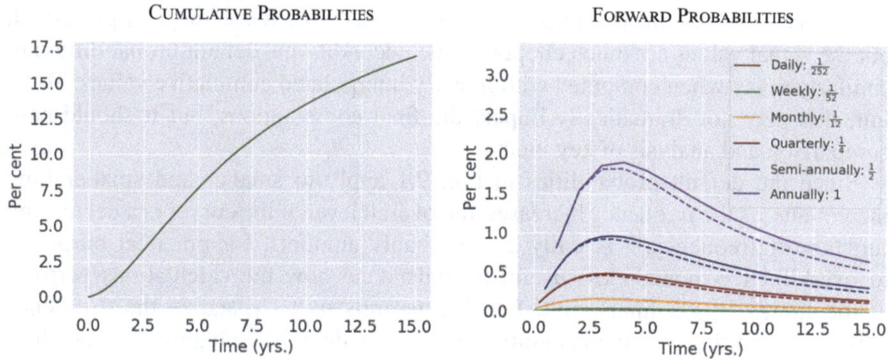


**Fig. 9.1** *Role of frequency*: The graphics above describe the interplay between our various default probability term structures. The left-hand graphic displays the PD12 cumulative through-the-cycle default-probability curve. The right-hand graphic illustrates both conditional (i.e., solid-lined) and unconditional (i.e., dash-lined) through-the-cycle default probabilities computed over a range of time grids from daily to annual frequency. All of the quantities in the right-hand graphic are computed via the left-hand graphic and Eqs. 9.17 and 9.18.

Unconditional forward default probabilities, the second possible definition, are rather easier to determine. We define the collection of these values as

$$p(t_{k-1}, t_k) = p(t_0, t_k) - p(t_0, t_{k-1}), \tag{9.18}$$

for $k = 1, .., n$. These are comfortably computed using the smoothed cumulative default probabilities.

Figure 9.1 provides a stylized description of the NIB master-scale PD12 through-the-cycle probabilities: the cumulative, conditional forward, and unconditional forward default term structures. Our internal non-homogeneous Markov chain model—based on Bluhm and Overbeck [6]'s work—was used to build the left-hand-graphic cumulative values. Using this cumulative quantity, the forward curves displayed in the right-hand side have been fit to a variety of partitions—ranging from daily to annual—over a 15-year horizon. The unconditional forward default probabilities—represented as dashed lines—simply use the smoothed cumulative likelihoods and Eq. 9.18. The associated conditional forward probabilities—appearing as solid lines in Fig. 9.1—are determined with the recursive algorithm outlined in Eqs. 9.15 to 9.17. The consequence is that, for every single grid point, the identity from Eq. 9.14 holds. Following the preceding steps, therefore, ensures that we have mathematical equivalency—irrespective of the time granularity—between these central default-probability definitions.

The form of the cumulative default probability curve, from Fig. 9.1, is basically invariant to the choice of default frequency. Since it is always defined relative to the starting point (i.e., $t_0$), the identical curve is used for every possible choice of end tenor (i.e., $t_k$). The only requirement is the ability to compute a value for any possible choice of $t_k$; we make use of a cubic-spline approximation for this purpose.

When one employs linear interpolation, by contrast, the basic shape is preserved, but the actual values are much choppier. The unconditional default probabilities are similarly noisy when computed with linearly interpolated cumulative values. To be fair, this may not dramatically impact the final computations, but it should ease comparison and analysis of key inputs.

Since the default probabilities in Fig. 9.1 apply to smaller and smaller time increments, as the frequency increases, the overall level of the curves is a decreasing function of frequency.[16] A daily grid probably amounts, for practical purposes, to overkill; it is nonetheless useful to understand how the calculations perform at the limit.[17] As a final point, Fig. 9.1 permits us to visualize the difference between conditional and unconditional forward default probabilities. For short tenors, deviations are almost imperceptible. As time passes, however, we see the distance between these two quantities gradually increases. This is the role of conditionality at work.

**Colour and Commentary 105** (DEFAULT PROBABILITY INGREDIENTS): *As seen in Chaps. 7 and 8, both through-the-cycle and point-in-time default-probability term structures are constructed at annual or quarterly frequencies. The expected-credit loss calculation, however, is typically based on a finer time partition. This raises the question of how one should determine these intermediate values. In principle, this is not an incredibly central choice, since it does not dramatically impact the final results; that said, there are a few possible traps for the unwary. It is also thus helpful to properly sort out the various quantities and have both clear mathematical formulae and computer sub-routines to move between them. Given more than one recipe for the final expected-credit loss computation, it is good practice to carefully organize the various ingredients. The cumulative default-probability curve—with its ease of interpretation and frequency invariance—is the recommended starting point. The conditional and unconditional forward default probabilities then follow naturally.*

### 9.1.4 The Simplest Example

While a consistently computed set of default probabilities across our time partition is an essential prerequisite for the expected-loss computation, there still remain a number of questions on our list that need to be answered. To help make things

[16] 252 business days per year over 15 years implies almost 3800 individual grid points. To satisfy the preceding equations, the default-probability level must necessarily fall with the frequency.

[17] A monthly partition of one's time interval will typically suffice for production work.

**Table 9.1** *Bullet-loan example details*: This table provides a quick overview of the main details associated with a simple bullet-loan example. Computing the expected credit loss of this loan in various ways will help us clarify a defensible computation algorithm.

| Characteristic | Value |
|---|---|
| Loan-amortization schedule | Bullet |
| Maturity $(T-t)$ | 15 years |
| Credit rating $(S_t)$ | PD12 |
| Loan notional amount $(\bar{c})$ | EUR 1,000,000 |
| Loss-given-default $(\bar{\gamma})$ | 0.30 |
| Coupon rate $(\upsilon)$ | 0.00% |
| Constant discount rate $(y)$ | 2.00% |

a bit less abstract, it is useful to introduce a simple example. This will assist in considering the implications of different calculation approaches and, ultimately, identification of a defensible algorithm. Table 9.1 introduces the details of an entirely fictitious, relatively plain-vanilla, EUR one million, 15-year, PD12, bullet-amortizing loan with a constant loss-given-default value of 0.3. The credit rating of our example loan was not selected randomly. It coincides with the default probabilities displayed in Fig. 9.1, permitting use of the values from our previous illustrative computations.

The bullet-bond form dramatically simplifies matters. Things are further improved by the use of a constant (i.e., time homogeneous) loss-given-default figure.[18] Finally, we initially make the (entirely unreasonable) simplifying assumption of a zero coupon rate. This unconscionable choice will be relaxed later, but helps us to avoid significant clutter in the early stages. Using Eq. 9.10, Fig. 9.1, and Table 9.1, the expected credit loss reduces to the product of *four* figures:[19]

$$
\begin{aligned}
\mathbb{E}_t^{\mathbb{P}}\Big(L_t(t,T)\Big) &= \underbrace{p(t,T)\cdot\bar{c}(t,T)\cdot\bar{\gamma}(t,T)\cdot\hat{\delta}(t,T)}_{\text{Eq. 9.10}}, \qquad (9.19)\\
&= p(t,T)\cdot\bar{c}\cdot\bar{\gamma}\cdot e^{-y(T-t)},\\
&= (0.170)\cdot(1,000,000)\cdot(0.30)\cdot(0.741)\\
&= 37,758,
\end{aligned}
$$

[18] We make this simplifying assumption for all of our loan-impairment calculations. In short, the loss-given-default value does not vary across the through-the-cycle and point-in-time perspectives. Such an assumption can naturally be relaxed, but it immediately raises significant parametrization challenges.

[19] We drop the $i$ obligor index to avoid notational clutter.

We may state without controversy—by virtue of the simplicity of our example—that the *true* loan-lifetime, expected credit loss for this instrument is thus approximately EUR 38,000. This amounts to about $3\frac{3}{4}\%$ of the initial notional amount, which is generally consistent with the highly skewed nature of default loss distributions examined at length in previous chapters.

While the true expected loss value is now known, it is not immediately obvious how one might replicate this calculation on our time partition. This may appear to be a waste of time and energy for this example, but loan-impairment calculations will involve more complex loans and other computational gymnastics necessitating a time partition. Our preference is to get the computation straight in the simplest possible setting before increasing the complexity. The key idea is that if our time-partition calculation works in this most straightforward of cases, it will generalize in a reasonable way. If not, at least we'll have an idea of where to look if things go astray.

A sensible starting point for replicating the computation in Eq. 9.19 over our time partition is

$$\begin{aligned} \mathbb{E}_t^{\mathbb{P}}\bigg(L_t(t,T)\bigg) \equiv \mathbb{E}_t^{\mathbb{P}}\bigg(L_t(t_0,t_n)\bigg) &= \sum_{k=1}^{n} p(t_0,t_{k-1},t_k)\cdot\bar{c}\cdot\bar{\gamma}\cdot\hat{\delta}(t_0,t_k), \qquad (9.20)\\ &= \bar{c}\cdot\bar{\gamma}\cdot\sum_{k=1}^{n} p(t_0,t_{k-1},t_k)\cdot\hat{\delta}(t_0,t_k). \end{aligned}$$

Here we use the conditional forward default probabilities for each time interval; to repeat, these are the default probability on each $(t_{k-1}, t_k]$, conditional on survival to $t_{k-1}$. Inspection of Eq. 9.20 reveals that each term in the sum involves the product of a default probability and a discount factor. This will be difficult to simplify. Let's ease matters, for the moment, by setting the discount rate identically to zero. The consequence is that $\hat{\delta}(t_0, t_k) = 1$ for all $k = 1, ..., n$. This permits some rearrangement

$$\begin{aligned} \mathbb{E}_t^{\mathbb{P}}\bigg(L_t(t_0,t_n)\bigg) &= \bar{c}\cdot\bar{\gamma}\cdot\sum_{k=1}^{n} p(t_0,t_{k-1},t_k), \qquad (9.21)\\ &= \bar{c}\cdot\bar{\gamma}\cdot\underbrace{\sum_{k=1}^{n}\frac{p(t_0,t_k)-p(t_0,t_{k-1})}{1-p(t_0,t_{k-1})}}_{p(t_0,t_n)?}, \end{aligned}$$

where the first-principle definition—derived in previous chapters—of the conditional forward default probability is used. If we could show that the sum in Eq. 9.21 is equal to $p(t_0, t_n)$, this would establish equivalence—at least under a zero discount factor—with the correct calculation in Eq. 9.19. The sum is not easily simplified—given that each term has a different denominator—and our identity from Eq. 9.14 indicates that the relationship between cumulative and conditional forward probabilities is multiplicative and not additive. Indeed, try as we might, our sum does not collapse to the desired conditional default probability. If we use the suggested approach from Eq. 9.20, we arrive at an expected credit loss of about EUR 49,000. The actual undiscounted outcome, calculated using Eq. 9.19, is almost EUR 51,000.

The use of conditional forward default probabilities is a failure. This would appear to be the consequence of two elements. First, the aggregation of expected credit losses is performed additively over the time partition; this creates an issue due to the multiplicative relationship between cumulative and conditional forward default probabilities. Second, and perhaps more importantly, the loan-impairment is unconditional—at least, with respect to time—and introduction of conditionality is inconsistent with the fundamental approach.[20] This suggests restating Eq. 9.20 with *unconditional* forward default probabilities as,

$$
\begin{aligned}
\mathbb{E}_t^{\mathbb{P}}\bigg(L_t(t_0, t_n)\bigg) &= \sum_{k=1}^{n} p(t_{k-1}, t_k) \cdot \bar{c} \cdot \bar{\gamma} \cdot \hat{\delta}(t_0, t_k), \\
&= \bar{c} \cdot \bar{\gamma} \cdot \sum_{k=1}^{n} p(t_{k-1}, t_k) \cdot \hat{\delta}(t_0, t_k).
\end{aligned}
\tag{9.22}
$$

Facing the same issue with managing the product of default probabilities and discount factors, we again deploy the trick of setting the discount rate to zero. The consequence is,

$$
\begin{aligned}
\mathbb{E}_t^{\mathbb{P}}\bigg(L_t(t_0, t_n)\bigg) &= \bar{c} \cdot \bar{\gamma} \cdot \sum_{k=1}^{n} p(t_{k-1}, t_k), \\
&= \bar{c} \cdot \bar{\gamma} \cdot \underbrace{\sum_{k=1}^{n} \bigg(p(t_0, t_k) - p(t_0, t_{k-1})\bigg)}_{\text{Telescoping sum}}, \\
&= \bar{c} \cdot \bar{\gamma} \cdot \left( p(t_0, t_n) - \underbrace{p(t_0, t_0)}_{=0} \right), \\
&= \bar{c} \cdot \bar{\gamma} \cdot p(t_0, t_n).
\end{aligned}
\tag{9.23}
$$

[20] Conditionality of expected losses will, in latter sections, be introduced with respect to macro-financial outcomes. This, however, is embedded in the point-in-time perspective and is a rather different style of conditionality.

This happy result stems from the first-principle definition of unconditional forward default probabilities and the telescoping nature of their sum over the time partition. Up to the discount factor, Eq. 9.22 and the true value—summarized in Eq. 9.19—look to be equivalent.

This is progress. If we set the discount rate back to its setting from Table 9.1, however, we encounter a slight setback. The expected-loss estimate, using Eq. 9.22, is about EUR 45,000. Despite the equivalence of Eqs. 9.19 and 9.23, a source of difference remains. As the only remaining difference, it must be related to the discount factor. The reason for this issue, in fact, stems from our assumptions about the magnitude of the exposure-at-default value. Fixing it at the final time point is perfectly acceptable, but fixing it over the entire time partition is not. If default occurs on interval $(t_{k-1}, t_k]$, then the size of the credit exposure is not $\bar{c}$. Instead, it is the present value of $\bar{c}$ at time, $t_k$. In other words, we need to write,

$$\dot{c}(t_k) = \bar{c}e^{-y(t_n - t_k)}, \tag{9.24}$$

for $k = 1, ..., n$. Two assumptions are quietly embedded in this representation: default occurs at time $t_k$ and interest rates may be continuously compounded. Neither are particularly defensible—and both may be relaxed—but for a reasonably large number of time steps, neither choice will make much of a difference on the final result.

Using this updated, or time-adjusted, exposure-at-default definition, we may return to Eq. 9.22 and simplify,

$$\begin{aligned}
\mathbb{E}_t^{\mathbb{P}}\Big(L_t(t_0, t_n)\Big) &= \sum_{k=1}^{n} p(t_{k-1}, t_k) \cdot \dot{c}(t_k) \cdot \bar{\gamma} \cdot \hat{\delta}(t_0, t_k), \qquad (9.25)\\
&= \bar{\gamma} \cdot \sum_{k=1}^{n} p(t_{k-1}, t_k) \cdot \underbrace{\bar{c}e^{-y(t_n - t_k)}}_{\dot{c}(t_k)} \cdot \underbrace{e^{-y(t_k - t_0)}}_{\hat{\delta}(t_0, t_k)},\\
&= \bar{c}\bar{\gamma} \cdot \sum_{k=1}^{n} p(t_{k-1}, t_k) \cdot e^{-y(t_n - \cancel{t_k}) - y(\cancel{t_k} - t_0)},\\
&= \bar{c}\bar{\gamma} \cdot \underbrace{e^{-y(t_n - t_0)}}_{\hat{\delta}(t_0, t_n)} \cdot \underbrace{\sum_{k=1}^{n} p(t_{k-1}, t_k)}_{p(t_0, t_n)},\\
&= \underbrace{p(t_0, t_n) \cdot \bar{c} \cdot \bar{\gamma} \cdot \hat{\delta}(t_0, t_n)}_{\text{Eq. 9.19}}.
\end{aligned}$$

We have another cheerful result. When we appropriately adjust the exposure-at-default for the time value of money, we find a direct correspondence between the true (cash-flow determined) and time-partitioned computations. It should be clear,

**Table 9.2** *Bullet-loan example results*: This table provides the results of a range of alternative approaches for the computation of the expected credit loss for the bullet-bond introduced in Table 9.1. Unconditional forward default probabilities and time-adjusted (i.e., discounted) loan exposures are required to correctly compute expected credit losses on a time partition.

| | $y = 0$ | $y = 2.00\%$ | |
|---|---|---|---|
| Approach | Flat $\bar{c}$ | Flat $\bar{c}$ | Adjusted $\bar{c}$ |
| Cumulative without partition | 50,958 | **37,751** | |
| Conditional forward on partition | 55,462 | 48,420 | 41,087 |
| Unconditional forward on partition | 50,958 | 44,674 | **37,751** |

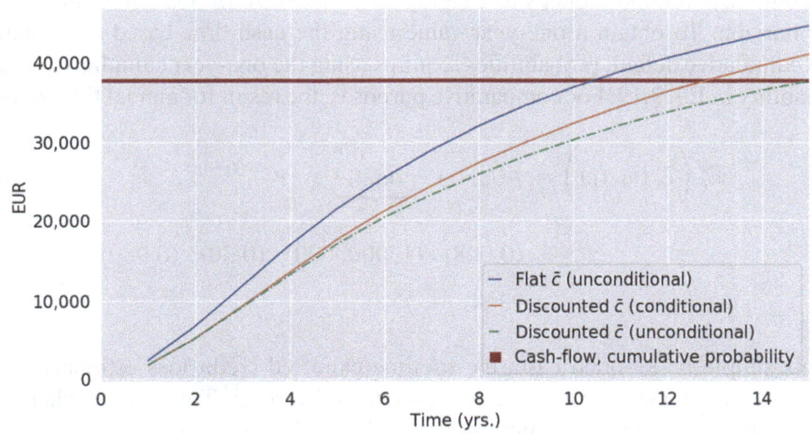


**Fig. 9.2** *ECL calculation alternatives*: This graphic, using the alternatives from Table 9.2 visually highlights the importance of the default-probability definition and proper discounting to the expected-credit-loss calculation.

from the development in Eq. 9.25, that this only works when there is a fixed and common discount rate, $y$.

Table 9.2 summarizes the various cases that we have examined. The first variation involves setting the discount factor to zero. We clearly see that use of cash-flows and cumulative default probabilities agrees perfectly when applying *unconditional* default probabilities to an exposure-based time partition. Use of *conditional* default probabilities simply does not work. Introducing a non-zero discount factor, however, leads to some additional complication. We need to adjust the individual exposures on our partition for the time value of money to reestablish equivalence between the cumulative-probability cash-flow and unconditional-probability, time-partitioned exposure calculations. This result is visually demonstrated in Fig. 9.2.

To really underscore our bullet-bond example, Table 9.3 illustrates all of the individual components, on an annual basis, associated with the actual computation.[21] Although it is not enormously interesting in this bullet-bond case, it sets the stage for detailed comparison with the more complicated upcoming cases. Table 9.3 nonetheless shows the unconditional forward probabilities, discount factors, and discounted outstanding amounts for each year over the 15-year time horizon. The discount factors decrease monotonically over the period, whereas there is a gradual increase in the discounted outstanding. The actual expected-credit loss values, however, are strongly influenced by the time profile of the unconditional forward default probabilities. This allows us, for the first but not the last time, to look at the evolution of expected-credit loss over time. The lifetime expected-credit loss of about EUR 38,000 reduces to roughly EUR 1800, if we examine only a one-year horizon. To obtain a one-year value using the cash-flow-based computation with cumulative default probabilities requires using the one-year cumulative default probability in Eq. 9.19. For comparative purposes, the result for annual time steps is

$$\begin{aligned} \mathbb{E}_t^{\mathbb{P}}\bigg(L_t(t_0,t_1)\bigg) &= p(t_0,t_1)\cdot\underbrace{\bar{c}(t_0,t_1)}_{\bar{c}}\cdot\bar{\gamma}\cdot e^{-y(t_1-t_0)}, \qquad (9.26) \\ &= (0.008)\cdot(1,000,000)\cdot(0.30)\cdot(0.980) \\ &= 2364. \end{aligned}$$

In this simple bullet-bond case, the lifetime expected-credit loss estimates agree perfectly. At the one-year horizon, however, they diverge.[22] This will not change as we relax the simplifying assumptions embedded in this example.

**Colour and Commentary 106** (CHOOSING A DEFAULT PROBABILITY): *Entering into our first example, it was unclear which flavour of default probability should be used in the expected-credit-loss calculation. When employing the instrument's cash-flows, the* cumulative *default probability is the most natural and appropriate choice. It treats each bond as a portfolio of separate zero-coupon bonds; each receiving their own discount factor and cumulative default probability. The IFRS 9 guidance strongly pushes us in the direction of employing a time partition and some notion of exposure-at-default for each increment. This implies that it will be difficult to use the intuitive cash-flow-based approach in a generic fashion. We demonstrated unequivocally in this section that, when using a time partition, one must*

(continued)

[21] We can do this for a much finer time partition, but Table 9.3 probably already has too many rows.

[22] Equation 9.26 can be *fixed* by appropriate discounting of the final exposure (i.e., setting $\bar{c} = 1{,}000{,}000 \cdot e^{-14 \cdot 0.02} = 755{,}784$), but this logically undermines the spirit of the cash-flow-based computation.

**Table 9.3** *Bullet-loan example calculation*: This table provides a highly detailed description of the various elements into the exposure-based, time-partition version of the expected-credit loss calculation for our bullet-bond example introduced in Table 9.1.

| Year | Forward probability | LGD | Discount factor | | Outstanding | Discounted outstanding | ECL |
|---|---|---|---|---|---|---|---|
| $k$ | $p(t_{k-1}, t_k)$ | $\bar{\gamma}$ | $\hat{d}(t_0, t_k)$ | Cash-flow | $\bar{c}$ | $\dot{c}(t_k)$ | $p(t_{k-1}, t_k) \cdot \bar{\gamma} \cdot \hat{d}(t_0, t_k) \cdot \dot{c}(t_k)$ |
| 1 | 0.0080 | 0.3 | 0.980 | 0 | 1,000,000 | 755,784 | 1787 |
| 2 | 0.0153 | 0.3 | 0.961 | 0 | 1,000,000 | 771,052 | 3395 |
| 3 | 0.0181 | 0.3 | 0.942 | 0 | 1,000,000 | 786,628 | 4022 |
| 4 | 0.0182 | 0.3 | 0.923 | 0 | 1,000,000 | 802,519 | 4038 |
| 5 | 0.0169 | 0.3 | 0.905 | 0 | 1,000,000 | 818,731 | 3749 |
| 6 | 0.0151 | 0.3 | 0.887 | 0 | 1,000,000 | 835,270 | 3364 |
| 7 | 0.0134 | 0.3 | 0.869 | 0 | 1,000,000 | 852,144 | 2977 |
| 8 | 0.0118 | 0.3 | 0.852 | 0 | 1,000,000 | 869,358 | 2623 |
| 9 | 0.0104 | 0.3 | 0.835 | 0 | 1,000,000 | 886,920 | 2313 |
| 10 | 0.0092 | 0.3 | 0.819 | 0 | 1,000,000 | 904,837 | 2046 |
| 11 | 0.0082 | 0.3 | 0.803 | 0 | 1,000,000 | 923,116 | 1819 |
| 12 | 0.0073 | 0.3 | 0.787 | 0 | 1,000,000 | 941,765 | 1626 |
| 13 | 0.0066 | 0.3 | 0.771 | 0 | 1,000,000 | 960,789 | 1463 |
| 14 | 0.0060 | 0.3 | 0.756 | 0 | 1,000,000 | 980,199 | 1324 |
| 15 | 0.0054 | 0.3 | 0.741 | 1, 000, 000 | 1,000,000 | 1,000,000 | 1205 |
| **Total** | | | | **1,000,000** | **15,000,000** | **13,089,112** | **37,751** |

**Colour and Commentary 106** (continued)
*employ the correctly discounted loan exposures along with* unconditional *forward default probabilities in the expected-loss calculation. This avoids problems with time conditionality while the additive form preserves the integrity of the computation. There are thus two equivalent avenues one might follow: use of cash-flows and cumulative default probabilities or appropriately discounted exposures on a time partition with unconditional forward default probabilities. Although there is perfect agreement—given a fixed and common discount rate—over the loan's lifetime, they will not generally agree for each sub-period.*

### 9.1.5 A More Realistic Example

The bullet loan example is somewhat oversimplified; many real-world loans exhibit an amortizing schedule. In other words, principal is gradually paid down over the loan's lifetime leading to a predicable decrease in exposure and associated credit risk. In this section, we'll extend our example to incorporate this dimension. Table 9.4 thus revises Table 9.1 to capture this amortizing dimension. In particular, after a five-year grace period, there is a linear reduction in loan principal.

Figure 9.3 helps us to envision the time profile—on a time partition with an annual frequency—of our amortizing loan. The exposure remains fixed for the first *six* years and then begins to decline in a linear fashion. Although the principal repayments occur from years 6 through 15, the exposure includes the actual repayment. This is because we are worried about default up to that point, which also includes the principal repayment.

The natural starting point is with the intuitive cash-flow-based approach. A bit more caution is required. First of all, we need to make a distinction between our time partition and the cash-flow pattern. In this first calculation, we will restrict ourselves to the cash-flow profile. Given $m \in \mathbb{N}$ cash-flows, we imagine that the cash-flows

**Table 9.4** *Amortizing-loan example details*: This table provides a quick overview of the main details associated with an extension to an amortizing-loan setting. This is one step towards full generalization of the expected-credit loss calculation.

| Characteristic | Value |
|---|---|
| Loan-amortization schedule | Amortizing (linear) |
| Maturity $(T-t)$ | 15 years |
| Credit rating $(S_t)$ | PD12 |
| Grace period | 5 years |
| Loan notional amount $(\bar{c})$ | EUR 1,000,000 |
| Loss-given-default $(\bar{\gamma})$ | 0.30 |
| Coupon rate $(\upsilon)$ | 0.00% |
| Constant discount rate $(y)$ | 2.00% |

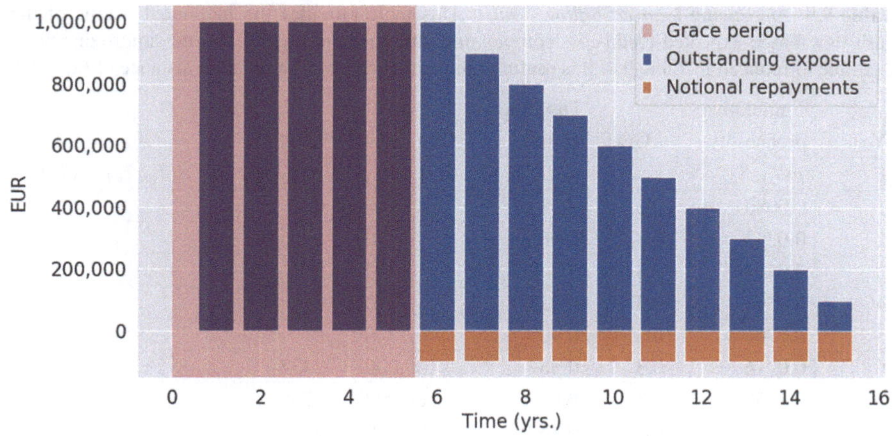


**Fig. 9.3** *Amortizing-loan profile*: This graphic, using the details from Table 9.4, outlines the exposure and cash-flow profile—using an annual time partition—associated with our amortizing-loan example.

are spread over time as

$$\left\{ t = T_0, T_1, \ldots, T_{m-1}, T_m = T \right\} \tag{9.27}$$

This compares logically with Eq. 9.11. They share the same beginning (i.e., time $t$) and ending (i.e., time $T$) points, but the frequencies can be rather different.[23] Unlike the original time partition from Eq. 9.11, the steps between the grid points need not be equal. That is, $T_m - T_{m-1}$ is not always constant.[24] This is a subtle, but important difference, which the notation tries to capture with the upper- and lower-case representations of time (i.e., $t$ versus $T$) and the distinction between $m$ and $n$.

Using the cash-flow partition from Eq. 9.27, and generalizing the initial calculation from Eq. 9.19, we arrive at the following expression:

$$\mathbb{E}_t^{\mathbb{P}}\left( L_t(t, T) \right) = \sum_{k=1}^{m} p(T_0, T_k) \cdot \bar{c}(T_k) \cdot \bar{\gamma} \cdot \hat{\delta}(T_0, T_k). \tag{9.28}$$

We can think of each individual cash-flow as being a separate instance of Eq. 9.19—each with its own cumulative default probability and discount factor—and Eq. 9.28 is simply adding them all together. The notation $\bar{c}(T_k)$ is a slight extension to refer to the treatment of each (i.e., $k$th) cash-flow as its own zero-coupon, or bullet, loan.

[23] Practically, for example, it is common that $n \gg m$.

[24] Indeed, this will only occur on cash-flow dates.

**Table 9.5** *Amortizing-loan cash-flow results*: This table provides the individual details of the cash-flow-based expected-credit-loss computation introduced in Eq. 9.28 for the amortizing bond example introduced in Table 9.4. It is useful to think of each row as a separate instance of Eq. 9.19.

| Year | Cumulative probability | LGD | Discount factor | Cash-flow | ECL |
|---|---|---|---|---|---|
| $k$ | $p(T_0, T_k)$ | $\bar{\gamma}$ | $\hat{d}(T_0, T_k)$ | $\bar{c}(T_k)$ | $p(T_0, T_k) \cdot \bar{\gamma} \cdot \hat{d}(T_0, T_k) \cdot \bar{c}(T_k)$ |
| 1 | 0.0080 | 0.3 | 0.980 | 0 | 0 |
| 2 | 0.0233 | 0.3 | 0.961 | 0 | 0 |
| 3 | 0.0414 | 0.3 | 0.942 | 0 | 0 |
| 4 | 0.0596 | 0.3 | 0.923 | 0 | 0 |
| 5 | 0.0764 | 0.3 | 0.905 | 0 | 0 |
| 6 | 0.0916 | 0.3 | 0.887 | 100,000 | 2437 |
| 7 | 0.1050 | 0.3 | 0.869 | 100,000 | 2738 |
| 8 | 0.1168 | 0.3 | 0.852 | 100,000 | 2985 |
| 9 | 0.1272 | 0.3 | 0.835 | 100,000 | 3187 |
| 10 | 0.1364 | 0.3 | 0.819 | 100,000 | 3350 |
| 11 | 0.1446 | 0.3 | 0.803 | 100,000 | 3481 |
| 12 | 0.1519 | 0.3 | 0.787 | 100,000 | 3585 |
| 13 | 0.1585 | 0.3 | 0.771 | 100,000 | 3666 |
| 14 | 0.1644 | 0.3 | 0.756 | 100,000 | 3728 |
| 15 | 0.1699 | 0.3 | 0.741 | 100,000 | 3775 |
| **Total** | | | | **1,000,000** | **32,932** |

Unlike the bullet-bond example, a bit more work is involved to arrive at the final expected-credit-loss estimate using Eq. 9.28. To ensure the maximal amount of clarity—as well as comparability—Table 9.5 chronicles all of the annual cumulative default probabilities, discount factors, and cash-flows involved in the computation. The final result is about EUR 33,000. Comparing this to the bullet-bond example in the preceding section, we observe a roughly EUR 5000 (i.e., 13%) decrease in expected-credit loss. This makes logical sense; the presence of gradual principal repayment over the loan's lifetime reduces credit risk and should manifest itself in lower expected credit losses.

Moving to the exposure-based calculation, even more machinery is required. First of all, for an arbitrary point along the equally spaced time partition $t_k$, we need to describe the outstanding loan amount. This is accomplished via a time-varying sum over the remaining cash-flows

$$X(t_k) = \sum_{T_j \geq t_k}^{T_m} \bar{c}(T_j). \tag{9.29}$$

Although the calculation occurs on the time partition from Eq. 9.11, the sum is taken over the cash-flow grid introduced in Eq. 9.27. $X(t_k)$, despite its rather ugly form, is essentially the sum of the remaining notional cash-flows from time $t_k$ until maturity (i.e., $T = T_m = t_n$).

Having learned our lesson from the previous bullet-bond example, we know that Eq. 9.29 will not quite work without some kind of discounting adjustment. More specifically, as at time $t_k$, each of the future cash-flows in our sum needs to be discounted back to the specific interval. This leads to the following modification of Eq. 9.29:

$$\dot{X}(t_k) = \sum_{T_j \geq t_k}^{T_m} \bar{c}(T_j)e^{-y(T_j - t_k)}. \tag{9.30}$$

This is the amortizing-bond analogue to the bullet-bond quantity from Eq. 9.24. The objective is to preserve the integrity of the time value of money across each of our time steps. Once again, time-homogeneity of the discount rate will be essential to maintain equivalence.

The exposure-based computation on our time partition is defined as

$$\mathbb{E}_t^{\mathbb{P}}\bigg(L_t(t_0, t_n)\bigg) = \sum_{k=1}^{n} p(t_{k-1}, t_k) \cdot \hat{\delta}(t_0, t_k) \cdot \dot{X}(t_k) \cdot \bar{\gamma}, \tag{9.31}$$

which compares directly to the bullet-loan definition from Eq. 9.25. Unlike Eq. 9.25, it is not particularly easy to establish a correspondence with the cash-flow-based computation. Working with the basic definitions, we can re-arrange Eq. 9.31 somewhat as

$$\begin{aligned}
\mathbb{E}_t^{\mathbb{P}}\bigg(L_t(t_0, t_n)\bigg) &= \underbrace{\sum_{k=1}^{n} p(t_{k-1}, t_k) \cdot \hat{\delta}(t_0, t_k) \cdot \dot{X}(t_k) \cdot \bar{\gamma}}_{\text{Eq. 9.31}}, \\
&= \bar{\gamma} \cdot \sum_{k=1}^{n} p(t_{k-1}, t_k) \cdot \underbrace{e^{-y(t_k - t_0)}}_{\hat{\delta}(t_0, t_k)} \cdot \underbrace{\sum_{T_j \geq t_k}^{T_m} \bar{c}(T_j)e^{-y(T_j - t_k)}}_{\text{Eq. 9.30}}, \\
&= \bar{\gamma} \cdot \sum_{k=1}^{n} p(t_{k-1}, t_k) \cdot \left(\sum_{T_j \geq t_k}^{T_m} \bar{c}(T_j) \cdot e^{-y(T_j - \cancel{t_k}) - y(\cancel{t_k} - t_0)}\right), \\
&= \bar{\gamma} \cdot \sum_{k=1}^{n} p(t_{k-1}, t_k) \cdot \left(\sum_{T_j \geq t_k}^{T_m} \bar{c}(T_j) \cdot e^{-y(T_j - t_0)}\right).
\end{aligned} \tag{9.32}$$

This is not a terribly promising path to establishing the analytic relationship between Eqs. 9.28 and 9.31. It will take a bit more patience and creativity. Let's, once again, set the discount rate $y = 0$ and force our equally spaced time and cash-flow partitions to agree perfectly; this basically means that $m = n$ and we are sitting at a cash-flow date. Also ignoring the loss-given-default, which is common to all terms in Eq. 9.32, we can organize each of the terms in our sum within the following matrix:

$$
\begin{array}{rcccccc}
1 & p(T_0, T_1)\cdot\bar{c}(T_1) & p(T_0, T_1)\cdot\bar{c}(T_2) & p(T_0, T_1)\cdot\bar{c}(T_3) & \cdots & p(T_0, T_1)\cdot\bar{c}(T_{m-1}) & p(T_0, T_1)\cdot\bar{c}(T_m) \\
2 & - & p(T_1, T_2)\cdot\bar{c}(T_2) & p(T_1, T_2)\cdot\bar{c}(T_3) & \cdots & p(T_1, T_2)\cdot\bar{c}(T_{m-1}) & p(T_1, T_2)\cdot\bar{c}(T_m) \\
3 & - & - & p(T_2, T_3)\cdot\bar{c}(T_3) & \cdots & p(T_2, T_3)\cdot\bar{c}(T_{m-1}) & p(T_2, T_3)\cdot\bar{c}(T_m) \\
\vdots & \vdots & \vdots & \vdots & \ddots & \vdots & \vdots \\
m-1 & - & - & - & \cdots & p(T_{m-2}, T_{m-1})\cdot\bar{c}(T_{m-1}) & p(T_{m-2}, T_{m-1})\cdot\bar{c}(T_m) \\
m & - & - & - & \cdots & - & p(T_{m-1}, T_m)\cdot\bar{c}(T_m) \\
\hline
 & p(T_0, T_1)\cdot\bar{c}(T_1) & p(T_0, T_2)\cdot\bar{c}(T_2) & p(T_0, T_3)\cdot\bar{c}(T_3) & \cdots & p(T_0, T_{m-1})\cdot\bar{c}(T_{m-1}) & p(T_0, T_m)\cdot\bar{c}(T_m) \\
\hline\hline
\end{array}
$$

Working from right to left, the $\bar{c}(T_m)$ cash-flow arises $m$ times across our double sum. If we sum all of its contributions we recover the cumulative default probability, $p(T_0, T_m)$. Similarly, the $\bar{c}(T_{m-1})$ cash-flow shows up on $m-1$ occasions permitting us to recover its product with $p(T_0, T_{m-1})$. This continues all the way down to the first cash-flow, $\bar{c}(T_0, T_1)$, which makes only a single appearance. Adding up all of these contributions, it is not hard to see the form of Eq. 9.28 albeit absent the discount factors and loss-given-default components.

This provides the intuition, but we can do a bit better. It requires some reordering of our sums. Admittedly somewhat painful and tedious, this is nonetheless really our only (rigorous) way forward. To see more clearly how this is done, let's simplify the form of Eq. 9.32 as,

$$
\overbrace{\sum_{k=1}^{n} \underbrace{p(t_{k-1}, t_k)}_{y_k} \sum_{j=k}^{n\equiv m} \underbrace{\bar{c}(T_j)e^{-y(T_j-T_0)}}_{x_j}}^{\text{Eq. 9.32}} = \sum_{k=1}^{n}\sum_{j=k}^{n} x_j y_k, \tag{9.33}
$$

where $x_j = \bar{c}(T_j)e^{-y(T_j-T_0)}$ and $y_k = p(t_{k-1}, t_k)$. Let's us now try expand, and then collapse, Eq. 9.33

$$
\sum_{k=1}^{n}\sum_{j=k}^{n} x_j y_k = \begin{array}{r} x_1y_1 + \\ x_2y_1 + x_2y_2 + \\ x_3y_1 + x_3y_2 + x_3y_3 +, \\ \vdots \\ x_ny_1 + x_ny_2 + x_ny_3 + \cdots x_ny_n \end{array} \tag{9.34}
$$

$$
\begin{aligned}
&= \begin{array}{r} x_1 y_1 + \\ x_2 (y_1 + y_2) + \\ x_3 (y_1 + y_2 + y_3) +, \\ \vdots \\ x_n (y_1 + y_2 + y_3 + \cdots y_n) \end{array} \\
&= x_1 \sum_{k=1}^{1} y_k + x_2 \sum_{k=1}^{2} y_k + x_3 \sum_{k=1}^{3} y_k + \cdots x_n \sum_{k=1}^{n} y_k \\
&= \sum_{j=1}^{n} \sum_{k=1}^{j} x_j y_k.
\end{aligned}
$$

Without changing the final value, we've essentially switched the order of our summations while simultaneously revising their starting and end points. This is the analytic equivalent of our previous matrix computation.

This turns out to be really quite useful. Let's return to Eq. 9.32 and—to keep from completely losing our minds—continue to force our time partition to perfectly agree with the cash-flow pattern (i.e., set $n = m$). Keeping this simplification and our trick at the ready, we have

$$
\begin{aligned}
\mathbb{E}_t^{\mathbb{P}}\bigg(L_t(t_0, t_n)\bigg) &= \underbrace{\bar{\gamma} \cdot \sum_{k=1}^{n} p(t_{k-1}, t_k) \cdot \left( \sum_{T_j \geq t_k}^{T_m} \bar{c}(T_j) \cdot e^{-y(T_j - t_0)} \right)}_{\text{Eq. 9.32}}, \qquad (9.35) \\
&= \bar{\gamma} \cdot \overbrace{\sum_{k=1}^{n} \underbrace{p(T_{k-1}, T_k)}_{y_k} \sum_{j=k}^{n=m} \underbrace{\bar{c}(T_j) \cdot \hat{\delta}(T_0, T_j)}_{x_j}}^{\text{Put into form of Eq. 9.33}}, \\
&= \underbrace{\bar{\gamma} \cdot \sum_{j=1}^{n} \sum_{k=1}^{j} p(T_{k-1}, T_k) \bar{c}(T_j) \cdot \hat{\delta}(T_0, T_j)}_{\text{Apply the result from Eq. 9.34}}, \\
&= \bar{\gamma} \cdot \sum_{j=1}^{n} \bar{c}(T_j) \cdot \hat{\delta}(T_0, T_j) \underbrace{\sum_{k=1}^{j} p(T_{k-1}, T_k)}_{\substack{\text{Telescoping} \\ \text{sum}}},
\end{aligned}
$$

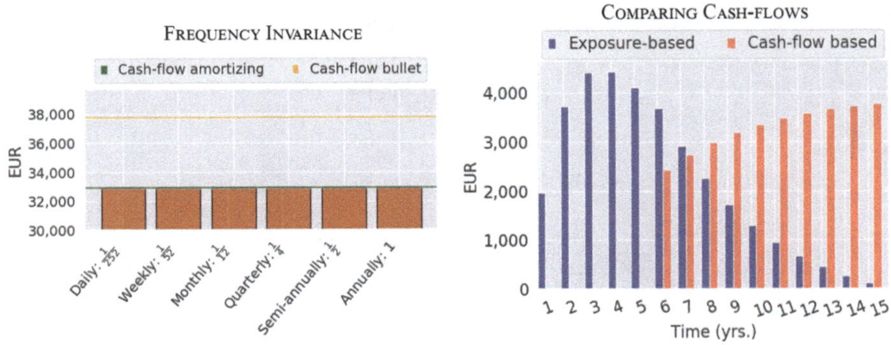


**Fig. 9.4** *Frequency and cash-flows*: The preceding graphics consider two separate elements of the expected-credit-loss computation. The left-hand graphic demonstrates the invariance of the results to the choice of time-partition granularity when using Eq. 9.31. The right-hand graphic, on an annual time partition, compares the periodic expected-credit-loss partitions associated with the exposure and cash-flow-based approaches.

$$= \underbrace{\bar{\gamma} \cdot \sum_{j=1}^{n} \bar{c}(T_j) \cdot \hat{\delta}(T_0, T_j) p(T_0, T_j)}_{\text{Eq. 9.28}} .$$

This returns us to the cash-flow definition introduced—for a zero-coupon bond—in Eq. 9.28. When our time-partitioned and cash-flows-based computations are put on a common grid, then the values should agree with one another. With some patience, and a bit of pain, it is presumably possible to demonstrate the more general result for differing time- and cash-flow grids.

Although it is reassuring to understand the analytical relationship between these two approaches—within the context of a zero discount factor—it is even better to numerically demonstrate their equivalence. Table 9.6 provides the gory details of the various inputs to the exposure-based expected-credit-loss computation—on an annual grid—stemming from Eq. 9.31 for the amortizing bond example. The agreement with the cash-flow-based results in Table 9.5 is evident. Our caution in managing the various discount rates has clearly paid dividends.

Figure 9.4 takes things a step further by attempting to address two open questions. The first relates to the granularity of the time partition in the exposure-based computation. Tables 9.5 and 9.6 illustrate equivalence when there is a common annual time partition for both exposures and cash-flows.[25] What happens when $n$ is much greater than $m$. The left-hand graphic of Fig. 9.4 shows, rather definitively, that the results are invariant to the fineness of our time partition. Breaking up each

[25] This was done to ease direct comparison and keep the overall number of rows (slightly) under control.

**Table 9.6** *Amortizing-loan exposure results*: This table provides the individual details of the exposure-based expected-credit-loss computation—on an annual grid—introduced in Eq. 9.31 for the amortizing bond example introduced in Table 9.4. We clearly see the agreement with the results in Table 9.5.

| Year | Forward probability | LGD | Discount factor | Cash-flow | Outstanding | Discounted outstanding | ECL |
|---|---|---|---|---|---|---|---|
| $k$ | $p(t_{k-1}, t_k)$ | $\bar{\gamma}$ | $\hat{d}(t_0, t_k)$ | $\bar{c}(t_k)$ | $X(t_k)$ | $\dot{X}(t_k)$ | $p(t_{k-1}, t_k) \cdot \bar{\gamma} \cdot \hat{d}(t_0, t_k) \cdot \dot{X}(t_k)$ |
| 1 | 0.0080 | 0.3 | 0.980 | 0 | 1,000,000 | 828,324 | 1959 |
| 2 | 0.0153 | 0.3 | 0.961 | 0 | 1,000,000 | 845,058 | 3721 |
| 3 | 0.0181 | 0.3 | 0.942 | 0 | 1,000,000 | 862,129 | 4408 |
| 4 | 0.0182 | 0.3 | 0.923 | 0 | 1,000,000 | 879,545 | 4425 |
| 5 | 0.0169 | 0.3 | 0.905 | 0 | 1,000,000 | 897,313 | 4109 |
| 6 | 0.0151 | 0.3 | 0.887 | 100,000 | 1,000,000 | 915,440 | 3687 |
| 7 | 0.0134 | 0.3 | 0.869 | 100,000 | 900,000 | 831,913 | 2906 |
| 8 | 0.0118 | 0.3 | 0.852 | 100,000 | 800,000 | 746,699 | 2253 |
| 9 | 0.0104 | 0.3 | 0.835 | 100,000 | 700,000 | 659,763 | 1721 |
| 10 | 0.0092 | 0.3 | 0.819 | 100,000 | 600,000 | 571,071 | 1292 |
| 11 | 0.0082 | 0.3 | 0.803 | 100,000 | 500,000 | 480,587 | 947 |
| 12 | 0.0073 | 0.3 | 0.787 | 100,000 | 400,000 | 388,275 | 671 |
| 13 | 0.0066 | 0.3 | 0.771 | 100,000 | 300,000 | 294,099 | 448 |
| 14 | 0.0060 | 0.3 | 0.756 | 100,000 | 200,000 | 198,020 | 267 |
| 15 | 0.0054 | 0.3 | 0.741 | 100,000 | 100,000 | 100,000 | 121 |
| **Total** | | | | **1,000,000** | **10,500,000** | **9,498,234** | **32,932** |

year into 252 daily time intervals or taking a single step yield the same result, which also perfectly matches the cash-flow-based value.

The right-hand graphic of Fig. 9.4 basically compares the final columns—representing the annual expected-credit-loss allocations—of Tables 9.5 and 9.6. This brings us back to the observation in the bullet-bond setting: although the lifetime expected-credit loss is identical in the cash-flow and exposure-based methods, the periodic amounts follow rather different patterns over the loan's maturity profile. When using loan exposures, as in Table 9.6, the annual contributions are skewed towards the early part of the loan. The cash-flow computation has the opposite effect; its contributions coincide unsurprisingly with the cash-flow incidence.[26] If our only interest was lifetime expected-credit loss, this would be irrelevant. As we'll see shortly, however, the IFRS 9 guidance takes a significant interest in the time dimension.

**Colour and Commentary 107** (CASH-FLOWS VERSUS EXPOSURES)*: In introducing this section, we posed a number of questions. One critical query related to whether or not one should employ cash-flows or exposures in the computation of expected credit loss. To answer this point we have examined, analytically and numerically, both approaches in the context of bullet and amortizing loans. The conclusion is rather clear: it does not matter. If one is sufficiently careful in one's treatment of the time value of money and choice of default probabilities, the two approaches are mathematically equivalent. There is one important caveat. This result only applies to the total expected-credit loss computed over the loan's entire lifetime. The periodic profile of exposure and cash-flows are not equivalent and, as a consequence, in any one period the values need not agree. While useful, therefore, the analytical equivalence between these approaches can only bring us so far. We will, rather soon, need to make a concrete choice taking into account the demands of the IFRS 9 accounting guidance.*

### *9.1.6 Coupon and Discount Rates*

To this point, we have been rather vague about the discount rate and essentially assumed away the loan's coupon rate. In practical settings, of course, loans bear coupons and this will turn out to have rather important implications for the discount factor.

[26] One could with appropriate discounting, of course, pull the cash-flows back into any given period. This may prove useful, but would also somewhat defeat the purpose.

The discount rate has, in fact, a rather fancy name. It is referred to as the effective interest rate and needs to be determined from the loan cash-flows. Indeed, it is a time-varying quantity and must be re-estimated for each new calculation date. This turns out to be rather straightforward, thankfully, since it is basically a form of bond-yield computation.

Let's begin with a generic non-zero coupon rate of $\upsilon$. Recall that $\sum_{k=1}^{m} \bar{c}(T_k)$ denotes the notional (or outstanding) value of our loan, or bond, at the current point in time. We then also need to add accrued interest at the calculation time, which we will represent as $a(T_0)$. The combination of these two quantities provides a description of the loan's gross carrying amount. The cash-flows are readily defined by our pre-defined principal repayment stream and the coupon rate. The effective interest rate is defined as the root—in our discount rate, $y$—of the following one-dimensional non-linear equation:

$$\underbrace{\left(\sum_{k=1}^{m} \bar{c}(T_k) + a(T_0)\right)}_{\text{Gross carrying amount}} - \underbrace{\sum_{k=1}^{m} \left((1+\upsilon) \cdot \bar{c}(T_k)\right) e^{-y(T_k - T_0)}}_{\text{Present value of cash-flows}} = 0. \tag{9.36}$$

$y$ is the *common* discount rate that equates the discounted loan cash-flows with its gross carrying amount. For each loan—depending on its cash-flow profile, principal structure, accrued interest, and coupon rate—it will be slightly different. To be frank, although Eq. 9.36 represents the spirit of the effective-interest-rate calculation, it is not quite correct. The reason relates to the compounding decision. Typically a continuously compounded discount factor is not employed, but rather some sort of discrete compounding. While these details are practically important, for sheer mathematical elegance and comparison to our previous development, we'll stay with continuous compounding.[27]

At this point, it is useful to recall why we use the notation $\hat{d}(t_0, t_k)$ to denote the discount factor over the time interval, $[t_0, t_k]$. It is the expectation of the continuously compounded integral of the instantaneous short-term interest rate over $[t_0, t_k]$ taken with respect to the physical probability measure, $\mathbb{P}$. It is decidedly *not* a risk-free rate and needs to incorporate the credit-risk dimension of one's loan. It is not obvious that Eq. 9.36 perfectly catches the risk dimension, but it also does not ignore it. To the extent that the coupon rate—or in the floating-rate case, the margin over the forecasted reference rate—embeds the credit riskiness of the underlying obligor, it can be considered a proxy for the appropriate discount rate. To be fair to the accounting guidance, such a quantity is not easily estimated.

Table 9.7 provides the final revision to our amortizing loan example originally introduced in Table 9.4. The first addition is a (arbitrarily selected) non-zero fixed coupon rate of 3%. This choice immediately allows us to formally compute the

[27] We can think of this as artistic license in the presentation of overall methodology. The actual differences are typically quite small.

**Table 9.7** *Full amortizing-loan example details*: This table revises (once again) our amortizing loan example from Table 9.4 through the addition of an actual coupon rate. This also allows us to formally compute the common discount rate by solving Eq. 9.36, which is referred to as the effective interest rate.

| Characteristic | Value |
|---|---|
| Loan-amortization schedule | Amortizing (linear) |
| Maturity $(T-t)$ | 15 years |
| Credit rating $(S_t)$ | PD12 |
| Grace period | 5 years |
| Loan notional amount $(\bar{c})$ | EUR 1,000,000 |
| Accrued interest $(a(T_0))$ | EUR 0 |
| Loss-given-default $(\bar{\gamma})$ | 0.30 |
| Coupon rate $(\upsilon)$ | 3.00% |
| Effective interest rate $(y)$ | 2.96% |

common discount rate by solving for the root of Eq. 9.36 in $y$. The result, which we now know is typically referred to as the effective interest rate, is 2.96%. If we had used discrete annual compounding—since we are computing the value at inception with no accrued interest—the coupon and effective interest rates would perfectly coincide. The small, immaterial difference arises from our choice of continuous compounding.

Table 9.8 immediately makes use of these new coupon and discount rate values to compute the expected-credit loss under both the cash-flow- and exposure-based approaches. As previously in Table 9.5 and 9.6, the time partition has been selected to be consistent with the cash-flow profile (i.e., $n = m$). As before, with the introduction of a non-zero coupon, the two methods generate precisely the same lifetime expected-loss results. At EUR 36,000, the outcome quite reasonably exceeds the zero-coupon result by about 10%. It remains, despite the 3% coupon, slightly south of the zero-coupon bullet bond example presented in Table 9.3. These variations on our simple example provide some interesting insight into the role of a loan's cash-flow structure on its lifetime expected-loss estimate.

The discounted outstanding column in Table 9.8 also helps explain the logic lying behind Eq. 9.36. For each time increment from years 1 to 6, the $\dot{X}(t_k)$ values are equivalent to the overall notional value plus the (as-yet-unpaid) annual coupon payment. The same occurs from years 7 to 15, but it is less easy to see. No other discount rate will generate this result.[28] This is another reason for the (slightly controversial) choice of continuous compounding; using discrete annual compounding, this effect would not have been visible. The effective interest rate

[28] Moreover, such an effect would be impossible absent the use of a single common discount factor to move cash-flows forward and backward in time.

was clearly explicitly selected, by those responsible for the accounting guidelines, to ensure consistency between cash-flow treatment and the gross carrying amounts found in the firm's balance sheet.

Table 9.8 also indicates that the addition of coupon payments does nothing to improve the temporal inconsistency of the cash-flow- and exposure-based computations. Results of the cash-flow method still push expected credit-loss further into the future, closer to the end of the loan's lifetime, while the exposure-based technique has the opposite behaviour. When we address some of the key aspects of the IFRS 9 standard, this seemingly modest distinction will take on a much higher degree of importance.

**Colour and Commentary 108** (THE EFFECTIVE INTEREST RATE)*: When performing computations that involve moving cash-flows both forward and backwards in time, as in the expected-loss setting, the choice of discount factor will inevitably play a central role. Given that a common discount rate is clearly essential to maintaining equivalence between the cash-flow- and exposure-based approaches, we cannot simply use the term structure of interest rates at the time of computation. Moreover, as we saw earlier, the discount factor involves the expectation under the physical probability measure, $\mathbb{P}$. As a consequence, it cannot be a risk-free interest rate, but needs to incorporate some dimension of risk. The effective-interest-rate computation, which stems from the more general treatment of non-marketable (i.e., non-traded) loans and bonds, can be considered to be a proxy from this credit-risky discount factor.*[a] *The double incidence of credit risk—through the separately determined default probabilities and discount factor—can be considered to be a feature of the expected-credit loss computation. In any event, the effective interest rate is the common, time-homogeneous discount rate that equates the present value of the instrument's cash-flows with its gross carrying amount. This definition appears to have been explicitly selected, by those responsible for the accounting guidelines, to ensure general consistency with other balance-sheet reporting and equivalence between cash-flow- and exposure-based versions of the expected-credit loss computations.*

[a] This occurs from the presence of credit risk within the coupon rate or lending margin.

### *9.1.7 Impact of Credit Rating*

Over a loan's lifetime, particularly one with a long tenor, there is a reasonable probability that it might experience a change in its credit rating. The expected-credit loss computation does not attempt to explicitly predict the incidence of credit

**Table 9.8** *Full amortizing-loan calculation*: This table provides the individual details of the cash-flow and exposure-based expected-credit-loss computation—on an annual grid—using the full amortizing-loan example as detailed in Table 9.7.

| Year | Forward probability | Forward probability | Discount factor | Cash-flow | Discounted outstanding | Cash-flow ECL | Exposure ECL |
|---|---|---|---|---|---|---|---|
| $k$ | $p(T_0, T_k)$ | $p(t_{k-1}, t_k)$ | $\hat{d}(t_0, t_k) \equiv \hat{d}(T_0, T_k)$ | $\bar{c}(T_k)$ | $\dot{X}(t_k)$ | | |
| 1 | 0.0080 | 0.0080 | 0.971 | 30,000 | 1,030,000 | 70 | 2412 |
| 2 | 0.0233 | 0.0153 | 0.943 | 30,000 | 1,030,000 | 198 | 4449 |
| 3 | 0.0414 | 0.0181 | 0.915 | 30,000 | 1,030,000 | 341 | 5117 |
| 4 | 0.0596 | 0.0182 | 0.888 | 30,000 | 1,030,000 | 476 | 4988 |
| 5 | 0.0764 | 0.0169 | 0.863 | 30,000 | 1,030,000 | 593 | 4496 |
| 6 | 0.0916 | 0.0151 | 0.837 | 130,000 | 1,030,000 | 2991 | 3917 |
| 7 | 0.1050 | 0.0134 | 0.813 | 127,000 | 927,000 | 3252 | 3029 |
| 8 | 0.1168 | 0.0118 | 0.789 | 124,000 | 824,000 | 3429 | 2303 |
| 9 | 0.1272 | 0.0104 | 0.766 | 121,000 | 721,000 | 3538 | 1725 |
| 10 | 0.1364 | 0.0092 | 0.744 | 118,000 | 618,000 | 3593 | 1270 |
| 11 | 0.1446 | 0.0082 | 0.722 | 115,000 | 515,000 | 3603 | 914 |
| 12 | 0.1519 | 0.0073 | 0.701 | 112,000 | 412,000 | 3580 | 634 |
| 13 | 0.1585 | 0.0066 | 0.681 | 109,000 | 309,000 | 3529 | 416 |
| 14 | 0.1644 | 0.0060 | 0.661 | 106,000 | 206,000 | 3457 | 243 |
| 15 | 0.1699 | 0.0054 | 0.642 | 103,000 | 103,000 | 3369 | 108 |
| **Total** | | | | **1,315,000** | **10,815,000** | **36,021** | **36,021** |

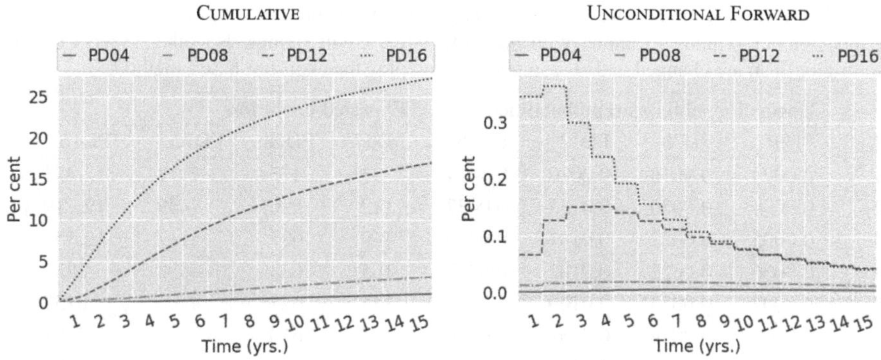


**Fig. 9.5** *Probability term structures by rating*: The graphics above display—for a selection of different internal ratings—the *through-the-cyle* cumulative and unconditional forward default probability term structures over a 15-year horizon. The construction of these curves is detailed in Chap. 7.

migration, but it readily permits adjustment for any possible rating change. The calculation simply jumps to another default-probability curve. Other than changing the underlying probabilities, therefore, nothing else changes in the details of our computation.

Figure 9.5 displays—for four distinct internal rating levels—the *through-the-cyle* cumulative and unconditional forward default probability term structures over our example loan's 15-year lifetime. Given the exponential nature of default on the rating scale, the differences between the various notches in Fig. 9.5 are enormous. As detailed in Chap. 7, the construction of such curves is not a trivial undertaking. Their current availability, however, makes determining the impact of rating transition very straightforward.

Table 9.9 employs the default-probability curves from Fig. 9.5—along with all of the previous cash-flow and discount-rate information—to compute the expected-credit loss for our coupon-bearing, amortizing bond example under *four* different rating levels. We see immediately, from the shading, the EUR 36,000 value from Table 9.8 under the original credit category, PD12. In the unlikely event of an eight-grade upgrade, this number would fall to roughly EUR 1800. This amounts to a reduction in excess of 90%. On the other hand, a four-notch downgrade almost doubles the expected-credit loss estimate.

Figure 9.6 allows us to visualize *all* possible rating levels for our concrete amortizing loan example. It includes, in explicit form, the values from Table 9.9 to help interpret the results. Interestingly, the expected-credit loss under the PD20 rating—amounting to about EUR 120,000 or 12% of our loan's notional value—is almost 70 times larger than the its PD01 equivalent. If we stay closer to home, and consider ± one credit-rating step, the expected-credit loss ranges from EUR 27,000 to 45,000. When considering the outcome as a percentage of loan notional amount, this amounts to a variation of about ± 1% in expected-credit loss associated with

**Table 9.9** *Expected-credit loss by rating class*: This table produces the expected-credit loss results, for our running example, with *four* alternative credit ratings. No other aspects of our amortizing-loan are changed and all computations employ the exposure-based method.

| | Unconditional forward probabilities | | | | Expected-credit loss | | | |
|---|---|---|---|---|---|---|---|---|
| $k$ | PD04 | PD08 | PD12 | PD16 | PD04 | PD08 | PD12 | PD16 |
| 1 | 0.0003 | 0.0016 | 0.0080 | 0.0414 | 83 | 475 | 2412 | 12,423 |
| 2 | 0.0004 | 0.0020 | 0.0153 | 0.0437 | 112 | 596 | 4449 | 12,719 |
| 3 | 0.0005 | 0.0022 | 0.0181 | 0.0359 | 140 | 627 | 5117 | 10,158 |
| 4 | 0.0006 | 0.0023 | 0.0182 | 0.0287 | 165 | 634 | 4988 | 7885 |
| 5 | 0.0007 | 0.0024 | 0.0169 | 0.0231 | 185 | 627 | 4496 | 6153 |
| 6 | 0.0008 | 0.0024 | 0.0151 | 0.0188 | 197 | 610 | 3917 | 4858 |
| 7 | 0.0008 | 0.0023 | 0.0134 | 0.0155 | 183 | 526 | 3029 | 3499 |
| 8 | 0.0008 | 0.0023 | 0.0118 | 0.0129 | 163 | 444 | 2303 | 2522 |
| 9 | 0.0009 | 0.0022 | 0.0104 | 0.0109 | 141 | 365 | 1725 | 1812 |
| 10 | 0.0009 | 0.0021 | 0.0092 | 0.0094 | 118 | 293 | 1270 | 1292 |
| 11 | 0.0008 | 0.0020 | 0.0082 | 0.0081 | 94 | 227 | 914 | 907 |
| 12 | 0.0008 | 0.0019 | 0.0073 | 0.0071 | 72 | 168 | 634 | 619 |
| 13 | 0.0008 | 0.0018 | 0.0066 | 0.0063 | 51 | 116 | 416 | 400 |
| 14 | 0.0008 | 0.0017 | 0.0060 | 0.0057 | 32 | 71 | 243 | 232 |
| 15 | 0.0008 | 0.0017 | 0.0054 | 0.0052 | 15 | 33 | 108 | 102 |
| **Total** | | | | | **1752** | **5814** | **36,021** | **65,581** |

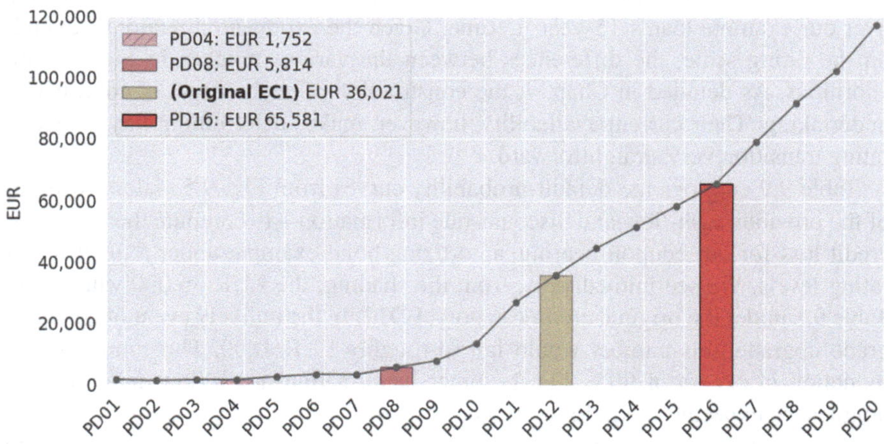


**Fig. 9.6** *Through-the-cycle expected-credit loss by rating*: This graphic shows the lifetime, through-the-cycle expected-credit loss—for our concrete amortizing loan—across every internal rating grade. The four specific cases from Table 9.9 are presented to aid interpretation.

a (rather probable) single notch movement. There is no way around it; an entity's credit rating plays a central role in its expected-credit loss estimate.

Figure 9.6 provides another useful insight. Visually, the evolution of expected-credit loss is relatively flat from PD01 to roughly PD08. At that point, it appears to increase in an approximately linear manner up to the final rating category, PD20. If our loan remains reasonably deep within investment-grade category, the expected-credit loss remains comfortably below 1% of its notional value. The broad conclusion from this observation is that expected-credit losses will be vanishingly small for high-quality instruments. If a default does occur, however, the actual loss—depending on the exposure profile of one's portfolio—is likely to be significantly larger. We will return to this idea later in our discussion.

**Colour and Commentary 109** (EXPECTED-CREDIT LOSS AND CREDIT RATING)*: While hardly a controversial statement, it nonetheless bears making: an entity's credit rating matters very importantly for the determination of its expected-credit loss. The details of the calculation, however, barely change. In the event of a rating upgrade or downgrade, one simply replaces the unconditional forward default probabilities with the new curve. Computational simplicity aside, even a one- or two-grade rating migration has a significant impact on the lifetime expected-credit loss estimate. Multiple step rating changes—which may accrue over a loan's lifetime—can lead to expected-credit losses being multiples (or fractions) of the original estimate. Longer-term loans will be particularly sensitive to such rating movement. As a final point, the sensitivity of (lifetime) expected-credit loss outcomes depends upon the instrument's location along the credit spectrum. Within investment grade, the economic impact of rating change is relatively flat.*[a] *As we move into speculative grade, however, there is a rather steep relationship between credit downgrades and expected-credit loss. If we imagine a portfolio of investment-grade loans, therefore, the expected-credit loss estimate will typically be rather small relative to the overall portfolio. If exposures are uneven, or lumpy, this could lead to a disconnect between any actual credit losses and the expected values. More on this important point later.*

[a] Strictly speaking, it is not flat, but the changes are so small in currency terms that they practically appear economically fairly indistinguishable.

### *9.1.8 Adding Macro-Financial Uncertainty*

Having addressed the main technicalities of the expected-credit loss calculation, we are finally in a position to answer our final question: how do we incorporate—as required by IFRS 9 guidance—the forward-looking element. This also involves a

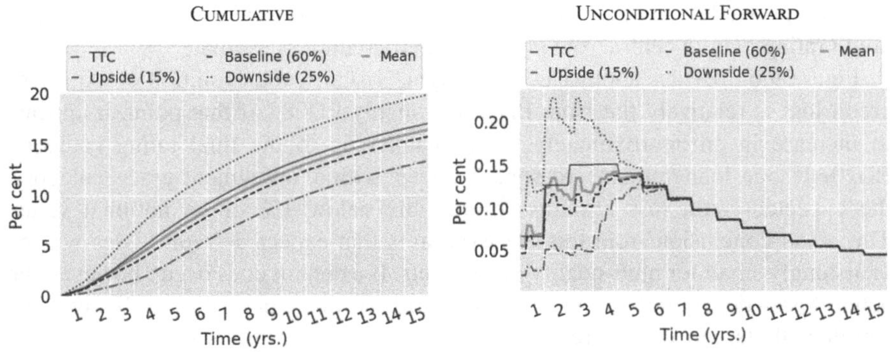


**Fig. 9.7** *Probability term structures by scenario*: The graphics above display—for three distinct macro-financial scenarios—the (PD12) *point-in-time* cumulative and unconditional forward default probability term structures over our 15-year horizon. The construction of these curves is detailed in Chap. 8. Weighted average and through-the-cycle default-probability term structures are included for comparison.

rather straightforward—when leaning upon the hard labour performed in Chap. 8—adjustment to our underlying default-probability term structures.

Figure 9.7 provides us—in a manner analogous to Fig. 9.5—with the raw ingredients. For rating category PD12, it illustrates the *point-in-time* cumulative and unconditional forward default probability term structures for three distinct macro-financial scenarios: upside, baseline, and downside.[29] IFRS 9 does not provide any direct guidance—beyond requiring a minimum amount of coverage—on the number of scenarios that one should utilize; the choice lies with the financial institution. That said, three scenarios—including a baseline bracketed by a positive and negative view—should be considered as the minimal necessary construction. It would be hard to argue for a balanced perspective on future outcomes absent, at least, three such scenarios.

Although perhaps minimalist, *three* forward-looking scenarios—with ten macro-financial state variables—nonetheless provide the analyst (and the financial institution) with significant flexibility. It becomes even more nuanced when we introduce the notion of scenario weights. Since expected-credit loss is a *single* number, some method for combining our three scenarios is necessary. These weights, rather unsurprisingly, determine the relative importance of each scenario in the final calculation. Naturally non-negative and summing to unity, these are not estimated quantities. We can think of them as subjective probabilities—calibrated during the forecasting process—associated with the various scenarios.[30] Logic also argues for a (conceptual) minimum of or 40–50% weight on the so-called *baseline* or central

[29] These are based on our variation of Yang [27]'s methodology. See Chap. 8 for a detailed discussion of how one constructs such curves.

[30] Subjectivity is *not* a requirement. It is also entirely possible, within one's modelling framework, to formally assign scenario probabilities.

scenario.[31] The reader will hopefully agree that ten macro-financial variables, three scenarios, and an equal number of scenario weights permits a rather rich characterization of the future.

To continue with our concrete example, we have concocted some imaginary scenarios weights. The baseline occurs with a 60% subjective probability, while the upside and downside cases receive 15% and 25%, respectively.[32] These values allow us to display the weighted average default-probability term structures in Fig. 9.7; it appears to come out, for most periods, just slightly below the through-the-cycle values. Not surprisingly, the associated upside forward default probabilities are the most optimistic, the downside are the most conservative, while the baseline values lie somewhere in between. While this need not always be the case—it will ultimately depend on the constellation of individual macro-financial scenarios—we would typically expect to observe this general pattern.

Table 9.10 highlights these individual forward probabilities for our example 15-year, fixed-coupon-bearing, amortizing loan. It also includes the expected-credit loss contributions associated with each of the scenarios along with the weighted-average outcome. The figures are presented so that one can simply sum the expected-credit loss upside, baseline, and downside figures to arrive at the final column. As we would have likely predicted, from the default-probability curves in Fig. 9.7, the forward-looking expected-credit loss is slightly below the through-the-cycle estimate. There is not much to read into this result. The distance between the through-the-cycle and point-in-time estimates can vary dramatically depending on the structure of the macro-financial scenarios—which are, in this example, symmetric by construction—or the scenario weights or both.[33]

Another perspective is provided in Fig. 9.8. It demonstrates each of the annual expected-credit loss values, for each of the macro-financial scenarios and their weighted average, over the entire 15-year lifetime of our concrete example.[34] Up until about four or five years, the downside estimates dominate the baseline, upside, and through-the-cycle values. As we move towards years eight to ten, however, the annual figures across all scenarios gradually converge to a common value. This is entirely driven by the convergence of the point-in-time scenarios to the through-the-cycle perspective over time. We also see the slight superiority of the through-the-cycle calculations over the weighted average outcomes; this supports the modest decrease in lifetime, point-in-time expected-credit loss. It bears

[31] Although not written in stone, it is hard to defend the centrality of the baseline view when it does *not* dominate one's scenario weights.

[32] This is a typical result when pessimistic risk managers are left to their own devices.

[33] There is, however, a clear relationship between the two perspectives. The horizontal line between year 10 and 11, in Table 9.10, describes the point beyond which all point-in-time scenarios have converged to the through-the-cycle estimate. This feature, and the value of information, is discussed in Chap. 8.

[34] In all cases, for Table 9.10 and Fig. 9.8, the exposure-based approach is used.

**Table 9.10** *Expected-credit loss by scenario*: Using our coupon-bearing amortizing loan example, this table summarizes the full forward-looking expected-credit loss computation. Annual cash-flows are provided for each scenario and the combined weighted-average outcome.

| | Unconditional forward probabilities | | | | | Expected-credit loss | | | | |
|---|---|---|---|---|---|---|---|---|---|---|
| $k$ | TTC | Upside (15%) | Baseline (60%) | Downside (25%) | Average | TTC | Upside (15%) | Baseline (60%) | Downside (25%) | Total |
| 1 | 0.0080 | 0.0032 | 0.0070 | 0.0143 | 0.0082 | 2412 | 146 | 1254 | 1070 | 2470 |
| 2 | 0.0153 | 0.0062 | 0.0128 | 0.0252 | 0.0149 | 4449 | 272 | 2244 | 1837 | 4352 |
| 3 | 0.0181 | 0.0061 | 0.0125 | 0.0246 | 0.0146 | 5117 | 257 | 2123 | 1741 | 4120 |
| 4 | 0.0182 | 0.0109 | 0.0154 | 0.0218 | 0.0163 | 4988 | 449 | 2539 | 1494 | 4482 |
| 5 | 0.0169 | 0.0145 | 0.0161 | 0.0180 | 0.0164 | 4496 | 578 | 2581 | 1201 | 4360 |
| 6 | 0.0151 | 0.0144 | 0.0149 | 0.0155 | 0.0150 | 3917 | 560 | 2319 | 1001 | 3880 |
| 7 | 0.0134 | 0.0132 | 0.0133 | 0.0135 | 0.0134 | 3029 | 447 | 1810 | 763 | 3020 |
| 8 | 0.0118 | 0.0117 | 0.0118 | 0.0118 | 0.0118 | 2303 | 344 | 1380 | 577 | 2301 |
| 9 | 0.0104 | 0.0104 | 0.0104 | 0.0104 | 0.0104 | 1725 | 258 | 1035 | 432 | 1725 |
| 10 | 0.0092 | 0.0092 | 0.0092 | 0.0092 | 0.0092 | 1270 | 190 | 762 | 318 | 1270 |
| 11 | 0.0082 | 0.0082 | 0.0082 | 0.0082 | 0.0082 | 914 | 137 | 548 | 228 | 914 |
| 12 | 0.0073 | 0.0073 | 0.0073 | 0.0073 | 0.0073 | 634 | 95 | 381 | 159 | 634 |
| 13 | 0.0066 | 0.0066 | 0.0066 | 0.0066 | 0.0066 | 416 | 62 | 249 | 104 | 416 |
| 14 | 0.0060 | 0.0060 | 0.0060 | 0.0060 | 0.0060 | 243 | 37 | 146 | 61 | 243 |
| 15 | 0.0054 | 0.0054 | 0.0054 | 0.0054 | 0.0054 | 108 | 16 | 65 | 27 | 108 |
| **Total** | | | | | | **36,021** | **3848** | **19,435** | **11,012** | **34,295** |

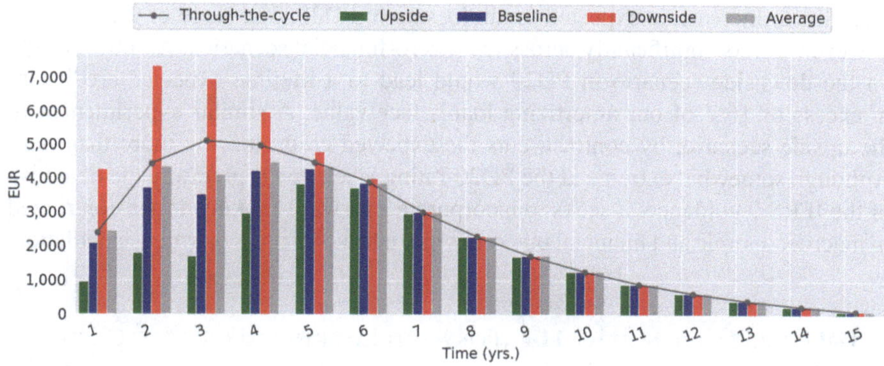


**Fig. 9.8** *Point-in-time expected-loss profile*: This graphic demonstrates each of the annual expected-credit loss values, for each of the macro-financial variables and their weighted average, over the entire 15-year lifetime of our concrete example. In all cases, the exposure-based approach is used. The through-the-cycle values are also provided for comparative purposes.

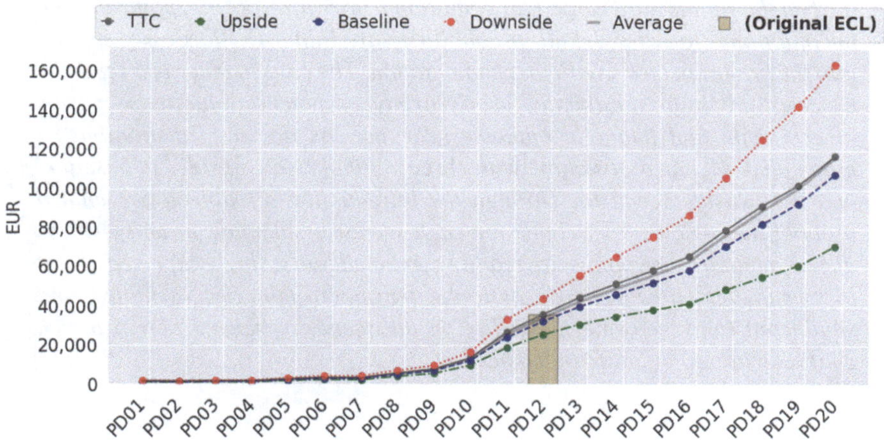


**Fig. 9.9** *Lifetime point-in-time expected-credit loss by scenario and rating*: This graphic shows the lifetime, point-in-time expected-credit loss—for our concrete amortizing loan—across every internal rating grade and macro-financial scenario. Our original through-the-cycle PD12 estimate is highlighted to help anchor our starting point.

repeating, because it will become important quite soon, that the difference between the macro-financial scenarios are highest in the first few years of the analysis.

Figure 9.9 takes this analysis to its logic limit by displaying the lifetime, point-in-time expected-credit loss—still for our concrete amortizing loan—across every internal rating grade and each macro-financial scenario. The original through-the-cycle PD12 estimate of EUR 36,000 is also highlighted to help us anchor to the previous analysis. Figure 9.9 is usefully compared to Fig. 9.6. The same low, roughly economically equivalent, expected-credit loss estimates are evident—across all scenarios—up to about PD08 or PD09. From that point, we again observe a fairly steep linear increase in expected-credit loss up to PD20. The slope of the increase, however, differs significantly across the macro-financial scenarios. A 100% weight on the downside scenario in PD20 would lead to a lifetime expected-credit loss in excess of 16% of our amortizing loan's face value. A similar experiment with the upside scenario, by contrast, cuts the expected-credit loss by more than half. Although somewhat extreme at the PD20-rating level, this is precisely the objective of the IFRS 9 guidance: it seeks to incorporate a forward-looking dimension rooted in macroeconomic and financial outcomes into a firm's loan-impairment calculation.

**Colour and Commentary 110** (FORWARD-LOOKING EXPECTED-CREDIT LOSS)*: Chapters 7 and 8 represented a long and laborious detour into the world of through-the-cycle default-probability term structures and mapping macro-financial scenarios into general credit conditions for the construction of a defensible point-in-time perspective. At times, the reader may have (legitimately) wondered where all this development was headed. We now reap the benefits of this hard work. Our conditional, forward-looking, point-in-time unconditional forward default probabilities are (almost) effortlessly slipped into the base expected-credit loss computation. The consequence is a separate expected-credit loss estimate for a variety of potential future scenarios of economic and financial outcomes. We use, as do many institutions, a minimalist scenario structure with* three *outlooks: an upside, a baseline, and a downside scenario. Through the introduction of subjective scenario probabilities—non-zero weights for each scenario summing to unity—these disparate future viewpoints are readily combined into a single expected-credit loss estimate. Three scenario outlooks, ten macro-financial variables, and significant (and welcome) flexibility on the scenario weights permit a rich characterization of future outcomes.*

### *9.1.9 Tying It All Together*

At the beginning of this section, we posed a range of questions concerning the loan-impairment computation. Over the preceding pages we have, in occasionally excessive detail, attempted to answer these queries. Table 9.11 seeks to collect our answers. It contains a surprising number of important practical details such as the probability measure, the distinction between use of cash-flows and exposures, the proper default-probability flavour to use, how to compute the correct discount factor, and the incorporation of point-in-time scenarios.

These lessons allow us to write down, with a reasonable amount of rigour, a mathematical definition of the overall portfolio lifetime expected-credit loss. This

**Table 9.11** *Loan-impairment questions and answers*: This table revisits the questions posed at the beginning of this section and attempts to provide—gleaned from the previous analysis—a set of succinct answers.

| Question | Answer |
|---|---|
| PROBABILITY MEASURE? | The physical measure, $\mathbb{P}$. |
| MANAGING EXPOSURE? | Cash-flows or (appropriately) discounted exposures. |
| TIME INCREMENTS? | Exposures can be placed on an arbitrary, equally spaced grid. |
| DISCOUNT FACTOR? | Common, numerically determined **effective interest rate**. |
| DEFAULT-PROBABILITY? (CASH-FLOW APPROACH) | Cumulative default probabilities. |
| DEFAULT-PROBABILITY? (EXPOSURE-BASED APPROACH) | Forward unconditional default probabilities. |
| INCORPORATING SCENARIOS? | Point-in-time perspectives combined with scenario weights. |

is an important step in the determination of the loan-impairment entry into a firm's balance sheet. It has the following form:

$$\begin{aligned}\text{Lifetime Portfolio ECL} &= \overbrace{\sum_{j=1}^{J} \omega_j \underbrace{\sum_{i=1}^{I} \underbrace{\sum_{k=1}^{n} p_{ij}(t_{k-1}, t_k) \cdot \hat{\delta}(y_i, t_0, t_k) \cdot \dot{X}_i(t_k) \cdot \bar{\gamma}_i}_{\text{Each individual loan: Eq. 9.31}}}_{\text{The portfolio viewpoint: all } I \text{ assets}}}^{\text{Averaging over all scenarios}}, \quad (9.37)\\ &= \sum_{j=1}^{J} \omega_j \sum_{i=1}^{I} \mathbb{E}_t^{\mathbb{P}}\Big( L_{ijt}(t_0, t_n) \Big).\end{aligned}$$

Although this has many familiar elements—and exploits Eq. 9.31 as its kernel—it still requires a bit of translation. The first point is that we make use of the exposure-based computation. Whatever the granularity of the time-partition, it is important to select a value of $n$ that captures the full lifetime of the longest maturity instrument in one's portfolio.[35] For short-tenor assets, the values of $\dot{X}$ will be simply be zero for the majority of the outer time steps. The second point is that we use the $i$ subscript to refer to each of the $I$ financial instruments in one's portfolio. Each will have a different effective interest rate (i.e., $y_i$) implying alternative discount rates. They will also have varying loss-given-default values, exposure profiles, and their forward unconditional default probabilities will depend on their current credit rating. Every element in Eq. 9.31 will thus potentially vary between individual loans or bonds.

[35] In our production implementation, we use a monthly time grid and set $n = 480$, which pushes us out 40 years into the future.

The final point is the presence of $J = 3$ macro-financial-motivated point-in-time scenarios with associated subjective weights, $\{\omega_j : j = 1, ..., J\}$.[36]

Equation 9.37 can also, of course, be written using the cash-flow approach. As we've seen, if done correctly, these two approaches are numerically equivalent. In the next section, we will finally explain the relevance of our time partition and our significant efforts to build an exposure-based loan-impairment estimator. This will bring us away from our heretofore mathematical perspective and introduce some important underlying accounting logic.

**Colour and Commentary 111** (MEASURE THRICE, CUT ONCE)*: Wood, stone, glass, or steel are expensive materials. When an experienced artisan is working with any of these materials, common practice is to take numerous measurements before actually proceeding to slice, grind, or cut. Measurement is cheap, but incorrect action can be costly. This section has taken this hard-earned practical advice to heart and tried to apply it—conceptually, at least—to the financial loan-impairment calculation.*[a] *We have carefully constructed the expected-credit loss computation from first principles, thought about the appropriate probability measure behind the expectation operator, wrestled with cash-flow exposures and their associated probabilities, identified a sensible common discount rate and examined its overall role, thought carefully about various time partitions, considered the importance of an instrument's ratings, and finally incorporated the macro-financial scenarios constructed in previous chapters. These myriad measurements, and their associated lessons, now permit us to move forward and confidently cut our materials.*

[a] One might argue that the costs of an incorrect mathematical computation are quite low. For figures that ultimately find their way into a firm's financial statements, however, this is not a terribly compelling argument.

[36] To be a bit pedantic, we require that $\omega_j > 0$ for $j = 1, ..., J$ and

$$\sum_{j=1}^{J} \omega_j = 1. \tag{9.38}$$

These fairly commonsensical subject-probability constraints should be explicitly mentioned (at least) once.

**Table 9.12** *IFRS 9 stage allocation*: The IFRS 9 guidance allocates financial instruments to *three* distinct stages with differing treatment. This table summarizes their key aspects.

| | | |
|---|---|---|
| Stage I | PERFORMING | No **significant increase in credit risk** since initial recognition |
| | | 12-month expected credit loss |
| Stage II | UNDER-PERFORMING | **Significant increase in credit risk** since initial recognition |
| | | Lifetime expected credit loss |
| Stage III | NON-PERFORMING | **Credit impaired** financial asset |
| | | Lifetime expected credit loss (or writedown) |

## 9.2 Introducing Stages

If we were considering FASB's current expected-credit loss methodology (CECL), then we could essentially move directly to the discussion of adjustments for portfolio composition. Under CECL, all loans are assigned their lifetime expected-credit loss using either the cash-flow- or exposure-based approaches highlighted in the previous development. Since we are interested in the IFRS 9 approach, however, another important step remains: stage allocation. Under IFRS 9, each financial asset subject to the loan-impairment calculation is assigned to one of *three* stages, which receive alternative expected-credit loss treatment. Loosely speaking, stages I to III deal with performing, under-performing, and non-performing assets, respectively.

Table 9.12 provides the key elements of IFRS 9 stage allocation definitions. In stage I, things are going according to plan with the credit obligor and the firm has no information to suggest any significant deterioration of credit quality. The consequence is that only *12 months* of expected-credit loss is provisioned for such loans.[37] Financial assets where, since initial recognition, the firm has ascertained a *significant increase in credit risk* are assigned to stage II. Such financial instruments are assigned a *lifetime* expected-credit loss provision. Finally, in the event of credit impairment, the assets are allocated to stage III. Again, lifetime ECL is necessary, but quite often a more conservative financial provision is taken. Typically, handling of these non-performing assets falls out of the responsibility of the quantitative risk analyst and moves to the domain of accountants and credit experts.

It is at this point that we may finally reveal the true reason for preference of an exposure-based expected-credit loss to the more natural, and intuitive cash-flow approach. It is possible to use cash-flows to produce 12-month stage I expected credit-loss estimates, but it is awkward. The heterogeneity of cash-flows patterns among various loans makes organization of the implementation—not to mention comparison of the final results—a confusing and error-prone task. The exposure-based method allows us to place all of our financial instruments onto a common grid for ease of calculation and interpretation. In fact, the stage-logic leads to two

[37] This stage differentiation is the principal difference—for a quantitative analyst—between IFRS' ECL and FASB's CECL. There are others and these distinctions are well described in Etheridge and Hsu [13].

separate grids: a 12 month partition for stage I and another lengthier time grid out to some distant point in the future for computation of stage-II estimates.[38]

Two key issues immediately arise when looking at the definitions found in Table 9.12: what are the implications for loan impairments and how does one actually decide on the stage allocations? Both questions are interesting and their answers yield important insight into the overall calculation. Let's consider each in turn.

## 9.2.1 Stage-Allocation Consequences

The first consequence of this stage allocation is that it makes a *large* difference in the provisioning amounts. Table 9.13 returns to our simple fixed-coupon, amortizing loan example from the previous example and illustrates the different estimates—across a variety of perspectives—for the 12-month (i.e., stage-I) and lifetime (i.e., stage-II) expected-credit losses. For our 15-year loan, the weighted-average, lifetime expected credit loss is almost 14 times smaller than its one-year equivalent.[39]

**Table 9.13** *The impact of stage allocation*: This table presents, again using our concrete fixed-coupon, amortizing loan, the expected-credit losses estimates across various perspectives employing both the stage I and II definitions. The stage-allocation decision, in this particular case, alters the fundamental relationship of the weighted-average estimate relative to the through-the-cycle value.

| Perspective | Stage I (1-Year) | Stage II (Lifetime) |
|---|---|---|
| Through-the-cycle | 2412 | 36,021 |
| Upside (15%) | 972 | 25,653 |
| Baseline (60%) | 2091 | 32,392 |
| Downside (25%) | 4281 | 44,047 |
| **Weighted Average (Total)** | **2470** | **34,295** |

A dramatic provisioning reduction is not the only by-product of stage allocation. While on a lifetime basis the through-the-cycle expected credit loss exceeds the weighted average value by about 5%, it is actually 2% lower on a one-year basis. The stage-allocation decision, in this particular case at least, alters the fundamental relationship of the weighted-average estimate relative to the through-the-cycle value. The reason stems from Fig. 9.7 and the time value of macro-financial

[38] The length and granularity of one's time grid, of course, will depend on an institution's lending maturity profile.

[39] Due to non-linearities associated with discounting, coupon payments, and amortizing notional, we should not expect the one-year expected credit-loss of a 15-year loan to be simply $\frac{1}{15}$th of the lifetime value.

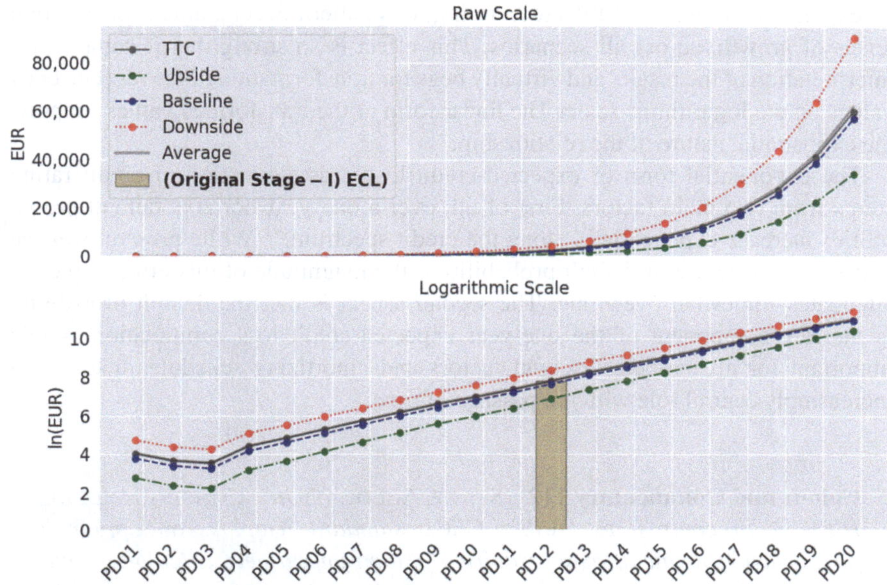


**Fig. 9.10** *Stage-I point-in-time expected-credit loss by scenario and rating*: The graphic above shows the stage-I, point-in-time expected-credit loss—for our concrete amortizing loan—across every internal rating grade and macro-financial scenario. These results are usefully compared with Fig. 9.9. Given its exponential raw form, it is also presented on a logarithmic scale. Our original through-the-cycle PD12 estimate is highlighted to help anchor our starting point.

forecasting information. Over the lifetime of a relatively long-tenored financial instrument, the forward-looking element will naturally converge to the through-the-cycle approach. The obvious reason is that our ability to forecast deteriorates with time and, ultimately, our best guess about the future is our long-term unconditional estimator. When solely examining the one-year expected-credit loss estimate, however, the full extent of these forecasting differences comes into play. A portfolio comprised of stage-I assets will thus, by logical extension, exhibit rather greater sensitivity to macro-financial conditions than a portfolio dominated by stage-II credits.[40]

To underscore this point, Fig. 9.10 displays the evolution of the one-year expected-credit loss across all credit-rating categories or the various scenarios. This result is best compared with the lifetime expected-credit loss results from Fig. 9.9. The deviations between the one-year and lifetime profiles are fairly dramatic for our 15-year maturity loan. Whereas the lifetime expected-credit loss is fairly flat out to about PD09 and then increases linearly thereafter, the one-year ECL looks to be

[40] How much of a difference, of course, will depend importantly on the maturity profile of the underlying assets. If all loans were to mature within the next year, for example, we would expect no difference.

an exponential function of the credit rating; this pattern occurs, albeit for different levels of growth, across all scenarios. This effect is so strong that it complicates interpretation of the results and virtually begs for transformation of the raw currency values onto a logarithmic scale. The linear form of the transformed values supports the exponential nature of the relationship.

The exponential form of expected-credit losses as a function of credit rating stems from two main factors. First of all, over a one-year horizon, default probabilities increase exponentially along the credit spectrum.[41] While present over the entire term structure of default probabilities, the magnitude of this effect typically attenuates somewhat over time. The second aspect is that the default probability is the key component of the one-year expected-credit loss computation. While important for all periods, discount factors and amortizing schedules take on an increasingly central role with the passage of time.

**Colour and Commentary 112** (STAGE-ALLOCATION CONSEQUENCES)*: IFRS 9—in contrast to FASB's CECL standard—employs an approach placing each financial asset requiring a loan-impairment calculation into* three *buckets or stages: performing (stage I), under-performing (stage II), and non-performing (stage III). Stage III assets typically fall outside of the quantitative analyst's purview.*[a] *The remaining stage-I and II financial instruments are treated rather differently from a loan-impairment perspective. Stage-I assets are assigned one-year of expected-credit loss, while the full lifetime value is allocated to stage-II instruments. For a portfolio comprised of medium to long-tenor loans, the differences in impairment values associated with stage allocation can be considerable. In particular, stage-I assets will typically receive only a fraction of the overall loan-impairment value and they will simultaneously exhibit a higher degree of sensitivity to macro-financial scenarios.*

[a] This is not to say that their treatment is unimportant, but rather that stage-III assets require a level of specificity and nuance that do not (usually) lend itself to mathematical modelling.

## 9.2.2 Stage-Allocation Logic

Like many accounting standards, IFRS 9 is not prescriptive, but rather directive. It does not tell you precisely what you need to do, but rather describes the general principles of how the task should be accomplished. This has both advantages and

[41] This fact has been demonstrated on many occasions in previous chapters; Chap. 7, in particular, delves into this idea.

disadvantages whose discussion are best left for those with a better understanding of accounting concepts. One challenge, for the quantitative analyst at least, relates to the non-prescriptive definition of under-performing stage-II assets. To properly distinguish between stage-I and stage-II instruments, one must somehow decipher the phrase "significant increase in credit risk since initial recognition." The main difficulty is that this principle can clearly be defined in a range of different ways.[42]

One common approach is the construction of a quantitatively motivated test to determine stage membership.[43] It needs to somehow measure the change in credit risk from initial recognition—in other words, since loan issuance—until the current point in time. A natural candidate for this task is the point-in-time default term structure. Defining $\tau_i$ as the default event of the $i$th asset, we set $\bar{t}_i$, $t$, and $T_i$ as the $i$th inception (i.e., issuance), current calculation, and maturity date, respectively. Our interest is the financial asset's cumulative default probability over $[t, T_i]$, computed at *two* different time points. In the first case, we introduce the following quantity based upon the inception point-in-time term structure:

$$\begin{aligned} d_i(t) &= \mathbb{P}_{\bar{t}_i}\bigg(\tau_i \in (t, T_i]\bigg), \\ &= \sum_{k=1}^{N_i} p_{\bar{t}_i}(t_{k-1}, t_k), \end{aligned} \tag{9.39}$$

where $N_i$ denotes the remaining number of grid points for the $i$th instrument as of time $t$. This is essentially the total probability mass over the loan's remaining time to maturity—captured by the interval, $[t, T_i]$—assessed at the loan-issuance date. The revised probability, at the calculation date, is written as

$$\begin{aligned} n_i(t) &= \mathbb{P}_t\bigg(\tau_i \in (t, T_i]\bigg), \\ &= \sum_{k=1}^{N_i} p_{t_i}(t_{k-1}, t_k). \end{aligned} \tag{9.40}$$

This is comparable to the quantity in Eq. 9.39, but it is updated to incorporate the default-probability estimate embedded in the latest point-in-time curve. It is, to be clear, entirely possible that the credit obligor may have experienced an upgrade or downgrade from inception (i.e., $\bar{t}_i$) to the current calculation date (i.e., $t$). In most cases, however, we would expect the credit rating to remain unchanged.

---

[42] Beerbaum and Ahmad [3] provide some useful insight into this question.

[43] One can, and should, also use *qualitative* criteria to determine if a significant increase in credit risk has occurred. Given the focus of this work, however, we will restrict our attention to the quantitative dimension.

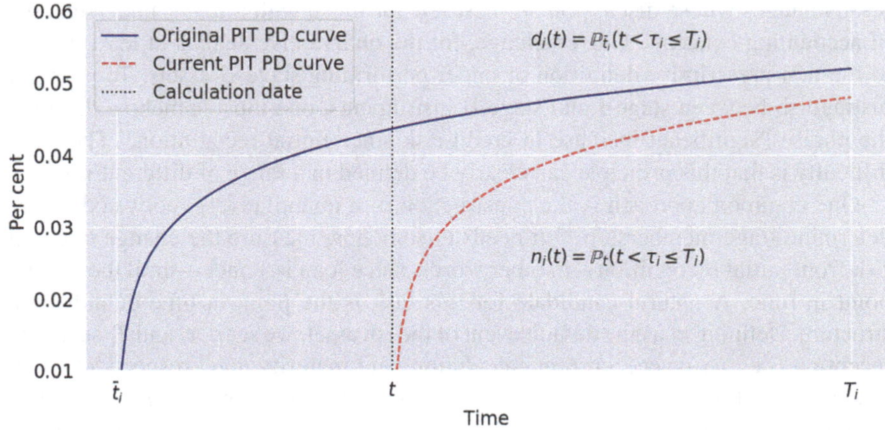


**Fig. 9.11** *A possible stage-allocation rule*: This graphic schematically describes a possible quantitative decision rule—following from Eqs. 9.39 to 9.41—to determine the stage membership of an individual loan.

Given the definitions from Eqs. 9.39 and 9.40, a proposed quantitative decision rule becomes

$$\text{(Possible) Stage Decision Rule}_i = \begin{cases} \frac{n_i(t)}{d_i(t)} \leq \epsilon: & \text{Stage 1} \\ \frac{n_i(t)}{d_i(t)} > \epsilon: & \text{Stage 2} \end{cases}, \tag{9.41}$$

for $i = 1, ..., I$ where $\epsilon \in \mathbb{R}_+$ is a predetermined boundary.[44] It is basically a ratio of current to original default-probability estimates over each loan's remaining term.

Figure 9.11 schematically describes the decision rule following from Eqs. 9.39 to 9.41. It is clear that our ratio $\frac{n_i(t)}{d_i(t)}$, under this construction, must exceed one to represent *any* degree of credit-risk increase. What specifically represents a *significant* increase is unclear. Does it need to double or triple (i.e., $\epsilon = 2$ or 3)? This is for the firm, and their auditors, to determine. In any event, it is a fairly important decision.

While this approach to stage-allocation has a sensible internal logic and provides some quantitative security, it is not without its flaws. From a modelling perspective, it does not receive high marks for parsimony. While we can conceptually understand what is going on, it is practically difficult to develop much intuition as to which specific firms will find their way into stage II. This lack of clarity can create interpretation and communication challenges.

The second, more serious, challenge relates to the passage of time and the value of information. The comparison of point-in-time default probabilities, formulated at

[44] It is also possible, and practically advisable, to require that $n_i(t) - d_i(t)$ exceeds some minimum value. This avoids large percentage changes in small numbers driving a stage-allocation decision.

two distinct moments, is a central aspect of the decision rule in Eq. 9.41. It is also its principal weakness. We are comparing a loan at two potentially very different points in its life cycle. If $\bar{t}_i \ll t$, for example, then the value of $d_i(t)$ will essentially be summing over through-the-cycle default probabilities.[45] In certain situations, our decision rule can find itself performing a pure comparison between point-in-time and through-the-cycle default curves. This undermines the logic of the quantitative test.

Following from the previous point, it is possible for a loan, when using the approach in Eq. 9.41, to move into stage II absent an actual credit-rating downgrade. Let's consider financial institutions computing expected-credit losses—and using our decision rule from Eq. 9.41—during the extreme macro-financial setting reigning in the spring of 2020 at the outset of the COVID-19 pandemic. Most macro-financial scenarios during this period were (quite rightly) dire. This led to a significant upwards shift in virtually all point-in-time default probabilities curves. The ratio of current to initial cumulative default probability consequently stepped up importantly forcing numerous firms—who had not experienced a downgrade—into stage II. In the limit, pushing this point to its logical extreme, a sufficiently sizable macro-financial shock could theoretically force the entire portfolio into stage II.

It is hard to tell if this is a feature or a shortcoming of Eq. 9.41's decision rule. We can, in a rough manner, view a loan's credit rating as mainly describing the idiosyncratic dimension. The point-in-time default probability, by contrast and construction, possesses a strong systemic element. Our decision rule—absent any credit migration—appears to be disproportionately focused on the systemic dimension. It is an open question, unfortunately not directly addressed in the IFRS 9 guidance, as to whether the stage-allocation decision should be driven by a loan's idiosyncratic or systemic risk characteristics. While somewhat out of the scope of this predominately practical quantitative discussion, the consequent macroeconomic pro-cyclicality of this decision rule is certainly of interest to financial regulators.[46]

Whether you find it compelling or not, the stage logic embedded in Eq. 9.41 is complex. It is difficult to understand, communicate, implement, and validate. Moreover, its heavy weight on the systemic dimension can lead to unwanted pro-cyclical loan-impairment dynamics. The systemic dimension aside, some may find it rather hard to argue for a **significant increase in credit risk** without any explicit (internal or external) credit downgrade. To this end, we offer a simplified alternative. It focuses entirely on the distance between the loan obligor's current and initial (i.e., at loan issuance) credit rating. By construction, a downgrade is necessary for movement to stage II and involves *four* disjoint cases. Specifically, a loan is classified depending on the magnitude and final location of any downgrade between

[45] This is because the macro-financial information will have long decayed and the associated default probabilities will have converged to their unconditional values.

[46] For those interested in an engaging discussion of these issues, please see ESRB [12].

the issue time (i.e., $\bar{t}_i$) and the current time (i.e., $t$) of

$$\text{(Alternative) Stage Decision Rule}_i = \begin{cases} \underbrace{\{S_i(t) - S_i(\bar{t}_i) \geq 1\}}_{\text{1+ notch downgrade}} \cap \underbrace{\{S_i(t) \geq 11\}}_{\substack{\text{Speculative}\\ \text{grade}}} : & \textbf{Stage 2} \text{ (Case 1)} \\ \underbrace{\{S_i(t) - S_i(\bar{t}_i) \geq 2\}}_{\text{2+ notch downgrade}} \cap \underbrace{\{6 \leq S_i(t) \leq 10\}}_{\substack{\text{Low investment}\\ \text{grade}}} : & \textbf{Stage 2} \text{ (Case 2)} \\ \underbrace{\{S_i(t) - S_i(\bar{t}_i) \geq 3\}}_{\text{3+ notch downgrade}} \cap \underbrace{\{1 \leq S_i(t) \leq 5\}}_{\substack{\text{High investment}\\ \text{grade}}} : & \textbf{Stage 2} \text{ (Case 3)} \\ \text{Otherwise}: & \textbf{Stage 1} \text{ (Case 4)} \end{cases} \tag{9.42}$$

for $i = 1, ..., I$ where $S_i(x)$ denotes the credit rating of the $i$ financial asset at time $x$. It is logically motivated by the form of the lifetime expected-credit loss, as a function of credit rating, illustrated in Fig. 9.9. A one-notch downgrade in speculative grade (i.e., PD11 to PD20) leads to a linear increase in expected-credit loss. This can be characterized as significant. A one-notch downgrade in the investment-grade sector, however, would not appear to rise to the level of "significant." Investment grade is itself split into two halves. From PD05 to PD10, where the slope of Fig. 9.9 is beginning to rise, a two-notch downgrade is considered significant. From PD01 to PD05, a downgrade of three steps is necessary for movement to stage II. Naturally, any four-notch downgrade is considered significant. One can naturally quibble with this logic, but it is less complex, easily verified, systemically independent, and dramatically easier to manage.[47] It also, strictly speaking, fulfils the IFRS 9 guidance insofar as it takes into account the initial recognition information and explicitly defines a *significant* credit event. It fails, however, to incorporate a forward-looking (or systemic) perspective.

**Colour and Commentary 113** (STAGE-ALLOCATION RULES)*: The principles-based IFRS 9 is not particularly concrete regarding the practical distinction between stage I and II assets. The phrase "a significant increase in credit risk" leaves much room for interpretation. Two possible alternatives are considered. The first involves a rather complex comparison of cumulative point-in-time default probabilities—constructed at both the initial (i.e. loan issuance) and current time points—over the remaining lifetime of the loan. The resulting quantitative test offers some benefits, but it makes it hard for loan-impairment consumers to predict, interpret, and verify stage-allocation decisions. The central role of systemic-driven elements—not to mention the*

(continued)

[47] One could also easily add different cases or change the boundaries in Eq. 9.42 without undermining the basic idea.

**Colour and Commentary 113** (continued)
*confusing combination of point-in-time and through-the-cycle perspectives—implies that a loan can potentially move to stage II absent an actual credit downgrade. Moreover, the same dynamics create a highly pro-cyclical expected-credit loss estimator. Depending on one's perspective, this may be considered either a feature or a bug. The second, less controversial alternative, employs the distance between inception and current credit ratings to make the stage-allocation decision. Requiring explicit downgrade, it also incorporates some of the lessons regarding the interaction between expected-credit loss and credit quality learned in the previous analysis. Any actual stage-allocation logic should probably combine a bit of both alternatives as well as any available qualitative criteria.*

## 9.3 Managing Portfolio Composition

Loan portfolios can look very different. A retail-debt portfolio—comprised of say credit-card, automobile, or student-loan obligations—involves a large number of similarly sized, relatively homogeneous credit obligors. Expected-credit losses are, in such cases, rather sensible estimators for true future credit losses. On the other end of the spectrum, one finds small to medium-sized commercial-lending portfolios. In this setting, there is typically only a moderate number of credit counterparties with rather disparate exposures—some small, some average, and others quite large—in the context of fairly heterogeneous credit characteristics. Given the inherent concentrations in such portfolios, expected-credit loss may need to be supplemented. In this final section, we propose a so-called portfolio-composition adjustment that—linking into the economic-capital ideas presented in the previous chapters—(imperfectly) attempts to address this situation.

Our objective is to construct an instrument-level add-on for concentration risks that is simultaneously conceptually defensible and relatively easy to compute. This is not an easy task and we do not claim to have the last word. Instead, the idea is to motivate the problem and transparently propose a possible solution.

### *9.3.1 Motivating Our Adjustment*

For reasonably concentrated commercial-loan portfolios, the expectation of the credit-loss distribution (i.e., the expected-credit loss) may *not* tell the whole story. To understand this point, let us return to our original 15-year, fixed-coupon, amortizing loan example. At PD12, its (lifetime) expected-credit loss was about EUR 36,000, while if assigned PD04 this falls to EUR 1800. If it actually defaults—and the loss-given-default value of 0.3 is realized—the actual loss would amount to EUR 300,000. Irrespective of the rating category, this is many multiples of the expected-credit loss; the situation only gets worse if it is a stage-I asset. If we had 250 such loans with similar characteristics, however, then the expected loss becomes a reasonable estimator of actual credit losses.

Let's make this a bit more precise. The (stage I) expected-loss estimate for a portfolio comprised of 250 identical loans to our amortizing example, from Table 9.7, would be about EUR $2470 \times 250 =$ EUR $617,500$. Realization of such an actual credit loss would necessitate $\frac{\text{EUR } 617,500}{\text{EUR } 300,000} \approx 2$ defaults. This is about 0.8% of the total loans, which agrees very well with the one-year default probability associated with the PD12 credit class.[48] One default would lead to an overestimate of our actual credit losses, while three defaults would move in the other direction. But anything from zero to four or five defaults would put expected and realized defaults roughly into the same ballpark.

To make a point about concentration, we'll now do something a bit unfair and extreme. Let's make one addition to our 150-loan portfolio. It has all of the same characteristics, but unlike the other it has a EUR 50 million notional value. The expected credit loss scales linearly so that we estimate it to be EUR $617,500 +$ EUR $2470 \times 50 =$ EUR $741,000$. There is a slight increase in expected-credit loss, but the concentration is ignored. Imagine now, and you probably saw this coming, that the single large EUR 50 million exposure was to default.[49] The consequence—again assuming a 0.3 loss-given-default—would be an actual credit loss of EUR 15 million, which is about 20 times the expected credit loss estimate.

Despite its inherent unfairness—and slight lack of realism—this example makes an important point. The presence of exposure-based concentrations can, given an unfortunate constellation of defaults, lead to spectacular deviations between estimated expected-credit and realized credit outcomes.[50] Given the lumpy nature of defaults, we do not require a perfect relationship between these two quantities. The problem is that important concentrations can lead to pathological differences. Such a potential wedge between loan impairments and actual credit losses essentially defeats the purpose of entire exercise.

[48] See the first row of the second column of Table 9.8 for this value.

[49] If we like, we can add zero to four defaults in the other instruments as well. It doesn't really matter; the large position is dominant.

[50] In a perfect world, with rich and informative firm-specific datasets, this issue might be addressed in the construction and calibration of the point-in-time stress scenarios. Medium-sized portfolios and rarity of default, however, conspire to force us to estimate loan impairments independently from portfolio concentration.

### 9.3.2 Building an Adjustment

Our concentration problem is intimately related to the right (or positive) skew of the credit-loss distribution.[51] Expected-credit loss is a measure of central tendency, but it has difficulties in the presence of skewness. It is an average loss outcome. Another, well-known and closely related, measure is the median credit loss, which is defined as

$$\mathbb{M}(L) = \inf\left(\ell : \mathbb{P}(L \leq \ell) \geq 0.5\right), \tag{9.43}$$

where $L$ simply denotes the portfolio-credit loss. In a sentence, half of the probability mass lies below (and above) the median. We can provide a more practical definition of Eq. 9.43, which will also look rather familiar. Letting $f_L(\ell)$ describe the portfolio credit-loss density, we have that

$$\int_{\mathbb{M}(L)}^{\infty} f_L(\ell)d\ell = 0.5, \tag{9.44}$$

and with some elementary manipulation, we may conclude that

$$\begin{aligned} \mathbb{P}(L \geq \mathbb{M}(L)) &= 0.5, \\ 1 - \mathbb{P}(L \geq \mathbb{M}(L)) &= 1 - 0.5, \\ \mathbb{P}(L \leq \mathbb{M}(L)) &= 0.5, \\ F_L(\mathbb{M}(L)) &= 0.5, \\ \mathbb{M}(L) &= F_L^{-1}(0.5). \end{aligned} \tag{9.45}$$

While concluding that $\mathbb{M}(L)$ is the 50th quantile of the credit-loss distribution is mostly a definitional exercise, it also explicitly pulls us back into the world of economic capital.

We might (reasonably) expect that $\mathbb{E}(L) \approx \mathbb{M}(L)$. It turns out that there is no specific link between skewness and the relationship between the mean and the median. Thus, although the median cannot directly help us with our concentration problem, it can nonetheless provide some direction. Generalizing Eq. 9.43, we can introduce the following quantity:

$$\mathbb{V}_\delta(L) = \inf\left(\ell : \mathbb{P}(L \leq \ell) \geq \delta\right), \tag{9.46}$$

---

[51] All credit-loss distributions, by their very nature, exhibit such behaviour. Concentration risk, however, exacerbates this situation.

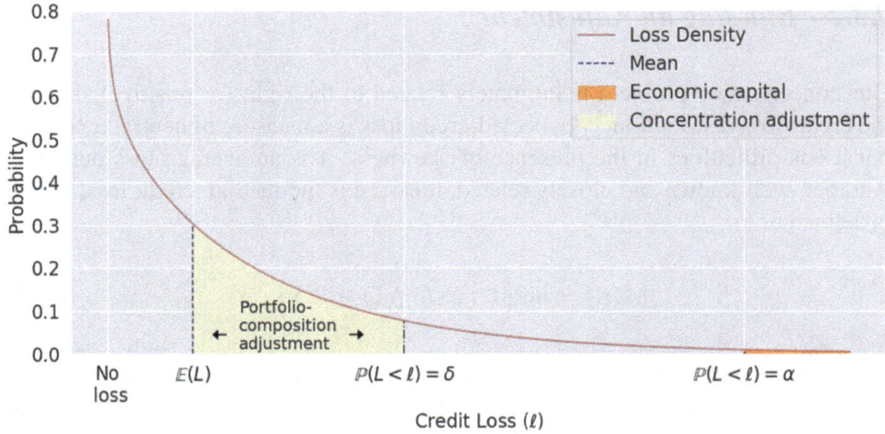


**Fig. 9.12** *A possible portfolio-composition adjustment*: This graphic displays a stylized credit-loss distribution. We see both the expected-credit loss and the $\alpha$-quantile economic capital. A possible portfolio-composition adjustment involves identifying a sensible $\delta$-quantile somewhere between these two extremes.

which allows to immediately conclude that

$$\begin{aligned}\mathbb{V}_{\delta}(L) &= F_L^{-1}(1-\delta), \\ &\equiv \text{VaR}_{\delta}(L),\end{aligned} \tag{9.47}$$

is nothing other than a familiar friend: the $1-\delta$ quantile Value-at-Risk (i.e., $\delta$-VaR) of the credit-loss distribution. This generalization of the median can be tailored to meet our needs.

The source of this concentration issue relates to the linear nature of the expected credit-loss computation. A doubling or tripling of credit exposure leads directly to a strict doubling or tripling of expected-credit loss. Faced with important exposure concentrations in one's portfolio, this characteristic is *not* entirely reasonable. Not all risk measures, however, have this property. Operating on the same underlying credit-loss distribution, a quantile-based risk metric (i.e., VaR) of a given loan position will scale non-linearly for changes in its exposure. If we double the exposure of a position, therefore, we should expect to more than double its VaR-related risk.[52]

Figure 9.12 displays a stylized credit-loss distribution in an effort to motivate our proposed portfolio-composition adjustment. We see both the expected-credit loss (i.e., $\mathbb{E}(L)$) and the $\alpha$-quantile Value-at-Risk (i.e., $\mathbb{V}_{\alpha}(L)$). The intuition is

[52] The degree of non-linearity will be a function of the position's concentration within the overall portfolio. For a coherent risk measure, exhibiting positive homogeneity as required by Artzner et al. [2], doubling one's *portfolio* will double its risk. At the instrument level, however, this does not generally hold.

fairly simple. In a concentrated portfolio, the mean (or the median) is likely to underestimate actual credit losses. A sufficiently high-level VaR figure will do a much better job of capturing worst-case losses, but is far too conservative a tool for loan-impairment purposes. The proposition is that there exists some quantile—let's call it $\delta$—that pulls us away from the expected-loss understatement and incorporates a meaningful degree of worst-case concentration-loss potential. There is no strictly objective way to determine $\delta$—it is an inherently subjective choice—but it is a promising conceptual path for our portfolio-composition adjustment.

To advance ideas, let's leave $\delta$ as an arbitrary value.[53] For each individual instrument, the $\delta$-VaR can be computed and summed to an overall portfolio value as

$$\mathbb{V}_\delta(L) = \sum_{i=1}^{I} \mathbb{V}_\delta(L_i). \tag{9.48}$$

We can view each of the terms in the right-hand side of Eq. 9.48, which are readily computed from the economic-capital model presented in Chap. 2, as the raw materials for our portfolio-composition adjustment. For our purposes, we simply employ a variation of the approximation model introduced in Chap. 5.

The portfolio-composition adjustment should be a non-negative, relatively stable add-on to our base model-derived expected-credit loss estimate. We propose the following structure:

$$\mathbb{O}_\delta(L_i) = \max\Big(\mathbb{V}_\delta(L_i) - \mathbb{E}(L_i), 0\Big) \tag{9.49}$$

for the $i = 1, ..., I$ exposures in the loan-impairment calculation. Equation 9.49 basically compares—on an individual loan basis—the expected-credit loss and $\delta$-VaR values. Should the $\delta$-VaR, with its focus on concentration, exceed our expected-credit loss the difference is allocated to the adjustment. If not, the adjustment is assigned a value of zero.

Combining these ideas with our original expected-credit loss computation, the total proposed loan-impairment of the $i$th instrument is thus,

$$\widetilde{\mathbb{E}(L_i)} = \underbrace{\mathbb{E}(L_i)}_{\substack{\text{Model}\\ \text{ECL}}} + \underbrace{\mathbb{O}_\delta(L_i)}_{\substack{\text{Concen-}\\ \text{tration}}}, \tag{9.50}$$

[53] The reader should feel free to mentally choose any value between about 0.55 and 0.9, depending on the desired degree of risk aversion and conservatism.

where the associated portfolio-level loan-impairment is

$$\widetilde{\mathbb{E}(L)} = \sum_{i=1}^{I} \underbrace{\left( \mathbb{E}(L_i) + \mathbb{O}_\delta(L_i) \right)}_{\widetilde{\mathbb{E}(L_i)}}. \tag{9.51}$$

We can clearly see the importance of one's choice of $\delta$. If we are too conservative, then it is entirely possible that $\mathbb{V}_\delta(L_i) > \mathbb{E}(L_i)$ for all $i$. The consequence would be that

$$\widetilde{\mathbb{E}(L)} = \sum_{i=1}^{N} \mathbb{O}_\delta(L_i) = \text{VaR}_\delta(L). \tag{9.52}$$

In other words, the entire expected-shortfall computation would be replaced with the $\delta$-quantile VaR measure. This would clearly undermine the entire exercise. The trick is to find a level of $\delta$ that is, for most financial assets, close to zero. Ideally, it would take a larger positive value for large concentration positions in one's portfolio. These are precisely the targeted assets, since they are culprits driving the concentration problem. As we saw in our (somewhat rigged) example, a well diversified portfolio typically has a relatively healthy relationship between expected and realized credit losses. If one's portfolio is absent any important concentrations, then optimally our adjustment would be quite small.

Some individuals, when considering the nature of this proposed portfolio-composition adjustment, might object to the inclusion of economic-capital (i.e., unexpected loss) information in the computation of an expected-loss quantity. This is understandable; it feels like mixing apples and pears. To the extent that we wish to correct the expected-loss downward bias arising from concentration, however, there is not an enormous range of useful alternatives. In Chap. 5, we did touch on the concentration literature, which includes concentration and Lorenz curves, Herfindahl-Hirschman indices and Gini coefficients.[54] While it is entirely possible to construct an alternative portfolio-composition adjustment using a variation of such measures, we logically prefer the proposed method. There are two main reasons for this view. First, classical concentration measures consider only the size of the exposure and do not readily simultaneously incorporate regional, industrial, and firm-size considerations. Our economic-capital quantile measures, by virtue of our extensive efforts in previous chapters, do this naturally in the context of our own lending portfolio. In short, it is very hard to find a better source regarding our internal portfolio concentrations than our economic-capital model. This brings us to the second, related point: quantile economic-capital measures are working with the same underlying credit-loss distribution as loan impairments. Admittedly, there are

[54] Yitzhaki and Olkin [28], Figini and Uberti [16], Bellalah et al. [4], Milanovic [24], and Lütkebohmert [22] are a range of helpful entry points into this discussion.

**Table 9.14** *Final amortizing-loan example details*: This table revises (one final time) our amortizing loan example from Table 9.4. It adds a number of additional fields required for the use of the economic-capital default-approximation model from Chap. 5.

| Characteristic | Value |
|---|---|
| Loan-amortization schedule | Amortizing (linear) |
| Maturity $(T - t)$ | 15 years |
| Credit rating $(S_t)$ | PD12 |
| Grace period | 5 years |
| Loan notional amount $(\bar{c})$ | EUR 1,000,000 |
| Loss-given-default $(\bar{\gamma})$ | 0.30 |
| Coupon rate $(\upsilon)$ | 3.00% |
| Effective interest rate $(y)$ | 2.96% |
| Concentration-index value | 0.75 |
| Systemic weight | 0.25 |
| Public-sector entity? | False |

potential differences in time horizon (i.e., one-year or lifetime) and conditionality (i.e., through-the-cycle or point-in-time), but they have a rather great deal in common. To make a sensible adjustment to the bias associated with an estimator to the central moment of any distribution, we necessarily need to incorporate higher moment information. There is simply no better, practical, available source of intelligence about the higher moments of our credit-loss distribution than our very own economic-capital model.

### *9.3.3 Retiring Our Concrete Example*

Our definition of the portfolio-composition adjustment is admittedly abstract. For the final time, before its official retirement, we will return to our imaginary 15-year, PD12, fixed-coupon, amortizing loan. Since we will find ourselves computing various $\delta$-VaR estimates for this instrument, we will require some additional information. Table 9.14 updates our example details to include a concentration-index value, a systemic-weight parameter, and its public-sector status.[55] These values are required—as we saw in Chap. 5—to use our economic-capital default-approximation model.[56]

While certainly computationally convenient, use of our approximation model does pose a few problems. The first is that it approximates economic capital, which is the difference between worst-case and expected credit loss. If we used economic-capital to estimate our $\delta$-VaR, then we'd essentially subtracting expected losses twice when applying Eq. 9.49. This is, fortunately, easily resolved. The default

[55] We've selected fairly average values for this example.

[56] Given the sole focus on the default dimension, we need not use the migration approximation methodology from Chap. 5.

approximation model explicitly includes expected loss; we need only add it back into our approximation.

The second point relates to the nature of the credit-loss distribution returned from our approximation model. The expected-credit loss from Eq. 9.49 will—depending on its stage allocation—be some combination of the point-in-time and through-the-cycle components. If allocated to stage II, then the expected-loss also considers the entire asset's lifetime. The approximation model—based upon daily production runs of the economic-capital model—focuses on a one-year horizon and unambiguously adopts the through-the-cycle perspective. This may appear to be a situation of combining apples and pears. A bit of reflection, however, suggests that this is not necessarily an issue. The base expected-loss calculation and the stage-allocation rules concern themselves with management of the time-perspective and macro-financial conditionality. The portfolio-composition adjustment, conversely, takes a stable, one-year, unconditional (i.e., through-the-cycle) standpoint; in doing so, it (reasonably) cleanly captures the exposure structure of the current portfolio.

The final shortcoming is a bit slippery. Our economic-capital model employs expected shortfall, while we require a VaR estimator for our proposed adjustment. The easiest—although computationally most expensive—solution would be to re-run one's credit-risk model to extract the associated VaR estimators. Since we'd prefer to use our base approximation model from Chap. 5, however, we'll need to do some additional work. The plan is to use the ratio of the multipliers from the parametric versions of the $t$-distributed VaR and expected-shortfall estimators. Our objective is to identify a sensible factor—or rather a number between zero and one—that we can use to scale down the expected-shortfall estimates to bring them closer to an associated VaR.[57] While conceptually straightforward, it involves a bit of tedious mathematics.

Our task is to derive analytic expressions for the VaR and expected shortfall measures under the assumption of $t$-distributed credit losses.[58] From Eq. 9.44, the $(1-\alpha)$-quantile of a standard t-distributed variate $L$ with $\nu$ degrees of freedom—which we'll call $q(\nu,\alpha)$—is written as

$$\int_{-\infty}^{q(\nu,\alpha)} \underbrace{\frac{\Gamma\left(\frac{n+1}{2}\right)}{\Gamma\left(\frac{\nu}{2}\right)\sqrt{\pi\nu}}\left(1+\frac{\ell^2}{\nu}\right)^{-\frac{(\nu+1)}{2}}}_{\text{Loss distribution}} d\ell = 1-\alpha, \tag{9.53}$$

$$\mathbb{P}\left(L \leq q(\nu,\alpha)\right) = 1-\alpha,$$

$$F_{\mathcal{T}_\nu}\left(q(\nu,\alpha)\right) = 1-\alpha,$$

[57] Recall that, by its very construction, the expected-shortfall must be greater than or equal to the VaR metric.

[58] See Kotz and Nadarajah [21] for a wealth of information on this statistical distribution.

where $F_{\mathcal{T}_\nu}(\cdot)$ denotes the standard $t$ cumulative distribution function with $\nu$ degrees of freedom. The solution, as we've seen, is merely

$$q(\nu, \alpha) = F_{\mathcal{T}_\nu}^{-1}(1 - \alpha). \tag{9.54}$$

The standard inverse $t$ cumulative distribution function, $F_{\mathcal{T}_\nu}^{-1}(\cdot)$, similar to its Gaussian counterpart, does not have a closed-form solution. Its value can be found in most statistical or mathematical software packages.[59]

To arrive at a parametric VaR estimator, we need to scale the outcome to the moments of our credit-loss distribution. If $Y$ is a one-dimensional $t$-distributed random variable with $\nu$ degrees of freedom, then $\hat{Y} = a + \sqrt{b}Y \sim \mathcal{T}_\nu\left(a, b \cdot \left(\frac{\nu}{\nu-2}\right)\right)$. We actually desire $\hat{Y} \sim \mathcal{T}_\nu(a, b)$, which is resolved by defining $\hat{Y} = a + \sqrt{\frac{\nu-2}{2}}\sqrt{b}Y$; in this case, then we have indeed $\hat{Y} \sim \mathcal{T}_\nu(a, b)$. This is easily verified

$$\begin{aligned} \hat{Y} &= a + \sqrt{\frac{n-2}{2}}\sqrt{b}Y, \qquad (9.55) \\ \text{var}(\hat{Y}) &= \text{var}\left(a + \sqrt{\frac{n-2}{2}}\sqrt{b}Y\right), \\ &= \left(\frac{n-2}{2}\right) \cdot b \cdot \text{var}(Y), \\ &= \cancel{\left(\frac{n-2}{2}\right)} \cdot b \cdot \cancel{\left(\frac{n}{n-2}\right)}, \\ &= b. \end{aligned}$$

The VaR of the credit-loss distribution is thus approximated as,

$$\begin{aligned} \text{VaR}_\alpha(\nu, L) &\approx \sqrt{\frac{n-2}{n}} q(n, \alpha) \sqrt{\text{var}(L)}, \qquad (9.56) \\ &= \overbrace{\sqrt{\frac{\nu-2}{\nu}} \underbrace{F_{\mathcal{T}_\nu}^{-1}(1-\alpha)}_{\text{Eq. 9.54}}}^{\chi_{\text{VaR}}(\alpha):\text{ VaR multiplier}} \sqrt{\text{var}(L)}. \end{aligned}$$

This is the basic idea behind the parametric estimator, where the term $\chi_{\text{VaR}}(\alpha)$ approximates the $\alpha$-VaR as a multiple of the loss variance.

[59] For a more detailed discussion of numerical and analytic approximations of the standard inverse $t$-distribution, see Shaw [25].

To complete our adjustment ratio, we also need to extend the $t$-distributed parametric credit loss to the notion of expected shortfall. The $(1-\alpha)$-quantile expected shortfall is readily defined as

$$\begin{aligned}
\mathbb{E}\left(L \middle| L \leq q(\nu,\alpha)\right) &= \frac{1}{1-\alpha}\int_{-\infty}^{q(\nu,\alpha)} y f_{\mathcal{T}_\nu}(\ell)d\ell, \qquad (9.57)\\
&= \frac{1}{1-\alpha}\int_{-\infty}^{F_{\mathcal{T}_\nu}^{-1}(1-\alpha)} \ell f_{\mathcal{T}_\nu}(\ell)d\ell,\\
&= \frac{1}{1-\alpha}\int_{-\infty}^{F_{\mathcal{T}_\nu}^{-1}(1-\alpha)} \ell \frac{\Gamma\left(\frac{\nu+1}{2}\right)}{\Gamma\left(\frac{\nu}{2}\right)\sqrt{\pi\nu}}\left(1+\frac{\ell^2}{\nu}\right)^{-\frac{(\nu+1)}{2}} d\ell,\\
&= \frac{\Gamma\left(\frac{\nu+1}{2}\right)}{(1-\alpha)\Gamma\left(\frac{\nu}{2}\right)\sqrt{\pi\nu}}\int_{-\infty}^{F_{\mathcal{T}_\nu}^{-1}(1-\alpha)} \ell\left(1+\frac{\ell^2}{\nu}\right)^{-\frac{(\nu+1)}{2}} d\ell,\\
&= \frac{\Gamma\left(\frac{\nu+1}{2}\right)}{(1-\alpha)\Gamma\left(\frac{\nu}{2}\right)\sqrt{\pi\nu}}\left[-\left(\frac{\nu}{\nu-1}\right)\left(1+\frac{\ell^2}{\nu}\right)^{-\left(\frac{\nu-1}{2}\right)}\right]_{-\infty}^{F_{\mathcal{T}_\nu}^{-1}(1-\alpha)},\\
&= -\frac{\left(\frac{\nu}{\nu-1}\right)\Gamma\left(\frac{\nu+1}{2}\right)}{(1-\alpha)\Gamma\left(\frac{\nu}{2}\right)\sqrt{\pi\nu}}\left(1+\frac{\left(F_{\mathcal{T}_\nu}^{-1}(1-\alpha)\right)^2}{\nu}\right)^{\frac{1-\nu}{2}},
\end{aligned}$$

where $\Gamma(\cdot)$ denotes the gamma-function.[60] This is a bit ugly, but it can be simplified somewhat by patiently collecting a few terms as

$$\begin{aligned}
\mathbb{E}\left(L \middle| L \leq q(\nu,\alpha)\right) &= -\frac{\left(\frac{\nu}{\nu-1}\right)\Gamma\left(\frac{\nu+1}{2}\right)}{(1-\alpha)\Gamma\left(\frac{\nu}{2}\right)\sqrt{\pi\nu}}\left(1+\frac{\left(F_{\mathcal{T}_\nu}^{-1}(1-\alpha)\right)^2}{\nu}\right)^{\frac{1-\nu}{2}}, \qquad (9.58)\\
&= -\frac{\nu^{-\frac{1}{2}}\left(\frac{\nu}{\nu-1}\right)\Gamma\left(\frac{\nu+1}{2}\right)}{(1-\alpha)\Gamma\left(\frac{\nu}{2}\right)\sqrt{\pi}}\left(\frac{1}{\nu}\right)^{-\frac{(\nu-1)}{2}}\left(\nu+\left(F_{\mathcal{T}_\nu}^{-1}(1-\alpha)\right)^2\right)^{\frac{1-\nu}{2}},\\
&= -\frac{2\nu^{\frac{1}{2}+\frac{\nu-1}{2}}\left(\frac{1}{\nu-1}\right)\Gamma\left(\frac{\nu+1}{2}\right)}{(1-\alpha)\Gamma\left(\frac{\nu}{2}\right)2\sqrt{\pi}}\left(\nu+\left(F_{\mathcal{T}_\nu}^{-1}(1-\alpha)\right)^2\right)^{\frac{1-\nu}{2}},
\end{aligned}$$

60 McNeil et al. [23] provide an excellent overview of various risk measures.

$$= -\frac{\nu^{\frac{\nu}{2}}\left(\frac{2}{\nu-1}\right)\Gamma\left(\frac{\nu+1}{2}\right)}{(1-\alpha)\Gamma\left(\frac{\nu}{2}\right)2\sqrt{\pi}}\left(1+\left(F_{\mathcal{T}_\nu}^{-1}(1-\alpha)\right)^2\right)^{\frac{1-\nu}{2}},$$

$$= -\frac{\nu^{\frac{\nu}{2}}\Gamma\left(\frac{\nu-1}{2}\right)}{(1-\alpha)\Gamma\left(\frac{\nu}{2}\right)2\sqrt{\pi}}\left(\nu+\left(F_{\mathcal{T}_\nu}^{-1}(1-\alpha)\right)^2\right)^{\frac{1-\nu}{2}}.$$

The last step follows from the, not terribly obvious, fact that $\left(\frac{\nu-1}{2}\right)\Gamma\left(\frac{\nu-1}{2}\right) = \Gamma\left(\frac{\nu+1}{2}\right)$.[61]

Returning to our running example, we may approximate the $t$-distributed $\alpha$-level expected shortfall as,

$$\mathcal{E}_\alpha(\alpha, L) \approx -\sqrt{\frac{\nu-2}{\nu}}\mathbb{E}\left(L \,\middle|\, L \leq q(\nu,\alpha)\right)\sqrt{\text{var}(L)}, \tag{9.60}$$

$$= \overbrace{\sqrt{\frac{\nu-2}{\nu}}\underbrace{\frac{\nu^{\frac{\nu}{2}}\Gamma\left(\frac{\nu-1}{2}\right)}{(1-\alpha)\Gamma\left(\frac{\nu}{2}\right)2\sqrt{\pi}}\left(\nu+\left(F_{\mathcal{T}_\nu}^{-1}(1-\alpha)\right)^2\right)^{\frac{1-\nu}{2}}}_{\text{Eq. 9.58}}}^{\chi_{\text{ES}}(\alpha):\text{ Expected-shortfall multiplier}}\sqrt{\text{var}(L)}.$$

This finally gets us to our desired quantity. If we combine the multipliers from Eqs. 9.56 and 9.60, we may construct the following *approximate* adjustment to our expected-shortfall estimates:

$$\text{Adjustment Factor}(\alpha) = \frac{\chi_{\text{VaR}}(\alpha)}{\chi_{\text{ES}}(\alpha)}. \tag{9.61}$$

If $\alpha = 0.9997$, then this amounts to about 0.92. That is, the VaR estimate is (approximately) 8% smaller than the equivalent expected-shortfall estimate. It falls to about 0.8 if we reduce $\alpha$ to 0.95. Unfortunately, this analytical approximation starts to break down as we reduce the value of $\alpha$ too far. For our purposes, in the spirit of approximation, we will simply fix $\alpha = 0.999$ and use an adjustment factor of roughly 0.85 to scale down our expected-shortfall estimates across all quantiles.

Figure 9.13 illustrates the application of our approximation model and Eq. 9.50 to our amortizing-bond example. Arbitrarily (but conservatively) setting $\delta = 0.85$,

[61] If you wish to convince yourself of this fact, start with the definition of the gamma function and the integration-by-parts formula,

$$\int_0^\infty u dv = uv|_0^\infty - \int_0^\infty v du, \tag{9.59}$$

where $u = x^{\frac{n-1}{2}}$ and $dv = e^{-t}dt$.

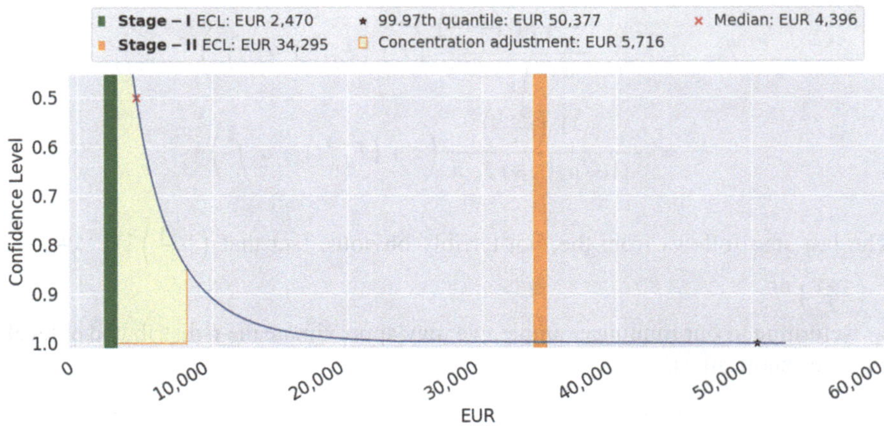


**Fig. 9.13** *Applying our proposed portfolio-composition adjustment*: This graphic summarizes the implications of applying our proposed portfolio-composition adjustment to our amortizing loan example. The displayed value is based, rather arbitrarily, on the 85th quantile. Stage I and II, median, and 99.97th quantile credit losses are included for context.

the portfolio-composition adjustment amounts to roughly EUR 6000. This leads to a roughly threefold increase in stage I loan-impairment allocation for this asset, but only a fraction of the stage-II figure. Interestingly, the median credit-loss is approximately twice the original one-year expected-credit loss of around EUR 2500. The 99.97th quantile VaR estimate, by way of comparison, is slightly less than twice the stage II allocation.

Table 9.15 numerically summarizes the portfolio-composition adjustment results—from both stage I and II perspectives—for a possible range of $\delta$ values from 0.5 to 0.999. What can we conclude? For most reasonable choices of $\delta$, the magnitude of the portfolio-composition adjustment is relatively modest—at least in absolute terms—assuming the loan is allocated to stage I. If our loan is classified

**Table 9.15** *Portfolio-composition adjustment by the numbers*: This table enhances Fig. 9.13 by including the numerical portfolio-composition adjustment values—from both stage I and II perspectives—for a range of alternative choices of $\delta$. Again, all the computations are performed using our running amortizing-bond example.

| | $\max\left(\mathbb{V}_\delta(L_i) - \mathbb{E}(L_i), 0\right)$ | |
|---|---|---|
| Perspective | Stage I | Stage II |
| (Model) expected-credit Loss | 2470 | 34,295 |
| 50.00th quantile adjustment | 2134 | 0 |
| 65.00th quantile adjustment | 3194 | 0 |
| 85.00th quantile adjustment | 5716 | 0 |
| 95.00th quantile adjustment | 10,419 | 0 |
| 99.90th quantile adjustment | 44,320 | 12,495 |

as a stage II credit, then a rather unrealistic setting of $\delta$ is required to generate a non-zero portfolio-composition adjustment.

One financial asset is clearly insufficient to inform one's selection of $\delta$. It needs to be calibrated through examination of one's portfolio concentrations and possible constellations of actual credit losses. Table 9.15 nonetheless provides a few insights. It supports the general idea. Within this fairly generic example, without shocking amounts of effort, it generates fairly reasonable outcomes. It also suggests that one might defensibly set $\delta$ to some value in the interval $[0.55, 0.85]$. Actually identifying a specific setting within this interval, unfortunately, remains a matter of judgement, discussion and potentially disagreement.

**Colour and Commentary 114** (A PORTFOLIO-COMPOSITION ADJUSTMENT): *The IFRS 9 guidance is predicated on the fundamental idea that loan impairments stemming from forward-looking expected-credit loss calculations are sensible predictors of actual portfolio credit losses. This need not be perfect, nor should we expect it to be. Forecast errors and timing issues can lead to significant differences between expected and observed credit losses. For small to medium-sized commercial loan portfolios with significant concentrations, however, the standard expected-credit loss methodology has a downward bias. A few large defaults can generate actual losses that are many multiples of forecasted loan impairments. Borrowing key concepts and tools from previous chapters, we propose a possible add-on to counteract this bias.*[a] *Consistent with the underlying, through-the-cycle credit-loss distribution, it operates on an instrument level to slightly increase the overall loan impairment and thereby counteract the concentration-related bias. Based on a single parameter, which is admittedly difficult to calibrate, this method is far from perfect. That said, although we are unsure of the magnitude of the adjustment, its direction is quite clear. We argue, however, that it is better to imperfectly address this fundamental shortcoming than to ignore it.*[b]

[a] The idea is to get as close as possible to an unbiased estimator.

[b] We are essentially trying to avoid Voltaire's famous observation that, in practical affairs, often "perfect is the enemy of the good."

## 9.4 Wrapping Up

In recent years, starting around 2017 or so, the computation of loan impairments has become a necessarily complicated business. This chapter—supported heavily by extensive foundational discussions in Chaps. 7 and 8—bears evidence to this claim. Derivation of a consistent forward-looking expected-loss estimator on an arbitrarily granular time partition raises a number of questions related to choice of probability measure, handling of the time value of money, determination of default-probability definition, scenario incorporation, and asset-exposure management. Formulating careful and proper responses to these questions—within the context of a concrete, illustrative example—consumed the majority of this chapter.

A second source of complexity relates to the notion of stage definition and allocation introduced in the IFRS 9 accounting standard. While conceptually easy to understand, the principle-based definition leaves substantial room for interpretation. As a consequence, we consider two possible avenues for stage allocation. Both are broadly consistent with the definition, but approach the problem in rather different ways. The final twist on the loan-impairment question stems from the relationship between expected- and realized-credit losses for small to medium-sized commercial loan portfolios with sizable exposure concentrations. In such cases, which coincide with our current situation, the expected-credit loss definition has a downward bias. In other words, the default of a few medium- or large-sized loans could lead to actual credit losses dramatically exceeding the loan-impairment value. Finding a defensible bias correction for this problem is difficult; ultimately, augmenting the central moment of the credit-loss distribution requires incorporation of information regarding one's portfolio composition. Making use of the previously described credit-loss distribution constructed within our economic-capital framework—a natural, well-suited, and available source of intelligence regarding our portfolio's structure—we offer a possible portfolio-composition adjustment to address this shortcoming. The complementarity between loan-impairments and economic capital should not be terribly surprising, since they both depend (albeit in different ways) upon our portfolio's underlying credit-loss distribution.

## References

1. E. I. Altman, B. Brady, A. Resti, and A. Sironi. The link between default and recovery rates: Theory, empirical evidence, and implications. *The Journal of Business*, 78(6):2203–2228, 2005.
2. P. Artzner, F. Delbaen, J.-M. Eber, and D. Heath. Coherent measures of risk. *Mathematical Finance*, 9(3):203–228, July 2001.
3. D. Beerbaum and S. Ahmad. Credit Risk According to IFRS 9: Significant Increase in Credit Risk and Implications for Financial Institutions. Social Science Research Network, January 2015.
4. M. Bellalah, M. Zouari, A. Sahli, and H. Miniaoui. Concentration measures in risk management. *International Journal of Business*, 20(2):110–127, 2015.
5. T. Björk. *Arbitrage Theory in Continuous Time*. Oxford University Press, Great Clarendon Street, Oxford, first edition, 1998.
6. C. Bluhm and L. Overbeck. Calibration of PD Term Structures: to be Markov or not to be. *Risk*, 20(11):98–103, November 2007.
7. D. J. Bolder. Affine Term-Structure Models: Theory and Implementation. Bank of Canada: Working Paper 2001-15, October 2001.
8. D. J. Bolder and D. Stréliski. *Yield Curve Modelling at the Bank of Canada*. Technical Report No. 84. Ottawa: Bank of Canada, 1999.

9. D. Duffie. *Dynamic Asset Pricing Theory*. Princeton University Press, Princeton, New Jersey, second edition, 1996.
10. D. Duffie and K. Singleton. *Credit Risk*. Princeton University Press, Princeton, first edition, 2003.
11. B. Efron. Bootstrap methods: Another look at the jackknife. *The Annals of Statistics*, 7(1): 1–26, Jan 1979.
12. ESRB. The Cyclical Behaviour of the ECL Model in IFRS 9. Technical report, European Systemic Risk Board: European System of Financial Supervision, March 2019.
13. H. Etheridge and K. H. Y. Hsu. Financial Instrument Credit Impairment Models - A Rift in the Convergence of IASB and FASB Accounting Standards. *Academy of Accounting and Financial Studies Journal*, 17(12):119–126, 2013.
14. EY. Impairment of financial instruments under IFRS 9. Ernst & Young Global Corporate Publication, December 2014.
15. EY. Impairment of financial instruments under IFRS 9. Ernst & Young Global Corporate Publication, April 2018.
16. S. Figini and P. Uberti. Concentration measures in risk management. *The Journal of the Operational Research Society*, 64(5):718–723, May 2013.
17. M. Gornjak. Literature Review of IFRS 9 and Its Key Parameters. International School for Social and Business Studies, Slovenia, May 2020.
18. J. Gregory. *Counterparty Credit Risk: The New Challenge for Global Financial Markets*. John Wiley & Sons Ltd., Chicester, UK, 2010.
19. J. Harrison and D. Kreps. Martingales and arbitrage in multiperiod security markets. *Journal of Economic Theory*, 20:381–408, 1979.
20. J. Harrison and S. Pliska. Martingales and stochastic integrals in the theory of continuous trading. *Stochastic Processes and Their Applications*, 11:215–260, 1981.
21. S. Kotz and S. Nadarajah. *Multivariate t Distributions and Their Applications*. Cambridge University Press, New York, 2004.
22. E. Lütkebohmert. *Concentration Risk in Credit Portfolios*. Springer Verlag, Berlin, 2008.
23. A. J. McNeil, R. Frey, and P. Embrechts. *Quantitative Risk Management: Concepts, Tools and Techniques*. Princeton University Press, New Jersey, 2015.
24. B. Milanovic. The Gini-type functions: An alternative derivation. *Bulletin of Economic Research*, 46(1):81–89, 1994.
25. W. T. Shaw. New methods for simulating the student t-distribution–direct use of the inverse cumulative distribution. Nomura Centre for Quantitative Finance, January 2006.
26. S. Tzu. *The Art of War*. Bantam Doubleday, Dell Publishing Group, 1983.
27. B. H. Yang. Point-in-time PD term structure models for multi-period scenario loss projection: Methodologies and implementations for IFRS 9 ECL and CCAR stress testing. MPRA Paper 76271, University Library of Munich, Germany, January 2017.
28. S. Yitzhaki and I. Olkin. Concentration indices and concentration cures. *Stochastic Orders and Decision under Risk*, IMS Lecture Notes – Monograph Series 1991.

# Part IV
# Other Practical Topics

# Chapter 10
# Measuring Derivative Exposure

*If a man tells you he knows a thing exactly, then you can be safe in inferring that you are speaking to an inexact man.*

*(Bertrand Russell)*

One of the central inputs in the computation of credit-risk economic capital, which is often somewhat taken for granted, is a position's expected exposure at default. In full generality, this is a random quantity following some (potentially complicated) probability law. For standard linear instruments—such as loans, deposits, or bonds—it is common practice to ignore their stochastic nature and assume deterministic exposures. This is (mostly) defensible, because the uncertainty surrounding future exposure outcomes is usually sufficiently small that the extra effort (and incremental complexity) is unwarranted. For some financial instruments, this argument is less compelling. Derivative contracts are the classic counterexample.

There is a fundamentally large amount of variability in the exposure associated with a future default event involving (interest-rate, cross-currency, or default) swaps, options, or forward contracts. Swaps and forward contracts are linear, but at any given point in time they may represent an asset or a liability to their holders; more importantly, their status can change quickly with market movements. The same cannot (typically) be said for option contracts, but their situation is often complicated by non-linear pay-off structures.[1] To be blunt, assuming deterministic exposure-at-default values for derivative contracts is a singularly bad idea.

This important realization, it turns out, opens something of a Pandora's box of incremental questions for consideration. Indeed, it is so involved that it has spawned a separate, albeit related, field of analysis: counterparty credit risk. The bilateral *counterparty* aspect is the deciding factor. Very often, collateral is exchanged to offset and mitigate risks associated with the swings in derivative contract values. Collateral exchange, of course, is governed by legal agreements and operates across multiple derivative contracts with a single counterparty. This fact, combined with the

[1] One can, of course, have swap contracts with embedded optionality. In this way, one has to juggle both sign change in exposures *and* non-linearities with respect to underlying risk factors.



D. Bolder, *Modelling Economic Capital*, Contributions to Finance and Accounting,
https://doi.org/10.1007/978-3-030-95096-5_10

multiplicity of derivative contracts and their associated features, gives rise to many special cases and detailed exceptions. To summarize, the world of counterparty credit risk is *not* simple.

It is nonetheless necessary to wade into the realm of counterparty credit risk to understand the techniques used to approximate (random) exposure-at-default amounts associated with one's derivative contracts. This chapter attempts to describe the basic challenge, briefly sketch out the *correct* way to address it, review a widely used (and surprisingly useful) regulatory derivative-exposure approximation, and thereby motivate NIB's approach.

## 10.1 The Big Picture

As the name strongly suggests, counterparty credit risk turns around the idea of a counterparty. There are many other possible filters through which one can examine this risk dimension, but this represents the highest level of aggregation. Exposure at default is defined by each individual counterparty. One might, however, have hundreds or even thousands of individual positions of various types, sizes, tenors, and currencies. Moreover, it is entirely possible that multiple legal agreements might be in place—for different sub-entities or instrument types—with a single counterparty. This immediately raises a second critical point: how should these various positions be aggregated? This falls under the category of questions that are notoriously easy to ask, but rather more difficult to answer.

A useful way to think about aggregation is to introduce the notion of a netting set. Duffie and Canabarro [11] refer to this helpful idea as a netting node, but the idea is identical. Closely related, although not necessarily identical, is the so-called margin set or node. Duffie and Canabarro [11] describe this as:

> a collection of trades whose values should be added in order to determine the collateral to be posted or received.

The central idea behind netting is to permit, within a collection of trades, market values to offset one another when aggregating credit exposures. If, for example, you have two trades—one negative and the other positive—netting permits the negative exposure to (at least, partly) nullify the positive component.[2] As clearly highlighted in Gregory [13], such an arrangement has value under *two* main conditions. First, some (or all) of the trades must potentially take negative values. A bit of reflection reveals that no netting benefit is possible if *all* market values are strictly positive (or negative). The second, perhaps less obvious, point touches upon the dependence between market-value outcomes. In the event of perfect (positive) correlation between current and future market values, there will be limited scope for

[2] When you think about it, this is far from obvious, since these represent two separate contracts. Salonen [20] provides an interesting and comprehensive discussion of how this notion developed, which is far outside of the author's area of expertise.

any difference in sign between individual positions; the consequence would, once again, be no netting benefit. Naturally, perfect correlation is somewhat exaggerated and rarely observed in practice, but it represents a limiting case. In general, the stronger the positive correlation between the underlying risk factors driving the valuation of the derivative trades in one's netting set, the lower the potential netting benefit.

Although the most natural form of aggregation occurs along netting sets, the margin set determines the collateral. Collateral levels, in turn, have important implications for one's exposure computations. A central divide, therefore, is between margined and unmargined netting sets. Unmargined netting sets are not, it should be stressed, completely absent of any collateral. Typically, some initial margin or independent amount is posted at the inception of these trades, which can often be adjusted in the event of a credit-migration event by either counterparty.[3] The distinction between margined and unmargined netting sets comes from the role of variation margin; these are amounts that are exchanged (usually on a daily basis) in the event of changes in the netting set's market value.

In straightforward cases—which happily coincides with NIB's situation—a counterparty can be mapped to a single, common netting and margin set. It is possible to have a margin set comprise multiple netting sets; that is, there may be a one-to-many mapping between margin and netting sets.[4] For the purposes of this discussion, we will assume a one-to-one mapping between netting sets and counterparties as well as between netting and margin sets. To be very explicit, all derivative trades (or positions) with a single counterparty are netted and follow a common margin policy. Deviations from this rule are practically essential to capture in one's portfolio—and most definitely should not be assumed away—but they do not add much to the overall narrative. They result in more dimensionality and logistical complexity, but their management mostly just requires careful bookkeeping.

Figure 10.1 tries to conceptualize our simplified view of the interaction between the counterparty, netting, margining, and our set of derivative trades. Practically, as indicated, there might be multiple hedging sets within each margin set and many margin sets for a given counterparty. The viewpoint in Fig. 10.1 will, however, be sufficient to address the main concepts associated with the determination of credit counterparty exposures.

[3] Initial margin and independent amount are conceptually the same thing, but the specific choice of term appears to depend on the situation and instrument type. See Gregory [13] for more background on basic collateral concepts.

[4] The reverse does not seem to be the case. That is, one does not (to the best of the author's knowledge) observe multiple margin sets within a single netting set.

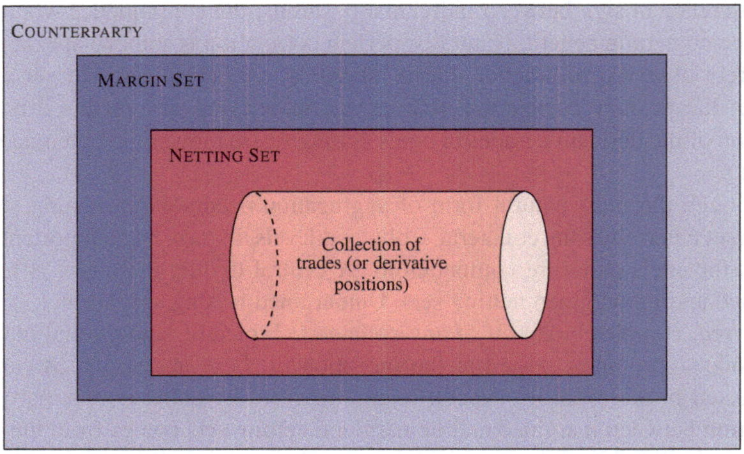


**Fig. 10.1** *A simplified hierarchy*: This schematic illustrates, in a high-level conceptual manner, the interactions between counterparty, margin and netting sets, and the collection of derivative trades. This is a simplified representation; in practice, there are often many netting and margin sets associated with a given counterparty.

**Colour and Commentary 115** (A KEY TASK IN CREDIT COUNTERPARTY RISK)*: Aggregation of exposures for plain-vanilla instruments—such as loans, bonds, or deposits—is dead simple: you just need to add them up. Moreover, their relative stability (typically) precludes the need to treat such exposures as stochastic. The exposure picture for derivative contracts is rather murkier due to their ability to quickly move from asset to liability, imperfect correlation structures, and pay-off non-linearities. Derivative exposures, as a consequence, cannot responsibly be treated in a deterministic fashion. The quantitative risk analyst's task is to determine a (defensible) derivative exposure-at-default amount for each of her institution's credit counterparties at a given point in time. This necessitates the aggregation of individual trade (or position) market values along netting relationships. It further involves the incorporation of collateral over each margin set. The entire point of collateral, of course, is to mitigate credit losses in the event of a counterparty default. There will be different amounts of collateral depending on the margining policy and this needs to be taken into consideration. The final, and not least complicated, issue involves making some adjustment for the fact that individual netting set market values can actually move against us. Despite the presence of collateral, market forces can (and do) lead to increased exposure and consequently larger potential default losses. Building a comprehensive framework to capture all of these moving parts is, in terms of a big picture, not particularly easy. We will have our hands full in the following discussion.*

## 10.2 Some Important Definitions

There are a number of fundamental definitions that need to be introduced to make any useful headway in this area. Almost as important as the definitions themselves is the establishment of a meaningful and descriptive notation. Given the numerous possible levels of aggregation, keeping track of the details will prove essential to success in this venture. There are many excellent sources on these basic definitions, but this treatment draws principally from Gregory [13] and Duffie and Canabarro [11]. Our notation has a few unique elements, but it is certainly inspired from these and other helpful sources.

We begin at the trade or position level. Although we use the terms trade and position interchangeably in this discussion, they are not precisely identical. One might buy a futures contract in a number of separate transactions, where each one would be a trade. The collection of these identical trades represents a position. Systems operate at either level, and occasionally both, so exactly how this is performed can vary. Whichever one uses, we can think of these as being (close to) the most atomistic level of derivative exposure definition. We define $V_{kt}(i)$ as the market value of the $k$th derivative position with the $i$th counterparty at time $t$.[5] The notation thus makes reference to the position, the counterparty, and the current point in time. Assuming a single netting and margin set for the $i$th counterparty, we can compute the netting-set market value as,

$$V_t(i) = \sum_{k=1}^{K_i} V_{kt}(i), \tag{10.1}$$

where $K_i$ represents the number of individual derivative trades in the $i$th counterparty's netting set.[6]

The notion of exposure comes in a variety of flavours in the field of counterparty credit risk. Counterparty *exposure* is typically written as,

$$\begin{aligned} E_t(i) &= \max\left(V_t(i), 0\right), \\ &\equiv \left(V_t(i)\right)^+. \end{aligned} \tag{10.2}$$

In plain English, the exposure is the positive part of the netting set's market value. The sole focus on positive outcomes is natural since, in the event of default, no

[5] Unless otherwise specified, as elsewhere in this book, we use $t$ to denote the current point in time.

[6] In the case of multiple netting sets, then one has multiple versions of Eq. 10.1.

loss is incurred in the face of negative market values.[7] Sometimes the term *current exposure* is used to refer to Eq. 10.2, because it denotes the time $t$ exposure.

The origin of most of the complexity in this area stems from precisely the fact that derivative transactions—and by extension derivative books—can take both positive and negative values. That one's current exposure is zero, by virtue of a negative netted market valuation, is *no* assurance that it will remain so tomorrow, the day after, or next week. Not being able to peek into the future, we cannot know what will happen. As prudent risk managers, however, we can try to prepare for the worst. This leads to the idea of future exposure, which we could denote as $E_{t+T}(i)$. This would be the (unknown) exposure to counterparty $i$ at time $T$ or $T - t$ units of time into the future.

The best we can do, absent a functioning crystal ball, is to treat $E_{t+T}(i)$ as a random variable. It is thus interesting to consider the mathematical expectation of this value as,

$$\mathbb{E}\left(E_{t+T}(i)\middle|\mathcal{F}_t\right) = \mathbb{E}\left(\underbrace{\max\left(V_{t+T}(i), 0\right)}_{\text{Eq. 10.2}}\middle|\mathcal{F}_t\right), \tag{10.3}$$

$$\mathbb{E}_t\left(E_{t+T}(i)\right) = \mathbb{E}_t\left(\left(V_{t+T}(i)\right)^+\right),$$

where $\mathcal{F}_t$ is the information set (or $\sigma$-algebra) at time $t$. Probabilistic details aside, the $\mathcal{F}_t$ explicitly captures the idea that such computations can only be performed with the information available at time $t$; anything else would be essentially cheating. To avoid the clutter of the conditioning set, however, we define the *expected exposure* (or EE) as $\mathbb{E}_t\left(E_{t+T}(i)\right)$. To actually evaluate Eq. 10.3, it is necessary to make some sort of distributional assumption about the market value of our counterparty's netting set, $V_{t+T}(i)$.

Equation 10.3 illustrates the expected exposure of counterparty $i$ for a given point of time in the future, $T$. Practically, for example, we might set $T - t$ to be one-year in the future. It is also interesting to consider the full time profile of expected exposures for $\tau \in (t, T]$. To boil this down to a single number, it is common to compute the average expected exposure over such a time interval. Mathematically, this would reduce to integrating Eq. 10.3 over the time dimension and dividing the result by

[7] It would be helpful to describe the quantity in Eq. 10.2 as *positive* exposure to avoid confusion. Sadly, this is not the case.

$T - t$. This yields

$$\mathbb{E}_t\Bigg(E(i,t,T)\Bigg) = \frac{1}{T-t}\int_t^T \mathbb{E}_t\Bigg(\Bigg(V_{t+\tau}(i)\Bigg)^+\Bigg)d\tau. \tag{10.4}$$

This quantity is generally referred to as the *expected positive exposure* or EPE. We opted to write it as $\mathbb{E}_t\Bigg(E(i,t,T)\Bigg)$ to illustrate the explicit dependence on the counterparty, the information set, and the time interval.

Another twist on counterparty exposure is the so-called *potential future exposure* or PFE measure. It may be defined as,

$$\text{PFE}_\alpha(i,t,T) = \inf_{x\in\mathbb{R}}\Bigg(x\Bigg|\mathbb{P}\Bigg(V_{t+T}(i)\geq x\Bigg)\geq 1-\alpha\Bigg). \tag{10.5}$$

where $\alpha$ is a predefined confidence level. Those familiar with the Value-at-Risk (or VaR) metric—or have already reviewed Chaps. 2 or 5 or even Chap. 7—will see a clear similarity. The key difference between PFE and VaR is which tail of the value distribution they focus upon. VaR is concerned with downside losses, whereas PFE attempts to describe upside derivative-valuation gains. The reason, of course, is that the larger the positive value of one's netted derivative exposure with a given counterparty, the larger the scope for losses in the event of default. As we will see in the next section, however, Eq. 10.5 might be the typical definition of PFE, but it is not the only way this quantity might be computed.

Expected and potential-future exposure (i.e., EE and PFE) are thus looking at the same underlying distribution; the former examines the expectation, while the latter concerns itself with a given quantile. The choice of exposure measure along with the specification of $\alpha$ and, not least, the determination of $T$ all depend on the specific application and one's desired degree of conservatism. For the reporting of one's exposure, it might make sense to use the expected exposure measure. Economic-capital—with its focus on worst-case events—might usefully employ the PFE perspective. Whatever one's selection, it requires some reflection and justification.

Figure 10.2 helps to turn the previous equations into visualizations by illustrating the interaction between netting set valuations, (positive) exposure, expected exposure, and potential future exposure. The left-hand side considers one-step into the future over the interval, $(t, T]$; here we clearly see the current, expected, and potential-future exposures. The right-hand graphic, conversely, takes *five* steps to span the time interval, $(t, T]$; many more steps, of course, are possible. This allows for the introduction of the expected positive exposure measure.

There are a few final concepts that are worth introducing to avoid confusion down the road. These ideas stem principally from the regulatory setting.[8] They

---

[8] See BIS [3] for more detailed background.

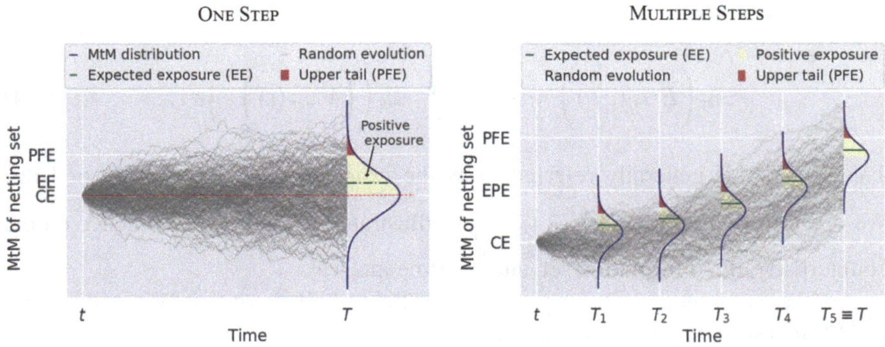


**Fig. 10.2** *Some useful visualizations*: The graphics above illustrate the interaction between netting set valuations, (positive) exposure, expected exposure, and potential future exposure. The two graphics examine both one- and multiple-step perspectives, which allow for the introduction of expected positive exposure.

all relate to the passage of time. Either the plain expected exposure (i.e., EE) or expected positive exposure (i.e., EPE) can be computed for a range of possible future points in time. As we move further out the horizon, there will be some maturities in one's derivative netting set. This will naturally lead to a gradual decrease in both the EE and EPE measures. Although, in practice, these positions are likely to be either rolled-over or otherwise replaced, such assumptions are complicated and typically not included in one's analysis. The regulatory solution was to introduce the idea of *effective* EE and EPE measures. The effective means that the EE and EPE profiles are computed, but then are adjusted so that they are (weakly) monotonically increasing (i.e., non-decreasing).[9] Imagine, for example, that you calculated the effective exposure in monthly time steps out to a year. If the highest EE estimate occurred during the seventh month, then the effective EE would fix all subsequent (lower) values to the maximal amount.

**Colour and Commentary 116** (Derivative Exposure Definitions)*: Counterparty credit risk can, and should, be viewed as a risk-management sub-field. Like all areas of endeavour, it has its own central ideas and vernacular. The preceding definitions represent essential groundwork for the computation of exposure-at-default values for one's derivative portfolios; while not entirely comprehensive, they do touch upon the core of counterparty credit-risk measurement. A few important commonalities arise. First, attention is strongly on the positive part of the future netting-set valuations.*

(continued)

[9] This is a fairly unfortunate choice of word, since *effective* does not usually, in the author's understanding of general English-language parlance, imply weak positive monotonicity.

**Colour and Commentary 116** (continued)
*This makes logical sense since this is where the risk lies. The second point is that there are both cross-sectional and time dimensions at play. There is a collection of derivative contracts for a given point in time (i.e., the cross section), but we are also interested in how the value of these contracts behaves over various periods (i.e., the time dimension). We will have to manage randomness of the underlying risk drivers associated with our derivative positions along both dimensions; this will necessarily involve implicitly or explicitly introducing stochastic processes. Given that netting effectiveness depends importantly on correlation assumptions, the joint distribution of the various marginal risk-factor dynamics will also play an important role.*

## 10.3 An Important Choice

Financial institutions with large derivative portfolios inevitably find themselves in the valuation business. To permit proper exchange of collateral, a market-consistent current value for all derivative contracts in one's portfolio is required. This necessitates implementation of pricing formulae (or numerical algorithms) linking the individual cash-flows of each instrument to its associated underlying risk factors: interest rates, exchange rates, commodity prices, and so on. Often embedded within these pricing approaches—or determined for relatively modest additional cost—are associated hedging ratios and risk-factor sensitivities. These quantities can help predict changes in the value of individual instruments—and by extension one's portfolio—for given movements in key risk factors. Development, construction, and maintenance of such valuation frameworks involve much work and significant resources. It is, however, basically a cost of being a player in derivative markets.

Linking this back to our previous definitions, we can see how this valuation infrastructure feeds into counterparty credit risk. Without proper and timely valuations, we cannot hope to reasonably exchange collateral or compute current exposure levels. Equations 10.1 and 10.2 are only knowable with the appropriate valuation machinery. This is good news, since part of what we need is, literally by construction, already available. As we move to Eq. 10.3, however, the situation changes. No matter how sophisticated one's valuation framework, it cannot tell you the value of individual derivative instruments in the future. These outcomes are unknown and depend, of course, on the stochastic evolution of multiple market-related random variables.

The *correct* solution to this problem involves the creation of a second forward-looking valuation framework, which lies on top of the base pricing infrastructure. It is an analytically and computationally intensive undertaking. Generally, it relies on simulation methods. This is partly due to the complexity of the underlying instruments, but principally due to the non-analytic nature of collateral exchange and the management of netting and margin sets. It begins with the calibration and simulation of a collection of correlated stochastic processes, over some pre-defined analysis horizon, describing the set of risk drivers for one's derivative portfolio.

Stepping forward into the future—for each sample path and along time grids of varying granularity—one revalues each individual instrument, revises cash-flow patterns as necessary, exchanges collateral (or not), and determines the time profile of the netting set for each credit counterparty.[10] This process helps to trace out the (simulated) evolution of derivative exposure for each counterparty in one's portfolio. With such an engine, (positive) exposure, expected exposure, expected positive exposure, potential future exposures, and many other possible variations are readily numerically approximated.

The ability to describe the future evolution and distribution of one's derivative portfolio—by individual instrument and counterparty—offers value beyond exposure computation. Following the great financial recession, there have been fairly dramatic changes in how credit risk is incorporated into derivative pricing.[11] This leads to the idea of the credit valuation adjustment (CVA) and its many related flavours, which is generally referred to as XVA.[12] Such simulation engines also play a central role in this derivative-pricing activity. As a consequence, it is common for financial institutions heavily involved with derivative instruments to have not only a valuation engine, but also a complex apparatus for PFE and XVA computations.

At first glance, the solution to our problem seems obvious. Given an army of quantitative analysts already computing exposure profiles for individual instruments and counterparties, we should simply borrow their results for our purposes. It is always pleasant to find someone competent to perform a difficult task for you. Ultimately, despite a few clear advantages, we have nonetheless opted *not* to follow this route. Instead, we make use of a regulatory approximation. There are *three* main reasons. First, and perhaps most importantly, our focus is on the risk-management dimension. Most forward-looking simulation engines are firmed focused on pricing; they work with different time horizons and probability measures. A second point relates to conditionality. We seek a through-the-cycle perspective in our economic-capital computations to avoid—as mentioned numerous times in previous chapters—pro-cyclicality. Any sensible forward-looking simulation model is calibrated to current market conditions—otherwise it cannot reproduce current valuations—and is thus, by its very construction, working under the point-in-time viewpoint. The final point relates back to our conceptual axioms introduced in the preface. It is a difficult, full-time job to maintain and run a forward-looking

[10] For some computations, particularly those over short periods, one may ignore the collateral exchange to understand just how bad one's exposure position could become with a given counterparty.

[11] The basic issue was that, prior to the 2008 crisis, most derivative pricing and hedging (more or less) structurally ignored default risk. See Brigo [10] for a much more eloquent and detailed description of this point.

[12] See Ruiz [19] for an excellent jumping off point into this world.

simulation platform; such an engine seeks to perform a complex array of tasks. Were we to simply borrow these results, there is a very real danger of it becoming a black box for risk-management staff. It seems more defensible to use a simpler, more easily understandable approach for our purposes.

**Colour and Commentary 117** (PICKING AN ANALYTIC LANE): *Treatment of derivative exposure as a random variable, for use in our economic-capital model, complicates our life. It turns out, however, that we are not the only group of quantitative analysts taking this perspective. Subsequent to the 2008 global financial crisis, a major rethink occurred in the area of derivative pricing. One of the (many) consequences has been the construction of forward-looking derivative exposure simulation engines to support the revised pricing algorithms. This infrastructure would, at first blush, seem to be tailor-made for our purposes. Sadly, it is not. Forward-looking engines have a pricing, and not risk-management, focus. They are also, by absolute necessity, firmed rooted in the point-in-time perspective. Finally, they embed a level of complexity rather far beyond what is required for our purposes. Such exposure estimates could, rather easily, become a black-box input into our economic-capital computations. From an economic-capital perspective, we require short-term, $\mathbb{P}$-measure, through-the-cycle, and relatively easily interpretable derivative-exposure estimates. With some reluctance, therefore, we have firmly elected to follow the simpler (pseudo-)analytic lane offered by the regulatory authorities.*[a]

[a] This choice, depending on one's organization and resources, certainly need not apply to all financial institutions.

## 10.4 A General, But Simplified Structure

To make any further progress, it is necessary to make some concrete assumptions about the underlying distributional dynamics of the market value of one's netting sets. As just discussed, the most direct way would be to begin by describing the joint behaviour of the underlying collection of (correlated) market risk factors—such as interest rates, exchange rates, commodity prices, or volatilities—that drive derivative valuations. While this approach is the most defensible, it also involves the largest degree of complexity. We have opted for an alternative strategy.

Understanding our requirements, there is a strong incentive to simplify. A useful approach involves working with the overall netting-set market value as a *single*, aggregated random variable. In other words, we exploit the fact that a netting set is a kind of sum of many other random variables. How might this work? Imagine that we define the following stochastic process on $(\Omega, \mathcal{F}, \mathbb{P})$ describing the intertemporal dynamics of the $i$th counterparty's netting set:

$$dV_t(i) = \mu_i dt + \sigma_i dW_t, \tag{10.6}$$

where $\mu_i \in \mathbb{R}$, $\sigma_i \in \mathbb{R}_+$ and $\{W_t, \mathcal{F}_t\}$ is a standard, scalar Wiener process on $(\Omega, \mathcal{F}, \mathbb{P})$. This is a drifted Brownian motion. If we would like to solve Eq. 10.6 for $V_t(i)$, then we need to make use of the underlying, rather famous, theorem from the stochastic calculus.[13]

**Theorem 10.1 (Itô)** *Let $X_t$ be a continuous semi-martingale taking values in an open subset $U \subset \mathbb{R}$. Then, for any twice continuously differentiable function $f : U \rightarrow \mathbb{R}$, $f(X_t)$ is a semi-martingale and,*

$$f(X_T) - f(X_t) = \int_t^T \frac{\partial f}{\partial X_u} dX_u + \frac{1}{2} \int_t^T \frac{\partial^2 f}{\partial X_u^2} d\langle X_u \rangle, \tag{10.7}$$

*where $d\langle X_t \rangle$ denotes the quadratic variation of the process $X_t$.*

This is a fairly trivial application, where we need only select the identity function $f(V_t(i)) \equiv V_t(i)$ to apply Theorem 10.1. This leads to:

$$\begin{aligned} V_T(i) - V_t(i) &= \int_t^T \frac{\partial f(V_u(i))}{\partial V_u(i)} dV_u(i) + \frac{1}{2} \int_t^T \frac{\partial^2 f(V_u(i))}{\partial V_u(i)^2} d\langle V_u(i) \rangle u, \quad (10.8) \\ &= \int_t^T 1 \left( \mu_i du + \sigma_i dW_u \right) - \cancel{\frac{1}{2} \int_t^T 0 \cdot d\langle \mu_i du + \sigma_i dW_u \rangle}, \\ &= \mu_i \int_t^T du + \sigma_i \int_t^T dW_u, \\ V_T(i) &= V_t(i) + \mu_i (T - t) + \sigma_i \left( W_T - W_t \right), \end{aligned}$$

where $W_T - W_t \sim \mathcal{N}(0, T - t)$ is a Gaussian-distributed, independent increment of the Wiener process. The consequence is that for any future time period, $T \geq t$, the market value of our netting set is distributed as

$$V_{t+T}(i) \equiv V_T(i) \sim \mathcal{N}\left( \underbrace{V_t(i) + \mu_i (T - t)}_{\mu_i(t,T)}, \underbrace{\sigma_i^2 \left( T - t \right)}_{\sigma_i(t,T)^2} \right), \tag{10.9}$$

for the $i$th credit counterparty where the functions $\mu_i(t, T)$ and $\sigma_i(t, T)$ are introduced to keep the notation moderately under control. In other words, starting

---

[13] This is only a very quick (and non-rigorous) peek into this vast array of mathematical endeavour. See Karatzas and Shreve [15], Oksendal [18], and Heunis [14] for much more information, rigour, and intuition.

from the current value of $V_t(i)$, it will grow at the rate of $\mu_i$ in a manner proportional to the passage of time. The volatility around this value is $\sigma_i$ scaled by the square-root of the time interval.

The consequence of this mathematical detour is a cohesive approach to the intertemporal dynamics of the total market value of the individual derivative positions with counterparty $i$.[14] Equation 10.9 basically tells us how we can describe the value of a given netting set for any time $\tau \in (t, T]$. All of the intricacy of underlying risk factors is embedded in the value of $\mu_i$ and $\sigma_i$. Information is certainly lost, but this foundational assumption allows us to put more structure—and specificity—to the exposure definitions introduced in the previous section.

### 10.4.1 Expected Exposure

Using Eq. 10.3 and the final result from Eq. 10.9, we may now proceed to put a face to the notion of expected exposure. At first glance, it might seem difficult to actually determine the expectation of only the positive part of $V_{t+T}(i)$. It turns out, however, to be relatively straightforward. Since $V_{t+T}(i)$ is a Gaussian random variable with support on $\mathbb{R}$, the positive expectation is determined by simply integrating over the positive part of this domain, $\mathbb{R}_+$. Practically, this reduces to:

$$\begin{aligned}
\mathbb{E}_t\left(E_{t+T}(i)\right) &= \underbrace{\mathbb{E}_t\left(\left(V_{t+T}(i)\right)^+\right)}_{\text{Eq. 10.3}}, \qquad (10.10)\\
&= \int_0^\infty v f_V(v)dv,\\
&= \int_0^\infty \frac{v}{\sigma_i(t,T)\sqrt{2\pi}} e^{\frac{-(v-\mu_i(t,T))^2}{2\sigma_i(t,T)^2}} dv.
\end{aligned}$$

Although this involves a wearisome bit of calculus, it is instructive to actually solve this integral.[15] It does, however, necessitate a few substitutions. Let us first define $g = v - \mu_i(t,T)$. This immediately implies that $v = g + \mu_i(t,T)$ and consequently

[14] Basically this approach paves over all of the underlying market-risk factors—such as interest rates, foreign-exchange, and key spreads—and operates immediately at the aggregate netting-set level.

[15] This is the type of exercise that is typically left for the reader, which always feels slightly unfair.

$dv = dg$ leading to:

$$\begin{aligned}
\mathbb{E}_t\bigg(E_{t+T}(i)\bigg) &= \int_0^{\infty} \frac{g+\mu_i(t,T)}{\sigma_i(t,T)\sqrt{2\pi}} e^{\frac{-g^2}{2\sigma_i(t,T)^2}}\,dg, \qquad (10.11)\\
&= \int_0^{\infty} \frac{g}{\sigma_i(t,T)\sqrt{2\pi}} e^{\frac{-g^2}{2\sigma_i(t,T)^2}}\,dg + \mu_i(t,T)\int_0^{\infty} \frac{1}{\sigma_i(t,T)\sqrt{2\pi}} e^{\frac{-g^2}{2\sigma_i(t,T)^2}}\,dg.
\end{aligned}$$

Resolution of the first integral in Eq. 10.11 requires a second substitution. Setting $u = \frac{-g^2}{2\sigma_i(t,T)^2}$ gives us $du = \frac{-gdg}{\sigma_i(t,T)^2}$ where $gdg = -\sigma_i(t,T)^2 du$. Plugging this back into Eq. 10.11 and using some basic properties of the normal distribution, we may simplify as:

$$\begin{aligned}
\mathbb{E}_t\bigg(E_{t+T}(i)\bigg) &= \frac{-\sigma_i(t,T)^{\cancel{2}}}{\cancel{\sigma_i(t,T)}\sqrt{2\pi}}\int_0^{\infty} e^u\,du\\
&\quad + \mu_i(t,T)\int_0^{\infty} \frac{1}{\sigma_i(t,T)\sqrt{2\pi}} e^{\frac{-(v-\mu_i(t,T))^2}{2\sigma_i(t,T)^2}}\,dv, \qquad (10.12)\\
&= \frac{-\sigma_i(t,T)}{\sqrt{2\pi}}\Big[e^u\Big]_0^{\infty} + \mu_i(t,T)\underbrace{\int_{\frac{\mu_i(t,T)}{\sigma_i(t,T)}}^{-\infty} \frac{1}{\sqrt{2\pi}} e^{\frac{-v^2}{2}}\,dv}_{\text{To standard normal}},\\
&= \frac{-\sigma_i(t,T)}{\sqrt{2\pi}}\Big[e^{\frac{-(v-\mu_i(t,T))^2}{2\sigma_i(t,T)^2}}\Big]_0^{-\infty} + \mu_i(t,T)\underbrace{\int_{-\infty}^{\frac{\mu_i(t,T)}{\sigma_i(t,T)}} \frac{1}{\sqrt{2\pi}} e^{\frac{-v^2}{2}}\,dv}_{\text{By symmetry}},\\
&= \frac{-\sigma_i(t,T)}{\sqrt{2\pi}}\left(\underbrace{\lim_{v\to\infty} e^{\frac{-(v-\mu_i(t,T))^2}{2\sigma_i(t,T)^2}}}_{=0} - e^{\frac{-\mu_i(t,T)^2}{2\sigma_i(t,T)^2}}\right)\\
&\quad + \underbrace{\mu_i(t,T)\,\Phi\left(\frac{\mu_i(t,T)}{\sigma_i(t,T)}\right)}_{\text{By definition}},\\
&= \frac{\sigma_i(t,T)e^{\frac{-\mu_i(t,T)^2}{2\sigma_i(t,T)^2}}}{\sqrt{2\pi}} + \mu_i(t,T)\Phi\left(\frac{\mu_i(t,T)}{\sigma_i(t,T)}\right),\\
&= \sigma_i(t,T)\phi\left(\frac{\mu_i(t,T)}{\sigma_i(t,T)}\right) + \mu_i(t,T)\Phi\left(\frac{\mu_i(t,T)}{\sigma_i(t,T)}\right),
\end{aligned}$$

where $\phi(\cdot)$ and $\Phi(\cdot)$ denote the standard normal probability density and cumulative distribution functions, respectively.

If we recall our definitions of $\mu_i(t, T)$ and $\sigma_i(t, T)$, the expected exposure (or EE) becomes, in its full glory,

$$\mathbb{E}_t\left(E_{t+T}(i)\right) = \sigma_i\sqrt{T-t}\phi\left(\frac{V_t(i)+\mu_i(T-t)}{\sigma_i\sqrt{T-t}}\right) + \left(V_t(i)+\mu_i(T-t)\right)\Phi\left(\frac{V_t(i)+\mu_i(T-t)}{\sigma_i\sqrt{T-t}}\right), \quad (10.13)$$

for the $i$th counterparty and any arbitrary choice of $T \in (t, \infty)$. This may not be the most pleasant looking or intuitive formula, but it is a concrete analytic consequence of assuming one's netting set's market value follows a drifted Brownian motion process and a firm focus on positive value outcomes. This expression also lies, as we will see in following discussion, at the heart of the suggested regulatory approach towards computation of derivative exposure-at-default estimates.[16]

### 10.4.2 Expected Positive Exposure

Given the form of Eq. 10.13, it would be convenient to derive another formula for the expected positive exposure. Unfortunately, it is not so straightforward. The cumulative distribution function, $\Phi(\cdot)$, is not integrable. Adding another time-related integral over $(t, T]$ does not help matters. In practical settings, it is common practice to analytically compute the expected exposure using Eq. 10.13 over a number of steps along a time partition of $(t, T]$; we then approximate the EPE as the average over this discrete partition of the time domain. This is not particularly satisfying, but it is reasonably manageable. If one desires more precision, then it is always entirely possible to numerically integrate Eq. 10.13 over any individual's time interval of interest.

Figure 10.3 attempts to provide a bit more colour by displaying the analytic expected exposure over a given time period. This example was (arbitrarily) computed using the formula in Eq. 10.13 with $V_t(i) = 5$, $\mu_i = 0.05$, $\sigma_i = 1.75$, and $T - t = 10$. The expected positive exposure is also computed in *two* ways: as a simple average of the expected exposure observations and via numerical integration.[17] There is little or no (practical) difference between these two approaches.

[16] Equation 10.13 plays, roughly speaking, the same role for regulatory counterparty risk exposure calculations as Gordy [12]'s ASRF model in the Basel IRB methodology. See Bolder [9, Chapter 6] for an introduction to these concepts. We'll also return to this point in Chap. 11 when we examine the broader regulatory capital perspective.

[17] For the average computation, *four* discrete steps are taken for each year over $T - t$ for a total of 40 expected-exposure evaluations. As we increase the granularity of the time grid, of course, these two approaches converge.

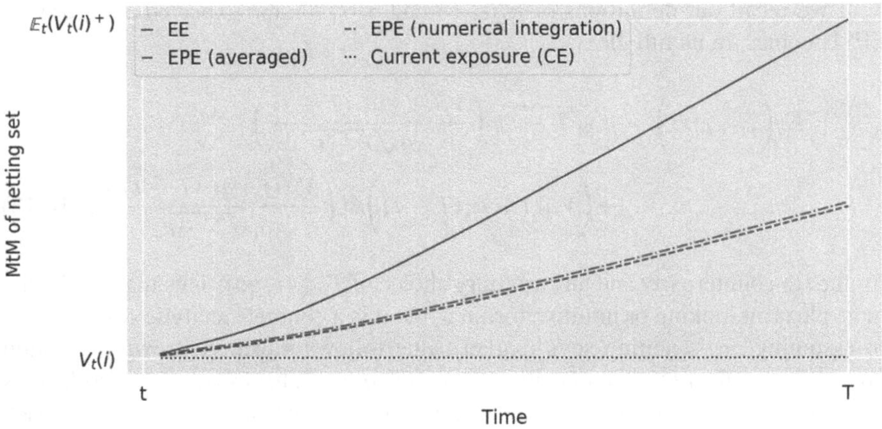


**Fig. 10.3** *Analytic exposure*: This graphic displays the analytic expected exposure over a given time period. The EPE is also computed as a simple average of the EE observations and via numerical integration; there is little or no economic difference. This example was (arbitrarily) computed with $V_t(i) = 5$, $\mu_i = 0.05$, $\sigma_i = 1.75$, and $T - t = 10$.

If one is willing to make an additional assumption, then it is possible to obtain an analytic expression for the expected positive exposure. We need to assume that $\mu_i(t, T) = V_t(i) + \mu_i(T - t) \equiv 0$. Practically, this means that we must eliminate the drift element from our Brownian motion in Eq. 10.6. This transforms Eq. 10.13 into

$$\begin{aligned}\mathbb{E}_t\bigg(E_{t+T}(i)\bigg) &= \underbrace{\sigma_i\sqrt{T-t}\phi\,(0) + (0)\cdot\Phi\left(\frac{0}{\sigma_i\sqrt{T-t}}\right)}_{\text{Eq. 10.13}}, \\ &= \frac{\sigma_i\sqrt{T-t}}{\sqrt{2\pi}}.\end{aligned} \tag{10.14}$$

This eliminates the annoying $\Phi(\cdot)$ term and easily allows us to determine an expected positive exposure expression as,

$$\begin{aligned}\frac{1}{T-t}\int_t^T \mathbb{E}_t\bigg(E_{t+\tau}(i)\bigg)d\tau &= \frac{1}{T-t}\int_t^T \frac{\sigma_i\sqrt{\tau-t}}{\sqrt{2\pi}}d\tau, \\ &= \frac{\sigma_i}{\sqrt{2\pi}(T-t)}\int_t^T \sqrt{\tau-t}\,d\tau, \\ &= \frac{\sigma_i}{\sqrt{2\pi}(T-t)}\left[\frac{2}{3}(\tau-t)^{\frac{3}{2}}\right]_t^T,\end{aligned} \tag{10.15}$$

$$
\begin{aligned}
&= \frac{2\sigma_i}{3\sqrt{2\pi}\cancel{(T-t)}}(\tau - t)^{\frac{\cancel{3}}{2}}, \\
&= \frac{2\sigma_i\sqrt{\tau - t}}{3\sqrt{2\pi}}.
\end{aligned}
$$

The conclusion is that if the netting-set market value follows a Brownian motion with a zero drift and time-homogeneous variance, then both the EE and EPE measures are simply multiples of the volatility and the passage of time. Admittedly, these are perhaps not the most reasonable possible assumptions one might take. They do, however, permit (mostly) analytic formulae and a point of comparison.

### 10.4.3 Potential Future Exposure

Morgan/Reuters [17] originally suggested the VaR measure in the context of portfolio loss. Equation 10.5 provides a twist on this idea. Let's repeat it here—in a slightly different form—to examine it in more detail, help consider alternatives, and understand under what conditions it might be determined analytically. The $\alpha$-VaR of the $i$th counterparty's netting-set exposure over the horizon $T - t$ can be written as,

$$
q_\alpha(i, t, T) = \inf_{x \in \mathbb{R}} \left( x \middle| \mathbb{P}\left( V_{t+T}(i) \geq x \right) \geq 1 - \alpha \right). \tag{10.16}
$$

The function depends on *two* parameters: $\alpha$, which a threshold for the probability on the right-hand side of Eq. 10.16 and the time horizon, $T - t$. Imagine that we set $\alpha$ to 0.95 and $T - t = \frac{1}{52}$ or one week. With these parameter choices, the VaR describes the smallest exposure outcome that exceeds 95% of possible valuations, but is less than 5% of them. In other words, $q_\alpha(i, t, T)$ is the upper $(1 - \alpha)$-quantile of the netting set's exposure distribution.[18] By common convention, the VaR is denoted as $q_\alpha(i, t, T)$ to describe how far, for the $i$th counterparty, out into the future and the distribution's tail one wishes to go.

A second, increasingly common risk measure, is defined as the following conditional expectation,

$$
\mathbb{E}\left( V_{t+T}(i) \middle| V_{t+T}(i) \geq q_\alpha(i, t, T) \right) = \frac{1}{1 - \alpha} \int_{q_\alpha(i,t,T)}^{\infty} v f_{V_{t+T}(i)}(v) dv. \tag{10.17}
$$

In words, Eq. 10.17 essentially describes the exposure given that one find's oneself at or beyond the $(1 - \alpha)$-quantile, or $q_\alpha(i, t, T)$, level. This quantity is, for this

[18] Quantiles are points in a distribution pertaining to the rank order of the distribution's values. It is a generalization of the notion of a percentile, which is defined on a scale of 0 to 100.

reason, often termed the conditional Value-at-Risk, the tail VaR, or the expected shortfall.[19] We will use the latter term and denote it as $\mathcal{E}_\alpha(i,t,T)$ to explicitly include the desired quantile defining the tail of the return distribution (as well as the time horizon and credit counterparty). Either Eq. 10.16 or 10.17 is a reasonable candidate for the potential future exposure.

Both of these quantities are fairly abstract. With a bit of additional effort and the assumption of Gaussianity, we may derive analytic expressions for both measures. From Eq. 10.16, the $(1-\alpha)$-quantile satisfies the following (by-now-quite-familiar) relation for a standard normal variate,

$$\begin{aligned}
\int_{q_\alpha(i,t,T)}^{\infty} f_{V_{t+T}(i)}(v)dv &= 1-\alpha, \qquad (10.18)\\
1-\int_{-\infty}^{q_\alpha(i,t,T)} f_{V_{t+T}(i)}(v)dv &= 1-\alpha,\\
\int_{-\infty}^{q_\alpha(i,t,T)} f_{V_{t+T}(i)}(v)dv &= \alpha,\\
\mathbb{P}\bigg(V_{t+T}(i) \le q_\alpha(i,t,T)\bigg) &= \alpha,\\
\Phi\bigg(q_\alpha(i,t,T)\bigg) &= \alpha,\\
q_\alpha(i,t,T) &= \Phi^{-1}(\alpha).
\end{aligned}$$

The standard inverse normal cumulative distribution function, $\Phi^{-1}(\cdot)$, does not have a closed-form solution, but through a variety of approximations, it is found in virtually any software package.[20]

Equation 10.18 summarizes the results for a standard normal random variable. All that remains is to scale the outcome to the moments of our portfolio-return distribution. Recall that if $Z \sim \mathcal{N}(0,1)$, then $X = a + \sqrt{b}Z \sim \mathcal{N}(a,b)$. Using this logic, it follows that

$$\begin{aligned}
q_p(\alpha, T-t) &= \mu_i(t,T) + q_\alpha(i,t,T)\sigma_i(t,T), \qquad (10.19)\\
&= V_t(i) + \mu_i(T-t) + \underbrace{\Phi^{-1}(\alpha)}_{\substack{\text{Eq.}\\ 10.18}}\sigma_i\sqrt{T-t}.
\end{aligned}$$

[19] The expected shortfall measure—a central metric for our economic-capital model—also fulfills all of the criteria for a co-called *coherent* risk measure. See Artzner et al. [1] for an introduction to this theoretically important notion.

[20] An $\alpha$ of 0.95, for example, leads to a constant value $\Phi^{-1}(0.95) \approx 1.65$, whereas an $\alpha$ of 0.99 leads to $\Phi^{-1}(0.99) \approx 2.33$.

Given an $\alpha$ of 0.99, $V_t(i) = 5$, $\mu_i = 0.05$, $\sigma_i = 1.75$, and $T - t = \frac{1}{52}$, a possible VaR-based PFE estimate takes the value,

$$\begin{aligned} q_\alpha(i, t, T) &= \underbrace{5 + 0.05 \cdot \left(\frac{1}{52}\right)}_{\mu_i(t,T)} + \Phi^{-1}(0.99) \cdot \underbrace{1.75 \cdot \sqrt{\frac{1}{52}}}_{\sigma_i(t,T)}, \\ &= 5.10 + 2.33 \cdot 0.24, \\ &= 5.66. \end{aligned} \tag{10.20}$$

In this setting, the 99% VaR would be 5.66 units of currency. Alternatively, we estimate that the worst-case increase in exposure over the next week, with a 99% degree of confidence, is $q_\alpha(i, t, T) - V_t(i) = 0.66$ units of currency. The computation itself is trivial. All of the effort is found in the identification of robust and sensible expected return and portfolio volatility estimates.

To find a workable expression for an expected-shortfall-based PFE, we again begin with a standard normal random variate, $V_{t+T}(i) \sim \mathcal{N}(0, 1)$. The average value in the tail beyond the $(1 - \alpha)$-quantile is defined as follows,

$$\begin{aligned} \mathbb{E}\left(V_{t+T}(i) \middle| V_{t+T}(i) \geq q_\alpha(i, t, T)\right) &= \frac{1}{1-\alpha} \int_{q_\alpha(i,t,T)}^{\infty} v f_{V_{t+T}(i)}(v) dv, \\ &= \frac{1}{1-\alpha} \int_{\Phi^{-1}(\alpha)}^{\infty} v \phi(v) dv, \\ &= \frac{1}{1-\alpha} \int_{\Phi^{-1}(\alpha)}^{\infty} \frac{v}{\sqrt{2\pi}} e^{-\frac{v^2}{2}} dv. \end{aligned} \tag{10.21}$$

This is not, at first glance, a terribly easy integral to solve. If one computes $\phi'(v)$, the solution presents itself directly. In particular,

$$\begin{aligned} \phi(v) &= \frac{1}{\sqrt{2\pi}} e^{-\frac{v^2}{2}}, \\ \phi'(v) &= \left(\frac{-2v}{2}\right) \frac{1}{\sqrt{2\pi}} e^{-\frac{v^2}{2}}, \\ &= \frac{-v}{\sqrt{2\pi}} e^{-\frac{v^2}{2}}, \\ &= -v\phi(v), \end{aligned} \tag{10.22}$$

where $\phi(\cdot)$ denotes the standard normal density function. Inserting Eq. 10.22 into 10.21, we have

$$\begin{aligned}
\mathbb{E}\left(V_{t+T}(i)\middle| V_{t+T}(i) \geq q_\alpha(i,t,T)\right) &= \frac{1}{1-\alpha}\int_{\Phi^{-1}(\alpha)}^{\infty} \underbrace{\frac{v}{\sqrt{2\pi}}e^{-\frac{v^2}{2}}\,dv}_{\text{Eq. 10.22}}, \qquad (10.23)\\
&= \frac{1}{1-\alpha}\int_{\Phi^{-1}(\alpha)}^{\infty} -\phi'(v)dv,\\
&= \frac{1}{1-\alpha}\bigg[-\phi(v)\bigg]_{\Phi^{-1}(\alpha)}^{\infty},\\
&= \frac{1}{1-\alpha}\bigg[-\underbrace{\lim_{v\to\infty}\phi(v)}_{=0} + \phi(\Phi^{-1}(\alpha))\bigg],\\
&= \frac{\phi\left(\Phi^{-1}(\alpha)\right)}{1-\alpha}.
\end{aligned}$$

Once again, this need only be scaled using our netting-set moments.

$$\begin{aligned}
\mathcal{E}_\alpha(i,t,T) &\equiv \mathbb{E}\left(V_{t+T}(i)\middle| V_{t+T}(i) \geq q_\alpha(i,t,T)\right), \qquad (10.24)\\
&= \mu_i(t,T) + \underbrace{\frac{\phi\left(\Phi^{-1}(\alpha)\right)}{1-\alpha}}_{\text{Eq. 10.23}}\sigma_i(t,T),\\
&= V_t(i) + \mu_i(T-t) + \frac{\phi\left(\Phi^{-1}(\alpha)\right)}{1-\alpha}\sigma_i\sqrt{T-t}.
\end{aligned}$$

Returning to our previous example with $\alpha = 0.99$ and the same set of parameter values used earlier in the VaR setting, we may compute

$$\begin{aligned}
\mathcal{E}_{0.99}(i,t,T) &= \underbrace{5 + 0.05\cdot\left(\frac{1}{52}\right)}_{\mu_i(t,T)} + \frac{\phi(\Phi^{-1}(0.99))}{1-0.99}\cdot\underbrace{1.75\cdot\sqrt{\frac{1}{52}}}_{\sigma_i(t,T)}, \qquad (10.25)\\
&= 5.10 + 2.67\cdot 0.24,\\
&= 5.74.
\end{aligned}$$

It makes logical sense that the expected shortfall should exceed the VaR for the same value of $\alpha$. Indeed, since the expected shortfall is the average of all values beyond the VaR values, it must logically be greater than (or, at the very least, equal to) the VaR computation. Conceptually, since we are already quite far out in the tail

**Table 10.1** *Simple example details*: This table summarizes, at a glance, the numerical details of various exposure measures in the context of a rather simple example.

| Characteristic | Notation | Value |
|---|---|---|
| Starting point | $V_t(i)$ | 5.00 |
| Drift (or trend) | $\mu_i$ | 0.05 |
| Diffusion (or volatility) | $\sigma_i$ | 1.75 |
| Time horizon | $T - t$ | 0.02 |
| Confidence level | $\alpha$ | 0.99 |
| VaR-based PFE | $q_\alpha(i, t, T)$ | 5.66 |
| Expected-shortfall-based PFE | $\mathcal{E}_\alpha(i, t, T)$ | 5.74 |

and the Gaussian distribution has relatively small amounts of probability mass in its extremes, it also makes sense that the expected shortfall is not dramatically larger than the VaR values—in this case, it exceeds it by about $\mathcal{E}_\alpha(i, t, T) - q_\alpha(i, t, T) = 0.08$ units of currency.[21]

Table 10.1 summarizes the results of this simple numerical exercise. Either the VaR measure from Eq. 10.19 or the expected shortfall metric in Eq. 10.24 is a reasonable choice for the $i$th counterparty's potential future exposure. The expected shortfall is, by construction, somewhat more conservative since it explicitly delves into the tail of the netting set's value distribution.[22]

**Colour and Commentary 118** (CREDIT COUNTERPARTY RISK ANALYTIC FORMULAE)*: This section has illustrated how far we can go, in terms of analytic expressions for important counterparty credit risk quantities, on the back of the assumption of drifted Brownian motion for one's netting set dynamics. Expected exposure, expected positive exposure (in the special case of $\mu_i(t, T) \equiv 0$), and potential future exposure all boil down to relatively concise formulae. While useful and insightful, it is important to keep our enthusiasm somewhat in check. The central assumption is, if we are honest with ourselves, quite likely flawed. Extensive empirical evidence indicates that few, if any, important financial risk factors follow a Gaussian distribution. The basic form and symmetry are consistent, but actual risk-factor and market-value distributions are significantly more heavy tailed than the assumption of normality would suggest. Perhaps more problematic is the underlying complexity of the true netting-set valuation process. Given the broad range of potential pay-off patterns and underlying risk factors, treating*

(continued)

[21] In the this Gaussian case, the parametric expected shortfall estimator simply amounts to a change in the magnitude of the multiplier constant. The VaR multiplier is, for the 99% confidence level, equal to about 87% of the expected-shortfall value.

[22] A similar expression can be derived for different assumptions regarding the stochastic dynamics of the netting-set process. Chapter 10, for example, provides similar computations under the $t$ distribution.

**Colour and Commentary 118** (continued)
*the overall netting-set as a single monolithic object is hard to defend. For this reason, as we've already highlighted, these various derivative exposures definitions are typically computed using rather complicated simulation engines. The previous investigation, however, remains pertinent since these formulae represent the foundation for our chosen path: simplified regulatory approximations. It is also useful as an easy-to-understand diagnostic and comparator for more complex derivative-exposure calculations performed in other parts of one's organization.*

## 10.5 The Regulatory Approach

Virtually every piece of regulatory guidance has a history; it can often prove surprisingly helpful in appreciating the general context and what the regulators seek to accomplish. It is nevertheless often difficult, for any given regulatory standard, to know how far in time one should go back. In the area of counterparty credit risk, perhaps the first reference is BIS [2] where the idea of a netted exposure add-on, to account for potential value increases, was first introduced. BIS [2] is a revision to the original 1988 Basel Accord. While interesting, this is probably a bit too far back into the past. A better starting point would be BIS [3, Part I], which was written about ten years after the first revision. This document provides a thorough description of the so-called current-exposure and standardized methods; referred to understandably as CEM and SM, respectively. These models are very useful background into the regulator's mindset with regard to counterparty credit risk.

The directives found in BIS [3] were nonetheless superseded about another decade later with BIS [5]. This paper contains an updated exposure-at-default measurement methodology, which has been catchily dubbed the *standard approach for counterparty credit risk*. This being rather a mouthful has led to the broad-based use of the unfortunate acronym, SA-CCR. Jumping into BIS [5] without any preparation can be a bit overwhelming; perhaps appreciating this fact, a helpful companion paper—see BIS [6]—was produced a few months later. BIS [7] provides further responses to frequently asked questions. This section seeks to provide a workable description of the Basel Committee on Banking Supervision's (BCBS) SA-CCR methodology. It makes ample use of BIS [2, 3, 5, 6, 7]—along with a number of other references mentioned along the way—to accomplish this task. It is precisely this so-called SA-CCR approach that we will use to describe our (non-deterministic) derivative exposures for the purposes of economic-capital computations.[23]

Like most regulatory guidance, the SA-CCR is highly prescriptive and stylized. This is, given regulatory objectives, both natural and understandable. It nonetheless consists of a sequence of formulae that require some unpacking and deciphering. Let's not lose sight of our principal objective: a reasonably realistic and parsimonious description of the current exposure-at-default (i.e., EAD) associated with an arbitrary counterparty $i$. The SA-CCR high-level, entry-point formula for this object has the following form:

$$\text{EAD}_t(i) = \alpha \cdot \bigg(\text{RC}_t(i) + \text{PFE}_{t+T}(i)\bigg), \tag{10.26}$$

where $\text{RC}_t(i)$ denotes the replacement cost of the $i$th credit counterparty at time $t$ and $\alpha \in \mathbb{R}_+$. We use the Greek letter $\alpha$ in this context to be consistent with the regulatory documentation. One should be careful to avoid confusion with the confidence level, which uses the same symbol.

Replacement cost is intended to represent the loss incurred in the event of *immediate* default. There is no lapse of time and, as a consequence, no possibility of upward movement in the market value of one's netting set. The PFE term, as you might expect, looks $T - t$ units of time into the future to capture possible value increases. The sum of these current and forward-looking effects are modified by a constant multiplier, $\alpha$. As of the writing of this document, $\alpha$ was set to a value of 1.4.[24] The rationale for $\alpha$ is, it would appear, to provide a cushion for increased conservatism. The replacement-cost and PFE computations are distinct pieces with different perspectives. Although obviously not unrelated, it is convenient to address them separately. We'll follow this strategy in the coming sections and then pull them back together to complete the picture.

### *10.5.1 Replacement Cost*

Of the two quantities in Eq. 10.26, the replacement cost is the least complicated to compute. The reason is simple; it only depends on the current point in time. In its basic form, the replacement cost is the sum of the market value of the individual trades in the $i$th countparty's netting set *less* the existing collateral. If the total market value is EUR 10 million and one holds EUR 8 million of collateral, then the replacement cost is EUR 2 million. Conversely, if you have a negative market

[23] Derivative exposure—as we'll soon see—also typically makes an appearance in leverage calculations.

[24] The constant $\alpha$ may take different values for different applications of the resulting exposure estimate. When, for example, computing leverage—see BIS [4]—the value of $\alpha$ is fixed at unity.

value of EUR −20 million and have posted EUR 15 million of collateral, then you have a EUR −5 million replacement cost. This logic is approximately correct, but also a bit faulty. We are not terribly interested in negative replacement costs and we need to be a bit more conservative in our treatment of collateral.

To address these issues, BIS [5] defines the replacement cost as

$$\text{RC}_t(i) = \begin{cases} \max\left(V_t(i) - \tilde{C}_{t+T}(i), 0\right) & : \text{No margin} \\ \max\left(V_t(i) - \tilde{C}_{t+T}(i), 0, \text{TH}_i + \text{MTA}_i - \text{NICA}_t(i)\right) & : \text{Margin} \end{cases} \tag{10.27}$$

This is fairly detailed definition that requires a bit of digestion. Indeed, Eq. 10.27 contains a number of acronyms that are desperately in need of explanation. The first point is that the replacement-cost definition differs by margin policy. For unmargined netting sets, the replacement cost is simply the positive part of the difference between the current market value and collateral holdings. Since there is always the danger that non-cash collateral can lose value—due to adverse market movements—$\tilde{C}_t(i)$ denotes the haircut value of any net collateral position.[25] It is, in a technical sense, described as,

$$\tilde{C}_{t+T}(i) = \begin{cases} C_t(i) \cdot \left(1 - h(t, T)\right) & : \text{Holding collateral where } C_t(i) > 0 \\ C_t(i) \cdot \left(1 + h(t, T)\right) & : \text{Posting collateral where } C_t(i) < 0 \end{cases}, \tag{10.28}$$

where $h(t, T)$ is the haircut value over the time interval $T - t$ and $C_t(i)$ represents the market value of the $i$th counterparty's net collateral position at time $t$.[26] The introduction of $T$, as an argument, is necessary to reflect the role of the time-horizon in the collateral haircut computation and our broader analysis.

The notion of *net* collateral will help us make sense of the second part of the replacement-cost definition for margined netting sets in Eq. 10.27. The initial margin or independent amount, given their similarity and the potential for confusion, are referred to as independent collateral amount (or ICA) in the regulatory setting. Unlike variation margin, the ICA can be simultaneously posted and received. This immediately leads to the idea of net ICA, or NICA, which represents the difference between received and posted initial collateral. The NICA value might be either positive or negative; it really depends on the magnitude of the ICA values associated with both counterparties. In the non-margin setting, therefore, the $\tilde{C}_{t+T}(i)$ value

[25] A haircut is a rather colourful, colloquial term used to describe any adjustment to the valuation of a collateral position to account for possible unfavourable market movements.

[26] This is a very simplified set of haircut rules; it can, in practice, be much more nuanced.

basically refers to the NICA amount with the appropriate application of haircuts as described in Eq. 10.28.

In the margined cases, the current collateral amount, $\tilde{C}_{t+T}(i)$, is related to variation margin. The second line of Eq. 10.28, however, has three arguments in the max operator. The third argument, $\text{TH}_i + \text{MTA}_i - \text{NICA}_t(i)$, includes the net independent collateral amount at the current time, $t$. This maintains a separation between the variation and initial margins. The TH and MTA variables are determined through the legal counterparty contracts governing the management of margins. TH is an acronym for the collateral threshold; this is a lower bound, below which collateral is not exchanged. For example, if there is a threshold of EUR 100,000 and the market value of the netting set is EUR 50,000, then no collateral would be received. The point of the threshold is to reduce the operational costs associated with calling and returning collateral. Naturally, this creates a trade-off between risk mitigation and logistical costs.[27]

MTA represents the minimum transfer amount, which unsurprisingly is the lowest amount of collateral that may be transferred between two entities. Much like the threshold, the intention is to reduce operational overhead. It probably doesn't make logical sense to exchange EUR 10 of collateral for a minuscule change in market value.[28] The threshold and minimum transfer amount should *not*, however, be considered separately. As clearly stated in Gregory [13]:

> The minimum transfer amount and threshold are additive in the sense that the exposure must exceed the sum of the two before any collateral can be called.

This succinctly explains why these two values enter jointly into the margined netting-set replacement cost in Eq. 10.27. This extra condition covers the situation where there is positive exposure, but it has not broken through the lower bound required for receipt of collateral. The net ICA is subtracted from this amount to account for the offsetting impact of the initial margin. In short, Eq. 10.27 is a rather conservative view of the current losses associated with immediate counterparty default.

### 10.5.2 The Add-On

Conservatism of its construction aside, the replacement cost does not tell the whole story. It completely ignores the possibility of future value increases in the counterparty's netting set. This is precisely the role of the second term in the high-level SA-CCR expression presented in Eq. 10.26. It has the following form,

$$\text{PFE}_t(i) = \mathcal{M}_i \cdot \mathbb{A}_i^{\Sigma}, \tag{10.29}$$

[27] One may, of course, set the threshold to zero to move completely towards the risk-mitigation direction.

[28] Such a value should be somehow related—logically, at least, if not practically—to the confidence interval around our valuation estimates.

where $\mathcal{M}_i \in (0.05, 1]$ is a multiplier with a reasonably complex form and $\mathbb{A}_i^{\Sigma}$ is referred to as the aggregate *add-on* for the $i$th credit counterparty. Putting the multiplier aside for the moment, a central point is that what SA-CCR refers to as PFE is actually something else. In fact, BIS [6] indicates that it is intended to represent a conservative estimate of the netting set's effective expected positive exposure. To repeat, it does *not* technically describe potential future exposure.

The aggregate add-on, as the name strongly suggests, is some kind of function of the underlying trades within the netting set designed to capture the risk of future derivative-value increases. This naturally involves a number of levels and, of course, a logical hierarchy to determine the proper order of aggregation. It is, quite frankly, a bit messy. Figure 10.4 provides, in an attempt to help matters, a visualization of the *five* levels associated with the SA-CCR methodology. Individual trades are first organized into *five* distinct asset classes. These are essentially flavours of derivative contracts: interest rate, currency, credit, equity, and commodity. This immediately raises an important question: what is done with derivatives that touch upon multiple asset classes?[29] BIS [5]'s answer reads:

> The designation should be made according to the nature of the primary risk factor. [...] For more complex trades, where it is difficult to determine a single primary risk factor, bank supervisors may require that trades be allocated to more than one asset class.

For the purposes of this discussion, we will assume that each derivative trade can be reasonably and defensibly assigned to a single asset class. The aggregate add-on is thus,

$$\mathbb{A}_i^{\Sigma} = \sum_{a \in \mathcal{A}_i} \mathbb{A}_i^{(a)}, \tag{10.30}$$

where $\mathcal{A}_i$ denotes the collection of asset classes associated with netting set $i$. One thus simply sums over the asset classes to get to the aggregate level.[30]

Within an asset class, the trades are further allocated into so-called hedging sets. Again BIS [5], who introduce the concept, offer the best definition:

> a hedging set is the largest collection of trades of a given asset class within a netting set for which netting benefits are recognized in the PFE add-on of the SA-CCR.

The corollary, of course, is that hedging sets within an asset class are not permitted to offset one another. If we write the collection of hedging sets within asset class $a$ and netting set $i$ as $\mathcal{H}_i^{(a)}$, then these hedging sets are aggregated as

$$\mathbb{A}_i^{(a)} = \sum_{h \in \mathcal{H}_i^{(a)}} \left| \mathbb{A}_i^{(a,h)} \right|, \tag{10.31}$$

[29] A cross-currency swap, for example, has both currency and interest rate exposure.

[30] To be crystal clear with this invented notation, if a netting set includes $N$ assets classes then $\mathcal{A}_i = \left\{ \mathcal{A}_i^{(1)}, \mathcal{A}_i^{(2)}, \cdots, \mathcal{A}_i^{(N)} \right\}$.

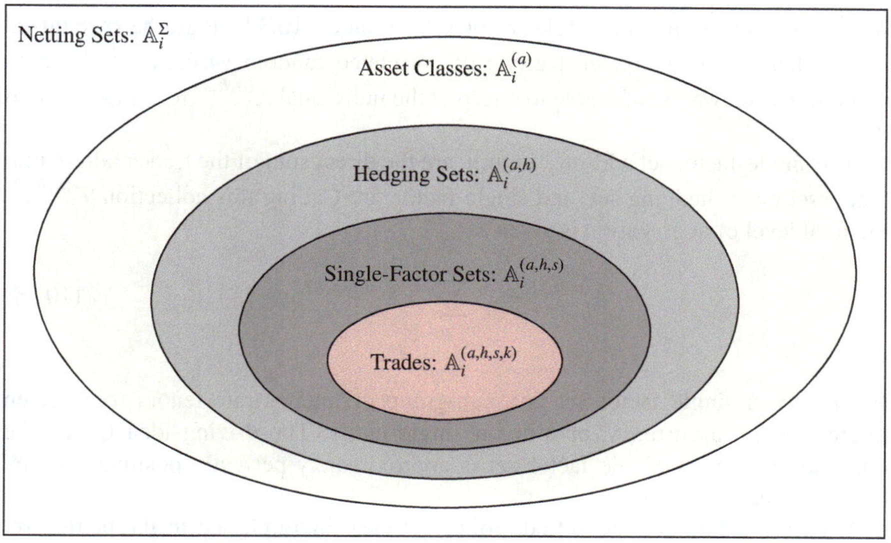


**Fig. 10.4** *The add-on hierarchy*: The schematic above outlines the five levels of aggregation embedded in the SA-CCR methodology. In addition to visualizing how the aggregate add-on is computed, it also introduces the notation used to describe the various components.

where $\mathbb{A}_i^{(a,h)}$ represents the calculated add-on for the $h$th hedging set of asset class $a$ associated with netting set $i$. $\mathcal{H}_i^{(a)}$ is the related collection of hedging sets. The notation is admittedly dreadful, but given the complexity of the hierarchy in Fig. 10.4, it will only get worse. The absolute value operator in Eq. 10.31 precludes any possible netting between these hedging sets.

The hedging set, as the name indicates, permits some form of diversification. This is captured through non-perfect positive correlation between the individual single factor sets comprising the hedging set. We further define the collection of hedging sets in asset class $a$ and netting set $i$ as $\mathcal{S}_i^{(a,h)}$. This allows us to write the aggregation of each hedging set as,

$$\mathbb{A}_i^{(a,h)} = \sqrt{\sum_{s \in \mathcal{S}_i^{(a,h)}} \sum_{r \in \mathcal{S}_i^{(a,h)}} \rho(s,r) \mathbb{A}_i^{(a,h,s)} \mathbb{A}_i^{(a,h,r)}}, \tag{10.32}$$

where $\mathbb{A}_i^{(a,h,s)}$ represents the $s$th single-factor set of hedging set $h$ in asset class $a$ and $\rho(r,s)$ is the (regulator determined) correlation between single factor sets $r$ and $s$. These latter values are explicitly provided by the regulatory authorities. Each

$\mathbb{A}_i^{(a,h,s)}$ is referred to as a single-factor set. Equation 10.32 should be recognized as the standard deviation of a group of correlated random variables.[31] For it to work, however, we must be able to interpret the individual $\mathbb{A}_i^{(a,h,s)}$ terms as standard deviations.

The single-factor set add-ons, in turn, are the direct sum of the trades falling into that asset class, hedging set, and single-factor set. Calling this collection $\mathcal{T}_i^{(a,h,s)}$, the final level of aggregation is given as,

$$\mathbb{A}_i^{(a,h,s)} = \sum_{k \in \mathcal{T}_i^{(a,h,s)}} \mathbb{A}_i^{(a,h,s,k)}. \tag{10.34}$$

Practically, a single factor set is a sub-group of interest-rate tenors for a given interest curve, a currency, or a credit single entity. The driving idea is that the correlation within a single factor set is approximately perfectly positive, so they can be directly summed.

Each individual derivative trade follows a clear hierarchy up to the netting set level. The underlying logical chain illustrates how each trade, single-risk-factor, hedging-set, and asset-class collection is nested,

$$\mathcal{T}_i^{(a,h,s)} \subseteq \mathcal{S}_i^{(a,h)} \subseteq \mathcal{H}_i^{(a)} \subseteq \mathcal{A}_i, \tag{10.35}$$

for the $i$th netting set.[32]

Just for fun, let's now combine all of these elements together to create a single, abstract representation of the aggregate add-on associated with the $i$th counterparty.

[31] If $X_1, ..., X_N$ are a collection of $N$ correlated random variables, then the variance of their sum can be represented as

$$\text{var}\bigg(X_1 + \cdots + X_N\bigg) = \underbrace{\sum_{i=1}^{N}\sum_{i=j}^{N} \text{corr}(X_i, X_j)\sqrt{\text{var}(X_i)}\sqrt{\text{var}(X_j)}}_{\sum_{i=1}^{N}\sum_{i=j}^{N} \text{cov}(X_i, X_j)}, \tag{10.33}$$

where we recover Eq. 10.32 by taking the square root of both sides.

[32] Or, if you prefer a word equation, we might describe the idea in Eq. 10.35 as

$$\underbrace{\text{Collection of Trades}}_{k \in \mathcal{T}_i^{(a,h,s)}} \subseteq \underbrace{\text{Single-Factor Sets}}_{s \in \mathcal{S}_i^{(a,h)}} \subseteq \underbrace{\text{Hedging Sets}}_{h \in \mathcal{H}_i^{(a)}} \subseteq \underbrace{\text{Asset Class}}_{a \in \mathcal{A}_i}. \tag{10.36}$$

Starting from Eq. 10.30, we have

$$
\begin{aligned}
\mathbb{A}_i^{\Sigma} &= \underbrace{\sum_{a\in\mathcal{A}_i} \mathbb{A}_i^{(a)}}_{\substack{\text{Eq.}\\ 10.30}}, \qquad (10.37)\\
&= \sum_{a\in\mathcal{A}_i} \underbrace{\sum_{h\in\mathcal{H}_i^{(a)}} \left|\mathbb{A}_i^{(a,h)}\right|}_{\text{Eq. 10.31}},\\
&= \sum_{a\in\mathcal{A}_i} \sum_{h\in\mathcal{H}_i^{(a)}} \left| \underbrace{\sqrt{\sum_{s\in\mathcal{S}_i^{(a,h)}} \sum_{r\in\mathcal{S}_i^{(a,h)}} \rho(s,r)\mathbb{A}_i^{(a,h,s)}\mathbb{A}_i^{(a,h,r)}}}_{\text{Eq. 10.32}} \right|,\\
&= \sum_{a\in\mathcal{A}_i} \sum_{h\in\mathcal{H}_i^{(a)}} \left| \sqrt{\sum_{s\in\mathcal{S}_i^{(a,h)}} \sum_{r\in\mathcal{S}_i^{(a,h)}} \rho(s,r) \underbrace{\sum_{k_s\in\mathcal{T}_i^{(a,h,s)}} \mathbb{A}_i^{(a,h,s,k_s)}}_{\text{Eq. 10.34}} \underbrace{\sum_{k_r\in\mathcal{T}_i^{(a,h,s)}} \mathbb{A}_i^{(a,h,r,k_r)}}_{\text{Eq. 10.34}}} \right|.
\end{aligned}
$$

With its almost frightening array of sums, Eq. 10.37, is not particularly easy to look at. It does, however, clearly chart out the path from individual trade to single-factor set to hedging set to asset class and, ultimately, to netting set as described in Fig. 10.4. Although slightly masochistic and certainly not the typical treatment of this material, this final expression does provide some useful intuition to a complex aggregation.

**Colour and Commentary 119** (SA-CCR AGGREGATION LOGIC)*: As anyone with a sock drawer can tell you, getting all of the right socks paired up correctly with their partner can be a lengthy and annoying undertaking. The SA-CCR regulatory guidance add-on calculations involve a five-level hierarchy with three alternative aggregation approaches. The aggregation logic is, to be blunt, ugly and rather hard to follow. Like a particularly untidy and convoluted sock drawer, a bit of organization can go a long way. The preceding discussion consequently introduces some (imperfect) notation and logic to help keep some order in this hierarchy. A netting set is comprised of a number of distinct asset classes. Within each asset class, trades are*

(continued)

**Colour and Commentary 119** (continued)
*allocated into hedging sets. The various single factor sets, within a hedging set, combine together in a manner similar to variance. Between hedging sets, no offsetting is permitted; aggregation occurs with absolute values. Trades within each single factor set, by virtue of their perfect positive correlation, can be simply summed. Perhaps somewhat ironically, the need to create a rather straightforward formulaic exposure calculation is the main driver of this relatively messy structure. In a classic potential-future-exposure computation, the complexity is embedded in the dependence structure underlying the risk factors and their mapping to derivative valuations. Netting set aggregation is, in this setting, comparatively trivial.*[a] *In the SA-CCR, the risk-factor structure is simplified. The cost is somewhat unwieldy aggregation logic.*

[a] The heavy-lifting has to be performed somewhere. In this case, it is performed by the forward-looking exposure engine.

### *10.5.3 The Trade Level*

The effective expected positive exposure form of the add-on needs to meet a central objective. As we saw in the previous section, to use the variance-motivated aggregation at the hedging-set level as in Eq. 10.32, it is necessary to view the individual (hedging-set) add-ons as a standard deviation. To accomplish this, a number of assumptions regarding the market value of each individual trade are required. These include—and are also outlined in both BIS [5, 6]—a zero current market value, an absence of collateral, no cash-flows over the next one-year time horizon, and undrifted Brownian-motion dynamics.[33]

We now reap the benefits of having worked through the details of the Brownian-motion case. Let us employ $k$ to denote an arbitrary trade with the $i$ credit counterparty. The market value of the $i$th trade at time $t + T$, following from the preceding assumptions, is given as

$$V_{t+T}(i,k) \sim \mathcal{N}\left(0, \underbrace{\mathbb{I}_{\{m_k \geq T\}}\sigma_k\sqrt{T-t}}_{\sigma_{ik}(t,T)}\right), \tag{10.38}$$

[33] These are fairly strong assumptions and, to a certain extent, they are relaxed through the multiplier. We will address this point in forthcoming discussion.

where $m_k$ is the remaining maturity. This is entirely consistent with the undrifted Brownian-motion case. The only real twist is that all trades maturing before time $t + T$ are excluded.

Equipped with the definition of an arbitrary trade's market-value, we observe that we are in the general, but simplified, structure described in the preceding sections. From Eqs. 10.13 and 10.14, the expected exposure associated with the $k$th trade is simply

$$\mathbb{E}_t\left(V_{t+T}(i,k)^+\right) = \frac{\mathbb{I}_{\{m_k \geq T\}}\sigma_k\sqrt{T-t}}{\sqrt{2\pi}}. \tag{10.39}$$

The actual value of $T$ will vary depending on whether or not the netting set is margined or non-margined. In the non-margined case, $T - t = 1$ year. For margined netting sets, one needs to define a margin period of risk, which we will refer to as $t + \tau_{M_i}$ to reflect its dependence on the netting set. As discussed earlier, we can compute the expected exposure profile by evaluating (and averaging) Eq. 10.39 for a number of choices of $T \in (t, t+1]$ or $T \in (t, t+\tau_{M_i}]$ for non-margined and margined netting sets, respectively.

The authors of the SA-CCR (understandably) wanted to avoid—as highlighted in BIS [6]—the need to partition the time interval and repeatedly compute (and average) Eq. 10.39. This leads to a restatement of our maturity indicator variable as

$$\mathbb{I}_{\{m_k \geq t\}} \equiv 1. \tag{10.40}$$

This is equivalent to forcing all trades in one's portfolio to have a minimum maturity of—depending on the margin policy—either one-year or the margin period of risk.

This assumption allows us, following directly from Eq. 10.15, to represent the expected positive exposure as

$$\frac{1}{T-t}\int_t^T \mathbb{E}_t\left(V_{t+\tau}(i,k)^+\right)d\tau = \frac{2\sigma_k\sqrt{T-t}}{3\sqrt{2\pi}}, \tag{10.41}$$

where $T = 1$ or $\tau_{M_i}$. Two features of Eq. 10.39 also make it the *effective* expected positive exposure: over $(0, T]$ there are neither cash-flows nor maturities and $\sigma_k \in \mathbb{R}$. The presence of these conditions ensures that the expression in Eq. 10.41 is (at least) weakly positively monotonic in $T$. Under this monotonicity condition the expected positive exposure (EPE) and effective expected positive exposure (EEPE) coincide.

Pulling this all together, the trade-level add-on has the following theoretical form,

$$\mathbb{A}_i^{(a,h,s,k)} = \underbrace{\frac{2\sigma_k\sqrt{T-t}}{3\sqrt{2\pi}}}_{\text{Eq. 10.41}}. \tag{10.42}$$

It is important to stress that this is not the final form of the trade-level add-on. Ultimately, as we'll see shortly, it has a rather different practical form. Nonetheless, following from BIS [6], Eq. 10.42 describes its origins.

**Colour and Commentary 120** (SA-CCR PFE COMPONENT)*: It should be clear by this point that what the SA-CCR refers to as the PFE component is not actually, in the typical definition of the term, potential future exposure. It is, to be clear,* not *a tail-based measure of the worst-case upside movement in a trade or netting set's market value. Instead, it is defined with regard to the expectation of the positive part of the trade or netting set's future exposure; in the non-margined case, this becomes effective positive exposure, whereas this reduces to expected exposure in the margined setting. In both cases, numerous assumptions are necessary to preserve analytic formulae for these quantities. This choice is perfectly within the purview of the regulatory authorities and, given their objectives, makes logical sense. Their characterization of PFE does, after all, respect the fundamental idea of incorporating some additional amount to accommodate the possibility of future value increases. It nonetheless bears stressing that the add-on element should* not *be strictly interpreted—relying on its name—as a quantile-based characterization of the future counterparty level value distribution. Understanding this fact may very well help to avoid unnecessary confusion.*

The next step is to adjust Eq. 10.42 so that it naturally handles both margin and non-margined netting sets. In principle, one could simply change the value of $T$ depending on the margin policy. As a practical matter, however, the EEPE form from Eq. 10.42 only really applies to non-margined netting sets. For margined netting sets, the margin period of risk is typically quite short: something between 10 to 20 working days. Averaging the expected positive exposure of this period would, according to the formula, reduce the add-on by one third. Apparently, this was judged to be insufficiently conservative. The SA-CCR consequently restates the trade-level add-on as,

$$\mathbb{A}_i^{(a,h,s,k)} = \begin{cases} \dfrac{2\sigma_k}{3\sqrt{2\pi}} & : \text{No margin (EEPE)} \\ \dfrac{\sigma_k\sqrt{\tau_{M_i} - t}}{\sqrt{2\pi}} & : \text{Margin (EE)} \end{cases}. \tag{10.43}$$

Again, this is not precisely how it is represented in the SA-CCR documentation. Instead, they express the trade-level add-on as,

$$\begin{aligned} \mathbb{A}_i^{(a,h,s,k)} &= \frac{2\sigma_k\sqrt{\text{1-year}}}{3\sqrt{2\pi}}\text{MF}_k, \\ &= \frac{2\sigma_k}{3\sqrt{2\pi}}\text{MF}_k, \end{aligned} \tag{10.44}$$

where $\text{MF}_k$ is called the maturity factor and it is defined as,

$$\text{MF}_k = \begin{cases} 1 & : \text{No margin (EEPE)} \\ \frac{3\sqrt{\tau_{M_i} - t}}{2} & : \text{Margin (EE)} \end{cases}. \tag{10.45}$$

Rather obviously, Eqs. 10.44 and 10.45 are entirely equivalent to the representation in Eq. 10.43. To avoid confusion in the application and discussion of the SA-CCR computation, it is probably best to make use of the maturity factor.

**Colour and Commentary 121** (THE SA-CCR MATURITY FACTOR)*: The maturity factor is intended to simplify the SA-CCR implementation by permitting a common form irrespective of a netting set's margin policy. It is a rather small point, but role of the maturity factor in the trade-level add-on obscures a fundamental modelling choice. Non-margined netting set add-on values are based on the effective expected positive exposure measure. Margined netting sets, conversely, use straight-up expected exposure. Given the dramatic difference between the time interval involved, this is an understandable and conservative regulatory choice. It is still useful to* see through *the maturity factor form and to be aware of this choice. If one is comparing SA-CCR results to a model-based implementation, this could potentially lead to some confusion.*

BIS [6] indicates clearly that "the SA-CCR does not directly operate with trade volatilities." The actual form of the trade-level add-on is given as,

$$\mathbb{A}_i^{(a,h,s,k)} = \delta_k \cdot d_k^{(a)} \cdot \text{SF}_k^{(a)} \cdot \text{MF}_k, \tag{10.46}$$

where $\delta_k$ is the directional delta, $d_k^{(a)}$ is the adjusted notional, and $\text{SF}_k^{(a)}$ is the supervisory factor. The $a$ subscript arises, because as we'll see shortly, some of these quantities are handled differently depending on their asset-class membership. $\delta_k$ essentially denotes the sign of the add-on, while $\delta_k$ describes its magnitude.[34] The supervisory factor provides the link back to the volatility structure found in Eq. 10.44. Indeed, if we equate Eqs. 10.44 and the absolute value of 10.46 and solve for $\sigma_k$ we arrive at

$$\underbrace{\frac{2\sigma_k}{3\sqrt{2\pi}} \cancel{\text{MF}_k}}_{\text{Eq. 10.44}} = \left| \underbrace{\delta_k \cdot d_k^{(a)} \cdot \text{SF}_k^{(a)} \cdot \cancel{\text{MF}_k}}_{\text{Eq. 10.46}} \right|, \tag{10.47}$$

[34] For option contracts, the directional delta captures the sign, but also tells us something about moneyness.

$$\sigma_k = \left(\frac{3\sqrt{\pi}\mathrm{SF}_k^{(a)}}{\sqrt{2}}\right)\left|\delta_k\right| \cdot d_k^{(a)},$$

$$\sigma_k \approx \left(2.66 \cdot \mathrm{SF}_k^{(a)}\right)\left|\delta_k\right| \cdot d_k^{(a)}.$$

The punchline is that the volatility of the trade is simply a scaled version of the supervisory factor. What is particularly useful to know is that the term $\left(2.66 \cdot \mathrm{SF}_k^{(a)}\right)$ should be interpreted, according to BIS [6], as

> the standard deviation of the primary risk factor at the one-year horizon.

The individual analyst does not determine these values; they are provided by one's friendly neighbourhood regulator. These supervisory factors are presumably determined by individual asset class and single risk-factor definitions as a combination of calibration to historical outcomes and regulatory judgement.

Once again, pulling together the high-level aggregate add-on viewpoint from Eq. 10.37 and incorporating Eq. 10.46, we arrive at:

$$\mathbb{A}_i^{\Sigma} = \underbrace{\sum_{a \in \mathcal{A}_i} \sum_{h \in \mathcal{H}_i^{(a)}} \left| \sqrt{\begin{array}{c} \sum\limits_{s \in \mathcal{S}_i^{(a,h)}} \sum\limits_{r \in \mathcal{S}_i^{(a,h)}} \rho(s,r) \sum\limits_{k_s \in \mathcal{T}_i^{(a,h,s)}} \mathbb{A}_i^{(a,h,s,k_s)} \\ \times \sum\limits_{k_r \in \mathcal{T}_i^{(a,h,s)}} \mathbb{A}_i^{(a,h,r,k_r)} \end{array}} \right|}_{\text{Eq. 10.37}}, \tag{10.48}$$

$$= \sum_{a \in \mathcal{A}_i} \sum_{h \in \mathcal{H}_i^{(a)}} \left| \sqrt{\begin{array}{c} \sum\limits_{s \in \mathcal{S}_i^{(a,h)}} \sum\limits_{r \in \mathcal{S}_i^{(a,h)}} \rho(s,r) \sum\limits_{k_s \in \mathcal{T}_i^{(a,h,s)}} \underbrace{\delta_{k_s} \cdot d_{k_s}^{(a,h,s)} \cdot \mathrm{SF}_{k_s}^{(a,h,s)} \cdot \mathrm{MF}_{k_s}}_{\text{Eq. 10.46}} \\ \times \sum\limits_{k_r \in \mathcal{T}_i^{(a,h,r)}} \underbrace{\delta_{k_r} \cdot d_{k_r}^{(a,h,s)} \cdot \mathrm{SF}_{k_r}^{(a,h,r)} \cdot \mathrm{MF}_{k_r}}_{\text{Eq. 10.46}} \end{array}} \right|.$$

Admittedly somewhat overwhelming, this representation nevertheless indicates how the various pieces fall into place. The rather puzzling application of the absolute-value operator to the result of a square root suggests differential treatment among certain asset classes. We will turn to this important point after completing the overall add-on computation.

### 10.5.4 The Multiplier

The multiplier is an attempt to attenuate the rather strong assumptions involved in the construction of the add-on. The most violent choices, from an add-on perspective at least, entail ignoring any future collateral and forcing the current market value to zero. Unlike the individual add-ons, however, the multiplier is defined at the netting-set level. A bit of reflection suggests that the starting point, of any given netting set, could be significantly negative for one (or a combination) of two reasons: the overall netting-set market value is large and negative and/or there is over-collateralization. Both situations can, and do, happen in practice. In the event that the starting point is significantly negative, it seems reasonable to adjust the aggregate add-on downwards to reflect this fact. To not do so, would be to unfairly overestimate the SA-CCR aggregate add-on component.

Quite simply, the multipler is a netting-set level value in the unit interval—that is, $\mathcal{M}_i \in [0, 1]$—that modifies the aggregate add-on for a negative starting position. As with many regulatory quantities, it is a bit funky, but it also follows a certain logic. The actual construction takes a few steps, but relies on elements already introduced and discussed in previous sections. The first step involves a distributional assumption regarding the value of the $i$th netting set. Similar in spirit, but different in level of aggregation, to Eq. 10.38 we have

$$V_{t+T}(i) \sim \mathcal{N}\left(\overbrace{V_t(i) - \tilde{C}_{t+T}(i)}^{\mu_i(t,T)}, \overbrace{\underbrace{\mathbb{I}_{\{m_k \geq t\}}}_{=1} \sigma_i \sqrt{T-t}}^{\sigma_i(t,T)}\right), \tag{10.49}$$

Basically the mean starting-level has been added back. Immediately, again with recourse to Eq. 10.13, we can write the expected exposure for the $i$th netting set as,

$$\begin{aligned}\mathbb{E}_t\bigg(E_{t+T}(i)\bigg) &= \sigma_i\sqrt{T-t}\phi\left(\frac{V_t(i) - \tilde{C}_{t+T}(i)}{\sigma_i\sqrt{T-t}}\right)\\ &\quad+\bigg(V_t(i) - \tilde{C}_{t+T}(i)\bigg)\Phi\left(\frac{V_t(i) - \tilde{C}_{t+T}(i)}{\sigma_i\sqrt{T-t}}\right).\end{aligned} \tag{10.50}$$

This form is not immediately helpful, since we do not actually work with the volatilities, but rather with add-ons. Equation 10.43 illustrates the theoretical link between the trade-level add-on and the volatility. Conceptually, for a margined netting set, this reduces to:

$$\begin{aligned}\mathbb{A}_i^{\Sigma} &= \frac{\sigma_i\sqrt{T-t}}{\sqrt{2\pi}}, \\ \sigma_i &= \frac{\mathbb{A}_i^{\Sigma}\sqrt{2\pi}}{\sqrt{T-t}}.\end{aligned} \tag{10.51}$$

We are, in this case, using the expected-exposure perspective add-on assumption associated with a margined netting set. This is an important point, because the expected positive exposure approach used for non-margined sets will not permit an analytic solution. We saw this result in an earlier section.

If we plug Eq. 10.51 back into Eq. 10.50 and simplify things a little bit, we arrive at

$$
\begin{aligned}
\mathbb{E}_t\left(E_{t+T}(i)\right) &= \underbrace{\begin{array}{c}\sigma_i\sqrt{T-t}\phi\left(\frac{V_t(i)-\tilde{C}_{t+T}(i)}{\sigma_i\sqrt{T-t}}\right)+\left(V_t(i)-\tilde{C}_{t+T}(i)\right)\\ \times\Phi\left(\frac{V_t(i)-\tilde{C}_{t+T}(i)}{\sigma_i\sqrt{T-t}}\right)\end{array}}_{\text{Eq. 10.13}}, \qquad (10.52)\\
&= \underbrace{\left(\frac{\mathbb{A}_i^{\Sigma}\sqrt{2\pi}}{\cancel{\sqrt{T-t}}}\right)}_{\text{Eq. 10.51}}\cancel{\sqrt{T-t}}\phi\left(\frac{V_t(i)-\tilde{C}_{t+T}(i)}{\underbrace{\left(\frac{\mathbb{A}_i^{\Sigma}\sqrt{2\pi}}{\cancel{\sqrt{T-t}}}\right)}_{\text{Eq. 10.51}}\cancel{\sqrt{T-t}}}\right)\\
&\quad+\left(V_t(i)-\tilde{C}_{t+T}(i)\right)\Phi\left(\frac{V_t(i)-\tilde{C}_{t+T}(i)}{\underbrace{\left(\frac{\mathbb{A}_i^{\Sigma}\sqrt{2\pi}}{\cancel{\sqrt{T-t}}}\right)}_{\text{Eq. 10.51}}\cancel{\sqrt{T-t}}}\right),\\
&= \mathbb{A}_i^{\Sigma}\sqrt{2\pi}\phi\left(\frac{V_t(i)-\tilde{C}_{t+T}(i)}{\mathbb{A}_i^{\Sigma}\sqrt{2\pi}}\right)\\
&\quad+\left(V_t(i)-\tilde{C}_{t+T}(i)\right)\Phi\left(\frac{V_t(i)-\tilde{C}_{t+T}(i)}{\mathbb{A}_i^{\Sigma}\sqrt{2\pi}}\right),\\
&= \mathbb{A}_i^{\Sigma}\left(\sqrt{2\pi}\cdot\phi\left(\frac{\upsilon}{\sqrt{2\pi}}\right)+\upsilon\cdot\Phi\left(\frac{\upsilon}{\sqrt{2\pi}}\right)\right),
\end{aligned}
$$

where

$$
\upsilon = \frac{V_t(i)-\tilde{C}_{t+T}(i)}{\mathbb{A}_i^{\Sigma}}. \qquad (10.53)
$$

The consequence is a (fairly) concise analytic representation of the expected exposure associated with the $i$th netting set written in terms of known quantities: the aggregate add-on, the current netting-set valuation, and the collateral position.

The central part, or kernel, of the SA-CCR multiplier is now defined as the quotient of the expected exposure representation in Eq. 10.52 and the aggregate add-on. In particular, this gives

$$\begin{aligned}\frac{\mathbb{E}_t\left(E_{t+T}(i)\right)}{\mathbb{A}_i^{\Sigma}} &= \frac{\overbrace{\cancel{\mathbb{A}_i^{\Sigma}}\left(\sqrt{2\pi}\cdot\phi\left(\frac{v}{\sqrt{2\pi}}\right)+v\cdot\Phi\left(\frac{v}{\sqrt{2\pi}}\right)\right)}^{\text{Eq. 10.52}}}{\cancel{\mathbb{A}_i^{\Sigma}}}, \\ &= \sqrt{2\pi}\cdot\phi\left(\frac{v}{\sqrt{2\pi}}\right)+v\cdot\Phi\left(\frac{v}{\sqrt{2\pi}}\right).\end{aligned} \tag{10.54}$$

We can think of this as a form of standardization. If the expected exposure—computed with the starting point and collateral in mind—exceeds the add-on (which is determined assuming a zero replacement cost), then the ratio in Eq. 10.54 will exceed one. This means the expected evolution of the netting set value is even more positive than the aggregate add-on would suggest. This is not the situation the regulators are interested in. The multiplier is intended to cover the opposite case where $\mathbb{E}_t\left(E_{t+T}(i)\right) < \mathbb{A}_i^{\Sigma}$ (or equivalently, where Eq. 10.54 is less than one). In this case, the aggregate add-on assumptions are too conservative and the multiplier's job is to mitigate this somewhat.

With this in mind, the *theoretical* form of the multiplier is expressed as,

$$\begin{aligned}\underbrace{\tilde{f}_i(v)}_{\tilde{\mathcal{M}}_i} &= \min\left(1, \frac{\mathbb{E}_t\left(E_{t+T}(i)\right)}{\mathbb{A}_i^{\Sigma}}\right), \\ \tilde{f}_i(v) &= \min\left(1, \underbrace{\sqrt{2\pi}\cdot\phi\left(\frac{v}{\sqrt{2\pi}}\right)+v\cdot\Phi\left(\frac{v}{\sqrt{2\pi}}\right)}_{\text{Eq. 10.54}}\right),\end{aligned} \tag{10.55}$$

where we can think of the multiplier as a function of $v$, denoted $\tilde{f}_i$. The role of the $\min(\cdot)$ operator is to ensure that the multiplier only considers those cases where the ratio is in the unit interval. A bit of reflection reveals that this occurs only when the numerator of $v$—the initial replacement cost $V_t(i) - \tilde{C}_{t+T}(i)$—is less than zero. This, in turn, only happens when the initial market value is out-of-the-money or overcollaterized.

At this point, the construction of the multiplier starts to get a bit weird. BIS [6] claims that:

> MTM values of real nettings sets are likely to exhibit heavier tail behaviour than the one of the normal distribution.

This is likely to be empirically true, but no other justification or motivation is provided. The proposed solution—which comes a bit out of thin air—is to select the following alternative multiplier function:

$$\underbrace{\breve{f}_i(v)}_{\breve{\mathcal{M}}_i} = \min\left(1, e^{\gamma v}\right), \tag{10.56}$$

where $\gamma \in \mathbb{R}_+$ is a parameter that requires specification. BIS [6] further indicates that $\gamma$ is determined by equating the derivatives of the theoretical and proposed multiplier ratios evaluated at zero. This is readily verified

$$\begin{aligned}
\frac{d}{dv}\underbrace{\left(e^{\gamma v}\right)}_{\substack{\text{Equation}\\ 10.56}}\Bigg|_{v=0} &= \frac{d}{dv}\underbrace{\left(\sqrt{2\pi}\cdot\phi\left(\frac{v}{\sqrt{2\pi}}\right) + v\cdot\Phi\left(\frac{v}{\sqrt{2\pi}}\right)\right)}_{\text{Eq. 10.52}}\Bigg|_{v=0}, \qquad (10.57)\\
\left(\gamma e^{\gamma v}\right)\Big|_{v=0} &= \left(\frac{\cancel{\sqrt{2\pi}}}{\cancel{\sqrt{2\pi}}}\cdot\phi'\left(\frac{v}{\sqrt{2\pi}}\right) + \Phi\left(\frac{v}{\sqrt{2\pi}}\right) + \frac{v}{\sqrt{2\pi}}\cdot\Phi'\left(\frac{v}{\sqrt{2\pi}}\right)\right)\Bigg|_{v=0},\\
\gamma &= \phi'(0) + \Phi(0),\\
\gamma &= \underbrace{\left(\frac{-x}{\sqrt{2\pi}}e^{-\frac{x^2}{2}}\right)\Bigg|_{x=0}}_{=0} + \frac{1}{2},\\
\gamma &= \frac{1}{2}.
\end{aligned}$$

This leads to updating the proposed multiplier function to

$$\breve{\mathcal{M}}_i \equiv \breve{f}_i(v) = \min\left(1, e^{\frac{v}{2}}\right). \tag{10.58}$$

This is *not*, confusingly, the end of the story. BIS [6], making reference to the fact that Eq. 10.58 "would still approach zero with infinite collateralization", impose a floored version with the following *final* form:

$$\underbrace{f_i(v)}_{\mathcal{M}_i} = \min\left(1, \vartheta + (1-\vartheta)\cdot e^{\frac{v}{2\cdot(1-\vartheta)}}\right), \tag{10.59}$$

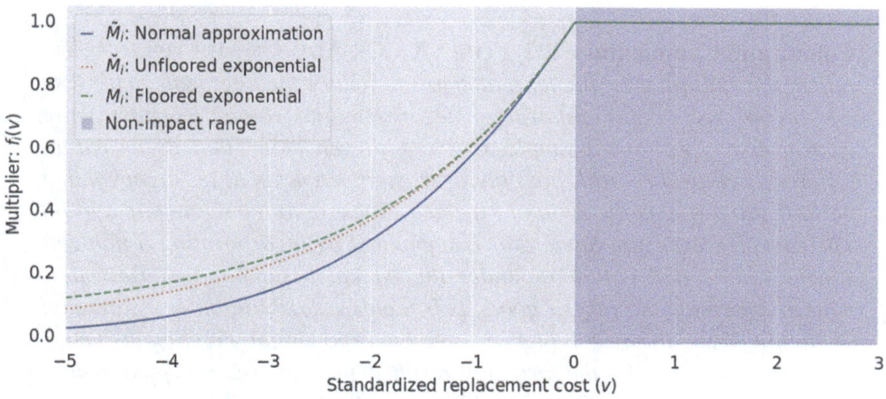


**Fig. 10.5** *The add-on multiplier*: This graphic illustrates three alternative forms of the add-on multiplier: the (theoretical) normal approximation from Eq. 10.55, the raw exponential form in Eq. 10.58, and the official floored exponential version from Eq. 10.59. The only real difference among these three choices is their speed of decrease in $-v$.

where, currently, $\vartheta = 0.05$. The idea of Eq. 10.59 is that as $v$ gets very large and negative, the multiplier tends to $\vartheta$ rather than zero. This appears to be a mathematical adjustment, rather than predicated on any theory.

Figure 10.5 illustrates *three* alternative forms of the add-on multiplier over the interval $[-5, 3]$. It includes the *theoretical* normal approximation from Eq. 10.55, the heuristic exponential form in Eq. 10.58, and the official floored exponential version from Eq. 10.59. The only practical difference among these three choices is their speed of decrease in $-v$. It is also quite clear, from Fig. 10.5, that none of the multipliers plays an role for positive realizations of Eq. 10.53.

As a final point, the only distinction between the multiplier in margined and non-margined netting sets relates to the treatment of the collateral in the definition of $v$. That is,

$$v = \begin{cases} \dfrac{V_t(i) - \tilde{C}_{t+1}(i)}{\mathbb{A}_i^{\Sigma}} & : \text{No margin} \\ \dfrac{V_t(i) - \tilde{C}_{t+\tau_{M_i}}(i)}{\mathbb{A}_i^{\Sigma}} & : \text{Margin} \end{cases}, \tag{10.60}$$

where the haircut period applies to one-year and the margin period of risk for non-margined, and margined netting sets, respectively. Although it is a bit difficult to see after the multiple interventions, both computations also share the same expected exposure foundation.

**Colour and Commentary 122** (THE SA-CCR ADD-ON MULTIPLIER)*: The role of the multiplier is simple: it attempts to reduce the aggregate netting-set add-on for excess collateral or large negative market values. Its construction is, conversely,* not *at all simple. One could even claim that its derivation follows a relatively weird, possibly over-engineered, or at least convoluted, path. It starts out as the ratio of expected exposure to the aggregate add-on. The expected-exposure numerator is computed by incorporating a non-zero starting value and collateral under the typical assumption of Brownian-motion dynamics. So far, so good. This yields a fairly intuitive expression. Then the basic form is replaced with an exponential function, which is vaguely calibrated to the original result. This can be accepted with a slight "suspension of disbelief." Finally, a floor is imposed for "infinite overcollateralization." The ultimate result is practical, workable, and appears to meet the key regulatory objectives. The weirdness, therefore, has no lasting consequences. One simply needs to invest some additional effort in understanding the origins and justification of the add-on multiplier. Without this background, examination of the final form might lead to a bit of head scratching.*

### *10.5.5 Bringing It All Together*

The preceding sections have been, quite frankly, jumping around somewhat. The idea has been to derive and motivate the various elements of the SA-CCR exposure methodology, which forms the basis of our derivative-exposure model. It is nonetheless admittedly hard to follow the thread connecting these diverse formulae. Figure 10.6 attempts to (at least partially) rectify this situation by offering a high-level overview of the main SA-CCR points. It begins from the derivative exposure (i.e., EAD) equation and then splits into *two* streams: the replacement cost and the add-on. Attempting to incorporate the margin and non-margin perspectives, it also chronicles the various levels of the add-on hierarchy and a number of miscellaneous definitions. It can be viewed as something of a cheat-sheet for anyone looking to implement (or understand) this important calculation.

The description in Fig. 10.6 does, however, remain somewhat abstract. It does not, for example, delve into the important instrument level details of the directional delta, adjusted notional and supervisory factors. To actually use the SA-CCR approach, it is necessary to grapple with these concepts. For this reason, these components, determined at the individual asset-class level, are the next topic of consideration.

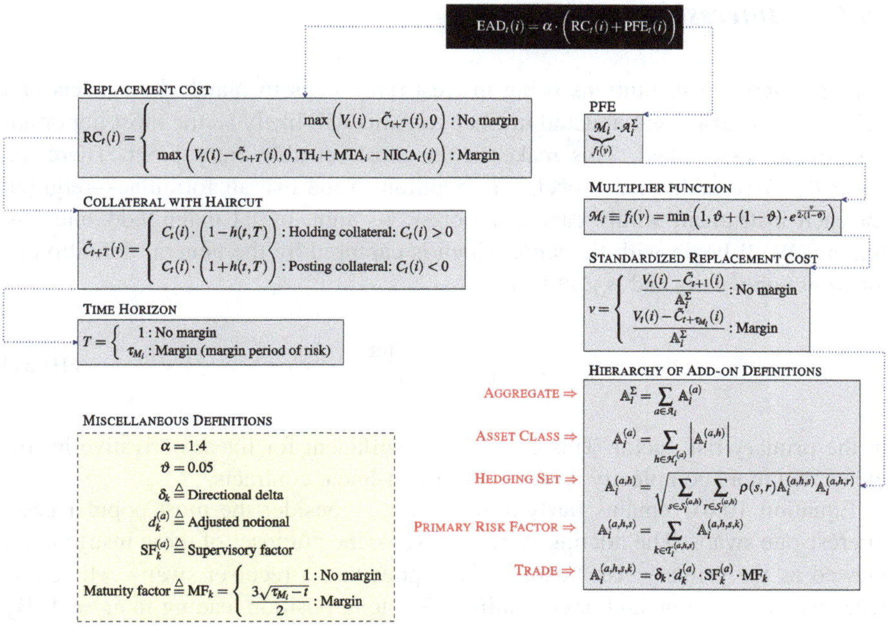


**Fig. 10.6** *SA-CCR cheat-sheet*: This schematic outlines, at a single glance, the principal formulae involved in the SA-CCR exposure calculation. It also attempts to highlight the most important relationships between the key elements.

## 10.6 The Asset-Class Perspective

The SA-CCR methodology decomposes the universe of derivative contracts into *five* distinct asset classes: interest rates, currency, credit, equity, and commodities. This is a challenging task. Much like peeling an onion, one could easily construct many other additional asset classes. There are also many sub-layers within a given asset class. The notions of primary risk factors and hedging sets are, in fact, an attempt to capture some of the complexity of these sub-layers.

To actually implement the SA-CCR methodology, Figs. 10.4 and 10.6, while hopefully useful, are not enough. Additional colour is required—regarding the directional deltas, adjusted notionals, and supervisory factors—to evaluate Eq. 10.46. Detailed direction, and helpful examples, are found in BIS [5, 7]. The following sections will walk through the key details in the area of interest-rate and currency derivatives; these are the two areas of principal interest to the NIB. They also coincide with the currently most popular and widely used OTC derivatives found in financial markets: interest-rate and cross-currency swaps.

### 10.6.1 Interest Rates

For most lending institutions using interest-rate swaps to match their assets and liabilities—as discussed in detail in Chap. 6—this will likely be the most important category of asset class. This makes it the most sensible entry point. There are basically *three* additional aspects—in addition to the overall formulae—required for each instrument within each asset class: its sign, initial magnitude, and risk scaling. We'll begin with the sign, which is captured by the general definition of the *directional* delta and is given as

$$\delta_k = \begin{cases} 1 : \text{Long} \\ -1 : \text{Short} \end{cases}, \tag{10.61}$$

in the primary risk factor. This definition is sufficient for linear derivative instruments, but more complexity is required for non-linear contracts.[35]

Equation 10.61 remains fairly abstract. Let's consider the most popular case: interest-rate swaps. The floating swap rate is, for the purposes of these instruments, viewed as the primary risk factor. This implies that a receiver swap—where one receives the fixed rate and pays floating—is a long position leading to $\delta_k = 1$. By the reverse logic, a payer swap is short in the primary risk factor leading to $\delta_k = -1$. Proper classification of one's swaps can thus help tremendously in determination of the directional delta. Basis swaps, where both legs represent alternative floating rates, are less obvious. According to BIS [7], each floating pair needs to be treated as a separate hedging set. In our implementation, we assume that the shortest reset frequency is the primary-risk factor. In those (very rare) cases where the frequencies of the floating components are equal, then the order of the indices determines the sign.[36]

The *adjusted* notional amount of an interest-rate derivative with a lifetime over the interval $[S_k, E_k]$ is given as,

$$d_k^{(\text{IR})} = N_k \cdot \text{SD}_k, \tag{10.62}$$

where $N_k$ denotes the *average* notional position over the instrument's lifetime and $\text{SD}_k$ represents the so-called supervisory duration. $S_k$ and $E_k$ are, as one might expect, the start and end dates of the derivative contract. Using $t$, as usual, to represent the current point in time, the remaining term to maturity (or tenor) is simply $E_k - t$.

[35] If the position possesses optionality, then the $\pm 1$ is replaced with the appropriately signed option deltas. The model that one must use to determine these quantities—and the key input parameters, such as implied volatility—is provided in the regulatory guidance. See BIS [5, 6] for more details.

[36] In this case, the assignment of a sign is arbitrary. It just needs to be consistent across all ordered pairs.

As usual for the SA-CCR model parameters, the supervisory duration is determined via regulator-provided formulae. It also applies to both interest-rate and credit derivatives. According to BIS [6] it stems from

$$\begin{aligned} \text{SD}_k &= \int_{\max(S_k,t)}^{E_k} e^{-r(\tau-t)} d\tau, \qquad (10.63)\\ &= \left[ -\frac{e^{-r(\tau-t)}}{r} \right]_{\max(S_k,t)}^{E_k}, \\ &= \frac{e^{-r\cdot(\max(S_k,t)-t)} - e^{-r(E_k-t)}}{r}, \end{aligned}$$

where $\max(S_k, t)$ is intended to handle ongoing and forward-start derivative contracts. In the current implementation of SA-CCR, the value of $r$ has been arbitrarily—and rather non-conservatively given current interest-rate levels—set to 5%.

Given that we typically think of the modified duration of a fixed-income instrument as a normalized partial derivative of its value function with respect to its yield, it is somewhat surprising to see the integral form in Eq. 10.63.[37] It is not, in fact, a classical estimate of duration, but rather the cumulative discount factor over the interval, $\left[ \max(S_k, t), E_k \right]$.

**Colour and Commentary 123** (SUPERVISORY DURATION)*: The term* supervisory duration, *in the context of SA-CCR, is not easily interpreted. As a (normalized) sensitivity to an interest-rate movement, duration is typically defined as a derivative taken with respect to some dimension of the yield curve. This could be a single rate, the instrument's yield, or a spread. Equation 10.63 illustrates the supervisory duration—rather uniquely in the author's experience—as the sum (or integral) of a continuously compounded discount factor—at a fixed rate of 5%—over the trade's lifetime. The consequence is a rather high "duration" estimate; for* $E_k - S_k = 10$*, for example, the result is approximately 7.9. Interestingly, as* $r \to 0$*, the supervisory duration estimate tends towards* $E_k - S_k$*. This leads to the conclusion that supervisory duration is, loosely speaking, constructed under the (rather conservative) treatment of a swap as something similar to the cumulative discount factor of a bond with tenor* $E_k - S_k$ *and a yield of 5%. Once again, as we've already seen on numerous occasions, there is a certain logic to this approach, but the rationale is not entirely clear from the outset.*

---

[37] See Bolder [8, Chapter 2] for rather more on the foundations of modified duration and related concepts.

An interest-rate hedging set encapsulates all trades in a given currency. As the tenor of fixed-income securities is quite important—short-term instruments can act rather differently, for example, than their long-term equivalents—this dimension is used to construct primary risk factors. In particular, the notion of a maturity bucket is introduced by BIS [5] and defined as,

$$\text{Maturity Bucket} \equiv \text{MB} = \begin{cases} \text{Short } (S) : E_k - t \in (0, 1] \\ \text{Medium } (M) : E_k - t \in (1, 5] \\ \text{Long } (L) : E_k - t \in (5, \infty) \end{cases} . \tag{10.64}$$

This partition of yield-curve space is not particularly granular, but it dramatically eases the implementation.

Although it is a bit tedious and repetitive, we will combine all of these elements together and explicitly write out the aggregate relations from the trade to the hedging-set level. This begins with the following trade description

$$\mathbb{A}_i^{(\text{IR,CCY,MB},k)} = \pm N_k \underbrace{\overbrace{\left( \frac{e^{-r\cdot(\max(S_k,t)-t)} - e^{-r(E_k-t)}}{r} \right)}^{\text{Eq. 10.62}}}_{\text{Eq. 10.63}} \cdot \text{MF}_k, \tag{10.65}$$

where the sign is determined by Eq. 10.61. The add-on by primary factor set, or rather maturity bucket in this case, is now

$$\mathbb{A}_i^{(\text{IR,CCY,MB})} = \sum_{k\in\text{MB}} \underbrace{\pm N_k \left( \frac{e^{-r\cdot(\max(S_k,t)-t)} - e^{-r(E_k-t)}}{r} \right) \cdot \text{MF}_k}_{\text{Eq. 10.65}} . \tag{10.66}$$

Each interest-rate hedging set is aggregated following the logic in Eq. 10.32 as

$$\mathbb{A}_i^{(\text{IR,CCY})} = \underbrace{0.05\%}_{\text{SF}_k} \sqrt{\sum_{s\in\{S,M,L\}} \sum_{r\in\{S,M,L\}} \rho(s,r) \underbrace{\mathbb{A}_i^{(\text{IR,CCY},s)} \mathbb{A}_i^{(\text{IR,CCY},r)}}_{\text{Eq. 10.66}}}, \tag{10.67}$$

where CCY denotes a given currency defined hedging set and the supervisory factor, $\text{SF}_k$ is given as 0.05% in BIS [5, Table 2].[38] Practically, the correlation coefficients are provided by the regulators and set to $\rho(S, M) = \rho(M, L) = 0.7$ and $\rho(S, L) = 0.3$. Although the absolute levels are not easily motivated across all currencies, the choice makes sense given that adjacent maturity categories tend to be significantly

[38] The previously discussed basis swaps, where each pair of floating indices are treated as separate hedging sets, receive a supervisory factor of 0.025%. Cutting the base interest-rate swap amount in half is explicitly indicated in BIS [7].

more highly correlated than more distant nodes along the yield curve. Finally, the sum over the currency hedging sets requires no application of the absolute-value operator, because the hedging-set aggregation in Eq. 10.67 always yields positive values.[39]

Computation of the interest-rate add-on, therefore, requires only a limited amount of information for each instrument: the average notional amount, position currency, start and end dates, and whether it is a short or long position. In line with typical regulatory calculations, this imposes a limited operational and data burden on the calculating agent.

### 10.6.2 Currencies

The currency asset class is a bit larger than one might initially imagine. This is because cross currency swaps are allocated to this category. This might seem somewhat odd, but given the significantly higher volatility of most currencies relative to interest rates, this seems like a judicious choice.[40] The ability of a proper forward-looking simulation engine to simultaneously manage all underlying risk factors associated with each position—by comparison—is definitely an advantage. This is one of the costs of parsimony.

In contrast to interest rates, the currency asset class is relatively straightforward. The adjusted notional amount is expressed as,

$$d_k^{(\text{CCY})} = N_k^{\text{LC}}, \tag{10.68}$$

where LC denotes the local-currency value of the foreign-currency claim. If both legs of the trade are in foreign currency, then BIS [5] recommends computing both in local currency terms and using the larger of the two estimates.[41] The directional delta has the same basic form as found in Eq. 10.61, while the supervisory duration is implicitly $\text{SD}_k \equiv 1$. The corollary of this choice is that the trade-level add-on is independent of the instrument's maturity.

In the currency asset class, a hedging set is defined as a currency pair; we will denote this by CP. The idea, it seems, is that each member of the hedging set's primary risk factor is the spot exchange rate associated with its currency pair. The key practical task is to get the correct directionality of the currency pairs. A EUR-

---

39 If it did not, with the presence of the square-root operator, we might find ourselves with a difficult-to-explain, complex-valued interest-rate add-on.

40 The regulators could, of course, have assigned them to both asset classes. This would, however, lead to more complexity and immediately break the general rule of assigning each instrument to a single asset class.

41 Our current implementation, incidentally, always conservatively uses the larger of the two legs in local-currency terms.

AUD pair is, of course, equivalent to an AUD-EUR position. What is important is to identify the set of unique currency pairs and determine long and short positions with respect to that combination.[42]

There is no primary risk factor sub-category in the aggregation, since it is already defined at the trade level by the choice of currency pair. The trade-level formula is given as,

$$\mathbb{A}_i^{(\text{CCY},\text{CP},k)} = \pm N_k^{\text{LC}} \cdot \underbrace{4.0\%}_{\text{SF}_k} \cdot \text{MF}_k, \tag{10.69}$$

where the supervisory factor is significantly (and understandably) much larger than in the interest-rate setting. Summing over all of the trades within a given currency pair yields,

$$\mathbb{A}_i^{(\text{CCY},\text{CP})} = \underbrace{\sum_{k\in\text{CP}} \pm N_k^{\text{LC}} \cdot \underbrace{4.0\%}_{\text{SF}_k} \cdot \text{MF}_k}_{\text{Eq. 10.69}}. \tag{10.70}$$

The currency asset class add-on then reduces to the following final aggregation over all of the individual currency pairs,

$$\mathbb{A}_i^{(\text{CCY})} = \sum_{c\in\text{CCY}} \underbrace{\left|\mathbb{A}_i^{(\text{CCY},c)}\right|}_{\text{Eq. 10.70}}. \tag{10.71}$$

The uniqueness of the currency asset class stems from the overlap between the trade and primary-risk factor levels. Equation 10.71 also reveals the reason for the presence of the absolute-value operator in Eqs. 10.37 and 10.48. If it were not present, then positive and negative exposures from different currencies would (rather indefensibly) be able to offset one another.

## 10.7 A Pair of Practical Applications

As usual, we would like to conclude with some concrete discussion to help solidify these ideas. Unfortunately, there are fundamental reasons that make it challenging in this case. As should be clear from the previous sections, the individual SA-CCR calculations are rather data-heavy and multi-layered; there is a real danger of spend-

[42] Ultimately, the actual sign assigned to long and short trades does not matter since absolute values will be imposed in a latter step. The key is consistency of sign treatment among short and long positions with each unique currency pair.

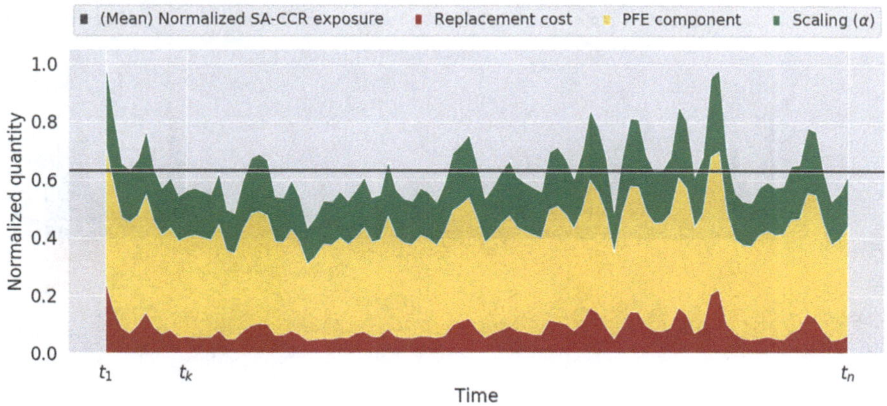


**Fig. 10.7** *Normalized portfolio-level derivative exposure*: This graphic traces our normalized portfolio-level SA-CCR derivative exposure estimate over a roughly six-month period in 2021. It should help to visualize the relative roles of replacement cost, the model-based PFE component, and the additional regulatory conservatism.

ing more time introducing the data than actually discussing the results. It is also impossible to directly use NIB-related inputs, because these derivative obligations represent rather sensitive internal data. Even if we could, the dimensionality of the data would be a bit overwhelming.

To counteract these shortcomings, we will look at a pair of, rather stylized, examples. The first examines a normalized view of our overall portfolio-level derivative exposure. These results generically describe the key relationships between the various elements of the SA-CCR computation. Our second example investigates a practical application—important for all financial institutions—of derivative exposure estimates: the so-called leverage ratio.

### *10.7.1 Normalized Derivative Exposures*

Derivative exposures are computed at the counterparty level; this is an unavoidable consequence of counterparty credit risk. When the exposures of all individual derivative counterparts are summed up, however, we arrive at a surprisingly interesting perspective on portfolio-level exposure.

Figure 10.7 provides, for an arbitrarily selected six-month time interval during 2021, the normalized view of our portfolio-level derivative exposure.[43] This vantage point allows us to establish a few basic facts about the SA-CCR computation.

[43] The normalization involves imposing unit volatility and scaling by the maximum observation. This allows us to abstract from the actual values and focus on trends and broad-based insights.

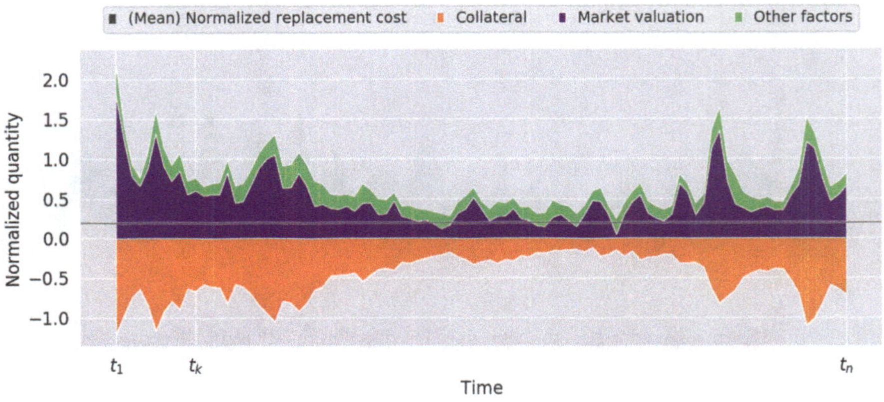


**Fig. 10.8** *Normalized portfolio-level replacement cost*: The graphic above traces the our normalized portfolio-level replacement cost over a roughly six-month period in 2021. This should be viewed as drilling deeper into the replacement-cost component presented in Fig. 10.7.

The portfolio-level values—which are a function of *three* main components—are relatively stable across time. Moreover, the replacement cost represents a fairly modest part of the overall picture. This is essentially the point of the SA-CCR; the add-on-related PFE component is an adjustment for risk placed on top of the collateralized current exposure. This PFE element, which is determined by the structure of the underlying derivative instruments, is naturally quite persistent.[44] The final component, stemming from the constant in Eq. 10.26, is a bit of additional conservatism provided by our regulators.

Figure 10.8 drills deeper into the replacement-cost component. As we learned in the previous discussion, the key replacement-cost drivers are market value and collateral. Again using a normalized, portfolio-level perspective, we see clearly that collateral and derivative valuations are essentially mirror images of one another.[45] This is, in fact, the entire point of the collateral process. As market values move in the financial institution's favour, collateral is received to offset the increasing counterparty credit risk.[46] The component called *Other factors* in Fig. 10.8 relates to the net initial collateral, collateral threshold, and minimum transfer amounts introduced in Eq. 10.27. These elements—which are simply the difference between the SA-CCR replacement cost and the residual market value after collateral—are uniformly positive. They represent an additional element of caution in the SA-CCR construction.

[44] A big part of the reason is the fixed regulatory parameters, which are not recalibrated on a daily basis as is the case with most forward-looking exposure engines.

[45] The offset is not perfect, but the correlation coefficient between these two series over this period is approximately −0.9.

[46] Over this period, NIB was a net receiver of collateral at the portfolio level. An institution's collateral position tends to ebb and flow over time with market movements and portfolio composition.

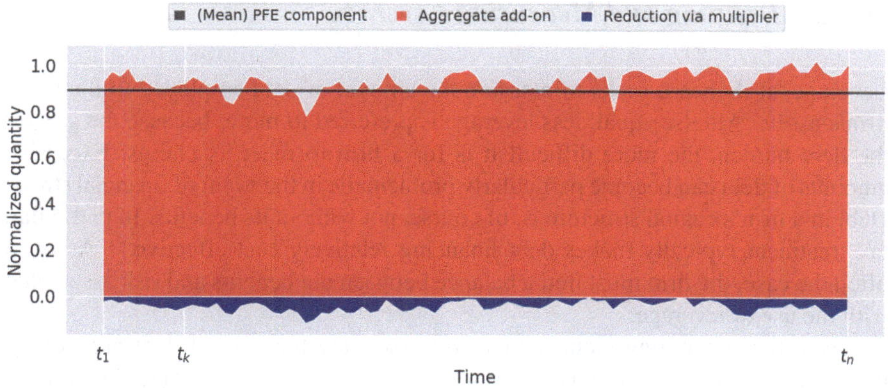


**Fig. 10.9** *Normalized portfolio-level SA-CCR PFE*: This graphic traces our normalized portfolio-level SA-CCR PFE over a roughly six-month period in 2021. This should, once again, be visualized as zooming in on the PFE component presented in Fig. 10.7.

Figure 10.9 concludes our high-level examination by zooming in on the PFE component. This normalized, portfolio-level risk-adjustment is decomposed into two sub-components: the aggregate add-on and the multiplier reduction. Recalling from Eq. 10.59, the multiplier acts to reduce the overall PFE component in cases of negative market values or overcollateralization. Over this period, the multiplier plays a comparatively limited role in the determination of the PFE contribution to overall portfolio derivative exposure. This is both typical and consistent with the regulatory guidance; the multiplier is an adjustment to handle a special case.

**Colour and Commentary 124** (INTERPRETING DERIVATIVE EXPOSURES)*: Much can be learned from a high-level analysis of one's own derivative portfolio. Using a normalized daily portfolio-level view, we consider values over a six-month period during 2021. This bird's eye perspective yields a number of interesting points. The total portfolio-level derivative exposure is generally quite stable over time; this is consistent with our desired through-the-cycle exposure estimate.*[a] *Replacement cost is, in general, only a relatively small fraction of the overall SA-CCR estimate; the risk-related PFE component represents the dominant contribution. Collateral and derivative market values, as one would expect, largely offset one another. This drives the stability and (relatively small) magnitude observed in the replacement cost. The add-on multiplier, while conceptually important, appears to play a fairly limited role. Finally, the presence of other (collateral-related) factors in the replacement cost and the scaling constant in the overall computation lend additional conservatism to the final result.*

[a] This is a direct consequence of fixed regulatory risk parameters.

### 10.7.2 Defining and Measuring Leverage

Leverage, at its heart, seeks to measure the amount of debt employed to finance a firm's assets. All else equal, less leverage is preferred to more, because the greater the debt burden, the more difficult it is for a firm to meet its claims. Excessive amounts of debt can become particularly problematic in the event of financial stress. Debt in a firm's capital structure is, of course, not without its benefits. In particular, tax treatment typically makes debt financing relatively cost effective.[47] As is so often the case, the firm must find a balance between the benefits and risk associated with the use of leverage.

Given the accounting identity that firm assets are the sum of debt and equity, there are a variety of (broadly equivalent) ways to estimate leverage. Sometimes it is represented as a debt-to-equity ratio, while in other cases one examines the ratio of debt to total assets. In the financial-institution setting, the leverage ratio is computed as

$$\text{Leverage Ratio} = \frac{\text{Available Financial Resources (Equity)}}{\text{Total Asset Exposure}}. \tag{10.72}$$

This particular definition is consistent with European Union banking regulation.[48] The benefit of the unit-less ratio format is that it is easy to interpret, enforce, and compare with other financial institutions.

It is natural to compare Eq. 10.72 to the concept of capital headroom discussed on numerous occasions in previous chapters. Both involve, after all, the firm's capital supply. When inspecting Eq. 10.72, we find that it is silent on the riskiness of the underlying assets. It depends solely on their overall magnitude or, as it is commonly referred to, volume. This is simultaneously a strength and a weakness. On the positive side, it is relatively easily described and computed. There is little scope for analytical freedom in determination of Eq. 10.72. More negatively, asset-risk composition matters. Two financial institutions might have the save leverage ratio, but vastly different asset-risk profiles. The leverage ratio provides no information on this dimension. A solid compromise is to avoid arguing about the relative merits of economic capital and leverage; instead, one can easily use both and thereby gain a broader complementary perspective.

The leverage ratio, while vastly simpler to compute than economic capital, still has a few tricky parts. While the numerator of the leverage-ratio definition in Eq. 10.72 is fairly clearly related to some variation on internal capital supply, the denominator remains somewhat vague. The regulation is, however, quite specific. In particular, the guidance stipulates that it must include:

---

[47] This fact has been appreciated for decades and is a key driver of capital-structure decisions; see, for example, Modigliani and Miller [16].

[48] Further background, from the regulatory side, is found in BIS [4].

1. an accounting representation of firm assets *excluding* derivative contracts and associated collateral;
2. an allocation for non-derivative-related off-balance sheet items; and
3. an allowance for derivative contracts incorporating **an add-on for counterparty credit risk**.

It is this final point that, in the context of this chapter, catches our interest. Pulling these directions together, we arrive at the following revised, and more precise, description of the leverage ratio:

$$\text{Leverage Ratio} = \frac{\text{Tier I Capital Position}}{\begin{array}{l}\text{Accounting Assets ex Derivatives} \\ \quad +\text{Off-Balance Sheet Items} + \text{Derivatives}\end{array}}. \tag{10.73}$$

Practically, most of the ingredients are relatively easily procured. Accounting asset values are sourced from internal systems. Off balance-sheet items relate exclusively to agreed, but not-yet-disbursed loans. Committed agreed, not disbursed loans are transformed with a 50% credit-conversion factor into loan equivalents; only 10% of uncommitted loans are included.[49] The wild-card in this calculation, however, relates to derivative exposure.

The regulatory term "allowance for derivative contracts" is a bit vague. Assuming a financial institution can convince its regulator of the reasonableness of its computation, then presumably it has a fairly broad range of alternatives. Common practice, and in this respect NIB is no exception, is to simply employ the SA-CCR methodology for this purpose. This completes Eq. 10.73 and readily permits its computation.[50]

**Colour and Commentary 125** (MEASURING LEVERAGE)*: Leverage seeks to describe the amount of debt employed to finance one's assets.*[a] *Unlike the risk-based economic-capital measure, which sits at the heart of this book, it focuses exclusively on volume. It can nonetheless provide a very useful complement to risk-based metrics. While leverage can be measured in many ways, it is common to construct ratios involving a firm's assets and equity (i.e., capital supply). The majority of the inputs into any leverage assessment are not particularly controversial and easily obtained from a firm's financial*

(continued)

[49] The credit-conversion factor is a regulatory invention, which we have already encountered in previous chapters. It is a value between zero and one that, when multiplied by the instrument's notional value, transforms an off-balance-sheet item into a balance-sheet equivalent.

[50] Somewhat ironically, given that it typically only represents a small fraction of a financial institution's total assets, much of the effort associated with the leverage-ratio computation relates directly to the derivative component.

**Colour and Commentary 125** (continued)
*statements. Derivatives, which may be either an asset or a liability depending on their mood, are the exception. Regulatory guidance on the measurement of leverage counsel excluding all derivative-related balance-sheet inputs—both collateral and valuations—and replacing them with* an allowance for derivative contracts. *Those wishing to measure leverage thus find themselves in the business of estimating derivative exposure. The SA-CCR computation jumps into this breach and offers a tailor-made solution to this problem.*

[a] Assets, in this context, go somewhat beyond the accounting view to consider off-balance sheet items.

## 10.8 Wrapping Up

There are many ways, of varying degrees of complexity, to compute forward-looking measures of derivative exposure. The most conceptually correct methods involve the construction of a high-dimensional instrument-level, simulation-based valuation engine that also incorporates time-varying collateral behaviour. For quantitative analysts involved in derivative pricing, complex simulation engines are a non-optional prerequisite. For economic-capital purposes, however, such complexity is neither necessary nor desired. The more stable, through-the-cycle, $\mathbb{P}$-measure-based regulatory capital calculations make for a more natural choice. They provide defensible risk-based derivative exposure estimates and, as a side benefit, represent a helpful input into the measurement of one's leverage position.

## References

1. P. Artzner, F. Delbaen, J.-M. Eber, and D. Heath. Coherent measures of risk. *Mathematical Finance*, 9(3):203–228, July 2001.
2. BIS. Treatment of potential exposure for off-balance-sheet items. Technical report, Bank for International Settlements, April 1995.
3. BIS. The application of Basel II to trading activities and the treatment of double default effects. Technical report, Bank for International Settlements, July 2005.
4. BIS. Basel III leverage ratio framework and disclosure requirements. Technical report, Bank for International Settlements, January 2014a.
5. BIS. The standardised approach for measuring counterparty credit exposures. Technical report, Bank for International Settlements, March (revised April 2014) 2014b.
6. BIS. Foundations of the standardised approach for measuring counterparty credit risk exposures. Technical report, Bank for International Settlements, August (revised June 2017) 2014c.

7. BIS. Calculation of RWA for credit risk: Standarized approach to counterparty credit risk. Technical report, Bank for International Settlements, December 2019.
8. D. J. Bolder. *Fixed Income Portfolio Analytics: A Practical Guide to Implementing, Monitoring and Understanding Fixed-Income Portfolios*. Springer, Heidelberg, Germany, 2015.
9. D. J. Bolder. *Credit-Risk Modelling: Theoretical Foundations, Diagnostic Tools, Practical Examples, and Numerical Recipes in Python*. Springer-Nature, Heidelberg, Germany, 2018.
10. D. Brigo. Counterparty risk faq; credit var, pfe, cva, dva, closeout, netting, collateral, re-hypothecation, wwr, basel, funding, CCDS and margin lending. In D. Brigo, editor, *Counterparty Credit Risk, Collateral and Funding*. Wiley Finance, 2012.
11. D. Duffie and E. Canabarro. *Measuring and marking counterparty risk*, chapter 9, pages 122–134. Euromoney Books, 2003.
12. M. B. Gordy. A risk-factor model foundation for ratings-based bank capital rules. *Journal of Financial Intermediation*, 12:199–232, 2003.
13. J. Gregory. *Counterparty Credit Risk: The New Challenge for Global Financial Markets*. John Wiley & Sons Ltd., Chicester, UK, 2010.
14. A. J. Heunis. Notes on stochastic calculus. University of Waterloo, Winter 2011.
15. I. Karatzas and S. E. Shreve. *Methods of Mathematical Finance*. Springer-Verlag, New York, NY, 1998.
16. F. Modigliani and M. H. Miller. The cost of capital, corporation finance and the theory of investment. *The American Economic Review*, 48(3):261–297, 1958.
17. J. Morgan/Reuters. *RiskMetrics — Technical Document*. Morgan Guaranty Trust Company, New York, 1996.
18. B. K. Oksendal. *Stochastic Differential Equations*. Springer Verlag, Berlin, fourth edition, 1995.
19. I. Ruiz. *XVA Desks: A New Era for Risk Management*. Palgrave Macmillan, New York, NY, 2015.
20. A. P. Salonen. *Transnational Law of the Over-the-Counter Derivatives Market: A Study of the Interactions of Law and Finance*. PhD thesis, Faculty of Law, University of Helsinki, 2019. Unpublished Thesis.

# Chapter 11
# Seeking External Comparison

*It does not do to leave a live dragon out of your calculations, if you live near him.*

*(J.R.R. Tolkien)*

Few things are done in isolation, and NIB's computation of economic capital is certainly not one of them. While an unregulated entity, we assign significant importance towards regulatory capital calculations for the benchmarking of internal methodologies. The Basel Committee on Banking Supervision (BCBS) and the European Banking Authority (EBA) support a two-pillared approach towards the estimation of regulatory capital requirements.[1] Pillar I refers to a collection of highly formulaic, portfolio-invariant approaches. Easy to compute, interpret, and compare, these are the bread-and-butter of the regulatory capital calculation. Pillar II deals with complexities surrounding the (necessary) simplifications made in Pillar I. It should come as no surprise, therefore, that Pillar II computations are hard work.

The supervisory community is not the only group interested in capital adequacy. Credit-rating agencies, in their quest to assess the credit quality of large numbers of institutions, also have a keen interest in this area and, to varying degrees, possess their own perspectives and methodologies. To be more concrete, on an semi-annual basis—in addition to ongoing monitoring—the Standard & Poor's (S&P) credit-rating agency performs a regular assessment of the creditworthiness of many corporate, supranational, and sovereign entities. NIB falls into this group. S&P examines myriad criteria to arrive at their final appraisal.[2] A key figure plays an important role: it is termed the S&P risk-adjusted capital (RAC) ratio. The objective of this S&P calculation—based on a comprehensive internally developed methodology—is to place global institutions on equal footing and facilitate their fair and independent comparison and ranking. In this respect, the objectives

[1] There is also a third pillar, but it is more concerned with the presentation rather than the computation of capital adequacy.

[2] S&P [32] is an excellent survey of the elements considered.



D. Bolder, *Modelling Economic Capital*, Contributions to Finance and Accounting,
https://doi.org/10.1007/978-3-030-95096-5_11

of credit-rating agencies and regulators coincide. Given the centrality of NIB's external-debt rating to its business model, this measure is worth investigating and understanding.

In quantitative modelling endeavours, multiplicity of perspective is highly valuable. Regulatory capital and key credit-rating agency measures represent crucially important points of comparison for our internal capital adequacy calculations. These alternative approaches also share some important similarities. S&P's RAC ratio computation is broken down into two pieces: calculation of risk-weighted assets and associated adjustments. These elements are conceptually analogous to the Pillar I and II processes. Interestingly, numerous underlying mathematical and statistical techniques are also shared. Their relationship thus goes beyond a conceptual level.

Pillar II computations and S&P risk-weighted asset adjustments are, unfortunately, *not* particularly trivial. Pillar I style risk weighting of an entity's assets are performed upon each exposure independently, thereby ignoring important portfolio concepts such as diversification and concentration. These simplifications need to be corrected in the second stage. Specific examples relate to the role of single-name concentration, geographic and sectoral diversification effects, and the role of multiple underlying systemic factors. Many of these computations are motivated from the regulatory and academic literature and encompass—to understand what is actually being done—reasonably involved mathematics. Working through these details and finding sensible implementations will require a heavy effort. This will be the main task of this chapter.

A second, and somewhat unique, source of complexity is the lack of complete clarity regarding the S&P approach. S&P [31, 33] provide a useful high-level overview of their RAC calculation, but, in many cases, they are short on the actual details. To a certain extent, therefore, the analyst performing this replication is required to operate in the dark. This is, in fact, by design. S&P is open about their desire to leave a degree of ambiguity with respect to their methodology. Their view is that this inherent opacity makes it difficult for rated entities to reverse-engineer their computation to achieve a desired rating outcome. Although entirely defensible, this practice complicates comparison.

In short, the techniques presented in this chapter are not easy. It is, however, a worthwhile and valuable exercise. The importance of credit ratings and regulatory capital-adequacy calculations notwithstanding, the principle benefit arises from their role as outside comparators. Every internal economic-capital framework is, by necessity, complex and involved. Any external methodology—be it from the credit-rating or regulatory perspectives—offers a unique opportunity to assess the consistency and deviations between these alternative approaches. Much is learned from such constant and explicit comparison.

## 11.1 Pillar I

Pillar I computations turn principally around the idea of risk-weighted assets. In its most general form, this quantity is, for the $i$th exposure, defined as,

$$\text{Risk-Weighted Assets}_i = \underbrace{\text{Exposure-at-Default}_i}_{c_i} \cdot \underbrace{12.5 \cdot \text{Risk Capital Weight}_i}_{\text{Risk Weight}_i}, \tag{11.1}$$

for $i = 1, \ldots, N$ individual asset exposures held by a given corporate entity.[3] At the risk of stating the painfully obvious, each asset is weighted by some measure of its risk. The secret sauce, of course, associated with any of these Pillar I based (or inspired) methodologies relates to precisely how one determines these weights. Two central properties of risk-weighted assets (or RWA) are their additivity and independence. Equation 11.1 can be computed independently for each exposure; to be clear, no other portfolio information is required. If one desires the total RWA figure, one need only sum over all individual exposures.[4] While theoretically shaky, these analytical properties dramatically simplify computations and foster comparison.[5] With this in mind, we will examine three alternative approaches to the Pillar I computation.

### 11.1.1 *The Standardized Regulatory Approach*

The most natural place to start is with the regulatory perspective. Within the regulatory world, it makes the most logical sense to begin with the so-called BCBS standardized approach. The gory details are found in BIS [6, Part 2, Section II]. The basic idea is, however, very simple: the risk weight from Eq. 11.1 is determined as a function of the type and credit quality of the underlying exposure. In practice, however, it is not quite as simple. There are a wealth of acronyms and exceptions to consider and manage. Getting to the actual implementation requires multiple careful readings of BIS [6] or the more recent publication, BIS [8].

Table 11.1 provides a high-level description of the standardized approach risk-weight guidance from BIS [6, Part 2, Section II]. There are basically three types of exposure: sovereign and central banks, banks and securities firms, and

[3] The factor 12.5 is merely the reciprocal of the classic 8% charge in the Basel setting.

[4] Naturally, it follows immediately from Eq. 11.1, that if we divide the risk-weighted assets by 12.5, we arrive at the risk-capital amount.

[5] The combination of these two characteristics is often referred to as portfolio invariance. The risk weight, for a given asset, is invariant to the portfolio composition. From first principles of portfolio theory, this cannot be correct.

**Table 11.1** *Standardized-model risk weights*: The underlying table describes the (high level) risk weights used, under the Basel II guidance, within the standardized model for the computation of risk-weighted assets (and regulatory capital). Each risk weight is a function of external rating and asset sector; there are many exceptions and, for a precise implementation, the Basel documentation should be consulted. These values will be replaced in January 2022 with a revised implementation.

| Sector | AAA to AA– | A+ to A– | BBB+ to BBB– | BB+ to BB– | B+ to B– | Below B– | Unrated |
|---|---|---|---|---|---|---|---|
| | 1 | 2 | 3 | 4 | 5 | 6 | 7 |
| Sovereigns[a] and Central Banks[b] | 0.0 | 0.2 | 0.5 | 1.0 | 1.0 | 1.5 | 1.0 |
| Banks and Securities Firms (Base)[c] | 0.2 | 0.5 | 0.5 | 1.0 | 1.0 | 1.5 | 0.5 |
| Banks and Securities Firms (Short-Term) | 0.2 | 0.2 | 0.2 | 0.5 | 0.5 | 1.5 | 0.2 |
| Corporations | 0.2 | 0.5 | 0.5 | 1.0 | 1.5 | 1.5 | 1.0 |

[a]For sovereign risk weights, there is another option. Country risk scores provided by export credit agencies (ECA)—who opt to follow a pre-determined OECD methodology—can also be used. This leads to another set of risk weights on a seven-point scale.
[b]Local and regional governments can qualify for the same treatment as sovereigns and central banks if certain conditions are met. Other public-sector entities may require different treatment.
[c]Not all regulatory jurisdictions permit the use of external ratings for bank exposures; for this reason, a separate standardized credit risk assessment (SCRA) approach is provided. Securities firms must be regulated as banks to qualify for this approach.

corporations. It is reasonable to distinguish between such exposure types due to underlying distinctions in how they are financed and meet their financial claims. Other sub-categories are mentioned and may either fall into the groups from Table 11.1 or be treated slightly differently. Using the S&P's credit rating scale, firm creditworthiness is partitioned into seven groups. The standardized risk weight is thus simply determined by looking up the appropriate value from Table 11.1.

As of 1 January 2022, the standardized approach is governed by BIS [8]. This leads to the revised risk weights found in Table 11.2. The most important distinction is that BIS [8] provides additional colour on a number of different asset types. In particular, the risk weights associated with multilateral development banks (MDBs), public-sector entities, and covered bonds are precisely detailed. As a second point, BIS [8] also involves some slight changes in weights. The largest differences occur with the, generally more conservative, treatment of unrated bonds. To briefly summarize, the standardized implementation will not change dramatically. There is, however, heightened clarity and slightly more conservatism.

**Table 11.2** *Forthcoming standardized-model risk weights*: The underlying table provides a (very high level) description of the forthcoming risk weights to be used, under the Basel III guidance, within the standardized model for the computation of risk-weighted assets (and regulatory capital). These values will take effect in January 2022. As is typically the case, there are many exceptions and, for a precise implementation, the Basel documentation should be consulted.

| Sector | AAA to AA– | A+ to A– | BBB+ to BBB– | BB+ to BB– | B+ to B– | Below B– | Unrated |
|---|---|---|---|---|---|---|---|
| | 1 | 2 | 3 | 4 | 5 | 6 | 7 |
| Central Banks and Sovereigns[a] | 0.0 | 0.2 | 0.5 | 1.0 | 1.0 | 1.5 | 1.0 |
| Multilateral Development Banks | 0.2 | 0.3 | 0.5 | 1.0 | 1.0 | 1.5 | 0.5 |
| Public-Sector Entity | 0.2 | 0.5 | 0.5 | 1.0 | 1.0 | 1.5 | 0.5 |
| Banks and Securities Firms (Base)[b] | 0.2 | 0.3 | 0.5 | 1.0 | 1.0 | 1.5 | 1.5 |
| Banks and Securities Firms (Short-Term) | 0.2 | 0.2 | 0.2 | 0.5 | 0.5 | 1.5 | 1.5 |
| Covered Bonds | 0.1 | 0.2 | 0.2 | 0.5 | 0.5 | 1.0 | [c] |
| Corporations | 0.2 | 0.5 | 0.75 | 1.0 | 1.5 | 1.5 | 1.0 |

[a]For sovereign risk weights, there is another option. Country risk scores provided by export credit agencies (ECA)—who opt to follow a pre-determined OECD methodology—can also be used. This leads to another set of risk weights on a seven-point scale.
[b]Not all regulatory jurisdictions permit the use of external ratings for bank exposures; for this reason, a separate standardized credit risk assessment (SCRA) approach is provided. Securities firms must be regulated as banks to qualify for this approach.
[c]A separate scale is provided for unrated covered bonds, which depends on the risk weight of the issuing bank.

The standardized approach places a relatively light burden on exposure-level data collection. One need only know the type of asset and its external rating.[6] Everything else is prescriptively provided by one's regulator. In terms of advantages, this approach offers simplicity of computation and interpretation and a relatively high degree of conservatism. On the other hand, the link to actual risk outcomes is fairly tenuous and the portfolio perspective is entirely absent. The next approach represents a comprehensive effort by the regulatory community to address some of the shortcomings of this standardized model.

[6] For internal implementation of this benchmarking model, we also make (sparse) use of a partition of our own 20-notch rating scale. In particular, in rare cases when S&P or equivalent external ratings are unavailable, we map as follows:

1. **AAA to AA**− to PD01–PD04;
2. **A+ to A**− to PD05–PD07;
3. **BBB+ to BBB**− to PD08–PD10;
4. **BB+ to BB**− to PD11–PD12;
5. **B+ to B**− to PD13–PD14;
6. **Below B**− to PD15–PD19; and
7. **Unrated** to PD20.

**Colour and Commentary 126** *(*THE STANDARDIZED APPROACH*): The idea of risk weighting does* not *appear to have been introduced by the BCBS, but BIS [2] looks to have been instrumental in popularizing and codifying its use. Although the standardized model treats risk weights associated with individual exposures in a very simple way, it is actually an interesting benchmark. The burden of information required is extremely low—only the magnitude, type, and external credit rating for each institution are employed—permitting straightforward computation and comparison. Maintaining the idea that minimum risk-capital requirements should be, at least, 8% of an entities risk-weighted assets permits one—with use of the factor 12.5—to easily move back and forth between these two quantities. Given its historical importance and continued relevance—simplicity and portfolio invariance aside—the standardized approach needs to be the starting point for any discussion of regulatory capital computations.*

### *11.1.2 The Internal Ratings-Based Approach*

The principal alternative to the standarized model is the BCBS' so-called Internal-Rating-Based (IRB) approach.[7] The risk weights, in this setting, are not simply derived from a regulatory matrix. Instead, the computation is supported by an explicit attempt to model the risk characteristics of each position, albeit in a restricted manner.

To be more specific, each risk weight is indexed to a given level of confidence and is closely related—although with some slight differences—to the popular risk measure, $\text{VaR}_\alpha(L)$.[8] This makes logical sense considering that economic capital is generically defined, for a given level of confidence, $\alpha$, as

$$\begin{aligned}\text{Unexpected Loss} &= \text{Worst-Case Loss} - \text{Expected Loss}, \\ &= \text{VaR}_\alpha(L) - \mathbb{E}(L).\end{aligned} \tag{11.2}$$

As we've seen in previous chapters, the unexpected loss is thus essentially the worst-case loss, for a given level of confidence, less the expected default loss. The expected default loss is subtracted, because it has already been explicitly considered in the pricing of the underlying obligation.

[7] See BIS [3, 4, 5] or Bolder [9, Chapter 6] for a (much) more detailed discussion.

[8] See Jorion [22] for detailed background on this risk metric.

According to current Basel IRB guidance, the risk weight associated with the $i$th obligor has the following form:

$$\text{Risk Weight}_i(\alpha) = \bar{\gamma}_i \cdot \underbrace{\text{Unexpected Loss}_i}_{\mathcal{K}_\alpha(i)}, \tag{11.3}$$

where $\bar{\gamma}_i$ denotes the *expected* loss-given-default and $\mathcal{K}_\alpha(i)$ represents the risk-capital contribution. This latter quantity is constructed to relate directly to the exposure's unexpected loss.

The BCBS faced a tricky question. Although there was a desire to incorporate more realistic risk characteristics into the IRB risk weights, the approach needed to remain formulaic and reasonable tractable. In particular, it was necessary to maintain the notion of portfolio invariance. To accomplish this, two rather strong assumptions were required. First of all, there could be only a single source of systemic risk; let's denote it as $G$. The actual implementation choice was a one-factor Gaussian threshold model.[9] Secondly, and perhaps more strongly, it was assumed that the only source of default risk is systematic so that,

$$\begin{aligned} \text{VaR}_\alpha(L) &\approx \mathbb{E}\left(L \,\middle|\, G = \Phi^{-1}(1-\alpha)\right), \\ &\approx \sum_{i=1}^{N} \mathbb{E}\left(L_i \,\middle|\, G = \Phi^{-1}(1-\alpha)\right). \end{aligned} \tag{11.4}$$

In words, therefore, the Value-at-Risk (for a given confidence level) is fully described by the conditional expectation of the portfolio loss given an extreme outcome of the systemic risk factor. This can only be true in the virtual absence of any idiosyncratic risk. A lack of idiosyncratic risk, in truth, can only occur when the portfolio is highly diversified. That is, the idiosyncratic elements have been fully diversified away. Gordy [14] first described this as the infinitely granular portfolio assumption. Under this condition, the overall conditional portfolio loss or Value-at-Risk—as shown in Eq. 11.4—can be expressed as the sum of the conditional expectations of each individual exposure given an extreme systemic risk-factor outcome.

To actually evaluate Eq. 11.4, a bit more structure is involved. Imagine that the composite state variable of our one-factor Gaussian threshold model looks like,

$$X_i = r_i G + \sqrt{1 - r_i^2}\,\epsilon_i, \tag{11.5}$$

[9] The choice of one-factor model, as we'll see when we move to Pillar II, is not so essential. Any one-factor threshold or mixture model will do the job.

for $i = 1, \ldots, N$ and where $G$ and $\epsilon_i$ are independent and identically distributed random normal variates. Moreover, as usual, the incidence of the $i$th default event, $\mathcal{D}_i$, is defined as

$$\mathbb{I}_{\mathcal{D}_i} = \mathbb{I}_{\{X_i \leq \Phi^{-1}(p_i)\}}. \tag{11.6}$$

The obvious corollary is that the $i$th exposure's loss is described as $L_i = c_i \gamma_i \mathbb{I}_{\mathcal{D}_i}$.

Equipped with all of the necessary (and familiar) elements to determine the risk weight and the unexpected loss, we have

$$\begin{aligned}
c_i \cdot \overbrace{\underbrace{\bar{\gamma}_i \cdot \text{Unexpected Loss}_i}_{\mathcal{K}_\alpha(i)}}^{\text{Risk Weight}_i(\alpha)} &\approx \underbrace{\mathbb{E}\left( L_i \,\middle|\, G = \Phi^{-1}(1-\alpha) \right)}_{\text{Eq. 11.4}} - \mathbb{E}(L_i), \qquad (11.7)\\
&\approx \mathbb{E}\left( c_i \gamma_i \mathbb{I}_{\mathcal{D}_i} \,\middle|\, G = \Phi^{-1}(1-\alpha) \right) - \mathbb{E}\left( c_i \gamma_i \mathbb{I}_{\mathcal{D}_i} \right),\\
&= c_i \mathbb{E}(\gamma_i)\, \mathbb{P}\left( \mathcal{D}_i \,\middle|\, G = \Phi^{-1}(1-\alpha) \right) - c_i \mathbb{E}(\gamma_i)\, \underbrace{\mathbb{P}\left( \mathcal{D}_i \right)}_{p_i},\\
&= c_i \bar{\gamma}_i \left( \mathbb{P}\left( \underbrace{X_i \leq \Phi^{-1}(p_i)}_{\text{Eq. 11.6}} \,\middle|\, G = \Phi^{-1}(1-\alpha) \right) - p_i \right),\\
&= c_i \bar{\gamma}_i \left( \mathbb{P}\left( \epsilon_i \leq \frac{\Phi^{-1}(p_i) - r_i \Phi^{-1}(1-\alpha)}{\sqrt{1-r_i^2}} \right) - p_i \right),\\
&= c_i \bar{\gamma}_i \left( \underbrace{\Phi\left( \frac{\Phi^{-1}(p_i) - r_i \Phi^{-1}(1-\alpha)}{\sqrt{1-r_i^2}} \right)}_{p_i(\Phi^{-1}(1-\alpha))} - p_i \right),\\
\cancel{c_i} \cdot \bar{\gamma}_i \cdot \text{Unexpected Loss}_i &= \cancel{c_i} \bar{\gamma}_i \left( p_i\left( \Phi^{-1}(1-\alpha) \right) - p_i \right),\\
\underbrace{\cancel{\bar{\gamma}_i} \cdot \text{Unexpected Loss}_i}_{\text{Risk Weight}_i(\alpha)} &= \cancel{\bar{\gamma}_i} \left( p_i\left( \Phi^{-1}(1-\alpha) \right) - p_i \right),\\
\underbrace{\text{Unexpected Loss}_i}_{\mathcal{K}_\alpha(i)} &= p_i\left( \Phi^{-1}(1-\alpha) \right) - p_i,
\end{aligned}$$

where $p_i(g) = \mathbb{E}(\mathbb{I}_{\mathcal{D}_i} | G = g) = \mathbb{P}(\mathcal{D}_i | G = g)$ is referred to as the conditional probability of default. The final two lines of Eq. 11.7 provide us with workable exposure-level expressions for the Basel IRB risk weight and unexpected loss, respectively.

In regulatory publications, the final line of Eq. 11.7 has a (slightly) different form. It is often written as a function of *two* main arguments: the unconditional default probability, $p_i$, and the tenor, or term to maturity, of the underlying credit obligation denoted $M_i$. The risk coefficient (or unexpected loss) is typically described as

$$\underbrace{\mathcal{K}_\alpha(\text{Tenor}_i, \text{Default probability}_i)}_{\text{Unexpected Loss}_i} = \begin{pmatrix} \text{Conditional} & & \text{Unconditional} \\ \text{Default} & - & \text{Default} \\ \text{Probability}_i & & \text{Probability}_i \end{pmatrix} \cdot \begin{matrix} \text{Maturity} \\ \text{Adjustment}_i \end{matrix}, \tag{11.8}$$

$$\begin{aligned} \mathcal{K}_\alpha(M_i, p_i) &= \left( p_i\left(\Phi^{-1}(\alpha)\right) - p_i \right)\tau(M_i, p_i), \\ &= \left( \underbrace{\Phi\left( \frac{\Phi^{-1}(p_i) + \sqrt{r_i^2(p_i)}\Phi^{-1}(\alpha)}{\sqrt{1 - r_i^2(p_i)}} \right)}_{p_i(\Phi^{-1}(\alpha))} - p_i \right) \tau(M_i, p_i), \end{aligned}$$

where $\tau(M_i, p_i)$ is a maturity adjustment or correction, which depends on the tenor of the credit exposure, $M_i$.

It is relatively easy to identify the similarities between Eqs. 11.7 and 11.8. There are also a few deviations. First of all, the systemic weights (i.e., $r_i$) are not selected by the financial institution, but rather specified by the regulator. The Basel IRB approach recommends a specific level of the state-variable (i.e., asset) correlation function, $r_i^2(p_i)$, as a function of its credit quality for each credit obligor as,

$$r_i^2(p_i) = \Lambda \cdot \left( \rho^- q(p_i) + \rho^+ \left( 1 - q(p_i) \right) \right), \tag{11.9}$$

where

$$q(p_i) = \frac{1 - e^{hp_i}}{1 - e^h}, \tag{11.10}$$

and

$$\Lambda = \begin{cases} 1.25 & \text{If firm } i \text{ is a large and regulated financial institution} \\ 1 & \text{otherwise} \end{cases}. \tag{11.11}$$

The actual choice of $r_i^2$ is thus a convex combination of the limiting values $\rho^-$ and $\rho^+$ in terms of $q(p_i)$. The value $q(p_i)$ is confined, by construction, to the unit interval, which ensures the asset-correlation coefficient lies in the interval, $\rho(p_i) \in [\rho^-, \rho^+]$.

The maturity adjustment, $\tau$, is a regulatory addition. Quite simply, long-term exposures are riskier than their shorter-term equivalents. To increase the risk weighting for longer-term maturities, an adjustment factor—once again incorporating the unconditional default probability—is included. The maturity adjustment is written as,

$$\tau(M_i, p_i) = \frac{1 + \left(M_i - \frac{5}{2}\right) b(p_i)}{1 - \frac{3}{2} b(p_i)}. \tag{11.12}$$

The embedded function, $b(p_i)$ is given a very specific form,

$$b(p_i) = \left(0.11852 - 0.05478 \ln(p_i)\right)^2, \tag{11.13}$$

and is usually referred to as the slope function. To collect the main points together, the maturity function is an increasing linear function of the instrument's tenor, larger (smaller) for high (low) quality credit obligations and is neutral when $M_i = 1$.[10]

There is also a final technical precision regarding the conditional default probability, $p_i(g)$. BCBS's idea, it appears, was to simplify the usage. When $g$ is evaluated at its worst-case $\alpha$-level outcome, the regulators have replaced $\Phi^{-1}(1-\alpha)$ with $\Phi^{-1}(\alpha)$. This changes the sign in the second term of the numerator, makes the formula easier to follow, and avoids the need to discuss the negative relationship between the systematic variable and default outcomes implicit in the one-factor Gaussian threshold model. The combination of these three differences—the systemic weight, the maturity adjustment, and the sign of the extreme systemic outcome—provides a complete reconciliation between Eqs. 11.7 and 11.8.

In a nutshell, the risk weight Basel IRB approach attempts to describe the expected loss under the assumption that one's portfolio is perfectly diversified. It also incorporates loss-given-default and a maturity adjustment to capture other dimensions of risk. Finally, it provides prescriptive guidance on the selection of systemic weights. It would thus have appeared to have achieved its objective: a relatively simple implementation requiring only a few straightforward formulae and a more realistic link to each exposure's risk characteristics.

It is important to stress, of course, that this places a higher burden on the firm. It requires a reliable internal production of firm ratings and loss-given-default values.

[10] This is easily verified,

$$\gamma(1, p_i) = \frac{1 + \left(1 - \frac{5}{2}\right) b(p_i)}{1 - \frac{3}{2} b(p_i)} = \frac{\cancel{1 - \frac{3}{2} b(p_i)}}{\cancel{1 - \frac{3}{2} b(p_i)}} = 1. \tag{11.14}$$

For this reason, it is not available to all regulated entities. Explicit permission, following extensive review and discussion with one's regulators, is required. NIB is not a regulated entity and, as a consequence, cannot presume to qualify for the Basel IRB approach. Whether or not we would receive permission to use Basel IRB is actually beside the point; our economic-capital requirements are managed via the internal model discussed in previous chapters. Practically, we do nevertheless compute regulatory capital requirement under both approaches—on a daily basis—to permit a broader scope of comparison.

**Colour and Commentary 127** (BASEL IRB): *The internal ratings based approach represents a monumental step forward in the notion of risk weighting and regulatory capital computation. It is built on the foundation of a structural credit-risk model—the one-factor Gaussian threshold model popularized by Vasicek [37, 38, 39]—that logically flows from Merton [26]'s original paper, which essentially founded the modern study of credit risk. In other words, it establishes an explicit link between risk and risk weights. To incorporate the risk dimension and yet simultaneously preserve portfolio invariance, some hard choices had to be made. The two principal elements—as highlighted by Gordy [14]—involve the necessity of a single-factor model and a sole and unique focus on systemic risk. In effect the Basel IRB approach takes some important elements of risk on board, but also sweeps other critical pieces under the rug. It is precisely these ignored items that lead to the necessity of the Pillar II process.*

### 11.1.3 S&P's Approach to Risk-Weighting

S&P, in the context of their RAC computation, have their own approach to risk weighting assets. The key ideas are summarized by two principal documents, S&P [31, 33].[11] In 2016, S&P updated and republished both documents as part of an effort to gather feedback from interested parties with regard to their suggested improvements and alterations. The combination of these two sources thus forms the basis of any external implementation or replication.

At the outset, it is important to understand that a single measure, even one as involved and useful as S&P's RAC ratio, does not drive the overall credit rating. Indeed, S&P [32] make it quite clear that a multiplicity of dimensions are considered in the establishment of a credit rating. S&P [32, Paragraph 20] states further that

[11] S&P [31] outlines the treatment of financial institutions in general, whereas S&P [33] provides some additional details for multilateral-lending institutions (MLIs). These will be important in the second (Pillar II) part of this discussion.

"the most important step in analyzing the creditworthiness of a corporate or governmental obligor is gauging the resources available to it for fulfilling its obligations." As a ratings agency, S&P faces some unique challenges. It is required to combine a broad range of both qualitative and quantitative factors together and distill them into an assessment of the relative credit quality of a vast array of obligors. Moreover, these entities are spread across the globe and face different accounting standards, regulatory environments, and disclosure requirements. Consistency of data inputs and treatment is, thus, a critical concern.

Capital-adequacy, while only one piece of the rating puzzle, remains important. To maintain consistency, independence and to avoid reliance upon modelling assumptions, S&P have created their own methodology for its measurement: the S&P-RAC framework. Conceptually, it is dead easy and critically linked to the idea of risk-weighted assets. In particular, the RAC ratio is merely,

$$\text{Risk-Adjusted Capital} = \frac{\text{Total Adjusted Capital}}{\text{Risk-Weighted Assets}}. \tag{11.15}$$

The larger the ratio, all else equal, the greater the creditworthiness of the obligor. It is easy to see that as the magnitude of the risk-weighted assets decreases, for a fixed amount of capital, the RAC ratio will increase. The RAC ratio is thus a deflated or normalized measure of a firm's base capital. One point is also abundantly clear; the RAC definition from Eq. 11.15 brings S&P into the business of estimating asset risk weights.

A firm's assets are organized by S&P into *three* main categories for the purposes of the RAC computation: credit, market, and operational. The credit risk component will be our focus in this chapter. The largest, and most complex, of these categories, which one would expect since we are dealing with financial institutions, relates to credit risk. It is comprised of *six* asset classes. The five *key* asset classes are schematically summarized in Fig. 11.1.

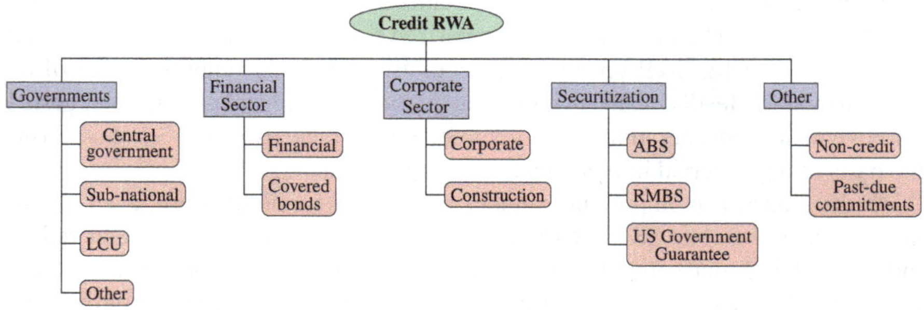


**Fig. 11.1** *Credit risk-weighted assets*: This schematic summaries the five key elements of the *credit* risk-weighed asset definition. Each aspect has numerous sub-elements requiring slightly different treatment. There is an additional sixth category, termed the retail sector, that arises in S&P [31, 33]. It is not, however, relevant for NIB.

The first asset class, termed governments or sovereigns, includes *four* sub classes: exposures related to central and sub-national governments, un-hedged local-currency bonds (i.e., LCU), and a fourth container for anything not fitting into the previous sub-classes. The next two asset classes relate to the financial and corporate sectors. Different nomenclature is possible, which can lead to some confusion. The financial sector sub-class is also sometimes referred to as institutions. Moreover, the corporate sector has a large number of additional sub-categories, but only the two presented groupings have any potential relevance for us.

There is also a retail sector, described in great detail in S&P [31], that is not pertinent for our analysis since NIB has neither a retail presence nor any retail activities. For typical financial institutions, however, this could involve quite a bit of work. Securitized assets are an additional asset class. The main areas of interest are covered bonds, asset-backed (ABS) and residential mortgage-backed (RMBS) securities. A separate sub-category was created for US government guarantees, since this has potentially important implications for the risk weights.

S&P [31] also highlights an additional exposure for asset classes related to collateral and other credit-risk mitigation. Sovereign and financial-sector collateral has already, for the most part, been netted from the reported credit positions. As such, the argument is that it need not be considered explicitly. S&P [31] does indeed hold that collateral, after an appropriate haircut, must be netted from the exposure position. Depending on the manner by which one's collateral is netted from reported exposures, there is the potential for some differences.

**Colour and Commentary 128** *(S&P TREATMENT OF COLLATERAL): There is the potential for divergent treatment of collateral between a given financial institution and S&P. S&P [31] requires that collateral, after an appropriate haircut, needs to be netted from the exposure position. The official formula, from S&P [31, Paragraph 75] is*

$$\text{Collateralized Exposure} = \text{Adjusted Exposure} - \text{Covered Exposure} \cdot \left(1 - \text{Haircut}\right). \tag{11.16}$$

*If S&P makes some adjustment for the haircut, while you do not, it could lead to differences. This is not a particularly deep point, but it is a common source of disagreement.*

The final asset class is another catch-all category termed "other." These include past-due and other non-credit-obligation assets. Past-due exposures are often subject to a constant, but non-standard risk weight. S&P [31, 33] provide no guidance on this question; this lack of detailed documentation represents one of the challenges associated with replicating the S&P-RAC methodology.

S&P's approach to determination of risk weights is, practically speaking, rather closer to the standardized than the Basel IRB approach. Asset class and quality are used to select from a broad range of possible weights. Actual choices are selected by S&P to represent the worst-case unexpected loss—which implies some choice of confidence interval—from a given risk scenario. The associated hypothetical stress scenarios are, organized by ratings categories AAA through B and described in S&P [30, Appendix IV]. There is, therefore, an underlying risk-weight calibration logic underlying the specific S&P choices. In particular, given a specific asset class, there are *three* main determinants of risk weights in S&P's methodology. These include:

**Credit Ratings** S&P uses a 25-notch alphabetic credit-rating scale ranging from AAA to C-.[12] For the purposes of the risk-weight determination, the *sovereign long-term* credit rating is employed.

**BICRA** S&P's Banking Industry Country Risk Assessment (or BICRA) is a 10-notch numeric scale ranging from 1 to 10 used by S&P to describe the relative riskiness of different countries' banking systems. S&P [34] indicates that "a BICRA score is a combination of multiple factors reflecting a country's economy, financial regulatory infrastructure, and the credit culture of its banking industry." A score of 1 denotes the lowest risk category, whereas 10 represents the highest level of riskiness.

**Equity Group** According to S&P [31, Paragraph 87], the S&P-RAC methodology places equity investments into one of four equity-market groups. These are defined—although the precise methodology is not described—using 30-year stock volatility measures from a country's major stock-market index. S&P [31, Table 13] merely allocates 100 countries to one of these four numeric categories ranging, in ascending order of riskiness, from 1 to 4.

The specific choice of risk-weight determinant is made by S&P.

The actual risk-weights are summarized, by asset class, in a number of tables found in S&P [31]. It is useful to examine these values graphically to gain some intuition into the underlying computation. The rating-based risk-weights are illustrated in Fig. 11.2. Quite reasonably, the magnitude of the risk weight is an inverse function of an asset's credit quality. AAA assets, for example, have very small risk-weight values. Moreover, the type of exposure also appears to matter. Securitized assets are clearly viewed as significantly more risky, particularly as we move out the credit spectrum, than exposure to central or local governments. Finally, unrated exposures, denoted as WR, are accorded the same risk weight as the lowest rating category.

Figure 11.3 takes our analysis of risk weights a step further and outlines, by asset class, the BICRA and equity-group values. Similar patterns to the ratings

[12] An additional notch can be added if one wishes to include default. Defaulted positions are, however, not typically treated as assets and thus can be ignored. We typically only focus on the first 17 non-default rating categories: the 16 typical categories from AAA to B− and places all of the CCC+ to C− classes into a single CCC category. This choice stems from the credit quality of our assets.

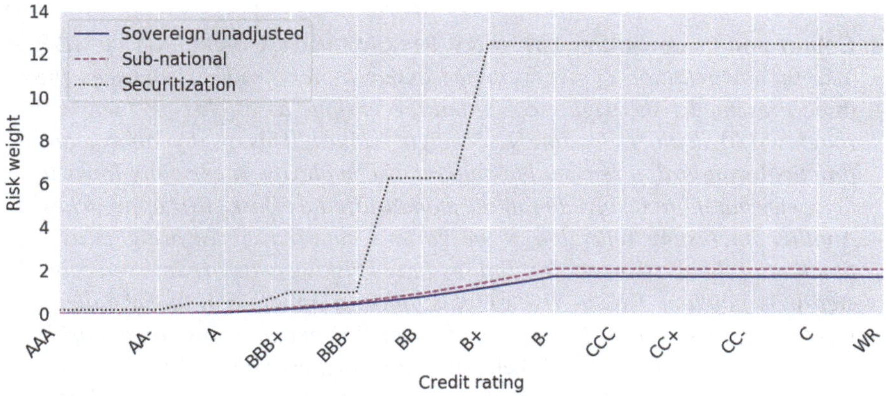


**Fig. 11.2** *Ratings-based risk weights*: This figure summarizes the S&P risk weights organized by asset class and credit ratings. The three main asset classes are sovereign unadjusted, sub-national, and securitization. These values are found in S&P [31, Tables 4 and 9].

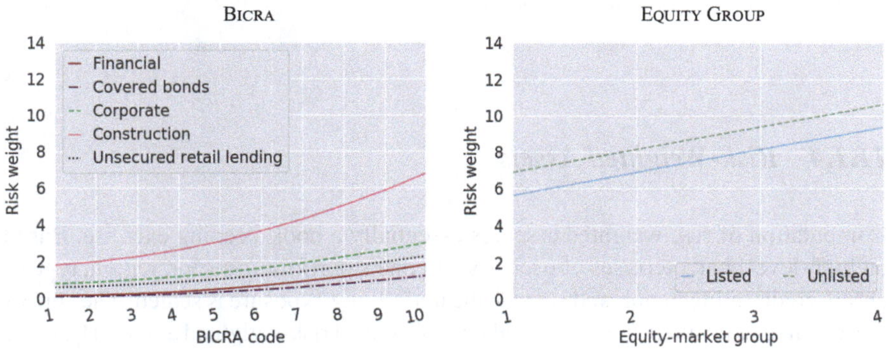


**Fig. 11.3** *Other risk-weight determinants*: This figure describes the relationship, for non-sovereign asset classes, between risk-weight and their underlying determinant. The BICRA ranking and the equity-group classification are used by S&P, rather than credit rating, to distinguish between different issuers.

classification are visible: risk weights increase as credit quality decreases and riskier asset classes are assigned higher values. All graphics in Figs. 11.2 and 11.3 are on the same scale, so we can see that securitized assets are viewed as the highest-risk assets. These are followed by listed and unlisted equity as well as construction. Indeed these assets possess risk weights that are many multiples of the base sovereign, institutional, and corporate assessments. Broadly speaking, we can think of Figs. 11.2 and 11.3 as being the S&P equivalent of Tables 11.1 and 11.2 describing the risk-weight choices from the standardized regulatory approach.

**Colour and Commentary 129** *(*S&P RISK-WEIGHT COMPLEXITY*): S&P take the computation of risk-weighted assets rather seriously. Between the* three *presented risk-weight scales and the various asset classes, there are roughly 130 distinct possible risk-weight values. This is, by almost any practical standard, a reasonable amount of complexity. It certainly looks to be somewhat more involved than the standardized or Basel IRB approaches. Another interesting reflection is the various patterns of risk weights as a function of their riskiness. The ratings-based risk weights are an increasing step-wise function, BICRA risk weights follow a smooth non-linear pattern, whereas equity-group risk weights are linear. This underscores, to an outside observer at least, the relatively* heuristic *nature of these values. There are most certainly good reasons for these differences, but they are not documented. This is, of course, entirely S&P's prerogative. The consequence, however, is that such specifications, without a firm foothold, can be easily changed suggesting that any firm, seeking to understand this approach, is well advised to keep a close eye on any and all S&P publications.*

### *11.1.4 Risk-Weighted Assets*

Computation of risk-weighted assets is essentially a book-keeping exercise. Based on high-level characteristics of each asset in one's portfolio—sector, region, type of entity, credit rating, tenor, and so on—the underlying exposure is scaled. The sum of these scaled exposures yields the total portfolio-level risk-weighted assets. The basic idea is clever and appealing; one's assets are transformed from raw currency terms into a risk-motivated representation. The ability to perform this computation on each individual asset independently of the other positions—while deeply unrealistic—drastically eases the complexity of these computations and facilitates aggregation across large portfolios distributed across the globe.

This simplicity has a flip side, which will become clearly evident in the following section. A price must be paid to adjust for the central simplifying assumption adopted in the Pillar I setting. In many discussions, these skeletons are left in the furthest reaches of our analytic closet. We will, however, follow a rather different strategy. For everyone who has ever been annoyed with a textbook leaving crucial elements as an exercise for the reader, the following section is for you. We've tried hard to include all of the important, technical bits in the most honest possible manner. That said, the minutiae can, at times, get a bit out of control. The reader should feel free to select the degree of detail that best fits her interests and purposes.

## 11.2 Pillar II

The first regulatory pillar is basically concerned—via the idea of asset risk weighting—with the notion of minimum regulatory capital requirements. Although perhaps taken somewhat for granted in recent years, this is a pretty important point. Creating a link between a firm's capital position and the riskiness of its assets—and thus establishing a capital floor—has rather fundamental consequences for financial stability. As should nonetheless have become clear in the previous pages, risk-weighted assets are, without some form of adjustment, a fairly blunt instrument. Into this breach enters Pillar II. This second step is basically about specializing the generic Pillar I analysis to a specific institution. It is much more flexible. As they say, however, "flexibility is the mother of all complexity." As a consequence, Pillar II is more difficult to precisely describe.

A working description of Pillar II is nevertheless found in BIS [7] and reads:

> Pillar 2 of the Basel Framework does not include prescriptive guidance or direction on supervisory approaches. Rather, it is principles-based and intended to be tailored to the risks, needs and circumstances of the respective jurisdictions.

Pillar II thus covers a significant amount of ground and does not necessarily follow a clear-cut form for each supervised entity. The headline aspects principally include concentration risks: single-name, sectoral, and geographical. These lend themselves to the most objective, quantitative style of analysis. Despite this viewpoint, it is important to stress that Pillar II is rather larger than simply concentration risks. It casts a much wider net by also including reputation-related, legal, and strategic business-model risks.[13] These are important risks, but they are rather more difficult to measure. Given that this book takes the perspective of the quantitative analyst working on the front lines of risk measurement, we will restrict our attention to the more technical elements of Pillar II.

The S&P RAC methodology does not, since it is obviously not a regulatory calculation, have any explicit link to Pillar II. S&P, despite having invested a significant amount of time and effort into their methodology for risk-weighted-asset estimation, fully appreciate that it has some shortcomings. It turns out that, since their basic approach is conceptually closely related to the Pillar I world, they share many of the same limitations with the regulatory approach. To improve the precision of their estimates and address the major issues, S&P performs a series of adjustments. These adjustments overlap in important ways with the Pillar II guidance. The relevant adjustments for a multilateral-lending institution (MLI) such as NIB are summarized in S&P [33].

There are multiple adjustments, each of varying degrees of complexity, but we will restrict our focus to the three most important. They are schematically described in Fig. 11.4. The principal deficiency of the risk-weighted asset approach is its

[13] It also contains a section relating to interest-rate risk in a regulated firm's banking book (or IRRBB).

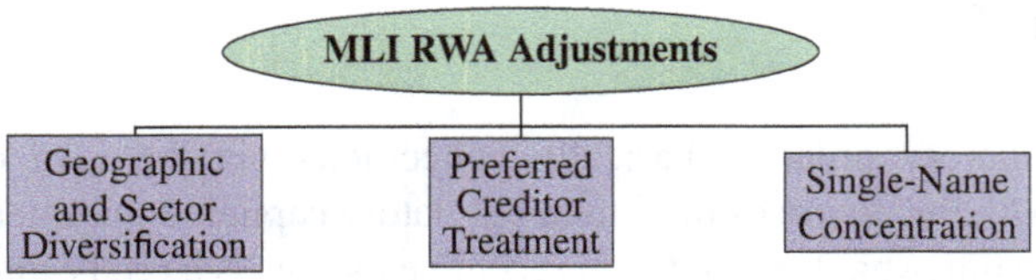


**Fig. 11.4** *Multilateral-lending institution adjustments*: This schematic outlines three risk-weighted asset adjustments required for the S&P-RAC computation. A significant amount of uncertainty surrounding the precise computation makes it difficult to precisely replicate the S&P calculations. These ideas also apply, albeit in potentially different ways, to Pillar II analysis.

instrument, or exposure, based perspective.[14] That is, as we've seen before, the composition of the overall portfolio is not considered in the base computation. This applies to all three previously discussed methods for the computation of risk-weighted assets: the standard, IRB, and S&P approaches. The geographic-diversification and single-name concentration adjustments, therefore, seek to incorporate this aspect by adopting a portfolio perspective. This is not completely trivial, which leads to a number of rather mathematically involved calculations.

The remaining adjustment is rather less technically involved, but nonetheless pertinent. As an MLI, NIB benefits in some cases from the so-called preferred-creditor treatment. Given the policy importance of these multilateral financial institutions, most countries will continue to service MLI debt even when they find themselves in financial distress.[15] The relative indebtedness of an MLI's obligors are considered and the risk weights are varied accordingly to account for this preferred-creditor status.

In the following discussion, we will work through each of these adjustments, derive the central results and explain how they are performed. This will set the stage for the examination of these various effects within the context of our portfolio.

**Colour and Commentary 130** (THE UGLY TRUTH ABOUT PILLAR II): *The notion of Pillar II introduced by the second round of the Basel Accord (i.e., Basel II) is a useful and welcome addition to the regulatory framework. As a catch-all category for residual risks not adequately captured in the Pillar I setting, it nonetheless finds itself facing some difficult tasks. Understanding this fact helps one to appreciate an important, and slightly ugly, truth about*

(continued)

[14] To be fair, this is simultaneously its greatest strength and weakness.

[15] They are a variety of reasons for this behaviour. Although far behind the scope of this technical modelling discussion, some entities may also have explicit (bilateral) framework agreements for lending operations with sovereigns, which protect and codify this preferred-creditor status. The basic concept is well introduced in S&P [33, Paragraph 25].

**Colour and Commentary 130** (continued)
*Pillar II: it is very complicated. Strategic, reputational, and legal risks—while quite real and vital to a firm's well being—are notoriously difficult to quantify. Concentration and diversification effects, the focus of the remainder of this chapter, necessitate rather heavy mathematical manipulations. The forthcoming pages will appear, to many readers, to be virtually indistinguishable from a treatise on mathematics. This is regrettable and unfortunate, but it is also an unavoidable consequence of the dramatic simplifying assumptions—most particularly, portfolio invariance—made in the Pillar I methodology. Sweeping these issues under the carpet in the first act simply implies their more intense, and furious, return in the second.*

### 11.2.1 Geographic and Industrial Diversification

Our emphasis is on specific techniques that will permit us to construct a meaningful benchmark comparison with our internal economic-capital computations. We will begin with the notion of geographical and sectoral diversification. This section, however, is principally concerned with the S&P approach to this question, although with minor adjustment this method could readily fulfill one's Pillar II requirements. There are other possible techniques that one might consider. Lütkebohmert [23] is, for example, an excellent starting point for a broad-based discussion of concentration effects. It provides a much wider and more nuanced discussion than what we can reasonably cover in this chapter.

Risk-weighted assets, as we saw in the previous sections, are computed individually ignoring the portfolio perspective and any associated diversification benefits. Diversification effects can stem from industrial or geographical elements. If exposures are spread across multiple regions or industries—as is the case for the majority of financial institutions—the net effect of incorporating diversification would be to somewhat reduce the risk-weighted assets. Diversification imposes, after all, downward pressure on one's risk estimates. Reducing risk-weighted assets will, all else equal, have the impact of increasing the S&P-RAC ratio or reducing the Pillar-I reported risk-weighted assets.

Let us focus, for the moment, on the geographic dimension since the industrial approach works in an analogous manner. In the S&P documentation—S&P [31, Paragraph 133-134]—the geographic adjustment has a basic quadratic form. The vector of $n = 1, \ldots, N$ distinct country weights is written as follows,

$$\zeta = \begin{bmatrix} K_1 \cdot C_1 & K_2 \cdot C_2 & \cdots & K_N \cdot C_N \end{bmatrix}^T, \tag{11.17}$$

where $K_n$ denotes the total risk-weighted assets associated with the $n$th geographical entity and $C_n$ denotes the $n$th concentration factor or coefficient. For typical financial institutions, these concentration factors are provided by S&P and determined using the volatility of the relevant country's gross domestic product.[16] For multilateral lending institutions, this is irrelevant, since S&P [33, Paragraph 46] reads "we remove penalization (to avoid double counting) for geographic concentration." This implies that $C_n = 1$ for all $n = 1, \ldots, N$. This allows us to redefine our vector of country weights as,

$$\zeta = \begin{bmatrix} K_1 \; K_2 \cdots K_N \end{bmatrix}^T. \tag{11.18}$$

$\zeta$ thus amounts to a vector of total risk-weighted assets organized by country. An analogous organization of risk-weighted assets is also possible following some industrial categorization.[17] The following development—presented here from the regional perspective—thus applies equally to both geographic and industrial Pillar-II effects.

To capture diversification effects, we will need to describe the dependence structure, or correlation, between individual geographic (or industrial) sectors. To motivate this idea, imagine that we define the following matrix,

$$\Omega(\gamma) = \begin{bmatrix} 1 & \gamma & \cdots & \gamma \\ \gamma & 1 & \cdots & \gamma \\ \vdots & \vdots & \ddots & \vdots \\ \gamma & \gamma & \cdots & 1 \end{bmatrix}. \tag{11.19}$$

This is simply a matrix with ones along the diagonal and the parameter, $\gamma \in [0, 1]$, populating all of the off-diagonal elements. Imagine that we set $\gamma = 1$ and compute the following quantity,

$$\sqrt{\zeta^T \Omega(1) \zeta} = \sqrt{\begin{bmatrix} K_1 \; K_2 \cdots K_N \end{bmatrix} \begin{bmatrix} 1 & 1 & \cdots & 1 \\ 1 & 1 & \cdots & 1 \\ \vdots & \vdots & \ddots & \vdots \\ 1 & 1 & \cdots & 1 \end{bmatrix} \begin{bmatrix} K_1 \\ K_2 \\ \vdots \\ K_N \end{bmatrix}}, \tag{11.20}$$

[16] The factors are normalized so that the USA takes a value of unity; lower total output values are assigned a larger concentration coefficient. See S&P [31, Table B.2].

[17] Here, as touched upon in Chap. 3, one might make use of one's internal or external industrial classification taxonomy.

$$
\begin{aligned}
&= \sqrt{\begin{bmatrix} \sum_{n=1}^{N} K_n & \sum_{n=1}^{N} K_n & \cdots & \sum_{n=1}^{N} K_n \end{bmatrix} \begin{bmatrix} K_1 \\ K_2 \\ \vdots \\ K_N \end{bmatrix}}, \\
&= \sqrt{K_1 \sum_{n=1}^{N} K_n + K_2 \sum_{n=1}^{N} K_n + \cdots + K_N \sum_{n=1}^{N} K_n}, \\
&= \sqrt{\Big(K_1 + K_2 + \cdots + K_N\Big) \sum_{n=1}^{N} K_n}, \\
&= \sqrt{\left(\sum_{n=1}^{N} K_n\right)\left(\sum_{n=1}^{N} K_n\right)}, \\
&= \sqrt{\left(\sum_{n=1}^{N} K_n\right)^2}, \\
&= \sum_{n=1}^{N} K_n.
\end{aligned}
$$

This might seem to be of limited interest, but it nevertheless demonstrates a point. The sum of the risk-weighted assets, when weighted in a quadratic form by a matrix of ones is unchanged. If the off-diagonal elements in $\Omega(\gamma)$, however, are no longer unity, then Eq. 11.20 is no longer true. What is true, however, is that

$$
\sqrt{\zeta^T \Omega(\gamma) \zeta} < \sqrt{\zeta^T \Omega(1) \zeta}, \tag{11.21}
$$

for all values of $\gamma \in [0, 1)$. That is, as long as $\gamma$ remains in the unit interval and takes a value of less than unity, the square-root of the quadratic weighting of the risk-weighted assets will be reduced.

The matrix, $\Omega$, is, of course, a correlation matrix and the off-diagonal elements represent the pairwise linear correlation coefficient between the $N$ geographical entities. Naturally, when this correlation matrix is estimated, it is not the case that all off-diagonal elements are equal to $\gamma$. Instead, the values should vary between $-1$ and 1. We used the notion of $\gamma$ to gain some intuition into the nature of the computation.[18] As long as we do not observe perfect correlation between any two countries, we should observe the phenomenon in Eq. 11.21.[19]

The geographic (industrial) diversification computation is thus,

$$\begin{aligned}\text{Geographic (industrial) diversification adjustment} &= \sqrt{\zeta^T \hat{\Omega} \zeta} - \sqrt{\zeta^T \Omega(1) \zeta}, \\ &= \sqrt{\zeta^T \hat{\Omega} \zeta} - \underbrace{\sum_{n=1}^{N} K_n}_{\substack{\text{Total}\\ \text{unadjusted}\\ \text{RWA}}},\end{aligned} \tag{11.22}$$

where $\hat{\Omega}$ denotes the empirically estimated correlation matrix between the various geographic (industrial) entities. Given this correlation matrix, therefore, the actual computation merely requires summing the risk-weighted assets by each geographic (or industrial) entity and performing some matrix multiplication.

A natural question is: what is the source of these correlations? Given $\hat{\Omega}$, the computation is easy, but obtaining $\hat{\Omega}$ is not so obvious. S&P [31, Paragraph 142] claim that "for correlations by geographic regions and industry sectors, we have used the MSCI stock indices." It is unclear what data-range is employed in S&P's computations and with what frequency it is updated. To perform this computation for the Pillar II diversification effect, however, we might simply make use of the same MSCI stock-return data to inform the correlation parameters of the collection of systemic risk factors introduced in previous chapters.[20]

### Fisher's $z$-Transformation

This is not the end of the geographic and industrial diversification story. Additional complexity lies in the determination of the individual entries of the correlation matrix. S&P [31, Paragraph 144], somewhat curtly reads "we stressed the results to capture more fat-tail risk. To do so, we use a Fisher transformation and stress the resulting value to a confidence interval of 99.5%." R.A. Fisher, one of the most

[18] We had to originally place some restrictions on the naive form of $\Omega(\gamma)$, because if all off-diagonals are the same negative number, it breaks the positive-definiteness of the matrix. In this case, it is not longer a correlation matrix. As long as $\Omega$ is a true correlation matrix, however, Eq. 11.21 will hold.

[19] Indeed, with negative correlation, which is empirically less common, the impact is even greater.

[20] This is the (annually updated) roughly 20-year collection of monthly stock-return values for 13 regions and 11 industrial categories introduced in Chap. 3.

prodigious statisticians of all time, has worked on many aspects of modern statistics.[21] We deduce that S&P is referring to Fisher's so-called $z$-transformation.[22]

The original reference is Fisher [13], but a more accessible discussion is found in Stuart and Ord [35, Sections 16.33–34] and Held and Bové [20, Example 4.16]. The original application of this result, as clearly suggested by the title of Fisher [13], was to understand the asymptotic behaviour of correlation-coefficient estimates for the purposes of statistical inference. McNeil et al. [25, Chapter 3] refer to the Fisher transform as a "variance-stabilizing transform."

The basic idea behind the technique is quite clever. Consider the (unknown) population correlation coefficient between two random variables, $X$ and $Y$, as $\rho$. In practice, we collect data on $X$ and $Y$ as the best we can. To approximate $\rho$, we then compute the sample correlation coefficient, which we will denote as $r$. The distribution of this estimatior, $r$, is practically difficult to use.[23] Fisher's method transforms $r$ such that the distribution of the revised value is approximately Gaussian. The resulting "stabilized" distribution for $r$ is correspondingly quite useful. From the cryptic quote in S&P [31, Paragraph 144], we infer that they transform each $r$, apply a normal shock to move to the top of the estimator's confidence interval, and then perform the inverse transformation to arrive at a revised estimate of the correlation coefficient. The remainder of this section works through the necessary, but fairly involved, technical details. It also provides some additional insight into the origin of this technique.

Let us return to our two random variables, $X$ and $Y$, and denote $\rho$ as their (unknown) correlation-coefficient population parameter. Assume that we have $N$ observations of each random variable. The population parameter, $\rho$, can be estimated by the Pearson correlation coefficient as,

$$
\begin{aligned}
r &= \frac{\frac{1}{N}\sum_{n=1}^{N}(X_n-\bar{X})(Y_n-\bar{Y})}{\sqrt{\sum_{n=1}^{N}\frac{(X_n-\bar{X})^2}{N}}\sqrt{\sum_{n=1}^{N}\frac{(Y_n-\bar{Y})^2}{N}}} \equiv \frac{\sum_{n=1}^{N}(X_n-\bar{X})(Y_n-\bar{Y})}{\sqrt{\sum_{n=1}^{N}(X_n-\bar{X})^2}\sqrt{\sum_{n=1}^{N}(Y_n-\bar{Y})^2}}, \\
&\equiv \frac{\widehat{\text{cov}(X,Y)}}{\widehat{\sigma(X)}\widehat{\sigma(Y)}},
\end{aligned} \tag{11.23}
$$

[21] See, for example, Savage [29] for an overview of his work.

[22] This is not to be confused with the discrete analogue of the Laplace transformation, which is also (regrettably) referred to as a $z$-transformation. See, for example, Harris and Stocker [19, Section 20.6].

[23] It is, in fact, skewed. For more information see, for example, Stuart and Ord [35, Chapter 13].

where $\widehat{\sigma(\cdot)}$ denotes the classic estimator of the standard deviation of a given random variable. The (large-sample) distribution of $r$ is, asymptotically,

$$r \sim \mathcal{N}\left(\rho, \frac{(1-\rho^2)^2}{N}\right). \tag{11.24}$$

This lovely form is *not* available to us, however, because it requires knowledge of the unknown population parameter, $\rho$. The small-sample version is, by contrast *not* particularly nice.[24] The consequence of this form is a serious challenge associated with the performance of any statistical inference on $r$.

To resolve these shortcomings, Fisher [13] offers a clever trick, which has come to be referred to as the Fisher $z$-transformation. It is described as,

$$z_{XY} = \frac{1}{2}\ln\left(\frac{1+r}{1-r}\right). \tag{11.25}$$

Examination of Eq. 11.25 may look somewhat familiar. If $|r| < 1$, then—see, for example, Harris and Stocker [19, Section 5.3]—this is the inverse hyperbolic tangent function, which allows us to rewrite Eq. 11.25 as,

$$z_{XY} = \text{arctanh}(r). \tag{11.26}$$

This quantity may also be written as $\tanh^{-1}(\cdot)$.

While this mathematical transformation may not seem to follow a specific purpose, it follows asymptotically that if $X$ and $Y$ are bivariate normal, then

$$z_{XY} \sim \mathcal{N}\left(\frac{1}{2}\ln\left(\frac{1+r}{1-r}\right), \frac{1}{N-3}\right). \tag{11.27}$$

Since the demonstration of this fact is not exactly straightforward, we will treat it as given. Equation 11.27 is precisely true if $X$ and $Y$ are bivariate Gaussian, but approximately true in cases where this assumption is not too egregiously violated. Financial returns are not, in general, Gaussian, but the distance from normality is not enormous. In this case, Eq. 11.27 can be considered a fairly reasonable approximation of the distribution of the transformed correlation-coefficient estimate.

Since $z_{XY}$ is Gaussian, we can construct an $\alpha$ shock to its value in the usual way. Let us define a perturbation of one $\alpha$ standard-deviation from the current value as,

$$\epsilon_\alpha = \Phi^{-1}(\alpha) \cdot \sqrt{\frac{1}{N-3}}, \tag{11.28}$$

[24] See Wishart [41] or Stuart and Ord [35, Sections 16.24–16.32] for treatment of the small-sample distribution of the correlation coefficient where both underlying random variables are normally distributed.

where $\Phi^{-1}(\cdot)$ is (as usual) the inverse standard normal cumulative distribution (or quantile) function. From Eq. 11.27, we can (reasonably) safely assume that the standard-error of the correlation coefficient—in this transformed space—is approximately $\sqrt{\frac{1}{N-3}}$. If we add $\epsilon_\alpha$ to our sample estimator, $r$, this amounts to an upper (or worst-case) bound on the correlation coefficient. This is sensible since, from S&P's perspective, the larger the correlation, the smaller the risk-weighted-asset adjustment.

The upper bound, again in transformed space, is thus simply,

$$\tilde{z}_{XY} = z_{XY} + \epsilon_\alpha. \tag{11.29}$$

Quite simply, $\tilde{z}_{XY}$ is an $\alpha$ standard-deviation shock to the expected (transformed) value of the correlation-coefficient estimate.

We now require the inverse transform to recover the actual (true) upper bound on our correlation-coefficient estimate. This is a simple algebra exercise where we solve Eq. 11.25 for $r$. More specifically,

$$\begin{aligned}
\underbrace{z_{XY} + \epsilon_\alpha}_{\tilde{z}_{XY}} &= \underbrace{\frac{1}{2}\ln\left(\frac{1+\tilde{r}}{1-\tilde{r}}\right)}_{\text{Eq. 11.25}}, \\
\frac{1+\tilde{r}}{1-\tilde{r}} &= e^{2\tilde{z}_{XY}}, \\
(1-\tilde{r})e^{2\tilde{z}_{XY}} &= 1+\tilde{r}, \\
e^{2\tilde{z}_{XY}} - 1 &= \tilde{r}\left(e^{2\tilde{z}_{XY}} + 1\right), \\
\tilde{r} &= \frac{e^{2\tilde{z}_{XY}} - 1}{e^{2\tilde{z}_{XY}} + 1}, \\
&= \frac{e^{2(z_{XY}+\epsilon_\alpha)} - 1}{e^{2(z_{XY}+\epsilon_\alpha)} + 1}.
\end{aligned} \tag{11.30}$$

Or, if you wish to use the trigonometric form from Eq. 11.26, then our upper bound is simply

$$\begin{aligned}
z_{XY} + \epsilon_\alpha &= \operatorname{arctanh}(\tilde{r}), \\
\tilde{r} &= \tanh\left(z_{XY} + \epsilon_\alpha\right).
\end{aligned} \tag{11.31}$$

The representations in Eqs. 11.30 and 11.31 are equivalent.

**Colour and Commentary 131** (THE POINT OF FISHER'S $z$-TRANSFORMATION): *Measurement of geographical or sectoral diversification effects essentially involves adjusting risk-weighted assets by the associated correlation structure. It is, in fact, the failure of the portfolio-invariant Pillar I approach to capture this (less-than-perfect) correlation that necessitates the adjustment. The question becomes a bit more interesting when we consider how to actually estimate the correlation coefficients. The simplest approach would be to apply the classic Pearson correlation coefficient estimator to a collection of historical data.*[a] *Although this would yield an unbiased estimator of pairwise correlation, S&P prefers a more conservative approach. This is the reason for employment of Fisher's so-called $z$-transformation. It offers a relatively simple formula—based upon a clever (and very useful) simplification of the distribution of the correlation coefficient estimator—to place an upper bound on the level of correlation between any two random variables. Thus instead of using a central estimate of the correlation coefficient, one uses a more conservative value. The level of conservatism is then determined by the choice of confidence level, $\alpha$. Setting $\alpha = 0.99$, for example, would imply that if one were to draw 100 independent samples, only once would one expect to find a larger estimate of one's correlation coefficient upper bound.*

[a] We are interested in asset correlation between geographic and industrial regions; since this is difficult to procure, stock-return data is typically employed as a proxy.

### *11.2.2 Preferred-Creditor Treatment*

In comparison to the complex geographical-industrial and (forthcoming) single-name-concentration adjustments, this element is relatively straightforward. The preferred-creditor-treatment adjustment attempts to take into account the policy importance of international institutions such as the NIB. Many sovereign borrowers will continue to service multilateral-lending institution debt even when they find themselves in financial distress. This applies, quite naturally, only to sovereign debt and, most importantly, it is not a contractual right. It is more a question of political economy. International financial institutions often act as lenders of last resort; knowing that in the worst case one might need to rely upon their support leads to a reluctance to default. S&P, realizing this fact, incorporate the preferred-creditor aspect by adjusting the risk weights of government debt. Such adjustments do not arise in the Pillar-II setting, because entities experiencing this effect are (as a rule) not regulated.

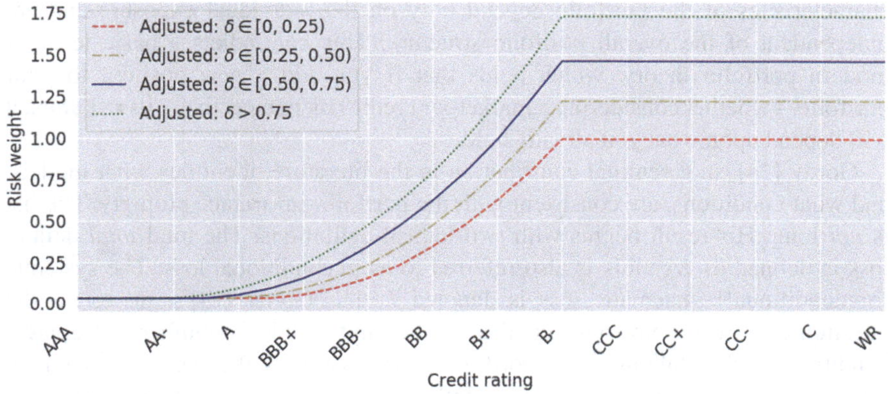


**Fig. 11.5** *Preferred-creditor adjusted risk weights*: This figure summarizes the adjusted risk-weights—assigned as a function of MDB debt and total debt—used to adjust for preferred-creditor status.

The level of adjustment is a function of the ratio of multilateral-development bank (MDB) to total indebtedness. Figure 11.5 summarizes the adjusted risk-weights—assigned as a function of MDB and total debt—used to adjust for preferred-creditor status. If the ratio of MDB to total debt exceeds 75%, then the risk weights default back to the base government risk weights. Otherwise, the S&P risk weights are a decreasing function of proportional MDB debt.

Practically, there is not much to be done. One needs to collect the MDB and total debt data, compute the appropriate ratio, find the associated risk weights, and adjust the government exposures. In our setting, given the currently relatively limited amount of sovereign lending, this is typically a rather small adjustment. If, conversely, you are working for a normal, garden-variety financial institution, you may happily ignore this element.

### *11.2.3 Single-Name Concentration*

This brings us to the final, and most complex, of the Pillar II quantitative adjustments: concentration. As we saw in the previous settings, Pillar I computations have a tendency to overstate the risk due to the presence of diversification effects. Simultaneously, however, there is an offsetting tendency to understate the risks associated with concentration. The techniques described in the following pages—despite their complexity—are attempts to find analytic formulae permitting us to describe the magnitude of this understatement of risk.

The Basel-IRB approach and the unadjusted S&P-RAC framework—as already highlighted on numerous occasions in this chapter—are based upon a very important, but unrealistic, assumption: portfolio invariance. This means that the risk characteristics of the portfolio depend only on the individual exposure and are independent of the overall portfolio structure. This contradicts a basic tenet of modern portfolio theory, which holds that if you add a new position to your portfolio—whether considering a market- or credit-risk perspective—its risk impact will depend upon what you already hold.

Gordy [14], in a seminal contribution to the literature, identifies what models, and what conditions, are consistent with the portfolio-invariance property. The list is *not* long. His result begins with two logical definitions. The total *total* default loss is defined as $L_N$; this is also referred to as unconditional loss. The systemic (or conditional) systematic loss is denoted $L_N|G$. Gordy [14]'s answer to the question of portfolio invariance is that, in the limit—under a number of technical conditions—when talking about portfolio invariance, only the systematic element matters. We can thus think of portfolio invariance as implying something like:

$$\lim_{N \to \infty} L_N \approx \mathbb{E}(L_N|G). \tag{11.32}$$

In other words, it assumes an infinite number of small positions. For large, well-diversified portfolios, total default loss tends towards systematic loss. Unfortunately, in practice, not all portfolios satisfy the large, well-diversified condition. This is not terribly precisely stated, but rather more an intuitive expression.[25]

The key finding of Gordy [14] is that portfolio invariance is possible *only* under what he refers to as an asymptotic single-factor risk (ASRF) model. No other model possesses this characteristic. It is typically represented as a type of limiting model, as $N \to \infty$, of the Gaussian threshold model forwarded by Vasicek [37, 38, 39]. Gordy [14] identifies the technical conditions under which unconditional and conditional VaR converge—this is roughly equivalent to applying the VaR operator to both sides of Eq. 11.32. For this to hold, *two* key assumptions are required:

1. one's portfolio must be infinitely grained; and
2. there can be only *one* systematic risk factor.

*Infinitely grained* means that no single exposure may dominate total portfolio exposure. It is an asymptotic result, which does not hold for any real portfolio, but may represent a reasonable approximation for large, well-diversified financial institutions. While neither assumption is particularly realistic, together they represent the price of portfolio invariance. The larger point is that the ASRF, the standarized model, the IRB approach, and the (unadjusted) S&P-RAC framework all studiously ignore idiosyncratic risk.[26] The only source of risk in these settings stems from systematic factors impacting, to varying degrees, all credit obligors.

[25] A rigorous and axiomatic treatment is found in Gordy [14].

[26] The case for sole focus on systemic risk is a bit less open-and-shut for non Basel-IRB approaches. The reason is that we do not know precisely how the risk weights are determined; they are simply provided. It is possible that some elements of idiosyncratic risk were employed

This leaves the many institutions who are far from the infinitely granular ideal with a need to perform some kind of adjustment for their portfolio concentrations. Indeed, Pillar II *requires* regulated financial institutions to address concentration risk. Easily required, this demand is rather more difficult to fulfil. Gordy [14], very aware of the inherent challenges of portfolio invariance, offers a solution. He suggests an *add-on* to account for concentration risk. While a fantastic idea that has gained widespread acceptance, it turns out to be, mathematically at least, a surprisingly complex undertaking. Creating an additive adjustment for concentration risk is not a completely natural process. The reason is simple; portfolio concentrations are complicated, non-linear functions of one's portfolio composition. In the following sections, we will describe the details behind the computation of such add-ons making liberal use of results from Gordy [14], Martin and Wilde [24], Emmer and Tasche [12], and Torell [36] among others.[27] Given our aversion to black boxes, we wade rather deep into the details to ensure a full understanding of what is behind these computations. The reader less interested in the technical details can restrict her attention to the gray boxes.

## A First Try

Following from Eq. 11.32, we redefine the total default loss as $L$ and the systematic loss as $\mathbb{E}(L|G)$. In this case, $G$ represents the global or systematic risk factor (or factors) impacting all credit obligors. Using a bit of algebraic slight of hand, we can construct a single identity including all of the key characters as follows,

$$\begin{aligned} L &= L + \underbrace{\mathbb{E}(L|G) - \mathbb{E}(L|G)}_{=0}, \\ \underbrace{L}_{\substack{\text{Total}\\\text{Loss}}} &= \underbrace{\mathbb{E}(L|G)}_{\substack{\text{Systematic}\\\text{Loss}}} + \underbrace{L - \mathbb{E}(L|G)}_{\substack{\text{Idiosyncratic}\\\text{Loss}}}. \end{aligned} \tag{11.33}$$

If the total loss is $L$ and the systematic loss is $\mathbb{E}(L|G)$, then it logically follows that $L - \mathbb{E}(L|G)$ represents the idiosyncratic risk. That is, the specific or idiosyncratic element of risk is merely the distance between total and systematic risk. As the idiosyncratic risk is diversified away, the distance $|L - \mathbb{E}(L|G)|$ becomes progressively smaller and, ultimately, tends to zero. This only happens if, as the portfolio grows, it becomes increasingly granular.

---

in their calibration. In the Basel IRB setting, the logic is clear and it excludes the idiosyncratic element.

[27] In the early parts of the discussion, there is also a significant overlap with Bolder [9, Chapter 6]. This treatment nevertheless goes rather deeper into the granularity adjustment.

**Colour and Commentary 132** (MODELLING CONCENTRATION): *For small and concentrated portfolios, idiosyncratic risk is probably quite large and requires one's consideration. To do so, however, we need some kind of analytic foothold. Gordy [14] comes to our rescue. He describes the total credit loss of the portfolio as L and represents the systemic credit loss as the conditional expectation of this loss given the systemic risk factor, G. We will, borrowing his notation, denote this quantity as $\mathbb{E}(L|G)$. Measuring concentration risk, therefore, amounts approximating the magnitude of the distance between these two quantities: $|L - \mathbb{E}(L|G)|$.*[a] *In plain English, subtracting systematic risk from total risk must necessarily yield the idiosyncratic (i.e., concentration) component. This is the fundamental form of the concentration add-on; the rest is just (unfortunately quite complicated) detail.*

[a] In practice, it is somewhat more involved, because we need to do this in terms of unexpected loss, which leads us to the Value-at-Risk (VaR) measure.

### A Complicated Add-On

We begin by assuming that we have a generic *one-factor* stochastic credit-risk model. $L$, as usual, represents the default loss and $G$ denotes the common systematic factor. We denote the VaR of our portfolio's default loss, for a given quantile $\alpha$, as $q_\alpha(L)$. This is a quantile at some point in the tail of the default-loss distribution and, by construction, includes both idiosyncratic and systematic elements.

We further define $q_\alpha^{\text{ASRF}}(L)$ as the diversified VaR estimate associated with the ASRF model. The *systematic* loss, to lighten somewhat the notation burden, is referred to in short form as $X = \mathbb{E}(L|G)$. Gordy [14], in one of its many contributions, showed us that

$$\begin{aligned} q_\alpha^{\text{ASRF}}(L) &= q_\alpha\left(\mathbb{E}(L|G)\right), \\ &= q_\alpha(X). \end{aligned} \tag{11.34}$$

This is the systematic VaR. In the limit, we know that, conditional (i.e., systematic) and unconditional (i.e., total) VaR converge. Our job, however, is to describe this difference,

$$\mid \text{Real-world VaR} - \text{Infinitely grained VaR} \mid = \mid q_\alpha(L) - q_\alpha(X) \mid. \tag{11.35}$$

The first (critical) step involves an ingenious trick that helps us isolate our distance of interest. We start with $q_\alpha(L)$, which is our total $\alpha$-level credit VaR, including both systematic and idiosyncratic elements. The idea is similar to the expansion from Eq. 11.32

$$\begin{aligned} q_\alpha(L) &= q_\alpha\left(L + \underbrace{X - X}_{=0}\right), \\ &= q_\alpha\left(X + (L - X)\right), \\ &= q_\alpha\left(X + \epsilon\,(L - X)\right)\big|_{\epsilon=1}, \\ &= q_\alpha\left(f(\epsilon)\right)\big|_{\epsilon=1}, \end{aligned} \tag{11.36}$$

where $L = f(1)$ conveniently contains both the idiosyncratic and systematic elements. This might not look like much; it is, in fact, simply a notational change. It does, however, introduce both the total and systematic VaR figures into a single expression. This is a surprisingly important first step.

The second task is to tease out the idiosyncratic and systematic elements. To do this, we will perform a second-order Taylor series expansion of $q_\alpha(L)$ around $\epsilon = 0$. This yields,

$$\begin{aligned} q_\alpha\left(f(\epsilon)\right)\big|_{\epsilon=1} &\approx q_\alpha\left(f(\epsilon)\right)\big|_{\epsilon=0} + \underbrace{\frac{\partial q_\alpha\left(f(\epsilon)\right)}{\partial \epsilon}\bigg|_{\epsilon=0}(1-0)^1}_{=0} \\ &\quad + \frac{1}{2}\frac{\partial^2 q_\alpha\left(f(\epsilon)\right)}{\partial \epsilon^2}\bigg|_{\epsilon=0}(1-0)^2, \\ q_\alpha\left(f(1)\right) &\approx q_\alpha\left(f(0)\right) + \frac{1}{2}\frac{\partial^2 q_\alpha\left(f(\epsilon)\right)}{\partial \epsilon^2}\bigg|_{\epsilon=0}, \\ q_\alpha(X + 1\cdot(L - X)) &\approx q_\alpha\left(X + 0\cdot(L - X)\right) + \frac{1}{2}\frac{\partial^2 q_\alpha\left(X + \epsilon\,(L - X)\right)}{\partial \epsilon^2}\bigg|_{\epsilon=0}, \\ \underbrace{q_\alpha(L) - q_\alpha(X)}_{\text{Eq. 11.35}} &\approx \frac{1}{2}\frac{\partial^2 q_\alpha\left(X + \epsilon\,(L - X)\right)}{\partial \epsilon^2}\bigg|_{\epsilon=0}. \end{aligned} \tag{11.37}$$

This is important progress. The Taylor expansion has allowed us to move from the, relatively unhelpful, VaR of the sum of two elements of risk—idiosyncratic and systematic—towards the (approximate) difference of the VaRs of these quantities. In other words, we have, using a mathematical trick, happily found a representation for Eq. 11.35. The result is that this difference is approximately one half of the second derivative of the VaR of $f(\epsilon)$ evaluated at $\epsilon = 0$. This an elegant result.

Further progress depends importantly on our ability to evaluate the second derivative of this VaR expression. Fortunately, this is a known result provided by Gourieroux et al. [17]. We must first explain why the first derivative vanishes. It is somewhat messy and depends on the structure of the first derivative of VaR—also found in Gourieroux et al. [17]. The formal development is,

$$\begin{aligned}
\left.\frac{\partial q_\alpha\left(X+\epsilon(L-X)\right)}{\partial \epsilon}\right|_{\epsilon=0} &= \mathbb{E}\left(L-X \,\middle|\, X=q_\alpha(X)\right), \qquad (11.38)\\
&= \mathbb{E}\left(L-\mathbb{E}\left(L|G\right) \,\middle|\, \mathbb{E}\left(L|G\right)=q_\alpha\left(\mathbb{E}\left(L|G\right)\right)\right),\\
&= \mathbb{E}\left(L-\mathbb{E}\left(L|G\right) \,\middle|\, \underbrace{G=q_{1-\alpha}\left(G\right)}_{X \text{ is monotonic in } G}\right),\\
&= \mathbb{E}\left(L \,\middle|\, G=q_{1-\alpha}\left(G\right)\right)-\mathbb{E}\left(\mathbb{E}\left(L|G\right) \,\middle|\, G=q_{1-\alpha}\left(G\right)\right),\\
&= \mathbb{E}\left(L \,\middle|\, G=q_{1-\alpha}\left(G\right)\right)-\underbrace{\mathbb{E}\left(L \,\middle|\, G=q_{1-\alpha}\left(G\right)\right)}_{\text{By iterated expectations}},\\
&= 0.
\end{aligned}$$

The first critical line stems from Gourieroux et al. [17].[28] It turns out that there is a close link between conditional expectation and the derivatives of VaR. We provide this result without derivation, but the interested reader is referred back to Chap. 2 where the concept of exposure-level risk decomposition is introduced. The second point, where the conditioning variable $X = q_\alpha(X)$ is replaced by $G = q_{1-\alpha}(G)$, stems from the relationship between default loss and the systematic risk variable. $L$ and $\mathbb{E}(L|G)$ are both strictly monotonically decreasing in $G$.[29] For this reason, the two conditioning sets are equivalent.

Having established that the first derivative of VaR vanishes in this setting, we now face the challenge of evaluating the second derivative. This requires a bit of additional heavy-lifting. Starting from the object of interest, we may perform the

[28] Rau-Bredow [28] also addresses this tricky issue in substantial detail.

[29] This is specialized to the Gaussian threshold setting, but in any one-factor setting this behaviour is prevalent. The systematic factor may be, of course, monotonically increasing in $G$. The key is that, in all one-factor models, default loss is a monotonic function of the systematic factor; the direction of this relationship is irrelevant.

following manipulations, using the definition of the second derivative of VaR, from Gourieroux et al. [17], as our starting point

$$\begin{aligned}
\left.\frac{\partial^2 q_\alpha(f(\epsilon))}{\partial \epsilon^2}\right|_{\epsilon=0} &\qquad (11.39)\\
&= \left.\frac{\partial^2 q_\alpha(X+\epsilon(L-X))}{\partial \epsilon^2}\right|_{\epsilon=0},\\
&= -\text{var}(L-X|X=x)\left.\frac{\partial \ln f_X(x)}{\partial x}\right|_{x=q_\alpha(X)} - \left.\frac{\partial \text{var}(L-X|X=x)}{\partial x}\right|_{x=q_\alpha(X)},\\
&= \left.\left(-\text{var}(L-X|X=x)\left(\frac{1}{f_X(x)}\right)\frac{\partial f_X(x)}{\partial x} - \frac{\partial \text{var}(L-X|X=x)}{\partial x}\right)\right|_{x=q_\alpha(X)},\\
&= -\frac{1}{f_X(x)}\left.\left(\text{var}(L-X|X=x)\frac{\partial f_X(x)}{\partial x} + \frac{\partial \text{var}(L-X|X=x)}{\partial x}f_X(x)\right)\right|_{x=q_\alpha(X)},\\
&= -\frac{1}{f_X(x)}\frac{\partial}{\partial x}\left.\left(\underbrace{\text{var}(L-X|X=x)f_X(x)}_{\text{By product rule}}\right)\right|_{x=q_\alpha(X)},\\
&= -\frac{1}{f_X(x)}\frac{\partial}{\partial x}\left.\left(\underbrace{\text{var}(L|X=x)f_X(x)}_{\text{var}(X|X=x)=0}\right)\right|_{x=q_\alpha(X)},
\end{aligned}$$

where the manipulation in the final step arises, because $\text{var}(X|X = x)$ is equal to zero—given the value of the random variable, $X$, there is no remaining uncertainty. This is a useful simplification, but we'd like to take it a step further. The conditioning, and differentiating, variable is $x = q_\alpha(X)$. We would like to perform a transformation of variables so that we replace $X$ with the global systematic variable, $G$. We have established already, through the monotonicity of $X$ in $G$, that the following two conditioning statements are equivalent,

$$\{x = q_\alpha(X)\} \equiv \{g = q_{1-\alpha}(G)\}. \qquad (11.40)$$

A critical consequence of this fact is that $\alpha$ quantile of the systematic VaR—that is, $q_\alpha(X)$—coincides with the expected loss when the systematic variable falls at its $1-\alpha$ quantile. Specifically, it is true that

$$q_\alpha(X) = \mathbb{E}(L|G = q_{1-\alpha}(G)). \qquad (11.41)$$

If we plan to change variables, then we will move from the density of $X$ to $G$. This will require the change-of-variables formula.[30] The density of $X$ can now be written as,

$$
\begin{aligned}
f_G(q_{1-\alpha}(G)) &= f_X(q_\alpha(X)) \left| \frac{\partial q_\alpha(X)}{\partial q_{1-\alpha}(G)} \right|, \\
&= f_X(q_\alpha(X)) \left| \frac{\partial \overbrace{\mathbb{E}(L|G = q_{1-\alpha}(G))}^{\text{Eq. 11.41}}}{\partial q_{1-\alpha}(G)} \right|, \\
f_X(q_\alpha(X)) &= f_G(q_{1-\alpha}(G)) \left( \left| \frac{\partial \mathbb{E}(L|G = q_{1-\alpha}(G))}{\partial q_{1-\alpha}(G)} \right| \right)^{-1}.
\end{aligned}
\tag{11.42}
$$

This allows us to write the second derivative in the following form,

$$
\left. \frac{\partial^2 q_\alpha(f(\epsilon))}{\partial \epsilon^2} \right|_{\epsilon=0} = - \frac{1}{f_G(g)} \frac{\partial}{\partial g} \left. \left( \frac{f_G(g)\mathrm{var}(L|G = g)}{\frac{\partial \mathbb{E}(L|G=g)}{\partial g}} \right) \right|_{g=q_{1-\alpha}(G)} \tag{11.43}
$$

This, recalling Eq. 11.37, leads us to the underlying approximation of the distance between total and systematic portfolio risk,

$$
\begin{aligned}
q_\alpha(L) - q_\alpha(\mathbb{E}(L|G)) &\approx \frac{1}{2} \left. \frac{\partial^2 q_\alpha(\mathbb{E}(L|G) + \epsilon(L - \mathbb{E}(L|G)))}{\partial \epsilon^2} \right|_{\epsilon=0}, \\
\mathcal{G}_\alpha(L) &= - \frac{1}{2 \cdot f_G(g)} \frac{\partial}{\partial g} \left. \left( \frac{f_G(g)\mathrm{var}(L|G = g)}{\frac{\partial \mathbb{E}(L|G=g)}{\partial g}} \right) \right|_{g=q_{1-\alpha}(G)}.
\end{aligned}
\tag{11.44}
$$

Commonly referred to as the granularity adjustment, this explains why we use the symbol $\mathcal{G}$ to describe it. We have eliminated any reference, through our change of variables, to the systematic loss variable, $\mathbb{E}(L|G)$. Although not directly applicable in this form, Eq. 11.44 is written completely in terms of the systematic global risk factor, $G$. With a specific choice of model, we may now obtain our objective: a practical, exposure-level add-on to approximate idiosyncratic risk.

[30] See Billingsley [1, Sections 16–17] for more colour on the change-of-variables technique. Torell [36] does this in a slightly different, but essentially, equivalent manner.

**Colour and Commentary 133** (A TAYLOR SERIES EXPANSION): *The kernel of the additive concentration risk adjustment stems from the combination of* three *immensely clever manipulations. The first begins with the first-principles definition of credit Value-at-Risk; by simply adding and subtracting the systemic element, one arrives at a workable expression for our object of interest,* $|L - \mathbb{E}(L|G)|$. *A dummy variable,* $\epsilon = 1$, *is then created to logically isolate* $|L - \mathbb{E}(L|G)|$. *In the second step, this expression is given concrete form as a second-order Taylor series expansion of the VaR function with* $\epsilon = 1$ *around the point* $\epsilon = 0$. *The corresponding derivatives of VaR are neither easy to look at nor particularly fun to work with. The third, and final, manipulation involves using the change-of-variables formula to move from the portfolio loss to the systemic risk-factor density. The overall result of these complex steps is nevertheless a tractable expression for our desired idiosyncratic dimension of risk.*

To get the granularity adjustment into a more practical form, we need to first evaluate the necessary derivatives. To ease the notation, let us define the following functions

$$\begin{aligned} f(g) &= f_G(g), \\ \mu(g) &= \mathbb{E}(L|G = g), \\ \nu(g) &= \text{var}(L|G = g). \end{aligned} \tag{11.45}$$

These are the density of the systematic risk factor and the conditional expectation and variance of the default loss given a specific value of the systematic risk factor, respectively. This allows us to re-state Eq. 11.44 as,

$$\mathcal{G}_\alpha(L) = -\frac{1}{2 \cdot f(g)} \frac{\partial}{\partial g} \left( \frac{f(g)\nu(g)}{\mu'(g)} \right) \Bigg|_{g=q_{1-\alpha}(G)}. \tag{11.46}$$

Recalling the quotient and product rules, it is a simple bookkeeping exercise to expand Eq. 11.46 into the following, more expedient form,

$$\mathcal{G}_\alpha(L) = -\frac{1}{2 \cdot f(g)} \left( \underbrace{\frac{\Big(f(g)\nu(g)\Big)' \mu'(g) - f(g)\nu(g)\mu''(g)}{(\mu'(g))^2}}_{\text{Quotient rule}} \right) \Bigg|_{g=q_{1-\alpha}(G)}, \tag{11.47}$$

$$
\begin{aligned}
&= -\frac{1}{2 \cdot f(g)} \left( \frac{\overbrace{\left( f'(g)\nu(g) + f(g)\nu'(g) \right)}^{\text{Product rule}} \mu'(g) - f(g)\nu(g)\mu''(g)}{(\mu'(g))^2} \right) \Bigg|_{g=q_{1-\alpha}(G)}, \\
&= -\frac{1}{2 \cdot f(g)} \left( \frac{f'(g)\nu(g)\mu'(g) + f(g)\nu'(g)\mu'(g) - f(g)\nu(g)\mu''(g)}{(\mu'(g))^2} \right) \Bigg|_{g=q_{1-\alpha}(G)}, \\
&= -\frac{1}{2} \left( \frac{f'(g)\nu(g)}{f(g)\mu'(g)} + \frac{\nu'(g)}{\mu'(g)} - \frac{\nu(g)\mu''(g)}{(\mu'(g))^2} \right) \Bigg|_{g=q_{1-\alpha}(G)}, \\
&= -\frac{1}{2} \left( \frac{1}{\mu'(g)} \left( \frac{f'(g)\nu(g)}{f(g)} + \nu'(g) \right) - \frac{\nu(g)\mu''(g)}{(\mu'(g))^2} \right) \Bigg|_{g=q_{1-\alpha}(G)}.
\end{aligned}
$$

Admittedly somewhat unwieldy, this expression is the starting point for the add-on to the ordinary Basel-IRB regulatory-capital amount. It is also the springboard for the single-name concentration adjustment in the S&P-RAC ratio.

**Colour and Commentary 134** (GRANULARITY ADJUSTMENT INGREDIENTS)*: Despite its complex form, the granularity adjustment has only* three *main ingredients: the density function of the systemic risk factor and the conditional expectation and variance of the systemic portfolio loss. The latter two quantities, in both cases, condition upon an extreme outcome—with confidence level α—of the systemic risk factor. Not coincidentally, this is consistent with the Basel IRB approach. Armed with these three elements and the second-order Taylor series expansion of portfolio VaR, some basic calculus permits development of a practical expression for the granularity adjustment. To actual implement it, however, one needs to choose a specific underlying credit-risk model. This choice will fix the identity of our three ingredients and lead to concrete granularity adjustment formulae. The final form, of course, will vary depending on the specific model one selects.*

### The CreditRisk+ Case

A popular, practical choice of granularity adjustment—following from Gordy and Lütkebohmert [15, 16]—is based on the one-factor CreditRisk+ model.[31] This credit-risk approach—introduced by Wilde [40] and covered in great detail in Gund-

[31] For more on concentration risk, the reader is referred to Lütkebohmert [23].

lach and Lehrbass [18]—is essentially a special case of a Poisson-Gamma model. This implementation is also used in the context of the S&P RAC methodology.

In the CreditRisk+ setting, the defaults in a portfolio of $N$ obligors are governed by $i = 1, \ldots, N$ independent and identically distributed Poisson random variables, $X_i \sim \mathcal{P}(\lambda_i(S))$. The $i$th default indicator is re-defined as,

$$\mathbb{I}_{\mathcal{D}_i} \equiv \mathbb{I}_{\{X_i \geq 1\}} = \begin{cases} 1: & \text{defaults occurs before time } T \text{ with probability } p_i(S) \\ 0: & \text{survival until time } T \text{ with probability } 1 - p_i(S) \end{cases}, \tag{11.48}$$

where $S \sim \Gamma(a, b)$ is an independent (common) gamma-distributed random variable. $S$, in this model, plays the role of the systematic state variable; it is the analogue of the variable, $G$, in the one-factor threshold setting.

Given the relatively small probability of default, it is further assumed that ,

$$\begin{aligned} p_i(S) &\equiv \mathbb{E}\left(\mathbb{I}_{\mathcal{D}_i} \,\middle|\, S\right), \\ &= \mathbb{P}\left(\mathcal{D}_i \,|\, S\right), \\ &\approx \lambda_i(S). \end{aligned} \tag{11.49}$$

In other words, the random Poisson arrival intensity of the default outcome and the conditional probability of default are assumed to coincide.[32]

Wilde [40] gave $p_i(S)$ an ingenious functional form,

$$p_i(S) = p_i\left(\omega_{i,0} + \omega_{i,1} S\right), \tag{11.50}$$

where $\omega_{i,0} + \omega_{i,1} = 1$ implying that we can restate Eq. 11.50 more succinctly as,

$$p_i(S) = p_i\left(1 - \omega_i + \omega_i S\right). \tag{11.51}$$

We can interpret the parameter $\omega_i$ as the factor loading on the systematic factor, while $1 - \omega_i$ denotes the importance of the idiosyncratic factor.[33] It is easy to show that, if we select the parameters of the gamma-distributed $S$ such that $\mathbb{E}(S) = 1$, then $\mathbb{E}(p_i(S)) = p_i$. That is, in expectation, the conditional default probability reduces to the unconditional default probability. If one assumes the shape-scale

[32] Practically, for small values of $\lambda_i(S)$, the random variable $X_i$ basically only takes two values: 0 and 1. The $\mathbb{P}(X_i > 1)$ is vanishingly small.

[33] If, for example, $\omega_i = 0$, then this reduces to an independent-default Poisson model.

parametrization of the gamma distribution, it is necessary to assume that $S \sim \Gamma\left(a, \frac{1}{a}\right)$.[34]

An excellent discussion of the granularity adjustment for the one-factor CreditRisk+ model is found in Gordy and Lütkebohmert [15, 16]. This work forms the foundation of many Pillar II implementations of single-name concentration risk. It is also the documented choice of S&P's single-name concentration RAC framework implementation.[35] Given this formulation, we will work through the general CreditRisk+ granularity adjustment and touch on the simplifications and calibrations suggested by Gordy and Lütkebohmert [15, 16].

Gordy and Lütkebohmert [15, 16] also allow for the incorporation of random recovery. In other words, the loss-given-default parameter for the $i$th obligor, still denoted as $\gamma_i$, is assumed to be stochastic. Its precise distribution is not given, but it is assumed to be independent of default and any other recovery events. Moreover, its first two moments are described as,

$$\begin{aligned}\mathbb{E}(\gamma_i) &= \bar{\gamma}_i, \\ \text{var}(\gamma_i) &= \nu_{\gamma_i}.\end{aligned} \tag{11.52}$$

The principal consequence of this modelling choice is that the default loss function is a bit more complicated as,

$$L = \sum_{i=1}^{N} \gamma_i c_i \mathbb{I}_{\mathcal{D}_i}. \tag{11.53}$$

With the (assumed) model details established, all that remains is the mundane task of extracting the conditional expectation, conditional variance, and state-variable density terms and their derivatives. We will begin with the conditional expectation of the default loss given a specific value of the systematic state variable, $S$. Working from first principles, we have

$$\begin{aligned}\mu(s) &= \mathbb{E}\left(L \,|\, S = s\right), \\ &= \mathbb{E}\left(\underbrace{\sum_{i=1}^{N} \gamma_i c_i \mathbb{I}_{\mathcal{D}_i}}_{\text{Eq. 11.53}} \middle| \, S = s\right), \\ &= \sum_{i=1}^{N} c_i \, \mathbb{E}\left(\gamma_i \mathbb{I}_{\mathcal{D}_i} \,\middle|\, S = s\right),\end{aligned} \tag{11.54}$$

[34] In the shape-rate parameterization, the density has a slightly different form. In this case, we assume that $S \sim \Gamma(a, a)$. Ultimately, there is no difference in the final results.

[35] See, for example, S&P [31, Paragraphs 148-151].

$$
\begin{aligned}
&= \sum_{i=1}^{N} c_i \, \mathbb{E}\left(\gamma_i \,|\, S = s\right) \mathbb{E}\left(\mathbb{I}_{\mathcal{D}_i} \,\middle|\, S = s\right), \\
&= \sum_{i=1}^{N} c_i \mathbb{E}\left(\gamma_i\right) \mathbb{P}\left(\mathcal{D}_i \,|\, S = s\right), \\
&= \sum_{i=1}^{N} c_i \bar{\gamma}_i p_i(s),
\end{aligned}
$$

where most of the preceding manipulations are definitional. We should stress that, since each $\gamma_i$ is independent of $S$, $\mathbb{E}(\gamma_i | S) = \mathbb{E}(\gamma_i)$; no information is provided by the conditioning set.

Recalling the definition of $p_i(S)$ from Eq. 11.51, we can readily determine the first derivative of $\mu(s)$ as,

$$
\begin{aligned}
\mu'(s) &= \frac{\partial}{\partial s}\left(\underbrace{\sum_{i=1}^{N} c_i \bar{\gamma}_i p_i(s)}_{\text{Eq. 11.54}}\right), \qquad (11.55) \\
&= \frac{\partial}{\partial s}\left(\sum_{i=1}^{N} c_i \bar{\gamma}_i \underbrace{p_i \left(1 - \omega_i + \omega_i s\right)}_{\text{Eq. 11.51}}\right), \\
&= \sum_{i=1}^{N} c_i \bar{\gamma}_i p_i \omega_i .
\end{aligned}
$$

It is easy to see—since $\mu(s)$ is a linear function of $s$—that the second derivative, $\mu''(s)$, vanishes. This simple fact has important implications since the second term in Eq. 11.47 conveniently disappears, significantly simplifying our task.

Determining the conditional variance is rather heavy. Two facts will prove quite useful in its determination. First, the default event, by Eq. 11.48, is Poisson-distributed. An interesting feature of the Poisson distribution is that its expectation and variance are equal: that is, in this case, $\mathbb{E}(\mathbb{I}_{\mathcal{D}_i}) = \text{var}(\mathbb{I}_{\mathcal{D}_i})$. The second fact is that, from first principles, if $X$ is a random variable with finite first two moments, then $\text{var}(X) = \mathbb{E}(X^2) - \mathbb{E}(X)^2$. This implies directly that $\mathbb{E}(X^2) = \text{var}(X) + \mathbb{E}(X)^2$. Both of these observations, which we will employ directly, apply unconditionally and conditionally.

The conditional variance can be written as,

$$
\begin{aligned}
\nu(s) &= \operatorname{var}\left(L \mid S = s\right), \qquad (11.56)\\
&= \operatorname{var}\left( \underbrace{\sum_{i=1}^{N} \gamma_i c_i \mathbb{I}_{\mathcal{D}_i}}_{\text{Eq. 11.53}} \middle| \, S = s \right),\\
&= \sum_{i=1}^{N} c_i^2 \operatorname{var}\left(\gamma_i \mathbb{I}_{\mathcal{D}_i} \mid S = s\right),\\
&= \sum_{i=1}^{N} c_i^2 \underbrace{\left( \mathbb{E}\left(\gamma_i^2 \mathbb{I}_{\mathcal{D}_i}^2 \middle| S = s\right) - \mathbb{E}\left(\gamma_i \mathbb{I}_{\mathcal{D}_i} \mid S = s\right)^2 \right)}_{\text{By definition}},\\
&= \sum_{i=1}^{N} c_i^2 \left( \mathbb{E}\left(\gamma_i^2 \middle| S = s\right) \mathbb{E}\left(\mathbb{I}_{\mathcal{D}_i}^2 \middle| S = s\right) - \mathbb{E}\left(\gamma_i \mid S = s\right)^2 \mathbb{E}\left(\mathbb{I}_{\mathcal{D}_i} \mid S = s\right)^2 \right),\\
&= \sum_{i=1}^{N} c_i^2 \left( \mathbb{E}\left(\gamma_i^2\right) \mathbb{E}\left(\mathbb{I}_{\mathcal{D}_i}^2 \middle| S = s\right) - \mathbb{E}\left(\gamma_i\right)^2 \mathbb{E}\left(\mathbb{I}_{\mathcal{D}_i} \mid S = s\right)^2 \right),\\
&= \sum_{i=1}^{N} c_i^2 \left( \underbrace{\left(\operatorname{var}(\gamma_i) + \mathbb{E}(\gamma_i)^2\right)}_{\nu_{\gamma_i} + \bar{\gamma}_i^2} \left( \operatorname{var}\left(\mathbb{I}_{\mathcal{D}_i} \mid S = s\right) + \mathbb{E}\left(\mathbb{I}_{\mathcal{D}_i} \mid S = s\right)^2 \right) - \bar{\gamma}_i^2 p_i(s)^2 \right),\\
&= \sum_{i=1}^{N} c_i^2 \left( \left(\nu_{\gamma_i} + \bar{\gamma}_i^2\right) \left( \mathbb{E}\left(\mathbb{I}_{\mathcal{D}_i} \mid S = s\right) + \mathbb{E}\left(\mathbb{I}_{\mathcal{D}_i} \mid S = s\right)^2 \right) - \bar{\gamma}_i^2 p_i(s)^2 \right),\\
&= \sum_{i=1}^{N} c_i^2 \left( \left(\nu_{\gamma_i} + \bar{\gamma}_i^2\right) \left( p_i(s) + p_i(s)^2 \right) - \bar{\gamma}_i^2 p_i(s)^2 \right),\\
&= \sum_{i=1}^{N} c_i^2 \left( \nu_{\gamma_i} p_i(s) + \nu_{\gamma_i} p_i(s)^2 + \bar{\gamma}_i^2 p_i(s) + \cancel{\bar{\gamma}_i^2 p_i(s)^2} - \cancel{\bar{\gamma}_i^2 p_i(s)^2} \right),\\
&= \sum_{i=1}^{N} c_i^2 p_i(s) \left( \bar{\gamma}_i^2 + \nu_{\gamma_i} \left(1 + p_i(s)\right) \right).
\end{aligned}
$$

We can now directly determine the required first derivative of the conditional variance. With the fairly succinct form of Eq. 11.56, it is readily written as

$$
\begin{aligned}
\nu'(s) &= \frac{\partial}{\partial s}\left(\underbrace{\sum_{i=1}^{N} c_i^2 p_i(s)\Big(\bar{\gamma}_i^2 + \nu_{\gamma_i}(1+p_i(s))\Big)}_{\text{Eq. 11.56}}\right), \qquad (11.57)\\
&= \frac{\partial}{\partial s}\left(\sum_{i=1}^{N} c_i^2\Big(\nu_{\gamma_i} p_i(s) + \nu_{\gamma_i} p_i(s)^2 + \bar{\gamma}_i^2 p_i(s)\Big)\right),\\
&= \sum_{i=1}^{N} c_i^2\Big(\nu_{\gamma_i} p_i\omega_i + \nu_{\gamma_i} 2p_i(s)p_i\omega_i + \bar{\gamma}_i^2 p_i\omega_i\Big),\\
&= \sum_{i=1}^{N} c_i^2 p_i\omega_i\Big(\bar{\gamma}_i^2 + \nu_{\gamma_i}\,(1+2p_i(s))\Big).
\end{aligned}
$$

The final remaining piece of the puzzle is the density function of the systematic state variable and its first derivative. Recall that, to meet the needs of the model, we require that $S \sim \Gamma\left(a, \frac{1}{a}\right)$. The shape-scale version of the density of the gamma distribution for these parameter choices is written as,

$$
f_S(s) = \frac{s^{a-1}e^{-sa}}{\Gamma(a)\left(\frac{1}{a}\right)^a}, \qquad (11.58)
$$

where $\Gamma(a)$ denotes the gamma function.[36] The first derivative with respect to $s$ has a convenient form,

$$
\begin{aligned}
f_S'(s) &= \frac{\partial}{\partial s}\left(\frac{s^{a-1}e^{-sa}}{\Gamma(a)\left(\frac{1}{a}\right)^a}\right), \qquad (11.59)\\
&= \frac{1}{\Gamma(a)\left(\frac{1}{a}\right)^a}\Big((a-1)s^{a-2}e^{-sa} - as^{a-1}e^{-sa}\Big),
\end{aligned}
$$

[36] See Casella and Berger [10, Chapter 3] or Johnson et al. [21, Chapter 17] for more information on the gamma distribution.

$$
\begin{aligned}
&= \underbrace{\frac{s^{a-1}e^{-sa}}{\Gamma(a)\left(\frac{1}{a}\right)^{a}}}_{f_S(s)} \left((a-1)s^{-1} - a\right), \\
&= f_S(s)\left(\frac{a-1}{s} - a\right).
\end{aligned}
$$

While the convenience might not be immediately clear, we will require the ratio of the first derivative of the gamma density to its raw density for the calculation of the granularity adjustment. This ratio, following from Eqs. 11.58 and 11.59, is thus

$$
\begin{aligned}
\frac{f_S'(s)}{f_S(s)} &= \frac{\cancel{f_S(s)}\left(\frac{a-1}{s} - a\right)}{\cancel{f_S(s)}}, \\
\mathcal{A} &= \frac{a-1}{s} - a.
\end{aligned}
\tag{11.60}
$$

This quantity depends only on the model and, more particularly, on the parametrization of the underlying gamma distribution. The density function itself happily cancels out.

We finally have all of the necessary elements to describe, at least in its raw form, the granularity adjustment for the one-factor CreditRisk+ model. Revisiting Eq. 11.47 we have,

$$
\begin{aligned}
\mathcal{G}_\alpha(L) &= \underbrace{-\frac{1}{2}\left(\frac{1}{\mu'(s)}\left(\frac{f'(s)\nu(s)}{f(s)} + \nu'(s)\right) - \underbrace{\frac{\nu(s)\mu''(s)}{(\mu'(s))^2}}_{=0}\right)}_{\text{Eq. 11.47}}\Bigg|_{s=q_\alpha(S)\equiv q_\alpha} \\
&= -\frac{1}{2}\left(\frac{\mathcal{A}\nu(q_\alpha) + \nu'(q_\alpha)}{\mu'(q_\alpha)}\right), \\
&= \frac{-\mathcal{A}\nu(q_\alpha) - \nu'(q_\alpha)}{2\mu'(q_\alpha)},
\end{aligned}
\tag{11.61}
$$

where $q_\alpha \equiv q_\alpha(S)$ and we use $\alpha$ instead of $1-\alpha$, because the probability of default is monotonically *increasing* as a function of the state-variable in the CreditRisk+ setting. If we select a parameter $a$ and determine the desired degree of confidence (i.e., $\alpha$), then we can input Eqs. 11.55–11.57 and 11.60 into the revised granularity-adjustment expression in Eq. 11.61. This would represent a practical concentration adjustment.

**Colour and Commentary 135** (SEEING THE FOREST THROUGH THE TREES): *A common choice of granularity adjustment stems from selection of the Poisson-gamma mixture model—with random recovery—referred to as the CreditRisk+ approach. A number of detailed computations are required to identify our three main ingredients—the systemic density and conditional expectation and variance—along with their derivatives. It is unfortunately rather easy to get lost in the detail. Gordy and Lütkebohmert [15, 16], appreciating this fact, invest a significant amount of effort to improve this situation. In particular, they perform three tasks: they simplify the notation, write the granularity adjustment in terms of exposure-level add-ons, and eliminate a few complex, but not terribly important terms.*[a] *We work through these, at times tedious calculations, in the following discussion. Understanding the helpfulness of this additional work helps make the forthcoming mathematical manipulations a bit more bearable.*

[a] This slightly reduces the sharpness of the approximation, but dramatically eases the presentation.

Equation 11.61 would, usually, be the end of the story. Gordy and Lütkebohmert [15, 16], in their desire to use this approach for regulatory purposes, quite reasonably seek to streamline the presentation and simplify the final result. This requires some additional manipulation. To accomplish their simplification, they introduce three new terms. The first is,

$$\mathcal{R}_i = \bar{\gamma}_i p_i. \tag{11.62}$$

The second is not merely a simplification, but also an expression in its own right. It is the amount of regulatory capital for the $i$th obligor required as a proportion of its total exposure. More specifically, it is given as,

$$\begin{aligned}
\mathcal{K}_i &= \frac{\text{Worst-Case Loss from Obligor } i - \text{Expected Loss from Obligor } i}{i\text{th Exposure}}, \\
&= \frac{\mathbb{E}\left(\gamma_i \cancel{c_i} \mathbb{I}_{\mathcal{D}_i} \,\middle|\, S = q_\alpha\right) - \mathbb{E}\left(\gamma_i \cancel{c_i} \mathbb{I}_{\mathcal{D}_i}\right)}{\cancel{c_i}}, \\
&= \mathbb{E}\left(\gamma_i \mathbb{I}_{\mathcal{D}_i} \,\middle|\, S = q_\alpha\right) - \mathbb{E}\left(\gamma_i \mathbb{I}_{\mathcal{D}_i}\right), \\
&= \mathbb{E}(\gamma_i)\, \mathbb{E}\left(\mathbb{I}_{\mathcal{D}_i} \,\middle|\, S = q_\alpha\right) - \mathbb{E}(\gamma_i)\, \mathbb{E}\left(\mathbb{I}_{\mathcal{D}_i}\right), \\
&= \bar{\gamma}_i p_i (1 - \omega_i + \omega_i q_\alpha) - \bar{\gamma}_i p_i, \\
&= \cancel{\bar{\gamma}_i p_i} - \bar{\gamma}_i p_i \omega_i + \bar{\gamma}_i p_i \omega_i q_\alpha - \cancel{\bar{\gamma}_i p_i}, \\
&= \bar{\gamma}_i p_i \omega_i (q_\alpha - 1).
\end{aligned} \tag{11.63}$$

The sum of $\mathcal{R}_i$ and $\mathcal{K}_i$ also has a relatively compact form,

$$\begin{aligned}
\mathcal{R}_i + \mathcal{K}_i &= \underbrace{\bar{\gamma}_i p_i}_{\substack{\text{Eq.}\\ 11.62}} + \underbrace{\bar{\gamma}_i p_i \omega_i (q_\alpha - 1)}_{\text{Eq. 11.63}}, \qquad (11.64)\\
&= \bar{\gamma}_i p_i + \bar{\gamma}_i p_i \omega_i q_\alpha - \bar{\gamma}_i p_i \omega_i,\\
&= \bar{\gamma}_i \underbrace{p_i \left( 1 - \omega_i + \omega_i q_\alpha \right)}_{p_i(q_\alpha)},\\
&= \bar{\gamma}_i p_i(q_\alpha).
\end{aligned}$$

The final definition involves the mean and variance of the loss-given-default parameter,

$$C_i = \frac{\bar{\gamma}_i^2 + \nu_{\gamma_i}}{\bar{\gamma}_i}. \qquad (11.65)$$

Outfitted with these definitions, we can follow the Gordy and Lütkebohmert [15, 16] approach to find a more parsimonious representation of the CreditRisk+ granularity adjustment. Starting with Eq. 11.61, this will take a number of steps. First, we begin with the following adjustment,

$$\begin{aligned}
\mathcal{G}_\alpha(L) &= \underbrace{\left( \frac{q_\alpha - 1}{q_\alpha - 1} \right)}_{=1} \underbrace{\frac{-\mathcal{A}\nu(q_\alpha) - \nu'(q_\alpha)}{2\mu'(q_\alpha)}}_{\text{Eq. 11.61}}, \qquad (11.66)\\
&= \frac{\delta_\alpha(a)\nu(q_\alpha) - (q_\alpha - 1)\nu'(q_\alpha)}{2(q_\alpha - 1)\mu'(q_\alpha)},
\end{aligned}$$

where the new, model-based constant $\delta_\alpha(a)$ is written as,

$$\begin{aligned}
\delta_\alpha(a) &= (q_\alpha - 1)\mathcal{A}, \qquad (11.67)\\
&= -(q_\alpha - 1) \left( \frac{a-1}{q_\alpha} - a \right),\\
&= (q_\alpha - 1) \left( a - \frac{a-1}{q_\alpha} \right),\\
&= (q_\alpha - 1) \left( a + \frac{1-a}{q_\alpha} \right).
\end{aligned}$$

We will return to this constant when we are ready to actually implement the model—Gordy and Lütkebohmert [15, 16] allocate a significant amount of time to its determination.

There are three distinct terms in Eq. 11.66. We will use the preceding definitions to simplify each in turn. Let's start with the denominator. From Eq. 11.55, we have that,

$$
\begin{aligned}
(q_\alpha - 1)\mu'(q_\alpha) &= (q_\alpha - 1)\underbrace{\sum_{i=1}^{N} c_i \bar{\gamma}_i p_i \omega_i}_{\text{Eq. 11.55}}, \qquad (11.68)\\
&= \sum_{i=1}^{N} c_i \underbrace{\bar{\gamma}_i p_i \omega_i (q_\alpha - 1)}_{\mathcal{K}_i \text{ (Eq. 11.63)}},\\
&= \sum_{i=1}^{N} c_i \mathcal{K}_i,\\
&= \mathcal{K}^*,
\end{aligned}
$$

which is the total regulatory capital under the CreditRisk+ model.

The first term in the numerator is reduced, using Eq. 11.56, to

$$
\begin{aligned}
\delta_\alpha(a)\nu(q_\alpha) &= \delta_\alpha(a)\underbrace{\sum_{i=1}^{N} c_i^2 p_i(q_\alpha)\bigg(\bar{\gamma}_i^2 + \nu_{\gamma_i}(1 + p_i(q_\alpha))\bigg)}_{\text{Eq. 11.56}}, \qquad (11.69)\\
&= \delta_\alpha(a)\underbrace{\left(\frac{\bar{\gamma}_i}{\bar{\gamma}_i}\right)}_{=1}\sum_{i=1}^{N} c_i^2 p_i(q_\alpha)\bigg(\bar{\gamma}_i^2 + \nu_{\gamma_i}(1 + p_i(q_\alpha))\bigg),\\
&= \delta_\alpha(a)\sum_{i=1}^{N} c_i^2 \underbrace{\bar{\gamma}_i p_i(q_\alpha)}_{\mathcal{R}_i + \mathcal{K}_i}\Bigg(\underbrace{\frac{\bar{\gamma}_i^2 + \nu_{\gamma_i}}{\bar{\gamma}_i}}_{C_i} + \frac{\nu_{\gamma_i}}{\bar{\gamma}_i}\underbrace{\left(\frac{\bar{\gamma}_i}{\bar{\gamma}_i}\right)}_{=1} p_i(q_\alpha))\Bigg),\\
&= \delta_\alpha(a)\sum_{i=1}^{N} c_i^2(\mathcal{R}_i + \mathcal{K}_i)\bigg(C_i + \frac{\nu_{\gamma_i}}{\bar{\gamma}_i^2}\underbrace{\bar{\gamma}_i p_i(q_\alpha))}_{\mathcal{R}_i + \mathcal{K}_i}\bigg),\\
&= \sum_{i=1}^{N} c_i^2\left(\delta_\alpha(a) C_i\,(\mathcal{R}_i + \mathcal{K}_i) + \delta_\alpha(a)\,(\mathcal{R}_i + \mathcal{K}_i)^2\frac{\nu_{\gamma_i}}{\bar{\gamma}_i^2}\right).
\end{aligned}
$$

Although this does not seem particularly concise, it does permit us to write everything in terms of the various definitions.

The second term in the numerator and the last term required to re-write the granularity adjustment, depend on our derivation in Eq. 11.57,

$$
\begin{aligned}
(q_\alpha - 1)\nu'(q_\alpha) &= \underbrace{(q_\alpha - 1)\sum_{i=1}^{N} c_i^2 p_i \omega_i \left(\bar{\gamma}_i^2 + \nu_{\gamma_i}\left(1 + 2p_i(q_\alpha)\right)\right)}_{\text{Eq. 11.57}}, \qquad (11.70)\\
&= \underbrace{\left(\frac{\bar{\gamma}_i}{\bar{\gamma}_i}\right)}_{=1} \sum_{i=1}^{N} c_i^2 p_i \omega_i (q_\alpha - 1)\left(\bar{\gamma}_i^2 + \nu_{\gamma_i}\left(1 + 2p_i(q_\alpha)\right)\right),\\
&= \sum_{i=1}^{N} c_i^2 \underbrace{\bar{\gamma}_i p_i \omega_i (q_\alpha - 1)}_{\mathcal{K}_i} \left( \underbrace{\frac{\bar{\gamma}_i^2 + \nu_{\gamma_i}}{\bar{\gamma}_i}}_{C_i} + 2\frac{\nu_{\gamma_i}}{\bar{\gamma}_i} \underbrace{\left(\frac{\bar{\gamma}_i}{\bar{\gamma}_i}\right)}_{=1} p_i(q_\alpha) \right),\\
&= \sum_{i=1}^{N} c_i^2 \mathcal{K}_i \left( C_i + 2\frac{\nu_{\gamma_i}}{\bar{\gamma}_i^2} \underbrace{\bar{\gamma}_i p_i(q_\alpha)}_{\mathcal{R}_i + \mathcal{K}_i} \right),\\
&= \sum_{i=1}^{N} c_i^2 \mathcal{K}_i \left( C_i + 2\left(\mathcal{R}_i + \mathcal{K}_i\right) \frac{\nu_{\gamma_i}}{\bar{\gamma}_i^2} \right).
\end{aligned}
$$

Collecting Eqs. 11.68 to 11.70 and plugging them into Eq. 11.66, we have the following lengthy expression for the granularity adjustment,

$$
\begin{aligned}
\mathcal{G}_\alpha(L) &= \underbrace{\frac{\delta_\alpha(a)\nu(q_\alpha) - (q_\alpha - 1)\nu'(q_\alpha)}{2(q_\alpha - 1)\mu'(q_\alpha)}}_{\text{Eq. 11.66}}, \qquad (11.71)\\
&= \frac{\overbrace{\sum_{i=1}^{N} c_i^2 \left( \delta_\alpha(a) C_i \left(\mathcal{R}_i + \mathcal{K}_i\right) + \delta_\alpha(a)\left(\mathcal{R}_i + \mathcal{K}_i\right)^2 \frac{\nu_{\gamma_i}}{\bar{\gamma}_i^2} \right)}^{\text{Eq. 11.69}} - \overbrace{\sum_{i=1}^{N} c_i^2 \mathcal{K}_i \left( C_i + 2\left(\mathcal{R}_i + \mathcal{K}_i\right)\frac{\nu_{\gamma_i}}{\bar{\gamma}_i^2} \right)}^{\text{Eq. 11.70}}}{2\underbrace{\mathcal{K}^*}_{\text{Eq. 11.68}}},\\
&= \frac{1}{2\mathcal{K}^*} \sum_{i=1}^{N} c_i^2 \left( \left( \delta_\alpha(a) C_i \left(\mathcal{R}_i + \mathcal{K}_i\right) + \delta_\alpha(a)\left(\mathcal{R}_i + \mathcal{K}_i\right)^2 \frac{\nu_{\gamma_i}}{\bar{\gamma}_i^2} \right) - \mathcal{K}_i \left( C_i + 2\left(\mathcal{R}_i + \mathcal{K}_i\right) \frac{\nu_{\gamma_i}}{\bar{\gamma}_i^2} \right) \right).
\end{aligned}
$$

Again, this does not seem like a dramatic improvement, in terms of parsimony at least, relative to the raw form found in Eq. 11.66. It is, however, the form summarized in equation 6 of Gordy and Lütkebohmert [15, Page 7]. Moreover, this is the structure quoted in most regulatory discussions of the granularity adjustment.

Some additional parametric details helps somewhat. Gordy and Lütkebohmert [15] suggest a specific form for $\nu_{\gamma_i}$ to "avoid the burden of a new data requirement." Their recommended choice is,

$$\nu_{\gamma_i} = \xi \bar{\gamma}_i (1 - \bar{\gamma}_i), \tag{11.72}$$

where $\xi \approx 0.25$.[37] This has some precedent in previous regulatory discussions. Our method-of-moments approach, from Chap. 3, to the calibration of individual recovery beta distributions is another potential source for specification of $\nu_{\gamma_i}$.

In their quest for parsimony, Gordy and Lütkebohmert [15] also offer a further simplification. They argue that, given the relative sizes of $\mathcal{R}_i$ and $\mathcal{K}_i$, products of these quantities are of second-order importance and—in the spirit of approximation—can be summarily dropped. Practically, this involves setting $(\mathcal{R}_i + \mathcal{K}_i)^2$ and $\mathcal{K}_i(\mathcal{R}_i + \mathcal{K}_i)$ equal to zero. The impact on Eq. 11.71 is quite substantial,

$$\begin{aligned}\mathcal{G}_\alpha(L) &= \frac{1}{2\mathcal{K}^*}\sum_{i=1}^{N} c_i^2 \Bigg(\bigg(\delta_\alpha(a) C_i \left(\mathcal{R}_i + \mathcal{K}_i\right) + \cancel{\delta_\alpha(a)\left(\mathcal{R}_i + \mathcal{K}_i\right)^2 \frac{\nu_{\gamma_i}}{\bar{\gamma}_i^2}}\bigg) \\ &\quad - \mathcal{K}_i \left(C_i + \cancel{2\left(\mathcal{R}_i + \mathcal{K}_i\right)\frac{\nu_{\gamma_i}}{\bar{\gamma}_i^2}}\right)\Bigg), \\ &= \frac{1}{2\mathcal{K}^*}\sum_{i=1}^{N} c_i^2 \Big( \left(\delta_\alpha(a) C_i \left(\mathcal{R}_i + \mathcal{K}_i\right)\right) - \mathcal{K}_i C_i \Big), \\ &= \frac{1}{2\mathcal{K}^*}\sum_{i=1}^{N} c_i^2 C_i \Big(\delta_\alpha(a)\left(\mathcal{R}_i + \mathcal{K}_i\right) - \mathcal{K}_i\Big). \end{aligned} \tag{11.73}$$

It is occasionally simplified even further to,

$$\mathcal{G}_\alpha(L) = \frac{1}{2\mathcal{K}^*}\sum_{i=1}^{N} c_i^2 C_i \mathcal{Q}_i, \tag{11.74}$$

where

$$\mathcal{Q}_i = \delta_\alpha(a)\left(\mathcal{R}_i + \mathcal{K}_i\right) - \mathcal{K}_i. \tag{11.75}$$

Ultimately, after much effort and tedium, we have achieved a reasonable degree of simplification. How good this granularity adjustment performs in an absolute sense,

[37] Incidentally, the fixed recovery volatility value from the legacy implementation of our credit-risk economic capital model was loosely motivated by this work.

and relative to the more precise form in Eq. 11.71, is an empirical question. It turns out, however, to be quite effective in many cases.[38]

**Colour and Commentary 136** (GRANULARITY-ADJUSTMENT MISMATCH): *A logical problem arises if one selects the CreditRisk+ model, as proposed by Gordy and Lütkebohmert [15], to build a single-name concentration adjustment. The Basel IRB approach is predicated on a one-factor Gaussian threshold model. This creates something of a mismatch between the threshold-based description of systemic risk and the mixture-based concentration model. While it is useful and important to be aware of this point, it is not an insurmountable issue. Gordy and Lütkebohmert [15] establish a certain degree of equivalency between the two approaches through the calibration of key model parameters. In particular, the factor loadings in the CreditRisk+ granularity adjustment are selected to be consistent with those found in the ASRF model.*

Establishing some form of equivalency between the ASRF and one-factor CreditRisk+ models is required. The Basel-IRB model is, for a given parameter $\rho$, roughly equivalent to the ASRF model. This permits us to use the ASRF model as our starting point. The appendix of Gordy and Lütkebohmert [15], in an effort to highlight their choice of $\xi$, presents an interesting method to identify the $\omega_i$ parameter. The authors do this by identifying the contribution to economic capital associated with the $i$th obligor in both the CreditRisk+ and the asymptotic one-factor Gaussian threshold (i.e., ASRF) approaches. In the CreditRisk+, we define this quantity as,

$$\begin{aligned}
\mathcal{K}_i^{(1)} &= \underbrace{\bar{\gamma}_i c_i p_i \left(q_\alpha(S)\right)}_{\text{Unexpected loss}} - \underbrace{\bar{\gamma}_i c_i p_i}_{\substack{\text{Expected}\\ \text{loss}}}, \qquad (11.76)\\
&= \bar{\gamma}_i c_i \left( p_i \left(1 - \omega_i + \omega_i q_\alpha(S)\right) - p_i \right),\\
&= \bar{\gamma}_i c_i \left( \cancel{p_i} - p_i\omega_i + p_i\omega_i q_\alpha(S) - \cancel{p_i} \right),\\
&= \underbrace{\bar{\gamma}_i c_i \omega_i p_i \left( q_\alpha(S) - 1 \right)}_{\text{Eq. 11.63}}.
\end{aligned}$$

[38] See Bolder [9, Chapter 6] for a practical analysis of this question.

This is a function of obligor data, but also the parameter $\omega_i$ and the degree of confidence, $\alpha$. The associated ASRF quantity is,

$$\mathcal{K}_i^{(2)} = \underbrace{\bar{\gamma}_i c_i p_i \left(q_{1-\alpha}(G)\right)}_{\text{Unexpected loss}} - \underbrace{\bar{\gamma}_i c_i p_i}_{\substack{\text{Expected}\\ \text{loss}}}, \tag{11.77}$$

$$= \underbrace{\bar{\gamma}_i c_i \left( \Phi\left( \frac{\Phi^{-1}(p_i) - r_i \Phi^{-1}(1-\alpha)}{\sqrt{1-r_i^2}} \right) - p_i \right)}_{\text{Eq. 11.7}}.$$

The ASRF expression depends on similar obligor data inputs, but also on the $r_i$ parameter and the degree of confidence.[39]

In the Basel framework, guidance is provided for the choice of $r_i$. Indeed, it is a predefined function of the credit counterparties unconditional default probability; that is, $r_i = f(p_i)$ from Eq. 11.9 on page 675. Given this choice, we seek the appropriate, and equivalent choice of $\omega_i$ in the CreditRisk+ model. Both are factor loadings on the systematic state variable. The (approximate) solution is to equate Eqs. 11.76 and 11.77 and to solve for $\omega_i$. The result is,

$$\mathcal{K}_i^{(1)} = \mathcal{K}_i^{(2)}, \tag{11.78}$$

$$\underbrace{\cancel{\bar{\gamma}_i c_i} \omega_i p_i \left( q_\alpha(S) - 1 \right)}_{\text{Eq. 11.76}} = \underbrace{\cancel{\bar{\gamma}_i c_i} \left( \Phi\left( \frac{\Phi^{-1}(p_i) - r_i \Phi^{-1}(1-\alpha)}{\sqrt{1-r_i^2}} \right) - p_i \right)}_{\text{Eq. 11.77}},$$

$$\omega_i = \frac{\left( \Phi\left( \frac{\Phi^{-1}(p_i) - r_i \Phi^{-1}(1-\alpha)}{\sqrt{1-r_i^2}} \right) - p_i \right)}{p_i \left( q_\alpha(S) - 1 \right)}.$$

While useful, this expression has a few drawbacks. Perhaps most importantly, it depends on the level of confidence, $\alpha$. A different level of $\omega_i$ is derived for each level of $\alpha$. The CreditRisk+ parameter has an additional parameter, $a$, summarizing the variance of the underlying gamma distribution used to describe the Poisson

[39] Recall that the monotonicity of conditional default probabilities runs in opposite directions for the CreditRisk+ and threshold methodologies. Thus, $q_{1-\alpha}(G)$ is (directionally) equivalent to $q_\alpha(S)$ where $G$ and $S$ denote the standard-normal and gamma distributed systematic state variables, respectively.

arrival intensity.[40] The $\alpha$ quantile of $S$, which shows up as $q_\alpha(S)$ in Eq. 11.78, also explicitly depends on $a$.

Determining $a$ is not an obvious task. An important, and very welcome, contribution of Gordy and Lütkebohmert [15, 16] was to provide some concrete suggestions regarding its value. They construct an equation where $a$ is set equal to the default-probability variance—this is accomplished using, among other things, the trick from Eq. 11.78. Fixing the other quantities in Eq. 11.78, they numerically find the value of $a$ that satisfies it. Gordy and Lütkebohmert [15] recommend a value of 0.25, which was revised in Gordy and Lütkebohmert [16] to 0.125. This choice, in addition to informing the choice of $\omega_i$, also has an important influence on the $\delta_\alpha(s)$ quantity described in Eq. 11.67. If one sets $a = 0.25$ and $\alpha = 0.999$, we arrive at an approximate value of 4.83 for $\delta_\alpha(a)$. This is commonly used in regulatory applications and, in our specific case, is the current value employed in the S&P-RAC framework.

Figure 11.6 collects together all of the key formulae from Gordy and Lütkebohmert [16]'s CreditRisk+ implementation of the granularity adjustment.[41] It is essentially this form that is employed in many Pillar II concentration risk calculations; it is also the foundation of S&P's single-name adjustment.

### 11.2.4 Working with Partial Information

Gordy and Lütkebohmert [16, Section 3] offer an additional contribution—which is employed in the S&P RAC computations—for handling situations with partial information. In particular, they argue that

> aggregation of multiple exposures into a single exposure per borrower is likely to be the only substantive challenge in implementing the granularity adjustment.

For very large banks with operations (and systems and data repositories) in jurisdictions across the globe, this is almost certainly the case. For small to medium-sized players, this may be somewhat less pertinent. There is nonetheless value in understanding Gordy and Lütkebohmert [16, Section 3]'s proposal, particularly since it is also required to better appreciate S&P risk-adjusted asset adjustments.

Gordy and Lütkebohmert [16, Section 3]'s specific suggestion, to address this potential challenge, is to construct an upper bound permitting the calculation of the granularity adjustment on "a subset consisting [of the firm's] largest exposures." They demonstrate how such an upper bound might be constructed—in the context of the CreditRisk+ implementation of the granularity adjustment—for both the

---

[40] $a$, in principle, also describes the expectation of $S$, but this has been set to unity.

[41] We could have, as many publications do, skipped directly to this final result. In doing so, however, we would have missed out on all the fun and insight.

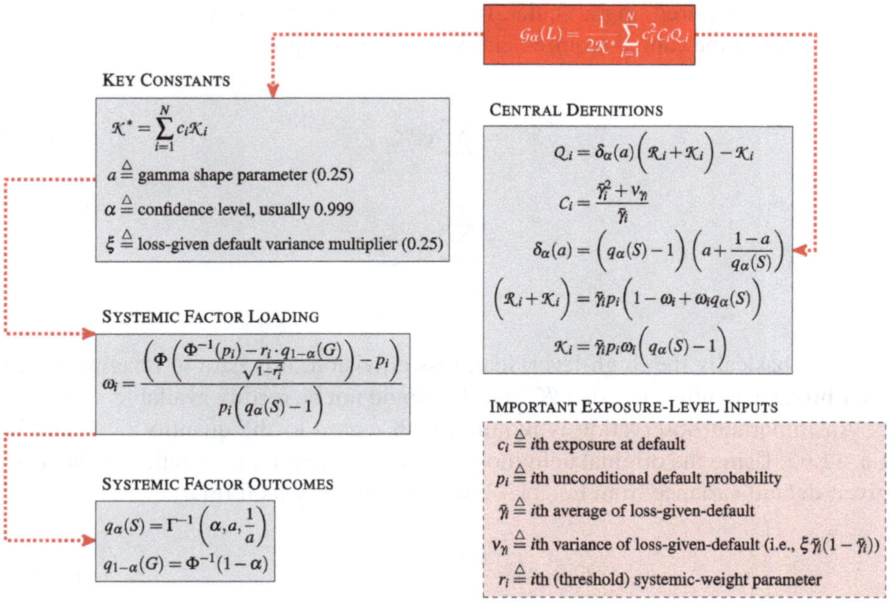


**Fig. 11.6** *Granularity adjustment cheat-sheet*: The schematic above outlines, at a single glance, the principal formulae involved in Gordy and Lütkebohmert [16]'s CreditRisk+ implementation of the granularity adjustment calculation. It also attempts to highlight the most important relationships between the key elements.

cases of homogeneous and heterogeneous exposures. While interesting from a motivational perspective, the homogeneous exposure case is not overly realistic. In our presentation of their upper bound, we will restrict our attention to the heterogeneous situation.

A bit of set-up is involved. First of all, we identify the $M$ distinct largest borrowers for whom we have complete information.[42] We will refer to this set of exposures as $\mathcal{M}$. By simple arithmetic, there exist $N - M$ remaining exposures outside of this set. We assume knowledge of an upper bound, $\bar{c}$, on their individual exposure. That is, $\bar{c} \geq c_i$ for all $i \notin \mathcal{M}$.[43] As a final step, some portfolio-level

[42] Complete information, in this context, is all the information to perform the computation summarized in Fig. 11.6.

[43] This should not be hard to find. One could simply order the exposures outside $\mathcal{M}$ and use the largest one. Alternatively, we could use the smallest exposure from $\mathcal{M}$.

constants are required. In particular, we need to know $\mathcal{K}^*$ as defined in Eq. 11.68; this quantity is the capital requirement. We will also require

$$\begin{aligned}\mathcal{R}^* &= \sum_{i=1}^{N} c_i \mathcal{R}_i, \\ &= \sum_{i=1}^{N} c_i \underbrace{\bar{\gamma}_i p_i}_{\substack{\text{Eq.}\\ 11.62}},\end{aligned} \tag{11.79}$$

which is basically the (high-level) loan-loss provision. It is hard to imagine, given their broader significance, that $\mathcal{K}^*$ and $\mathcal{R}^*$ would not be readily available.

An important observation is required with regard to the quantity $C_i$ found in Eq. 11.65. Using the original definition and the proposed representation of the loss-given-default variance from Eq. 11.72, we may simplify its form as

$$\begin{aligned}C_i &= \underbrace{\frac{\bar{\gamma}_i^2 + \nu_{\gamma_i}}{\bar{\gamma}_i}}_{\substack{\text{Eq.}\\ 11.65}}, \\ &= \frac{\bar{\gamma}_i^2 + \overbrace{\xi\bar{\gamma}_i(1-\bar{\gamma}_i)}^{\text{Eq. 11.72}}}{\bar{\gamma}_i}, \\ &= \frac{\cancel{\bar{\gamma}_i}\Big(\bar{\gamma}_i + \xi(1-\bar{\gamma}_i)\Big)}{\cancel{\bar{\gamma}_i}}, \\ &= \xi + \bar{\gamma}_i(1-\xi).\end{aligned} \tag{11.80}$$

Given that values of $\bar{\gamma}_i \in (0,1)$, Eq. 11.80 permits us to show that $C_i \in (\xi, 1)$. Moreover, since practical values of $\xi$ are in the neighbourhood of 0.1 to 0.3, we can comfortably conclude that $C_i \leq 1$ for any choice of loss-given-default parameters (and for all $i = 1, \ldots, N$). This fact will prove helpful in the derivation of the upper bound.

The final step in our preparation of Gordy and Lütkebohmert [16, Section 3]'s upper bound involves the definition of some important constants. Let us denote the total capital requirement within the observable set as,

$$\mathcal{K}^*_{\mathcal{M}} = \sum_{i\in\mathcal{M}} c_i \mathcal{K}_i. \tag{11.81}$$

We then introduce the observable loan-loss reserve requirement as,[44]

$$\mathcal{R}^*_{\mathcal{M}} = \sum_{i\in\mathcal{M}} c_i \mathcal{R}_i. \tag{11.82}$$

These two quantities turn out to be quite useful, since if one knows the total amount and the observable amount, then the unobservable quantity must be their difference.

Collecting all of these pieces together, Gordy and Lütkebohmert [16, Section 3]'s upper bound, when given partial information about the composition of one's portfolio, is derived as

$$\begin{aligned}
\mathcal{G}_\alpha(L) &= \underbrace{\frac{1}{2\mathcal{K}^*}\sum_{i=1}^{N} c_i^2 C_i Q_i}_{\text{Eq. 11.74}}, \qquad (11.83)\\
&= \frac{1}{2\mathcal{K}^*}\left(\underbrace{\sum_{i\in\mathcal{M}} c_i^2 C_i Q_i}_{\text{Observable set}} + \underbrace{\sum_{i\notin\mathcal{M}} c_i^2 C_i Q_i}_{\text{Unobservable set}}\right),\\
&\leq \frac{1}{2\mathcal{K}^*}\left(\sum_{i\in\mathcal{M}} c_i^2 C_i Q_i + \sum_{i\notin\mathcal{M}} \underbrace{\bar{c}c_i}_{\leq c_i^2}\underbrace{C_i}_{\leq 1} Q_i\right),\\
&\leq \frac{1}{2\mathcal{K}^*}\left(\sum_{i\in\mathcal{M}} c_i^2 C_i Q_i + \bar{c}\sum_{i\notin\mathcal{M}} c_i \underbrace{\left(\delta_\alpha(a)\left(\mathcal{R}_i + \mathcal{K}_i\right) - \mathcal{K}_i\right)}_{Q_i}\right),\\
&\leq \frac{1}{2\mathcal{K}^*}\left(\sum_{i\in\mathcal{M}} c_i^2 C_i Q_i + \bar{c}\sum_{i\notin\mathcal{M}} c_i \Big( (\delta_\alpha(a) - 1)\,\mathcal{K}_i + \delta_\alpha(a)\mathcal{R}_i\Big)\right),\\
&\leq \frac{1}{2\mathcal{K}^*}\left(\sum_{i\in\mathcal{M}} c_i^2 C_i Q_i + \bar{c}\Big( (\delta_\alpha(a) - 1)\sum_{i\notin\mathcal{M}} c_i\mathcal{K}_i + \delta_\alpha(a)\sum_{i\notin\mathcal{M}} c_i\mathcal{R}_i\Big)\right),
\end{aligned}$$

[44] This notion of loan-loss reserve (or loan impairment) is not as general as the expected-credit loss calculation addressed in Chap. 9. It simply provides a more classic assessment of the unconditional expectation of portfolio credit loss over a one-year horizon.

$$
\leq \frac{1}{2\mathcal{K}^*}\left(\sum_{i\in\mathcal{M}} c_i^2 C_i Q_i + \bar{c}\Bigg( (\delta_\alpha(a)-1)\underbrace{\left(\mathcal{K}^* - \mathcal{K}^*_{\mathcal{M}}\right)}_{\sum_{i\notin\mathcal{M}} c_i\mathcal{K}_i} + \delta_\alpha(a)\underbrace{\left(\mathcal{R}^* - \mathcal{R}^*_{\mathcal{M}}\right)}_{\sum_{i\notin\mathcal{M}} c_i\mathcal{R}_i}\Bigg)\right),
$$

$$
\leq \frac{1}{2\mathcal{K}^*}\left(\sum_{i\in\mathcal{M}} c_i^2 C_i Q_i + \bar{c}\Big( (\delta_\alpha(a)-1)\left(\mathcal{K}^* - \mathcal{K}^*_{\mathcal{M}}\right) + \delta_\alpha(a)\left(\mathcal{R}^* - \mathcal{R}^*_{\mathcal{M}}\right)\Big)\right).
$$

It is also relatively easy to see that as the observable set $\mathcal{M}$ converges to the total collection of portfolios, then the two terms $\mathcal{K}^* - \mathcal{K}^*_{\mathcal{M}}$ and $\mathcal{R}^* - \mathcal{R}^*_{\mathcal{M}}$ tend to zero. The result is that the upper bound converges, as one would logically expect, to the usual granularity adjustment.

**Colour and Commentary 137** (AN UPPER BOUND ON THE GRANULARITY ADJUSTMENT): *Large financial institutions might find it challenging to (affordably) collect all of the diverse exposures—spread over multiple branches over the globe—into a single place. Gordy and Lütkebohmert [16, Section 3] provide, for just such an eventuality, an upper bound on the granularity adjustment. The idea is simple; one focuses on the largest, most important, exposures in the portfolio. Partial information regarding the portfolio is sufficient for construction of this upper bound. One needs full information regarding the main exposures, some modest portfolio-wide quantities as well as a cap on the magnitude of the unobserved exposures. The form of the upper bound is intuitive and, as we tend towards full information about the portfolio, it collapses to the usual granularity adjustment. A small- or medium-sized institution may not find this particularly important, but its occasional use by S&P in their RAC methodology argues for investing some effort towards understanding its construction.*

### *11.2.5 A Multi-Factor Adjustment*

The preceding granularity adjustment—offered by Gordy and Lütkebohmert [15, 16]—is not the only approach to this question. Pykhtin [27] proposes an alternative that essentially permits expanding our treatment to include two distinct elements: the usual single-name and a new multi-factor adjustment. Unlike the previous section, this effort restricts its focus to the Gaussian threshold—or what we could also refer to as CreditMetrics—methodology. There are only a few twists over the preceding discussion, but the discussion remains rather heavy from a technical perspective. It is nonetheless a useful exercise to solidify the key ideas in the granularity adjustment and, in many ways, better comprehend our credit-risk economic-capital model.

Again, the less enthusiastic reader is advised to keep to the figures and gray boxes (or skip immediately to Chap. 12).

### A Generic Multi-Factor Model

As with all granularity adjustments, the following development involves a high level of complexity. To avoid potential confusion and to permit easy comparison, we'll endeavour to derive the key relationships using the broad strokes of Pykhtin [27]'s notation. The approach begins with the definition of a fairly generic multi-factor Gaussian threshold model. The $i$th credit obligor has the following structural composite latent state variable,

$$X_i = r_i Y_i + \sqrt{1 - r_i^2}\xi_i, \tag{11.84}$$

where $\xi_i \sim \mathcal{N}(0, 1)$ and

$$Y_i = \sum_{k=1}^{K} \alpha_{ik} Z_k, \tag{11.85}$$

for $i = 1, \ldots, N$. The systemic component is thus a linear combination of $K$ (i.e., $\{Z_k; k = 1, \ldots, K\}$) independent, identically distributed $\mathcal{N}(0, 1)$ random variates. We further wish that $X_i \sim \mathcal{N}(0, 1)$ for $i = 1, \ldots, N$, which requires the following condition on the form of each $Y_i$:

$$\sum_{k=1}^{K} \alpha_{ik}^2 = 1. \tag{11.86}$$

This condition is readily met in our credit-risk economic-capital implementation, where we denote the $\alpha_{ik}$ coefficients as

$$\alpha_{ik} = \frac{\beta_{ik}}{\sqrt{\beta_i \Omega \beta_i^T}}, \tag{11.87}$$

where $\beta_{ik}$ is the $i$th counterparty's loading on the $k$th factor and $\Omega \in \mathbb{R}^{K \times K}$ represents the factor correlation matrix. These are not directly comparable, however, because the underlying state variables in our approach are not orthogonal. To get our model into this form entails orthogonalization of our industrial and geographical factor space.[45]

[45] We achieve this by performing a Cholesky decomposition on $\Omega = UU^T$ and then rewriting the factor-loaded system as $(\beta U)I(U^T\beta^T)$. The numerator in Eq. 11.87 is simply replaced with $(\beta_i U)_k$. That is, it is the $k$th element of the product of the $i$th obligor's raw factor loadings and

The (asset) correlation between any two arbitrary entities—which will make an appearance in latter discussion—is given as,

$$
\begin{aligned}
\operatorname{corr}(X_i, X_j) &= \frac{\operatorname{cov}(X_i, X_j)}{\underbrace{\sqrt{\operatorname{var} X_i}}_{=1}\underbrace{\sqrt{\operatorname{var} X_j}}_{=1}}, \qquad (11.88)\\
&= \mathbb{E}\left(\left(X_i - \underbrace{\mathbb{E}(X_i)}_{=0}\right)\left(X_j - \underbrace{\mathbb{E}(X_j)}_{=0}\right)\right),\\
&= \mathbb{E}\left(X_i X_j\right),\\
&= \mathbb{E}\left(\left(r_i Y_i + \sqrt{1-r_i^2}\xi_i\right)\left(r_j Y_j + \sqrt{1-r_j^2}\xi_j\right)\right),\\
&= r_i r_j \mathbb{E}\left(Y_i Y_j\right),\\
&= r_i r_j \mathbb{E}\left(\left(\sum_{k=1}^{K} \alpha_{ik} Z_k\right)\left(\sum_{k=1}^{K} \alpha_{jk} Z_k\right)\right)\\
&= \underbrace{r_i r_j\, \mathbb{E}\left(\sum_{k=1}^{K} \alpha_{ik}\alpha_{jk} Z_k^2\right),}_{\text{By independence}},\\
&= r_i r_j \sum_{k=1}^{K} \alpha_{ik}\alpha_{jk} \underbrace{\mathbb{E}\left(Z_k^2\right)}_{=\operatorname{var}(Z_k)=1},\\
&= r_i r_j \sum_{k=1}^{K} \alpha_{ik}\alpha_{jk}.
\end{aligned}
$$

That is, the asset correlation is a function of the systemic weights of both counterparties and their factor loadings on the latent systemic state variables.

The portfolio loss function is thus readily written as,

$$
L = \sum_{i=1}^{N} c_i \bar{\gamma}_i \mathbb{I}_{\{X_i \leq \Phi^{-1}(p_i)\}}. \qquad (11.89)
$$

the upper-diagonal matrix stemming from the Cholesky decomposition of the systemic-factor correlation matrix; everything else remains unchanged. See Chap. 2 for more on this point.

When $K > 3$ or 4, we need to take recourse with simulation methods to solve this problem.[46] Following the lead from Gordy [14], we can write the limiting loss of the infinitely granular version of our portfolio as,

$$L^{\infty} = \mathbb{E}(L|\vec{Z}), \tag{11.90}$$

where $\vec{Z}$ denotes our collection of systemic state variables. In plain English, the infinitely granular portfolio loss is the systemic part of $L$; it is what is left once the idiosyncratic aspect has been diversified away. This is conceptually identical to the previous setting with one important distinction: we are not conditioning on a single systemic risk factor, but rather a collection of them. Evaluating Eq. 11.90 in the usual way results in the very familiar

$$L^{\infty} = \sum_{i=1}^{N} c_i \bar{\gamma}_i \underbrace{\Phi\left(\frac{\Phi^{-1}(p_i) - r_i \sum_{k=1}^{K} \alpha_{ik} Z_k}{\sqrt{1 - r_i^2}}\right)}_{\hat{p}_i(y) \equiv \hat{p}_i\left(\sum_{k=1}^{K} \alpha_{ik} Z_k\right)}, \tag{11.91}$$

where $\hat{p}_i(y)$ is the conditional default probability associated with the multi-factor model. Since the granularity adjustment relies on the single-factor structure, these ideas cannot be used directly.

## Introducing a One-Factor Model

To this point, we have not done anything particularly new. The basic notation of a generic multi-factor Gaussian threshold has been advanced. Building on this foundation, Pykhtin [27] then introduces a one-factor model. He does so, however, in a clever manner. In particular, the latent state variable is written as

$$X_i = a_i \bar{Y} + \sqrt{1 - a_i^2} \epsilon_i, \tag{11.92}$$

where $\epsilon_i \sim \mathcal{N}(0, 1)$ and

$$\bar{Y} = \sum_{k=1}^{K} b_k Z_k. \tag{11.93}$$

46 The saddlepoint method, see Bolder [9, Chapter 7] and the many useful references therein, offers a very effective pseudo-analytic solution for low-dimensional credit-risk models.

Again, we desire $X_i$ to be standard normally distributed so we impose the condition

$$\sum_{k=1}^{K} b_k^2 = 1. \tag{11.94}$$

to maintain unit variance of $\bar{Y}$ and, by extension, $X_i$. The trick is that the one-factor model is also a function of the (same) multidimensional set of systemic factors, but the weights are fixed for all obligors. This implies that $\bar{Y}$ is a single, global systemic factor. Quite naturally, it is some linear combination of a larger set of underlying factors. This makes sense. The real world is obviously multidimensional. Reducing it to a single dimension will invariably involve averaging over existing dimensions.[47] It also, via its one-factor structure, provides us access to the usual granularity adjustment logic.

We may now introduce the conditional portfolio loss associated with the one-factor model given $\bar{Y}$ as

$$\underbrace{\mathbb{E}(L|\bar{Y})}_{\bar{L}} = \sum_{i=1}^{N} c_i \bar{\gamma}_i \underbrace{\Phi\left(\frac{\Phi^{-1}(p_i) - a_i \bar{Y}}{\sqrt{1-a_i^2}}\right)}_{p_i(\bar{Y})}, \tag{11.95}$$

where we typically approximate the $\alpha$th quantile of the one-factor loss distribution by replacing $\bar{Y}$ with $\Phi^{-1}(1-\alpha)$. Note that $p_i(\cdot)$ represents the one-factor conditional default probability; we'll need to be careful to keep $\hat{p}_i(\cdot)$ and $p_i(\cdot)$ distinct. To be crystal clear, they are associated with the single- and multi-factor models, respectively. This concentrated (or granular) one-factor model will be used, with some modifications, in the forthcoming concentration adjustment.

The next part of the set-up is the classic granularity adjustment approach. We attempt to estimate the distance $\left| \, q_\alpha(L) - q_\alpha(\bar{L}) \, \right|$ using the surprisingly effective manipulation:

$$\begin{aligned} q_\alpha(L) &= q_\alpha\left(L + \underbrace{\bar{L} - \bar{L}}_{=0}\right), \\ &= q_\alpha\left(\underbrace{\bar{L} + \epsilon\left(L - \bar{L}\right)}_{L_\epsilon}\right)\Bigg|_{\epsilon=1}, \end{aligned} \tag{11.96}$$

[47] An analogous situation arises with the one-dimensional Capital Asset Pricing Model (CAPM) and the multi-dimensional Arbitrage Pricing Theorem (APT).

The leads to the Taylor series expansion around $\epsilon = 0$ and

$$\underbrace{q_\alpha(L) - q_\alpha\left(\bar{L}\right)}_{\mathcal{G}_\alpha(L)} \approx \left.\frac{\partial q_\alpha\left(\bar{L}+\epsilon\left(L-\bar{L}\right)\right)}{\partial\epsilon}\right|_{\epsilon=0} + \frac{1}{2}\left.\frac{\partial^2 q_\alpha\left(\bar{L}+\epsilon\left(L-\bar{L}\right)\right)}{\partial\epsilon^2}\right|_{\epsilon=0},$$

$$\approx \underbrace{\mathbb{E}\left(L-\bar{L}\,\middle|\,\bar{L}=\Phi^{-1}(1-\alpha)\right)}_{=0?}$$

$$-\frac{1}{2}\frac{1}{\phi(y)}\frac{\partial}{\partial y}\left.\left(\frac{\phi(y)\mathrm{var}\left(L-\bar{L}|\bar{Y}=y\right)}{\frac{\partial\mathbb{E}(L-\bar{L}|\bar{Y}=y)}{\partial y}}\right)\right|_{y=\Phi^{-1}(1-\alpha)} \tag{11.97}$$

where we use the (extensive and laborious) logic from the preceding section to get to this point. To ease the notation, we use $\phi(y)$ to describe the Gaussian density function of the one-factor state variable and set

$$\mu(y) = \mathbb{E}(L-\bar{L}|\bar{Y}=y), \tag{11.98}$$

and

$$\nu(y) = \mathrm{var}(L-\bar{L}|\bar{Y}=y). \tag{11.99}$$

Again, this is all entirely consistent with the development in the previous sections. The only difference is that we are working with an alternative definition of the one-factor model. In other words, we have previously spoken of a blanket systemic risk factor, $G$. In this case, we denote it as $\bar{Y}$ and assign it the specific construction in Eq. 11.93.

### Calibrating the Multi- and Single-Factor Worlds

The principal job at hand, and the challenge that Pykhtin [27] resolves, is to use the connection between $\bar{Y}$ and $\vec{Z}$—that is, the single global source of risk and the underlying collection of systemic risk factors—to describe the difference between $L$ and $\bar{L}$. In this formulation, there are two elements of difference: the number of factors and the level of portfolio granularity. Pykhtin [27]'s method permits us to capture both.

To do this, a central requirement is to determine the coefficients $\{a_i; i = 1, \ldots, N\}$ and $\{b_k; k = 1, \ldots, K\}$. These are the factor loadings on the one-factor state variable and the fixed linear combination of the multiple underlying risk factors, respectively. Identification of these parameters is thus essentially a calibration exercise. The driving idea is to create a form of equivalency between these multi- and single-factor credit-risk models.

Accomplishing this begins with the definition of another representation of the systemic state variable, $Y_i$. Pykhtin [27] writes it as,

$$Y_i = \underbrace{\rho_i \bar{Y} + \sqrt{1-\rho_i^2}\eta_i}_{\substack{\text{Also } \sum_{k=1}^{K} \alpha_{ik} Z_k \text{ by} \\ \text{Eq. 11.85}}}, \tag{11.100}$$

where, as usual, $\eta_i \sim \mathcal{N}(0,1)$ and $\rho_i$ is the $i$th obligor's loading on the single global factor. There is, nonetheless, a twist. Each $\eta_i$ is independent of $\bar{Y}$, but they are *not* mutually independent. That is, $\text{cov}(\eta_i, \eta_j) \neq 0$ for each $i, j = 1, \ldots, N$. This basically decomposes the composite latent state variable, in the multiple risk-factor setting, into two main components: the single-factor component and the residual from the other state variables. This is the reason that the residual components, embedded in the $\eta$ terms, are not independent. It is basically a risk decomposition between the single- and multi-factor perspectives.

The $\rho_i$ coefficients, as one would expect, represent the correlation between each $Y_i$ variable and $\bar{Y}$. This is readily demonstrated:

$$\begin{aligned}
\text{corr}(Y_i, \bar{Y}) &= \frac{\mathbb{E}\left(\left(Y_i - \overbrace{\mathbb{E}(Y_i)}^{=0}\right)\left(\bar{Y} - \overbrace{\mathbb{E}(\bar{Y})}^{=0}\right)\right)}{\underbrace{\sqrt{\text{var}(Y_i)}}_{=1}\underbrace{\sqrt{\text{var}(\bar{Y})}}_{=1}}, \qquad (11.101)\\
&= \mathbb{E}(Y_i \bar{Y}),\\
&= \mathbb{E}\left(\left(\rho_i \bar{Y} + \sqrt{1-\rho_i^2}\eta_i\right)\bar{Y}\right),\\
&= \rho_i \underbrace{\mathbb{E}(\bar{Y}^2)}_{=\text{var}(\bar{Y})=1} + \underbrace{\sqrt{1-\rho_i^2}\mathbb{E}(\eta_i)\mathbb{E}(\bar{Y})}_{=0},\\
&= \rho_i.
\end{aligned}$$

Using our alternative definition of $Y_i$, we can find an equivalence between $\rho_i$ and other important model coefficients. In particular,

$$\begin{aligned}
\text{corr}(Y_i, \bar{Y}) &= \mathbb{E}(Y_i \bar{Y}), \qquad (11.102)\\
&= \mathbb{E}\left(\underbrace{\left(\sum_{i=1}^{K} \alpha_{ik} Z_k\right)}_{Y_i}\underbrace{\left(\sum_{i=1}^{K} b_k Z_k\right)}_{\bar{Y}}\right),
\end{aligned}$$

$$
= \underbrace{\sum_{i=1}^{K} \alpha_{ik} b_k \overbrace{\mathbb{E}\left(Z_k^2\right)}^{=\text{var}(Z_k)=1}}_{\substack{\text{By independence} \\ \text{of } \{Z_k;\, k=1,\ldots,K\}}},
$$

$$
= \sum_{i=1}^{K} \alpha_{ik} b_k .
$$

This naturally implies that $\rho_i = \sum_{i=1}^{K} \alpha_{ik} b_k$. While essentially just a consequence of the various definitions, these relationships will prove useful later in the development.

Even more interesting is what happens when we plug in this revised definition of $Y_i$ into our original multi-factor composite latent state variable, $X_i$. The development is a bit less obvious and looks as follows:

$$
\begin{aligned}
X_i &= \underbrace{r_i Y_i + \sqrt{1 - r_i^2}\xi_i}_{\text{Eq. 11.84}}, \qquad (11.103) \\
&= \underbrace{r_i \left( \rho_i \bar{Y} + \sqrt{1 - \rho_i^2}\eta_i \right)}_{\text{Eq. 11.100}} + \sqrt{1 - r_i^2}\xi_i, \\
&= r_i \rho_i \bar{Y} + r_i \sqrt{1 - \rho_i^2}\eta_i + \sqrt{1 - r_i^2}\xi_i, \\
&= r_i \rho_i \bar{Y} + \sqrt{r_i^2 - r_i^2 \rho_i^2}\eta_i + \sqrt{1 - r_i^2}\xi_i.
\end{aligned}
$$

With three sources of risk, this does not appear terribly easy to get this into a tractable form. Reading between the lines—since it is not explicitly demonstrated—Pykhtin [27] opts for a representation that preserves the standard normality of $X_i$. The expectation is uninteresting; it will remain zero in virtually all cases. This brings us to the variance. We need to recall that each individual variable (i.e., $\bar{Y}$, $\eta_i$, and $\xi_i$) is statistically independent. We begin with

$$
\begin{aligned}
\text{var}(X_i) &= \text{var}\left( r_i \rho_i \bar{Y} + \sqrt{r_i^2 - r_i^2 \rho_i^2}\eta_i + \sqrt{1 - r_i^2}\xi_i \right), \qquad (11.104) \\
&= r_i^2 \rho_i^2 \text{var}(\bar{Y}) + (r_i^2 - r_i^2 \rho_i^2)\text{var}(\eta_i) + (1 - r_i^2)\text{var}(\xi_i).
\end{aligned}
$$

Now, since $\text{var}(\eta_i) = \text{var}(\xi_i) = 1$, we will replace it with another standard normal random variable, $\zeta_i \in \mathcal{N}(0, 1)$. This leads to

$$\begin{aligned}
\text{var}(X_i) &= r_i^2\rho_i^2\text{var}(\bar{Y}) + (r_i^2 - r_i^2\rho_i^2)\underbrace{\text{var}(\zeta_i)}_{=\text{var}(\eta_i)} + (1 - r_i^2)\underbrace{\text{var}(\zeta_i)}_{\text{var}(\xi_i)}, \quad (11.105)\\
&= r_i^2\rho_i^2\text{var}(\bar{Y}) + \left(\cancel{r_i^2} - r_i^2\rho_i^2 + 1 - \cancel{r_i^2}\right)\text{var}(\zeta_i),\\
&= r_i^2\rho_i^2\underbrace{\text{var}(\bar{Y})}_{=1} + (1 - r_i^2\rho_i^2)\underbrace{\text{var}(\zeta_i)}_{=1},\\
&= 1.
\end{aligned}$$

The corollary is that we may write $X_i$ much more succinctly as,

$$X_i = r_i\rho_i\bar{Y} + \sqrt{1 - r_i^2\rho_i^2}\,\zeta_i, \tag{11.106}$$

without any loss of generality. This allows us to re-write the conditional portfolio loss as,

$$\underbrace{\mathbb{E}(L|\bar{Y})}_{\bar{L}} = \underbrace{\sum_{i=1}^{N} c_i\gamma_i\Phi\left(\frac{\Phi^{-1}(p_i) - r_i\rho_i\bar{Y}}{\sqrt{1 - r_i^2\rho_i^2}}\right)}_{\text{Same form as Eq. 11.95}}, \tag{11.107}$$

and immediately infer from Eq. 11.95 that $a_i = r_i\rho_i$. Indeed, collecting our previous definitions, we have established that

$$a_i = r_i\underbrace{\sum_{i=1}^{K}\alpha_{ik}b_k}_{\rho_i}. \tag{11.108}$$

The $\{a_i; i = 1, \ldots, N\}$ and $\{\rho_i; i = 1, \ldots, N\}$ parameters are thus a function of three deeper components: the $r_i$'s, the $\alpha_{ik}$'s, and the $b_k$'s.

It is useful, at this point, to take stock of the various model parameters. The $\{r_i; i = 1, \ldots, N\}$ are the systemic-weight parameters. These are determined to capture the importance of the systemic and idiosyncratic elements of each credit obligor, which are estimated outside of this procedure. The $\{\alpha_{ik}; i = 1, \ldots, N\}$ parameters denote the factor loadings. Again, computed outside this approach, these describe the importance of the individual sectoral and geographical state variables to a given credit counterpart. This leaves us with the set of $\{b_k; i = 1, \ldots, N\}$ parameters; this is the only area where we have some choice. At this point, however, our sole available insight regarding the $b_k$'s is that they must meet the condition that $\sum_{k=1}^{K} b_k^2 = 1$. Beyond this meagre restriction, the set of options is rather broad.

Pykhtin [27] indicates that, conceptually, we would like to select the $\{b_k; i = 1, \ldots, N\}$ parameters to minimize the distance between $q_\alpha(L)$ and $q_\alpha(\bar{L})$. Since $L$ is unknown, and ultimately the object we are attempting to approximate, this understandably turns out to be a difficult task.[48] Instead, Pykhtin [27] proposes a proxy. He recommends selecting the $b_k$'s to generate the largest possible positive correlation between the single risk factor and the composite risk factors. That is, to maximize $\text{corr}(Y_i, \bar{Y})$.

To be rather more specific, this leads to the following constrained optimization problem:

$$\max_{b_1,\ldots,b_K} \sum_{i=1}^{N} \omega_i \overbrace{\underbrace{\sum_{k=1}^{K} \alpha_{ik} b_k}_{\text{corr}(Y_i,\bar{Y})}}^{\text{Eq. } 11.102}, \tag{11.109}$$

$$\text{subject to: } \sum_{k=1}^{K} b_k^2 = 1 \text{ (from Eq. 11.94).}$$

The role of the $\omega_i$'s is essentially to combine, or weight, the pairwise correlation coefficients between the single and multi-factor perspectives. This problem can be happily solved analytically using the method of Lagrange multipliers. If we formulate the associated Lagrangian, we have

$$\mathcal{L} = \sum_{i=1}^{N} \omega_i \sum_{k=1}^{K} \alpha_{ik} b_k - \lambda \left( \sum_{k=1}^{K} b_k^2 - 1 \right), \tag{11.110}$$

for $k = 1, \ldots, K$ and where $\lambda$ denotes the Lagrange multiplier. The first-order conditions are given by

$$\begin{aligned} \frac{\partial \mathcal{L}}{\partial b_k} &= \frac{\partial}{\partial b_k} \left( \sum_{i=1}^{N} \omega_i \sum_{k=1}^{K} \alpha_{ik} b_k - \lambda \left( \sum_{k=1}^{K} b_k^2 - 1 \right) \right), \\ &= \sum_{i=1}^{N} \omega_i \alpha_{ik} - 2\lambda b_k, \end{aligned} \tag{11.111}$$

[48] Indeed, if we could readily solve this problem, we wouldn't need the approximation in the first place.

for $k = 1, \ldots, K$. This, in turn, implies that for each $k$

$$b_k = \sum_{i=1}^{N} \frac{\omega_i \alpha_{ik}}{2\lambda}. \tag{11.112}$$

This is a good first step, but we need now to specify both $\lambda$ and the $\omega_i$'s. To determine the Lagrange multiplier, we differentiate the Lagrangian with respect to $\lambda$ as

$$\begin{aligned} \frac{\partial \mathcal{L}}{\partial \lambda} &= \frac{\partial}{\partial \lambda}\left(\sum_{i=1}^{N} \omega_i \sum_{k=1}^{K} \alpha_{ik} b_k - \lambda\left(\sum_{k=1}^{K} b_k^2 - 1\right)\right), \qquad (11.113)\\ &= \sum_{k=1}^{K} b_k^2 - 1. \end{aligned}$$

Setting this second condition to zero and plugging in our intermediate value of $b_k$ yields

$$\begin{aligned} \sum_{k=1}^{K}\left(\sum_{i=1}^{N} \frac{\omega_i \alpha_{ik}}{2\lambda}\right)^2 &= 1, \qquad (11.114)\\ \lambda &= \frac{1}{2}\sqrt{\sum_{k=1}^{K}\left(\sum_{i=1}^{N} \omega_i \alpha_{ik}\right)^2}. \end{aligned}$$

Introducing this back into our original quantity provides us with an estimate for each $b_k$ parameter

$$b_k = \frac{\sum_{i=1}^{N} \omega_i \alpha_{ik}}{\sqrt{\sum_{m=1}^{K}\left(\sum_{i=1}^{N} \omega_i \alpha_{im}\right)^2}}. \tag{11.115}$$

This leaves us with the thorny question of selecting the $\omega_i$'s. Pykhtin [27] suggests the following choice:

$$\begin{aligned} \omega_i &= c_i \bar{\gamma}_i \Phi\left(\frac{\Phi^{-1}(p_i) - r_i \Phi^{-1}(1-\alpha)}{\sqrt{1-r_i^2}}\right), \qquad (11.116)\\ &= \underbrace{c_i \bar{\gamma}_i \hat{p}_i\left(\Phi^{-1}(1-\alpha)\right)}_{\text{See Eq. 11.91}}, \end{aligned}$$

for $i = 1, \ldots, N$. This is essentially the conditional expected loss for the $i$th obligor given an adverse (i.e., $1 - \alpha$ confidence level) systemic risk-factor outcome. The final result is a fairly unwieldy, but entirely calculable expression for each of our $b_k$'s

$$b_k = \frac{\sum_{i=1}^{N} c_i \bar{\gamma}_i \hat{p}\left(\Phi^{-1}(1-\alpha)\right)\alpha_{ik}}{\sqrt{\sum_{m=1}^{K}\left(\sum_{i=1}^{N} c_i \bar{\gamma}_i \hat{p}\left(\Phi^{-1}(1-\alpha)\right)\alpha_{im}\right)^2}}. \tag{11.117}$$

Each $b_k$ parameter, therefore, is a function of the portfolio exposures, loss-given-defaults, systemic weights, and factor loadings. It is a complicated function of the expected loss of each credit obligor conditional on the underlying state variable being realized at an $\alpha$ level.

**Colour and Commentary 138** (CALIBRATING THE PYKHTIN [27] MODEL)*: To actually use any model, a practical strategy is required to determine its parameters. There are basically* five *groups of model coefficients: the* $r_i$*'s, the* $\alpha_{ik}$*'s, the* $\rho_i$*'s, the* $a_i$*'s and the* $b_k$*'s for* $i = 1, \ldots, N$ *credit obligors and* $k = 1, \ldots, K$ *systemic risk factors. The first two are given by the multi-factor model: the* $r_i$*'s and* $\alpha_{ik}$*'s represent its systemic weights and factor loadings, respectively. These are readily available; indeed, we discuss their estimation in Chap. 3. The* $\rho_i$ *coefficients represent the correlation between the single systemic risk factor,* $\bar{Y}$*, and Pykhtin [27]'s alternative representation of the one factor state variable. This is basically a stepping stone between the single- and multi-factor models. It turns out that the* $\rho_i$*'s are a function of the* $\alpha_{ik}$*'s and the* $b_k$*'s. The* $a_i$ *parameters are the systemic weights associated with the equivalent one-factor model. They can be written as a function of the* $r_i$*'s,* $\alpha_{ik}$*'s and the* $b_k$*'s. The only missing remaining unspecified piece, therefore, relates to the* $b_k$*'s; these are the (fixed) combination of the systemic system of risk factors* $\{Z_k; k = 1, \ldots, K\}$ *yielding the single-factor,* $\bar{Y}$*. As long as the constraints are preserved, any choice of* $b_k$*'s is possible. Practically, however, we wish to use this opportunity to bring the single- and multi-factor models maximally together. Pykhtin [27] thus suggests that the* $b_k$*'s are selected to generate the largest possible positive correlation between the single risk factor and the composite risk factors.*

(continued)

**Colour and Commentary 138** (continued)
*That is, to maximize* $\text{corr}(Y_i, \bar{Y})$. *This leads to a maximization problem and explicit closed-form expressions for the* $b_k$*'s. In many ways, this is the most important step in the practical implementation of Pykhtin [27]'s granularity adjustment.*

## Granularity Adjustment Revisited

We can now return to our Taylor-series expansion. Since we have imposed the condition that $\bar{L} = \mathbb{E}(L|\bar{Y})$, the first derivative vanishes. We saw the same result in the previously analyzed standard granularity adjustment. This allows us to describe our approximation as,

$$q_\alpha(L) - q_\alpha(\bar{L}) \approx \underbrace{-\frac{1}{2\cdot\phi(y)}\frac{\partial}{\partial y}\left(\frac{\phi(y)\nu(y)}{\mu'(y)}\right)\Bigg|_{y=\Phi^{-1}(1-\alpha)}}_{\text{Eq. 11.97}}, \tag{11.118}$$

$$\approx -\frac{1}{2}\left(\frac{1}{\mu'(y)}\left(\frac{\phi'(y)\nu(y)}{\phi(y)} + \nu'(y)\right) - \frac{\nu(y)\mu''(y)}{(\mu'(y))^2}\right)\Bigg|_{y=\Phi^{-1}(1-\alpha)},$$

which is precisely the same form as in Gordy and Lütkebohmert [15, 16]'s granularity adjustment. One important difference, however, is that in this case the density of the underlying latent risk factor follows a standard-normal Gaussian distribution; that is, $f(y) = \phi(y)$. We may cheerfully take advantage of the convenient fact that, for this specific density function, $\phi'(y) = -y\phi(y)$. This (again) allows us to practically eliminate the density component from this expression. It also permits a slight rearrangement of the terms to agree with Pykhtin [27]'s representation. This is a small point, but it turns out to be important in subsequent analysis when the approximation is decomposed into two distinct parts. The starting point is thus,

$$q_\alpha(L) - q_\alpha(\bar{L}) \approx -\frac{1}{2}\left(\frac{1}{\mu'(y)}\left(\frac{\overbrace{-y\cancel{\phi(y)}}^{\phi'(y)}\nu(y)}{\cancel{\phi(y)}} + \nu'(y)\right) - \frac{\nu(y)\mu''(y)}{(\mu'(y))^2}\right)\Bigg|_{y=\Phi^{-1}(1-\alpha)} \tag{11.119}$$

$$\mathcal{G}_\alpha(L) = -\frac{1}{2\mu'(y)}\left(\nu'(y) - \nu(y)\left(\frac{\mu''(y)}{\mu'(y)} + y\right)\right)\Bigg|_{y=\Phi^{-1}(1-\alpha)}.$$

Since we would like to use this method to perform practical computations, we now need to identify the individual characters in our approximation. Let us begin with the conditional loss term $\mu(y)$ and its derivatives. These are, with the exception of the revised density, identical to the standard CreditRisk+ based Gordy and Lütkebohmert [16] granularity adjustment. In particular, we have that

$$
\begin{aligned}
\mu(y) &= \mathbb{E}\left(L \mid \bar{Y} = y\right), \qquad (11.120)\\
&= \mathbb{E}\left(\sum_{i=1}^{N} c_i \gamma_i \mathbb{I}_{\mathcal{D}_i} \middle| \bar{Y} = y\right),\\
&= \sum_{i=1}^{N} c_i \bar{\gamma}_i \Phi\left(\frac{\Phi^{-1}(p_i) - a_i y}{\sqrt{1-a_i^2}}\right),\\
&= \sum_{i=1}^{N} c_i \bar{\gamma}_i p_i(y).
\end{aligned}
$$

As we've seen many times before, the conditional default loss is the sum of the exposure-weighted *conditional* default probabilities: $p_i(y)$ for $i = 1, \ldots, N$. What is new, however, is the need to evaluate both the first and second derivatives of this equation. The first derivative is,

$$
\begin{aligned}
\mu'(y) &= \frac{\partial}{\partial y}\left(\underbrace{\sum_{i=1}^{N} c_i \bar{\gamma}_i \Phi\left(\frac{\Phi^{-1}(p_i) - a_i y}{\sqrt{1-a_i^2}}\right)}_{\text{Eq. 11.120}}\right), \qquad (11.121)\\
&= -\sum_{i=1}^{N} c_i \bar{\gamma}_i \frac{a_i}{\sqrt{1-a_i^2}} \phi\left(\frac{\Phi^{-1}(p_i) - a_i y}{\sqrt{1-a_i^2}}\right),\\
&= -\sum_{i=1}^{N} c_i \bar{\gamma}_i \underbrace{\frac{a_i}{\sqrt{1-a_i^2}} \phi\left(\Phi^{-1}\left(p_i(y)\right)\right)}_{p_i'(y)}.
\end{aligned}
$$

The final line is a bit of shorthand. We have already defined the conditional default probability more succinctly as $p_i(y)$. If we only want the argument evaluated in the Gaussian cumulative distribution function in $p_i(y)$, we need merely apply the Gaussian quantile function. That is,

$$
\Phi^{-1}\left(p_i(y)\right) = \Phi^{-1}\left(\Phi\left(\frac{\Phi^{-1}(p_i) - a_i y}{\sqrt{1-a_i^2}}\right)\right), \qquad (11.122)
$$

$$= \frac{\Phi^{-1}(p_i) - a_i y}{\sqrt{1 - a_i^2}}.$$

This allows us to shorten some of our expressions and (happily) recycle existing computer code; it also makes the expressions slightly easier on the eyes.

The second derivative involves a tad more effort, but can ultimately be written as

$$\mu''(y) = \frac{\partial}{\partial y}\left(\underbrace{-\sum_{i=1}^{N} c_i \bar{\gamma}_i \frac{a_i}{\sqrt{1-a_i^2}} \phi\left(\frac{\Phi^{-1}(p_i) - a_i y}{\sqrt{1-a_i^2}}\right)}_{\text{Eq. 11.121}}\right), \tag{11.123}$$

$$= \frac{\partial}{\partial y}\left(-\sum_{i=1}^{N} c_i \bar{\gamma}_i \frac{a_i}{\sqrt{1-a_i^2}} \frac{1}{\sqrt{2\pi}} \exp\left(\frac{-\left(\frac{\Phi^{-1}(p_i)-a_i y}{\sqrt{1-a_i^2}}\right)^2}{2}\right)\right),$$

$$= -\sum_{i=1}^{N} c_i \bar{\gamma}_i \frac{a_i}{\sqrt{1-a_i^2}} \left(-\frac{a_i}{\sqrt{1-a_i^2}}\right)\left(-\frac{\Phi^{-1}(p_i) - a_i y}{\sqrt{1-a_i^2}}\right)$$

$$\frac{1}{\sqrt{2\pi}} \exp\left(\frac{-\left(\frac{\Phi^{-1}(p_i)-a_i y}{\sqrt{1-a_i^2}}\right)^2}{2}\right),$$

$$= -\sum_{i=1}^{N} c_i \bar{\gamma}_i \frac{a_i^2}{1-a_i^2} \frac{\Phi^{-1}(p_i) - a_i y}{\sqrt{1-a_i^2}} \phi\left(\frac{\Phi^{-1}(p_i) - a_i y}{\sqrt{1-a_i^2}}\right),$$

$$= -\sum_{i=1}^{N} c_i \bar{\gamma}_i \underbrace{\frac{a_i^2}{1-a_i^2} \Phi^{-1}\left(p_i(y)\right) \phi\Big(\Phi^{-1}\left(p_i(y)\right)\Big)}_{p_i''(y)}.$$

At this point, things start to deviate importantly from the standard Gordy and Lütkebohmert [16] granularity adjustment calculation. Let's begin with the usual form of the conditional variance of the default loss. Using similar ideas to those developed so far and exploiting the conditional independence of the default events, we have

$$\begin{aligned}\nu(y) &= \text{var}\left(L_i \,|\, \bar{Y} = y\right), \qquad (11.124)\\ &= \text{var}\left(\sum_{i=1}^{N} c_i \gamma_i \mathbb{I}_{\mathcal{D}_i} \,\middle|\, \bar{Y} = y\right),\\ &= \underbrace{\sum_{i=1}^{N} c_i^2 \text{var}\left(\gamma_i \mathbb{I}_{\mathcal{D}_i} \,|\, \bar{Y} = y\right)}_{\text{By independence}}.\end{aligned}$$

Although $\gamma_i$ and $\mathbb{I}_{\mathcal{D}_i}$ are independent, the variance of their product is not particularly easy to compute. It requires first removing the conditioning set, performing a few manipulations, and then adding it back. The consequence will be a more workable expression. This tedious operation begins with the first-principles definition of variance as

$$\text{var}\left(\gamma_i \mathbb{I}_{\mathcal{D}_i}\right) = \mathbb{E}\Big(\left(\gamma_i \mathbb{I}_{\mathcal{D}_i}\right)^2\Big) - \mathbb{E}\Big(\gamma_i \mathbb{I}_{\mathcal{D}_i}\Big)^2, \qquad (11.125)$$

$$\text{var}\left(\gamma_i \mathbb{I}_{\mathcal{D}_i} \,|\, \gamma_i\right) = \mathbb{E}\left(\left(\gamma_i \mathbb{I}_{\mathcal{D}_i}\right)^2 \,\middle|\, \gamma_i\right) - \mathbb{E}\left(\gamma_i \mathbb{I}_{\mathcal{D}_i} \,\middle|\, \gamma_i\right)^2,$$

$$\mathbb{E}\left(\left(\gamma_i \mathbb{I}_{\mathcal{D}_i}\right)^2 \,\middle|\, \gamma_i\right) = \text{var}\left(\gamma_i \mathbb{I}_{\mathcal{D}_i} \,|\, \gamma_i\right) + \mathbb{E}\left(\gamma_i \mathbb{I}_{\mathcal{D}_i} \,\middle|\, \gamma_i\right)^2,$$

$$\mathbb{E}\left(\mathbb{E}\left(\left(\gamma_i \mathbb{I}_{\mathcal{D}_i}\right)^2 \,\middle|\, \gamma_i\right)\right) = \underbrace{\mathbb{E}\left(\text{var}\left(\gamma_i \mathbb{I}_{\mathcal{D}_i} \,|\, \gamma_i\right) + \mathbb{E}\left(\gamma_i \mathbb{I}_{\mathcal{D}_i} \,\middle|\, \gamma_i\right)^2\right)}_{\text{Taking expectation of both sides}},$$

$$\underbrace{\mathbb{E}\Big(\left(\gamma_i \mathbb{I}_{\mathcal{D}_i}\right)^2\Big)}_{\substack{\text{By iterated}\\ \text{expectations}}} = \mathbb{E}\left(\text{var}\left(\gamma_i \mathbb{I}_{\mathcal{D}_i} \,|\, \gamma_i\right) + \mathbb{E}\left(\gamma_i \mathbb{I}_{\mathcal{D}_i} \,\middle|\, \gamma_i\right)^2\right),$$

$$\mathbb{E}\Big(\left(\gamma_i \mathbb{I}_{\mathcal{D}_i}\right)^2\Big) - \underbrace{\mathbb{E}(\gamma_i \mathbb{I}_{\mathcal{D}_i})^2}_{\substack{\text{Subtract from}\\ \text{both sides}}} = \mathbb{E}\left(\text{var}\left(\gamma_i \mathbb{I}_{\mathcal{D}_i} \,|\, \gamma_i\right) + \mathbb{E}\left(\gamma_i \mathbb{I}_{\mathcal{D}_i} \,\middle|\, \gamma_i\right)^2\right) - \underbrace{\mathbb{E}(\gamma_i \mathbb{I}_{\mathcal{D}_i})^2}_{\substack{\text{Subtract from}\\ \text{both sides}}},$$

$$\underbrace{\mathbb{E}\Big(\left(\gamma_i \mathbb{I}_{\mathcal{D}_i}\right)^2\Big) - \mathbb{E}(\gamma_i \mathbb{I}_{\mathcal{D}_i})^2}_{\text{var}(\gamma_i \mathbb{I}_{\mathcal{D}_i})} = \mathbb{E}\left(\text{var}\left(\gamma_i \mathbb{I}_{\mathcal{D}_i} \,|\, \gamma_i\right) + \mathbb{E}\left(\gamma_i \mathbb{I}_{\mathcal{D}_i} \,\middle|\, \gamma_i\right)^2\right) - \underbrace{\mathbb{E}\left(\mathbb{E}\left(\gamma_i \mathbb{I}_{\mathcal{D}_i} \,\middle|\, \gamma_i\right)\right)^2}_{\substack{\text{By iterated}\\ \text{expectations}}},$$

$$\text{var}(\gamma_i \mathbb{I}_{\mathcal{D}_i}) = \mathbb{E}\Big(\text{var}\left(\gamma_i \mathbb{I}_{\mathcal{D}_i} \,|\, \gamma_i\right)\Big) + \underbrace{\mathbb{E}\left(\mathbb{E}\left(\gamma_i \mathbb{I}_{\mathcal{D}_i} \,\middle|\, \gamma_i\right)^2\right) - \mathbb{E}\left(\mathbb{E}\left(\gamma_i \mathbb{I}_{\mathcal{D}_i} \,\middle|\, \gamma_i\right)\right)^2}_{\text{var}\left(\mathbb{E}\left(\gamma_i \mathbb{I}_{\mathcal{D}_i} | \gamma_i\right)\right)},$$

$$\text{var}(\gamma_i \mathbb{I}_{\mathcal{D}_i}) = \mathbb{E}\bigg(\text{var}\left(\gamma_i \mathbb{I}_{\mathcal{D}_i} \,\middle|\, \gamma_i\right)\bigg) + \text{var}\bigg(\mathbb{E}\left(\gamma_i \mathbb{I}_{\mathcal{D}_i} \,\middle|\, \gamma_i\right)\bigg),$$

$$\text{var}\left(\gamma_i \mathbb{I}_{\mathcal{D}_i} \,\middle|\, \bar{Y} = y\right) = \underbrace{\mathbb{E}\left(\text{var}\left(\gamma_i \mathbb{I}_{\mathcal{D}_i} \,\middle|\, \gamma_i\right) \middle| \bar{Y} = y\right) + \text{var}\left(\mathbb{E}\left(\gamma_i \mathbb{I}_{\mathcal{D}_i} \,\middle|\, \gamma_i\right) \middle| \bar{Y} = y\right)}_{\text{Reintroduce original conditioning information}}.$$

Thus after a significant amount of manipulation, we have an alternative expression for the conditional variance of the product of our (independent) loss-given-default and default-event variables. At this point, we can exploit the independence of these variables along with the conditioning information to, if not simplify, rearrange this expression into known quantities. In particular,

$$\begin{aligned}
&\text{var}\left(\gamma_i \mathbb{I}_{\mathcal{D}_i} \,\middle|\, \bar{Y} = y\right) \qquad (11.126)\\
&= \mathbb{E}\left(\gamma_i^2 \text{var}\left(\mathbb{I}_{\mathcal{D}_i} \,\middle|\, \gamma_i\right) \middle| \bar{Y} = y\right) + \text{var}\left(\gamma_i \mathbb{E}\left(\mathbb{I}_{\mathcal{D}_i} \,\middle|\, \gamma_i\right) \middle| \bar{Y} = y\right),\\
&= \mathbb{E}\left(\gamma_i^2 \text{var}\left(\mathbb{I}_{\mathcal{D}_i}\right) \middle| \bar{Y} = y\right) + \text{var}\left(\gamma_i \mathbb{E}\left(\mathbb{I}_{\mathcal{D}_i}\right) \middle| \bar{Y} = y\right),\\
&= \mathbb{E}\left(\gamma_i^2 \middle| \bar{Y} = y\right) \mathbb{E}\left(\text{var}\left(\mathbb{I}_{\mathcal{D}_i}\right) \middle| \bar{Y} = y\right) + \mathbb{E}\left(\mathbb{I}_{\mathcal{D}_i} \,\middle|\, \bar{Y} = y\right)^2 \text{var}\left(\gamma_i \middle| \bar{Y} = y\right),\\
&= \mathbb{E}\left(\gamma_i^2\right) \text{var}\left(\mathbb{I}_{\mathcal{D}_i} \,\middle|\, \bar{Y} = y\right) + \mathbb{E}\left(\mathbb{I}_{\mathcal{D}_i} \,\middle|\, \bar{Y} = y\right)^2 \text{var}\left(\gamma_i\right),\\
&= \underbrace{\left(\mathbb{E}\left(\gamma_i\right)^2 + \text{var}\left(\gamma_i\right)\right)}_{\mathbb{E}(\gamma_i^2)} \text{var}\left(\mathbb{I}_{\mathcal{D}_i} \,\middle|\, \bar{Y} = y\right) + \mathbb{E}\left(\mathbb{I}_{\mathcal{D}_i} \,\middle|\, \bar{Y} = y\right)^2 \text{var}\left(\gamma_i\right),\\
&= \mathbb{E}\left(\gamma_i\right)^2 \text{var}\left(\mathbb{I}_{\mathcal{D}_i} \,\middle|\, \bar{Y} = y\right) + \text{var}\left(\gamma_i\right) \text{var}\left(\mathbb{I}_{\mathcal{D}_i} \,\middle|\, \bar{Y} = y\right) + \mathbb{E}\left(\mathbb{I}_{\mathcal{D}_i} \,\middle|\, \bar{Y} = y\right)^2 \text{var}\left(\gamma_i\right),
\end{aligned}$$

which includes a number of familiar characters. Plugging this back into our original conditional variance expression, we arrive at

$$\begin{aligned}
&\nu(y) \qquad (11.127)\\
&= \overbrace{\sum_{i=1}^{N} c_i^2 \underbrace{\left(\mathbb{E}\left(\gamma_i\right)^2 \text{var}\left(\mathbb{I}_{\mathcal{D}_i} \,\middle|\, \bar{Y} = y\right) + \text{var}\left(\gamma_i\right) \text{var}\left(\mathbb{I}_{\mathcal{D}_i} \,\middle|\, \bar{Y} = y\right) + \mathbb{E}\left(\mathbb{I}_{\mathcal{D}_i} \,\middle|\, \bar{Y} = y\right)^2 \text{var}\left(\gamma_i\right)\right)}_{\text{Eq. 11.126}}}^{\text{Eq. 11.124}},\\
&= \sum_{i=1}^{N} c_i^2 \left(\bar{\gamma}_i^2 p_i(y)\left(1 - p_i(y)\right) + \nu_{\gamma_i} p_i(y)\left(1 - p_i(y)\right) + p_i(y)^2 \nu_{\gamma_i}\right),\\
&= \sum_{i=1}^{N} c_i^2 \left(\bar{\gamma}_i^2 \left(p_i(y) - p_i(y)^2\right) + \nu_{\gamma_i} p_i(y) - \cancel{p_i(y)^2 \nu_{\gamma_i}} + \cancel{p_i(y)^2 \nu_{\gamma_i}}\right),
\end{aligned}$$

$$
= \sum_{i=1}^{N} c_i^2 \left( \bar{\gamma}_i^2 \left( p_i(y) - p_i(y)^2 \right) + \nu_{\gamma_i} p_i(y) \right) \equiv \underbrace{\sum_{i=1}^{N} c_i^2 p_i(y) \left( \nu_{\gamma_i} + \bar{\gamma}_i^2 \left( 1 - p_i(y) \right) \right)}_{\substack{\text{Put aside for (future) comparison} \\ \text{to Eq. 11.149}}}.
$$

Finally, after a lengthy and wearisome computation, we have an expression for the conditional variance.[49] While interesting, and most definitely an important part of the foundation for future computations, this definition of conditional variance is *not* directly employed in the Pykhtin [27] model.

Very quickly, before we move on, and because it will prove interesting, we compute the first derivative of this (unused) version of conditional variance. It is given as,

$$
\begin{aligned}
\nu'(y) &= \frac{d}{dy} \left( \sum_{i=1}^{N} c_i^2 \left( \bar{\gamma}_i^2 \left( p_i(y) - p_i(y)^2 \right) + \nu_{\gamma_i} p_i(y) \right) \right), \qquad (11.128) \\
&= \sum_{i=1}^{N} c_i^2 \left( \bar{\gamma}_i^2 \left( p_i'(y) - 2p_i(y) p_i'(y) \right) + \nu_{\gamma_i} p_i'(y) \right), \\
&= \sum_{i=1}^{N} c_i^2 p_i'(y) \left( \bar{\gamma}_i^2 \left( 1 - 2p_i(y) \right) + \nu_{\gamma_i} \right).
\end{aligned}
$$

We will keep this mind when interpreting a key part of the final result proposed by Pykhtin [27].

Without perhaps realizing it, we have actually developed all of the formulae and machinery required for the computation of Gordy and Lütkebohmert [16]'s granularity adjustment in the one-factor Gaussian threshold model setting. Figure 11.7 collects all of the loose ends from the previous derivations and presents the final result. While perhaps not packaged as neatly as the construction in Fig. 11.6, this is nonetheless a legitimate Pillar II option for one's concentration adjustment. The remaining discussion in this section examines how Pykhtin [27] extends this basic construction to a more ambitious description of concentration effects.

### The Big Reveal

Pykhtin [27] does not seek to replicate the standard granularity adjustment. His objective is to incorporate both concentration and multi-factor effects. To achieve this difficult feat, Pykhtin [27] relies on the so-called law of total variance. Imagine

[49] The complexity of this result likely explains, at least in part, Gordy and Lütkebohmert [16]'s preference for use of the CreditRisk+ model in their granularity adjustment. Bolder [9, Chapter 6] considers the constant loss-given-default case of the one-factor, Gaussian threshold model; this relatively unrealistic choice nonetheless dramatically eases the mathematics.

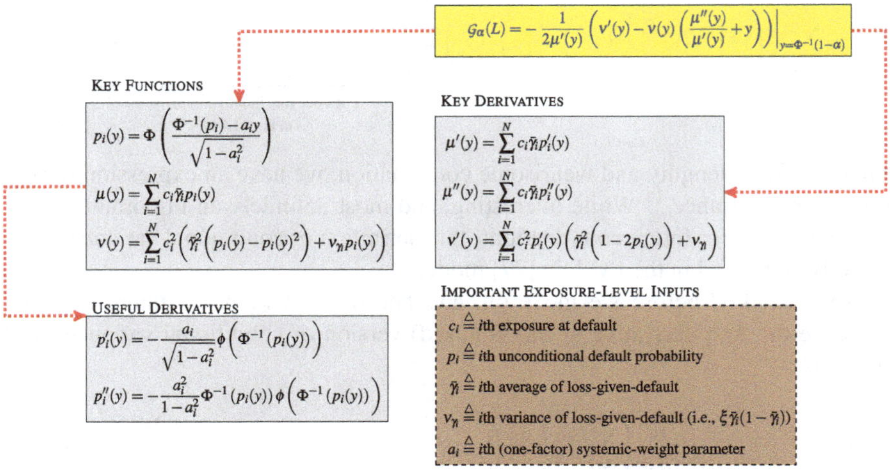


**Fig. 11.7** *Gaussian threshold granularity adjustment*: This schematic outlines, at a single glance, the principal formulae involved in Gordy and Lütkebohmert [16]'s granularity adjustment calculation. The key difference is that, in this case, it is applied to the one-factor Gaussian threshold model rather than the CreditRisk+ mixture approach from Fig. 11.6.

that we have two random variables, $X$ and $Y$. The law of total variance holds that[50]

$$\text{var}(X) = \mathbb{E}\bigg(\text{var}(X|Y)\bigg) + \text{var}\bigg(\mathbb{E}(X|Y)\bigg). \tag{11.129}$$

Pykhtin [27] essentially takes this one level deeper and adds a third conditioning variable; let's call it $Z$.[51] This leads to:

$$\text{var}(X|Z) = \underbrace{\text{var}\left(\mathbb{E}(X|Y)\bigg| Z\right)}_{\substack{\text{Explained (systemic)}\\ \text{component}}} + \underbrace{\mathbb{E}\left(\text{var}(X|Y)\bigg| Z\right)}_{\substack{\text{Unexplained (idiosyncratic)}\\ \text{component}}}. \tag{11.130}$$

In practical statistical applications—when, for example, one is decomposing variance—these two components are often referred to as the explained and unexplained components. Linking this back to finance theory, we cannot escape the systemic or explained component, but as the portfolio tends to infinite granularity,

[50] This is a well-known result in probability theory. For more on this idea, see Durrett [11, Section 4.1, Exercise 1.9]. Indeed, the attentive reader will have noticed that we have already derived it, from first principles, during the construction of $\nu(\cdot)$ in Eq. 11.125.

[51] Of course, as is typical in finance applications, we are being rather loose with the notion of conditioning set. More technically, we are conditioning on the $\sigma$-algebra generated by $Z$ or $\sigma\{Z\}$.

the idiosyncratic element can be diversified away. This foreshadows their respective role in describing the multi-factor and concentration effects.

Application of this idea to the conditional variance arising in this problem, $\nu(\cdot)$, leads to the following very important decomposition:

$$\underbrace{\operatorname{var}(L|\bar{Y}=y)}_{\nu(y)} = \underbrace{\operatorname{var}\left(\mathbb{E}(L|\{Z_k\})\middle|\bar{Y}=y\right)}_{\nu_\infty(y)} + \underbrace{\mathbb{E}\left(\operatorname{var}(L|\{Z_k\})\middle|\bar{Y}=y\right)}_{\nu_{\mathcal{G}}(y)}, \tag{11.131}$$

where $\nu_\infty(y)$ and $\nu_{\mathcal{G}}(y)$ denote the conditional variance associated with the multi-factor and concentration effects, respectively.

If we plug this decomposition into our originally derived approximation, this yields

$$q_\alpha(L) - q_\alpha(\bar{L}) \approx \overbrace{-\frac{1}{2\mu'(y)}\left(\underbrace{\left(\nu'_\infty(y)+\nu'_{\mathcal{G}}(y)\right)}_{\nu'(y)} - \underbrace{\left(\nu_\infty(y)+\nu_{\mathcal{G}}(y)\right)}_{\nu(y)}\left(\frac{\mu''(y)}{\mu'(y)}+y\right)\right)}^{\text{Eq. 11.119}}\Bigg|_{y=\Phi^{-1}(1-\alpha)}, \tag{11.132}$$

$$\mathcal{G}_\alpha(L) = -\frac{1}{2\mu'(y)}\left[\underbrace{\left(\nu'_\infty(y)-\nu_\infty(y)\left(\frac{\mu''(y)}{\mu'(y)}+y\right)\right)}_{\text{Multi-factor component}} - \underbrace{\left(\nu'_{\mathcal{G}}(y)-\nu_{\mathcal{G}}(y)\left(\frac{\mu''(y)}{\mu'(y)}+y\right)\right)}_{\text{Concentration component}}\right]\Bigg|_{y=\Phi^{-1}(1-\alpha)},$$

which explains why it was important to re-arrange and isolate the conditional variance terms. This is possible due to the linearity of the original decomposition and the linear properties of first derivatives. Pykhtin [27] refers to this as the quantile correction or multi-factor adjustment.

**Colour and Commentary 139** (VARIANCE DECOMPOSITION)*: The "reveal" is a literary term used to describe when a piece of information, critical to a book or play or movie's plot, is finally exposed to the audience or reader. Pykhtin [27]'s big reveal stems from an astute application of the law of total variance. He uses this well-known variance decomposition method to place the conditional variance of credit loss into two categories: systemic and idiosyncratic components. The idiosyncratic element is broadly consistent with the usual concentration adjustment. As the portfolio tends to infinite granularity, it will tend to zero. The systemic component, however, cannot be diversified away. Moreover, since single- and multi-factor models use alternative approaches to describe the nature of systemic risk, this component captures the multivariate dimension. The linearity of this breakdown and*

(continued)

**Colour and Commentary 139** (continued)
*its derivatives also permit the maintenance of the linear form of this add-on. Each effect can be computed and measured separately. Their relative magnitude is an interesting empirical question.*

### The Drudgery

The final task, before we can actually implement this approximation, is to determine the specific form of our conditional variance terms and their first derivatives. This turns out, rather unfortunately but not terribly surprisingly, to be a relatively unpleasant undertaking. Simply put, it is mathematical drudgery. It should perhaps be relegated to an appendix, but it is included here to appease our intense aversion to black boxes.

The first step is to find an alternative expression for $X_i$, our original multi-factor composite state variable, in terms of Pykhtin [27]'s alternative representation of the systemic state variable. This amounts to,

$$
\begin{aligned}
X_i &= r_i Y_i + \sqrt{1-r_i^2}\xi_i, \qquad (11.133)\\
&= r_i \underbrace{\left(\rho_i \bar{Y} + \sqrt{1-\rho_i^2}\eta_i\right)}_{\substack{\text{Alternative representation}\\ \text{of } Y_i = \sum_{k=1}^K \alpha_{ik} Z_k}} + \sqrt{1-r_i^2}\xi_i,\\
&= r_i\rho_i\bar{Y} + r_i\sqrt{1-\rho_i^2}\eta_i + \sqrt{1-r_i^2}\xi_i,\\
&= \underbrace{r_i\rho_i}_{a_i}\bar{Y} + r_i\cancel{\sqrt{1-\rho_i^2}}\underbrace{\left(\frac{Y_i-\rho_i\bar{Y}}{\cancel{\sqrt{1-\rho_i^2}}}\right)}_{\eta_i} + \sqrt{1-r_i^2}\xi_i,\\
&= a_i\bar{Y} + r_i\left(Y_i - \rho_i\bar{Y}\right) + \sqrt{1-r_i^2}\xi_i,\\
&= a_i\bar{Y} + r_i\underbrace{\sum_{k=1}^K \alpha_{ik}Z_k}_{Y_i} - \underbrace{r_i\rho_i}_{a_i}\underbrace{\sum_{k=1}^K b_k Z_k}_{\bar{Y}} + \sqrt{1-r_i^2}\xi_i,\\
&= a_i\bar{Y} + \sum_{k=1}^K\left(r_i\alpha_{ik} - a_i b_k\right)Z_k + \sqrt{1-r_i^2}\xi_i.
\end{aligned}
$$

It is perhaps tempting to conclude that this is yet another manipulation of definitions. It is not. It turns out to be an essential component of computing the asset correlation between any two credit obligors. To see this, let's first determine the conditional expectation and variance (given $\bar{Y}$) of this revised version of $X_i$. The expectation is given as,

$$\begin{aligned}
\mathbb{E}(X_i|\bar{Y}) &= \mathbb{E}\left(a_i\bar{Y} + \sum_{k=1}^{K}\left(r_i\alpha_{ik} - a_ib_k\right)Z_k + \sqrt{1-r_i^2}\xi_i \,\middle|\, \bar{Y}\right), \qquad (11.134)\\
&= \mathbb{E}\left(a_i\bar{Y}|\,\bar{Y}\right) + \sum_{k=1}^{K}\left(r_i\alpha_{ik} - a_ib_k\right)\underbrace{\mathbb{E}\left(Z_k|\,\bar{Y}\right)}_{=0} + \sqrt{1-r_i^2}\,\underbrace{\mathbb{E}\left(\xi_i\,|\,\bar{Y}\right)}_{=0},\\
&= a_i\bar{Y},
\end{aligned}$$

while the conditional variance is

$$\begin{aligned}
\text{var}(X_i|\bar{Y}) &= \text{var}\left(a_i\bar{Y} + \sum_{k=1}^{K}\left(r_i\alpha_{ik} - a_ib_k\right)Z_k + \sqrt{1-r_i^2}\xi_i \,\middle|\, \bar{Y}\right), \qquad (11.135)\\
&= a_i^2\underbrace{\text{var}\left(\bar{Y}|\,\bar{Y}\right)}_{=0} + \text{var}\left(\sum_{k=1}^{K}\left(r_i\alpha_{ik} - a_ib_k\right)Z_k \,\middle|\, \bar{Y}\right) + (1-r_i^2)\underbrace{\text{var}\left(\xi_i\,|\,\bar{Y}\right)}_{=1},\\
&= \sum_{k=1}^{K}\left(r_i\alpha_{ik} - a_ib_k\right)^2\underbrace{\text{var}\left(Z_k|\,\bar{Y}\right)}_{=1} + (1-r_i^2),\\
&= \sum_{k=1}^{K}\left(r_i^2\alpha_{ik}^2 - 2a_ir_i\alpha_{ik}b_k + a_i^2b_k^2\right) + (1-r_i^2),\\
&= r_i^2\underbrace{\sum_{k=1}^{K}\alpha_{ik}^2}_{=1} - 2a_i\,r_i\underbrace{\sum_{k=1}^{K}\alpha_{ik}b_k}_{a_i} + a_i^2\underbrace{\sum_{k=1}^{K}b_k^2}_{=1} + (1-r_i^2),\\
&= \cancel{r_i^2} - 2a_i^2 + a_i^2 + 1 - \cancel{r_i^2},\\
&= 1 - a_i^2.
\end{aligned}$$

The consequence is that $X_i \sim \mathcal{N}(a_i\bar{Y}, 1-a_i^2)$.

Now we have the various pieces required to compute the correlation between the composite latent state variables of two arbitrarily selected credit obligors, $i$ and $j$.

Let us begin with the covariance term:

$$
\begin{aligned}
\operatorname{cov}\left(X_i, X_j \middle| \bar{Y}\right) &= \mathbb{E}\left(\left(X_i - \mathbb{E}(X_i)\right)\left(X_j - \mathbb{E}(X_j)\right)\middle| \bar{Y}\right), \\
&= \mathbb{E}\left(X_i X_j \middle| \bar{Y}\right) - \mathbb{E}\left(X_i \middle| \bar{Y}\right)\mathbb{E}\left(X_j \middle| \bar{Y}\right), \\
&= \mathbb{E}\left(X_i X_j \middle| \bar{Y}\right) - a_i a_j \mathbb{E}\left(\bar{Y}^2 \middle| \bar{Y}\right), \\
&= \mathbb{E}\left(X_i X_j \middle| \bar{Y}\right) - a_i a_j \mathbb{E}\left(\underbrace{\left(\sum_{k=1}^{K} b_k Z_k\right)^2}_{\bar{Y}^2} \middle| \bar{Y}\right), \\
&= \mathbb{E}\left(X_i X_j \middle| \bar{Y}\right) - a_i a_j \sum_{k=1}^{K} b_k^2 \underbrace{\mathbb{E}\left(Z_k \middle| \bar{Y}\right)}_{=\operatorname{var}(Z_k)=1}, \\
&= \mathbb{E}\left(X_i X_j \middle| \bar{Y}\right) - a_i a_j \underbrace{\sum_{k=1}^{K} b_k^2}_{=1}, \\
&= \mathbb{E}\left(X_i X_j \middle| \bar{Y}\right) - a_i a_j.
\end{aligned}
\tag{11.136}
$$

The first term on the right-hand side merits special attention.

$$
\begin{aligned}
&\mathbb{E}\left(X_i X_j \middle| \bar{Y}\right) \\
&= \mathbb{E}\left(\prod_{n=i,j} \underbrace{\left(a_n \bar{Y} + \sum_{k=1}^{K}\left(r_n \alpha_{nk} - a_n b_k\right) Z_k + \sqrt{1 - r_n^2}\xi_n\right)}_{\text{Eq. 11.133}} \middle| \bar{Y}\right), \\
&= \mathbb{E}\Bigg(a_i a_j \bar{Y}^2 + a_i \bar{Y}\sum_{k=1}^{K}\left(r_j \alpha_{jk} - a_j b_k\right) Z_k + a_j \bar{Y}\sum_{k=1}^{K}\left(r_i \alpha_{ik} - a_i b_k\right) Z_k \\
&\quad + \prod_{n=i,j}\sum_{k=1}^{K}\left(r_n \alpha_{nk} - a_n b_k\right) Z_k \Bigg| \bar{Y}\Bigg), \\
&= a_i a_j \bar{Y}^2 + \mathbb{E}\left(a_i \bar{Y}\left(r_j \underbrace{\sum_{k=1}^{K}\alpha_{jk} Z_k}_{Y_j} - a_j \underbrace{\sum_{k=1}^{K} b_k Z_k}_{\bar{Y}}\right) + a_j \bar{Y}\left(r_i \underbrace{\sum_{k=1}^{K}\alpha_{ik} Z_k}_{Y_i} - a_i \underbrace{\sum_{k=1}^{K} b_k Z_k}_{\bar{Y}}\right) \middle| \bar{Y}\right)
\end{aligned}
\tag{11.137}
$$

$$
\begin{aligned}
&+\mathbb{E}\left(\prod_{n=i,j}\left(r_n \underbrace{\sum_{k=1}^{K}\alpha_{nk}Z_k}_{Y_n} - a_n \underbrace{\sum_{k=1}^{K} b_k Z_k}_{\bar{Y}}\right)\middle|\,\bar{Y}\right),\\
&= \cancel{a_i a_j \bar{Y}^2} + \mathbb{E}\left(a_i r_j \bar{Y} Y_j - \cancel{a_i a_j \bar{Y}^2} + a_j r_i \bar{Y} Y_i - a_i a_j \bar{Y}^2 + \prod_{n=i,j}\sum_{k=1}^{K}\left(r_n Y_n - a_n \bar{Y}\right)\middle|\,\bar{Y}\right),\\
&= \mathbb{E}\left(a_i r_j \bar{Y} Y_j + a_j r_i \bar{Y} Y_i - a_i a_j \bar{Y}^2 + \left(r_i Y_i - a_i \bar{Y}\right)\left(r_j Y_j - a_j \bar{Y}\right)\middle|\,\bar{Y}\right),\\
&= \mathbb{E}\left(\cancel{a_i r_j \bar{Y} Y_j} + \cancel{a_j r_i \bar{Y} Y_i} - \cancel{a_i a_j \bar{Y}^2} + \left(r_i r_j Y_i Y_j - \cancel{a_j r_i Y_i \bar{Y}} - \cancel{a_i r_j Y_j \bar{Y}} + \cancel{a_i a_j \bar{Y}^2}\right)\middle|\,\bar{Y}\right),\\
&= r_i r_j \mathbb{E}\left(\underbrace{\left(\sum_{k=1}^{K}\alpha_{ik}Z_k\right)}_{Y_i}\underbrace{\left(\sum_{k=1}^{K}\alpha_{jk}Z_k\right)}_{Y_j}\middle|\,\bar{Y}\right),\\
&= r_i r_j \sum_{k=1}^{K}\alpha_{ik}\alpha_{jk}\underbrace{\mathbb{E}\left(Z_k^2\,\middle|\,\bar{Y}\right)}_{=\text{var}(Z_k)=1},\\
&= r_i r_j \sum_{k=1}^{K}\alpha_{ik}\alpha_{jk}.
\end{aligned}
$$

Pulling all of the pieces together finally gets us to the desired conditional correlation coefficient. It is given as

$$
\begin{aligned}
\underbrace{\text{corr}\left(X_i, X_j \,\middle|\, \bar{Y}\right)}_{\rho_{ij}} &= \frac{\text{cov}\left(X_i, X_j \,\middle|\, \bar{Y}\right)}{\sqrt{\text{var}(X_i|\bar{Y})}\sqrt{\text{var}(X_j|\bar{Y})}}, \qquad (11.138)\\
\rho_{ij} &= \frac{r_i r_j \displaystyle\sum_{k=1}^{K}\alpha_{ik}\alpha_{jk} - a_i a_j}{\sqrt{1-a_i^2}\sqrt{1-a_j^2}}.
\end{aligned}
$$

This gives us the necessary pieces to find concrete expressions for the two elements of conditional variance. Beginning with the systemic component, we have

$$
\nu_\infty(y) = \underbrace{\text{var}\left(\mathbb{E}(L|\{Z_k\})\,\middle|\,\bar{Y} = y\right)}_{\text{First term of Eq. 11.131}}, \qquad (11.139)
$$

$$
\begin{aligned}
&= \text{var}\left(\sum_{i=1}^{N} c_i\bar{\gamma}_i\mathbb{E}\left(\mathbb{I}_{\{X_i\leq\Phi^{-1}(p_i)\}}\Big|\{Z_k\}\right)\Bigg|\bar{Y}=y\right),\\
&= \sum_{i=1}^{N}\sum_{j=1}^{N} c_ic_j\bar{\gamma}_i\bar{\gamma}_j \underbrace{\text{cov}\left(\mathbb{E}\left(\mathbb{I}_{\{X_i\leq\Phi^{-1}(p_i)\}}\Big|\{Z_k\}\right),\mathbb{E}\left(\mathbb{I}_{\{X_j\leq\Phi^{-1}(p_j)\}}\Big|\{Z_k\}\right)\Big|\bar{Y}=y\right)}_{\mathcal{X}}.
\end{aligned}
$$

This leads us to the fairly nasty looking covariance term. To ease the notation when deriving this term, let's define $H_i = \mathbb{I}_{\{X_i\leq\Phi^{-1}(p_i)\}}$. This allows us to write our covariance term (reasonably succinctly) as

$$
\mathcal{X} = \mathbb{E}\left(\Big(\mathbb{E}\left(H_i|\{Z_k\}\right)-\mathbb{E}(\mathbb{E}\left(H_i|\{Z_k\}\right))\Big)\Big(\mathbb{E}\left(H_j|\{Z_k\}\right)-\mathbb{E}\left(\mathbb{E}\left(H_j|\{Z_k\}\right)\right)\Big)\Big|\bar{Y}=y\right), \tag{11.140}
$$

$$
\begin{aligned}
&= \mathbb{E}\left(\Big(\mathbb{E}\left(H_i|\{Z_k\}\right)-\mathbb{E}(H_i)\Big)\Big(\mathbb{E}\left(H_j|\{Z_k\}\right)-\mathbb{E}\left(H_j\right)\Big)\Big|\bar{Y}=y\right),\\
&= \mathbb{E}\Big(\mathbb{E}\left(H_i|\{Z_k\}\right)\mathbb{E}\left(H_j|\{Z_k\}\right)-\mathbb{E}\left(H_i|\{Z_k\}\right)\mathbb{E}\left(H_j\right)-\mathbb{E}\left(H_j|\{Z_k\}\right)\mathbb{E}(H_i)\\
&\qquad +\mathbb{E}(H_i)\mathbb{E}\left(H_j\right)\Big|\bar{Y}=y\Big),\\
&= \mathbb{E}\left(\mathbb{E}\left(H_iH_j|\{Z_k\}\right)-\mathbb{E}\left(H_i|\{Z_k\}\right)\mathbb{E}\left(H_j\right)-\mathbb{E}\left(H_j|\{Z_k\}\right)\mathbb{E}(H_i)+\mathbb{E}(H_i)\mathbb{E}\left(H_j\right)\Big|\bar{Y}=y\right),\\
&= \mathbb{E}\left(H_iH_j|\bar{Y}=y\right)-\mathbb{E}\left(H_i|\bar{Y}=y\right)\mathbb{E}\left(H_j|\bar{Y}=y\right)-\cancel{\mathbb{E}\left(H_j|\bar{Y}=y\right)\mathbb{E}\left(H_i|\bar{Y}=y\right)}\\
&\qquad \cancel{+\mathbb{E}\left(H_i|\bar{Y}=y\right)\mathbb{E}\left(H_j|\bar{Y}=y\right)},\\
&= \mathbb{E}\left(\mathbb{I}_{\{X_i\leq\Phi^{-1}(p_i)\}}\mathbb{I}_{\{X_j\leq\Phi^{-1}(p_j)\}}\Big|\bar{Y}=y\right)\\
&\qquad -\underbrace{\mathbb{E}\left(\mathbb{I}_{\{X_i\leq\Phi^{-1}(p_i)\}}\Big|\bar{Y}=y\right)}_{p_i(y)}\underbrace{\mathbb{E}\left(\mathbb{I}_{\{X_j\leq\Phi^{-1}(p_j)\}}\Big|\bar{Y}=y\right)}_{p_j(y)},\\
&= \mathbb{P}\left(\{X_i\leq\Phi^{-1}(p_i)\}\cap\{X_j\leq\Phi^{-1}(p_j)\}\Big|\bar{Y}=y\right)-p_i(y)p_j(y),\\
&= \mathbb{P}\left(\left\{\xi_i\leq\underbrace{\frac{\Phi^{-1}(p_i)-a_iy}{\sqrt{1-a_i^2}}}_{\Phi^{-1}(p_i(y))}\right\}\bigcap\left\{\xi_j\leq\underbrace{\frac{\Phi^{-1}(p_j)-a_jy}{\sqrt{1-a_j^2}}}_{\Phi^{-1}(p_j(y))}\right\}\right)-p_i(y)p_j(y),\\
&= \mathbb{P}\Big(\left\{\xi_i\leq\Phi^{-1}(p_i(y))\right\}\cap\left\{\xi_j\leq\Phi^{-1}(p_j(y))\right\}\Big)-p_i(y)p_j(y).
\end{aligned}
$$

This is progress. The final stumbling block is the first joint probability term. This is, of course, the joint conditional probability of default; or rather the probability of simultaneous occurrence of both default events: $\mathcal{D}_i$ and $\mathcal{D}_j$. In the

Gaussian threshold model, this is conveniently characterized by the bivariate normal distribution. It has the following specific form,

$$\begin{aligned}\mathbb{P}\left(\mathcal{D}_i \cap \mathcal{D}_j \middle| \bar{Y} = y\right) &= \mathbb{P}\Big(\xi_i \leq \Phi^{-1}(p_i(y)), \xi_j \leq \Phi^{-1}(p_j(y))\Big), \qquad (11.141)\\ &= \int_{-\infty}^{\Phi^{-1}(p_i(y))}\int_{-\infty}^{\Phi^{-1}(p_j(y))} \frac{1}{2\pi\sqrt{1-\rho_{ij}^2}} e^{-\frac{\left(u^2-2\rho_{ij}uv+v^2\right)}{2(1-\rho_{ij}^2)}} dv du,\\ &= \Phi\Big(\Phi^{-1}(p_i(y)), \Phi^{-1}(p_j(y)); \rho_{ij}\Big).\end{aligned}$$

This value is easily and directly computed using numerical integration. Collecting all of these pieces together, the conditional variance of the systemic component is written as

$$\nu_\infty(y) = \sum_{i=1}^N \sum_{j=1}^N c_i c_j \bar{\gamma}_i \bar{\gamma}_j \underbrace{\left(\Phi\Big(\Phi^{-1}(p_i(y)), \Phi^{-1}(p_j(y)); \rho_{ij}\Big) - p_i(y)p_j(y)\right)}_{\text{Eqs. 11.140 and 11.141}}. \qquad (11.142)$$

This then brings us to the next step: calculation of the first derivative of the systemic aspect of conditional variance with respect to $y$. This is, to be blunt, rather a handful.

$$\nu'_\infty(y) = \frac{d}{dy}\left(\underbrace{\sum_{i=1}^N \sum_{j=1}^N c_i c_j \bar{\gamma}_i \bar{\gamma}_j \left(\Phi\Big(\Phi^{-1}(p_i(y)), \Phi^{-1}(p_j(y)); \rho_{ij}\Big) - p_i(y)p_j(y)\right)}_{\text{Eq. 11.142}}\right), \qquad (11.143)$$

$$= \sum_{i=1}^N \sum_{j=1}^N c_i c_j \bar{\gamma}_i \bar{\gamma}_j \left(\underbrace{\frac{d}{dy}\left(\Phi\Big(\Phi^{-1}(p_i(y)), \Phi^{-1}(p_j(y)); \rho_{ij}\Big)\right)}_{\mathcal{A}} - \underbrace{\frac{d}{dy}\Big(p_i(y)p_j(y)\Big)}_{\mathcal{B}}\right).$$

This is sufficiently messy that it will be necessary to divide and conquer by separately handling each of the $\mathcal{A}$ and $\mathcal{B}$ components of the previous expression. As will become obvious in a moment, $y$ enters into the bivariate density through both arguments of the double integral. This implies that there are two derivatives to resolve:

$$\mathcal{A} = \mathcal{A}_i + \mathcal{A}_j, \qquad (11.144)$$

$$
= \underbrace{\frac{d}{dy}\left(\Phi\left(\Phi^{-1}(p_i(y)), \Phi^{-1}(p_j(y)); \rho_{ij}\right)\right)}_{\mathcal{A}_i}
$$

$$
+ \underbrace{\frac{d}{dy}\left(\Phi\left(\Phi^{-1}(p_j(y)), \Phi^{-1}(p_i(y)); \rho_{ij}\right)\right)}_{\mathcal{A}_j}.
$$

Let's begin with the first term and, since they are symmetric, this will be sufficient to specify both. In particular,

$$
\begin{aligned}
\mathcal{A}_i &= \frac{d}{dy}\left(\Phi\left(\Phi^{-1}(p_i(y)), \Phi^{-1}(p_j(y)); \rho_{ij}\right)\right), \qquad (11.145)\\
&= \frac{d}{dy}\left(\underbrace{\int_{-\infty}^{\Phi^{-1}(p_i(y))}\int_{-\infty}^{\Phi^{-1}(p_j(y))}\frac{1}{2\pi\sqrt{1-\rho_{ij}^2}}e^{-\frac{\left(u^2-2\rho_{ij}uv+v^2\right)}{2(1-\rho_{ij}^2)}}dvdu}_{\text{Eq. 11.141}}\right),\\
&= \left(\int_{-\infty}^{\Phi^{-1}(p_j(y))}\frac{1}{2\pi\sqrt{1-\rho_{ij}^2}}e^{-\frac{\left(\Phi^{-1}(p_i(y))^2-2\rho_{ij}\Phi^{-1}(p_i(y))v+v^2\right)}{2(1-\rho_{ij}^2)}}dv\right)\frac{d}{dy}\left(\Phi^{-1}(p_i(y))\right),\\
&= \left(\int_{-\infty}^{\Phi^{-1}(p_j(y))}\frac{1}{2\pi\sqrt{1-\rho_{ij}^2}}e^{-\frac{\left(\Phi^{-1}(p_i(y))^2-2\rho_{ij}\Phi^{-1}(p_i(y))v+v^2+\Phi^{-1}(p_i(y))^2\rho_{ij}^2-\Phi^{-1}(p_i(y))^2\rho_{ij}^2\right)}{2(1-\rho_{ij}^2)}}dv\right)\\
&\quad\times\frac{d}{dy}\left(\frac{\Phi^{-1}(p_i)-a_iy}{\sqrt{1-a_i^2}}\right),\\
&= \left(\int_{-\infty}^{\phi\left(\Phi^{-1}(p_j(y))\right)}\frac{1}{2\pi\sqrt{1-\rho_{ij}^2}}e^{-\frac{\Phi^{-1}(p_i(y))^2\cancel{(1-\rho_{ij}^2)}}{2\cancel{(1-\rho_{ij}^2)}}-\frac{\left(v-\rho_{ij}\Phi^{-1}(p_i(y))\right)^2}{2(1-\rho_{ij}^2)}}dv\right)\left(-\frac{a_i}{\sqrt{1-a_i^2}}\right),\\
&= \underbrace{\left(\frac{1}{\sqrt{2\pi}}e^{-\frac{\Phi^{-1}(p_i(y))^2}{2}}\right)}_{\phi\left(\Phi^{-1}(p_i(y))\right)}\underbrace{\left(\int_{-\infty}^{\frac{\Phi^{-1}(p_j(y))-\rho_{ij}\Phi^{-1}(p_i(y))}{\sqrt{1-\rho_{ij}^2}}}\frac{1}{\sqrt{2\pi}}e^{-\frac{v^2}{2}}dv\right)}_{\Phi\left(\frac{\Phi^{-1}(p_j(y))-\rho_{ij}\Phi^{-1}(p_i(y))}{\sqrt{1-\rho_{ij}^2}}\right)}\left(-\frac{a_i}{\sqrt{1-a_i^2}}\right),
\end{aligned}
$$

$$
\begin{aligned}
&= \Phi\left(\frac{\Phi^{-1}(p_j(y)) - \rho_{ij}\Phi^{-1}(p_i(y))}{\sqrt{1-\rho_{ij}^2}}\right)\underbrace{\left(-\frac{a_i}{\sqrt{1-a_i^2}}\phi\Big(\Phi^{-1}(p_i(y))\Big)\right)}_{p_i'(y)},\\
&= \underbrace{\Phi\left(\frac{\Phi^{-1}(p_j(y)) - \rho_{ij}\Phi^{-1}(p_i(y))}{\sqrt{1-\rho_{ij}^2}}\right)}_{\Phi_{ji}(y)} p_i'(y).
\end{aligned}
$$

This settles the first part. It immediately implies that

$$
\begin{aligned}
\mathcal{A} &= \underbrace{\overbrace{\Phi\left(\frac{\Phi^{-1}(p_j(y)) - \rho_{ij}\Phi^{-1}(p_i(y))}{\sqrt{1-\rho_{ij}^2}}\right)}^{\Phi_{ji}(y)} p_i'(y)}_{\mathcal{A}_i} \qquad (11.146)\\
&\quad + \underbrace{\overbrace{\Phi\left(\frac{\Phi^{-1}(p_i(y)) - \rho_{ij}\Phi^{-1}(p_j(y))}{\sqrt{1-\rho_{ij}^2}}\right)}^{\Phi_{ij}(y)} p_j'(y)}_{\mathcal{A}_j}.
\end{aligned}
$$

The second piece is easily resolved as

$$
\begin{aligned}
\mathcal{B} &= \frac{d}{dy}\Big(p_i(y)p_j(y)\Big), \qquad (11.147)\\
&= p_i'(y)p_j(y) + p_i(y)p_j'(y),
\end{aligned}
$$

This leads to the final result as,

$$
\begin{aligned}
\nu_\infty'(y) &= \sum_{i=1}^{N}\sum_{j=1}^{N} c_i c_j \bar{\gamma}_i\bar{\gamma}_j\,(\mathcal{A}-\mathcal{B}), \qquad (11.148)\\
&= \sum_{i=1}^{N}\sum_{j=1}^{N} c_i c_j \bar{\gamma}_i\bar{\gamma}_j\left(p_i'(y)\Big(\Phi_{ji}(y) - p_j(y)\Big) + p_j'(y)\Big(\Phi_{ij}(y) - p_i(y)\Big)\right),\\
&= \underbrace{2\sum_{i=1}^{N}\sum_{j=1}^{N} c_i c_j \bar{\gamma}_i\bar{\gamma}_j p_i'(y)\Big(\Phi_{ji}(y) - p_j(y)\Big)}_{\text{By symmetry}},
\end{aligned}
$$

where the final step, in this exhausting calculation, stems from the symmetry of the problem and the double summation.[52]

This brings us to the second component of our conditional variance decomposition. We need to recall that $\sigma\{\bar{Y}\} \subset \sigma\{Z_k\}$ and, in the memorable words of Durrett [11], "the smaller $\sigma$-field always wins."

$$
\begin{aligned}
\nu_{\mathcal{G}}(y) &= \underbrace{\mathbb{E}\left(\operatorname{var}(L|\{Z_k\})\middle| \bar{Y} = y\right)}_{\text{Second term of Eq. 11.131}}, \qquad (11.149)\\
&= \mathbb{E}\left(\operatorname{var}\left(\sum_{i=1}^{N} c_i \gamma_i \mathbb{I}_{D_i} |\{Z_k\}\right)\middle| \bar{Y} = y\right),\\
&= \mathbb{E}\left(\sum_{i=1}^{N} c_i^2 \operatorname{var}\left(\gamma_i \mathbb{I}_{D_i} |\{Z_k\}\right)\middle| \bar{Y} = y\right),\\
&= \mathbb{E}\left(\sum_{i=1}^{N} c_i^2 \left(\mathbb{E}\left(\gamma_i^2 \mathbb{I}_{D_i}^2 |\{Z_k\}\right) - \mathbb{E}\left(\gamma_i \mathbb{I}_{D_i} |\{Z_k\}\right)^2\right)\middle| \bar{Y} = y\right),\\
&= \sum_{i=1}^{N} c_i^2 \mathbb{E}\left(\left(\mathbb{E}(\gamma_i^2)\mathbb{E}\left(\mathbb{I}_{D_i} |\{Z_k\}\right) - \mathbb{E}(\gamma_i)^2 \mathbb{E}\left(\mathbb{I}_{D_i} |\{Z_k\}\right)^2\right)\middle| \bar{Y} = y\right),\\
&= \sum_{i=1}^{N} c_i^2 \left(\mathbb{E}(\gamma_i^2)\mathbb{E}\left(\mathbb{I}_{D_i} | \bar{Y} = y\right) - \mathbb{E}\left(\left(\mathbb{E}(\gamma_i)^2 \mathbb{E}\left(\mathbb{I}_{D_i} |\{Z_k\}\right)^2\right)\middle| \bar{Y} = y\right)\right),\\
&= \sum_{i=1}^{N} c_i^2 \left(\left(\nu_{\gamma_i} + \bar{\gamma}_i^2\right) p_i(y) - \bar{\gamma}_i^2 \underbrace{\mathbb{E}\left(\left(\mathbb{E}\left(\mathbb{I}_{D_i} |\{Z_k\}\right)^2\right)\middle| \bar{Y} = y\right)}_{\text{Smaller } \sigma\text{-algebra wins!}}\right),\\
&= \sum_{i=1}^{N} c_i^2 \left(\left(\nu_{\gamma_i} + \bar{\gamma}_i^2\right) p_i(y) - \bar{\gamma}_i^2 \mathbb{E}\left(\mathbb{I}_{D_i} \cdot \mathbb{I}_{D_i} \middle| \bar{Y} = y\right)\right),\\
&= \sum_{i=1}^{N} c_i^2 \left(\left(\nu_{\gamma_i} + \bar{\gamma}_i^2\right) p_i(y) - \bar{\gamma}_i^2 \mathbb{P}\left(D_i \cap D_i \middle| \bar{Y} = y\right)\right),\\
&= \sum_{i=1}^{N} c_i^2 \left(\left(\nu_{\gamma_i} + \bar{\gamma}_i^2\right) p_i(y) - \bar{\gamma}_i^2 \mathbb{P}\left(\{X_i \leq \Phi^{-1}(p_i)\} \cap \{X_i \leq \Phi^{-1}(p_i)\} \middle| \bar{Y} = y\right)\right),\\
&= \sum_{i=1}^{N} c_i^2 \left(\left(\nu_{\gamma_i} + \bar{\gamma}_i^2\right) p_i(y) - \bar{\gamma}_i^2 \mathbb{P}\left(\left\{ \xi_i \leq \frac{\Phi^{-1}(p_i) - a_i y}{\sqrt{1 - a_i^2}} \right\}\right.\right.
\end{aligned}
$$

[52] We have tested both formulations—from the second and third lines of Eq. 11.148—numerically and they are indeed, as expected, equal.

$$
\bigcap\left\{\xi_i \leq \frac{\Phi^{-1}(p_i) - a_i y}{\sqrt{1-a_i^2}}\right\}\Bigg)\Bigg),
$$

$$
= \sum_{i=1}^{N} c_i^2 \left( \left(\nu_{\gamma_i} + \bar{\gamma}_i^2\right) p_i(y) - \bar{\gamma}_i^2 \Phi\left(\Phi^{-1}(p_i(y)), \Phi^{-1}(p_i(y)); \rho_{ii}\right)\right),
$$

$$
= \underbrace{\sum_{i=1}^{N} c_i^2 p_i(y) \left( \nu_{\gamma_i} + \bar{\gamma}_i^2 \left( 1 - \frac{\Phi\left(\Phi^{-1}(p_i(y)), \Phi^{-1}(p_i(y)); \rho_{ii}\right)}{p_i(y)} \right)\right)}_{\text{Now's a good time to return for comparison to Eq. 11.127}},
$$

where,

$$
\begin{aligned}
\rho_{ii} &= \frac{r_i^2 \overbrace{\sum_{k=1}^{K} \alpha_{ik}^2}^{=1} - a_i^2}{1 - a_i^2}, \\
&= \frac{r_i^2 - a_i^2}{1 - a_i^2}.
\end{aligned} \tag{11.150}
$$

On its own, Eq. 11.149 is difficult to interpret. Setting an important set of parameters to an extreme value can sometimes be helpful. In this case, if we set $\rho_{ii} = 0$, something interesting happens. The bivariate Gaussian distribution term collapses to

$$
\begin{aligned}
&\Phi\left(\Phi^{-1}(p_i(y)), \Phi^{-1}(p_i(y)); \rho_{ii}\right) \\
&= \int_{-\infty}^{\Phi^{-1}(p_i(y))} \int_{-\infty}^{\Phi^{-1}(p_i(y))} \frac{1}{2\pi\sqrt{1-\rho_{ii}^2}} e^{-\frac{\left(u^2 - 2\rho_{ii} uv + v^2\right)}{2(1-\rho_{ii}^2)}} dv du, \\
&\Phi\left(\Phi^{-1}(p_i(y)), \Phi^{-1}(p_i(y)); 0\right) \\
&= \int_{-\infty}^{\Phi^{-1}(p_i(y))} \int_{-\infty}^{\Phi^{-1}(p_i(y))} \frac{1}{2\pi} e^{-\frac{(u^2+v^2)}{2}} dv du, \\
&= \left( \int_{-\infty}^{\Phi^{-1}(p_i(y))} \frac{1}{\sqrt{2\pi}} e^{\frac{-v^2}{2}} dv \right) \left( \int_{-\infty}^{\Phi^{-1}(p_i(y))} \frac{1}{\sqrt{2\pi}} e^{\frac{-u^2}{2}} du \right), \\
&= \Phi\left(\Phi^{-1}(p_i(y))\right) \Phi\left(\Phi^{-1}(p_i(y))\right),
\end{aligned} \tag{11.151}
$$

$$= p_i(y)^2.$$

The consequence is that $\nu_{\mathcal{G}}(y)$ reduces to our original conditional variance term, $\nu(y)$. This quantity was previously derived, without Pykhtin [27]'s variance-decomposition, in Eq. 11.127. We actually put an explicit note on this value so that we could come back to it later. Plugging Eq. 11.151 into Eq. 11.149 permits us to establish—naturally under the assumption of $\rho_{ii} \equiv 0$—equivalence with the basic conditional variance found in Eq. 11.127. This condition provides a useful link between the standard one-dimensional Gaussian threshold model granularity adjustment summarized in Fig. 11.7 and Pykhtin [27]'s method.[53]

Moving on to the derivative of this second flavour of conditional variance, we are one step away from completion. Rather exceptionally—and mostly because of our previous efforts—this turns out to be rather straightforward to compute. We have

$$\nu'_{\mathcal{G}}(y) = \frac{d}{dy}\left(\sum_{i=1}^{N} c_i^2\left(\left(\nu_{\gamma_i} + \bar{\gamma}_i^2\right)p_i(y) - \bar{\gamma}_i^2\Phi\left(\Phi^{-1}(p_i(y)), \Phi^{-1}(p_i(y)); \rho_{ii}\right)\right)\right), \tag{11.152}$$

$$= \sum_{i=1}^{N} c_i^2\left(\left(\nu_{\gamma_i} + \bar{\gamma}_i^2\right)p'_i(y) - \bar{\gamma}_i^2\frac{d}{dy}\left(\Phi\left(\Phi^{-1}(p_i(y)), \Phi^{-1}(p_i(y)); \rho_{ii}\right)\right)\right),$$

$$= \sum_{i=1}^{N} c_i^2\left(\left(\nu_{\gamma_i} + \bar{\gamma}_i^2\right)p'_i(y) - \bar{\gamma}_i^2\left(\Phi_{ii}(y)p'_i(y) + \Phi_{ii}(y)p'_i(y)\right)\right),$$

$$= \sum_{i=1}^{N} c_i^2 p'_i(y)\left(\nu_{\gamma_i} + \bar{\gamma}_i^2\left(1 - 2\Phi_{ii}(y)\right)\right).$$

Recalling that $\Phi_{ii}(y) = \Phi\left(\frac{\Phi^{-1}(p_i(y)) - \rho_{ii}\Phi^{-1}(p_i(y))}{\sqrt{1-\rho_{ii}^2}}\right)$ and setting $\rho_{ii} = 0$, $\Phi_{ii}(y)$ collapses to $p_i(y)$. In this case, we again establish equivalency between $\nu'(y)$ in Eq. 11.128 and $\nu'_{\mathcal{G}}(y)$. The actual value of $\rho_{ii}$ depends upon the interaction between the $r_i$, $a_i$, and $\rho_i$ parameters. It does not, however, typically take the value of zero and that is precisely the point.

Figure 11.8 completes our analysis with a high-level summary of the principal formulae involved in Pykhtin [27]'s granularity adjustment calculation. It has many logical similarities to the one-factor Gaussian threshold model from Fig. 11.7, but capturing the multi-factor dimension leads to a significant increase in complexity. Although it deepens our appreciation of the granularity adjustment, it is not difficult to imagine why this approach might not have caught on as a regulatory standard. There is also a much higher parametric burden with Pykhtin [27]'s proposal.

[53] The simplest interpretation is that, in the one-factor setting, the $a$ and $r$ parameters are equal.

$$\mathcal{G}_\alpha(L) = -\frac{1}{2\mu'(y)}\left[\underbrace{\left(\nu'_\infty(y) - \nu_\infty(y)\left(\frac{\mu''(y)}{\mu'(y)} + y\right)\right)}_{\text{Multi-factor component}} - \underbrace{\left(\nu'_{\mathcal{G}}(y) - \nu_{\mathcal{G}}(y)\left(\frac{\mu''(y)}{\mu'(y)} + y\right)\right)}_{\text{Concentration component}}\right]\Bigg|_{y=\Phi^{-1}(1-\alpha)}$$

KEY FUNCTIONS

$$p_i(y) = \Phi\left(\frac{\Phi^{-1}(p_i) - a_i y}{\sqrt{1-a_i^2}}\right) \text{ and } \hat{p}_i(y) = \Phi\left(\frac{\Phi^{-1}(p_i) - r_i y}{\sqrt{1-r_i^2}}\right)$$

$$\mu(y) = \sum_{i=1}^{N} c_i \bar{\gamma}_i p_i(y)$$

$$\nu_\infty(y) = \sum_{i=1}^{N}\sum_{j=1}^{N} c_i c_j \bar{\gamma}_i \bar{\gamma}_j \left(\Phi\left(\Phi^{-1}(p_i(y)), \Phi^{-1}(p_j(y)); \rho_{ij}\right) - p_i(y) p_j(y)\right)$$

$$\nu_{\mathcal{G}}(y) = \sum_{i=1}^{N} c_i^2 \left(\left(\nu_{\gamma_i} + \bar{\gamma}_i^2\right) p_i(y) - \bar{\gamma}_i^2 \Phi\left(\Phi^{-1}(p_i(y)), \Phi^{-1}(p_i(y)); \rho_{ii}\right)\right)$$

KEY DERIVATIVES

$$\mu'(y) = \sum_{i=1}^{N} c_i \bar{\gamma}_i p'_i(y)$$

$$\mu''(y) = \sum_{i=1}^{N} c_i \bar{\gamma}_i p''_i(y)$$

$$\nu'_\infty(y) = 2\sum_{i=1}^{N}\sum_{j=1}^{N} c_i c_j \bar{\gamma}_i \bar{\gamma}_j p'_i(y)\left(\Phi_{ji}(y) - p_j(y)\right)$$

$$\nu'_{\mathcal{G}}(y) = \sum_{i=1}^{N} c_i^2 p'_i(y)\left(\nu_{\gamma_i} + \bar{\gamma}_i^2\left(1 - 2\Phi_{ii}(y)\right)\right)$$

USEFUL QUANTITIES

$$p'_i(y) = -\frac{a_i}{\sqrt{1-a_i^2}}\phi\left(\Phi^{-1}(p_i(y))\right)$$

$$p''_i(y) = -\frac{a_i^2}{1-a_i^2}\Phi^{-1}(p_i(y))\,\phi\left(\Phi^{-1}(p_i(y))\right)$$

$$\Phi\left(x, y; \rho\right) = \int_{-\infty}^{x}\int_{-\infty}^{y} \frac{1}{2\pi\sqrt{1-\rho^2}} e^{-\frac{\left(u^2 - 2\rho uv + v^2\right)}{2(1-\rho^2)}} dv du$$

$$\Phi_{ji}(y) = \Phi\left(\frac{\Phi^{-1}(p_j(y)) - \rho_{ij}\Phi^{-1}(p_i(y))}{\sqrt{1-\rho_{ij}^2}}\right)$$

$$\rho_{ij} = \frac{r_i r_j \sum_{k=1}^{K} \alpha_{ik}\alpha_{jk} - a_i a_j}{\sqrt{1-a_i^2}\sqrt{1-a_j^2}} \text{ and } \rho_{ii} = \frac{r_i^2 - a_i^2}{1-a_i^2}$$

$$a_i = r_i \sum_{i=1}^{K} \alpha_{ik} b_k$$

$$b_k = \frac{\sum_{i=1}^{N} c_i \bar{\gamma}_i \hat{p}_i\left(\Phi^{-1}(1-\alpha)\right)\alpha_{ik}}{\sqrt{\sum_{m=1}^{K}\left(\sum_{i=1}^{N} c_i \bar{\gamma}_i \hat{p}_i\left(\Phi^{-1}(1-\alpha)\right)\alpha_{im}\right)^2}}$$

IMPORTANT EXPOSURE-LEVEL INPUTS

$c_i \triangleq$ $i$th exposure at default
$p_i \triangleq$ $i$th unconditional default probability
$\bar{\gamma}_i \triangleq$ $i$th average of loss-given-default
$\nu_{\gamma_i} \triangleq$ $i$th variance of loss-given-default (i.e., $\xi\bar{\gamma}_i(1-\bar{\gamma}_i)$)
$r_i \triangleq$ $i$th (multi-factor) systemic-weight parameter
$\alpha_{ik} \triangleq$ $i$th obligor's factor loading on $k$th factor
$b_k \triangleq$ $k$th (fixed) weight on systemic factor $Z_k$
$a_i \triangleq$ $i$th (one-factor) systemic-weight parameter

**Fig. 11.8** *Pykhtin [27]'s Granularity adjustment*: This schematic outlines, at a single glance, the principal formulae involved in Pykhtin [27]'s granularity adjustment calculation. It has many logical similarities to the one-factor Gaussian threshold model from Fig. 11.7, but capturing the multi-factor dimension leads to a significant increase in complexity.

Keeping this in mind, the results in Fig. 11.8 also can be fruitfully compared to Gordy and Lütkebohmert [16]'s CreditRisk+ implementation in Fig. 11.6.

**Colour and Commentary 140** (FIGHTING AGAINST BLACK BOXES): *Derivation of the previous concentration adjustment results represents, it must be admitted, something of a mathematical marathon. By assuming portfolio-invariance, a quite indefensible assumption, the Basel-IRB and S&P-RAC approaches hoped to avoid some complexity and reduce the regulatory burden. The intricacies of credit-risk modelling, however, return in full force when trying, in the context of Pillar II, to adjust for concentration risk.*

(continued)

**Colour and Commentary 140** (continued)
*One could (half seriously) argue that it remains straightforward; one need, after all, only skip to the final formulae so generously derived by Gordy and Lütkebohmert [15], Pykhtin [27], and colleagues, to arrive at the result. A responsible quantitative analyst, however, is obliged to work through the details to understand what assumptions and simplifications are embedded in these regulatory formulae. Using the final result without understanding amounts to the construction of a black box. This might save time in the short run, but sooner or later, reliance on black boxes always ends in tears.*

### *11.2.6 Practical Granularity-Adjustment Results*

Actual implementation of Pykhtin [27]'s model will depend importantly on one's portfolio and critical assumptions about the factor structure of one's economic-capital model. In this final section, we will nonetheless provide a quick comparison of the three alternative versions of the granularity adjustment considered in the previous discussion: the one-factor Gaussian threshold, the multi-factor Pykhtin [27], and Gordy and Lütkebohmert [16]'s CreditRisk+ implementations. This will help to underscore the lengthy abstract discussion in the previous sections.

The plan is to address the various steps required to obtain a reasonable working version of our granularity adjustment. The first bit involves determination of the various Pykhtin [27] model parameters. A large number of model coefficients—and some useful summary statistics—are provided in Table 11.3. The central choice relates to the so-called $b$ parameters linking the one- and multi-factor models. Unsurprisingly, the multi-factor systemic weights (i.e., the $r$'s) fall somewhat on average when moving from the single-factor setting (i.e., the $a$'s). This is related to the concentration of all systemic risk into a single factor; when there are many factors, it is spread out and individual factor sensitivities can be higher. Figure 11.9 provides a graphical description of the centrally important $b$ coefficients governing this transformation into a (roughly) equivalent one-factor model.[54]

Using the common equivalent one-factor model $a$ parameters from Table 11.3, we can compute a reasonably fair comparison of the granularity adjustment across our three models. All use the same exposures, loss-given-default, unconditional default probabilities, and systemic weights. They differ in terms of the number and distribution of the systemic factors. The high-level results are summarized in

[54] These values are computed by solving the optimization problem presented in Eq. 11.109, but a bit of trial-and-error reveals that the final results are rather sensitive to these parameter values. We'd thus recommend, when actually implementing Pykhtin [27], experimenting with different approaches to the selection of $b$.

**Table 11.3** *Pykhtin [27] Parameter overview*: This table summarizes a set of selected summary statistics associated with the main Pykhtin [27] model parameters derived from our economic-capital model using an arbitrarily selected date in 2020. In all cases, where relevant, $y = \Phi^{-1}(1-\alpha)$ given a confidence level of $\alpha = 0.999$.

| | Selected statistics | | | |
|---|---|---|---|---|
| Parameter | Mean | Volatility | Minimum | Maximum |
| $\bar{\gamma}_i$ | 0.314 | 0.161 | 0.100 | 0.990 |
| $r_i$ | 0.590 | 0.080 | 0.346 | 0.632 |
| $b_k$ | 0.142 | 0.147 | 0.000 | 0.614 |
| $\rho_i$ | 0.307 | 0.154 | 0.003 | 0.614 |
| $a_i$ | 0.185 | 0.102 | 0.002 | 0.388 |
| $p_i$ | 0.003 | 0.010 | 0.000 | 0.200 |
| $\hat{p}_i(y)$ | 0.071 | 0.102 | 0.006 | 0.925 |
| $p_i(y)$ | 0.009 | 0.024 | 0.000 | 0.444 |
| $\mathbb{P}\left(\mathcal{D}_i \cap \mathcal{D}_j \middle\| \bar{Y} = y\right)$ | 0.000 | 0.001 | 0.000 | 0.221 |
| $\rho_{ij}$ | 0.013 | 0.103 | -0.099 | 0.400 |

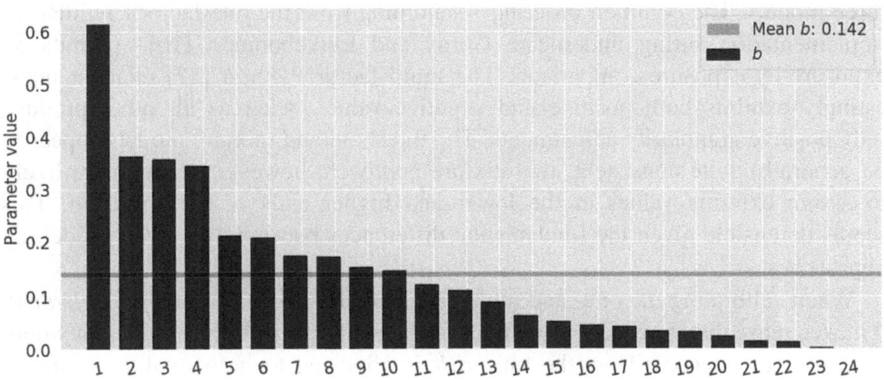


**Fig. 11.9** *The $b_k$ coefficients*: This figure outlines the $K = 24$ individual (ordered) fixed weights used to transform the multi-factor structure our internal production model—for an arbitrary date in 2020—into a one-factor model. These values are a complicated function of the portfolio structure, the factor loadings, and the systemic-weight correlations from Eq. 11.117.

Table 11.4; all values are computed using a $\alpha = 0.999$ confidence level for an arbitrarily selected date. Moreover, since the actual currency values are unimportant, we have simply normalized the results so that the classic Gordy and Lütkebohmert [16] model yields 100 units. This permits easy comparison of the final outcomes.

The standard, one-factor Gaussian threshold model granularity adjustment amounts to—for this example and parametrization—a roughly 50% larger outcome than in the CreditRisk+ implementation. As we would hope, the Gaussian model compares favourably to the Pykhtin [27] granularity adjustment. The Pykhtin [27] multi-factor adjustment is only about 7% of the base CreditRisk+ figure. This is a relatively modest amount suggesting that, for this parametrization, there is

**Table 11.4** *Flavours of granularity adjustment*: This table illustrates, again for our arbitrarily selected date, *three* different flavours of granularity adjustment: the standard one-factor Gaussian-threshold and Poisson-gamma mixture models as well as Pykhtin [27] multi-factor approach. All figures are normalized so that the Gordy and Lütkebohmert [16] model yields an estimate of 100 units. The $a$ parameters from Table 11.4 are employed for all models to permit better comparison.

| Granularity adjustment | Normalized estimate |
|---|---|
| Standard one-factor Gaussian threshold model | 153.1 |
| Pykhtin multi-factor element | 7.4 |
| Pykhtin concentration element | 151.2 |
| Total Pykhtin approach | 158.7 |
| CreditRisk+ one-factor Poisson-gamma mixture model | 100.0 |

not a particularly large *overall* difference between the single- and multi-factor implementations (at least in terms of impact on the concentration adjustment).

Figure 11.10 closes this analysis with an exposure-level presentation of the three models. The common ordering—stemming from the one-factor CreditRisk+ implementation sitting underneath Gordy and Lütkebohmert [16]—permits an exposure-by-exposure comparison. The multi-factor Pykhtin [27] element interestingly exhibits both positive and negative values, whereas all other produce only positive granularity adjustments. The threshold and mixture models appear to be generally quite consistent; the mixture approach, however, seems more likely to assign extreme values at the lower and higher ends of the spectrum. This seems defensible given the fundamental differences between these two modelling approaches.

When calibrating the one- and multi-factor models to be essentially *equivalent*, it makes sense that they yield roughly the same total results. If they did not, it would be cause for concern. How the total risk is allocated to individual exposures—as described in Fig. 11.10—would seem to be the main avenue of difference. Pykhtin [27]'s multi-factor adjustment thus appears to provide useful help along this dimension.

## 11.3 Wrapping Up

More than 200 years ago, the famous British mathematician and scientist Lord Kelvin commented that "when you can measure what you are speaking about, and express it in numbers, you know something about it." This captures the essence of seeking external comparison. We compute a broad range of economic-capital measures using our internally developed modelling framework. Although we have confidence in these figures, it is enormously helpful to establish explicit points of comparison. Challenger models represent one important touchstone for this strategy. The various flavours of regulatory guidance—within both Pillar I and II—

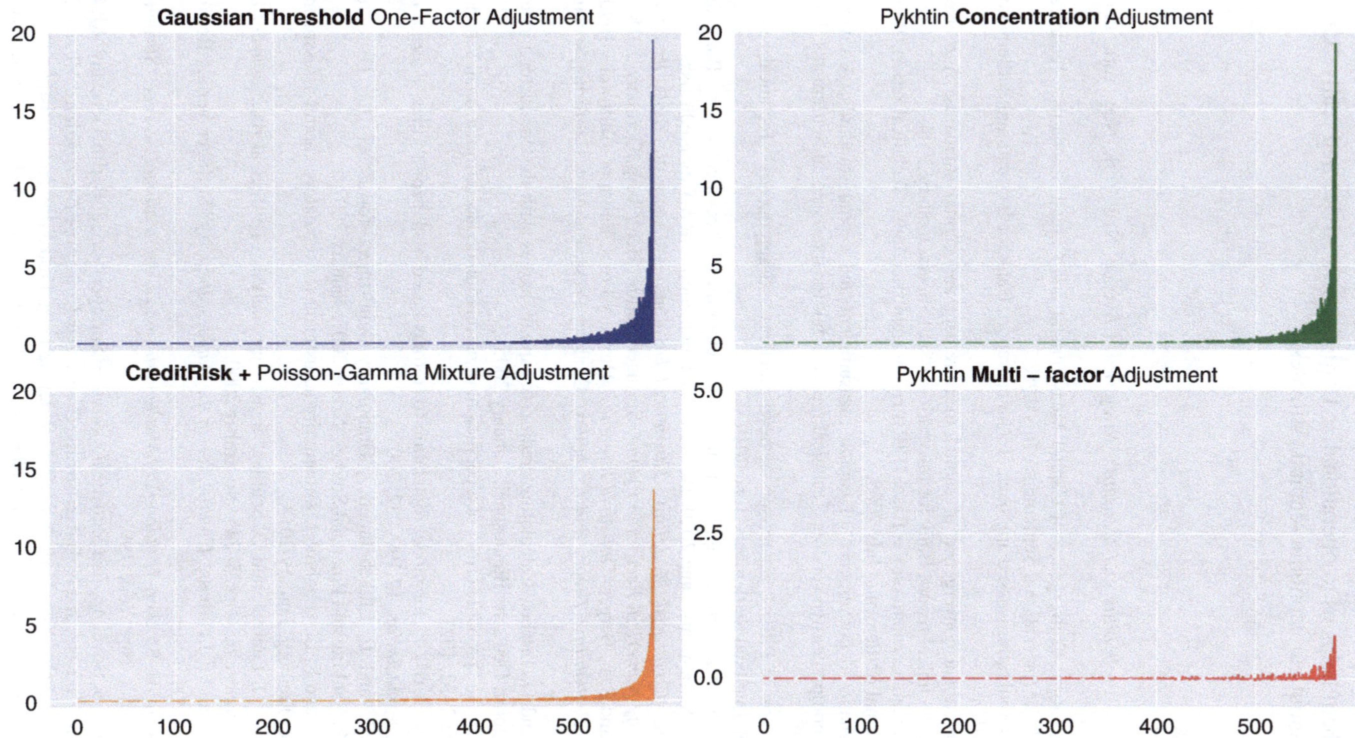


**Fig. 11.10** *Exposure-level granularity-adjustment comparison*: This figure illustrates the ordered exposure-level granularity adjustment values for the three models illustrated in Table 11.4. The common ordering stems from the one-factor CreditRisk+ implementation; this model, as in Table 11.4, also normalizes all of the presented results.

and the external-rating agencies represent another essential benchmark. Expressing this wide range of possible capital perspectives as concrete numbers and regularly contrasting them helps us to operationalize Lord Kelvin's advice and really "know something" about our economic-capital estimates.

## References

1. P. Billingsley. *Probability and Measure*. Wiley, Third Avenue, New York, New York, third edition, 1995.
2. BIS. International Convergence of Capital Measurement and Capital Standards. Technical report, Bank for International Settlements, July 1988.
3. BIS. The internal ratings-based approach. Technical report, Bank for International Settlements, January 2001.
4. BIS. International convergence of capital measurement and capital standards: A revised framework. Technical report, Bank for International Settlements, January 2004.
5. BIS. An explanatory note on the Basel II IRB risk weight functions. Technical report, Bank for International Settlements, July 2005.
6. BIS. International convergence of capital measurement and capital standards: A revised framework comprehensive version. Technical report, Bank for International Settlements, June 2006.
7. BIS. Overview of Pillar 2 supervisory review: practices and approaches. Technical report, Bank for International Settlements, June 2019.
8. BIS. (CRE20) Standardized approach: individual exposures. Technical report, Bank for International Settlements, June 2020. Part of CRE: Calculation of RWA for credit risk.
9. D. J. Bolder. *Credit-Risk Modelling: Theoretical Foundations, Diagnostic Tools, Practical Examples, and Numerical Recipes in Python*. Springer-Nature, Heidelberg, Germany, 2018.
10. G. Casella and R. L. Berger. *Statistical Inference*. Duxbury Press, Belmont, California, 1990.
11. R. Durrett. *Probability: Theory and Examples*. Duxbury Press, Belmont, California, second edition, 1996.
12. S. Emmer and D. Tasche. Calculating credit risk capital charges with the one-factor model. Technical report, Deutsche Bundesbank, January 2005.
13. R. Fisher. On the "probable error" of a coefficient of correlation deduced from a small sample. *Metron*, 1(4):3–32, 1921.
14. M. B. Gordy. A risk-factor model foundation for ratings-based bank capital rules. *Journal of Financial Intermediation*, 12:199–232, 2003.
15. M. B. Gordy and E. Lütkebohmert. Granularity Adjustment for Basel II. Deutsche Bundesbank, Banking and Financial Studies, No 01-2007, January 2007.
16. M. B. Gordy and E. Lütkebohmert. Granularity adjustment for regulatory capital assessment. University of Freiburg, January 2013.
17. C. Gourieroux, J. Laurent, and O. Scaillet. Sensitivity analysis of values at risk. *Journal of Empirical Finance*, 7(3-4):225–245, November 2000.
18. M. Gundlach and F. Lehrbass. *CreditRisk+ in the Banking Industry*. Springer Verlag, Berlin, first edition, 2004.
19. J. W. Harris and H. Stocker. *Handbook of Mathematics and Computational Science*. Springer Verlag, New York, New York, 1998.
20. L. Held and D. S. Bové. *Applied Statistical Inference*. Springer-Verlag, Berlin, Germany, 2014.
21. N. L. Johnson, S. Kotz, and N. Balakrishnan. *Continuous Univariate Distributions: Volume 2*. John Wiley and Sons, New York, NY, 1997. Wiley Series in Probability and Statistics.
22. P. Jorion. *Value at Risk: The New Benchmark for Managing Financial Risk*. McGraw-Hill Ryerson Limited, New York, NY, 2006.

23. E. Lütkebohmert. *Concentration Risk in Credit Portfolios*. Springer Verlag, Berlin, 2008.
24. R. J. Martin and T. Wilde. Unsystematic credit risk. *Risk*, pages 123–128, November 2002.
25. A. J. McNeil, R. Frey, and P. Embrechts. *Quantitative Risk Management: Concepts, Tools and Techniques*. Princeton University Press, New Jersey, 2015.
26. R. Merton. On the pricing of corporate debt: The risk structure of interest rates. *Journal of Finance*, 29:449–470, 1974.
27. M. Pykhtin. Multi-factor adjustment. *Risk*, (3):85–90, March 2004.
28. H. Rau-Bredow. Value-at-risk, expected shortfall, and marginal risk contribution. In G. Szegö, editor, *Risk Measures for the 21st Century*. John Wiley & Sons, 2004.
29. L. J. Savage. On rereading R.A. Fisher. *The Annals of Statistics*, 4(3):441–500, May 1976.
30. S&P. Understanding standard & poor's rating definitions. Technical report, Standard & Poor's Global Inc., June 2009.
31. S&P. Bank capital methodology and assumptions. Technical report, Standard & Poor's Global Inc., December 2010.
32. S&P. General criteria: Principles of credit ratings. Technical report, Standard & Poor's Global Inc., February 2011.
33. S&P. Multilateral lending institutions and other supranational institutions ratings methodology. Technical report, Standard & Poor's Global Inc., November 2012.
34. S&P. CreditModel Financial Institutions: A state-of-the-art scoring model for banks and insurance companies. Technical report, Standard & Poor's Global Inc., May 2017.
35. A. Stuart and J. K. Ord. *Kendall's Advanced Theory of Statistics*, volume 1. Oxford University Press, New York, 5 edition, 1987.
36. B. Torell. Name concentration risk and pillar 2 compliance: The granularity adjustment. Technical report, Royal Institute of Technology, Stockholm, Sweden, January 2013.
37. O. A. Vasicek. Probability of loss on loan distribution. KMV Corporation, February 1987.
38. O. A. Vasicek. Limiting loan loss probability distribution. KMV Corporation, August 1991.
39. O. A. Vasicek. The distribution of loan portfolio value. *Risk*, (12):160–162, December 2002.
40. T. Wilde. CreditRisk+: A credit risk management framework. Credit Suisse First Boston, January 1997.
41. J. Wishart. The Correlation between Product Moments of any Order in Samples from a Normal Population. *Proceedings of the Royal Society of Edinburgh*, 49:78–90, 1930.

# Chapter 12
# Thoughts on Stress Testing

*Reality is the leading cause of stress.*

*(Lily Tomlin)*

There are a number of good reasons why stress-testing analysis finds itself as the final topic considered in this book: it is difficult, somewhat awkward, and requires a bird's eye view of one's portfolio and modelling techniques. This, perhaps slightly controversial, opening statement requires some additional colour and justification. Stress-testing's difficulty is easily explained. There is always a range of choice in any financial modelling exercise, but stress-testing is rather extreme. There are at least two fundamental perspectives that one might follow and, within each of these approaches, literally an infinity of possible stress scenarios that one might select, employ, and analyze. There is, in fact, basically too much choice. Creating some kind of logical order and structure, in face of this potential chaos, is one of the fundamental tasks that we will face in the following discussion.

Onto the awkwardness. The words of Rebonato [26] express this sentiment rather well, stating that stress testing

> has always been the poor relation in the family of analytical techniques to control risk.

Rather harsh words, but the underlying reason stems from the fundamental structure of stress-testing. It proposes outcomes or events—which are typically extreme and lead to rather adverse portfolio effects—without an associated assessment of their probability. This stands in sharp contrast to classical risk metrics—such as VaR or expected shortfall—that structurally involve the combination of events and their associated likelihoods. Prowling in the background of both worlds, as we've seen in previous chapters, is necessarily an underlying (and unknown) loss distribution. We can envisage a stress scenario as a set (or event) in one's probability space. Unfortunately, we do not know how to assign a measure to it.[1] The consequence is an inherent degree of subjectivity in any stress-testing analysis.

[1] At the same time, we (rather keenly) hope that it is not a set of measure zero.

 
D. Bolder, *Modelling Economic Capital*, Contributions to Finance and Accounting,
https://doi.org/10.1007/978-3-030-95096-5_12

This situation creates an incongruity between standard risk measures on the one hand and stress-testing results on the other; it feels like a situation of comparing apples and pears. Aragonés et al. [2] summarize this sentiment very well with the following question:

> How can we combine a probabilistic risk estimate with an estimate that such-and-such a loss will occur if such-and-such happens?

At the same time, however, there appears to be a real need for stress-testing. Quantitative analysts should not start patting one another on the back because of the logical consistency of event and probability treatment within their models. Time and again, over recent decades, probabilistic risk estimates have failed to predict a dismaying number of crises associated with realizations of extreme financial outcomes. Why is this the case? It may stem from over-optimism in one's parametrization, leading to insufficient weight on severely adverse outcomes. Part of the explanation is certainly, as argued by Taleb [31], that unknown unknowns driving financial crises structurally elude our models until it is too late.[2] It is also entirely possible that asking our models to accurately predict inherently unpredictable financial shocks, driven by complex human behaviour, is simply too tall an order. Whatever the reason, it is useful to (once again) underscore the fallibility of probabilistic models.

Stress-testing, when done well, is thus a complement and not a competitor to our probabilistic models. The key objective of stress-testing analysis is not necessarily the construction of extreme scenarios not fully captured in our base models—although this is certainly part of it—but rather to identify vulnerabilities in our portfolios. Where, for example, are the weak spots? What constellation of events would be particularly troublesome for our portfolio? Such information, despite its subjectivity and lack of probability assignment, is useful. When combined with our standard modelling framework, it tells a more nuanced and complete story.

The final claim—the need for a bird's eye view—is the strongest reason for treating stress-testing analysis in our final chapter. "If such-and-such happens", to borrow again the expression from Aragonés et al. [2], we need to understand the implications for our portfolio. For our purposes, this basically amounts to estimating the impact on our firm's capital position. Such an assessment requires understanding the big picture. We need to incorporate dimensions—introduced in Chap. 1—of both capital demand and supply. The capital-demand impact will necessarily flow through our economic-capital model addressed in Chaps. 2 to 4; as a result, we need to understand how precisely this will happen and how to estimate it. Capital-supply effects arise via the profit-and-loss statement; our loan-impairment computations from Chap. 9 will play a central role in this respect. We will also recycle—and, in some ways, extend—many of the earlier ideas associated with stress-scenario generation introduced in Chaps. 7 and 8. Faced with the need to

[2] Such never-before-observed events cannot, by their very nature, be incorporated into our parameter estimates.

estimate large number of computationally intensive economic-capital values, we will again rely upon our approximation model from Chap. 5. Thus, while it might be an exaggeration to state that this final discussion relies on all of the previous chapters, it does lean heavily on most of them.

To summarize, stress-testing is not easy and requires a broader perspective. It is, however, useful and represents a welcome companion to the classical, probabilistic models presented in previous chapters. In the following sections, we will consider a range of alternative approaches—with our usual focus on the credit-risk perspective—towards the incorporation of stress scenarios into our analysis.

**Colour and Commentary 141** (THE ROLE OF STRESS-TESTING ANALYSIS): *Among quantitative analysts, stress-testing has something of a bad reputation. Its very structure—involving specification of an extreme event without an associated probability—is somewhat awkward. Such analysis can be hard to interpret and difficult to combine with traditional probabilistic models. Since the great financial crisis, however, there has been a groundswell of support for stress-testing. Failure of probabilistic models to predict numerous past crises have undermined their credibility; some even argue that such models should be entirely replaced with stress-testing analysis. These arguments, for and against stress-testing, both have some merit. Stress-testing certainly deserves more credit and attention, but it is* not *a replacement for more holistic financial models.*[a] *In practice, there is ample room for both approaches in the assessment of financial risk. Stress-testing, in short, is an effective complement to probabilistic models and a powerful tool for the identification of vulnerabilities in one's portfolio.*

[a] To entirely replace probabilistic models with stress-testing would essentially amount to "throwing the baby out with the bath water." One can certainly improve basic modelling techniques (i.e., eliminate the dirty water) while maintaining their fundamental usefulness (i.e., keeping the baby).

## 12.1 Organizing Stress-Testing

Before jumping into the technical details and considering practical examples, we first need to organize our thinking. As is often the case, it is useful to highlight the key issues as a catechism. We thus raise *three* important questions:

1. What pathways do stress-scenarios follow on their way to impact the firm's capital position?
2. What logical approach should we take in our construction of a stress-testing framework?

3. How do we manage, in a stress-testing setting, the passage of time and our portfolio composition?

Reflecting upon these questions and providing detailed answers will help immensely in clarifying a possible, and pragmatic, way of thinking about stress-testing. Let's address each in turn.

### 12.1.1 The Main Risk Pathway

Our first question can basically be translated as: what does stress-testing actually even mean within our context? We are considering the firm's economic-capital position—and associated measures—from a predominately credit-risk perspective. Economic-capital, as we've indicated and discussed numerous times, is fundamentally based on a long-term, unconditional, through-the-cycle parametrization. This assumption permeates our basic credit-risk model and, as we saw in Chap. 11, underscores most of the regulatory guidance. This is logically rather problematic; to be frank, it feels like a deal-breaker. The very structure of our economic-capital computations would appear to preclude the role of stress scenarios. The long-term, through-the-cycle view presumably incorporates numerous, extreme stress outcomes, but when averaged over many, more normal events, their individual-parameter influence is strongly diluted.

If our model parameters cannot change, then what is effected by stress scenarios? A bit of reflection suggests that, although the through-the-cycle perspective needs to be maintained, stress outcomes can indeed have an important impact on our portfolio's risk profile. Since the beginning of Chap. 2, we have focused on the *three* key credit-risk variables: default probability (i.e., credit rating), loss-given-default, and exposure. All three aspects can be altered from a specific stress scenario. The most obvious, and important, relates to the credit ratings of one's obligors. An adverse event may not change the model parameters, but if it creates broad-based rating downgrade of one's credit counterparties, the impact can be quite severe.

Economic-capital is, in fact, influenced via *two* main avenues associated with the downgrade of a given credit obligor. The first is quite direct. In most cases, a downgrade will lead to an increase in the amount of economic-capital associated with a given credit counterpart.[3] Downgrades, all else equal, will lead to an increase in capital demand. The result is thus a reduction of the firm's capital headroom.

[3] This is not always true. Since default and migration risk often move in opposite directions, the net impact of a downgrade can sometimes lead to small decreases in economic capital. While possible, however, such outcomes are not typical and, when they occur, are generally small in magnitude.

The second avenue depends on the accounting treatment of the counterparty's exposure. If the underlying instruments are fair-valued, there will be a valuation impact associated with the downgrade.[4] Should the underlying instruments be held at amortized cost—as is typical for a loan portfolio—then there will be consequences for loan impairments. The expected-credit loss will move to a new (higher) default-probability term structure and, depending on the magnitude of the downgrade, may even involve stage-II lifetime treatment. Either way, the loan-impairment balance will rise. Although the magnitude of the effects will differ depending on fair-value or amortized-cost treatment, the logical consequences are the same. The resulting losses will pass through the profit-and-loss statement and lead to a reduction in capital supply and, as an unwelcome side-effect, a decrease in capital headroom.

A credit downgrade basically creates a squeeze-play for firm's capital position. Capital demand is pushed upwards, capital supply is pushed downwards, and the capital headroom is caught in the middle. A sufficient number of credit downgrades of sizable magnitude can—depending on the firm's capital position—lead to complete erosion of the firm's capital position. The result may involve a credit downgrade of its own or, in the worst case, reduced confidence in the firm, triggering a chain of events leading to default. All of this occurs within the through-the-cycle perspective without any impact on the model parameters. The entire adjustment occurs through the stress-induced deterioration of credit quality of one's portfolio.

This is, of course, a very credit-risk-centric view of stress-testing. Large, adverse shocks to market-risk factors will also—even in the through-the-cycle setting—generate negative valuation effects impacting capital supply. One might wish to revisit operational-risk capital estimates or even adjust capital buffers. These effects matter and are important—although they tend to play a lesser role in most lending institutions—but will *not* be addressed in our treatment. Our focus will—in a manner consistent with previous development—lie firmly upon the credit-risk dimension.

[4] Given increased risk, we should expect a higher discount factor, a lower value, and thus a valuation loss.

**Colour and Commentary 142** (CREDIT-RISK STRESS-TESTING PATHWAYS)*: Crime dramas, investigative journalists, and political actors are fond of using the phrase* "follow the money."[a] *As exciting as it sounds, it sadly doesn't typically come up too often in quantitative modelling. In this case, however, we have identified a possible exception. The fundamental through-the-cycle perspective of economic-capital computations—with its stable, long-term, unconditional parameters—precludes any direct modelling impact from adverse stress scenarios. At first glance, one might reasonably conclude that stress analysis is misplaced in this context. An important indirect pathway nonetheless exists. Should a stress scenario lead to broad-based credit-obligor downgrade, two capital effects present themselves. The first is a direct increase in capital demand associated with lower portfolio credit quality. The second is—via either valuations or loan-impairments—a decrease in capital supply.* Following the money *through our modelling frameworks and financial statements, we can identify a consequent squeeze in one's capital headroom. A severe stress scenario can thus, without impacting our model parameters, lead to dramatic weakening of a firm's capital-adequacy position. Portfolio downgrade, through economic-capital, market valuation, and loan impairments, represents the (principal) risk pathway of our stress-testing analysis.*

[a] Apparently, this dangerous-sounding expression originated from the 1970's movie "All the President's Men" surrounding the Watergate scandal starring Robert Redford and Dustin Hoffman.

### *12.1.2 Competing Approaches*

Most authors on stress-testing—see, for example, Rebonato [26], Bellini [4] or Rösch and Scheule [28]—would agree that there are *two* broad-based approaches to the topic: top-down or bottom-up. Within each class, there are many variations and there are presumably arguments to be made for an alternative organization. For our purposes—that is, examining how external stress can generate portfolio downgrades and capital degradation—this structure is perfectly sufficient.

Figure 12.1 schematically illustrates these two ideas. As the name suggests, the top-down approach takes a macro perspective. The stress scenarios are defined, in a global sense, through adverse changes in economic output, inflation, monetary policy, commodities prices, and so on. This comfortably links back to our discussion of stress-scenario construction in Chap. 8.

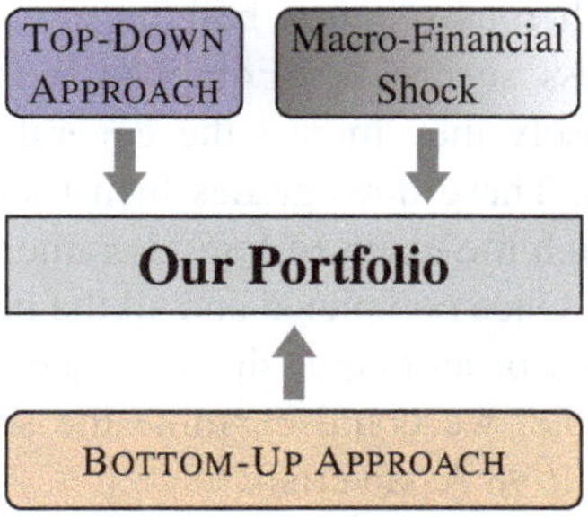


**Fig. 12.1** *Attacking the stress-testing problem*: This schematic illustrates the two broad-based approaches to the stress-testing problem. One may approach from either a top-down or bottom-up perspective. The top-down viewpoint necessarily works through macro-financial outcomes, whereas the bottom-up method is rather less obviously defined.

The top-down approach to the stress-testing problem is, in many ways, the most natural viewpoint. It easily allows us to construct interesting, and topical, narratives. What are the implications, one might ask, of prolonged lower output and higher inflation following the resolution of the COVID-19 pandemic? What if inflationary expectations get out of hand leading to a secular increase in commodity prices and interest rates? Constructing a story for each stress-testing scenario helps to practically narrow down the, literally infinite, number of potential options.

There are other ways to identify top-down stress scenarios. It is possible, and indeed fairly common practice, to *borrow* extreme outcomes from the past to inform one's macro-financial shocks. We could go back as far as the bond-market sell-off in 1994, the Asian crisis, the dot-com bubble, the events surrounding the Lehman Brothers bankruptcy, or the most recent COVID-19 pandemic. There is no shortage of choice.[5] The significant advantage is that the analyst need not construct an explicit macro-financial outcome, nor does she need to worry whether it could potentially occur.[6] The downside is that, because it already took place, the likelihood of a repeat performance is vanishingly small.

There is also an entire industry dedicated to the collection, processing, and forecasting of key financial variables. Such firms are quite competent at shuffling through all of the complexity of economic conditions and financial markets. They not only provide baseline point forecasts and uncertainty bounds, but also stress scenarios of varying degrees of uncertainty. For those institutions with sufficient resources, this is a sensible path to scenario identification.

[5] Reinhart and Rogoff [27] is an excellent source of inspiration for past crises.

[6] This is because it has, in fact, already happened.

The top-down approach thus requires building, buying or borrowing one or more macro-financial stress scenarios.[7] Equipped with these events, one must then determine how precisely they impact the general credit quality (i.e., credit ratings) of one's portfolio. These downgrades then translate into capital demand and supply effects. Although the chain of logic is rather long and complex, it is a very compelling approach. Once completed and all the intermediate steps arranged, one can examine the impact of an output shock on the firm's capital position. Or, as another possible example, we could examine the sensitivity of one's current portfolio to a repeat of the 1998 Asian crisis.

The bottom-up approach attacks the stress-testing problem from the opposite direction. One asks, in a micro fashion, what would be the impact of a direct downgrade to a specific subset of counterparties. The location of downgrade could be determined by individual identity, rating level, industrial sector, region, or it might even be randomized. There is no logical link—at least, directly—to the state of the macroeconomy or financial markets. Instead, it looks to the portfolio structure and seeks to understand the vulnerabilities associated with key concentrations.

This bottom-up perspective appears rather less structured, and thereby less conceptually compelling, than the top-down approach. While entirely true, it also relies less upon the (at times) tenuous set of statistical relationships for its computation. As we've seen in Chap. 8—and will see again in later discussion—establishing a robust relationship between general credit conditions and a set of macro-financial variables is *not* an easy or unequivocal task. Although we may be rather interested in determining the impact of an output shock on our capital position, our ability to accurately measure such an effect will be limited. Rather less sexy, the bottom-up approach makes up in honesty what it lacks in conceptual appeal.

While not precisely the same thing, there is, in our case at least, a link between the bottom-up approach and the idea of reverse stress-testing. The basic idea of reverse stress testing is to identify those scenarios that create headaches for the firm. There is a relatively small, but growing quantitative literature on this topic—see, for example, Albanese et al. [1] in the market-risk setting—and it appears to be increasingly popular in regulatory circles.[8]

[7] Given the difficulty of identifying sensible stress scenarios, it may even be preferable to source them from multiple places.

[8] It finds, for example, explicit mention in BIS [6].

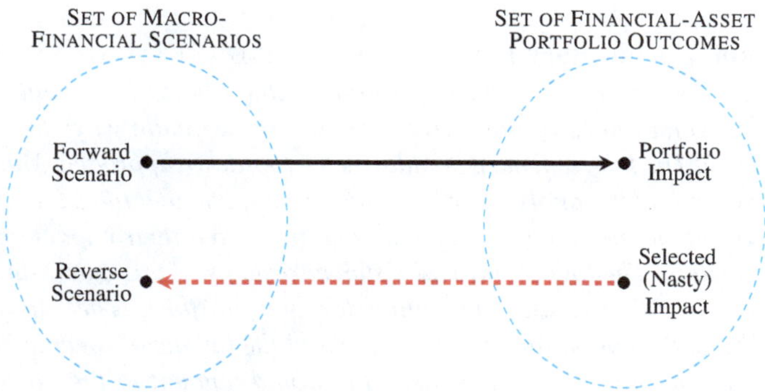


**Fig. 12.2** *Forward and reverse stress-testing*: This schematic illustrates, in a highly stylized fashion, the logical distinction between forward and reverse stress testing. The forward direction follows the standard approach of translating a macro-financial shock into a portfolio result. Reverse stress-testing tries to work backwards from a particularly unpleasant portfolio outcome to the original macro-financial shock. This helps to identify vulnerabilities.

Figure 12.2 provides a visualization of the notion of reverse stress testing. The forward direction follows the standard, top-down approach of translating a macro-financial shock into a portfolio result. Reverse stress-testing works backwards from a particularly unpleasant (i.e., nasty) portfolio outcome to the original macro-financial shock. Thinking a bit more mathematically, the set of macro-financial scenarios can be seen as the domain. Each stress scenario, or function argument, is passed through some (usually unknown) stress-testing function to determine the portfolio impact (i.e., the function target or image). Reverse stress-testing essentially involves selecting some portfolio loss from the image of the stress-testing function and trying to infer its pre-image.[9] Notice that we explicitly avoid the term *inverse*, but instead use pre-image; there is no reason to expect a unique one-to-one correspondence between portfolio outcomes and macro-financial scenarios. A bad portfolio outcome could occur through many different possible constellations of adverse macro-financial variables (and vice versa).

By focusing on adverse portfolio outcomes, the reverse stress-testing process can help to identify vulnerabilities. Once again, this is not quite equivalent to a bottom-up approach. In the forthcoming practical discussion, however, it will come tantalizingly close.

[9] Since we don't really know the true form of the stress-testing function, this can be a challenging task.

**Colour and Commentary 143** (STRESS-TESTING STRATEGIES): *Stress-testing analysis seeks to identify portfolio vulnerabilities associated with extreme, adverse states of the world.*[a] *There are two main ways to address this problem. The first, and most popular, is the top-down approach. Motivated from forward-looking analysis or historical crises, one identifies a collection of unpleasant macro-financial outcomes and traces out their impact on one's capital position. The logic is basically summarized as: if this macro-financial event happens, this is the implication for our portfolio. The alternative, referred to as the bottom-up approach, looks at the impact of specific adverse portfolio events. In our specific case, this would amount to the downgrade of a given set of obligors or those within a geographic region or sector. Related to the bottom-up approach, but nonetheless distinct, is the notion of reverse stress-testing. This basically takes the bottom-up method a step further by trying to identify the macro-financial shock (or shocks) that might have created it. Although the context differs, the conceptual idea of stress-testing is identical in engineering settings. When building a bridge, for example, the engineer seeks to understand the vulnerability in her design and construction to various wind sheers, weight loads, and a variety of other dimensions beyond a financial analyst's expertise. Instead of physical structures, our objective is to explore and identify important vulnerabilities in our asset portfolios that might jeopardize the firm's capital adequacy position.*

[a] The creditworthiness state variable in our credit-risk economic capital model incidentally uses a similar idea, but maps out the entire credit loss distribution (including many extreme outcomes).

### *12.1.3 Managing Time*

In stress-testing analysis, time can be a bit tricky. When, for example, does a scenario actually occur? We cannot simply (without some reflection, at least) snap our fingers and impose a large-scale, negative shock to our asset portfolio. Granted, some adverse situations can occur quickly, but often they unfold over multiple quarters or even years. Even if the effect is instantaneous (or close to it), the aftermath is also important for our analysis.

The consequence is that we should expect our macro-financial scenarios to unfold over time. For argument's sake, let's fix our stress horizon to one year.[10] This immediately raises a second question: how do we describe the portfolio? It is exceedingly unlikely that the portfolio remains fixed over a one-year period. Even

[10] This is at the lower end of the scale. It is not uncommon to see two- to five-year stress horizons.

in the unlikely case that it did, multiple aspects of the portfolio will nonetheless change. At a minimum, there will be principal repayments reducing exposures and all instruments will have a shorter tenor.[11] In short, the passage of time creates a number of thorny issues.

There is no single correct way to solve this problem. It basically involves a trade-off between granularity and accuracy on one hand and parsimony and manageability on the other. Looking out numerous years into the future makes it logistically almost impossible to maintain the full details of one's current portfolio structure. There are simply too many moving parts associated with the roll-down of the current portfolio and assumptions regarding the details of new assets. The only workable approach involves dimension reduction. One creates a stylized, low-dimensional view of one's portfolio and builds a model to describe its intertemporal evolution.[12] The top-down or bottom-up scenarios are then applied to this stylized portfolio. Corners nonetheless need to be cut and overall accuracy suffers.

The alternative, which is only tenable for reasonable short time horizons, involves assuming that the current portfolio remains fixed in its current state. As unrealistic as this might appear, it does offer some important advantages. The full granularity of the portfolio is preserved. The regional and industry identities along with credit ratings, loss-given-defaults, tenors, and exposures are known with precision. This permits continued use of our detailed economic-capital and loan-impairment frameworks in the computation. If one looks too far into the future or expects imminent portfolio changes, then this tactic will break down.

This issue basically brings us to the distinction between risk-management and strategic analysis. The risk-management viewpoint takes the portfolio as it is, operates at the highest level of detail, and restricts its attention to relatively short time periods. Strategic analysis extends over longer horizons and provides the analyst with flexibility over the portfolio structure. The ability to dial up or down risk attributes to meet strategic objectives is, after all, the main point of the exercise. To do this, one needs to stylize the portfolio construction. Generally speaking, since one cannot legitimately do both, it is necessary to pick a lane.

With these ideas in mind, we will consciously take the risk-management pathway. Preservation of full portfolio dimensionality is critical, because it allows us to borrow from the various helpful ideas presented in previous chapters. Digging into the minutiae of the portfolio, from both top-down and bottom-up perspectives, also permits us to more definitely identify vulnerabilities. There is a price. We cannot defensibly look too far into the future. A one-year time horizon is thus a fairly tight constraint for our analysis.

---

[11] All else equal, this roll-down effect will reduce migration risk.

[12] This is common in strategic portfolio-choice problems. See, for example, Bolder [7, 8] or Bolder and Deeley [9] for a practical example demonstrating just how involved such exercises can become.

### 12.1.4 Remaining Gameplan

We asked *three* fundamental questions and have provided detailed answers for each of them. Our first question enquires about the practical link between stress and portfolio outcomes. The principal risk pathway for our stress scenarios towards the firm's capital position—within economic capital's through-the-cycle goggles—is via downgrade of individual credit obligors. This provides us with a fairly clear idea of the capital demand and supply effects to be considered.

The second question is strategic: how does one actually go about stress testing? There are two fairly broadly defined alternative avenues for the investigation of stress-scenario impact on our portfolios: the top-down and bottom-up approaches. Rather than choosing a specific track, we will, as we've done throughout this entire book, consider *both* approaches to this problem. There is no compelling reason to specialize our stress-testing framework when much can be learned from exploration of both alternatives

The final question relates to management of the time dimension. We will make use of the current portfolio—in all of its detail—for our analysis. This critically assumes that the portfolio structure remains unchanged as we advance in time. To avoid this assumption turning into conceptual abuse, we must constrain our time horizon to a single year.[13] In making this choice, we have explicitly adopted a high-dimensional, risk-management perspective in our stress-testing analysis.[14]

The remaining discussion in this chapter is relatively easily described. In the context of a small (fictitious) portfolio, we will proceed to examine both the theory and implementation associated with both the top-down and bottom-up approaches to stress-testing analysis. This exercise will not only underscore the key ideas, it will also uncover the many links to the discussion from previous chapters. In this manner, it pulls the (occasionally) disparate material in this book together for the reader.

## 12.2 The Top-Down, or Macro, Approach

The top-down approach is the proper starting point. When most people think about stress-testing analysis, it is the top-down perspective that they have in mind. Figure 12.3 gets right to the point with a description of the various steps involved in our specific capital-focused, credit-risk implementation of a top-down stress analysis.

[13] This, to be perfectly frank, is already pushing things somewhat. Its defensibility will turn on whether or not one believes that the current portfolio is a reasonable estimator for the future portfolio one year hence.

[14] The longer-term, strategic perspective is also entirely sensible. It does, however, bring us closer to the important (strategic) question of capital forecasting and planning.

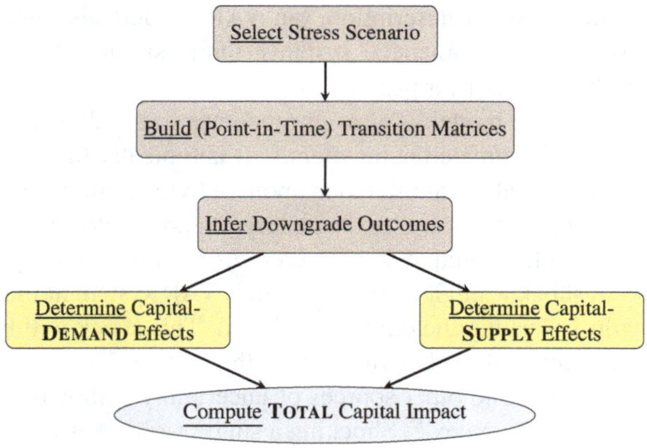


**Fig. 12.3** *Top-down sequencing*: This graphic walks through the sequence of steps—from selection of stress scenarios to computation of the total capital impact—involved in the performance of a top-down stress-testing analysis. It is a relatively complex multi-step undertaking.

The sequence of steps in Fig. 12.3 is surprisingly long. Selection of one's stress scenario—which is of utmost importance—is only the beginning. One then needs to establish a link between these adverse macro-financial outcomes and individual credit-obligor downgrades. Fortunately, in Chap. 8 we constructed a methodology for mapping stress outcomes into point-in-time default and transition probabilities. The basic loan impairment calculation—from Chap. 9—relied heavily upon the default-probability dimension. Our top-down stress-testing efforts, by contrast, will exploit the full point-in-time transition matrices to infer portfolio downgrades.[15]

Given the resulting portfolio downgrades, the remaining effort is rather straightforward. We simply determine the valuation, loan-impairment and economic-capital consequences, organize the results, and compute the capital impact. The lower boxes in Fig. 12.3 are common in both the top-down and bottom-up approaches. This is the good news. The bad news is that there is an infinity of possible stress scenarios that one might potentially select. We require some way to make sense of this bewildering array of choice.

Some useful guidance can be found in the field of macroeconomics. More than 40 years ago, in a path-breaking paper, Sims [29] introduced the vector auto-regression (VAR) model to the economics profession.[16] VAR models remain, to this day, a critical element of the economist's toolkit. The reason is that this approach is surprisingly flexible in its ability to capture the complex interactions between a system (i.e., vector) of correlated, time-indexed random variables. Not only does

[15] The through-the-cycle matrix is still used to compute credit-migration economic capital given each obligor's (shocked or current) credit state.

[16] Christiano [10] is a fascinating look into the history and repercussions of Sims [29] and related work.

it provide a useful statistical description, but VAR models also permit generally effective forecasts of macro-financial systems. Quite simply, the VAR model is basically custom-built for our purposes.

Vector auto-regressive models—of even moderate size—almost invariably possess a large number of estimated parameters.[17] It is typically fairly hopeless to try to interpret, or perform statistical inference upon, individual model coefficients. For this reason, different strategies are used to interpret and employ VAR models. One common, and powerful, technique is referred to as the impulse-response function. The core idea is to shock a single variable in one's VAR system at the current time, while simultaneously leaving the others unaffected. This shock will typically exert an instantaneous effect on the other variables in the system. The VAR model is then forecasted forward—with no other sources of uncertainty—allowing it to return to its long-term equilibrium values.[18] Shocking a single variable is the *impulse*, while the forecasting results represent the *response*.

While not a definitive solution, the VAR framework and its associated impulse-response functions offer a helpful strategy for organizing the vast array of possible stress scenarios. The first step is to transform our collection of macro-financial variables—we will continue to use the specific variable choices introduced in Chap. 8—into vector-auto-regressive form. We then build the appropriate impulse-response functions. Using these quantities, we may then investigate, for each of our macro-financial state variables, the joint impact of a multiple standard-deviation shock over a one-year stress horizon. Following the sequence of steps outlined in Fig. 12.3, we may then compute a separate capital impact for each macro-financial shock. Instead of a single stress scenario, we produce an logically organized collection of them. This provides some semblance of order to the confusing task of stress-scenario selection. It need not be the end of the line. One can use this information to construct more global stress scenarios, but this analysis will help identify key vulnerabilities. In this way, it lends a bit of direction to any subsequent investigation.

**Colour and Commentary 144** (THE IMPULSE-RESPONSE FUNCTION)*: It is simultaneously easy and difficult to select a macro-financial stress scenario. It is practically easy, since one need only mix and match some random set of movements in one's collection of state variables. It is difficult, because there are infinitely many possible choices and it's not* a priori

(continued)

[17] This is not always true, since one can impose numerous clever constraints to control and guide variable interactions. In these cases, individual parameters can become quite important. The sizable parameter dimensionality, the previous point notwithstanding, typically holds.

[18] Although the term through-the-cycle is not actively used in macroeconomics, the long-term equilibrium of a VAR model is essentially the same idea.

**Colour and Commentary 144** (continued)
*clear how to identify a meaningful one. The field of macroeconomics offers a clue towards resolving this impasse. Introduced decades ago by Sims [29], the vector auto-regressive model admirably captures the dynamics of high-dimensional, correlated, macroeconomic and financial time series. The vector-auto-regressive framework also offers a tool—termed the impulse-response function—that describes the system-wide impact of a shock to a single variable in one's system. Capturing the correlation effects, the impulse-response function traces out the system's return to its long-term equilibrium. Shocking each macro-financial variable and applying the associated impulse-response function in a systematic fashion allows us to examine our portfolio's vulnerabilities one source of uncertainty at a time. The results might represent one's final analysis or a stepping stone to the construction of a more detailed stress scenario. In either case, this strategy lends some welcome structure to a difficult choice.*

### 12.2.1 Introducing the Vector Auto-Regressive Model

Nothing in life is free. To effectively employ impulse-response functions in our exploration of our macro-financial scenario space, we first need to fully understand how they work. This requires an associated appreciation of the vector auto-regressive model. Accomplishing this task, which will require a bit of work and patience, is the objective of this section.

### 12.2.2 The Basic Idea

Given their general popularity in economic circles, there is no shortage of superb sources on vector auto-regressive models. A central resource, for time-series analysis in general and vector auto-regressions in particular, is Hamilton [16].[19] We will lean heavily on his treatment and, indeed, borrow his general notation to sketch out the main elements required for our purposes.[20] We begin with a time-indexed, vector-valued collection of random variables, $y_t \in \mathbb{R}^{\kappa \times 1}$. For our purposes, this will be our set of macro-financial variables introduced in Chap. 8. More generally, they could be anything. As the name strongly suggests, we are basically regressing the

[19] Judge et al. [18] and Lütkepohl [20] are two other excellent alternative choices.

[20] The reader is, of course, recommended to return to the source. Hamilton [16] is a much more complete, nuanced, and thoughtful exposition.

current values of the system on their previous values. That is, we are regressing the vector $y_t$ on previous versions of itself. More specifically, we postulate a description of $y_t$ as a linear function of its previous values. In general, it can be written as

$$y_t = c + \sum_{i=1}^{p} \Phi_i y_{t-i} + \epsilon_t, \tag{12.1}$$

where $c \in \mathbb{R}^{\kappa \times 1}$ is a vector of constants, each $\Phi_i \in \mathbb{R}^{\kappa \times \kappa}$ is a parameter matrix, and $\epsilon_t \in \mathbb{R}^{\kappa \times 1}$ is an error vector. $p \in \mathbb{N}$ is the number of lags, or time steps into the past, used to describe the current $y_t$ outcome. This model arises very naturally. If we perform, as we did in Chap. 2, a standard discretization of a Markov process (such as a drifted geometric Brownian motion) we will recover something conceptually similar to Eq. 12.1. There is, therefore, a clear link between these econometric ideas and the study of stochastic processes.

To keep the notational clutter under control—and to specialize to our specific application—we will set $p = 1$ leading to:[21]

$$y_t = c + \Phi y_{t-1} + \epsilon_t. \tag{12.2}$$

In this case, we have a single matrix, $\Phi \in \mathbb{R}^{\kappa \times \kappa}$, of coefficients in addition to the constant vector, $c$. The structure of the error term is crucially important. In particular, we assume that $\mathbb{E}(\epsilon_s) = 0$ for all $s$ and

$$\mathbb{E}\left(\epsilon_t \epsilon_s^T\right) = \begin{cases} \Omega : t = s \\ 0 : t \neq s \end{cases}, \tag{12.3}$$

where $\Omega$ is a real-valued, positive-definite, symmetric covariance matrix. This basically means that there is a fixed error structure at each point in time, but these errors are not serially correlated throughout time.

[21] All of the following results generalize readily the $p$-lag case. In fact, with a bit of cleverness, any vector auto-regressive process can be written with a first-order structure. This is referred to as the so-called companion form. Again, Hamilton [16] is a good starting place for this discussion.

If we take expectations of both sides of Eq. 12.2, we can determine the long-term unconditional average value of $y_t$. The consequence is:

$$\mathbb{E}(y_t) = \mathbb{E}\Big(c + \Phi y_{t-1} + \epsilon_t\Big), \tag{12.4}$$
$$\mathbb{E}(y_t) = c + \Phi\mathbb{E}(y_{t-1}) + \underbrace{\mathbb{E}(\epsilon_t)}_{=0},$$
$$\underbrace{\mathbb{E}(y_t)}_{\mu} - \Phi\,\underbrace{\mathbb{E}(y_{t-1})}_{\mu} = c,$$
$$\mu = (I - \Phi)^{-1}c,$$

where $\mu$ represents the (unconditional) mean of our vector auto-regressive process. This is the multivariate analogue of the one-dimensional average, $\frac{c}{1-\Phi}$. In the univariate case, it is clear that $\Phi \in \mathbb{R}$ has to be less than unity or the long-term mean is undefined. The same intuition applies to Eq. 12.4, but the condition is a bit more complicated. We rather obviously require that the $\kappa \times \kappa$ matrix, $(I - \Phi)$, be non-singular. The constraint is that all of the $\kappa$ eigenvalues of $\Phi$ must lie in the unit circle.[22]. Vector auto-regressions satisfying this constraint are referred to as covariance-stationary. In practice, this is essentially a non-negotiable condition.

Our principal interest lies with the forecasting of $y_t$ several periods into the future. This is accomplished with the use of the natural recurrence in the vector auto-regression. Let us begin, again from Eq. 12.2, with the conditional expectation of $y_{t+1}$,

$$y_{t+1} = c + \Phi y_t + \epsilon_t, \tag{12.5}$$
$$\mathbb{E}\left(y_{t+1}\,\middle|\,\sigma\{y_t\}\right) = \mathbb{E}\left(c + \Phi y_t + \epsilon_t\,\middle|\,\sigma\{y_t\}\right),$$
$$= c + \Phi\underbrace{\mathbb{E}\left(y_t\,\middle|\,\sigma\{y_t\}\right)}_{y_t} + \underbrace{\mathbb{E}\left(\epsilon_t\,\middle|\,\sigma\{y_t\}\right)}_{=0},$$
$$= c + \Phi y_t,$$

where $\sigma\{y_t\}$ denotes the $\sigma$-algebra—or as econometricians refer to it, the information set—generated by $y_t$. This result is relatively unsurprising: the conditional one-step forward expectation is a linear function of the lagged values, $y_t$. Trying

[22] Or, equivalently, that the eigenvalues of $(I - \Phi)$ are all *outside* the unit circle. We refer to the unit circle because eigenvalues may occasionally take complex values. We thus consider the complex norm or modulus of the eigenvalue. If $\lambda$ denotes the eigenvalue, then the general condition is $|\lambda| = |r + zi| = \sqrt{r^2 + z^2} < 1$ for any $r, z \in \mathbb{R}$ where $i = \sqrt{-1}$. For more on the complex norm, see Harris and Stocker [17, Chapter 17]

two steps forward—with the same information set—and using similar arguments, yields

$$
\begin{aligned}
y_{t+2} &= c + \Phi y_{t+1} + \epsilon_{t+1}, \qquad (12.6)\\
\mathbb{E}\left(y_{t+2}\middle|\sigma\{y_t\}\right) &= \mathbb{E}\left(c + \Phi y_{t+1} + \epsilon_{t+1}\middle|\sigma\{y_t\}\right),\\
&= c + \Phi \underbrace{\mathbb{E}\left(y_{t+1}\middle|\sigma\{y_t\}\right)}_{\text{Eq. 12.5}} + \underbrace{\mathbb{E}\left(\epsilon_{t+1}\middle|\sigma\{y_t\}\right)}_{=0},\\
&= c + \Phi\Big(c + \Phi y_t\Big),\\
&= c + \Phi c + \Phi^2 y_t.
\end{aligned}
$$

We can, of course, continue to play this game as long as we like. Ultimately, the general term for $k$ steps into the future is described as

$$
\begin{aligned}
y_{t+k} &= c + \Phi c + \cdots + \Phi^{k-1}c + \Phi^k y_t, \qquad (12.7)\\
&= (I + \Phi + \cdots + \Phi^{k-1}\Big)c + \Phi^k y_t,\\
&= \sum_{i=0}^{k-1} \Phi^i c + \Phi^k y_t.
\end{aligned}
$$

This yields a rather elegant result. If we continue to the limit and let $k$ tends towards infinity, then two things happen. First, given that all of the eigenvalues of $\Phi$ are in the unit circle, for sufficiently large $k$, $\Phi^k$ tends to zero. This means that the impact of the conditioning information, $y_t$, disappears over time. Using the same properties of $\Phi$, the first term in Eq. 12.7 converges to $(I - \Phi)^{-1}c$, which is none other than the long-term unconditional mean from Eq. 12.4. To be very definitive, using the fact that the limit of the sum is the sum of the limits, the result is:

$$
\begin{aligned}
\lim_{k\to\infty} y_{t+k} &= \lim_{k\to\infty}\left(\sum_{i=0}^{k-1}\Phi^i c + \Phi^k y_t\right), \qquad (12.8)\\
&= \underbrace{\lim_{k\to\infty}\left(\sum_{i=0}^{k-1}\Phi^i c\right)}_{(I-\Phi)^{-1}c} + \underbrace{\lim_{k\to\infty}\Phi^k y_t}_{=0},\\
&= \mu.
\end{aligned}
$$

**Table 12.1** *Vector auto-regression details*: The underlying table highlights a number of interesting details associated with a VAR(1) implementation of our $\kappa = 10$ macro-financial variables. We observe, by virtue of the eigenvalues of $\Phi$, that it is covariance stationary. The volatility of the error term and the long-term mean values are also displayed for each state variable.

| Macro-financial variable | $\Phi$ Eigen-values | $\Omega$ Error volatility | Long-term mean ($\mu$) | Series mean |
|---|---|---|---|---|
| Credit spreads ($\varphi_t$) | 0.32 | 0.34 | 2.03 | 2.01 |
| Inflation ($\pi_t$) | 0.82 | 0.20 | 0.43 | 0.42 |
| Fed Funds ($r_t$) | 0.82 | 0.27 | −0.03 | −0.04 |
| GDP ($\theta_t$) | 0.62 | 4.17 | 2.45 | 2.57 |
| Unemployment ($k_t$) | 0.51 | 0.90 | 5.88 | 5.89 |
| (Non-Fuel) Commodities ($w_t$) | 0.51 | 5.29 | 0.79 | 0.79 |
| S&P 500 ($m_t$) | 0.33 | 5.38 | 1.82 | 1.97 |
| Oil ($h_t$) | 0.33 | 0.15 | 0.01 | 0.01 |
| Curve slope ($s_t$) | 0.13 | 0.34 | −0.02 | −0.01 |
| VIX ($\sigma_t$) | 0.07 | 5.07 | 0.10 | 0.05 |

In other words, as we move into the future, our forecasted values of $y_{t+k}$ ultimately tend towards the unconditional mean of our vector auto-regressive process. As a practical matter, this convergence can occur rather quickly, often with a few years. This is precisely the same logic—indeed, borrowed from this fundamental aspect of time-series analysis—used in Chap. 8 to motivate the notion of time decay.

At this point, let's quickly return to our concrete situation. We introduced a $\kappa = 10$ system of macro-financial variables in Chap. 8. While perhaps somewhat USA-centric, they do represent a fairly broad view of the global macroeconomy and financial markets. It is a good idea, at this early stage, to fit a VAR(1) specification to this data-set.[23] Table 12.1 provides some key values for each macro-financial variable. The first point is that all of the eigenvalues of the slope coefficient matrix, $\Phi$, are comfortably below unity. We may thus, with some relief, conclude that a VAR(1) model of our macro-financial system is covariance stationary. Using Eq. 12.8, we also display the long-term equilibrium values for each variable. In the column immediately beside it, we find the average value for each time series across our three-decade data-set. While not precisely the same, the individual $\mu$ values are generally quite close to their simple, long-term mean. This should underscore the conceptual link between equilibrium VAR values and the through-the-cycle perspective. The final element in Table 12.1, from the diagonal of $\Omega$, is an estimate of each macro-financial variable's error volatility. This provides some insight into the typical magnitude of a shock.

[23] Recall that our quarterly data spans almost 30 years from the early 1990s until 2021; it thus comprises about 120 observations for each macro-financial variable.

**Colour and Commentary 145** (A VECTOR AUTO-REGRESSIVE STARTING POINT): *In Chap. 8, when introducing our system of 10 macro-financial variables, we took pains to ensure that none of the individual components was non-stationary.*[a] *This was important for estimation of Yang [33]'s structural model linking through-the-cycle and point-in-time probabilities, but it also proves helpful in the stress-testing setting. Estimating a VAR(1) specification for our macro-financial system reveals a covariance-stationary result.*[b] *This basically ensures that our statistical model is stable. Moreover, when left to its own devices, it will tend back towards its well-defined long-term equilibrium values. These equilibrium outcomes, not coincidentally, are not far from the long-term unconditional mean estimates for each individual time series. The VAR model equilibrium is thus closely coupled with the idea of a through-the-cycle perspective.*

[a] We relied on the work of Dickey and Fuller [11] to test this condition.

[b] Or, in other words, all of the eigenvalues of the slope coefficient matrix, $\Phi$, are comfortably within the unit circle.

### 12.2.3 An Important Link

There is an equivalent representation of the vector auto-regression, which is particularly important for our purposes. It is based on a recursive argument and, to be honest, is a bit tedious to construct. It nevertheless relies on a number of the basic ideas introduced in the preceding discussion. Let's again begin with Eq. 12.2,

$$\begin{aligned} y_t &= \overbrace{c + \Phi \underbrace{\left(c + \Phi y_{t-2} + \epsilon_{t-1}\right)}_{y_{t-1}} + \epsilon_t}^{\text{Eq. 12.2}}, \qquad (12.9) \\ &= c + \Phi c + \Phi^2 y_{t-2} + \Phi \epsilon_{t-1} + \epsilon_t, \\ &= c + \Phi c + \Phi^2 \underbrace{\left(c + \Phi y_{t-3} + \epsilon_{t-2}\right)}_{y_{t-2}} + \Phi \epsilon_{t-1} + \epsilon_t, \\ &= c + \Phi c + \Phi^2 c + \Phi^3 y_{t-3} + \Phi^2 \epsilon_{t-2} + \Phi \epsilon_{t-1} + \epsilon_t, \\ &= \sum_{i=0}^{2} \Phi^i c + \Phi^3 y_{t-3} + \sum_{i=0}^{2} B_i \epsilon_{t-i}, \end{aligned}$$

where $B_i = \Phi^i$ denotes the $i$th moving-average coefficient matrix. After two recursions, we begin to see the general pattern. If we push this out indefinitely, we arrive at the following structure with two main components,

$$y_t = \underbrace{\sum_{i=0}^{\infty} \Phi^i c}_{(I-\Phi)^{-1}c} + \sum_{i=0}^{\infty} B_i \epsilon_{t-i}, \tag{12.10}$$
$$= \mu + \sum_{i=0}^{\infty} B_i \epsilon_{t-i},$$

which, as we saw before, is only possible if $y_t$ is covariance stationary. This is sometimes called the Wold representation of the vector auto-regression; it is basically a vector moving-average process with an infinite number of lags. The idea is that the current value of our random vector (i.e., $y_t$) can be described as its long-term average plus the sum of all of the past $B_i$-weighted shocks going back as far as one can imagine. Because all of the eigenvalues of $\Phi$ are restricted to the unit circle, however, the importance of these past errors, shocks or innovations gradually decays and, ultimately, disappears over time. Thus, the long-term unconditional average plays a central role whether we are looking forward as in Eq. 12.8 or backwards as in Eq. 12.10.

From a stress-testing perspective, our interest is in the consequences of a specific (adverse) shock to one of the key elements of $y_t$. Specifically, we might ask about the impact of a three standard deviation downward movement in economic output. It is very interesting to consider, on a standalone basis, what this might mean for our portfolio? Equation 12.10 shows us, rather clearly, that the mechanism to construct such a shock is through a perturbation of one or more elements in $\epsilon_t$. Let's consider a concrete one-period forward version of Eq. 12.10

$$y_{t+1} = \mu + \sum_{i=0}^{\infty} B_i \epsilon_{t+1-i}. \tag{12.11}$$

What if we compute the derivative of $y_{t+1}$ with respect to $\epsilon_t$? That is, the sensitivity of our vector process to a change in the innovation term. The result is

$$\frac{\partial y_{t+1}}{\partial \epsilon_t} = \frac{\partial}{\partial \epsilon_t}\left(\mu + \sum_{i=0}^{\infty} B_i \epsilon_{t+1-i}\right), \tag{12.12}$$
$$= B_1.$$

This immediately allows us to describe the impact of our perturbation on $y_{t+1}$ as

$$\begin{aligned}\underbrace{y_{t+1} - y_t}_{\Delta y_{t+1}} &= \frac{\partial y_{t+1}}{\partial \epsilon_t}\epsilon_t, \\ &= B_1 \epsilon_t.\end{aligned} \tag{12.13}$$

Repeating this same chain of logic leads to the following general version of Eq. 12.11

$$y_{t+n} = \mu + B_n \epsilon_t, \tag{12.14}$$

for an arbitrary choice of $n$. This immediately suggests that we can categorize our time $t$ shock to $\epsilon_t$ as

$$\begin{aligned}\underbrace{y_{t+n} - y_t}_{\Delta y_{t+n}} &\approx \frac{\partial y_{t+n}}{\partial \epsilon_t}\epsilon_t, \\ &\approx B_n \epsilon_t.\end{aligned} \tag{12.15}$$

Given that each of the moving-average coefficients is intimately related to powers of the $\Phi$ matrix, as discussed previously, the impact of the $\epsilon_t$ shock ultimately dissipates to zero.

It is rather interesting to think about a shock at time $t$ of magnitude $\epsilon_t$, but zero for all other future periods (i.e., $\epsilon_{t+1}, \cdots, \epsilon_{t+n} \equiv 0$). To make it more specific, we could give a special structure to $\epsilon_t$; in particular, we might define it as a one standard-deviation shock to the $j$th element of $\epsilon_t$ and zero for all other factors. Following Eq. 12.15, the system impact going forward in time is simply,

$$B_1\epsilon_t, B_2\epsilon_t, \cdots, B_n\epsilon_t, \cdots. \tag{12.16}$$

The specific shock could be to output, employment, or the oil price. Indeed, we could perform a sequence of such shocks, in an organized sequential fashion, for each of our macro-financial variables. This powerful idea is called the impulse-response function. It helps us identify—within the context of a large number of variables and parameters—the impact of a shock to inflation on, for example, the oil price in three periods.

### 12.2.4 The Impulse-Response Function

There is, however, a catch. Since $\epsilon_t$ is a correlated system of errors, it becomes very difficult to disentangle the effects of a given shock. The consequence is that Eq. 12.15—since it is not really telling us what we would like to know—is not typically directly used for this task. Instead, econometricians use some clever tricks to orthogonalize the covariance matrix of $\epsilon_t$. The consequence of this adjustment is that we can interpret a modified version of Eq. 12.15 as a true partial derivative.

The general approach is to revise somewhat the Wold representation from Eq. 12.14—under the assumption of a single time-$t$ shock—as

$$\begin{aligned} y_{t+n} &= \underbrace{\mu + B_n \overbrace{H^{-1} H}^{I} \epsilon_t}_{\text{Eq. 12.14}}, \\ &= \mu + B_n H^{-1} u_t, \end{aligned} \tag{12.17}$$

where $u_t = H\epsilon_t$ and $H \in \mathbb{R}^{\kappa \times \kappa}$ is non-singular. This mathematical sleight of hand—essentially multiplying by the matrix equivalent of one—permits us to treat our revised error vector as a projection.

While this might not seem like progress, it all depends on the choice of $H$. The objective is to find an $H$ such that the covariance matrix of $u_t$ is diagonal. From Eq. 12.3, the error-covariance matrix of $\epsilon_t$ is denoted as $\Omega$, which represents a fairly natural jumping-off point. In particular, given its real-valued, symmetric and positive-definite form, we may write this error covariance matrix as,

$$\Omega = P P^T, \tag{12.18}$$

where $P \in \mathbb{R}^{\kappa \times \kappa}$ is a lower-triangular matrix.[24] The direct corollary of Eq. 12.18 is that

$$P^{-1}\Omega(P^{-1})^T = I. \tag{12.19}$$

With $H = P^{-1}$, or equivalently $u_t = P^{-1}\epsilon_t$, the variance of $u_t$ immediately becomes

$$\begin{aligned} \text{var}(u_t) &= \text{var}\Big(P^{-1}\epsilon_t\Big), \\ &= P^{-1} \underbrace{\text{var}(\epsilon_t)}_{\Omega} (P^{-1})^T, \\ &= \underbrace{P^{-1}\Omega(P^{-1})^T}_{\text{Eq. 12.19}}, \\ &= I. \end{aligned} \tag{12.20}$$

[24] This is referred to as the Cholesky factorization or decomposition, which has already made multiple appearances in previous chapters. Loosely speaking—although, not technically quite true—it feels a bit like the square-root of a matrix. See Golub and Loan [14, Chapter 4] and Press et al. [25, Section 2.9] for much more detailed background.

This is a pretty convenient choice of $H$, because the covariance matrix of $u_t$ is now the identity matrix. This amounts to an orthogonalization of the macro-financial shock dimension.

To introduce our (now independent) shocks, we let $\delta_j$ denote a $\kappa$-dimensional vector with a value of 1 at element $j$ and zero everywhere else. The value of $\delta_1$, for example, is simply

$$\delta_1 = \begin{bmatrix} 1 \\ 0 \\ \vdots \\ 0 \end{bmatrix} \tag{12.21}$$

By iterating over $\delta_j$ for $j = 1, \ldots, 10$, we can induce consecutive one-standard-deviation shocks for each of our individual macro-financial variables. Should we wish to generate larger shocks, we need only scale up the value of each $\delta_j$ by the appropriate constant.

We now have all of the moving parts needed to construct our impulse-response function. For the $i$th step into the future, it is usefully conceptualized as the difference of two conditional expectations. The first involves a shock of $\delta_j$ at time $t$, while the second is business as usual where we have no information on the shock. In both cases, we condition on the information available at time $t-1$. The distance between these conditional expectations brings us to the following orthogonalized form of the impulse-response function:

$$\begin{aligned} \text{irf}(i,j) &= \underbrace{\mathbb{E}\left(y_{t+i} \,\middle|\, u_t = \delta_j, \sigma\{\epsilon_{t-1}\}\right)}_{\substack{\text{Conditional expection given} \\ \text{shock to variable } j}} - \underbrace{\mathbb{E}\left(y_{t+i} \,\middle|\, \sigma\{\epsilon_{t-1}\}\right)}_{\substack{\text{Normal conditional} \\ \text{expectation}}}, \\ &= \mathbb{E}\left(\underbrace{\cancel{\mu} + B_i P u_t}_{\text{Eq. 12.17}} \,\middle|\, u_t = \delta_j, \sigma\{\epsilon_{t-1}\}\right) - \mathbb{E}\left(\underbrace{\cancel{\mu} + B_i P u_t}_{\text{Eq. 12.17}} \,\middle|\, \sigma\{\epsilon_{t-1}\}\right), \\ &= B_i P \delta_j - \cancel{B_i P P^{-1} \underbrace{\mathbb{E}\left(\epsilon_t \,\middle|\, \sigma\{\epsilon_{t-1}\}\right)}_{=0}}, \\ &= B_i P \delta_j. \end{aligned} \tag{12.22}$$

for $i = 0, \ldots, n$ and $j = 1, \ldots, \kappa$ where $B_i$ is the $i$th moving-average coefficient matrix and $P$ is the lower-diagonal factorization of $\Omega$. Given that $B_i, P \in \mathbb{R}^{\kappa \times \kappa}$ and $\delta_j \in \mathbb{R}^{\kappa \times 1}$ the result of Eq. 12.21 is a $\kappa$-dimensional vector for each time step. Tracing out Eq. 12.22 for each $i = 1, \ldots, n$ describes the adjustment of our macro-financial system associated with a one-standard-deviation innovation to the $j$th variable.

The orthogonalized impulse-response function is a huge step forward, but it still has an important shortcoming. The order of the shocks still matters. Slightly annoying, this requires us to reflect on issues of causality and essentially increases our number of cases from $\kappa$ to something rather larger. Koop et al. [19] and Pesaran and Shin [24]—with a significant amount of additional effort—offer a solution to this problem. Referred to as the *generalized* impulse-response function, they offer the following twist on Eq. 12.22

$$
\begin{aligned}
\text{girf}(i, j) &= \underbrace{\mathbb{E}\left(y_{t+i} \middle| \epsilon_t = \delta_j \sqrt{\omega_{jj}}, \sigma\{\epsilon_{t-1}\}\right)}_{\substack{\text{Conditional expection given} \\ \text{shock to variable } j}} - \underbrace{\mathbb{E}\left(y_{t+i} \middle| \sigma\{\epsilon_{t-1}\}\right)}_{\substack{\text{Normal conditional} \\ \text{expectation}}}, \qquad (12.23)\\
&= \mathbb{E}\left(\underbrace{\cancel{\mu} + B_i \epsilon_t}_{\text{Eq. 12.14}} \middle| \epsilon_t = \delta_j \sqrt{\omega_{jj}}, \sigma\{\epsilon_{t-1}\}\right) - \mathbb{E}\left(\underbrace{\cancel{\mu} + B_i \epsilon_t}_{\text{Eq. 12.14}} \middle| \sigma\{\epsilon_{t-1}\}\right), \\
&= B_i \mathbb{E}\left(\epsilon_t \middle| \epsilon_t = \delta_j \sqrt{\omega_{jj}}, \sigma\{\epsilon_{t-1}\}\right) - \cancel{\underbrace{B_i \,\mathbb{E}\left(\epsilon_t \middle| \sigma\{\epsilon_{t-1}\}\right)}_{=0}}, \\
&= \frac{B_i \Omega \delta_j \sqrt{\omega_{jj}}}{\omega_{jj}}, \\
&= \underbrace{\frac{B_i \Omega \delta_j}{\sqrt{\omega_{jj}}} \overbrace{\frac{\cancel{\sqrt{\omega_{jj}}}}{\cancel{\sqrt{\omega_{jj}}}}}^{=1}}_{\omega_{jj}}, \\
&= \frac{1}{\sqrt{\underbrace{\delta_j^T \Omega \delta_j}_{\omega_{jj}}}} B_i \Omega \delta_j,
\end{aligned}
$$

which is invariant to the ordering of the macro-financial shocks for $i = 0, \ldots, n$ and $j = 1, \ldots, \kappa$. This result relies on the fact that $\epsilon_t$ is multivariate normally distributed and requires setting the shock to $\epsilon_{jt}$ to the volatility of the $j$th element in our vector auto-regression.

We can immediately turn this, relatively abstract, discussion into practical, useable outputs. Figure 12.4, for each of our 10 macro-financial variables, illustrates the impact of a multiple standard-deviation downward shock to the Fed-funds rate over a 16-quarter (i.e., 4-year time horizon). The entire three-decade history and fitted

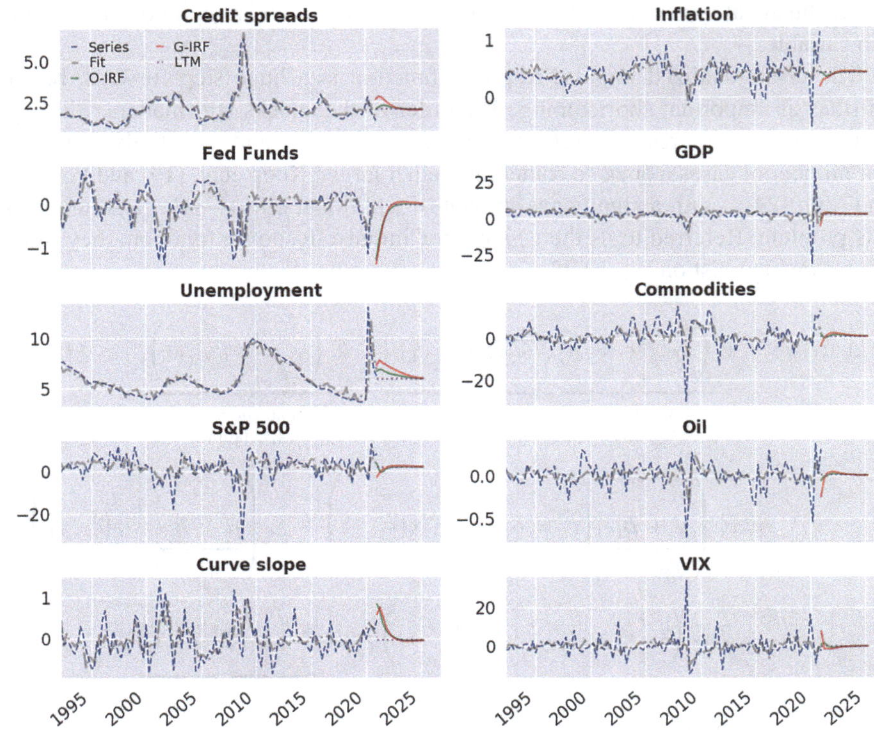


**Fig. 12.4** *Fed-funds impulse response functions*: These graphics illustrate the impact of a multiple standard-deviation downward shock to the Fed-funds rate variable. We observe the simultaneous impact to the other macro-financial variables and the gradual return—over a four-year period—back to their long-term values. Both the orthogonalized (O-IRF) and generalized (G-IRF) impulse-response functions are provided for comparison.

VAR(1) values are also presented. The orthogonalized and generalized impulse-response functions—from Eqs. 12.22 and 12.23, respectively—are naturally both included. Although they provide relatively similar results, there are a few notable points of deviation. In the following analysis, we will use the generalized method, from Eq. 12.23, since it is independent of the ordering.

The utility of the impulse-response function is clearly visible in Fig. 12.4. A large downward shock to the Fed-funds rate leads to instantaneous adjustment to all factors. Particularly effected are the credit spreads, unemployment, output, oil prices, and the slope of the yield curve. The magnitude, direction, and duration of the effects are interesting to examine. Figure 12.4 starkly illustrates why Sims [29]'s suggested use of VAR models found such success. It permits us to assess the plausibility of the model dynamics within an intuitive framework. It seems

**Table 12.2** *An imaginary portfolio*: To examine the various flavours of stress-testing analysis that one may perform, it is easier to conceptualize with a concrete portfolio. This entirely fictitious example, summarized in the underlying table, is hopefully small enough to see what is going on, but large enough to illustrate key trends.

| # | PD | Exposure (EUR) | LGD | Tenor (yrs.) | Grace (yrs.) | Bullet Loan ? | Coupon Rate | Fair-Valued ? | Systemic Weight | Concentr. Index |
|---|---|---|---|---|---|---|---|---|---|---|
| 1 | 3 | 3,500,000 | 0.40 | 6 | 0 | True | 1.50% | True | 0.24 | 0.75 |
| 2 | 4 | 1,500,000 | 0.35 | 4 | 0 | True | 1.75% | True | 0.19 | 0.72 |
| 3 | 7 | 2,000,000 | 0.45 | 3 | 1 | False | 1.00% | False | 0.22 | 0.80 |
| 4 | 9 | 1,750,000 | 0.55 | 2 | 0 | True | 2.25% | False | 0.30 | 0.85 |
| 5 | 13 | 1,500,000 | 0.60 | 5 | 2 | False | 3.50% | False | 0.15 | 0.70 |
| 6 | 14 | 3,000,000 | 0.15 | 18 | 6 | False | 3.00% | False | 0.40 | 0.95 |
| 7 | 15 | 1,000,000 | 0.35 | 3 | 1 | False | 4.00% | False | 0.28 | 0.90 |
| 8 | 17 | 4,500,000 | 0.30 | 15 | 5 | True | 5.00% | False | 0.22 | 0.75 |
| 9 | 18 | 750,000 | 0.40 | 5 | 2 | False | 6.50% | False | 0.20 | 0.80 |
| 10 | 20 | 500,000 | 0.20 | 4 | 1 | False | 6.00% | False | 0.40 | 0.90 |
| Total/Mean | 11.1 | 20,000,000 | 0.36 | 8.7 | 2.4 | 56% | 3.12% | 25% | 0.26 | 0.80 |

rather plausible that a dramatic downward movement in interest rates would be accompanied with falling output, commodity and equity prices, a widening of credit spreads, lower inflation, higher unemployment, a steeper yield curve, and enhanced financial-market volatility. The behaviour of each individual member of our macro-financial system can be examined in this manner. For our purposes, therefore, it makes for an excellent stress-testing tool. In the coming sections, we'll investigate the portfolio and capital consequences associated with 10 separate versions of Fig. 12.4.

## 12.2.5 A Base Sample Portfolio

Equipped with all of the necessary technical elements to perform a top-down stress-testing analysis, all we need is a portfolio. For obvious reasons, the examination of the vulnerabilities of NIB's actual portfolio is a bad idea. Even if we could, the expositional and pedagogical value would be limited by the portfolio size. It is simply too hard to see precisely what is going on in the face of hundreds, or even thousands, of individual positions. Our solution, as in a few previous chapters, is to consider a fabricated example.

Table 12.2 displays a fictitious portfolio comprised of ten distinct positions with an equal number of credit obligors.[25] The number of positions is intended to form a happy compromise along the size dimension. Too many instruments and it is

[25] This abstracts from many complicating real-world factors such as multiple loans and instruments with a single credit counterparty, guarantees, and derivative contracts.

difficult to follow, but too few limits the possible dynamics and interesting cases to be examined. The total portfolio is EUR 20 million with an average PD—along our internal scale—of roughly 11, a mean tenor of roughly 9 years, and a weighted-average loss-given-default of about 0.35. The elements have an assortment of coupon rates and about half of the total notional amounts have a bullet-repayment profile. Two high-quality instruments—allocated to an internal trading portfolio—are fair-valued, while the remainder are accounted for via amortized cost. This creates some distinction between valuation and loan-impairment effects. Finally, Table 12.2 also includes (randomly assigned) systemic weights and concentration-index values to permit easy use of the economic-capital approximation model from Chap. 5.

Using Tables 12.2, 12.3 demonstrates the base, un-shocked, risk position for our imaginary portfolio. It includes both the stage-I and II through-the-cycle expected-credit loss amounts as well as the default, migration, and total economic-capital estimates. We assume that all obligors, at inception, find themselves in stage I.[26] The consequence is that the total loan-impairment is less than one percent of the overall portfolio.[27] Credit-risk economic capital, by contrast, represents almost 9% of the portfolio value. This ranges from a few percent, at the upper end of the credit scale, to about 15% at the bottom end.

Table 12.3 is our baseline. These results will be our point of comparison for all future stress-testing shocks, whether from the top-down or bottom-up approaches. A couple of simplifications need to be mentioned. First, we use the economic-capital approximation with the parameters described in Chap. 5. This is, of course, a slight abuse because these parameters apply to a rather different underlying portfolio. Hopefully the reader will excuse this discretion in the name of simplicity. The second issue, relating to the expected-credit loss, is a bit harder to justify. Chapter 9 indicated clearly that the overall expected-credit loss estimate is a (subjectively) weighted average of three forward-looking macro-financial scenarios. With plans to systematically shock each of our macro-financial variables, it is difficult to imagine the consequence for our forward-looking scenarios. With some patience and imagination, one could attempt to reconstruct a set of macro-financial shock consistent with the forward-looking point-in-time default-probability term structures. In this analysis, however, we have taken the easy way out. The expected-loss calculation is proxied with the shock-invariant through-the-cycle default curves. Given its centrality to the forward-looking construction, it will do a sensible job

---

[26] This implies that they have not experienced any significant decrease in credit quality since inception. See Chap. 9 for more discussion on IFRS 9 stage-allocation logic.

[27] The fair-valued instruments do not contribute to this overall ECL amount. These positions are excluded from the loan impairments; any valuation effects associated with credit-spread movements flow directly through the profit-and-loss statement.

**Table 12.3** *Our risk baseline*: It is centrally important to have a clear starting point, or baseline, for one's stress analysis. This table summarizes the initial loan-impairment and economic-capital values for each instrument in our portfolio. Across all of the downgrade shocks—from both top-down and bottom-up perspectives—this will be our comparison point.

| | Trade details | | | | Risk estimates | | | | |
|---|---|---|---|---|---|---|---|---|---|
| | | | | | Expected-credit loss | | Economic capital | | |
| # | PD | EAD | LGD | Tenor | Stage I | Stage II | Default | Migration | Total |
| 1 | 3 | 3, 500, 000 | 0.40 | 6 | 0 | 0 | 20, 895 | 83, 690 | 104, 585 |
| 2 | 4 | 1, 500, 000 | 0.35 | 4 | 0 | 0 | 6638 | 14, 064 | 20, 702 |
| 3 | 7 | 2, 000, 000 | 0.45 | 3 | 920 | 2469 | 41, 510 | 13, 434 | 54, 944 |
| 4 | 9 | 1, 750, 000 | 0.55 | 2 | 2371 | 4936 | 123, 618 | 11, 630 | 135, 248 |
| 5 | 13 | 1, 500, 000 | 0.60 | 5 | 11, 187 | 68, 130 | 82, 369 | 19, 207 | 101, 576 |
| 6 | 14 | 3, 000, 000 | 0.15 | 18 | 8261 | 83, 035 | 247, 514 | 168, 848 | 416, 361 |
| 7 | 15 | 1, 000, 000 | 0.35 | 3 | 9584 | 26, 952 | 143, 230 | 10, 145 | 153, 375 |
| 8 | 17 | 4, 500, 000 | 0.30 | 15 | 84, 324 | 364, 675 | 467, 692 | 60, 674 | 528, 366 |
| 9 | 18 | 750, 000 | 0.40 | 5 | 27, 700 | 66, 725 | 98, 595 | 2360 | 100, 955 |
| 10 | 20 | 500, 000 | 0.20 | 4 | 19, 996 | 29, 538 | 71, 339 | 2676 | 74, 016 |
| Total/Mean | 11.1 | 20, 000, 000 | 0.36 | 8.7 | 164, 344 | 646, 459 | 1, 303, 401 | 386, 727 | 1, 690, 128 |
| Percent of portfolio | | | | | 0.8% | 3.2% | 6.5% | 1.9% | 8.5% |

of capturing the downgrade and stage-allocation effects. It ignores, and this is important to stress, any macro-financial-related shock consequences.[28]

**Colour and Commentary 146** (A MINIMAL WORKING PORTFOLIO): *Internally, as do all financial institutions, we naturally perform our stress-testing analysis using our current portfolio in all of its (gory) detail. This nonetheless creates two problems for the present discussion. The specific structure and vulnerabilities of our actual portfolio contain numerous proprietary and confidential elements. As such, it cannot really be used. Even if it was useable, its sheer size and complexity would certainly make it sub-optimal for our pedagogical discussion. To resolve this problem, we invented a small portfolio comprised of 10 positions each associated with a different credit obligor. Although entirely fictitious, it does cover a reasonable range of credit ratings, position sizes, tenors, notional repayment profiles, accounting treatments, and recovery values. It is big enough to illustrate reasonably complex effects, but small enough to actually see what is going on. As such, it strikes a workable compromise between parsimony and realism.*

### 12.2.6 From Macro Shock to Our Portfolio

Given a specific macro-financial shock, the link to an associated transition matrix is described in Chap. 8. In brief, there are three steps in the construction of a point-in-time transition matrix. The first is the impact upon the default probabilities in the final column. The second involves the so-called upgrade and downgrade ratios. These are factors, centred on unity, that scale up or down the (non-default) off-diagonal, through-the-cycle, quarterly transition matrix elements. In this way, a given macro-financial shock impacts the likelihood of default and relative probability of upgrade and downgrade. The final step is the necessary adjustment of the diagonal elements to ensure each row still sums to unity.[29]

Figure 12.5, to underscore the link to our transition matrices, shows these upgrade and downgrade ratios for each of our 10 macro-financial-variable shocks *four* quarters into the future. We observe rather important differences among the various shocks as well as throughout time. As we would expect, the distance from zero appears to be gradually decreasing with each time step. Eventually, as the shock dissipates, we recover our through-the-cycle transition matrix.

[28] Such effects can, with some additional effort and assumptions, be incorporated into one's analysis.

[29] This is a kind of conservation-of-(probability-)mass constraint.

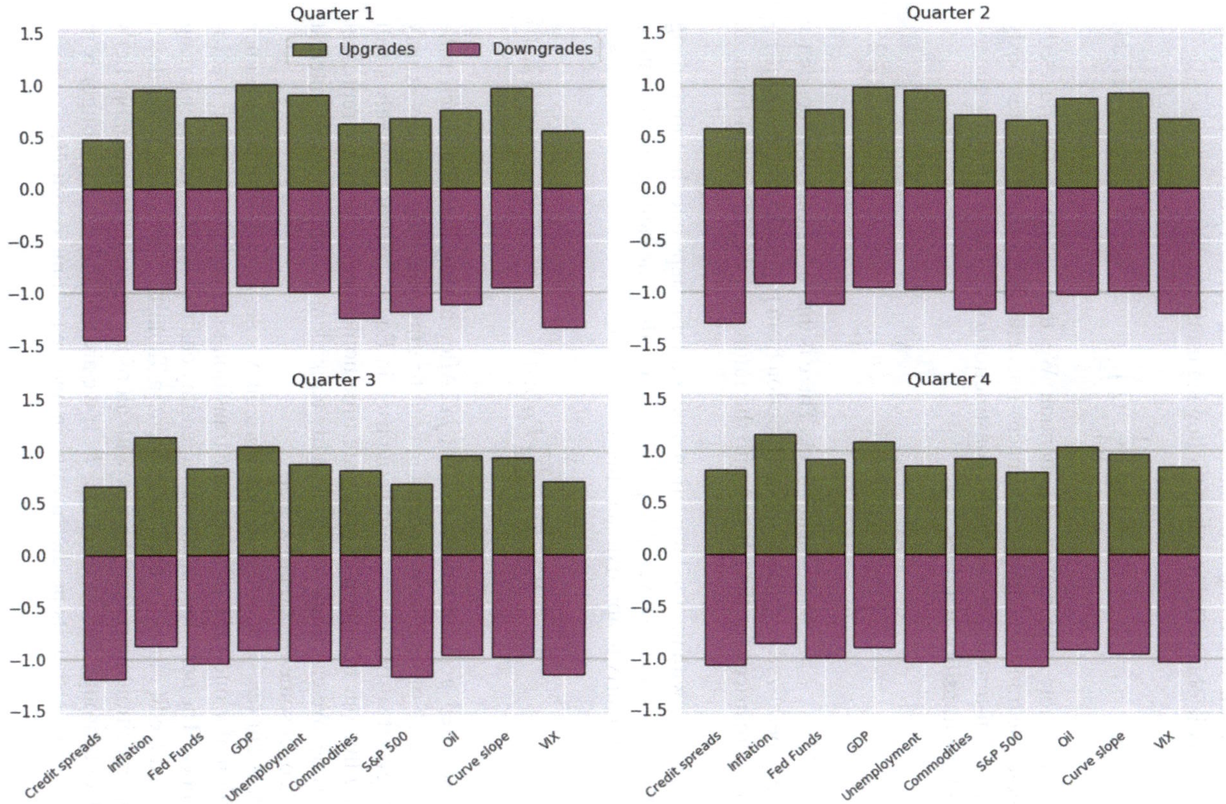


**Fig. 12.5** *Upgrade and downgrade multipliers*: This graphic displays the evolution of the quarterly upgrade and downgrade multipliers—out to our one-year stress-testing horizon—associated with a multiple standard-deviation shock to each of our macro-financial state variables. These outcomes play a central role in the structure of the subsequent point-in-time transition matrices.

Some time-related book-keeping is required. With a quarterly model of macro-financial movements, it is also necessary to work with a quarterly transition matrix. To address this point, we need the generator matrix $G$, which is computed from the (annual) through-the-cycle transition matrix, $P$.[30] The quarterly through-the-cycle transition matrix is obtained through the following transformation:

$$P_Q = \exp\left(\frac{1}{4} \cdot G\right), \tag{12.24}$$

where $\exp(\cdot)$ denotes the matrix exponential. We then combine the quarterly through-the-cycle transition matrix, our macro-financial shocks, and the previously described point-in-time transition-matrix construction logic. The result is a sequence of point-in-time transition matrices,

$$\left\{P_Q(i, j) : i = 1, \ldots, n\right\}, \tag{12.25}$$

for each $j = 1, \ldots, \kappa$ macro-financial shock. There is thus a logical correspondence between the generalized impulse-response function from Eq. 12.23 and the point-in-time transition matrices for the $i$th step into the future and the $j$th macro-financial shock.

Our interest lies with the final transition matrix after $n$ steps into the future along our shocked macro-financial variable paths. We use the time-homogeneity feature of the transition matrix to approximate this quantity as,

$$P(n, j) = \prod_{i=1}^{n} P_Q(i, j) \tag{12.26}$$

with an associated generator matrix, $G(n, j)$. After having invested much time maligning the lack of time homogeneity in credit-rating transition matrices, it may appear somewhat suspicious to see it being used in Eq. 12.26. For relatively small $n$, assuming that our transition-matrices are time-homogeneous does not represent a serious crime. We can think of it as roughly equivalent to annualizing an interest rate applied over some fraction of a year.

To respect our one-year stress-testing horizon, we set $n = 4$. The consequence is a collection of $\kappa$ one-year, point-in-time transition matrices: one for each macro-financial shock. The next step, in our rather lengthy chain of logic, involves inferring the associated credit rating for each instrument in Table 12.2 across each top-down shock. The transition matrix provides us with all of the requisite information. Let's begin with our through-the-cycle matrix, $P$. If we are told that a credit obligor is in state $S_k(t)$ at time $t$, then its predicted value in one-year's time is simply,

$$S_k(t + 1) = \sum_{m=1}^{21} P_{k,m} \cdot m. \tag{12.27}$$

[30] These ideas were also introduced in Chap. 8.

We exploited this trick in Chap. 5 when constructing our migration economic-capital estimator. To determine the natural progression of the portfolio, over a one-year horizon, we need only apply Eq. 12.27 for $k = 1, \ldots, 20$. We then compare the set of distances,

$$\Upsilon_k = S_k(t+1) - S_k(t), \tag{12.28}$$

for $k = 1, \ldots, 20$. The sign and magnitude of $\Upsilon_k$ determine the downgrade outcome. If $\Upsilon_k = 0.1$, this suggests a tendency towards credit deterioration, but it is not large enough to predict an actual downgrade. Although debatable, we set the threshold at 0.5. That is, there is a one-notch downgrade if $\Upsilon_k > 0.5$, a two-notch downgrade if $\Upsilon > 1.5$, and so on. Interestingly, using this criterion, the one-year, through-the-cycle transition matrix does not predict a downgrade for any credit rating.[31]

To concretely establish the link from macro-financial shocks to transition matrix matrices to attendant rating outcomes, we arrive at

$$\Upsilon_k(n,j) = \underbrace{\overbrace{\sum_{m=1}^{21} P_{k,m}(n,j) \cdot m}^{S_k(t+1,j)}}_{\text{Shocked rating}} - \underbrace{S_k(t+1)}_{\text{TTC forecast}}, \tag{12.29}$$

for $n = 4$ and $j = 1, \ldots, \kappa$. To suit our purposes, we have slightly modified the definition of Eq. 12.28. We are comparing the one-year shocked credit-rating outcome to the one-year, through-the-cycle forecast. This ensures an apples-to-apples comparison. If, for example, the shocked rating forecast is 9.6, but the through-the-cycle downgrade expectation is 9.7, we can hardly attribute a downgrade to the macro-financial shock.

### *12.2.7 The Portfolio Consequences*

Having delineated the path from macro-financial system to impulse-response function to point-in-time transition matrix to portfolio downgrades, we may now reap the benefits. Table 12.4 provides a concrete point of comparison to the base results in Table 12.3 associated with a multiple standard-deviation shock to the Fed Funds rate—as described in Fig. 12.4—over our one-year stress-testing horizon.

---

[31] Naturally, given its structure, it eventually pulls all credit counterparties to downgrade, and ultimately default, as we move sufficiently far into the future.

**Table 12.4** *A (first) macro-financial shock analysis*: The underlying table illustrates the impact—via portfolio downgrades—of a multiple standard-deviation shock to the Fed Funds rate as summarized in Fig. 12.4. The default-probability, valuation losses, expected-credit loss (including stage-allocations), and economic-capital implications are presented.

| # | Trade Details | | | | | Capital Supply | | Capital Demand | | |
|---|---|---|---|---|---|---|---|---|---|---|
| | | | | | | ECL | MTM | Economic Capital | | |
| | $PD_0$ | $PD_1$ | EAD | LGD | TTM | Stage I/II | Δ-Spread | Default | Migration | Total |
| 1 | 3 | 4 | 3,500,000 | 0.40 | 6 | 0 | 10,139 | 27,281 | 57,606 | 84,886 |
| 2 | 4 | 5 | 1,500,000 | 0.35 | 4 | 0 | 3,512 | 8,742 | 13,358 | 22,100 |
| 3 | 7 | 7 | 2,000,000 | 0.45 | 3 | 920 | 0 | 41,510 | 13,434 | 54,944 |
| 4 | 9 | 9 | 1,750,000 | 0.55 | 2 | 2,371 | 0 | 123,618 | 11,630 | 135,248 |
| 5 | 13 | 15 | 1,500,000 | 0.60 | 5 | 104,016 | 0 | 118,496 | 12,373 | 130,868 |
| 6 | 14 | 16 | 3,000,000 | 0.15 | 18 | 103,158 | 0 | 308,689 | 94,721 | 403,410 |
| 7 | 15 | 17 | 1,000,000 | 0.35 | 3 | 47,882 | 0 | 183,635 | 5,040 | 188,676 |
| 8 | 17 | 19 | 4,500,000 | 0.30 | 15 | 470,857 | 0 | 541,849 | 250,467 | 792,315 |
| 9 | 18 | 19 | 750,000 | 0.40 | 5 | 79,747 | 0 | 104,040 | 16,456 | 120,496 |
| 10 | 20 | 20 | 500,000 | 0.20 | 4 | 19,996 | 0 | 71,339 | 2,676 | 74,016 |
| Total/Mean | 11.1 | 12.4 | 20,000,000 | 0.36 | 8.7 | 828,947 | 13,650 | 1,529,199 | 477,762 | 2,006,960 |
| Percent of Portfolio | | | | | | 4.1% | 0.1% | 7.6% | 2.4% | 10.0% |

Seven of our ten credit obligors experienced a downgrade; three of these were downgraded by a single notch, while the other four experienced a two-grade movement. The credit-risk economic capital allotment rose by about EUR 300,000 or $1\frac{1}{2}$ percentage points of the portfolio's notional amount. Although both the migration and default dimensions were impacted, around three quarters of the increase can be attributed to default risk. One-notch downgrades to our two high-quality fair-valued securities lead to a modest valuation loss. The largest impact, by a significant margin, stems from the loan-impairment side. The expected-credit loss rise by almost EUR 700,000—about twice the economic-capital movement—amounting to more than 3% of the total portfolio. The lion's share of the loan-impairment result stems from the allocation of five positions—comprising more than one half of the portfolio's value—to IFRS 9's stage II. The corresponding lifetime expected-credit loss values represent a sizable, non-linear hit to the firm's capital position.

Combining the figures in Table 12.4 gets us to the ultimate prize: the capital impact of a given macro-financial shock. The total increase in capital demand is, as mentioned, about EUR 300,000. The corresponding capital-supply result approaches EUR 700,000. Together they squeeze the firm's capital headroom by a total of approximately EUR 1 million. This represents about 5% of the total assets and—although we have not specified the original capital position—would be a tough blow for any financial institution.

Table 12.4 is a critical milestone, but Fig. 12.6 is the end game. It illustrates—for a multiple standard-deviation shock of each macro-financial variable—the combined impact of the five capital drivers associated with credit risk: default and migration economic capital, stage I and II expected-credit losses, and valuation adjustments. The red, downward-trending, bars in Fig. 12.6 cut to the chase. They provide the overall impact to the firm's capital associated when we combined the one-two punch of capital demand and supply effects.

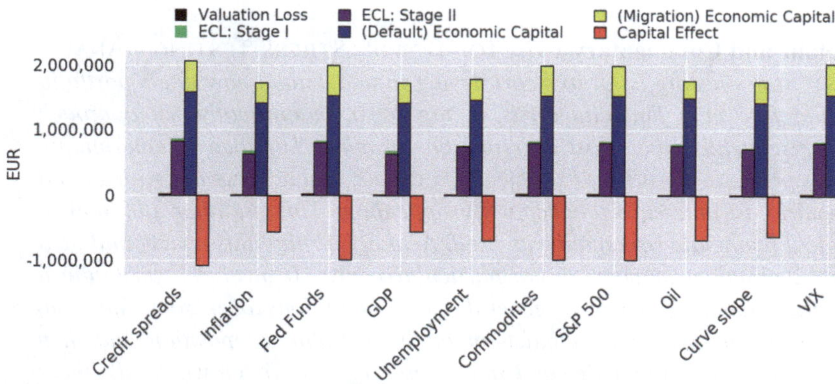


**Fig. 12.6** *Impulse-response-function intuition*: The preceding graphic provides—in a systematic fashion—the expected-credit loss and economic-capital outcomes associated with a multiple standard-deviation shock to each of our $\kappa = 10$ macro-financial variables. The net capital impact, combining both capital supply and demand effects, is also presented.

Given the extreme nature of the shocks, none of our $\kappa$ stress scenarios looks particularly appealing. The advantage of this visualization—indeed, the entire exercise—is that it allows us to classify our portfolio's sensitivity to the various macro-financial factors. Overall, credit spreads seem to exhibit the largest capital impact, while the portfolio is least sensitive to inflation. Examining Fig. 12.6 we could, in fact, put our macro-financial factors into three groups. The highest impact group—with a capital squeeze in the neighbourhood of EUR 1 million—include credit spreads, the Fed Funds rate, commodity and equity prices, and finally financial-market volatility. A medium impact group would include unemployment, oil prices, and the yield-curve slope. The capital consequence for this group is in the neighbourhood of EUR 600,000 to 700,000. Output and inflation appear to be the final, *lower*-effect, macro-financial variables with capital reduction about half of the magnitude of the high-impact group.

While there are clearly limits to the potential interpretation of an imaginary portfolio, Table 12.4 and Fig. 12.6 illustrate the cornerstones of a larger, broader top-down analysis. It is perfectly reasonable to augment this analysis with a few forward- or backward-looking macro-financial stress scenarios. The technical steps in moving from scenario to portfolio impact remain unchanged. Most importantly, our systematic, variable-by-variable, shock-based assessment provides valuable insight into portfolio vulnerabilities and dramatically eases interpretation and communication of the results from more global stress scenarios.

**Colour and Commentary 147** (TOP-DOWN STRESS-TESTING ANALYSIS): *Stress testing is, at its heart, trying to understand how one's portfolio would fare in a financial crisis. A top-down, macro-motivated approach is consequently what most everyone has in mind. The idea of determining one's portfolio sensitivity to a specific, extreme, and adverse macro-financial scenario is inherently conceptually appealing. This is, after all, how a typical financial crisis manifests itself. Actually turning this conceptual idea into a practical outcome is not particularly easy. It involves translating a macro-financial shock into general credit conditions over some horizon, inferring the associated impact on one's portfolio composition and then computing the capital demand and supply effects. To crown it all, there are an infinity of possible stress scenarios from which to choose. Using a workhorse model from macroeconomics, we propose a systemic approach to examine macro-financial shocks—of various degrees of severity—one macro-financial variable at a time. This helps to manage the complexity of stress-scenario selection. The long and tenuous chain of logic from scenario to capital impact, however, is simply a feature of top-down analysis. It is also a weakness, which suggests a motive to intellectually diversify. For this reason, the top-down approach to the stress-testing problem is sensibly complemented with a bottom-up perspective.*

## 12.3 The Bottom-Up, or Micro, Approach

As discussed, it is possible to come at the stress-testing question from another angle. The bottom-up approach side-steps the macro-financial dimension and jumps straight to the downgrade outcomes. Figure 12.7 provides a visualization of the sequencing associated with this alternative strategy. Comparing it to the top-down logic from Fig. 12.3, we see *two* main differences. First, the macro-financial stress scenarios and point-in-time transition matrices disappear. Second, we identify portfolio downgrades rather than *infer* them from macro-financial shocks. We are basically imagining that, at the snap of our fingers, we can change the credit state of any (and every) credit obligor in our current portfolio. This is not very realistic, of course, but we can view this as the essence of the bottom-up thought experiment.

The bottom-up approach liberates us somewhat, but also creates its own challenges. The change of viewpoint does not, to be clear, resolve many of the fundamental issues associated with stress-testing analysis. Direct identification of portfolio downgrades remains absent any probability assignment and there are many—indeed, far too many—possible combinations of downgrade that one might select for consideration. The objective is nonetheless the same: to identify important

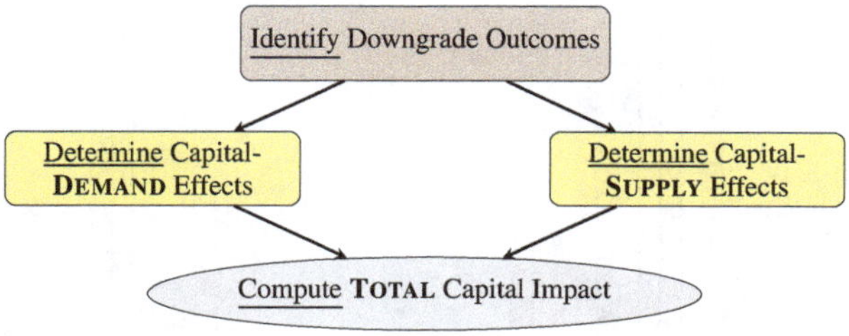


**Fig. 12.7** *Bottom-up sequencing*: This graphic describes the sequence of steps—as compared to the schematic in Fig. 12.3—involved in the performance of a bottom-up stress-testing analysis. Conceptually, at least, it is rather less involved than the top-down case.

vulnerabilities in one's portfolio. Like the top-down setting, effective use of the bottom-up approach will require some structure and organization. To the best of the author's knowledge, there is no *correct* way to perform this task. In the remainder of this chapter, we will instead consider a number of practical variations of the bottom-up approach and, in doing so, help to complement the preceding top-down results. The first order of business is to motivate the need for a master plan.

### *12.3.1 The Limits of Brute Force*

Although we've eliminated the thorny question of selecting macro-financial scenarios, we immediately face another problem.[32] How precisely do we identify downgrade cases? The simple, and naive, answer is *all of them*. This essentially means looking at all possible combinations of downgrades one's portfolio might experience. While it has a certain appeal, for even a moderate number of credit obligors, this implies an enormous number of possible future combinations and permutations of different credit migrations. The number of combinations of credit ratings—across our 20-notch non-default scale—associated with several hundred different credit obligors is simply staggering.[33]

One might argue that the full power set of downgrade permutations is excessive.[34] Perhaps we might wish to consider the set of all possible one-notch

[32] This situation brings to mind the old proverb, which is used in Tolkien [32], about moving "out of the frying pan and into the fire." It describes going from a bad situation to a worse one.

[33] Even with $n = 10$ counterparties and $k = 20$ credit states, there are some

$$\binom{n+k-1}{k-1} \approx 20,000,000, \tag{12.30}$$

possible combinations of portfolio credit ratings. For any meaningful number of obligors, this is an insurmountable hurdle.

[34] We use the term power set to represent the set of all subsets of downgrades.

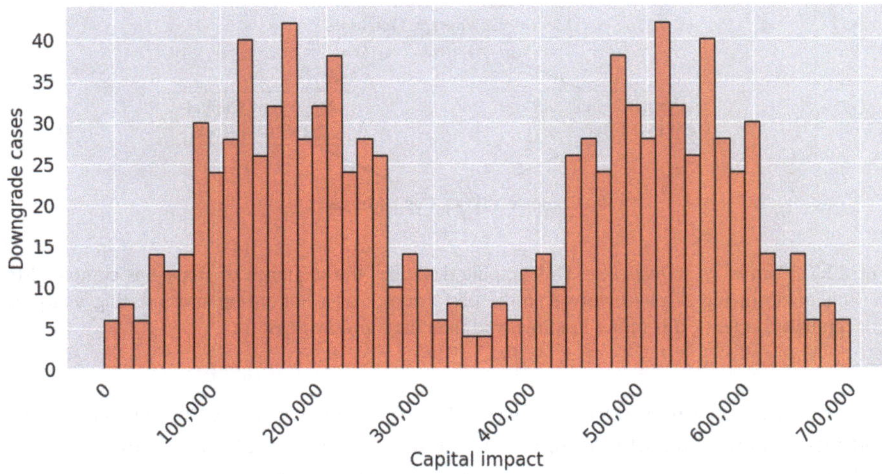


**Fig. 12.8** *One-notch downgrade distribution*: The preceding histogram maps out the capital impact of the set of 1023 possible downgrade combinations for our 10-counterparty example introduced in Table 12.2. While interesting, such analysis is not possible outside of unrealistically small portfolio examples.

downgrades. With two counterparties, this is a very small set: each downgrade and both downgrade. It contains only *three* cases. If we add another counterparty, the set grows to seven elements, but it is still manageable. As a general rule, the number outcomes is

$$n\text{-notch downgrade outcomes} = (n+1)^{\text{Number of counterparties}} - 1, \quad (12.31)$$

using basic combinatorial logic and subtracting off the single case where no obligor downgrades. Applying Eq. 12.31 to our 10-obligor portfolio from Table 12.2, where $n = 1$ yields 1023 different possible combinations of one-notch downgrade. Again, while not small, this seems like something we can handle. If we increase the number of obligors to a modest 100, however, the number becomes simply too large to reasonably write down.[35]

Figure 12.8 provides a histogram of the capital impact associated with the set of 1023 possible one-notch downgrades for our small example in Table 12.2. There is no denying that this is an interesting object. It has two modes: one around EUR 200,000 and another in the neighbourhood of EUR 550,000. Many possible combinations of downgrades can generate such reductions in capital. There are only very few constellations of one-notch downgrades, by contrast, that can generate

[35] Some readers might recognize this idea from the story about a clever inventor, a King, a chessboard, and many grains of rice. See Tahan [30] for more on this ancient take on Bellman [5]'s curse of dimensionality.

capital decreases of EUR 700,000. Although a bit cumbersome—given the relatively large number of cases—one could drill into Fig. 12.8 and try to identify trends and patterns within the downgrades.

The bottom line is that, however interesting it may be, Fig. 12.8 is simply *not* available. No matter how much we might wish to perform such an analysis, the dimensionality of the power set of downgrades in a real-life portfolio—even for a single notch—is just too big to tame. Another solution needs to be found.

### 12.3.2 The Extreme Cases

When faced with such a complex problem, one's first thought is typically try to reduce dimensionality. How might we start? While it might sound a bit silly at first, one option is to look at the extremes. By *extreme* we mean placing *all* of our credit obligor into the same rating category. The result is a portfolio entirely comprised of PD01 ratings, another completely in PD02 and so on out until PD20; this assignment occurs irrespective of an obligor's starting point.[36] We can organize this idea in the form of a matrix, which we'll call $E$. If we place the $I$ instruments in one's portfolio along the horizontal axis and map the columns to the rating categories, we have $E \in \mathbb{R}^{I \times 20}$. Computing the capital-demand and supply effects for each element in this matrix, $(I-1) \times N$ instrument-level computations are involved.[37] For a medium-sized portfolio with 500 credit obligors, this amounts to approximately 10,000 sets of calculations. The main takeaway is that only 20 (extreme) portfolios are considered: one for each credit rating. There is much to criticize, but the huge advantage of this perspective is its invariance to the size of the portfolio.

It is admittedly somewhat artificial and unnatural to assign all of the credit obligors in one's portfolio simultaneously to the *same* credit category. Information is clearly being lost, but that is the price of dimension reduction. The litmus test is the helpfulness of this approach and the associated insights it provides into one's portfolio.

For our sample portfolio where $I = 10$, this dimension-reduction idea involves 20 new portfolios with only 180 instrument-level calculations. As a consequence, the figures are quickly computed. As in all of the previous analysis, we employ our default and migration economic-capital approximation model. This is not without some drawbacks. Our approximations are estimated using the current portfolio with a broad mixture of rating outcomes. It is rather unfair to then ask the approximation framework to provide entirely sensible results for such extreme portfolios. It will, in particular, have difficulty with the corner cases; that is, where all obligors

[36] Each counterparty will thus experience—depending on its starting point—an upgrade, a downgrade, or no change at all.

[37] This is specialized to our 20-notch (non-default) credit-rating scale. It naturally generalizes to any finite number of credit ratings.

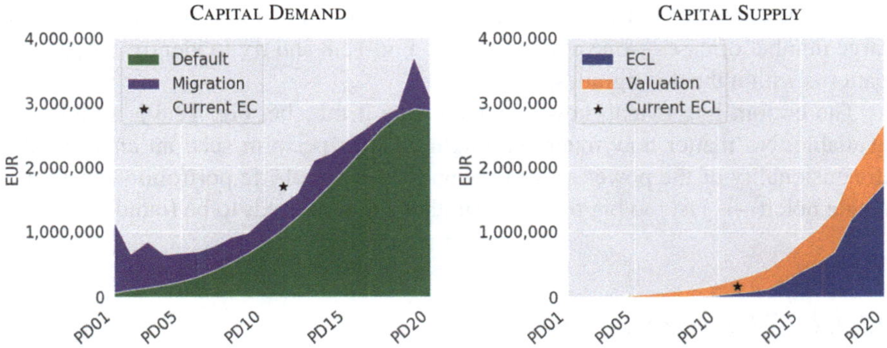


**Fig. 12.9** *An extreme portfolio perspective*: These graphics summarize the capital demand and supply effects associated with a rather extreme *what-if* exercise. All positions are simultaneously moved into the same, common credit rating.

are assigned either the highest or lowest credit quality. This situation is readily resolved by simply re-running the simulation model either for all 20 portfolios or, if computational resources are constrained, for the most extreme portfolios.

Figure 12.9 highlights the capital-demand and supply implications of—starting from our baseline—moving all positions into our 20 extreme-rating configurations. On the capital-demand side, default economic capital is a rather smooth increasing function of the credit state. Migration, however, is a bit less well-behaved. This is partly due to difficulty on the part of the approximation model and lumpiness in our small portfolio. Positions #6 and #8 with their large exposures—together representing close to 40% of the portfolio—have rather long tenors. At the corners, this can lead to odd behaviour. This could be partly resolved with proper portfolio simulations, but perhaps not completely eliminated.

The right-hand graphic of Fig. 12.9 illustrates the capital-supply consequences for these extreme portfolios. The loan-impairment allocation ranges from effectively zero to more than 8% of the overall portfolio value.[38] The valuation impact, which influences only *two* securities, are surprisingly large. These are nonetheless relatively sizable, reasonably long-tenor positions currently situated at the upper echelon of the credit spectrum. Dramatic downgrade—below PD12 or so—would

[38] The reasonableness of this figure is easily verified by calculating:

$$\begin{aligned}\text{Extreme PD20 ECL} &\approx \text{Total Exposure} \cdot \text{PD20 Default Probability} \cdot \text{Average LGD}, \\ &\approx \text{EUR } 20,000,000 \cdot 20\% \cdot 0.36, \\ &\approx 1,440,000,\end{aligned} \tag{12.32}$$

which is slightly more than 7% of the portfolio.

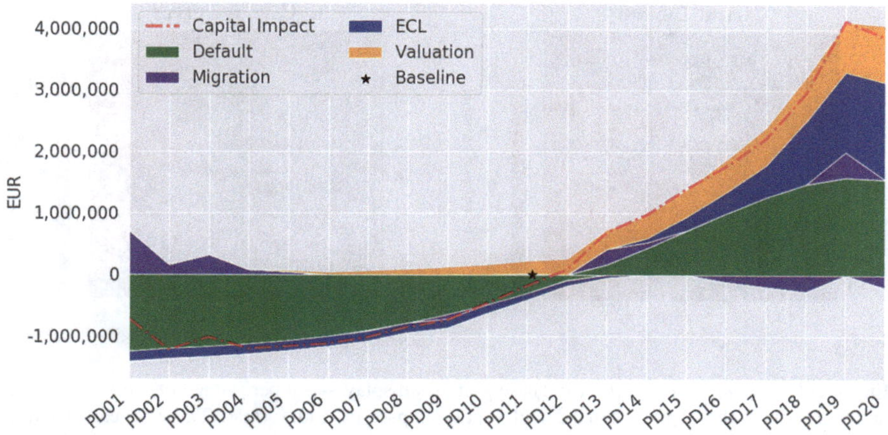


**Fig. 12.10** *Capital impact at the extremes*: This graphic combines the capital demand and supply effects—across our extreme views of the portfolio—and illustrates the associated capital impact relative to our baseline setting.

involve significant spread widening with attendant valuation consequences. For small shocks of one or two credit notches, this effect is *not* visible.

Combining the capital demand and supply graphics from Fig. 12.9 and incorporating the baseline perspective, Fig. 12.10 lays out the capital impact of these extreme portfolios. It tells an interesting story. Moving south of the current portfolio—with an average credit rating of about PD11—there is an increasing reduction of capital headroom. At PD19 or PD20, this amounts to roughly EUR 4 million. At the other end of the spectrum, up to about EUR 1 million of capital is actually released. There is thus a certain asymmetry around the baseline portfolio.

Figure 12.11 provides a final perspective on our extreme-portfolio construction. At the position level—as a percentage of its notional value—the individual capital demand and supply results are presented. A heat-map format is employed to incorporate the three dimensions of position, credit rating, and capital percentage. The current baseline portfolio is represented as the shaded line running roughly through the diagonal of our heat maps. The objects in Fig. 12.11 are basically capital demand and supply versions of the previously introduced matrix, $E$. For lack of a better term, we refer to these as stress matrices.

In a real-world portfolio, such matrices can be quite large.[39] If one orders the positions from highest to lowest credit category, however, an interesting pattern emerges. Everything to the right of the shaded baseline-portfolio line represents various combinations of portfolio downgrade, whereas everything to the left of

[39] To manage the sheer size of these stress matrices, it is also entirely possible to collect the individual positions into meaningful sub-categories. Good examples would include regions, industries, firm-size, or initial credit rating. Indeed, the organization is limited only by the analyst's creativity (and data availability).

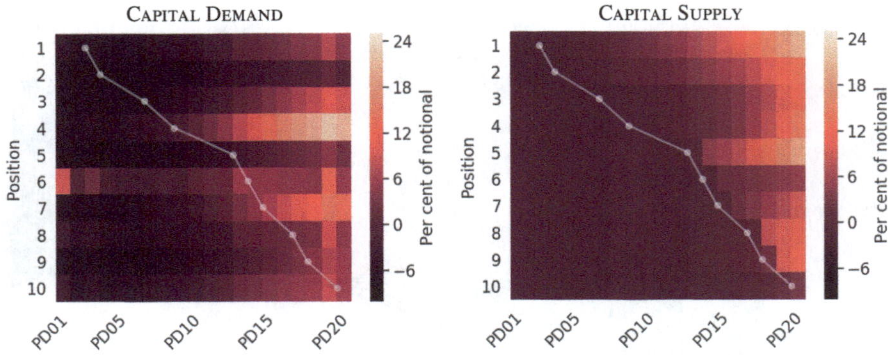


**Fig. 12.11** *Extreme stress matrices*: These graphics display—as a percentage of their underlying notional value—the capital demand and supply impact in grid format. These so-called stress matrices permit identification of particularly sensitive instruments. The true portfolio is highlighted in white.

the demarcation denotes upgrade. As pessimistic risk managers, we naturally focus on the right-hand side, but both provide insights into one's portfolio. The capital-supply heat map suggests, for example, that there is little scope for capital relief associated with upgrade along this dimension; everything left of the shaded line has essentially the same colour. On the capital-demand side, the picture is a bit more subtle. Some positions—such as #4 and #7—are relatively stable for a one- or two-notch downgrade. As we move to multiple downward steps, however, their capital-demand requirements increase substantially. Moreover, something funny (and possibly incorrect) is occurring for extreme upgrades of position #6. The visualization in Fig. 12.11, while certainly imperfect, does provide a slightly different perspective on one's portfolio.

**Colour and Commentary 148** (Brute-Force and Extremes)*: A brute-force examination of the power set of one- or two-notch downgrades—despite its intellectual and practical appeal—is unfortunately off the table. The combinatorics tell the merciless story of a mind-bogglingly large set of possibilities. When the dimensionality is too large, common practice is to identify ways that it might be reduced. A simple approach, which involves a computational burden that is roughly invariant to one's portfolio size, involves consideration of so-called extreme portfolios. This basically means placing all of one's position sequentially into each of the rating buckets. The result is a collection of highly stylized extreme portfolios. The truth is that this is probably an excess of dimension reduction. Much information is lost and the associated portfolio outcomes are* not *realistic. There is, however, some insight to be gained. Our extreme-portfolio construction, while it cannot be*

(continued)

**Colour and Commentary 148** (continued)
*the sole bottom-up strategy for our stress-testing analysis, allows for rather informative visualization of our portfolio. Portfolios are complicated high-dimensional objects. Anything we can do to visualize these sensitivities and vulnerabilities is thus both helpful and entirely welcome.*

### *12.3.3 Traditional Bottom-Up Cases*

While a useful starting point, the extreme-portfolio perspective should rather be viewed as exploratory analysis. We can learn a few high-level vulnerabilities of our portfolio, which might be incorporated into more realistic cases. Analogous to the top-down setting, when it comes down to it, stress-testing basically boils down to subjective selection of shocks. In this section, we will investigate a few alternative (and perhaps more typical) ways to proceed.

The term chestnut, beside its obvious meaning, is used by (typically fairly old) English-speakers to describe an over-used joke, story, or example.[40] Our first choice of standalone bottom-up scenario definitely falls into this definition. It involves a case of a global and simultaneous one- or two-notch downgrade to all of the positions in one's portfolio. Its conceptual shortcomings are (partially) offset by its simplicity. No deep reflection or complex logic is required; each position is treated in the same manner.

Table 12.5 summarizes the aggregate, instrument-level, capital-related results of this type of global one- and two-notch portfolio downgrade. The reduction to the firm's capital headroom is displayed in both currency and percentage terms and ordered, in descending fashion, by the two-notch downgrade percentage impact. A global one-grade downgrade leads to a roughly EUR 700,000 headroom squeeze, which corresponds to a medium-impact macro-financial impulse-response function shock. At two notches, the EUR 1.1 million headroom exceeds any of our macro-financial scenarios. This comparison of bottom-up shocks to our top-down macro-financial outcomes is not precisely reverse stress-testing, but it is rather close.

Table 12.5 also provides useful information about our individual positions that, in some cases, overlaps with the extreme-portfolio analysis from the previous section. In the final column, for example, we observe that the average capital effect—when moving from one to two notches of downgrade—is about +70%. This varies wildly across individual positions. One instrument experiences, in fact, a negative

[40] See Merriam-Webster [22, page 231].

**Table 12.5** *An analytic chestnut*: This table summarizes the (ordered) capital-headroom results of the classic (and perhaps slightly overused) trick of applying a broad one- or two-notch downgrade to one's entire portfolio. While not particularly nuanced, it does help identify the most capital-sensitive sensible instruments in both currency and percentage terms.

| # | Trade Details | | | | One Notch | | Two Notches | | Notch Increase Percentage |
|---|---|---|---|---|---|---|---|---|---|
| | PD | EAD | LGD | Tenor | EUR | Per cent | EUR | Per cent | |
| 8 | 17 | 4,500,000 | 0.30 | 15 | 354,571 | 7.9% | 650,482 | 14.5% | **83%** |
| 9 | 18 | 750,000 | 0.40 | 5 | 71,587 | 9.5% | 74,701 | 10.0% | **4%** |
| 5 | 13 | 1,500,000 | 0.60 | 5 | 86,020 | 5.7% | 122,121 | 8.1% | **42%** |
| 7 | 15 | 1,000,000 | 0.35 | 3 | 43,079 | 4.3% | 73,599 | 7.4% | **71%** |
| 4 | 9 | 1,750,000 | 0.55 | 2 | 32,885 | 1.9% | 79,270 | 4.5% | **141%** |
| 6 | 14 | 3,000,000 | 0.15 | 18 | 82,577 | 2.8% | 81,946 | 2.7% | **-1%** |
| 3 | 7 | 2,000,000 | 0.45 | 3 | 14,018 | 0.7% | 31,113 | 1.6% | **122%** |
| 2 | 4 | 1,500,000 | 0.35 | 4 | 4,911 | 0.3% | 10,587 | 0.7% | **116%** |
| 1 | 3 | 3,500,000 | 0.40 | 6 | -9,560 | -0.3% | 7,960 | 0.2% | **183%** |
| 10 | 20 | 500,000 | 0.20 | 4 | 0 | 0.0% | 0 | 0.0% | **0%** |
| Total/Mean | 11.1 | 20,000,000 | 0.36 | 8.7 | 680,087 | 3.3% | 1,131,779 | 5.0% | **72%** |
| Percent of Portfolio | | | | | 3.4% | – | 5.7% | – | – |

movement.[41] Another exhibits no movement at all.[42] A handful of instruments encounter increases of around twice the portfolio average. These are, from a risk-management perspective at least, quite interesting cases.

Credit analysts work with *watch* lists of firms that appear close to downgrade or even default. Figure 12.12 runs with this idea and extends it—using the information in Table 12.5—to a create a quantitatively motivated *danger* list. These firms may be in fine financial shape, in contrast to the watch list, but were they to be downgraded, they would exert the greatest negative capital impact on the financial institution. Figure 12.12 restricts this to the top-four most sensitive instruments in our small, fictitious portfolio. In a real-life portfolio, this idea can be made much more precise and refined. It nonetheless represents a pragmatic application of the chestnut one- or two-notch downgrade scenarios, which can aid in the identification of real portfolio vulnerabilities.

If a global one- or two-notch downgrade bottom-up strategy lacks finesse, then how might we do better? Again, the challenge is the sheer number of possible combinations. There is, however, an entire class of bottom-up scenarios that are constructed using portfolio-level knowledge. There are many possible examples. One might consider downgrades, of various magnitude, for a given industrial

[41] This is related to the vagaries of migration risk for long-tenor, high-quality securities.

[42] Since position #10 is already in PD20, it can no longer downgrade without moving into default. We have precluded this possibility and held it fixed. Alternatively, of course, one could move it into default and compute the loss. It is a question of preference.

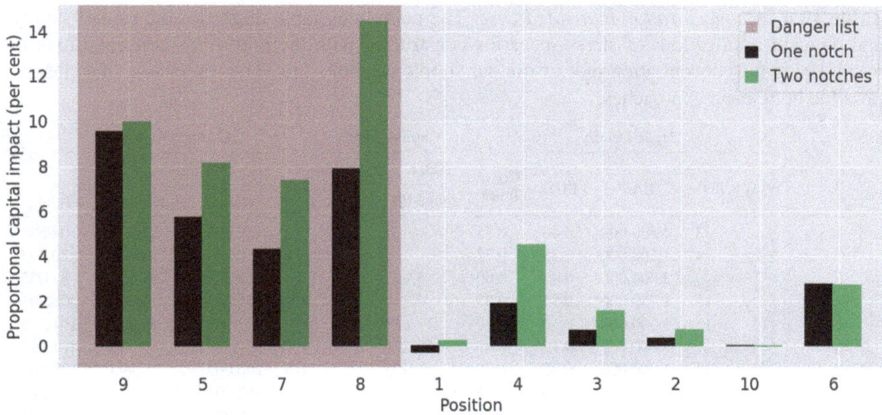


**Fig. 12.12** *Creating a quantitative danger list*: This graphic uses 7th and 8th columns of Table 12.5 to construct a quantitatively motivated danger list. These are securities with the highest capital sensitivity to one- or two-notch downgrade.

sector, or firm size, or geographical region. These might be supported by portfolio concentrations, macro-financial reasoning, or a gut feeling. Typically, there is a story associated with such scenarios. The deteriorating prospects of a particular industry, as an example, may have been treated extensively in the media or identified by one's credit analysts. A natural bottom-up stress scenario would involve a broad-based, or more complex, set of downgrades to one's obligors in this industry.[43]

To illustrate and motivate this idea, we will construct a fairly artificial example for our sample portfolio. The idea is to use the concentration index from Table 12.2. These, completely invented, values shouldn't really be taken very seriously when thinking about these ideas and interpreting the results. Instead, we should view them as a proxy for something more complicated in the underlying structure of the portfolio. In particular, we propose the following bottom-up stress scenario:

$$\text{Downgrade}_i = \begin{cases} \text{Concentration Index}_i \geq 0.9 : +3 \\ \text{Concentration Index}_i \in [0.8, 0.9) : +2 \\ \text{Concentration Index}_i < 0.8 : 0 \end{cases}, \tag{12.33}$$

[43] This might feel a bit like a macro-financial scenario, and to a certain extent it is, but such situations are typically too granular (or micro-focused) for treatment within a macro-financial model.

**Table 12.6** *A concentration-motivated case*: The underlying table illustrates the capital supply and demand implications of stress scenarios constructed with the portfolio's concentrations in mind. Using the concentration index from our simple example, this is representative of a class of possible bottom-up approaches.

| # | Trade Details | | | | | Capital Supply | | Capital Demand | | |
|---|---|---|---|---|---|---|---|---|---|---|
| | | | | | | ECL | MTM | Economic Capital | | |
| | $PD_0$ | $PD_1$ | EAD | LGD | Conc. Index | Stage I/II | Δ-Spread | Default | Migration | Total |
| 1 | 3 | 3 | 3,500,000 | 0.40 | 0.75 | 0 | 0 | 20,895 | 83,690 | 104,585 |
| 2 | 4 | 4 | 1,500,000 | 0.35 | 0.72 | 0 | 0 | 6,638 | 14,064 | 20,702 |
| 3 | 7 | 9 | 2,000,000 | 0.45 | 0.80 | 5,942 | 0 | 69,383 | 11,652 | 81,035 |
| 4 | 9 | 11 | 1,750,000 | 0.55 | 0.85 | 16,398 | 0 | 185,515 | 14,976 | 200,491 |
| 5 | 13 | 13 | 1,500,000 | 0.60 | 0.70 | 11,187 | 0 | 82,369 | 19,207 | 101,576 |
| 6 | 14 | 17 | 3,000,000 | 0.15 | 0.95 | 123,291 | 0 | 334,819 | 67,071 | 401,890 |
| 7 | 15 | 18 | 1,000,000 | 0.35 | 0.90 | 62,826 | 0 | 200,007 | 2,993 | 203,000 |
| 8 | 17 | 17 | 4,500,000 | 0.30 | 0.75 | 84,324 | 0 | 467,692 | 60,674 | 528,366 |
| 9 | 18 | 20 | 750,000 | 0.40 | 0.80 | 95,166 | 0 | 103,871 | 4,320 | 108,191 |
| 10 | 20 | 20 | 500,000 | 0.20 | 0.90 | 19,996 | 0 | 71,339 | 2,676 | 74,016 |
| Total/Mean | 11.1 | 12.2 | 20,000,000 | 0.36 | 0.80 | 419,129 | 0 | 1,542,529 | 281,322 | 1,823,851 |
| Percent of Portfolio | | | | | | 2.1% | 0.0% | 7.7% | 1.4% | 9.1% |

for $i = 1, \ldots, I$. Equation 12.33 consequently applies a three-notch downgrade to the most concentrated aspects of the portfolio, two grades for moderate concentration, and no change for everything else. In this way, specific positions or obligors are *not* targeted. Instead, some set of downgrade criteria are applied and investigated. Equation 12.33 is simply one example of a very large, probably countably infinite, class of stress scenarios. The trick is to identify a few that are meaningful and useful for one's purposes.

Following the usual format, Table 12.6 provides the capital implications of the stress scenario from Eq. 12.33 for our example portfolio. There are three cases with a three-step downgrade; position #10, already being at the very bottom of the scale, is nonetheless left unaffected. Another three cases are downgraded by two notches, while all other positions remain unchanged. Comparing to the baseline in Table 12.3, the total capital headroom reduction is slightly less than EUR 400,000. Roughly $\frac{2}{3}$ of the impact can be attributed to the capital-supply effects stemming from the loan-impairment calculation. Since only about 40% of the portfolio is hit by this stress scenario, the results are relatively less severe than we've seen in previous bottom-up and top-down cases. In a real-life portfolio, the depth of analysis and insight are potentially more significant than with our imaginary example. Equation 12.33 and Table 12.6 nonetheless provide a concrete illustration of the more traditional class of bottom-up scenarios.

**Colour and Commentary 149** (CLASSIC BOTTOM-UP STRESS SCENARIOS)*: Top-down macro-financial related stress-testing scenarios, to be effective, usually involves an associated narrative. One envisions the outcome* as a consequence *of some forward- or backward-looking sequence of events. Bottom-up scenario construction, albeit in a different way, is similarly constrained. We can ignore this point via global n-notch portfolio downgrades.*[a] *This provides some useful insight in a more realistic manner than in our extreme-portfolio experiment. It can even help to build danger lists of instruments with particular capital sensitivity to downgrade. To really gain traction in bottom-up analysis, however, a narrative is indispensable. Classical bottom-up scenarios involve identifying downgrade stories for different aspects of one's portfolio. Related to elements such as firm size, industry, or region, they are typically inspired by intimate portfolio knowledge. A good start is the well-known risk-management question: what keeps you up at night? Practical examples are related to concentrations, known weaknesses, or specific public information too granular for inclusion in one's macro-financial model.*

[a] Usually, we set $n = 1, 2$, although there are no fast rules. For sufficiently large $n$, however, the results converge to the lower end of our extreme-portfolio analysis.

### *12.3.4 Randomization*

Our final flavour of bottom-up stress-testing scenario construction is less conventional, but has a long and successful history in quantitative analysis: randomization. It has been used to solve intractable high-dimensional problems via Monte Carlo simulation,[44] to identify useful search directions in complex non-linear optimization problems,[45] and to improve the efficiency of solutions to stochastic optimal-control problems.[46] All of these examples have something in common; they involve trying to solve problems in the face of potentially crippling dimensionality. As we quickly learned when attacking the selection of bottom-up scenarios via brute force, we face a similar challenge in this setting. It thus stands to reason that we might also benefit from this technique.

[44] Indeed, we already investigated these ideas extensively in Chap. 4.

[45] See, for example, McCall [21].

[46] There are multiple possible references for this field, all widely outside the author's area of competence, with increasing levels of technical complexity. Ono et al. [23] is a deeply cool example—to give the reader a sense of the broad applicability of randomized strategies—involving planning trajectories of entry, descent, and landing for future Mars missions.

While randomization of downgrade outcomes might be employed in any number of ways, we will examine it in a rather specific manner. Our interest is in the significant—let's call it catastrophic—downgrade of a small number of important credit obligors in one's portfolio. It could also be restricted to some subset of the portfolio such as the largest exposures, those obligors with the highest loss-given-default uncertainty, or those with generally excellent credit credentials. Assigning downgrade to a handful of members of such a portfolio subset—as a specific stress scenario—is problematic. The analyst will inevitably be asked: why did you pick this obligor and not another one? The question is entirely justified. Our response is to abstract from any one (or several) obligors and select *all of them*. The difference with the brute-force setting is that we will randomly downgrade a few counterparties—by numerous credit notches—and compute the capital-headroom implications. We will then reset the portfolio and repeat the process. Performing this randomized action many times and averaging across the results will—integrating across all the possibilities—approximate the capital impact of catastrophic downgrade in a subset of one's portfolio. It will do so, however, in a global sense without explicitly identifying any specific credit counterparties.

Let's assume that we have $I$ members in our portfolio and we wish to consider all possible combinations of catastrophic downgrade by $n$ credit counterparts. This is a well known counting problem with the solution,

$$\binom{I}{n} = \frac{I!}{n!(I-n)!}. \tag{12.34}$$

For small $I$ and $n$, this number of combinations is quite manageable. Imagine that you have 100 large exposures and wanted to consider all combinations of *two* multiple-step downgrades. Using Eq. 12.34 with these values generates 4950 possibilities. Randomization hardly seems necessary. We could compute the capital impact for each case and take the average. Once again, however, dimensionality becomes a problem. For $I = 100$, Eq. 12.34 grows very fast in $n$.[47] Setting $n = 3$ yields more than 150,000 combinations, while $n = 5$ already puts the total to more than 75 million. Examining all possible combinations is thus not a suitable general strategy; randomization, in such cases, can get us to good answers with much less computational effort.

We'll use our small portfolio to make this idea a bit more tangible. Given that $I = 10$, a value of $n = 5$ generates the largest number of possible combinations: 210 cases. As a consequence, a randomization strategy is not really necessary for any choice of $n$. Setting $n = 2$, however, does allows us to investigate the interplay between randomization and simply examining all possible instances of catastrophic default.

[47] Given that Pascal's triangle is lurking in the background, Eq. 12.33 reaches a maximum when $n = \frac{I}{2}$—if $I$ is an even number—and then starts to decrease again.

| | 1 | 2 | 3 | 4 | 5 | 6 | 7 | 8 | 9 | 10 |
|---|---|---|---|---|---|---|---|---|---|---|
| 1 | (1, 1) | (1, 2) | (1, 3) | (1, 4) | (1, 5) | (1, 6) | (1, 7) | (1, 8) | (1, 9) | (1, 10) |
| 2 | (2, 1) | (2, 2) | (2, 3) | (2, 4) | (2, 5) | (2, 6) | (2, 7) | (2, 8) | (2, 9) | (2, 10) |
| 3 | (3, 1) | (3, 2) | (3, 3) | (3, 4) | (3, 5) | (3, 6) | (3, 7) | (3, 8) | (3, 9) | (3, 10) |
| 4 | (4, 1) | (4, 2) | (4, 3) | (4, 4) | (4, 5) | (4, 6) | (4, 7) | (4, 8) | (4, 9) | (4, 10) |
| 5 | (5, 1) | (5, 2) | (5, 3) | (5, 4) | (5, 5) | (5, 6) | (5, 7) | (5, 8) | (5, 9) | (5, 10) |
| 6 | (6, 1) | (6, 2) | (6, 3) | (6, 4) | (6, 5) | (6, 6) | (6, 7) | (6, 8) | (6, 9) | (6, 10) |
| 7 | (7, 1) | (7, 2) | (7, 3) | (7, 4) | (7, 5) | (7, 6) | (7, 7) | (7, 8) | (7, 9) | (7, 10) |
| 8 | (8, 1) | (8, 2) | (8, 3) | (8, 4) | (8, 5) | (8, 6) | (8, 7) | (8, 8) | (8, 9) | (8, 10) |
| 9 | (9, 1) | (9, 2) | (9, 3) | (9, 4) | (9, 5) | (9, 6) | (9, 7) | (9, 8) | (9, 9) | (9, 10) |
| 10 | (10, 1) | (10, 2) | (10, 3) | (10, 4) | (10, 5) | (10, 6) | (10, 7) | (10, 8) | (10, 9) | (10, 10) |

**Fig. 12.13** *Partitioning the unit square*: To motivate the randomization strategy among our $I = 10$ exposures, this square allows us to visualize the set of all possible combinations of $n = 2$ catastrophic downgrades. By symmetry, the values above and below the diagonal have an identical portfolio impact.

We will also use a rather simple method for random selection of our two downgrade candidates. There are other, rather more clever ways to do this, but the presented method helps us see clearly what is going on. Our plan is to choose, in a uniformly random manner, two of $I = 10$ obligors.[48] This can be accomplished by partitioning the unit square into $I \times I$ sub-squares, where each square is described by two integer coordinates.[49] This object is presented in Fig. 12.13. There are $K \times K = 100$ sub-squares. Due to the inherent symmetry of our problem—the order of the pair has no importance—and a need to avoid the diagonal, there are only $\frac{I^2-I}{2} = 45$ unique combinations.[50]

48 The technique we present is conceptually related to the more general stratified sampling method termed Latin-hypercube sampling. See, for example, Glasserman [13, Section 4.3], Fishman [12, Section 4.3], and Asmussen and Glynn [3, Section V.7]. The basic idea is to divide the one's sample space into a disjoint set of sub-regions—typically referred to as *strata*—and to ensure that simulated random variates fall into each of these strata. This partitioning of the sample space ultimately leads to reduction of variance in one's simulation estimators without biasing its convergence.

49 For $n = 3$, this becomes the unit cube, while for larger values it generalizes to the unit hypercube.

50 This happily coincides, as it must, with evaluation of $\binom{10}{2} = 45$ from Eq. 12.34.

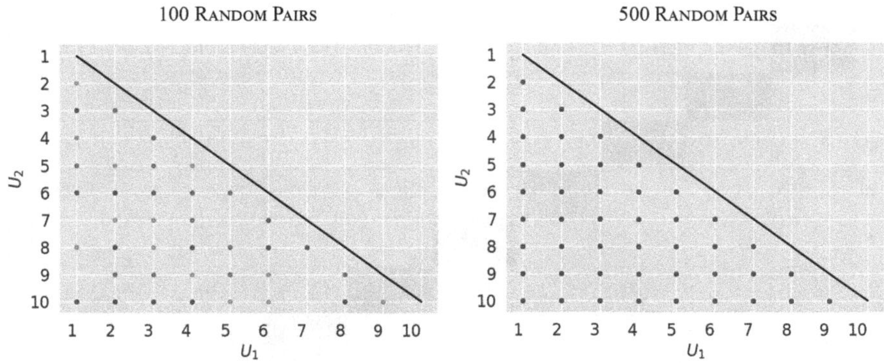


**Fig. 12.14** *Unit-square coverage*: By uniform random selection of downgrade pairs, it takes a rather large number of draws to cover the lower-diagonal of our partitioned unit square. 100 draws is not enough, while 500 seems to do the job. Considering there are only 45 combinations, this is not very efficient. As we add dimensions to our hypercube and increase $I$, however, this becomes a viable strategy.

Randomly selecting a pair of obligor downgrades thus reduces to picking a single sub-square. This is operationalized by selecting uniformly distributed random variates, $U_1, U_2 \sim \mathcal{U}[0, 1]$. The corresponding square is given by

$$\left(\underbrace{\lceil I \cdot U_1 \rceil}_{\text{Row}}, \underbrace{\lceil I \cdot U_2 \rceil}_{\text{Column}}\right) \equiv \left(\underbrace{\lceil I \cdot U_2 \rceil}_{\text{Row}}, \underbrace{\lceil I \cdot U_1 \rceil}_{\text{Column}}\right). \tag{12.35}$$

where $\lceil \cdot \rceil$ denotes the ceiling operator to ensure that we obtain integer coordinates.[51] The only constraint is that we need to ensure that no draw falls along the diagonal, since this amounts to having a single counterpart downgrading twice.[52]

How well does repeated draws from Eq. 12.34 fill in the unit square? Not particularly well. Figure 12.14 displays—for 100 and 500 randomly drawn pairs of downgrades—the coverage of the lower-diagonal of our partitioned unit square from Fig. 12.13. 100 draws is not enough, while 500 seems enough to do the job. Considering there are only 45 combinations, this is fairly inefficient. For our (very small) sample portfolio, this is clearly overkill. As we add dimensions to our hypercube (i.e., $n > 4$ or so) and increase the number of counterparties (i.e., $I > 50$), however, this becomes an entirely (indeed, perhaps the only) viable strategy.

[51] This is readily generalized for arbitrary $n$ by selecting $n$ independent uniform variates and adjusting Eq. 12.35 accordingly.

[52] Practically, this means we toss out any randomized draws from the diagonal. This is admittedly not very elegant and a bit computationally wasteful.

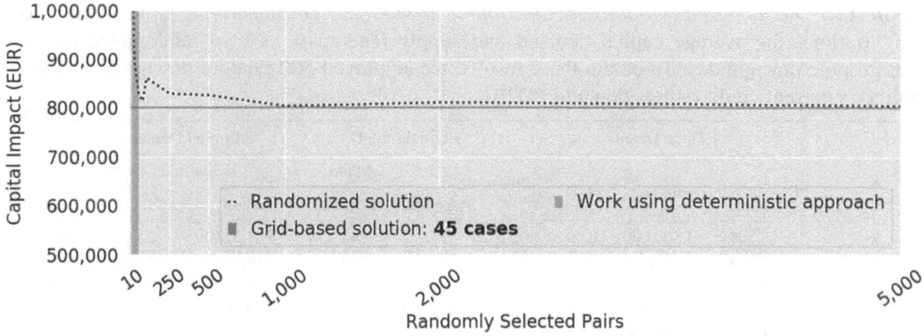


**Fig. 12.15** *Randomized convergence*: After a few hundred randomly drawn downgrade pairs, the average capital impact converges rather closely to the grid-based solution involving the (known) 45 possible combinations. Once again, as we increase both $I$ and $n$, randomization strategies represent our only hope of solving this problem.

Figure 12.15 submits the (rather sad) results of comparing various numbers of random pairs of downgrades to the average across all of the known combinations for our simple 10-security portfolio. It takes a few hundred random samples to get near to the final figure, which is just south of about EUR 800,000. This is rather typical. In low dimensions, randomization is a poor, inefficient strategy. Numerical approaches using grids or working with the power set routinely dominate in terms of accuracy and speed. A randomized approach, for all its shortcomings, does have an important advantage. It is roughly invariant to dimensionality; that is, its (slow) convergence rate does not change (much) for very large problems.

At this point in our discussion, we should take a moment to underscore the importance of Chap. 5. While the expected-credit-loss and credit-spread-valuation computations are fast, estimating economic capital consequences are not. If we had to turn to our simulation engine to estimate the implications of every downgrade, the majority of the ideas we've considered in our bottom-up analysis would be infeasible. Our economic-capital approximation models thus open up broad avenues of investigation, which were previously inaccessible. This is a huge analytic advantage. The approximation does, of course, have some shortcomings. In particular, for extreme changes to our portfolio, we should be somewhat cautious in interpreting the result.[53] Indeed, in such cases, there is certainly value in turning back to the simulation engine to *verify* the approximation-model results.

[53] Handling the downgrade of a few positions within the overall portfolio, by contrast, is an entirely natural application of the approximation model.

**Table 12.7** *Randomized two-obligor catastrophic downgrade*: The underlying table, in the usual way, outlines the average capital demand and supply repercussions of a randomized pair of catastrophic downgrades. To obtain these results, we employed 500 random downgrades of two obligor's current credit ratings down to PD20.

| # | Trade Details | | | | | Capital Supply | | Capital Demand | | |
|---|---|---|---|---|---|---|---|---|---|---|
| | | | | | | ECL | MTM | Economic Capital | | |
| | $PD_0$ | $\overline{PD}_1$ | EAD | LGD | Conc. Index | Stage I/II | Δ-Spread | Default | Migration | Total |
| 1 | 3 | **6.4** | 3,500,000 | 0.40 | 0.75 | 0 | 144,538 | 103,273 | 72,440 | 175,713 |
| 2 | 4 | **7.3** | 1,500,000 | 0.35 | 0.72 | 0 | 43,217 | 29,968 | 12,809 | 42,777 |
| 3 | 7 | **9.1** | 2,000,000 | 0.45 | 0.80 | 42,765 | 0 | 90,146 | 12,586 | 102,733 |
| 4 | 9 | **11.8** | 1,750,000 | 0.55 | 0.85 | 67,623 | 0 | 220,890 | 10,296 | 231,185 |
| 5 | 13 | **14.4** | 1,500,000 | 0.60 | 0.70 | 66,505 | 0 | 98,620 | 16,927 | 115,547 |
| 6 | 14 | **15.1** | 3,000,000 | 0.15 | 0.95 | 40,289 | 0 | 269,501 | 147,059 | 416,560 |
| 7 | 15 | **16.1** | 1,000,000 | 0.35 | 0.90 | 28,698 | 0 | 158,317 | 8,981 | 167,298 |
| 8 | 17 | **17.6** | 4,500,000 | 0.30 | 0.75 | 178,757 | 0 | 483,600 | 61,142 | 544,742 |
| 9 | 18 | **18.4** | 750,000 | 0.40 | 0.80 | 40,384 | 0 | 99,587 | 2,728 | 102,315 |
| 10 | 20 | **20.0** | 500,000 | 0.20 | 0.90 | 19,996 | 0 | 71,339 | 2,676 | 74,016 |
| Total/Mean | 11.1 | **12.9** | 20,000,000 | 0.36 | 0.80 | 485,017 | 187,755 | 1,625,242 | 347,645 | 1,972,888 |
| Pecent of Portfolio | | | | | | 2.4% | 0.9% | 8.1% | 1.7% | 9.9% |

Table 12.7 outlines, in the now familiar format, the detail capital demand and supply results associated with many randomized pairs of catastrophic downgrades. As in Fig. 12.15, catastrophic implies an obligor being downgraded from its current credit rating all the way down to PD20.[54] The average increase in capital demand is a bit over EUR 250,000, while the loan-impairment impact comes to around EUR 300,000. Interestingly, the valuation repercussions total almost EUR 200,000. This stems from the current high quality of the fair-valued securities in our portfolio. Overall, as we saw in Fig. 12.15, the total capital squeeze amounts to just shy of EUR 800,000. As always in a stress-testing analysis, we cannot assign a probability to this outcome. We can, however, state that it is twice our concentration-motivated, bottom-up scenario from Table 12.6, it is roughly equivalent to an extreme portfolio with all obligors assigned about PD13, and it lies at the upper end of our medium-impact impulse-response function macro-financial shocks.

[54] As before, for credit counterparties already at PD20, we do not force default.

**Colour and Commentary 150** (THE POWER OF RANDOMIZATION)*: Traditional bottom-up stress-testing, in contrast to the top-down approach, places higher importance on the idiosyncratic dimension. These are risks specific to the financial institution's portfolio. They consider downgrades—in terms of concentrations, industries, and regions—that may really do harm to one's capital position. Taking idiosyncratic risk to its logical limit, we should also consider a small number of individual obligors experiencing severe deterioration in their credit quality. Independent of macro-financial shocks and portfolio structure, this basically captures* bad luck. *While tempting, it is not a good idea to simply pick a handful of names from one's portfolio, downgrade them by multiple notches, and call it misfortune. You will naturally be asked: how did you come to choose those particular names? It also represents a single, extremely low probability, case. An alternative solution is to use a randomization strategy. One thus computes the average capital demand and supply outcomes over many randomly selected sets of hard-luck (or catastrophic) downgrades.*[a] *The results shine a different light on (more global) idiosyncratic vulnerabilities in one's portfolio.*

[a] One can make this even more meaningful by focusing on subsets of one's portfolio. Selecting a small number of obligors from the firm's 100 largest exposures or a particularly important industry or region.

### 12.3.5 Collecting Our Bottom-Up Alternatives

The various alternatives examined in the previous sections should *not* be viewed as an exhaustive review of the entire universe of bottom-up stress scenarios. Instead, they represent some practical ideas for getting a handle on the complexity associated with scenario selection. Whatever strategy one follows to identify meaningful bottom-up stress scenarios, however, it is important to impose some structure and organization. Failure to do so does not immediately imply disaster, but does substantially increase the chances of losing the forest for the trees.

To close out our bottom-up stress-testing analysis, Fig. 12.16 presents *four* of the main scenarios examined in this section. Designed analogously to the macro-financial results presented in Fig. 12.6, it allows comparison of capital demand and supply effects in a single glance. Our simple portfolio example does not permit incredibly complex dynamics, but there is nonetheless a surprising amount of intra-scenario deviation among the individual components. The loan-impairment stage allocation and valuation effects are rather more nuanced in the concentration-index and randomized-downgrade scenarios.

Stress-testing, as the preceding discussion hopefully makes clear, is hard work. There are no short cuts; it is inherently a bit messy, hard to manage, and high

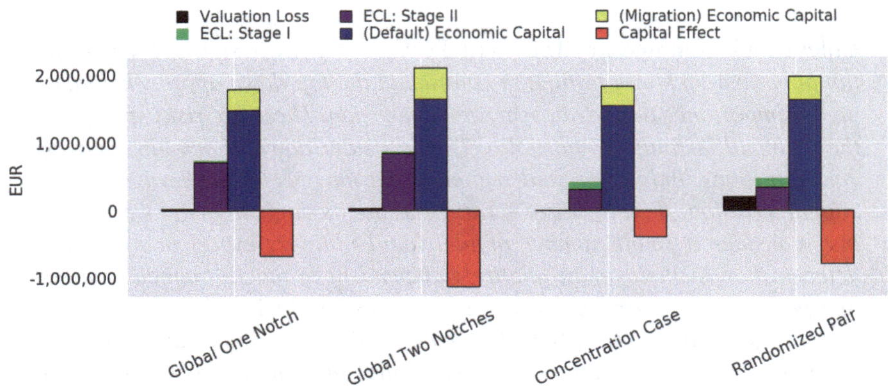


**Fig. 12.16** *Bottom-up intuition*: This graphic illustrates, in a manner analogous to the macro-financial results from Fig. 12.6, the individual capital demand and supply consequences for *four* of the bottom-up scenarios considered in this section. It is enlightening to inspect the capital impact and its various sources across the different stress-tests.

dimensional. It is precisely such multifaceted analysis of alternative bottom-up—and, of course, also top-down—scenarios that contributes to a deeper understanding of the vulnerabilities in one's portfolio. No one scenario provides the full picture. It is rather through the judicious selection and comparison of various scenarios, constructed following different strategies, that stress-testing analysis adds value.

## 12.4 Wrapping Up

In the banking world over the last few decades, much (entirely warranted) emphasis has been placed on the notion of *know-your-customer* to help minimize money laundering activities and other financial crimes.[55] The core idea is that more knowledge about a phenomenon leads to improved understanding and management of associated risks. This excellent and uncontroversial point is readily extended to our stress-testing discussion in the form of the snappy, but entirely pertinent, catchphrase: *know your portfolio*.

Our risk-management models, as we've seen in previous chapters, provide us with a wealth of information. Much of it, however, is embedded in the through-the-cycle perspective with the assumption of a constant portfolio. Stress-testing expands our horizon by examining—from a rich array of perspectives—the repercussions of downgrade-related portfolio changes. Although broadly defined and difficult to organize, the principal contribution of stress-testing is portfolio knowledge. Better comprehension and classification of portfolio weaknesses and vulnerabilities

[55] There are many sources on this area, but Graham [15] provides an interesting introduction.

**Table 12.8** *A stress-testing menu*: The underlying table, like an *à la carte* menu, illustrates the seven alternative top-down and bottom-up stress-testing techniques treated in this chapter. While certainly non-exhaustive, hopefully it can help readers design and execute their own menus.

| | |
|---|---|
| I. TOP-DOWN | I.1 Forward-looking adverse scenarios |
| | I.2 Historical backward-looking crisis outcomes |
| | I.3 Structured impulse-response-function motivated analysis |
| II. BOTTOM-UP | II.1 The power set of all downgrades |
| | II.2 Extreme (all in one credit class) portfolios |
| | II.3 The $n$-notch global downgrade chestnut |
| | II.4 Classic portfolio-knowledge motivated scenarios |
| | II.5 Randomized catastrophic defaults |

complement traditional probabilistic models and help stakeholders take better decisions.

Table 12.8 is given the last word. Organized like an *à la carte* menu from a fancy restaurant, it summarizes the *seven* alternative top-down and bottom-up stress-testing techniques examined in the previous sections. While certainly not an exhaustive list, it does provide a reasonable amount of choice. Hopefully, when combined with the ideas presented in preceding chapters, it can help the reader design and execute her own stress-testing menu.

## References


1. C. Albanese, S. Crépey, and S. Iabichino. Reverse Stress Testing. Social Science Research Network, February 2021.
2. J. R. Aragonés, C. Blanco, and K. Dowd. Incorporating stress tests into market risk modeling. *Institutional Investor*, pages 44–49, Spring 2001.
3. S. Asmussen and P. W. Glynn. *Stochastic Simulation: Algorithms and Analysis*. Springer-Verlag, Heidelberg, Germany, first edition, 2007. Stochastic Modelling and Applied Probability.
4. T. Bellini. *Stress Testing and Risk Integration in Banks: A Statistical Framework and Practical Software Guide*. Elsevier Inc., London, UK, 2017.
5. R. Bellman. *Adaptive Control Processes: A Guided Tour*. Princeton University Press, 1961.
6. BIS. Stress testing principles. Technical report, Bank for International Settlements, October 2018.
7. D. J. Bolder. A Proposed Stochastic Simulation Framework for the Government of Canada's Debt Strategy Problem. Bank of Canada: Working Paper 2003-10, April 2003.
8. D. J. Bolder. The Canadian Debt Strategy Model. Bank of Canada Review: Summer 2008, October 2008.
9. D. J. Bolder and S. Deeley. The Canadian Debt-Strategy Model: An Overview of the Principal Elements. Bank of Canada: Discussion Paper 2011-3, May 2011.
10. L. J. Christiano. Christopher A. Sims and Vector Autoregressions. *Scandinavian Journal of Economics*, 114(4):1082–1104, 2012.
11. D. A. Dickey and W. A. Fuller. Distribution of the estimators for autoregressive time series with a unit root. *Journal of the American Statistical Association*, 74(366):427–431, 1979.

12. G. S. Fishman. *Monte Carlo: Concepts, Algorithms, and Applications*. Springer-Verlag, 175 Fifth Avenue, New York, NY, 1995. Springer Series in Operations Research.
13. P. Glasserman. *Monte Carlo Methods in Financial Engineering*. Springer, Berlin, first edition, 2004.
14. G. H. Golub and C. F. V. Loan. *Matrix Computations*. The John Hopkins University Press, Baltimore, Maryland, 2012.
15. N. M. Graham. Know your customer: Good for compliance, great for client service. *Journal of Investment Compliance*, 4(3), 2003.
16. J. D. Hamilton. *Time Series Analysis*. Princeton University Press, Princeton, New Jersey, 1994.
17. J. W. Harris and H. Stocker. *Handbook of Mathematics and Computational Science*. Springer Verlag, New York, New York, 1998.
18. G. G. Judge, W. Griffiths, R. C. Hill, H. Lütkepohl, and T.-C. Lee. *The Theory and Practice of Econometrics*. John Wiley and Sons, New York, New York, second edition, 1985.
19. G. Koop, M. Pesaran, and S. M. Potter. Impulse response analysis in nonlinear multivariate models. *Journal of Econometrics*, 74(1):119–147, 1996.
20. H. Lütkepohl. *New Introduction to Multiple Time Series Analysis*. Springer, Heidelberg, Germany, 2005.
21. J. McCall. Genetic algorithms for modelling and optimisation. *Journal of Computational and Applied Mathematics*, 184(1):205–222, 2005.
22. Merriam-Webster. *Webster's Ninth New Collegiate Dictionary*. Merriam-Webster, 9th edition, 1991.
23. M. Ono, M. E. Chamie, M. Pavone, and B. Açikmese. Mixed strategy for constrained stochastic optimal control. *CoRR*, abs/1607.01478, 2016.
24. M. Pesaran and Y. Shin. Generalized impulse response analysis in linear multivariate models. *Economics Letters*, 58(1):17–29, 1998.
25. W. H. Press, S. A. Teukolsky, W. T. Vetterling, and B. P. Flannery. *Numerical Recipes in C: The Art of Scientific Computing*. Cambridge University Press, Trumpington Street, Cambridge, second edition, 1992.
26. R. Rebonato. *Coherent Stress Testing: A Bayesian Approach to the Analysis of Financial Stress*. John Wiley & Sons, West Sussex, UK, 2010.
27. C. M. Reinhart and K. S. Rogoff. *This Time Is Different: Eight Centuries of Financial Folly*. Princeton University Press, Princeton, New Jersey, 2009.
28. D. Rösch and H. Scheule. *Stress Testing for Financial Institutions: Applications, Regulations, and Techniques*. Risk Books, London, UK, 2008.
29. C. A. Sims. Macroeconomics and reality. *Econometrica*, 48(1):1–48, 1980.
30. M. Tahan. *The Man Who Counted: A Collection of Mathematical Adventures*. W.W. Norton & Co., New York, NY, 1993.
31. N. N. Taleb. *The Black Swan: The Impact of the Highly Improbable*. Random House, New York, NY, 2007.
32. J. Tolkien. *The Hobbit*. Harper Collins, Hammersmith, London, 1937.
33. B. H. Yang. Point-in-time PD term structure models for multi-period scenario loss projection: Methodologies and implementations for IFRS 9 ECL and CCAR stress testing. MPRA Paper 76271, University Library of Munich, Germany, January 2017.

# Index





D. Bolder, *Modelling Economic Capital*, Contributions to Finance and Accounting,
https://doi.org/10.1007/978-3-030-95096-5

# Author Index





D. Bolder, *Modelling Economic Capital*, Contributions to Finance and Accounting,
https://doi.org/10.1007/978-3-030-95096-5